Mac® OS X Bible
Panther Edition

D1743567

Mac® OS X Bible
Panther Edition

**Sam A. Litt, Kevin C. Boland, Thomas Clancy Jr.,
Warren G. Gottlieb, Douglas B. Heyman,
and Craig Zimmerman**

Wiley Publishing, Inc.

Mac® OS X Bible Panther Edition

Published by
Wiley Publishing, Inc.
111 River St.
Hoboken, NJ 07030-5774
www.wiley.com

Copyright © 2004 by Wiley Publishing, Inc., Indianapolis, Indiana

Published simultaneously in Canada

Library of Congress Control Number available from publisher.

ISBN: 0-7645-4399-7

Manufactured in the United States of America

10 9 8 7 6 5 4 3 2 1

1B/SR/QR/QU/IN

About the Authors

Samuel A. Litt is an Apple Certified Technical Coordinator as well as a member of the Apple Solutions Experts program. He has provided Macintosh service and support for a diverse client base, including the Computer Investigations unit at the NYPD, Ralph Lauren, Swatch, Messener Vetere Berger McNamee Schmetterer, Time Warner, MTV Networks, Hearst Publishing, Scholastic Publications, and TBWA/Chiat/Day. He is currently Director of IT for the Blue Rock Editing Company — Manhattan's premier post-production editorial company. His works published to date include the *Mac OS X Administration Basics Exam Cram* as well as several articles for Element K's *Mac Administrator Journal*.

Kevin Boland is a former Apple Senior Systems Engineer. He has worked as a Systems Analyst, Macintosh Systems Administrator, and Technical Consultant with Mac-based companies in the New York City area, including Martha Stewart Living Omnimedia, Siegel and Gale, Bankers Trust, Deutsche Bank, Phillip Morris USA, and Bantam Doubleday Dell. He has been proud to use Macintosh computers intensively since their introduction in 1984.

Craig Zimmerman has actively pursued his passion for technology and communication since he was 13 years old. His career started as SYSOP of Apple Castle, a BBS for Apple II enthusiasts. He later worked a Chiat/Day, where he helped build the world's most famous virtual advertising agency, managing and networking UNIX and Macintosh systems in multiple offices. Currently, Craig manages both UNIX and Macintosh systems for Spontaneous, a top post-production company in New York City.

Thomas Clancy, Jr. attended Queens College (CUNY) and received his bachelor's degree in European history. Tom's love of computers blossomed into a great career, especially under the guidance of Sam Litt as his diabolical mentor and manager. Tom is one of the three founding partners of Valiant Technology LLC, a consulting and support company, along with Douglas Heyman and Gene McMurray. Tom currently lives in New York with his wife Alice and their two cats, Zeta and Mo. Tom would like to point out that he is NOT related to "the" Tom Clancy, although he is happy to be related to another Tom Clancy, Sr., his dad, a New York City Firefighter (which is a better job than "world-famous-author" any day, although the pay isn't as good).

Douglas Heyman is a longtime Mac user, having cut his teeth on the venerable System 6. Early in his career, Doug worked as a writer and managing editor on numerous literary projects. Shifting his focus to technology, he spent the next few years as in-house IT staff for a major New York advertising agency and then in the IT consulting world working for a leading Apple Authorized Service Provider. He currently works as a founding partner of Valiant Technology, a New York–based technology solutions provider. Born and raised in New Jersey, he resides in Hoboken with his loving wife, Suzanne.

Warren G. Gottlieb has been using Macs since 1988. It all started when his dad brought a Mac home one day after having enough to do with PCs, even before Windows was around. A Macintosh was later purchased for him under the guise of having it used for schoolwork, yet in actuality it was a (successful) attempt to foil his television watching. When Warren was in college he was more likely to be found helping friends with their Macs and working at the Help Desk than doing his assigned schoolwork. Eventually his propensity for interacting with people and their Macs led him to spend several years working at two of the top Macintosh tech houses in New York City, as a full time specialist and consultant. Warren would like to coin the term "Mac Factor" as a statement defining the influence of Macintosh culture on individuals, and this feels like a good place to do so. Warren was born and raised in Queens, New York, where he currently resides.

Credits

Acquisitions Editor
Michael Roney

Project Editor
Beth Taylor

Technical Editor
Debbie Gates

Copy Editor
Maarten Reilingh

Editorial Manager
Robyn Siesky

Vice President & Executive Group Publisher
Richard Swadley

Vice President and Executive Publisher
Bob Ipsen

Vice President and Publisher
Barry Pruett

Project Coordinator
Ryan Steffen

Graphics and Production Specialists
Amanda Carter, Lauren Goddard,
Denny Hager, Joyce Haughey,
Jennifer Heleine, Stephanie D. Jumper,
Kristin McMullan, Lynsey Osborn,
Heather Ryan, Melanie Wolven

Quality Control Technicians
John Greenough, Andy Hollandbeck,
Carl William Pierce, Kathy Simpson

Special Help
Steve Arany

Proofreading
Nancy Reinhardt

Indexing
TECHBOOKS Production Services

For Mom and Dad

Foreword

Mac OS X version 10.3 "Panther" is the fourth major release of Mac OS X in just over three years and the most ground-breaking version of Apple's UNIX-based operating system to date. Panther delivers more than 150 breakthrough new features, including a completely new Finder that provides one-click access to a user's favorite files and folders; Exposé, a revolutionary new way to instantly see all open windows at once; and iChat AV, a complete desktop videoconferencing solution for business, education, and consumers. We're delivering innovations today that will not be seen in any other operating system for years to come.

Whether you're using a Mac for managing pictures or making movies, designing a magazine or researching for your finals, the newly revised Mac OS X Bible offers a legion of tips and techniques that make it an invaluable resource for getting the most out of Panther and the most out of your Mac.

With over 900 pages of detailed information, author Sam Litt has created a comprehensive reference for Mac OS X users.

Jon Rubenstein

Senior Vice President, Hardware Engineering

Apple Computer, Inc.

Acknowledgments

Sam Litt: I would like to thank the women in my life, Jodi and Peri, for their patience and support. I would also like to thank my friends and coauthors (The Fab 5) for their contributions to this project. A special thanks to my author agent David Fugate, as well as Mike Roney and Beth Taylor at Wiley for having faith. I am grateful to John Palestrini, Ethel Rubinstein, David Rosen, and Ted Dunn for their encouragement and support as well. This book was an intense effort and many people contributed to its publication; many thanks to all who labored tirelessly on my behalf. Lastly, I would like to thank Jon Rubinstein for not only his genius but his kindness as well.

Kevin Boland: I would like to thank the following people for their invaluable support during this project: Laura M. Mango and the Mango family, Geraldine G. Boland, Ellen Boland, Jean and Owen Boland, Marianne and Owen Boland, Eiline and Douglas Miller, John J.M. Hussar IV, Jack Musella, Jim Dunleavy, Emily Kuenstler, Brenna McCarthy, Andy Espo, Nicole and Steve Gustavesson, Alicia Milosz, Sheila Vaccaro, Jarrett Garcia, Jason Myers, Dr. Joel Mausner, and Sam Litt.

Craig Zimmerman: I would like to thank all the people whose support, encouragement, and contacts made this book possible. Thanks especially to Calamity Jane for selling me a Hayes 300-baud modem for the Apple][+ and getting me online way back when, and Franz "System 7 is going to change everything" Oehler, for bringing me back 10 years later. To Mom, Dad, and Kimberly for always supporting my interests and putting up with modem calls to the house at all hours of the night. Special thanks to my lovely wife Aimee for being there with a smile.

Tom Clancy: I would like to thank my wife Alice for her unflagging support and for my Xbox reward. Thanks to my Mom, Clancy McKenna, for inspiring me to fight, scrape, and scrabble to build a career (you are a great inspiration). Thanks to my Dad, Tom Clancy, Sr., for teaching me how to critically analyze and get at the heart of a problem and fix it. Thanks to Uncle Ed McCann for being a great friend, peer, and role model. Thanks to my best man, Rich Douek, for letting me hang out and play with his old Atari ST. Thanks to Georg Dauterman for keeping me inspired to "talk-tech" whenever possible. And BIG thanks to Gene McMurray for keeping our company rolling while Doug and I worked on this book.

Douglas Heyman: I would like to thank my beautiful wife for putting up with me while I wrote this book, all of my family for being so supportive, the software developers who granted permission to reproduce their works, Andrew Montgomery for his help hashing out ideas, Gene for always thinking critically, Tom for putting up with me, Warren, Kevin, and Craig for their collaboration and kindness, and a special thanks to Sam for being a colleague, mentor, and most importantly, a good friend.

Warren Gottlieb: I would like to thank Andrew Montgomery for his substantial, invaluable written and technical contributions to the networking section. His friendship, kindness, and guidance have been an amazing help.

Thanks Scott Schaefer for giving me my start into this Mac world to which I belong, and to Sam for his guidance and for signing me onto this project.

Contents at a Glance

Contents

Part II: At Work with Mac OS X   263

Chapter 9: Printing and Faxing 265

Chapter 10: Accessing Files over a Network 281

Part III: Beyond the Basics of Mac OS X   409

Chapter 14: Managing User Accounts and Privileges 411

Part IV: Making the Most of Mac OS X   601

Chapter 19: Working with Included Programs 603

Introduction

According to popular legend, a Mac is so easy to use that you don't need to read books about it. Alas, if only that were true. The fact is, to harness all the power of Mac OS X would take a substantial amount of time of exploring and tinkering. The reality is, not everyone has the time, the inclination, or the patience to devote to the mastery of an operating system. Save your time for having fun with games, surfing the Internet, or perhaps getting some work done. Benefit from the experience of others (in this case, we the authors)! Read this book so that you can leverage the full power of OS X without a lot of ambling around the desktop.

You might be under the impression that you don't need this book because of Apple's supplied Mac OS X Getting Started Guide and onscreen help. Though these are good sources of information, the *Mac OS X Bible Panther Edition* contains a great deal of information and how-to that you won't find anywhere else.

Getting to Know Mac OS X

Introduction and Installation of Mac OS X

From the moment you see Mac OS X, you know that it's different from any other computer operating system on the planet, including earlier iterations of Mac OS. Nothing else looks quite like it. Yet, use it a bit and you will see that there is familiarity about its operation. Apple has made great efforts to ensure that Macintosh users can leverage their OS 9 skill sets. Although on the surface Mac OS X may seem familiar, its internal workings have no relation to any Apple desktop OS to date.

This chapter provides an overview of the core technologies that comprise Mac OS X. Knowing the core technologies can help you master the overall operation of OS X. We conclude this chapter by examining the system requirements of Mac OS X and its installation.

What Is Mac OS X?

Mac OS X is Apple's answer to the quest for a modern operating system. It combines the power and stability of Unix with the simplicity of the Macintosh. In 1996, after continual failed attempts to develop its own next-generation operating system, Apple management looked outside the company and acquired NeXT Software Inc. NeXT's OS at the time was called OpenStep. It had all the features that Apple desired in a modern OS: protected memory, preemptive multitasking, multithreading, and symmetric multiprocessing. With OpenStep as the foundation, Apple initially designated the code name Rhapsody for the its new OS, but as the project matured, it was renamed to Mac OS X, keeping in line with the progression of Apple's existing system software monikers. Apple has enjoyed phenomenal success with Mac OS X, which has been adopted by over 5 million users and is now generally considered the largest vendor of Unix-based systems on the planet.

Mac OS 10.3 is an evolutionary step in the OS X product line. It has numerous user enhancements that are covered throughout this book. One of the more prolific enhancements is that the OS has been updated to run on the IBM PowerPC 970 processor, which is the heart of Apple's G5 64-bit computer. But Mac OS 10.3 is not a true 64-bit OS; rather, it's what's referred to as a hybrid OS. This means that while

Mac OS 10.3 has been optimized to take advantage of the 64-bit data paths of the G5 processor and is capable of utilizing up to 8GB of memory access and native double-precision (64-bit) arithmetic, it still allows 32-bit applications to run.

Core Technologies of Mac OS X

The most important thing to know about Mac OS X is that it is based on open standards. This is because at the heart of OS X is Unix, which has played a major role in the development of the Internet. Because Unix is so Internet centric, OS X can be integrated in virtually any computing environment. In fact, the X in Mac OS X represents the X in Unix. But fear not, although Mac OS X is a Unix operating system, its operation does not require the mastery of complex Unix command syntax. As Apple publicizes, the command line is there for those who would like to use it, but it is not required for day-to-day operations. One can make as much or as little use of it as desired.

If OS X were to be compared to an automobile, we would see a similarity in that both are comprised of many parts. All these parts have very distinct functions, and yet, all make up a greater whole. Metaphorically speaking, the intention of Apple was to design a vehicle akin to a Formula 1 racing car. When the engineers at Apple set out to build OS X, they pulled together world-class technologies in an effort to build the most advanced consumer operating system the world has ever seen. Let's take a closer look at these parts.

Darwin

The foundation of OS X is Darwin, which is an open source community/Apple joint effort. Though Darwin is a complete OS in and of itself, the primary objective of the Darwin project was to build an industrial-strength Unix-based operating system core that would provide greater stability and performance compared to all existing iterations of the Mac OS. To review Darwin in detail is beyond the scope of this book. Instead, we shall review some of Darwin's more marketed features.

Mach microkernel

At the center of Darwin is the Mach microkernel, which is the foundation that provides basic services for all other parts of the operating system. Mach was developed at Carnegie-Mellon University, and it has a closely tied history with BSD Unix (Berkeley Software Distribution). It is Mach that gives OS X the features of protected memory architecture, preemptive multitasking, and symmetric multiprocessing.

Protected memory

Protected memory isolates applications in their own individual memory workspaces. When an application crashes, the program can be terminated without having a negative effect on other running applications or requiring a restart of the computer.

Advance memory management

Advance memory management automatically manages physical RAM and virtual memory dynamically as needed. Virtual memory uses hard disk space in lieu of physical RAM. Information that would normally sit in RAM, but is not currently needed, is transferred to the hard disk to free up physical RAM for the demands of data/applications that need it. This alleviates out-of-memory conditions and eliminates the need, experienced by users of previous Macintosh desktop operating systems, of having to manually adjust memory allocations.

Preemptive multitasking

Mac OS X, like all Mac OS versions since System 7, allows more than one application to be open and operating at the same time. This capability is known as multitasking. Prior to OS X, the Mac OS employed a version of multitasking referred to as *cooperative* multitasking. In cooperative multitasking, applications sometimes seemed unresponsive, because the system software could not efficiently manage the concurrent demands of multiple running programs. Mac OS X remedies this by implementing *preemptive* multitasking. Preemptive multitasking prioritizes processor tasks by order of importance. This more efficient method of managing processor tasks allows the computer to remain responsive, even during the most processor-intensive tasks.

Symmetric multiprocessing

Symmetric multiprocessing provides support for multiprocessor Macintosh computer systems. This allows applications to take advantage of two or more processors by assigning applications to specific processors or by splitting parts of applications known as threads between multiple processors simultaneously. By contrast, Mac OS 9 uses one processor for the majority of its tasks and programs need to be explicitly written to take advantage of multiprocessor Macs. These programs are limited to a few graphics and scientific applications.

Graphics technologies in Mac OS X

When it comes to graphics Mac OS X is one of the most powerful operating systems on the planet. To achieve this power, Mac OS X employs several standards-based technologies that are best-of-class. These technologies include Quartz, OpenGL, and QuickTime.

Quartz

Quartz is a powerful two-dimensional (2D) graphics-rendering system. It has built-in support for the Portable Document Format (PDF), on-the-fly rendering, compositing, and antialiasing. It supports multiple font formats, including TrueType, Postscript Type 1, and OpenType. Quartz supports Apple's ColorSync color-management technology, allowing for consistent and accurate color in the print/graphics environment.

OpenGL

Open Graphics Library (OpenGL) started out as a technology initiative by Silicon Graphics Inc., a manufacturer of high-end graphics workstations. It has since become an industry standard for three-dimensional (3D) graphics rendering. It provides a standard graphics application programming interface (API) by which software and hardware manufacturers can build 3D applications and hardware across multiple platforms on a common standard. OpenGL is very prevalent in gaming, computer-aided design (CAD), professional 3D animation/modeling, and graphic design.

QuickTime

QuickTime is Apple's cross-platform multimedia authoring and distribution engine. QuickTime is both a file format and a suite of applications. QuickTime has been around since 1991 and has matured into a very powerful technology. QuickTime supports over 50 media file formats encompassing audio, video, and still images. Some examples of these file formats include AIFF, AVI, JPEG, MIDI, MP3, MPEG-1, PICT, and TIFF. QuickTime has support for real-time video streaming, allowing viewers to tune in to live or prerecorded content on demand.

Aqua

Though Aqua is not a graphics technology in Mac OS X, it is its graphical user interface (GUI). Appearance-wise, it is a dramatic departure from OS 9's Platinum interface, although it retains certain common elements. This allows for greater familiarity for legacy Macintosh operators, thus making the transition to OS X a more intuitive experience.

Mac OS X's application environments

Application environments allow Mac OS X to run its modern OS-enabled applications while simultaneously supporting legacy Mac OS software. An application environment consists of various system resources, components, and services that allow an application to function. Mac OS X has five application environments: Cocoa, Carbon, Java, BSD, and Classic.

Cocoa

Cocoa applications are specifically developed for Mac OS X. Cocoa applications are incompatible with older Macintosh operating systems and therefore will not run on Mac OS 9. Cocoa applications take advantage of all of Mac OS X's modern OS features, such as advance memory management, preemptive multitasking, symmetric multiprocessing, and the Aqua interface. Apple evangelizes Cocoa for its modern object-oriented programming techniques and rapid application development tools, which make application development significantly faster and easier than for Carbon. Some examples of Cocoa applications are OS X's Mail and Preview applications as well as Netopia's Timbuktu for Mac OS X.

Carbon

The greatest advantage of the Carbon application environment is that developers can build applications that run in either Mac OS 9 or OS X. When running within OS X, Carbon applications take advantage of most of OS X's modern OS features, including the Aqua interface. In order for Carbon applications to run within Mac OS 9, the CarbonLib library must be present within the Extensions folder within the Mac OS 9 System Folder. Some examples of Carbon applications are AppleWorks 6.1, Acrobat Reader 5.0, and Quicken 2003. Ironically, some Carbon applications do not run under Mac OS 9. The most prominent is Microsoft's Office Version X for Mac.

Packages and bundles

A package, sometimes referred to as a bundle, is a single-icon, point-and-click representation of an application. Just like previous Classic applications, Mac OS X's Carbon and Cocoa applications can be comprised of multiple subordinate files and resources. In the GUI, all these subordinate pieces are neatly wrapped up into a representation of a single executable file for the end user. To view the contents of an application package, simply hold down the Control key while highlighting the Carbon or Cocoa application icon. You are then provided the option to show the package's contents. For illustration purposes, Figure 1-1 depicts the contents of Internet Explorer for Mac OS X.

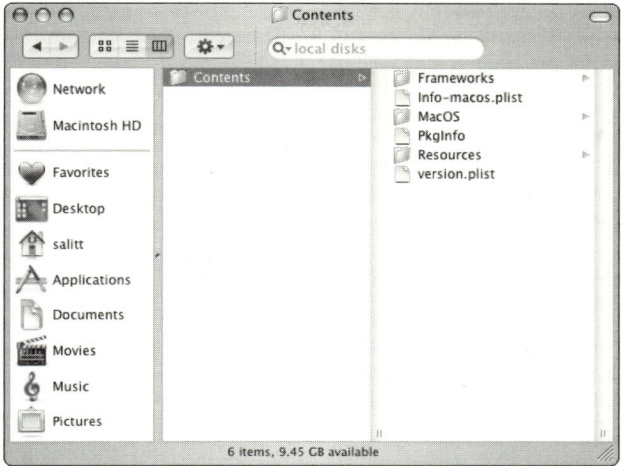

Figure 1-1: Internet Explorer's package contents.

Frameworks

Mac OS X frameworks are analogous to Mac OS 9 shared libraries in that they both contain dynamically loading code that is shared by multiple applications. Frameworks alleviate the need for applications that contain common code to individually load that code for each instance of those applications running simultaneously. Mac OS 9's shared libraries can be found within the Extensions folder inside the System Folder. Examples of shared libraries are AppleScript and CarbonLib.

Java

The Mac OS X Java environment is Java 2 Standard Edition–compliant. It can run both Java applications and applets. The key advantage of Java development is that Java applications can run on any platform that contains a cross-compatible Java Virtual Machine.

BSD

The BSD application environment usually deals with command-line executable shell scripts. A shell script is similar to an MS-DOS batch file in that they are both text files that contain a sequence of commands. Interestingly enough, shell scripts do not necessarily have to be executed from the command line. Shell scripts can be implemented within Cocoa applications, allowing them to be executed from the GUI.

Classic

Classic provides OS X with the ability to run a full version of Mac OS 9 in a protected memory space. This compatibility environment enables the user to run most Macintosh legacy software that has not been updated to run natively in OS X. Just as in OS 9, if you have more than one Classic application open at the same time, it is possible that other Classic applications that are working in the background may bog each other down. That is because, just like in Mac OS 9, Classic applications share the Classic environment by using cooperative multitasking.

Additionally, Classic applications do not benefit from protected memory, at least not from each other. This lack of protected memory means that if one Classic application fails, it may make other Classic programs that are open fail as well (or make them unreliable). But, thanks to Darwin, in the event that an offending program within Classic causes the application environment to crash, the Mach microkernel safely terminates the process without negative consequences for other native OS X applications that are running. Conversely, a problem in a Mac OS X application does not affect the Classic environment or any Classic applications. When a Classic program fails, Apple states that you need to restart the entire Classic environment and all the Classic programs you were using.

Note   According to Apple, the Classic application environment will function with a minimum installation of Mac OS 9.1. However, Apple strongly recommends that Mac OS 9 be upgraded to its latest iteration, which at the time of this writing is Mac OS 9.2.2. If not, you will minimally need to update the Mac OS 9 Startup Disk control panel. This update is located on the Mac OS X Installer Disc 1 CD in a folder titled Utilities. This update provides the ability to select a Mac OS X system folder as a valid startup OS. Also, if you intend to use QuickTime within Classic, you will need to update it to Version 6.0.3.

Installation Considerations for Mac OS X

Now that we have reviewed the core technologies of Mac OS X, let's focus on its installation process. Although Mac OS X has a very structured installation process, several variations of installation are available. The user's needs dictate the appropriate installation strategy. However, before any Mac OS X implementation can take place, it is necessary to evaluate the target computer to see whether it meets Apple's official hardware requirements.

Hardware requirements of OS 10.3

Apple's minimum hardware requirements for Mac OS 10.3 include a factory-shipped NewWorld Architecture G3 Macintosh CPU with 128MB of RAM, 2GB of available hard disk space, and Apple-supplied video option. In Mac OS 10.3, Apple has dropped support for beige hardware and PowerBooks that do not have built-in USB ports. The Apple factory-shipped video display cards/options are IXMicro, ATI, and nVidia. As for third-party hardware, Apple states that OS X natively supports many third-party hardware devices, although some devices may require additional driver updates from their respective manufacturers to utilize a products full feature set. Also, if the Classic environment is used, Mac OS 9.2.*x* requires another 320MB hard drive space and another 64MB of RAM.

Note   A SCSI chain that works with Mac OS 9 may not work with Mac OS X. AppleCare Knowledge Base article 106147 states that OS X is less tolerant to improper SCSI termination than OS 9. Additionally, if a hard disk of greater capacity than 8GB is installed in a Revision A, B, C, or D iMac, Mac OS X must be installed within the first 8GB of the primary hard disk.

Qualified Mac models

Mac OS X can be installed on the following models if they have enough RAM and disk space:

   ✦ Power Mac G5 (all)

   ✦ Power Mac G4 (all)

   ✦ Power Mac G4 cube

- ✦ Power Mac G3 (Blue & White only)
- ✦ PowerBook G4
- ✦ PowerBook G3 (must include built-in USB port)
- ✦ iMac (all)
- ✦ iBook (all)

Preparing for the installation of OS X

After you have deemed that the target hardware meets OS X's minimum hardware requirements, you need to verify that the target computer's firmware is up to date. Firmware is programming that tells a computer's hardware how to behave. Starting with the iMac, Macintosh computers have used a firmware-upgradeable hardware design. This design element is a component of what is referred to as NewWorld Architecture. The Power Mac's firmware is inserted into a programmable (flashable) read-only memory (PROM). This programmable firmware approach enables Apple to fix technical issues via patches and upgrades like any other software. As a result, this innovation allows Apple to achieve greater hardware stability and overall improved system performance. Using a utility referred to as a Flash-ROM updater, firmware can be upgraded (sometimes referred to as revved). The Mac OS 10.3 installer alerts you if your systems firmware is out of date. You can also determine your systems firmware by running Apple System Profiler. Apple's latest firmware may be included on the Mac OS X Install Disc 1 CD. It can also be obtained either through Mac OS 9's built-in Software Update mechanism or the following Web address www.info.apple.com/support/downloads.html.

Note　All system firmware updaters released to date by Apple are available via Mac OS 9 applications only. It is not recommended to update a system's firmware using the Classic application environment in lieu of booting directly from Mac OS 9.

Installation strategies for OS X

OS X has three installation strategies, each with its own advantages and disadvantages. Common to all three strategies is the requirement that the install partition needs to be formatted as an Extended (HFS+) or a Unix File System (UFS) volume. An HFS+-formatted volume's single biggest advantage is that it is *case preserving*. All Macintosh desktop OSs to date have used file systems that have been dependent on case-preserving formatted volumes (this includes the old HFS format as well).

The opposite of the case-preserving format is the case-sensitive format. With the case-sensitive format, it is possible to have multiple files named identically in the same location/folder/directory. The only thing that would differentiate the files to the naked eye is the varied use of uppercase characters. For example, it is possible to have individual files named DOG, DoG, Dog, dOg, doG, dOG, and dog located in the same folder.

As mentioned previously, OS X also supports another format referred to as the Unix File System (UFS), although it isn't the preferred format because it does not support AirPort networking and is case sensitive. In addition, UFS volumes do not show up when booted from Mac OS 9, their volume names cannot be customized, and, in order to run the Classic application environment, Mac OS 9 and its applications must be installed on a separate HFS+ formatted volume. Apple states that "a UFS format may be desired for developing Unix-based applications *within* OS X," and you should not choose this format unless you specifically need it. Apple also states that the UFS format should not be used if your Mac OS X installation destination is a G3 Blue & White. Finally, bootable UFS volumes can be made via the Mac OS X installer only, and not via Disk Utility.

Single partition

A single-partition installation combines OS X and OS 9 on the same partition/logical volume. Its primary advantage is that it is the quickest and easiest of the Mac OS X installation strategies. Another advantage of the single-partition installation is that Mac OS X can be installed on top of an existing Mac OS 9–prepared hard drive. Apple ships OS X–installed Macs in a single-partition installation.

Separate partitions

A separate-partition installation installs OS X and OS 9 on two separate partitions on the same hard drive or on two entirely separate hard disks. The main advantage of the separate partition strategy is that it provides a safety net in the event that the OS X portion becomes damaged. By separating OS 9 and OS X, you can easily erase and reinstall the OS X portion while preserving the OS 9 portion. This modular approach was initially Apple's recommended strategy for OS X installation prior to shipping OS X–preinstalled Macs.

The separate-partitions strategy is the most cautious way to migrate from Mac OS 9 to OS X, although it does require the greatest effort. To set up a separate-partitions system, you need to back up all data on your existing hard disk and reformat it into two partitions using the Disk Utility application included on the Mac OS X Install Disc 1 CD.

An alternate way to build a separate-partitions system is to install a second hard drive, if your Mac has built-in support for it. If your Mac does not have built-in support for this, it may be possible to install a second hard drive by means of a third-party OS X–compatible SCSI or IDE PCI host adapter card. Never take for granted that you have the latest firmware for your third-party or Apple-supplied SCSI or IDE PCI host adapter card. You should always check with the manufacturer's Web site. Lastly, installation of OS X on USB or FireWire hard drives and on removable media is unsupported.

Note   Article 106220 in the AppleCare Knowledge Base, states that if multiple versions of OS X are installed on the same Mac, the computer may be unable to select a desired startup system folder.

Mac OS X only

A Mac OS X–only installation is identical to a single-partition installation, with the exception that this install strategy does not include an OS 9 installation. Although you only have to deal with one operating system, you face some limitations. Not only is the Classic environment gone, but also some system functionality from OS 9 is still missing from OS X. In addition, some troubleshooting and administration tasks are better suited to OS 9 than to OS X.

Tip   You can install Mac OS 9 separately, after OS X has been installed. If, after you install OS X only, you change your mind and decide that you want to use the Classic application environment, you will need to do as follows. If your system can boot OS 9, first, run the Mac OS 9 Installer that came with your Macintosh, and select the Clean Installation option. This will not harm any existing data on you hard disk. After the installation is complete, you will want to boot your system selecting your newly installed Mac OS 9 System Folder and run the Software Update control panel in order to acquire any recent OS 9 updates. For those systems that can't boot Mac OS 9, you will need to use the Software Restore CD that shipped with your computer. Any Mac OS 9 updates will need to be downloaded from Apple Software Updates Web site and installed manually.

Gather setup information

Regardless if you are upgrading from Mac OS 9 or Mac OS X, if you want your computer to use the same Internet and network settings before you install Mac OS X on it, you need to make a note of your system's current preferences. Depending upon how you connect to the Internet, one or more of the following settings may need to be recorded. In Mac OS 9, the settings are located in the AppleTalk, File Sharing, TCP/IP, Remote Access, Modem, and Internet control panels. In Mac OS X, the settings are located in the Internet, Network, and Sharing Preference panes as well as in the Internet Connect application. Additionally, you may need to get the settings for your email account from your email reader application.

Hard drive backup

To back up today's large hard drives, you need some type of storage device that can accommodate the capacity of your backup. These devices can include, but are not limited to, another internal IDE or SCSI hard drive, a FireWire or USB hard drive, a tape drive, or a recordable optical or magnetic media drive. It is possible to back up to a Finder-accessible volume by simply dragging the desired contents to the destination disk. But it's more reliable to use a dedicated backup utility, such as Retrospect from Dantz Development, because it can verify the successful outcome of a backup. Another benefit of Retrospect is that it can compress the contents of a backup, increasing overall storage efficiency, requiring less backup media. Finally, depending upon the type of backup being implemented, Retrospect can also provide a search catalog that simplifies the task of locating and restoring specific contents from a backup.

Preparing the destination volume

After you've backed up, you are ready to prepare your intended destination volume for Mac OS X installation, employing one of the installation strategies previously described. To do so, you need to use the Disk Utility application located on the Mac OS X Install Disc 1 CD. Disk Utility is covered in Chapter 19. Otherwise, you simply need to update your hard disk's existing driver.

A driver is a piece of software that enables an operating system to interface or control a hardware device. In general, the operation of driver software is requires no action from the end user. All hard drives use driver software. It is imperative that the hard disk driver is compatible with the Mac OS version in use or problems will result. Updating driver software is a quick process and generally doesn't adversely affect drive contents. Though for safety's sake remember to back up, before updating your hard disk's driver.

If you elect to use the single partition strategy with a preexisting installation of Mac OS 9 on an Apple factory supplied hard drive, the Mac OS X Installer updates the driver for you. If you're not installing on an Apple-branded hard disk, and third-party formatting software was used to prepare it, you need investigate if the formatting software is Mac OS X–compatible. If not, you need to use formatting software that is compatible. Typically, an initialization is required, but some third-party formatting software can update and overwrite an existing driver without the need of an initialization.

Mac OS X installation CDs

After the destination volume is prepared, you are ready to run the Mac OS X Installer application. The Mac OS X installer is comprised of three CDs. The first disk is the only disk that can install a bootable Mac OS X system. The first disk can install all available installation components. The subsequent other two disks can be run independently of the first disk on an existing installation of Mac OS X, but they only facilitate an installation on a subset of the components available when using the first installer disk. Disk 2 provides facility to install Additional Applications, Print Drivers, Language Translations, Additional Asian Fonts, and the BSD Subsystem. Disk 3 provides facility to install Fonts for Additional Languages, Additional Speech Voices, and the X11 Window System that is used by some Unix applications.

Running the Mac OS X installer

To install OS X you are required to boot from the Mac OS X Install CD Disc 1. You can boot from the Mac OS X install CD in the following four ways:

✦ Boot the Macintosh while holding down the C key.

✦ Use the Startup Manager. To activate the Startup Manager, hold down the Option key at startup. You are then presented with a graphical interface that enables you to select it as a startup disk.

✦ Select the Mac OS X Install CD Disc 1 by using either Mac OS 9's Startup Disk control panel or Mac OS X's Startup Disk Preference pane.

✦ You can boot from a OS X install CD by inserting the CD while running either OS 9 or OS X and locating and double-clicking the Install Mac OS X application that requires the authorization of an administrator's account.

Figure 1-2 shows the Restart button in the Install Mac OS X window. When the computer starts from the Mac OS X Install CD Disc 1, the Installer program starts automatically and presents a series of screens that ask you to make certain choices as described in the following text.

Figure 1-2: The Restart button in the Install Mac OS X program restarts the computer with the Mac OS X Install CD to begin installation.

Select Language

The Mac OS X installer supports installations for many languages. Select the appropriate language for the remainder of the installation process and click the Continue button.

Introduction

The Introduction screen is a welcome screen that acts as a prelude to the rest of the installation process. No action is required except for clicking the Continue button.

Read Me

The Read Me screen presents the same contents that can be found in the Read Before You Install document on the Mac OS X install CD Disc 1. Skipping this document is tempting, but the information provided may be important, so you should at least skim it. After reading the information, click the Continue button.

License

The License screen presents you with OS X's Software Licensing Agreement. The license agreement is filled with legalese, but you may want to look through it so that you know what you're agreeing to. For example, one provision states that you may only install the software on one computer at a time. You must click the Continue button, and a second confirmation screen appears, requesting you to click Agree before you can continue forward with the installation process.

Tip Apple's lawyers think that the License Agreement is important, so they provide the convenience of a pop-up menu where you can choose to view it in a language other than English.

Select Destination

The Select Destination screen enables you to choose the destination volume for your Mac OS X installation. This screen also contains a button that says Options as shown in Figure 1-3. Click the Options button and a sheet appears, providing the choices to Upgrade Mac OS X, Archive and Install, and Erase and Install. Here's what those options mean:

✦ **Upgrade Mac OS X:** Upgrades an existing installation of Mac OS X, while preserving current applications, fonts, and preferences.

✦ **Archive and Install:** Moves existing System files to a folder named Previous System and then installs a fresh copy of Mac OS X. On the surface, it looks similar to the Mac OS 9 Installer's Clean Install option. Though similar to Mac OS 9, once a system folder has been designated as previous, it can't be used as a valid startup OS. The Preserve Users and Network Settings is a suboption under Archive and Install, which facilitates the preservation of user accounts and home folders and network settings.

✦ **Erase and Install:** Provides a clean slate. As with the Disk Utility, it erases your hard disk. *Be warned*, when installing OS X on a preexisting installation of OS 9, do not select the option to erase and format the disk from within the OS X installer. Doing this erases the existing Mac OS 9 installation as well as all your user's applications and documents. The Erase and Install option also allows you to choose your disk format: MAC OS Extended (Journaled) or Unix File System. Selecting the journaling option may help protect the data on your hard disk from unforeseen failures such as system freezing or power outages. The downsides are that it slightly slows down hard disk performance and may be incompatible with some disk utilities. As of this writing to recover data that is on a hard disk that employs journaling, you will need to do so from the command line, which is covered in the Apple Knowledge Base Article 107248.

Tip According to Apple Knowledge Base Article 106442, if there is a sole ATA/IDE hard drive in your Mac and the Select a Destination screen does not display an available hard disk to install to, you need to verify that the intended target ATA/IDE drive is configured as a master drive on the bus.

After making your selections, click the Continue button.

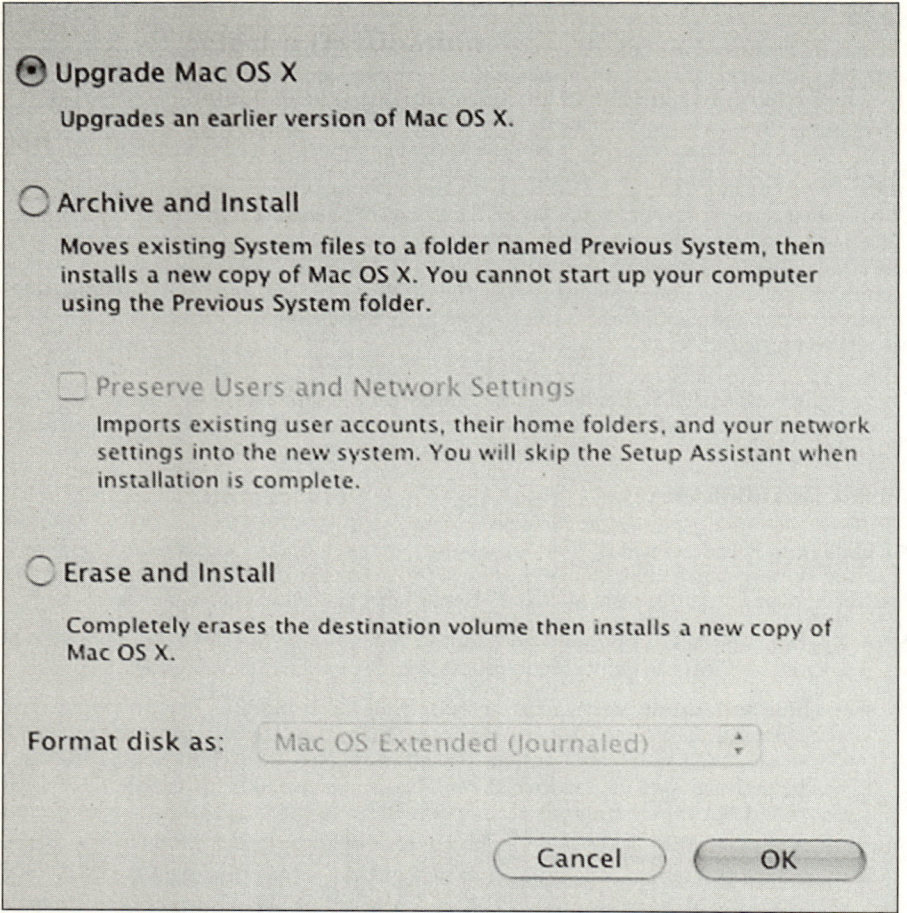

Figure 1-3: Though the Options pane does not provide the partition customizing abilities of the Disk Utility, it is the only place that you can make a bootable volume.

Installation Types

The Installation Types screen provides two choices for installation types. The choices are Easy Install and Custom Install. By default, the Mac OS X installer starts with Easy Install that is comprised of the packages essential System Software, BSD Subsystem, Additional Applications, Print Drivers, Additional Asian Fonts, and Language Translations. After choosing your Install type, click the Continue button.

> **Note**   Custom Install gives you the option of installing Essential System Software only. Remember that the BSD Subsystem option is a required component for proper network functionality in Mac OS X. If you do not install the BSD Subsystem initially, it can be installed from the Mac OS X Install Disc 2 CD as noted previously.

Stopping the Mac OS X Installer

Until you click the Install button to get the installation process under way, you can stop installation by choosing Installer⇨Quit Installer. If you do this, the installer displays a dialog that asks you to confirm that you really want to stop installation. Click the Restart button in this dialog to have installation stop and your computer restart. When you hear your computer's startup chime, hold down the Option key to select a valid startup disk other than the Mac OS X Install CD Disk 1. To start up using the Mac OS X CD, hold down the C key as the computer starts up. You can also eject the Mac OS X Install CD Disk 1, by depressing the mouse button during restart.

Caution After the installation process has begun, terminating the Installer intentionally or unintentionally may leave your computer in an unstable state. The Installer displays an alert informing you of this danger and provides a chance to resume installation.

Installing

The OS X installer will now begin to verify the condition of the destination hard disk. This process can be skipped by clicking the Skip button. Once the disk has been verified or skipped, the installer will commence the actual OS install, which will last between fifteen minutes to an hour. For the most part, this is an automated process. Depending upon the installation type and what is being installed, the installer will prompt you when necessary for the insertion of the other two Mac OS X Install CDs.

Finish Up

At this point, the installer performs several optimization and cleanup tasks to complete the installation process.

Using the Setup Assistant

After the Mac OS X install process has been completed, the computer automatically reboots. Next, Mac OS X's Setup Assistant automatically launches. A presented welcome screen appears to guide you through the process of procuring an Apple ID for purchasing Apple products and services online, registering your OS software, and connecting to the Internet.

Welcome

The Welcome screen is where you select the country or region in which the Macintosh will be used. After making your selection, click the Continue button.

Personalize your settings

The Personalize Your Settings screen is where you select the keyboard layout that is appropriate for the country or region in which the Macintosh will be used. You can change the preference later, after you are into the computer. Make your language selection and click the Continue button.

Your Apple ID

Eerily, reminiscent of Microsoft's Passport, an Apple ID lets you make one-click purchases from the iTunes Music, iPhoto, and the Apple Stores. If you already possess a .Mac membership, use that as your Apple ID. Otherwise you can specify your own ID, have the Setup Assistant create one for you, or skip the process entirely. If you do elect to create an Apple ID, you will also be provided a 60-day trial membership to .Mac. .Mac is a combination of software and online tools that can enhance your "Internet experience," while using your Mac. After making your selections, click the Continue button.

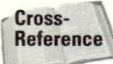

Cross-Reference For more details on .Mac see Chapter 18.

Registration information

This is the product registration that is automatically sent to Apple when you connect the Mac to the Internet. You cannot leave anything blank except the email address and the company or school. You skip this screen by typing the ⌘-Q key combination, which takes you directly to the Create Your Account screen and automatically configures your network settings for DHCP. You are also reminded to register your product. Otherwise, after completing the Registration Information screen, click the Continue button.

A Few More Questions

The screen is comprised of a demographic survey, asking whether you use the computer at home, school, business, and so on; what you do; and whether you want Apple and other companies to contact you. After making your selections, click the Continue button.

Thank You

The Thank You screen apprises you that your registration information will be sent once you connect to the Internet. At this point, if you need to make any modifications to any of the information input in any previous Setup Assistant screen click the Go Back button and do so; otherwise, click the Continue button.

Create Your Account

After you have submitted the necessary registration information, you will need to set up your user account. Chapter 14 reviews user accounts in detail, but for now suffice it to say that the information you provide will be necessary to perform administrative functions within Mac OS X. When creating your account, you will need to specify both a Name and a Short Name. A Short Name is exactly what it sounds like—a short name. It alleviates the need for typing out your whole name. You will appreciate your short name when user authentication is requested by certain applications or during certain administrative functions within OS X.

A Short Name is automatically generated when you tab from the Name field to the Short Name field. But don't worry; it can be changed. A short name is all lowercase, has a maximum of eight characters, and cannot contain any spaces or the following characters: < > ' " * { } [ ] ( ) ^ ! \ # | & $? ~

Make sure to pick a Short Name you like, because it can't be changed after the fact. Once you have chosen your short name, you will need to provide a password. Although OS X will accept more than eight characters for this field, it only checks the first eight. The entry last field allows you to provide yourself an optional password hint if desired. Finally, you will need to select a picture that serves as an iconic representation your user account. After making your selections, click the Continue button.

Get Internet Ready

The Get Internet Ready portion of the Setup Assistant provides the option to configure your Mac for Internet access. This screen gives you the choice of setting up trial Internet service with EarthLink, setting up Mac OS X to use your existing Internet service, or not setting up for the Internet at this time. If you choose to set up for your existing Internet service, the Assistant asks for the following information:

✦ **How you connect.** Connect by telephone modem, local network, cable modem, DSL, or AirPort wireless.

✦ **Your Internet Selection.** These details vary depending on your connection method. Use the information gathered earlier from before you installed Mac OS X to help you here.

Get .Mac

Next, the Assistant offers to set up a .Mac account for you. Some of the features a .Mac account provides include an email address, a personal Web site, and storage space on the Internet. You can create a .Mac trial account on the spot, enter a member name and password for an existing .Mac account, or skip the process entirely. After making your selection, click the Continue button.

Now you're ready to connect

After dealing with .Mac, the Assistant advises that it's ready to send your registration and configure your computer. Click Continue. The Assistant connects with Apple to send your registration information. You can cancel the connection and stop sending the registration information by quickly clicking the Cancel button.

Set Up Mail

By default, the Set Up Mail portion of the Setup Assistant uses your .Mac account information for email client configuration. If you do not want to use .Mac as your email service provider, you can manually enter the account information for an alternate email service, or you can skip the process altogether. Once configured, click the Continue button.

Select Time Zone

The Select Time Zone allows you to specify the time zone the computer will be operating in. Clicking your geographic location or typing the name of the closest city where the computer will be located accomplishes this. After making your selection, click the Continue button.

Set the Date and Time

The Set the Date and Time screen lets you to set your computer's clock and calendar. Once completed, click the Continue button.

Thank You

Upon successful registration of the computer, you will be greeted with a screen informing you of such and urging you to enjoy your computer and the Internet.

Running Software Update

It is not uncommon to find that the installer CDs in hand does not contain the most recent version of a software product. Usually, software updates can be obtained via a manufacturer's Web site. Apple simplifies this process by automating the update process upon initial OS X startup. If by some chance this does not occur, the process can be manually activated via the Software Update preference panel. This will be reviewed in detail in Chapter 13. Figure 1-4 shows OS X's Software Update preference panel, an excellent tool for obtaining the latest updates for Mac OS X.

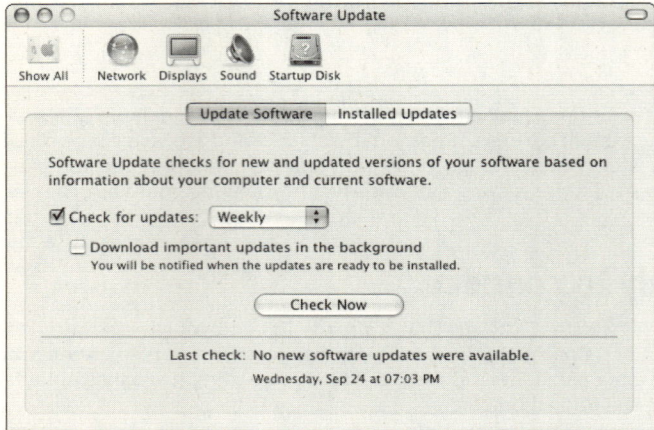

Figure 1-4: No installation is complete without checking for product updates.

As you can see, it is not a difficult task to build an OS X box. Taking the time to evaluate your installation considerations and applying the appropriate OS X installation strategy goes a long way toward ensuring a smooth migration from a previous Mac OS version.

Summary

Mac OS X is a Unix operating system. It is built upon open standards, providing preemptive multitasking, symmetric multiprocessing, protected memory, and advanced memory management, as well as world-class graphics capabilities. Though it may be complex in design on the inside, on the surface, it retains its world-class usability and visual appearance that customers expect of the Mac OS.

✦   ✦   ✦

Exploring Aqua GUI

This chapter familiarizes you with the basic environment of Mac OS X. As with all Graphical User Interfaces (GUIs), Mac OS X consists of windows, menus, icons, and controls. Apple calls this environment *Aqua*. It is a consistent, elegant interface, rich in color and depth; yet it is possible to get lost as you explore the world of Aqua. In addition to the Aqua environment, Mac OS X enables you to work concurrently in Classic, an emulation of the environment from Mac OS 9. In the Classic environment, the menu bar, windows, and controls look and operate somewhat differently than their Mac OS X counterparts.

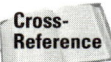
Cross-Reference   Classic is covered in greater depth in Chapter 17.

By the conclusion of this chapter, you will have a greater understanding of the basic elements of the OS, and most importantly, a stronger grasp of the terms and phrases used in following chapters. Before describing menus, windows, icons, and controls, this chapter explains how you start a session in the Mac OS X environment and concludes by explaining how you log out, restart, or shut down to end a Mac OS X session.

Starting Up and Logging In

Of course, when you first turn on your computer, it must go through a startup process. Startup begins with the Apple startup chime, a signal that the most basic hardware elements are operational. After the chime, the remaining hardware tests continue as the computer tests the hard drive for basic errors. After this, the remaining hardware elements activate as the full operating system software loads into RAM from a disk.

Starting up your computer

You start up a Macintosh by pressing any of the following:

- ✦ The Power button on the computer

- ✦ The Power key on the keyboard, if the keyboard has one

- ✦ The Power button on most Apple flat-panel displays (on some older display models, the power button only turns the display on or off)

Once upon a time, the familiar Happy Mac icon was displayed in the center of the screen while the Mac OS loaded. Mac OS 10.2 retired Happy Mac, replacing it with a solid grey Apple logo. A spinning set of bars below the Apple logo indicates that the computer is busy loading the core OS elements. Figure 2-1 illustrates this stage of the startup process.

Figure 2-1: A gray Apple logo with a spinning set of bars is among the first stages of the startup process.

Soon a Mac OS X greeting appears together with a gauge that measures startup progress, and a sequence of brief messages reports steps in the startup process. The spinning disk changes to an arrow-shaped pointer. This pointer tracks mouse movement, but clicking the mouse button has no effect at this time. Figure 2-2 illustrates this part of the startup process.

Note   You can set some older Macintosh computer models to start up with Mac OS 9 instead of Mac OS X. In this case, a Mac OS 9 greeting appears during startup and the Mac OS X environment is not available after startup. Chapter 13 explains how to select the system you want to use for startup.

Figure 2-2: A progress gauge and a series of messages report on later stages of the startup process.

Logging in to Mac OS X

After the startup process has begun, OS X loads all basic system elements, and completes activation of kernel (background) operations, a login procedure begins. The login procedure is a means of identifying yourself to your computer. This is both a means of ensuring that your computer activates your particular environment (called your user account), and it's an effort to keep unauthorized people from using the computer. The login procedure is mandatory but can be automated. In fact, Mac OS X is initially configured for automatic login and remains that way unless someone sets it for manual login. Upon completion of the login process, the appropriate user account is activated and the user can interact with his or her OS X environment.

What login accomplishes

The login procedure accomplishes two things.

- ✦ It proves that you are authorized to use the computer.

- ✦ It establishes which user you are, and this user identity determines what you can see and do on the computer.

Your user identity is especially important if you or an administrator has set up your computer for multiple users, such as members of a family or several workers in an office, because each user has personal preference settings and private storage areas. For example, you may prefer a different background picture on the screen, and you may not want other users to have access to the data you store on the computer or all the application programs you use. As mentioned in the opening chapter, Mac OS X is a truly multi-user operating system. Since more that one user account can be set up on a particular computer, it's important to identify each user via a login. You can find information on setting up Mac OS X for multiple users in Chapter 14.

If you have left your computer configured for the default automatic login, you do not get the distinct honor of seeing the login screen. After the startup sequence, the computer just activates your user account, and all elements of your account are available. If you have configured your computer for manual login, Mac OS X displays a login window, and you must provide a user account name and password before the startup process can continue. Instead of logging in, you may shut down or restart your computer by clicking the appropriate button in the window. The login window will show one of two screens. Each is covered under the following headings. Figure 2-3 shows examples of both types of login window.

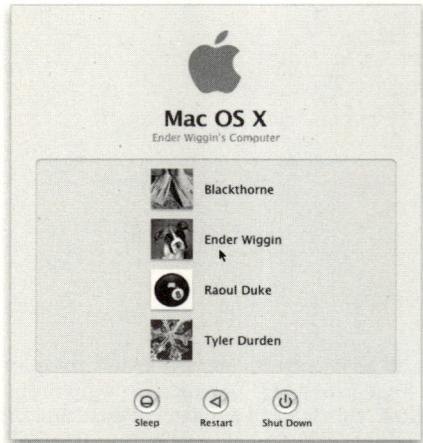

Login window with user choices

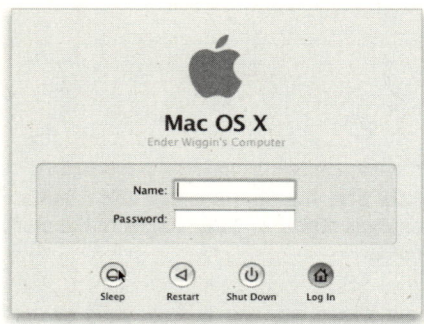

Login window without user choices

Figure 2-3: When logging in to Mac OS X, you may get to select a user account from a list (left) or you may have to type a valid account name (right).

Logging in with a list of user accounts

If the login window shows a list of users, log in by following these steps:

1. **Use the mouse to click your account name.** The initial login window contents change to show your account only, along with a space for entering a password. Figure 2-4 shows an example of this phase of the login process.

Note
   If your user account name is not listed, you can still log in. To do this, click Other at the bottom of the list of account names and continue at Step 1 in the next procedure. If the account list doesn't include Other, you can't log in by entering an account name. Get help from the person who configured the computer for multiple users.

2. **Type your password.** You can't read what you type because, for privacy, the password displays it as a sequence of dots. Capitalization counts in the password; upper and lowercase letters are not interchangeable. If you don't know the password for the selected user account, click the Go Back button to return to the initial login window and select a different user. If you don't know the password for any account, check with the person who configured your computer for multiple users.

3. **Press Return (or Enter) on the keyboard or use the mouse to click Log In.** The login window fades, and soon the Mac OS X desktop and menu bar appear, possibly together with windows, icons, and the Dock. You can read more about the menu bar and the other objects in later sections of this chapter.

Figure 2-4: After clicking one of the account names listed in the initial login window, you must enter the password for the account.

Logging in without a list of user accounts

If the login window shows blank spaces for user account name and password, as shown previously in Figure 2-3, follow these steps to log in:

1. **Type your user account name, press the Tab key, and then type your password.** You can read the name you type, but for privacy, the password displays as a sequence of dots. Capitalization matters only in the password field. If you don't know both your account name and password, check with the person who configured your computer for multiple users.

2. **Press Return (or Enter) on the keyboard or use the mouse to click Log In.** The login window goes away, and soon the Mac OS X menu bar appears, possibly together with windows, icons, and the Dock. You can read more about the menu bar and the other objects in later sections of this chapter.

Dealing with login problems

If the login window shakes back and forth (like someone shaking his head no), either you entered an incorrect password for your specified user account name, or Mac OS X did not recognize the user account name you entered. The Password space clears so that you can retype the password and press Return or click Log In. If you typed a user account name and you need to retype it, press the tab key to highlight the Name space. If you selected a user account from a list, you can select a different account by clicking the Go Back button.

Note   Even if you're the only person who uses your computer, some of the data stored on it is protected so that you can't change it or remove it. This protects the integrity of the operating system (often referred to as protecting users from themselves).

Why Is Security Important?

As you do more and more important work on your computers, such as banking, reviewing credit reports, submitting proposals to clients, trading stocks, or writing Mac OS X guidebooks, your computer fills up with critically important and very sensitive information. In addition, most types of high-speed Internet connections keep your Mac available via the Internet 24 hours a day.

Through your DSL or Cable Modem or (cough cough) dial-up service, your Mac is open and available to countless computers around the world. Because of its basis in Unix (a fact that Apple marketing brings up at every turn), the security options you have with OS X are varied and powerful. That being said, Mac OS X is more open to misuse *because* of its Unix base. Unix has had over 30 years of evolution to enable the discovery of both loopholes and solutions to security.

Other users can turn the security options on or off; configure your computer for total remote control via the Internet, and guess your password more easily than you might imagine. As a result, your hot new Mac can become the new best friend of a hacker, who can steal or erase your documents as well as launch attacks that crash your machine or network,. Unix is a very powerful tool. Like a hammer or circular saw, Unix can build, but it can also destroy. The first line of defense against any type of unauthorized access is a tough password that you keep secret. For advice on picking a good password, see Appendix A.

Meeting Your Environment

Once you complete login, you are ushered into the world of Mac OS X. Mac presents that world to you — complete with icons, folders, menus, and the desktop — through an application known as the Finder. The Finder, which is the core application at the heart of a user's interaction with the OS is covered in detail in Chapter 3. The following headings explore the various commonly seen elements throughout the operating system.

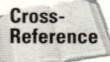

Cross-Reference   The Dock is covered in more detail later in this chapter. For more on applications, see Chapters 4 and 5. For more on system settings, see Chapter 13. To learn more about relaunching the Finder, see Chapter 22.

Note   The Finder is not the same as Find. Find is a search application, designed to help users find documents, whereas the Finder is the system's main program that helps launch other applications (like Find or Safari), and allows for exploration and viewing of drives, disks, and the folders they contain.

Investigating Menus

The Mac OS uses menus to present lists of commands or attributes. You can issue a command or put an attribute into effect by choosing it from its menu using the mouse. Menus can take up a lot of space on the screen, so they're normally hidden except for their titles. When you want to see one, click its title with the mouse.

Choosing a command or attribute generally changes the state of an object. This object may be something you selected in advance, such as some text that you want to make a different size. The object of a menu command may instead be an implicit part of the command, such as displaying a list of general preference settings when you choose the Preferences command from an available menu.

Although you always see menu titles in the menu bar at the top of the screen, menus can also appear outside the menu bar. For example, a pop-up menu may appear inside of a dialog. You can see that these menus are available through the clever display of a distinctive arrow. See Figure 2-7 for an example. In addition, the Mac OS can display contextual menus as a response to a Control-click on a particular object. The options and actions presented in the contextual menu are populated according to what the selected object is.

Using the menu bar

The menus in the menu bar at the top of the screen contain commands that are relevant to the application you are using at the time. The menus may also contain attributes that apply to objects that you work with in the application. Menu titles appear in the menu bar, and you can use the mouse to display one menu at a time beneath its title. Figure 2-5 shows the menu bar as it appears initially in Mac OS X, with the application menu displayed.

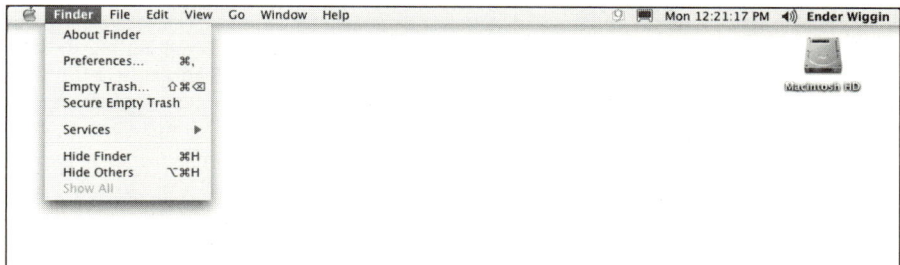

Figure 2-5: The menu bar is a permanent fixture at the top of the screen. Note the application menu's title shows the name of the active application, in this case Finder.

To use the menu bar, you position the mouse pointer over a menu title and click or press the mouse button. The menu opens beneath the menu title so that you can see the items in it and choose one, if you like.

To choose a menu item, position the pointer over it, highlighting it. Then click the mouse button. The menu item you choose flashes briefly and then the menu fades away. The menu item's effect is then applied.

Some menus have submenus within them. These menus are known as pullout menus. They are indicated by a distinctive black arrow pointing to the right. When your mouse navigates over a menu the arrow, the pullout menu appears, displaying its options. Figure 2-6 shows a pullout menu at work.

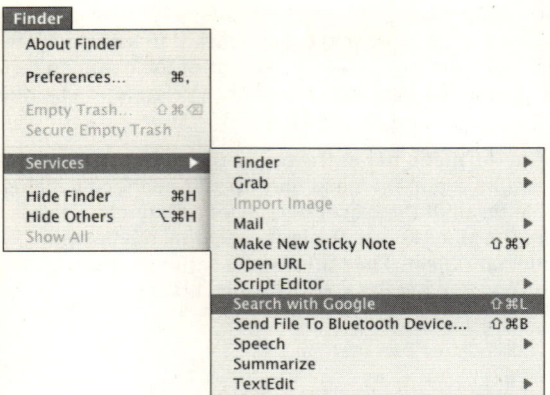

Figure 2-6: Pullout menus are a useful addendum to standard menus.

When a command is not available or applicable to the current circumstances, it is dimmed out. A dimmed item's text is a faded translucent gray, rather than the normal black solid text. An example of an unavailable command.

In Mac OS X, unlike previous Mac OS versions, an active menu stays open indefinitely until you click again. With a menu displayed, you can leave your finger off the mouse button and move the pointer up and down the menu, highlighting each menu item as the pointer passes over it. You can close a menu without choosing an item from it by clicking the mouse button when the pointer is on the menu's title or anywhere outside the menu.

While looking at any menu in the menu bar, you can activate a different menu by moving the pointer over the menu's title. You can click any menu item you see to choose it, or click outside any menu to stop looking at menus in the menu bar.

Tip   If you're used to the way Macintosh menus originally worked, you can still use them that way. If you click a menu title and keep holding down the mouse button while moving the pointer, the menu goes away as soon as you release the mouse button. To choose a menu item, just click and hold, move to the menu item, and release. With this method, you click only once, but you have to keep pressing the mouse button.

Understanding standard Mac OS X menus

In most Mac OS X applications, the left side of the menu bar includes several of the following standard menus:

Why One Menu Bar?

The Mac OS has a permanent menu bar at the top of the screen for several reasons. One reason is that a menu bar at the top of the screen is an easy target to hit with the mouse. You can quickly slide the mouse pointer to the top of the screen, where it automatically stops at the menu bar. If the menu bar were at the top of a window in the middle of the screen (as in Microsoft Windows), you would have to take more time to position the pointer carefully over the menu bar.

A second reason is that having a permanent menu bar at the top of the screen gives you a reliable place for every application's commands. If each window on the screen had its own menu bar, you'd have to think about which one you wanted to use. Of course, Apple's method can also result in confusion, as users must keep track of which application is active and responding to menu commands.

✦ **Apple:** At the left end of the menu bar and has a miniature solid Apple logo for its title (as compared to the six-color striped Apple menu logo in OS 9). Use this menu to get basic information about your Macintosh, change system preference settings, change Dock preference settings, or change the network location. You can also use this menu to open a recently used application or document, or to force applications to quit. In addition, the Apple menu has commands for putting the computer into sleep mode, restarting it, shutting it down, or logging out of your user account.

✦ **Application menu:** Next to the Apple menu and has the name of the application that you are currently using as its title. This menu includes commands that apply to the application as a whole. Use the application menu to get information about the current application, change preference settings, get services from other applications (as described in Chapter 11), hide the current application or all others, or quit the application when you are done using it.

✦ **File:** Next to the application menu and contains commands that affect a whole document (or file), such as New, Open, Close, Save, and Print. Usually, applications that don't have documents don't have a File menu. More information on most of these commands is available in Chapter 5; the Print command is covered in Chapter 9.

✦ **Edit:** To the right of the File menu and contains commands that you can use to change a document's contents, such as Undo, Cut, Copy, Paste, and Select All. Read more about these commands in Chapter 5.

✦ **Window:** Enables you to zoom (maximize) or minimize the active window, or bring all the listed windows in front of windows belonging to other applications. The Window menu lists other windows that belong to the same application and also may have additional commands for window manipulation. Zooming and minimizing windows are discussed later in this chapter.

✦ **Help:** Gives you access to onscreen help. This menu is located immediately to the right of the last application-specific menu in the menu bar. In some cases, the application may have its own help menu and the OS X Help menu may not be present. If this is true and you want to open the OS X Help, you can either switch to an Apple-made application such as the Finder, or use the keyboard shortcut of the Command-? keys. Chapter 8 has more information on the Help menu.

The right side of the menu bar is typically populated with these system-specific menus:

✦ **Clock menu:** On the right side of the menu bar and has a digital clock or an analog clock as its title. Click this menu to see the current date as well as the time, to switch between digital and analog clocks, and to open the Date & Time pane of the System Preferences application, which is covered in Chapter 13.

✦ **Sound menu:** Normally appears next to the clock in the menu bar and enables you to adjust the computer's volume. This menu has a speaker icon as its title, and it indicates the current sound level. A setting in the Sound pane of the System Preferences application determines whether the sound menu appears in the menu bar, as described in Chapter 13.

✦ **AirPort menu:** Normally appears if your computer has an AirPort wireless networking card installed. This menu's title icon shows four arcs (resembling a baseball diamond) that indicate the strength of the wireless network signal. You can use the AirPort menu to join a wireless network, create a wireless network, or turn the AirPort card off and on. You can also use this menu to open the Internet Connect application, which we cover in Chapter 6. Chapter 16 covers AirPort in much greater detail.

Each application may omit some of these menus and may add its own menus on the left side, between the Edit menu and the Help menu. The menus on the right side of the menu bar may appear in a different order, and you can reorganize them according to your preference. In addition, the menu bar may have more icons with menus on the right side of the menu bar. For example, the menu bar may have a modem icon with a menu and a PPPoE icon, each with a menu for monitoring and controlling Internet connections via modem and PPPoE, as described in Chapter 6.

Tip   Because menu positions are less predictable in Mac OS X than in previous Mac OS versions, be sure to read the menu titles before opening them up! All menus to the right of the application menu may appear in slightly different positions on the menu bar depending on the application you are currently using, because the width of the application menu's title varies according to the length of the application's name. If you aren't careful, you end up searching for Edit commands in the Window menu and vice versa.

Using pop-up menus

A *pop-up menu* appears within a dialog or a control palette when you click the pop-up menu's title. The title may be a text label or an icon, and is marked with a pair of selection arrows to indicate that clicking it displays a pop-up menu. The menu may also be marked with a single arrow pointing to the right. As with the menus in the menu bar, you can only display one pop-up menu at a time. If a pop-up menu is open, it goes away automatically if you click the title of another pop-up menu. Figure 2-7 shows examples of a pop-up menu.

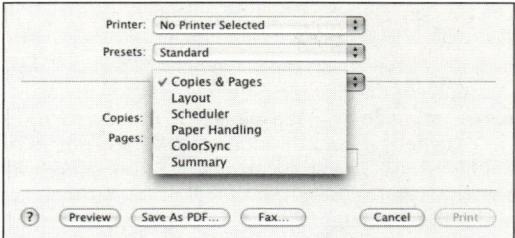

Figure 2-7: An arrowhead marks a pop-up menu in the Print dialog.

Using contextual menus

Rooting through menus to find a particular command isn't much fun. Wouldn't it be better if all you saw were relevant commands? That's the beauty of contextual menus — they offer commands that make sense in a given context. You can display a contextual menu by holding down the Control key while clicking an icon, a window, or some selected text for which you want to choose a command or attribute. The contextual menu lists commands relevant to the item that you Control-click. Figure 2-8 shows an example of a contextual menu for an icon.

You can Control-click one item or a selection of several items. Control-clicking a selection of several items displays a contextual menu of commands that pertain to the whole group. You learn how to make a selection of several items later in this chapter.

Figure 2-8: Pressing the Control key while clicking an item may display a contextual menu.

Tip

With a multibutton mouse or trackball, you can display contextual menus by simply pressing the right button. If your multibutton mouse or trackball does not already work this way, you can program it to simulate a Control-click whenever you press the right button. For instructions on programming a multibutton mouse or trackball, see the manufacturer's documentation. These alternative pointing devices are made by many manufacturers, like Kensington Technology (`www.kensington.com/`), Logitech (`www.logitech.com/`), and others. As of yet, Apple does not make a mulitbutton mouse (Don't ask us why). Before purchasing a multi-button mouse, check with the manufacturer to ensure that Mac OS X supports the device. Third-party multibutton mice are strongly recommended, as a user's speed and control within the OS improves by consolidating control under one hand. This is especially true with the addition of Exposé, which is explored in Chapter 4.

Menu symbols

A variety of symbols may accompany a menu item. A triangle pointing to the right at the end of an item indicates that the menu has a submenu. An ellipsis (...) at the end of the item name indicates that choosing the item brings up a dialog in which you must supply additional information before the command can be completed. The following list summarizes these symbols and their meanings:

✓ **Blue**   Designates an item that is currently selected or an attribute that applies to everything that is currently selected.

— **Italic**   Designates an attribute that applies only to some things that are currently selected.

● **Great**   Designates a document that has unsaved changes; some applications use it instead of ✓ to designate an attribute that applies to everything that is currently selected.

◆ **Docu**   Designates, in some applications, a window that is minimized in the Dock; designates, in the Classic environment's application menu, an application that requires your attention.

▶   Designates a menu item with a submenu.

Other symbols are used to specify keyboard shortcuts for menu items. Pressing a specified combination of keys has the same effect as choosing the menu item. For example, pressing Command-X is equivalent to choosing the Cut command from the Edit menu. The following symbols represent keys:

⌘   Represents the Command key

⇧   Represents the Shift key

⌥   Represents the Option key

⌃   Represents the Control key

⌦   Represents the Delete key

When you use a keyboard shortcut for a command in a menu, the title of the menu may flash briefly to indicate that the command has been issued. Learning these keyboard shortcuts is critical to improving your control over the OS (and impressing your coworkers).

Looking into Windows

A window is literally a portal that displays information for your perusal. There are many different kinds of windows. Each serves a particular function; each offers options for control and interaction. Some windows show the contents of disks and folders. Some windows show the text of a written document, or the content of a photograph. Certain windows alert you to conditions requiring your input. Other windows even offer interaction with tools that are used to modify the contents of other windows. Most windows are rectangular and many are malleable. You can reshape them to maximize your screen real estate. This section describes how different types of Mac OS windows look and operate.

Recognizing different window types

There are several types of Mac OS X windows, and each is designed to display a specific kind of information. Some windows display the files and other items stored on disks. Other window types display the actual contents of files, which may be text, pictures, movies, or other kinds of information. Figure 2-9 shows examples of the different types of Aqua windows. The different types of windows are as follows:

✦ **Finder windows:** A window that shows the content of folders and disks. These windows are generated by the Finder, covered in Chapter 3.

✦ **Document:** A document window displays the content of a particular document, be it a photograph, a movie or text.

✦ **Dialogs:** Windows that display options that you can set and actions you can perform.

✦ **Sheets:** A dialog that applies to, and is attached to, another window. A sheet ensures you won't lose track of which window the dialog applies to.

✦ **Alerts:** Dialogs in which the Mac OS or an application program notifies you of a hazardous situation, a limitation in your proposed course of action, or an error condition.

✦ **Palettes:** Also called panels or utility windows, palettes contain controls or tools or display auxiliary information for the application that you're currently using.

Window controls

As mentioned, windows are portals that display important data. They are made up of numerous control surfaces and other objects, including buttons and more. There are many different types of windows in Mac OS X, as was discussed in the previous chapter, but there are a slew of common control surfaces and buttons available within most windows. Of course, you won't find all types window controls on every kind of window. For example, document windows have all or most of the available controls, whereas dialogs generally have fewer window controls available, and alerts have fewer still. Figure 2-10 shows a standard document window with the most commonly found items indicated.

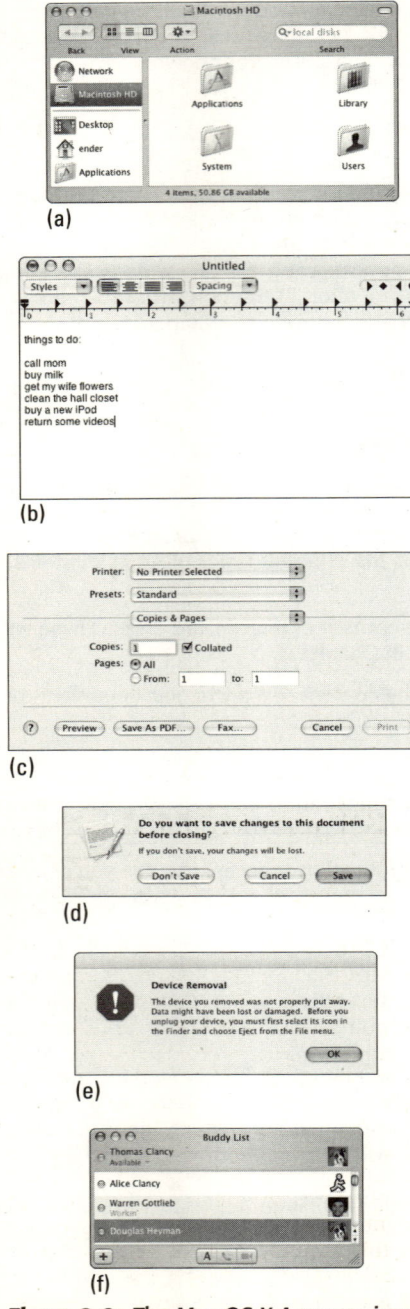

(a)

(b)

(c)

(d)

(e)

(f)

Figure 2-9: The Mac OS X Aqua environment has
several different types of windows: a Finder
window (a), a document (b) a dialog (c), a sheet (d),
an alert (e), and a palette (f).

Close minimize buttons   Title bar

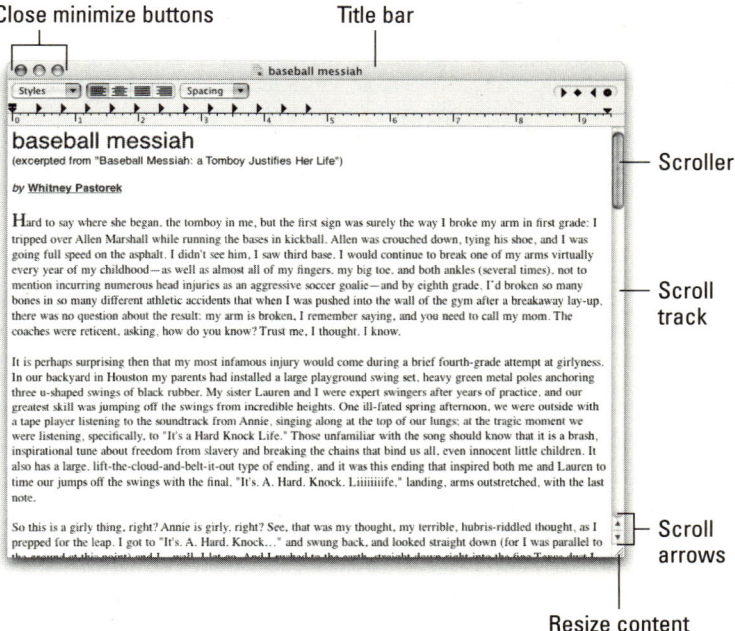

Scroller

Scroll track

Scroll arrows

Resize content

Figure 2-10: Windows are made up of numerous controls and objects. Learning what they all do is crucial to an efficient computing experience. These highlighted items are common to many windows.

✦ **Title bar:** The title bar is the usually the home of the stoplight cluster of close, minimize and zoom on the left side, as well as the location of the name of the active window (the Title). The title indicates which document is currently being displayed (or which folder is being displayed in the case of a Finder window, discussed later in this chapter). Click and drag on the title bar to move the window. Double-clicking the title bar minimizes the window into the Dock just as the minimize button described below.

✦ **Close:** The close button is the uppermost and leftmost item in every window. The color scheme of the close button and his two partners, the minimize and the zoom buttons, are based on a stoplight. The close button is typically a round red button found at the top left of a window and when you move the pointer near this button, an X appears in its center. Red usually means stop after all, and this button will close the window to which it is attached. In some applications, notably the Finder, press the Option key and click this button to close all of the application's windows. Please note that unlike Microsoft Windows, this will NOT usually quit the active application, but will simply close the displayed window. Quitting applications is covered in Chapter 5.

✦ **Minimize:** The minimize button is usually a round yellow button, found to the right of the close button, and when you move the pointer near it, a minus sign (–) appears in it. In keeping with the stoplight theme, clicking this button will minimize the attached window, sucking it down into the Dock, for easy retrieval later (its sort of like "slow down", isn't it?). Minimizing too many windows will result in a cluttered Dock, so be careful!

✦ **Zoom:** The zoom button is typically a round green button, found to the right of the minimize button, and when moving the pointer near it, a plus sign (+) appears inside it. Its function is to make a window first as large as is required to display all items within, or to make that window as large as possible, without stretching off screen if too many items are present to be displayed at once. A zoomed window may leave a margin at the bottom or sides of the screen for the Dock. After the first zoom-button click, this button will then reduce the window to its original size. If a window cannot be resized, its zoom button is dim, and a plus sign does not appear in its center. (This fits into the stoplight theme of these three buttons as in "Zoom! Hit the gas!")

✦ **Scroller:** The scroller is both an indicator as well as a control item. The scroller indicates a given window's current focused position of the displayed folder contents with both its size as well as its position in the Scroll Track. For example: If the scroller is at the top of the Scroll Track, and is taking up about one third of the scroll track, the window is displaying on third of the total folder's viewable material, and is showing the top third portion. Click and drag the scroller to move quickly to a desired position within a displayed folder. This is the fastest way to shift your window's list of displayed items. Like Scroll Arrows, the scroller will not be available if all of a folder's contents are displayed by the current window's size.

✦ **Scroll track:** The scroll track is the container for the scroller. As with the scroller, the Scroll Track is an indicator as well as a control surface. The scroll track can be clicked to refocus the window one full window display area at a time. For example: If the scroller is half the size of the scroll track and at the top of the scroll track, a single click in the scroll track will move the window's focus to the bottom half. This method is useful to quickly scan a folder's contents.

✦ **Scroll arrow:** The scroll arrows will shift a windows focus in the arrow's indicated direction slightly with each mouse click. Clicking and holding on a scroll arrow will shift the window's focus both smoothly and more quickly. These buttons are useful when trying to slowly scan through a large grouping of items. Note: Scroll arrows will only be available for use if the window is not large enough to display all items within it.

✦ **Resize control:** The bottom-right corner of a window is typically the resize control surface. This is usually indicated with a slightly rougher texture or indentation to that corner that would suggest grabbing it. Click and drag the resize corner to adjust the size of the window. Hold down shift before clicking to resize the window equally in both length and width, forming a neat square.

Note   The color of the Close, Minimize, Zoom, and Scroller controls may be gray instead of red, yellow, green, and blue. You set the color by using the General pane of System Preferences application, as described in Chapter 4.

Buttons and other controls

Window controls, as covered in the previous heading, afford you means of controlling the window itself. But, within many of the windows encountered day to day are a wide variety of controls that you also operate by clicking or dragging with the mouse. These other controls perform various functions, hopefully clearly labeled by the software designers! Examples of these other controls include push buttons, checkboxes, radio buttons, sliders, little arrows for increasing or decreasing numeric values, disclosure triangles, scrolling lists, and tabs.

Using push buttons

A *push button* causes an action to take place when clicked. A label on the button indicates the action that the button performs. The label may be text or graphic. Push buttons with text labels are generally rectangular with rounded ends. Buttons with graphic labels may be any shape. Figure 2-11 illustrates push buttons.

Figure 2-11: Click a push button in an Aqua window to cause an action to take place.

Using standard OK and Cancel buttons

Many dialogs have buttons labeled OK and Cancel. Clicking OK accepts all the settings and entries in the dialog. Clicking Cancel rejects any changes you may have made in the dialog and restores all settings and entries to their state before the dialog appeared. A shortcut for clicking the Cancel button is pressing the Escape key (the Escape key is labeled esc) or pressing the ⌘ and Period (.) keys in combination.

Using radio buttons

Radio buttons let you select one setting from a group. They're called radio buttons because they work like the station presets on a car radio. Just as you can select only one radio station at a time, you can select only one radio button from a group. To select a radio button, click it. The selected radio button is darker than its unselected neighbors. Figure 2-12 illustrates radio buttons.

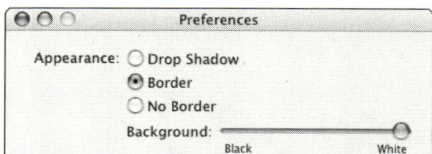

Figure 2-12: Click a radio button in an Aqua window to select one setting from a group.

Recognizing the Default button

One button in an Aqua dialog, alert, or sheet may pulsate, going from light gray to a darker color (initially blue, but you can change colors as described in Chapter 13). The other buttons are all light gray. This is the *default button*.

The default button represents the action that you most often want to take. However, if the most common action is dangerous, then a button representing a safer action may be the default button. As a shortcut for clicking the default button, you can press the Return key or the Enter key.

Using checkboxes

A *checkbox* lets you turn a setting on or off. When a setting is on (or selected), a check mark appears in the checkbox. When a setting is off (or deselected), the checkbox is empty. When a setting is partly on and partly off because it indicates the state of more than one thing, such as the format of a range of text, a dash appears in the checkbox. Unlike radio buttons, checkboxes are not mutually exclusive. You can turn on checkboxes in any combination. That being said, some applications may use check symbols in their radio button fields, allowing only one check to be seen at a time, just to confuse us all. Be careful. Clicking a checkbox reverses its state. Figure 2-13 shows examples of checkboxes.

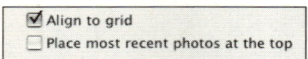

Figure 2-13: Click checkboxes in Aqua windows to turn settings on and off individually.

Using sliders

A *slider* consists of a track that displays a range of values or magnitudes and the slider itself, also known as the *thumb,* which indicates the current setting. You can change the setting by dragging the slider. An Aqua slider is a dark color (initially blue, but you can change colors as described in Chapter 4). Figure 2-14 shows examples of sliders.

Figure 2-14: Drag a slider in an Aqua window to change a setting across a range of values.

Using little arrows

Little arrows, which point in opposite directions, let you raise or lower a value incrementally. Clicking an arrow changes the value one increment at a time. Pressing an arrow continuously changes the value until it reaches the end of its range. Figure 2-15 illustrates little arrows.

Using disclosure triangles

A *disclosure triangle* controls how much detail you see in a window. When the window is displaying minimal detail, clicking a disclosure triangle reveals additional detail and may automatically enlarge the window to accommodate it. Clicking the same triangle again hides detail and may automatically shrink the window to fit. Figure 2-16 shows an example of disclosure triangles.

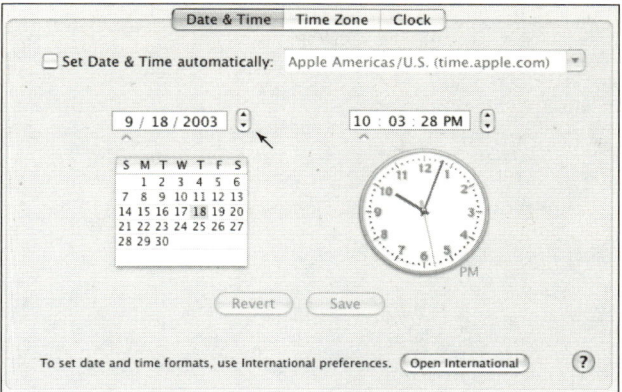

Figure 2-15: Click or press a little arrow in an Aqua window to change a value incrementally.

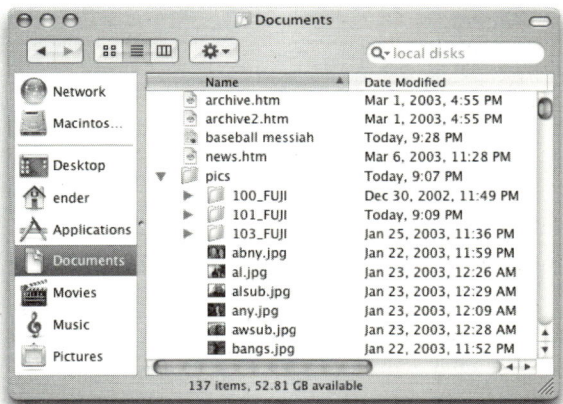

Figure 2-16: Click a disclosure triangle to adjust the amount of detail shown.

Using scrolling lists

A *scrolling list* displays a list of values in a box with an adjacent scroll bar. If there are more values than can be displayed at once, the scroll bar becomes active and you can use it to see other values in the list. Clicking a listed item selects it. You may be able to select multiple items by pressing Shift or ⌘ while clicking. Figure 2-17 illustrates scrolling lists.

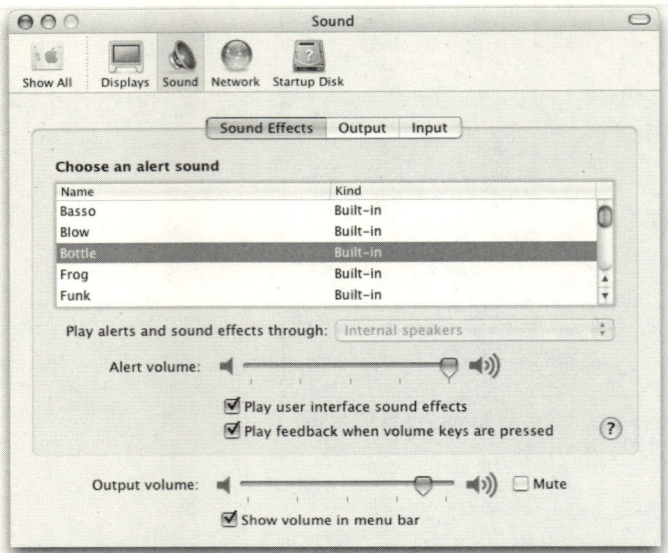

Figure 2-17: Scroll a list to see an item you want and then click to select it (Shift-click or ⌘-click to select multiple items) in an Aqua window.

Using tabs

Tabs in Mac OS windows perform the same function as tabs on dividers used in card files or ring binders. They divide the contents of a window into discrete pages or sections, with each tab presenting one section of window content. Apple calls each tabbed section a *pane*. You can see only one pane at a time, and users switch to a different pane by clicking the appropriate tab. Figure 2-18 shows an example of tabs.

Using Icons

Icons are small pictures that represent many objects in the Mac OS. You work with the objects by manipulating their representative icons. For example, you work with the applications, documents, folders, and disks in your computer by manipulating icons on the computer screen. This section explains what the look of an icon tells you about it and how you use icons.

Mac OS X icons have a different look from icons in previous Mac OS versions. They are typically larger and much more photo-realistic. Unlike the fixed-size icons in previous Mac OS versions, you can size Mac OS X icons up to 128 x 128 pixels. In some contexts, you decide how large you want Mac OS X to display icons. In other contexts, Mac OS X scales icons to fit the available space.

Note   A *pixel*, or *pic*ture *el*ement, is equivalent to a single dot on the screen. These dots make up all the text and graphics that appear on your computer's screen.

An icon's basic appearance often gives you some idea of what kind of item it represents. You can usually identify icons for applications, documents, and folders by common characteristics of each type.

Identifying application icons

Application icons come in three basic varieties:

✦ **Regular Mac OS X applications:** Icons of regular Mac OS X applications have several distinctive characteristics. An application icon depicts the kind of information it creates or views, such as pictures, notes, or a particular type of document. Application icons usually include a tool that suggests the type of task the application helps you perform, such as a pen for writing or a pair of glasses for viewing. Figure 2-18 shows several Mac OS X application icons.

Figure 2-18: Icons of Mac OS X applications depict the kind of information the application creates or views and what you can do with it.

✦ **Mac OS X utilities:** The icon of a utility application communicates the auxiliary function it performs. An icon showing a doctor's stethoscope over a hard drive suggests a hard drive doctor, and in fact is the icon for Apple's Disk First Aid repair utility. Utility icons typically use color sparingly; they are predominantly shades of gray. Figure 2-19 shows some icons of Mac OS X utilities.

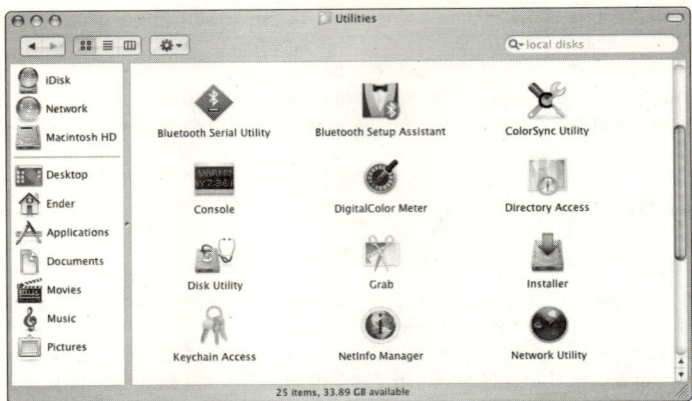

Figure 2-19: A utility application's icon in Mac OS X depicts the function that the utility performs.

> ✦ **Classic applications:** Icons of Classic applications generally have much simpler designs than Mac OS X application icons. They also appear somewhat jagged or grainy, especially when they are scaled larger than their original dimensions, which are usually 32 x 32 pixels.

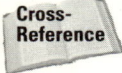
Cross-
Reference

For more information on the Classic application icons, see Chapter 17.

Identifying document icons

Icons that look like a sheet of paper with a dog-eared corner generally represent document files. Document files can contain the text, pictures, sounds, and other kinds of data stored on your computer. The icon may depict the kind of data in a document. In addition, a document icon may indicate which application created it by including a derivative of the application's icon. Figure 2-20 shows several document icons.

Figure 2-20: Document icons represent files that contain music, address information, stories, or other data.

Identifying folder icons

Icons that look like folders represent the folders in which programs, documents, and other items are organized on your disks. A folder with a special purpose may incorporate an image that indicates the particular kind of items the folder contains. Figure 2-21 shows some folder icons.

Figure 2-21: Folder icons may indicate the kind of items inside. This is a view of a user's home folder (covered later in this chapter).

Identifying disk icons

The easiest items to spot are disk icons. They usually look like the type of disk they are. For example, hard drives look like real hard drives, CD-ROMs look like an actual CD. Network drives may be depicted with a distinctive starscape sphere, or may appear as hard drives with wires emerging from the bottom, symbolizing the network connection to the drive. See Figure 2-22.

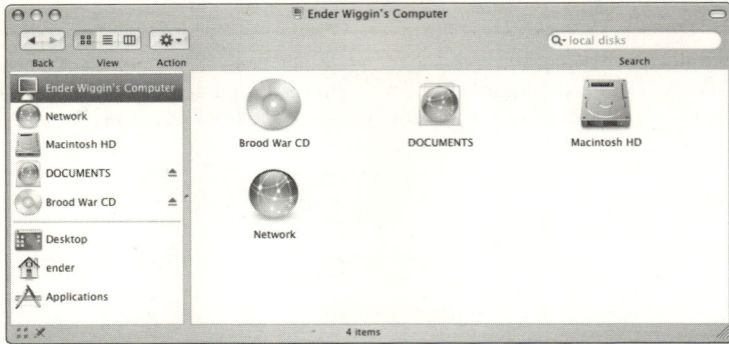

Figure 2-22: Disk icons represent the type of disks mounted.

Identifying alias icons

Aliases are shortcuts to a document, folder or application. These items often reside deep inside a hard drive, or even on a server drive. By using aliases, users can navigate quickly to desired locations quickly, with less clicking (more on aliases in Chapter 4). The alias icon is typically a copy of the original item's icon, with a small black arrow in the lower-left corner, indicating the icon "points" to that original item. Figure 2-23 shows a few aliases.

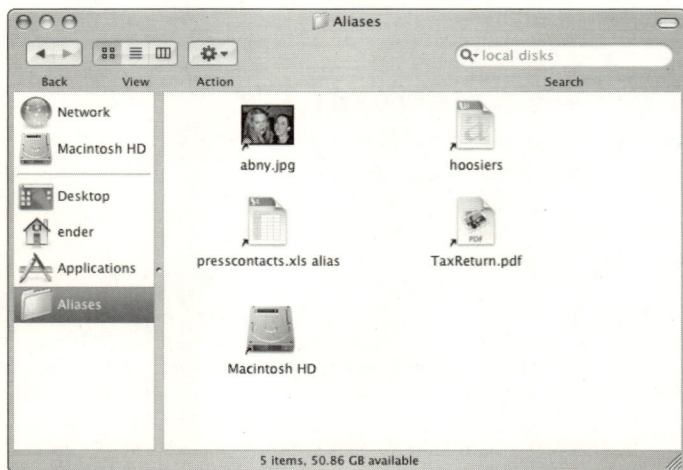

Figure 2-23: Aliases are shortcuts to other files, enabling users to access files easily without removing them from their original location.

Identifying restricted folders

Some folders on your computer or on servers are restricted to particular users. This is particularly true of items within home folders (covered later in this chapter). You cannot access and edit another user's folders or their contents when logged in with your account. You can spot restricted folders easily because they are marked with the European "wrong way" symbol, a red circle with a white dash. Figure 2-24 shows an inactive user's home folder, and all of its restricted folders.

Figure 2-24: Restricted folders are inaccessible to the current user. This is a view of another user's home folder. Notice that Public and Sites are not restricted.

Looking at the Dock

The Dock, arguably the single most useful and unique feature of Mac OS X, gives users fast access to frequently used items within their environment. The Dock contains shortcuts to your favorite applications and documents, shows active applications, and minimized windows. You can easily edit the Dock to more accurately represent your needs. The Dock is shown in Figure 2-25.

Figure 2-25: The Dock contains icons for frequently used applications, files, minimized windows, and so forth.

The Dock contains an initial set of icons, which you can rearrange to suit your needs. (We explain how to add, remove, and move Dock icons in Chapter 4.) The initial set of Dock icons includes the following:

✦ **Finder:** An application for managing the files and folders stored on your computer, always at the left end of the Dock

✦ **Mail:** An application for sending and receiving email

✦ **iChat:** An instant messaging (IM) client compatible with AOL's AIM client

✦ **Address Book:** A contact list for people, business, and so on, integrated with Apple's Mail application and the rest of Mac OS

✦ **Microsoft Internet Explorer:** An application for browsing the Internet

✦ **iTunes:** An application for playing, organizing, and recording digital music from CDs, MP3 files, and Internet radio

✦ **iPhoto:** An application for transferring and organizing photos from digital still cameras

✦ **iMovie:** An application for working with digital video

✦ **Sherlock:** An application for searching your computer, your network, and the Internet

✦ **QuickTime Player:** An application for viewing digital movies

✦ **System Preferences:** An application for customizing Mac OS X on your computer

✦ **Apple – Mac OS X:** A link to the Mac OS X page on Apple's Web site

✦ **Trash:** A container for discarding files and folders that you no longer need

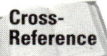

Trash is covered in detail in Chapter 3.

More icons are temporarily added to the Dock automatically as you use your computer. When you open an application, its icon bounces up and down in the Dock and remains there while the application is open. An open application's icon has a small black triangle underneath it to represent that the application is open. When you minimize an Aqua window, it shrinks to the size of an icon and appears in the Dock. A window shrinks to the Dock with a wavering visual effect that Apple likens to a genie going into a bottle, or the application can shrink in a linear scale progression.

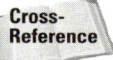

You can learn how to minimize an Aqua window by clicking its Minimize button, as described in Chapter 3. You can change the visual effect by choosing Dock Preferences from the Dock submenu of the Apple menu, as described in Chapter 4.

Appreciating Dock niceties

The Dock is divided into two sections, separated by a thin vertical line. The items to the left of the line are applications. The right section contains the trash along with all other item types, such as minimized windows, files, and folders. As you open new applications, they appear in the Dock to the left of the vertical line between the System Preferences and Apple – Mac OS X icons. New documents and windows minimized to the Dock appear between the vertical separator and the Trash icon.

The icons of items in the Dock sometimes provide feedback. For example, an application that requires attention can bounce up and down, as if it was excitedly raising its hand in class. Another example: The Mail icon indicates the number of new messages waiting for you.

Identifying Dock icons

When you move the mouse pointer to a Dock icon, the icon's name appears above it. Clicking a Dock icon opens the item. When you click a minimized window in the Dock, the window emerges and becomes full-sized again.

Recognizing the Desktop

The vast expanse of swirling blue that's displayed below the menu bar and behind the Dock is called the *desktop*. Initially, the only items on the desktop are your installed hard drives and any inserted disks, but other icons may appear. For example, an icon appears on your desktop for each file server, if any, to which your computer is connected. All these different icons normally appear on the desktop, but you can suppress them by changing settings in Finder Preferences.

The desktop is actually a folder, stored in your home folder. The contents of the Desktop folder are always displayed onscreen, so users always have a location to store and retrieve items quickly. Mac OS X keeps your desktop's contents and appearance separate from users who log in with other user account names. Each user account has its own Desktop folder. Figure 2-26 shows the Desktop in all its glory.

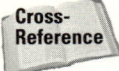

Cross-Reference For more on changing settings in the Finder Preferences, see Chapter 4. You can also learn how to place icons on the desktop, change the picture displayed on the desktop, and customize other aspects of the desktop in Chapter 4.

Note Although the icons of hard drives, CDs, and other disk volumes may appear on the desktop, your Desktop folder does not contain these items. The icons of disk volumes appear on the desktop simply because the Finder displays them there (together with other items actually stored in your desktop folder). This can be confusing, as it goes against our understanding of folders *containing* the items they display, but it is the only exception to this rule.

Figure 2-26: Each user account has its own private desktop, and items you put on your desktop are kept in your Desktop folder.

Discovering Your Inner Hard Drive

Now that you are aware of the basic elements of your environment, it's time to become familiar with the most important area of your computer. All of the data stored on your computer, from the letters your write to the digital photos your take to the actual operating system itself are all sorted and organized on various disks. Most of the data is on your hard drive, some may be stored on removable CD-ROMs, some maybe stored on your digital camera, or on other types of media. On your Desktop, you will see a disk icon for Macintosh HD in the top-right corner. That drive is the main system drive, and contains the operating system, your applications, and your user account information. All of this information is sorted in various sub-folders. Figure 2-27 shows the contents of a standard Macintosh OS X hard drive.

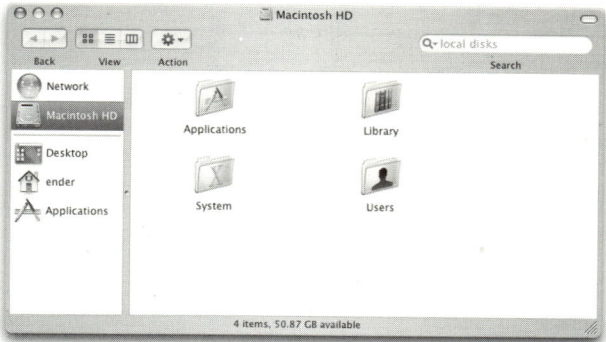

Figure 2-27: The first level of a standard Mac OS X hard drive, known as the *root* level, contains various subfolders that perform very important functions.

✦ **Applications:** as its name implies, this folder contains applications. Applications are the tools that you use to review, create, or edit documents.

✦ **System:** This folder contains the actual files that comprise the heart of Mac OS X. Many of pieces of the complex jigsaw puzzle that make your computer work are stored here. This folder is explorable by users, but is not editable. Users cannot erase, edit, or add files within the System folder. Essentially, you can see behind the wizard's curtain, but you cannot interrupt him while he's working.

✦ **Library:** the Library folder contains system-wide settings files, as well as some additional files that help the computer operate. All of the settings saved in this Library folder apply to all users. For example, any fonts that are installed within this Library are available for all users to access. Mac OS X actually has 3 library folders. Each performing a similar function, but at a different level of *priority*. Chapter 23 has more on this.

✦ **Users:** within this folder are a number of subfolders. One for each user of the computer. Each of these folders is the central storage area for users. These subfolders are known as a user's home folder or simply "home." As this folder is of great import, it is covered in greater detail in the following heading.

Living at home

As Mac OS X is a truly multi-user operating system, each user needs to have a private storage area. The operating system itself also needs a place to store settings, preferences and other information for each user. This area is appropriately named "home." Each user has a home of their own, represented by a folder in Users folder. Each user's home is named for the user, and each is protected from the prying eyes and fingers of the other users on the system. When you create or save documents, the documents are stored within the creating user's home folder. When you make changes to your environment, or adjust settings influencing the behavior of your computer, the operating system stores the settings in your home as well. Figure 2-28 shows the home folders on a system. The currently logged in user's home is represented by an icon that looks like a house. The inactive user's homes are simply folders.

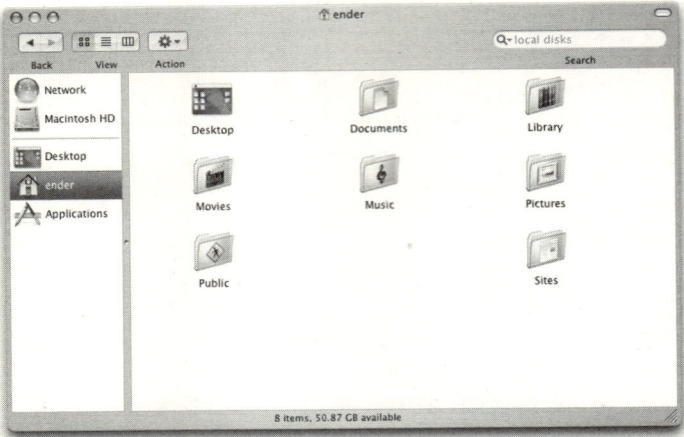

Figure 2-28: The home folders.

Each user's home contains subfolders that are designed to help keep information sorted out by its purpose. Table 2-2 covers these sub-folders.

Table 2-2: Home Folder Contents

Name	Contents
Desktop	Contains all items on display on the desktop, with the exception of disks.
Documents	A catch-all folder where a user's miscellaneous documents are stored by default.
Library	Contains application preferences, environmental settings, and other system elements unique to the user account. The settings in this Library are NOT system-wide. They only apply to this user.
Movies	The default save location for Apple's iMovie application, and a convenient place to store any other movie files.
Music	The default location for the iTunes music library, and a convenient place to store any other music files.
Pictures	The default location for the iPhoto picture library, and a convenient place to store any other image files.
Public	The default location for a user to place items that are meant to be shared across the network or between user accounts. Sharing files between users is covered in Chapter 5.
Sites	The default location for Web sites that a user may want to save, and a convenient location to place created Web pages.

Note Only the currently logged in user can access his or her home. This security measure is designed to keep users documents and settings separate. That said, there is a built-in method to share information with the other users on your system. The method of sharing is a one-way street though. You can *give* files to other users, and they can *give* files to you, but you cannot *take* files from each other. To learn more about sharing files between local users, tune in to Chapter 5.

Sleeping, Shutting Down, Restarting, or Logging Out

When you want to conclude a session with your computer, you need to do one of the following:

✦ Make the computer sleep to save energy.

✦ Log out so someone else won't have access to your data. They can log in and use the computer with their own account (assuming the computer is configured for multiple users).

✦ Restart the computer to complete the installation of some updates or new applications, or to allow the computer to run its self-tests on startup.

✦ Shut down the computer to save energy, ensure greater safety in case of power failure, and prolong the lifespan of components.

Caution If you shut down your Mac improperly, for example by disconnecting the power, you risk damaging your files. Such damage may be minor and not readily apparent, but an accumulation of minor damage may lead to mysterious, serious problems later. You can find some maintenance procedures in Chapter 22.

To Shut Down or Not To Shut Down

You do not need to regularly shut down a Mac OS X-based computer, because its Unix foundation operates much more cleanly than Mac OS 9 and earlier. What does this mean? In the old days of Mac OS 9, the computer's performance would degrade over time, requiring regular restarts just to shake out the cobwebs. OS X is so clean, these digital cobwebs never get a chance to form. However, some useful maintenance operations may not happen according to schedule if you only have your computer sleep every night, as we explain in Chapter 22. Most technicians will recommend shutting down your computer instead of putting it to sleep. As we noted earlier, during startup, your computer performs a basic self-test, where it verifies that all hardware is functioning normally. The computer's self-test functions are very useful indicators of upcoming problems, and they happen during startup. Another factor in the recommendation is the possibility of local power problems. The computer is much safer being shut down normally rather than having the power fail while you're away from the machine for the weekend. This is also not to mention the electric bill! You wouldn't leave the television on when you go out, would you?

Making the computer sleep (and wake up)

If you're not going to use your computer for a while, you can save energy and reduce wear and tear on the computer by making it sleep. When you're ready to use your computer again, you can wake it quickly. Waking from sleep is much faster than starting up.

Going to sleep

To make your computer sleep, do one of the following:

✦ If you have a PowerBook or iBook, close the lid.

✦ Choose Sleep from the Apple menu.

✦ If your keyboard has a Power key, press it briefly and then press the S key or click the Sleep button in the resulting dialog, which is shown in Figure 2-30.

✦ If your keyboard has an Eject key, you can shut down by pressing the Option ⌘-Eject combination.

✦ If your keyboard has an Eject key, press Control while pressing the Eject key, and then press the S key or click the Sleep button in the resulting dialog, which is shown in Figure 2-29.

Note   The Eject key is in the upper-right corner of the PowerBook, iBook, and Apple Pro keyboard. This symbol is an up-pointing triangle with a line underneath.

✦ If you have an Apple Cinema display, or Apple Studio LCD display, press its power button.

✦ Configure your computer to sleep automatically after a period of inactivity by using the Energy Saver pane of System Preferences.

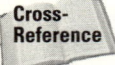

Cross-Reference   For more on the System Preferences, see Chapter 13.

Note   You can't put some Power Mac G4 models to sleep if you have particular PCI cards installed. When this is the case, the Apple menu's Sleep command is dim. You can still configure the computer to sleep when it's idle.

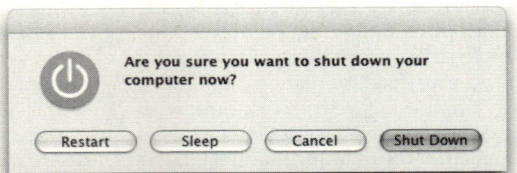

Figure 2-29: An alert appears when you press the power key on some keyboards, the Control and Eject keys on some other keyboards, or the power button on some Apple displays. Alternately, the computer may just go to Sleep mode, with little or no warning.

Waking up

To make your computer wake up from sleep, do one of the following:

✦ If you have a PowerBook or iBook, open its lid. This action doesn't wake all PowerBook models.

✦ Press any key on the keyboard.

✦ Click the mouse.

Logging out of Mac OS X

You can log out of Mac OS X so that someone else can log in, or just to protect your data's security. To log out, choose Log Out from the Apple menu. A dialog appears in which you must confirm or cancel your intention to log out. Figure 2-30 shows this dialog.

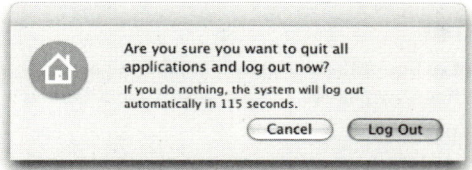

Figure 2-30: After choosing Log Out from the Apple menu, you must confirm or cancel your intention to log out.

If you click Log Out in the dialog, Mac OS X instructs all open applications to quit. If any open application has a document with unsaved changes, the affected application asks whether you want to save the changes before quitting. After all applications have quit, the login window appears, as previously shown in Figure 2-3.

In this case, the login window appears after you log out even if your computer is configured to log in automatically. That said, you can have the computer log in automatically by clicking the Restart button in the login window.

Tip   You can configure your computer so that the Restart and Shut Down buttons don't work in the login window. This makes it more difficult, although not impossible, for someone to restart the computer with Mac OS 9 or a CD, which may allow them to access your Mac OS X files. You learn how to disable these buttons in Chapter 13.

Restarting the computer

You need to restart your computer far less often with Mac OS X because it doesn't crash as often as earlier Mac OS versions. Nevertheless, you may need to restart your computer after installing new software or to get the computer to recognize a newly connected device.

Use any of the following methods to restart your computer:

✦ If your keyboard has a Power key, press it; then press the R key or click the Restart button in the dialog that appears, which was previously shown in Figure 2-29.

✦ If your keyboard has an Eject key, press Control while pressing Eject and then press the R key or click the Restart button in the dialog that appears, which was previously shown in Figure 2-30.

✦ Log out and then click the Restart button in the login window.

✦ Choose Restart from the Apple menu. This displays a dialog as shown in Figure 2-29.

With any of these methods, Mac OS X tells all open applications to quit. As with logging out, any open applications that have a document with unsaved changes asks whether you want to save the changes before quitting. After all applications have quit, the computer shuts down and then automatically starts up as described at the beginning of this chapter.

Shutting down the computer

Although you can leave the computer running indefinitely and just make it sleep when no one is using it, you can also shut it down. Shutting down saves more energy than sleeping.

You can use any of these methods to shut down:

✦ If your keyboard has a Power key, press it and then press the Enter key or click the Shut Down button in the dialog that appears, which was previously shown in Figure 2-29.

✦ If your keyboard has an Eject key, press Control while pressing Eject and then press the Enter key or click the Shut Down button in the dialog that appears (previously shown in Figure 2-29).

✦ Log out, and then click the Shut Down button in the login window.

✦ Choose Shut Down from the Apple menu. This displays the dialog seen in Figure 2-29.

When you shut down your computer, Mac OS X tells all open applications to quit. If an open application has a document with unsaved changes, it asks whether you want to save the changes before quitting. After all applications have quit, the computer shuts off its power.

Note   In the event of a hard system crash, you may need to power your computer down manually, as opposed to using these safer methods of restarting, logging out, or shutting down. When a hard crash occurs, push and hold the power button on your computer for 5 seconds. This shuts down your computer, but it does so without saving any open documents and may result in damage to the system. Refer to Chapter 23 for more notes on crashes and recommended repair schemes.

Summary

Here's what you know after reading this chapter:

✦ After pushing the power button, your computer loads Mac OS X into its memory from disk.

✦ During startup, Mac OS X goes through a login procedure in an effort to keep unauthorized people from using the computer. The login procedure is mandatory but can be automated.

✦ Menus present lists of commands or attributes for you to choose from. Menus always appear in the menu bar at the top of the screen. Elsewhere, distinctive arrows indicate pop-up menus, and Control-clicking an item may display a contextual menu for it.

✦ Mac OS X has several types of Aqua windows: Finder windows, document windows, dialogs, sheets, alerts, and palettes.

✦ Icons represent applications, documents, folders, disks, and other items in your computer. An icon's basic appearance tells you which type of item it represents.

✦ The home folder is each user's default file store, and it contains that user's settings and preferences. Home folders are inaccessible to unauthorized users.

✦ The Dock contains icons of items you use often, in addition to items that are currently open or hidden.

✦ When you are ready to finish a session with your computer, you need to make it sleep, log out of Mac OS X, restart the computer, or shut down.

✦   ✦   ✦

Managing Your Workspace

In this chapter, you learn how to use the objects and controls introduced in Chapter 2. You learn how to open, close, and resize windows. You learn how to select, move, and modify groups of icons easily. You learn how to erase files. You learn how to use Apple's undo command and how to create optical discs. In this chapter, you are introduced to Exposé, Apple's awesome (yes, awesome) new window management system. Most importantly, the Finder is explored in detail, and you learn how use to Finder-specific windows, menus, and control methods.

Finding Out about the Finder

Ask most Mac users which application they use most often, you will receive answers like "Adobe Photoshop" or "Microsoft Word" or "Internet Explorer." These answers are all incorrect. What's the correct answer? The Finder! The Finder is the most accessed application in the Mac OS because it is at the heart of your environmental experience. Unlike most other applications, you don't have to do anything to make it start running. The Finder starts running automatically when you log in and keeps running until you log out. Represented by a blue smiling computer face (which looks like a cartoon Steve Jobs, sans glasses, in our opinion), the Finder's icon is always first in the Dock. As mentioned in Chapter 2, the Finder is responsible for generating the desktop, maintaining its own windows, and controlling the interaction between files, their host applications, and the hard drive. Of course, this makes the Finder not only the most commonly used, but also the most important and potentially most fragile application. The old Macintosh OS 9 Finder was less of an application, and more of a system function. Any attempts to recover from a Finder problem would typically be met with a user shouting at the screen and/or punching the keyboard as the last few hours of work disappeared in a reboot. The Mac OS X Finder though, operates much like other applications; able to recover from errors — even able to relaunch when needed — on the fly, without forcing a reboot or damaging a user's work in other applications. Finder crashes and methods of recovery are discussed in greater depth in Chapter 22.

Finder-specific menus

In Chapter 2, we discuss the menu bar in general. Most applications make their own additions to the menu bar, or they may eliminate some menu items, or remove the menu bar altogether! Yes, even the Finder, the core system application has its own unique menus that are added to the menu bar.

Finder menu

The Finder menu is the most common Application menu you will encounter. The application menu is the first menu after the Apple menu, and is named for the active application. Thus, while in the Finder, the menu is named Finder. As with all application menus, this menu is populated with commands that pertain to the application as a whole. Selecting the About Finder option opens a window containing copyright information on the Finder as well as stating which version of the Finder you are using (Apple releases updates all the time, which you should keep up with via your Software Update preference pane as covered in Chapter 13.). Other menu options in the Finder menu include the command to Empty the Trash, and the Services pullout menu that contains various additional features and commands. The Services menu and its various elements are covered in Chapter 11.

Go menu

The Go menu is one of two Finder-specific menus available in the menu bar. The Go menu is designed to offer the user a few convenient shortcuts to commonly used locations or items. By selecting these items, a new Finder window opens, displaying the selected location. Figure 3-1 shows the Go menu.

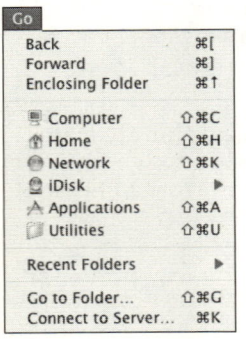

Figure 3-1: The Go menu contains shortcuts to numerous commonly used locations.

Choose Computer, Home, iDisk, or Applications from the Go menu to display the contents of the corresponding folder in the front Finder window. (If no Finder window is currently displayed, a new Finder window appears.) All these Go menu items have handy keyboard shortcuts. Computer is ⌘-Shift-C, Home is ⌘-Shift-H, iDisk is ⌘-Shift-I, and Applications is ⌘-Shift-A.

Recent Folders

The Recent Folders submenu of the Go menu lists the last 10 folders that you displayed in the Finder. This submenu is similar in concept to the Recent Items menu in the Apple menu, which lists applications and documents that you have recently used. Like the Apple ➪ Recent Items submenu, the Go ➪ Recent Folders submenu has a menu choice for clearing the current list of recent folders. (The Apple ➪ Recent Items submenu is described in more detail in Chapter 5.)

Go to Folder

If you know the exact name and path to the folder you want (and you type well), choose Go ➪ Go To Folder (or press the keyboard shortcut ⌘-Shift-G). The Finder displays a dialog in which you type the path and name of the folder desired. This is far from the traditional Macintosh graphical interface, but it is one near and dear to the hearts of folks coming from Unix and MS-DOS.

A complete path to a folder begins with a slash character (/) and is followed by the names of every folder from the outermost folder to the folder that you want to open, with an additional slash between folder names. For example, /Applications/Utilities is the path to the Utilities folder within the Applications folder.

If you don't start the pathname with a /, the Finder looks for a relative path, one which starts in the current folder. For example, if the Applications folder is open in the front Finder window, you can open the Utilities folder by typing just Utilities in the Go to Folder dialog.

> **Tip** Unix pathname shortcuts all work in the Go To Folder dialog. For example, if you're in a folder on another volume and wish to be in the Sites folder of your home folder, just press ⌘-Shift-G to display the Go To Folder dialog and type **~/Sites** to be transported. Similarly, to get to the Public folder of another user named spenser, you would type **~spenser/Public**. Confused? See Chapters 24–26 for more on Unix.

Back

If you want the front Finder window to go back to the folder or disk that it last displayed, choose Go ➪ Back (or press ⌘-[). You can continue going back by choosing Go ➪ Back again. When the front Finder window can't go back any more because it is displaying the first folder or disk that it ever displayed, the Back item is disabled (dim) in the Go menu. The Back item in the Go menu is equivalent to the Back button in the Finder window toolbar.

Connect to Server

The Go menu's final choice provides access to file servers, either on your own network or on the Internet. Choosing Go ➪ Connect to Server (or press ⌘-K) displays a dialog in which you specify the server that you want to connect to. This dialog provides a pop-up menu of recent servers, in addition to a browser area in which you find available servers on your local network. We discuss the Connect to Server dialog in much more detail in Chapter 15.

View menu

The View menu contains commands that change the style and method of items presented via the Finder. In addition to switching between view modes (covered later in this chapter), the View menu enables users to edit some specific view details for each view mode. The commands apply to Finder windows and the desktop, and will typically only affect the foremost window (or the desktop if no windows are selected or open). Figure 3-2 shows the view menu.

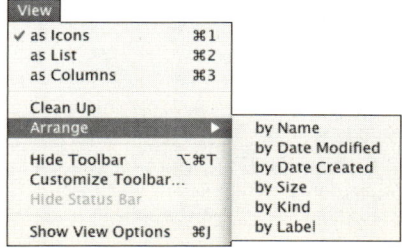

Figure 3-2: The View menu includes options to adjust the appearance of items in a Finder window or on the desktop.

The View menu contains the following commands:

✦ **as Icons:** This switches the current Finder window to the icon view mode. The keyboard shortcut to perform this command is ⌘-1. This command is only available if a Finder window is open and active.

✦ **as List:** This switches the current Finder window to the list view mode. The keyboard shortcut to perform this command is ⌘-2. This command is only available if a Finder window is open and active.

✦ **as Columns:** This switches the current Finder window to the column view mode. The keyboard shortcut to perform this command is ⌘-3. This command is only available if a Finder window is open and active.

✦ **Clean Up:** This command is available in icon view mode only. Clean Up neatens up the current window's contents by aligning the items on a grid.

✦ **Arrange:** This command is also available in icon view mode only. Arrange reorganizes a window's contents both to a grid and to a specified factor. You specify the sorting factor via the submenu: the options are By Name, By Date Modified, By Date Created, By Size, and By Kind.

✦ **Hide Toolbar:** This command will do more than just turn off the toolbar in the active Finder window. In fact, hiding the Toolbar results in a very different looking and much simpler Finder window. If the toolbar is already hidden, the menu option will read Show Toolbar, and selecting it returns the toolbar to view. The keyboard shortcut for this command is ⌘-Option-T. This command is only available if a Finder window is open and active.

✦ **Customize Toolbar:** This command brings up a dialog that enables users to customize the toolbar according to their needs. This operation is covered in Chapter 4. This command is only available if a Finder window is open and active.

✦ **Hide Status Bar:** This command is only available for Finder windows that are in the simpler "Hide Toolbar" view. This command will turn off the status bar in the active Finder window. If the status bar is already hidden, the menu option will read Show Status Bar, and selecting it returns the status bar to view.

✦ **Show View Options:** This menu command opens a dialog where the current view mode can be edited and adjusted. This is covered in Chapter 4.

Finder windows

Typically, you navigate your computer's myriad files and folders via Finder windows. Finder windows graphically represent the contents of particular folders or disks, and can present this information in many ways, each with its own characteristics and advantages. Figure 3-3 shows a basic Finder window, and points out its unique elements. A standard Finder window is a good place to review many of the most common objects.

Mac OS X gives you a few ways to create new Finder windows:

✦ Choose File ➪ New Finder Window.

✦ Click on any folder or disk icon and select Open from the Finder menu.

✦ Click on the Finder icon in the Dock (if no Finder window is currently displayed, not counting minimized Finder windows in the Dock).

- ✦ If the Finder is the active application, press ⌘-N (identifying active applications is discussed later in this chapter).

- ✦ Double-click on any folder or disk icon visible on the desktop.

- ✦ Double-click on any folder or disk icon in another Finder window with the toolbar suppressed (turned off).

- ✦ Press ⌘ while opening (double-clicking) a folder or disk displayed in a Finder window with the toolbar visible.

In this newly minted Finder window, you are confronted with a number of interesting controls and surfaces. Some are large and obvious, the sidebar, the toolbar (both discussed later in this chapter), a few icons in the main window pane (either the elements of your Home folder or the root-level of your hard disk).

Note   Root-level is geek-talk for the topmost or outermost layer. Think of root-level as the candy coating on an M&M, with all your files living beneath, in a chocolate haven.

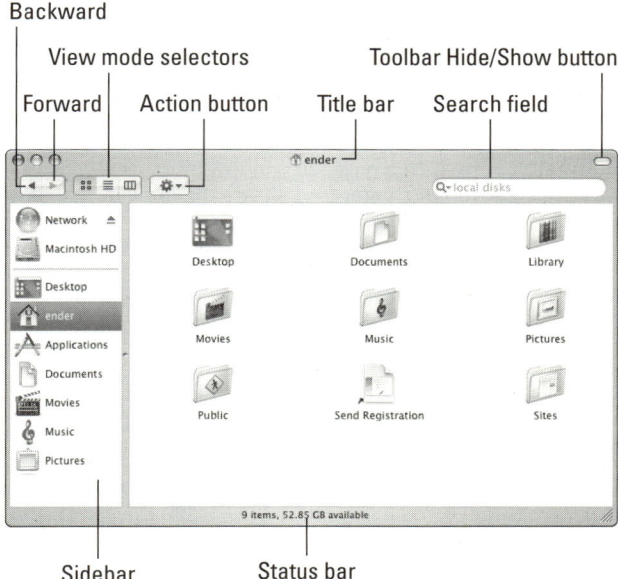

Figure 3-3: Finder windows are the primary tools used to view available files within folders or disks. These are some items unique to Finder windows.

Finder windows are comprised of the standard window controls described in the previous chapter in addition to a number of unique additional tools to modify the window's appearance and behavior.

✦ **Sidebar:** New in Mac OS 10.3, the sidebar is the area on the left side of a Finder window that contains commonly needed destinations within a user's system. The Sidebar can be edited to suit your needs. Editing the Sidebar is discussed in Chapter 4. To use a Sidebar item, simply click on its icon. The current window will display the Sidebar item's contents. For example, if you are currently reviewing your home folder in a Finder window, and then click on the Macintosh HD icon in the Sidebar, the contents of the root level of the hard disk will be displayed in the main window, rather than the home folder. Holding down ⌘ when clicking a Sidebar item opens a completely new Finder window in front of the original window. The new window displays the selected item's contents. Holding down option while clicking on an item closes the original window and opens a new one with the selected item displayed.

✦ **Toolbar:** The toolbar is located just below the title bar, and contains very useful tools to perform commonly used functions with a single click, rather than through complex commands. It functions as an adjunct to the menu bar (described in Chapter 2). With Mac OS 10.3's brushed metal look, there is no dividing line between the title bar and the toolbar any longer in Panther. They are now more like areas than they are actual separate bars. The toolbar can be edited to suit your needs or style. We discuss how to change the toolbar to suit your needs in Chapter 4.

✦ **Toolbar Hide/Show button:** An added element to the title bar in all Finder windows, the toolbar Hide/Show button is shaped like a grey pill. It is located in the top right portion of the title bar. Click this button to hide the toolbar, and to eliminate most of the finder-specific elements of the window. The result of turning off the toolbar is to produce a radically different looking Finder window, with no toolbar, no sidebar, and no brushed metal border. The look is very minimal, which will probably make the clean-freaks or OS 9 addicts out there happy. If this reduced window mode is already in effect, click this button to show the toolbar. Figure 3-4 shows the appearance of a standard window, and the same window with the toolbar turned off.

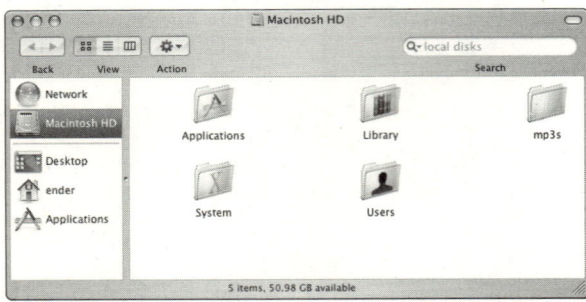

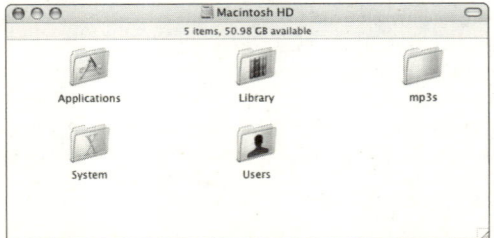

Figure 3-4: A standard Finder window (top) changes to a much simpler look (bottom) after clicking the Hide/Show button.

✦ **Action button:** New in OS 10.3, the Action button looks like a gear with a downward facing black triangle next to it. The action button performs functions nearly identical to a contextual menu. By clicking the Action button, a list of commands is presented based on the type of item selected.

✦ **Back:** A standard button in the toolbar, the Back button will rewind the Finder window to the previous folder that was opened.

✦ **Forward:** A standard button in the toolbar, the Forward button will move forward into a selected folder, or will undo a click of the Back button.

✦ **Status bar:** The status bar is displayed within the bottom of every Finder window's brushed metal frame. When a window is displayed with the Toolbar suppressed, the Status bar appears directly beneath the Titlebar. It presents information concerning the window's contents. The status bar also displays the amount of unused storage space on the disk or other volume that contains the folder whose contents appear in the window. (The space available is omitted in a window that shows the Computer level.) Also, if you do not have Write privileges for the folder, disk, or other item whose contents appear in the window, a small icon that looks like a crossed-out pencil appears near the left end of the status bar. Privileges are covered in Chapter 14. If the window is currently in icon view mode and is set up for automatic icon arrangement, an icon at the left end of the status bar indicates the type of arrangement. An icon that looks like a grid means icons always snap to an invisible grid. An icon that depicts four tiny aligned icons means icons in the window are kept arranged by name or another criterion. We describe how to set up automatic icon arrangement.

✦ **View mode selectors:** The view mode selectors are three buttons to the right of the Forward and Back buttons. This cluster of three items enables easy switching between the three possible Finder window view modes: Icon View, List View, and Column View. Each mode is represented by a unique icon. The icon view selector looks like four icons arranged in a square, the list view selector shows a list of information, and the column view selector shows three columns. Click on any of these three buttons to switch the current Finder window to the desired mode of view. These view modes are discussed in detail later in this chapter.

✦ **Search field:** It's all too easy to lose track of files or folders within the maze of your computer's files. This tool makes finding the lost files easy. Located at the top right of each Finder window, the Search field performs a dynamic file search. Start by clicking on the magnifying glass symbol next to the empty text field and select where you want to begin searching. The options are Local Disks (to scour all disks within your system), Home (to search only your Home), Selection (to search the currently displayed folder), and Everywhere (to search local disks and mounted server volumes). Select the most accurate place possible from this list, as the search will be completed faster the more accurately you define your search area. After selecting the search area, click within the search field to insert the cursor there. If you are looking for a file named, for example, Dog and Pony Show 01.doc, begin typing the name of the file, DOG. The current window will depopulate, and begin displaying all files and folders that contain the letters typed. This search field works dynamically, so each letter typed refines the displayed content. When you can see the file desired, simply stop typing and double-click on the file to open it, or open the file using any of the other methods covered in Chapter 5. Figure 3-5 shows the dynamic search in action, although it's difficult to capture the dynamic action occurring onscreen in a still photo.

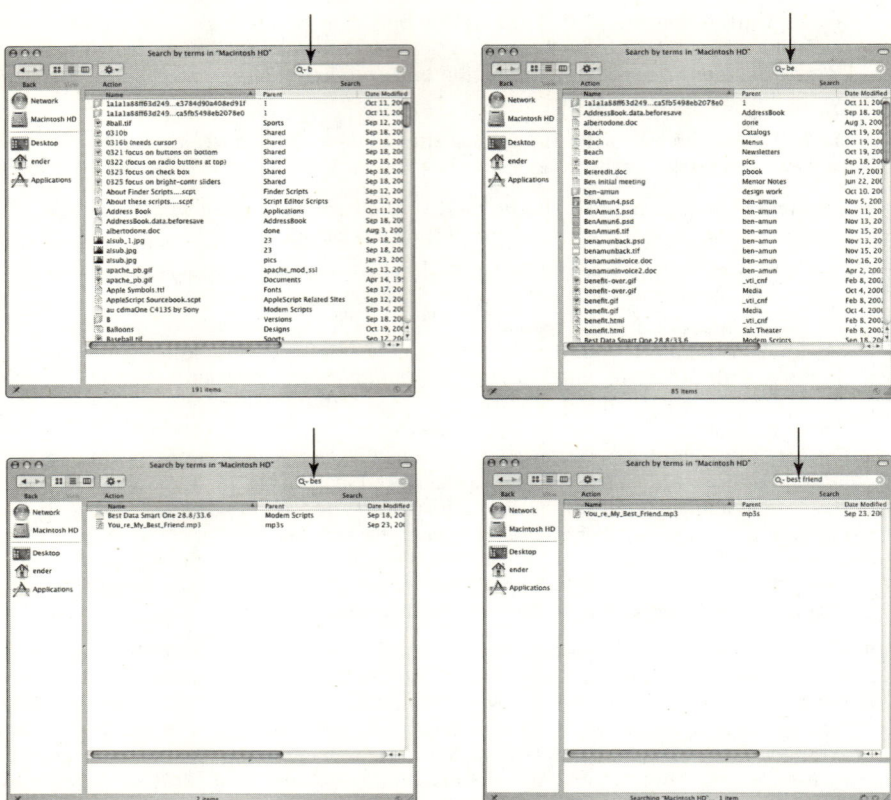

Figure 3-5: The Search field enables users to quickly search for items. As you enter text, the search refines, reducing the amount of displayed items.

Finder window views

Each Finder window can be viewed in one of three view modes, each with its own advantages and disadvantages. These choices are Icon View, List View, and Column View. Which mode or modes are used is completely up to a user's taste or the circumstances.

Choosing a view

You can choose your view format for the active Finder window in one of two ways:

✦ **Choose a view style from the Finder's View menu.** Select one of the three choices: as Icons, as List, or as Columns.

✦ **Click the appropriate part of the View Mode Selector button in the window's toolbar.** Click the left part of the button to view as icons, the middle part to view as a list, or the right part to view as columns.

Working in an icon view

The icon view is the original Finder view, dating back to the very first Macs shipped in 1984. Since then, this view has been enhanced in many small ways, but it is fundamentally the same view. You select an icon by clicking it, typing the first part of its name, pressing Tab or Shift-Tab, or pressing arrow keys. You can select multiple icons by clicking and dragging your pointer across them or by ⌘-clicking or Shift-clicking each icon in turn. The biggest advantage of the icon view is a visual sense. It is prettiest, after all. Also, graphic design applications (like Adobe Photoshop) create custom icons for each of their documents, representing the contents. Icon view shows these custom icons at their fullest, so a user can visually find a desired picture. The disadvantage is primarily the difficulty in managing many items in one window. Trying to navigate when it is difficult to find desired folders is painful!

Cleaning up

If the icons in an icon view are in disarray, you can have the Finder align them in neat rows and columns. You clean up the active window by choosing View ➪ Clean Up. You can clean up individual icons by holding down the ⌘ key while dragging them singly or in groups. Figure 3-6 shows a Finder window before and after being cleaned up.

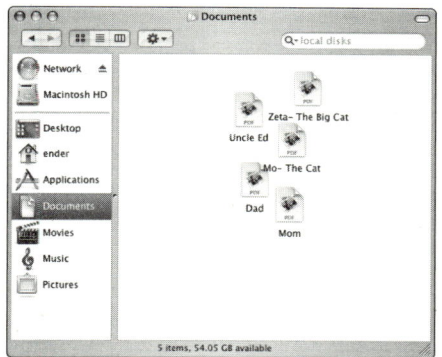 

Figure 3-6: A Finder window before (left) and after (right) the icons are arranged neatly.

Arrange by Name

You can also have the Finder alphabetize the icons and align them in rows and columns. Do this by choosing View ➪ Arrange by Name. Figure 3-7 shows a Finder window before and after being arranged by icon name.

The Finder can also keep the icons in a window arranged for you. You set up automatic icon arrangement in the Finder's View Options window as described in Chapter 4.

Working in a list view

List views can pack a lot of information in a window, and you can use all that information to help sort and organize the items. You can sort the list by any of the column headings at the top of the view. You can see the contents of enclosed folders in an indented outline format. Also, you can simultaneously select items contained in more than one enclosed folder. The primary advantage of list view is the variety of navigation tools available, and the ability to sort lists by more than just name. The disadvantage is the look and feel is a bit stifling. It feels very computer-ish, frankly. This, of course, is a matter of taste. Also, icons are smaller in list view, so visual scanning of icons for a particular document is more difficult.

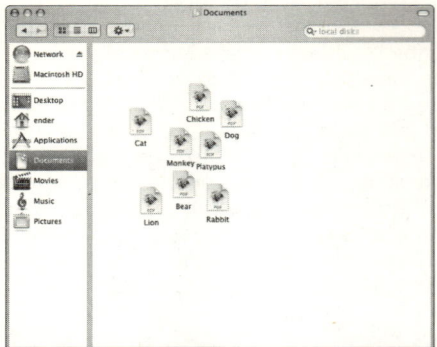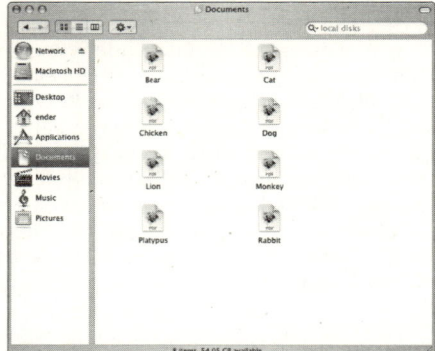

Figure 3-7: A Finder window before (left) and after (right) the icons are arranged alphabetically.

Changing the sort order

When you initially view a window as a list, the items are arranged alphabetically by name. A quick glance at the column headings tells you the sorting characteristic. The darker heading indicates the sorting characteristic. In a Finder window, you can sort the list in a different order by clicking one of the column headings near the top of the window. For example, to list the items in the order in which they were last modified, click the Date Modified heading. Click the heading again to reverse the sort. An arrowhead at the right end of the heading indicates the sort direction.

Rearranging and resizing columns

The columns of a list view are adjustable in a Finder window. This is helpful if an item's name is too long to be displayed in the current layout (indicated by the name truncated by an ellipsis [...]).

To change the size of a column:

1. **Move the mouse pointer to the right edge of a column heading.** (The pointer is in the right place for resizing a column when the pointer transforms into a thin upright with left and right pointing arrows coming out of it).

2. **Click and hold the mouse button.**

3. **Drag left or right.** Figure 3-8 is an example of resizing a column in a list view.

> **Tip**
>
> You don't have to widen a column in a list view just to read one long name. You can display the entire name in a help tag by moving the pointer over the name and waiting a few seconds. If you can't wait, point at the name and press Option to see the help tag immediately.

You can also change the order in which columns appear. Simply click and drag the column heading to the left or right. As you drag, the pointer looks like a hand and you see a pale image of the column you are moving. You can't move the Name column. Figure 3-9 is an example of rearranged columns.

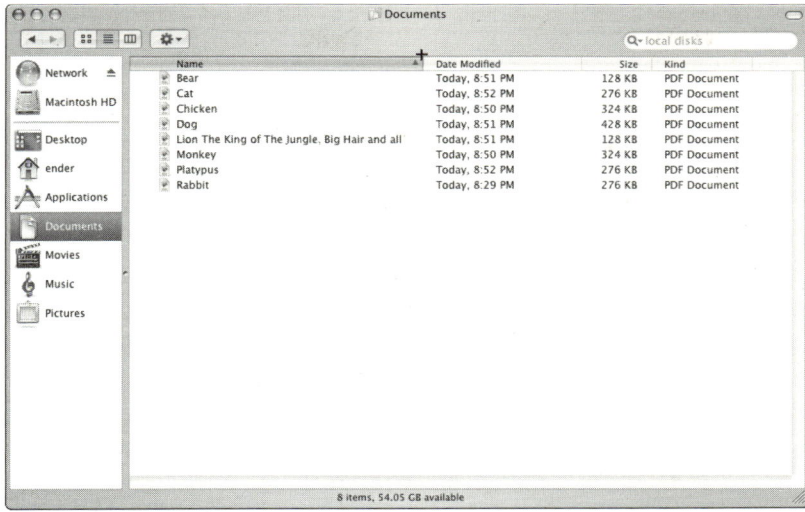

Figure 3-8: Drag a column heading's borderline to resize the column.

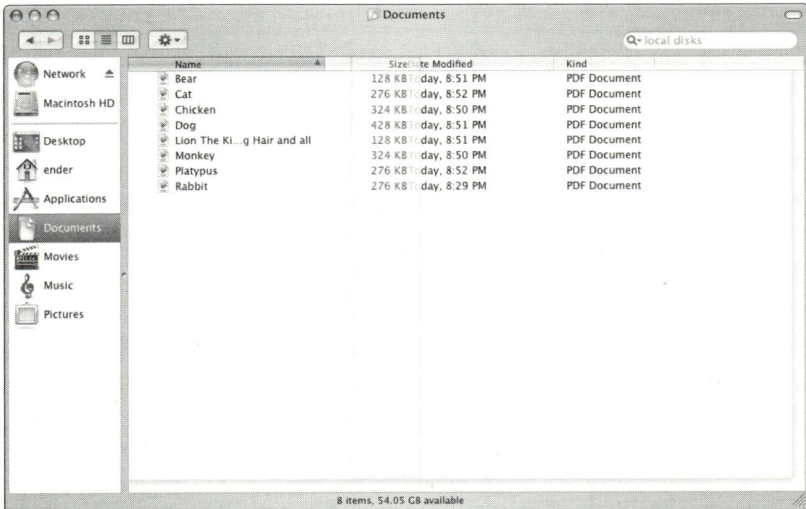

Figure 3-9: Drag a column heading to move the column.

Navigating a list view with disclosure triangles

When reviewing a folder's contents in List view, you don't have to open disks or folders in new windows to navigate deeper into your folder structure. A list view provides the additional technique of expanding the folders via a method similar to an indented outline. Instead of opening a folder or disk in a new window, you can see the contents of a disk or folder by clicking the disclosure triangle next to its icon.

Disclosure triangles next to folder names tell you whether the folders are expanded or collapsed. If a triangle points to the right, the folder next to it is collapsed, and you cannot see its contents. If the triangle points down, the folder is expanded, and below the folder name, you can see a list of the items in the folder. The Finder displays list views in an indented outline format. The levels of indentation in the outline show how folders are nested. The indented outline provides a graphical representation of a folder's organization. You can look through and reorganize several folders all in one window. Figure 3-10 shows an example of a list view with both expanded and collapsed folders.

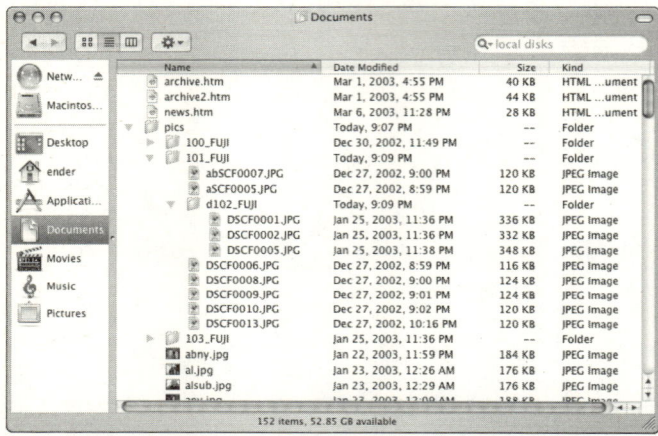

Figure 3-10: A list view with expanded and collapsed folders.

To expand a folder, click the triangle to the left of the folder's icon. When you expand a folder, the Finder remembers whether folders nested within it were previously expanded or collapsed and restores each to its former state. Figure 3-11 shows a folder after expanding it.

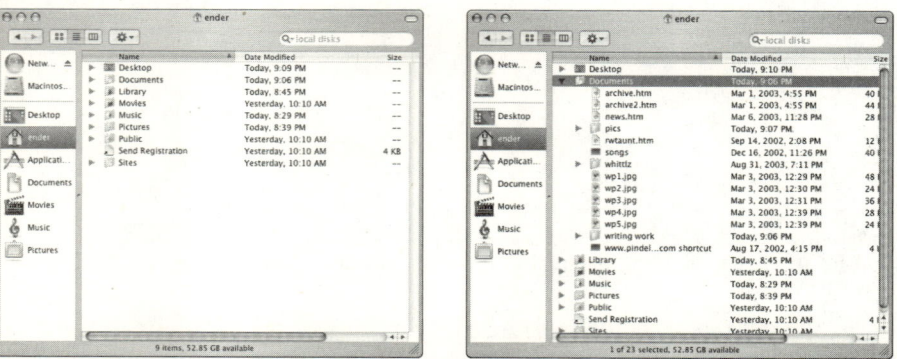

Figure 3-11: Click a disclosure triangle to expand a folder and display its contents.

To collapse a folder, click the down-pointing triangle to the left of the folder's icon. It returns to the right-pointing orientation, and the contents are no longer displayed.

To collapse a folder and any open subfolders within it, press Option while clicking the disclosure triangle of the outer folder. To expand a folder and all the subfolders within it, press Option while clicking the disclosure triangle.

 Tip   If you have a folder or multiple folders selected, you can press ⌘-→ to expand them or ⌘-Option-→ to expand them and all their nested subfolders. To collapse folders from the keyboard, ⌘-← collapses the outline to that level.

Working in a column view

Like list views, column views pack a lot of information into one window. This view's heritage is the NeXT browser view, and it first appeared on the Mac in the shareware utility, Greg's Browser, back in 1989. Understanding the column view and becoming comfortable with its use is relatively important because you see column views in the dialogs for opening and saving documents within applications (as explained in Chapter 5). The main advantage of column view is the ease of reviewing the path to a particular item. Knowing where your data is at all times is a very good thing! The disadvantage is the lack of additional visible data and the various sorting options present in List view.

A column view shows a folder and its contents in the same window through the use of limitless replicating columns. When you select a folder in a column view, that folder's contents appear in the next column to the right. The deeper you explore, the more columns become available. When you select an alias of a folder, Mac OS X resolves the alias and the Finder displays the original folder's contents in the next column to the right. (Aliases are discussed later in this chapter.) When you select a file, some basic information about the item, as well as its icon or a preview of its contents appears in the next column to the right. Whether you see a file's icon or a preview of its contents depends on the type of file. For an application, you always see an icon and some facts about the application. For some types of documents that contain text or graphics, you see a preview. Figure 3-12 shows a column view.

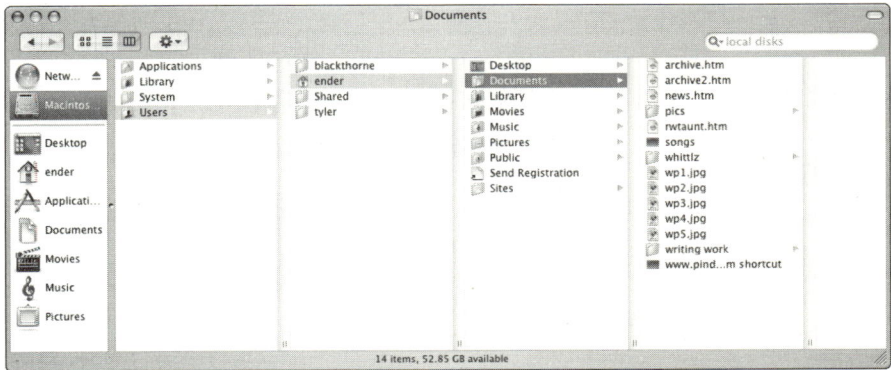

Figure 3-12: A column view shows the folder structure on a disk

A column view differs markedly from an icon view or a list view in how much of your folder structure you can see. Where an icon view shows only one folder and a list view shows one folder plus the folders it contains, every column view can show any part of the folder structure on any disk that's available on your computer. By scrolling a column view to the left, you can traverse the folder hierarchy to the Computer level. By scrolling to the right, you can traverse the folder hierarchy the other direction until you reach the currently selected folder or file.

Unlike list or icon views, you have no control over the sorting order in a column view. Items in each column are always listed alphabetically. (Actually, the order of items is based on the character-set ordering established for your system and language.)

Resizing columns

Column width is adjustable in a column view. You can adjust the widths of all columns uniformly or the width of a single column, as follows:

✦ To resize one column, drag the handle found at the bottom of the column divider.

✦ To resize *all* columns at once uniformly, hold Option while dragging the handle at the bottom of any column divider to the right or left.

Previewing files in a column view

One of the column view's nicest features is that, when you select certain types of document files, you see a preview of that document's contents in the rightmost column. Previews display for several types of documents, including plain text, PDF, sound, movie, and graphics files. For a document with multiple pages, the preview shows the first page. The preview for a sound or movie appears with a small QuickTime controller, which you use to hear the sound or see the movie. We cover QuickTime extensively in Chapters 20 and 21. For now, just know that you can click the Play button at the left end of the controller to play the movie or sound preview. The small Play button looks like a right-pointing arrowhead, as shown in Figure 3-13.

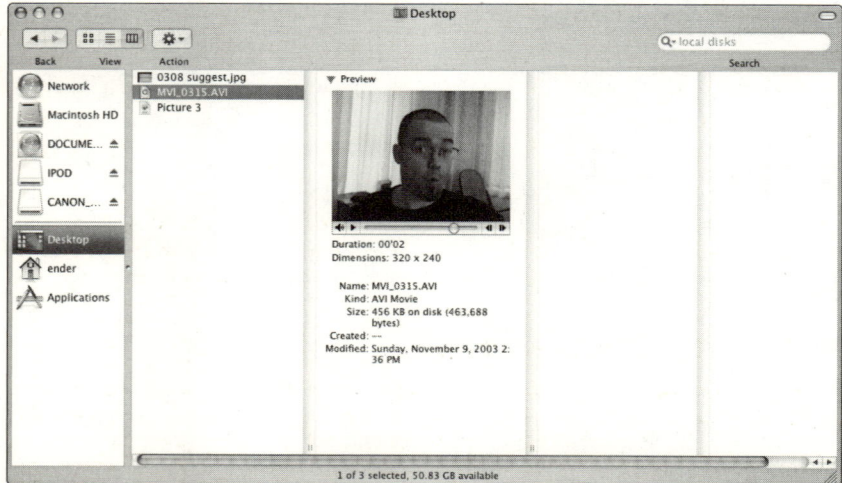

Figure 3-13: Preview your movie, sound, graphics, and text files in a Finder window viewed as columns.

Note   Preparing the preview for a long PDF document or even a very large plain text document can take a long time and cause the Mac to be unresponsive. To guard against extreme delays, the Finder doesn't show a preview for text and multiple-page PDF documents larger than about 500K.

Pathfinding alternative

As noted, a column view gives you a quick look at the path through the folder structure from the Computer level to the item or items displayed in the rightmost column. You don't have to be in a column view to obtain this path information, though. At the top of any Finder window, you see an icon for the folder you're in, accompanied by its name. When you press the ⌘ key and click the name, a menu pops up, showing the hierarchy of folders traversed to get back to the Computer level. The current folder is at the top of the pop-up menu and the Computer level is at the bottom, as shown in Figure 3-14.

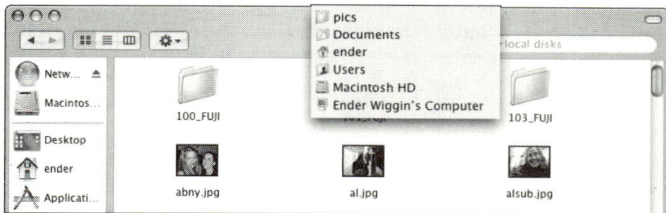

Figure 3-14: See the path through your folder structure by ⌘-clicking the title of a Finder window.

Interacting with Windows

Having described Finder windows in detail, it's important to remember that there are many additional types of windows in Mac OS X, but they all adhere to standards of command and have many of the same control surfaces. In this section, you learn how to create and control windows. You work mostly with Finder windows, as they tend to have the most tools for control.

A new window please

As noted earlier in this chapter, to open a new Finder window, simply double-click on a folder or a disk icon. Alternately, you can single click to select folder or disk and then press ⌘-O or select Open from the File menu (or use any of the host of other options described).

Active and inactive windows

When more than one standard window is open, only one window is considered active, meaning that you can interact with all the items in it, and control surfaces it is comprised of. You may be able to interact with some window controls and other items in inactive windows (for example, you can close inactive windows by clicking their respective close buttons), but you can't interact with everything in inactive windows.

Recognizing the active window

You can tell the active window because it is in front of inactive windows. Therefore, the active window overlaps all other windows except palettes belonging to the same application as the active window. (Palettes float in a layer above the active window.) In addition, the active window is conspicuous because all its controls are full color and available for use, whereas the controls of inactive windows are dim. Figure 3-15 shows active and inactive windows.

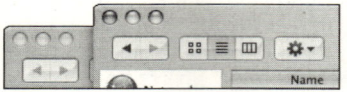

Figure 3-15: The active window is in front of inactive windows, and its controls are more conspicuous (especially when you see the windows in color).

Making another window active

You can make any visible window the active window by clicking any visible part of it. Making a window active brings it in front of the window that was previously active. If the new active window belongs to an application with palettes, they all come to the front, as well. To make all the windows of a Mac OS X application come forward together, click the application's icon in the Dock.

Note   If an alert or a dialog other than a sheet is displayed, you may need to dismiss it (by clicking its OK button or Cancel button) before you can make another window active in the same application program.

Interacting with inactive windows

If you want to interact with something in an inactive window, you can always click the window to make it active and then click again to interact with the object of your desire in the window. In some cases, you don't have to click twice to interact with items in an inactive window. For instance, you can operate the Close, Minimize, and Zoom buttons in most inactive Aqua windows, and they perform their standard functions, closing, minimizing, or in the case of Zoom, changing the window's size. In addition, some applications bring a window to the front when you click the window's Zoom button. The Finder does not behave this way; a Finder window that's in the background stays in the background when you click the window's Zoom button. If you think about what the Close and Minimize buttons do, you can see why clicking one of these in an inactive window does not bring the window to the front. The ability to interact directly with an item in an inactive window is called click-through.

Some items in inactive Aqua windows respond when you interact with them, while other items in the same windows don't respond. A responsive window control in an inactive Aqua window becomes more pronounced when the mouse pointer passes over it. A responsive item labeled with text or a symbol (such as an arrow) is supposed to have a dark label to indicate that it is enabled. An unresponsive item is supposed to have a dim label to indicate that it is disabled. However, Mac OS X applications don't follow these rules uniformly. You will have to learn by trial and error which items are responsive in inactive windows. Figure 3-16 illustrates the difference between responsive and unresponsive items in inactive Aqua windows.

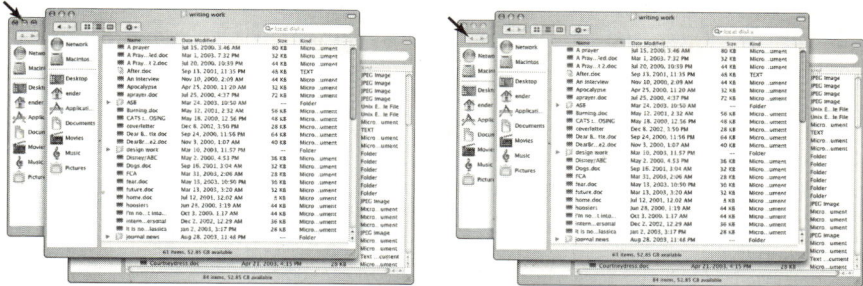

Figure 3-16: As the pointer passes over items in an Aqua background window, responsive items become more pronounced (left), but unresponsive items don't (right).

Using the Window menu

When you have multiple Finder windows displayed and want to use one in particular, figuring out which of them is the one you want can often be difficult. In Mac OS X, the Finder sports a Window menu that lists all the open Finder windows by name. You can quickly bring a particular Finder window to the front by choosing it from the Window menu. Figure 3-17 shows an example of the Finder's Window menu.

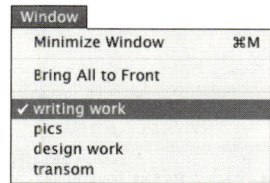

Figure 3-17: Bring a Finder window to the front by choosing it from the Window menu.

In Mac OS X, Finder windows can become intermingled with windows belonging to other applications. Clicking a window belonging to a particular Mac OS X application brings just that one window to the front. If you click Finder windows alternately with windows belonging to other Mac OS X applications, the windows end up stacked in the order you clicked them regardless of application, as shown in Figure 3-18.

Bringing just the clicked window forward is a consistent and flexible behavior, but there are times when you will want to bring all of a particular application's windows to the fore. This is the raison d'être of Bring All to Front in the Window menu. Choose Window ➪ Bring All to Front, and all the Finder windows will now be in front of all other applications' windows, while retaining their own front-to-back ordering. Choosing Window ➪ Bring All to Front does not bring any minimized windows to the front; they stay in the Dock. Let us hope that developers of other Mac OS X applications follow the Finder's lead, and build this function into all applications. Many already have it, but some don't. Some applications don't even have a Window menu!

Tip   You can also bring all the Finder's windows to the front by clicking the Finder's icon in the Dock. To bring all Finder windows to the front while hiding all other windows, ⌘-Option-click the Finder's icon in the Dock.

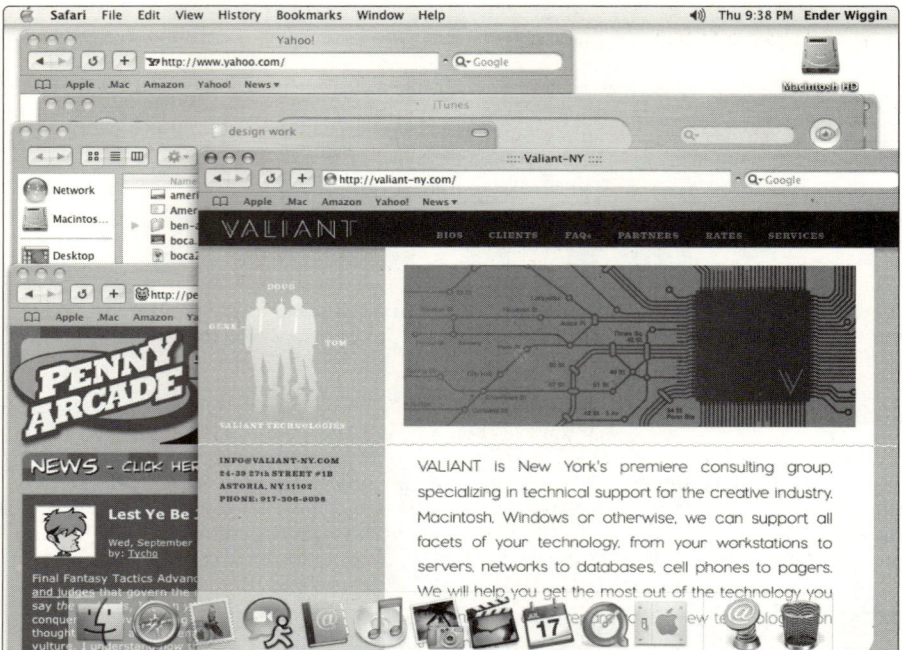

Figure 3-18: Finder windows can become intermingled with windows belonging to other Mac OS X applications.

Window Tricks

You can move and minimize most inactive windows without bringing them to the front. The following window tricks work even on windows that don't have visible controls:

✦ To move an inactive window, press ⌘ while dragging the window's title bar. Alternatively, you can ⌘-drag the frame of an inactive window to move the window.

✦ To minimize all windows that belong to the same application as the active window, press Option while clicking the active window's Minimize button. In some cases, you get the same effect by pressing Option and ⌘ while double-clicking the title bar of any window that belongs to the same Mac OS X application as the active window.

✦ To minimize an inactive window, press ⌘ while double-clicking its title bar. (Or just click the minimize button, which of course is easier.)

Interacting with Icons

Whether you are viewing your windows in list mode, column mode, or icon mode, the items you interact with day-to-day are all icons. All icons respond universally to a few standard interactive techniques. This section explores some of them, preparing you for a more in-depth look at your environment in the following chapters. Modifying the appearance of items is covered in Chapter 4. Opening applications and creating/editing documents is covered in Chapter 5.

Selecting icons

Everyone who uses a Mac quickly learns to select an icon by clicking on it with the mouse, but even some seasoned veterans don't know that you can select icons individually by typing instead of clicking. In addition, you can select more than one icon at a time using various techniques.

When you select an icon, the Mac OS highlights it by creating a border around it and by highlighting the item's name. Figure 3-19 shows an example of an icon that is highlighted and one that isn't.

Figure 3-19: Mac OS X highlights the selected icon by surrounding it with a shadow and highlighting the title.

Selecting multiple icons by clicking

Ordinarily, clicking an icon selects it (highlights it) and deselects the icon that was previously highlighted. After selecting the first icon, you can select a group of icons in the same window by pressing the ⌘ key while clicking each icon in turn. At any time, you can deselect a selected icon by holding down the ⌘ key and clicking it again.

Selecting multiple items in a column view

In a window where icons are displayed in a list or column, you can select a whole range of icons with two clicks. First, you click one icon to select it; then you press and hold the Shift key while clicking another icon to select it and all the icons between the first icon and the one you just selected. In a Column View, when multiple items are selected, preview data in the right-most column is not shown, nor do selected folders expand in the next column.

Selecting from multiple folders in a list view

In a list view, you are afforded an additional technique for selecting with ⌘-clicks. After expanding several folders in a list view, you can simultaneously select items in any of the expanded folders. To select an additional item, press ⌘ while clicking it. If you want to select consecutive items, drag a selection rectangle across the consecutive items or select the first item and Shift-click the last item. If you need to deselect a few items, ⌘-click each item. Figure 3-20 shows a list view with items selected from two folders.

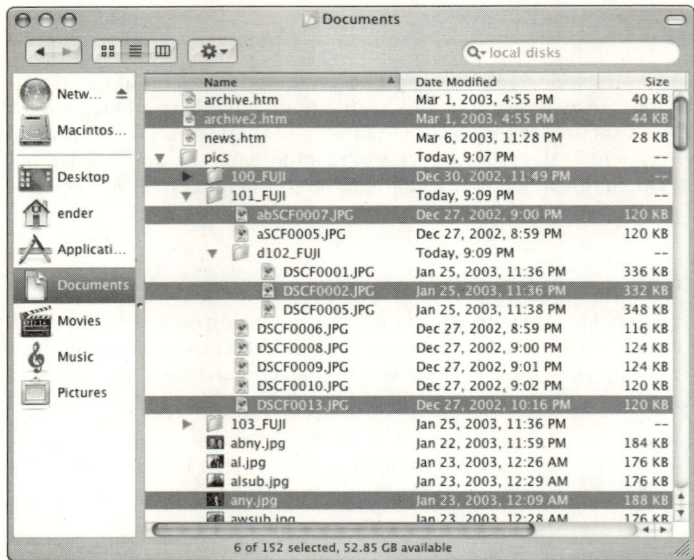

Figure 3-20: In a list view, you can select items from multiple folders.

Selected items remain selected if you expand or close other folders in the same window. Note that any selected items in a folder you collapse are no longer selected.

Selecting multiple icons by dragging

In addition to selecting multiple icons by clicking with the ⌘ or Shift keys, you can select adjacent icons by dragging the mouse pointer across them. As you drag, the Mac OS displays a shaded rectangle, called a selection rectangle, and every icon it touches or encloses is selected. Icons are highlighted one-by-one as you drag over them, not en masse after you stop dragging. All icons must be in a single window. Figure 3-21 is an example of selecting several icons with a selection rectangle.

You can combine dragging with the use of the ⌘ key. Pressing ⌘ while dragging a selection rectangle across unselected icons adds the enclosed icons to the current selection. Conversely, pressing ⌘ while dragging a selection rectangle across selected icons deselects the enclosed group without deselecting other icons (if any).

Selecting by typing

When you know the name of an icon that you want to select but aren't sure where it is in a window, you can quickly select it by typing. Typing may be faster than clicking if the icon you want to select requires lots of scrolling to bring it into view.

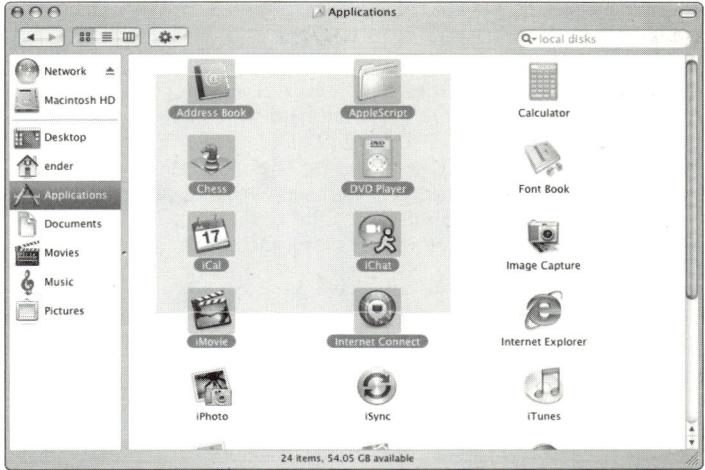

Figure 3-21: Drag across adjacent icons to select all of them.

To select an icon in the active window by typing, simply type the first part of its name. You need to type only enough of the name to identify the icon you want uniquely. In a window in which every icon has a completely different name, for example, you need to type only the first letter of a name to select an icon. By contrast, in a folder where every item name begins with Mac, you have to type those three letters plus enough additional letters to single out the icon you want. This typing must be done reasonably quickly, as any lengthy delays will result in the computer assuming you are searching for a new file. This will frustrate slower typists. (And, perhaps, serve as inspiration for some intense typing practice?) When selecting by typing, capitalization doesn't matter.

Also, pressing one of the arrow keys selects the icon nearest the one currently selected in the arrow's direction. In a window where icons are not displayed in a list, pressing Tab selects the next icon alphabetically and Shift-Tab selects the previous icon alphabetically. Table 2-1 summarizes keyboard selection techniques.

Table 2-1: Selecting Icons by Typing

To Select This	Do This
An icon	Type the icon's partial or full name.
Next icon up or down*	Press Up or Down Arrow ($\uparrow$) or ($\downarrow$).
Next icon left or right*	Press Left or Right Arrow ($\leftarrow$) or ($\rightarrow$)
Next icon alphabetically*	Press Tab.
Previous icon alphabetically*	Press Shift-Tab.

*Applies only to a window where icons are not displayed in a list.

Contextual Menus

Through a simple Control-click on an item, the contextual menu is revealed. Each item's contextual menu is different, depending on the item's type (thus the name, contextual). Folders, documents, aliases, disks, and applications all get their own suite of options. All the commands made available in a contextual menu are available elsewhere, via the File menu, the Apple menu, or some other way, but the contextual menu is a convenient and fast way to apply commonly used commands to an item. Bringing up the contextual menu for the desktop and selecting Change Desktop Background brings up the Desktop & Screen saver preference pane, which enables you to change the desktop background. The contextual menu for a standard document has an Open With option. This expands via a submenu to show compatible applications. It's a convenient way to open a document with a different application. We refer to contextual menus often, and strongly recommend purchasing a two-button mouse and using the right-button. The two-button method is much easier and faster than the "Steve-Jobs-two-handed" control-click method.

Moving icons

After selecting a few items, you may wish to move them around. To move files from folder to folder, simply select the files, then drag any of the items to the new desired location. You can drag an item by its icon or its name. In a list view, you can also drag an item by any text on the same line as the item's icon, such as its modification date or kind. The new location for your item can be the desktop, an open Finder window or a closed folder. When you position the item you are moving over a folder icon, the Finder highlights the destination icon by making it darker. When you drag an item over a Finder window, the Finder highlights the window by drawing a heavy border inside the window frame. The highlight visually confirms your target.

When you release the mouse button, the item will be moved from its original location to the newly selected one. There is one exception: if you are attempting to move a file to a different disk, the mouse pointer changes from a black arrow to a plus sign within a green dot. This symbol signifies that you are not moving the file to the new location, but rather making a copy of the file to the new location. The original item will be unaffected.

If a folder or disk is open, you can move it by dragging the small proxy icon in the title bar of its window. To drag a proxy icon, you must place the pointer over it and hold down the mouse button for a second before dragging the icon away. Proxy icons are handy when you want to move a folder that is already open. Even if you can't see the folder's regular icon, you can move the folder by dragging its proxy icon to a Finder window, the desktop, a different folder's icon, or the Dock.

Replacing items

If you move an item into a folder that contains another item of the same name, you are confronted with an alert, asking if you want to replace the file at the destination. (If you copy a group of items and more than one of them has the same name as items at the destination, you are alerted one-by-one for each of the duplicates.) Clicking Replace will erase the items noted in the alert window from the destination folder and replace them with the moved items. Clicking Stop will cancel the move operation. Figure 3-22 shows an example of the alert the Finder displays to verify replacement.

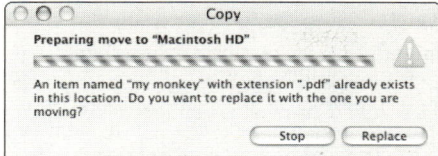

Figure 3-22: The Mac OS X Finder lets you decide whether to replace existing files of the same name.

Spring loaded folders

To move an item from one folder to another, you do not need to have both folders open in separate windows simultaneously. You can deposit an item directly on top of another folder. This will place the item within the folder. If you want to delve deeper, use Apple's extra-nifty Spring Loaded Folders feature. Drag an item over a folder to highlight it and hold it there. After a brief delay, the folder blinks twice as if double-clicked and opens to display its contents. If there wasn't a window already opened, a new one will open. You can then place the item within the folder that has been sprung, or repeat the process with more and more subfolders as they are revealed. If you open the wrong folder with this method, either move the item out of the window (which will close the window), or move the item over a location in the sidebar to navigate there. For example, if you delve too deeply into your Documents folder, go back to the root level of your Documents folder by dragging over its icon in the sidebar. After the brief Spring Loaded Folder delay, your window will now display the Documents folder, and you can reattempt the moving process. After you release the item into its new location, the item is placed there. It is worth noting that if the window was created by the Spring Loaded Folders function, releasing the item places it in its new location and also closes the window.

This technique works for disks as well; dragging an item directly on top a disk (and waiting for the term of the prescribed delay) will open a new Finder window displaying the contents of the root level of the selected drive. The length of delay time before springing is set in the Finder preferences, as covered in Chapter 4.

Replicating your files

There will be times when you may need to replicate a file, either to make changes to one while preserving the original version, or to copy the file from one disk to another. The commands Copy or Duplicate are typically used, and are interchangeable in this context for all intents and purposes. In either case, there are a few simple techniques available.

Making Corrections with Undo

If you move a file to an incorrect location, assign the wrong file name, or incorrectly label a file with a color, pressing ⌘-Z (or selecting Undo from the Edit menu) will undo the erroneous move/name/color. The function will undo only the last action performed, and the Undo operation will *not* undo an item replacement or deletion. It will simply restore items to their original location or name or color, but replaced or deleted items are gone for good! Of course, it's still a powerful tool to use. In fact, after using the Finder's Undo feature a few times, we all wish the other aspects of our lives had an "undo."

Duplicating an item

To generate an identical copy of a selected item in the same location as the original, use the Duplicate command. To perform a duplicate operation, single-click on an item and select Duplicate from the File menu. If the item chosen is a folder, the duplicate contains duplicates of everything in the original folder. The newly created item will be placed in the same folder as the original, but with the word copy tagged onto the end of its name. This phrase is added to the end to help distinguish between the original and the copy, and because two files with the same name cannot exist simultaneously in the same folder. (The computer would have no way to know which one is which.) Additional copies of the same item also have a serial number added after the word copy. If the name does have a file extension, the word copy and the serial number appear before the extension. For example, the first duplicate of a folder named Untitled Folder is Untitled Folder copy, but the first duplicate of a file named Readme.txt is Readme copy.txt. The keyboard shortcut for Duplicate is ⌘-D. You can also duplicate a file with the contextual menu, selecting the Duplicate option when control-clicking on an item.

Copying an item

The main difference between Duplicate and Copy is that Duplicate creates the new item in the same location as the original and tinkers with the new item's name, whereas Copy does not. A copy can create items in the same folder, forcing the name change, but it can also create files in new locations, with no need to change the name, due to the alternative location (i.e., no name conflict).

To copy a file, select the item, and then choose Copy from the Edit menu (or contextual menu). Then, navigate to the new desired location and make it active. Select Paste from the Edit (or contextual) menu to initiate the copy. This method works best with a two-button mouse, as all copies can be done with one hand.

Another method is to hold down the Option key and then drag the file. The pointer will switch from its normal status as an arrow to becoming a plus symbol in a green dot. This signifies that you are about to copy the file to the selected location, rather than just move it there.

The Finder always copies an item when you drag it to a folder that's on another disk. Again, the Finder displays a little plus sign on the pointer when you position an item over a folder of a different disk.

Replacing an item

Much as with moving files, when you copy an item to a folder that already contains an item by the same name, an alert asks whether you want to replace the item at the destination. If you copy a group of items and more than one of them has the same name as items at the destination, you are alerted one by one for each of the duplicates. Clicking Replace will erase the items in the destination folder and replace them with the new copies. Clicking Stop will halt the copy operation.

Renaming Files

After an item is selected, you can rename the item to better reflect your needs. For example, you may need to reflect changes in the document by tacking on a "revised" to the name, or you may just want to rename an item to reflect its creator or content "Story from Mom" or "Picture of Famke Jannsen." Some items can be renamed with impunity, while other items are best left unmodified. Documents can be renamed with total freedom. Applications and system files should not be renamed on a whim. (If you aren't sure, don't rename them!) Disks can be renamed with freedom, although the new name may goof up some external things, like aliases and path shortcuts. (Aliases are covered in detail in Chapter 4, network paths are covered in Chapter 15.)

Creating an Archive

Archive creation is a new standard feature in Panther. This was once handled by third-party software, but now the OS does it internally. What is archiving? Archiving compiles and compresses any number of files selected into a single, smaller, more protected file. Select any folder, disk, item (or group of items), and select Create Archive of <filename> from the File menu (or from the contextual menu). When using the archive command, a progress bar will briefly appear as the system is creating the archive. Archiving is often necessary to email files to friends, as email really kicks your files around in transit (much like the post office does with your mail), and often corrupts them. This is especially true when trying to email more than one item at a time. By compressing the files into a single archive, you protect them from harm as they zoom around the Internet. This archiving is also a form of compression. Compression makes a file smaller without actually reducing any of the quality (when the file is uncompressed it goes back to its original size). Compression is obviously useful if you want to preserve space on your disk, or if you just want to make a particular cluster of files into a single, easily manageable item. After the archive is created, you can un-archive the files by simply double clicking on it. The archive will be opened and the files safely extracted by any of a number of available tools. After extraction, the archive will remain in its original form, still full of your files.

To rename a folder, file, or other item, you must explicitly select its name. After you have performed the selection correctly, the item's name will be highlighted with a lighter shade of the selection color (remember, when items are selected, the icon is highlighted, and the name is surrounded by a color). The lighter shade highlighting the name indicates that the entire text is selected and ready for replacement. There are a few different methods to achieve this, depending on the way your items are displayed.

✦ **In any view mode:** First select the item, and then strike the Return or Enter key.

✦ **In Icon view:** Single-click on the *text* of the name, rather than the icon. After a brief delay, the name will be highlighted with the lighter shade.

✦ **In the List view or Column view:** You must first select the item using any method you choose, then *wait* briefly and click the selected item's name. If you issue the second click too quickly, the computer will think you are double-clicking though, and open the document rather than selecting the name for editing. In either case, after a brief delay, the name will be selected for your editing pleasure.

✦ **In the Get Info window:** You can change the name in the Name and Extension panes. When the name is first selected, the entire name is highlighted. With the whole name selected this way, you replace it completely by typing a new name. If you want to change only part of the name, you can select that part and replace or delete it. You can also place an insertion point and type additional text. Figure 3-23 shows one icon name entirely selected, another name partially selected, and an insertion point in a third name.

Figure 3-23: Select all of an icon name (left), part of an icon name (middle), or simply type new text from an insertion point (right).

To replace or delete part of an item name, do the following:

1. **Select the name for editing.** Use any of the methods just described.

2. **Position the pointer where you want to begin selecting in the name.** When the pointer is over the selected text, it should be shaped like the letter *I*.

3. **Hold down the mouse button and drag the pointer to select part of the name.** As you drag, Mac OS X highlights the text you are selecting.

   To select one particular word in a name, you can double-click the word instead of dragging across it.

4. **Release the mouse button to stop selecting.**

5. **Type a replacement for the selected part of the name or press Delete to remove the selected text.**

6. **Press Return to end your editing.** Alternatively, you can click outside the name that you're editing.

To insert text in an item name, follow these steps:

1. **Select the name for editing.** Use any of the proscribed methods.

2. **Position the pointer where you want to make an insertion.** When the pointer is over the selected text, it should be shaped like the letter *I*.

3. **Click to place an insertion point.** A thin flashing line (known as the *cursor*) marks the position of the insertion point.

4. **Type your additional text.**

5. **Press Return to end your editing.** Alternatively, you can click outside the name that you're editing.

When the desired name is entered, press return or enter to complete the renaming. If you decide you don't want to rename the item, but have already accidentally erased the original name, don't panic! Press the Escape key before pressing return and the original name will be restored. If you have already pressed Return and applied the name, all is still not lost. Use the Finder's Undo feature to revert the name. To use the Undo, press ⌘-Z. The Undo feature is covered in greater detail later in this chapter.

Naming with Cut, Copy, and Paste

While editing a name, instead of typing the name from scratch, you can use the Cut, Copy, and Paste commands in the Edit menu. To copy all or part of an icon name, select the part that you want to copy and choose Copy from the Edit menu. The Copy command places the selected text on the Clipboard, which is an internal holding area. Then you can paste what you copied by selecting all or part of another icon's name and choosing Paste from the Edit menu. At this point, you can make changes to the name that you pasted. Whatever text you copied remains on the Clipboard until you use the Copy command again or the Cut command. The Cut command works just like the Copy command, but Cut also removes the initially selected text while placing it on the Clipboard. Cut, Copy, and Paste operations are covered in greater detail in Chapter 5.

Selecting Text with the Keyboard

With an icon name selected for editing, you can also move the insertion point or change the selection by using the arrow keys.

↑	Moves the insertion point to the beginning of the name
↓	Moves the insertion point to the end of the name
→	Moves the insertion point to the right
←	Moves the insertion point to the left
Shift-→	Selects more (or less) of the name to the right
Shift-←	Selects more (or less) of the name to the left

Whether Shift-→ and Shift-← selects more or less depends on the direction that you dragged when you initially selected part of the name.

Note

Some item names cannot be selected for editing. You can't rename such an item because it is locked or you don't have Write privileges for the item. You may be able to unlock the item, but you probably can't give yourself Write privileges. We discuss locking and unlocking later in this chapter. Privileges are covered in detail later in Chapter 14.

Some notes on naming

Mac OS X is very forgiving with regards to naming rules. With support for 255 character-long names and all the funky symbols you can imagine, names in the Mac OS X world are only limited by your imagination. That said, your friends and their Windows machines are not so forgiving. If you ever intend to share your documents or submit them for publication or review, then you should obey certain rules.

✦ Avoid special characters, like the infinity symbol (∞), the bullet symbol (•) or the euro symbol (€) in the file name, because the Windows OS may not render these characters correctly. Because of having incorrectly represented characters in a name, the files may come up as unreadable for others.

✦ Names can't include colons because the Mac OS uses colons internally to specify the *path* through your folder structure to a file. A pathname consists of a disk name, a succession of folder names, and a file name, with a colon separating each name. For example, the pathname `Macintosh HD:Applications:Chess` specifies the location of the Chess application on a startup disk named Macintosh HD. Putting a colon in a file name would interfere with the computer's scheme for specifying paths, so the Finder won't let you do it.

✦ Although the Finder won't let you use colons in a file name, it *will* let you use slashes. It is strongly advised that you *never* use slash characters (/ or \) in your file names. Windows machines read these characters as indicating the path on their disks, and the computer will be looking to folders that do not exist, resulting in a completely inaccessible document (unless your friend is smart enough to figure out how to rename the files).

I'm sorry Dave, I cannot allow you to do that...

Mac OS X doesn't permit you to move, rename, or copy everything, and it won't let you put stuff anywhere you want. For example, you can't move or copy your items into another user's home folder. Conversely, you can't move or rename items that belong to other users, although you may be able to copy other users' items into your folders.

The Finder won't let you move an item from its current location or rename it unless you have Write privileges for the item. If you try to move an item for which you don't have Write privileges but do have Read privileges, the Finder makes a copy of the item instead. If you don't have Write or Read privileges for an item, the Finder doesn't let you move, rename, or copy the item.

Regardless of your Write privileges for an item that you want to move or copy, you must also have Write privileges for the destination folder. If you try to move or copy an item to a folder for which you don't have Write privileges, the Finder displays an alert, saying the destination folder cannot be modified.

We cover privileges in Chapter 14.

✦ Periods are also not recommended as both Mac OS X and Windows use the information following the period to determine a file's type. In the Mac OS, this information, called the file *extension,* is hidden by default. Of course, you can place a period in the name if you want to specify the file extension, or if you just want to take the chance.

✦ A few things that *are* okay: All alphabetic letters (capital or not, i.e., A–Z, a–z), Hindu-Arabic numbers (0–9), The symbols in the number row (`~!@#$%^&*()=+), blank spaces, hyphens (-) and underscores (_) are universally acceptable, as are commas (,).

Get Info

Mac OS X keeps a great deal of detailed information about your files, folders, and disks beyond what's available in regular Finder windows. A time may come when you want to see or change some of this information. Hidden in the Info window (also known as the Get Info pane; or just Get Info) is the area that displays the additional critical information and enables some interesting changes to be performed on most selected items. To bring this powerful window to light, select an item and select Show Info from the File menu, or press ⌘-I. The Get Info window opens, complete with basic information and bearing multiple disclosure triangles hiding various information and control repositories, as shown in Figure 3-24. These are described in the following text.

General

General is the main area of the Get Info window. The item's icon, its name, type, location, creation date, modification data, and size are all shown in this area. Depending on the item's type, additional or alternate information will be displayed. For example, if the selected item is a disk, as shown on the left side of Figure 3-24, information on the Format method applied to the disk will be shown, and the size information will be replaced and supplemented with total capacity, available space remaining on the disk, and the amount of space currently in use.

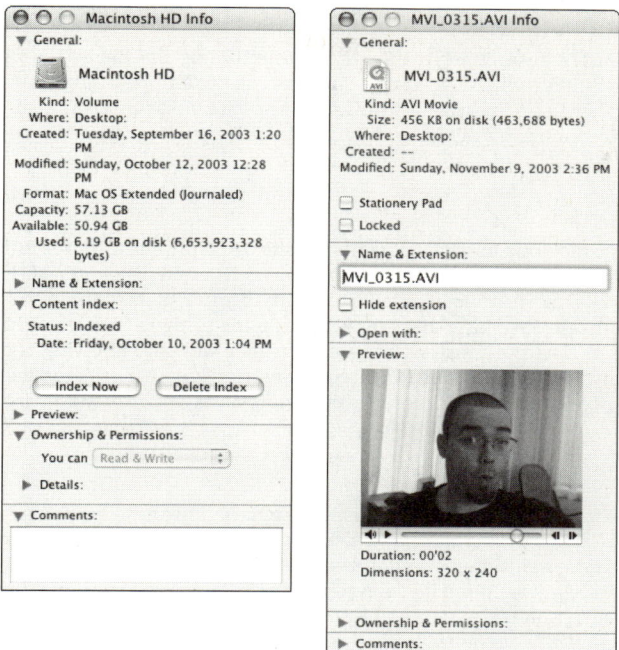

Figure 3-24: The Get Info windows a disk (left) and a movie file (right), each with different disclosure triangles exposed.

Name & Extension

The name of the selected item is shown in the Name & Extension section. Clicking in the box containing the item's name allows you to edit the name of the item. It is worth noticing that the name of the item is shown with its extension here. The file name extension is a three or four letter code that delineates the document's type. Changing this extension is not recommended, as it has the potential to confuse the Finder's ability to choose the appropriate application to open for the document. See "Some notes on naming" earlier in this chapter regarding some general tips on naming files.

Preview

If the item is a graphic file, this area will show a preview of the image here. If the file is a movie file, the preview will be a miniature version of the movie, complete with controls to play it, as shown on the right side of Figure 3-24. Some items cannot be previewed in this area, either because they cannot be rendered by the preview engine or because there is nothing to preview. Items that cannot be previewed include but are not limited to text documents, folders, and disks. In this case, the Preview field will just be populated with a full size rendering of the item's icon.

Open With

Each document has a parent application, that is, the application that by default will attempt to open it. In this area, that default application can be changed. For example, many types of images can be opened by Apple's built-in Preview application or by Photoshop. Choose which application you'd like to open the document with by default by using the convenient pop-up menu.

Ownership & Permissions

Ownership of a file and the permissions associated with the file are complex and potentially confusing. The basic concept is as follows: The creator of a file is the default owner of that file. The owner can do as he pleases with his files, editing, copying, or deleting them to his or her heart's delight. Permissions are the rules that an owner applies to their files, enabling other people to work with them. The permissions can be very specific, only allowing visitors to read files, and not to edit or delete them. The permissions can be cut and dried as well, allowing total control or complete lock-out. Ownership & Permissions are covered in greater detail in Chapter 14.

Comments

This field can be populated with any information you care to insert. This field can be helpful when managing a large host of files with similar names, as users can enter information there to help distinguish files. Also, information can be entered in the Comments field for the benefit of others that may be using the files. The Comments field also gets automatically populated with information at certain times. For example, if you download a file off the Internet, the Web address that the file came from is often entered here, depending on the Web browser used.

Stationery Pad

Many items have the stationery pad checkbox. Checking this box turns the item into a template. More on stationery pads and templates can be found in Chapter 5.

Locking or unlocking an item

You can use the Info window to lock files individually so that they can't be changed. After locking a file, you can open the file and copy it, but you can't change its name or its contents. In addition, the Finder does not let you move locked files into the Trash. You can tell a file is locked by the small, lock-shaped badge on its icon. Lock a file by following these steps:

1. **Select the file that you want to lock.** Information for the selected item appears in the Info window.

2. **Select the Locked option in the Info window.** The Locked option appears at the bottom of the Info window. You can't change an item's Locked option if you're not the item's owner.

Working with Folders

Having discussed some generic, universal commands to interact with icons and windows, including resizing, renaming, getting info, and selecting, the following sections cover some specific techniques for a few different item types.

Creating folders

Folders are very small files that create branches on the data storage tree within a volume. All they do is partition the files into smaller clutches of information that you organize yourself. Apple provides you with a host of useful folders within the user's home folder, but you will certainly need to create more finely tuned subdivisions. To create new folders, the Finder must be the active application. Simply click Create New Folder in the File menu, or press ⌘-Shift-N. This creates a new folder named Untitled Folder in the currently active window. If no window is active, the folder will be created on the desktop. When the new folder is created, its name will be automatically selected and ready for editing. (Unless you are in column view, in which case the folder's name is not automatically selected. Just click on the name itself to edit it.) Type a desired name, and press Enter or Return or click the mouse somewhere else onscreen. At this point, the folder is ready for action and itchy to receive any and all files you throw at it. There is no limit to how much data a given folder can hold, although it makes sense to organize your data in a way that makes finding files easy. There is certainly no need to create a folder for every individual item, but it makes sense to create new folders for documents of particular types or files containing data on similar topics. Some applications have the capability to create new folders, particularly during the Save process.

Tip　A quick way to create a new folder on the desktop or in a background window is to Control-click the place where you want the new folder and choose New Folder from the contextual menu that pops up. You can do this one-handed if you have a two-button mouse; just right-click to get to the contextual menu.

Opening folders and disks

One way to navigate the folder structure of your disks is by opening disks and folders. You can open any disk or folder that you can see in a Finder window or on the desktop (with the exception of restricted folders and disks, discussed in Chapter 14). When you open a disk or a folder, you see its contents in a Finder window. If these contents include folders, you can open one of them to see its contents in a Finder window. By opening folders within folders, you make your way through the folder structure. If you open the right sequence of folders, eventually you open the folder that contains the document or application that you're looking for.

Places You Cannot Create New Folders

You cannot create a new folder inside some folders because you do not have Write privileges for all folders. For example, you cannot create a new folder in the System folder, the Users folder, or another user's home folder. These folders are off limits to protect their contents. We discuss privileges in more detail later in Chapter 14. If you do not have Write privileges for the folder that's displayed in the active Finder window, the New Folder command is disabled (dim) in the File menu and is not included at all in the window's contextual menu. The easiest way to keep an eye on your Write privileges is to have the Finder window status bar showing (choose View ➪ Show Status Bar). If you see an icon that looks like a pencil with a line through it at the left end of the status bar, you don't have Write privileges for the folder displayed in the window.

To open a disk or folder that you have located in a Finder window or on the desktop, you can use any of these methods:

✦ Double-click the icon or the name of the item.

✦ Click the item's icon to select it, and then choose File ➪ Open.

✦ Click the item's icon to select it, and then press ⌘-O.

✦ Control-click the item's icon to display its contextual menu, and then choose Open from the contextual menu.

All these methods for opening items work in any Finder window viewed as icons, lists, or columns. The methods also work for opening items on the desktop (which is always viewed as icons).

Note   In a list view of Mac OS X 10.1.1 and earlier, you must first click an item to select it before you can display its contextual menu by Control-clicking the item. Of course, we recommend Apple's Panther (Mac OS 10.3) for many reasons, this being one of them.

When you open a folder shown in an already open window, its contents appear in the same Finder window. Folders open in new Finder window if the window's toolbar is suppressed. You can reverse this behavior by pressing the ⌘ key while opening a folder. For example, if you ⌘-double-click a folder in a Finder window whose toolbar is showing, the folder's contents appear in a new Finder window. You can also change a Finder preference setting to make the Finder normally display a new window when you open a folder; we cover setting Finder preferences in Chapter 4.

Opening the alias of a folder or disk has exactly the same effect as opening the folder or disk that the alias represents. If you open an alias of a folder or disk, Mac OS X resolves the alias and the Finder displays the contents of the original folder or disk.

Folder Actions

With Panther, Apple has added quite a few new tools to make your computing more efficient. A collection of AppleScripts, known as Folder Actions have been added, so that your folders themselves can perform actions for you — making your day-to-day work easier. Folder Actions are actually AppleScripts that run when the Folder is accessed in some fashion. Some Folder Actions perform operations on documents that are dropped within them. Some Folder Actions simply edit the way a folder behaves, closing all folders within, or by displaying more or less information, basically Folder Actions do whatever the chosen AppleScript demands.

Enable Folder Actions

To enable Folder Actions, bring up the contextual menu on any folder or disk, and select Enable Folder Actions from the list. Selecting this option will make the Folder Action system active, enabling you to attach and remove actions to particular folders or volumes. After you select it, this menu option becomes Disable Folder Actions, which when selected, will turn off all Folder Actions system-wide.

Attach action

To attach an action to a folder, bring up the contextual menu for the item, and select the desired action from the dialog that follows. Apple provides a collection of scripts that perform various functions, most relating to file conversion. The dialog is shown in Figure 3-25.

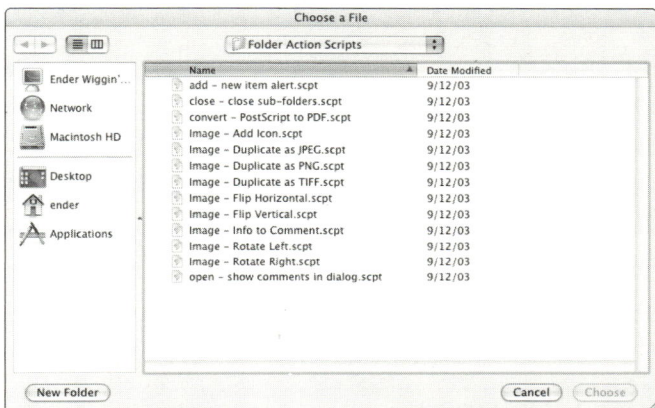

Figure 3-25: Folder Actions are a convenient way to make folders into tools that perform certain selected operations when items are placed within.

Select the action you want to apply to the folder, and click Choose. This will close the dialog and make the selected Folder Action active on the folder. The Folder Action is now ready for use!

Using actions

The standard method to use a Folder Action is simply to drag an item (or items) onto the icon of the folder. This will activate the Folder Action script, and perform the programmed action on the items selected. Most of the standard Apple-made Folder Actions simply convert images. These types of scripts also create two subfolders within their parent folder: one called Original Images and another called <type> Images (where <type> is the chosen destination format for the images). To use these actions, place images of certain types onto the folder, the script runs, converts images from one format to another. The script then places the original unedited item into the Original Images folder, and creates the converted file in the <type> Images folder. This is a vastly easier way to save a large cluster of files in an alternate format.

Folder Actions are of course not limited to simply reformatting images, and don't always require that items be dropped in to activate. You can create your own Folder Actions that perform other operations, like emailing dropped-in files to certain people, or renaming files according to a certain standard, or automatically uploading the files to a server and then securely deleting them from your computer. You are limited only by your imagination and your knowledge (and the capabilities) of AppleScript. To learn how to use AppleScript, tune in to Chapter 23.

Configure Actions

To add, remove, temporarily deactivate, or edit Folder Actions all in one convenient window, use the Configure Actions command. Select Configure Actions from the contextual menu from any folder or disk. The Folder Actions Setup application opens, as shown in Figure 3-26.

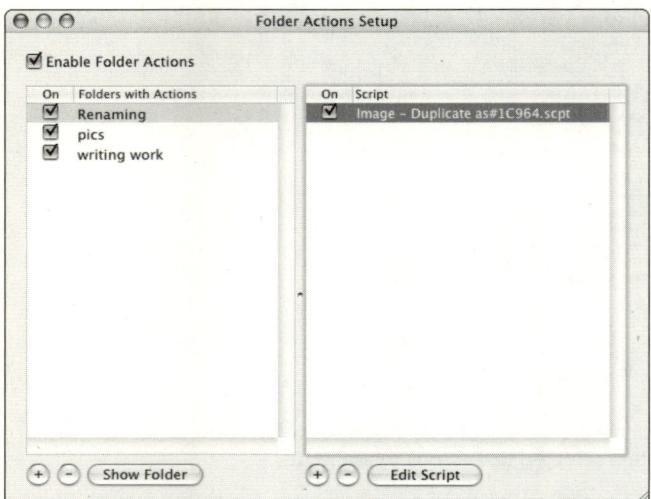

Figure 3-26: Configure Actions is a convenient way to turn off actions without removing them from folders; it's also a helpful tool to see how many actions are currently in place.

After applying a number of Folder Actions, it is possible to lose track of which actions have been applied where. The Folder Actions Setup application also is helpful in this eventuality. The list on the left side shows all folders that have Folder Actions applied. Selecting any folder on the left side will populate the right side of the window with a list of the actions applied to that folder. Each item has a checkbox next to it. Uncheck any folder to temporarily turn off all applied actions for that folder. Uncheck individual actions from the right side of the window if you wish to temporarily deactivate only some of the actions applied to a folder.

At the top of the Folder Actions Setup window is a checkbox labeled Enable Actions. Unchecking this box will deactivate all Folder Actions. (You can get this result more easily by simply selecting Disable Actions from the contextual menu from any folder or disk.)

At the bottom of the left side (the folder side) of the Folder Actions Setup application are plus (+), minus (-), and Show Folder button. Click the plus sign to select a new folder to which you want to attach actions. This action generates a dialog from which you select a new folder to which you wish to attach Folder Actions. Navigate through your drive hierarchy in this dialog, select the folder you wish, and click Open. This dialog is shown in Figure 3-27.

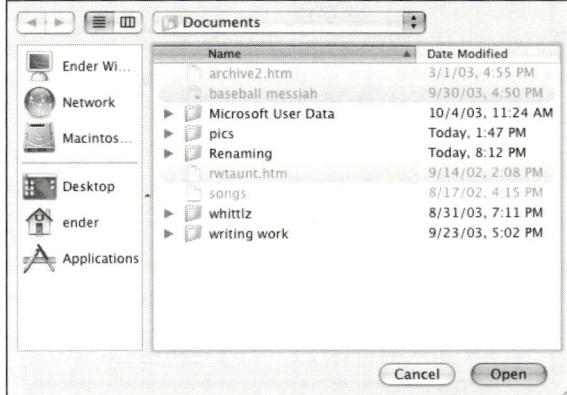

Figure 3-27: To select a new folder for Folder Actions, select it from this dialog.

The newly selected folder will appear in the left side of the main window. Select any item in the left side of the window, and the minus sign and the Show Folder button become active. To remove all Folder Actions on a folder, click the minus sign. An alert will come up after clicking the button, confirming your intention to remove all Folder Actions. To see a folder that has actions applied to it, click the Show Folder button and a new Finder window will open displaying content of the selected folder's parent (that is, the folder that the selected item lives inside of).

At the bottom of the right side (the action side) of the Folder Actions Setup window are plus (+), minus (-), and Edit Script buttons. These items will be active only when an item is selected on the left side (as the right side will not be populated with any actions to edit without first choosing a folder). To add an action to a folder, click the plus sign. A dialog box appears containing the list of valid Folder Actions. Select the desired action and click Attach. This dialog is shown in Figure 3-28.

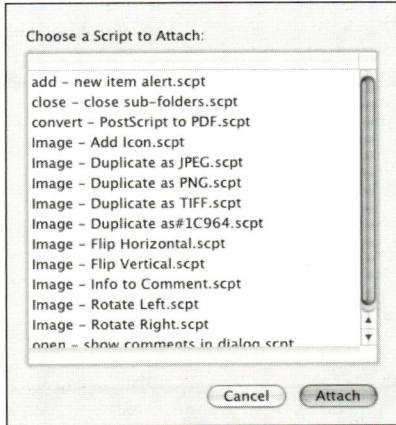

Figure 3-28: To add actions to a folder, select one from this dialog.

To remove an action from a folder, select the action and then click the minus sign. A dialog will appear, confirming your intention to remove the selected script.

To edit a Folder Action, select the action and then click on the Edit Script button. The ScriptEditor application will open, allowing you to tinker with or simply review the content of the action. AppleScript is covered in Chapter 23.

Remove Action

You don't need to go to Folder Actions Setup to remove an action from a folder. To do this more quickly, use your contextual menus! From the contextual menu of a folder with Folder Actions attached, select Remove Action to reveal a pull-out menu. The pull-out menu is populated with all actions attached to this folder, selecting any of them will remove that action from the folder.

Edit Action

You can also Edit the actions applied to a folder via your contextual menus. From the contextual menu of an item with Folder Actions applied, select Edit Action to reveal the pull-out menu that contains the list of attached scripts. Select the script you wish to edit, and the ScriptEditor Application will open, with your script ready for edit or review. AppleScript is covered in detail in Chapter 23.

Working with Disks and Other Volumes

A volume is a fixed amount of storage. Typically volumes exist on disks, but they can also exist on tapes or even on memory sticks or USB keys. A volume is a location in which data can be placed. The terms disk and volume are often used interchangeably, but volumes are areas within a disk, and there can be more than one volume per disk. For our purposes in this book though, the terms can be transposed with some freedom.

Looking at drives, partitions, and volumes

When you click the Computer button in the sidebar, the window will reveal all the volumes currently available on your computer. The simplest example of a volume is a disk, such as your internal hard drive, a Zip disk, or a CD-ROM. However, as we mentioned, a disk can be partitioned so that it contains two or more volumes. A partitioned disk is like a duplex or apartment building; one building holds two or more separate residences, and one disk can have two or more independent volumes. If you want to partition your hard drive into multiple volumes, you'll need to use the Disk Utility application as described in Chapter 22.

A mounted disk image is also a volume. A disk image is actually a file that when opened creates a virtual disk available to your system. The content stored on these virtual disks is typically application installers or upgrades. Many software developers distribute software updates in a disk image file. You are able to make your own disk image files with the Disk Utility application, which is also described in Chapter 21.

File server drives and iDisks are also volumes. We explain how to access these volumes in Chapter 10.

Mac OS X represents each type of volume with a distinctive icon. For example, hard drives and partitions have an icon that looks like an internal hard drive, while network drives look like something from a science fiction movie, to represent the ethereal and high-tech network connection between the server and your machine. Figure 3-29 shows several different volume icons.

Figure 3-29: Various types of volumes have different icons.

You decide whether volume icons show on your desktop. This is set in Finder preferences (covered in Chapter 4). The default setting is to show all disks on your desktop.

Ejecting disks

Server volumes, disk images, CD-ROM's, Zip/Jaz Disks, and Floppy disks have one very important thing in common, they are all removable. Remove disk icons by unmounting (also known as ejecting) the disk. Although ejecting really only applies to removable disks, such as Zip disks or CDs, the same term is used throughout the Mac OS for consistency. Eject a volume by using one of the following methods:

✦ **Drag the disks to the Trash (the last item in the Dock).** The Trash icon becomes an Eject symbol, when dragging a disk, to reassure users that you are not "Trashing" a disk, just removing it.

✦ **Control-click the volume's icon, either in the Computer window or on the desktop, and choose Eject from the contextual menu.**

✦ **Select the volume's icon and choose File ➪ Eject *<name>*.** (*<name>* is the name of the disk selected.) The keyboard equivalent for this command is ⌘-E.

✦ **Click the Eject symbol that appears in the sidebar next to the desired disk.**

✦ **Select the volume's icon and press the Eject key on your keyboard.** (If your keyboard doesn't have an eject key, the F12 key works.) This method doesn't work for server volumes.

If the volume isn't in use (in use refers to the volume containing open files), the Finder removes it from the desktop and the Computer window. Because the System volume (the one containing the active copy of Mac OS X) is in use, you cannot eject it.

Removable disks, such as Zips and CDs, are remounted by inserting them back in their drives. Disk images are remounted by double-clicking the images and allowing the Disk Utility application to mount them. Hard drives and partitions can be remounted by logging out and logging back in to Mac OS X or by using the Disk Utility application.

Erasing volumes

Sometimes, particularly with removable volumes like Zip disks or USB keys, you may want to return a disk to its original condition, before it contained any data. This process is called initializing or erasing a disk. You accomplish this with the Disk Utility application. The procedure is described in Chapter 21.

Burning discs

Most modern computers have the capability to write data to optical media. This is most commonly known as burning a disc (spelled d-i-s-c when referring to optical media, and d-i-s-k when referring to hard drives, network drives, or other removable media types). Burnable optical media includes CD-R, CD-RW, DVD-R, DVD-R+, DVD-RAM, DVD-RW. The mad scientists at Apple realized that as more people got access to this technology, it would be nice if it was easy to use! To this end, Mac OS X supports the ultra-easy and intuitive Finder-based burning.

To get the process started, insert one piece of blank optical media of your choice. (Do make sure the media is compatible with your drive. Check the documentation that came with your system and/or Apple System Profiler as described in Chapter 22.) After inserting the disc, an alert will appear, as shown in Figure 3-30.

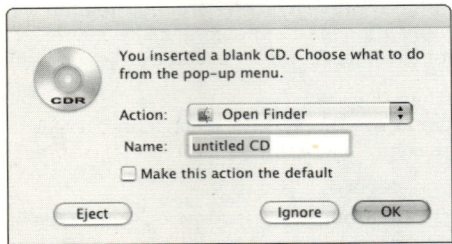

Figure 3-30: The alert when a blank or burnable disc is inserted.

The alert window gives you choices about how to use the disc. Enter a name for the disc in the Name field, and select your desired application to prepare the disc. The default setting is Open Finder. You'll notice the Make this action the default checkbox. If you first check this box, your computer will always prepare a blank disc the way you select. It's not advisable to check this box, simply because you may want to prepare discs differently later on. If you accidentally set the wrong default action, or want to edit the settings, open the CDs & DVDs preference pane and choose the appropriate actions from the pull-down menus. The preference pane is shown in Figure 3-31.

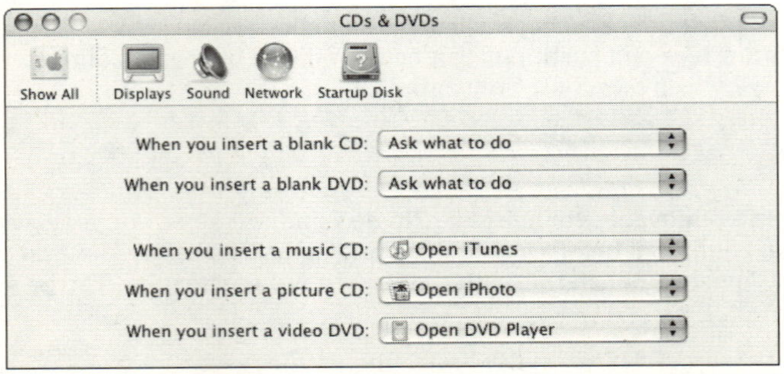

Figure 3-31: The CDs & DVDs preference pane gives you control of the Finder's behavior when discs are inserted. The window contains controls for blank media as well as formatted media.

Selecting Open Finder tells the Finder to take responsibility for making your new disc. The Finder first prepares a virtual version of the disc on your desktop. Though the virtual disc looks like a real disc, it's just a pseudo-CD, and it functions just like a hard drive. (It actually is a small piece of your hard drive that gets dynamically set aside for this process.) Double-click the virtual disc to reveal its contents. Because the Finder sees this virtual disc as a different disc than your hard drive, all you have to do is drag items over to copy items to it. Copy any items that you wish to burn onto the disc (limited, of course, by the storage capacity of the chosen blank media) and then organize them as you like. When you are satisfied with the setup of the disc, select Burn Disc from the Finder menu (or from the contextual menu for the disc itself), or drag the disc to the Trash. You'll notice the Trash icon, which would become the Eject symbol when removing a disc, becomes a type of fallout shelter/nuclear waste warning symbol, which is Apple's clever Burn icon.

Regardless of how you initiate the burn, the result is another alert window, requesting confirmation of your intent to burn the disc as shown in Figure 3-32.

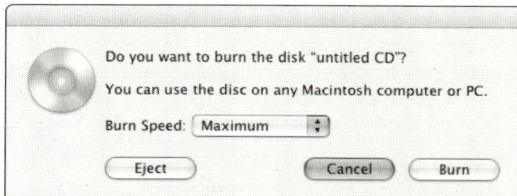

Figure 3-32: After selecting Burn Disc in the File menu, this dialog box appears to confirm your intention.

 If you prematurely selected Burn Disc, and want to continue editing the disc's contents, select Ignore. That will ignore the Burn command, and allow you to continue. If you want to cancel the whole disc-burning project, select Eject. This will remove the virtual disc from the desktop, and eject your unmodified blank disc from the drive.

A Burn Speed pull-down menu is also present in the burn confirmation dialog. Though the default speed is Maximum, you can choose a slower speed from the pull-down menu. These slower speed options are useful if your media is of lesser quality or if your drive is misbehaving.

After selecting Burn from the confirmation dialog, the burn process begins. A progress meter appears, displaying information on what's happening behind the scenes: The Finder prepares the data, initiates the writing process, and then verifies the condition of the newly created CD, as seen in Figure 3-33.

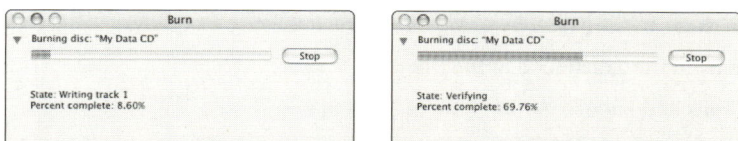

Figure 3-33: During the burn process, this progress meter appears to assure you that all is well. First the disc gets burned (left), then the Mac OS verifies the data (right).

When complete, the drive will eject your fresh-off-the-presses disc. You can put this disc away for storage or reinsert it into the computer to go through it personally.

At nearly any time during the process, you can click the Stop button in the progress meter. This may result in a partially burned disc, which is useless. Your computer can't deal with a disc that's only half done.

The aforementioned process is used to create data discs. If you want to create a music CD, the process is different. You would select iTunes from the initial disc-preparation window's pop-up menu. Similarly, select iMovie or iDVD to create a movie disc, or select iPhoto to create a disc full of images. After selecting the appropriate application for your project, the chosen application launches and initiates its own burn controls and dialogs. These processes are discussed further for each application in Chapters 19 and 20.

Using Aliases

An alias is a shortcut that points to another item. The alias looks and functions much like the original item, but it can be placed wherever you like, and the original can stay put in its original place. An important visual cue to help differentiate between the alias and the original is a small black arrow in the lower-left corner of all aliases. (The arrow signifies that the item points to the original.) Methods of creating and modifying aliases are covered in Chapter 4.

To use an alias, simply double-click on it. The Finder will open the original item. Alternately, if you drag an item to an alias, the Finder resolves the alias (that is, figures out what the alias points to), and then takes the appropriate action. The resulting action is just as if you dragged directly to the alias's original item. For example, dragging an item to an alias of a folder puts the dragged item into the original folder, or if you drag a document to an alias for an application, the application will attempt to open the document. Dragging an alias to a folder moves just the alias.

Taking out the Trash

At the opposite end of the Dock from the Finder icon, you see an icon resembling a wire-mesh wastepaper basket. This is the Trash, the receptacle into which you place items you want to be rid of. Deleting files and folders is a two-step process. First, you need to move them to the Trash and then you need to empty the Trash. Before emptying the Trash, you can still change your mind, open the Trash and remove items from it.

Moving items to the Trash

Move one or more items to the Trash by using one of the following four ways:

✦ Drag the items to the Trash icon in the Dock.

✦ Select the items and choose Finder ➪ Move To Trash.

✦ Select the items and press ⌘-Delete (which is the keyboard shortcut for choosing Finder ➪ Move to Trash).

✦ Control-click an item, or select several items and Control-click one of them, and then choose Move To Trash from the contextual menu that appears.

After moving an item to the Trash, the Trash icon will change from an empty wire mesh basket to a basket full of crumpled up papers. The documents are not deleted yet though. They are merely in your trash pail. To actually delete them, much like your kitchen trash pail, you have to take out the trash. In the Finder menu, select Empty Trash, or press ⌘-Shift-Delete. A click or swish sound will be heard and your files will be deleted. Do not get in the habit storing items in the Trash. Not only will the trash file get bloated storing all the unwanted garbage, it's also very easy to accidentally empty the trash when trying to send an item to the trash (especially with the keyboard shortcut, it's only a Shift key's difference). If you intend to trash something, do so. If you think you want to trash something, but aren't sure yet, store the files somewhere else. We'll talk more about file organization in Chapter 5.

Viewing and removing Trash contents

You can see the contents of the Trash by clicking the Trash icon in the Dock. The Trash contents appear in a Finder window. You can remove items from the Trash by dragging them out of this Finder window and placing them in another folder or on the desktop. (As you observed in Chapter 3, the items you put on the Mac OS X desktop are actually located in the Desktop folder of your home folder.)

Note   When you view the Trash contents, you see only items that you have moved to the Trash since you last emptied it. If other people use your computer with different login accounts, you do not see items that they have moved to the Trash. Mac OS X keeps a separate Trash for each user.

Emptying the Trash

Empty the Trash by using one of the following methods:

✦ Choose Finder ➪ Empty Trash.

✦ Press ⌘-Shift-Delete.

✦ Control-click the Trash icon (or click it and hold) and when the pop-up Dock menu appears, choose Empty Trash.

In the first two methods, the Finder displays a warning, asking if you really want to permanently delete the items that are in the Trash. If you use the pop-up Dock menu, the Trash is emptied without warning. Figure 3-34 shows the warning.

Tip   If you find the Trash warning annoying, you can eliminate it by changing a setting in Finder Preferences, as described in Chapter 4. The warning also does not appear if you press ⌘-Shift-Option-Delete.

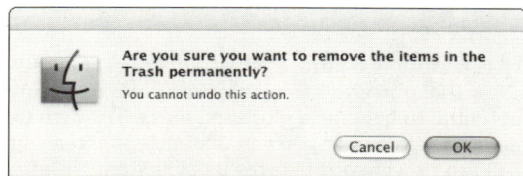

Figure 3-34: If you choose File ➪ Empty Trash or press ⌘-Shift-Delete, the Finder confirms that you really want to empty the Trash.

Note   If you put a file in the Trash by accident, you can remove it from the Trash by using the Finder undo feature, pressing ⌘-Z. This will work only if putting the item in the Trash was the last thing you did (as the undo will only undo the last thing you did) and, most important, if you *haven't emptied the Trash yet.* The emphasis is there for a reason! Emptying the Trash normally means "bye-bye files." To recover files that have been erased accidentally or prematurely (or to rescue files from disks that are damaged) you will need to call in a team of professionals. Check out www.DriveSavers.com and www.OnTrack.com if you need help recovering files. Get your checkbook ready, as file recovery prices range from $100–$3000, depending on disk size, disk condition, and how quickly you need the files back. To avoid this unfortunate situation happening to you, back up your work often, as discussed in Chapter 23.

Secure Empty Trash

If you are selling your computer, or have very sensitive information on your computer, simply emptying the Trash is not an effective way to remove the data. As noted above, it is indeed possible to get your work back! This may be a bad thing if you really want the files gone. To this end, Apple has added the Secure Empty Trash option, which will truly purge the trashed files from your computer by overwriting them with meaningless junk data. This is significant because what actually happens when a file gets simply trashed is the computer erases its record of where the file was. Because the computer no longer recognizes that there is a file there, it will write over the (still extant) file eventually, as you create more work. The problem is, this may take a while, or never occur at all. A good technician (or evil hacker) may be able to restore Trashed files with third-party software. By first erasing the file record, and then overwriting the file's location with meaningless data, Mac OS X makes it much more difficult if not impossible to recover the work. To use this erasure method, simply select Secure Empty Trash from the Finder menu or contextual menu. Figure 3-35 shows the alert when selecting the Secure Empty Trash option.

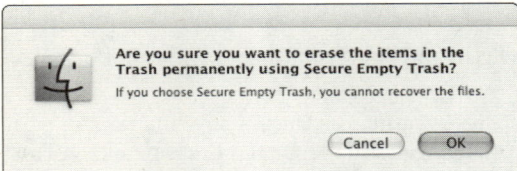

Figure 3-35: Secure Empty Trash is a better way to ensure that your unwanted data is erased permanently, as a determined person can often very easily undo the normal Empty Trash command.

Exposé

The most exciting new feature of OS 10.3 is a window control system Apple's Francophile marketing people have named Exposé. Now that you know how to create Finder windows and open documents, your screen has the potential to become a cluttered mess. Through using the Window menu you can manage some of the clutter, or you can minimize the items into the Dock with the Minimize button, but it's all too slow! Exposé makes its all instant with the click of one of three buttons. Please note that part of the beauty of this product is the animated nature of the action. To see it in action is much more impressive than these screenshots can convey! Figure 3-36 shows a typical screen after a few hours of working, Web surfing, and iTunes-ing.

Figure 3-36: Window Clutter!

Show all windows

When there are two or more applications and multiple documents open, the screen will get cluttered very quickly. Exposé's first command is the All Windows command. Click the F9 key, and all the open windows shrink and rearrange themselves spread around the screen (accompanied by an impressive animation) so all windows can be visible at once. Hover your mouse over any of the reduced windows, and the window is highlighted and reveals the application's name. (Documents and Web pages reveal their name, rather than the application.) Clicking on any of these reduced windows brings that window to the foreground. If you don't want to change your active window, clicking F9 again returns all windows to full size and restores the previous active window to the foreground. Figure 3-37 shows the results of Exposé's All Windows command.

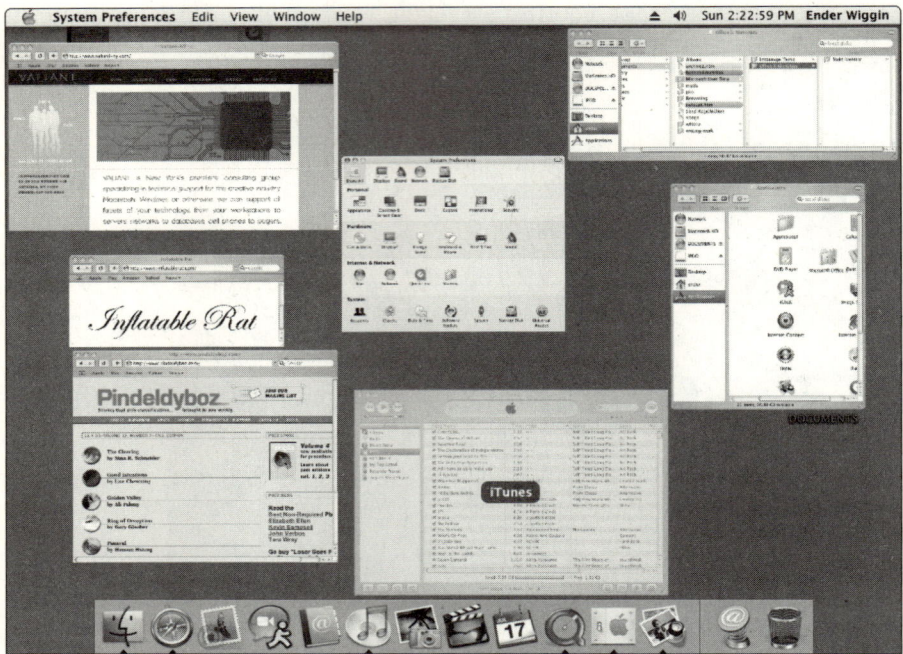

Figure 3-37: Exposé is a very easy way to switch between applications and any open windows.

Show active application's windows

Many applications support multiple windows. Web browsers for example often have multiple Web pages open at once. For example, consider when a user who reviews a rare car part for their car (a 1968 Dodge Charger, let's say) on eBay, checks a local mechanic's Web page to determine the street value of the part, compares that price to a Dodge Charger enthusiast organization's notes on their Web page. It would be easy to get lost switching between just those three windows, much less any other applications that may be open. Exposé's first command works, but when a user just wants to find a window within the current active application, the Application Windows command is the solution. With a click of F10, all the user's open Web pages shrink and align themselves (while dimming all other application windows). Moving the pointer over a window shows the Web page's name, making it easy to pick which window is desired. Clicking the desired window causes all windows to restore to normal size and make the clicked window active in the foreground. Pressing F-10 again restores all application windows to their previous position, restoring the previous active window to the foreground. Figure 3-38 shows the results of the Active Application Windows command.

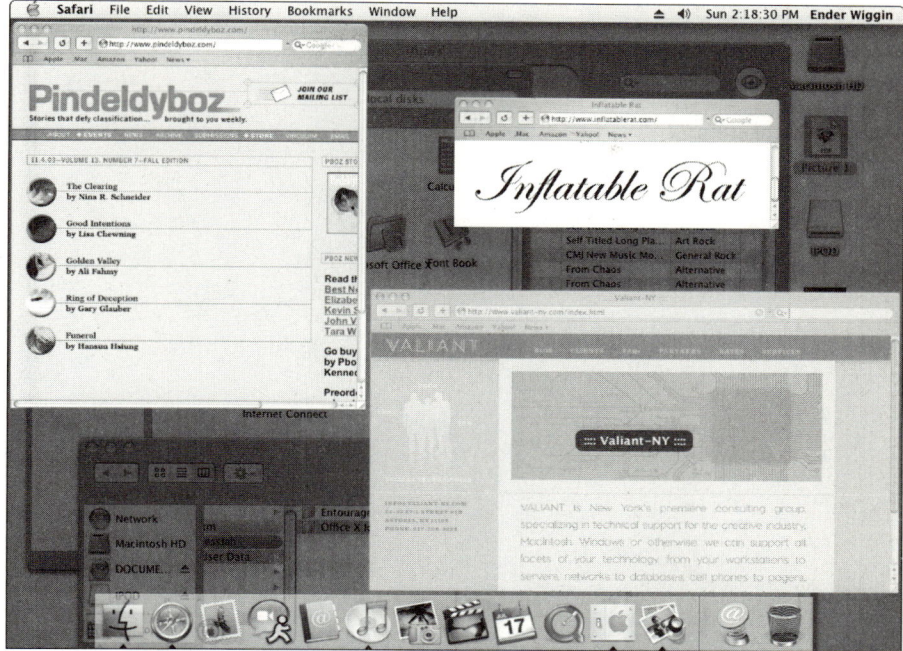

Figure 3-38: Within one application, many windows can be open at once, Exposé makes finding a desired window within a particular application easy to find.

Show desktop

Even with ten windows open, there may be a need to open more documents. Getting to your desktop or opening your hard drive to open a particular document or folder can be troublesome with so many windows already open. Exposé's third command, the Desktop command, makes it easy. Click F11, and all open windows retreat to the beyond the edges of the screen, leaving only a small bit remaining, and thus revealing the desktop. Disks and folders can be opened and searched for the desired document, all without restoring the clutter. After a document or application is opened, the windows return to their original position, with your newly opened item as the active window. Alternatively, clicking on the visible edges of the retracted applications (or pressing F11 again) restores them to their original positions. Figure 3-39 shows the results of the Show Desktop command.

Figure 3-39: A very helpful way to carve through the clutter to open an item hidden on the desktop.

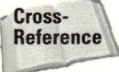

Cross-Reference   You can enhance and adjust your Exposé experience. Customization of the Exposé controls is covered in Chapter 4.

Summary

This chapter presented you with an introduction to the Finder, your main tool to access the data hidden on your machine. You learned how to interact with the windows and folders that display the applications and documents within your Mac. You learned how to work with volumes, ejecting and even burning new ones! Also, Exposé, Apple's new window control tool has been introduced, making it possible to switch between open windows and applications with ease, as well as enabling you to open items on your desktop with minimal clicking. After reading this chapter, you know how to do the following:

✦ Use the Finder-specific menus, Finder, Go, and View.

✦ Create new Finder windows.

✦ Switch among Finder's icon, list, and column view modes.

✦ Recognize the active window and make other windows active.

✦ Interact with icons in all view modes — selecting them by typing or with the mouse, selecting multiple items.

✦ Interact with folders, opening, resizing, and applying Folder Actions.

✦ Burn CDs and DVDs using the Finder.

✦ Put unwanted items in the Trash, and empty the Trash to delete them and use Secure Delete to eradicate files from prying techs or hackers.

✦ Use Exposé to manage the many possible open windows and applications presented by Mac OS X.

To learn about adjusting Mac OS X's appearance to suit your needs and match your style, proceed to Chapter 4.

✦　　✦　　✦

Enhancing Your Workspace

You received an introduction to Mac OS X, the Finder, documents, the Dock, Exposé, and the desktop in Chapters 2 and 3. Now you're going to find out how to *customize* all the elements of the Mac OS X environment to suit your tastes and to improve your enjoyment and productivity. In this chapter, you learn how to customize the overall appearance of the environment, and how to change the toolbar in Finder windows. You learn how to set View Options that affect the look of each Finder window and how to change the picture on the desktop. You also learn about screen savers, and how to change their options to suit your needs. You also explore ways to get the most from Exposé and the Dock.

In addition, this chapter describes techniques for working with aliases and labels. These techniques include applying labels and modifying label titles. You learn how to make aliases work for you-how to create them, change them, fix them if they break, and more.

The Desktop

The desktop, as you know, is the large expanse of color that comprises the background of your Mac OS environment. By default, this area has a swirling blue color, ostensibly to soothe your jangled nerves as you slave away at your computer. Of course, blue is a relaxing color, but it can be *boring*. You may want to change the color to black, red, or your favorite color. Or you may want to place a picture of your cat or your motorcycle as a desktop picture. To do so, you must delve into the System Preferences.

Desktop background customization

You can cover the Desktop with a solid color or a picture by choosing an image file as follows:

1. **Click the System Preferences icon in the Dock (or System Preferences menu item in the Apple menu).** The System Preferences window appears, showing buttons for different types of settings.

2. **In System Preferences, click the Desktop & Screen Saver button or choose View ⇨ Desktop & Screen Saver.** The System Preferences window changes to show one of the two panes in this preference panel. The settings for changing the desktop

background are of course under the Desktop pane. Click on the Desktop button if it isn't already selected (top left) to reveal the Desktop pane. Divided into two distinct frames, the left side contains a list of options, while the right side is populated dynamically according to which list item you select on the left. The Desktop pane is shown in Figure 4-1.

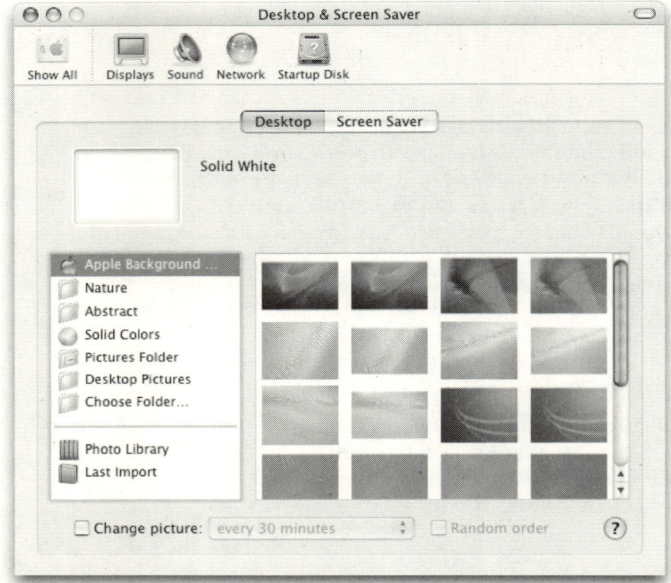

Figure 4-1: Set the Desktop background in the Desktop & Screen Saver pane of System Preferences.

3. **Select either a color or a picture for your background.**

4. **Close the window with the red Close button to complete setting the preference. Alternately, you can select Quit System Preferences from the System Preferences menu.**

When choosing a background, you have a number of preinstalled options available to pick from. You can set your background as a solid color, or as one of many attractive pictures or patterns.

✦ **To choose a color:** click the Solid Colors list item and then choose one of the preselected colors available in the right-side window pane.

✦ **To choose a picture, click any of the following list items:**

• **Apple Background Images:** A collection of swirly patterns. Typically these are attractive patterns, usually comprised of a single color. Click any patterns in the right-side frame to set it as the desktop.

• **Nature:** A standardized preselected list of nature-themes pictures. The pictures include Snowy Hills, Water, Faux Fur, Ladybug, and more. Click any picture in the right frame to set it as the desktop.

- **Abstract:** Another collection of swirly patterns. These are typically much more colorful, with two, three, or more colors per pattern (i.e., ugly). Click any picture in the right frame to set it as the desktop.

- **Pictures Folder:** If your Pictures folder (found in your Home Folder) contains any images, they appear in the right-side pane. Click any picture displayed in the right frame to set it as the desktop.

- **Desktop Pictures:** This contains the same images as the Apple Background Images folder.

- **Choose Folder:** A dialog appears with this option. This dialog is like a column view of a Finder window. In this dialog, select a folder containing images you want to use, and click the Open button. Images from the selected folder appear in the right-side pane. Click any of the pictures in the right frame to set it as the desktop.

- **Photo Library:** A nice tie-in feature to iPhoto. This list item displays all of the available photos from your iPhoto library. (iPhoto is covered in Chapter 20). Please note, if your iPhoto library contains many photos, this option will potentially make your computer slow down while it renders all the pictures. Click any picture in the right frame to set it as the desktop.

- **Last Import:** Another nice tie-in to iPhoto, this option displays the last grouping of images imported into iPhoto in the right-side pane. This is a helpful option if your iPhoto library contains numerous images and you desire a recently imported image. Click any picture in the right frame to set it as the desktop.

Tip   If you check the Change Picture checkbox, the operating system will cycle through pictures at the specified rate. To choose the change rate, select from the pull-down menu of time options. At the specified interval, your desktop image will change. The change picture option will use images from the same folder as your initially chosen image. Checking the Random button causes the system to randomly display your choices from the folder instead of displaying them in alphabetical order. The time interval options range from five seconds to every day, with additional options for changing at each login or after waking from sleep.

Saving the Screen

Originally designed as a method of preserving displays from damage, screen savers are now as much a form of entertainment as they are a hardware-protection measure. Early Cathode Ray Tube (CRT) displays were victimized by an unfortunate condition known as phosphor burn-in. Phosphor burn-in occurs when a display shows the same image for too long. After a few days of displaying the same static image, the display is permanently scarred with a shadow of the image. That said, fundamental changes wrought in CRT display technology in the mid 1990s reduced the risk of phosphor burn-in to practically nil. Phosphor burn-in is also no longer a concern for CRT owners simply because lower prices and more demanding users result in the replacement of displays much more often. These factors combined to practically eliminate the need for screen savers. A new factor has arisen though. Many users are migrating to the Liquid Crystal Displays (LCD), which are again susceptible to a form of image burn-in. Screen savers are again a useful piece of software. In general though, the best protection for your screen and of your electric bill is to have your monitor completely switch off after a period of inactivity. This option is found in the Energy Saver preference pane.

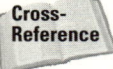

Cross-Reference   For more on the Energy Saver preference pane, see Chapter 13.

To use a screen saver, or to change the settings of the currently selected screen saver, follow these steps:

1. **Click the System Preferences icon in the Dock (or System Preferences menu item in the Apple menu).** The System Preferences window appears, showing buttons for many different settings. (Most are covered in Chapter 13.)

2. **In System Preferences, click the Desktop & Screen Saver button or choose View ➪ Desktop & Screen Saver.** The System Preferences window changes to show one of the two available panes in this preference panel. Screen saver controls are of course under the Screen Saver pane. Click the Screen Saver button (top right) to reveal the Screen Saver pane. Much like the Desktop pane, the Screen Saver pane is divided into two distinct panels. The left side has a list of available screen savers; the right side shows a preview display of the screen saver in action.

3. **Choose the screen saver desired from the left panel.**

4. **Close the Desktop & Screen Saver preference pane with the Close button or quit system preferences via the Application menu to enable the screen saver.**

The Screen Saver pane is shown in Figure 4-2. The standard preinstalled screen savers include the following:

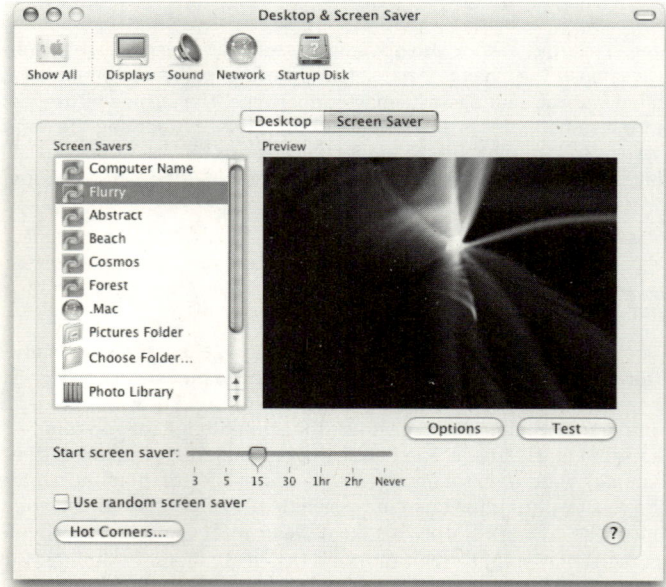

Figure 4-2: Screen savers engage after a set period of inactivity, replacing your screen's displayed items by showing photos, cycling interesting patterns, or changing colors.

✦ **Computer Name:** A simple display of a platinum-looking Apple logo, with an overlay of your computer's name on a black background. The logo and name fade and reappear, each centered at different points onscreen. Your computer's name is set during the installation process.

✦ **Flurry:** The only truly animated screen saver provided by Apple. While Flurry may or may not be the most popular, it is definitely the most hypnotic! Flurry is perhaps best described as a single point of light erupting and spewing forth colorful streams of light while moving around the screen. ... you will buy apple computers... you will buy apple computers...

Cross-Reference

To change your computer's name, consult Chapter 13.

✦ **Abstract:** A collection of colorful patterns and swirls, cross-fading and panning across the screen. This is the first of the Ken Burns–style slideshow screen savers. (Ken Burns directed a series of famous documentaries, and is very creative in the use of still images throughout.)

✦ **Beach:** Another of the slideshow-style screen savers. Rather than abstract images of color swirls, Beach is comprised of photos of various beach locations. Consider it inspiration for your next vacation.

✦ **Cosmos:** Like the Beach screen saver, but designed by a Star Trek fan, Cosmos is comprised of various deep space photos.

✦ **Forest:** Another of the slideshow-style screen savers, Forest is a collection of images of various wilderness locations.

✦ **.mac:** allows you to access and display images from your .mac account, as well as any public images from your friends or family's .mac accounts.

✦ **Pictures Folder:** Any images stored in your Pictures folder (found in your Home Folder) will become the slides in the screen saver slideshow as they pan, zoom, crossfade, and are randomized. Moving items to and from folders is discussed in detail in Chapter 5.

✦ **Choose Folder:** Just as with the Choose Folder option for the Desktop Picture, a dialog opens. Choose a folder containing images you desire to have as a screen saver. Click Open once you find the folder, and the dialog box closes. The screen saver will display images from the selected folder.

✦ **Photo Library:** A tie-in to iPhoto, this screen saver option uses your entire iPhoto library as the slides in the screen saver.

✦ **Last Import:** This is also a tie-in to iPhoto, but this option only uses images from your last import as the available elements of the slideshow.

Screen saver general settings

In addition to selecting a screen saver, there are a few settings available to optimize each screen saver's functionality.

✦ **Test:** Click the Test button under the preview area of the screen saver pane to preview your screen saver in full-screen mode. Move the mouse or click any key to return to the preference pane.

✦ **Start Screen saver:** This slider, located at the bottom of the Desktop & Screen Saver window, allows you to set the screen saver's activation time. The activation time is how long the computer will sit idle before engaging the screen saver. The slider ranges from 3 minutes to 2 hours, with Never at the far right. Setting activation to Never prevents any screen saver from engaging.

✦ **Random:** If you click the Use random screen saver checkbox in the lower-left area of the pane, Mac OS X will choose one of the installed screen savers at random before each screen saver activation.

✦ **Hot Corners:** When clicking on this push button in the lower-left corner, a dialog box appears. In the dialog, four pull-down menus in the corners surround a small window representing the Desktop. Clicking on any of these menus reveals options that engage when a user moves the mouse to that corner of the screen. The options include Activate Screen Saver, Disable Screen Saver, and any of the three modes of Exposé. You can assign each corner one of these commands. Moving the pointer to the specified corner initiates that action. Activate Screen Saver immediately engages the screen saver. Disable Screen Saver prevents the screen saver from engaging at the specified activation time. The Exposé features are covered in the Customizing Exposé heading later in this chapter. Figure 4-3 shows the Hot Corners dialog box, as well as the one of the pop-up menu's options.

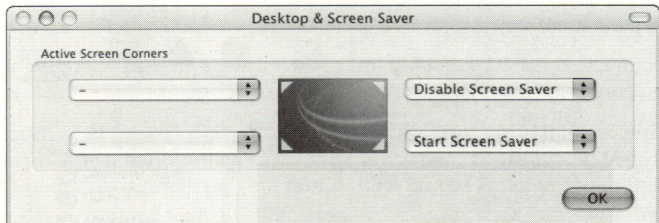

Figure 4-3: The Hot Corners dialog enables instant activation of screen savers, or a quick way to disable all screen savers, simply by moving the pointer to the appropriate corner.

Screen saver options

Each screen saver may have a series of options available to modify its performance. When you select a screen saver on the left side of the Desktop & Screen Saver dialog, click the Options button that sits underneath the preview. If the Options button is dimmed out, there are no available options. (For example, the Computer Name screen saver has no available options.)

Flurry's options include the following:

✦ **Color:** A pull-down menu with many options. There are six colors to choose from (each of which roots the Flurry's eruptions in a particular color space), alternately; there are four cycle speeds (each sets the Flurry's eruptions to cycle through all colors at varying speeds); and lastly, there are three brightness levels to choose from (each keeps the Flurry and its eruptions rooted at a particular degree of brightness). These options are mutually exclusive. The Flurry is set by default to Cycle, an average brightness setting, and cycling through all colors.

✦ **Streams:** A slider ranging from Few to Many, Streams sets how many eruptions of color come from the Flurry. By default, this is set in the middle.

✦ **Thickness:** A slider ranging from Thin to Thick, Thickness sets the width of the emerging streams of color. By default, this is set in the middle.

✦ **Speed:** Another slider, ranging from Slow to Fast, Speed sets the pace at which the Flurry itself moves about the screen. By default, this is set in the middle.

All the slideshow-style screen savers have the same options set, with checkboxes to engage/disengage each option.

✦ **Cross-Fade between slides:** This option enables the selected slides to cross-fade from one to the next; as one image is fading away, another is fading in. When not selected, each image fades to black before another fades in.

✦ **Zoom Back and Forth:** Selecting this option causes the screen saver to zoom in and out on images, as well as to pan left and right.

✦ **Crop to Fit:** This option ensures that your images displayed full screen, as opposed to displaying too small or radically oversized.

✦ **Centered Onscreen:** This option modifies the Zoom Back and Forth option, as the slides will zoom in and out only, and will no longer move left to right. Having Zoom Back and Forth and Centered Onscreen unchecked disables all zooming and panning, and results in a more static (boring) screen saver.

✦ **Randomize:** This option randomly selects the images from the available slides. In the case of large image collections, this option helps to alleviate boredom. (After all, screen savers are supposed to be fun!)

Tip   Screen savers are also a very convenient way to secure your workstation if you walk away and forget to log out, as you can set the screen saver to lock down your workstation in the Security preference pane. The Security preference pane and this option are discussed in Chapter 13.

Appearance Preferences

In addition to setting the colors or pictures displayed on your desktop, you can also set the color scheme and some of the standard control features the OS uses. The Appearance preference pane controls many of these general appearance elements. To open the Appearance preference pane, click the System Preferences icon in the Dock (or System Preferences menu item in the Apple menu), then select the Appearance preference pane. Alternatively, you can choose View ➪ Appearance. Figure 4-4 shows the Appearance preference pane, and the options are listed as follows:

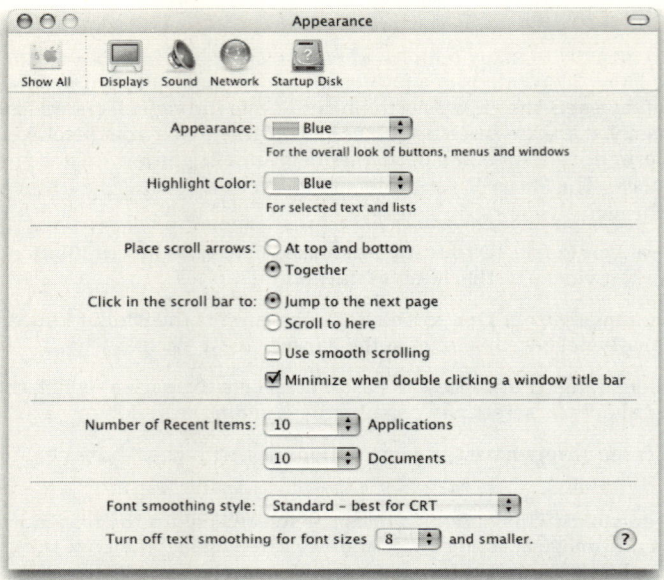

Figure 4-4: The Appearance preference pane is the location of many options adjusting the general look and feel of the Mac OS X environment.

✦ **Appearance:** A pull-down menu with two options, Graphite and Blue. The default setting is Blue. Switching to Graphite changes the color of certain system control elements: the Scroller, highlighted push buttons, and the Close/Minimize/Zoom buttons become a graphite grey color.

✦ **Highlight Color:** A pull-down menu with eight color options and an intriguing item named Other. The color you select from this list becomes the color used to highlight selected text. You can choose any of these Highlight Color options to change your highlight color from blue (the default) to any of the eight preselected colors. Selecting Other brings up the Color Picker. See the final item under this heading for more information about the Color Picker.

✦ **Place scroll arrows:** The two options available are At top and bottom, or Together (default). The scroll arrows shown in all windows when needed will be placed according to this setting. When set to At top and bottom, the up arrow will be at the top of the scroll bar, the down arrow at the bottom, the left arrow on the left side and the right arrow on the right side. The default keeps the up and down buttons together at the bottom and the left/right buttons on the right side.

✦ **Click in the scroll bar to:** The two available options are Jump to the next page (default) or Scroll to here. The default is the preferred mode, as it is consistent and predictable. Clicking in the scroll bar shifts the window one page or screen of data at a time. The alternative method, Scroll to here, causes the window to jump to the position you clicked, rather than one page at a time.

✦ **Use smooth scrolling:** This option causes the scrolling of data in windows to be slightly more smooth when holding down on the scroll arrow or when using a mouse with a scroll wheel. The difference is very subtle.

✦ **Minimize when double-clicking a window title bar:** Rather than being forced to click the minimize button, this option allows (as the title suggests) you to double click on the title bar to minimize.

✦ **Number of Recent Items:** Recently used applications and documents are displayed in the Apple menu in a pull-out menu. Increasing or decreasing the numbers here will lengthen or shorten the lists. The default is 10 each.

✦ **Font smoothing style:** Onscreen fonts are smoothed out (called *antialiasing*) by OS X to create a more appealing experience. The styles available here tailor the degree of smoothing. The default is Standard-best for CRT, as most users still use CRT displays. The other options are Light, Strong, and Medium-best for LCD displays. If you have an LCD, select Medium. Selecting any of these options will result in very subtle changes that you may not notice.

✦ **Turn off text smoothing for font sizes:** Because font smoothing can result in smaller type being very difficult to read (the fonts get too gooey looking, and letters blend together or get blurry), this option enables you to deactivate antialiasing on fonts at a certain threshold and below.

The Color Picker

The Color Picker is a tool designed to afford users the option of choosing any color under the sun. In the Appearance pane, it is used to pick a custom highlight color. The Color Picker comes up in other areas of the Finder, with the same controls, applying the custom color to other itemss. In the Color Picker, five subpanes are available, each with its own method of choosing colors. Common elements include a magnifying glass that when clicked enables users to choose a color from any visible area on screen, and the white box next to the magnifying glass. This white box fills with the chosen color. Close the Color Picker to choose the color in the box. Figure 4-5 shows each of the 5 subpanes.

✦ **Color picker subpane 1, A color wheel:** Click in any area of the color wheel to choose that color. The slider to the right adjusts the overall brightness of the color wheel.

✦ **Color picker subpane 2, A slider-based color selector:** The pull-down menu offers different types of sliders, from CMYK (shown in Figure 4-5) to RGB to HSB. The different sliders are useful if you have to reproduce a specific color by its numeric value, rather than finding it by eye.

✦ **Color picker subpane 3, A list-based color selector:** The standard Apple list has 11 colors. Other lists are available, and custom lists can be created. The search field can be used to find a color by name.

✦ **Color picker subpane 4, The picture-based color selector:** It is by default populated with the Spectrum image, containing a wide range of colors. The pull-down menu at the bottom has a New from file option, enabling you to open an image in that window, and then select the desired color from the image.

✦ **Color picker subpane 5, Crayons!** This pane has a collection of crayons available. Pick your favorite crayon color.

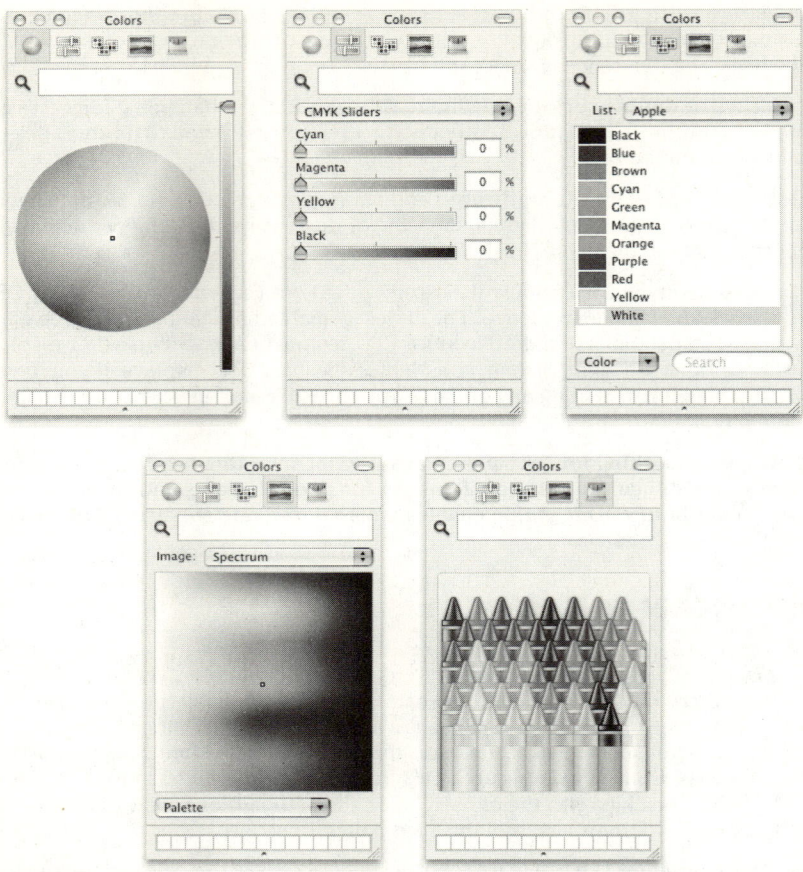

Figure 4-5: The Color Picker is the primary tool provided by Apple to allow users to choose a color using a number of different methods.

Customize the Dock

By default, the Dock is located on the bottom of your display and is quite large. In addition to changing the location and size, the Dock has a few additional tricks up its sleeve, all available in the Dock preference pane. Many of the Dock's settings can also be changed via a contextual menu or through direct clicking on the Dock. The different ways to initiate all of the commands is discussed under each heading. That said, to gain access to all of the Dock's available options in one place, open the Dock preference pane, shown in Figure 4-6. Choose Apple ➪ Dock ➪ Dock Preferences (or Apple ➪ System Preferences ➪ Dock). The Dock pane of System Preferences appears, as shown in Figure 4-6.

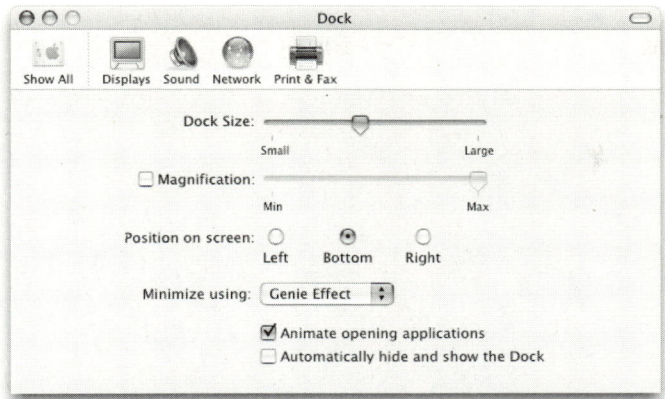

Figure 4-6: Change Dock size, magnification, hiding, position, and visual effect in the Dock pane of System Preferences.

Resizing the Dock

The Dock resizes automatically as items are added to or removed from it, but you can also manually resize the Dock (and the icons in it) yourself. To do this, move the Dock Size slider from Small to Large and release at the desired size. Alternately, move the pointer to the vertical line that separates application icons from folder and document icons. When the pointer changes to look like a two-headed arrow, drag down to make the Dock smaller or up to make the Dock larger. Figure 4-7 illustrates the difference between a large and a small Dock.

Tip

To scale the Dock up or down incrementally, so the icon size is always a multiple of 16 pixels, press Option while you drag the separator line.

Setting the Dock position and hiding

The Dock can be at the bottom of the screen or at either side. The bottom of the screen is longer than the sides and has room for more Dock icons. That said, the Dock will get in your way more at the bottom than on a side. At the bottom of the screen, the Dock interferes with making windows the full height of the screen to minimize vertical scrolling. This has become obvious as more and more users migrate to widescreen-style displays. The increased room left to right translates to less room top to bottom, and the dock takes up a healthy portion of that top to bottom space!

The Dock, when permanently displayed, is least obtrusive on the right side of the screen, because most applications display windows aligned with the left side of the screen. To reposition the Dock on the left or right side of the screen, select the appropriate radio button in the Dock preference pane. As an alternative method to reposition the Dock, hold the control key and click on the vertical separator in the Dock, and click to check the desired location from the Dock position onscreen pull-out menu.

Figure 4-7: The Dock at maximum size, filling the width of the screen (top), the Dock at minimum size (bottom).

Regardless of the Dock position, to conserve space, the most desirable option is to have the Dock stay out of your way altogether. This is accomplished by having it hide until you move the pointer to one of the edges of the screen. In the Dock preference pane, select the Automatically hide and show the Dock option. (Alternatively, you can Control-click on the vertical line that separates application icons from folder and document icons, and select Turn Hiding On.) This option will cause the Dock to retreat beyond the edge of the screen. When your mouse is moved to the area where the Dock should normally be, the Dock emerges from hiding, ready for use. This is the best way to get the most out of your available screen real estate.

Setting Dock magnification

When you resize the Dock to make the icons very small, it becomes difficult to distinguish between the various items. As a solution to this, the Dock can magnify icons as the pointer approaches so they are easier to recognize. To enable this feature, click the Magnification checkbox. The Magnification slider will no longer be dimmed out. This slider adjusts the amount of magnification that occurs when your pointer rolls over a particular item in the Dock. Alternatively, you can Control-click the Dock's separator line to display its contextual menu, and choose Turn Magnification On. When magnification is turned on, the menu commands change to Turn Magnification Off. Figure 4-8 shows the results of magnification active and set to the middle rate.

Figure 4-8: Magnification is a way to better see the items in the Dock as the pointer approaches.

Choosing a visual effect

When you minimize a window, the Dock normally shows a visual effect that resembles a genie being sucked into a bottle.

The genie-in-a-bottle visual effect that occurs when you minimize a window is impressive, but after a while, you may get tired of it and wish the window would just minimize more quickly. For this purpose, Apple has made the Scale Effect. It's simpler and faster than the Genie Effect (in which the window gradually gets smaller as it minimizes). You can set the visual effect by choosing Scale Effect in the Minimize using pull-down menu in the Dock preferences pane, or you can Control-click the separator line in the Dock and then choose Scale Effect in the pop-up menu.

Adding items to the Dock

Add any item to the Dock by simply dragging it to the Dock. This creates a Dock-based alias of the item. Note that there is no small arrow in the lower left nor the word *alias* in its name to signify its alias status, but since the actual item remains in its original location, and this Dock item merely points to it, the icon in the Dock is a kind of alias. Applications must be placed on the same side of the separator line as the Finder; documents, folders, and other disks must be placed on the other side of the line. Placing an application's icon in the Dock gives you one-click access to the application regardless of what application is currently active. When you place a document or folder icon in the Dock, it is quickly available with a single click.

Removing Dock icons

Removing an item from the Dock is also extremely simple. Drag the icon out of the Dock, let go, and it disappears in a puff of smoke. You can't remove the Finder or the Trash from the Dock.

Moving icons in the Dock

You can rearrange icons in the Dock by dragging them to different positions. As you drag an icon across the Dock, the other icons move apart to make room for the icon you're dragging. You can place the icon you're dragging in any space that opens up by releasing the mouse button.

Using Dock folder navigation

The real convenience and power of the Dock is felt when you place a folder or disk icon in the Dock. As with all items in the Dock, clicking it opens it. An application when clicked will open; a document when clicked will open in its target application. Click a folder, its contents appear in a new Finder window. But if you click and hold (or Control-click) a folder icon in the Dock, you see a hierarchical menu that enables you to traverse the folder structure and navigate down deeper into the folder's contents. Release the mouse button after this menu appears, navigate through it, and then click any item in the menu to open it. If you prefer, click and hold the mouse button the whole time you navigate, and release the mouse button on the desired item. A folder's pop-up Dock menu also contains a Show in Finder command. Choose Show in Finder to see the folder in a Finder window. Figure 4-9 shows an example of a folder's pop-up Dock menu.

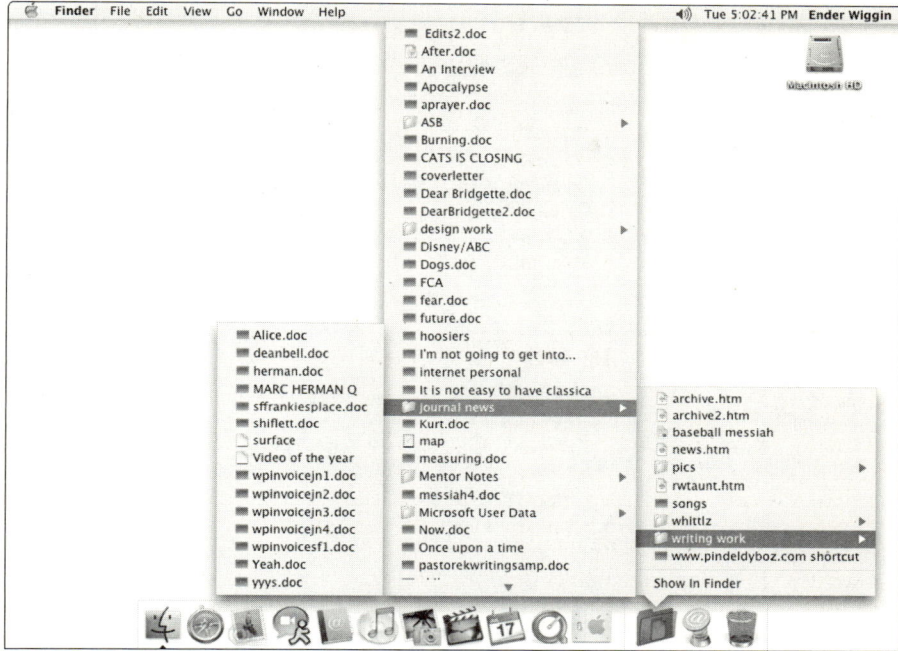

Figure 4-9: Get to any part of a folder when its icon is in the Dock.

Applications in the Dock

In addition to the shortcuts that are already in the Dock, every open application adds its own icon to the Dock temporarily. When these applications quit, the icon will fade, shrinking the Dock back to its original state. All open applications are identifiable by a small black triangle-shaped marker that appears below the application's icon in the Dock. When you click and hold (or Control-click) the icon of an open application in the Dock, a pop-up menu appears, giving you application-specific choices. For example, the Finder's pop-up Dock menu presents a list of available windows, and you can choose one to bring it to the front. Other applications list different commands and items in their pop-up Dock menus. Figure 4-10 shows an example of the iTunes pop-up Dock menu, displaying options to Quit, Hide (which banishes all open windows off screen, to help free up screen space), Show in Finder (which opens a new Finder window displaying the item in its location on the disk), and all the open windows that can be brought to the front by selecting them from the pop-up menu. If the application is not perma-nently added to the Dock, another option will appear: Keep in Dock. Selecting this option is another convenient way to prevent an application from leaving the Dock after quitting the application.

Figure 4-10: The pop-up Dock menu of an open application may include items that are specific to the application.

Minimizing windows in the Dock

When you minimize a window by clicking its Minimize button, the Genie or Scale effect occurs, leaving you a miniature version of the window in the Dock (on the right side of the vertical separator). Whatever was displayed in that window is also displayed, but reduced in size, in the minimized window. Furthermore, the window belongs to an application that is still running, and the application may continue updating the minimized window in the Dock. For example, Apple loves to demonstrate this capability by playing miniature QuickTime movies in the Dock. (Chapter 20 describes how to work with QuickTime movies.) Click a minimized window icon in the Dock to restore the window to full size and its original position.

Enhancing Exposé

The three modes of Exposé can be activated with the F9, F10, and F11 keys. Through the Exposé preference pane, you can make any of the modes activate by moving your pointer to a particular corner of the screen (this is called *using a hot corner*). However, the most effective method of using Exposé is only available if you have a multibutton mouse. Apple's standard mice all have only one button. (Steve Jobs, Apple's CEO hates multiple buttons for some weird reason.) With a multibutton mouse, you can map desired Exposé modes to particular mouse buttons, radically improving speed. Figure 4-11 shows the Exposé control panel.

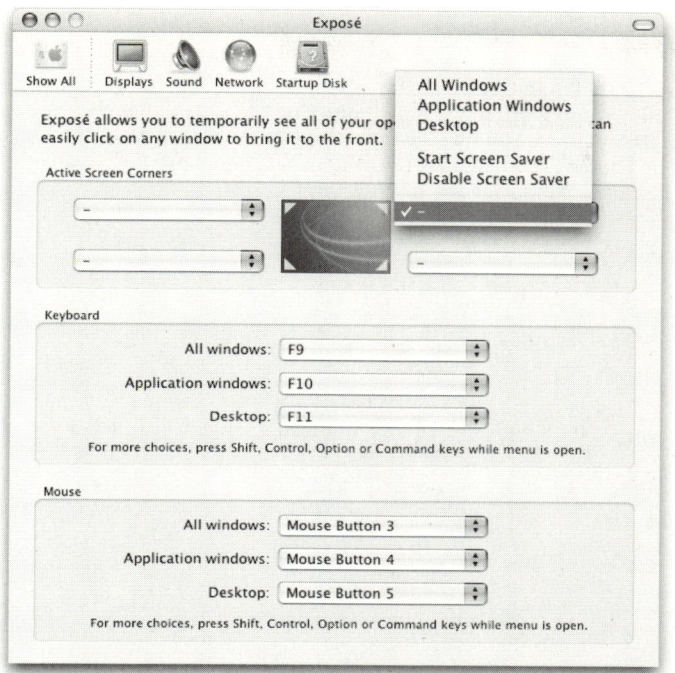

Figure 4-11: Exposé's preference pane offers options to change the keys, hot corners, or mouse buttons assigned to activate each of Exposé's modes.

The Exposé preference pane allows you to change the keys that activate the three different modes. The keyboard area has a pull-down menu available for each mode of Exposé. Each pull-down menu is populated with a list of keys that can activate Exposé. When accessing the pull-down menu, the Shift, Option, Control, and Command keys all modify the list. Holding any of those keys while selecting the items in the list will result in that combination activating Exposé. For example, holding down Option and selecting F10 will result in the Exposé mode being activated only when pressing Option and F10 together. The mouse area has a pull-down menu populated with all available mouse buttons. Each hot corner's menu offers each of the three Exposé modes. They will engage when the pointer is pointed to that corner.

Note

Each hot corner's pull-down menu in the Exposé preference pane also has two screen saver commands available, as the other function of hot corners can be to activate or disable screen savers. After all, a hot corner can only do one thing at a time.

Setting Finder Preferences

The Finder has a number of preference settings that affect the appearance of icons on the Desktop, behavior of Finder windows, Label colors, emptying the Trash, and showing extensions on the names of files and more You change these preference settings by choosing Finder ➪ Preferences. The Finder Preferences window appears. There are four available subpanes to the Finder Preferences window. Each is shown in Figure 4-12.

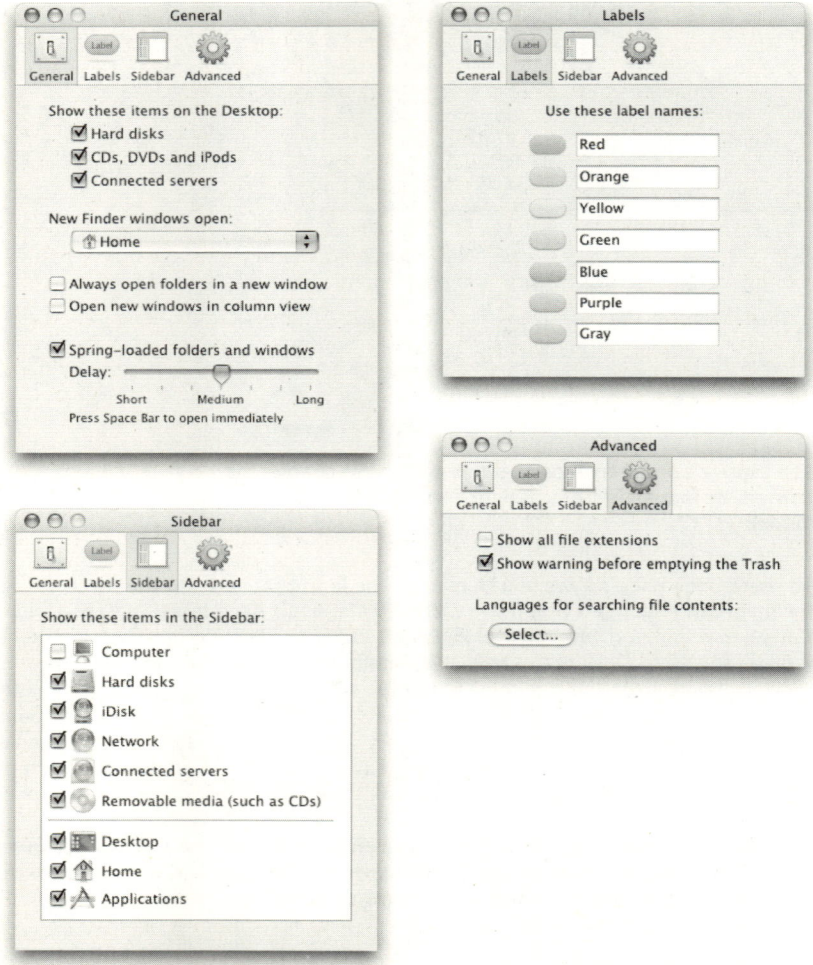

Figure 4-12: The Finder's preference settings affect desktop icons, Finder windows, the Trash, and file extensions.

Finder Preferences offers the following options:

✦ **Show these items on the Desktop:** Select the types of items that you want the Finder to display on your desktop. These items are displayed together with any additional items located in the Desktop folder of your Home folder. All items appear at the Computer level of your workspace regardless of the settings here.

✦ **New Finder windows open:** Select what folder you want displayed when you create a new Finder window. The default, and recommended, option is the contents of your Home folder. Other options include the Documents folder, Macintosh HD (root level of the disk), iDisk (if available), the Computer level of your folder structure, or Other. Selecting Other will bring up a dialog box. Select the desired folder and click Open. The Home folder is recommended, as this is the main repository for all of your personal data, including documents, music, pictures, and more.

✦ **Always open folders in a new window:** Select this option to reverse the Mac OS X Finder's practice of navigating within a single window. This makes the Mac OS X Finder spawn windows in the same way as the old Mac OS 9 Finder.

✦ **Open new windows in column view:** Select this option, and the Finder opens all new windows in column view. Of course, once the window is opened, you can switch to any desired view mode through the methods covered in Chapter 3.

✦ **Spring-loaded folders and windows:** If you drag an icon over a closed folder, the folder will automatically open after a brief delay. This delayed opening is called *spring-loading*. This slider sets the time delay between when you drag an icon over a folder and when that folder springs open. As the note below the slider points out, if you want a folder to open immediately, drag the icon over the folder, then press the Space bar on the keyboard.

✦ **Labels:** Each individual file in Mac OS X can have a colored label applied to it, affording users another way of visually sorting through their files. In the second subpane of the Finder Preferences pane, the Labels can be named to more accurately reflect their purpose. By default, the names are simply the name of the color. Read the "Labels" section later in this chapter for more on labels.

✦ **Sidebar:** This subpane of the Finder Preference pane displays the list of standard items shown in the sidebar. Deselecting items here will remove them from the sidebar.

✦ **Show all file extensions:** Select this option if you want to see the three or four character name extensions (suffixes) for all files that have them. Viewing file extensions is useful for users that share files with others, as files may be delivered to you and be unidentifiable by your computer. Displaying the file extension gives you a clue as to what *type* of file you may have been given.

✦ **Show warning before emptying the Trash:** Deselect this option if you want the Finder to empty the Trash without first having you confirm the action. If this option is off, the Finder also deletes locked items from the Trash without any warning. It is recommended to leave this option selected, to prevent accidental erasure of files.

Sidebar is in; Favorites is Out

Apple's new Sidebar feature is a great way to have easy access to your favorite files, folders, applications and locations. Just drag an item over any blank space in the Sidebar and presto! The item is now added to the Sidebar. To remove items, you can just drag them out of the Sidebar and they disappear. This convenient storage area operates very nicely in conjunction with the Dock, and as such, Apple seems to have forgotten the Favorites menu. The Favorites menu was a menu populated with aliases that were placed in the Favorites folder. This was a useful method of keeping all commonly used elements in one easy-to-find place. But, it became largely unneeded with the advent of the Dock in OS X, and apparently even less needed with the integration of the Sidebar in OS 10.3. The Favorites folder still exists in a user's Library folder though, and Favorites still serves one purpose. When logging into a server, you can opt to "Add to Favorites," which will place an alias in the Favorites folder. The server aliases in the folder appear as shortcuts in the Server Connection window. Read more on server connections in Chapter 16.

Finder Window Modification

You already know how to view a Finder window as icons, a list, or columns. You also know how to clean up an icon view and change the sorting of a list view. In addition, you know how to show and hide the toolbar at the top of any Finder window (which results in a rather different look!). We covered all these operations in Chapter 3. These are only some of the ways you can customize Finder windows. Other methods for tuning Finder windows include suppressing the sidebar and customizing the toolbar. These methods are covered in this section.

Customizing the toolbar

The default toolbar consists of a number of buttons with their names beneath them: Back, Forward, View Mode Selectors, and Action Buttons, and the Search field. Apple enables you to remove any of these buttons, add others, and arrange them any way you want. You can also set the toolbar to display the buttons as named icons (the default), icons without names, or names alone. To make these changes, with any Finder window active, choose View ⇨ Customize Toolbar. The active Finder window changes to display the Customize Toolbar dialog box shown in Figure 4-13.

With the Customize Toolbar dialog displayed, change the toolbar by doing the following:

✦ **Add buttons:** Drag any of the optional buttons to the toolbar from the main part of the dialog. You don't have to add buttons only at the right end of the toolbar. If you drag a button between two buttons in the toolbar, they move apart to make room for the button you're dragging. If the toolbar is full of buttons and you drag another button to the toolbar, buttons that don't fit on the toolbar appear in a pop-up menu. To see this menu, click the arrow that appears at the right end of the toolbar. Click the Done button to complete your toolbar customization. All of the additional tools are described in the section "Additional Toolbar buttons."

✦ **Remove buttons:** Drag buttons away from the toolbar.

✦ **Rearrange buttons:** Drag buttons to different places on the toolbar.

✦ **Revert to default buttons:** If you've customized the toolbar and want to get back to the default set of buttons, drag the boxed default set from the lower part of the dialog to the toolbar to replace whatever is currently there.

✦ **Change toolbar mode:** Show items as icons with names, icons only, or names only by choosing from the Show pop-up menu at the bottom of the dialog. Figure 4-14 shows the three toolbar modes. The Use Small Size checkbox makes the toolbar icons smaller, conserving space.

Figure 4-13: Add, remove, and rearrange buttons in a Finder window's toolbar by using the Customize Toolbar dialog box.

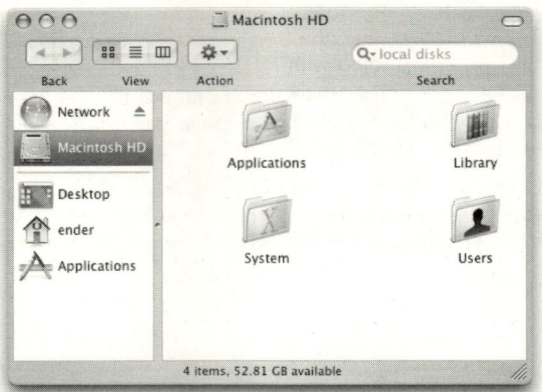

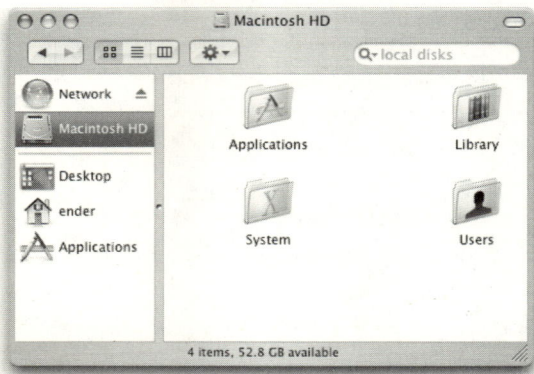

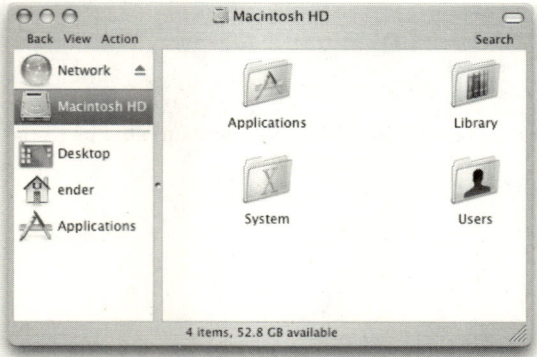

Figure 4-14: A Finder window's toolbar displaying both icons and text (top), only icons without text (middle), and only text (bottom).

Note   Add icons as buttons. Even without the Customize Toolbar dialog open, if you drag folders, files, or disks from Finder windows to the toolbar, the items become buttons there. For example, if you create a folder for a particular project within your Documents folder, drag its icon to the toolbar to make it accessible with a single click. To remove items, use the Customize Toolbar dialog. Although, the easiest way to remove items is to hold down ⌘ and drag the item out of the toolbar. The item will disappear in a puff of smoke.

Tip   Clicking a folder button in the toolbar opens the folder in the same window. If you ⌘-click a folder button in the toolbar, the folder opens in a new Finder window.

Additional toolbar buttons

As shown in Figure 4-13, there are numerous additional tools available for the toolbar. Each has its uses:

✦ **Path:** The Path tool when clicked displays a pop-up menu showing the file hierarchy path to the current folder. Selecting any of the folders in the path will open that folder within the active window. This can also be performed by ⌘-clicking the title bar.

✦ **Eject:** This tool will eject any selected disks or disconnect server volumes. The contextual menu for each disk or volume offers the same option.

✦ **Burn:** If your computer is equipped with a CD or DVD burner, this tool will open the Burn disk dialog (as covered in Chapter 3).

✦ **Customize:** This tool when clicked will bring up the Customize Toolbar window.

✦ **Separator:** The Separator is a simply vertical line that serves as a visual dividing line between items.

✦ **Space/Flexible Space:** The Space item is a simply a blank space, approximately the same width as other tools. The Flexible Space item will fill all space available in the toolbar. Placing a flexible space between items will push items on both sides to the far-left and far-right sides.

✦ **New Folder:** Clicking this tool will create a new folder in the active window. This action can also be performed by pressing Shift-⌘-N.

✦ **Delete:** This tool will move selected items to the Trash.

✦ **Connect:** Clicking this tool will open the Connect dialog. This dialog can also be opened via the Go menu, or by pressing ⌘-K. The connect dialog is discussed in Chapter 10.

✦ **Find:** This tool brings up the Find dialog window.

✦ **Get Info:** This tool will open the Get Info window for any selected item. This window can also be opened by pressing ⌘-I.

✦ **iDisk:** Click on this tool to open your iDisk (a feature of Apple's .Mac service, covered in Chapter 18).

Setting View Options

The Finder in Mac OS X provides still more ways to tweak the basic icon and list views. In this section, we discuss the adjustments you can make to icon and list views in the View Options window, which you display for an active window by choosing View ⇨ Show View Options. The options in this window are different for icon view and list view, as shown in Figure 4-15.

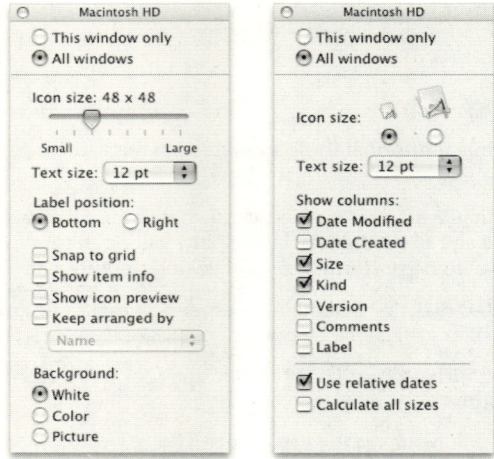

Figure 4-15: The View Options windows for icon view (left), and list view (right).

The View Options window displays the settings of the folder, disk, or other item whose name appears in the title bar of the active Finder window. To reinforce this fact, the same name appears in the title bar of the View Options window. If you make another Finder window active (bring it to the front), the View Options window changes to show settings for the item named in this Finder window's title. Therefore, you can only see the View Options settings for one folder at a time.

The View Options settings don't actually apply to the active Finder window. The View Options settings actually apply to the folder, disk, or other item that is *displayed* in the active Finder window. The settings for the folder shown in a Finder window remain applied even when you close the window. If you open the same folder in another Finder window later, the Finder uses that folder's previously established View Options settings. (You can alter this behavior by changing an option in Finder Preferences, as described later in this chapter.) If a background Finder window is displaying the contents of the same folder as the active Finder window, then both windows have the same title and changes you make to the View Options settings affect both windows.

Setting icon view options

In a Finder window set to icon view, you can set the icon size, text size, automatic snap to grid, or arrangement of icons, label position, item info, item preview, and background color or picture.

Changing the icon size in an icon view

To change the icon size in an icon view, use the Icon Size slider in the View Options window. If you set the slider for the smallest size, the icon's name displays next to the icon rather than below it. The icons of most Mac OS X applications and their documents are designed to look great at any size. Figure 4-16 illustrates the minimum, standard, and maximum sizes icons available in icon views.

Setting text size

An item's name is displayed in 12-point text by default. The Text Size pull-down menu offers other options.

Label position

The name of an item is displayed beneath its icon by default. These radio buttons will maintain this setting or force the text to be placed to the right at all times.

Snap To Grid, Item Info, Icon Preview

These three checkboxes alter the behavior of the items much as their names imply. Snap to Grid causes all icons to automatically align to an invisible grid. This option is a great help keeping icons neatly organized. The Item Info checkbox will display important information about many items, such as the number of items in a folder or a disk's size and available space remaining. Not all items display any additional information. Icon preview forces the operating system to generate a icon-sized preview of graphic image files. This is helpful as many graphic files don't have a preview pregenerated, especially items downloaded from the Web.

Changing the icon arrangement in icon view

The icon arrangement setting in the View Options window determines if and how the Finder automatically aligns icons in an icon view. Check the Keep Arranged checkbox and then select one of the following six options in the pull-down menu: Name, Date modified, Date created, Size, Kind, and Label. The Finder then aligns icons on the invisible grid and places them in order according to the chosen factor.

Changing the background in icon view

In addition to specifying icon size and arrangement, you can specify the background for a folder displayed in an icon view. Figure 4-17 shows the results of the different options. Here are your options:

✦ **White:** The standard white appears in the background behind your icons.

✦ **Color:** Makes the background a solid color, which you can specify by following these steps:

1. **After selecting the Color setting, click the small swatch of the currently selected color that appears in the View Options window.** This action displays the standard Mac OS X Color Picker window, shown earlier in Figure 4-5.

2. **Pick the background color you want.** Depending on the type of Color Picker you selected, you pick a color for your background (as described earlier in this chapter).

3. **Click OK.**

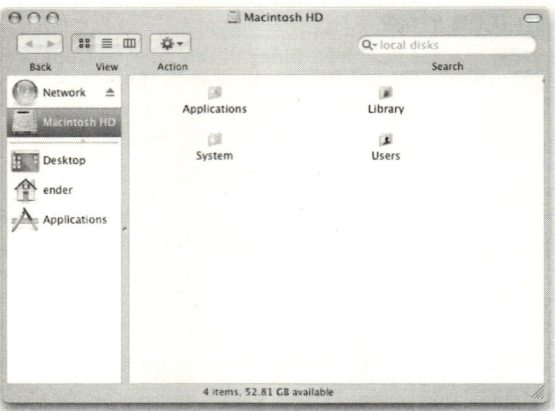

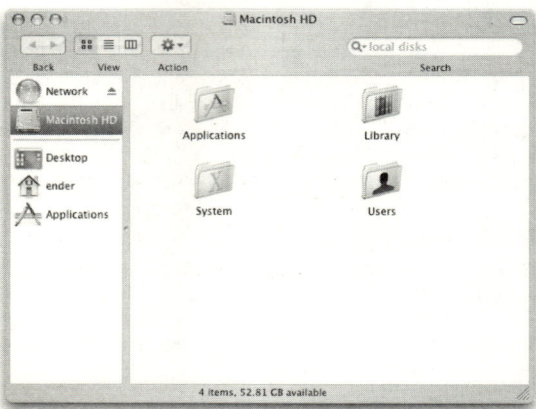

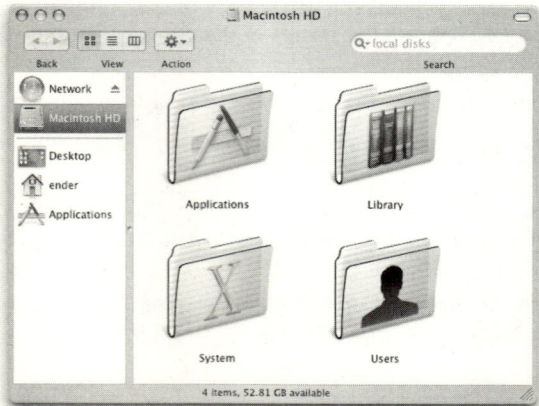

Figure 4-16: Icons in a Finder window at minimum
(16 x 16 pixels) size (top), at standard (48 x 48 pixels) size
(middle), and at maximum (128 x 128 pixels) size (bottom).

✦ **Picture:** Makes the background a picture, as seen in Figure 4-17. To set an image as the background, follow these steps:

1. **After selecting the Picture setting, click the Select button that appears in the View Options window.**

2. **In the resulting dialog box, select a graphics file that contains an appropriate picture and click Select.** This dialog box is a standard Open dialog box, which we cover in more detail in Chapter 5.

Figure 4-17: The background of icon view windows can be a color or a picture. While fun, this can get distracting.

> **Note**   If you'd like to change the settings for the desktop's icons, select View ➪ Show View Options with the desktop active (i.e., no active windows). The desktop's view options appear in the View Options window. To be sure you are editing the correct View Options, check the title of the View Options window. (It will say Desktop.)

Setting list view options

For a list view, you can set the icon and text size (with the radio buttons and pull-down menu, respectively) and select which of seven optional columns you want shown. By selecting just the columns you need to see in a window, you can see most or all columns without scrolling the window. Of course, you can make more columns fit in a window by widening the window or reducing column widths, as described in Chapter 3.

A list view always includes the Name column. The columns that you can show or hide are the following:

✦ Date Modified (selected by default)

✦ Date Created

✦ Size (selected by default)

✦ Kind (selected by default)

✦ Version

✦ CommentsLabel

Another option for list views determines whether the Finder displays relative dates (yesterday, today, tomorrow) rather than the actual month, day, and year. For dates other than yesterday, today, and tomorrow, the Finder uses the date and time formats that are set in the International pane of System Preferences (as described in Chapter 13). The column's width determines whether the Finder uses the long date format or short date format from System Preferences. For example, a standard-width column that shows Tue, Jan 2, 2001 12:00 PM would show 1/2/01 12:00 PM in a narrower column or Tuesday, January 2, 2001 12:00 PM in a wider column.

You can also set an option to have the Finder calculate folder sizes and display them in a list view. Folder size calculation takes place in the background, while you're doing other things. This is a helpful way to monitor your folder sizes, but the information is not only slow to appear, having this option checked can cause your computer to slow down when displaying a list containing many folders, as it has to calculate this information for all folders shown.

Setting column view options

Column view has three options. Set text size, Show icon, and Show preview column. Set text size changes the size of text names. If Show Icon is deselected, the column view will simply show the text names of items, with no icons. The Show preview column checkbox enables the preview column to display the item preview when a single item is selected.

Using global or individual view options

Each folder can be displayed in a Finder window according to global View Options settings or the folder's individual View Options settings. The option at the top of the View Options window determines which settings the displayed folder in the active Finder window uses.

✦ **This window only:** The settings changed only modify the currently displayed folder.

✦ **All windows:** The settings modified will apply to all folders viewed in the currently selected mode. Thus, if the active folder is in list view, all folders viewed in list view will refer to these settings as their starting point.

The wording of these settings is a bit misleading. Like all other options in the View Options window, the option at the top of the View Options window applies to the *folder* (or all folders) displayed in a Finder window, not to the Finder window itself.

The Finder keeps track of the option at the top of the View Options window separately for icon view and list view. For example, a folder's list view can use global settings while the same folder's icon view uses individual settings.

Note   If the View Options window is closed, some changes you make in a Finder window affect whether the folder that is displayed in the window is set to use global or individual View Options settings. If you rearrange or resize columns in a list view, the folder is automatically set to use individual View Options settings for list view. When you open the View Options window for this folder, you see that the option at the top of the window has been set to This window only.

Get in the habit of double-checking the option at the top of the View Options window before you change any settings in the window. Unless you're sure that you want to change the global settings many folders use, set the option at the top of the View Options window to This window only.

Using Custom Icons

If you don't want all of your folder icons to look the same, or if you don't like the default icons provided by applications for either the application itself or the documents they create, you can (on a file-by-file basis) attach custom icons of your choosing to those files through the Get Info window.

Attaching a custom icon

To attach a custom icon, follow these steps:

1. **Copy an image that you want to use as an icon.** You can do this by opening an image file and choosing Edit ➪ Copy (⌘-C). This command puts a copy of the picture on the Clipboard, a temporary system storage area. It is recommended you try to copy a square image that is as close as possible to 128 x 128 pixels. If the image is larger, the Finder scales it down, if it is too small, the icon will appear jagged or fuzzy if it is displayed at a size larger than its native size.

2. **In the Finder, make sure that the Info window is showing (⌘-I) and select the file or folder whose icon you want to replace.** The selected item's information and icon appear in the General section of the Info window.

3. **In the General section of the Info window, click the displayed icon to select it.** When the icon is selected, a border appears around it. You can't select the icon if the item is locked or you don't have Write privileges for the item.

4. **Choose Edit ➪ Paste (⌘-V).** The Finder pastes the image from the Clipboard into the item's icon, as shown in Figure 4-18.

Removing a custom icon

You can remove a custom icon as follows:

1. **Select the file or folder whose custom icon you want to remove.** The selected item's icon appears in the corner of the Info window.

2. **In the General section of the Info window, click the icon to select it.** You can't select the icon if the item is locked or you don't have Write privileges for the item.

3. **Press the Delete key.** The custom icon disappears and the standard icon for the selected file or folder returns.

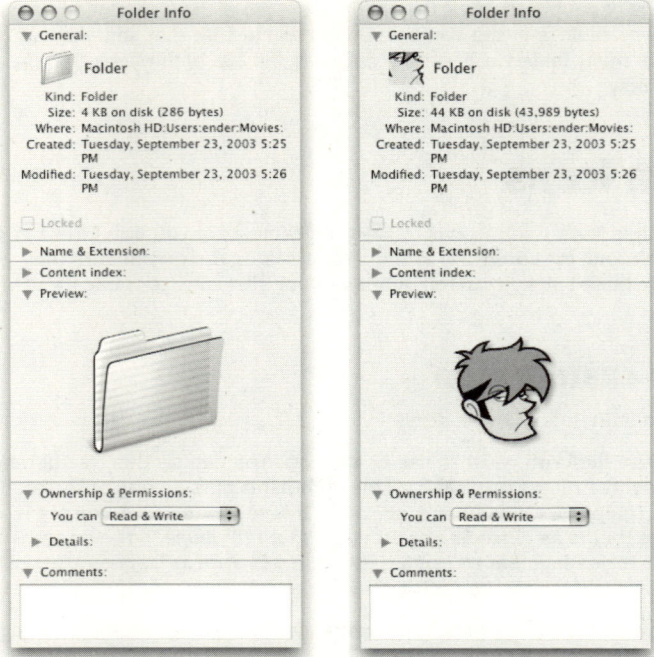

Figure 4-18: After copying an image, you can paste it as a custom icon in the Info window.

Labels

Labels are a tool used to color-code various items on a user's hard drive. Items have no label applied by default. To apply a label, single-click on an item to select it, then open the File menu, and select the desired label color from the list at the bottom of the menu. To be more individually tailored, labels can be renamed according to priority, or named for particular clients. This is done in the Finder preferences window, as described earlier in this chapter. Applying the priority or client named label to a file marks it visually for quick recognition. Figure 4-19 shows the File menu.

In icon view, a colored border will surround a labeled item's name. The items almost look as if they are selected (as selecting an item also surrounds the name with a color). The key difference to note is that selected item's actual *icons* are also highlighted with a gray box, as shown in Figure 4-20. When selecting an item that is labeled, the label color still remains as a slight border around the selection color.

Figure 4-19: To help items visually stand out, apply colored labels to them with the File menu.

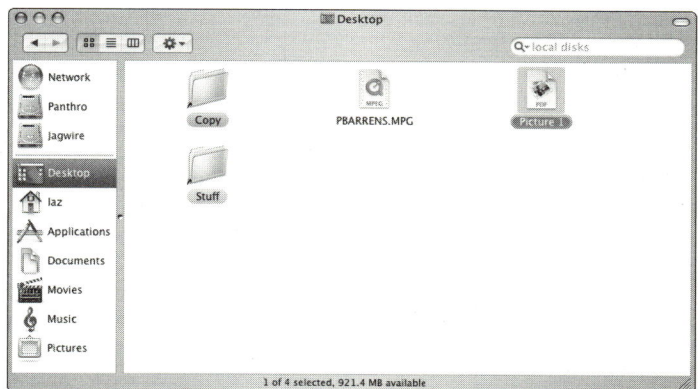

Figure 4-20: Labeled item's names are surrounded with a colored border. A selected and labeled item's text is surrounded with the selection color, plus the label's color as a border, and in addition, he icon is highlighted.

In list view, a labeled item's entire line will be surrounded with the colored border. Turn on the label column in the List View Options to enable sorting by label color (as described in Chapter 3). Figure 4-21 shows the list view with three different label colors applied to different items.

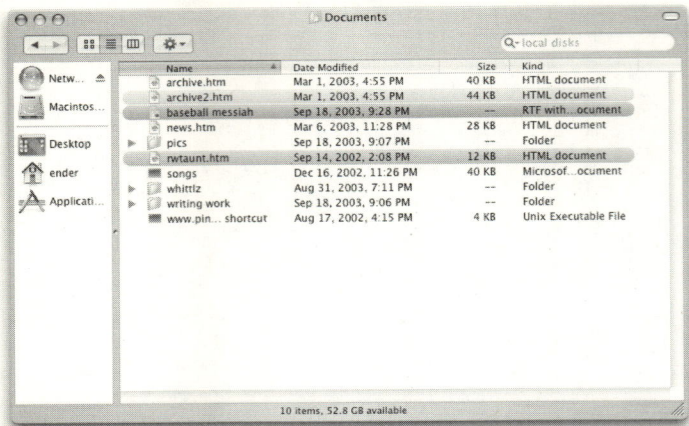

Figure 4-21: Labels are especially noticeable in list view.

Working with Aliases

As described earlier, aliases are shortcut files that when opened point to and open another file. In some ways, aliases act just like the files or folders they represent. In other ways, aliases may act like the independent files they actually are. Accordingly, you use many of the same techniques when working with aliases that you do when working with files and folders, although some differences do exist. In this section, we cover many techniques for working with aliases.

Making an alias

You can make an alias for files, folders, or disks. You can make more than one alias for the same original item and put each alias in a different location.

Making an alias is a simple procedure. Do one of the following:

✦ **Select an item and then choose File ➪ Make Alias or press ⌘-L.** This will create the alias in the same folder as the original item.

✦ **Control-click an item to pop up its contextual menu and choose Make Alias from there.** This will create the alias in the same folder as the original item.

✦ **Press ⌘-Option while dragging an item to the place where you want an alias of it.** You can start pressing ⌘-Option at any time while dragging, but you must hold down the keys while you release the mouse button to make an alias. While you press ⌘-Option, the pointer changes, and acquires a small right-pointing arrow in addition to its normal large left-pointing arrow. This method allows you to simultaneously create an alias and place it in the desired location, saving you the step of moving the alias required by the previous two methods.

An alias has the same icon as the original item, except that the icon has a small curved arrow superimposed to indicate it is an alias. The alias also inherits the name of the original item. If the alias is created in the same folder as the original, the Finder adds the word *alias* to the alias name. The Finder also adds a number to the name as needed (to prevent a new alias from having the same name as another alias in the same folder). The word *alias* is not added when you make an alias by ⌘-dragging the original item to another folder. Figure 4-22 illustrates the subtle differences between an alias and an original.

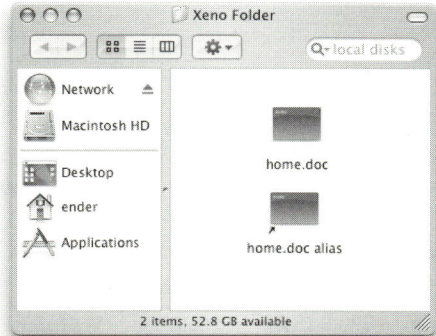

Figure 4-22: Be aware that the alias of an item (bottom) is primarily differentiated from the original (top) by the small arrow in the corner (always present), rather than by the word *alias* which can be removed.

Tip The small icons in Finder window title bars can also be used to make aliases. Just press ⌘-Option while dragging the small icon to make an alias of the original folder.

Renaming an alias

Immediately after you create an alias, its name is selected for editing. You can change the name by typing a replacement or by using the other name-editing techniques described in Chapter 3. For example, you may want to remove the word *alias* from an alias name so the alias has the same name as its original item. An alias can have exactly the same name as its original item as long as they are in different folders. If an alias is in the same folder as its original item, move the alias somewhere else before you try to make the alias's name the same as the original item's name. Of course, an alias and its original can be in the same folder if their names are very similar but not identical.

Dragging items to an alias

Aliases function like their original item when items are dragged to them. For example, if you drag an item to an alias of a folder, Mac OS X resolves the alias and the Finder puts the dragged item into the original folder. Dragging a document to an alias of an application will cause the original application to attempt to open the document. Please note that dragging an *alias* to a folder or application just moves the alias or causes the application to attempt to interact with the alias.

Moving, copying, and deleting an alias

After you make an alias, you can manipulate it as you would any other item. You can move it, copy it, and delete it.

✦ **If you move an alias to a different folder,** its original item is not affected. Only the alias is moved, and the alias still knows where to find its original item.

✦ **If you make copies of an alias,** all the copies of the alias refer to the same original item.

✦ **If you delete an alias,** its original item is not deleted.

Finding an original item

You can find an alias's original item by choosing File ➪ Show Original (⌘-R). The Show Original command displays a Finder window that contains the original item, scrolls the original item into view, and selects it. Alternately, Control-clicking on an alias (bringing up its contextual menu) also offers an option to Show Original.

Fixing broken aliases

If you try to show an alias's original item but the original item has been deleted or moved to a disk that has been ejected or removed, the Finder tells you that the original item can't be found. Figure 4-23 shows the alert that you see in the Finder if Mac OS X can't resolve an alias.

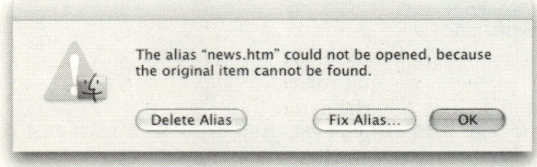

Figure 4-23: The Finder displays an alert when it can't find an alias's original item.

Note   You may not get the alert shown in Figure 4-23 if you try to use a broken alias in an application other than the Finder. In certain Mac OS X applications, the alert you see may simply state the item could not be opened.

The Finder's alert has an OK button, a Delete Alias button, and a Fix Alias button. Clicking OK will cancel the attempt to use the alias for now. Clicking Delete Alias moves the alias to the Trash. Clicking Fix Alias displays a Fix Alias dialog in which you can choose a new original for the alias. This dialog is like the column view of a Finder window. In this dialog, select a file or folder to be the new original item and click the Choose button. (Of course, you can select the old original item to be the new original item, if you know where it is.) Figure 4-24 shows the Fix Alias dialog in which you choose a new alias.

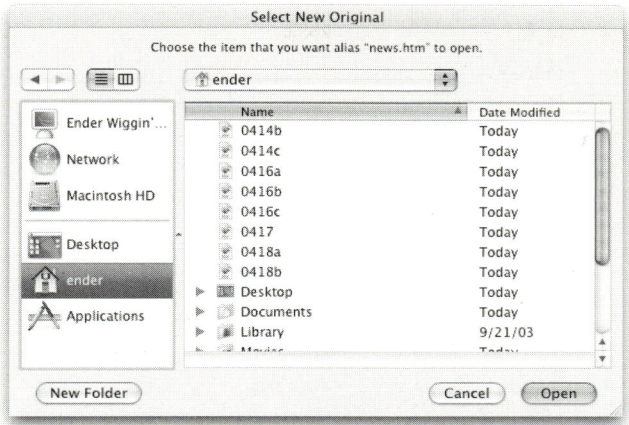

Figure 4-24: Choose a new original for a broken alias.

Selecting a new original for an alias

Instead of throwing away an obsolete or broken alias and making a new one, you can recycle the old alias by assigning it a new original item. Frankly, creating a new alias and discarding an old one is easier than assigning the old one a new original item, and recycling old aliases certainly has no positive environmental impact. Nevertheless, you may have an alias on which you have lavished great attention (having applied a fancy custom icon, elaborate comments, or a clever name) and repurposing such a work of art may be easier than recreating it. Perhaps you have an alias in your Favorites folder that refers to a project folder buried inside your Documents folder, and you want to keep using the same alias when you move on to a new project folder. It is also possible that when fixing a broken alias you selected the wrong original item, and rather than recreate the alias, you can just select a different item. Whatever your reason for taking advantage of the power that the Info window grants you to redirect an alias, here is the procedure for doing the deed:

1. **Select the alias to which you want to assign a new original item.**

2. **Open the Get Info window.** A Select New Original button appears in the General section of the Info window. This button is disabled if the alias is locked or you don't have Write privileges for the alias.

3. **Click the Select New Original button.** The Fix Alias dialog box appears. This dialog box is like the column view of a Finder window and is shown previously in Figure 4-24.

4. **In the Fix Alias dialog, select a file or folder to be the new original item and click the Choose button.**

Summary

In this chapter, you learned how to modify the behavior and appearance of your Finder windows, icons, Exposé, the Desktop, screen savers, and the Dock. In addition, you learned how to work with labels and aliases. The next chapter covers working with documents and applications more in depth.

✦   ✦   ✦

Working with Applications and Documents

You found out just how useful the Finder is in the last two chapters, but you can spend only so much time tinkering with your look and feel, browsing your drive, and organizing files and folders. Pretty soon, it's time to get some real work done. When that time comes, you need to open some applications and work with some documents. Applications provide the tools. Documents are the result of doing the work.

In this chapter, we look at the different types of applications you can use in Mac OS X and explore how you open applications to start using them. We also talk about opening documents with the Finder and with other applications that are open. We discuss how to manage having several applications open at the same time. Then we delve into some basic methods of editing documents — copy-and-paste, drag-and-drop. We cover the ways you can create new documents and save the documents you have created or changed. Finally, we describe how to quit using applications when you're finished.

This chapter covers general techniques that apply to almost all applications and documents. Other chapters get specific about particular applications that are included with Mac OS X. You can find out where we cover each application by scanning the table of contents or checking out the index.

Looking at Mac OS X Applications

With Mac OS X, you use applications built on any of three different frameworks: Cocoa, Carbon, or Classic. The diversity of these frameworks reflects the parentage of Mac OS X: the traditional Mac OS wedded with NeXT's Unix genealogy. The different frameworks exist because each enables an important type of applications to work with Mac OS X.

This state of bliss did not always exist. For many years, Apple wanted to move to a completely new style of Mac OS but couldn't. Apple couldn't just orphan the applications upon which Mac users had come to rely. Plus, Apple could not get enough application developers to agree to completely rewrite all their software for a new Mac OS that required them to use development tools and programming languages not in common use.

Regardless of the merits of the two programming languages best supported by these new development tools, Objective C and Java, neither is used for such mainstream applications as Microsoft Office, Adobe Photoshop, Macromedia Flash, Internet Explorer, Netscape Communicator/Navigator, and so forth. The developers of these applications were unwilling to invest time, human resources, and money to rewrite their products from the ground up for a new Mac OS, and then commit to maintaining the new Mac OS version in parallel with a Microsoft Windows version written in a different programming language. Doing this would wipe out a core reason that the developers remained committed to the Mac platform, namely that each application's Mac OS and Windows versions share a great deal of program code. Typically, only about 20 percent of the application needs to be written specifically for Mac OS or Windows; the rest is shared.

Apple has addressed these concerns in Mac OS X. Developers now have a choice. They can update their existing applications to benefit from the new Mac OS X features. They can develop innovative applications by using the new development tools. They can also do nothing, at least for a while, because most existing Mac OS 9 applications still work in Mac OS X just like they do in Mac OS 9.

Some may quibble as to whether there are two, three, four, or even more types of Mac OS X applications. The conservative, literal quibblers say that there are two application types: *Cocoa* and *Carbon*. Most of the rest say that there are three (including *Classic* as the third type). Some split the Cocoa family into Objective C and Java. Finally, some include BSD Unix command-line applications as another variety. In this chapter, we discuss the following types of applications that you can use in Mac OS X:

✦ **Cocoa applications** are programs written from the ground up by using the new development tools provided by Mac OS X; these Cocoa applications require Mac OS X to run. No one really expects to make Windows versions of Cocoa applications.

✦ **Carbon applications** typically are programs that have been around for a while. Most likely originally developed for Mac OS 9 or earlier, Carbon applications can still run in Mac OS 9 (with the addition of the CarbonLib system extension) in addition to Mac OS X.

✦ **Classic applications** are applications originally made for Mac OS 9 or earlier. Classic applications run in the Classic environment of Mac OS X, an emulator of sorts, known also simply as Classic. Most, but not all, Mac OS 9–compatible applications work well in the Classic environment. Those applications that require extensions (not the shared library kind) may be either fully or partially incompatible. Turn to Chapter 17 for information on Classic.

Cocoa and Carbon applications benefit from the major new features of Mac OS X, including protected memory, preemptive multitasking, multithreading, and built-in multiprocessor support. Because Classic applications do not have these features, it is strongly recommended that Classic applications be abandoned in favor of Cocoa or Carbon applications as quickly as possible. (This means you Quark users!)

Preinstalled applications

Apple preinstalls various useful applications with Mac OS X. Some of these applications are in the AppleScript folder or the Utilities folder, which are inside the Applications folder. Table 5-1 lists the applications provided with Mac OS X 10.3 and identifies the applications that are normally located in an interior folder of the Applications folder. The contents of your Applications folder may be different, because Apple adds and subtracts from the bundled software as time passes, and someone else who uses your computer may install additional applications.

Understanding Packages

Although all Mac OS X applications appear in the Finder as a single icon, many of them actually consist of a collection of folders and files. These compound applications are variously known as *packages, bundles,* or *application wrappers*. The terms are synonymous. Examples of such applications are as close as your Applications folder. Almost every application included with Mac OS X in the Applications folder is one of these application packages. Put simply, a package is a structured collection of files and folders that looks to users like a single file.

In Mac OS X, application packages have the name extension .app. You don't ordinarily see this name extension because Mac OS X hides it (unless you deactivate that option in the Finder Preferences window, as discussed in Chapter 4). You can also see the name extension in the Finder's Info window. (Choose View ⇨ Show Info and then choose Name & Extension from the Info window's pop-up menu.)

Packages can be stored on volumes that have the Unix File System (UFS) format as well as on volumes that have the Mac OS Extended format (also known as HFS Plus). Thus, they are considerably more flexible than traditional Mac applications, which aren't packages. An application that isn't a package generally has a two-part file and extensive Finder information, with the part known as the resource fork being equivalent to an application package's Resources folder. The problem with two-fork files with extensive Finder information is that they must be stored on volumes that have the Mac OS Extended format. The traditional two-forked applications can't be stored on volumes that use the UFS format. Because of this, Apple hopes to wean application developers away from the use of resource forks, and packages are the means to do so.

When you double-click an application package, say, Preview, it opens and runs; however, Preview is not a single file. You can see what we mean if you Control-click the Preview icon in the Finder and choose Show Package Contents from the contextual menu. Doing this presents a Finder window with a folder icon named Contents. Opening the Contents folder, you see that it contains a Resources folder, and opening the Resources folder reveals the various files and folders containing the resources used by Preview, as shown in the following figure.

Continued

Continued

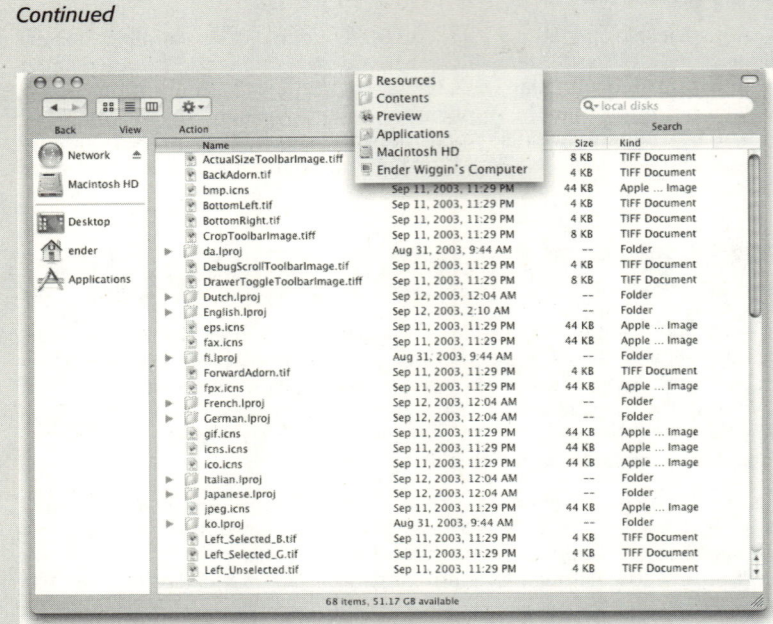

The Mac OS folder of the Contents folder contains the file that actually runs when you double-click the application icon in the Finder. The PkgInfo file contains the Type and Creator information so familiar to experienced Mac users. The really interesting file is the one named Info.plist in the Contents folder. Info.plist is an *XML* (eXtensible Markup Language) property list, hence, the extension .plist. This property list includes much of the information traditionally found in Macintosh application resource forks, such as type, creator, version string, short version string, and language.

For Cocoa applications, the resource folder contains a number of files ending in .nib. These are NeXT Interface Builder files. NIB files contain the interface description information (such as window dimensions, buttons, and the like) in a classes file and the actual binary data in an objects file, both named with the .nib extension.

You also see a file called COPYING—that's just a license file from an organization named GNU (Gnu's Not Unix), which is required to be included with any code distributed based upon their libraries and tools, such as the libraries and Objective C compiler that NeXT brought to the party.

Table 5-1: Included Applications

Name	Folder	Brief Description
Address Book	Applications	Lets you manage an address (postal and email) and phone book. Integrated with LDAP (Lightweight Directory Access Protocol) directory searches and linked to Mail and iChat. (See later in this table.)
Calculator	Applications	A very basic calculator, controlled from the keypad or with the mouse.
Chess	Applications	A graphical front end for GNU Chess; a pretty decent chess program with multiple difficulty settings and both 2-D and 3-D views.
DVD Player	Applications	The default application to play DVDs. Will not work if your computer doesn't have a DVD drive.
Font Book	Applications	A font management program. Use it to preview, activate, and deactivate fonts.
iCal	Applications	A calendar management app; basically, a digital appointment book.
iChat	Applications	Instant messaging (IM) client.
Image Capture	Applications	Download photos from compatible (USB) digital cameras. Comes with a series of AppleScripts to automatically reformat and arrange pictures.
iMovie	Applications	Digital video editing application.
Internet Connect	Applications	Manage PPP application for dial-up Internet connections.
Internet Explorer	Applications	Microsoft's Web browser.
iPhoto	Applications	Still video editing and cataloging application.
iSync	Applications	Used to synchronize data between cell phones, palm pilots and your computer.
iTunes	Applications	Play songs from audio CDs, MP3 files, and Internet radio stations. Burn recordable CDs on Macs equipped with CDRW drives.
Mail	Applications	Flexible email application. Supports multiple accounts and personalities; links to Address Book.
Preview	Applications	View graphic and PDF files. Also used to access print preview from applications.
QuickTime Player	Applications	Apple's application to play, create, and edit multimedia files.
Safari	Applications	Apple's Web browser.
Sherlock	Applications	Searches various Internet locations for information. Sherlock can search for movie times, plane tickets and more.
Stickies	Applications	Create and manage notes windows.

Continued

Table 5-1 *(continued)*

Name	Folder	Brief Description
System Preferences	Applications	Control Panel application for your System Preference settings.
TextEdit	Applications	Styled-text editor (a miniword processor).
Script Editor	AppleScript	Record, create, and edit AppleScript (and other OSA scripting system) files.
Activity Monitor	Utilities	Shows processor, memory, and network usage and currently running processors. Allows for termination of processes to help with troubleshooting and repair.
AirPort Admin Utility	Utilities	Change individual settings of an AirPort base station device, including settings that aren't changed by the AirPort Setup Assistant application (described next).
AirPort Setup Assistant	Utilities	Guides you through providing an AirPort base station device with the settings it needs to get a wireless AirPort network connected to the Internet.
Audio MIDI Setup	Utilities	Central control for routing audio and MIDI.
Bluetooth File Exchange	Utilities	Bluetooth short-range wireless data transfer utility.
Bluetooth Serial Utility	Utilities	Utility to create serial connections between devices: often used to access modems in palmtop computers or cell phones.
Bluetooth Setup Assistant	Utilities	An assistant designed to help set up Bluetooth.
ColorSync Utility	Utilities	Verifies and repairs ColorSync ICC (International Color Consortium) profiles. These profiles are used to synchronize color input and output between various device types (monitors, scanners, printers, and the like).
Console	Utilities	Presents a window to the Unix console log for your session, letting you see messages from Mac OS X and applications. This tool is primarily useful to programmers and system administrators only. Remember that underlying everything you do in Mac OS X, you are really running a Unix system.
DigitalColor Meter	Utilities	Presents the RGB (or other) color information for the pixels under the pointer.
Directory Access	Utilities	Set up the LDAP services and authentication protocols used by Directory Services and Mac OS X.
Disk Utility	Utilities	The Swiss Army knife of disk control applications. Used to burn discs, verify, repair, and format disk volumes, create disk images.
Grab	Utilities	Used to take screen pictures, either of the entire screen or a selection.

Name	Folder	Brief Description
Installer	Utilities	Used by Apple and some software developers to install new software and updates to your computer.
Keychain Access	Utilities	Used to store and retrieve your user IDs and passwords for files, remote sites, servers, and so forth.
NetInfo Manager	Utilities	Used to administer a NetInfo server configuration.
Network Utility	Utilities	A collection of network and Internet utility programs.
ODBC Administrator	Utilities	ODBC (Open Database Connectivity) configuration.
Print Setup Utility	Utilities	Configure, register, and monitor printers.
StuffIt Expander	Utilities	Freeware utility that expands StuffIt and Zip archives, as well as a number of other formats.
System Profiler	Utilities	Utility to report how your hardware is configured and what software you have installed. This is a handy diagnostic tool when tracking down hardware and software problems.
Terminal	Utilities	This is your window into the Unix command line environment. See Chapters 25-27 for further information.

Installing applications

In addition to these preinstalled applications, there will come a time to add new tools to this digital toolbox. Installing additional applications is a great way to expand your options. There are a few different methods of application installations, although most are very self-explanatory. Typically, a set of paper instructions or a digital text file will accompany the application. The text file usually has a name like Read me or Installation instructions. Read these instructions carefully, because there may be exceptions to the rules we present here.

The easiest method of installation is the *drag-install*. This method is commonly used when installing an application from removable media (CD-ROM, DVD, etc....) and from downloaded disk images. If a drag installation is called for, it will be indicated in the instructions or via a visible note within the disk that says "drag this folder to your hard drive to install." Simply drag the specified folder to your applications folder to copy the required data there. You do not need to copy the application to the applications folder, although that location makes the most sense. Regardless of the location to which you copied the files, after the copy is complete, launch the newly copied application. If the application has to perform any additional setup functions, it should do so at this time. The application will copy files to various locations within your system and then proceed to ask for a serial number if needed, in addition to bugging you with the ubiquitous registration page. (We hate those things too.) Figure 5-1 shows the Microsoft Office install disk's contents. It's pretty obvious what to do from the window's instructions.

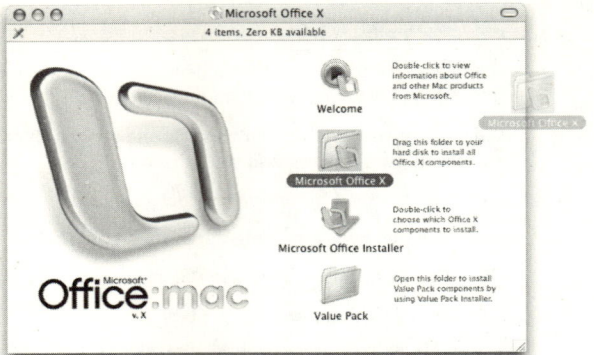

Figure 5-1: The drag-install is the easiest install method available. Simply drag the folder to the desired location, and go to work!

The old-fashioned method of installation is the installation program. Normally titled something like Setup or Install, they are programs that go through the install process, querying for various bits of input from the user as they do. Each installation program is unique, but most require users to agree to a legal copyright agreement, insert serial numbers, and then select the destination drive to complete the process. Figure 5-2 shows the Adobe Photoshop installation screen in action.

Figure 5-2: The installation program method is a commonly used technique for adding programs, although it tends to feel a bit old-fashioned.

Removing applications

In the event that you no longer want to have an application stored on your hard drive, simply drag the application item out of the Applications folder, and deposit it into the Trash icon in the Dock. After emptying the Trash (Apple Menu ⇨ Empty Trash), the application in question will be gone. Just as with trashing a document you no longer want, be *sure* that you really want to throw it away. The item won't come back from the digital graveyard very easily. Many applications spread various bits of themselves around in other folders in the system. You usually don't have to worry about them, but you may want to fully eradicate an application. The best place to look is in the Application Support folder. This folder is the standard dumping ground for extra files generated by an application. You will find Application Support just inside the main Library folder (Hard Drive/Library/Application Support). Inside Application Support, you may find some items related to the deleted application. You can trash these files, but again, be careful, as you may be deleting files that are affiliated with the wrong application.

Opening Applications and Documents

You open an application when you want to work with it. This action is also called *launching* an application. You open a document when you want to view or edit its contents. For example, you can open TextEdit when you want to view, edit, or create a text document. (You can also work with text documents by opening a variety of other applications.) Numerous ways to open applications, documents, and other types of files and folders are available. This section discusses a variety of ways to open applications and documents.

Opening items with the Finder

The methods presented in Chapter 3 for opening folders in the Finder can also be used for opening an application or document with the Finder:

✦ Double-click the program or document icon that you want to open.

✦ Select the application or document that you want to open and then choose File ⇨ Open (⌘-O).

✦ Control-click the item that you want to open and choose Open from the contextual menu that appears.

Opening a document by using any of these methods automatically opens an application to handle the document. The Finder determines which application handles the document, opens that application, and then tells that application to open the document.

Suppose that you want to open multiple documents. No problem! Just select them all and then double-click one of them or use the Open command. If the documents are handled by different applications, the Finder opens each application and tells it which documents to open.

Opening documents with an application

Drag a document directly onto the icon of a compatible application, and the application's icon will highlight, and releasing the item will result in the document opening within the selected application. You can also open documents from within an application by choosing Open from that application's File menu. Choosing File ⇨ Open displays an Open dialog. This dialog enables you to go through your folders and select a file that you want to open.

Mac OS X Open dialog

When you choose File ⇨ Open in a Mac OS X application, you see an Open dialog containing a pane reminiscent of the Finder's list or column view, as shown in Figure 5-3. The view can be switched between list or column view with the two familiar buttons in the top left of the window.

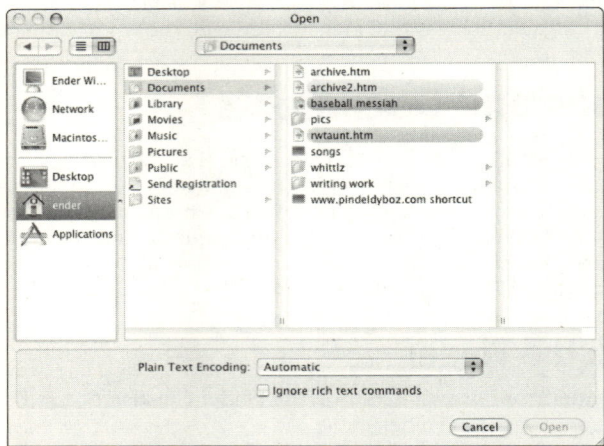

Figure 5-3: In Mac OS X applications, the Open dialog is like a list or column view in the Finder.

You can use the file browser to navigate through your folders to find the item you want to open, just as you do in the Finder. In column view, each column shows the contents of a folder, and clicking a folder causes its contents to appear in the next column to the right. You can scroll left to see folders closer to the Computer level or scroll right to see the currently selected folder. In list view, double-clicking folders takes you deeper within the hierarchy. The pull-down menu available at the top of the window populates with the file hierarchy in addition to a few standard items. As you go deeper, the pull-down extends to offer you a way up to higher levels.

You can quickly go to a file or a folder in an Open dialog's file browser if you can see the file or folder outside the dialog on the Desktop or in a Finder window. All you do is drag the file or folder to the dialog.

Initially the Open dialog shows two columns, but you can widen the dialog to see more columns. Drag the resize control at the lower-right corner to make the dialog larger or smaller.

You can move the Open dialog to see items under it. Move the dialog by dragging its title bar.

If you like to type and you can remember the full path to the file you seek, you can type the path in the Go to text box and click Open (or press Return) to open the file. Similarly, if you don't recall the file's exact name but do recall the full path to the file's folder, you can type the path in the Go to text box and press Return to have the Open dialog reposition into the folder, revealing the files within.

The Open dialog has two buttons at the bottom of the dialog:

✦ **Cancel:** Dismisses the dialog without opening anything.

✦ **Open:** Tells the application to open the selected file. This is the default button, so pressing Return is the equivalent of clicking Open.

Applications may customize the Open dialog by placing their own controls near the bottom of the dialog. As the example shown in Figure 5-4 shows, TextEdit adds a pop-up menu for choosing a text encoding method and a checkbox for ignoring rich text formatting when it opens the document you select.

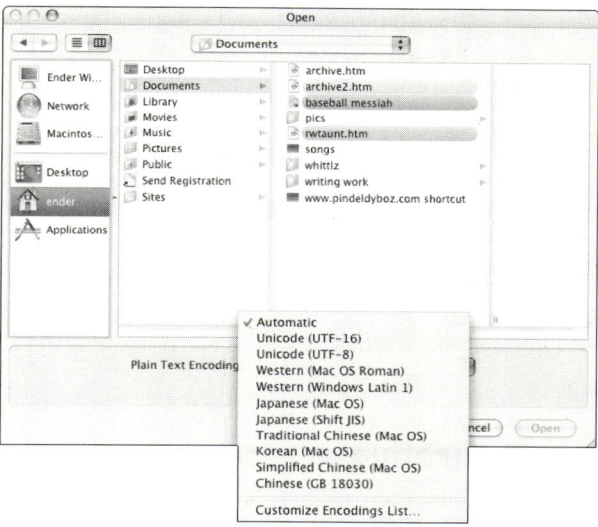

Figure 5-4: While opening a file, the open dialog may offer numerous options.

You will notice that some documents presented in the list may be dimmed out. This is because the application is not compatible with the dimmed out files, and will not be able to open them.

To open a document, you select it in the list and click the Open button. Alternatively, you can double-click the document in the list, or click it and press Return or Enter.

Opening a document with another compatible application

Instead of opening a document with the application that usually handles it, you can also open it with any compatible application. For example, the Preview application can open documents that are usually handled by Adobe Acrobat.

To do this, open the desired application, and select Open from that application's File menu. Select the document from the dialog window that appears. The dialog window will only show documents that the application knows it can open. Other documents are automatically made invisible in the dialog.

Another method to accomplish this is to drag the document's icon onto the icon of the application that you want to use (or to an alias of the application). For example, if you have a Web page you saved from Internet Explorer that you want to edit in TextEdit, drag the document icon onto the TextEdit icon (or onto an alias to TextEdit). In most cases, if the application is compatible with the document, the application's icon becomes highlighted. Release the mouse button while the application icon is highlighted, and the application opens the document. If the application is not already open, the Finder opens it automatically. If an application can't open a document you drag to it, nothing happens—no highlighting, no opening. Figure 5-5 shows how an application icon looks if it can open a document that you drag to it.

Note Some applications can't really open certain documents with which they appear to be compatible. For example, TextEdit tries to open a picture or movie file that you drag to the TextEdit icon, but displays a window full of gibberish instead of a picture or a movie. This happens because TextEdit interprets the picture or movie data as if it were text characters, and displays this as text. Strangely enough, TextEdit can display pictures and movies that are included in document files that are saved by TextEdit.

Figure 5-5: When you drag a document to a compatible application, the application's icon becomes highlighted.

Setting a new default application

Documents are set to open with a default application, depending on their type. For example, movie files most likely will open with QuickTime Player, pictures will open with Preview and text files will open with TextEdit. (Or they'll open with a real word processor like Microsoft Word or AppleWorks, if installed.) The Mac OS offers controls to change the default for one document or even to have alternate applications open all files of a particular type. Select an item that you want to open with a new default application and open the Get Info window (⌘-I). The Open With area is hidden with a disclosure triangle. Figure 5-6 shows the Open With area.

The Open With area contains a pull-down menu and a Change All button. The pull-down menu is populated with compatible applications and an Other option. Selecting one of the applications listed will change the file's parent application to the new selection. Selecting Other will bring up a dialog box in which you will select a new parent application. This dialog is helpful if the Mac OS doesn't recognize an application as compatible, which would preclude it from being in the pull-down list, or if you want to experiment with what happens when you open an audio file with a text editor. (Lots and lots of gibberish appear within a text document.) Figure 5-7 shows the dialog.

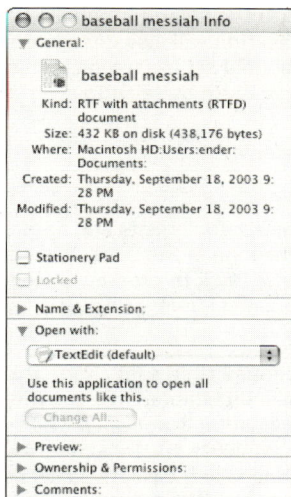

Figure 5-6: The Info window contains the means to switch a document's parent application.

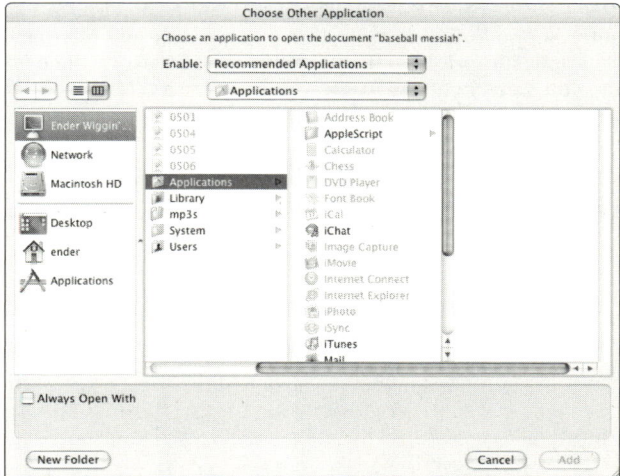

Figure 5-7: The select new parent application dialog is helpful when the Mac OS doesn't recognize your desired parent application as being compatible with a particular document.

After selecting a new application, you can make this application the default for all files of this type by clicking the Change All button. Switching parent application will also change document icons to reflect the new parent application. If you goof up and set the wrong application, it's easy enough to do undo your mistake. Just reverse the procedure by selecting the original parent application and selecting Change All.

Opening items in the Dock

As discussed in Chapter 4, you can place icons of frequently used documents and applications in the Dock and then open them simply by clicking on the icon in the Dock. You can also place a folder in the Dock; then click and hold on the icon in the Dock to produce a menu of files and folders you can traverse to find the item you want to open (Dock navigation, as covered in Chapter 4).

You can also open a document by dragging it to the icon of a compatible application that is already in the Dock. When the application's Dock icon becomes highlighted, release the item. If the application is running, it opens the document. If the application is not open, the application opens and then opens the document. As with opening documents via drag-and-drop in the Finder, the application icon in the Dock may not highlight, in which case, the selected application cannot open the selected item.

Opening with the Apple menu

Choosing Apple ➪ Recent Items displays a submenu with labeled sections for Applications and Documents. The Recent Items submenu enables you to easily reopen an application or document that you used recently. Suppose, for example, that you recently quit Microsoft Word. Rather than opening the Applications folder, then opening the Microsoft Office folder, and finally opening Word again, you merely choose Apple ➪ Recent Items ➪ Microsoft Word, and the application reopens. Figure 5-8 shows the Recent Items submenu.

Figure 5-8: The Recent Items submenu is a helpful shortcut to find recently opened documents and applications.

While useful for applications, Apple ➪ Recent Items is even more desirable for reopening documents because you are far more likely to have your documents distributed throughout a hierarchy of folders. (Users typically just add their favorite applications to the Dock, eliminating the need to access them in Recent Items.) Obviously, navigating your folder structure to reopen a document that you recently used takes much longer than choosing the document from the Recent Items submenu.

The Recent Items submenu in Mac OS X keeps track of 5 to 50 recent applications and 5 to 50 recent documents. You can change the numbers of items tracked in the Appearance Preference Pane, as described in Chapter 4.

In the Mac OS X Apple menu, the Recent Items submenu has an additional and a very handy menu choice: Clear Menu. This choice empties out the Recent Items submenu (but doesn't affect the actual items that were listed).

Managing Multiple Open Applications

This ability to have multiple applications open simultaneously is called *multitasking.* In Mac OS 9 and earlier, this multitasking is *cooperative,* meaning that the various open applications have to voluntarily take turns using the computer's processor, memory, and other hardware. Mac OS X has *preemptive* multitasking, which means that Mac OS X dynamically parcels out chunks of time to the various open applications.

Multitasking is convenient but can be disorienting. For example, a stray mouse click may make another open program active, bringing its windows to the front and covering the windows of the program you were using. If this happens unexpectedly, you may think that the program you're using has crashed when it is actually still open and healthy, albeit in the background. You must get used to having multiple layers of open programs like piles of paper on a desk. Fortunately, you instantly sort through and organize your open applications with Exposé (as covered in Chapter 3), plus you can hide applications on the Mac (unlike the layers of paper on your desk) as discussed later in this section.

As mentioned in Chapter 2, only one application has control of the menu bar, no matter how many applications you have open. The application currently in control is called the *active application.*

Switching programs

When you have more than one application open, you can switch to another application by simply clicking its icon in the Dock. You can also use Exposé to show all of the application windows with F9, and then select the desired application. You can also switch to another application by clicking any of its visible windows (or a window minimized in the Dock). Another method is to use the application switch command. Figure 5-9 shows this function in action. Here's how to do it:

1. Press and hold ⌘, then press Tab. Striking this keyboard combination displays a list of open applications across the screen.

2. Continue holding ⌘, and with each additional press of Tab, a highlight window migrates to the different open applications.

3. Release ⌘ when the desired application is highlighted. This application becomes the active application.

Figure 5-9: The application switch command in action.

Tip

When you switch to another application, its menus take over the menu bar. Its name appears as the title of the application menu, which is next to the Apple menu.

If you switch applications by clicking an application icon in the Dock, all of the application's open windows come forward as a group. (Windows that are minimized in the Dock remain there.) If you're a Mac OS 9 veteran, this layered window behavior is what you expect.

If you switch to a Mac OS X application by clicking one of its windows, *only that window comes forward*. Other windows belonging to the same application remain where they are in the layered hierarchy. You can bring them all to the front by clicking the application's icon in the Dock or by choosing Window ➪ Bring All to Front. (Some applications don't have this menu command.) For Mac OS 9 veterans, this window behavior will take some getting used to.

Hide and Seek

With many applications open, the screen quickly becomes a visual Tower of Babel. You can eliminate the clutter by using the Hide feature. Using Hide is different than clicking the Minimize button (which you will recall puts a small version of the window in the Dock). When you hide an application, the application and all of its open windows disappear! This reduces clutter onscreen and in the Dock. To activate Hide, choose Hide Others from the application menu. This command hides the windows of all applications except the currently active one. Alternatively, you can hide only the currently active application's windows and simultaneously switch to the most recently active application by choosing Hide *Application* (where

Application is the name of the active application) from the application menu. Additionally, you can Option-click anywhere on the Desktop to hide the currently active application. To restore any applications from Hide, click their icons in the Dock. (Remember, open applications have a small black triangle under their icon.) To make the windows of all applications visible with one click, choose Show All from the application menu.

Tip   A quick way to hide all background applications is to ⌘-Option-click the active application's icon in the Dock. If you ⌘-Option-click another application's icon in the Dock, it becomes active and all other applications' windows are hidden. To hide the active application while switching to another application, Option-click the other application's icon in the Dock or Option-click a window belonging to the other application.

Attending to background applications

If a Mac OS X application that's open in the background needs your attention, its icon starts jumping up and down in the Dock (like a little kid in class waving his hand excitedly for attention). The icon jumps far enough that you can see it even if the Dock is hidden. To find out what has made the application so excited, click its icon in the Dock. When the application's windows come forward, look for an alert, sheet or dialog that you need to attend to. Figure 5-10 shows an example of an application jumping for attention.

Figure 5-10: When an application's icon jumps out of the Dock, the application needs your attention.

Tinkering with Document Contents

While a document is open, you can generally tinker with its contents. Create new content, move existing content around to different locations within the same document, or even move content to other documents. Each application has its own content type — Microsoft Word works with text, Adobe Photoshop with pictures, iMovie with video, for examples — and each has its own methods of content creation and editing. For details on this, consult some of the other excellent Wiley Publishing titles available for your application of choice. This section covers the established standard techniques that many applications use, regardless of data type. For example, the traditional method to shuffle a document's content is via the Edit menu's Copy, Cut, and Paste commands. Additionally, most programs also let you drag content from one place to another or, by holding down the Option key while dragging, copy the content from one spot to another.

Copy, Cut, and Paste

One of the first things a Mac user learns is to use the Cut, Copy, and Paste commands in an application's Edit menu to transfer data from one place to another within a document or between documents. The first thing you do is select the data you wish to move. Next, you choose what to do with that data.Choose Edit ➪ Cut (if you wish to *move* the original data) or Edit ➪ Copy (if you wish to place a copy of the data in another location). Either of these actions places the data on the *Clipboard,* a temporary virtual storage area for data being moved. After deciding your method of gathering the data, select the location the data is to be placed. Finally, you choose Edit ➪ Paste to put it there.

Pasting does not remove the data from the Clipboard. The data remains there until you use Cut or Copy again to place new content on the Clipboard or you log out. This also means you only get one contiguous Cut or Copy at a time. If you select and Copy some data, and then Copy something else, the original Copy is gone. The two Copy contents are not stored in the Clipboard; rather the original is overwritten with the new Copy.

You can Cut, Copy, and Paste within a single document, between multiple documents of a given application, or between the documents of different applications. This technique rapidly becomes second nature, especially after you start using the keyboard shortcuts: ⌘-X for Cut, ⌘-C for Copy, and ⌘-V for Paste (and ⌘-A to select All of the data in a document).

Drag and Drop

The Mac OS provides a more direct way to copy text, graphics, and other material. This capability, called *drag-and-drop editing,* only works with programs that are designed to take advantage of it. Fortunately for you, this includes most Mac OS X applications that open documents.

To move material within a document, open the document and select the text, graphic, or other data you wish to move. Then, position the mouse pointer over the selected material, press and hold the mouse button and then drag the selected material to its new location. As you drag, a lightened, ghostlike version of the selected material follows the pointer, and typically, an insertion point shows where the material appears after you stop dragging. If you want to copy rather than move the material, press Option before releasing the mouse button. Figure 5-11 shows some text being moved within a TextEdit document.

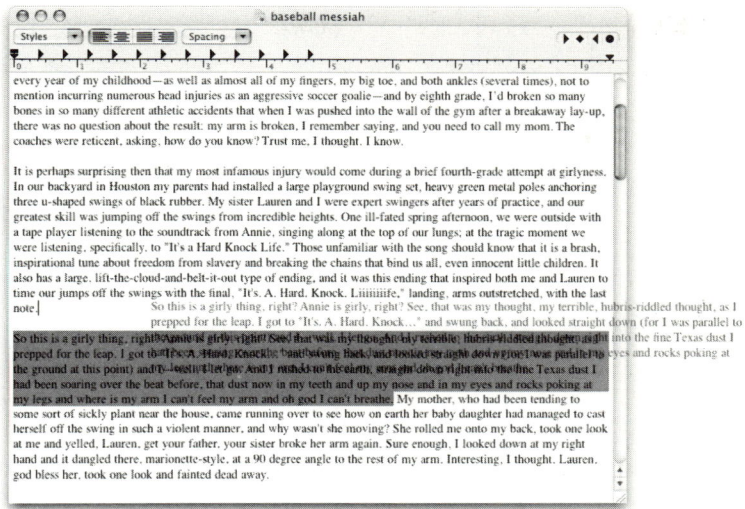

Figure 5-11: With drag-and-drop editing, you can move data within a document.

Tip
If you have trouble dragging selected material, try holding down the mouse button a moment longer before you start to drag.

To drag-copy material between documents, first open both documents and position them so that you can see the source material and the place where you want to drop a copy of it. Select the text, graphic, or other source material and then drag the selected material to the place in the second document where you want the copy. As you drag, an outline of the selected material follows the mouse pointer. When the pointer enters the destination window, a border appears around the content area of the window; and if you're dragging text, an insertion point shows where the copy appears when you stop dragging. Note that you do not have to press Option to make a copy when dragging between documents. You can use the same method to copy between two documents in the same application or between documents or windows in different applications. The only requirement is that the destination window be capable of handling the type of material you are dragging. Figure 5-12 shows some text being copied from a TextEdit window into a Stickies note.

Some people prefer drag-and-drop to cut-and-paste editing because they find it easier to use. Drag-and-drop editing has one clear advantage: It doesn't use or wipe out the contents of the Clipboard, so it's a good method to use when the Clipboard contains important material that you're not ready to replace. It is best to know how to use both methods in tandem, as they each have their benefits, and knowing more techniques is the key to being a better computer user.

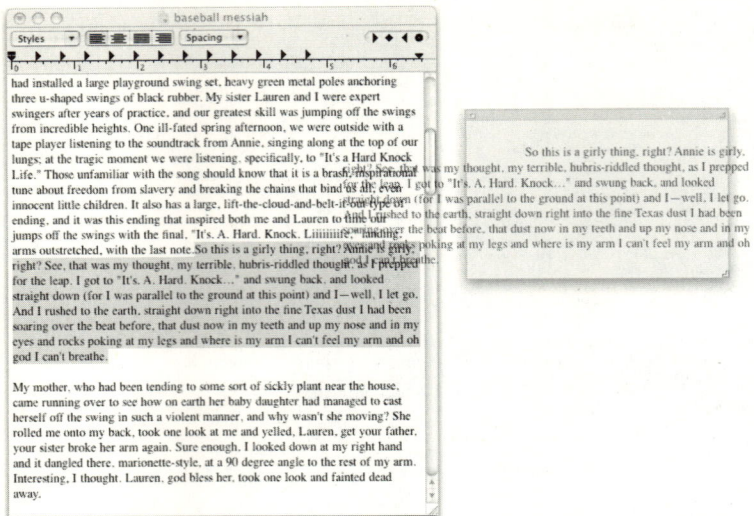

Figure 5-12: With drag-and-drop editing, you can also move text, images, and other data between windows and even other applications.

Clipping files

You can also drag selected material from a document to the Desktop or to a folder, where the Finder creates a clipping file that contains a copy of the dragged material. Clipping files can contain text, pictures, QuickTime movies, or sound, but a single clipping file can contain only one type of data. You can open a clipping file to see it in the Finder, but you can't select anything in a clipping file. To copy the contents of a clipping file to a document, drag the clipping-file icon to an open document's window. The contents will be inserted when you release the mouse button.

You can use a clipping file over and over. For example, you can keep clippings that contain your letterhead, the company logo, your signature, a list of email addresses, or any other element that you use frequently.

Creating Documents

You won't always be opening documents that already exist. Sometimes you need to create new ones. Many application programs automatically create a brand-new, untitled document when you double-click the application icon. In addition, most applications let you create a new document any time you want one by choosing File ➪ New.

Creating copies of documents

You can also create a document by making a copy of an existing document. This method is especially useful if the existing document contains something you want to include in a new document, such as a letterhead or some boilerplate text. To make a copy of a document, use the Finder's Duplicate command or one of the other methods described in Chapter 3.

Creating documents with stationery pads

Rather than duplicating a document each time you want a copy of it, you can make a frequently used document into a *stationery pad*. (Most software developers call these items *templates* but Apple calls them stationery pads. Go figure.) When you open a stationery pad, you get a new document with a preset format and contents. It's like tearing a sheet off an endless pad of preprinted stationery (hence the name). Some stationery pads have a distinctive icon that looks like a stack of documents and indicates which application opens the stationery pad. Other stationery pads have blank document icons or icons indistinguishable from those of standard documents.

Some applications allow you to save an ordinary document as a stationery pad or template. We explain how in the next section. You can also convert any document into a stationery pad in the Finder's Info window, as shown in Figure 5-13, by following these steps:

1. **In the Finder, select the document you want to make into a stationery pad.**

2. **Choose File ➪ Get Info (⌘-I).** This command brings up the Info window.

3. **Select the Stationery Pad checkbox.**

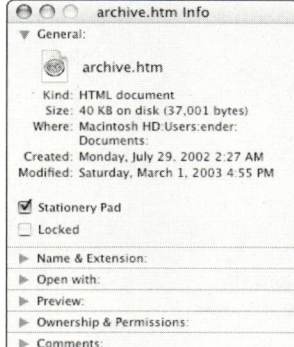

Figure 5-13: You can make a stationery pad in the Finder's Info window.

What happens when you open a stationery pad depends on whether the application that opens it knows the difference between stationery pads and regular documents. If the application is programmed to work with stationery pads, it will create a new untitled document with the format and content of the stationery pad. If the application is not compatible with stationery pads, the Finder should create a new document by making a copy from the stationery pad and having the application open the copy.

Saving Documents

After creating a new document or making changes to a document you opened, you need to save the document on disk for the changes to persist. Make sure that the document's window is active (in front of other document windows) and choose File ➪ Save or File ➪ Save As. For a new document, either of these commands displays a dialog in which you name the document and select the folder where you want it saved. For a previously saved document, the Save command does not bring up a dialog; the application automatically saves the changed document in place of the previously saved document (replacing the original with this modified version). The Save As command always brings up the dialog so that you can rename and/or relocate the edited version, so that you can preserve the original and the modified file.

Tip   While you are entering a name for the document to save in a Save dialog, the Cut, Copy, and Paste commands are available from the Edit menu. This means that you can copy a name for a document from within the document before choosing the Save command, and then you can paste the copied name into the dialog. Instead of using the Edit menu, you can also use the keyboard equivalents: ⌘-X for Cut, ⌘-C for Copy, and ⌘-V for Paste.

The Save dialog has a simple form and an expanded form. You switch between the simple form and the expanded form by clicking the disclosure triangle, which is next to the pop-up menu labeled Where. Figure 5-14 shows an example of a simple Save dialog and an expanded Save dialog.

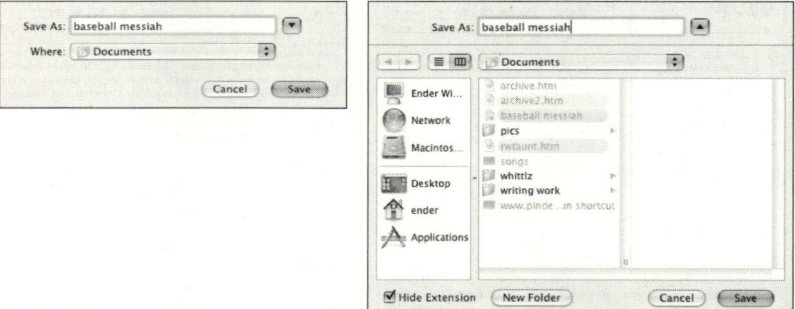

Figure 5-14: Click the disclosure button to switch between the simple Save dialog (first image) and the expanded Save dialog (second image).

A Save dialog has a pop-up menu giving you the choice of the current folder, the desktop, your home folder, and a hierarchical menu to your iDisk. This pop-up menu also lists recently used folders. In addition, the Save dialog has a text box where you enter the name for the document. The Save dialog may have an option for hiding the name extension, and the dialog may have other controls for setting document format options.

The location browser visible in the expanded Save dialog works just like the browser in the Open dialog. The option exists to navigate in list view or column view. In column view, each column shows the contents of a folder, and clicking a folder causes its contents to appear in the next column to the right. You can scroll left to see folders closer to the Computer level or scroll right to see the currently selected folder. In list view, double clicking folders will take you deeper within the hierarchy. The pull-down menu available at the top of the window will populate with the file hierarchy in addition to a few standard items. As you go deeper, the pull-down extends to offer you a way up to higher levels.

You can quickly go to a file or a folder in a Save dialog's file browser if you can see the file or folder outside the dialog on the Desktop or in a Finder window. All you need to do is drag the file or folder to the dialog.

The Save dialog is also resizable. Drag the resize control at the lower-right corner to make the dialog larger or smaller.

In some applications, the Save dialog is a sheet that's attached to the window of the document being saved. In other applications the Save dialog is independent, and you can move it by dragging its title bar.

Tip   Some Mac OS X applications indicate that a document has unsaved changes by displaying a small dot at the center of the document window's Close button. (Applications built on the Cocoa framework do this.)

Saving a Stationery Pad

In many applications, you can designate in the Save dialog whether to save a document as a stationery pad (template), or as a regular document. Some applications offer this choice with two radio buttons; one labeled with a regular document icon, and the other labeled with a stationery pad icon. Other applications offer many document format options, including stationery or template, in a pop-up menu in the dialog. Figure 5-15 shows a Microsoft Word Save dialog with Document and Template radio buttons — you click Template if you wish the document saved as a stationery pad.

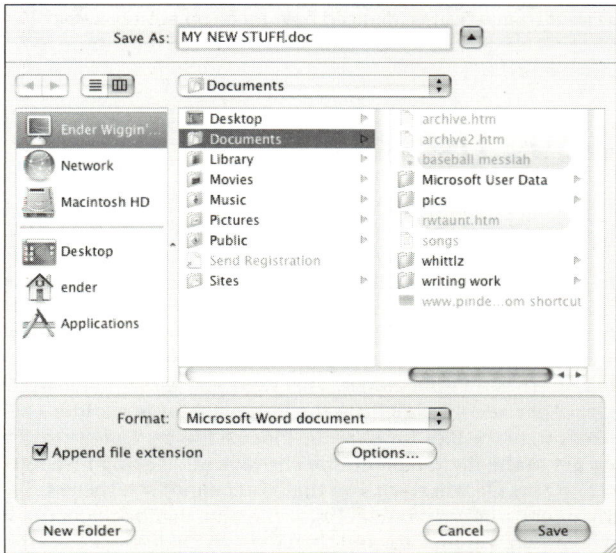

Figure 5-15: Some applications let you save a document as a stationery pad, also called a template.

A Word on Home

Your home folder has a collection of various useful sub-folders for convenient organization of your data. It contains a Pictures folder for your images, a Movies folder for movies, etc. It is recommended by Apple and by most technicians that you use these folders as much as possible, and store as much of your data as possible within your Home. Remember, items on your Desktop are actually already within your Home, as the Desktop is actually a folder stored within your Home. You can create as many folders as you'd like within your Home, although its wise to place created sub-folders within the Documents folder, so as to avoid cluttering up your Home's root level. Storing your work within your Home makes it very easy to protect your data, as you only need to create a backup of one folder to protect your most important information. Applications can be reinstalled, even the OS can be reinstalled, but your documents are much more difficult to re-create.

Moving Documents

After creating and then saving a document, you may wish to move that item to a different location within your disk or to a removable disk or server volume. The Mac OS makes this very easy. Simply drag the item from its original location to a new one. You can drag the item to an item in the Sidebar, to a folder represented in the Dock, to any area of your Desktop, to the root level of your hard drive, or to any area of your user folder. This drag-and-drop method of moving should be very familiar to you by now. A new feature of Mac OS X is Cut and Paste moves. After selecting an item, select Cut from the Edit menu (or from the contextual menu of a particular item), and then with the desired new location active, select Paste from the Edit menu and the item will be moved to the new location. This technique will be very familiar to former Windows users.

Playing Well with Other Users

As Mac OS X is a secure multi-user environment, the elements of each user account are only available to that user account. When logged in as Frank, you can get at Frank's files, but you cannot get access to Tammy's files. To get at Tammy's files, you'd need to prove to the Mac that you were Tammy by logging out of Frank's account and then entering Tammy's password at the login screen. However, as Frank, it is possible to give files to Tammy, and for her to give files to you. You can't *take* files from each other, but you can *give* them to each other. To share work with other users on your computer, you will need to use the pre-made Drop Boxes. Within each user's Home, there is a Public folder. This folder is- as the name implies, a Public area- that is accessible by other accounts. Within the Public folder is a folder called Drop Box. This folder allows users to place files for sharing. Place a file for Tammy into her Drop Box, and Tammy can then get at the file the next time she logs in. Placing files into drop boxes is a blind event though. The Mac OS will warn you that you cannot see the results of placing the file. It's similar to dropping mail into one of those big blue mailboxes in the street. You just have to trust that the Postman will pick up and then deliver the letter. Please note that dropping a file into a Drop Box does not move the file, but rather *copies* it there. Your original file remains in its original location.

Quitting Applications

When you are done working with an application for a while, you can issue a Quit command, to terminate it. Mac OS X provides a number of ways to quit from a running program. Some are for normal situations; others are for use when a program stops responding.

Using an application's Quit command

Nearly every application menu has a Quit command at the bottom of the Application menu, with a standard keyboard equivalent of ⌘-Q. Using the Quit command is the preferred method for quitting from an application. When you choose this command, the application asks whether to save each unsaved document, as shown in Figure 5-16, before closing that document's window. This is the same dialog that you see if you click the Close button of an unsaved document's window. In this dialog, the Save and Don't Save buttons are self-explanatory. The Cancel button tells the application that you've changed your mind about quitting. If you click Cancel, the application *doesn't* quit and the document it was asking you about saving remains in the forefront.

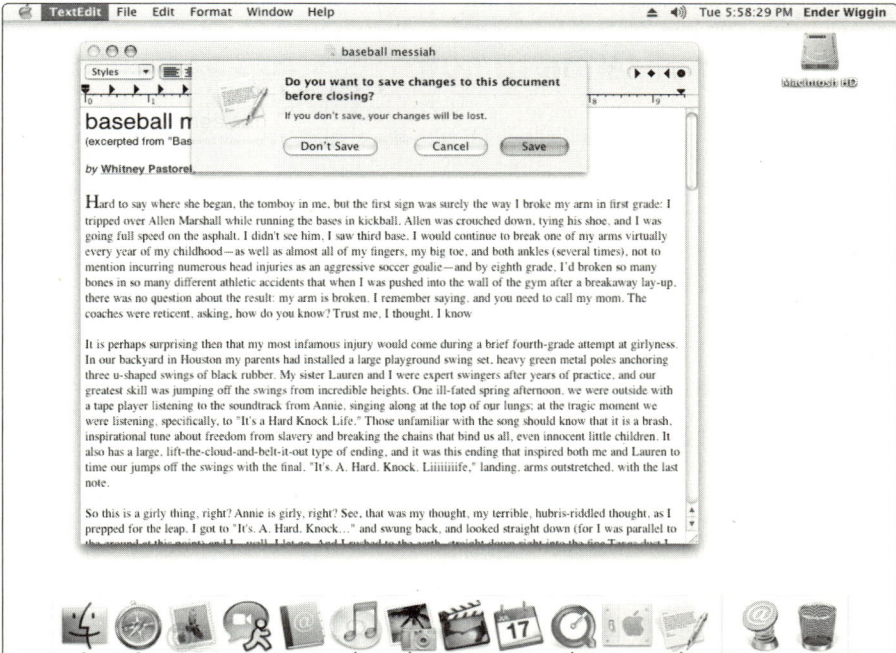

Figure 5-16: You're asked to save open documents when you quit an application.

Quitting with a pop-up Dock menu

You can also quit an application by Control-clicking (or right-clicking, or clicking and holding) its icon in the Dock. When the pop-up Dock menu appears, choose Quit from it. This method is handy for quitting an application that's open in the background, because you can quit the background application without making it active.

If you quit an application in this manner, the application's icon may start jumping out of the Dock. This behavior indicates that the application needs your attention. It probably wants to ask you what to do about documents with unsaved changes. Address the application's warnings as appropriate.

Quitting by logging out, shutting down, or restarting

Another way is to quit all open applications is by choosing Apple ➪ Log Out (⌘-Shift-Q) or Apple ➪ Shut Down or Apple ➪ Restart. After choosing any of these commands, you are asked whether you really wish to quit from all open applications. If you answer affirmatively, each application quits in turn, asking what to do about unsaved changes as shown in Figure 5-16. Canceling the save dialog in any document's Close dialog cancels both the Quit command in addition to the logout, restart, or shutdown.

Forcing an application to quit

Inevitably, occasions arise when an application stops, stalls, or fails to respond to input, preventing you from doing anything meaningful with the application, including quitting. Mac OS X gives you a number of ways to force the offending application to quit. Choosing Apple ➪ Force Quit or pressing ⌘-Option-Esc presents the window shown in Figure 5-17. Select the unresponsive application in the Force Quit Applications window and click the Force Quit button.

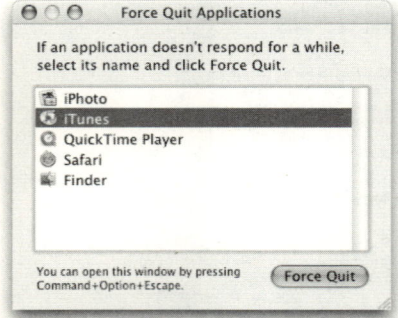

Figure 5-17: Select a runaway application you wish to have quit.

Alternatively, you could launch the Activity Monitor utility, which is located in the Utilities folder of the Applications folder (path /Applications/Utilities). Activity monitor presents a list of all active processes, as shown in Figure 5-18. Select the process you wish to terminate and choose Processes ➪ Quit Process. Selecting this method bypasses any save dialogs, and unsaved changes are lost.

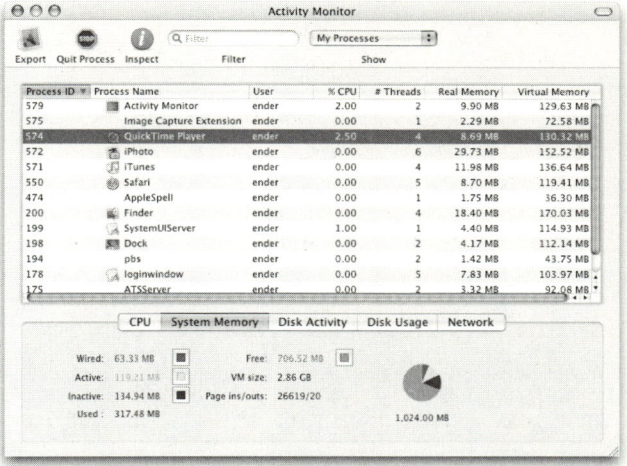

Figure 5-18: The process listing in the Activity Monitor provides the opportunity to view allocation of system resources, and to quit stalled processes and applications.

Cross-Reference

If you are frequently experiencing stalled application issues, turn to Chapter 23 for help on maintaining the Mac OS X.

Summary

In this chapter, you learned how to do the following:

✦ Open applications with the Finder, Dock, and Apple menu.

✦ Open documents from the Open dialog in applications.

✦ Switch between several open applications.

✦ Edit documents with copy-and-paste and drag-and-drop editing.

✦ Create new documents, copies of documents, and stationery pads.

✦ Save documents with the Save dialog.

✦ How to move files around on your drive.

✦ How to share files with other local users.

✦ Quit applications and force unresponsive applications to quit.

✦   ✦   ✦

Going on the Internet

CHAPTER 6

If your Macintosh is running OS X, and especially if you have made the effort to read this book (whether you're browsing in the computer section of a Barnes and Noble or perusing the pages in the comfort of your living room), there is no doubt about it: your computer needs an Internet connection. Having access to the World Wide Web is an essential component of the OS X experience, not only for information and communication, but also for downloading Apple's frequently provided and often massively sized software updates.

This chapter discusses the very basics of getting your Mac onto the Internet, and how to use the Internet after you are successfully connected to it. This chapter walks you through the Internet Setup Assistant as the means to configure your Mac for Internet connectivity. For advanced configuration and setup, see Chapter 15. The Internet Connect application is described here, as well as Mac OS X's menu bar icons that are related to connecting you to the Internet. This chapter also gives a detailed run through of Apple's Safari Web browser and Mail application, for surfing the Web and sending and receiving email, and a brief description of newsgroups and news readers.

Why You Need the Internet

Using the Internet used to be less than enjoyable. Access was slow, clumsy, and expensive. Information was erratic, unreliable, and difficult to find. Although certain difficulties still exist, lately, the Net is a pleasure to use. Information is readily available. Access is cheaper and faster than it has ever been. Often, it is faster and easier to find things on the Web than by using more-traditional methods, and often the case turns out to be that certain information is available by Web only. Nowadays, it's almost unheard of that any company or business (or for that matter, anyone or anything that wants attention) does not have a Web site. Companies have spent intense time and money on informative and well-designed sites that provide support and details. The Web makes information and communication almost instantaneous. Newspapers and magazines publish articles and stories and have them online, viewable to millions of readers, seconds later. People who can't place the face of that one character in a lazy Sunday afternoon movie can find out who it is in seconds by searching the Internet Movie Database (www.imdb.com). When the Gap doesn't have the correct size in their stores, you can get clothing shipped (free!) to your house, ordered off of the Web. Email has

Apple and the Internet

Apple is very aware of all the advantages that the Internet offers, and has been gradually and more intensely centering the Mac user experience around the Internet. In the summer of 1998, Apple released the original iMac, which at the time was a revolutionarily designed, low cost, and peppy machine. The first in a long-standing and still-existing tradition of their consumer machine monikers, the *i* in iMac, iBook, iTunes, and so on, stands for Internet. Since that time, which spans the introduction and release of OS X, Apple has been making it easy for OS X users to get on the Internet, including step-by-step software setup assistants, free trials with Internet service providers (ISPs), and television commercials touting the Mac's ease of use and setup. Recently Mac users are able to purchase prints of digital photography and purchase and download music, straight from their Macs, using the Internet.

evolved into an extremely popular method of communication, thanks largely to its speed and worldwide span. It is common for people to spend several hours a day on the Web, for both business and pleasure reasons. Online banking has changed the way people pay their bills and manage their money. With just a few clicks, the credit cards and the electric company get paid! These are just some of the reasons that you need Internet access.

Connecting to the Internet

Getting on the Internet can be a relatively simple process; and, after initial setup, no configuration from that point forward is usually needed. Still, understanding the concepts and some basic behind-the-scenes action will make using and troubleshooting your Mac and the Internet a much more positive experience.

The first thing you really need to access the Internet is an agreement with an Internet service provider, or ISP. Much like the way your phone company provides the services necessary to make telephone calls, an ISP provides the services necessary to access the Internet from your computer. The Internet is essentially a huge, worldwide network of people's computers, with many different types of services available. The concept of the World Wide Web (www) stems from this worldwide network concept, and refers to the Internet service that you are likely most familiar with, reading Web pages. This giant network exists regardless if you have an agreement with an ISP, which is where one gets the ability to access it. Whenever a Web browser is launched, or an email sent, your ISP is responsible for your computer's ability to communicate with this world of computers. EarthLink (www.earthlink.net) and AT&T (www.att.net) are examples of ISPs. Usually an ISP charges you a monthly flat rate for their services and provides you with unlimited usage. You can find ISP services advertised on television and in local newspapers. Changing your ISP for better and/or less expensive service can be a healthy move, but keep in mind that an ISP switch usually means that your email address changes as well. For this reason it can be advantageous to have an email address that is ISP independent, such as Apple's .Mac services, which we cover in Chapter 18. In the past, services were usually billed on a per-minute basis, which quickly got expensive, and discouraged frequent partaking. There are still some pay-as-you-go plans for travelers on portables using services throughout the country or worldwide, and for people who use the Net infrequently. America Online (AOL) is another example of an ISP, but AOL is a special case, because it does more than just provide an Internet connection service, as we describe later in this chapter.

Types of Internet Connections

Presently, there are two main categories of Internet connection types, especially for the consideration of the home user: broadband, or dial-up. Dial-up has been around in its current form for many years. A dial-up connection is initiated by an analog modem, (MOdulator/DEModulator), which actually dials a telephone number in order to contact the ISP. Modem signals travel over regular telephone lines, the same ones that voice conversations go over, and the function of the device (there will be one on either end of the connection) is to translate the digital information coming from the computer, send it over the analog phone lines, and retranslate the signals back to digital. Every time a dial-up connection is made, there is a waiting period while the connection is initiated and authenticated. When you initiate a disconnect, there is a wait lag as well. Dial-up is slow, and because the signals are often traveling over antique telephone lines, often unreliable. Because dial-up monopolizes the phone line it is using, most frequenters of dial-up connections obtain a dedicated phone line. In many locations, especially ones away from larger urban areas, dial-up is all that is available. Dial-up is however well suited for the traveler and portable owner — anywhere there is a phone line, an Internet connection can be initiated. Because a dial-up connection is not always on, there are also security advantages as well, because your computer is not connected to the Internet full time.

Broadband is so named because of its speed, which is usually around fifty times faster than a dial-up connection. This means that a three-megabyte music file which would take twenty minutes to download over an analog modem would take just seconds to transfer using a broadband connection. If broadband is available to you, get it. Mac OS X thrives with it; it's the way the Internet was meant to be experienced. Pages load instantaneously, movie previews come up in seconds, there is very little waiting or frustration overall. Gone are the days or reading a magazine and waiting for a Web page to load. Broadband typically comes in two flavors: cable or DSL.

Cable services are usually provided by the same company that provides your cable television; and the Internet signals usually arrive over the same lines that the television is sent over. When cable Internet is installed, a splitter is used to divide the incoming cable TV wire into two separate leads. One goes to the television, as before, and the other goes to a cable modem. The cable modem is then connected to the computer. Although a modem is used, there is no phone number to dial and no lag time in initiating a connection. Cable's inherent advantages are its "instant on" connection (no waiting to dial-up), its ease of setup, and its speed. Disadvantages are that it's usually more expensive than dial-up, it's not as widely available, and that because it's a shared connection (with other subscribers in your neighborhood) its speeds can decrease with heavy usage. To find out if cable service is available in your area, contact your cable television provider.

Broadband also comes in the form of the Digital Subscriber Line, or DSL. Like dial-up, DSL uses the same phone lines that voice travels over, but uses different protocols to substantiate a much faster connection. Like cable, DSL is fast connection. DSL can be used at the same time the telephone is used, so a separate phone line is not needed. A telephone cable is run from a wall jack to the DSL modem, and then the modem is connected to the computer. DSL's advantages are that its minimum speed is guaranteed (unlike cable which can slow down under heavy neighborhood usage) and that it's fast. Its disadvantages are that its setup is marginally more difficult (on the computer configuring side) and that, because its lines are the old telephone copper in the streets, you are left at the mercy of the phone company — which may or may not be the ISP — for repairs and maintenance. On a consumer level, DSL is comparable to cable in the services that are provided, so we do not recommend one over the other. On a professional or enthusiast level, DSL offers more options and more flexibility than cable, which we discuss further in Chapter 10.

Continued

Continued

Two other connection types worth mentioning are ISDN (Integrated Services Digital Network) and satellite. ISDN is technically a dial-up connection, and is configured in the same manner. Years ago, it was a faster and much more expensive alternative to dial-up, but today it is rarely seen or available. Satellite is a form of broadband and an alternative to cable or DSL, especially if neither is available in your area. Satellite can be provided by companies that also provide satellite television, or by independent providers. Satellite's advantage is that it is often available in more remote areas. However, it is often slower than its other broadband counterparts and can be adversely affected by the weather.

It is important to make a distinction between general network connectivity and true Internet connection types. Connecting to a local network in an office, or in a school's computer lab, might provide you with an Internet access, but the network itself is not the Internet connection type. The network is being provided with an Internet signal by a connection that is distributed among all the machines (usually a high-end DSL). The same goes for connecting to an AirPort wireless network; this is not your connection type to the Internet, it's a bridge that's connecting you to the network, which in turn is being provided with an Internet connection shared among its devices.

Making the connection

After you have the capability for Internet access, the next step is to configure your Mac. To help you configure your computer for an Internet connection, Mac OS X includes a Setup Assistant application that leads you through a series of decisions and questions to gather your Internet information. This Setup Assistant runs automatically after installation of Mac OS X, after the registration process is completed (or skipped).

If you are not sure if you have a Net connection, the easiest way to figure that out is to launch a Web browser. Click on the Safari icon in the dock. If the home page loads then you are all connected, and your computer does not need to be configured. If not, read onwards!

Internet setup without the Setup Assistant is an advanced skill that lies outside the scope of this chapter. If you skipped the Setup Assistant when you installed, you can launch the Setup Assistant manually. There are three places it might be found:

✦ If you clicked "I'm not ready to connect to the Internet" when you installed, there should have been a Setup Assistant alias placed inside the Utilities folder. Double-click the alias to launch.

✦ If there no alias in the Utilities folder, you can still get to the application, but it's a bit buried and requires delving deep into the System folder. In the System folder there is a Library folder, and in the Library folder lies a CoreServices folder. In this folder there is an application called Setup Assistant. Double-click this to launch it.

✦ A slightly different setup assistant, called the Network Setup Assistant, can also be accessed by clicking Assist Me in the Network Preferences pane.

Internet configuration via the Setup Assistant

The following section walks you through using the Internet Setup Assistant. The Internet Setup has a number of different screens, which correspond to the following section headings, like "Get Internet ready" and "How do you connect?"

Get Internet ready

Figure 6-1 shows the first screen of the Setup Assistan. You see four options:

✦ Setting up a free trial account with EarthLink

✦ Using a special activation code for EarthLink

✦ Using your existing Internet connection

✦ Connecting later (skipping it)

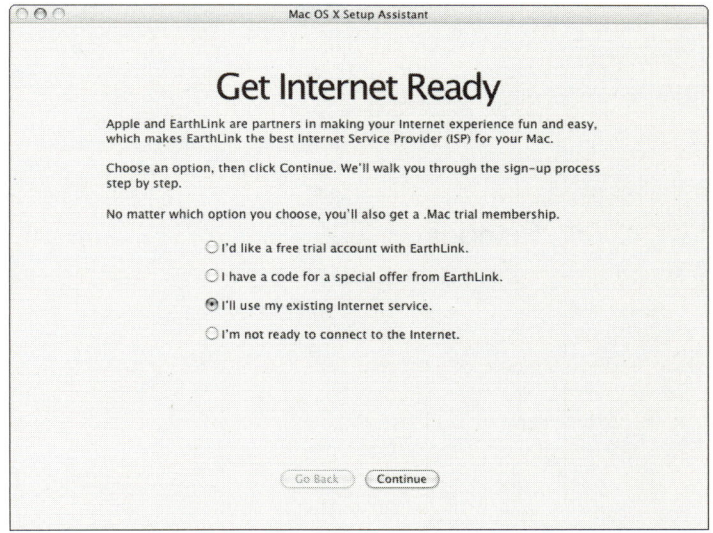

Figure 6-1: This is the first screen of the Setup Assistant.

EarthLink

Using EarthLink as an ISP will provide you with a dial-up connection. If you have broadband available in your area, you should get it; it's worth the extra expense, especially considering the cost of adding/maintaining a second phone line and the regular dial-up service costs (in the neighborhood of twenty dollars a month).

If you do not have broadband available to you, then dial-up may be your only option, and EarthLink is a great choice. Besides the fact that the Setup Assistant walks you through creating a new EarthLink account, EarthLink has great service and excellent support. Following the Setup Assistant to create a new EarthLink account requires a credit card, even though it will not charge you if you cancel the account before a charge is incurred. If you have an activation code (which you might have gotten by email or by snail mail) you might be entitled to some free access, but a credit card is still required; choose the I have a code for a special offer from Earthlink option for this. Either way, EarthLink setup will walk you through payment, retrieving EarthLink-specific dial-up settings (such as access phone numbers) and then configuring your computer to make the connection. While it is beyond the scope of this book to walk you through every EarthLink-specific step, the process is straightforward and easy to follow.

Setting up an existing service

If you already have an agreement with an Internet Service Provider, then choose the I'll use my existing Internet service option.

How do you connect?

You can connect using the five following options (see Figure 6-2):

✦ Telephone modem

✦ Cable modem

✦ DSL modem

✦ Local network (Ethernet)

✦ Local network (AirPort wireless)

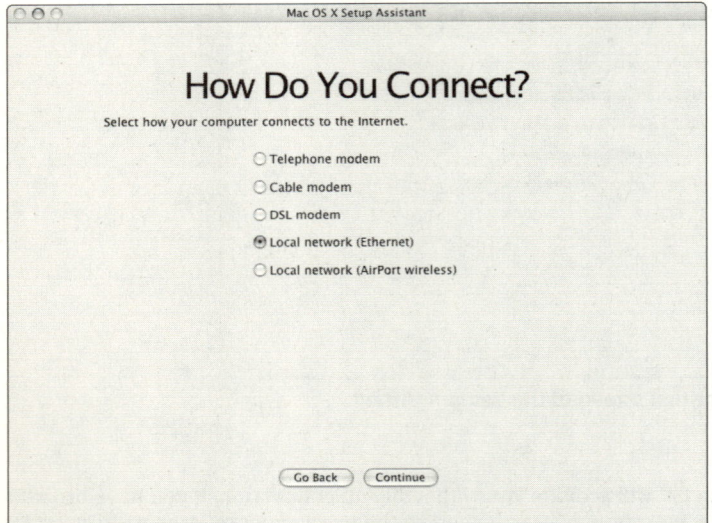

Figure 6-2: Tell the Setup Assistant how your computer is connected to the Internet in the "How Do You Connect" section.

Each of these should sound familiar, as they were discussed in the beginning of the chapter. We'll go through each of the possibilities. Most of these configurations require login and/or account information relating to your ISP.

Tip   Each of these connections, except for the AirPort, is a physical connection to the Internet. A wire needs to be plugged into your computer on one end, and the Internet connection device on the other. Just keep the make-sure-it's-plugged-in concept in mind when your computer refuses to connect for you; it's a great first troubleshooting step.

All Macs that support OS X have modems built in, unless you specifically elected not to have included one (it makes the computer cheaper, and in some cases it's never needed, like Macs in school labs). The modem port has a picture of a telephone handset with some diagonal dots. Think of it as a phone jack; it accepts a regular phone cable, and its official name is RJ-11. All Macs that support OS X have built in Ethernet. The Ethernet port has a picture of three dots with arrows pointing outwards on either end. It looks similar to a phone jack, except wider. Its official name is RJ-45.

If you have a telephone modem connection (dial-up)

Welcome aboard! Plug that phone cable in and follow along. The first screen, as shown in Figure 6-3, asks for your account username, password, ISP phone number, and if you need to dial a number for an outside line, necessary in some offices and schools. If you have call waiting, you can select the Yes box, and the following screen will give you the option to turn call waiting off by typing in a code (*70) while you are on the Internet. This is useful if the phone line you are using is not a dedicated Internet line, and do not want a telephone call to interrupt your Internet session. The next screen asks you what kind of modem you have; unless you are using something other than the internal modem, the answer should be the default, Apple Internal 56K Modem (V.92). Choosing to ignore the dial tone is useful if you are using an infra-red or Bluetooth modem (see Chapter 15) or if you have a phone service with an inconsistent dial tone, such as a phone system that changes dial tone to alert you of a new voicemail. Next comes the .Mac setup, which comes after every configuration option. See the separate ".Mac" section later in this chapter. The You're Finished screen is the last to appear. Click the Go button and Setup Assistant transposes your information into the Mac OS for you, and you are ready to go!

Caution   Modems are analog. Many telephone systems are digital. Although there is no physical difference in the jacks, plugging your computer into a digital telephone jack is a surefire way of ruining your modem. Hotels often have dedicated analog lines for modems to circumvent this. Many buildings are all digital. If you're not sure, don't risk it, and use a digital line tester, available from resellers like CDW (www.cdw.com).

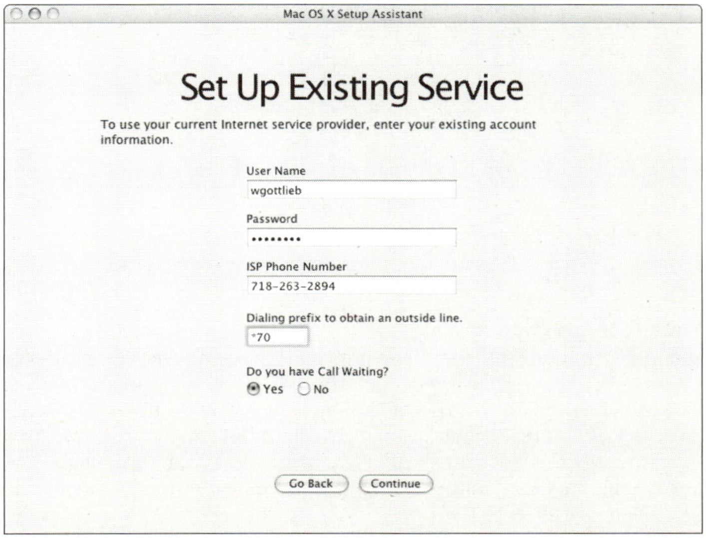

Figure 6-3: Set your Mac to dial-up by typing in your name, password, and telephone information.

If you have a cable modem connection

What a fast connection you have! String that Ethernet cord from the cable modem to your Mac and you're almost there. Clicking on the Continue button takes you to the Your Internet Connection screen, as shown in Figure 6-4. The most commonly used connection method for cable modem is via the Dynamic Host Configuration Protocol, or DHCP. If it's not set to that already, select Using DHCP in the TCP/IP Connection Type pull-down menu. If you are familiar with the term, you can enter a DHCP client ID, otherwise don't worry about it and leave it blank. Using DHCP usually means that you don't have to enter any other information, like the DNS Host, Domain name, or Proxy Server, that the assistant displays. If you are in possession of this information, you should enter it; otherwise leave it blank. In rare cases, your cable modem will use PPPoE to connect. If that is so, check the box and follow the steps in the next section, for configuring a DSL modem. If you are having problems with the aforementioned DHCP setting, check with your cable provider. Next comes the .Mac screen, and then, that's it. You're finished! Click the Go button to transpose the settings to your computer, and you're ready for some surfin'.

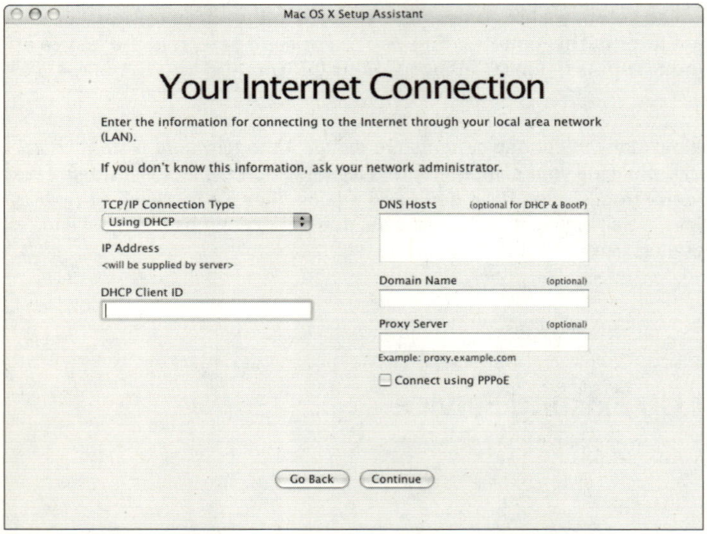

Figure 6-4: Using DHCP is the most common method for connecting with a cable modem.

If you have a DSL modem connection

You have a need for speed! Click that Ethernet cable into your Mac and the DSL modem, and hold on. Back at the How Do You Connect screen, click the DSL modem option, and click Continue. The following screen is the Your Internet Connection screen, (shown in Figure 6-5), which asks you to enter the DSL connection method. Almost all DSL modems connect using the Point-to-Point Protocol over Ethernet, or PPPoE. Pull down the TCP/IP connection type and choose PPP. Make sure the checkbox under the Proxy server window that says Connect using PPPoE is selected. Click Continue to the Connect Using PPPoE screen shown in Figure 6-6). Typing in your service provider is optional and is not part of the connection settings; it's useful for future reference, so if you know it, type it in. The same goes for the service name. The necessary information is the account name and password. If you do not know these, you will need to retrieve them from your ISP. Clicking Continue takes you to the .Mac screen. After your .Mac choices are made, the last screen, You're Finished! appears. Click Go to configure your Mac and start some browsin'.

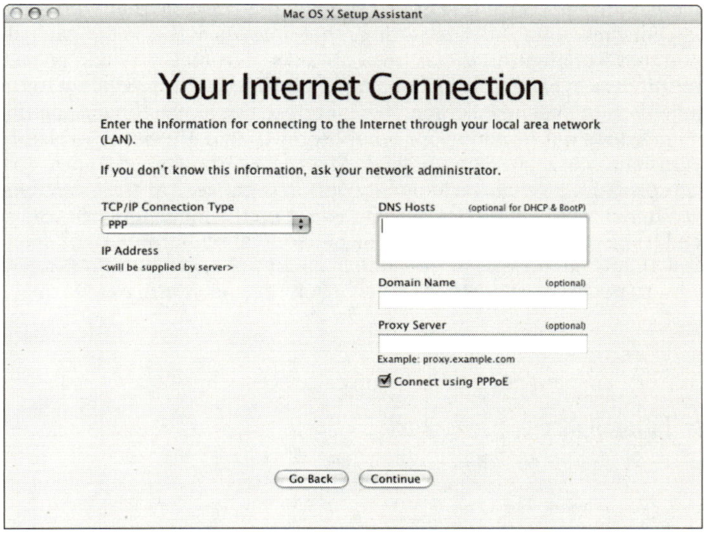

Figure 6-5: DSL usually uses the Point-to-Point Protocol over Ethernet (PPPoE).

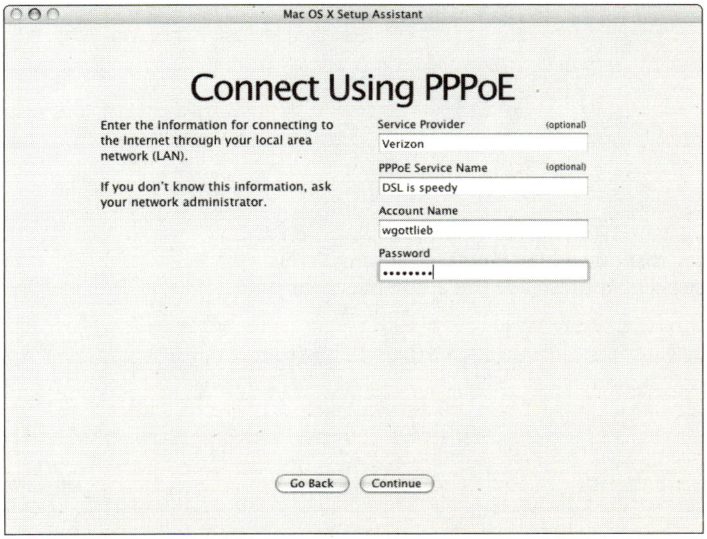

Figure 6-6: After choosing PPPoE, the next screen asks you for your login information.

If you have a local Ethernet network connection

Plug that Ethernet cable into your machine and get started. If you've already got a network setup (see Chapter 15 for more on networks), whether it is in your home, office, or elsewhere, you'll need to configure the Mac to access that network's services. Clicking Continue from the How Do You Connect screen brings you to one of two screens. It's possible that your network is configured to provide your machine with the settings that it needs. If this is the case, the Setup Assistant tells you that a configuration has been obtained automatically and gives the option of using it or not (shown in Figure 6-7). Choosing Yes brings you immediately to the .Mac screen, and then the You're Finished! screen. If you choose not to use the automatic configuration, or your network does not provide your computer with one, the Setup Assistant will ask you to enter the information in manually (shown in Figure 6-8). You'll need to pull down the TCP/IP connection type menu so that the Manually option is chosen. At this point, you'll need to enter in a whole bunch of numbers. Unless you've set up the local network yourself, these numbers will need to be provided to you by your network administrator, or at least someone who may know them, like the guy in the cubicle next to yours. Continue along to the .Mac screen, and then on to the You're Finished! screen, click Go, and you're ready...to go.

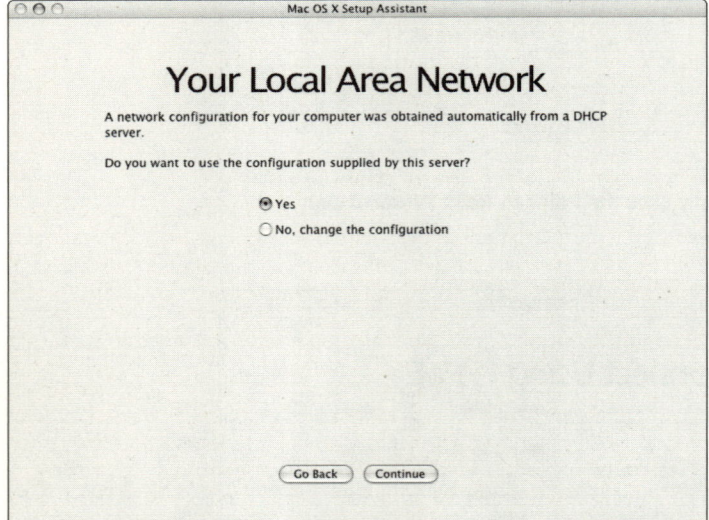

Figure 6-7: This display is shown when your Mac automatically retrieves its network settings. You can use the automatic ones, or set them manually.

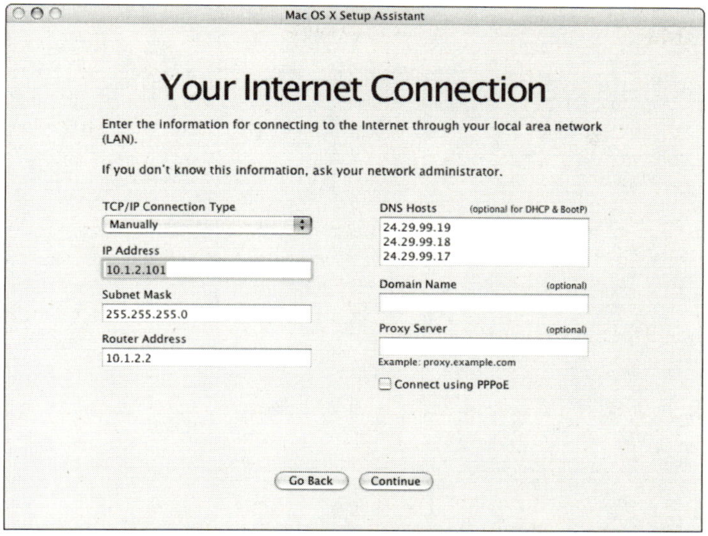

Figure 6-8: Setting up your local Ethernet connection manually looks something like this.

If you have an AirPort wireless network connection

Lucky you, no cables to plug in! Choosing the AirPort option at the How Do You Connect screen and clicking Continue presents you with the Wireless Service screen (shown in Figure 6-9), which lets you choose the wireless network that you wish to join. Networks that are within your signal range should show up in the list. When you see the one you want, select it by clicking once on it. If the network requires a password, a password field will be provided for you to type it in. For security purposes, some networks are not readily visible, and only the privileged that know its name can have access. If that is the case, you'll need to select Other Network and type in the invisible network's name and password. Clicking Continue brings you to the Your Internet Connection screen. The most common AirPort connection method is DHCP; if the TCP/IP Connection Type pull-down menu does not say that, choose Using DHCP. If the network requires a manual connection, you'll need to pull down to Manually and track down the network administrator (or a computer-savvy coworker) to find out what numbers to type in. After that's set, click Continue for the .Mac screen, make your choice, and click Continue once more to bring you to the final screen. Hit Go and you're home free.

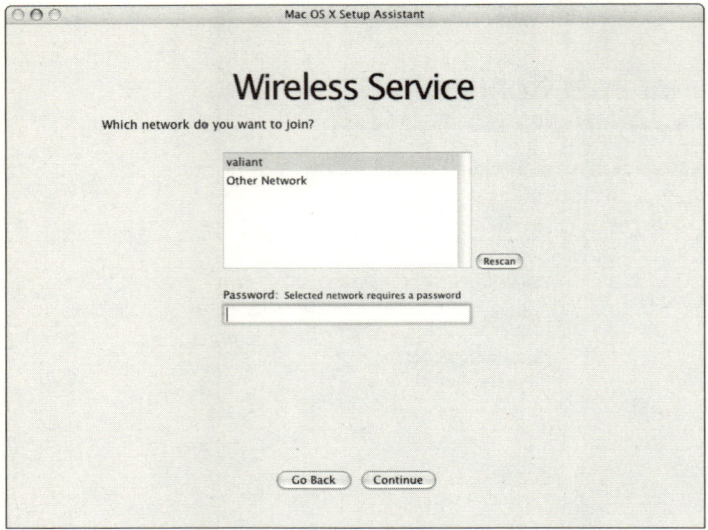

Figure 6-9: Choose your wireless network from the list.

Get .Mac

The Get .Mac configuration screen, shown in Figure 6-10, appears after each setup option. It's where you can type in your existing .Mac account information or create a new trial account. (Apple creates an Apple ID from these, used to login to many Apple Web services, such as purchasing prints in iPhoto and buying music through iTunes). You can also choose the set up later option. Click the Learn More button for an overview of .Mac services. The short story on .Mac is that it's email, homepage hosting, Internet drive storage space, a backup solution, and virus protection for $99.95 a year. Signing up for the trial version is a great way to see if .Mac is for you. The plus side is that it's a lot of services that are extremely well integrated into Mac OS X. The minus side is that it costs you money, every year. This could be a great segue into the reality of nothing being free on the Internet anymore, but we digress.

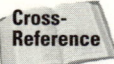

Cross-Reference   For an in-depth look at .Mac, see Chapter 18.

So, that's the Setup Assistant, which provides an easy way to configure the most common Internet settings. For a more in-depth look at networking, and for what all those terms like DHCP and PPPoE actually mean, please look in Chapter 10.

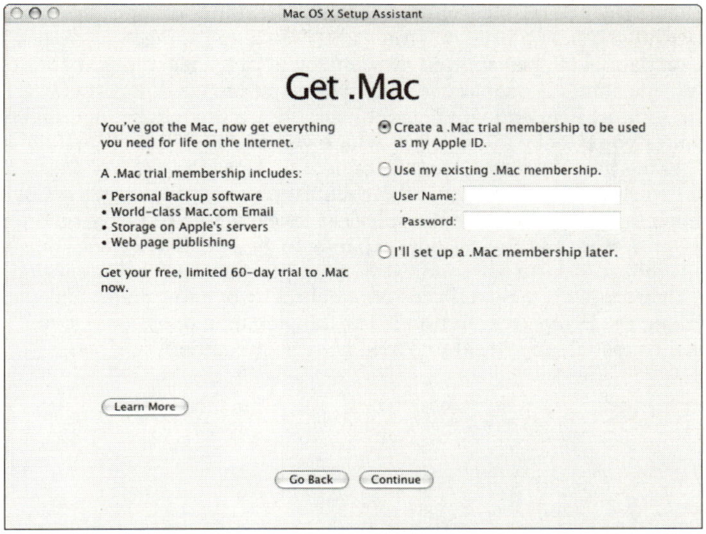

Figure 6-10: Apple presents this Get .Mac options screen after each setup is finished.

Making and breaking the connection

Mac OS X provides multiple interfaces and locations for controlling your Internet connection. Depending on how you see it, this can be a great flexibility or a confusing redundancy. Ahead we discuss the uses of the Internet Connect application (found in the Applications folder) and the menu bar icons as they pertain to managing your Internet connections. The menu bar icons will only be effective if you have already configured your Mac for Internet access — they are just pointers that affect underlying settings. It should be noted that cable and local Ethernet connections are handled automatically by the Mac OS. These are considered to be *instant-on* connections, and do not require user intervention to connect; you are permanently online. Dial-up, AirPort, and DSL connections do (or can) involve some user intervention, and therefore, they are what the following sections cover. For future reference, it should also be noted that defaults for dial-up and DSL are such that you must manually make the connection, but it is a common choice to automate this by configuring it in the Network preferences pane, covered in Chapter 15. You can also choose to have the session disconnect automatically or manually. Disconnecting from your Internet service when you are done is a good idea if you pay for service based on your time spent online, or if you are paying phone-number charges to connect.

Going through the numbers with dial-up

Open the Internet Connect application by double-clicking its icon from the Applications folder. Depending on your configuration and your hardware, the display might look slightly different then the one shown. You should, however, see an icon labeled Internal Modem. Clicking on this icon brings you to the modem screen; if you have already configured a dial-up account, the information fields should be filled, as they are in Figure 6-11. If they are not, and you are in possession of said information, you can fill it in now. When you are satisfied that the information is present, you can hit the Connect button. The status changes from Idle to Contacting PPP Server, and you hear a brief dial tone, and then some screeching noises. What you are hearing is digital data being transmitted over analog phone lines. It might sound terrible, but it's perfectly normal, and it's a great cue as to what your Mac is doing. (In fact, if you're in the computer support field and you're troubleshooting a modem connection, that screeching noise becomes your Rocky theme song, which you can even dance to, if no one is looking.) Continue watching the status area for the connection's progress. While the connection is advancing, you can stop it by clicking the Cancel button (which replaces the Connect button). When the connection is made (the entire process takes twenty to thirty seconds), the status changes to Connected, and the window expands to give details of the connection, such as the time connected, and status bars indicating that information is being sent and received, as shown in Figure 6-12. You can test the connection by opening Safari and seeing if a Web page loads. Clicking the Disconnect button is like hanging up a telephone; your Internet connection is terminated, and the status field goes back to Idle.

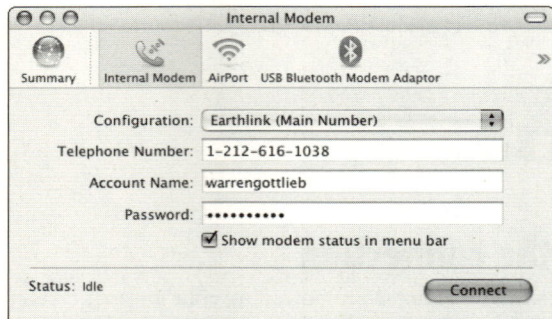

Figure 6-11: This is the Internet Connect application showing what the internal modem screen looks like.

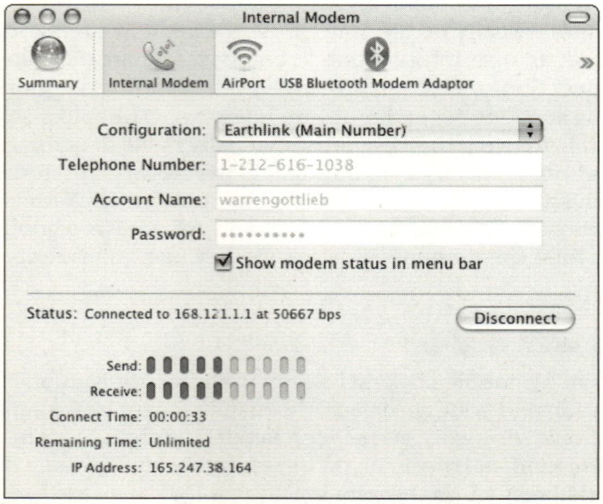

Figure 6-12: A successful dial-up connection yields a display like this.

Instead of opening the Internet Connect application every time you want to connect, a preferred way can be to have the Mac OS display a modem icon in the menu bar, and use the menu to initiate a connection. The Internal Modem section of the Internet Connect application gives you access to a Show modem status in menu bar option. When you select this option, a modem pull-down menu, with an icon just like the modem icon on the back of your computer, displays in the menu bar. Pulling down the menu displays some nifty options, but most importantly it displays the Connect option, shown in Figure 6-13. Choosing Connect initiates a connection, and is equal to clicking the Connect button in the Internet Connect application. Choosing the show time and/or show status option causes the information to be displayed in the menu bar along with the icon. When you are connected, the Connect command changes to a Disconnect command and you can choose that to end your session.

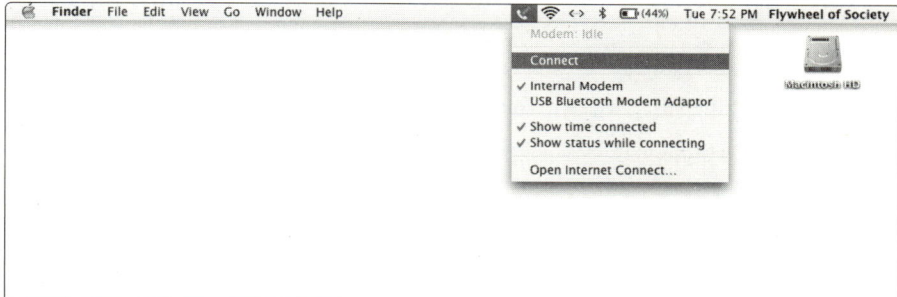

Figure 6-13: Click the telephone icon in the menu bar to display modem connection commands and options without opening a separate application.

Zoom through the phone lines with DSL

Open the Internet Connect application by double-clicking its icon from the Applications folder. If you have configured a DSL connection with the Setup Assistant, a Built-In Ethernet tab will be at the top of the window. Clicking on it displays a window similar to the Internal Modem screen, however the only required fields are the Account Name and Password (see Figure 6-14). If these are not present, enter them, and click Connect. There is a slight lag of a few seconds as the connection is made, but that's about it. Watch the status display to check progress. When you are successfully connected you'll be presented with a status display with the condition of your connection, displaying relevant information. Clicking Disconnect ends your Internet session.

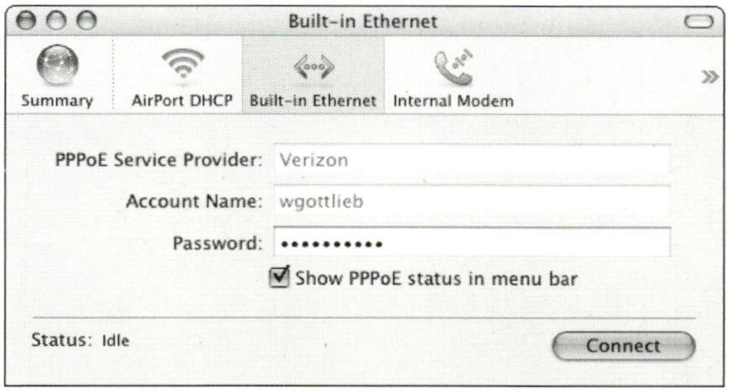

Figure 6-14: Select the Built-in Ethernet option if you want to connect through a DSL.

A DSL connection can be initiated from the menu bar, as well. In the Internet Connect application, when the DSL configuration is selected (Built-In Ethernet), a Show PPPoE status in menu bar option appears in the form of a checkbox. Selecting this option puts an Ethernet port icon in the menu bar, which can be used to initiate a connection without the use of Internet Connect (see Figure 6-15). Pull down and select Connect, and within a few seconds, you should be wired to go. A successful connection displays a Disconnect option in the pull-down menu; select this to terminate the session. Connectivity can be verified by launching Safari and seeing if a Web page loads.

Figure 6-15: Click the little picture of the Ethernet symbol in the menu bar to see its options.

Ditch your cables and head for the AirPort

Open the Internet Connect application by double-clicking its icon from the Applications folder. If your computer has an AirPort card installed, you will see an AirPort icon in the window. Selecting it brings you to the configuration screen, which provides you with options and information respective to wireless network connections (see Figure 6-16). The first option is the most basic: powering AirPort off or on, which disables or enables your computer's wireless capability. Connecting via AirPort requires that this capability be turned on. Powering AirPort off is useful on a portable machine, to save battery power if it's not being used. Click the Turn AirPort On button, if it's powered off. The next option is Network — use this menu to select the wireless network to which you want to connect. Because wireless networking is a standard, it means that your AirPort-equipped Mac should be able to connect to any wireless network that it sees; an AirPort Base Station is but one way to make a wireless network, and there are many other companies besides Apple whose products produce a wireless network signal that the Mac can access.

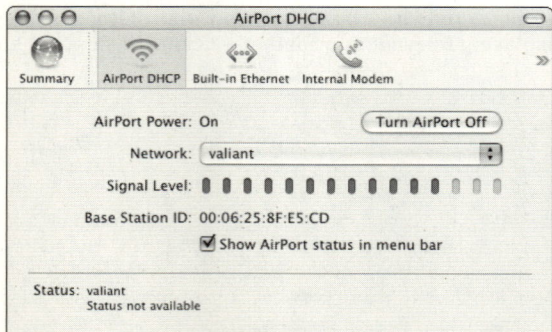

Figure 6-16: The AirPort configuration screen of the Internet Connect Application looks like this.

Often, in large buildings, or if you're lucky, if you're outside in a park, multiple networks will be in range and you'll need to choose one. If the network is password protected, you'll need to type that in when asked. An error message stating, "There was an error connecting to the AirPort Network" can mean an incorrect password was typed in or that you're too far out of range to sustain a connection. Below Network, the Signal Strength is displayed. The farther the bars are to the right-hand side, the better the base station's signal strength is. Weak signal strength will manifest itself in the form of dropped connections to the base station and slow Web speeds. The base station ID gives you the hardware identification number of the base station; don't worry about what that is for now. The status field at the bottom of the window tells you what network you are connected to, and how you are connected to the Net.

Also in the AirPort section of the Internet Connect window is a Show AirPort status in menu bar option. Selecting this option places an AirPort signal-strength indicator in the menu bar. Clicking on the icon brings down a menu that gives similar functionality of the Internet Connect application, including the ability to choose your network and to turn AirPort on or off. Solid black curved lines indicate signal strength; a muted gray display of lines indicates little or no signal. If AirPort is powered off the icon appears as an outline. The AirPort signals are shown in Figures 6-17, 6-18, and 6-19.

Figure 6-17: Full AirPort signal is displayed as thick black lines.

Figure 6-18: No AirPort signal is shown with gray lines in place of black ones.

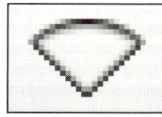

Figure 6-19: AirPort powered off is displayed as an outline of the signal strength indicator.

Tip

Hold down the command key and then drag a menu bar icon out and away from the menu bar will remove it. You can enable it again by rechecking the box that you checked to put it there in the first place. Have confidence, you can find it again.

Note

Although opening a Web browser is the quickest way to diagnose a successful connection, just because a browser is not loading Web pages does not mean that the computer is configured incorrectly. Your ISP could be having service interruptions, or there could be a problem with OS X. (Hey, it's not perfect.) When a connection that appears to be configured correctly fails to connect, a deeper delve (the Network preference pane) is necessary.

Browsing the World Wide Web

Of course, the whole point of learning and configuring all the previous stuff is to gain access to the wealth of information and communication known as the Internet.

One service available through this giant, globe-spanning Internet is known as the World Wide Web. Emerging gradually and booming within the mid-nineties, it is this technology that shook the Internet to public prominence, and made terms such as "surfin' the Web," or "browsin' the Net" household phrases of the previously nongeeky. Using the World Wide Web implies somehow experiencing and perusing this cacophony of information, whether it is a newspaper article or a movie preview.

Safari in the Web jungle

You can access the Web with a program called a *Web browser*. Recently Apple released its own Web browser, called Safari, which is now part of the Mac OS. Since its release, it has soared in popularity; it's fast and lean, and has a fantastic interface. We discuss Safari in more detail later in the "Taking a Safari through the Wild Web" section. Until Safari's takeover, Microsoft's Internet Explorer was the reigning browser king in OS X. As of this writing Microsoft canceled development of IE, a planned occurrence coinciding with Safari's official release, although Microsoft is still supporting its own product. If you were comfortable with Internet Explorer, you'll love Safari. As usual, Apple's interface engineers have mega-upped Microsoft, and made a functional product fantastic. A key truth that will make your Web life much better, is this: always have more than one browser handy. A secondary browser is an essential tool. Not all Web sites are created equal (nor are the browsers), and what looks fine in one browser may look terrible in another.

Note　Different browsers use different rendering engines to decode and display Web pages, which is why certain pages will look different in different browsers. Safari and OmniWeb use Apple's WebCore library, based on the KHTML engine. Netscape, and the Mozilla family, and the new AOL are based on the Netscape Gecko engine. Internet Explorer uses its own proprietary Microsoft engine, which, of course, is different from the Windows version.

Other browsers for your toolkit

A great advantage of the OS X platform is that many different browsers are available. You don't need all of them, but they're all worth a look. Each can be downloaded by using Safari.

✦ **Mozilla browsers** (you can read about them on their Web site) are available for download at `http://mozilla.org`. They include Mozilla, Firebird, and Camino.

✦ **Netscape** is alive and well and downloadable at `www.netscape.net`.

✦ **iCab** takes a unique approach, at `www.icab.de/index.html`.

✦ **OmniWeb,** among other awesome programs, comes from the Omni group. Get it at `www.omnigroup.com`.

✦ **Opera** has been recently optimized for Mac OS X 10.3 and can be downloaded from `www.opera.com`.

Understanding Web terminology

To use the Web, it helps to know a bit of its terminology. Web browser programs display information in *Web pages,* which can contain text, pictures, and animation as well as audio and video clips. The machines that store all this information and that serve it to you on request are called *Web servers*. On a Web page, the underlined text usually indicates one or more *links,* which are also known as *hyperlinks*. Pictures can also be links. A link can be discovered by moving the pointer over it; if it's a link, the arrow changes into a pointing hand. Clicking a link takes you to another Web page. The intriguing thing about a link is that it can take you to a Web page on the same Web server or a page on any other Web server on the planet. So, it's possible to click your way around the world and not even know it!

Taking a Safari through the Wild Web

Open Safari by clicking its icon in the Dock. When Safari opens, it displays a browser window and goes to a Web page that has been previously designated as the home page. With Mac OS X, the home page is initially set to an Apple-enhanced Netscape page, filled with news and links. Go to Apple's Web site Type in `www.apple.com` and hit the Return key. Besides being a Web site that every Mac-head should know and love, it is a great example page for demonstration. You can even go as far as to set this to your home page, by going under the Safari menu and choosing the Preferences option. (An example of this is shown in Figure 6-20.) Where it says Home Page, type in `www.apple.com`. If Safari is displaying the Apple Web site already, because you've typed its name into the address field, you can click the Set to Current Page button, which changes the homepage to whatever the browser is displaying. Click OK to save the change.

Figure 6-20: Safari displays a Web page. Note the icons of Safari's toolbar buttons, and the placement of the address field and Google search bar.

Navigation basics (Features immediately visible)

All the buttons and fields you see in front of you are tools designed to help you navigate the Web. You can type in the names of the Web sites that you want to visit, do searches, travel to your previously saved bookmarks, and shuffle backward and forward to places you have recently been. If you haven't noticed, the toolbars in Finder windows have a similar look to them. Apple has actually taken the Web browsing concept and applied its logical simplicity for browsing the files in Mac OS X as well. A walk-through of Safari's toolbar and basic features follows:

Backward and Forward buttons

Say that you're At Apple's Web site, and Wow! You've simply got to read more about that 15-inch PowerBook that was just released. So you click on its picture, a link, which takes you to Apple's hardware section where you can read more about said PowerBook. The overview, however, just isn't enough, and you've got to click on the Tech Specs section to get a nice feature comparison between all the models. When you're done with that, how can you get back to Apple's main page? Clicking the Back button (the one with the left-pointing arrowhead on it) once will take you one page back, from the tech specs back to the overview. Clicking Back again will take you from the overview back to Apple's main page. Want to go back to the overview? Click on the Forward button (with the right-pointing arrowhead) to take you forward to the page you just came back from. If you are buried many pages deep in a Web browsing session, you can click and hold on either the Back or the Forward button, and a list of pages that you have been to will appear. Scroll down the list and click on the page that you want to go to.

Stop and Reload buttons

Perhaps you are browsing the homepage of the *New York Times*. You've read a bunch of articles, clicked your way back to the main page, but it's an hour later, and you've got a hunch that a new tidbit of information might have been posted to the site. Clicking the Reload button (the one with the circle-arrow) will reload the Web site from the NYT server, and if anything new has posted, your display will reflect that. Shift-clicking on the Reload button fully reloads the page from the server, which is sometimes more effective than a regular reload.

As it often happens while browsing the Web, you clicked on a link, and man, that page is taking forever to load. You've gotten through a full email to your boss with the top ten reasons why you should be able to work from home, and that page isn't quite halfway done. You can see bits and pieces of text and graphics, but nothing useful, and you just can feel it. That page just isn't coming along. Look at the toolbar. Instead of a circle-arrow indicating a reload, the button has changed to display an X. In fact, anytime a page is loading, even if it's not stuck, an X will be displayed instead of a reload symbol. The X is the Stop button. Clicking on it ceases the download of whatever page load you were attempting. After the page has stopped, you can attempt to do a reload, or just move on in life.

Bookmark button

It's happened. You've found the definitive Web home of Arlo Guthrie, and you need to save that page for future reference. Click on the Add Book Marks bar (shown in Figure 6-21), and Safari will not only save it for you, but first asks you just where you want to save it to, and what name to give it. You can choose to save it in the bookmarks bar (which places it on the toolbar next to the currently displaying Amazon and eBay ones), the Bookmarks menu (you can get to it by going to the Bookmarks menu), or any number of folders that exist within Safari's unique bookmark management system. This system is covered a bit later in the chapter. For now, you can save it to the toolbar or in the menu.

Figure 6-21: Clicking on the Add Bookmark button presents you with the option to name your bookmark and save it to the location of your choice.

Address field

As it often happens, you need to go to a Web site, it's not bookmarked, but you know its address. Typing in its full name (like `www.apple.com`) and hitting the Return key on the keyboard gets you there. A Web address is officially called a URL, or Uniform Resource Locator. Many times, you do not need to type in the full name of the site, for instance, just typing in the word **macaddict** should take you to *MacAddict* magazine's Web site (`www.macaddict.com`). If you have been there before, and if it's bookmarked and you don't know it, Safari might try to fill in the name for you. This can be helpful at times and irritating when you don't want Safari to think for you.

The address field serves another purpose, a visual one, in Safari. As a Web page is loading, the background of the address turns into a page-load status bar; as the page loads further, the blue background gradually makes it all the way across the field. When a page has finished loading, the background turns back to white, as shown in Figure 6-22.

Just Google it

For a noun to make its way into verb status (at least in common language) is an esteemed achievement. Google is the very popular and very effective Web search engine (`www.google.com`) and now has become an action as well. If you ever hear someone tell you to just Google something, they're asking you to go to Google's Web page, type in the term, and hit Return. It's so popular and effective, in fact, that Apple has built this capability directly into the Safari toolbar. Typing something into the Google field and hitting Return is identical to first going to the actual Web site and searching from there. Safari's field even stores recently searched-for items, accessible by clicking on the magnifying glass inside of the field. If something is typed into the field and you wish to remove it, click on the *x* that appears in the right-hand side.

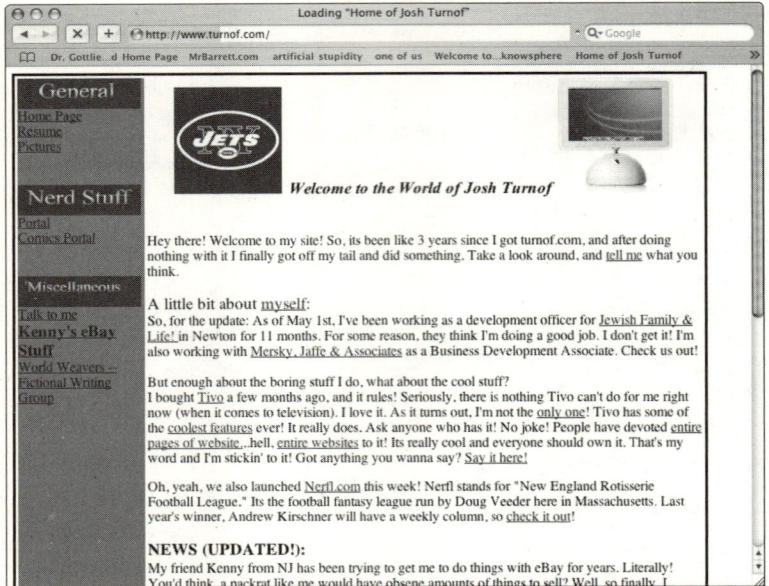

Figure 6-22: A page in the process of loading displays a progress bar in the address field.

Bookmarks bar

Below the toolbar with the above-mentioned features lies the bookmarks bar. When you save a page by clicking on the Add button, Safari gives you the option of saving the location in this always visible and easily accessible location. Once in the bookmarks bar, its name—that is, the name that you have specified (shorter names are ideal for the bookmarks bar)—becomes a button that you can click to bring the Web site up. Folders of bookmarks can be displayed in the toolbar as well and are evident by the presence of a disclosure triangle next to the folder's name. Clicking on the name displays a list of items residing in the folder.

More features, plus customization (Features not visible)

Now that you know the basics of Web navigation and of Safari's visible features , it's time to hike around to where Safari really shines: all its special features and customization. Apple has included many slick features, original or not, to make your Web browsing experience quick and enjoyable.

Preferences

Sometimes, the best way to get to know a program is to go poking around in its Preferences window. Safari's are located under the Safari menu.

Understanding URLs

The technical name for a Web address is called a *URL,* which stands for Uniform Resource Locator. An example of a URL is `http://www.macworld.com`. A URL begins with a code that specifies a kind of Internet protocol. The `http` stands for hypertext transfer protocol, which is the protocol for viewing Web pages. Often a Web URL is shown without the `http://` portion, and beginning with `www`. This is because most browsers are smart enough to assume that anything beginning with a `www` implies the `http` protocol, and the browser inserts that automatically. Another protocol is the file transfer protocol, which is signified by `ftp`, and is used for transferring files over the Internet. Protocols also exist for local networking; for example `afp` signifies AppleTalk Filing Protocol, used by many Mac OS fileservers. The remainder of the URL specifies the domain name, (`macworld.com`) and the specific server to access (`www`). Internet addresses are all based on numbers. The names you type in exist because they are easier to remember than the numbers. The catch is that the name has to resolve, or be properly tied into, the proper number, in order for the Web site to be located. This kind of information is stored on *DNS*, or Domain Name Service servers.

General

The first option is the General preferences, shown in Figure 6-23. Here, you can change your Mac's default Web browser to something other than Safari, using the pull-down menu. If you hate that your homepage opens every time you make a new window, you can set Safari to do something else, like to open nothing. You can also change which folder to save your down-loaded files to, and whether to automatically remove items from the download list or not. A checkbox lets you decide whether to let Safari automatically launch certain files after you download them, which is easier than double-clicking every file you save from the Web. Sometimes other applications link to Safari, like an email program; the last option lets you choose to have Web sites from linked applications open in a new window, or in the current window. Having links load in the current window runs the risk of taking you off of the page you were just reading, so many people like to have links open in a new one.

Appearance

The Appearance section lets you choose the fonts in which to view the World Wide Web. When pages don't specify in their formatting what font to use, Safari will use the ones that you can specify here. The standard font will be what you see the most, the fixed width will be used less often. If you have a really slow connection, or just hate pictures, you can choose not to have Safari load any graphics (meaning you'll just see text and colors).

Bookmarks

This section lets you choose what bookmark features show up where. In the bookmarks bar, you can choose to display a link that will access the bookmarks found in the Address Book (see Chapter 19) or from Rendezvous, Apple's zero-configuration networking technology (check out Chapter 15). You also have similar options for the Bookmarks menu (with the added option to display the bookmarks also appearing in the bar) and in the bookmark col-lection, which we discuss ahead.

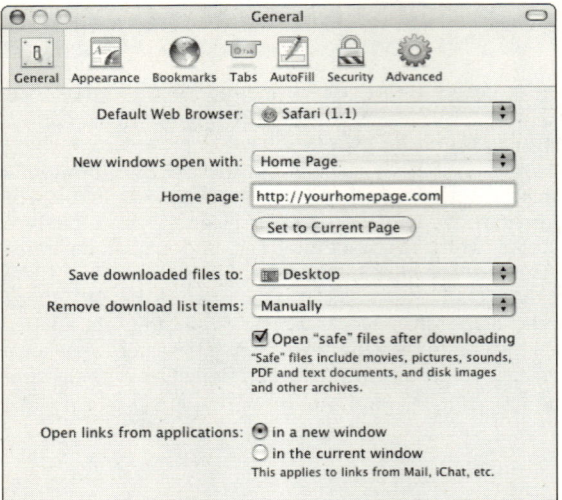

Figure 6-23: Change the default Web browser or your homepage in Safari's General preferences.

Tabs

Tabs are just plain fantastic, and are described ahead. Choose to enable tabbed browsing, and to always show the tab bar. Briefly, tabbed browsing lets you view multiple Web pages within the same window, instead of having 20 or so open Web pages cluttering your screen at once. Glorious. Choose New Tab from the file menu (⌘-T) to watch them in action.

AutoFill

Instead of typing in your name and address every single time you buy something, Safari can do it for you, if the AutoFill options are checked. Choose the names and passwords box to have all your names and passwords saved; they will show up automatically every time you visit the site. This can be a great time saver, but it's potentially hazardous if many people have access to your machine — they'll be able to get into anything you'd normally have to use a password for, like your Web-based email or your online banking. When you enter a password for the first time, or change an existing one, Safari asks you if you want to save passwords for that particular site. You can select Never for this Website, Not Now, meaning that you can decide to choose later on, or Yes, as shown in Figure 6-24.

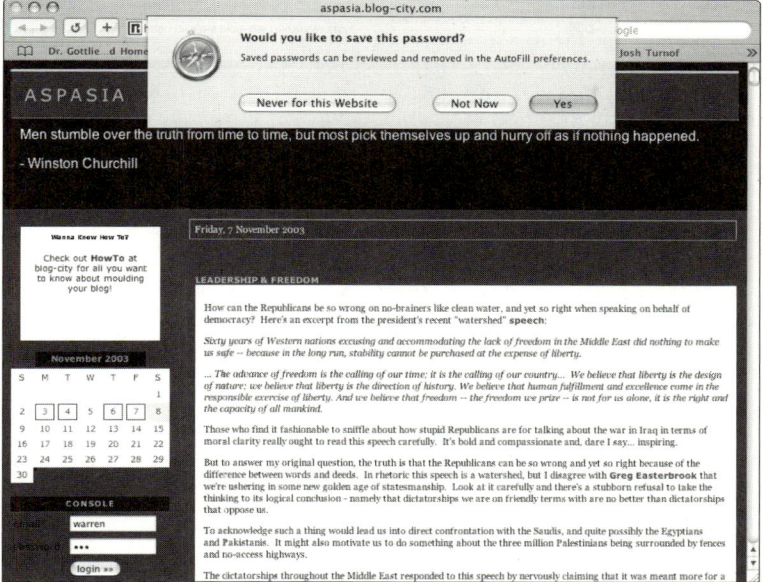

Figure 6-24: When you tell Safari to save names and passwords in the AutoFill preferences, it lets you choose how to handle individual pages when you enter or change a password.

Security

The fewer things you load onto your Mac from the Web, the less risk you open your Mac to. In general, you should feel free to leave all the Java options enabled; they affect your ability to view certain Java-programmed Web sites. If you only customize one thing about Safari (and we *do* tell you this more than once) make sure it's the Block Pop-up windows option. If this is checked (it can also be enabled from the file menu) you'll never again see another of those maddening, frustrating, and annoying pop-up advertisements that assault your screen. A *cookie* is a bit of information your computer stores when you have visited some Web sites. Amazon.com knows you've been there before (and might greet you by name) because it's being provided with that information from your computer. Selecting the option to accept cookies from only the sites that you navigate to will prevent cookies from advertisements and sites that you have not elected to visit from installing themselves on your computer. If you choose the option to "ask before sending a non-secure form to a secure Web site," you will be alerted every time this happens, as can occur when you switch, for example, from a secure online banking site to a Macintosh news site.

Advanced

Selecting a custom style sheet overrides the look and feel of the sites that you go to. If you know HTML (hypertext markup language), the language that Web pages are written in, you can code your own. Clicking the button to change proxies settings sends you to the Network Preferences pane.

Security

Most Web surfers are lax about security. Internet security, as it relates to you, is the idea that other Web users do or do not have access to information that you don't want them to see. This includes any information that you transmit, from your birth date, to your email password, to your credit card numbers. In general, when typing sensitive information into a Web page (like when you are buying something), make sure of two things in Safari: one is that the URL begins with `https://`, instead of just `http://`. The *s* means secure. Also, in the upper-right corner of Safari's window, you see a little icon of a locked padlock. If these two indicators are present, consider the site safe. See Figure 6-25.

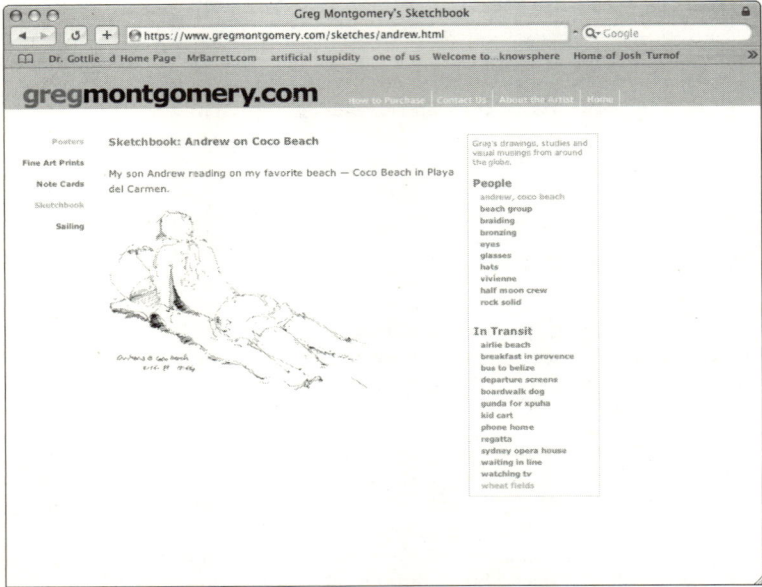

Figure 6-25: You know you're in a secure site by the presence of the lock icon in the upper-right-hand corner, and by the `https://` instead of just `http://` in the address field.

Apple Cares!

Apple Cares about how Safari's doing, plowing along through all those Web pages. Under the Safari menu, there's a Report Bugs to Apple command. Choosing this brings up a screen that inputs the name of the active Web page, a field for your comments, and a Submit button. Click on more options for greater specificity. If something doesn't work right, or a Web page that you go to doesn't load properly, tell Apple! They'll fix it.

Other ways to customize Safari

Safari's customization can go even further than we have discussed. By using Safari's menus, you can do things like change the items you see in the toolbar, see pages you have previously visited, and manage your bookmarks.

View menu

If you don't like some of the things you see in Safari's toolbar, or want to add some things that you don't see, the View menu is your method. Anything that is already visible in the toolbar will have a checkmark next to its name in the menu. Un-checking something removes it from the toolbar, and vice versa. Choosing to show the status bar is a recommendation. This places a thin bar at the bottom of every window. When you mouse over a link, the full URL will display in the status bar. When a page is loading it will keep you apprised of its progress. If you'd like to go behind the scenes, the View menu also incorporates a View Source option; choosing this lets you see the source code (HTML) of the active Web page. If you've got no programming experience, it'll look like gobbledygook, but it's a good window into what makes up a Web page, whether written out by hand or laid out in an application like Adobe GoLive or Macromedia's Dreamweaver.

History menu

This menu's main function is to provide an interface for your browsing history. Safari keeps track of all the sites you have visited, for a week at a time. Its true usefulness is only appreciated through experience. When you forget that great site that you were just at the other day, you can scroll through the pages that show up in the history, and find it. Clearing the history deletes all the locations that Safari has saved, useful if you don't want another person poking around where you've been. The History menu also lets you mark a page for snapback. Snapback is discussed in a little bit.

Bookmarks menu

Helps you manage your... bookmarks! This is the most convenient spot to access bookmarks that you have saved to the menu. Select a location on this menu and Safari takes you there.

Window menu

Gains you access to any open Safari windows, which will appear in a list at the bottom of the menu. Here, you can select to view the Activity window, which will show you more information than you probably wanted to know. The downloads window keeps track of all your downloads and pops up whenever a file is downloaded.

The coolness that is Safari

Some of the following features are unique to Safari, and others can be found in other browsers, but as usual, the interface wizards at Apple just know how to do it better. Read on to learn time-saving and easier ways to browse.

Avoiding the Back button

Web browsing can be a bit stressful. There's so much information, so many links, and the lurking fear of something getting lost in the searching! Using the Back button is a tried and true hallmark of Web navigation, but there are better and more organized ways; here are Safari's.

Snapback

You've Googled something (through Safari's toolbar, of course), say, an ex-boy or ex-girl-friend's name. Convince yourself that you're not a stalker. You've found some great sites and lots of useless information. In fact, you want to keep reading from the list that Google gave you, but you're currently eight clicks deep into a fascinating read on how llamas make great pets.

Instead of clicking the Back button a whole bunch of times, you might have noticed the little orange arrow that appeared in the Google search field (shown in Figure 6-26). Clicking the arrow takes you back to the original list of search results that Google returned, without back-tracking for a few dozen hits to the Back button. Safari accomplishes this by marking the first page you visit on a site. And, if you visit a page that you know you will be returning to, you can manually mark the page for snapback, by choosing to do so under the history menu.

Figure 6-26: Click on the orange arrow to snapback to your original list of search results.

Tabs

You're reading the *New York Times* site. There are tons of great articles. You can either open each one in a new window, which gets cluttered and unorganized pretty rapidly, or make generous use of the Back button, and only have one article loading at a time, or, you can use Safari's tabs feature. Using tabs gives you the ability to open multiple Web pages in a single browser window, separated by little tabs that protrude down from the toolbar (shown in Figure 6-27).

Tabs are enabled in the Tabs section of the Safari Preferences. You can create a new tab by selecting that option from the file menu, or typing ⌘-T. Notice that the tab displays a progress wheel to show that a page is loading. Holding down the Command key while clicking on a link opens the link as a new tab, as opposed to in the same window, obscuring what you were just viewing. If you've chosen to select new tabs as they are created (in Preferences), the tab will open in the foreground. If you have not, it will open in the background without taking the current page off of the screen. You can also Control-click a link to display a contextual menu, which, among other options, will give you an opportunity for opening it in a new tab. If the status bar is being displayed, mousing over the link while the Control or Option keys are held down reveals what will happen when the mouse button is clicked. Opening tabs in the background is a great strategy for managing links that you have come across while still browsing. Instead of interrupting your reading, you can open as many links as you like as tabs in the background, and read them all as you choose.

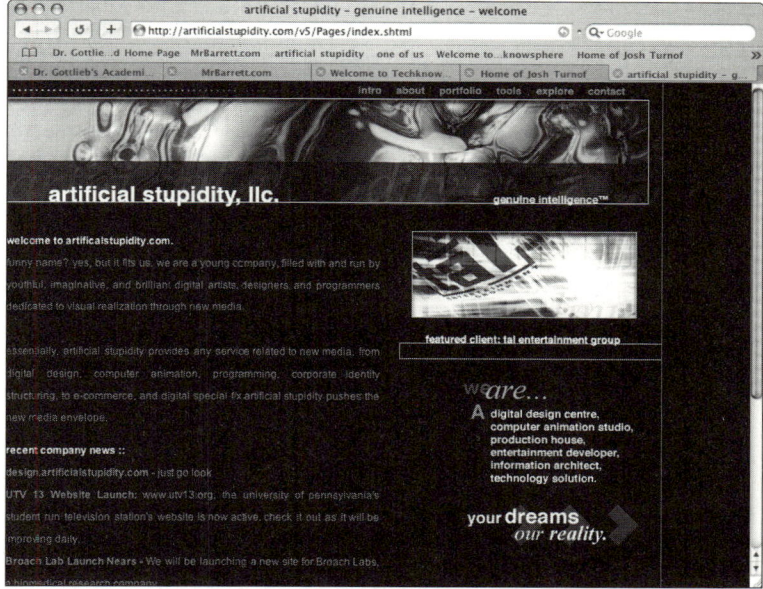

Figure 6-27: Tabbed windows look like this.

After all your tabs are open, you can click among them with reckless abandon. Cycle through them by holding down ⌘-Shift and either of the arrow keys. If there are too many tabs to view onscreen at once, Safari displays a double arrow in the toolbar to indicate more tabs to the right. Tabs can be closed by clicking the little *x* that appears on each tab, or by typing ⌘-W. If no tabs are open, ⌘-W closes the whole window. In addition, Control-clicking on a tab brings up a contextual menu with the option to close all tabs, or even reload them.

Keeping organized

A Great strength of Safari is it's capability to keep your Web browsing organized. By Blocking your pop-ups, managing your bookmarks, and keeping your downloads managed, Safari can reduce your Web clutter.

Block those pop-ups

Pop-ups are windows that jump to the front of the screen when you are browsing the Web. You haven't asked to see these windows. They just appear. They are advertisements. They slow down your Web browser and your Mac. With Safari, you can banish annoying pop-ups forever, by choosing to do so, under the Safari menu. That's it. Select that option, and Safari blocks them all automatically, simply by refusing to display information from a site that you have not chosen to visit. You can also choose to enable this feature in the Security Preferences; in this case, Safari warns you that some Web sites might use pop-ups for legitimate reasons, and those will be disabled as well. This is true, but very rare, and a small price to pay for the blocking of all the illegitimate ones.

Bookmark management

Safari has a concept of bookmarking that goes way beyond the ordinary. *Bookmarking* means saving a current page location for future visitation. Safari gives you two immediately visible places to put them — in the bookmarks bar, for pages you access very frequently, or the Bookmarks menu, for pages visited every so often. But, when you choose to save a bookmark, you are greeted with another option, in the form of a bunch of listed folders. Saving a bookmark in one of these folders obviously saves it there, but to retrieve it? Choose Show All Bookmarks from the Bookmarks menu, or click the little book icon in the bookmarks bar. What is displayed is Safari's bookmark manager (shown in Figure 6-28) — an iTunes-like interface for complete control and organization of your bookmarks — because, let's face it, they're hard to organize. You tend to accumulate lots of them, and don't even want them all in that menu all the time. If you've been using Internet Explorer (it's okay to admit that), then Safari will have automatically imported all your favorites into its IE Favorites folder.

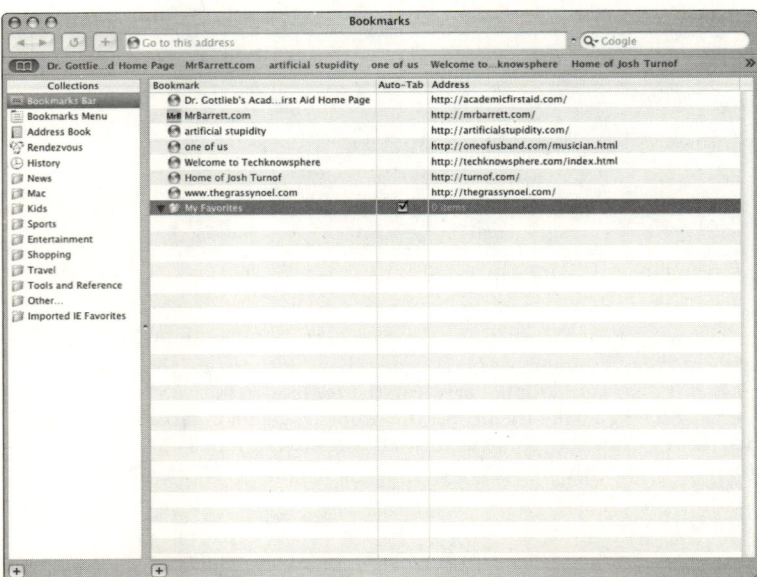

Figure 6-28: Keep your bookmarks out of the menu and the toolbar with Safari's bookmark manager.

What's great about this is that it's a way to save tons of bookmarks without having a Bookmarks menu that scrolls down and off of your screen for five solid minutes. Bookmarks stored in the folders of the Bookmarks window get themselves out of the menu but remain easily accessible. Clicking on the plus sign at the bottom creates a new folder, which you can rename and drag any of your existing bookmarks into. Apple has created a bunch of folders — you can choose to keep them, or get rid of them by clicking on them and hitting the Delete key. If you select a number of bookmarks in the right-hand pane, and Option-click on the plus sign in the right-hand window to make a new folder, Safari will make a new folder and move the selected bookmarks into it. From now on, when creating a bookmark, you can choose to file it in a categorized folder, as opposed to slapping it on to the end of a menu.

URLs (whether in the address bar, or in the form of a bookmark) in Safari are draggable. You can drag an address by its icon, either into a folder when it's being viewed in the bookmark manager, or into the bookmarks bar directly from the address field. Shift-clicking on the Add bookmark button (the plus sign) is a shortcut for adding a bookmark directly to the bookmarks bar. To make use of your bookmarks, go to the bookmark manager and double-click on a bookmark. You can also ⌘-click to open them in tabs.

Storing folders in the bookmarks bar is a great way to have easy access to a bunch of sites at a time. A great customization to this feature is Auto-Tab, which, instead of displaying a list of the bookmarks in the folder when you click on it in the bookmarks bar, will open every bookmark in there as a separate tab (shown in Figures 6-29 and 6-30). This option is available only when viewing the "Bookmarks Bar" collection within the Bookmark Manager. Check the box in the Auto-Tab column to activate. Beware, because clicking an auto-tabbed folder will override any tabs currently being viewed in that window.

Figure 6-29: Auto-Tab takes you from this...

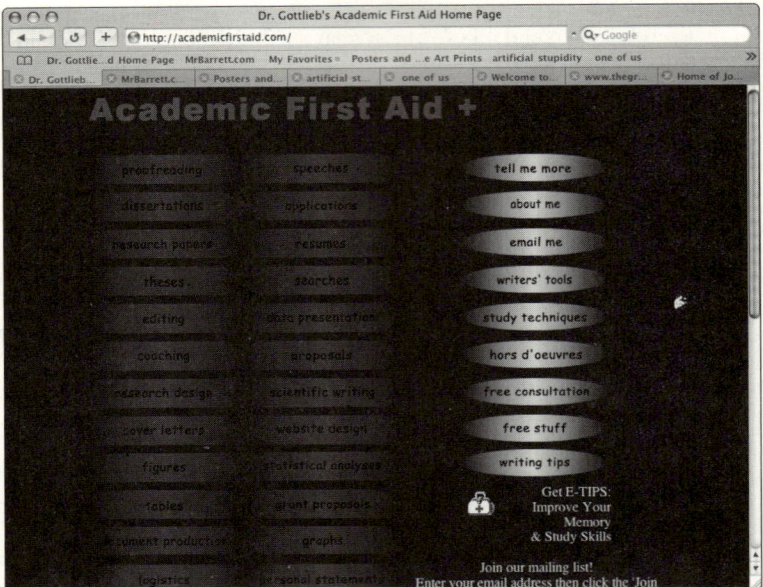

Figure 6-30: ...to this!

Safari, with the aid of a .Mac account, gives you the ability to sync your bookmarks between your different Macs, eliminating the frustration of managing and remembering different sets of saved locations between different computers, and keeping a single set constant among all your machines.

Download window

Downloading a file is a common practice, whether it is an instruction manual for your new outdoor grill, a new piece of software, or a movie preview. To *download* is to save a file to your computer. In most cases, clicking on the download link will bring up Safari's download window, simply a list of recently downloaded items. While an item is being transferred, an *x* will appear next to its name in the list, which will cancel the download if clicked. After it's downloaded, the *x* changes to a magnifying glass, which when clicked will show the file's location in the Finder. You can choose the default location in the preferences. At the bottom is a Clear button, which removes all the items in the list. Some items seem stubborn when their links are clicked, and refuse to download, and instead open a new Web page filled with text and code. What you see is the results of a browser opening the file instead of saving it to your Mac. Try Option-clicking the link, which forces Safari to download.

Caching Out

Safari stores the pages you visit in a cache (pronounced cash, not caché), which is a store of information located on your hard drive. Instead of reloading the page fully from the server each time, a revisit to the page will usually cause Safari to access this cache, which is faster than downloading the page again, because accessing your local hard drive is faster than accessing the Net. Information that changes frequently might be hindered by this cache, and necessitate a manual reload of a page by hitting the reload button. In some cases, hitting the Shift key and then the Reload button is necessary, it forces the browser to take a brand new copy of the page and not just poll the server for changed information. In rarer cases, a page becomes stuck in the cache and not even a reload will load the page's contents from the Internet properly. If this is the case, it is necessary to empty the cache, which deletes all locally saved Web pages from your computer's hard drive. Go to the Safari menu and choose to empty the cache. You'll be given a warning, but click on empty. Resume browsing with a clear cache.

Using the Debug Menu

Safari has a hidden feature called the Debug menu. It's got a lot of information for troubleshooting things like JavaScript exceptions and World Leaks, and consequently a lot of not-so-useful features for your everyday user. There are, however, a few cool things, and for the not-faint-of-heart, it's pretty easy to get to. Try the following:

1. **Open the Terminal,** from the Utilities folder.

2. **Type the following after the prompt:**

   ```
   defaults write com.apple.Safari IncludeDebugMenu 1
   ```

3. **Hit return.** (Later on, you can substitute a zero for the one and remove the debug menu.)

That should be it! The next time you open Safari, you should see a Debug menu to the right of the Help menu. One cool thing you can do with this is to fool a Web site into thinking that you are a non-Safari user, even a PC user! Why? Some Web sites consciously block access to certain platforms and browsers, whether out of spite or incompatibility worries. Under the Debug menu, choose the User Agent option, and tell the Internet what browser you want to masquerade as, even Internet Explorer for Windows (Windows MSIE 6.0). Other neat options are the ability to display a window with all of Safari's keyboard and mouse shortcuts, and to manually import bookmarks from another Web browser.

Searching the Internet

Google, though a popular favorite, is not the only search engine in town. Here are a few more, along with their URLs, to get the searches going:

✦ **Teoma** at `www.teoma.com`

✦ **Vivísimo** at `www.vivisimo.com`

- ✦ **WiseNut** at `www.wisenut.com`

- ✦ **Daypop** at `www.daypop.com`

- ✦ **Yahoo!** at `www.yahoo.com`

- ✦ **Excite** at `www.excite.com`

- ✦ **InfoSeek** at `infoseek.go.com`

- ✦ **Lycos** at `www.lycos.com`

- ✦ **AltaVista** at `www.altavista.com`

- ✦ **Northern Light** at `www.northernlight.com`

- ✦ **Ask Jeeves** at `www.ask.com`

- ✦ **Metacrawler** at `www.metacrawler.com`

Internet search engines all use different methodologies for searching, so the same search with different engines will likely yield different results. Google's accuracy is derived from its underpinnings; it displays results partly based on a Web site's frequency of access.

Apple's included application, Sherlock, provides a unique method of searching the Internet, by gathering information without having to actually launch a Web browser and view a Web page, and by providing a GUI (Graphical User Interface) for the Internet. More on Sherlock in Chapter 7. Other non-Web browsers that use the Internet to access information are OmniDictionary (`www.omnigroup.com`) and Watson (`http://karelia.com`).

The explosion in the number and popularity of Web pages has spawned a corresponding increase in the number of search sites. These sites use different methods for collecting and displaying pages. Sites such as Yahoo! are primarily directories; Yahoo! lists Web sites, organized hierarchically by category, that have been submitted by Web site developers and manually reviewed by Yahoo!'s staff. Other popular search sites, such as Google and AltaVista, use *robots* or *spiders* to automatically crawl through the Web and gather information, which is collected in a database and made available for searching via keywords or phrases. Many robot-driven sites also feature part of their database of Web sites in directory-style lists of links, for those users who prefer browsing rather than searching on keywords. The directory-style sites take advantage of the automated sites' technology as well. As of this writing, if a search turns up nothing in Yahoo!'s categories, Yahoo! automatically forwards the search to Google.

All Web sites need to pay the bills, and search sites are no exception. In addition to the usual banner advertisements, many search sites are becoming *portals,* which provide not only search functionality but also links to online shopping, weather, news, and just about any other kind of information they think you might need. The search sites partner with other providers, such as online bookstores. You can continue your search for information or products at that provider's site.

Don't be disappointed if a favorite site of yours doesn't show up in searches. It takes awhile for automated robots to crawl through the billions of pages on the Web, and directory sites make editorial decisions about which sites to include.

AOL Is Not the Internet

America Online deserves special mention here. It's an interesting concept, and a unique case. Instead of separating your ISP, your Web browser, your email, your text chatting, and your content into separate entities, AOL is all these things combined. With an EarthLink dial-up connection, EarthLink connects you to the Internet, but you browse the Web with Safari. You check your email with Entourage. You chat with iChat, and you search with Google. AOL, however, *is* your ISP. When you open the AOL application, *they* dial you up. AOL is *also* your Web browser, *and* your chat application. While this sounds okay, the downside stems from the fact that AOL *also* provides you with their own content. This content is *not* the World Wide Web. It's stuff that AOL generates; and because they make money when you view it, they try to keep you in their world as much as possible, and it's not the same thing as being truly on the Web. You can, however, use AOL as *just* your ISP, your connector, and use another browser, email program, and so on, just like you normally might, with a non-AOL type of connection.

It's easy to feel trapped by AOL. It's your email address, your screen name, and it's a pain to give that up. The good news is that AOL offers a little-known plan called the bring your own access plan, where you can pay AOL a small monthly fee to retain your AOL world, without using them as your ISP, that is, to dial you up. For example, if you have a cable connection, you can use AOL as your email application by telling AOL to *not* dial you up and to connect instead over your cable service.

AOL *does* have some plusses. They have local dial-up access numbers in some of the remotest areas on the globe (Siberia!), so if you travel a lot, an AOL account can be very handy. It also provides a level of content filtering, for blocking offensive material. The point is that AOL is okay to use, just don't be fooled: AOL is not the Internet.

Sending and Receiving Email

Although not as flashy as the Web, electronic mail is the most popular reason people use the Internet. Email lets you communicate with people all over the world. Unlike regular mail, your correspondents can be reading your messages within second after you send them, no matter whether the recipients are across the street or halfway around the world.

Mac OS X includes an email application simply named Mail (also called Mail.app, pronounced "mail-dot-app" to distinguish its application status), and it has an icon in the Dock for easy one-click access. With Mail you can check mail from multiple Internet email accounts, send and receive messages formatted with styled text and embedded pictures, and set up rules to automatically filter your mail based on content. Mail even has Safari's KHTML rendering engine built right in, which will display HTML-formatted email easily.

Setting up email information and preferences

Before Mail can send and receive email for you, it must know your email address, password, and other information. If you've preconfigured a .Mac account, either by using the Setup Assistant or via the Internet Preferences pane, then Mail should open and begin to check said account. If not, then the first time you open Mail, it displays a dialog asking you to enter the necessary information (shown in Figure 6-31).

Selecting an Email Application

Although Mac OS X includes the Mail application, you don't have to use it. You may prefer to stick with another email application that you're already using, or your company may require that you use a particular application. Email applications have their respective strength and weaknesses. Mail has an excellent junk-mail filtering capability. Microsoft's Entourage is great all-around, but isn't free. Other email apps include Eudora, Mulberry, Netscape, Mozilla, Thunderbird, and Zoe. If you access an exchange server, you'll need that capability built in—both Entourage and Mail.app include this feature-set.

Figure 6-31: The first time you launch Mail, you are asked to type in your email settings.

Here's the email information that Mail needs so it can send and receive your email:

✦ **Full Name:** The name you want people to see in their inbox when you send them an email.

✦ **Email Address:** The address where people send you email, for example: warren@ notmyrealemailaddress.com.

✦ **Incoming Mail Server:** The Internet name for the server from which Mail receives your email, for example: pop.earthlink.net.

✦ **Account Type:** This is determined by the provider of your email account, as explained in the sidebar "POP versus IMAP Email." Choose the Exchange option if your email is provided by an exchange server. Exchange servers are usually reserved for business email, especially if you're in a Windows environment; if you use one, you usually know. Average users, don't worry about this.

✦ **User Name:** This item is usually the first part of your email address (the part before the @ symbol). In some cases, it might be different, so check if you are unsure.

✦ **Password:** This item is optional here. If you omit the password here, you must enter it every time you open Mail. But you are less likely to forget it if you need to check your mail from another computer and no one else will be able to get your email if you let them use your Mac OS X account.

✦ **Outgoing Mail Server (SMTP):** The Internet name for the computer through which Mail sends your email, for example: `smtp.earthlink.net`.

After the above information is entered, Mail will verify the information by trying to contact your email servers. If this fails, you will be given a warning asking you to double-check your information. If it still won't go through properly, Mail lets you continue anyway, but warns you that you won't be able to send or receive mail. If you don't know the information that Mail needs, check with your Internet service provider or other organization that provides your email service, such as Apple for a .Mac account, or EarthLink if you've got an EarthLink address. Don't forget to make sure that your Mac has a valid Internet connection while setting up Mail.

When Mail opens for the first time, it asks you if you want to import any email from a previous email application. If you choose yes, you will be walked through this process, which involves telling Mail what your old email application was, and finding its relevant information. Entourage, Eudora, and Netscape are all importable to Mail. Don't sweat it if you've skipped, or want to skip this step: you can choose to import old email at any time, by choosing to Import Mailboxes... under the File menu.

Also, after Mail is open, you can add additional email accounts; having more than one is common for lots of people nowadays. Choose Preferences under the Mail menu, and click on the accounts section. Click the plus sign button on the bottom of the window to add another account. To update or add information to an existing account, highlight its name in the column and click away at the options, as shown in Figure 6-32.

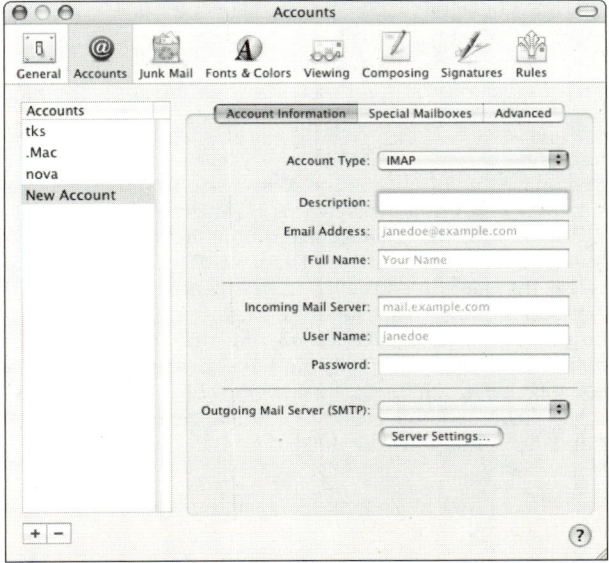

Figure 6-32: Customize your account in Mail's preferences.

The Preferences window includes many other settings. Under the General section is where you tell OS X what its default email application is — so even if you don't use Mail, you'll still need to configure this here. Use the Junk Mail area to heavily customize how Mail deals with Junk Mail, or Spam. It can be turned off, or tweaked to very complicated levels. Mail's fonts and colors can be played with here, as well as settings concerning Mail's column views, what happens when you compose an email, and configuring a signature and rules for messages.

Using Mail's viewer window

After your email information is set up, Mail displays a viewer window. It has a toolbar at the top, a list of messages below, and a message preview area at the bottom. A panel on the right side of the window lists mailboxes, which contain your messages (shown in Figure 6-33).

POP versus IMAP Email

The provider of your email account may let you set it up as a POP account or an IMAP account. With a POP account (Post Office Protocol), you transfer (download) your incoming messages from the POP server on the provider's computer to the Mail application's database on your computer's hard drive. Normally, your messages are deleted from the server after they have been transferred to your computer. Call your computer "Mac A." This means that if you then check your email from a second computer (call it "Mac B"), the new messages that just showed up on the original computer (Mac A) will not show up on the second (Mac B), because they have been removed from the provider's computer and are now only on Mac A. To help alleviate this disappearing email problem, now that many people check their email from more than one machine, most email programs let you choose to leave your POP messages on the server. Because the messages are still on the server, after they are checked, Mac A and Mac B will both get the messages. Doing this can, however, be quite hazardous to your email health, manifested by messages never, ever being deleted from the server, not for years and years. It's often not obvious, but deleting a message from your inbox will often not actually delete it from the server, and messages that might not appear in any of your inboxes will sit on the server anyway. Guarding against this requires maintenance: the best thing you can do is have your email program automatically delete messages from the server after a certain period of time.

Does all that sound like pain in the rear? Enter IMAP, the Internet Message Access Protocol. With an IMAP account, all the mail is stored on the server, all the time. Mail is also stored on your computer, all the time, in fact, your computer and the IMAP server stay synchronized; they mirror each other. If you delete a message from your computer, it's deleted from the server as well. This means that you can configure any number of computers to read your IMAP mail, and your inbox will look the same each time. Messages that have been replied to or forwarded will continue to show up that way, on machines that you didn't actually send the message from. Furthermore, you can also store other folders on the server, so that items like drafts or sent messages are always present. IMAP is often defaulted to downloading only the email headers (subject lines) until you specify to read an entire message. While it makes for a fast inbox download, you can get stuck if you're offline and haven't fully downloaded a message that you need to read. And of course, if you accidentally delete your entire inbox, it will be deleted from the server too, and any of your other computers, when they connect.

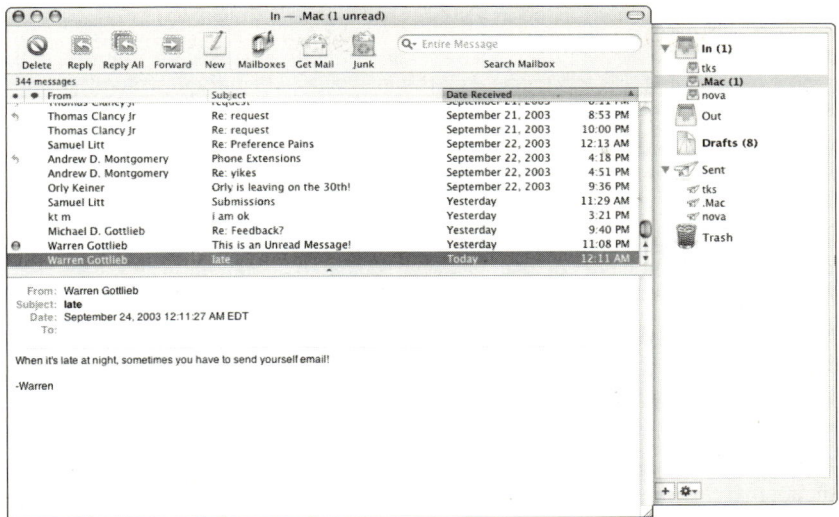

Figure 6-33: Mail's main window. Notice the toolbar, the mailboxes drawer, and the one unread message.

To see a list of messages in any mailbox, select the mailbox by clicking its name in the mailbox pane. If you see only the message "No mailbox is selected" in the title bar of the Mail window, it means that nothing is selected. If you have more than one account set up, you'll see a disclosure triangle next to the inbox, and in some cases the other folders. Instead of lumping all your messages from multiple accounts into one inbox, Mail gives you the option to view them each separately, by selecting each of the individual mini-inboxes independently. If you want to see everything at once, do click on the main inbox icon. Use the plus button to add a folder to the list. If you've got an IMAP account, you have the option of storing the folder on the server, or on your Mac, as shown in Figure 6-34. Use folders for organization and for storage. Click the action button for general control, like creating new message, or taking an account on- or offline manually. Mail shows the status of your connection right below the toolbar. Normally it displays the number of messages and the size of your inbox, or folder. When Mail senses that your computer has lost its Internet connection, it will change to read Offline.

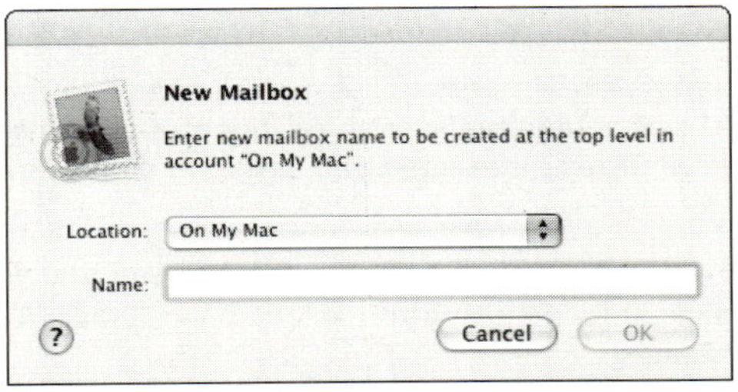

Figure 6-34: If you've got an IMAP account, Mail gives you the option to save a folder on the server, or locally on your Mac, as shown here.

You can work with the messages listed in a viewer window as follows:

✦ **Preview a listed message.** Clicking a message in the list displays its contents in the preview pane. Doing this will cause an IMAP message to be fully downloaded, and change status to "read" if the message was new.

✦ **Select messages in the list.** Click any information listed for a message. Command-click additional messages to select them also, or Shift-click to select a range of messages. After messages are selected they can be dragged into different folders.

✦ **Search the messages.** Type in the toolbar's Search box and use the adjacent pop-up menu to specify which part of each message to search. If Mail finds messages that meet your search criteria, it lists only those messages.

✦ **Resize the list and preview areas.** Drag the divider bar at the bottom of the list up or down.

✦ **Hide or show the message preview area.** Double-click the divider bar at the bottom of the list.

✦ **Sort the list by a column.** Click a column heading. The heading becomes highlighted to indicate that it is the sort key. Click the highlighted column heading to switch between forward and reverse sort order. Alternatively, you can choose a sort column and direction from the Sort submenu of the View menu.

✦ **Rearrange columns.** Drag a column heading left or right to move the column.

✦ **Resize columns.** Drag a column heading's right borderline left or right to make the column narrower or wider.

✦ **Show or hide columns.** In the View menu, choose the appropriate command to show or hide the Number, Flags, Contents, or Message Sizes columns. The Read Status, From, and Date & Time columns always appear. The Buddy Availability column will bullet messages whose sender is signed into iChat, if they are in your address book.

✦ **See more or fewer columns at once.** Click the window's Zoom button or resize the window.

Receiving mail

To get your mail, click the Get Mail button at the top of the viewer window, in the toolbar (or choose Get New Mail from the Mailbox menu). If you want to monitor the progress, choose Window ⇨ Activity Viewer. You can also have Mail check for new mail automatically by setting how often you want this to happen in the Accounts section of Mail's Preferences dialog.

The number of unread messages appears in parentheses next to the mailbox name in the mailbox panel. Unread messages are marked with a blue bullet in the list of messages below the buttons in a viewer window. The number of unread messages also appears superimposed, in red, on the Mail icon in the Dock.

You can read a message in the preview area at the bottom of a viewer window, but you won't have to scroll as much if you open the message in its own window. To read a message in its own window, double-click it in the list of messages.

Composing messages

Of course, receiving messages is only half the fun. Mail gives you several options for dealing with your email correspondence. You can reply to messages you receive, forward them to other people, or compose new messages.

Replying to messages

To reply to a message you are reading, click the Reply button or the Reply All button at the top of the window. Reply and Reply All both create a new message. Reply addresses the new message only to the sender, and Reply All addresses the new message to the sender and everyone else who received the original message. Instead of clicking these buttons, you can choose equivalent commands from the Message menu.

The new message appears in a separate window. It has the same subject as the original message, except that "Re:" is prefixed to the reply subject. The body of the reply includes the text of the original message.

Type your reply message above the original message, and click the Send button (or choose Message ⇨ Send Message) to send your message flying to its destination. If you've got the sound on, there's a satisfying rocket-swoosh that accompanies a sent message.

Note   When replying to a message, especially a long one, it's generally considered good *netiquette* (etiquette on the Internet) to trim the text of the original message down to the essentials. You can adjust how the text from the original message appears in the Fonts & Colors section of Mail's Preferences dialog.

Forwarding messages

Forwarding a message sends a message that you have received to somebody else. If you've got to share a message with someone, click the Forward button at the top of the window (or choose Message ⇨ Forward Message). The original message appears in a new window, with "Fwd:" prefixed to the subject. You need to supply the email address of the person to whom you are forwarding the message. You may want to add some introductory text above the forwarded message. Click the Send button (or choose Message ⇨ Send Message) to send the message on its way.

Composing new messages

To compose a new message, as shown in Figure 6-35, click the Compose button at the top of a viewer window or choose File ⇨ New Compose Window.. Type each recipient's email address separated by commas on the To line. On the Cc (carbon copy) line, add any additional recipients who should receive a copy of the message (but aren't necessarily expected to reply). Type a subject on the Subject line and type the message in the bottom pane. If you want to get fancy, you can select different text styles, colors, and fonts from the Format menu. When you're done, click Send.

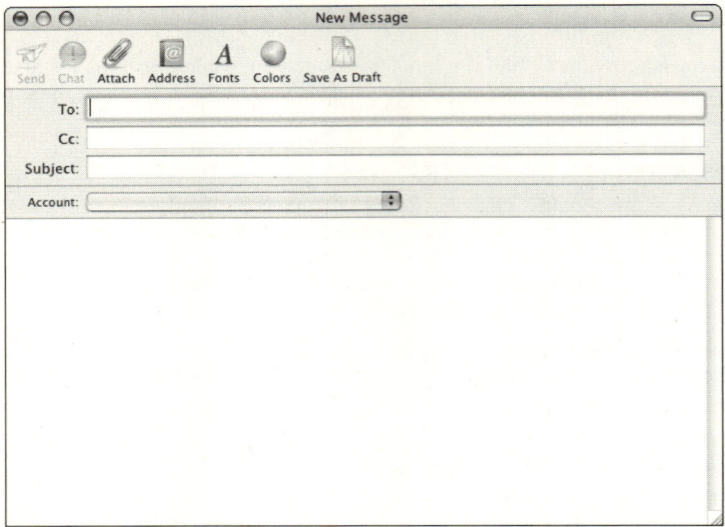

Figure 6-35: A new message (click on the Compose button) looks like this.

Tip   Mail remembers the addresses of people to whom you have recently sent email. When you start to type an address on the To line, Mail autocompletes the address for you or provides a drop-down list if more than one address matches what you're typing. If you don't want to use Mail's suggested address, just type over it. Mail also makes addresses draggable items — you can drag addresses, even from the body of an email text, into any of the sending fields that you wish.

Note   By default, Mail uses Rich Text Format (RTF) to compose messages so that you can send messages with styled text and inset pictures. Not all email programs can read this format, however. To change the format of an individual message, choose Make Plain Text from the Format menu when you are composing the message. If you know most of the people you send email to use email programs that don't support formatted messages, you may want to change your preferred message format to plain text. Choose Mail ⇨ Preferences, click Composing, and choose Plain Text from the Default message format pop-up menu.

Using the Address Book

The Mail application is linked to the Address Book application, which you can use to store frequently used email addresses and related contact information (such as phone numbers and birthdays). You can access the Address Book data by choosing Address Panel from the Window menu or by clicking the Address button in a message composition window. The Address Book can contain individual contacts, also know as virtual address cards (V-cards), and groups of contacts. Mail, along with applications like iChat and iCal, directly interfaces with the Address Book without actually launching the application, it instead accesses its database and reads the information. You can either choose the person's name or group contact from the address list, as shown in Figure 6-36, or just start typing the name into the address field in your email, and the person will pop up. More on the address book in Chapter 18.

Modifying Toolbars in Mail

Many windows in the Mail application have toolbars, and these toolbars normally have buttons and other items displayed as icons with names. You can hide a toolbar or modify it in other ways by using the toolbar's contextual menu or a toolbar item's contextual menu. (You can display the toolbar's contextual menu by Control-clicking the toolbar, and you can display a toolbar item's contextual menu by Control-clicking the item.) You can modify the toolbars in Mail as follows:

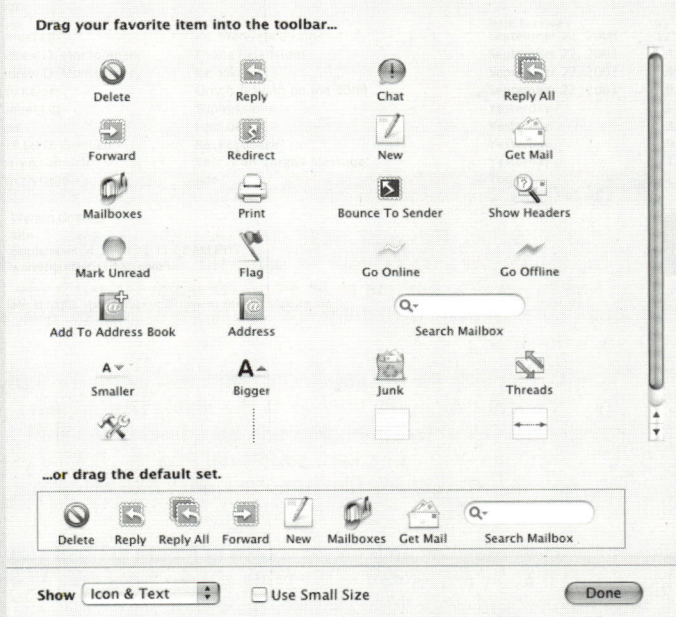

✦ **Hide the toolbar, or show it if it is hidden.** Click the lozenge-shaped toolbar button in the upper-right corner of the window.

✦ **Show items as icons with names, icons only, or names only.** Choose the style you want from the toolbar's contextual menu, or ⌘-click the lozenge-shaped toolbar button in succession to view all the different options.

✦ **Add items.** Choose Customize Toolbar from the toolbar's contextual menu, or from the View menu, or ⌘-Option-click the lozenge-shaped toolbar button. Either action displays a dialog that contains items you can drag into the toolbar.

✦ **Remove items.** Choose Remove Item from the button's contextual menu. Alternatively, ⌘-drag an item away from the toolbar to see it vanish in a puff of smoke. If the Customize Toolbar dialog is displayed (as described in "Add items." in this list), you don't have to press Command to drag an item away from the toolbar.

✦ **Move items.** ⌘-drag an item right or left to a different place on the toolbar. If the Customize Toolbar dialog is displayed (as described in "Add items." in this list), you don't have to press ⌘ to drag an item to another place on the toolbar.

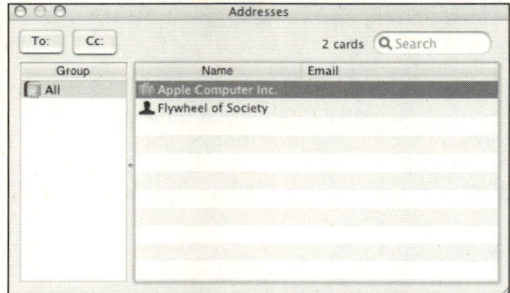

Figure 6-36: Choose an address from your Address Book by clicking the address button in the messages' toolbar.

Sending email attachments

In addition to text messages, you can send files with your email messages. Documents, archives of multiple files (which you can create in the Finder by using the Archive command), and other programs and files can be sent as attachments to an email message by using special protocols. Sending files as attachments can be useful if you'd like to send, for example, a Word document or a picture to somebody.

Adding an attachment in Mail is simple; just look for the paper clip. With new email (or reply email) open in its window, click the Attach button in the toolbar. In the dialog that appears, select the file you want to attach, and click Open. To attach multiple files, hold down Shift while selecting each one before clicking Open. You can attach additional files by clicking the Attach button again. Alternatively, you can just drag any file from the Finder into an open composition window, and Mail will attach the file.

Your attachment is represented in your message by an icon, as shown in Figure 6-37). If you select a picture to attach, that picture may be embedded in the body of your message. When you send the email message, attachments and embedded pictures go with it.

Note   It's generally considered good netiquette to send an attachment only to recipients who expect it or would want it. Large files can cause trouble when sent through email, whether it be the time it takes to download over a slow connection, or size limit restrictions imposed by someone's email service provider.

Receiving attachments

When you receive a message containing an attachment, you see the icon of the attachment in the body of the message. If the attachment is a multimedia file (picture, sound, or video clip), you may see it embedded in the body of the message, depending on the format of the attached file. Double-click the icon or single-click the name to open the attachment. Control-clicking brings up a menu with the option to save the attachment to your hard drive, as opposed to just opening it. You can also drag an attachment icon or embedded picture from the body of the email message to the Desktop or a Finder window to save the file.

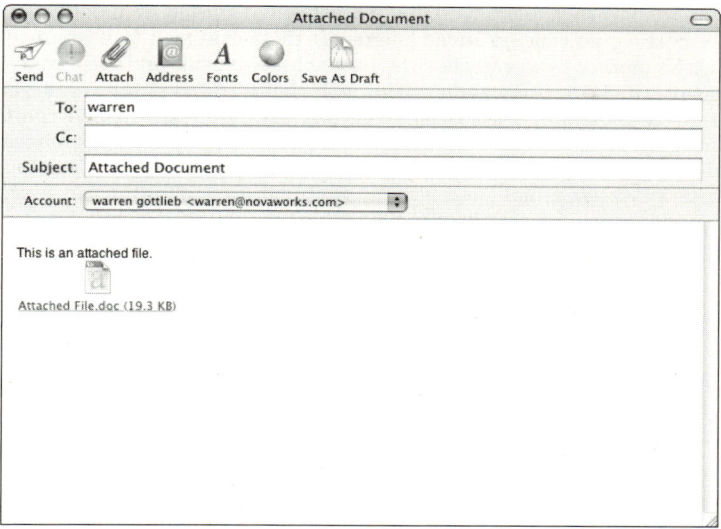

Figure 6-37: Mail displays attachments that you are sending inline with the text of the email.

 Note

In the Windows world, opening emails and their attachments is a risky business; it's the most common way for a virus to be transmitted to a computer. Companies invest millions in email and virus protection. The top selling software for Windows machines are Virus protection utilities. Because most viruses are actually mini-Windows applications, on a Mac, they are completely harmless, and can't harm your computer. Viruses that Macs catch are called Word macro viruses and come in the form of infected Microsoft Word documents. If you transfer a lot of these files with Windows users, some virus protection software like Symantec's Norton AntiVirus is a good idea.

Junk mail

Junk mail in the form of email, or spam, stinks. It clogs up your inbox. It forces you to see offensive material. Worst of all, when your email application beeps to inform you of your new message, it's a false alarm, just an advertisement for augmenting... something. Spammers can retrieve your email address from many places: anywhere you've posted it on the Web is searchable, and they'll find it. Anything you've subscribed to or signed up for has probably sold a list with your name on it, to spammers. The only way to completely rid yourself of spam is to get a new email address, but this isn't an option, or is just too inconvenient, for most. Because of the back-door techniques spammers use, there's no real way of stopping them... yet. Even so, most email providers, even free ones like Yahoo! mail (`http://mail.yahoo.com`), have some protection. But it's often not enough, and the junk still makes it to the inbox in droves.

Mail provides protection at the inbox level, that is, it employs a filter that identifies messages as junk before they make it there. Mail's junk mail filter starts off in *Training Mode*. Under training mode, a message that Mail thinks is junk appears in brown in your inbox, and has a header displayed with the message telling you that it has been identified as junk (shown in Figure 6-38). If Mail is correct, you can go ahead and delete the message. If Mail is not correct (a situation called a *false-positive*) you can click the button for Not Junk, and Mail will categorize it as a regular email. The great thing about the filter, is that it learns. After a while, its accuracy should be pretty good, and it shouldn't be getting any false positives. When this is the case, you can switch from Training Mode to Automatic mode (under the Preferences) by telling Mail to put all its junk mail in a special junk mail inbox, and you shouldn't see too much junk mail in your inbox after that. For advanced customization, click the Advanced button in the Junk Mail preferences to manually edit the junk rules (shown in Figure 6-39).

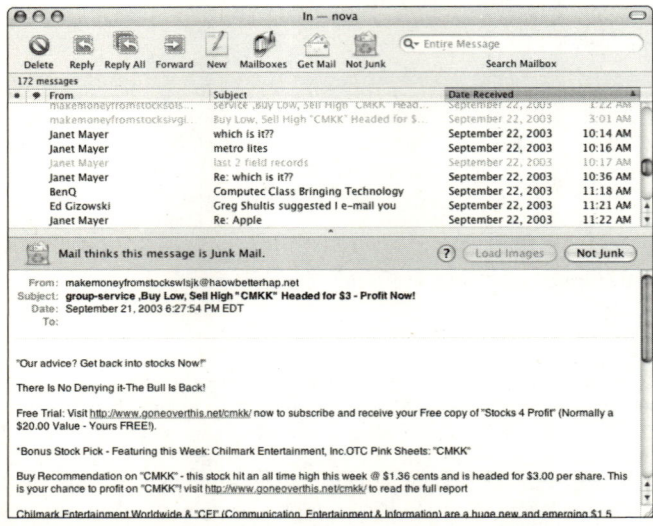

Figure 6-38: Mail thinks this is a junk-mail message.

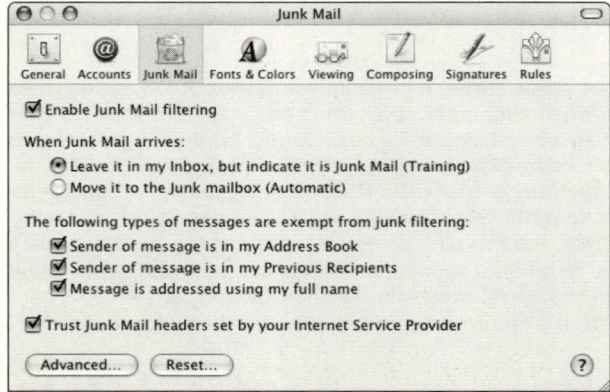

Figure 6-39: Change the junk-mail filter from training mode to automatic by choosing the option in the junk-mail preferences.

If you've been clicking on all those "take-me-off-your-list-and-you'll-never-get-spam-again" links at the bottom of your junk mails, congrats-you've just informed the spammer that there is a warm body at the end of your email address, and inadvertently subscribed to even more junk mail. In most cases, spam comes from a fake address, meaning you can't reply to it. If the address is legitimate, Mail provides a way of *bouncing* the message back to the sender; on the spammer side it appears that your email address is not a valid one, and you might get taken off of the list. To enable easy bouncing, customize the toolbar to show the Bounce button. To bounce a message to the sender, click the Bounce button while the offending message is selected, heed the warning Mail gives you, and off it goes. If you get a message saying that you got a returned mail, the bounce didn't work.

Threading

One of the more frustrating organizational issues is to easily locate all the messages from a single email conversation. Mail incorporates a feature called *threading:* when any message in a conversation is selected, all the others are highlighted as well! You can turn this feature on or off in the View section of Mail's preferences as well as change the highlight color, as shown in Figure 6-40.

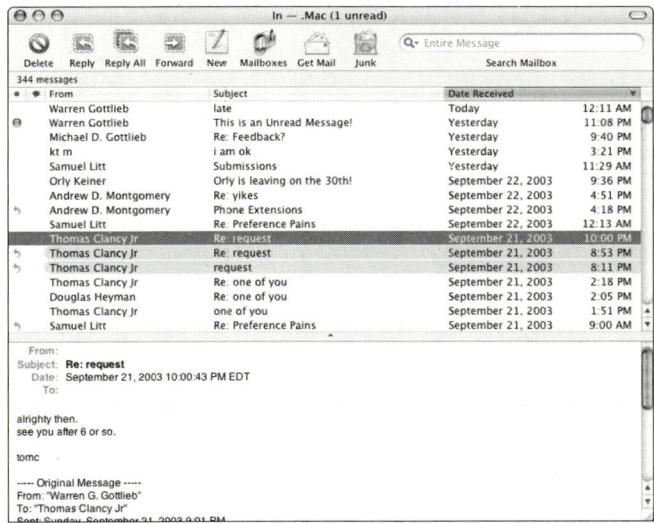

Figure 6-40: Selecting one message will subtly highlight other messages from the same email conversation.

Participating in Newsgroups

In addition to email and the Web, Usenet is another part of the Internet. You can think of Usenet as a worldwide bulletin board system, where people from everywhere can post messages and join discussions about subjects that interest them. Each subject is called a newsgroup. More than 25,000 newsgroups cover virtually every subject imaginable.

Finding newsgroups

To find a newsgroup that interests you, you have to know a little about the structure of newsgroup names. A newsgroup name has several parts separated by periods. The first part specifies the general subject, the next part narrows the subject, and subsequent parts narrow the subject still further. Table 6-1 shows the most common top-level newsgroup names, and Table 6-2 shows examples of full names of newsgroups.

Table 6-1: Common Top-Level Newsgroup Names

Identifier	Included subjects
alt	Subjects that don't fit into one of the other official categories
biz	Business
comp	Computers
misc	Miscellaneous subjects
news	News and other topical information
rec	Recreational hobbies and arts
sci	Scientific
soc	Social
talk	Debates

Table 6-2: Sample Full Names of Newsgroups

Newsgroup name	Subject
alt.tv.simpsons	Adventures in Springfield
comp.sys.mac.advocacy	Let's hear it for the Mac
rec.sport.triathlon	For the Iron man in all of us
sci.med.nutrition	Scrutinize your diet here

Accessing the news

You can find the newsgroup of your dreams using a variety of programs. Two Mac OS X newsreaders are Thoth, available at www.thothsw.com, and Microsoft's Entourage (which has a built in newsreader). You can also browse and search newsgroups from your Web browser by going to the Google Groups site (http://groups.google.com).

Summary

Mac OS X makes it easy to harness the incredible power of the Internet.

✦ Getting on the Internet with Mac OS X is simple. All it takes is a quick walk through the initial Mac OS X Setup Assistant.

✦ If you skip the Internet setup steps in the Setup Assistant, you can run it manually through the Network Preferences pane.

✦ After you've set up an Internet connection via cable modem, DSL, local network, or AirPort wireless, you're ready to browse the Web, get your email, and use other Internet services.

✦ Mac OS X provides easy means of making a Net connection, through the Internet Connect application, or the menu bar icons.

✦ Mac OS X includes Safari for browsing the Web, although other browsers are available.

✦ Mac OS X also includes an email application named Mail, which you can use to send, receive, and organize your email messages. Mail coordinates with the included Address Book application, which stores email addresses and other contact information.

✦ You can get on the Usenet and participate in the thousands of discussion groups that are available on nearly any topic imaginable. Two newsreader applications for Mac OS X are Thoth and Entourage.

✦   ✦   ✦

Searching with Find and Sherlock

Mac OS X includes two powerful tools to search for information: the Find command and the Sherlock application. Find searches for files or folders on your disks, and Sherlock searches the Internet for information.

In either case, a search can be extremely simple or very sophisticated. For example, Find can simply search for a file by name, or it can search by a complex combination of over a dozen other attributes, such as date, size, and kind. Find can also search for text inside documents.

When it comes to searching the Internet, Sherlock can search one site or a group of related sites, such as popular Web search engines (About, Lycos, LookSmart, and so on), people-search sites, reference sites, auction sites, and many others.

This chapter explains the uses of the Find command and Sherlock.

Searching for Files and Folders

No matter how carefully you organize your folders and disks, the time will come when you can't find a file or folder without a lot of digging through layers of folders. The Find command fetches lost or buried items with less effort. Using Find, you can search by name, text content, or a combination of name, content, and other criteria, such as file size or modification date. You determine which folders and volumes (disks) Find searches. When a search ends, Find displays a list of the files, folders, and volumes that match your search criteria. You can do a lot with items on this list, including seeing folder locations, opening them, and putting them in the Trash.

Searching by name

Searching for files, folders, and volumes by name is a simple matter. You specify the name or part of the name you want to find and where you want Find to look for it.

There are two ways to search using Find — by using the stand-alone Find window and by using the Search field in the Finder window toolbar.

Finder window Search

In Mac OS 10.3, every Finder window has a built-in Search field in its toolbar. Refer to Figure 7-1 for an example.

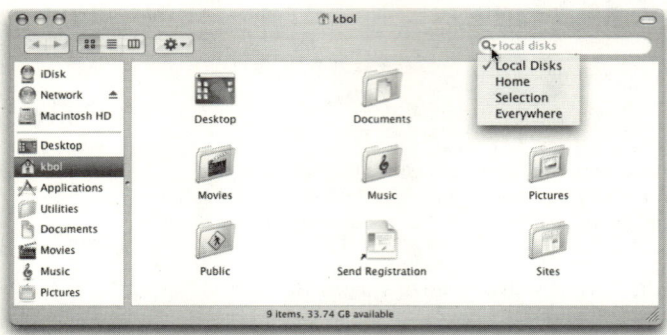

Figure 7-1: Every Finder window includes a Search field in its toolbar.

If the toolbar is hidden, show it by clicking the lozenge-shaped button in the upper-right corner of the window. If the window is not wide enough to display the Search field in the toolbar, click the double-arrowhead at the right end of the toolbar and select Search from the pop-up menu, as shown in Figure 7-2, to display the Find window shown in Figure 7-3.

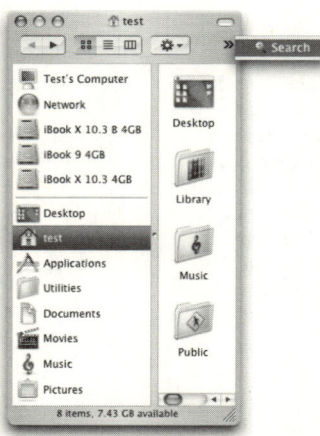

Figure 7-2: Narrow Finder windows place the Search command in a pop-up menu on the right side of the toolbar.

By default, the Search field contains the words "local disks" in gray, denoting where the search will take place, as shown in Figure 7-1. Clicking on the magnifying glass icon just to the left will show a pop-up menu with other locations you can choose for the search: home, selection, and everywhere (explained in more detail later in the chapter). Your selection will appear in the Search field in gray.

To enter text into the Search field, click inside it to make the search location selection disappear, and a flashing insertion point appears. Then type the name you are searching for.

As you type the first letter, changes start to happen:

✦ Items containing that letter begin to appear, listed in the large pane of the window.

✦ An icon of a white *X* in a gray circle appears on the right of the Search field; clicking this clears the search results from the large pane.

✦ In the middle of the bottom of the window, Find tells you how many places are being searched and how many items have been found.

✦ In the lower right of the window, you may see (if the search takes long enough) the clock icon spinning to show Find is working.

✦ To the right of the clock initially appears a tiny white counterclockwise arrow in a gray circle, which can be clicked to halt the search. As you type the second letter, this halt arrow icon turns into an *X* that more properly symbolizes its function.

With each successive letter typed, Find narrows its search. When the search is done, the clock in the lower right disappears, and the halt *X* icon in the lower right turns back into a clockwise arrow; clicking on it will perform the search again. If you add new letters to the field, the search begins again. If you subtract letters, the list alters to reflect the change.

The Find command and window

To see a Find window, as shown in Figure 7-3, first click anywhere on the desktop or on the Finder icon in the Dock to switch the active application to the Finder; then use the File ➪ Find command. The keyboard shortcut Command-F opens the Find window.

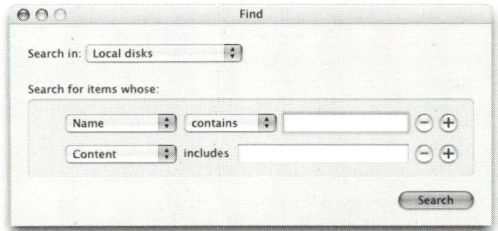

Figure 7-3: Use the Find window to search for files.

The Find window is set up by default to quickly perform a file search by name on all local disks. Follow these steps:

1. **Open the Find window.**

2. **In the first text field, enter the name or part of the name that you want to find.** To enter text in the text box, you can click inside the box or press Tab as needed to place an insertion point in the box. If the box already contains text from a previous search request, pressing Tab selects this text so that you can replace it simply by typing.

It doesn't matter how you capitalize the name or partial name that you type. Find considers the lowercase and uppercase forms of letters to be the same; *ReadMe* is the same as *readme, Readme,* or *README.*

3. **Click the Search button or press Return to begin the search.**

Looking at found items

When you click the Search button, the Search Results window immediately opens, showing the list of items as they are found. If your search lasts long enough, you may see the clock icon spinning in the top right. To its right, you see the counter-clockwise arrow icon; click it to halt the search.

When the clock icon disappears, the search is complete, and the window appears as shown in Figure 7-4. Find displays the total number of items it found just below the window's title bar. If Find doesn't find any items that match the name you specify, the message "No items were found" appears here.

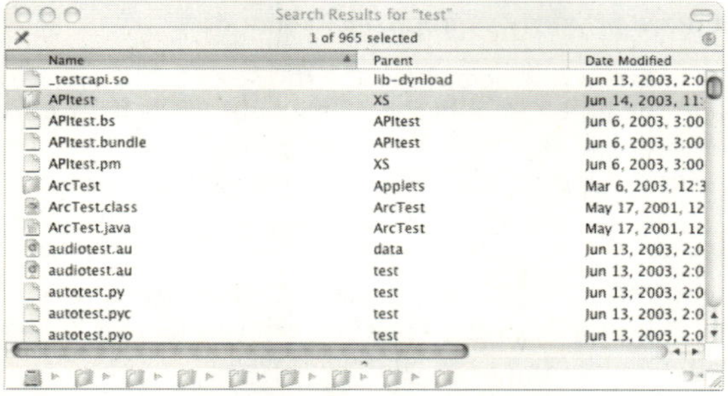

Figure 7-4: Search results display in a separate Search Results window.

You can scroll through the list of found items to see if it includes the file or folder you are seeking.

If you see a likely item, click it once to see its folder location path appear in the information area at the bottom of the Search Results window. New in Mac OS 10.3, by default this path is shown as a single row of folders separated by arrowheads, starting with drive icon on the left and ending with the selected item on the right. You can view the name of a folder by positioning your cursor over it. You can also expand the information area to see the path represented in two other ways, first with the names of each item showing, and then as you make the area bigger, with each item listed below the item enclosing it and indented to the right. (These path-viewing options are shown and described in greater detail later in this chapter.)

Double-click any item in the list of searchable sources or any item in the information area to open the item. If you double-click a folder, a new Finder window opens to display the folder's contents. If you double-click an application, it launches or opens. If you double-click a document file, the associated application launches or opens and displays the document contents in a window.

You can do other things with files and folders in the found items list, such as find other items that are similar to one of the found items. We discuss these options later in this chapter, under the heading "Working with Found Files and Folders."

Stopping and restarting a search

You may happen to specify a search that takes a long time to complete, and you may realize you don't want to wait any more, especially if you already see what you are looking for. You can stop the search by clicking the small round gray button just below the lozenge-shaped toolbar button in the upper right of the Search Results window. As noted previously, this button contains a counter-clockwise arrow as the search is occurring. If you stop the search, and click this button again to restart it, the arrow is replaced by an *X*. When the search is complete, the *X* reverts back to the arrow icon.

Yes, this button behavior is slightly different from the similar button behavior that appears in a Finder window if you use it to do a search, as described previously. If you find this discrepancy a little strange, be assured you are not alone! It must have made sense to the developers.

If you stop a search in progress, Find displays the list of items it found before you stopped the search.

Revising or repeating a search

If you want to repeat a search and possibly revise the name to search for or the sources to search, click the Find window behind the Search Results window to bring the Find window to the front. To expand your search, shorten the name entered in Find's text box or turn on more searchable sources. To narrow your search, lengthen the name to search for or turn off some sources.

Searching in Particular Folders

Initially, the Find command is set to search "Everywhere," which includes your home folder and the storage volumes connected to your computer, such as its internal hard drive, CD-ROM, and external disks connected to the computer's ports. You may be searching entire disks when all you need to search is a folder or two.

Adding a folder to the Find command

If you want to search only in particular folders (including these folders' enclosed folders and files) you can add these folders to the list of searchable sources in the Find command. Then you can turn on only the particular folders in the list that you want to search. If you turn on only one folder, Find searches only that folder. If you turn on multiple folders in the list of searchable sources, Find searches all of the folders.

 Note   When Find searches a folder, it must visit each item that the folder contains. When searching an entire volume, Find can quickly search a catalog of the volume's contents instead. Although an individual folder takes longer to search, you may not notice, unless the folder contains many items. The catalog is not something you can normally see; Mac OS X maintains it and makes it invisible to people using the computer.

To add a folder to the list of searchable sources, follow these steps:

1. **Open the Find window.**

2. **Choose Specific places from the pop-up menu, as shown in Figure 7-5.**

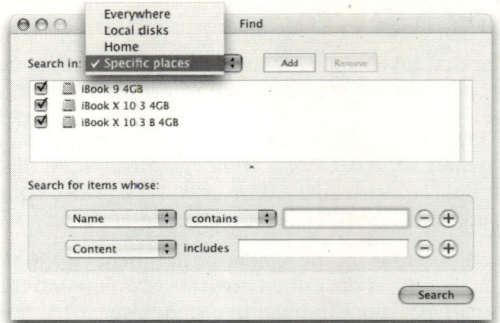

Figure 7-5: Choose "Specific places" from the Search In pop-up menu of the Find window.

3. **Click the Add button to the right of the Search In pop-up menu to show the Choose a Folder window shown in Figure 7-6.** As a shortcut, you can double-click the folder that you want to add.

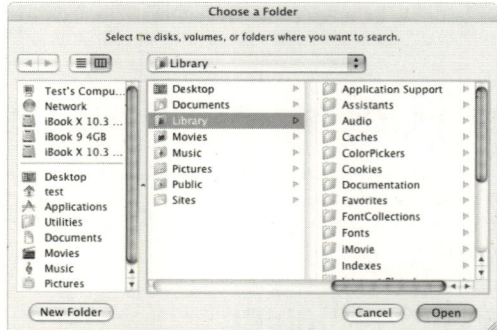

Figure 7-6: Select the folder you want to add to Find's list of searchable sources and then click Choose.

Mac OS X remembers these added places. The added places appear when you open Specific Places in the future.

In the Finder window, Search, a version of this Specific Places, option is available. It appears as Selection in the pop-up menu that opens when you click the magnifying glass icon in the Search field. With Selection chosen, Find searches the item or items you select. You can click once on a folder to select it or drag a rectangle around several folders. If you choose to do neither, Find will search the item selected in the Finder window sidebar.

Removing a folder from the Find command preferences

Not only can you add folders to the Find window's list of sources, but you can also remove folders from the list. To remove a folder from the list of searchable sources:

1. **Select one or more folders in the Find window's list of sources.** To select a folder, click its icon or name. Find highlights the folder's name and icon to indicate that it is selected. (The checkbox in the On column does not indicate whether a folder is selected for this purpose.)

   To select an additional folder, Command-click its icon or name. To select a range of folders, click the first one and then Shift-click the last one. You can also select a range of folders by dragging across their icons or names.

   Selecting a folder or folders enables the Remove button.

2. **Click the Remove button.** The selected folders are removed immediately. If you accidentally remove a folder, you can add it to the list again as described earlier.

Searching for Text in Files

Instead of searching for files by name, you can search the text contents of your document files. Find has the ability to look inside certain kinds of documents and search them for keywords. You don't have to laboriously open and search files one by one for the text information you want. By using Find, you can quickly and easily find the files that contain the information you seek. In addition, you can use Find to find a file when you don't remember its name but do remember what it contains.

What can Find search?

By necessity, Find can only search documents that contain text, and it can't get into every kind of document that contains text. In general, you'll have success searching the following kinds of documents:

✦ **Plain text documents,** such as those you can edit in the TextEdit application

✦ **HTML documents** are plain text documents with codes that are used to create Web pages.

✦ **PDF files** (Adobe's Portable Document Format)

✦ **Microsoft Word documents**

✦ **AppleWorks word processing documents**

✦ **WordPerfect documents**

✦ **Email** stored by Eudora, Outlook Express, and some other email applications

In addition to searching document contents for key words, Find also searches file, folder, and disk names for the same keywords.

Note   When searching the text contents of HTML and PDF documents, Find intelligently ignores the text-formatting commands that occur naturally throughout these documents. Special Text Extractor plug-in files make this possible. These plug-in files are in the Plugins folder at /System/Library/Find/Plugins/.

Specifying contents to find

Generally, you get the best results when searching by contents if you specify the least common keywords that you think will be in the documents that you want to find. If instead you specify common words that occur in many of your documents, the results of your search by contents will be a long list of mostly extraneous documents. To find the fewest extraneous documents, try to think of one or two unusual words that occur in only the documents that you want to find, and have Find search for those unusual words.

To search by contents, follow these steps:

1. **Open the Find window.**

2. **In the Content includes text field, enter the keywords that you want to find as shown in Figure 7-7.** To enter text, the text box must be selected. If necessary, you can accomplish this by clicking inside the box or pressing Tab as needed to place an insertion point in the box. If the box already contains text from a previous search request, pressing Tab selects this text so that you can replace it simply by typing.

   It doesn't matter how you capitalize keywords. Find is not case-sensitive, for example, *iMac* is the same as *imac, Imac,* or *IMAC.*

3. **Click the Search button or press Return to begin the search.**

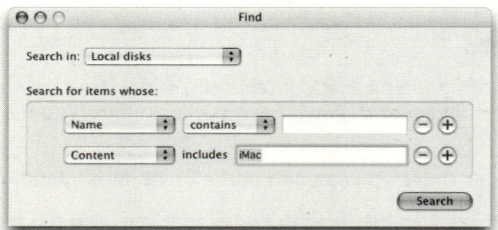

Figure 7-7: The Find window can search contents of several types of files in volumes of the computer that have been indexed.

Note   Find can search document contents only in folders and volumes (disks) that have been indexed. Indexing is described later in this chapter.

Looking at found documents

When Find finishes searching by contents, a list of the documents it has found is displayed. Find displays the number of documents it found below the list. If Find doesn't find any documents that match the keywords you specify, it displays a message to that effect.

Ranking the relevance of found documents

Find lists the found documents according to their relevance. A document's relevance is determined by how often the keywords occur in it and how close together they are in it. The more often the keywords occur and the closer their proximity, the higher the document's relevance. This method of evaluating relevance is not always 100 percent accurate. The document you're looking for may not have the very highest relevance. Even so, the document you want probably will be nearer the top of the list than the bottom. Find indicates the degree of each found document's relevance with the length of a bar in the list of found documents. The longer the bar, the more relevant Find judges a document to be. Figure 7-8 shows how Find ranks found documents by relevance when it displays the results of searching by contents.

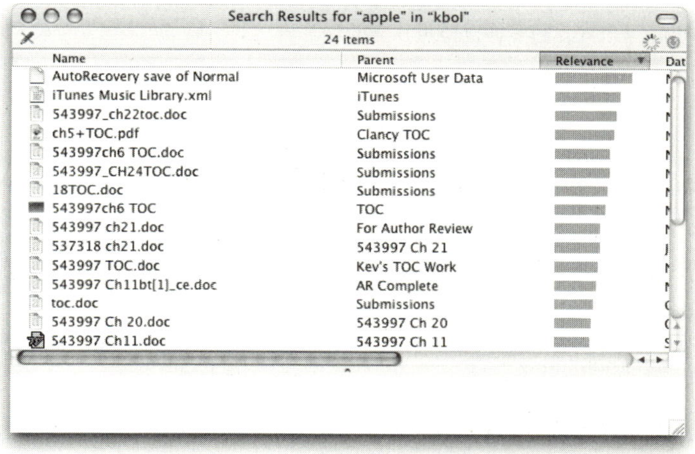

Figure 7-8: After searching by contents, Find ranks found documents by their relevance to the keywords.

Doing more with found documents

Aside from the relevance ranking, the list of found documents that results from a search by contents is similar to the list of found items that results from a search by name. If you click a listed document once, its folder location appears in the information area at the bottom of the Find window. Double-clicking a document opens it. You can discover what else you can do with files and folders in the found documents list, such as finding similar documents, later in this chapter.

Indexing folders

Searching the contents of documents seems almost magical but isn't. It requires some advanced preparation. Before Find can search document contents, it must index them. The Finder can create an index for each folder that you add to its list of searchable sources (as described earlier in this chapter). It stores each folder's index in an invisible file inside the folder. This file contains a database of words from the documents in the folder.

Given an index database, the Finder can determine whether the words in your search request exist in the indexed files by quickly searching the database. This search happens quickly because the database is much smaller than the aggregate length of the files it indexes. In addition, searching the index database is faster because the words in it are arranged in order. The first time you search a volume that is not indexed, Find begins by creating an index for that volume and then searching the index. Therefore, your first search of a new volume takes longer than any subsequent searches.

Note The Finder indexes only the first 2,000 unique words of each document to keep the index database file from becoming too large and bogging down searching by contents. Therefore, the Finder does not index all the words in a document that contains more than 2,000 unique words. The closer a unique word is to the end of such a long document, the less likely the Finder is to include it in the index. If the Finder doesn't index some words in a long document due to this limitation, you won't be able to find that document by searching for those words.

Creating indexes

The Finder initially indexes your home folder, and it automatically indexes other folders when you add them to the list of searchable sources. You can also have Find index some volumes, such as removable disks and network volumes, but it doesn't index entire volumes automatically. The Finder cannot index all folders and volumes.

Note Actually, the Finder does not prepare content indexes. It hands off this task to an application named ContentIndexing. ContentIndexing hides while it is operating and quits automatically when it finishes indexing. If you want to see ContentIndexing at work, open the Process Viewer application (in the Utilities folder) while the Finder is reporting that indexing is under way and look for ContentIndexing in Process Viewer's list of running processes.

What can and can't be indexed

The folders and volumes you index can be located on your computer, another computer on your network, or a network file server. To index a folder, you must have the privilege to save items in it.

Cross-Reference For more information about using folders from file servers and other computers on your network, see Chapter 10.

Find cannot index some types of folders and volumes because it cannot write (save) their index files. As you may expect, Find cannot write an index file on a write-protected disk, such as a CD-ROM or a locked Zip disk. What's more, Find cannot index a folder for which you do not have Write privilege, which is the privilege to make changes. Many such folders are on your Mac OS X startup disk. It's also common not to have Write privileges for folders from network file servers and other computers on your network.

Note Although you can't create an index on an existing CD-ROM, you may have CD-ROMs that are indexed. The index for such a CD-ROM was created in advance and recorded as part of the CD-ROM's contents. If you have a CD-R or CD-RW recorder, also known as a CD burner, you can provide a Find index for it by creating an index of the folder or disk whose contents will be recorded on the CD.

Tip You may be able to index a folder that Find says can't be indexed. Try logging in as a user who has administrator privileges and indexing again. If you still can't index the folder, log in as the root user (System Administrator) and try again. Note that Find maintains separate lists of searchable sources for each user. So any folders you add while logged in as one user you will have to add again after logging in as another user. We cover administrator and root user privileges in Chapter 14.

Updating indexes

The Finder updates indexes every time you search that folder or volume. Updating an index generally takes much less time than creating the index initially.

Find determines which indexes to update by going through the list of searchable sources. An index becomes out of date when you change the contents of an indexed document, add documents to an indexed folder or volume, or remove documents from an indexed folder or volume. Find can't search a folder accurately by contents if the folder's index is out-of-date. The more outdated an index is, the less accurate the search will be.

Manually updating or creating an index

You can manually update the index for any indexable folder or volume listed in the Files channel, or you can create the index for an indexable folder or volume that doesn't have one. Follow these steps to start indexing manually:

1. **Select the item you want to index by clicking its icon or name in a Finder window.**

2. **Choose File ⇨ Get Info.** The Get Info window appears as shown in Figure 7-9.

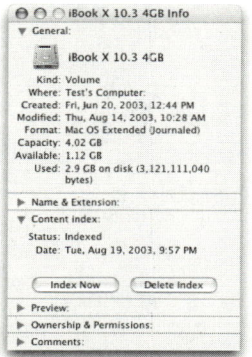

Figure 7-9: Indexes can be updated using the Content index pane of the Get Info window.

3. **Click the disclosure triangle to the right of the Content index pane to show the Content Index pane of the Get Info window.** The Content index pane displays.

4. **Click the Index Now button.** The index for the volume, folder, or disk is updated.

Indexing in the background

Indexing a folder or volume that contains many documents may take many minutes or even hours. You can let the Finder continue indexing in the background while you use the computer for other tasks. This background indexing is usually unobtrusive thanks to Mac OS X's preemptive multitasking.

Adjusting indexing speed and disk use

The speed at which the Finder creates and updates indexes depends on the number of languages it uses. The amount of disk space required for index files also depends on the number of languages. Fewer languages yield faster and smaller indexes.

To select which languages Find uses, follow these steps:

1. **Choose Finder ➪ Preferences to display the Preferences window.**

2. **Click the Advanced icon in the window's toolbar.**

3. **Click the Select... button under "Languages for searching file contents:" to display the Languages window.** Figure 7-10 shows the Languages window.

4. **Select the languages that you want the Finder to use when it creates and updates indexes.**

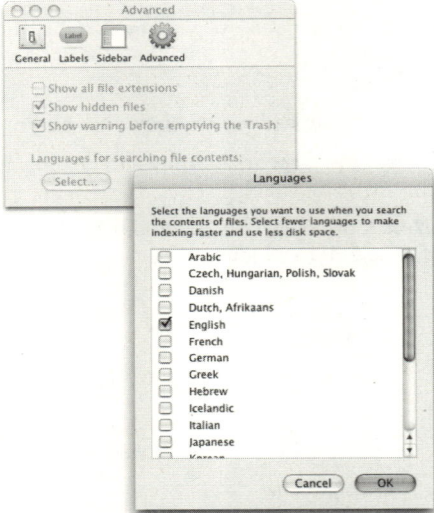

Figure 7-10: Make indexing faster and make indexes smaller by selecting fewer languages.

Deleting indexes

If you want to create a completely new index for a folder that already has one, you can delete the existing index. It's a good idea to delete a folder's existing index and create a new one if you make major changes to the folder or if you notice Find becoming noticeably slower at searching the folder by contents.

Follow these steps to delete an index:

1. **Select the item you want to index by clicking its icon or name in a Finder window.**

2. **Choose File ➪ Get Info.** The Get Info window appears, as shown earlier in Figure 7-9.

3. **Click the disclosure triangle to the right of the Content index.** The Content index pane displays.

4. **Click the Delete Index button.**

5. **Click OK when asked to confirm that you really want to delete.**

If the Delete Index button is grayed-out—not available—it is because the item has not yet been indexed. In this case, the Status line in the Content index pane will read Not Indexed.

Searching by Multiple File Attributes

Sometimes you can't find what you're looking for by searching the text contents or the names of files, folders, and volumes. You may need to take into account such other attributes as the age, size, or kind of item that you're looking for. Under these circumstances, you need to perform a custom search in the Find window.

Performing a custom search

To perform a custom search, open the Find window and click one of the plus sign buttons. Doing this adds a search criteria item to the window just underneath.

By pulling down the criteria item's pop-up menu, you can pick from several kinds of criteria. After you pick a criterion, the subsequent qualifier phrase will alter to go with your choice, often presenting a second pop-up menu with alternatives, including a text entry field when appropriate.

To remove an item, click the minus button to the right of the field. Clicking a plus button adds another search criteria just underneath. As you add additional criteria, Find helps you by removing previously set criteria from the new criteria's pop-up menu. Find sets the next criteria for you by picking from the remaining possibilities.

Figure 7-11 shows examples of these additional search criteria and controls.

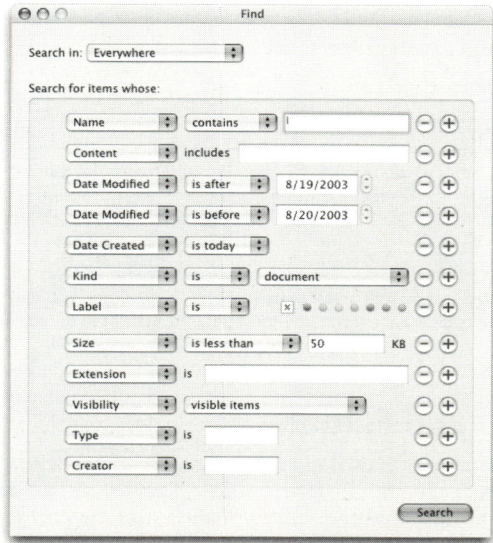

Figure 7-11: Adding criteria to the Find window can narrow the search results to more precise results.

Table 7-1 explains the additional criteria usable for searching.

Table 7-1: Settings for Find's More Search Options

Attribute	What Find looks for
Name	A file, folder, or volume whose name contains/starts with/ends with/is/is not/doesn't contain the text you enter
Content includes	Text within documents, such as the search by contents described earlier in this chapter
Date Created	A file, folder, or volume whose creation date is/is before/is after/is not; is today; is within 1/2/3 days of; is within 1/2/3 weeks of; is within 1/2/3/6 months of the date you enter
Date Modified	A file, folder, or volume whose modification date is/is before/is after; is today; is within 1/2/3 days of; is within 1/2/3 weeks of; is within 1/2/3/6 months of the date you enter
Size	A file whose size is less than/is greater than the number of KB you enter (1024KB = 1MB)
Label	A file whose label is/is not the color you choose, or if you click on the X box to the left of the label color dots, a file which does not have a label assigned
Kind	A file whose kind is/is not alias/application/document /folder /audio/ image/movie
Extension	A file whose three-character extension (also known as the file name suffix) is the character set you enter
Visibility	A file or folder that is invisible, or visible, as you choose
Type	A file that possesses a Type code[1]
Creator	A file that possesses a Creator code[2]

[1] Type and Creator codes were used in Mac OS 9 and before; Mac OS X can understand them. The four-letter Type code tells the operating system if the file is an application, a document, a system file, and so on. For instance, the type code APPL signifies the file is an application. The Type code also determines which files get displayed in an application's Open window.

[2] Type and Creator codes were used in Mac OS 9 and before; Mac OS X can understand them. The four-letter Creator code is used to link documents to the application that created them. For instance, when you double-click on a Microsoft Excel document, the Creator code XCEL is what tells the operating system to launch Excel.

Working with Found Files and Folders

When a search of the volumes on your computer ends, Find displays a list of files, folders, and disks that match your search criteria in a Search Results window. This list of found items appears in a separate window from the Find window, the Search Results window, and you can go back to the Find window to change your search criteria.

Obviously, you can browse the list of found items for items that particularly interest you. Less obviously, you can see the volume and folders in which a found item is located, and you can copy the name of a found item to the Clipboard. You can move or copy found items to any Finder window or the Desktop, make aliases of found items, and move found items to the Trash.

In addition, you can open found items or the folders that enclose them. If a found item is a document, you can print it. If a found item is an alias, you can show its original in a Finder window. With some types of found files, you can have Find find similar files. This section describes how to do all these tasks.

Seeing the path to a found item

Mac OS X will display the path to a found item through the hierarchy of its enclosing folders. The path is shown in an area at the bottom of the Search Results window.

As mentioned earlier in this chapter, in Mac OS 10.3, this path-viewing area features three different modes of display. Which mode is shown is based on the size of the viewing area, which you can change.

The path-viewing area is located just below the bottom scroll bar of the Search Results window, by default minimized to a single line, as shown in Figure 7-12. When the window first opens, nothing shows in this area, because you must select an item for its path to be shown.

When you select an item, a row of items appears in the path area, separated by arrowheads, starting with drive icon on the left and ending with the selected item on the right. This is the simplest mode of the path display, and is meant to show how many levels deep in the hierarchy your selected item is located.

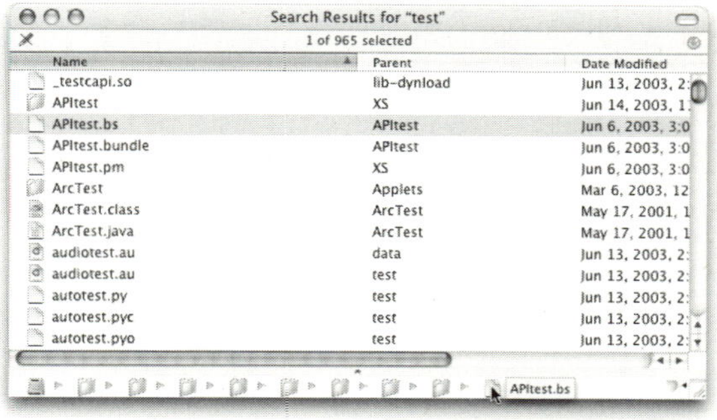

Figure 7-12: The initial, simple path view takes up only one line at the bottom of the Search Results window.

You can view the name of a folder in this mode by positioning your cursor over it; it takes a little longer than a second for the name to appear in a faintly yellow box, and it will disappear after about eight seconds.

In this simplified viewing mode, it is still easy to perform one of the more common actions you may wish to take while viewing a path: opening the folder that encloses your selected item. Simply double-click on the folder just to the left of the item, and a Finder window will open to display the contents of the folder, including your selected item.

Just above the path area, in the center of the bar that separates it from the window's bottom scroll bar, you find an indented dot, the path area's drag handle. Moving your cursor over this dot turns the cursor into a horizontal bar with arrowheads pointing up and down; if you hold down the mouse button, you can drag the separation and scroll bars upward, expanding the path area.

When you have expanded the path area to a little more than double its initial height, the path display switches to its second mode. Now the names of the folders appear, and the path can take up two lines, as shown in Figure 7-13. If the path is long, the folder names will appear abbreviated, with an ellipsis (...) in the middle. You can make the full name appear in a light yellow box by positioning the cursor over the abbreviated name.

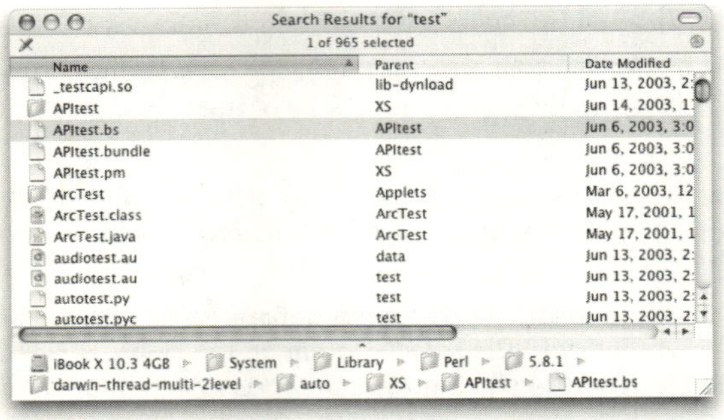

Figure 7-13: Expanding the path-viewing area allows the item names to be seen.

As you expand the path area further, the path is displayed on three lines, and the names are less abbreviated.

Expanding the path area a little beyond this causes the display to switch to its third mode, in which the successive folders appear indented to the right as you go deeper into the hierarchy, with your selection appearing at the bottom, as shown in Figure 7-14. This path view was used in versions of Mac OS X before Panther. Note that in this view, the path takes one line for each level, and is therefore a fixed number of lines; if the area is not expanded enough, you will not be able to see the entire path.

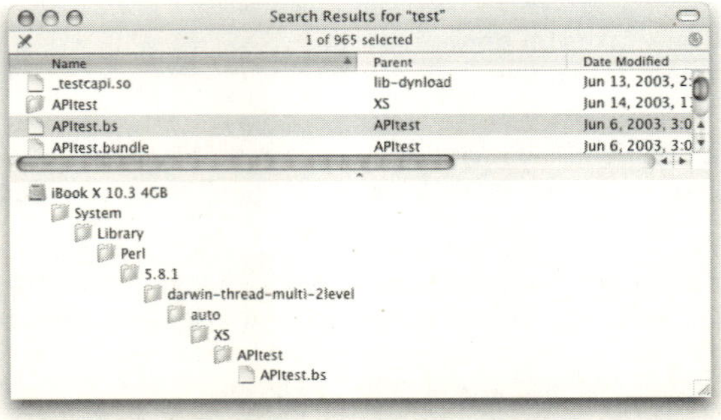

Figure 7-14: Expanding the path-viewing area reveals each hierarchy level on its own line.

Copying the name of a found item

You can copy the name of a found item by selecting it in the Search Results window's path area when the path is displayed in its most expanded mode, and choosing Edit ➪ Copy. Note that when you select the item, the name itself does not highlight, only the item's icon. Then you can insert the name in the TextEdit application or anywhere else you can edit text by going to that application and choosing Edit ➪ Paste.

Moving or copying a found item

You can move a found item by dragging it from the list of found items (not from the path area) to a Finder window, the Desktop, or a folder icon in either of these places. If you want to copy an item instead of moving it, simply press the Option key while you drag it from Find's list of found items. You don't need to press Option if the place you're dragging an item is on a different volume than the item's current location. Items are always copied, not moved, when you drag them to a different volume. You can tell that an item will be drag-copied when you see a green dot with a plus sign next to the cursor as you drag it.

If you change your mind about moving or copying a folder while in the midst of dragging it, you can cancel the operation by dragging to the menu bar and releasing the mouse button. Alternatively, you can drag the folder back where it came from or to the title bar of Find's window, but the menu bar is an easier target to hit. If you change your mind after you've dragged it, you can undo the move by choosing Edit ➪ Undo Move of [file name] — Find supplies the file name to help you remember what you just did — or use the keyboard shortcut Command-Z.

When you move an item, if it is still selected in the Search Results window, you will see the path display change to reflect its new position.

If you can't move or copy any items to a particular folder, then you may not have the privilege to make changes to that folder. If you can't move or copy one particular item to any folder, you do not have privileges to change that item or the folder it's in. Either your privileges for the item don't allow moving it from its folder or your privileges for the folder don't allow moving anything out of it. (We cover the effect of privileges on moving and copying in Chapter 4.)

 **Tip**   Instead of moving, copying, or performing another operation on found items one at a time, select multiple items and act on them all at once. Click one item to select it and then Command-click each additional item that you want to select. Select a range of items by dragging across them or by clicking the first item and then Shift-clicking the last one.

Making an alias of a found item

You can make an alias of a found item by pressing the Option and Command keys while you drag it from Find's list of found items to a Finder window or the Desktop.

Opening a found item

You can open a found item by double-clicking it or by selecting it and choosing File ➪ Open Item. The item you open can be in the list of found items or it can be in the hierarchical path displayed at the bottom of the Find window. Opening a folder displays its contents in a Finder window. Opening a document file opens the associated application and displays the document contents in a window.

Tip   While opening a found item from a Find window, you can simultaneously close the Find window by holding down the Option key as you double-click or choosing File ⇨ Open Item.

Opening a found item's enclosing folder

You can open the folder that encloses a found item by selecting the found item and choosing File ⇨ Open Enclosing Folder. A Finder window opens, showing the found item selected among the other contents of the enclosing folder.

Alternately, as noted above, you may also double-click on the enclosing folder in the path area.

Moving a found item to the Trash

You can move a found item to the Trash by dragging it from the list of found items to the Trash icon in the Dock or by selecting the item and choosing File ⇨ Move to Trash.

You can also select the item and press Command-Delete. Hearing a click means that the item's path has changed to show that the item is now in the Trash, and the item will be removed from any Finder window, or the Desktop, and appear in the Trash window. If you remove the file from the Trash, the path will change to show its new location.

Seeing the original of an alias

You can see the original of an alias in the list of found items by selecting the alias and choosing File ⇨ Get Info. A Get Info window opens for the alias, with the path to the original shown in the General pane of the Get Info window.

Searching the Internet with Sherlock

You can think of Sherlock as a specialized Web browser that is optimized for searching the Internet for particular kinds of useful information, such as Yellow Pages listings, tracking the latest stock prices, movie locations and show times, and eBay auction activity. To simplify the search, this information is organized into *channels,* and each channel displays the found information in a more helpful way than a HTML browser could.

Due to its immense size, searching the Internet can usually be a real chore. Online search engines and directories abound — AltaVista, Ask Jeeves, Excite, Google, HotBot, LookSmart, Lycos, and Yahoo! are just a few — but you often have to search several of them to find what you want. With Sherlock, you can conduct a search utilizing many of these search engines at once, and Sherlock displays the combined results in its window. You can see a brief summary of any found site in the Sherlock window, and with one or two clicks in Sherlock, you can have your Web browser go to a found site.

Sherlock gains access to each Web site through a plug-in file created by Apple, other companies, or individuals. These plug-ins make it possible for Sherlock to search not only Web search engines, such as those mentioned in the previous paragraph, but searchable Web sites including Amazon, eBay, Apple, and other e-commerce sites. News sites and Web magazines also supply Sherlock plug-ins that enable you to search their sites with Sherlock.

Each plug-in appears as a Sherlock channel. Sherlock initially has several Internet channels in its toolbar, with each channel containing a different category of search sites. Besides the basic Internet channel for search engines and directories, by default Sherlock has channels for picture searches, stocks, movies, Yellow Pages, eBay, flights, dictionary, translation, and the AppleCare site. You can reorganize and add your own channels.

Note To see and use any of Sherlock's Internet channels, you must be connected to the Internet. If you didn't set up your computer for an Internet connection during the initial Mac OS X setup procedure, see Chapter 18 to find out how to set up a connection now. If your computer uses a modem to connect to the Internet, you should make sure that your computer is set to dial up and make a connection automatically or that a connection is already made before you start an Internet search in Sherlock. Chapter 6 tells you how to make an Internet connection with a modem.

Tip The basic functionality of Sherlock, as implemented in Mac OS 10.2 and later, is based on a third-party application known as Watson. Watson offers an expanded list of channels and other bells and whistles not featured in Sherlock. If you find Sherlock useful, you may want to check out Watson. To find Watson, do a search for it at the OS X tab of www.versiontracker.com.

Opening Sherlock

To begin your search, you can open Sherlock and display its main window by using two different methods.

✦ **Open Sherlock from the Dock.** You can open Sherlock and display its window by clicking the Sherlock icon in the Dock at the bottom of the screen. This action opens the Sherlock application, displaying its window. Of course, you won't be able to open Sherlock from the Dock if someone has removed its icon. (Removing and adding items to the Dock is mentioned in Chapter 4.) Figure 7-15 shows the Sherlock icon in the Dock and in a Finder window.

✦ **Open Sherlock from a Finder window.** You can also open Sherlock by double-clicking its icon wherever it appears in a Finder window or even on the Desktop, if someone has put it there. For example, normally a Sherlock icon is in your Applications folder, which you can open by clicking the Applications item in the sidebar of a Finder window.

Figure 7-15: Sherlock's hat and magnifying glass icon appears in the Applications folder and the Dock.

Exploring the Sherlock window

Sherlock, like so many included applications in Panther, has received a redesign. The layout of the Channels panel has been improved. Figure 7-16 gives you a look at the new Sherlock 3.6 Channels panel.

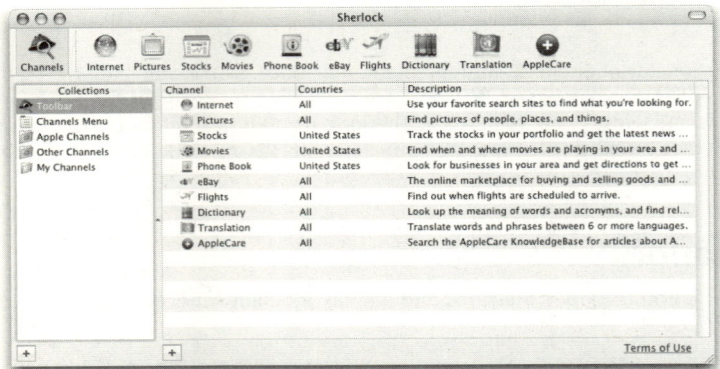

Figure 7-16: The Sherlock Channels panel in its default state, showing the Channel toolbar, Collections sidebar, and channel information list.

At the top of the Sherlock window is the Channel toolbar. It initially contains the default set of channels that Apple has chosen, but you can change the channels to your liking, as described next.

On the left side of the Channels window you see the Collections sidebar, which allows you to organize your channels into *collections*. A collection is essentially a folder that contains a set of channels. By default, the sidebar shows five collections.

Click a collection to view its contents in the large list area to the right. To add a channel to a particular collection, you can drag channel icons from the list area to that collection's folder.

The first collection listed is the Toolbar collection, containing the channels that appear in the Sherlock toolbar. Instead of a folder icon, this collection uses the Sherlock's hat and magnifying glass icon. To add or remove channels to the toolbar, drag them to or from this folder, or directly to or from the toolbar.

The next collection listed is the Channels Menu, with an icon representing a menu. Collections placed in this folder appear in the Sherlock's Channels menu.

Below this you find the Apple Channels collection folder. This folder contains the original set of channels that appear in the toolbar.

The Other Channels collection contains a bunch of interesting channels to choose from, provided by Apple. They are fun to look through and to try. You may prefer to have some of them in your toolbar.

 Note   You will only see this folder if you boot Sherlock while you have a connection to the Internet.

My Channels is an empty collections folder provided for you to fill with whatever channels you wish.

You can create additional collections by clicking on the plus sign button below the Collections side bar. A new collections folder appears with the default name "untitled" highlighted; type a new name for the collection and press the Return key, the Enter key, or click anywhere on the window to rename the collection.

To delete a collection, click on the collection to highlight it and then press the Delete key.

You can drag any collection folder to a new position in the list—just click and hold on the folder and drag it to its new position, which is marked by a black bar.

The channel to search

Each channel icon specifies the type of information you can search for, including files and folders, Web pages, products, people, or news. Each channel also specifies a group of sources you can search, and in this regard, most channels are actually groups of Internet sites.

You change search channels by selecting a channel icon. When you do, Sherlock reconfigures its window to list the channel's searchable sources across the bottom of the window and to display appropriate search criteria for the type of information that the channel can search for. Sherlock shows which channel is currently selected by adding the channel name to the title of the Sherlock window.

Every channel has a different pane or panel layout, but many of the elements are shared with other channel panes. Some of the more commonly seen elements are described below.

Tip   Clicking the icon for one of the channel's searchable sources on the bottom left edge of the Sherlock window (following the words "Content provided by") causes the URL for that source to load in your default Web browser.

What to search for

Below the channel toolbar is usually a text box in which you enter a search request. The search request consists of words that you want Sherlock to search for. To enter your search request in this text box, click inside it and begin typing. You can also press Tab; however, you may need to press Tab more than once to select this text box and see an insertion point blinking there. To further indicate when the text box is selected, Sherlock highlights it by drawing a blue border around it. Figure 7-17 shows a search request being entered in the text box.

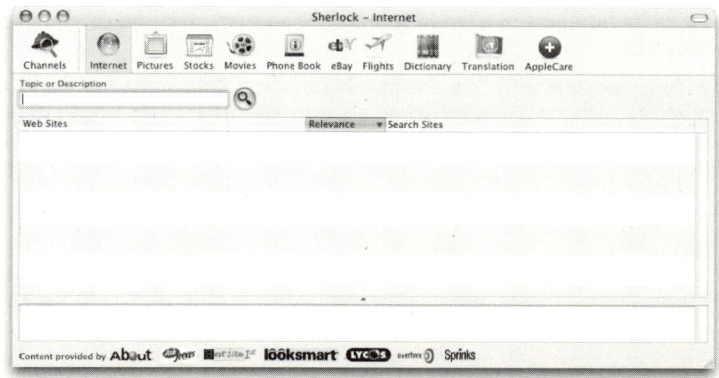

Figure 7-17: The Internet channel window with the text box highlighted.

Below the text box for entering a search request, you may see options for additional search criteria. The combination of options — in fact, whether there are any options — depends on the channel.

The Search and Back buttons

The large round Search button, which is labeled with a picture of a magnifying glass, starts a search and can stop a search that is under way. When the Search button is colored green, clicking it starts a search. When the Search button is colored red, a search is under way and clicking the button stops the search.

The list area

The middle of the channel window usually has a list area. After a search, Sherlock places the list of items it has found in this area. We explore what you can do with found items later in this chapter. Figure 7-18 shows an example list of found items in the Internet channel window.

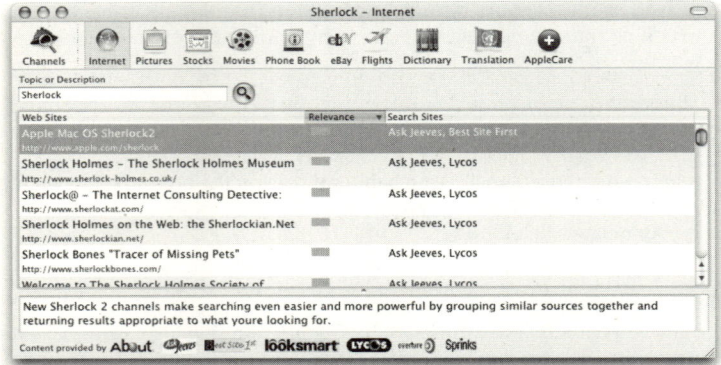

Figure 7-18: The Internet channel window after a successful search, listing the found Web sites in order of relevance.

Rearranging Sherlock's list area

Whether you see a list of found items or a list of searchable sources, you can rearrange the list in several ways. You can

- ✦ **Resize the list.** Drag the drag grip (it looks like an indented dot) in the bar that separates the list from the information area below it to change the relative height of both areas. Resizing the Sherlock window also changes the size of the information area.

- ✦ **Sort the list.** Click the heading of the column by which you want Sherlock to sort the list. Sherlock highlights the column heading.

- ✦ **Reverse the sort order.** Click the column heading that is currently highlighted to change from a descending order to an ascending order or vice versa. The small arrow to the right of the column heading points down for a descending sort or up for an ascending sort.

✦ **Move a column.** Drag the column's heading left or right to move the column. While you drag a column heading, the mouse pointer looks like a clutching hand.

✦ **Resize a column.** Drag the borderline on the right side of a column's heading to resize the column. The mouse pointer looks like a two-headed arrow when you place it over the borderline.

Tip You can't remove a column from a list of found items, but you can effectively hide it. Simply resize the column to its minimum width and move it to the right side of the list.

The information area

The bottom part of the Sherlock channel window generally displays information about whatever is selected in the list above it. For example, if you select an Internet site from the list of searchable sources, information about that site is displayed. (Information is not available for all Internet sites.) The information area may be blank if nothing is selected in the list. Figure 7-19 shows an example of the information area with a found item selected in the search area.

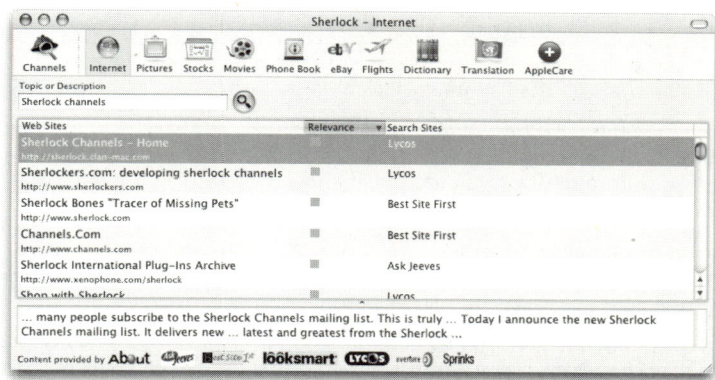

Figure 7-19: The information area at the bottom of the Sherlock window tells you more about the item selected in the list above it.

Searching Web pages

When you switch Sherlock to the Internet channel, Sherlock reconfigures its window to accommodate the different requirements of an Internet search. Figures 7-17 and 7-18 show Sherlock set to the Internet channel.

Searching the Internet channel

1. **Click the Internet channel button if it's not already selected.**

2. **In the text box, enter one or more words that describe the information you want to find.**

   To enter text, the text box must be selected. If necessary, you can accomplish this by clicking inside the box or pressing Tab as needed to place an insertion point in the box.

If the box already contains text from a previous search request, pressing Tab selects this text so that you can replace it simply by typing.

The search request you enter is interpreted differently by various Web search engines, directories, and other Internet search sites. Sherlock will not attempt to revise or adjust your request to accommodate these different interpretations. In general, you can simply enter a series of words that you think may generate results, such as *Olympic bobsled trials* or *outdoor camping*. You can also try interposing words that express a logical relationship, such as *and, or,* and *not*. You have to experiment with different combinations of words to see what generates the best results with different Internet search sites.

3. **Click the Search button or press Return to begin the search.**

Getting Better Web Search Results

The way you phrase your request when searching the Internet can profoundly affect the results. Each search engine, directory, and other site that you search on the Internet may take into account word order, punctuation, capitalization, and logical relationships, such as *and, or,* and *not*. Making matters even more complicated, the various search sites do not all follow the same rules for evaluating a search request. Nevertheless, these general guidelines can help you phrase your request so that your Internet searches in Sherlock turn up the results you want:

✦ **Word order:** Try putting the most important words first, even if you have to enter them in an unnatural order. Many search engines, directories, and other search sites consider the order of words in your request when determining how well each Web page matches your request. For example, you may get better results with *Stooges Three* than with *Three Stooges.*

✦ **Logical relationships:** Use the words *and, or,* and *not* to express logical relationships between words and phrases as follows:

- **and** before a word means that you want information that includes the word; between two words means that you want only information that contains both the words.

- **or** between two words means that you want information that contains either one or both of the words.

- **not** or **–** (a minus sign) before a word means that you want information that does not include the word.

For example, searching for *Aztec and Toltec* finds information that includes both terms. If you search for *Aztec or Toltec,* you'll get a lot more results because your results will include information that contains either term. Search for *Aztec not Toltec* and you'll get results that include the first term but don't include the second term. Most Internet search engines and directories recognize logical relationships expressed by *and, or,* and *not.*

✦ **Commas:** Try using commas between words and phrases. Although many search engines, directories, and other search sites don't require commas, some work better if you separate each keyword or phrase with a comma. A comma has generally the same effect as the word *or,* but commas cause some search sites to consider a Web page to better match your request when the site contains more of the words or phrases in your request.

✦ **Capitalization:** Some search engines, directories, and other search sites notice whether you capitalize words. If you don't capitalize, they ignore capitalization while searching; if you do capitalize, they look for the same capitalization as yours.

✦ **Quotation marks:** Some search sites prefer that you put phrases or proper names between quotation marks, such as "tape recorder" or "Huckleberry Finn." Additionally, some search sites find variations of unquoted words but not of quoted words. For example, searching these sites for *international* finds variations including intern, national, internationals, and so on; searching these sites for "international" finds only the literal quoted word.

Looking at Internet search results

Sherlock begins displaying the results of searching the Internet channel as soon as it receives them from any of the search sites. As other search sites return their results, Sherlock merges them in the list area. For each Web page that matches your search request, Sherlock displays an icon indicating the search site that found the page together with the page's name, relevance to your search request, and Web site. You can rearrange the list of results as described earlier.

You can see a summary of any listed Web page by clicking its icon, name, or site. The summary appears in the information area below the list of results. The summary is provided by the search site, and its composition varies from one search site to the next.

Seeing a listed Web page

You can see all of a Web page that appears in Sherlock's list of results by doing either of the following:

✦ Double-click the name of a listed Web page that you want to see.

✦ Drag the name of a listed Web page to a Web browser window.

Whichever method you use, Sherlock sends the page's Web address to your Web browser, which takes over and attempts to load the page via your Internet connection.

Copying a listed Web page's summary

You can copy part of the summary by selecting the Web page in the list area, clicking in the information area of the Sherlock window, and choosing Edit ➪ Select All, then Edit ➪ Copy. Sherlock places about 140 characters of the summary onto the Clipboard. Then you can go to TextEdit or any other application that lets you edit text and insert the partial summary by choosing Edit ➪ Paste.

Alternatively, you can select the text and drag it to its destination.

Copying a listed Web page's address

You can copy the address of a Web page by selecting the page in the list of search results and dragging the Web page listing from Sherlock's window to the window of a text document or other place where you can edit text. Dragging a Web page listing from Sherlock inserts the page's address, not its name.

Saving a link to a listed Web page

If you'd like to create a file that links to one of the Web pages from Sherlock's list of Internet search results so that you can see the page later, drag the page's name from Sherlock's list to any Finder window, the Desktop, or a folder icon in either of these places. This causes the Finder to create an Internet Location file, which you can open any time you want to see the Web page. You can recognize an Internet Location file by its distinctive icon, featuring the at-sign (@) symbol.

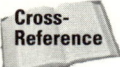

Cross-Reference   You'll find more information about Internet Location files in Chapter 6.

Searching other Internet channels

As previously mentioned, besides the basic Internet channel for searching the Web, Sherlock has several other predefined Internet channels loaded into its toolbar by default. You can switch to any of the following Internet channels by clicking the icon in the toolbar: Pictures, Stocks, Movies, Yellow Pages, eBay, Flights, Dictionary, Translation, and AppleCare. These channels are described in the following paragraphs.

Pictures channel

The Pictures channel includes search sites for finding pictures on the Internet. To use it, enter a subject you want to find pictures of in the text box, and click the Search button. To see the Internet address of a found picture, click the picture once to select the picture. The Internet address shows in the bottom of the Sherlock window. Double-clicking a picture sends the Internet address to your Web browser.

Stocks channel

The Stocks channel provides the ability to track stocks you are interested in. You can see a close-to-real-time price (delayed 15 minutes), see a summary of recent news headlines if any exist for the company, and view a graph of the stock's performance over time. If you select a news article in the news pane, a link will appear in the information area at the bottom of the window. Clicking that link shows the story in the Web browser. To add a new stock to the list, enter the company's name or stock abbreviation in the search field and click the magnifying glass to start the search. A view of the Stocks channel is shown in Figure 7-20.

Movies channel

The Movies channel has movie, theater, and show time information provided by Moviefone.com. To use this channel, choose to organize either by movies or theaters, enter a zip code, and choose a date from the pop-up menu on the right, and then press Return. When the list of movies appears, choose the movie you are interested in, and the middle pane will show the theaters the movie is playing at. Choose a theater to see the show times for the selected date. The results include movie name, theater, show times, summary, poster, and the movie trailer, as shown in Figure 7-21.

A nifty new feature of Sherlock 3.6 is the group of links in the lower-right corner of the Movies channel window. After you have selected a theatre, click on the Restaurants, Shopping, Bars, or Hotels link to "auto-magically" see information about those businesses nearest the theater, as listed in the Phone Book channel. The other link also takes you to the Phone Book channel, but allows you to choose from a long list of business categories.

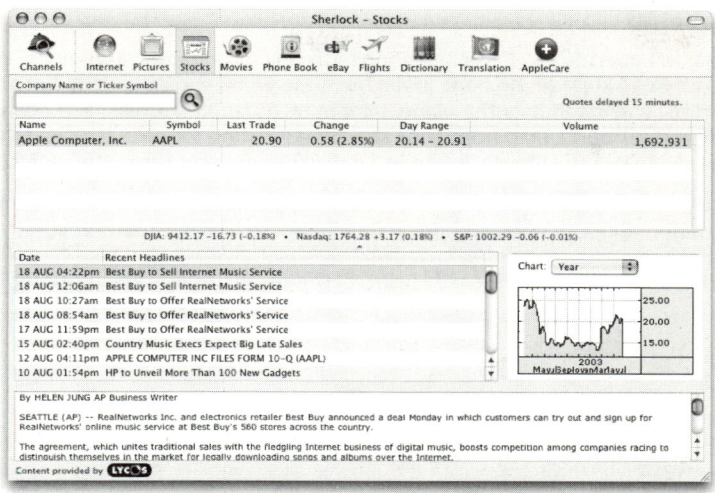

Figure 7-20: Use the Stocks channel to track stocks and see financial news.

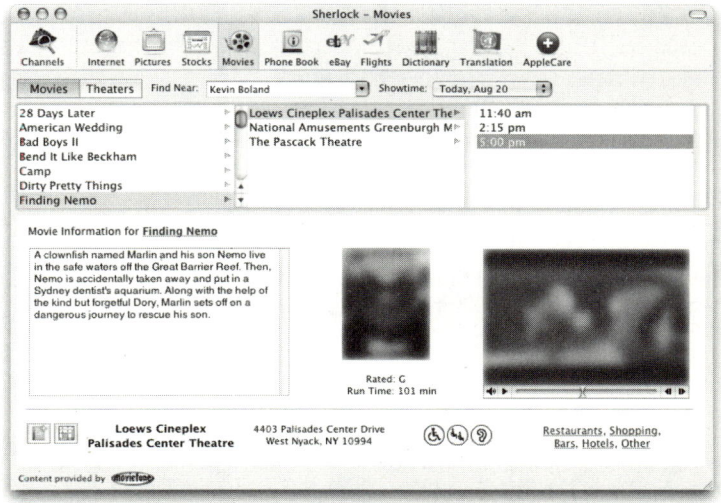

Figure 7-21: When Sherlock searches the Movies channel, the results include movies currently playing, theatres, show times, a synopsis, a poster, and the movie's trailer.

Phone Book channel

The Phone Book channel provides address, telephone, driving information, and maps for businesses. Enter a city and state or zip code and a business name you're looking for, and click the Search button. The result lists the name, telephone number, address, and distance as well as driving directions and a map from your specified location for each that matches your search request. A view of the Sherlock Phone Book channel is shown in Figure 7-22.

A new feature is the white or yellow pages switch at the top left of the window; use the white pages to find information about people, and the yellow pages to find information about businesses. Also new are the pop-up menus for Business Name or Category, and Find Near (Name, City or State, and Zip). And you can now easily print all the results from a small printer button on the right.

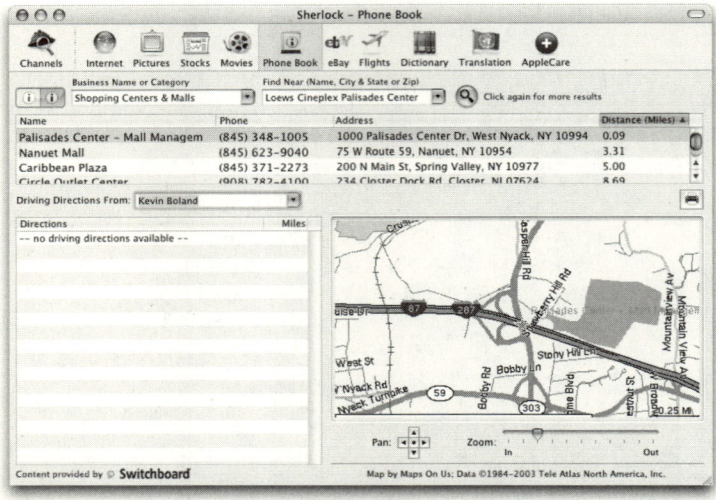

Figure 7-22: Use the Phone Book channel to find contact information for people or businesses, and see their locations automatically displayed on a map.

eBay channel

The eBay channel can be used to shop and to bid on auctions, just as though you were using a Web browser. You can track auctions through Sherlock, which is probably the easiest way for Mac user to do so. A view of the Sherlock eBay channel is shown in Figure 7-23.

Flights channel

The Flights channel lets you search for information on flight status of current flights, provided by FlyteComm.com. You can search either for a specific flight by airline and number, or you can search with departure and arrival city. When you find the flight you are interested in, click it and view its arrival or departure status and other information, as shown in Figure 7-24.

One of the niftiest bits of information is a chart, available for certain flights, which tracks the flight's progress on a weather map!

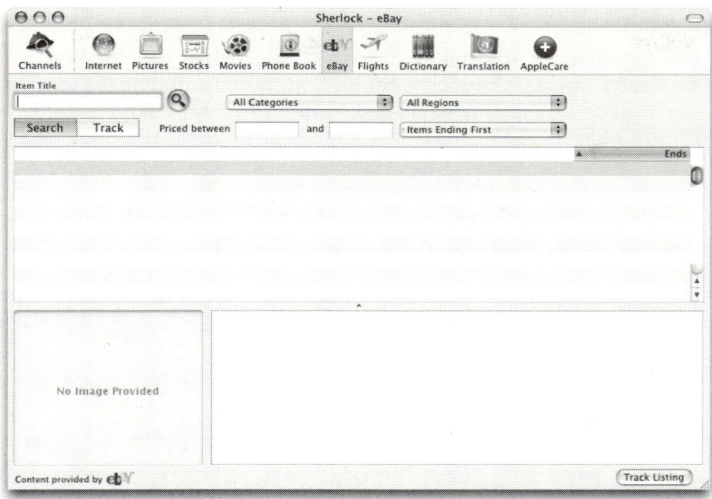

Figure 7-23: Use the eBay channel to shop and bid on auctions.

Notice the small button in the lower-right corner with a switch icon. This button is the Show Channel Preferences switch for Flights. Click it, and the Channel Preferences for Flights sheet comes down, allowing you to select what continent you want to search in for airlines and airports.

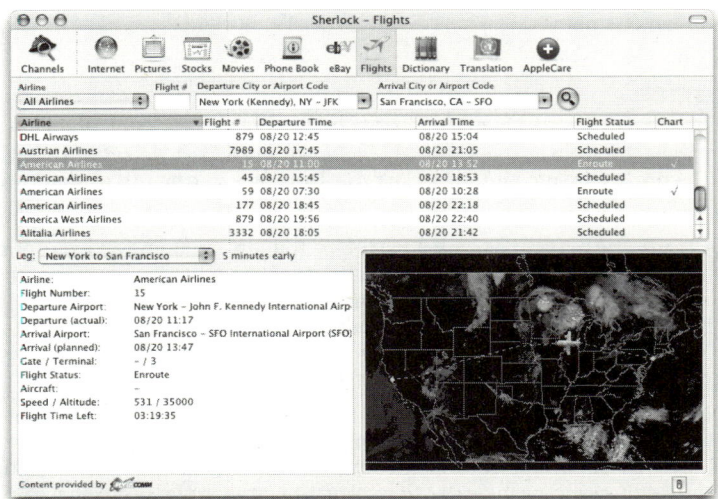

Figure 7-24: Use the Flights channel to search for information on current flight status.

Dictionary channel

The Dictionary channel searches for information on words, acronyms, and the names of famous people. To use the Dictionary channel, enter a word, name, acronym, or term in the text field and then click the Search button. Synonyms, definitions, and other information appear, as shown in Figure 7-25.

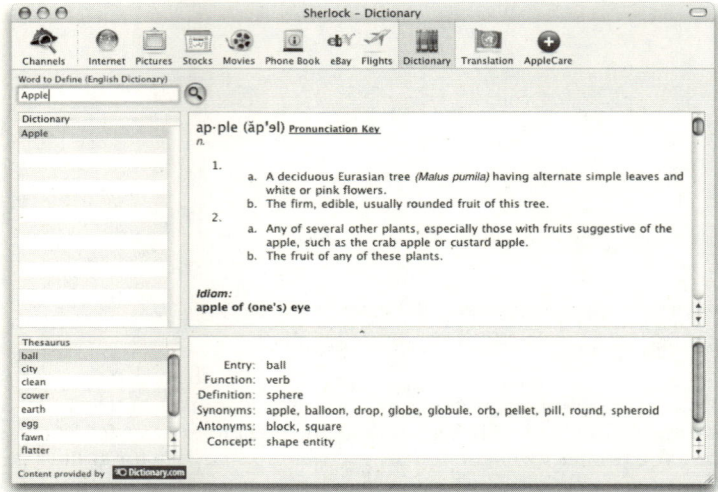

Figure 7-25: Use the Dictionary channel to search for information on words, acronyms, and famous names.

Translation channel

Need something translated from one language to another? Try the Translation channel. Enter the text you wish to translate from in the top field labeled Original Text, select a "to and from" language pair from the pop-up menu, and then click the Translate button. An example is shown in Figure 7-26.

Please note that the Translation channel is most useful for roughly decoding an excerpt so you can get the gist of the meaning; or for the simple translation of short phrases and sentences. Do not depend upon it for flawlessly accurate translations; remember, it's only a computer! However, its sometimes barely intelligible translations can provide an excellent laugh....

AppleCare channel

The AppleCare channel lets you search Apple's Knowledge Base of information on Apple hardware and software. Enter a topic or description of the item or issue in the text field in the upper-left and click the Search button. Knowledge Base articles appear in the main field. Clicking a Document title shows the article in the information area at the bottom of the Sherlock window. An example is shown in Figure 7-27.

The Knowledge Base articles frequently contain links to other articles, which may offer more information about your technical issue. If you click on a link, your default Web browser will open to display the linked Web page.

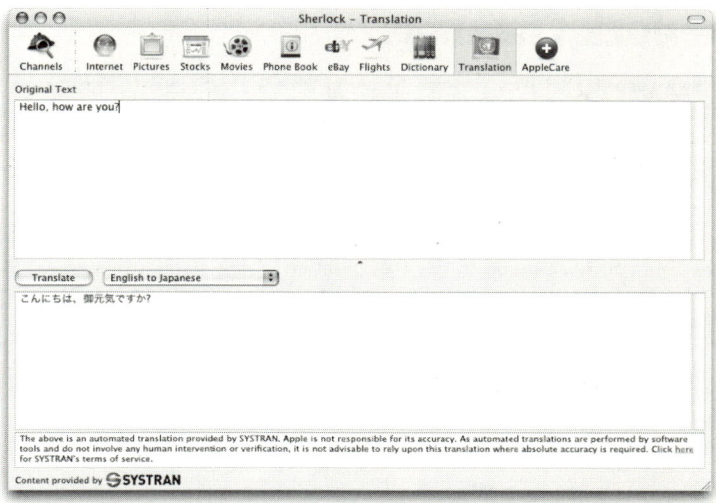

Figure 7-26: Use the Translation channel to translate text to and from languages.

Every Mac user should become familiar with the AppleCare channel, because it is sometimes very helpful when you encounter a technical problem. However, expect to find the solution to only some problems, not all.

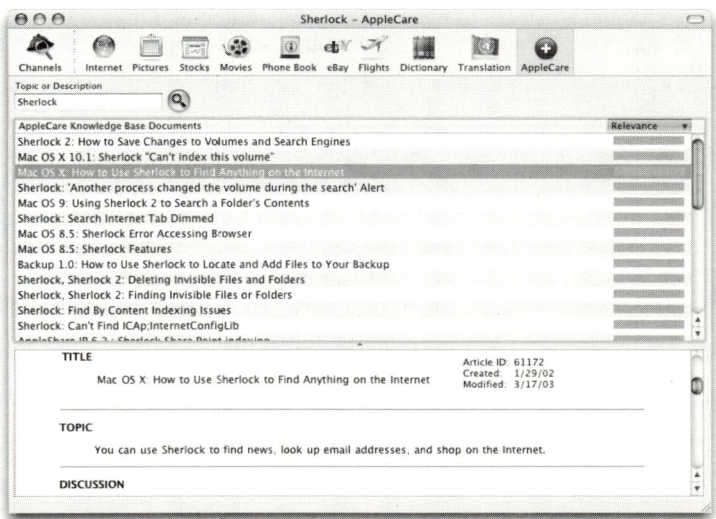

Figure 7-27: Use Sherlock to access Apple's helpful online Knowledge Base articles.

Modifying Sherlock Channels

The default channels (Internet, Pictures, Stocks, Movies, Yellow Pages, eBay, Flights, Dictionary, Translation, and AppleCare) may be all you need, but if not, you can add to and reorganize these 10 channels. You can add new channels for Internet search sites, and you can delete the channels you add. You can customize the look of the Sherlock toolbar and adjust the Sherlock Preferences.

Note   Sherlock repairs and updates its standard Internet channels periodically, and in so doing could undo changes you have made to the configuration of the standard channels. Every time you open Sherlock, it verifies that each standard channel exists and has its standard search sites. If channels or search sites are missing, it restores them from the Internet. In addition, Sherlock periodically checks the Internet for newer versions of standard search sites and channels, and it automatically updates your system as needed. If you move search sites out of a standard channel or remove a standard channel altogether, Sherlock's automatic update and repair mechanisms will eventually restore the standard search sites and channels you moved or removed.

Adding a channel to Sherlock

When you find a Web site with a Sherlock 3.6 and above–compatible channel, click the link on the Web site for the channel, and the new channel should appear in the Sherlock toolbar.

Deleting a channel

If you want to delete a channel, choose View ➪ Customize Toolbar to show the customizing toolbar pane. Click the channel you want to remove from the toolbar and drag it into the customizing pane. The channel icon will vanish in a small puff of smoke. Figure 7-28 shows the Customize Toolbar sheet.

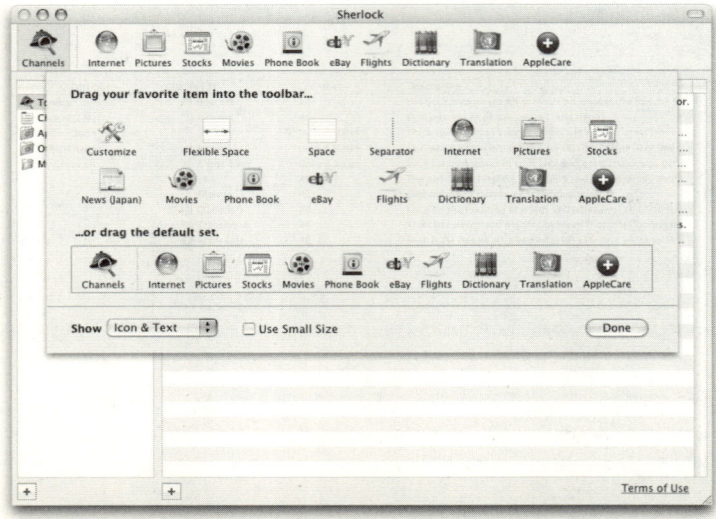

Figure 7-28:
Use the Customize Toolbar sheet to rearrange and delete the channels in the toolbar.

Rearranging and replacing channels

The channel buttons at the top of the Sherlock window are not permanently fixed in their initial positions. You can move them around, and you can replace one channel with another.

To move a channel button, simply open the Customize Toolbar and drag a channel icon to the right or left in the toolbar until it is where you want it to be, then release it. The other icons will reorder themselves to fit the space.

Editing cookies preferences

Sherlock's channels sometimes make use of cookies, which in this case are small text files that are automatically sent to your Mac by the Web server used by the channel. Cookies, which are also used with standard Web browsers, contain information that identifies you to the Web site, such as your name, passwords, preferences, and so on.

Most of the time, cookies are harmless. They are often convenient, ensuring that you do not need to reenter this information whenever you use the Channel or site. However, since they can also be used to track your online activities and otherwise violate your privacy, a good modern Web browser gives you the ability to turn them on or off, to review a list of cookies on your computer, and to delete the ones you don't want or no longer need. And of course, Sherlock belongs to the club of good modern Web browsers.

To set cookies preferences for Sherlock, follow these steps:

1. **Open Sherlock if it hasn't been opened already.**

2. **Choose File ➪ Preferences to open the Sherlock Preferences window.** It should initially appear with the Accept Cookies Always radio button selected, as shown in Figure 7-29.

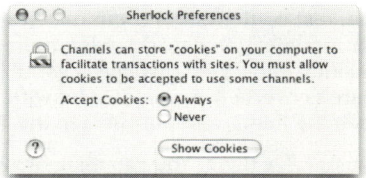

Figure 7-29: The Sherlock Preferences window lets you view and change settings for cookies.

3. **Click on the Show Cookies button** to see a list of the cookies Sherlock has accepted, or were preloaded to accompany the included channels, as shown in Figure 7-30.

4. **Click a cookie in the list to enable the Remove button; click the button to remove the cookie.** You may also click the **Remove All button** to delete all the cookies. Or, if you wish to make no changes, click **Done.**

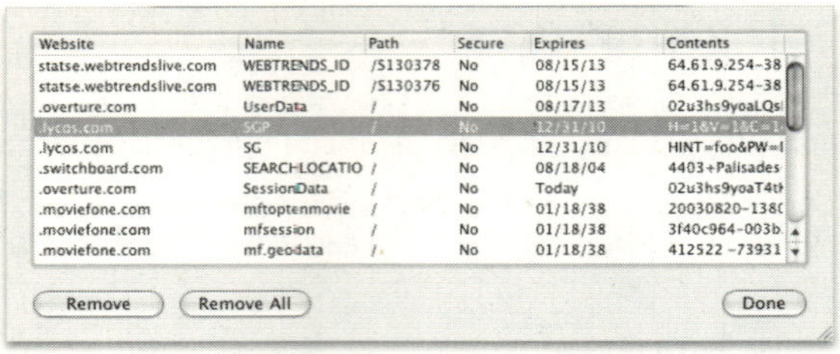

Figure 7-30: You can view a list of the cookies Sherlock uses and delete whichever ones you wish.

Making Multiple Searches

Sherlock can have a number of searches set up at the same time, each in a separate window. You can switch to a different Sherlock window or create a new window whenever Sherlock is not in the midst of conducting a search. Each window can have a different search that is completed or is in the process of being set up. To create a new Sherlock window, choose File ➪ New Window.

Summary

Here's what you should know after reading this chapter:

✦ Use Find to search files and folders on volumes and disks attached to your computer. Use Sherlock to search the Internet for other information.

✦ Use the Find command to search by name, text content, or a combination of name, content, and other criteria such as file size or modification date. You determine which folders and volumes Find searches. When a search ends, Find displays a list of the files, folders, and volumes that match your search criteria. You can do a lot with items on this list, including see their locations, open the items, and put them in the Trash.

✦ Before Find can search file contents, it must index them. You can manually start indexing a given folder or volume.

✦ You can open the Sherlock application from the Dock or from a Finder window.

✦ You switch channels by clicking channel icons in the toolbar at the top of the Sherlock window.

✦ You enter the words that you want Sherlock to search for in the text box below the channel toolbar.

✦ The Search button to the right of the text box starts a search and can stop a search that is underway.

✦ In the middle of its window, Sherlock lists items it has found. You can resize these lists, sort them in a different order, and move and resize their columns.

✦ The bottom part of the Sherlock window displays information about whatever is selected in the list above it.

✦ Sherlock has 10 standard channels for searching the Internet — Internet, Pictures, Stocks, Movies, Yellow Pages, eBay, Flights, Dictionary, Translation, and AppleCare — and you can add more. Each channel lets you search multiple Web search engines, directories, and other search sites all at once. Sherlock displays the combined results of the simultaneous searches in its window. You can see a brief summary of any found site in the Sherlock window, and with one or two clicks in Sherlock, you can have your Web browser go to a found site.

✦ You can move and copy Internet search sites between channels, add your own search sites, rearrange the channels, and add your own channels.

✦ Each Internet search site in a Sherlock channel corresponds to a search site plug-in file. Sherlock includes a number of search site plug-ins, and you can get more from various Web sites.

✦ Sherlock can have a number of searches going at the same time, each in a separate window.

✦   ✦   ✦

Getting Help

In this chapter, you find out how to take advantage of Mac OS X's built-in help systems. Figuratively or literally, anyone who has ever used a computer at one time or another needs help. When the need arises Mac OS X provides several types of built-in assistance. The principal help system is integrated into the OS, and the contents are displayed through a browser, aptly named the Help Viewer. The Help Viewer application provides explanations for most basic tasks. Another type of assistance within Mac OS X is help tags. When provided, help tags, are labels that are displayed when the mouse is pointed at various GUI elements. Typically these GUI elements are unlabeled buttons such as the ones found in AppleWorks or Microsoft Office's toolbars. Another form of built-in assistance is the man pages. Man pages provide help with the command-line tasks and are accessed through the Terminal application. In addition to the built-in help systems of Mac OS, many applications also provide their own built-in help. If all else fails, you can always break out the manuals or visit a products support site, if one is provided. Let's take a closer look at the various Mac OS X help systems.

Using the Help Viewer Application

The Help Viewer is the main source of general how-to help for Mac OS X. It also provides separate sections of specialized help on Apple technologies, such as AppleScript and QuickTime. In addition, some applications add their own sections of specialized help to the Help Viewer. In the Help Viewer, help is available by browsing a table of contents or by searching for words that describe the help you need. Some of the articles include links that you click to see related material as well as shortcuts to System Preference panes or OS X–included applications related to the assistance being sought. All the available help sections are listed in an table of contents in the Help Viewer, as explained in the following paragraphs.

To display onscreen help in the Help Viewer application, select Help from the menu bar or click the Help button. The application you're using determines what you see in the Help Viewer. You may see a list of all available help contents or a list of help article titles or a single help article related to the product in which help is being sought.

As a convenience, some windows include a Help button that you can click to get help for that window. When available, the Help button is the round button with a question mark on it. Clicking a Mac OS X Help button opens the Help Viewer application and displays a relevant help article or a list of relevant articles. For example, while using the Print dialog in a Mac OS X application, click the Help button to display the article about using the Print dialog.

Getting help within Mac OS X

While using the Finder, the Help Viewer provides the ability to browse a list of common Mac help topics. It also provides the ability to see what's new to Panther (Mac OS 10.3), help with top customer issues, and a starting point of assistance for those who are new to Mac OS. To use the help viewer follow these steps:

1. **If you're not currently using the Finder, switch to it.** For example, click any Finder window or click the Finder icon at the end of the Dock.

2. **Choose Help ⇨ Mac OS Help to display a list of Mac Help topics in the Help Viewer, as shown in Figure 8-1.**

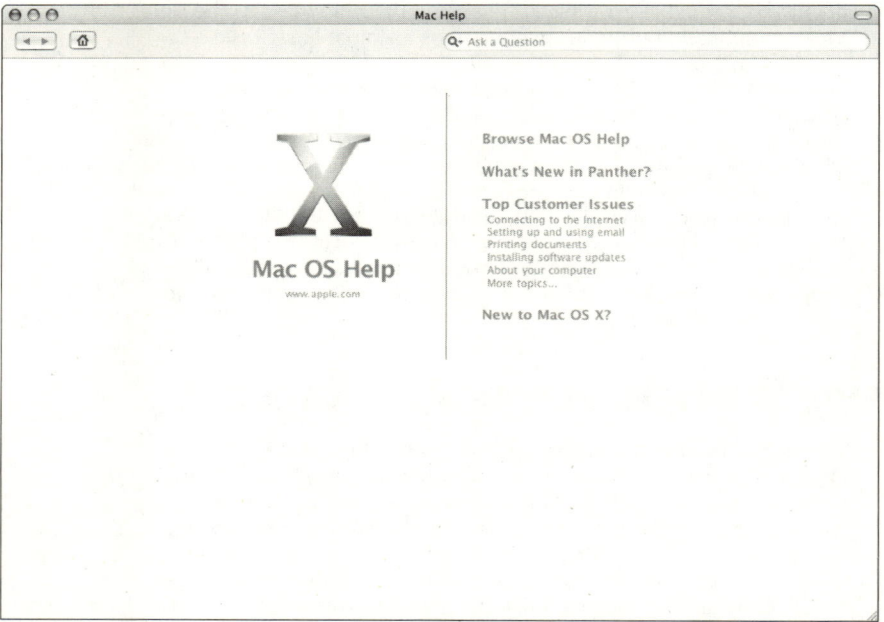

Figure 8-1: You can also open the Help Viewer application within the Finder using the key combination Command-?.

Browsing Mac OS Help

The Help Viewer application has a pseudo table of contents titled Browse Mac OS Help. The contents are based on subject matter that Apple has determined are the most commonly queried Mac OS X help issues. To view the list of central topics of help, click Browse Mac OS Help on the right side of the Help Viewer window. A list of help topics included by default with Mac OS X appears. Figure 8-2 shows the contents of Browse Mac OS Help.

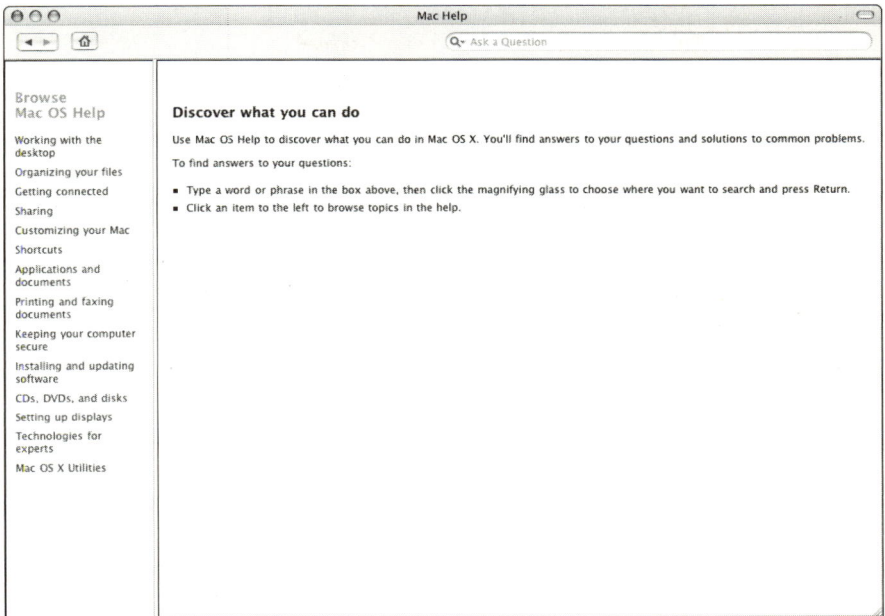

Figure 8-2: Browse Mac OS Help displays a consolidated list of help topics that are based on most common and frequent help inquiries.

Getting help for the active application

If the application you're using provides onscreen help via the Help Viewer, you can generally display this help by choosing a command from the Help menu. For example, while using Sherlock choose Help ➪ Sherlock Help to display a list of Sherlock-related topics in the Help Viewer, as shown in Figure 8-3.

Browsing Help Viewer links

The way that the Help Viewer works is similar to the way that a Web browser works. The blue underlined words in Help Viewer are links that you can click to see related material. For example, if you click on Browse Mac OS Help in the Help Viewer, while in the Finder, a list of relevant articles will be displayed. Clicking an underlined article's title displays the actual article. Articles themselves may also contain links to view related material as well as short-cuts to System Preference panes or OS X–included applications related to the assistance being sought. Figure 8-4 shows an example of searching for the words *keychain* and *password* with the second link selected, and Figure 8-5 shows that help article.

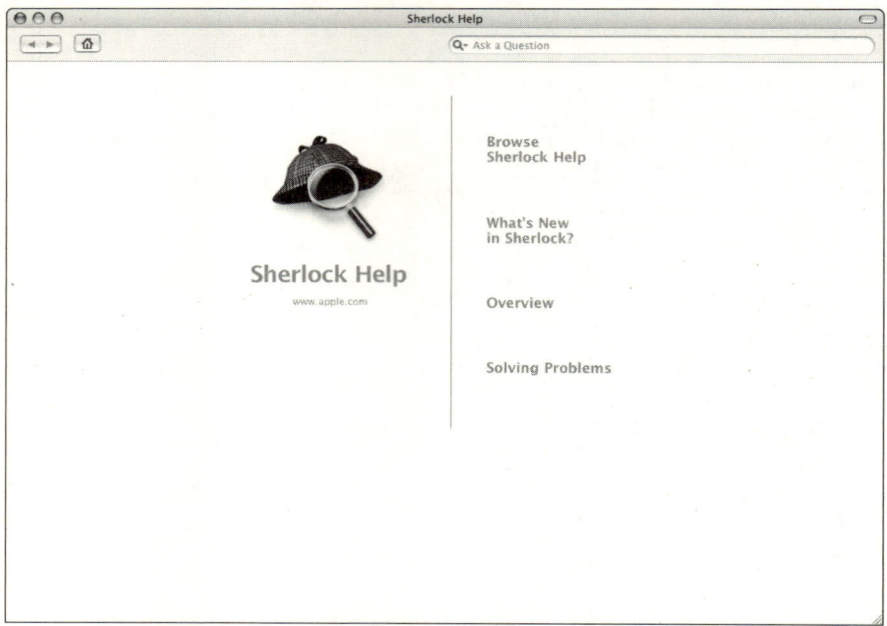

Figure 8-3: Opening the Help Viewer from Sherlock shows Sherlock-specific help. As with the Finder, you can also open the Help Viewer application within the Sherlock using the key combination Command-?.

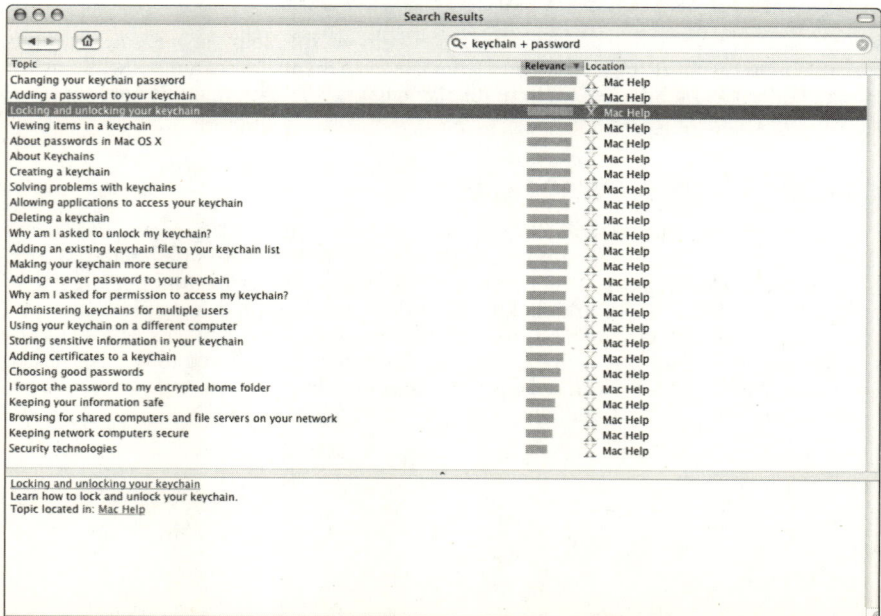

Figure 8-4: Click an underlined link to see related material in the Help Viewer.

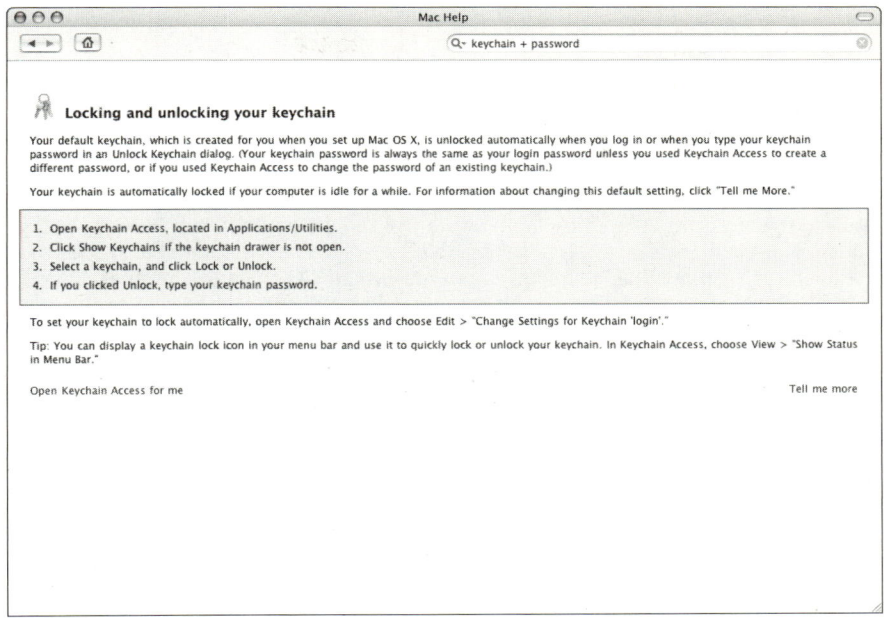

Figure 8-5: Depending upon the Help article, it may contain shortcuts to System Preference or OS X–included applications related to the assistance being sought.

Using Help Viewer Quick Clicks

Quick Clicks are links in articles that take you to many places inside and outside the Help Viewer. If the author of the help article writes clearly, you should have a good idea about where the link takes you. The possibilities include the following:

✦ A link may show you another article in the Help Viewer window.

✦ An Open... link probably opens the application that the article describes.

✦ A Tell me more link displays a list of articles that are related to the current article.

✦ A More link at the bottom of a list of article titles takes you to a continuation of the list.

✦ A Go to the website link shows you a related Web site in your Web browser. Other links may also go to Web sites, which is especially likely if the link includes an Internet address or is near an Internet address in the help article. However, clicking an Internet address that is not underlined in a help article does nothing. Text that is not underlined is not a link in the Help Viewer.

Tip   Links visited since you opened the Help Viewer are red instead of blue.

Retrieving Help from the Internet

At times, the Help Viewer must retrieve help articles from the Internet. For example, an application may initially have only its most popular help articles installed on your computer and keep less commonly read articles on the Internet. If you click a link to an article that's on the Internet, the Help Viewer automatically caches it on your computer. If you later want to read an article that the Help Viewer has already retrieved from the Internet, the Help Viewer displays the cached article on your computer. If there is an updated version of the article, the Help Viewer checks the Internet and will retrieve the newer version. The Help viewer also adds additional articles as they become available. Of course, the Help Viewer can retrieve articles from the Internet only if your computer has an Internet connection. If your computer has a dial-up connection to the Internet or you must go through an authentication procedure to make an Internet connection, the Help Viewer displays a dialog asking whether you want to make the connection.

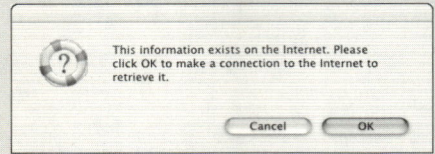

This information exists on the Internet. Please click OK to make a connection to the Internet to retrieve it.

Cancel   OK

If your computer isn't connected to the Internet, and the Help Viewer needs to retrieve an article, you must approve the connection.

Navigating using the Help Viewer buttons

Besides clicking links, you can go places in the Help Viewer by clicking buttons.

✦ Click the Back button (left-arrow) to go back to the previous page in the Help Viewer.

✦ After going back, click the Forward button (right-arrow) to go forward.

✦ Click the home button to return to the opening screen of the topic being viewed within the Help Viewer application and see its list of available help selections.

Searching within the Help Viewer

If you're looking for help on a specific subject and don't want to browse through links until you find it, use the search function to query for the help you need. The Help Viewer uses Sherlock search technology; to do a query, you type some words that are associated with a subject you need help with in the Ask a Question search field at the top of the Help Viewer window, and then press the Return key on your keyboard. When typing words to search for, you can include special characters to describe the help you need more precisely. Table 8-1 describes these special characters.

Tip   If your search words don't turn up the help articles you want, try different forms or combinations of the words you used or use other words to describe the topic you are looking for.

Table 8-1: Special Characters for Help Viewer Searching

Character	Meaning	Search example	Search results
+	and	desktop + Finder	This example finds articles that include both "desktop" and "Finder."
|	or	desktop | Finder	This example finds articles that include either "desktop" or "Finder."
!	not	desktop ! Finder	This example finds articles that include "desktop" but exclude "Finder."
( )	grouping	picture + (Finder | desktop)	This example finds articles that include "picture" and either "desktop" or "Finder."

Displaying Help Tags

Help tags are another form of help. Some applications allow you to get immediate information about GUI elements on the screen by displaying their help tags. If an object has a help tag, it automatically appears when you position the mouse pointer over the object and wait a couple seconds. You can recognize a help tag by its distinctive small yellow box, which contains a very short description of the object under the pointer. If no such box appears when you hover the pointer over an object onscreen, the object has no help tag. You do not have to click anything or press any keys to make a help tag appear. Figure 8-6 shows an example help tag.

Figure 8-6: A help tag describes the object under the pointer in a Mac OS X application.

Mac OS X provides help tag capability, but not all objects have help tags. Commonplace objects, such as window controls and scroll bars, have no help tags. Menus and menu items never have help tags. Buttons and other objects have help tags only if the application that they are part of provides descriptions to be displayed inside the help tags. Classic applications cannot provide help tags at all, and many Mac OS X applications do not provide any help tags.

If you have used Balloon Help in Mac OS 9 or earlier, you probably realize that the help tags are the Mac OS X equivalent of Balloon Help. On the downside, help tags provide much less detailed information than Balloon Help. On the upside, help tags are less intrusive and don't need to be turned on and off.

Getting Command-Line Help

In addition to the various GUI based help systems, Mac OS X's command line has an integrated help system referred to as the man pages. The man pages is accessed with the man command, which is short for manual. The Man pages it provide an online manual that contains information on just about every command available when using the command line.

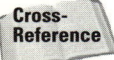

Cross-Reference   The man command and its use are reviewed in detail in Chapter 25.

Exploring Other Avenues of Help

Many applications add how-to help, onscreen reference material, or other items to the Help menu. For example, many applications published by Adobe, FileMaker, and Microsoft list onscreen help commands in the Help menu. The help may appear in the Help Viewer or in your Web browser. Some applications use other help systems to display their onscreen help. For instructions on an application's own help system, check the documentation that came with the application.

On the Web, you can find additional help for your Macintosh computer, Mac OS X, popular applications, and add-on hardware. Check the following sites:

✦ **AppleCare Service and Support:** www.apple.com/support/

✦ **AppleCare Knowledge Base:** http://kbase.info.apple.com/

✦ **Apple Manuals:** www.info.apple.com/manuals/manuals.taf

✦ **Apple Mac OS X Support:** www.info.apple.com/usen/macosx/

✦ **MacFixIt:** www.macfixit.com

✦ **The Web site of the company** that makes the software or hardware for which you need help

Summary

Here's what you should know after reading this chapter:

✦ Mac OS X displays onscreen help in the form of help tags and Help Viewer articles.

✦ The Help Viewer application displays short how-to articles, and you can display them by choosing items from the Help menu or by clicking a Help button in a window that has one. The kind of help that you get varies from application to application.

✦ Some Help Viewer articles include links that you click to see related articles, open related applications, or connect to an Internet site.

✦ You can search all Help Viewer articles for words you specify, optionally using the special characters +, |, !, and ( ) to pinpoint what you want to find.

✦ If an object has a help tag, you view it by positioning the mouse pointer on the object and waiting a few seconds. A help tag appears in a small yellow box and succinctly describes the object under the pointer.

✦ Some applications use help systems not provided by Mac OS X.

✦ As a last resort, one can always turn to the manual or to the product's Web site.

✦　　✦　　✦

At Work with Mac OS X

Printing and Faxing

This chapter covers how to print and fax in Mac OS X. Aside from what is being displayed on a monitor, printing is one of the most common forms of output in computing. Because Mac OS is a preferred platform in print and graphics industries, Apple did everything in its power to equal and often surpass the capabilities of its predecessors and its competition. Not only does Mac OS X deliver print connectivity options superior to any other shipping OS, it also provides built-in faxing and PDF capabilities.

Overview of Mac OS X Printing

Regardless of printing needs — from graphic artists, Apple Certified Technical Coordinators (ACTCs), book or newsletter editors, to home use printers of letters and birthday cards — understanding the underlying technology that comprises the Mac OS X print architecture is helpful in its operation. Mac OS X's printing services are based on the Common UNIX Printing System, better known as CUPS. CUPS is a cross-platform open source printing architecture that supports both PostScript and raster printers.

Mac OS X supports six types of printer connectivity: AppleTalk, Directory Services, IP Printing, Rendezvous, USB, and Windows Printing.

In order to print, Mac OS X requires a driver. A driver is a piece of software that allows the operating system to control a hardware device. If the additional Print Drivers were installed during the initial installation of Mac OS X, the OS supplies by default a sizable collection of third-party printer drivers for popular printers, including printers from Canon, Epson, Hewlett-Packard, and Lexmark. All of these print drivers are located in the top Library folder of your startup disk, grouped into folders by manufacturer. If, by chance, the required driver is not present for your printer, check the printer manufacturer's Web site for availability and the most recent iteration.

In theory, USB printers should provide the path of least resistance for installation (provided that the appropriate printer driver has been installed). If you have a printer connected that matches one of the supplied USB printer drivers, Mac OS X recognizes it automatically and that printer is set as the default choice in the Print dialog.

Note   You may have noticed that the Mac OS X Finder does not include a Print command in its File menu (or any other Finder menu for that matter). If you want to print a Finder window or the Desktop, you will need to take a snapshot of the screen using ⌘-Shift-3, ⌘-Shift-4, or the Grab utility. Then you will need to print it from the Preview application or Grab utility, respectively. Another way to deal with this feature deficiency is to use the third-party shareware utility Print Window, which we cover in Chapter 22.

Overview of Printers

Parallel, serial, USB, network, PostScript, raster, inkjet, laser, LED, dye sublimation, thermal wax, dot matrix, and impact are all ways to categorize printers. There are overlaps between the categories. For example, just because many PostScript printers are networked and laser-based doesn't mean that a USB inkjet printer can't be networked or PostScript enabled. Also, although Macintosh computers do not include the parallel ports required for many popular printers (for Windows), that doesn't rule out the use of a Windows printer by a Mac. Several third-party manufacturers sell USB-to-parallel converter cables that enable Macs to print to a select number of supported printers.

A quick review of the printer technology scene is as follows: Networked printers are printers accessed via a network connection such as Ethernet or AirPort using either IP or AppleTalk networking protocols. USB printers are physically connected to your Mac or to a USB hub, which in turn is connected to your Mac. Printers that use serial connectivity are literally and figuratively dinosaurs in the sense that they are being replaced by USB connectivity, and as such no recently manufactured Macintosh computers even include a serial port.

PostScript is a *page description language* (PDL) developed by Adobe Systems. PostScript is a mathematical language that has operators, variables, and commands that control precise shape and placement information for everything that gets drawn on a page, not just the fonts, although they are the most obvious example people see. A PostScript printer has a *raster image processor* (RIP), which translates the PostScript code into a *raster image* (set of discrete dots) that represents the data on the printed page at the current printer resolution. Thus, a one-inch line that is 1/6 of an inch thick is translated into 15,000 dots at 300 dpi, and into 240,000 dots at 1200 dpi. Because the RIP is an embedded computer requiring its own memory, PostScript printers are generally more expensive than non-PostScript printers. (And add the fee charged by Adobe or another RIP vendor to the printer manufacturer for using their RIP.) Although more common on laser printers, you can also find PostScript-enabled inkjet printers and dye-sublimation printers.

An alternative to PostScript RIPs are raster RIPs. A raster image processor uses a combination of hardware and software that converts images described in the form of vector graphics statements into raster graphics images or bitmaps.

Inkjet printers produce their output by spraying streams of ink through tiny nozzles onto the paper, transparency, or other media. Laser printers use heat to affix tiny particles of toner to the output medium.

On the surface, the least expensive printer type, at least initially, is the inkjet. However, if you're going to be producing a lot of output you'll find that the cost of consumables (ink cartridges) is fairly high. A single cartridge typically lasts about 500 pages and costs approximately $20 (some less, some more). In contrast, a typical laser printer produces about 4,000 pages from one toner cartridge that costs approximately $100.

Mac OS X ships with the ability to use most of the currently shipping printers; to verify if your printer is compatible visit http://www.apple.com/macosx/upgrade/printers.html.

Configuring Page Setup

Before a document can be printed, page parameters must be established. In Mac OS X, this is handled through the Page Setup sheet located in an application's File menu. The Page Setup sheet is where you specify the size paper to print on, whether you are going to print *portrait* (taller than wide) or *landscape* (wider than tall), the direction of the paper feed, and whether your document is going to be reduced or enlarged. All of these options are called *page attributes* and are managed through one screen, as shown in Figure 9-1.

The Settings pop-up menu has two other choices, Custom Paper Size and Summary. As the name implies, Custom Paper Size allows for the specification of custom paper sizes. The Summary choice is a consolidated report of the various choices made under Page Attributes. The Summary pane is handy when you have made a lot of changes in different panes and want to verify the settings without having to go through the panes one at a time.

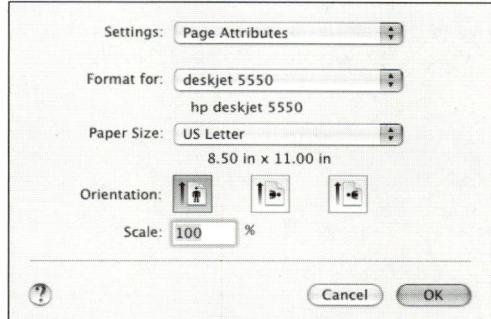

Figure 9-1: General document printing parameters are set in the Page Setup sheet.

Applications use the information from Page Setup to establish the parameters for margins and where page breaks occur.

When you select Page Attributes from the Settings pop-up menu, the following options appear:

✦ **Format for:** Enables you to select a specific or a generic printer for which your software will format a document. A generic printer has a limited set of capabilities — essentially those that would be available on any printer. When you choose a specific printer, its printer type is displayed beneath the pop-up menu.

✦ **Paper Size:** Enables you to select from the various paper sizes. A generic printer supports only US Letter, US Legal, A4, and B5 paper sizes, but specific printers will generally support a wider range, possibly including such things as #10 envelopes or 3 x 5-inch index cards. The physical dimensions of the paper size are displayed below the Paper Size pop-up, as shown in Figure 9-1.

✦ **Orientation:** Determines whether the top of the printed page is on the short edge of the paper (portrait), the bottom of the long edge (landscape), or the top of the long edge (also landscape).

✦ **Scale:** Reduces or enlarges the printed document according to the percentage you enter based on the documents original size. Full size is 100%. Because the page image is rendered in resolution-independent PDF, you don't have rigid minimum and maximum values imposed for scale. However, as a general rule, you should keep in mind the physical limitations of your printer and the resolutions it can print.

Printing and Printing Options

After the page parameters have been established, you will need to select Print... from an application's File menu (⌘-P), which produces the Print dialog, a GUI interface for configuring printing options. The Print dialog lets you select printers and their configuration options as well as preview, print, fax, or create a PDF of a document.

Adding a printer

If you don't have a local USB printer recognized by Mac OS X, the first time you print, the Print dialog says No Printer Selected in the Printer pop-up menu, as shown in Figure 9-2. Proceed as follows:

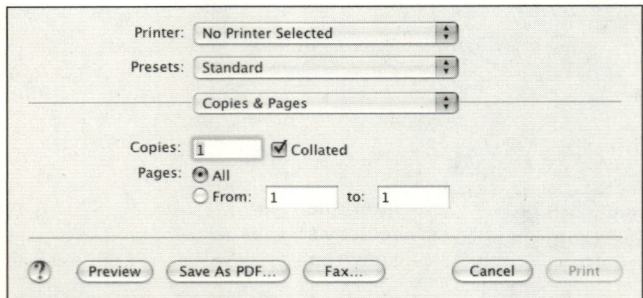

Figure 9-2: Add a printer.

1. **Select Edit Printer List...** from the Printer pop-up menu to open the Print Setup Utility. You will be presented with a dialog that states: You have no printers available. Would you like to add to your printer list now?

2. **Click the Add...** button to display the available printers, as shown in Figure 9-3.

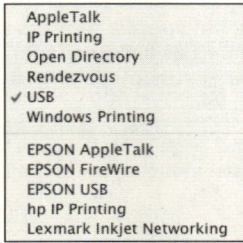

Figure 9-3: The Printer List sheet facilitates the selection of printers.

3. From the top pop-up menu, select one of the following:

- **AppleTalk** to connect to an AppleTalk enabled printer over a network as depicted in Figure 9-4. In order to connect to an AppleTalk-based printer, the AppleTalk networking protocol must first be enabled within the Network pane of System Preferences. If it is not, Mac OS 10.3 will automatically enable AppleTalk on your behalf. When you select a printer, the print Setup utility will then attempt to determine the printer type and bind the corresponding printer description to your selection. You can also manually select the appropriate printer description or, if your network is configured for it, a different AppleTalk zone.

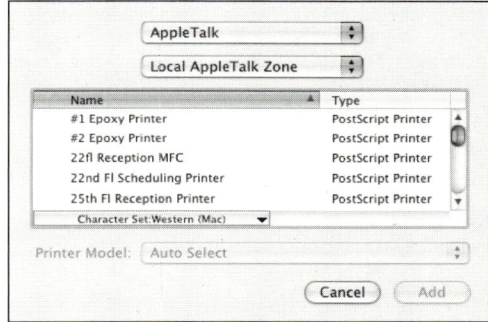

Figure 9-4: AppleTalk may be getting long in the tooth, but it's still a common protocol found on most Macintosh networks.

- **Open Directory** to list printers and printer queues that are available through NetInfo or LDAP directory services. Directory services should come into play in larger and more structured networking environments only.

- **IP Printing** if you wish to connect to a printer via Internet protocols such as *line printer daemon* (LPD), *line print remote* (LPR), and *Internet printing protocol* (IPP). To use IP Printing, your Mac will require a valid IP address, which is configured in the Network pane of System Preferences. We cover this maneuver in Chapter 13. You will also be required to input the intended printer's IP address or *domain name server* (DNS) name, as well as specify the model of the printer. Figure 9-5 shows the IP Printing window.

- **Rendezvous** to connect to Rendezvous-equipped printers connected to a network. Rendezvous is a networking protocol that allows automatic discovery, connectivity, and configuration of Rendezvous-aware applications and devices via the Zeroconf standard.

- **USB** if your Mac is connected to a USB printer and the printer requires manual configuration.

- **Windows Printing** to utilize a windows (SMB) printer on a network.

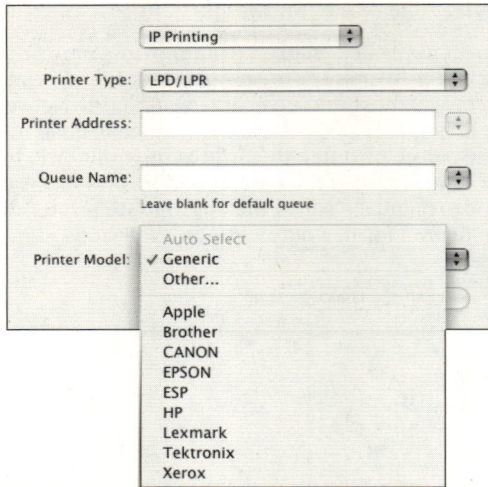

Figure 9-5: Select IP Printing from the pop-up menu to connect to a printer by specifying the printers DNS name.

4. **Click the Add button to add the printer to your available printer list.** The bottom portion of the menu provides the ability to select various manufacturer-specific modes of connectivity. The choices include, but are not limited to, Epson AppleTalk, Epson FireWire, Epson USB, HP IP Printing, and Lexmark Inkjet Networking.

To remove a printer, just select the printer you want to delete in the Print Center's list and click the Delete button.

Setting print options

After the printer has been configured, clicking on the unlabeled pop-up menu in the Print dialog, displays a list of print options that are for your selected printer, as shown in Figure 9-6.

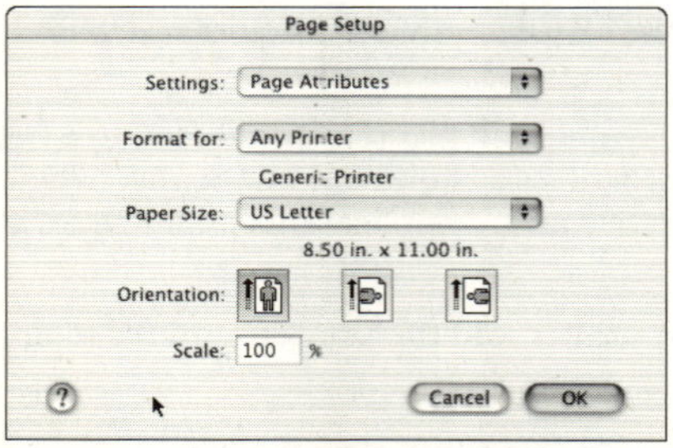

Figure 9-6: Although I do not have a name, I am central to printing!

Depending upon the option selected, the Print dialog changes its vertical size similarly to the behavior of the panes in the System Preferences application. The choices presented in this pop-up menu vary depending on the model of printer selected in the Printer pop-up menu. The following selections are likely to be present, in addition to a number of application-specific and printer-specific choices:

✦ **Copies & Pages:** Allows you to specify the number of copies desired. You can also indicate whether to collate the printout, and in what manner it should be output — one full copy followed by the next, or all the copies of each page to print together. Here you can also specify whether you want all pages of the document printed, just a specific range, or reverse the order of how a document should print. For example, you can just specify the ending page in the From box and beginning page in the To box to print from the last page to the first page of a document.

✦ **Output Options:** Allows you to save a file as a PDF (.pdf) or, if the printer you are using supports PostScript, save a file as a PostScript file (.ps). Using proprietary software supplied by the printer's manufacturer, some printers support the ability to print PostScript files independently of any print command. PostScript files can also be converted into PDFs using the Preview application. You can use PDF files as a means of distributing documents electronically via email and file servers.

Tip

If you don't have access to a PostScript printer and you desire to output a PostScript file, it is possible to still create one. You will need to create a virtual PostScript printer. To do so, open the Print Setup utility, add an IP printer, and type **localhost** in the Printer Address field. Name your virtual PostScript printer accordingly in the Queue Name field.

✦ **Imaging Options:** Allows you to select paper size and scale the image or crop the image to fit the indicated paper size.

✦ **Scheduler:** Allows you to specify at what time a printout should occur.

✦ **ColorSync:** Allows you to configure ColorSync output options without modifying the colors in a document.

✦ **Cover Page:** Allows you to select a preconfigured print-job cover page, indicate whether to print it before or after the document, and indicate billing info.

✦ **Error Handling:** Allows you to configure Mac OS X to print error reports, which may be useful in troubleshooting PostScript errors.

✦ **Two-Sided Printing/Duplex:** Allows you to indicate the use of both sides of the paper as well as the orientation of the output for binding purposes.

✦ **Paper Type/Quality:** Allows you to tell the printer whether to print in color or black and white, what type of media (paper, film, or transparencies) is being used, and whether to emphasize speed or quality.

✦ **Print Driver Information:** Allows you to obtain information about the version of the print driver that is being used.

✦ **Summary:** Allows you to see a summarized report of your settings for all the printer options that are available.

Most LaserWriter drivers will offer at least some of the following additional choices:

✦ **Paper Feed:** Allows you to specify the location from where the paper feeds. Set the pages to come from the same source or click the "First page from" radio button to choose a specific source for the first page, as well as a source for the remaining pages.

✦ **Error Handling:** Enables you to indicate whether you want a detailed report of any PostScript errors. You can also specify whether to switch trays if one runs out of paper and the printer has more than one tray available.

Applications often have at least one application-specific print option choice. For example, when printing from Microsoft's Word, there is a Microsoft Word option in the unlabeled pop-up menu in the Print dialog. In this instance, the applications-specific option provides a more granular control over what is being printed, as shown in Figure 9-7.

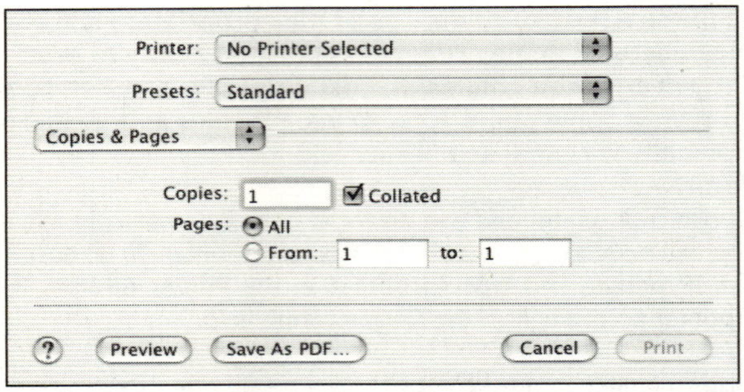

Figure 9-7: All pages, odd pages, even pages, it's all good.

In addition to the selections available in the unlabeled pop-up menu, the Print dialog also contains the following:

✦ **Presets:** This pop-up menu allows you to save and name groups of print options from the unlabeled menu in the Print dialog. This permits the quick selection of a group of print options without individually selecting them. To save the current settings for the print job, click the Presets pop-up menu and choose Save As.... You can use the Rename command on the Presets pop-up menu to rename a saved preset if you want to change its name. In future print sessions, that choice appears in the Presets pop-up menu at the top of the Print dialog.

✦ **Preview:** This button creates a temporary PDF file, which is then opened in the Preview application for perusal. If you like, you can save the file from within Preview as either a TIFF or PDF file or you can simply print it. Previews do not display the effects of print options such as Front and Back printing or printing several pages per sheet.

✦ **Save as PDF...:** Allows you to save the document as a PDF. Click the Save as PDF... button to show a Save to File window, shown in Figure 9-8, which you use to choose where on the computer to save the PDF. The only difference between saving a PDF via Output Options within the unlabeled menu in the Print dialog and the Save as PDF... button is that the configuration of the former can be contained within custom presets for easy access.

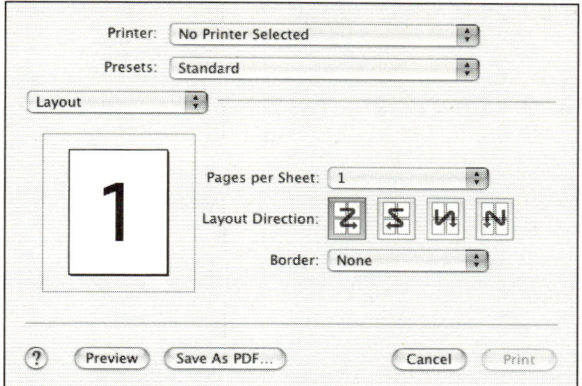

Figure 9-8: Use the Save to File dialog to save the PDF of your document to your computer.

Using the Print & Fax preferences pane

The Print & Fax preferences pane is a new addition to Mac OS 10.3. Although, it certainly aids in the simplification of printer configuration, its design was motivated by the need to make the operating system more intuitive to the Windows' user experience. To access the Print & Fax preference pane you will need to open the System Preferences located in the Applications folder. One way to do this is to select System Preferences from the Apple Menu. Another way to access the Print & Fax preferences pane is to select Preferences form the Print Setup Utility's Printer Setup Menu. The Print & Fax preferences pane is divided into two panels, Printing and Faxing. The Printing Panel has a button title Set Up Printers, which is a shortcut to the Printer Setup Utility. The Printing panel also allows you to specify a default printer and a default paper size within a Print dialog, and enable USB printer sharing as depicted in Figure 9-9.

Receiving a fax

The Faxing panel as shown in Figure 9-10, allows for the configuration of receipt of faxes. To receive a fax, follow these steps:

1. **Place a checkmark in the box next to Receive faxes on this computer.**

2. **Specify the desired number of rings to answer on in the field adjacent to When a Fax Arrives: Answer after (entry field) rings.**

   - **Specify the location to save faxes to...** in the Save to pop-up menu.

   - **Place a checkmark...** in the box next to Email to and specify an email address to forward received faxes to an email account.

   - **Place a checkmark...** in the box to the left of Print on printer and to the right specify the desired printer using the pop-up menu.

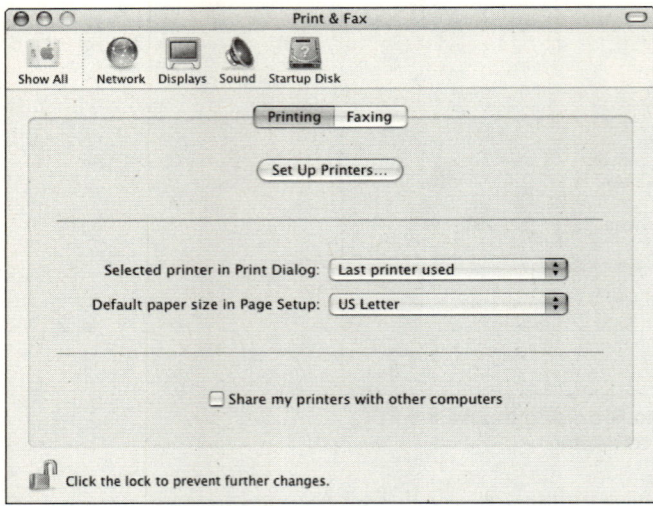

Figure 9-9: To make locally attached printers and fax modems available to other users via a network, place a checkmark in the box to left of Share my printers with other computers.

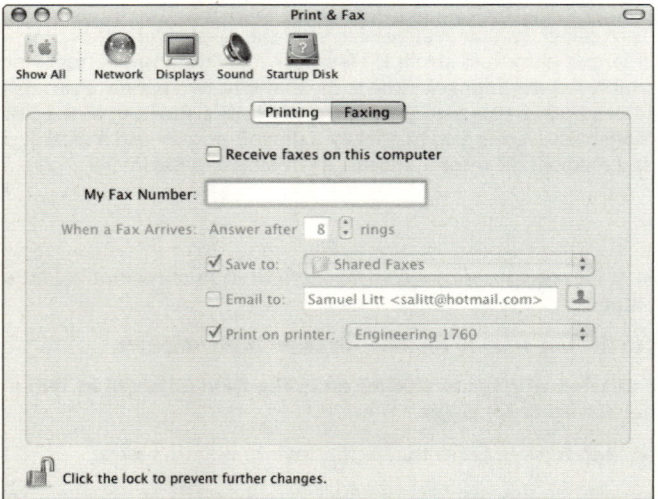

Figure 9-10: The Email to feature is dependent on Mac OS X's included Mail application.

Sending a fax

Although Microsoft's Window's operating systems has had integrated faxing capability for years, this is a new addition to Mac OS. Traditionally, faxing on Mac platform has always been handled by means of third-party software or services, such as FaxSTF or eFax. In fact, up until recently, Apple included a copy of SmithMicro Software's FaxSTF as part its software bundle with most shipping Macs. If you have used FaxSTF on Mac OS X in the past, you will undoubtedly find Panther's integrated faxing to be similar in operation. Although the usefulness of faxing has been somewhat nullified by email, faxing can be handy in communicating with computer challenged and as a means of printing when on the road and no printer is available. Mac OS 10.3 faxing operation is as follows:

✦ **Fax button:** Allows you to fax the document utilizing a local or shared analogue modem. Click the Fax button to show the Fax dialog as depicted in Figure 9-11.

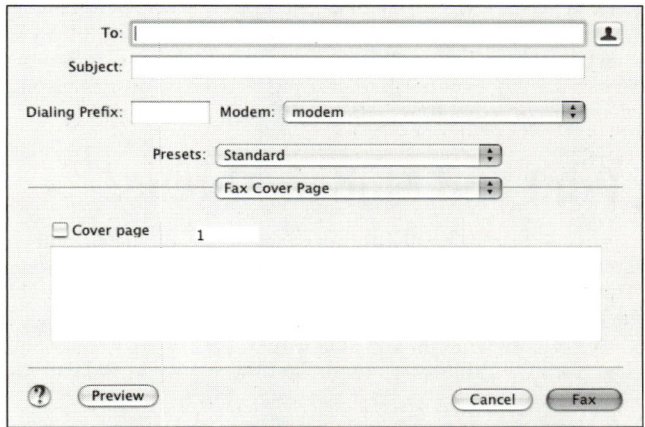

Figure 9-11: The operation of Mac OS X's built-in faxing is similar to that of FaxSTF.

✦ The **Fax** dialog operates in similar fashion to the Print dialog with a few exceptions; the most obvious being the To, the Subject, and the Dialing Prefix fields, and the Modem menu. The To field is where you specify the recipient of the fax. This can be done manually or via the fax Address book. To the right of the To field, is a button with an exclamation mark on it. This button opens up a fax Addresses window as shown in Figure 9-12, which lists the entries that have been input into the Address Book application located in the Applications folder.

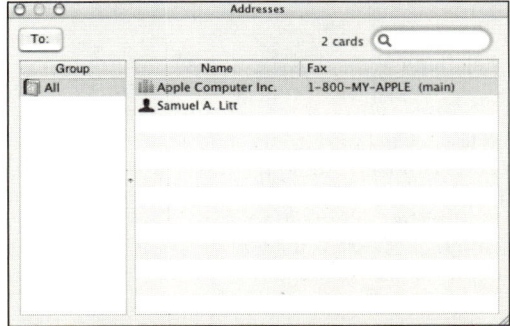

Figure 9-12: Use fax address book to select your Fax recipients.

✦ The **Subject** entry field is where you specify the subject of the fax.

✦ The **Prefix** field is where you would specify a dialing prefix such as disable call waiting (*70), and/or a country code such as (01144) for the United Kingdom.

✦ The **Modem field** is where you specify the modem that will be used to transmit the fax. There is also an option titled Show Fax List.... This is a shortcut that will open the Fax List window within the Print Setup Utility.

Cover Page and Modem are two noteworthy selections that appear under the unlabeled Print dialog menu when faxing. In Cover Page, you can select a predefined cover page as well as input the message you want to include on the cover page. This option enables you to select a cover page, specify where the cover page will be ordered in the fax, and assign billing information. In Modem, you can specify whether to dial using tone or pulse, if the sound should be on or off, and whether to wait for a dial tone before printing.

Administering Print and Modem Queues

In Mac OS 10.3, the majority of printer configuration is administered via a single application called the Printer Setup Utility, shown in Figure 9-13. There are three ways to access the Printer Setup Utility. The first and most direct way is to open it from inside the Utilities folder within the Applications folder. Another way is to open it via the Set Up Printers... button located in the Print & Fax Preference pane. The final way to access the Printer Setup Utility is to select Edit Printer List from the Printer pop-up menu that resides in all Print dialogs.

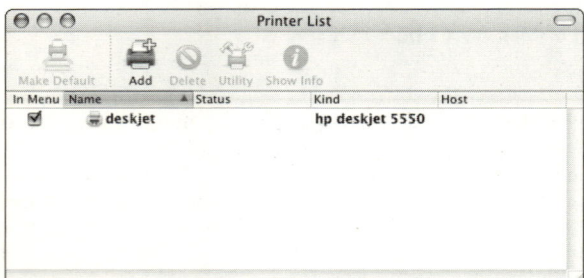

Figure 9-13: Printer configuration occurs in the Printer Setup Utility.

The Printer Setup Utility also has the ability to display the status of all print and fax jobs pending; this information can be found in what is referred to as the printer's print queue or a fax's Modem queue. Open the Printer Setup Utility (located in the Utilities folder in the Applications folder) and either double-click on a printer in the Printer List whose queue you want to manage or select the printer and choose Printers ➪ Show Jobs (⌘-O) to open a window for that printer's queue, as shown in Figure 9-14. Here you can delete a job, hold a job, resume a job, or stop the queue entirely. The Utility button displays printer-specific maintenance software if available. Printer utility software is usually supplied by the printer manufacturer and typically performs operations such as alignment and cleaning of inkjet print heads.

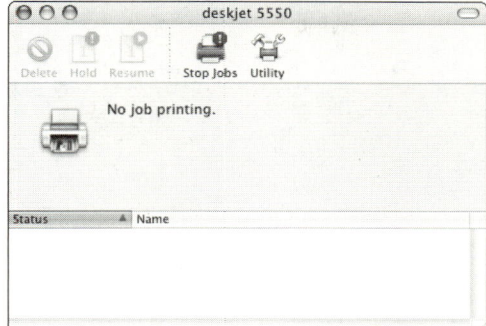

Figure 9-14: The queue depicted above is from a HP DeskJet 5550.

 **Tip**

If you are on the road and you want to print, but your printer is unavailable, you can stop the print queue and then issue the print command. Even if you turn off the computer, print jobs are retained. When you can connect back to the printer the document will be automatically printed.

To view the Modem queue, select Show Fax List from the View menu in the Printer Setup Utility and either double-click on a modem in the Modem List whose queue you want to manage or select the modem and choose Printers ⇨ Show Jobs (⌘-O) to open a window for that modem's queue as seen in Figure 9-15.

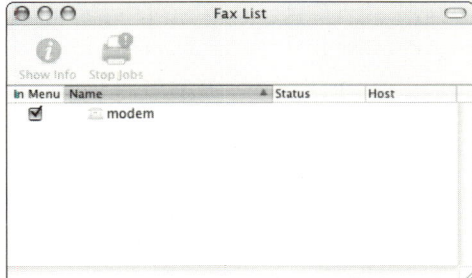

Figure 9-15 Except that it is managing modem queues, the administration of the Fax List is identical in operation to a Printer List.

For those of us who are not satisfied with status quos, the toolbars on the Printer and Fax Lists, as well as those on the print and modem queues, can all be customized in a similar fashion to a toolbar in a Finder window. To do so select Customize Toolbar... from the View menu and a custom options pane will materialize out of the corresponding window, as depicted in Figure 9-16.

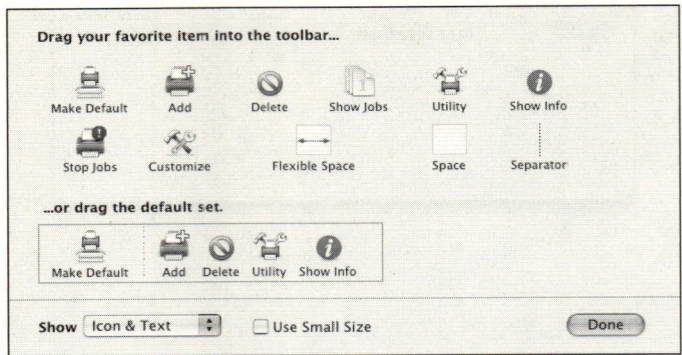

Figure 9-16: You can choose from many options.

You can also customize the columns in the Printer List and Fax List to contain any of the following headings: Kind (inkjet, PostScript, and so on.), Host (a computer sharing a printer), Status (Stopped, Printing, and so on.), Location (location of printer), and Jobs (name of current job printing). To do so, open the desired Printer List or the Fax List and make your selections under the Columns option in the View menu.

Other abilities of interest in the Printer Setup Utility include the following:

✦ **Make Default:** Determines from a list of printers which one will be the default. To select a default printer, highlight the desired printer in the Printer List and select Make Default from either the toolbar or the Printers menu. You can also use the key combination ⌘-D.

✦ **In Menu:** Provides the option to choose which printers will appear in the Printer menu in the Print dialog. To remove the printer, deselect it under the menu column in the Printer List.

✦ **Show Info:** Where you specify the printer's name and location, specify the Printer Model, and configure any installable options if available. To display currently selected options, highlight the desired printer in the Printer List and click on Show Info in the toolbar or select Show Info from the Printers menu or use the key combination ⌘-I.

Maximizing OS X Printing

Aside from the obvious ability to send faxes, a number of new features have been added to Mac OS 10.3 print capabilities. One of the most highly requested features to be added is the return of Mac OS 9's Desktop Printer functionality. A Desktop Printer is an iconic representation of a print queue or a modem queue that can be accessed via the GUI. This icon can be saved anywhere the user account has access to. By clicking on the Desktop Printer you will be directly able to administer the queue that you want to manage, circumventing the need to first open the Printer Setup Utility and then selecting the queue that you want to administer. To make a Desktop Printer, click on the intended queue from within the Printer Setup Utility and select Create Desktop Printer... from the Printers menu. The queues that Desktop Printers represent also temporarily manifest themselves in the Dock when jobs are being printed to them. As with Mac OS 9's Desktop Printers, Mac OS X's allows for dragging a document to print. You can also open the Desktop Printer and drag the desired document into the print queue, as well as drag jobs between print queues.

Pooling printers

Also new to Mac OS X printing is the Pool Printers feature. Pool Printers enables you to create a collection of printers, called a printer pool. A printer pool helps avoid printing delays by channeling a print job away from a busy printer to one that is not. If all printers in a printer pool are busy, the print job prints to the first available printer. To make a printer pool, select two or more printers in the Printer List by clicking on a desired printer and subsequently ⌘-clicking on any additional printers. Select Pool Printers from the Printer menu. Enter a name for the printer pool in the Printer Pool Name field. Drag the printers in order of priority to check for printing availability.

Checking for updates

One last printing addition to Max OS X worth noting is the Check for Printer Updates feature. Check for Printer Updates provides the ability to check for updated printer software from the Printer menu in the Print dialog. When selected, it will open up and run Mac OS X's built-in software update mechanism. These updates are provided by Apple and are supplied via an Internet connection. If updates are found, you can select and install them. Software Update is covered in greater detail in Chapter 22.

Tip   An alternate way you can administer the print services of Mac OS X is via the CUPS Web interface. As mentioned at the beginning of this chapter, CUPS (Common UNIX Printing System) is a cross-platform open-source printing architecture that is the heart of Mac OS X's print services. The CUPS Web interface is accessed through a Web browser utilizing the internal host address of the system (127.0.0.1) on port 631. Although not as intuitive as the Printer Setup Utility, the CUPS Web interface provides another GUI way to administer Mac OS X print services.

Summary

In this chapter, you've seen how to print, fax, and make PDFs as well as configure printers and manage print and modem queues using Printer Setup Utility. Mac OS X is a modern OS, and its CUPS-based print services reflect that. With its built-in support for numerous print connectivity options, in addition to its built-in faxing and on-the-fly PDF capabilities, Mac OS X's print services are an evolutionary leap over its predecessors and its competition.

✦   ✦   ✦

Accessing Files over a Network

Viewing Web pages over the Internet is just one type of network service that you can access with your computer. Just as the Internet is one way of obtaining information and viewing files, so is file sharing over a network and the Internet. Using different types of connection protocols and interfacing with Mac, Windows, and Internet servers, your Mac can connect to an abundance of devices and trade files back and forth between them all. This chapter explains first how to access files from other people's machines, how to use Mac OS X's keychains to keep track of all your passwords for you, and finally how to set up your own Mac for sharing files so that other users can get them from you.

Accessing Files

The sharing part of file sharing implies a give-and-take scenario. On a network, and over the Internet, you can take and use files from other people's computers, and, if you set your computer to allow it, they can do the same from you. Computers that provide files and storage space are known as *file servers*. A file server is said to be a dedicated server when it's a computer that is not used for personal work. Its primary job is to share files. A file server can also be someone's personal computer (also called a workstation) that, aside from being used for regular work, is set up to share its files with other network computers. For files to be moved between the machines, a specific client-server protocol must be used. These protocols are the language with which different hardware and different operating systems can speak to each other. Mac OS X supports quite a few of them. All are accessible through the Finder.

Apple has had its own file sharing protocol called AFP, or Apple Filing Protocol. Macintosh file servers use the AFP protocol. The address of an AFP server begins with `afp://`.

Windows servers typically use the SMB (Server Message Block) or CIFS (Common Internet File System) protocols for file sharing. Your Mac can connect to these without issue. Windows file server addresses usually begin with `smb://`.

Sharing files over the Internet is often done through FTP, or File Transfer Protocol. `ftp://` at the beginning of a server address designates it as an FTP server.

Other protocols that are supported in OS X include WebDAV and NFS. WebDAV stands for Web-based Distributed Authoring and Versioning, and is usually used in Web server applications where live changes need to be made to online material. NFS stands for Network File System, and is the native file sharing protocol that Unix uses.

The great thing about OS X is that Apple has made connecting to all these different kinds of servers and protocols extremely uniform in method. While specific messages and dialog boxes might be different, the basics are the same. To use any of these kinds of file servers or protocols, all you need is the Finder. With the Finder, you can connect to a file server, mount server volumes, see your access privileges on the server volumes, and copy files. You can also use the Finder to open files from a server, or you can open server files directly from within other applications. When you're finished using a server, you use the Finder to disconnect from it.

Tip   You can also connect to AFP and FTP shares by typing their addresses into the address field in Safari. When you hit the return key to connect, Mac OS X brings you an authentication dialog box, just as if you connected through the Finder.

Connecting to a file server

In previous versions of Mac OS X, the only way to connect to a server was to pull down the Finder's Go menu, and choose the Connect to Server option (⌘-K). This presents you with a dialog box in which you can both browse the network for local servers, or type an address and connect to a remote one. Puzzling to many people was that there was a "Network" globe visible at the Computer level of the Finder, which seemed as though it would be a convenient way to browse the local network. This was true in special circumstances only (when in the presence of a NetInfo server) and was often left unused.

In Mac OS X 10.3, Apple separates the methods for connecting to servers. The Connect to Server dialog box still exists, but it is mainly for specifying a known or remote server. Local servers are now accessible through the Network globe in the Finder, as it was commonly assumed in previous OS X versions. If you are in the Connect to Server dialog, you can hit the Browse button to open a new Finder window with the Network globe selected. Designating a server as local merely means that it is part of your network. The usual side-effect of this is that a local server will be visible when browsing for servers; you don't have to specify its location. A remote server, however, will not show up when browsing, and its location must be specified. Yes, it is possible to connect "remotely" to a local server by using the Connect To Server box and not browsing, but for our purposes, local servers will be accessed through the Finder's Network icon and remote servers will be accessed by choosing the Connect To Server command. Choosing the Connect to Server option from the Go menu presents you with the dialog box shown in Figure 10-1.

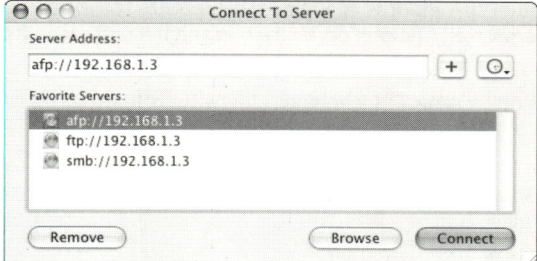

Figure 10-1: Your journey to a file server connection begins with this box.

Connecting remotely

The main idea here is to type in the address of a server and hit the Connect button to engage. If you want to view the servers that are available locally, click the Browse button. Although there are a bunch of different servers that you can connect to, the basic way in which you do so is the same. The following list is a breakdown of the elements found within the Connect to Server box:

✦ **Server Address:** This is the field in which you specify the location of your server. Just as you type in a URL for connecting to a Web site through Safari, you also must type in a URL to connect to a server. A Web site is specified by its http beginnings. When connecting to a file server, instead of specifying the hypertext transfer protocol, you need to specify a files sharing protocol, like FTP. For example, take the server at address 192.168.1.3. It is possible for this machine to have services active for connecting over many different protocols. The URL that you type in (for example ftp://192.168.1.3 for an FTP connection) is what specifies which service to connect to.

✦ **Add to Favorites:** The Add to Favorites button (the button with the plus sign) is used to save server addresses for future connection. Essentially, you are bookmarking the address, just as if you were bookmarking a Web site. If you are about to connect to a server and feel that you will want to visit it later, click the plus sign to add it to your list of favorite servers. Doing so also places a double-clickable file in your Favorites folder that you can launch to reconnect as well.

Note

If your Mac has file sharing turned on, you see your Mac listed as one of the file servers on the network. If you try to connect to it, Mac OS X will politely tell you that you need to access those files locally and not over the network.

✦ **Recent Servers:** Clicking on the Choose a Recent Server button (the button with a clock face icon) pulls down a list and displays the servers to which you have recently connected. The Mac OS saves your recent connections so you don't have to. If you have never connected to a server before, the list will be empty.

✦ **Favorite Servers:** In this portion of the window is a list of the servers that you saved by clicking on the Add to Favorites button. Clicking on an item in the list will place its address into the address field.

✦ **Remove:** Clicking the Remove button removes a selected favorite from the favorites list.

✦ **Browse:** Use the Browse button if you don't know the address of the server that you want to connect to, or if you just want to view all of the servers that are available over the network. Clicking on the Browse button takes you to a new Finder window within the network.

✦ **Connect:** Click the Connect button to initiate your connection to the server.

In all cases, if the address is valid and the server is online, after you hit the Connect button, you are presented with another dialog. This box confirms that a connection has been achieved, and has places for entering your name and password so that you can authenticate to the server. Depending on whether you are connecting to an AFP, FTP, or SMB volume, the box will look slightly different. In any case, the end goal is to access the files of these volumes from within the graphical interface of the Finder. Ahead, we look at the different possibilities.

Connecting to AppleTalk File Servers

Mac OS X normally uses the TCP/IP protocol to communicate with AppleShare file servers and file-sharing computers. However, many AppleShare file servers still use the AppleTalk protocol that was the standard for Mac file servers during the 15 years prior to Mac OS X. Beginning with Version 10.1, Mac OS X can use both TCP/IP and AppleTalk for file servers and file sharing. But Mac OS X does not use AppleTalk unless it was activated when your computer was set up for a network. If you don't see AppleTalk listed above Local Network in the Connect to Server dialog, then you need to activate AppleTalk before you can connect to file servers and file-sharing computers that use it. You make AppleTalk active in the Network pane of System Preferences, as described in Chapter 15.

The AppleTalk address of a file server is different from a TCP/IP address, because AppleTalk identifies file servers by name. If a file server's AppleTalk name includes spaces or symbols, these elements have to be encoded in the Address box of the Connect to Server dialog. For example, the AppleTalk address of a file server whose name is Aphrodite's G4 would appear as `afp:/at/Aphrodite%d5s%20G4` in the Address box. The code `%d5` stands for an apostrophe, and the code `%20` stands for a space. (These codes are based on ASCII code of the character, expressed as a hexadecimal number.)

Note that the AppleTalk address of an AppleShare file server or file-sharing computer begins with `afp:/` protocol identifier. This is similar to the `afp://` protocol identifier that begins the TCP/IP address of an AppleShare file server. However, the AppleTalk address has only one slash after the colon.

Connecting to AppleTalk-TCP/IP File Servers

Some file servers can communicate using AppleTalk and TCP/IP at the same time. This is referred to *AFP over IP* meaning that Apple's filing protocol is traveling over the TCP/IP protocol. Anytime you type in an address that begins with `afp://`, this will be the case. You need both AppleTalk and TCP/IP to be active in order to connect to one of these servers on a network; without AppleTalk active, the servers usually will not be visible while browsing. Without TCP/IP active, your Mac will not connect, and will display an error message when you try.

AFP connections

After typing in the URL of the Apple File Protocol server that you want to connect to, and hitting the Connect button, you are presented with an untitled dialog box that prompts you to connect either as a guest or a registered user of the server, as shown in Figure 10-2.

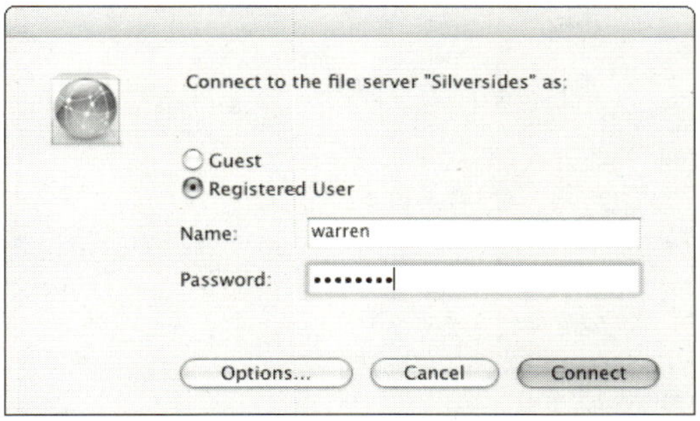

Connect to the file server "Silversides" as:

○ Guest
⦿ Registered User

Name: warren

Password: ••••••••

Options...   Cancel   Connect

Figure 10-2: Establish your identity as a guest or registered user of a file server.

To connect as a registered user, select the Registered User option and enter your registered name and password in the dialog. To be a registered user means that the owner of the server has set up a user account for you with the proper access privileges, and assigned this name and password to you. If your own computer is set up as a file server (later in this chapter) and you're connecting to it from another computer, enter your Mac OS X account name and password. When you enter your password, you must type it exactly right, including uppercase and lowercase letters. (It's case-sensitive.) Then click OK.

Enabling people to log in as a guest user means that anyone, including those without a user account and a password, can log into the server and access certain files. If you're not a registered user and the Guest option isn't disabled (grayed out), you can select the guest option to connect that way. However, guests usually have far fewer privileges on a file server than registered users. If the Guest option is disabled, guests are not permitted to access the file server. If you don't have a registered name and password for the file server, ask its owner to give you one.

Setting preferences for file server connections

While identifying yourself as a registered user or guest, you have the opportunity to set some preferences concerning the handling of your password and your connection. Clicking on the Options button shown in Figure 10-2 presents you with another dialog box, shown in Figure 10-3. This dialog provides you with a number of options. You can change your password by clicking on the Change Password button. You are then asked to type in your old password once, and the new one twice, for confirmation. Clicking OK saves the new password. You can also decide whether you want the password added to your keychain, which saves you the trouble of entering them every time you connect to the server. Check the box next to Add Password to Keychain to do this. (The keychain is discussed in detail later in this chapter.) If you click the Save Preferences button, the current settings become the default settings for future file server connections. Click OK to return to the identification dialog. Figure 10-3 shows the preference settings dialog.

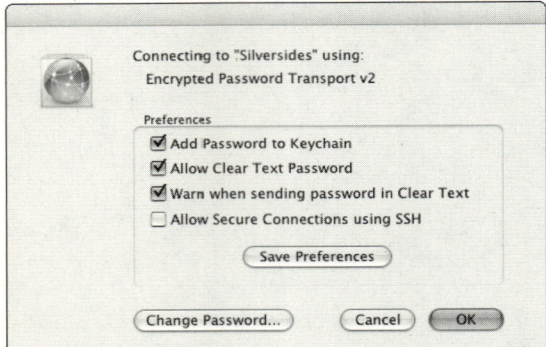

Figure 10-3: Set preferences for your password and your connection.

Selecting network volumes

After you hit the connect button from the identification screen, you see another dialog. This dialog tells you the name of the server to which you're connecting and the various volumes on that server that you can mount, as shown in Figure 10-4.

Connecting as a registered user gives you the choice of any folders or volumes to which you have access as one of the following:

✦ Any folders or volumes to which the owner or a member of the access group has access

✦ Any folders or volumes to which everybody else has access

✦ The Public folders of all other accounts on that Mac OS X machine

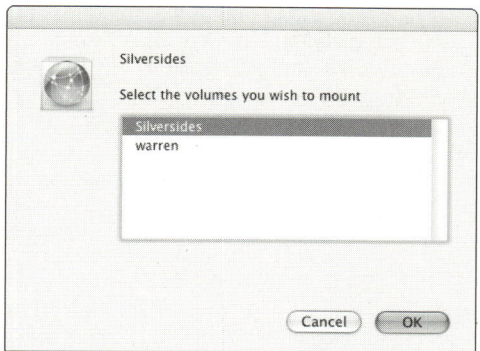

Figure 10-4: Select the volumes you want to mount from the file server.

If you are connecting to your own machine, you will typically see two volumes available to you. One is the name of your hard drive; because you are its owner, you have full access to it. The other volume will be your user folder, which you are also the owner of. If the server allows Guest access and you choose to connect as a Guest, you'll see a separate volume for each user that has a public folder. You'll also see any folders or volumes specifically set up for Guest access. You can double-click on the volumes you want to mount or select them (⌘-click or Shift-click for multiple items) and hit the OK button. Servers connected to through the Connect to Server dialog will show up in the Finder's sidebar, and mount on the desktop if you have your Finder preferences set that way.

After the volumes are mounted, you can treat them like any other disk, and begin working with the files. Refer to Chapter 3 for more discussion of access privileges, which are set through the Get Info windows in the Finder (or by Unix commands in the Terminal application).

Connecting to Microsoft Windows file servers

In a world dominated by Microsoft Windows (at least on the computing front), being able to access files on a Windows file server is important. Beginning with Mac OS X Version 10.1, you can use the Connect to Server dialog to connect to Microsoft Windows file servers. These include Windows NT file servers, Windows 2000 file servers, and Windows 98 computers with file sharing turned on.

A Windows server address gets entered in the Server Address box. The address of a Windows file server has the form `smb://server/share/` where *server* is the name or IP address of the file server and *share* is the name of the volume or folder that you want to connect to. For example, the address `smb://192.168.1.2/Public/` would connect to the Public folder of the Windows file server whose IP address is `192.168.1.2`. If you use a file server's name instead of its IP address, you may need to type the name in all capital letters. If you do not know the specific share, you can just type in the name or IP address of the server.

After entering the address of a Windows file server and clicking Connect in the Connect to Server dialog, another dialog appears in which you specify your workgroup or domain, username, and password on the Windows file server, as shown in the Figure 10-5. If you want to save your password, select the Add to Keychain option.

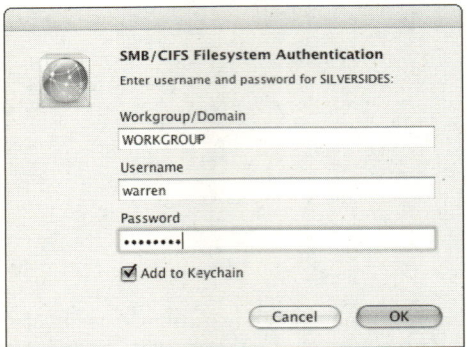

Figure 10-5: The login screen for a Windows file server.

If any problems occur that prevent connecting to a Windows file server, an alert appears saying no file services are available at the address you specified. This message may indeed mean the Windows file server is not available. The message also occurs if you simply mistype the address, workgroup, username, or password. Note that Mac OS X 10.1 can't connect to a Windows file server if the server name or share name includes any spaces, even if you encode them as %20, but 10.2 and 10.3 do not suffer from that ailment.

Connecting to an FTP server

On the Internet, files are commonly sent using File Transfer Protocol (FTP). A computer can make files available using this protocol by running a type of program called an *FTP server*. This term also refers to the combination of the server program and the computer that's running it. You may sometimes hear people refer to an *FTP site,* which is a collection of files on an FTP server that are available for downloading. An FTP site has the same function on the Internet as a file server on your network.

In Mac OS X, you can connect to FTP servers directly from the Finder. For more advanced functionality you can use a program specially made for FTP transactions, called an *FTP client.* One such application is called Transmit, and is covered in Chapter 21.

An FTP server address goes into the server address field, just like AFP and SMB addresses. Hitting connect brings up the FTP authentication screen, where you'll need to type in your name and password, as shown in Figure 10-6.

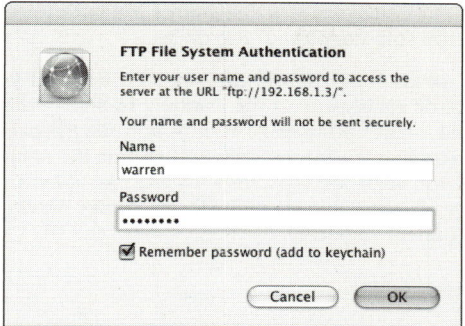

Figure 10-6: The login screen for an FTP server.

When you log in successfully and hit the OK button, the Connect to Server box disappears and the FTP volume is mounted in the Finder, free for your perusal.

Tip   Because Mac OS X has full Unix underpinnings, you can use the command line to access FTP servers, by launching the terminal and using the FTP command.

Connecting locally

Local servers are servers that appear on your network without having to initially specify their location. Local servers are great because you can browse for their existence. You can browse for local servers directly from the Finder. If you are already in the Connect to Server dialog, clicking the Browse button opens a new Finder window, with the Network globe selected. All the servers that are accessible on your network will show up in the Network globe window. You can also access the Network globe directly by opening a new Finder window and clicking on it, or by selecting the Network option from the Go menu. Look at Figure 10-7 to see how browsing in the Finder looks.

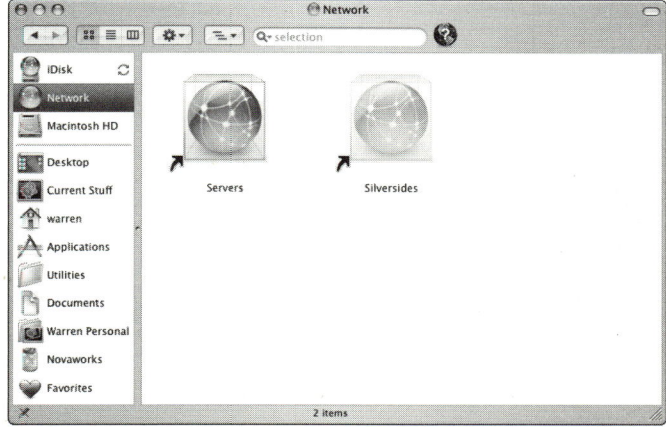

Figure 10-7: Browsing for local network servers. This network has one server available, called Silversides.

The Servers option that appears within the list of local servers designates the path for accessing NetInfo servers, which used to be the sole purpose of the globe.

Whichever Finder view you are in, (icon, list, or column) double-clicking on the server you wish to access immediately brings up a pared-down version of the Connect to Server dialog, (see Figure 10-8) with places for typing in your name and password only, and the option to connect as a guest. Clicking Connect brings you to a Finder window that serves the same purpose as Figure 10-4 shown earlier, which lets you view the volumes that you can access. When browsing and connecting locally, the volumes are available straight from a Finder window, and not a separate dialog box as when you connect remotely.

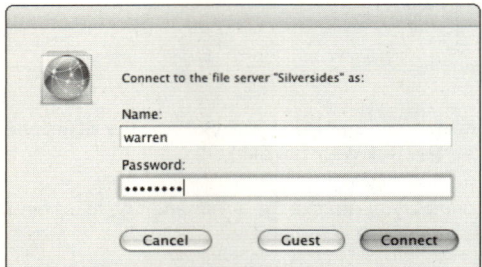

Figure 10-8: The pared-down Connect to Server dialog that appears when you connect to a local server.

When you are in the column view, you can click once on a server to select. The preview icon contains a Connect button. Clicking Connect brings up the pared-down connect-to-server box, and after you are connected, the volumes of the server extend through the column view, as shown in Figures 10-9 and 10-10.

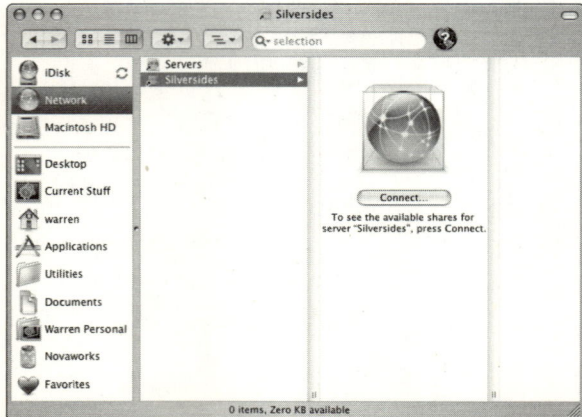

Figure 10-9: Click the Connect button from the column view to access the server.

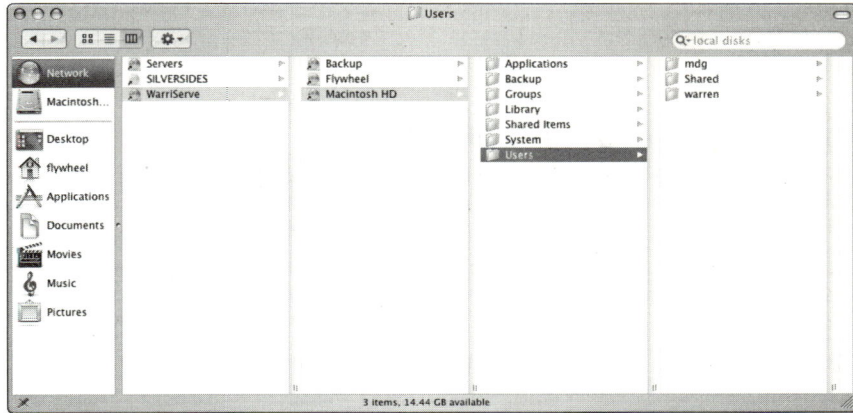

Figure 10-10: The server volumes and their contents appear directly in the Finder.

Connecting with a favorite

When you are in the Connect to Server dialog, or after the volume is mounted and you are in the Finder, you can create a favorite from a server location for more streamlined connections in the future. Opening a server location from a favorite skips the Connect to Server box and takes you right to the identification screen. If your password is saved in the keychain, you don't even have to type anything in. You can make a favorite by clicking the plus sign as discussed earlier in the chapter, or by dragging the mounted server's icon into your Favorites folder. The server favorites show up in the finder as documents, named with either the name or the IP address of its server. (See Figure 10-11.) These documents can be double-clicked, placed in the Dock, or even set as login items in order to connect to the servers.

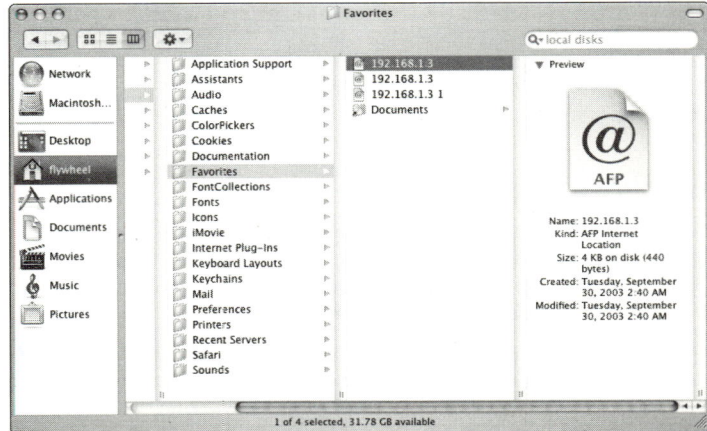

Figure 10-11: Mac OS X Finder can store the locations of servers in individual documents that can be launched with a double-click.

While making an alias for a server is possible, because of the way Mac OS X's Unix underpinnings deal with alias links across networks, making a favorite is the proper way to save a server's location.

Recognizing your access privileges

Just as you can recognize your access privileges to folders on your Mac in the Finder, the same indicators are present for server volumes and the folders they contain. The symbols for each type of privilege and description of access are as follows:

✦ **Read Only:** A small icon that looks like a pencil with a line through it appears in the status bar for a folder or volume where you can see the contents but may not change them.

✦ **No Access:** A folder icon with a circled red do-not-enter sign in the lower-right corner is a volume or folder that you cannot open or otherwise manipulate.

✦ **Write-only access:** A circled blue down arrow in the lower-right corner marks a *drop box* folder. You can put files into a drop box, but you cannot open it.

Figure 10-12 shows examples of these folder icons and the Read-only indicator in the bottom left-hand corner of the Finder window, the pencil with the line through it.

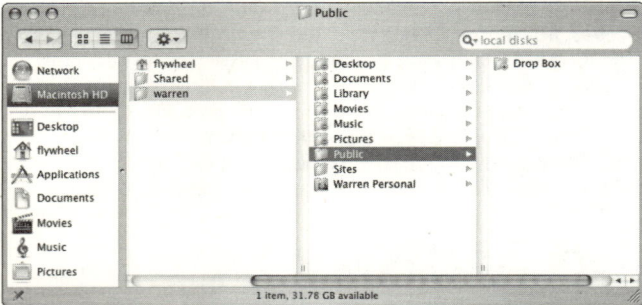

Figure 10-12: Special folder icons and an icon in the status bar indicate your access privileges.

Transferring network files

When you've got a server volume mounted in the Finder, OS X treats it like any other disk; that is, you can copy files to and from it (if you have the correct access privileges), you can open files from it in Open/Save dialog boxes from any application, or, you can open files directly from the server without copying them to your drive first.

Depending on your network, and the types and sizes of the files that you are working on, opening and editing files directly from the server can be a great way to streamline work, or it can be a huge, slow, crash-prone nightmare. In general, the faster your network is, the more reliable your connection is, and the smaller your files are, the better shape you will be in. For example, on a network of even very modest speeds, opening and saving Microsoft Word documents off of the server can be fine, and this eliminates the need for always first copying the file to your hard drive, and then copying it back when you are finished with your work. If you are working on a file locally (after copying it to your machine), it's possible for another coworker to also work on the same file without you knowing. You'd then run the risk of copying over her saved changes when you copy the file back. If, however, you are editing gigabyte-sized Photoshop files, working over the network would be a slow and frustrating process, and prone to data loss. In more advanced setups with OS X Server, it is possible to have your entire home folder located on the server, and not locally on your machine. In this case, all your work is being done off of the server, even when applications request preferences and fonts.

Opening network files

Because Mac OS X treats mounted server volumes exactly as though they are local disks, you can navigate to them in an Open dialog, as shown in Figure 10-13, and open them. Similarly, you can save to the network server in a Save dialog.

Disconnecting from network volumes and servers

When you finish using a network volume, you can remove it from the Finder by using any of the following methods:

✦ If the server is mounted on the desktop, you can drag the volume's icon to the Disconnect icon in the Dock. (The Trash icon changes to a Disconnect icon when you're dragging a network volume.) You can also Control-click the volume's icon and choose Eject from the contextual menu.

✦ Select the volume's icon and choose File ➪ Eject *(Name of Disk)* or press ⌘-E on the keyboard.

✦ Click on the eject icon that is visible from the sidebar in Finder windows.

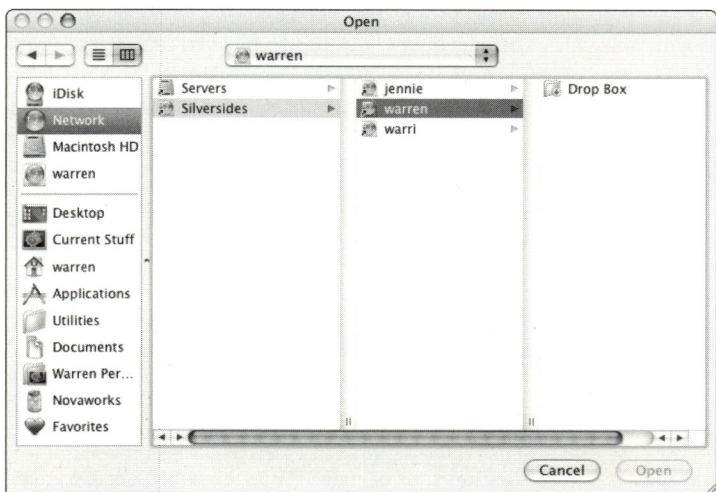

Figure 10-13: Open a file from a server just as though it is a local disk.

Removing a network volume from the Finder is also known as *unmounting* (not dismounting) the volume.

Disconnecting from a network file server involves no more than removing all that server's volumes from the Finder. It can be common to get errors upon attempting to unmount a network volume; these errors generally say something to the effect that the volume is still in use. A volume is in use as long as a file or application is open directly from it. If this is the case, quit any of your open programs and try again. If it *still* won't unmount, it's quite possible something is being used off of the disk, but it's nothing you can see or close. Often, relaunching the Finder (hit ⌘-Option-Escape or go to Apple menu ➪ Force Quit) will fix this problem.

Using the Keychain

Virtually every file server to which you connect, some of the Web sites you visit, and any number of network services you invoke require you to identify yourself with a name and a password. These combinations of name and password are called *access keys,* or just *keys* for short. If other people can guess your keys easily, the main reason for having them has failed. Similarly, if you use the same key for more than one account, anyone who obtains the key to one account can access the rest of your accounts — again, not a good thing. The difficulty with using multiple keys is the inconvenience of having to remember multiple not-easily-guessed keys and further, to remember which keys go with which account.

Because of this, Apple developed a *keychain* technology to help you keep track of your various account names and passwords. In fact, the keychain can automatically provide your name and password as needed. Apple first introduced the concept of a keychain with System 7 Pro's AOCE (Apple Open Collaborative Environment), also known as PowerTalk, a decade ago. Because AOCE's acceptance was less than inspiring, even the well-liked pieces, such as the keychain, were not widely used. PowerTalk disappeared from Apple System Software releases after System 7.5.5. Apple revived the keychain in Mac OS 9 and, because it didn't bring with it the overhead and clumsiness of AOCE, many more users started taking advantage of it. Now, with Mac OS X, the keychain continues to be even better integrated with Mac OS and its software.

You can use keychains to hold passwords for applications, Web sites, and servers. When you launch the application or connect to the server or Web site, your keychain supplies the password so that you don't have to type it, providing that you are using keychain-aware software.

Note   As discussed in Chapter 6, Safari has the capability of saving names and passwords for the Web sites that you have logins for. Safari stores these passwords in the keychain that we are discussing.

Initially, Mac OS X creates a default keychain, whose name is the same as your login account's short name, and a password that matches your login password. When you log in to Mac OS X, this keychain is automatically unlocked for you. You're not limited to just this one keychain, though. You can create multiple keychains to store password information for different purposes if you desire. One reason to create multiple keychains is if you wish to segregate some groups of keys from the rest and not have all your keys accessible at the same time. You may not want your spouse to know your keys for certain FTP sites, but might also need to make the keys for other sites available. In general, the keychain functions in the background, and many people will never even need to open it. For those who want extra control and customization, follow along!

Copying a keychain to another computer

If you want to use a keychain from your computer on another Mac OS X computer, you simply copy the keychain file. The usual location for keychain files is the Keychains folder in the Library folder of your home folder (path ~/Library/Keychains).

1. **Copy your keychain to a location (such as a network server) that you can access from the other computer.**

2. **Open Keychain Access on the other computer (in the Utilities folder of its Applications folder).**

3. **Choose File ⇨ Add Keychain.**

4. **Select your keychain and click Open.**

Creating a keychain

If you want to create additional keychains, you do so with the Keychain Access application (located in the Utilities folder of your Applications folder.) To use the Keychain Access application, choose File ⇨ New Keychain. In the regular Save As dialog that appears, enter a name for your new keychain, select a location to save it in, and click the Create button. Figure 10-14 shows the Save As dialog for creating a keychain.

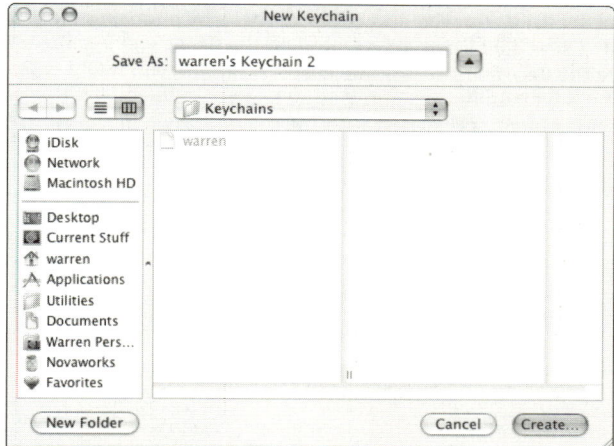

Figure 10-14: Saving a new keychain.

After you click Create, the New Keychain Password dialog appears. Decide on a password or phrase that you want to unlock the keychain, and enter it in both text boxes. The password can be up to 255 characters in length and is case-sensitive. As with all passwords, this should be something that you can remember and that you can type blind but will not be easily guessed by others. Click the disclosure triangle labeled Details to see the location of the keychain and the identity of the application that is creating it. Figure 10-15 shows the New Keychain Password dialog.

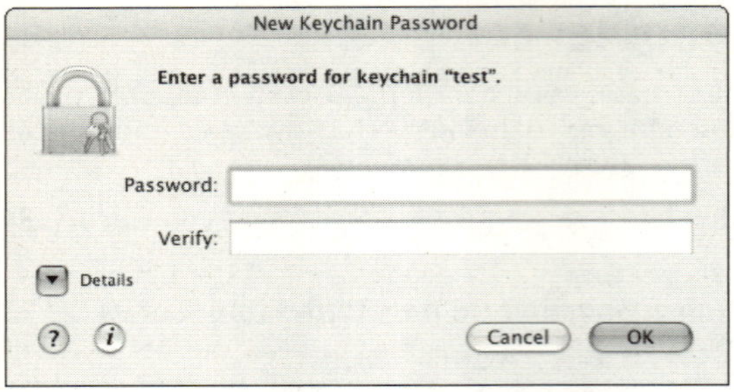

Figure 10-15: Enter the password for your new keychain twice.

Adding an item to your keychain

After you enter the identical password twice and clicked OK, Keychain Access displays your new keychain's window. Initially, it is empty. More commonly, you'll want to view your already existing keychain by clicking on it. If you've been using your system for a while, chances are you'll see at least one or two saved keychain items in the list. Items appear in the list when parts of your Mac OS, for example, Safari, save your passwords. This is where they get saved.

You can also add items to your existing keychain. In Mac OS X 10.3, you can add two kinds of items, a password item, or a secure note. You can add either of these by choosing their commands under the File menu. Most keychain items are created on the fly, as you log into sites and servers and choose to save the information. In some cases, however, you might want to manually create an item, and the Keychain Access application lets you. When you choose New Password Item from the File menu, you are presented with the dialog shown in Figure 10-16.

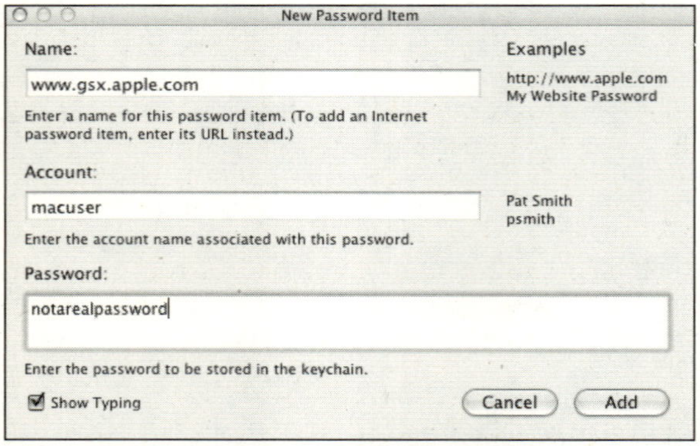

Figure 10-16: Creating a new password item.

To create a new keychain item:

1. **Type in the location of the Web site or server in the Name field.**

2. **Enter your account username in the Account field.**

3. **Enter your password in the password field.**

If the checkbox is checked, Keychain Access will display your password in clear text. If you type a Web site's location in, the next time you visit that site, Safari will make an attempt to use the information provided by this new password item. If you type in the location of a file server, the Finder will attempt to use the provided information the next time you connect to that server. Click the Add button to save it.

You can also choose to make a secure note in the Keychain Access application, which is a way of storing sensitive information that you might need to retrieve at a later date. Choosing New Secure Note Item from the file menu presents you with the screen shown in Figure 10-17.

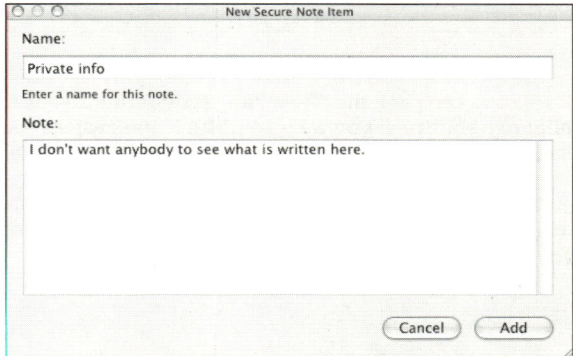

Figure 10-17: Creating a new secure note item.

Next, type in both a name to call your secure note and the information that you want to store. When this is accomplished, click the Add button to save it. Later, you can customize the level of access to this, but the idea behind the secure note item is to save sensitive information in a secure form.

Tip   If you want the keychain that is selected to be your default keychain (the one automatically unlocked when you log in to Mac OS X), choose File ⇨ Make "*keychain name*" Default. If the selected keychain is the default already, then this option is grayed out.

Locking and unlocking your keychain

When a keychain is unlocked, all items in it are available to keychain-aware applications; however, if the keychain is locked, the items are unavailable until you unlock the keychain by entering the passphrase when prompted.

Locking a keychain is simple. In the main window in the Keychain Access application, click the Lock button to lock the selected keychain. When the keychain is locked, the detail information is hidden and the button's name changes to Unlock. You can also lock a keychain by choosing File ➪ Lock "keychain name" (⌘-L) and can lock all keychains by choosing File ➪ Lock All Keychains.

Managing keychain items

After adding items to your keychain, you need to consider keeping them up-to-date. For example, periodically changing your passwords is considered good practice for security reasons. Alternatively, you may want to remove keys to file servers or Web sites that no longer exist.

Removing a keychain item is easy. In the Keychain Access window, select the item you want to delete and click the Delete button.

As in the Finder, Keychain Access enables you to view information for keychain items. Select the item (click on it) to view its information in the bottom of the Keychain window. The two subpanes are Attributes and Access Control.

Attributes tab

In the Attributes tab (see Figure 10-18), you can click the Show Password button to see the item's password. Use the copy to clipboard button if you want to paste it somewhere else. In this pane, you are also shown the kind of item it is (application, Internet, AppleShare, and so on), where it is located, to which account it belongs, when it was created, and when last modified. You also are presented with a Comments text box where you can enter information about the item (such as a URL for named Web server items). Make sure to click the Save Changes button if you make any changes to any of the fields in the window.

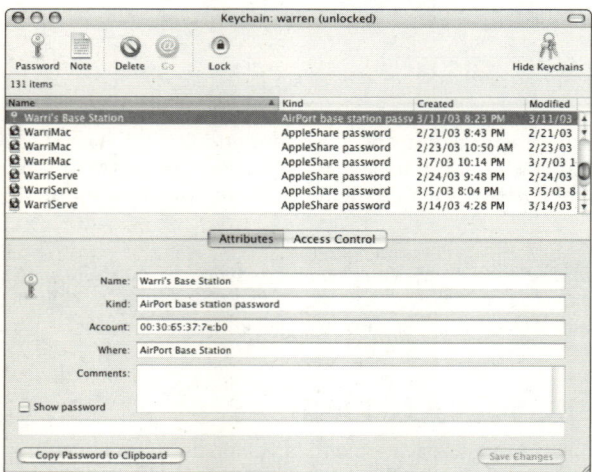

Figure 10-18: Click the Show password button to see an item's password.

Access Control tab

In the Access Control tab, shown in Figure 10-19, you find an option labeled Allow all applications to access this item. If this option is not selected, you are always prompted for keychain confirmation anytime something attempts to access this item. If you don't want all applications to have access, you can specify select applications that always have access to this keychain item by adding the applications to the Always allow access by these applications list. Click the Add and Remove buttons as appropriate.

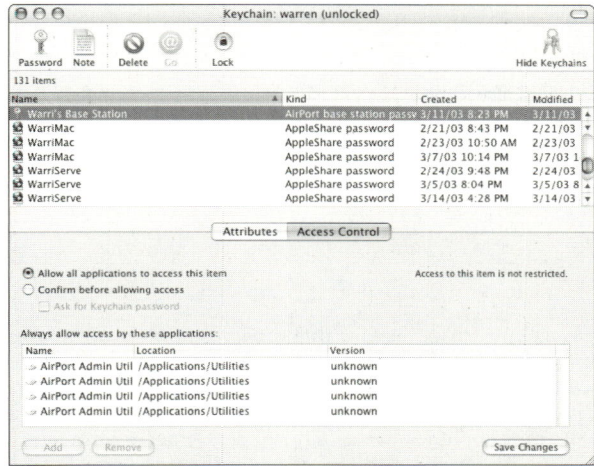

Figure 10-19: The Access Control pane of Keychain Access allows different levels of security for keychain items in the same keychain.

Changing keychain settings

You can set conditions under which your keychain automatically locks. You can also change the password of an existing keychain.

To change locking conditions of a keychain, choose Change Settings for Keychain "keychain name" from the Edit menu. This brings up the dialog box shown in Figure 10-20. From this dialog, you can choose to automatically lock the keychain after a specified number of minutes of computer inactivity, or to lock the keychain when the computer goes to sleep.

To change the password of a keychain, make sure it is selected from the list, and choose Change Password for Keychain "keychain name" from the Edit menu. This presents a dialog identical to the one shown previously in Figure 10-15 where you set the password for a new keychain.

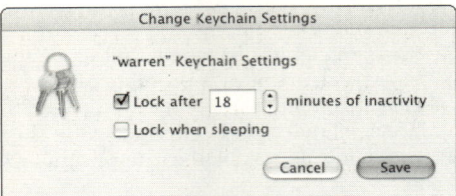

Figure 10-20: Control the settings for automatically locking a keychain.

Tip   You can have easy access to locking and unlocking your keychain at will, without ever having to open the Keychain Access application again. From the View menu, you can choose Show Status in Menu Bar. Choosing this option puts a little lock icon in the menu bar, which is a pull down menu that gives you the option to lock and unlock the keychain, lock the screen, and to open both the keychain and security preferences.

Sharing Your Files

The beginning of this chapter explains how to access files that other computers are sharing. This section of the chapter explains how to do the opposite: to make your files available for other people to access. First, you plan for file sharing and identify your computer on the network. Next, you start the file-sharing feature in Mac OS X, and then you can make files available for sharing and create user accounts for people you want to have greater access to your files. For folders that contain shared files, you can restrict the type of access some people have.

Using file sharing in a small network allows all or some of the computers on that network to function as both personal computer and file server, saving the cost and space of a dedicated machine functioning as a server.

Planning for file sharing

The personal file-sharing capabilities of Mac OS X make sharing items across a network surprisingly easy but not without some cost. This section discusses the capabilities and limitations of Mac OS X file sharing to help you decide in advance whether it meets your needs. The alternative to file sharing is a dedicated, centralized file server.

Deciding between distributed or centralized file sharing

Your network can implement file sharing in a distributed or centralized fashion. With distributed file sharing, also known as *peer-to-peer file sharing*, each computer makes files, folders, and disks available to other computers on the network. While your computer shares your files with other computers, you are free to use your computer for other tasks. The price you pay for making files from your computer available does lead to a reduced performance of your computer while other computers are accessing it. In addition, Mac OS X file sharing limits the number of people that can share the same folder or disk at the same time, making file sharing unsuitable for serving files to large numbers of computers.

By contrast, a network with centralized file sharing dedicates one computer (or more) to providing file-sharing services. The file sharing occurs between the centralized computer and the individual computers, not between the individual computers themselves. The dedicated computer runs file server software, such as Apple's Mac OS X Server, enabling the computer to serve files to a large number of other computers. A dedicated file server needs to be fast and needs to have one or more large hard disks. Although the underpinnings are the same in both Mac OS X Client and Mac OS X Server, the huge difference lies in the management tools that OS X Server provides. Mac OS X Server costs $499 for up to 10 simultaneous users, or $999 for an unlimited number of users. If you purchase an XServe, Apple's specially designed enterprise level rack-mountable server, OS X Server is included with the hardware purchase.

Although Mac OS X Client file-sharing capabilities are designed for distributed file sharing, you can use file sharing on a dedicated computer to create a file server for a small network. Folders or entire hard disks on that file-server computer can be made available to other computers on the network as described in the remainder of this chapter. (Going forward, any mention of "Mac OS X" is referring to the client [the one that ships on your Mac] version. The server version is specifically referenced as "Mac OS X Server.")

The problem with such a file server is its performance. Mac OS X assumes someone is using the dedicated computer for more than sharing files. As a result, Mac OS reserves more than 50 percent of the dedicated computer's processing power for tasks other than file sharing and runs the file-sharing activities at a lower priority than other tasks.

Mac OS X Server

The newest solution from Apple for centralized serving is Mac OS X Server. This server package, built on the Unix underpinnings of Mac OS X, offers Apple File Services support as well as sharing of many Ethernet-capable PostScript printers. Designed as a full-service Web, Internet, mail, and network server as well as an Apple File Services server, Mac OS X Server offers impressive performance and capabilities. One of those capabilities called NetBoot actually allows most late-model Macs to start up from the Mac OS X server machine, making it possible for a room full of such Macs to receive their system software and applications from a centralized server. You can choose to boot from a Network Startup volume in the Startup Disk pane of System Preferences. Another impressive capability is OS X Server's client management, offering individualized control over the user environments of the clients that connect to it, through the use of its NetInfo databases and Directory Services.

Centralized disk storage reduces the amount of local disk storage required by each networked computer while providing a way for people who work together to share information. People can store files on the server's disks where other people can open or copy them. Many people can access the server's disks and folders simultaneously, and new files become available to everyone instantly. Unlike the file sharing provided by Mac OS X, no one uses the server's computer to do personal work because it is dedicated to providing network services. Conversely, your computer is not burdened when someone else on the network accesses one of your shared items on the AppleShare server's disks.

A centralized file server is set up and maintained by a trained person called a *network administrator*. Mac OS X Server includes organizational, administrative, and security features to manage file access on the network. The network administrator does not control access to folders and files on the server's disks; that is the responsibility of each person who puts items on the disks.

The Mac OS X Server software runs on any Macintosh that came with built-in USB ports, as long as there is a minimum of 256 MB RAM and 2.5 GB free on the hard drive. These are however, the bare minimum requirements. OS X Server is quite RAM hungry, and the more you give it, the happier it is. Beige G3s are no longer supported in 10.3 Server.

Guidelines for file sharing

These guidelines and tips for sharing folders and disks help optimize file sharing and help prevent problems:

✦ **To share a Write-only folder (a drop box), it must be inside another shared folder that has read permission.**

✦ **The greater the number of accessed shared folders, the greater the memory and processing demands on your computer.** Too many sharing connections slow your system to a crawl.

✦ **Check or review any applicable licensing agreements before sharing programs, artwork, or sounds.** Often, licensing agreements or copyright laws restrict use of such items to a single computer.

✦ **Select a single computer and dedicate it to acting as a file server for the shared information.** Create an ordinary user account (not an administrator account) on this computer for everyone to use when connecting for file sharing. Everyone who connects for file sharing with this account's name and password has access to the contents of the account's home folder. This method is often the most efficient way to share numerous files or to share folders with several users simultaneously.

✦ **Use a router rather than a hub if your network has a DSL or cable modem connection to the Internet and each network computer has a public IP addressed assigned by your ISP.** If you use a hub, network traffic from one machine travels to another machine on your network via your ISP. In addition to upsetting most ISPs, this can result in significant performance degradation. This situation does not occur if the computers on your network have private IP addresses and your network has an Internet connection that shares a public IP address among the network computers.

Identifying your computer

Before your Mac can share files, it requires a network identity. There are two components to a network identity:

✦ **Computer name:** You establish the computer name in the Services tab of the Sharing pane of System Preferences, as shown in Figure 10-21.

✦ **Computer IP address:** The current IP address is also displayed in Sharing preferences (only is file sharing is enabled) but is established or changed in the Network pane of System Preferences.

Tip

After you have your settings the way you want them in Sharing preferences and Network preferences, you may want to click the lock button to prevent accidental changes. You are asked for your password to unlock the settings if you want to make changes later.

Turning file sharing on and off

After you establish your computer's network identity in Sharing preferences, and Network preferences if necessary, you are ready to turn on file sharing in the same Sharing preferences window. You don't need to turn on file sharing to access files from other computers, for example by using the Finder's Go ➪ Connect to Server command. However, you do need to turn on file sharing to allow users of other network computers to access the shared files on your computer. If some other computer users need to access your shared files via the AppleTalk protocol, you also need to turn on this protocol in Network preferences.

Unlike previous versions of Mac OS (Versions 9.2.2 and earlier), simply turning on file sharing does not significantly slow down your Mac OS X computer. You may, however notice your computer performing more slowly while other computers are opening or copying your shared files. During this activity, your attempts to open, save, or copy files as well as network activities of your own take a bit longer.

Starting and stopping file sharing

To start file sharing, simply check the On box to the left of Personal File Sharing in the services list. The right side of the preference pane will change to tell you that file sharing is starting up, and then it will change to say that it is turned on. Uncheck the box to stop personal file sharing. Alternatively, you can select the service, Personal File Sharing, from the list, and click on the button on the right-hand side to start file sharing, and click on the same button to stop file sharing after it has started. You can turn FTP access on as well as the capability for Windows users to access your Mac files by the same processes as for personal file sharing.

Enabling file sharing via AppleTalk

Mac OS X normally uses the TCP/IP protocol for file-sharing services, but it can also use the AppleTalk protocol simultaneously. If some other computer users need or prefer to use the AppleTalk protocol for file sharing, you can configure Mac OS X to use it. You turn on AppleTalk in the Network pane of System Preferences, as described in Chapter 18.

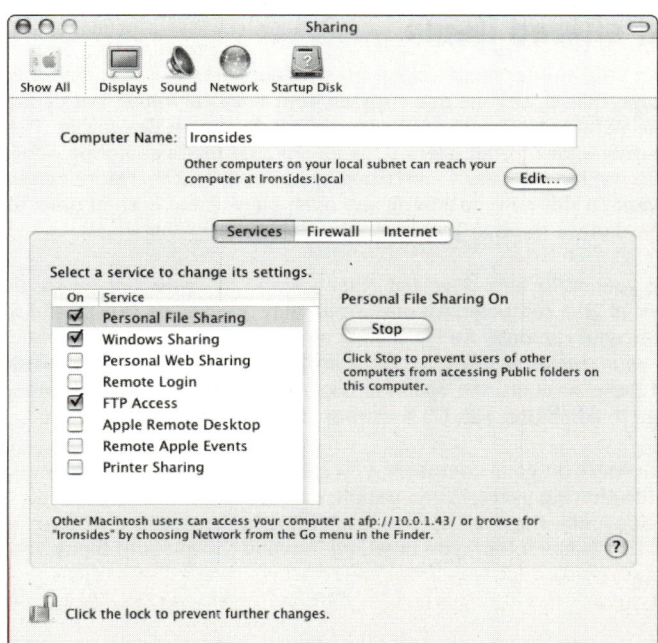

Figure 10-21: The Sharing preference pane.

Sharing with Microsoft Windows

For whatever reasons, far more people use Windows PCs than all other personal computers combined. Because the Windows PC is the lowest common denominator, other operating systems need to be able to coexist—something the Mac operating system has done well for quite some time. Not only can Mac OS X read and write PC-formatted disks, use Windows-format fonts, and share many hardware peripherals with Windows PCs, but it can also share files with Windows PCs. You can also enable SMB/CIFS file sharing by choosing to turn on Windows File Sharing in the Services tab of the Sharing pane of System Preferences.

Identifying who can connect for file sharing

In Mac OS X, unlike Mac OS 9 and earlier, you do not create users, groups, and passwords specifically for file sharing. In Mac OS X, the user accounts that are created in the Accounts preference pane are the same user accounts that people log into your Mac for accessing file sharing services. As soon as you turn file sharing on, any administrator level user will have full access to the hard drive, as well as his or her user folder. As long as file sharing is on, anyone will be able to log in as a guest and have access to every users public folder.

Mac OS X automatically puts all administrator users in groups named wheel and admin. All users who have login accounts, including administrators, are automatically members of a group named staff.

Designating your shared items

Inside every user account's home folder is a Public folder. By default, the Public folder is a Read-only folder for all users, that is, anyone can copy an item *from* the folder, but cannot copy anything *to* the folder. Within the Public folder, by default, is a Drop Box folder. The Drop Box folder is a Write-only folder for all users. This means that users can copy information *to* the drop box, but do not have access to anything inside of it, and therefore cannot take items *from* it. If you want to share items among any user, place them in the Public folder. People who give items to you place them in your Drop Box folder.

Caution   A user gains access to your entire hard drive and other volumes by connecting for file sharing as an administrator of your computer. For obvious security reasons, be very careful who you allow to connect to your computer for file sharing as an administrator. Ensure that user accounts created on your computer solely for file sharing purposes are not administrator accounts. For each of these accounts, the option in Users pane of your System Preferences that allows the account to administer Mac OS X on your computer should be turned off.

If you want to share more folders on your computer, you can create login accounts on your computer specifically for file-sharing users. When people connect to your computer for file sharing with one of these accounts, they can access everything in the account's home folder. If you want to put items in this home folder, you must log in using the account name and password. Then you can copy items into the account's home folder. Thereafter, other users can access the items in this home folder by connecting for file sharing with the account's name and password.

A special folder called Shared exists in the Users folder in Mac OS X. All registered users of a Mac OS X machine have access to this folder. If you want to make items accessible to all users of the machine but not to guests, place them in the Shared folder that is in the Users folder.

Setting specific access privileges

This section explains how to use the Finder's Info window to set separate access privileges for the owner, owner's group, and everyone else.

You set access privileges for a folder or volume in its Get Info window. Select a folder or volume in the Finder and Choose File ➪ Get Info (⌘-I) to display the Info window. (⌘-Option-I brings up the inspector window that will show information for whatever is selected in the Finder.) By default, the ownership and permissions section is partially disclosed, and a summary of the privileges that you have are displayed, which are usually read and write. Clicking the disclosure triangle next to the word "Details:" brings down the full permissions area, giving you the option to set privileges for owner, for group, and for everyone. (See Figure 10-22.)

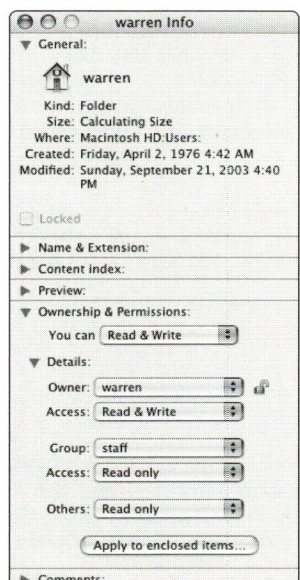

Figure 10-22: Each of your files and folders can have different privilege levels in three user categories.

As discussed in Chapter 4, each file and folder in Mac OS X can have different access privileges for three user categories: Owner, Group, and Others. Anyone connecting to your Mac without a name and password falls into the Others category. Even if a person connects with the name and password of a login account on your computer, this person falls in the Others category for every file and folder unless they are either the owner of the file or part of the owner's group.

You can set one of four privilege levels for each user category in the access privileges pop-up menus:

✦ **Read & Write:** Permits users to open and copy the file or folder. In the case of a folder, users can also see enclosed files and folders and can put items into the folder. In the case of a file, users can also make changes to the file.

✦ **Read only:** Permits users to open and copy the file or folder. In the case of a folder, users can see also enclosed files and folders.

✦ **Write only (drop box):** Permits users to put files and folders into the folder, but does not allow users to open the folder. (Files can't have Write-only permission.)

✦ **None:** This level denies access to the file or folder. Users can see the item but can't open it or change it.

To establish Write-only access to a folder, you must give the person or group Read privileges or Read & Write privileges to the folder containing the folder. For example, your Public folder has Read-only privileges for Others. Inside the Read-only Public folder is a folder named Drop Box, which has Write-only privileges for Others. Other users couldn't access the Drop Box folder if you put it inside another folder with Write-only privileges. That would defeat the purpose.

The Owner privileges must be at least as broad as the Group privileges, and the Group privileges must be at least as broad as the Others privileges. In other words, if you give Others Read & Write privileges, then both the Group and the Owner are automatically set to Read & Write.

If you wish to set the same privileges for all folders enclosed within the current folder, click the Apply to enclosed items button. Remember that this is an all-or-nothing operation.

Dealing with Security Risks

File sharing poses security risks. Allowing other users to connect as guests is a relatively low risk if you are careful. If your computer has multiple administrator login accounts, the risk is much greater. The risks are magnified if your computer has a public IP address and is thus directly exposed to the Internet, as opposed to being Network Address Translated and having a private IP address.

Assessing the risks of guest access

Mac OS X normally allows everyone on your network to access your Public folder as a guest, without supplying a name and password (if file sharing is turned on). Therefore, you should be careful what you put in your Public folder. The Public folder itself is normally Read-only, and you can set restricted access privileges individually for items that you put into your Public folder. However, if everyone has Write access to a folder inside your Public folder, such as to the Drop Box folder, a guest can still cause mischief by filling your disk with file after file.

Assessing the risks of administrator access

An administrator's special ability to connect to all disks and work without certain restrictions can threaten the computer's security much more than guest access does. In Mac OS X 10.1 and earlier, someone who connects to your computer for file sharing with an administrator's name and password can actually access the contents of all home folders and the main Library folder on your computer. This is more freedom than Mac OS X allows when you log in as an administrator. Under Mac OS X 10.2 and higher, an administrator logged in through file sharing has the same privileges and restrictions as that user would if logged into the machine locally.

Assessing the risk of your Internet connection

The security risks of file sharing are amplified by the fact that file sharing is normally available via the Internet's TCP/IP protocol. A potential hacker does not have to be physically near your Macs. The hacker could enter over an Internet connection. If your computer is connected directly to the Internet, anyone in the world who learns your computer's IP address can access your Public folder anonymously via the Internet. Someone who also knows the name and password of an administrator account on your computer has very broad access via the Internet. The Internet exposure is relatively high if your computer has a static IP address from your ISP. The Internet exposure is relatively low if your ISP assigns your computer a different IP address every time you connect, as is usually the case with a modem connection, a cable modem connection, or a PPPoE connection. If you share a connection via an Internet router, your computer may have a private IP address that can't be accessed from the Internet unless the router is explicitly configured to allow such access.

Improving file-sharing security

Here are some techniques you can employ to improve file-sharing security:

✦ **Be very sure to turn off the administrator option on any account that does not absolutely require it.**

✦ **Don't allow Write permission for guests, even to Drop Box folders.** Set the Others category of every shared folder to read only.

✦ **Do not overvalue the security of passwords.** Someone may connect to your computer with a password and then leave his or her computer without disconnecting. A passerby can then use this computer to access all your shared files (subject to the access privileges you set). Remind people who connect to your computer for file sharing that they must put away all your shared folders (by ejecting them) when they are finished. Also, remind users to lock their keychains or log out of the Mac when they leave it unattended. If they do not, unauthorized users may be able to access shared folders using their account, even if they do not know the password.

Particularly if you have high-speed Internet access, such as cable-modem, or DSL, you might want to set up a firewall to protect your local network. Firewalls provide a barrier to unauthorized access from outside your local network.

Cross-Reference   The Internet gateways covered in Chapter 15, including the Apple AirPort Base Station, generally can be configured to provide some forms of firewall protection.

Using a personal firewall to improve security

A firewall is an application that runs on a computer or a piece of separate network hardware that exists to improve security by blocking access to that computer or network. Mac OS X includes a firewall application that is integrated in the Sharing preference pane. To see the firewall configuration, open System Preferences, open the Sharing pane, and then click the Firewall subpane, as shown in Figure 10-23.

To turn on the firewall, click the Start button. The firewall automatically stops all incoming network traffic for all services, such as Personal File Sharing, that are not turned on in the Services tab. Turning on a service in the Services tab opens the port in the firewall to allow incoming connections for that service. If you want to allow access through the firewall for a given port, either select the checkbox in the Firewall list to open that port or (if what you are looking for isn't there) click the New button. A dialog sheet appears, as shown in Figure 10-24, in which you can add less-common access or custom access to ports that Mac OS X does not specify outright.

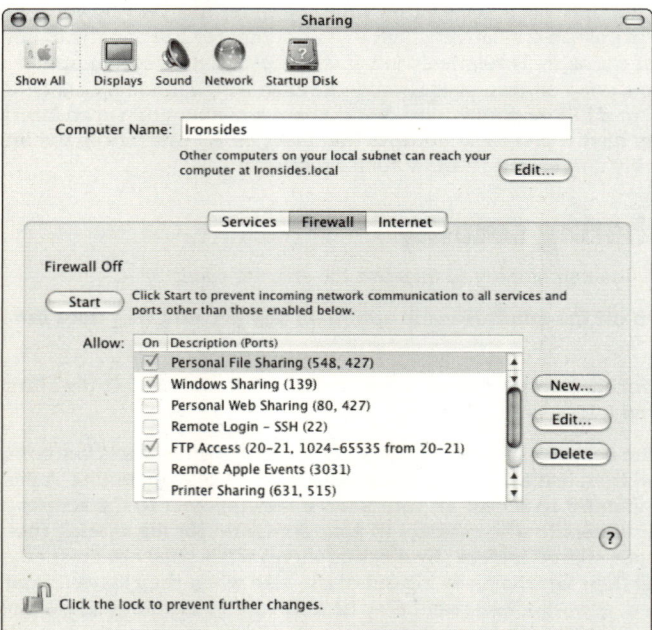

Figure 10-23: Use the Firewall subpane of the Sharing pane to turn the built-in firewall on and off and to change its settings.

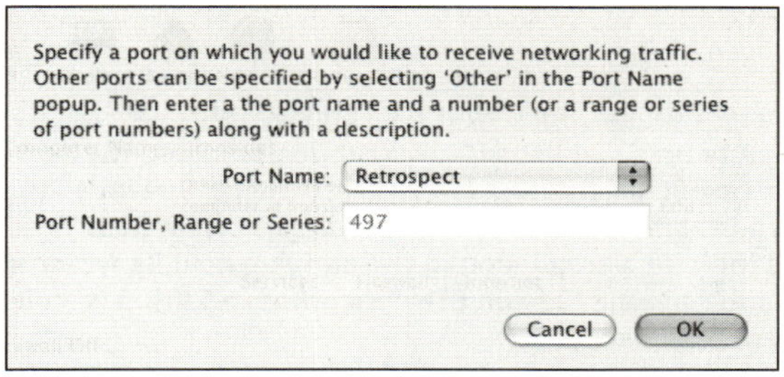

Specify a port on which you would like to receive networking traffic. Other ports can be specified by selecting 'Other' in the Port Name popup. Then enter a the port name and a number (or a range or series of port numbers) along with a description.

Port Name: Retrospect

Port Number, Range or Series: 497

Cancel | OK

Figure 10-24: The New button on the Firewall tab of the Sharing pane enables you to add specific ports to be opened through your system's firewall.

Sharing Your Internet Connection

A nifty feature of the OS X Sharing preference pane is the ability to share an Internet connection between more than one Mac. Under the Internet pane, you choose what connection of yours other Macs share *from,* and what connections of your Mac they can connect *to*. For example, if you are using a Bluetooth cell phone to give your laptop an Internet connection, you specify that you are sharing *from* a Bluetooth modem. If you have an AirPort card, you can allow other Macs to wirelessly connect to your Mac, and therefore share your Bluetooth Internet connection among them, over a self-created AirPort network. To do this, choose to share your connection from your Bluetooth modem, and check the box next to the AirPort connection that shows up in the To computers using list, shown in Figure 10-25. This is but one of many different possibilities.

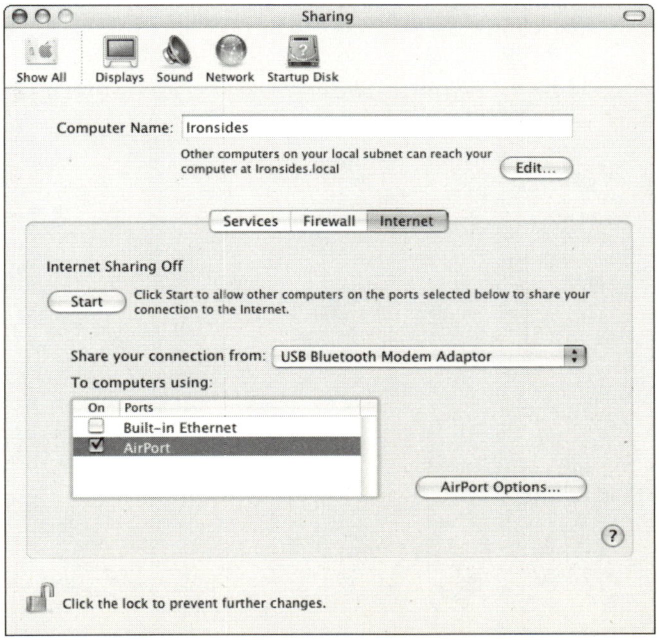

Sharing

Show All | Displays | Sound | Network | Startup Disk

Computer Name: Ironsides

Other computers on your local subnet can reach your computer at Ironsides.local

Edit...

Services | Firewall | Internet

Internet Sharing Off

Start | Click Start to allow other computers on the ports selected below to share your connection to the Internet.

Share your connection from: USB Bluetooth Modem Adaptor

To computers using:

On	Ports
☐	Built-in Ethernet
☑	AirPort

AirPort Options...

Click the lock to prevent further changes.

Figure 10-25: Share your Internet connection with other Macs.

Summary

This chapter showed you how to connect to and work with files and use storage space located on file servers on your local network. The file servers can be dedicated file servers, or they can be personal computers running file sharing. We covered using the Finder to connect to AFP, SMB, and FTP servers. To determine your access privileges to a folder, you can look at the folder's icon, open it, and look for a small icon in the status bar of its window. This chapter also discussed transferring and opening files on the network. In addition, you learned how to disconnect from shared folders and disks.

You can use the Mac OS X keychain to automatically provide your name and password when you connect to a file server. And you can streamline subsequent connections to a file server by making a favorite.

This chapter discussed the peer-to-peer (distributed) file sharing provided by Mac OS X. Peer-to-peer file sharing in Mac OS X is great for small groups, but a dedicated file server (such as AppleShare IP or Mac OS X Server) is generally better in a large environment.

You learned how to activate and deactivate file sharing, specify privileges for folders, and take basic security precautions.

You also learned how to share your Internet connection between other Macs.

✦   ✦   ✦

Taking Advantage of Services

In Mac OS X, certain applications are able to share useful functions with other applications. Apple refers to these functions as services (yes, with a small *s*), and they can save you time and effort. However, using them can seem a little tricky, because the way services are set up is somewhat counterintuitive until you know what you are doing. Here, our objective is to provide you with all the information you need to make use of services.

In this chapter, we'll take a look at the services available in Panther, and show you how to work with them. We spotlight the services provided by the Finder, Grab, Mail, Stickies, Speech, Summarize, and Text Edit. The other services available in Mac OS X are described at the end of the chapter.

About Services

Services appear as an item in the Application menu of every Mac OS X compatible application. (The Application menu is the one that appears when you click on the application's name in the menu bar. But you knew that.)

Choosing Services in Panther opens a submenu containing twelve items, none of which seem to work! But looks can be deceiving. Yes, at first glance, some of these items appear grayed-out, most of their commands are inaccessible, and their functions are not immediately apparent. How very mysterious! No wonder many move on and do not give the Services item a second thought.

The idea of services is to allow the applications and functions listed in the Services submenu to share their capabilities with other, compatible applications.

Here's how it works: First, you select some data in an application, such as the string of text, "We're coming to visit on Sunday." Then you choose a command from the Services submenu, such as the Mail application's Mail Text command. The command is executed on the selection, invoking Mail to create a new mail message with "We're coming to visit on Sunday," already placed in the message body. Very convenient!

For another example, in TextEdit you could invoke the Grab service's Selection command to allow you to select a part of the screen to be inserted as an image in your TextEdit document.

Using services often seems as though Mac OS X invisibly copies your selected data from one application and pastes it into another; the latter application modifies the data and most often copies the result back into the original application before you know it.

The content you can use with services may include text, graphics, pictures, or movies.

There's just one catch. It is important to note that services mainly work with applications and utilities written to run in Mac OS X's Cocoa environment, such as Safari, Mail, TextEdit, and many of the other programs included with Mac OS X. There are also hundreds of third-party Cocoa applications and utilities.

Carbon applications cannot take advantage of services, except in the rare event they are written to support services. Most commercial Carbon apps such as the Microsoft Office applications, Adobe Photoshop and Illustrator, and QuarkXPress, do not currently support services. This may have something to do with the fact that it is reportedly quite difficult for developers to adapt a Carbon application to use services. Perhaps they will eventually get around to it... or perhaps not.

Now you can guess why the Services submenu items often have their commands dimmed; if you are looking at them from a typical Carbon application, none of them will work. But just one second now, I hear someone say. They will also appear unavailable from inside a Cocoa application! Correct, unless you *first highlight the content you want the services to work on*! Aha, a critical point; the not-quite-so-intuitive "secret" trick to taking advantage of services. Only Grab's Services commands will be typically available before you select anything, because the entire screen is available to choose from. Also, a service will appear dimmed in the submenu if you have selected a type of content that the service does not work with.

You may find that after taking all this into account, the services command you want to use is still dimmed! The explanation: Some applications may not support every service. The application's developer decides which services will be supported.

Here's another critical point to keep in mind: services can't create documents. They can only work with a document that is open in a services-compatible application. For example, the Grab *utility* can create documents, but the Grab *service* can only work with an open document in a Cocoa or services-compatible application. That is why the Grab service commands remain dimmed if you access them from the Finder; the Finder cannot create a document for the service to place results in.

Mac OS X services will (hopefully? should? with any luck?) become increasingly useful as more and more Cocoa applications are developed that can use them, and as Apple and third parties develop more programs which make services available.

Services are really the current continuation of Apple's longtime dream of fostering communication and data exchange between individual applications. Some old-timers may still have enough functioning memory on their personal motherboards to recall the ancient notions called Publish and Subscribe. Another example would be Apple Events, still used in Mac OS X by those who make AppleScripts. Services are but a modest echo of such ambitious schemes; then again, services are more accessible and helpful.

The Finder

The Finder application provides three services to other applications, Open, Reveal, and Show Info, as shown in Figure 11-1.

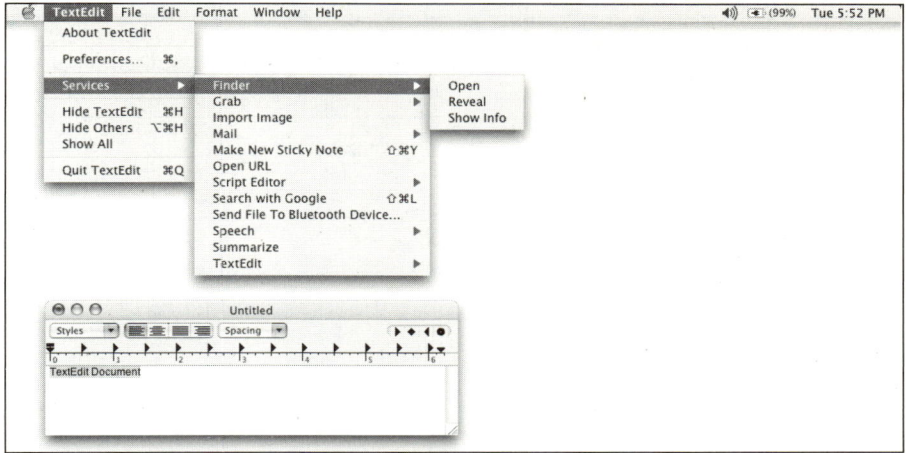

Figure 11-1: After content is selected, here the name of a file highlighted in TextEdit, use the Finder's services to Open, Reveal, and Show Info.

✦ **Open:** Opens the file with its default application, opens a selected folder or volume and displays the contents in a Finder window, or launches an application. Essentially, the Open command in a menu acts the same way as a double-click on the item's icon. If you type the path to a folder in a text file, highlight the pathname and select Services ➪ File ➪ Open, the folder will open in a new Finder window.

✦ **Reveal:** Reveals the item in the Finder by opening a Finder window and selecting the item.

✦ **Show Info:** Displays the Info window for the selected item.

Grab

Apple has long made it easy to "take snapshots" of your Mac screen and parts thereof. Mac OS X provides this capability via the Grab utility. The Grab utility is fully described in Chapter 6.

Grab lends its services to other applications, allowing you to take a snapshot of the entire screen, a selection, or a timed screen shot, as shown in Figure 11-2.

Screen Capture without Grab

Incidentally, you can capture the full screen or a selected area without using the Grab utility. This has nothing to do with services, but is such a helpful thing to know, it is included here for your convenience. The following keystrokes do the trick:

✦ Command-Shift-3 captures the full screen.

✦ Command-Shift-4 provides a crosshairs pointer to select the area you want captured. Drag the pointer diagonally to define the selection rectangle.

With either keystroke, the screen shot is saved as a PDF file on the Desktop.

For example, while working in TextEdit, you can choose TextEdit ➪ Services ➪ Grab ➪ Screen and a full-screen picture would be inserted in your TextEdit document at the current insertion point. Figure 11-3 shows a partial screen capture inserted into a Text Edit document.

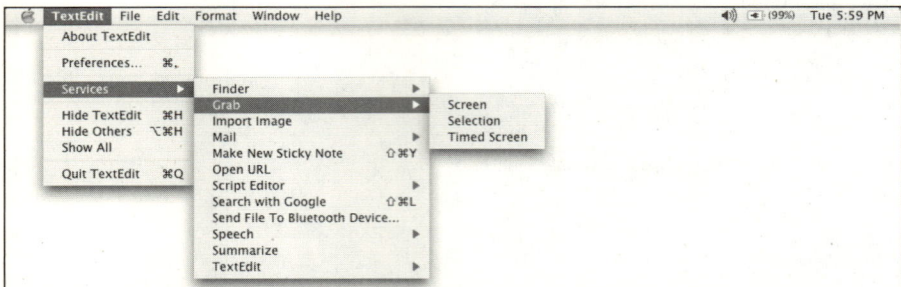

Figure 11-2: Grab Services include full screen, screen selection, and timed full-screen captures.

As mentioned previously, the Grab service's commands appear dimmed when you try to access them from the Finder. Many users have found this a tad confusing. But the Finder cannot produce a document for the Grab service to place its results in; it only produces Finder windows. Instead, use the Grab utility with the Finder; or use Mac OS X's screen capture commands, described in the sidebar "Screen Capture without Grab."

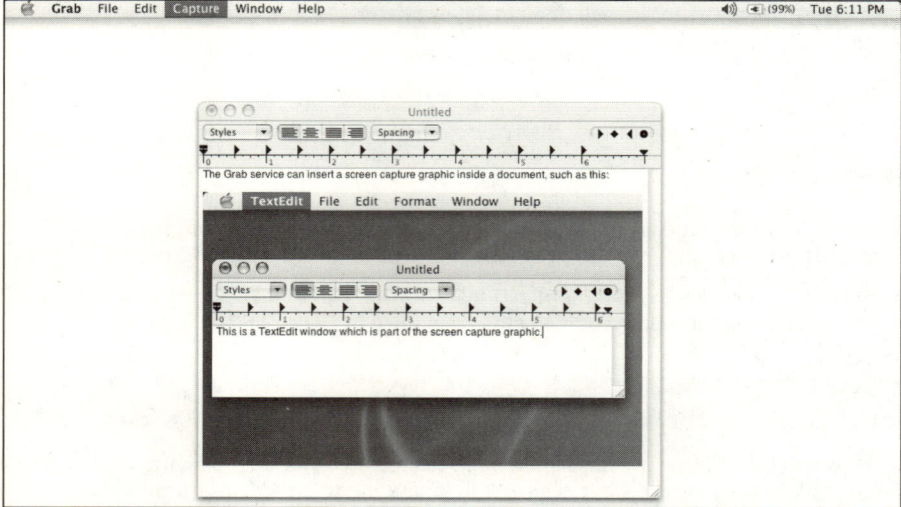

Figure 11-3: The Grab service has captured part of the screen and inserted it into a TextEdit document.

Mail

The Mail application supplied by Mac OS X provides two services to other applications: Send Selection and Send To.

✦ **Send Selection.** Your selection will appear in the body of a new email message.

✦ **Send To.** Your selection will appear in the address of a new email message.

A typical use of the Mail service is as follows:

1. **Select a name or email address in the body of your TextEdit document (or other word processor — it has to support Services).**

2. **Select Services ➪ Mail ➪ Send To from the Application menu.** The Mac OS X Mail application opens with a new email message addressed as you specified, shown in Figure 11-4.

Be aware that the Mail ➪ Send To service does not check for a valid email address or name. It merely takes the text you provide and places that text into the To: field of a new mail message.

Similarly, select a block of text, an image, or other material and choose Services ➪ Mail ➪ Send Selection from the application menu to create a new email message in Mail with the selected text or image in the body of the email message, as shown in Figure 11-5.

In addition to the Send Selection and Send to commands available to all compatible applications, Mail also provides a Send File service to mail an entire file from the Finder. To use this service, select a file or an entire folder in the Finder and then choose the Finder ➪ Services ➪ Mail ➪ Send File command, as shown in Figure 11-6. This command will not be visible in the Finder unless a file is selected.

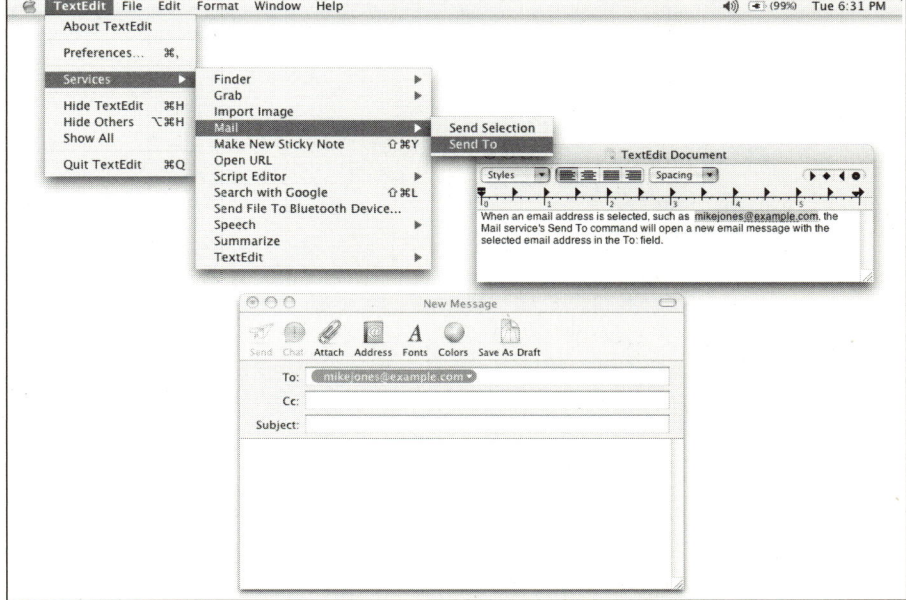

Figure 11-4: Use Mail's Send To service to create a mail message addressed to the selected name.

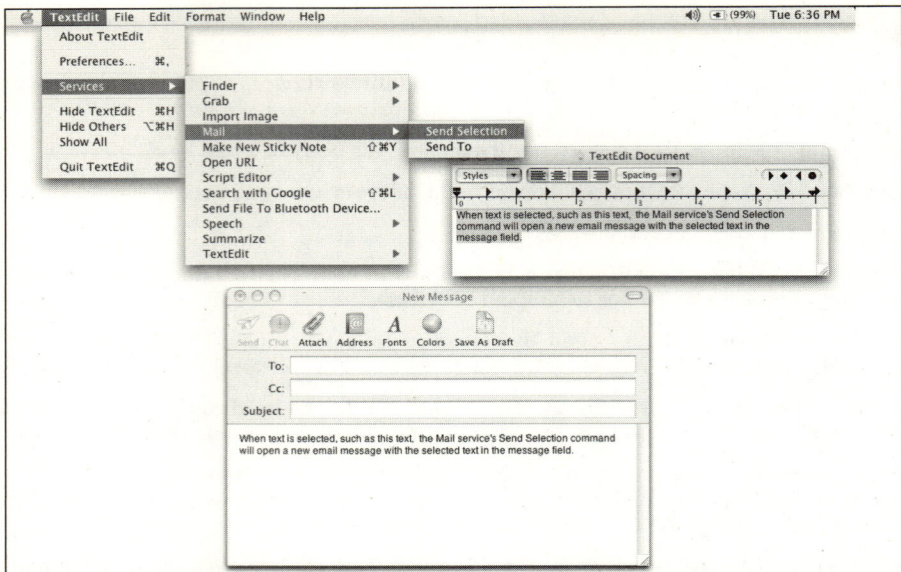

Figure 11-5: Use Mail's Send Selection service to make an email message from selected text, as seen here, or from other media.

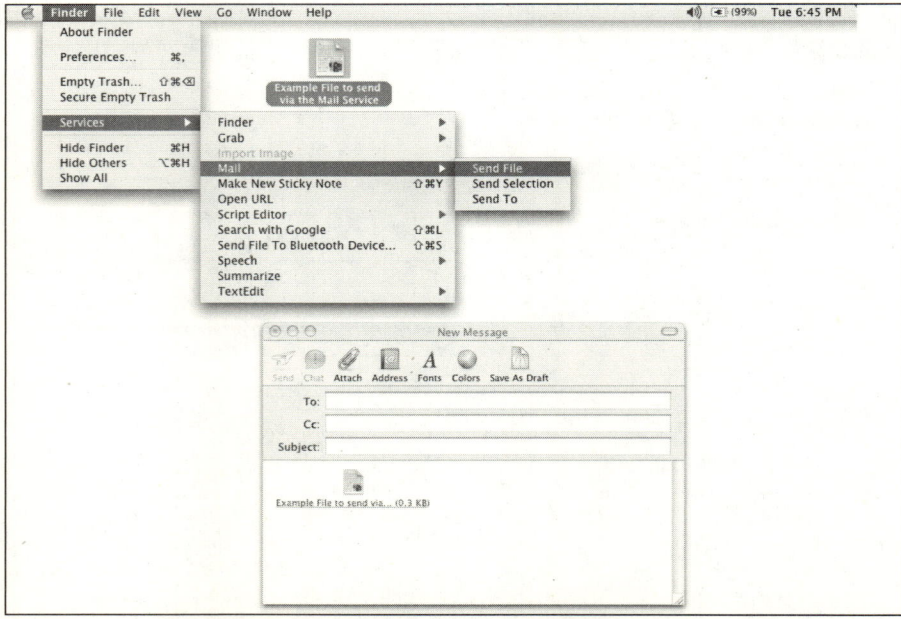

Figure 11-6: From the Finder, select a file (top); select the Mail service's Send File command (middle) and a new message will open with the file included as an attachment (bottom).

Using Stickies

For those fans of Post-It Notes and their digital counterpart, Mac OS X Stickies offers a service. Any selected text in an application that supports services can be made into a Sticky note by choosing Services ➪ Make New Sticky Note (Command-Shift-Y) from the application menu. Stickies is launched, if it isn't already, and a new Sticky note containing your selected text (up to the maximum size of a Sticky note) appears, as shown in Figure 11-7.

Note   Although Stickies can contain graphics in Mac OS X, the service ignores any graphics within the selection when it creates the Sticky note.

You can also access any of the supported services from within the Stickies application.

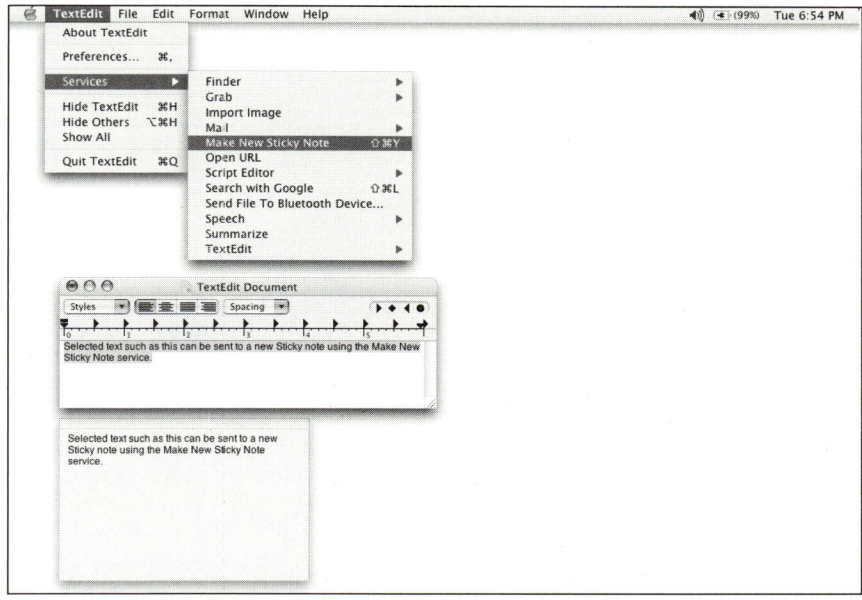

Figure 11-7: Use the Make New Sticky Note service to turn any selected text into a Sticky note.

Speech

In a Cocoa or services-compatible application, any selected text can be sent to the Speech service to be read aloud, by selecting the text and choosing the Services ➪ Start Speaking Text command as shown in Figure 11-8. To stop, use the Services ➪ Stop Speaking command. To change the settings for Speech, use the Speech pane in System Preferences. (System Preferences are covered in more detail in Chapter 13.) This service is helpful for comparing long numbers or exact wording (listen to one as you look at the other).

If you select an icon in the Finder and choose the Start Speaking Text command, Speech will speak the item's path! For example, if you select the application that makes this possible, System/Library/Services/SpeechService.service, and invoke Start Speaking Text, you will hear "System, Library, Services, SpeechService.services." This is mostly just a nifty trick, because you could more easily hold down the Command key and click on the title of the Finder window to see the path. Perhaps if you have to type the path, it would be helpful to hear it as you do so.

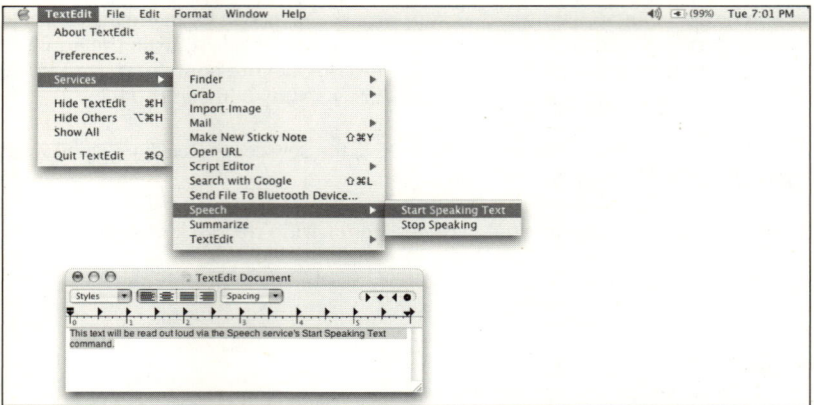

Figure 11-8: Use Speech's Start Speaking Text command to hear the text, notes, or email read aloud.

Summarize

An interesting service takes selected text and quickly summarizes it by extracting key sentences or paragraphs. This service is unusual because it's provided by an application that you don't use otherwise. The service is called Summarize, and it's provided by the Summary Service application, which you will not find in the Applications folder. It is located in the System/Library/Services folder.

To use this service, you select some text in a document and choose Services ➪ Summarize from the application menu. The Summary Service application opens, prepares a summary of the selected text, and displays the summary in a window. Figure 11-9 shows an example of the Summarize service.

Tip   If you select some text but the Summarize choice is disabled (dim) in the Services submenu, the Summarize service is not available in the application you're using. You can summarize the selected text by copying it to a document in the TextEdit application. Then select the text in the TextEdit document and choose TextEdit ➪ Services ➪ Summarize. You can use this same basic concept to use the other services, too.

When the Summary window appears, you can control the degree to which the text is summarized by sliding the Summary Size pointer; dragging it to the left causes the results to become shorter and less detailed. Slide the pointer and you will see the text dynamically respond, growing or shrinking as you do so. This way you can easily pick the perfect length for your summary.

The two radio buttons, Sentences and Paragraphs, control the style of summary produced. When Sentences is selected, Summarize will extract key sentences from within paragraphs in your selected text. When Paragraphs is selected, Summarize extracts the key paragraphs from the text, keeping them intact in the result. You can switch back and forth to see which style suits your needs.

Click the Clear All button to clear the contents of the Summary window and begin a new summary.

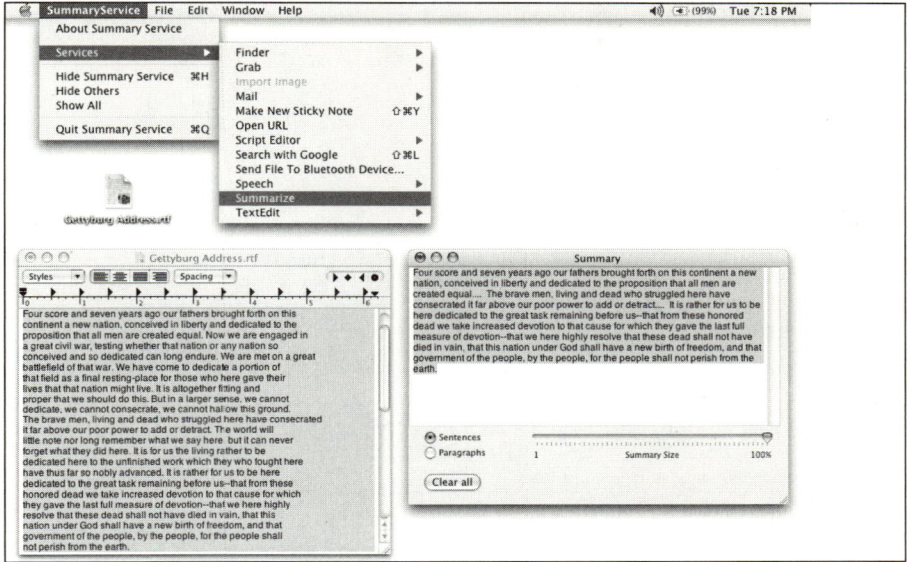

Figure 11-9: Use the Summarize service (top) to prepare a summary (bottom right) of selected text (bottom left).

You can save the summary as a text document by choosing File ⇨ Save As. In addition, you can edit the summary by using the Edit menu and other regular text editing methods. You can even check the spelling in the summary by choosing Edit ⇨ Spelling or Edit ⇨ Check Spelling.

Does the Summarize service use some new advance in Artificial Intelligence to do what heretofore one required a human to do? Disappointingly, no. A statistical analysis is performed on key-word frequency, parts of speech usage, sentence structure, and the like. Rules are applied, voodoo occurs, and the results spit out — all apparently within the realm of what current computer technology can do. No wonder the results can sometimes be of somewhat less quality than a human editor could achieve; but then again, *that* takes *work*...

TextEdit

The TextEdit application, the versatile text editor and word processor included with Mac OS X (covered in more detail in Chapter 6), provides two services:

✦ Open a file by name

✦ Create a new file containing selected content

To open a file by name, as shown in Figure 11-10, you select text that specifies a full path to the file and then choose Services ⇨ TextEdit ⇨ Open Selected File from the Application menu. If the file cannot be found, an error message appears stating that the file could not be opened; however, the error message doesn't tell you why the attempt failed. Note that the selection must be a file that TextEdit can open.

You can also select a block of text and other media. Then choose Services ⇨ TextEdit ⇨ New Window Containing Selection from the Application menu to create a new TextEdit document using the selected media, as shown in Figure 11-11. Because both text and other media are combined, you can edit the result. This service is a useful adjunct to clipping files.

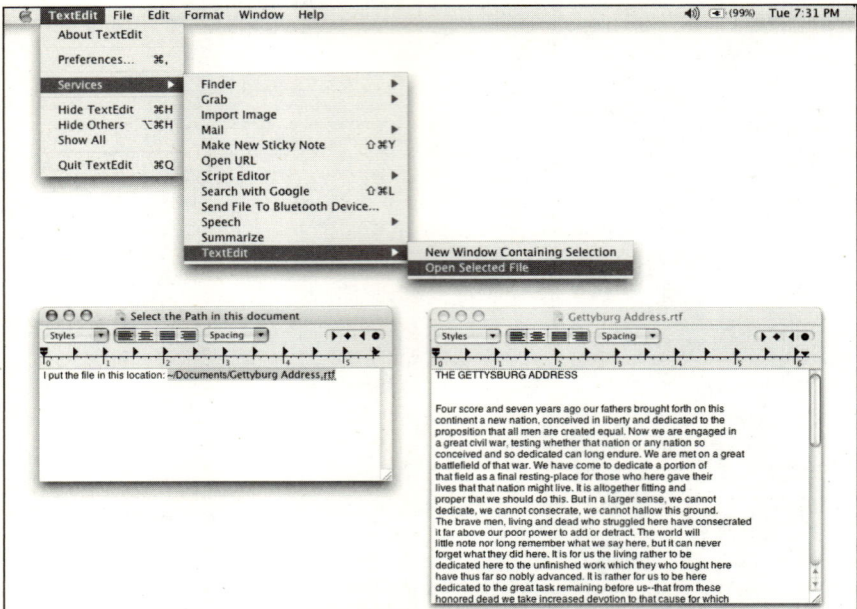

Figure 11-10: Select a full path (lower left), choose the Open Selected File command (top), and the file opens (bottom right).

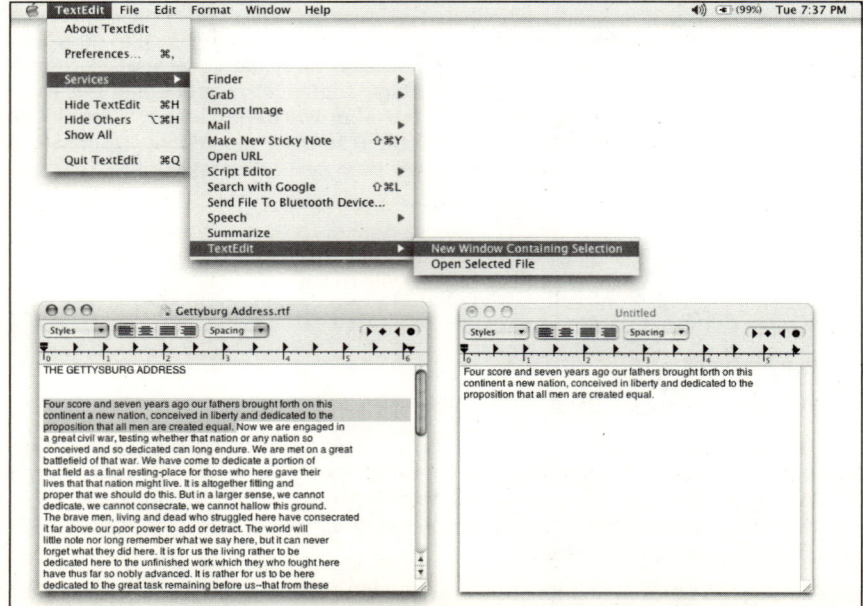

Figure 11-11: Use the New Window Containing Selection command (top) to create a TextEdit document (bottom right) from selected text (bottom left).

Other Services

These services also appear in the Panther Services submenu:

✦ **Import Image:** Works only when you have a device, connected to the computer that can be accessed through the Image Capture application (described in Chapter 21). This device will typically be a digital camera or a scanner. Select the image you wish to import via the Image Capture interface, and it will be imported into your document. This service is helpful for quickly emailing a few photos you just took without importing all the photos in the camera.

✦ **Open URL:** Highlight a URL in your document, and select this command to open your default Cocoa Web browser (usually Safari) to show the Web page in a new window. Nominee for the Most Useful New Service award.

✦ **Script Editor:** Uses services provided by the Script Editor application for working with AppleScripts. These commands are meant for AppleScript developers (which could, and perhaps should, be you! See Chapter 23 for more on AppleScript). Three commands are available:

• The **Get Result of AppleScript** command can be invoked by pressing Command-Shift-*. This command will replace the selected text, which must be an executable AppleScript, with the result of the executed script. For instance, type **123/45 * pi** into a TextEdit document, select it, and run this command. The text will be replaced with the result of the AppleScript calculation, in this case 8.587019919812. Throw those calculators away!

• The **Make New AppleScript** command will transfer the selected text, which should be part or all of an AppleScript, to a new script window in the Script Editor application.

• The **Run As AppleScript** command will execute the selected text, which must be an executable AppleScript.

✦ **Search with Google:** Highlight any text, select this command, and your default Cocoa Web browser (usually Safari) will open to display the results of a Google search using your text.

✦ **Send File to Bluetooth Device:** This service is provided by the Bluetooth File Exchange utility, and is enabled only when you have a Bluetooth transmitter/receiver, either inside your Mac or connected to a USB port. Selecting this command opens the Bluetooth File Exchange utility to the Select File to Send window for you to navigate to the desired file. Clicking Send opens the Select Bluetooth Device window for you to pick the device to send to. Click Send to transmit the file to the device. (See Chapter 15 to read all about these Bluetooth utilities.)

Other Cocoa applications that you install may provide additional services. Services provided by a newly installed application may not become available until the next time you log in.

You can also obtain third-party services to install on your Mac OS X machine; many of them are freeware. Perhaps the best way to browse for them is to visit VersionTracker.com, click the Mac OS X tab, and enter *services* in the search field.

A good example of a third-party service is AtYourService, which allows you to add a selection of items to your Services menu. This shareware can look up selected text at Dictionary.com, AcronymFinder.com, VersionTracker, Yahoo Stocks, and the Internet Movie Data Base (IMDB).

Third-party services will install to the System/Library/Services folder, where the icons of four services installed with Mac OS X 10.3 live. They are AppleSpellService, ImageCaptureService, SpeechService.service, and SummaryService.

Summary

In this chapter, you learned that services allow the applications and functions listed in the Services submenu of the Application menu to share certain helpful capabilities with other applications. Usually only Cocoa applications can utilize these services. To enable the services commands in the menu, you must first select content in an open document. The services perform varied actions on this selected content, which were described in detail for each service available by default in Panther. You can also install third-party services.

Refer to Chapter 5 for more information on the applications and utilities that come with Mac OS X.

✦ ✦ ✦

Wrestling Fonts into Submission

The vast majority of the world's graphic design, printing, and publishing companies are virtually standardized on the Macintosh as their main engine of creation. If it was printed, it almost certainly was designed on a Mac, and if you are reading it, you are likely looking at Mac fonts. In fact, you are looking at Mac fonts at this moment.

Mac OS X carries the Mac platform's leadership position in font display and reproduction capabilities to new extremes. And Panther features Font Book, the new utility that enables the user for the first time to preview and turn fonts on and off without dependency on a third-party font manager.

Practically every Mac user works with fonts in a basic way, by selecting a particular font to use in their documents. But few users, even many professional graphic artists, have a comprehensive understanding of how fonts work in Mac OS X, and how best to work with them!

In this chapter, you learn what exactly a font is, and what font technologies the Mac employs. We examine what features are designed into Mac OS X for working with fonts. The font types supported by Mac OS X are listed and described, and where to put your fonts is demystified. We look at managing fonts with font management software and how Font Book fits into the picture. You can find information on font utilities, tips for working with fonts, and how to deal with fonts in the Classic environment.

About Fonts

A *font* is a design for a complete set of type characters in a particular style and size. That's the quick and easy definition, but to understand how fonts fit in to the worlds of typography and computers, you have to know a couple of other terms.

The word *font* is very often incorrectly used as a synonym for *typeface*. Here's the difference: A typeface is a distinctive, visually consistent design for the symbols in an alphabet, and a font is how a typeface appears when it includes specific characteristics such as size, weight, spacing, and so on. For example, *Times-Roman Bold Oblique* is a typeface, and *Times-Roman 12 Bold Oblique* is a font.

Times-Roman is an example of a *family,* a set of fonts of the same typeface, but in different sizes and variations of style such as plain, bold, italic, oblique, bold italic, demibold, and so on.

In the predigital era, fascinatingly, each character was cast in its own block of metal, and these blocks were arranged in a row in the correct order to make words when inked and pressed into paper. In this world of metal type, a font is the alphabet and its accessory characters, cast into the blocks in a given typeface and size. In this sense, a printer could carry a box full of a font, or physically load a font into a typesetting machine. (And this also explains why companies that design fonts are still called *foundries*.)

Similarly, in our computer era, *font* has come to mean not only the typeface and its character set, but also the digital information encoding it. The files that contain this information are commonly referred to as fonts. In this sense, you could ask someone to copy fonts from a CD to a folder on a hard drive.

The word *font* has also come to be used in place of *typeface* and *family,* much to the bewilderment of typography purists. This is because today a single computer file can contain all the typefaces in a font family, and create them in any size desired.

So, in general usage today, font has come to mean a digital file that contains the information necessary for a computer to create characters of a unique, unified design on the screen and in print.

A *character* is an abstract visual symbol for a letter, number, punctuation mark, or mathematical sign. But in computer-speak, a *character* is any symbol that requires one byte of storage, as well as its representation within the computer in a numerical code system such as ASCII or Unicode (more about this later). Even an empty space between words is a character in these systems, the character that is sent when you press the space bar on your keyboard.

The height of characters in a font is measured in *points,* with each point measuring about $\frac{1}{72}$ inch. Selecting a point size in a program changes the displayed size of the font.

A *glyph* is the actual shape of a character's image; it represents the character visually and graphically. The first letter of the English alphabet is the character *A,* but the *A* can be drawn as a capital or a lowercase, a plain or an italic, in one typeface or another; and they would all be different glyphs. Some fonts have alternate glyphs for the same character, to be used in different circumstances, for instance to provide a choice between a fancier or plainer letter *A.*

Mac Font Formats

Digital fonts come in different *formats;* these are also known as font *types*. Font formats incorporate different technologies for producing fonts on a computer and, as a result, all formats are not supported by all computer platforms or operating systems. The following formats are supported by Mac OS X:

✦ PostScript Type

✦ Multiple Master

✦ Mac and Windows TrueType

✦ Mac and Windows OpenType

✦ Mac OS X System dfont

Bitmap fonts

Bitmap fonts (sometimes referred to as *bitmapped* or *fixed-size* fonts) are the original fonts used on the very first Macs in 1984. Mac OS X does not use bitmap fonts. But Mac OS 9 and, therefore, the Classic environment, still work with them, although hopefully most users have switched to more-advanced font types. The fonts you use today are almost certainly not bitmap fonts.

Although bitmap fonts are fast becoming a historical curiosity, knowing something about them is helpful in understanding font technology.

In a bitmap font, every character is represented by an arrangement of dots. Figure 12-1 shows the dots in an enlarged view of two characters of a bitmapped font.

Figure 12-1: Bitmap fonts contain dot-for-dot pictures of characters. (Times capital *A* and *G* at 12-, 14-, and 18-point sizes enlarged to show detail.)

The name *bitmap* refers to each dot's value (filled in or not) being stored in one or more *bits* of data. For monochrome fonts (and images), one bit is sufficient to record each dot's value. For shades of gray or colors, each dot requires more than one bit of data.

The computer translates the bitmap into *pixels* (picture elements) to display it on a monitor, or into ink dots to print it. The way each font looks on the screen, or after printing, depends on how its point size relates to the *resolution,* that is, the density of dots displayed on the monitor or produced by the printer.

Each bitmap font is designed for display in one size only, so bitmap fonts usually are installed in sets. A typical set includes 9-, 10-, 12-, 14-, 18-, and 24-point font sizes. If you need text in a size for which no bitmap font is installed, the Mac OS must scale a bitmap font's character bitmaps up or down to the size you want. The results are misshapen or blocky, as shown in Figure 12-2.

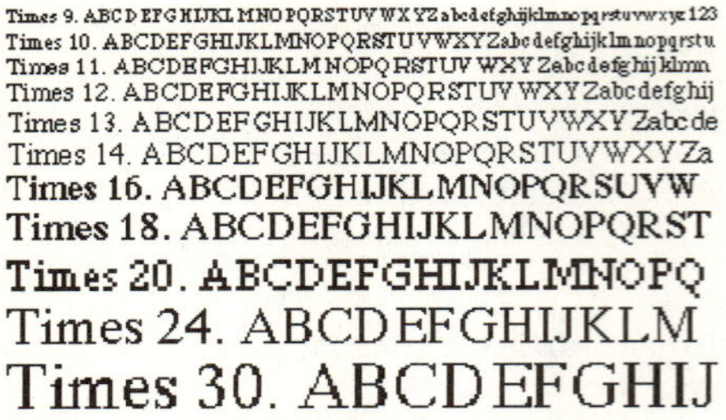

Times 9. ABCDEFGHIJKLMNOPQRSTUVWXYZ abcdefghijklmnopqrstuvwxyz 123
Times 10. ABCDEFGHIJKLMNOPQRSTUVWXYZabcdefghijklmnopqrstu
Times 11. ABCDEFGHIJKLMNOPQRSTUVWXYZabcdefghijklmn
Times 12. ABCDEFGHIJKLMNOPQRSTUVWXYZabcdefghij
Times 13. ABCDEFGHIJKLMNOPQRSTUVWXYZabcde
Times 14. ABCDEFGHIJKLMNOPQRSTUVWXYZa
Times 16. ABCDEFGHIJKLMNOPQRSUVW
Times 18. ABCDEFGHIJKLMNOPQRST
Times 20. ABCDEFGHIJKLMNOPQ
Times 24. ABCDEFGHIJKLM
Times 30. ABCDEFGHIJ

Figure 12-2: Bitmap fonts look best at installed sizes; in this scaling of the Times 24 font, note the blockiness of the 20- and 30-point font sizes. (Enlarged to show detail.)

PostScript fonts

PostScript fonts were the innovation that started the professional desktop publishing industry. Invented by Adobe Systems in 1984, they were the first fonts to look great at any size and any resolution. For this reason they are known as *scaleable* or *variable-size* fonts.

Instead of fixed-size bit maps, PostScript fonts use curves and straight lines to outline each character's shape, as shown in Figure 12-3. PostScript fonts were the first of the many types of *outline fonts*.

Figure 12-3: PostScript fonts are based on outlines. (Times capital *G* shown.)

This outline is a special kind of *vector graphic,* defined by mathematical instructions known as Bezier curves in the PostScript computer language. You may be familiar with vector graphics if you use an application such as Adobe Illustrator. In fact, Illustrator can be used to create or alter PostScript fonts.

Unlike other types of fonts, in which each font resides within a single file, the original Type 1 PostScript fonts have two files that must be properly installed for the font to function properly. Each PostScript font has a screen font file, and its associated printer font file. The screen font file contains a bitmap representation of the font in at least one point size; the printer font file contains the scalable outline font.

Although a PostScript screen font appears in font menus and onscreen correctly without its associated printer font installed, the screen font does not print correctly. In addition, a font does not appear in a font menu, nor does text previously formatted with that font appear correctly onscreen, without its associated screen font installed, because the screen font file contains the font metrics data. This is true whether Adobe Type Manager (described in a moment) is being used or not.

PostScript fonts are divided into two main categories: Type 1 and Type 3. (Type 2 was the font format used to embed fonts in Acrobat 3 PDF files, and so is no longer widely used.) Most PostScript fonts that you see are Type 1, because they yield better results at small font sizes and low resolutions. Although Type 1 fonts generally look better, Type 3 fonts are more elaborate. The characters in Type 3 fonts have variable stroke weights and are filled with something other than a solid color, such as shades of gray or blends that go from white to black. Type 3 fonts were popular in the late 1980s, and are still used for custom fonts and special effects. Mac OS X does not provide support for Type 3 fonts.

PostScript fonts were originally designed for printing on Apple LaserWriter printers and other PostScript output devices. In Mac OS 9, and hence in the Classic environment, Adobe Type Manager (ATM) software smoothly scales PostScript fonts to any size for non-PostScript printers and the display screen. With ATM and PostScript fonts, you didn't need a *set* of bitmap or TrueType fonts for the screen display. Just one bitmap size would suffice. ATM was included on the Mac OS 9 CD that came with Mac OS X 10.2 for awhile, in the Adobe Software folder. ATM Light is also available for free from Adobe's Web site.

Mac OS X, on the other hand, includes built-in support for Type 1 fonts in three variations:

✦ Screen font files, optionally in a font suitcase, plus corresponding PostScript Type 1 outline fonts

✦ QuickDraw GX–enabled font suitcases

✦ QuickDraw GX–enabled MultiMaster font suitcases

TrueType fonts (described later) cannot entirely replace PostScript fonts for a number of reasons. For one, PostScript fonts include a lot of information in the font file — kerning information and hints that help the font look better at different sizes — that TrueType fonts do not. Additionally, PostScript offers more than just outline fonts. It's a *page description language* that precisely specifies the location and other characteristics of every text and graphic item on the page.

PostScript fonts are still commonly used, especially in graphic production, and many organizations have large collections of them that will not be replaced with another format in the foreseeable future.

Multiple Master fonts

Multiple Master (or MM) fonts are special versions of certain PostScript Type 1 fonts that allow variation of one or more font parameters, most often weight (bold or light), style (italic or plain), or width (condensed or extended). This enables the creation of an unlimited number of different styles, known as *instances,* from the same font file, a unique advantage.

However, the MM technology was not entirely a success. Not all applications support it, and the MM fonts can be difficult to output correctly. There are only about 50 MM fonts, and most are from Adobe. In late 1999, Adobe announced it would no longer develop MM fonts. However, the technology behind MM fonts is still used in ATM and Adobe Acrobat.

Mac OS 10.2 and above can activate existing instances of this font type, but cannot create instances. (To *activate* a font means to make it available to applications for use.)

TrueType fonts

TrueType fonts are outline fonts that contain both screen and printer font information in a single font file — an advance over PostScript fonts.

TrueType fonts look good at all sizes. They work with all Mac OS applications and all types of printers, including PostScript printers. The Mac OS smoothly scales a TrueType font's character outlines to any size on a display screen and on printers of any resolution, all with equally good results. Figure 12-4 is an example of TrueType font scaling.

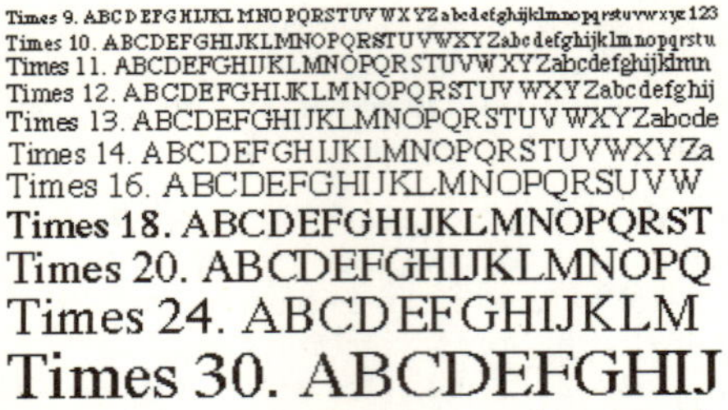

Times 9. ABCD EFG HIJKL MNO PQRSTUV WX YZ abcdefghijklmnopqrstuvwxyz 123
Times 10. ABCDEFGHIJKLMNOPQRSTUVWXYZ abcdefghijklmnopqrstu
Times 11. ABCDEFGHIJKLMNOPQRSTUVWXYZabcdefghijklmn
Times 12. ABCDEFGHIJKLMNOPQRSTUVWXYZabcdefghij
Times 13. ABCDEFGHIJKLMNOPQRSTUVWXYZabcde
Times 14. ABCDEFGHIJKLMNOPQRSTUVWXYZa
Times 16. ABCDEFGHIJKLMNOPQRSUVW

Times 18. ABCDEFGHIJKLMNOPQRST

Times 20. ABCDEFGHIJKLMNOPQ

Times 24. ABCDEFGHIJKLM

Times 30. ABCDEFGHIJ

Figure 12-4: TrueType fonts scale smoothly to all sizes and resolutions. (Enlarged to show detail.)

TrueType differs from PostScript in how it mathematically specifies font outlines and adjusts the outlines for small font sizes and low resolutions.

TrueType was developed by Apple and Microsoft initially as a response to the closed nature of PostScript fonts and the exceedingly high license fees charged by Adobe to include a PostScript rendering engine in LaserWriters. TrueType was introduced in 1991 as an integral part of Mac System 7 and Microsoft Windows 3.1. Adobe responded to this assault on the turf it controlled by releasing Adobe Type Manager to improve the onscreen appearance of PostScript Type 1 fonts, and by disclosing the PostScript Type 1 definition, allowing competition in the marketplace for PostScript fonts. TrueType was only a limited success. Font foundries were reluctant to develop TrueType fonts, concentrating instead on PostScript Type 1.

Mac OS X can recognize traditional Mac TrueType files and font suitcases, which are folder-like containers of traditional Mac font files. Because traditional Mac font files have two forks (parts), called the data fork and the resource fork, these font files and font suitcases must be stored on disks or other volumes that have the Mac OS Extended format (also known as HFS Plus).

Mac OS X also recognizes Windows TrueType font files, which have the file name extension of .ttf or .ttc. Windows TrueType font files, like all other Windows files, don't have two forks.

TrueType fonts are commonly used in home or office environments. They are infrequently used in graphic production; however, they are supported by most current RIPs. (A RIP is a raster image processor, hardware or software which prepares digital files for printing on a PostScript printer.) If you are a designer using TrueType fonts, be sure to embed them when making a PDF or PostScript file to avoid problems during the RIP process.

OpenType fonts

An extension of the TrueType format, the OpenType format supports PostScript font data in the same file with TrueType font data. You can think of OpenType as a wrapper around PostScript or TrueType font data.

Adobe and Microsoft worked jointly to create the OpenType font format, which was announced in 1996. The first OpenType fonts appeared on the market in 2000. It is too early to tell if OpenType will become popular, but it is a powerful and promising technology.

OpenType fonts and the operating system services that support them provide users with a simple way to install and use fonts, whether the fonts contain TrueType outlines or PostScript outlines.

The OpenType font format addresses the following goals:

✦ Broader multiplatform support

✦ Better support for international character sets

✦ Better protection for font data

✦ Smaller file sizes to make font distribution more efficient

✦ Broader support for advanced typographic control

An OpenType font is a single file and works across platforms, unlike PostScript and TrueType fonts that are made in separate Mac and PC versions. However, not all applications support OpenType fonts.

OpenType fonts also have the advantage of supporting extended character sets. OpenType fonts support the Unicode standard used in Mac OS X, which encodes characters for over 65,000 different glyphs in a single font. Compare this with PostScript and TrueType fonts, which can only handle the 256 glyphs of the ASCII standard, not enough for many languages.

OpenType fonts are also referred to as TrueType Open v.2.0 fonts because they use the TrueType font file format (which the Mac OS identifies internally with the file type code sfnt). PostScript data included in OpenType fonts may be directly rasterized, or converted, to the TrueType outline format for rendering, depending on which rasterizers have been installed in the host operating system. But the user experience is the same: OpenType fonts just work. Users do not need to be aware of the type of outline data in OpenType fonts. And font creators can use whichever outline format they feel provides the best set of features for their work, without worrying about limiting a font's usability.

OpenType fonts enable font creators to design better international and high-end fonts by including OpenType Layout tables. These tables contain information on glyph (character) substitution, glyph positioning, justification, and baseline positioning, which enables text-processing applications to improve text layout by making minute adjustments to the kerning and tracking.

In Mac OS X, OpenType fonts typically have a file name extension of .otf.

Mac OS X System dfonts

Mac OS X introduced the *dfont* format, a special Apple version of TrueType fonts that contain their information in the data fork instead of a separate resource fork like previous Mac font files did. This way they are compatible with Unix file systems, such as the Unified File System (UFS) that can be installed optionally with Mac OS X.

The system software uses the dfonts internally, and they are located in the System/Library/Fonts folder.

Some of the dfonts are high-quality fonts with extensive glyph sets, so graphic designers may be interested in using them. If you are installing PostScript or TrueType fonts on your system, be aware that some of their names conflict with some of the dfont names. As described later in this chapter, you should remove the conflicting fonts you don't want.

Also, if you are a designer and use dfonts, make sure your service provider is also using Mac OS X to output your documents, as they will not work with earlier versions of the Mac OS. You can get around this problem by creating a PDF to send instead of the application file.

Mac OS X Font Facts and Features

Mac OS X is full of font-related features and technologies. To introduce them, here are some facts you should know:

✦ Mac OS X 10.3 provides support for more font types than any other operating system. (You will find the types listed and described previously.) As a result, cross-platform file exchange is simplified.

✦ Unlike other operating systems, there is no limit to the number of fonts you can have open at one time in Mac OS X. If you wanted to, you could put an immense library of fonts in a single Fonts folder, and nothing would break; the operating system would automatically find the necessary memory. But as you see later in this chapter, there are better alternatives for managing large numbers of fonts.

✦ If you used Adobe Type Manager in Mac OS 9 to render your fonts, you will not need it in Mac OS X. In fact, Adobe does not provide a version of ATM for Mac OS X. Mac OS X contains a built-in rasterizer technology, Apple Type Services, to automatically render all font formats, including PostScript. But if you used ATM Deluxe, you may wonder how you can replace its font management features; read on, as your options are discussed later.

✦ Mac OS X uses subpixel filtering to increase the perceived resolution of fonts rendered on screen; Apple calls this Font Smoothing. The readability of fonts displayed by Mac OS X 10.3 can be controlled in the Appearance pane of System Preferences. In the Font Smoothing style pop-up menu, you may choose Standard (best for CRT displays), Light, Medium (best for flat-panel displays), and Strong. At very small font sizes, the smoothed fonts can seem fuzzy, so you can set the font size below which the operating system turns off text smoothing in the pop-up menu at the bottom of the Appearance pane.

✦ Mac OS X provides multiple font locations, with different access privileges for each location. This gives you better control and more options to organize fonts for different users and uses.

✦ With every new version of Mac OS X, Apple seems to provide more professional-quality fonts, and support for more non-Roman languages. Mac OS 10.3 currently includes 100 font families, almost double the number included with 10.2. To see the new fonts, you have to allow them to be added when you install Mac OS 10.3.

✦ Mac OS X protects itself by checking the integrity of a font when it is displayed or printed. Apple calls this Font Validation. If the operating system detects a corrupt font, it will be automatically deactivated.

✦ Apple Advanced Typography (AAT) is a Mac OS X system–level feature that supports (for programs written to make use of it) sophisticated typographic capabilities previously found only in typesetting applications such as QuarkXpress. Included in these capabilities: kerning (customizing the spacing between certain pairs of letters), tracking (adjusting the spacing between groups of letters and entire blocks of text), ligatures (two or more letters combined into one character), and a mind-boggling list of others. And all this is available even to humble applications like TextEdit.

✦ Font Book. Panther contains this new font management utility, described in detail later in this chapter.

✦ Mac OS X protects against the font corruption that plagued Mac OS 9. In Mac OS 9, if two fonts happened to have the same font ID number, the operating system attempted to resolve the conflict by assigning a new number to one of them. However, sometimes more than just the number would get changed, and the font file became corrupted, leading to mysterious problems, crashed systems, and much sadness.

But Mac OS X does not try to alter fonts, so the chance of corruption is greatly reduced. Font corruption can still happen in Mac OS X, but at least the OS is not a contributing factor. Check any fonts for corruption that you import from an older system, as well as those purchased from smaller font foundries, using one of the font utilities mentioned later in this chapter. And it's not a bad precaution to periodically check all the fonts on your system, just in case.

Mac OS X Font Locations

In Mac OS X, you can store fonts in six locations. Multiple font locations enable you to have more control over your fonts than if there was only a single location. If several users share the same machine, you can choose to keep their fonts separate and inaccessible from each other, so they cannot steal or change another user's fonts. You can also make certain fonts available to be shared by all the users of the machine. If you want to share fonts over a network with other machines, you can do that. And all this can be done by placing fonts in different locations.

Additionally, certain locations are used to store fonts reserved for a particular function. For example, some applications come with special fonts they need, so these fonts must be accessible in a separate location. The system software needs its own very secure place for its essential fonts, where users are not permitted to change them. And the Classic environment needs its own separate place for fonts to support its applications.

There is a background reason, too. The Unix operating system features multiple font directories, for many of the same purposes mentioned above. Mac OS X is Unix based, so it was a natural decision to take advantage of its very useful font locations scheme and build on it.

When a Mac OS X application asks the system to find a font, the system looks through these locations in the sequence they are numbered below. It uses the first font match it finds. So, if you have different versions of the same font in different locations, Mac OS X will use whichever is in the highest folder in the following list:

1. **Application's own fonts folder (if it has one):** Certain applications have private font folders inside the application's folder. If they do, this folder is the first to be checked, and any fonts found here will be used instead of duplicate fonts in other folders, but only for that specific application.

2. **User's Home fonts folder at /Users/*username*/Library/Fonts:** No one but the user can access these fonts. This is the most common location for fonts to be kept for most users.

3. **Main font folder at /Library/Fonts:** Fonts kept here can be accessed by all users with accounts on the machine. Only a user with an administrator login can change the contents of this folder.

4. **Network fonts at /Network/Library/Fonts:** This folder is inside the Network icon — in Mac OS 10.3, a shiny gray ball with stars inside a clear cube that can be found on the top level of the hierarchy, along with the machine's hard drive(s). The contents of this Fonts folder are actually located on another computer on your network, for instance a Mac OS X server running NetInfo, in order to share a consistent set of fonts with many users. All the fonts in this location are always in the activated state.

5. **System fonts at /System/Library/Fonts:** This location stores the fonts used by the system software to be used in menus, dialogs, and icons. You can see the fonts, but you cannot ordinarily change them. Later in the chapter a method for modifying these fonts under certain situations is described. No additions of user fonts should be added to this folder.

6. **Classic fonts at Mac OS 9/System Folder/Fonts:** This is the Fonts folder for the copy of Mac OS 9 that is used to run the Classic environment. This is the only folder that Classic applications can access fonts from. Mac OS X applications can also make use of fonts in this location.

So, with all these possible locations, where do you put your fonts? The answer to this question varies, depending on your situation. Find the situation below which best describes yours:

✦ If you are the only user of the machine and you will not be running any Classic applications, put your fonts in the /Users/*username*/Library/Fonts folder. This solution is perhaps the easiest and the one that most users of Mac OS X utilize. In this situation, you could also put fonts in the /Library/Fonts folder, but the system checks this location after the User's fonts folder, and if you ever decide to create new user accounts, they will be able to access all your fonts. Stick with the first one.

✦ If you expect to be running Classic applications as well as Mac OS X applications, you can put your fonts in the System Folder:Fonts folder of the copy of Mac OS 9 you will use to run Classic.

The System Folder/Fonts folder is the only fonts folder that applications running in the Classic environment can get fonts from, and Mac OS X applications can also use these fonts. This solution makes it easy for a Mac OS 9 user to upgrade to Mac OS X, because they have to do exactly nothing to have all their present fonts work with Mac OS X.

Tip   If you manage your fonts by putting them in the Classic Fonts folder, be aware that font name conflicts can occur with fonts in locations higher in the search order. For example, if you have a PostScript version of Times in the Classic Fonts folder, it will work with Classic applications with no problem. But for all Mac OS X applications, it will be overridden by the Times in Mac OS X's /System/Library/Fonts folder. To solve this problem, remove the duplicate Mac OS X system fonts, as explained later in this chapter.

✦ You can do a combination of the two previous solutions. Keep the fonts your Classic apps need in the Classic Fonts folder, and the fonts you will use with your Mac OS X apps in the /Users/*username*/Library/Fonts folder.

✦ If you expect to share the machine with multiple users, you can install the fonts they all will share in the /Library/Fonts folder. As the machine's administrator, you can create their user accounts with regular user privileges (not administrator privileges). This way, if they want to install personal fonts, the users can install them to the Fonts folder in their Home directory only, at /Users/*username*/Library/Fonts. They cannot steal or change each other's fonts, or alter the shared fonts, because they do not have permission to access these locations. This is the best solution for schools sharing a machine among many students, or for machines used by graphic design freelancers who have been known to bring their own personal fonts on the job.

✦ If you want many users to access the same Universal set of fonts, which you as the administrator can change at will, you can share the fonts with a Mac OS X file server running NetInfo, and your users can be set up to access the fonts in the Network/Library/Fonts location. This solution is good for schools and computer labs, and is best for managing a relatively small number of fonts that you want to be consistently available for the users. There are better solutions for graphic production and large numbers of fonts. Be aware that if the font server goes down, or the network goes down, users will not be able to access the fonts.

✦ If you are a graphic designer and have zillions of fonts, you probably use font management software now, and will want to use one in Mac OS X. In which case, read on; the next section will discuss how to do this.

Please note that wherever you put your fonts in Mac OS X 10.2 and above, you may nest your fonts inside subfolders, and Mac OS X can activate them. Many users were not happy with the inability of previous versions to do this; it is no longer an issue.

Managing Fonts in Mac OS X

You may never need to manage your fonts, especially if you use only a modest number of fonts. Most users use the 100 fonts included with Mac OS X 10.3 and never need more, and these fonts are, by default, always available.

But many users need a font manager, because they may use a larger amount of fonts, need to activate and deactivate them as they work, and group them into collections. Graphic design and production pros especially depend upon these capabilities.

For Mac OS 9, several third-party font manager utilities are available, including Adobe Type Manager Deluxe, Extensis Suitcase, Extensis Font Reserve, Insider Software's Font Agent, and Alsoft's MasterJuggler. Each of these utilities has its loyal fans, and each now has a version that works with Mac OS X.

Before Mac OS X 10.3, users were pretty much constrained to these third-party solutions as they slowly became available. It is possible in Mac OS X 10.2 to manage fonts by dragging them in and out of the fonts folders, creating subfolders, for example, to organize them by job or name, but this is really only feasible for relatively small font libraries or occasional use. Some applications such as TextEdit make use of Mac OS X's Font panel, which lets you change font sizes and group fonts into set-like collections, but it can't enable or disable collections, which is necessary when you have a large number of fonts.

This section describes the font management software included with Mac OS X 10.3.

Font Book

Mac OS X 10.3 includes a new application called Font Book. Font Book is not a full-fledged font manager, but it is close enough for most users who are not graphic design professionals.

With Font Book, you can accomplish the following tasks:

✦ Install fonts to your Home fonts folder or the Main fonts folder.

✦ Preview fonts.

✦ Turn a font on or off.

✦ Create, edit, and manage font collections.

✦ Turn font collections on or off.

✦ Detect and resolve duplicate fonts.

✦ Search for installed fonts in collections and in the six font locations.

Open Font Book by double-clicking its icon in the Applications folder. Figure 12-5 shows the Font Book window as it looks when you open it for the first time. The following sections describe how you use FontBook.

Font Book and the Font panel

When you make changes in Font Book, you can see some of them reflected in the font menus of applications. An easy way to check the changes is to look in the previously mentioned Mac OS X Font panel. Certain changes will only show up in the Font panel, such as changes in the Collection column.

The best way to call up the Font panel is to launch TextEdit and navigate the menu by choosing Format ➪ Font ➪ Show Fonts. The Font panel is more fully described later in this chapter.

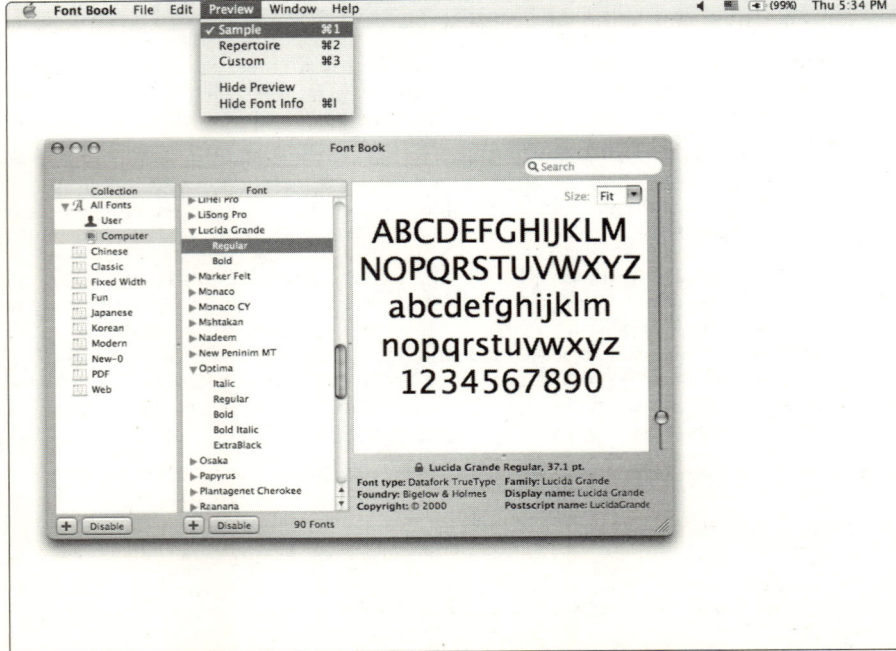

Figure 12-5: Font Book's interface, showing the Sample style of font preview.

Working with Font Book

In Font Book, the terms *on* and *enabled* are synonymous, as are *off* and *disabled*. On or enabled mean that the fonts appear in the Font menus of applications and appear in the Font panel. Off or disabled mean that the fonts will not appear in the Font menus of applications or in the Font panel.

When using Font Book, all properly installed fonts in Mac OS X actually remain available for use. What Font Book does is analogous to hiding them or showing them! This concept is very different from the concepts of *activation* and *deactivation,* long used by the third-party font manager utilities, where fonts are made available or unavailable for use, as if they had been uninstalled or reinstalled. Nevertheless, in Font Book you cannot use fonts that you cannot see.

Changes you make in Font Book stick after you quit. All the fonts stay in their enabled or disabled states until you launch Font Book again to make more changes. Font Book cannot perform the helpful and sometimes critical *autoactivation* of fonts as an application calls for them, a key feature of the third-party font manager utilities.

Font Book Preferences

You open the Font Book Preferences pane, shown in Figure 12-6, by choosing Font Book ⇨ Preferences.

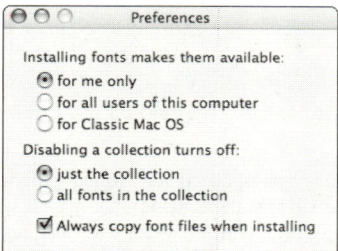

Figure 12-6: Font Book's Preferences pane.

Under Installing fonts makes them available: you have three choices — for me only, for all users of this computer, and for Classic Mac OS. Use this preference setting to determine the location the fonts are installed to. Note that the last choice is an easy way to install to the Fonts folder in the Mac OS 9 system used for Classic.

Under Disabling a collection turns off: you can choose just the collection or all fonts in the collection. If you choose to turn off just the collection, the fonts it contains remain enabled. The other choice turns the fonts contained in the disabled collection off, and these fonts will appear dimmed in all the other collections containing them.

At the bottom is a checkbox, Always copy font files when installing. If this is unchecked, as it is by default, the fonts will be moved, not copied, whenever possible. It is not possible to move fonts off of a CD or from a folder you have read-only access to.

Installing new fonts

To install new fonts to your system using Font Book, follow these steps:

1. **Copy the new fonts to your hard disk or insert the disc that contains the new fonts.**

2. **In the Finder, double-click on the font's icon.** Font Book opens and displays the font.

3. **Click the Install Font button.** The font is installed by default to the logged-in user's Home fonts folder at /Users/*username*/Library/Fonts. The font is available only to this user. Where the font is installed can be changed in the Font Book Preference pane. You do not have to quit Font Book for the changes to occur.

To make the font available to all users of the computer, drag it to the Computer folder in Font Book's Collection column. The font is installed to the Main fonts folder at /Library/Fonts. You must have administrator privileges to do this.

After it is installed, the font appears in the Font panel and in the list of available fonts in your applications.

Previewing fonts

To preview any font and all of its glyphs in Font Book, follow these steps:

1. **Open Font Book.**

2. **In the Collection column, select a collection.**

3. **In the Font column, select the font family you want to preview.**

4. **Click the disclosure triangle next to the font family name to reveal which typefaces are available.**

5. **Select a typeface.** All the characters available in that typeface appear in the preview area. Hold the cursor over any of them to see more information appear in a yellow box, including the full font file name, the font's type, the version number of the font, and its location in path form.

6. **Select a font size by using the Size pop-up menu, or choose Fit from the menu to fit the preview into the area.** You can also drag the font size slider on the right side of the preview area.

Choose from the following additional options in the Preview menu:

✦ **Sample** (the default): Shows font's the alphabet in upper- and lowercase with the ten digits.

✦ **Repertoire:** Shows the entire glyph set for the font, as shown in Figure 12-7.

✦ **Custom:** Allows you to type what you wish into the preview area.

✦ **Show** or **Hide Preview:** Hides or shows the preview area.

✦ **Show** or **Hide Font Info:** Adds an information area to the bottom of the Preview area. Information includes Font type, Foundry, Copyright year, Family, Display name, and PostScript Name.

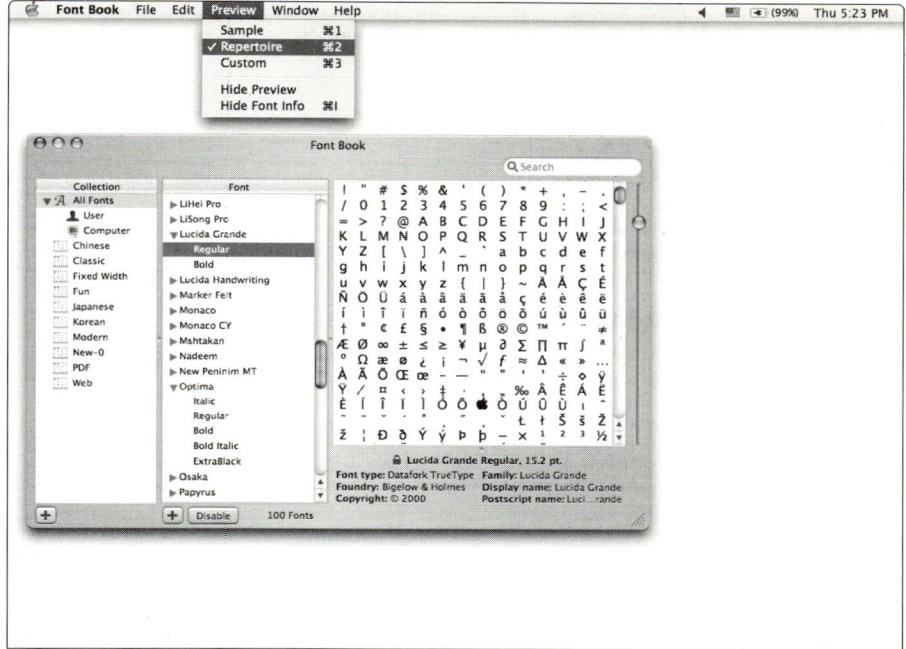

Figure 12-7: Font Book's preview feature set to Repertoire, showing part of the complete glyph set for Lucinda Grande Regular.

Turning a font on or off

In Font Book, turning on a font makes it appear in the Font panel or in an application's list of available fonts. Turning off a font makes it disappear from the Font panel or from an application's list of available fonts.

To turn a font on or off, follow these steps:

1. **Open Font Book.**

2. **In the Collection column, select a collection.**

3. **In the Font column, select the font family that you want to turn off or on.**

   • **To turn a font on,** click the Enable button and then click the Enable button again in the sheet that appears. In the Font window, you can see that the font name is undimmed and is no longer marked Off.

   • **To turn a font off,** click the Disable button and then Disable again in the sheet that appears, as shown in Figure 12-8. In the Font column, you see that the font name is dimmed and marked Off.

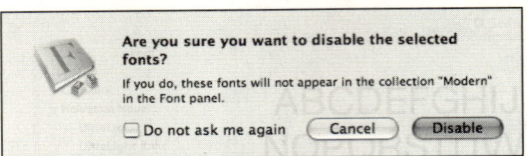

Figure 12-8: Clicking on the Font column's Disable button (at bottom) causes this sheet to appear; clicking the Disable button will disable the selected font, Helvetica Neue Regular.

Creating, editing, and managing font collections

Use font collections to gather the fonts you need for particular projects. Follow these steps to create and/or add fonts to a collection:

1. **Open Font Book.**

2. **Click the plus sign button at the bottom of the Collection column.** A collection appears in the Collection column named New-0 (or another number if there are other new collections). This step is illustrated in Figure 12-9.

3. **Type a name for the new collection.**

4. **In the Collection column, click the disclosure triangle next to All Fonts to reveal User and Computer.**

5. **Click User to see fonts from your Home fonts folder listed in the Font column; or click Computer to see fonts from your Main fonts folder.**

6. **Drag the fonts you want from the Font column to the new collection.**

You can add fonts in a similar way to any of the default collections. The fonts in all collections except User are available to all users of the computer; fonts in the User collection are available only to the logged-in user.

If you have Mac OS 9 installed to run Classic applications, or if you access fonts from the Network location, the fonts in these locations will appear in the Computer collection. The fonts in the System and Main locations also appear there. The only fonts that do not appear in the Computer collection are those in the User collection.

To remove fonts from a collection:

1. **Select the collection in the Collection column.**

2. **Select the fonts you want to remove in the Fonts column.**

3. **Press the Delete key on the keyboard and then the Remove button on the sheet that appears, shown in Figure 12-10.** The font disappears from the Fonts column.

To delete a collection:

1. **In the Collection column, select the collection you want to delete.**

2. **Press the delete key on the keyboard and then the Remove button on the sheet that appears.** The collection disappears from the Collections column.

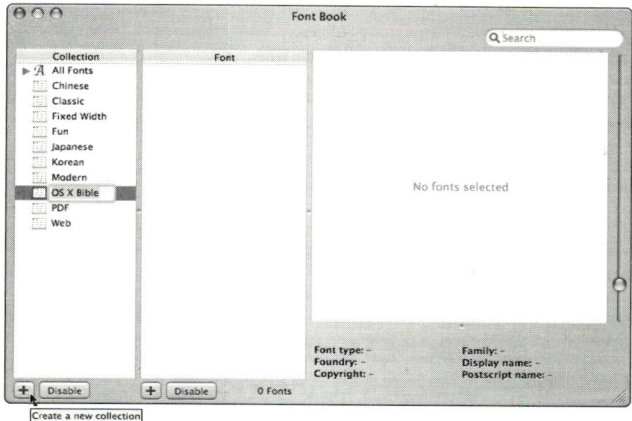

Figure 12-9: Clicking the plus sign button at the bottom of Font Book's Collection column creates a new collection, which can be renamed from New-*x* to any name you wish, here OS X Bible.

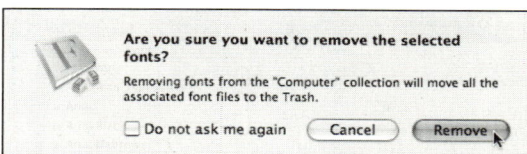

Figure 12-10: Fonts to be removed from a collection have been selected, the delete key pressed, and this sheet appears. Press the Remove button to complete the process.

Turning a font collection on or off

Turning a font collection on makes it appear in the Font panel. Turning it off makes it disappear from the Font panel. Here's how:

✦ To turn a font collection on or off, open Font Book and then select a collection from the Collection column.

✦ Turn the collection on by selecting all the fonts that the collection contains in the Font column. Then, click the Enable button at the bottom of the Font column.

✦ To turn the selected collection off, click the Disable button at the bottom of the Collection column. Then click Disable again in the sheet that appears.

Detecting and resolving duplicate fonts

Duplicate copies of installed fonts detected by Font Book are marked with a square bullet to the right of the font family name in the Fonts column, as shown in Figure 12-11.

To resolve duplicate fonts:

1. **Select the version of the font family that you wish to use.**

2. **Choose Edit ⇨ Resolve Duplicates.** The selected version of the font is turned on, and the other version(s) are turned off.

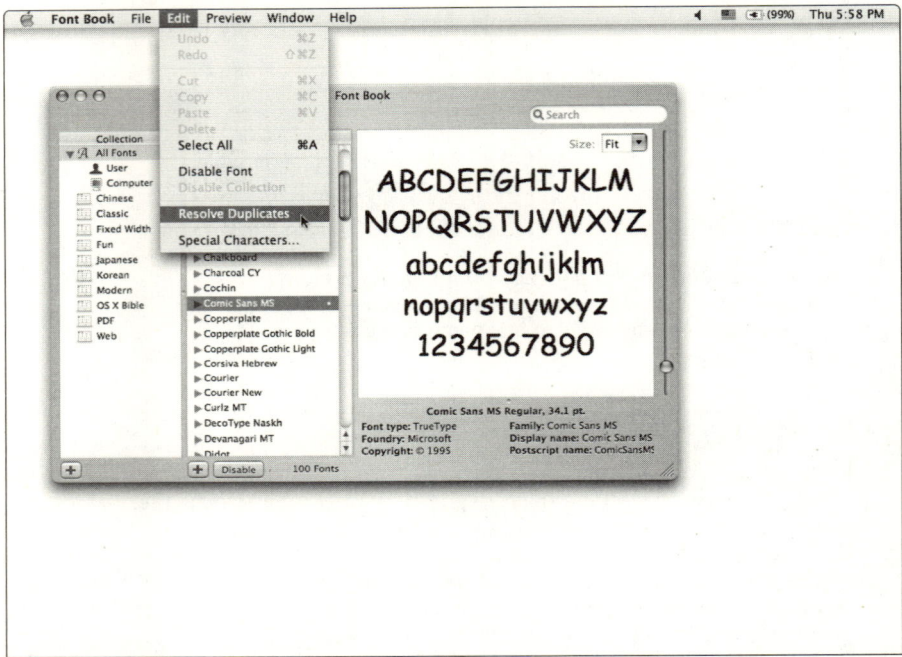

Figure 12-11: Here, the font Comic Sans MS is marked with a bullet to its right as having one or more duplicates. The Resolve Duplicates command straightens out the problem.

Searching for fonts

The Font Book window's search field works in a similar way to the one in every Finder window.

First, select the collection or font family you want to search in and then type the name (such as *Arial*) or part of the name (such as *italic*) in the search field in the upper right of the Font Book window.

As you type each letter, the search results appear almost instantly in the Font column. Fonts that match your entry appear under their family name for easy identification, as shown in Figure 12-12.

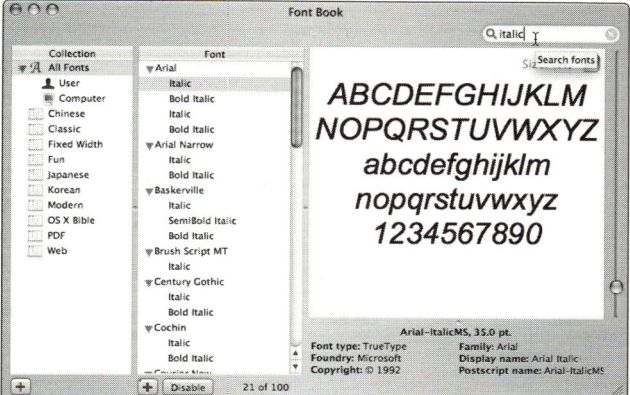

Figure 12-12: Entering the word *italic* into the Search field at the top-right of the Font Book window causes the selected collection (here, All Fonts) to be searched for fonts that match, and the results displayed in the Font column. Note that every font listed is an italic.

The Font panel

The Font panel has been a feature of Mac OS X from its first version. Apple includes it as a helpful feature that software developers, if they wish, can include in their programs. Many applications use their own way of working with fonts, and do not use the Font panel. Font Book is really a development of the Font panel, and they have similar interfaces. The redesigned Font panel of Mac OS X 10.3 is shown in Figure 12-13.

To see the Font panel, launch TextEdit and navigate the menu to Format ➪ Font ➪ Show Fonts. The Font panel can be accessed in a similar way in other applications that use it. You will not find the Font panel in the Application or Utilities folder, because it is a system-level facility that can only be accessed from inside a compatible, usually Cocoa, application.

The Font panel and Font Book interoperate to some degree — certain changes made in one are almost instantly reflected in the other. For example, if you create a collection in the Font panel, the new collection will appear in Font Book, and vice versa.

The Font panel can do many things that Font Book cannot, but it lacks Font Book's font management features.

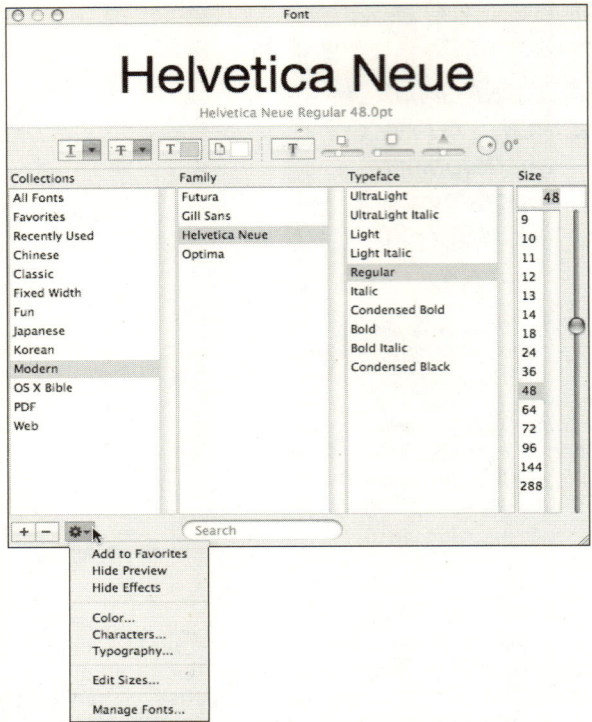

Figure 12-13: Mac OS X 10.3's Font panel. The Action pop-up menu is shown at the bottom.

With the Font panel, you can accomplish the following:

✦ View collections, families, typefaces, and sizes of fonts.

✦ Preview fonts in their font family name.

✦ Set font sizes.

✦ Create font collections and add fonts to them, including a Favorites collection.

✦ View recently used fonts.

✦ Add various visual effects to selected fonts.

✦ Add color to document backgrounds.

✦ Turn common font ligatures on or off, as shown in Figure 12-14.

✦ Adjust space between fonts.

✦ Adjust the font baseline.

✦ Search for fonts.

✦ Open Font Book.

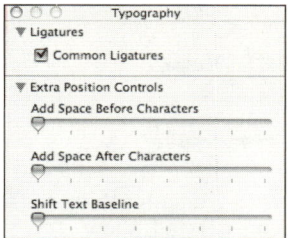

Figure 12-14: The Typography dialog, summoned from Font panel's Action menu, provides an easy way to control ligatures, tracking, and to shift the text baseline to a higher position.

The Character Palette

The Character Palette is a Mac OS X feature that you use to enter special characters, such as various symbols and dingbats, Chinese, Korean, and Japanese characters, and characters from other languages. The Character Palette is shown in Figure 12-15.

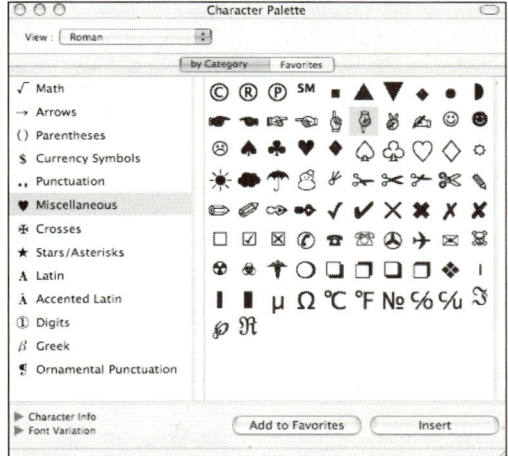

Figure 12-15: The Character Palette, set to view Roman characters and symbols by Category, with the Miscellaneous category selected and displayed.

Like the Font panel, the Character Palette is not an application or utility, but a system-level facility. Like the Font panel, it can only be opened from applications that support it. If you need to enter a special character in an application that does not support Character Palette, open it in TextEdit, enter the character into a TextEdit document, then cut and paste the character into your application's document.

In Mac OS X 10.3, the Character Palette is on by default, and can be turned on or off in the International System Preference's Input menu subpane.

To open Character Palette in Mac OS X 10.3, click its icon, usually a flag or a distinctive character (letter) in the menu bar. This is the Input menu, shown in Figure 12-16. From the Input menu, choose Show Character Palette. To open Character Palette in TextEdit or Font Book, or in most Cocoa applications, navigate the menus to Edit ➪ Special Characters.

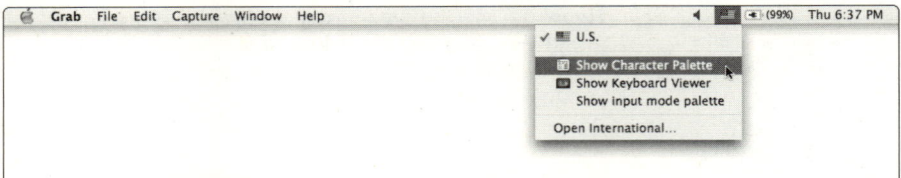

Figure 12-16: The Input Menu can be turned on or off, and have its contents selected, from the International Preference pane. Here two items have been selected, Show Character Palette and Show Keyboard Viewer.

To enter a special character or symbol with Character Palette:

1. **Place the insertion point in your document where you want to enter the character or symbol.**

2. **Open the Character Palette.**

3. **From the View pop-up menu at the top of the Character Palette window, choose the type of characters you want to enter.** (If you don't see the View pop-up menu, click the clear oval button in the upper-right corner of the window; click it again to hide the menu.)

   The View pop-up menu choices and their subsequent selector-button activated panes (otherwise known as tabs) are described here:

   • **Roman** allows you to pick characters by 13 categories of symbols, or from Favorites you define.

   • **Japanese** allows you to pick characters by Radical, by 22 categories of symbols, from 2 Code Tables, or from Favorites you define.

   • **Traditional Chinese** allows you to pick characters by Radical, by 16 categories of symbols, from 2 Code Tables, or from Favorites you define.

   • **Korean** allows you to pick characters by Radical, by 18 categories of symbols, or from Favorites you define.

   • **Simplified Chinese** allows you to pick characters by Radical, by 47 categories of symbols, from 2 Code Tables, or from Favorites you define.

   • **Unicode** allows you to pick by 122 categories of characters and symbols, from the entire Unicode Table, or from Favorites you define.

   • **Glyph** allows you to pick from the Glyph Catalog, or from Favorites you define.

4. **In the pane of your choice, select the category, radical, or Unicode block in the list column on the left and double-click the character or symbol you want to enter on the right.**

   Or if there is no list column in the pane, find and double-click the character or symbol.

5. **The double-clicked character or symbol will appear in your document at the insertion point.**

   Alternately, you can click the Insert button at the bottom of the window, or simply drag the character to the document window.

   If the current application does not support the character, an alert appears at the bottom of the window.

The Character Palette interface can be expanded by clicking on the Character Info or Font Variation disclosure triangles in the lower-left of the window, as shown in Figure 12-17.

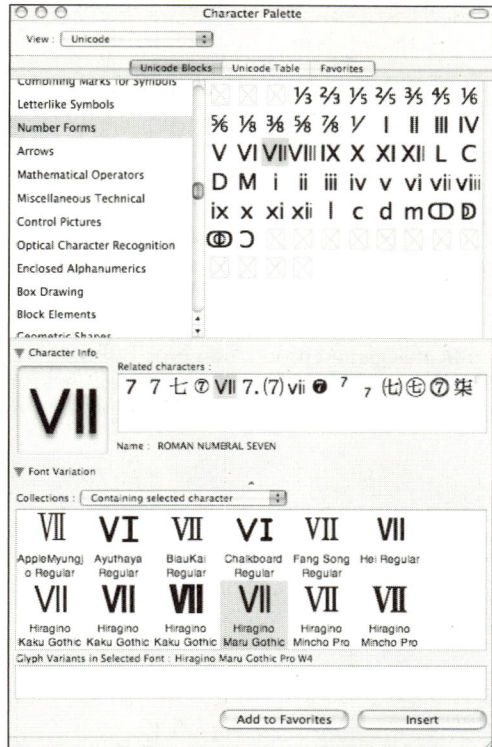

Figure 12-17: The Character Palette with the Character Info and Font Variation disclosure triangles turned down to reveal its extended interface. The Roman numeral seven is selected from the Unicode block Number Forms, revealing its Related Characters and Glyph Variations.

The Character Info area displays a close-up of the selected character or symbol along with any related characters, readings, or other information.

The Font Variation area shows variations of the selected character or symbol in available fonts, whose names appear below the symbol. Select one, and the Insert button changes to Insert with Font; you can click this button, double-click the character or symbol, or drag it to the document to insert it. The Font Variation area also contains a pop-up menu of the current default and user-created collections.

At any time, you can add any selected character or symbol to a Favorites collection that is kept with the View you are in, by clicking the Add to Favorites button. The Favorites list can be accessed by clicking the Favorites selector button (tab) in any of the views.

Using third-party font manager utilities

At the time of writing, these were the third-party font management utilities available for Mac OS X:

✦ **Extensis Suitcase X1,** shown in Figures 12-18 and 12-19

✦ **Extensis Font Reserve** (formerly DiamondSoft Font Reserve), shown in Figures 12-20 and 12-21; and Font Reserve Server

✦ **Insider Software FontAgent**

✦ **Alsoft MasterJuggler**

Notice that Adobe Type Manager Deluxe does not appear on this list. Adobe has announced that it will not be developing a version of ATM for Mac OS X. So if you use ATM Deluxe to manage your fonts in Mac OS 9, you must pick one of these font managers to work with. Some can import you fonts and sets from ATM Deluxe.

Despite the advent of Font Book, many graphic design and production pros will want to use a third-party font management utility with Mac OS X. This is because these professionals must manage hundreds and sometimes thousands of fonts, for which they need industrial-strength features.

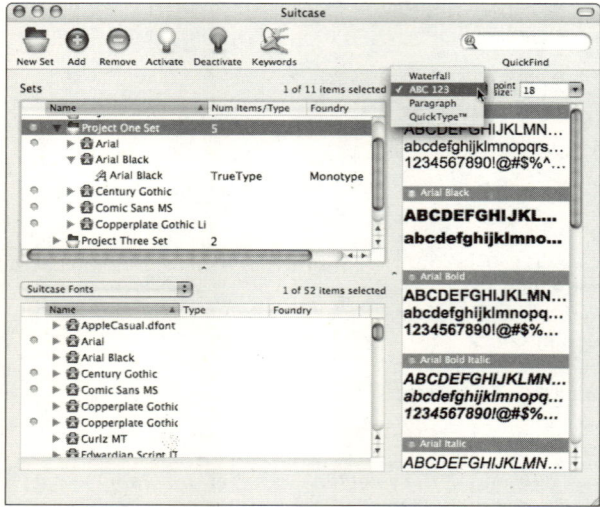

Figure 12-18: The Suitcase X1 interface, previewing the fonts in the Project One Set in 18 points, showing the preview style pop-up menu set to ABC 123.

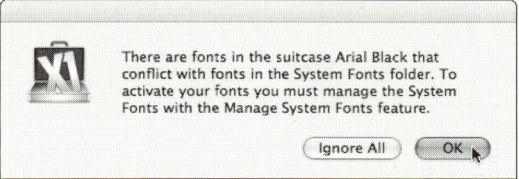

There are fonts in the suitcase Arial Black that conflict with fonts in the System Fonts folder. To activate your fonts you must manage the System Fonts with the Manage System Fonts feature.

Ignore All   OK

Figure 12-19: This sheet appears in Suitcase X1 when you try to activate a font suitcase that contains fonts in conflict with those in your Mac OS X System Folder. You could use the very helpful Manage System Fonts feature in this situation.

Font managers allow you to control your fonts so that only the ones you need are active at any one time. Mac OS 9 crashed if you had too many fonts open; Mac OS X does not crash, but scrolling through a mile long font menu is a poor use of time.

Third-Party Font Manager Utilities

Here are some commonly found features of third-party font manager utilities:

✦ Store fonts in any user-defined location.

✦ Import the Mac OS 9 ATM Deluxe font and set database.

✦ Add fonts and share them by dragging them.

✦ Preview and compare several fonts side by side, as a single line, three lines in different sizes (*waterfall* style), paragraph, or the alphabet with numerals.

✦ Print font specimen sheets and type books of entire font libraries.

✦ Activate or deactivate fonts by clicking selected fonts, font families, or font sets. (Font sets are similar to Apple's categories.)

✦ Automatically activate fonts. (When an application calls for a font, the utility automatically activates it.) This feature is provided for many common graphic design applications via plug-in software. (Business apps do not need plug-ins.)

✦ Remove nonessential fonts from system font folders.

✦ Scan for duplicate fonts by particular characteristics, and delete them.

✦ Automatically check fonts for corruption.

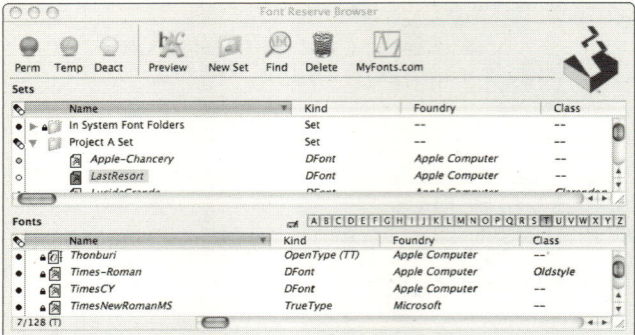

Figure 12-20: The Font Reserve Browser with a set, Project A, disclosed to show the fonts it contains; to their left are dots that indicate their activation status.

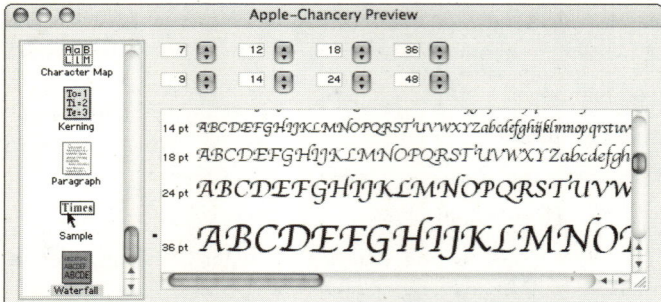

Figure 12-21: The Font Reserve Browser's Preview window showing the Apple-Chancery font in a Waterfall-style preview.

Organizing fonts for a font manager

Because you don't have to keep fonts in one of the six locations that Mac OS X looks in, you are free to store them in any location, and organize them in any way you wish. You can store them on your local machine, in folders named for clients, jobs, projects, or in alphabetical folders.

If you have a robust network (100 Mbps Ethernet or Gigabit Ethernet) you can centralize the fonts on a file server (which can be a Mac running either Mac OS X client or server), mount the server volume on your local machine's desktop and then point your font manager at the fonts to open them. This way you can reduce administrative time by managing everyone's fonts at once on the server.

Consider using Font Reserve Server if you need an industrial-strength network font server. This server enables administrators to create sets that all users can access, control which users can load fonts to the server or create and change font sets, and cache the fonts on client machines to cut down on network traffic. You can even manage font access rights in workgroups, so there are never more copies of a font in use than its license permits.

Removing duplicate System fonts

If you use your Mac to prepare files for professional printing, you will likely have installed the commonly used fonts Courier, Helvetica, Symbol, Times, and Zapf Dingbats; maybe you are even using special versions supplied by a client.

However, dfont versions of these fonts are already installed with Mac OS X in the System/Library/Fonts folder. For many users who would never install other versions of these fonts, their inclusion in the OS is a big advantage.

Figure 12-22 shows the location of these fonts.

Unfortunately, if other versions are installed, this situation creates the possibility of an accidental font substitution occurring, something that graphics people want to avoid. There can be subtle differences between different versions or formats of fonts with the same name.

For example, the System font Times might be accidentally opened and used to design the document instead of the customer's requested Times font, and a preflight tool would miss the distinction between the two. Result: The document needs to be laid out all over again.

Or, a client may submit a file to your print shop for printing, without the specially kerned version of Helvetica they used to design the document, and your system uses the System version of Helvetica instead, and nobody notices, resulting in a text reflow that causes the critical last sentence to be cut off in the middle.

Mistakes like these are all too common, and a lot of time and money go down the drain.

But there is a simple remedy: remove the duplicate System fonts.

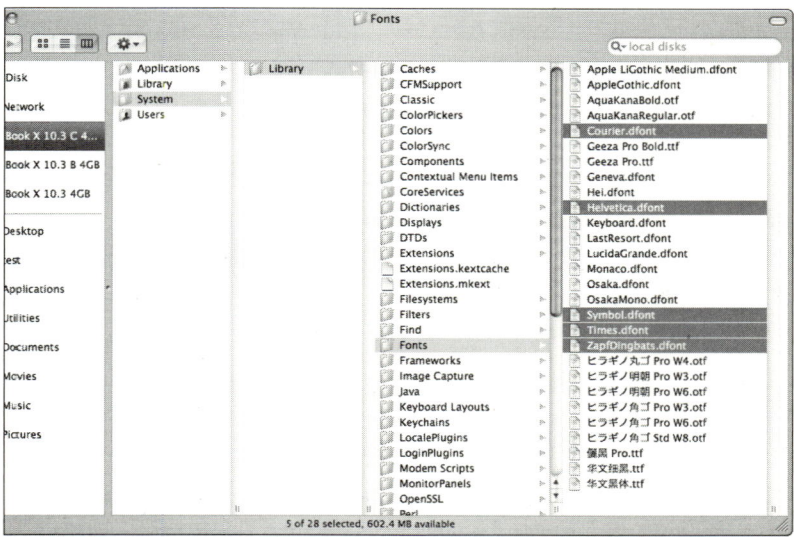

Figure 12-22: A Mac OS X 10.3 Finder window set to column view, showing the path to the System fonts. The fonts to be optionally removed, as mentioned in this section, are highlighted.

This was easy to do in Mac OS 9. Graphics and publishing pros would remove most of the fonts installed with Mac OS 9 in the System Folder, leaving only Charcoal, Chicago, Geneva, Monaco, and New York. The system needed these, and they were almost never used in designed documents, so chances of a font conflict were minimized. And any user could simply drag the fonts out of the System Folder; the system did not prevent this.

But in Mac OS X, the fonts in the System/Library/Fonts folder are protected by the system; not even a user with administrator rights can remove them. This is because Mac OS X will become inoperable if a user accidentally removes a vital system font. For instance, the main font used by the Finder, Lucida Grande, must never be removed under any circumstances; if it is, Mac OS X will have to be reinstalled. So, these System fonts are made off limits to the casual user, who can see them but not change them.

The best way to deal with System fonts that duplicate the fonts you would like to use is to use one of the font managers utilities mentioned above to deactivate the System fonts. For instance, Font Reserve has a feature called System Fonts Handler that makes it easy to do just that.

If you are comfortable with Unix commands, you could remove the fonts by using the Terminal utility. You would use the sudo command to temporarily become the root user, in order to get around the rights restriction.

You could log in as the root user and move the fonts. (For a description of how to turn on the root account, see the description of the NetInfo utility in Chapter 6.)

If you use Classic, you can boot from Mac OS 9, which gives the equivalent of root privileges to all files on your system. You could navigate to the System/Library/Fonts folder and remove the fonts.

Here is a technique to remove the System fonts from inside Mac OS X, without a font manager:

1. **In the Finder, select the System/Library/Fonts folder.**

2. **Press Command-I or select Get Info from the File menu.** The Fonts Info window opens.

3. **Open the Ownership & Permissions area by clicking its disclosure triangle.**

4. **Click on the Details disclosure triangle and then click the lock icon.**

5. **In the Owner pop-up menu, change the owner from *system* to the item just under it with your login name.**

You may now remove the fonts from the folder.

Tip   Make sure you save all the fonts you are removing in a safe place, in case you ever need to restore them.

Tip   If you are removing fonts from the System/Library/Fonts folder as described above, and you run Classic, you must also remove the same fonts from the Classic System Folder's Fonts folder. This is because Mac OS X applications can also see these fonts. The fonts usually removed are Courier, Helvetica, Times, Symbol, and Zapf Dingbats. Make sure the following fonts are left in at all times, because they are needed by Classic applications: Charcoal, Chicago, Geneva, Monaco, and New York.

Tip Always keep a Helvetica and Helvetica Neue active because some Mac OS X functions require them. These include Mail, iCal, TextEdit, the Sound preference pane, and certain third-party menu bar items. It does not matter what font format the Helveticas belong to; it just matters that one is always available to the system.

Font utilities

Mac OS X 10.3 includes a utility called Keyboard Viewer, which is an improvement on the Key Caps utility included in previous versions of the Mac OS. Key Caps did not understand Unicode, so many of the characters in fine Unicode fonts such as Lucida Grande and Zapfino were inaccessible. Keyboard Viewer supports Unicode fonts. Figure 12-23 shows the Keyboard Viewer interface.

Figure 12-23: The Mac OS X Keyboard Viewer, doing something the previous utility Key Caps could never do: showing the lowercase characters of the Unicode font Zapfino on the keys.

Keyboard Viewer can be turned on in the Input pane of International preferences.

To use Keyboard Viewer, choose Show Keyboard Viewer from the Input menu in the menu bar. Pick a font family from the pop-up menu and its typeface style from the submenu. The glyphs of the font now appear on the keys they are assigned to. By holding down the Shift, Option, Option-shift, or function keys, you can see how the glyphs change, and learn how to type the glyphs you want. You can also click with your cursor on any key in the Keyboard Viewer window, and that glyph will appear at the insertion point in your document.

Many useful commercial, shareware, and freeware font utilities are available. They tend to fall into the following categories:

✦ **Key Caps–style viewers** let you view the glyphs corresponding to the keys.

✦ **Waterfall–style viewers** display fonts in text samples, sometimes for multiple fonts.

✦ **Spec-sheet printers** display or print a list of fonts with text samples.

✦ **Analysis and repair utilities** can reorganize font libraries and repair damaged fonts.

✦ **Font Managers** activate or deactivate fonts (see the section describing them above).

To find current font utilities, check the Macintosh Products Guide at `www.apple.com/guide` and Version Tracker at `www.versiontracker.com`.

Fonts in the Classic Environment

When you use a Classic application, fonts installed in your Mac OS 9 System Folder (or managed by a Classic font management utility) are used rather than the fonts installed for Mac OS X.

Classic cannot see or use fonts in Mac OS X locations, but Mac OS X can see and use the Classic fonts.

For a discussion of fonts in the Classic environment, please turn to Chapter 17.

Summary

In this chapter, you learned that the term *font* has come to mean a digital file that contains the information necessary for the computer to create characters on the screen and in print.

You learned details about each of the Mac font formats, or font types: bitmap, PostScript, Multiple Master, TrueType, OpenType, and the Mac OS X dfont.

We reviewed the font-related features of Mac OS X, such as that you can use an unlimited number of fonts; you no longer need Adobe Type Manager; and that Mac OS X provides font smoothing, font validation, and protects against font corruption.

The six possible locations for fonts in Mac OS X were described: Application, Home, Main, Network, System, and Classic. This arrangement gives more control over fonts, protects essential fonts, and provides continuity with Unix. Where to put your fonts in various situations was discussed.

The new Mac OS X 10.3 application Font Book was examined in detail. Font Book enables most users to manage fonts in Mac OS X without having to purchase a third-party font management utility. We also looked at Mac OS X 10.3's Font panel (mainly for Cocoa apps), the Character Palette, and the Keyboard Viewer.

We listed the third-party font management utilities available for Mac OS X and discussed what they can do and in what situations their use is recommended. We also listed the general capabilities of other font utilities.

The necessity of removing fonts from the Mac OS X System folder under certain situations was covered, as well as techniques for removing them.

✦   ✦   ✦

Setting System Preferences

Computers are highly configurable. Numerous settings let you adjust most aspects of a computer's operation. You can adjust interface, hardware, and network settings, among others, as well as overall system preferences. Within Mac OS X, system software configuration and settings are managed by a central program known as the System Preferences application. Configuration of system settings within the System Preferences application are done through a Quartz GUI element, known as a pane. When a specific system preference is selected, the corresponding preference pane is loaded within the System Preferences application. Preference panes redraw themselves within the confines of the initial System Preferences application's window. The System Preferences application's window has a fixed width, but it resizes vertically to accommodate the contents of the preference pane being viewed.

The contents of the System Preferences application are divided in up to five preconfigured categories: Personal, Hardware, Internet & Network, System, and Other. The Personal section contains the preferences for Appearance, Desktop & Screen Saver, Dock, Exposé, International, and Security. Through the Hardware section, Bluetooth, CDs & DVDs, Displays, Energy Saver, Ink, Keyboard & Mouse, Print & Fax, and Sound preferences can be configured. Within the Internet & Network section, .Mac, Network, QuickTime, and Sharing preferences can be configured. The System section contains the Accounts, Classic, Date & Time, Software Update, Speech, Startup Disk, and Universal Access preferences. The other section only appears if there are preferences to set that fall outside of the previous four categories. With the exception of Apple's Remote Desktop centralized desktop management software, these preference panes are typically for third-party-supplied applications.

In addition to these categories, you also find a user customizable toolbar, similar to the one found in a Finder window. This toolbar is located at the top of the System Preferences application screen. This section contains user-selected preference pane shortcuts that can be accessed from any point within the System Preference application. By default, the following system preference shortcuts reside in this section: Displays, Sound, Network, and Startup Disk. Any of the default system preference shortcuts can be deleted, as desired. Also, any of the preferences within the System Preferences application can have shortcuts in the user-customizable toolbar.

In this chapter, you find out details about System Preferences that are not covered in other chapters of this book. Table 13-1 specifies where each System Preference pane is covered in the book.

Table 13-1: Coverage of System Preferences

System Preferences Pane	Covered In
Accounts	Chapter 14
Appearance	Chapter 4
Bluetooth	Chapter 15
CDs & DVDs	This chapter
Classic	Chapter 17
Date & Time	This chapter
Desktop & Screen Saver	Chapter 4
Displays	This chapter
Dock	Chapter 4
Energy Saver	This chapter
Exposé	Chapter 4
Ink	This chapter
International	This chapter
Keyboard & Mouse	This chapter
.Mac	Chapter 18
Network	Chapter 15
Print & Fax	Chapter 9
QuickTime	Chapter 20
Security	Chapter 27
Sharing	Chapter 16
Software Update	Chapter 22
Sound	This chapter
Speech	This chapter
Startup Disk	This chapter
Universal Access	This chapter

Using the System Preferences Application

This section describes the scope of Preference Settings, how to open System Preferences, display a pane whose settings you want to see or change, configure the System Preferences toolbar, and deal with locked settings in System Preferences.

Opening System Preferences

You can either click the System Preferences icon in the Dock or you can choose System Preferences from the Apple menu. When the System Preferences application opens, it displays a window that shows buttons for the different panes of settings. Figure 13-1 shows the contents of the System Preferences application.

Each button in the System Preferences application corresponds to a pane of preference settings. To see a pane, click its button or choose the pane by name from the View menu. The System Preferences application changes to show the settings for the pane that was clicked, and the title of the window changes to the name of the corresponding pane. If you want to return to the display of buttons for all panes, click the Show All button in the upper-left corner of the window or choose View ➪ Show All.

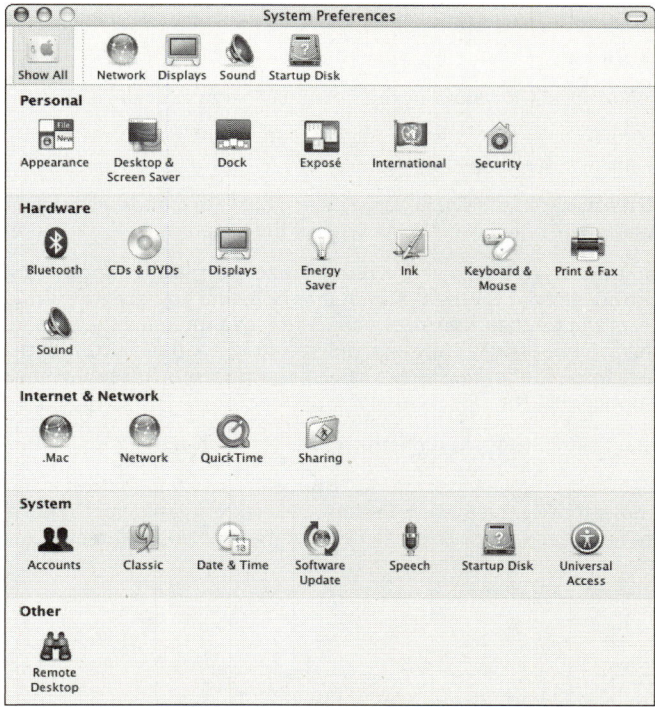

Figure 13-1: When the System Preferences application opens, the window displays buttons for all available preference panes.

Configuring the System Preferences toolbar

The System Preferences application contains a customizable toolbar at the top of its window that is continuously accessible no matter which preference pane the System Preferences application is currently displaying. The toolbar is intended to contain buttons for frequently used System Preferences panes. The toolbar can be customized to contain System Preferences shortcuts that you use most often. You can also hide the toolbar or set it to display buttons as named icons, icons without names, or names alone. You configure the System Preferences toolbar as follows:

✦ **Hide or show toolbar:** Hide the toolbar or show it if it is hidden, by clicking the lozenge-shaped toolbar button in the upper-right corner of the window. Alternatively, choose View ➪ Hide Toolbar or View ➪ Show Toolbar.

✦ **Change toolbar mode:** Show items as icons with names, icons only, or names only, as well as large or small versions, by ⌘-clicking the lozenge-shaped toolbar button one to five times.

- Start with the default view, with icons and names.

- One ⌘-click shrinks the icons and names to a smaller size.

- A second ⌘-click restores the icons to the original (large) size, but removes the names.

- A third ⌘-click shrinks the icon-only view to the smaller icon size.

- A fourth ⌘-click returns the names at their original (large) size, but deletes the icons.

- A fifth ⌘-click shrinks the name-only view.

- A sixth ⌘-click returns to the original (large) size icons and names view. Figure 13-2 shows the three primary (icons and names, icons only, names only) toolbar modes.

✦ **To add buttons:** Drag buttons to the toolbar from the main part of the window. You don't have to add buttons only at the right end of the toolbar. If you drag a button between two buttons in the toolbar, they move apart to make room for the button you're dragging. If the toolbar is full of buttons and you drag another button to the toolbar, buttons that don't fit on the toolbar appear in a pop-up menu. To see this menu, click the arrow that appears at the right end of the toolbar.

✦ **To rearrange buttons:** Drag buttons to different places on the toolbar.

✦ **To remove buttons:** Drag buttons away from the toolbar. Removing a button from the toolbar does not remove it from the System Preferences window. You can't remove the Show All button from its special place at the left end of the System Preferences toolbar.

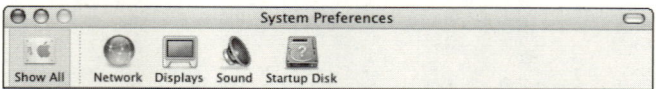

Figure 13-2: Change the toolbar mode in System Preferences by Command-clicking the toolbar button.

Unlocking preference settings

The settings in some System Preference panes can be locked. You can tell whether settings are locked in two ways.

✦ The locked settings are dim (displayed in gray text rather than black text).

✦ The security button padlock icon near the bottom-left corner of the window appears locked.

Table 13-2 lists the system settings that can be locked.

Table 13-2: Preference Settings That Can Be Locked

System Preferences Pane	Settings That Can Be Locked
Accounts	All settings except Picture and Startup Items
Date & Time	All settings except the menu bar clock settings
Energy Saver	All settings
Network	All settings except choosing a different location
Print & Fax	All settings except Set Up Printers, Selected printer in print Dialogue, and Default paper size in Page Setup
Security	All settings except Set Master Password & Turn On FileVault. These two items require independent authentication and authorization.
Sharing	All settings
Startup Disk	All settings

To change locked settings, you have access to the name and password of an administrator account. In Chapter 1, we note that an admin account is created via the Setup Assistant during the installation of Mac OS X. You can find more information about the administrator account in Chapter 14. To unlock preference settings, follow these steps:

1. **Click the locked security button denoted by the icon of the padlock in the lower-left corner of the preference pane.**

2. **In the dialog that appears, enter the name and password of an administrator account.** By default the current logged-in user's account name is pre-entered in this dialog, so if the account you are logged into is that of an administrator, simply enter the corresponding password. If you are logged in to an ordinary account, you have to enter the password and also change the name. Figure 13-3 shows the dialog in which you enter the name and password to unlock preference settings.

3. **Click OK.**

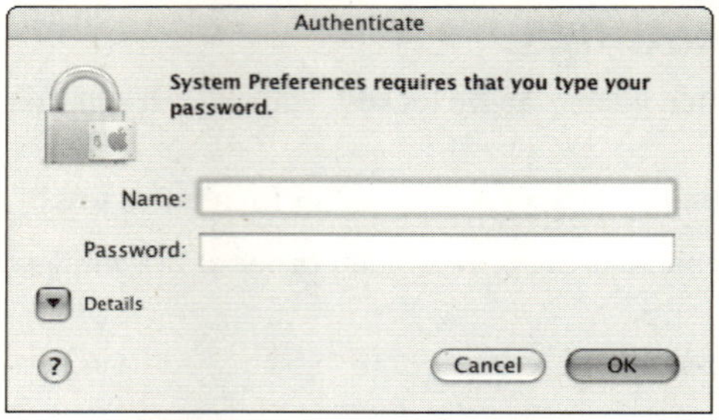

Figure 13-3: Unlock protected preference settings by entering the name and password of an administrator account.

Configuring CDs & DVDs Preferences

The CDs & DVDs preference pane allows you to configure the behavior of Mac OS X when a CD or DVD is inserted into the computer's optical drive. The options that are available are configured in accordance to the type of optical media being inserted into the drive. There are five menus based upon optical media type, blank CD, blank DVD, music CD, picture CD, and video DVD, as shown in Figure 13-4. Details on each of the five menus are listed as follows:

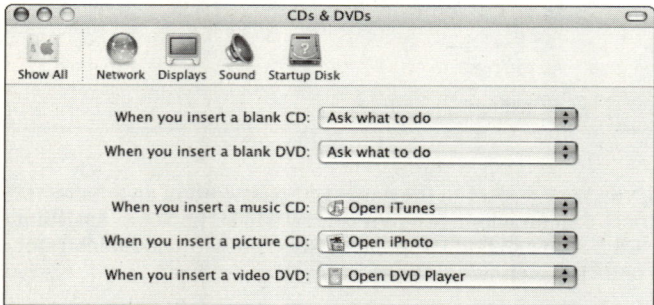

Figure 13-4: The CDs & DVDs pane determines the behavior of Mac OS X upon optical media insertion.

✦ **The When you insert blank CD pop-up menu provides the following choices:** Ask what to do, Open Finder, Open iTunes, Open other application, Run script, Ignore.

✦ **The When you insert blank DVD pop-up menu provides the following choices:** Ask what to do, Open Finder, Open iDVD, Open other application, Run script, Ignore.

✦ **The When you insert music CD pop-up menu provides the following choices:** Open iTunes, Open other application, Run script, Ignore.

✦ **The When you insert picture CD pop-up menu provides the following choices:** Open iPhoto, Open other application, Run script, Ignore.

✦ **The When you insert video DVD pop-up menu provides the following choices:** Open DVD Player, Open other application, Run script, Ignore.

With respect to the five different media types, the options tell Mac OS how to behave when the media is inserted, as follows:

✦ **Ask what to do:** Tells Mac OS X that you want to be queried on how to deal with the disk.

✦ **Open Finder:** Tells Mac OS X that the disk should be accessible via the Finder. Selecting Open Finder facilitates the copying of files and folders to given optical media for drag-and-drop disk burning.

✦ **Open iTunes, Open iPhoto, and Open DVD Player:** Tell Mac OS X to open one of those applications respectively.

✦ **Open other application:** Tells Mac OS X to open a predefined application, such as Roxio's Toast or the Mac OS X Disk Utility.

✦ **Run script:** Tells Mac OS X to run a specified AppleScript that can execute a sequence of actions. Although no actual scripts are provided with Mac OS X, you could make your own script. An example of such a script would be one that executed an automatic Finder backup of specified content to given optical media.

✦ **Ignore:** Tells Mac OS X that upon insertion of given optical media, do nothing.

Configuring Date & Time Preferences

In addition to displaying a clock on your menu bar, your computer uses date and time information for a variety of operations. For example, your computer uses date and time information to provide files with creation and modification dates and to time-stamp email. You can configure your computer's clock and calendar settings in the Date & Time preferences pane.

The Date & Time preferences pane is divided into three panels:

✦ Date & Time

✦ Time Zone

✦ Clock

Each panel is accessed by clicking on the button with the corresponding name at the top of the Date & Time preferences pane.

Date & Time panel

Click the Date & Time button to set your computer's current date and time.

✦ **To set the date and time automatically:** Select the Set Date & Time automatically option. This allows OS X to automatically synchronize the computer's internal clock to a time server over a network or the Internet using Network Time Protocol (NTP). The Set Date & Time automatically pop-up menu allows you to select an Apple time server that is based in the Americas, Asia, or Europe. It also allows for the manual input of a NTP server other than the ones that Apple provides.

✦ **To change the date:** Click the little arrows next to the month and year and click a day in the monthly calendar.

✦ **To change the time:** Drag the hands of the analog clock and click the AM/PM indicator next to this clock. Alternatively, click the digital hour, minute, or second and then either type a new value or click the little arrows next to the digital clock.

You must click Save to put the new time and date into effect. Figure 13-5 shows the clock and calendar settings in the Date & Time panel of Date & Time preferences.

Note   If the controls arrows for changing the date and time are absent, you need to deselect the option labeled Set Date & Time automatically.

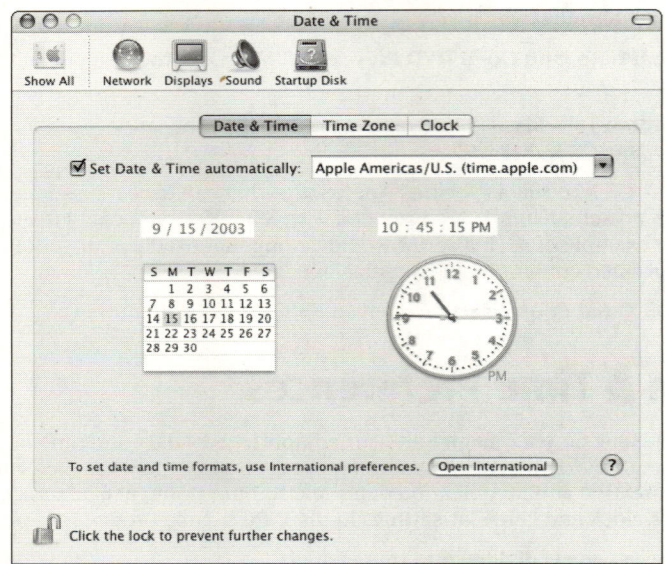

Figure 13-5: Date & Time panel also contains an Open International button that is a shortcut to the International preferences pane.

Tip   Besides the Apple time servers in the NTP Server drop-down list, you can use many public time servers. Check the list on the NTP (network time protocol) Web site at www.eecis.udel.edu/~mills/ntp/servers.htm.

Time Zone panel

Click the Time Zone button to set your time zone. The pop-up menu lists regions that may have different time zones in the highlighted part of the world. You can click another part of the world to highlight it. If daylight-saving time is in effect for the currently selected time zone, a sunburst graphic appears in the lower-left corner of the map next to the time zone's abbreviation. Figure 13-6 shows the Time Zone panel of the Date & Time preferences pane.

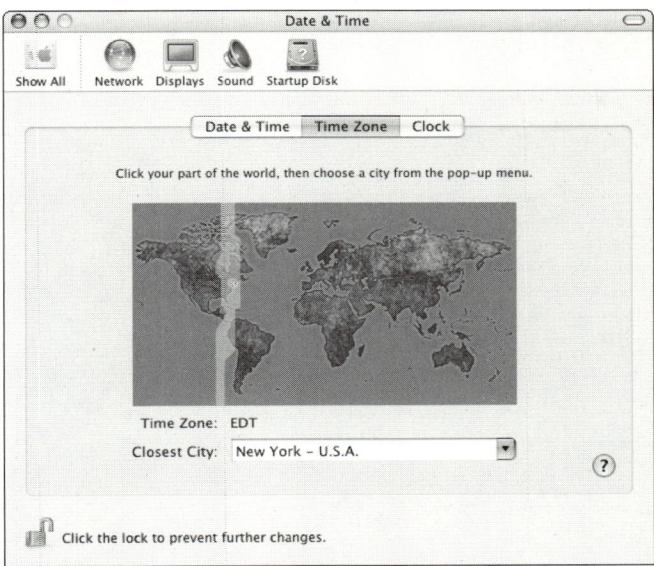

Figure 13-6: Set your time zone in the Time Zone panel of Date & Time preferences.

Tip   Even if you never move your computer, you should set its time zone so that people receiving your email in a different time zone can tell what time you sent the email.

Clock panel

Click the Clock button to configure the appearance of the clock, as shown in Figure 13-7.

By default Mac OS X places a clock in the Finder's menu bar. You can see the date by clicking the clock in the menu bar. This action displays a menu with the date at the top of it. In addition, this menu has choices for viewing the clock in analog or digital format and for opening the Date & Time pane of System Preferences.

The menu bar clock initially appears at the right end of the menu bar. You can move it by pressing ⌘ and dragging it. You can remove the menu bar clock by ⌘-dragging it off the menu bar.

In addition to configuring the appearance of the clock in the Finder's menu bar, the Clock panel allows the clock to be viewed in a separate window, as shown in Figure 13-8. As with the menu bar clock you can configure the window clock's display in either analog or digital format.

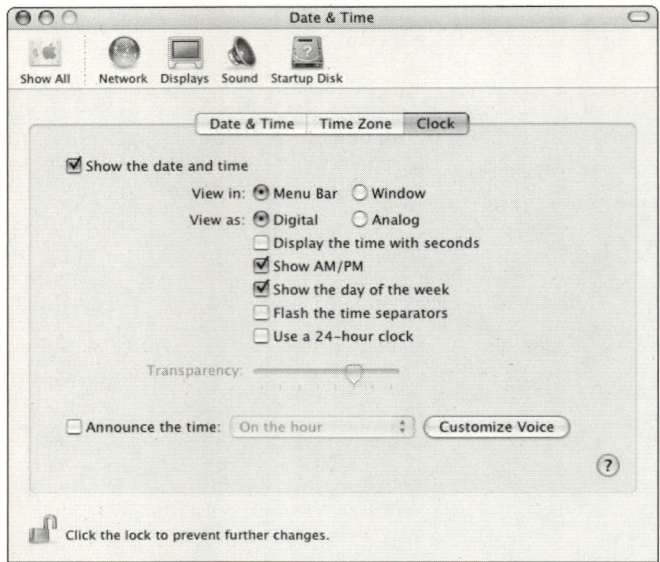

Figure 13-7: The Clock panel allows for the configuration of the appearance of the clock in Mac OS X.

Figure 13-8: Unlike the Clock application included with iterations of Mac OS X prior to Version 10.3, the view clock in window option can't be dragged into the Dock.

At the very bottom of the Clock panel, you can elect to have the clock announce the time on the hour, the half-hour, and the quarter-hour. You can also use the Customize Voice button to open the sheet that allows for the configuration of the voice in which the time will be announced, as shown in Figure 13-9.

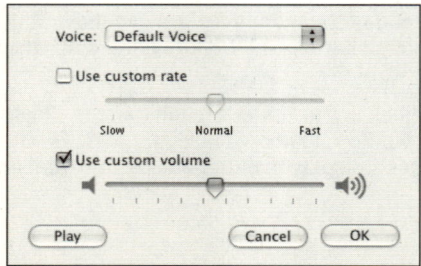

Figure 13-9: The Customize Voice sheet has every possible option except sound normal.

Configuring Display Preferences

If you stare at your display screen for hours on end, you want the view to be crisp and easy on the eyes. If you work with color, you want your screen to display colors as accurately and consistently as possible. If you work with more than one display screen on your computer, you need to have control over how the two work together. If your display is not a flat-panel type, you can set up a screen saver to protect the display against image burn-in.

Toward these goals, you can adjust your display by using the Displays and Screen Saver panes of System Preferences. You can also make quick adjustments with the Displays menu icon.

Like the Date & Time preferences pane, the Displays preferences pane is divided up into several panels, which are accessed via buttons at the top of Displays preferences pane. Depending upon your hardware configuration, the Displays Preferences may provide some or all of the following panels:

✦ **Display:** Settings for screen resolution, number of colors, refresh rate, contrast, brightness, and Finder menu bar access.

✦ **Geometry:** Settings for adjusting the shape and position of the screen image (not present for all makes and models of displays).

✦ **Color:** Settings for selecting a color profile and calibrating your display.

✦ **Arrange:** Settings for adjusting how multiple screens work together (present only if you have more than one display and your computer can work with them independently).

Display panel

Click the Display button to adjust the resolution, number of colors, refresh rate, contrast, or brightness of your display, as shown in Figure 13-10. You can also change a setting to show or hide the Displays icon in the menu bar. Some settings are not available with some types of displays. For example, no contrast setting for the LCDs (liquid crystal displays) is used in PowerBooks, iBooks, and flat-panel displays.

Resolutions and colors

The two most basic display settings are resolution and number of colors. *Resolution* is the size of the rectangular screen image — the number of pixels (picture elements or dots) wide by the number of pixels high. The number of colors, often called *color depth,* is the number of different colors that can be displayed for each pixel of the screen image. Color depth is sometimes referred to as *bit depth*, which is a measure of the amount of memory it takes to store each pixel (more colors require more bits of memory per pixel).

The higher the number of colors, the more realistic the screen image can look. However, increasing the number of colors doesn't necessarily make the screen display better, because the picture displayed onscreen may not make use of all of the available colors. For example, a black-and-white photograph is still black, white, and shades of gray when displayed on a screen capable of displaying millions of colors per pixel.

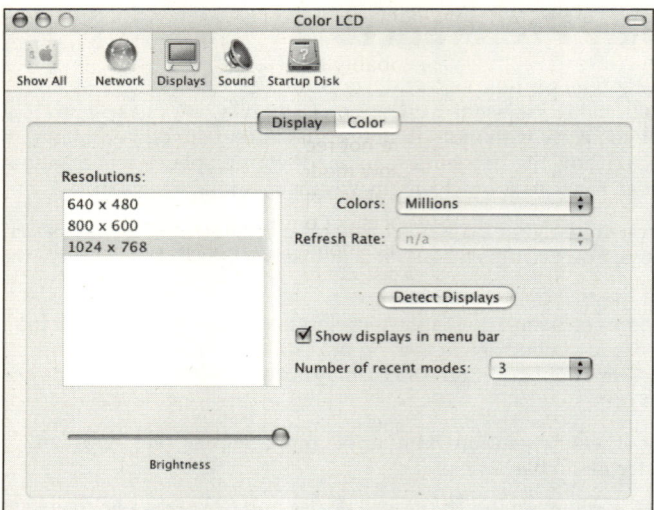

Figure 13-10: When using an iBook or a PowerBook that is attached to an external monitor, use the Detect Displays button to have OS X recognize that display.

Although you are provided with three choices, for all intents and purposes you have two practical choices of color depth in Mac OS X: thousands or millions of colors per pixel. Mac OS X can't accurately render its Aqua interface with a lower color depth. However, some old Classic applications may require a color depth of 256 colors.

The settings for resolution depend on the capabilities of the display and the computer's video card, but in general range from 800 x 600 pixels (the size of the original iBook display) up to 1900 x 1200 pixels (the size of a 23-inch Apple Cinema Display). Some displays can show only one resolution, while most new displays can show multiple resolutions.

Resolution and number of colors are related because increasing either requires more video memory. If you increase the resolution, Mac OS X may have to automatically reduce the number of colors. Conversely, you may be able to set a higher number of colors by decreasing the resolution.

Refresh rate

The significance of the refresh rate setting gets into the mechanics of displaying an image on the screen. The video card sends the screen image to the display one thin line of pixels at a time. After the video card sends the last line, it starts over again with the first line. The refresh rate is a measure of how fast the video card sends lines of the screen image to the display. A higher refresh rate means the entire screen image gets redisplayed more often. The refresh rate is of concern on a display with a CRT (cathode ray tube, or picture tube). If the refresh rate is below about 75 Hertz, the CRT's glowing phosphors may fade perceptibly before they are refreshed. Your eyes perceive this as a flickering of the video image, and the flickering can lead to eye fatigue and headache. A display with an LCD (liquid crystal display) doesn't flicker regardless of the refresh rate.

Each make and model of display has certain combinations of resolution and refresh rate that produce a clear, bright image with minimum flicker. If you set the refresh rate to a value that is not recommended for the display, the image probably is distorted or dark.

Tip When used in conjunction with an LCD monitor some choices of settings for resolution, colors, and refresh rate are dim to indicate they are not recommended. If you want to choose one of these, deselect the checkbox labeled Show modes recommended by display. If you choose a mode that is not recommended, an alert appears in which you must click the Confirm button to retain the mode. If you do not click Confirm within 10 seconds, Mac OS X automatically reverts to the previous mode. This automatic reversion is necessary because some modes may cause the display to show a distorted or black image, which prevents you from reverting to the previous mode by yourself.

Display settings in the menu bar

Besides using the Displays preference pane to adjust the resolution and colors of your display, you can also enable a Displays menu in the Finder's menu bar. Do this by placing a check mark in the box adjacent to Show displays in menu bar. A pop-up menu allows you to select how many choices are presented in the Displays menu. The increments are 0, 3, 5, and 10. After you've enabled it, you can click the Displays icon in the Finder's menu bar to see a menu of available screen resolutions and numbers of colors. This menu lists all your displays and has a command for turning mirroring on or off. The menu also has a command for opening the Displays pane of System Preferences. Figure 13-11 shows the contents of the Displays menu on an iBook.

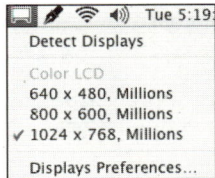

Figure 13-11: Use the Displays menu to directly open the Displays preferences pane without having to first open the System Preference application.

Tip You can move the Displays icon by pressing the ⌘ key and dragging the icon. Drag the icon left or right to change its position relative to other icons on the right side of the menu bar. Drag the icon off the menu bar to make it vanish in a puff of smoke.

Geometry panel

With some displays, such as the built-in display of an iMac or an eMac, the Displays preferences pane has a Geometry panel that allows you to adjust the shape and position of the image seen on the screen. You can expand the display area, so that less black border is visible. You can also change the pincushion (how concave the sides of the picture are) and the rotation of the display. Figure 13-12 shows the settings you see when you click the Geometry panel in the Displays preferences pane on an eMac.

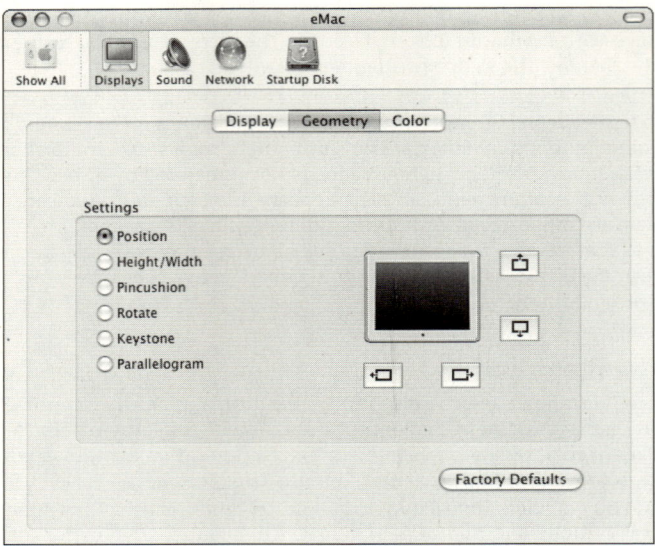

Figure 13-12: If your screen image isn't centered, use the Geometry panel to adjust the shape and position of image on the screen.

The graphic buttons on the right side of the panel reflect the various adjustments that you can make. These buttons change according to which setting you have selected to adjust. You can also make adjustments by dragging edges or the center of the small screen; the shape of the pointer tells you which way to drag. If you wreak havoc on your display by experimenting with the geometry settings, click the Factory Defaults button to returns the settings to their factory presets.

Color panel

The Color panel allows you to select a color profile for your display or to calibrate the display. After you calibrate the display, the Mac OS requires you to name and store the new settings as a color profile. Figure 13-13 shows the selections you see when you view the Color panel on an eMac.

You can create a custom profile for your display by clicking the Calibrate button in the Color panel. A custom profile accounts for your display's age and individual manufacturing variations. What's more, you can configure custom profiles for different resolutions, white points, and gamma corrections. With most displays, clicking the Calibrate button opens the Display Calibrator Assistant. The Calibrator walks you through the process that calibrates your display and creates a new ColorSync profile.

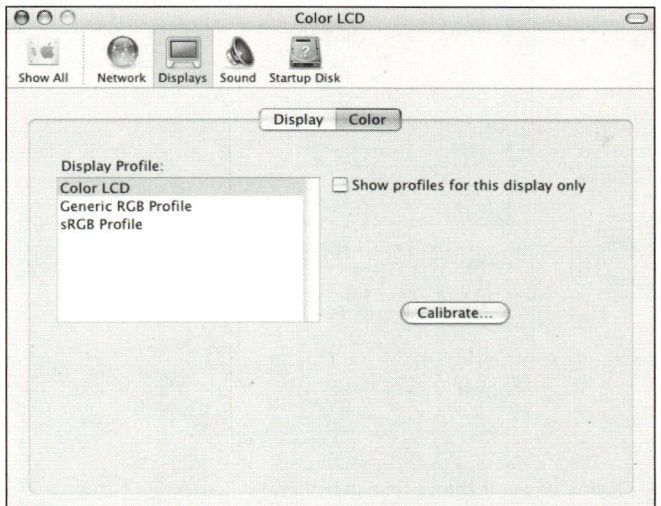

Figure 13-13: You can set the display's color profile or calibrate the display by clicking the Color panel of the Displays preferences pane.

Note   If you have an Apple ColorSync display, AppleVision display, or 21-inch Apple Studio Display, then a Recalibrate button may appear in lieu of the Calibrate button. Clicking Recalibrate activates the self-calibrating hardware built into these displays.

Display Calibrator Assistant

The Display Calibrator is actually a stand-alone application that acts as an Assistant (those coming from the Windows world call it a Wizard) that walks you through the process of creating a custom ColorSync profile for your display. If your ColorSync profile accurately reflects the behavior of your display, applications that take advantage of ColorSync can better display images in their intended colors. Similarly, if you have a proper profile for your printer, the colors match when printed — that's the *sync* in ColorSync.

You can use Display Calibrator to create a custom profile for your display and your viewing preferences. A custom profile accounts for your display's age and individual manufacturing variations. What's more, you can configure custom profiles for different resolutions, white points, and gamma corrections (more on all these terms shortly). Display Calibrator walks you through the process that calibrates your display and creates a new ColorSync profile. Figure 13-14 shows the Display Calibrator's introduction.

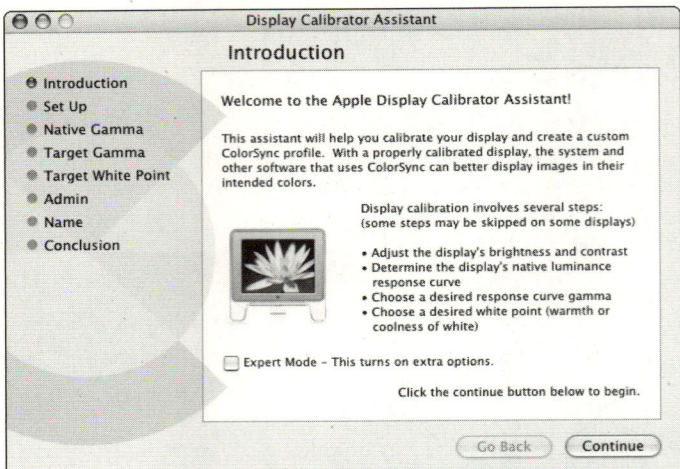

Figure 13-14: Display Calibrator walks you through calibrating a display and creating a custom profile.

Depending upon the type of display being calibrated, the Display Calibrator Assistant takes you through some or all of the following steps:

1. **Introduction:** Decide whether to use expert calibration settings instead of basic settings. There isn't much difference to the casual user, but graphics professionals who use ColorSync for color-correct output may find it useful to select Expert Mode before moving on to the next step. (Expert mode gives you more granular control over the settings in Display Calibrator, although for all intents and purposes it doesn't change the operation of the Display Calibrator dramatically.)

2. **Set Up:** Set your display to its highest contrast setting and then adjust the brightness. A test image helps you find the proper setting. This step is omitted on some displays.

3. **Native Gamma:** Provide information about the display's current gamma correction. *Gamma* refers to the relationship between the intensity of color and its luminance. Gamma correction compensates for the loss of detail that the human eye perceives in dark areas. In regular mode, you make adjustments to a gray image; in Expert mode, you determine the current gamma by adjusting sliders until red, green, and blue test images look right. This step is omitted on some displays.

4. **Target Gamma:** Specify the gamma correction that you want the display to use:

   • 1.8 is the standard gamma for Mac displays.

   • 2.2 is the standard gamma for television displays, video editing equipment, and Windows computers.

   • Native is gamma that is determined between input voltage and display brightness. Typically this feature is not available with LCD displays due to the fact the backlight runs at a constant level of illumination.

A low gamma setting makes colors appear more washed out. A high gamma setting makes colors appear more brilliant and with higher contrast. In this step, the Expert mode allows you to use a slider to choose a very specific gamma setting.

5. **Target White Point:** Select your preferred *white point,* which determines whether colors look warm (reddish) or cool (bluish). You can also choose to make no white-point correction. In Expert mode, you can use a slider to choose a specific white point measured in degrees Kelvin, which is a temperature scale commonly used in science.

6. **Name:** Name and save the custom profile for future use.

7. **Conclusion:** Close the Display Calibrator Assistant and select your newly created display profile under the Display Profile menu in the Color panel.

You can repeat the calibration process to create a number of profiles if you use your display at different resolutions or for different purposes.

Arrange panel

If your computer has two displays or more, you may be able to arrange how they work together. In one arrangement, called *display mirroring* or *video mirroring,* the second display shows exactly the same image as the first display. The other arrangement treats each display as part of an extended Desktop — as you move the pointer across the Desktop, it goes from one display to the next. Some Mac models, such as the iMac DV, can use two displays only for display mirroring not for an extended Desktop. Multiple displays are configured using the Arrangement panel, as shown in Figure 13-15.

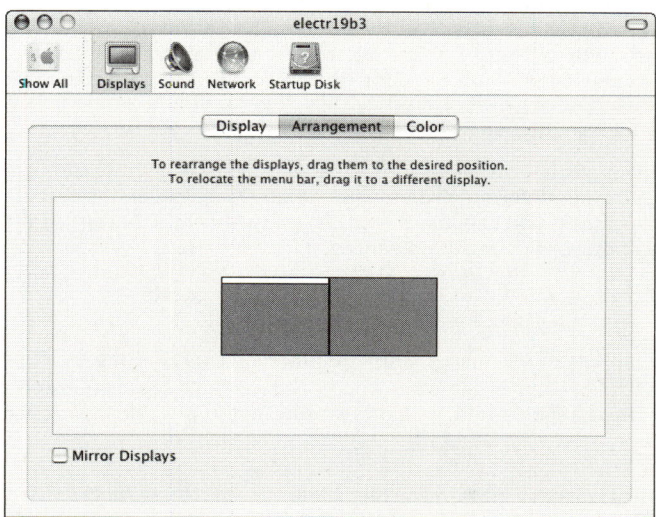

Figure 13-15: Use the Arrangement panel to move the menu bar from one screen to another.

You can change the relative positions of the displays in an extended Desktop by dragging the small screens in Displays preferences. You can also set which display has the menu bar by dragging the little menu bar to the appropriate small screen in Displays preferences. When you have two or more displays in an extended Desktop, Displays preferences has a separate window on each display. Each window has a Display panel, Color panel, and other panel for adjusting the display where the window is located. Only the primary display's preference pane contains an Arrange panel.

Note   To turn on the display mirroring setting, both displays must be set to the same resolution and number of colors.

Configuring Energy Saver Preferences

All Macs capable of using Mac OS X can save energy while they are inactive by taking advantage of sleep mode. Using sleep mode, a typical Desktop computer uses between 13 and 30 watts, and a display made after the middle of 1999 uses between 8 and 13 watts. These numbers reflect the requirements to comply with the U.S. Environmental Protection Agency's Energy Star program. Most Macs that can use Mac OS X comply with the Energy Star requirements, and all Apple displays made since the middle of July 1999 comply. Using the sleep mode is advantageous in two ways. The first benefit is that when waking from sleep the computer is usable sooner than from a cold start. Not only is the computer already powered on, but the sleep state keeps applications and documents open so that when you wake the computer, you can start work from where you left off. Second, the computer can still wake up via network or modem if configured to do so while in sleep mode.

Naturally, you can save even more energy by switching off your display when you leave your computer for a while. (You cannot switch off an Apple display that has the ADC connector without shutting down the computer.) While shutting down your computer would conserve even more energy, you would lose the quick start advantage.

The Energy Saver preference pane is divided into three panels: Sleep, Schedule, and Options. Their controls and settings let you determine when your computer sleeps and wakes. If your computer is a PowerBook or iBook, you can also set an option to show the battery status in the menu bar. The battery status option is not present on a Desktop Mac.

Sleep panel

Use the Sleep panel to adjust how much energy your computer saves by setting how long it remains inactive before going to sleep. As shown in Figure 13-16, you can set separate sleep timings for the whole system and the display, and choose whether to put the hard disk to sleep when possible.

Note   Installing a PCI card may prevent a Power Mac from going to sleep according to the timing for system sleep as set in Energy Saver Preferences. This behavior depends on the particular make and model of the PCI card. Some cards can be upgraded to eliminate this behavior. Even if the system can't sleep, you can still set separate timings for display sleep and hard disk sleep.

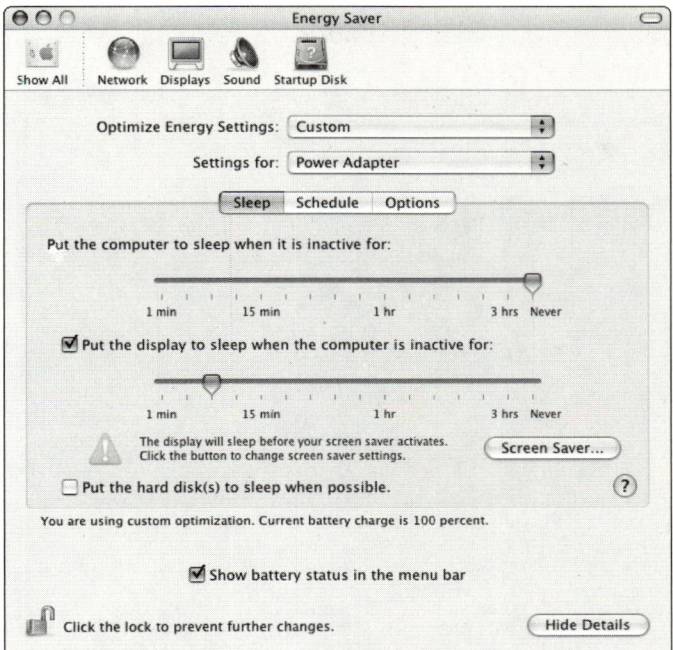

Figure 13-16: The Screen Saver button is a shortcut that opens the Screen Saver panel of the Desktop & Screen Saver preferences pane.

Schedule panel

The Schedule panel, shown in Figure 13-17, is used to configure the computer to start up and/or shut down or sleep automatically. The utility of the Schedule panel provides the convenience and assurance that a given system is on at a specified time and off at a specified time. By definition start up can mean either turn on or wake up. Selecting Start up the computer will enable you to select the frequency and what time the computer should start up. The frequency pop-up contains the following selections: Everyday, Weekdays, Weekends, and the days of the week. Selecting Shut Down enables you to specify when the computer shuts down. Shut Down is a pop-up menu, and you can select Sleep if a complete shutdown is undesired. As with the Start up option, the frequency pop-up menu contains frequency settings.

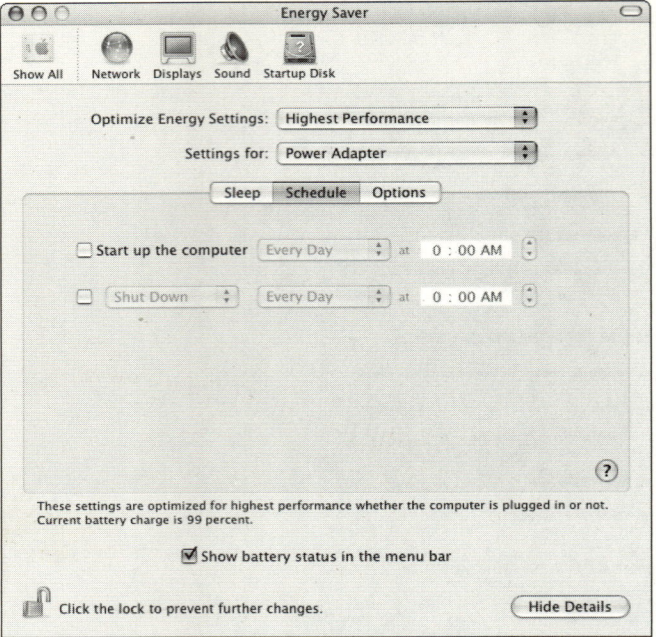

Figure 13-17: Use the Schedule pane to set your computer to start up and shut down automatically.

Options panel

As shown in Figure 13-18, the Options panel's principal function is to configure when your computer wakes from sleep. The ancillary function is to configure Mac OS X to restart the computer after a power failure.

Options for portables

When used with iBook and PowerBook computers, Energy Saver provides a number of features intended to help road warriors improve the performance of their portable computers. The majority of these features are managed via a combination of two pop-up menus: Optimize Energy Settings and Settings for. The Optimize Energy Settings pop-up menu contains a number of predefined energy saver settings optimized by task, as well as the ability to specify a custom configuration of settings. As an example, the Apple supplied Presentations setting ensures the display will not black out and sleep, whether the PowerBook is using a power adaptor or is on battery. The Settings for pop-up menu allows you to apply your settings based whether you are running off the power adapter or the battery. Last, when administrating the Energy Saver preference pane on portables, the Options panel contains a processor performance pop-up menu. As the name implies, this menu enables you to increase and reduce the overall performance of the processor in the computer. The benefits of reducing processor performance include extended battery life and a reduction of operating temperature.

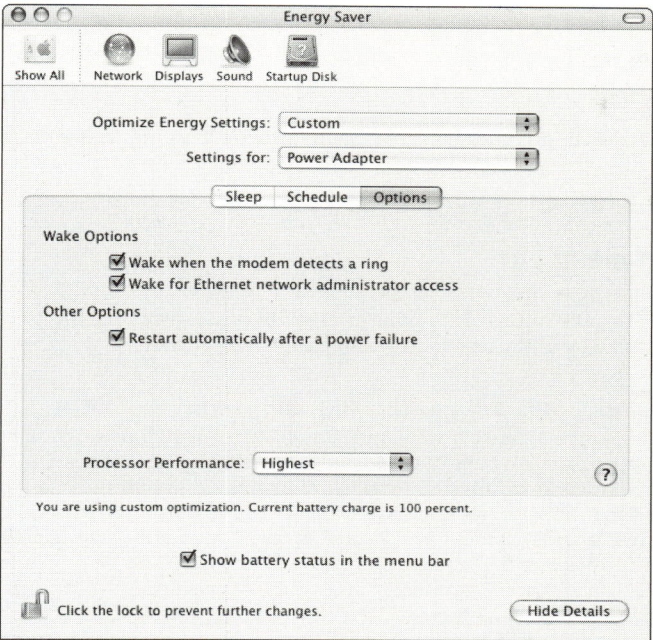

Figure 13-18: Use the Energy Saver preferences pane's Option panel to specify wake options.

Starting sleep manually

Although Mac OS X puts your computer to sleep after a period of inactivity, you gain additional energy savings by putting it to sleep manually if you know that you won't use it for a while. Some of the following methods may work on your computer:

✦ **Choose Sleep from the Apple menu.** (The Sleep command is dim on a Power Mac with a PCI card that prevents system sleep.)

✦ **Press the Power key on a keyboard that has one.** On an Apple Pro keyboard, which has no power key, press the Control and Eject keys at the same time. (The Eject key is in the upper-right corner of the numeric keypad.) After pressing Power or Control-Eject, a dialog appears asking whether you want to restart, sleep, cancel, or shut down. Click Sleep or press the S key.

✦ **Close the lid on a PowerBook or iBook.**

✦ **Press the power button on the computer on newer Mac models** — such as a Power Mac G5 or a Power Mac G4.

✦ **Press the power button on the display on newer Apple displays** — such as an Apple Studio Display with LCD screen and USB ports or an Apple Cinema Display. (On other Apple displays, pressing the power button simply turns off the display.)

Waking up your computer

To make your Mac wake up, try the following methods:

✦ **Click the mouse button.**

✦ **Press any key on the keyboard** (the Caps Lock and function keys may not work for this purpose).

✦ **Open a PowerBook or iBook.**

Battery status in the menu bar

If the Battery icon is showing in the menu bar, you can use it to monitor the condition of your computer's battery. The appearance of the Battery icon indicates whether the computer is using or recharging the battery, and how much battery capacity remains, as detailed in Table 13-3.

Besides indicating the battery condition graphically, the Battery icon can report the battery condition in words. You can see this information by clicking the Battery icon and looking at the top of the menu that appears. If the computer is using the battery, the first item in the Battery menu reports the hours and minutes of life remaining. If the computer is charging the battery, the menu reports the hours and minutes until the battery is fully charged. You can show the hours and minutes or an equivalent percentage in the menu bar by choosing from the Show submenu of the Battery menu.

Table 13-3: Battery Icon Appearance

Battery icon	Meaning
	Battery fully charged and computer operating on AC power
	Battery charging and computer operating on AC power
	Battery in use and partly depleted
	No battery; computer operating on AC power

Tip   You can move the Battery status icon by pressing the ⌘ key and dragging the icon. Drag the icon left or right to change its position relative to other icons on the right side of the menu bar. Drag the icon off the menu bar to make it vanish.

Configuring Ink Preferences

Culled from the now defunct Newton PDA, Inkwell is Mac OS X's stylus-based input technology. Inkwell facilitates the input of digital ink (drawings, signatures, and so on), the conversion of handwriting into text, and the execution of commands via the stylus. The latter differentiates itself from the use of the stylus as a mouse, by permitting the operator to input Command-key shortcuts without the use of the keyboard.

To utilize Inkwell, you need to use a third-party graphics tablet because Apple does not manufacture one of its own. Wacom Technology (`www.wacom.com`) provides the most popular options. After you acquire a tablet, make sure to download and install the latest drivers from the manufacturer's Web site.

Ink preferences pane

To configuration of Inkwell is done for the Ink preferences pane located in the Hardware section of the System Preferences application as shown in Figure 13-1. The Ink Preference pane is divided up into three panels Settings, Gestures, and Word List as shown in Figure 13-19.

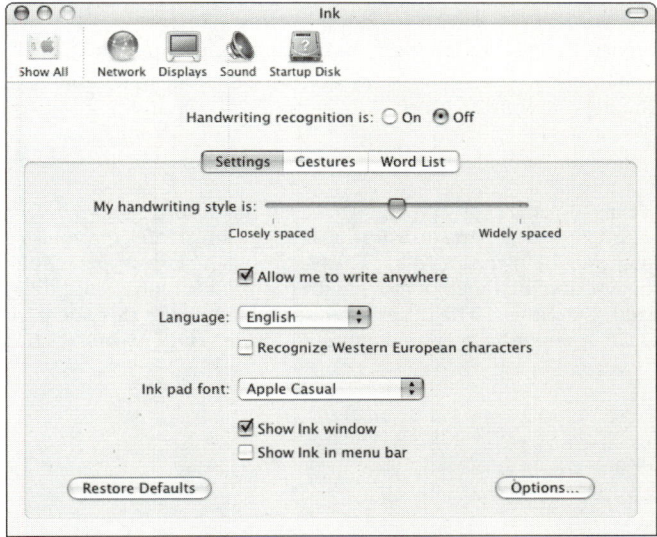

Figure 13-19: Before Inkwell can be used, click the On button to the right of Handwriting recognition is, at the top of the Ink preferences pane.

Note The Ink preferences pane will present itself in the System Preferences application only if a graphics tablet is attached to the Macintosh being administered.

Settings

The principal functions of the Settings panel depicted in Figure 13-19, are to configure Inkwell to accommodate a users writing style and to increase reliability for handwriting to text conversion. The panel contains adjustments for spacing of characters and words, the selection of language (English, French, German), and the selection of the font to be used to display recognized text in the Ink pad. Apple recommends using the Apple Casual font and to emulate its style for handwriting input to increase reliability of character recognition.

In addition to the previously mentioned selections, other options are Allow me to write any-where, recognize Western European characters, Show Ink window, and Show Ink in menu bar.

✦ **Allow me to write anywhere** specifies whether your writing is to be used solely with the Ink Pad, or in any application that supports handwriting input. The Inkpad is con-tained in the Ink window, a floating toolbar/palette that is available in any application and is the principal interface for handwriting input.

✦ **Recognize Western European characters** specifies whether to recognize language-specific marks incorporated into various western European languages.

✦ **Show Ink window** specifies whether the Ink widow should be present while using Mac OS X.

✦ **Show Ink in menu bar** specifies whether the Finder's menu bar should contain an Ink menu, as shown in Figure 13-20.

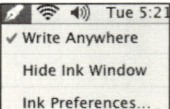

Figure 13-20: The Ink menu provides the ability to enable or disable Write Anywhere, Show or Hide Ink Window, and open the Ink preferences pane.

Using the Restore Defaults button reverts any changes made in the Settings panel back to fac-tory defaults, while the Options button opens an additional sheet for greater granular control of handwriting recognition as shown in Figure 13-21. These settings include speed controls for delay of handwriting recognition, distance of movement required for input, and delay before the stylus can be used as a mouse. The other selections available in this sheet include Recognize my handwriting when pen moves away from tablet, Hide pointer while writing, and Play sound while writing.

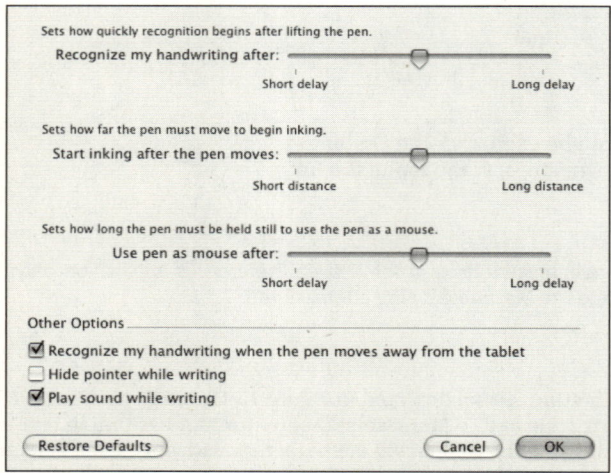

Figure 13-21: Consider the Restore Defaults button as your insurance policy against wreaking havoc in the Settings panel Options sheet.

Gestures

The Gestures panel, shown in Figure 13-22, contains a predefined list of characters that can be enabled or disabled on an item-by-item basis that is used in lieu of entering nonprintable characters such as spaces and tabs and performing actions such as undo, copy, and paste.

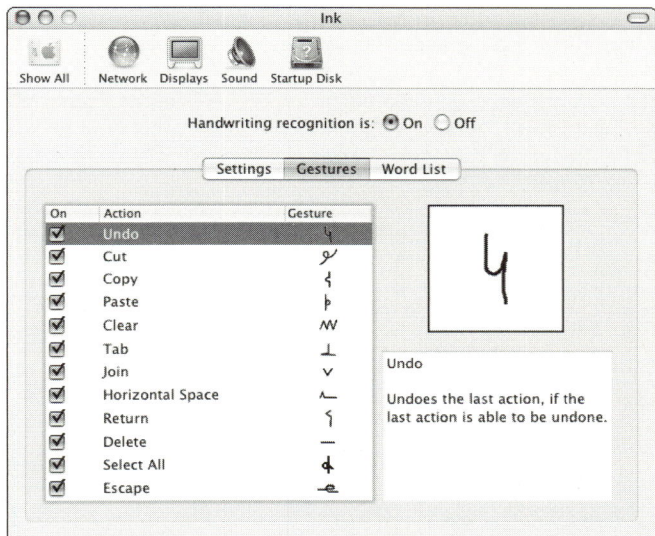

Figure 13-22: Though not as complex as using Palm's Graffiti method of data input, one must avail themselves of gestures in order to properly use Inkwell's handwriting recognition.

> **Tip**   Take a screen shot of the Gestures preference pane and print it out.

Word List

The Word List panel allows for the input of words that Inkwell has difficulty recognizing. This list is typically used for the input of names of people and places, foreign words incorporated into the specified language in the setting panel, and out-of-the ordinary lexicon.

Ink window

As stated previously, the Ink window is a floating toolbar/palette that is available in any application and is the principal interface for handwriting input. The toolbar, aptly titled Ink, contains a series of icons that run horizontally across it. These clickable icons facilitate the switching between using the stylus for handwriting recognition or as a mouse, the selection of modifier keys such as ⌘, Shift, Option, and Control, and the opening and closing of the Ink pad. It also contains a pop-up menu that opens the Ink contents within Mac OS X's help system or the Ink preference pane.

The Ink pad as depicted in Figure 13-23, is a predefined scratchpad where you can write text, enter gestures, and draw simple pictures. There are two buttons at the bottom-left side of the Ink pad to change between writing and drawing input. There are also two buttons on the right side titled Clear and Send. The Clear button clears out any contents entered in the Ink pad, and the Send button enters the contents of the Ink pad in the document you are working on. Finally, if a word is not recognized properly, hold the Control key and click on the word intended for correction. A pop-up list of words will appear that contain of Inkwell's handwriting recognition dictionary and words that were entered in the Word List panel.

Figure 13-23: Given enough time, Mac OS X's Ink pad will have you *gesturing* at the computer.

Configuring International Preferences

Mac OS X is a multilingual and multiregional operating system. It can display menus, dialogs, and other text in a variety of languages. These include not only languages that use the Roman alphabet, such as English, Spanish, French, and German, but also languages with much larger sets of characters, such as Japanese. Besides accommodating differences in language structure, writing direction, and alphabetical sorting, Mac OS X can also adjust for regional differences in formats for displaying dates, times, numbers, and currency. With Mac OS X, you're not limited to working in one language at a time. You can work in multiple languages and switch languages while you work. However, you may need to install special applications to create documents in different languages.

Choosing a language

Most but not all Mac OS X applications are able to display their menus, dialogs, and other text in a number of different languages. Applications with this ability include the Finder and the majority of the applications preinstalled in the Applications and Utilities folders. You can choose the language you want these Mac OS X applications to use.

Language Script Systems and Keyboard Layouts

The world's languages have many different alphabets and methods of writing (vertical or horizontal, left-to-right, or right-to-left). The software that defines a method of writing is called a language script system, or simply a script. Do not confuse this kind of script with the kind of script you create with AppleScript (as described in Chapter 23.

A language script system specifies which character in the specified language each keystroke produces as well as how the characters should behave—for example, the direction in which text flows. The script also specifies sort order, number and currency formats, and date and time formats.

Multiple languages can use one language script system. For example, the Roman script is used in most Western languages, such as English, French, Italian, Spanish, and German.

Associated with each language script system are one or more keyboard layouts. A keyboard layout defines the relationship between keys you press and characters entered. For example, the keyboard layout for U.S. English produces a # symbol when you press Shift-3, but the same keystroke produces a £ symbol with the British English keyboard layout.

The selection of language preference for menus and dialogs for Mac OS X's Finder and applications is done in the Language panel. The Language panel contains a Languages list of available languages, as shown in Figure 13-24. Each time you open an application, Mac OS X tells it to use the languages in the list specified in order of preference from top to bottom. If the application doesn't support menus in that language, Mac OS X tells it to use the next language in the list, and so on down the list. Not all languages are available with a default installation of Mac OS X; some languages may require you to install additional fonts before you can view the characters for those languages. Check the Mac OS X Install Disc 3 CD for the availability of additional fonts.

You change the order of preference for the language that Mac OS X applications use by rearranging the order in the Languages list. Drag your first language choice to the top of the list. Drag your second language choice to the second spot on the list and continue in this manner so that the languages are in descending order of preference. Language changes take effect in the Finder the next time you log in.

You can add languages to the list and remove them from it. Click the Edit button to see a dialog that lists all installed languages. In this sheet, select the checkbox of each language that you want to appear in the Languages list. You can change the sorting in the dialog by clicking a column heading.

The somewhat trickier task is to apply and configure the language preferences for a specific application. This is done within the Show Info window of a selected application from within the Finder. Figure 13-25 illustrates the languages portion of the Show Info window of the QuickTime Player application. Within the Languages section of the Show Info window, you also see a list of available system languages. The list of languages is alphabetized and cannot be reordered. Checking and unchecking the boxes adjacent to the languages can alter the application's language selection.

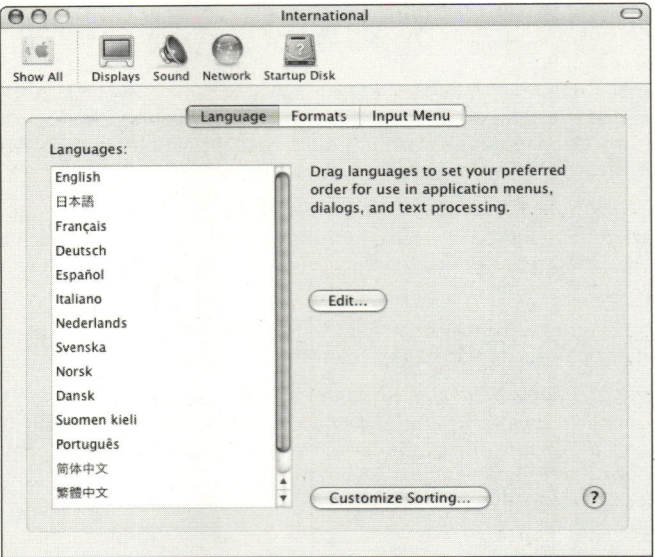

Figure 13-24: Set the language you want for Mac OS X menus and dialogs in the Language panel.

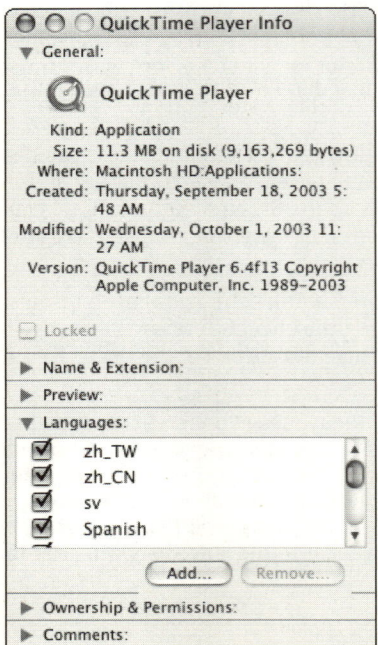

Figure 13-25: The Languages portion of the Show Info window of an application allows you to select your preferred language for that application.

For example, say that you want to open QuickTime up in French, but only QuickTime. You would need to highlight the QuickTime player within the Finder, choose Show Info from the File menu, and select Languages from the pop-up menu. Next, you would uncheck the all the languages except for French. This task can be executed regardless of whether the application is active, but in order for the language change to take effect for an application that is active, you need to quit and then relaunch the application. Upon restart, the application will open in the desired language, which in this instance is French, as shown in Figure 13-26.

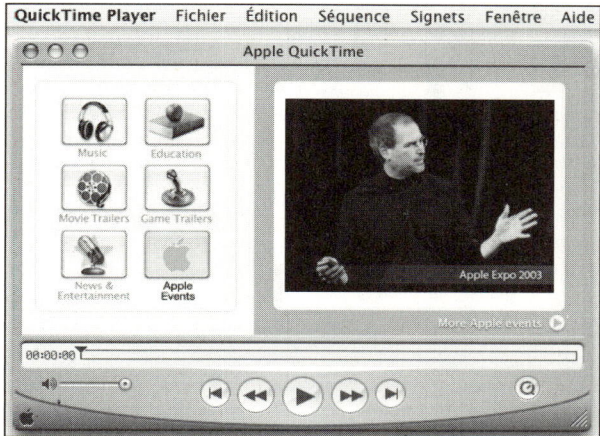

Figure 13-26: SACRÉ BLEU — QuickTime en Français!

In the event that more than one language is checked within the Language section of the Show Info window, the preferred language of the application will be determined by the order of the languages within the Language panel of the International preference pane. For example, say that both Spanish and French are checked within the Show Info window of the QuickTime Player (refer to Figure 13-25), and the order of languages within the Language panel of the International preference pane is as follows: English, Deutsch, Español, Français, Nederlands, Italiano, and Chinese (refer to Figure 13-24). Upon launching, QuickTime's default language would be Spanish (see Figure 13-27).

Customize Sorting

As stated previously, the software that defines a method of writing is called a language script system, or simply a script. Languages may use the same script, yet have different rules for alphabetizing, capitalizing, and distinguishing words. In Mac OS X, this set of rules is called a *text behavior*. You choose a text behavior for Mac OS X applications by clicking the Customize Sorting button. In this sheet, select one of the installed language script systems from the list on the left and then choose one of the script's regional languages from the adjacent pop-up menu on the right. For example, the Roman script system in Mac OS X has different text behavior rules for Austrian, Brazilian, Canadian French, Catalan, Danish, Dutch, English, Finnish, French, German, Italian, Norwegian, Portuguese, Spanish, and Swedish.

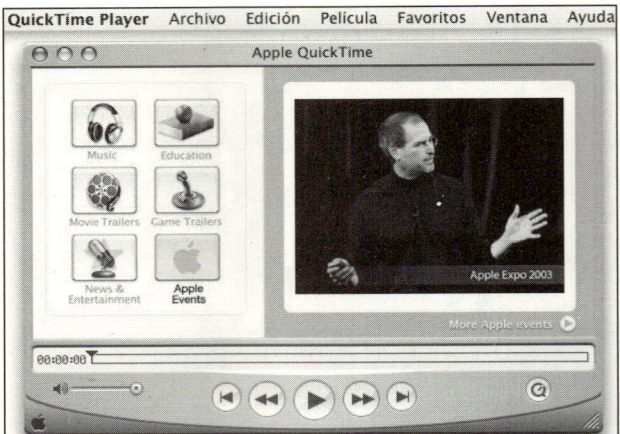

Figure 13-27: El Queso es viejo y mojado — QuickTime en Español.

Formats panel

You can set up standard formats for displaying dates, times and numbers. The Finder uses these formats in list views, the Info window, and elsewhere. Other applications may use these formats, or they may have their own preference settings.

Dates, Time, and Numbers

You set date, time, and numbers formats for Mac OS X applications in the Formats panel, as shown in Figure 13-28. This is accomplished by selecting the region the computer will be used for, such as Botswana or Zimbabwe. You can also create a custom format by using the customize buttons.

Input Menu panel

Each language has a different keyboard layout. For example, on the keyboard layout for Spanish, you can type the letter n with a tilde (ñ) by pressing one key instead of the two keys required for the same letter on a U.S. English keyboard layout. In addition, the question mark is in a different location, with an upside down question mark next to it on the Spanish keyboard layout, and the keys for adding accents to vowels are more accessible. Regions with the same language, such as Australia, Britain, Canada, and the U.S. have different keyboard layouts. You can even find special keyboard layouts for alternate typing methods, such as the Dvorak layout for typing English.

You can switch to a different keyboard layout or input method to facilitate entering or editing text in another language. You can switch keyboard layouts by using several different methods. If you regularly use multiple languages, you can set up the keyboard menu. You can also employ keyboard shortcuts for switching keyboard layouts, and you can have Mac OS X automatically switch the keyboard layout when you select text that uses a different script. For Mac OS X applications, you configure this using the Options sheet of the Input Menu panel.

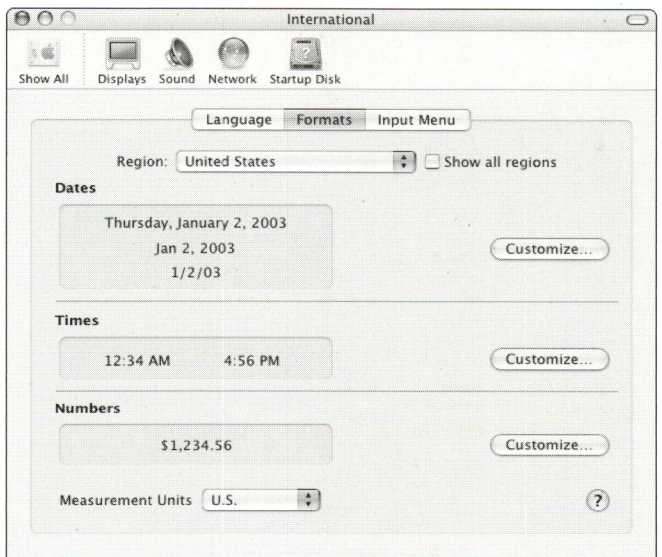

Figure 13-28: The Measurement Units pop-up menu allows for the selection of U.S. and Metric units.

Note   Keep in mind that the key labels printed on your keyboard do not change when you switch keyboard layouts. If you change to a different layout, some keys no longer generate the characters printed on them.

If your computer has more than one language script system, switching keyboard layouts may also change script systems. Each keyboard layout implicitly designates a script system. For example, switching from the U.S. keyboard layout to the Japanese keyboard layout implicitly switches from the Roman script system to the Japanese script system.

You set up a keyboard menu and configure other keyboard options for Mac OS X applications by clicking the Input Menu panel, which displays a list of available keyboard layouts. You can change the sorting in the list of keyboard layouts by clicking a column heading, as shown in Figure 13-29.

By checking Show input in menu bar or by turning on more than one keyboard layout, a keyboard input menu appears in the Finder's menu bar, as shown in Figure 13-30. The keyboard input menu lists the keyboard layouts that are turned on in the Input Menu panel. You can change the active keyboard layouts by choosing a different one from the list in this menu.

To view keyboard layouts place a check in the box next to keyboard viewer in the Input Menu panel and select Show Keyboard Viewer (located in the Input menu on the Finder's menu bar) shown in Figure 13-31.

Figure 13-29: Select keyboard layouts for the Mac OS X Keyboard menu in the Input Menu panel.

Figure 13-30: Switch Mac OS X's keyboard layout by choosing another one from the Keyboard menu.

Figure 13-31: Use the Keyboard Viewer to identify what key combinations generate which characters.

Character palettes

Depending upon the languages that are selected, the keyboard menu will display character palettes. Character palettes, are floating windows that facilitate the use of difficult-to-remember or difficult-to-reproduce foreign language characters. The last item in the keyboard input menu is Open International, which is a shortcut for opening the International preferences pane. Languages with large character sets augment the keyboard with other methods of inputting characters. For example, Japanese has input methods that involve a control palette, additional windows, and a menu, as shown in Figure 13-32.

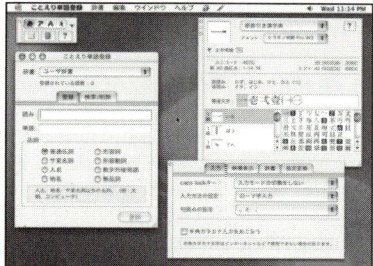

Figure 13-32: Japanese and other languages with many characters offer additional input methods besides a keyboard.

As mentioned previously, there are several ways you can switch between input methods. Aside from the Finder's input Menu, you can use the Input mode palette, which is enabled from the Input Menu. A floating pallet will appear on the screen containing all of the selected keyboard layouts from the Input Menu pane. This palette, in theory, should be available in all applications. If you want to be able to rapidly switch between the last two used scripts in the input, use the key combination ⌘-Option-Spacebar or have Mac OS X automatically switch layouts when you select text that uses a different script. You can always cycle through all of. the language scripts available in Mac OS X by pressing ⌘-Spacebar. Figure 13-33 shows the dialog in which you set the options for switching keyboard layouts. To enable or disable the latter two of these abilities, click the Options button in the Input Menu panel, which displays a sheet in which these items can be configured.

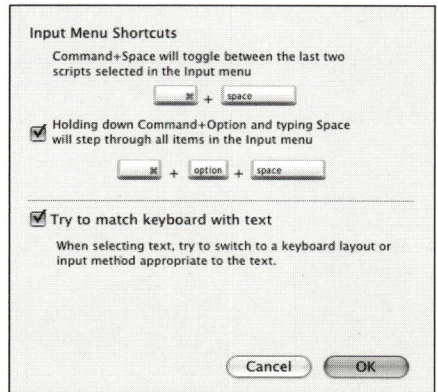

Figure 13-33: Set optional methods of switching the Mac OS X keyboard layout by clicking Options in the Input Menu panel.

Configuring Keyboard and Mouse Preferences

Although you may think of Mac OS X as something you look at, you also touch it by means of the keyboard, mouse, or trackpad. The behavior of the keyboard, mouse, or trackpad is adjustable to allow for differences among users. If you have trouble double-clicking or if you feel that the mouse pointer moves too slowly or too quickly, you can adjust the mouse or trackpad sensitivity. Likewise, if you end up typing characters repeatedly when you mean to type them only once, adjust the keyboard sensitivity. You adjust the sensitivity of the keyboard, mouse, or trackpad by using the Keyboard & Mouse preferences pane.

Keyboard panel

When you press almost any key on the keyboard and hold it down, the computer types that character repeatedly as long as you keep the key pressed. (The ⌘, Option, Control, Caps Lock, and Esc keys don't repeat.) Use the Keyboard panel, to change how quickly the characters repeat and how long you must hold down a key before the repeat feature kicks in. If you find repeating keys annoying rather than handy, disable the repeat by setting the Delay Until Repeat control to Off as seen in Figure 13-34.

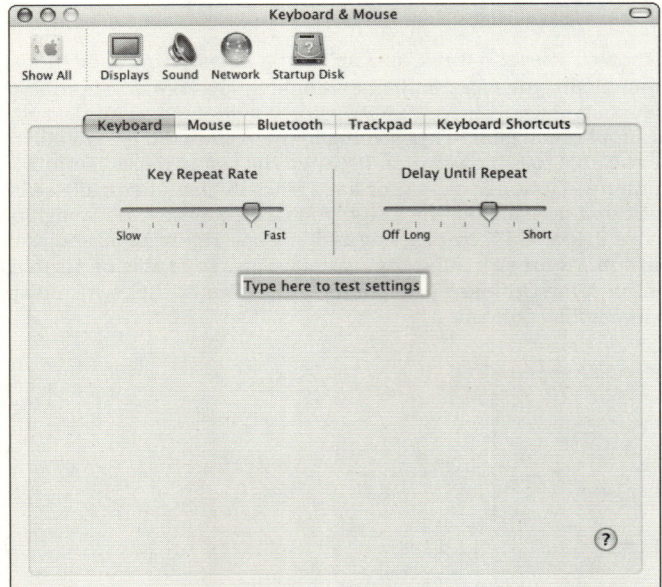

Figure 13-34: The field that contains Type here to test settings allows for you to immediately test your settings without having leaving the Keyboard & Mouse preferences pane.

Mouse and Trackpad panels

Depending upon if your computer is a desktop or a laptop, you can change the way Mac OS X responds to your manipulation of your computer's mouse or trackpad by setting options in the Mouse and/or Trackpad panels. Trackpad options are typically only available on a PowerBook or iBook computer, because they contain options specific to a trackpad, as shown in Figure 13-35.

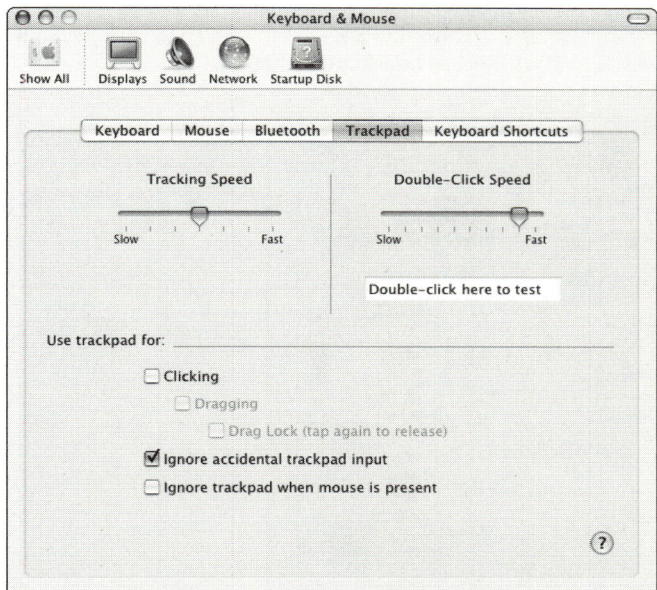

Figure 13-35: Use the Ignore accidental trackpad input to minimize unintentional mouse movement while using a trackpad as an input device.

The settings in common in the Mouse and Trackpad panels have the following effects:

✦ **Tracking Speed:** Determines how fast the pointer moves as you glide the mouse or trackpad. You may want to adjust the tracking speed if you change the display resolution. For example, if you change from the display resolution from 1024 x 768 to 800 x 600 pixels, you may want a slower tracking speed because the pointer has a shorter distance across the display screen.

✦ **Double-Click Speed:** Determines how quickly you must double-click for Mac OS X to perceive your two clicks as one double-click rather than two separate, unrelated clicks.

Bluetooth panel

If you computer is equipped with Bluetooth capability, the Bluetooth panel is where you manage Bluetooth keyboards and mice. To mate a Bluetooth-enabled peripheral such as keyboard or mouse you need to click the Set Up New Device button, which opens the Bluetooth Setup Assistant (covered in Chapter in 21). As with the Bluetooth preferences pane, there is an option for showing Bluetooth status in the Finder's menu bar.

Keyboard Shortcuts panel

Using the keyboard is sometimes faster or more convenient than using the mouse, trackball, or trackpad. The Keyboard Shortcuts panel, as shown in Figure 13-36, contains a list of predefined keyboard shortcuts. You can add or delete items from this list as well as change key combinations for the predefined list. Some shortcuts are solely to be used with keyboard navigation and Universal Access, which we discuss later in this chapter.

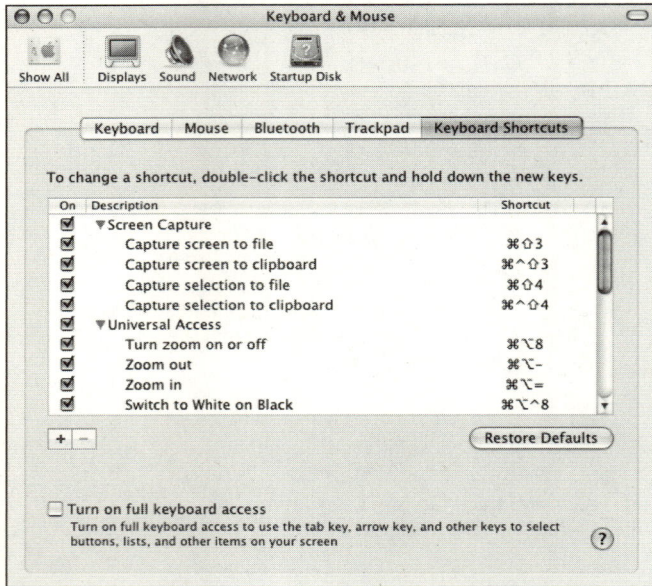

Figure 13-36: Keyboard shortcuts can be of great utility for those who have difficulties using a mouse.

To add a keyboard shortcut

To add a keyboard shortcut, take the following steps:

1. **Click the Add (+) button.**

2. **From the newly drawn sheet, choose an application from the Applications pop-up menu.** To apply a keyboard shortcut to all applications select All Applications from the pop-up menu. If your application is not listed, select other to specify.

3. **Specify the menu command as it exactly appears in the applications menu in the Title field.**

4. **Enter the key combination you want to assign the menu command in the Shortcut menu.**

5. **Click the Add button.**

How Keyboard Shortcuts Work

If you've ever wondered why ⌘-N with the Caps Lock key down isn't equivalent to pressing ⌘-Shift-N or similar things, the reason is fairly straightforward, if a bit geeky.

Mac applications (including Mac OS X applications) respond to *events,* such as a window activating or pressing a key. One such event is the *keydown event.* Keys such as Shift, Option, Control, and Caps Lock do not generate an event—their state (up or down) is recorded in what is called the *modifier field* of the event record. Therefore, when you press the N key, the programmer writing the code needs to check the state of the various modifier keys to determine whether it is just text being typed or whether it is some sort of a command. Every key on the keyboard has a separate state entry in the modifier field.

This method is not peculiar to Macs. The same techniques are used in Windows programming.

To remove a shortcut

Conversely to delete a keyboard shortcut, highlight the shortcut in list in the Keyboard Shortcuts panel and click the Delete (–) button.

Remember that no matter how badly you mess up here, you can always revert back to the default configuration by clicking on the Restore Defaults button.

 Note   When it comes to keyboard shortcuts, not all are listed in the Keyboard Shortcuts panel. The Mac OS X Finder has numerous keyboard shortcuts that may facilitate your Finder experiences. These keyboard shortcuts are covered in Chapter 3.

Full keyboard access

For those who have difficulty using the mouse, Mac OS X provides ability to use the keyboard for navigation. Full keyboard access enables you to use the keyboard to navigate to an item in a folder, operate menus in the Finder, and operate push buttons, checkboxes, radio buttons, sliders, and other controls in some windows and dialogs. Some Mac OS X applications respond more completely to full keyboard access than others. To give yourself full keyboard access, go to the bottom of the Keyboard Shortcuts panel and select Turn on full keyboard access. Under the Keyboard heading in the list of keyboard shortcuts, you can enable and disable as well as designate the key combinations that allow the keyboard to perform actions in lieu of the mouse. When full keyboard access is turned on, you press certain keys to navigate the menu bar, the Dock, the active window's toolbar, a palette, a window, or a dialog. Table 13-4 lists the keystrokes that determine the actions using full keyboard access.

Note   After you turn on full keyboard access, you may need to quit a Mac OS X application and open it again before it responds to keyboard control.

Table 13-4: Changing the Focus of Full Keyboard Access

Action	Function Keys
Full keyboard access on or off	Control-F1
Highlight menu bar	Control-F2
Highlight on Dock	Control-F3
Highlight on toolbar	Control-F5
Highlight on a palette (utility window) and then on each palette in turn	Control-F6
Focus on next window of the same application	Control-F7

You press other keys to navigate and highlight one of the items on which the keyboard is currently focused, such as a menu item, an icon in the Dock, a toolbar button, or a control setting in a dialog. The highlighted item has a dark border. You press yet another key to select the highlighted item or take another action. Table 13-5 lists the key combinations that highlight items, select items, and take other actions.

Table 13-5: Highlighting and Taking Action with Full Keyboard Access

Action	Keystroke
Highlight the next icon, button, menu, or control	Tab
Highlight the previous icon, button, menu, or control	Shift-Tab
Highlight the next control when a text box is selected	Control-Tab
Highlight a control next to a text box	Control-arrow keys
Highlight the next menu item, tab, item in a list, or radio button	Arrow keys
Move slider	Arrow keys
Restrict highlighting in the current window to text boxes and lists, or allow highlighting of any control in the current window	Control-F7
Select the highlighted item, or deselect it if it is already selected	Space bar
Click the default (pulsating) button or the default action in a dialog	Return or Enter
Click the Cancel button in a dialog	Esc
Close menu without selecting highlighted item	Esc
Cancel menu bar, Dock, or toolbar highlight	Esc

Configuring Sound Preferences

You can adjust the alert sound and other sound settings for Mac OS X applications in the Sound pane of System Preferences. The Sound Preferences pane consists of three panels to access its settings: Sound Effects, Output, and Input. No matter which panel you're in, you can adjust the main system volume or mute it altogether. You can also turn on an option to adjust the volume from a volume menu in the Finder's menu bar. After the volume slider in the menu bar has been enabled, click on its menu bar icon and use it to raise and lower the overall system sound output volume, as shown in Figure 13-37.

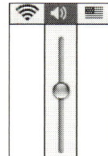

Figure 13-37: Use the Sound icon to adjust the main volume level.

Tip   You can move the Sound icon by pressing the ⌘ key and dragging the icon. Drag the icon left or right to change its position relative to other icons on the right side of the menu bar. Drag the icon off the menu bar to make it vanish.

Sound Effects panel

Use the Sound Effects panel to select an alert sound and set its volume to be as loud as or quieter than other sounds. You can also enable and disable interface sound effects and audio feedback when the volume keys are pressed. If an additional sound output is available other than the one that shipped with you Macintosh, you will also be provided the option to select that audio output device to play alerts and sound effects through. The alert sound settings affect only Mac OS X applications. Figure 13-38 shows the sound effects panel.

You can add more alert sounds by placing sound files of the AIFF format in the Sounds folder inside your home folder's Library folder. If System Preferences is open when you add or remove sounds from your Sounds folder, you must quit System Preferences and open it again to see the effect of your changes.

Output panel

The Output panel, shown in Figure 13-39, controls audio out. Use this panel, to select and control the audio hardware for sound output. Within this panel, you can also set the stereo channel balance if your output hardware supports it.

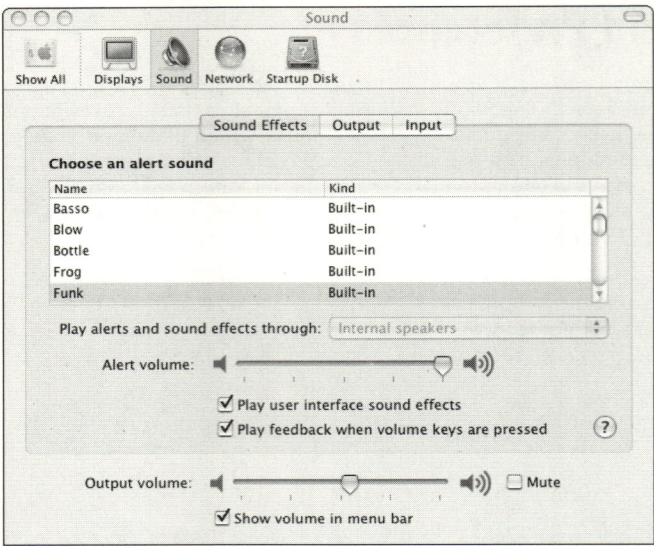

Figure 13-38: Adjust volume and balance controls and select an alert using this Sound Effects panel.

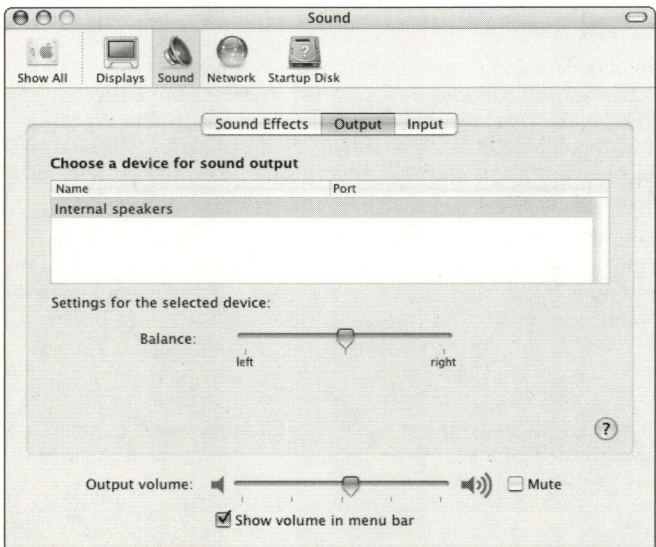

Figure 13-39: Choose an audio output device and set its stereo balance by using the Output panel.

Input panel

Use the Input panel as seen in Figure 13-40, to select the audio device you want used for sound input and set the input volume for the device.

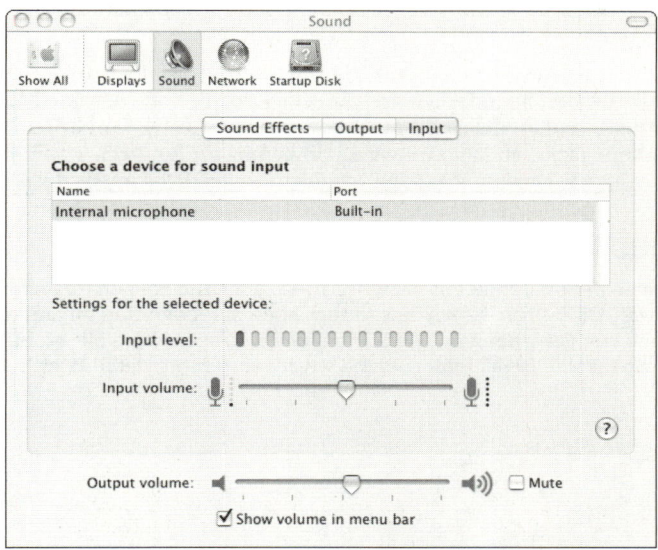

Figure 13-40: Choose an audio input device and set its input volume using the Input panel.

Configuring Speech Preferences

Many works of science fiction have depicted humans interfacing with computers by means of natural verbal communication. Macs have been capable of speaking text aloud since 1984, but it wasn't until 1993 that Apple introduced the ability for humans to speak to Macintoshes; although some would argue the Macs are still not listening.

Mac OS X's built-in English Speech Recognition is designed to understand a few dozen commands for controlling your computer. You can add to and remove some of the commands that the speech recognition system understands, but you can't turn it into a general dictation system. If voice dictation interests you, check out IBM's Via Voice for Macintosh (www.ibm.com/software/speech/mac/) and MacSpeech's iListen (www.macspeech.com).

Note   Speech recognition does not work in the Classic environment. Even if you install the Mac OS 9 version of the Apple speech recognition software, which is an optional component, it does not work in the Classic environment. You are not able to set it up in the Classic Speech control panel.

Getting a speech recognition microphone

Typically, speech recognition requires a special microphone. If you use a current-shipping iMac, eMac, iBook, or PowerBook, the built-in microphone may work for speech recognition. However, the microphone built into some older iMacs and PowerBooks does not work for speech recognition. Apple is characteristically vague about exactly which iMac and PowerBook microphones don't work, so you just have to try your own.

Consider upgrading your input hardware; you'll probably get the best results with speech recognition if you use a headset that includes a noise-canceling microphone designed for voice recognition. Many brands and models are available. Some have a standard 3.5mm mini-plug for Macs with microphone jacks, and some have a USB connector for Macs with USB ports. If you don't have any luck with your Mac's built-in microphone, try a headset instead.

Configuring speech recognition

Open the Speech preferences pane as depicted in Figure 13-41, click the Speech Recognition button, and then click the On/Off button. Now you can turn speech recognition on and off and specify the kind of feedback you get when you speak commands. You can also click a button to see the contents of the Speakable Items folder, which we cover in more detail later in this chapter.

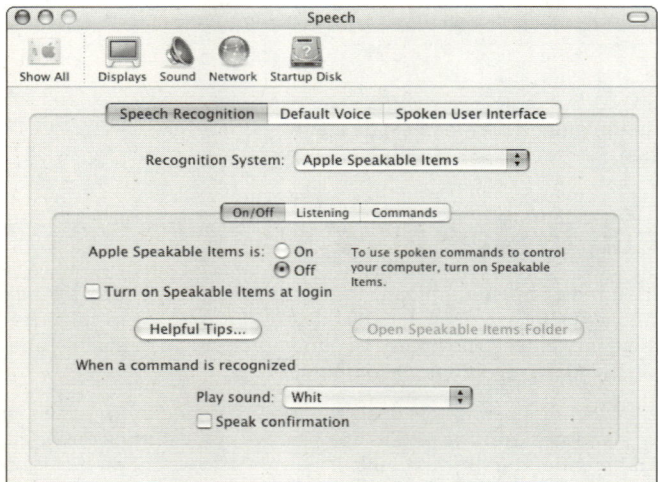

Figure 13-41: Whether you live on the Aleutian Islands or you're just a lonely soul turning on speech recognition is not the answer.

Turning on speech recognition

When you turn on speech recognition, a round feedback window appears. The first time you turn on speech recognition, it displays a welcome message that explains how speech recognition works. (You can read this message again by clicking the Helpful Tips button in Speech Preferences.)

If you want to have speech recognition turned on automatically every time you log in, select the option labeled Open Speakable Items at log in. This setting, like all others in the Speech Recognition panel, is user account–specific and does not have an effect on other user accounts.

Setting feedback options

Below the On/Off controls in the Speech Recognition panel are settings that affect the feedback you get while using speech recognition. You can turn the Speak confirmation option on or off using the Speak Confirmation checkbox to have Mac OS X speak an acknowledgement to your commands.

You can also change the sound that indicates the computer has recognized a spoken command. Choose a sound from the pop-up menu or choose None if you don't want to hear a sound signifying recognition. This pop-up menu lists the sounds from System/Library/Sounds; the Sounds folder of the main Library folder; and two special sounds, Single Click and Whit, which are part of the speech recognition software. If you put any sounds in ~/Library/Sounds, these sounds are not included in the speech feedback pop-up menu.

Using the feedback window

The speech feedback window appears when you turn on speech recognition and has several unusual attributes. First, the window is round. It floats above most other windows. What's more, this window has no close button, minimize button, or zoom button. Figure 13-42 shows the speech feedback window in several states.

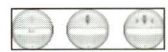 **Figure 13-42:** A feedback window indicates when speech recognition is idle (left), listening for a command (middle), or hearing a command (right).

Interpreting feedback

The speech feedback window provides the following information about speech recognition:

✦ **Attention mode:** Indicates whether the computer is listening for or recognizing spoken commands, as follows:

- **Not listening for spoken commands:** The small microphone at the top of the feedback window looks dim.

- **Listening for a command:** The small microphone at the top of the feedback window looks dark.

- **Recognizing to a command you are speaking:** You see arrowheads move from the edges of the feedback window toward the microphone picture.

✦ **Listening method:** Indicates how to make the computer listen for spoken commands. You may see the name of a key you must press or a word you must speak to let the computer know that you want it to interpret what you are saying as a command.

✦ **Loudness:** Colored bars on the bottom part of the window theoretically measure the loudness of your voice. In practice, there seems to be no relationship between the indicated loudness level and successful speech recognition. If you see no bars or one blue bar, you're speaking relatively quietly; a blue bar and one or two green bars mean you're speaking louder; and these three bars plus a red bar mean that you're speaking very loudly. Apple recommends you speak loudly enough to keep green bars showing but rarely should the red bar appear.

✦ **Recognition results:** When the computer recognizes a command that you have spoken, it displays the recognized command in a help tag above the speech feedback window. The displayed command may not exactly match what you said, because speech recognition interprets what you say with some degree of flexibility. For example, if you say, "Close window," speech recognition probably displays the command it recognized as "Close this window." If speech recognition has a response to your command, it generally displays it in a help tag below the feedback window. Figure 13-43 shows how speech recognition displays the recognized command and its feedback in help tags.

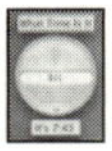

Figure 13-43: Help tags above and below the speech feedback window display the command that the computer recognized and its response, if any.

Using feedback window controls

The only control in the speech feedback window is a pop-up menu, which you can see by clicking the small arrow at the bottom of the window. One menu command opens Speech Preferences, previously shown in Figure 13-41. Another command in the pop-up menu opens a window that lists available speech commands.

You can move the feedback window by clicking it almost anywhere and dragging. You can't drag from the bottom of the window because clicking there makes the pop-up menu appear.

Minimizing the feedback window

Although the speech feedback window has no minimize button, you can minimize it with a spoken command, which is "Minimize speech feedback window." While minimized in the Dock, this window continues to provide most of the same feedback as it does when it is not minimized. While the feedback window is minimized, you don't see help tags containing the recognized command and response. In addition, the window's pop-up menu is not available in the Dock. Figure 13-44 shows the speech feedback window in the Dock.

Figure 13-44: While minimized in the Dock, the speech feedback window continues to indicate speech recognition status.

After minimizing the speech feedback window, you can open the window by clicking it in the Dock. You can also open the window by speaking the command, "Open speech feedback window."

Looking at the Speech Commands window

Instead of seeing your spoken command and the computer's response to it displayed briefly in help tags, you can see a list of all your recent spoken commands and the responses to them. The list of commands appears in the Speech Commands window, and also lists the commands you can speak in the current context. You can display this window by choosing Open Speech Commands Window from the pop-up menu at the bottom of the round speech feedback window. You can also open the Speech Commands window with the spoken command, "Open Speech Commands window." Figure 13-45 shows the Speech Commands window when the Finder is the active application.

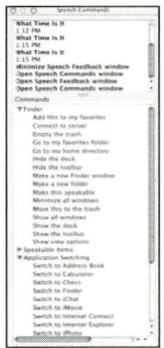

Figure 13-45: The Speech Commands window lists commands you have spoken, responses to them, and commands you can speak.

The commands you have spoken appear at the top of the speech commands window in bold, and any responses appear below each command in plain text. The bottom part of the window displays the commands you can speak in the current context. The list is organized in the following categories:

✦ **Name of current application:** Appears only if the application you're currently using has its own speakable commands.

✦ **Speakable Items:** Includes commands that are available no matter which application you're currently using.

✦ **Applications:** Lists commands for switching to specific applications. (Switching to an application opens it if necessary.)

You can hide or show the commands for a category by clicking the disclosure triangle next to the category name. You can adjust the relative sizes of the top and bottom parts of the speech commands window by dragging the handle located on the bar between the two parts of the window. You find out how to add speakable commands later in this chapter.

Setting the listening method

The Listening panel of the Speech panel facilitates the configuration of when the computer should listen for spoken commands:

✦ **Push-to-talk method:** This is the most reliable method because the computer listens for commands only when you are pressing a key that you designate.

✦ **Code name method:** The computer listens for its code name and tries to interpret the words that follow it as a command.

Setting the push-to-talk method

To set the push-to-talk method and the key that makes speech recognition listen for spoken commands, follow these steps:

1. **Click the Speech Recognition button.** The Speech Recognition panel is organized into three smaller subpanels: On/Off, Listening, and Commands.

2. **Click the Listening button.** You see the options for setting the speech recognition listening method. Figure 13-46 shows the listening panel set for the push-to-talk method with the Esc key, which is the initial setting.

3. **Set the Listening Method option to Listen only while key is pressed.** This setting means you can hold down the listening key to make speech recognition recognize your spoken commands.

4. **If you want to change the listening key, click the Change Key button.** A dialog appears in which you can type the key or combination of keys that you want to use as the listening key. You can use the Esc key, Delete key, any key on the numeric keypad, one of the function keys F5 through F12, or most punctuation keys. You can combine one of these keys with any one or more of the Shift, Option, Control, or Command keys. You can't use letter keys or number keys on the main part of the keyboard.

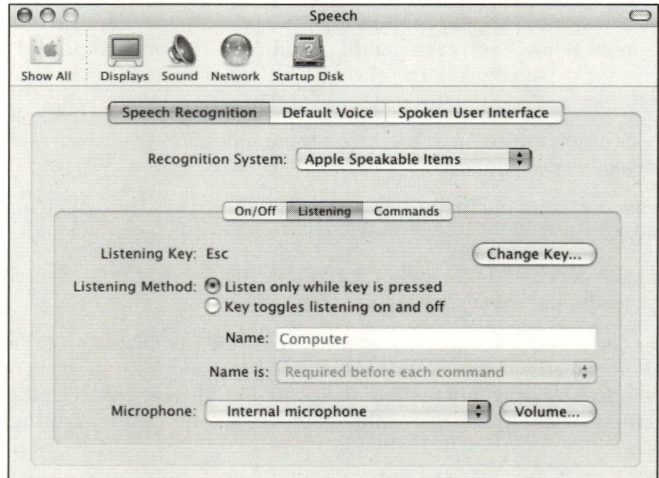

Figure 13-46: Speech recognition can be set for push-to-talk listening, but *be warned,* prolonged use of speech may also push your buttons.

Setting the code name method

If you prefer to have the computer listen for a code name that you say before speaking a command, use these steps:

1. **Click the Speech Recognition button.** The Speech Recognition panel is organized into three subpanels: On/Off, Listening, and Commands.

2. **Click the Listening button.** You see the options for setting the speech recognition listening method. Figure 13-47 shows the listening panel set for the code name method.

3. **Set the Listening Method option to Key toggles listening on and off.** This setting means pressing the listening key alternately turns listening on and off. Turning listening off puts speech recognition on standby, which may improve the performance of the computer.

4. **If you want to change the listening key, click the Change Key button.** A dialog appears in which you can type the key or combination of keys that you want to use as the key. You can use the Esc key, Delete key, any key on the numeric keypad, one of the function keys F5 through F12, or most punctuation keys. You can combine one of these keys with any one or more of the Shift, Option, Control, or ⌘ keys. You can't use letter keys or number keys on the main part of the keyboard.

5. **Specify a code name.** Type a code name for speech recognition in the text box; the default name is Computer. (The text box is not case-sensitive.) Use the nearby pop-up menu to specify when you must speak the name.

In the pop-up menu that specifies when you must speak the code name, one of the choices makes the code name optional but not without risk: The computer could interpret something you say in conversation as a voice command.

Other choices in the pop-up menu make the code name optional if you spoke the last command less than 13 seconds ago or 30 seconds ago. The idea is that when you have the computer's attention, you shouldn't have to get its attention immediately following the previous command. You can tell whether you need to speak the code name by looking at the round speech feedback window. If you see the code name displayed in the middle of the feedback window, you have to speak the name before the next command.

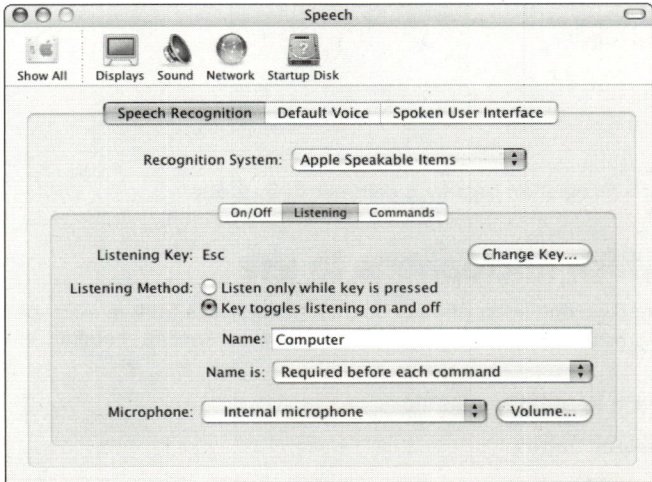

Figure 13-47: Speech recognition set for code name listening.

Specifying what commands to listen for

Speech has commands organized by group. You choose which groups of commands Speech will listen for in the Commands panel shown in Figure 13-48. To choose commands by group:

1. **Click the Speech Recognition button.**

2. **Click the Commands button.**

3. **Click the checkboxes to select and deselect groups of commands.** To activate the Front Windows commands group and the Menu Bar commands group, you must select Using Assistive Features in the Universal Access preferences pane. As you add and remove groups of commands, the groups appear and disappear in the Speech Commands window.

4. **Select or clear the checkbox next to Require exact wording of Speakable Item command names.** Requiring the speaker to use the exact name of the command improves recognition accuracy and response time. If this is deselected, Mac OS X will attempt to identify a command from more relaxed, casual speech.

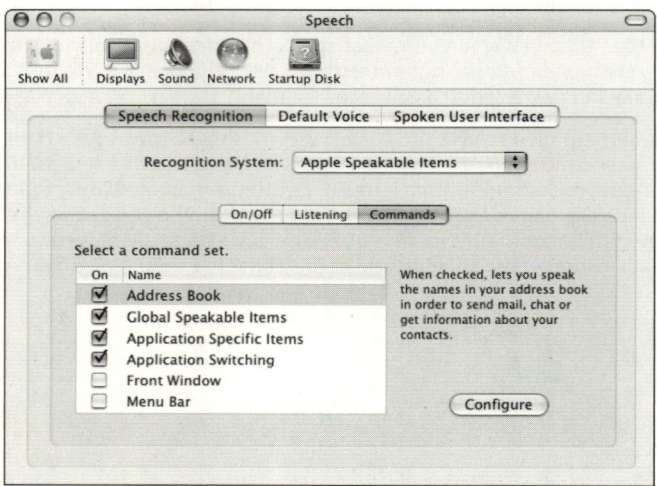

Figure 13-48: Speech recognition organizes commands by group.

Specifying which microphone to use

If your Mac has more than one microphone connected, such as a built-in microphone and an external microphone, you can specify which option you want speech recognition to use. Follow these steps:

1. **Click the Speech Recognition button.**

2. **Click the Listening button.**

3. **Choose an available microphone from the Microphone pop-up menu.** If your computer has a microphone jack, the pop-up menu includes it as a choice even if no microphone is plugged into the jack.

Specifying the spoken user interface

Mac OS X speaking ability is not just a one-way conversation. Speech can be used to vocalize OS X's responses back to the user. This capability is configured in the Spoken User Interface panel, as shown in Figure 13-49. Click the Spoken User Interface button within the Speech preferences pane. You can choose what phrase, such as "Alert!" or "Excuse me" to use as a signal phrase. You can edit the list of alert phrases and add your own phrases, too. You can choose a voice just for alert messages that's a different voice than the default voice; you can specify the time delay before the alert is spoken. You can also choose to have Speech read text under the mouse cursor as you move the cursor over text.

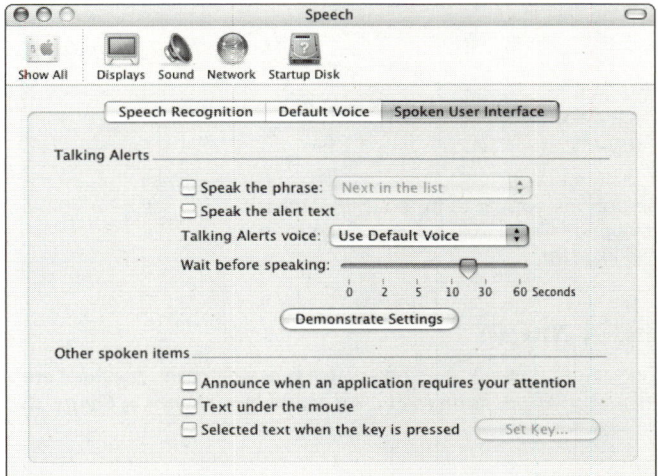

Figure 13-49: Before closing the Spoken User Interface panel, try out your settings by using the Demonstrate Settings button.

Choosing a voice for Mac OS X

The voices that the Speech preferences pane employs are highly configurable. You set the default voice and speaking rate for Mac OS X in the Default Voice panel as shown in Figure 13-50.

To set a voice and a speaking rate for Mac OS X, follow these steps:

1. **Click the Default Voice button.**

2. **Select any voice from the list on the left side of the Speech preferences pane.** You hear a sample of the voice, and a description of it appears next to the list.

3. **Optionally, change the speaking rate by adjusting the Rate slider.** Each voice has a preset speaking rate. You can hear a sample of the voice at the current rate by clicking the Play button.

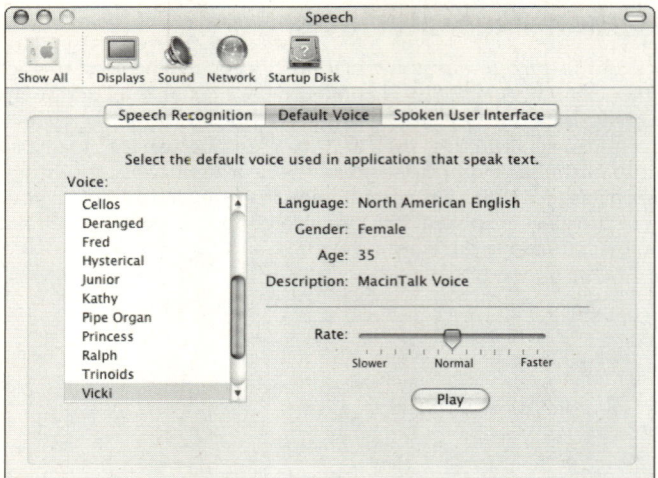

Figure 13-50: Although the options appear to be bountiful, try as you may, no combination of options here, will get you close to having your computer sound like HAL.

Reading documents aloud

If you are using an OS X application, Speech may be available as a Service. Services are available to OS X applications from the Application menu. An example is shown in Figure 13-51. Refer to Chapter 11 for more on Services.

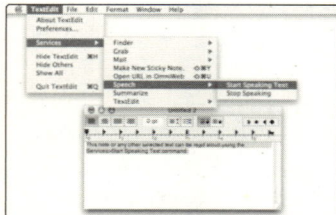

Figure 13-51 Speech is available as a Service to many OS X applications.

Configuring Startup Disk Preferences

Selecting an alternate startup system for your computer is an easy process. The only real requirement for selecting an alternate system folder is that it is a *valid boot system* for startup. Depending upon your Mac OS X install strategy and if your system supports Mac OS 9 booting, you may have alternate boot capable Mac OS System Folders on a single partition or on entirely different volumes. You can select any of the eligible System Folders in the Startup Disk preferences pane, or choose the Network Startup option to search for any available NetBoot Volumes to start up from, as shown in Figure 13-52.

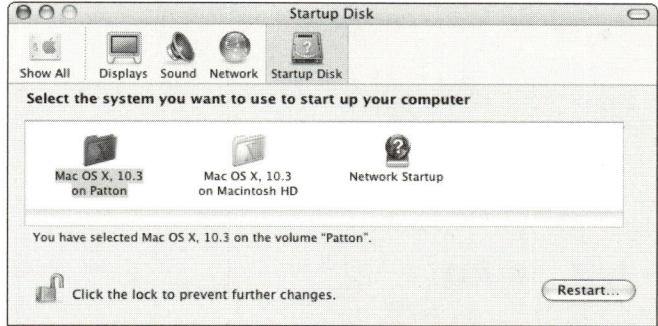

Figure 13-52: The Startup Disk preferences pane is used to designate which Mac OS System Folder is used the next time your computer starts up.

After selecting a valid System for startup, you can restart using the newly selected System right away by clicking the Restart button at the bottom of the preference pane. If you don't want to restart yet, you can close the Startup Disk preferences pane, quit the System Preferences application, or switch to another application. Regardless if you click Restart or not, an alert appears asking you to confirm that you want to change the System Folder for the next startup.

Configuring Universal Access Preferences

In the Universal Access pane, you can adjust the display and behavior of OS X to accommodate for different needs of sight and sound as well as to set up alternative methods of using the keyboard and mouse for individuals who have disabilities that preclude them from using the computer in standard configuration. *Mouse Keys* lets you use the numeric keypad portion of the keyboard to move the pointer on the screen and to click as if you were using the mouse button. *Sticky Keys* lets you type combination keystrokes such as ⌘-O one key at a time. The Universal Access pane was introduced with Mac OS X 10.1. All four panels of the Universal Access pane show the same two checkboxes at the bottom of the window:

> ✦ **Enable access for assistive devices:** Enables OS X to work with equipment, such as a screen reader.

> ✦ **Enable text-to-speech for Universal Access preferences:** Placing the mouse cursor over labels and options in the Universal Access window causes OS X Speech to read that option aloud.

Enable access for assistive devices is off by default; Enable text-to-speech for Universal Access preference is on by default. The checkboxes for these two items are shown at the bottom of Figures 13-53, 13-54, 13-55, and 13-56.

Seeing panel

The Seeing panel, as shown in Figure 13-53, provides options to benefit people with different vision-oriented limitations. You can turn Zoom on and off, reverse the display to show white text on black background instead of black on white, and set the display to grayscale.

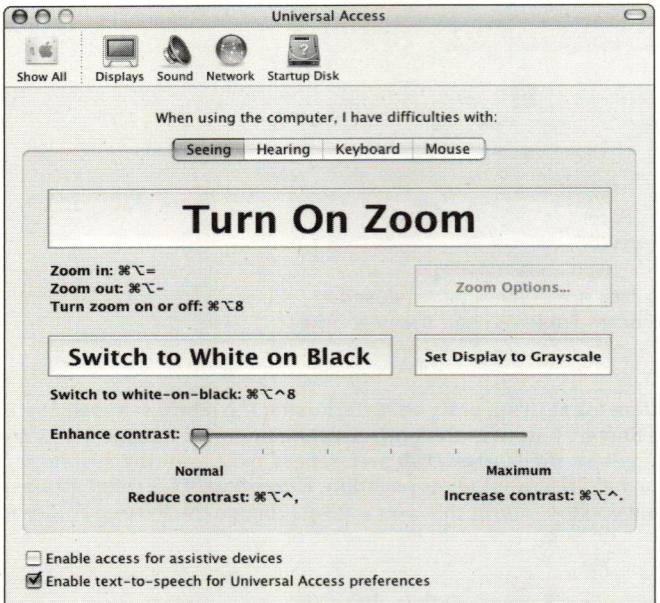

Figure 13-53: For individuals with difficulty seeing, the Seeing panel of Universal Access provides vision-oriented display options.

Hearing panel

The Hearing panel, as shown in Figure 13-54, offers a full-screen flash option as a substitute for alert sounds, provides a test of the flash screen substitute, and provides a button to open the Sound System Preferences to adjust the sound volume.

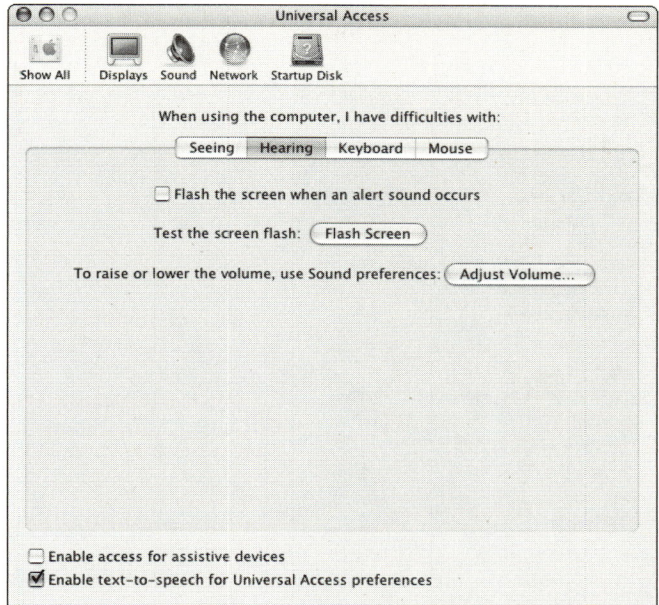

Figure 13-54: For individuals with difficulty hearing, the Hearing panel of Universal Access provides hearing-oriented display options.

Keyboard panel

Use the Keyboard panel, as shown in Figure 13-55, to set up the Sticky Keys feature for Mac OS X and Classic applications. If you turn on this feature, you can type a combination of modifier keys — ⌘, Shift, Option, or Control — one key at a time. For example, you can type ⌘-Shift-S (the standard keyboard shortcut for File ➪ Save As) by pressing the ⌘, Shift, S one at a time.

Besides turning Sticky Keys on or off, you can set an option to hear a beep, not the system alert sound, when you press a modifier key. You can also set an option to see the symbols of modifier keys superimposed on the screen. If the option to use keyboard shortcuts is turned on at the top of Universal Access Preferences, you can turn Sticky Keys on or off by pressing Shift five times in succession.

When Sticky Keys is turned on, and the option to show modifier keys onscreen is also on, pressing a modifier key causes the key's symbol to be superimposed on the screen. Press another modifier key, and its symbol is superimposed as well. Press the same modifier key a second time, and its symbol is removed. Press any other key to have it combined with the modifier keys whose symbols are currently superimposed on the screen. Press Esc to cancel all the modifier keys whose symbols are currently superimposed on the screen.

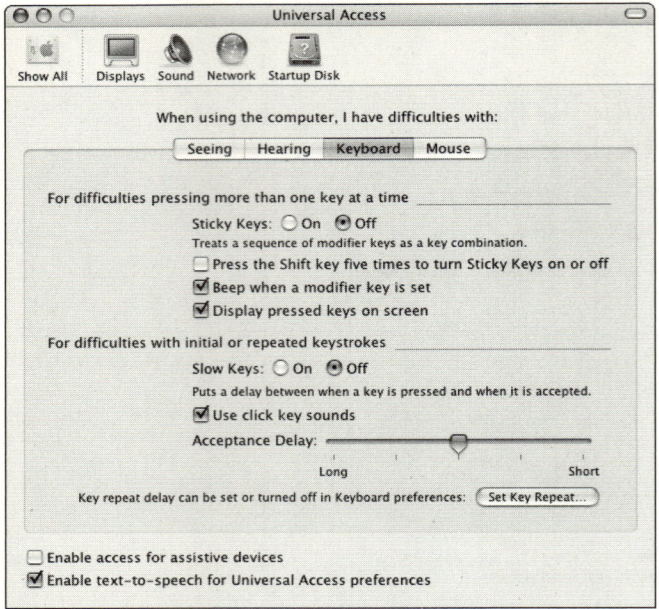

Figure 13-55: Use the Set Key Repeat button as a shortcut for opening the Keyboard & Mouse preferences pane to adjust the key repeat delay time.

Mouse panel

Use the Mouse panel, as shown in Figure 13-56, to set up the Mouse Keys feature. If you turn on this feature, you can click, drag, and move the pointer with the numeric keypad instead of the mouse or trackpad.

Tip   Mouse Keys is a very handy feature for moving graphic objects precisely. For this use, try setting the Initial Delay to Short.

The Mouse panel has the following settings:

✦ **On and Off:** If the option to use keyboard shortcuts is selected at the top of Universal Access Preferences, you can turn Mouse Keys on or off by pressing the Option key five times.

✦ **Initial Delay:** Determines how long you must hold down a keypad key before the pointer starts responding. As long as you keep pressing keypad keys to control the pointer, the delay does not recur. The delay occurs only with the first press of a key after a period during which you have not used the keypad for pointer control.

✦ **Maximum Speed:** Determines how fast the pointer gets going if you keep holding down a key. You have better control with a slow speed, but moving the pointer across the screen takes longer.

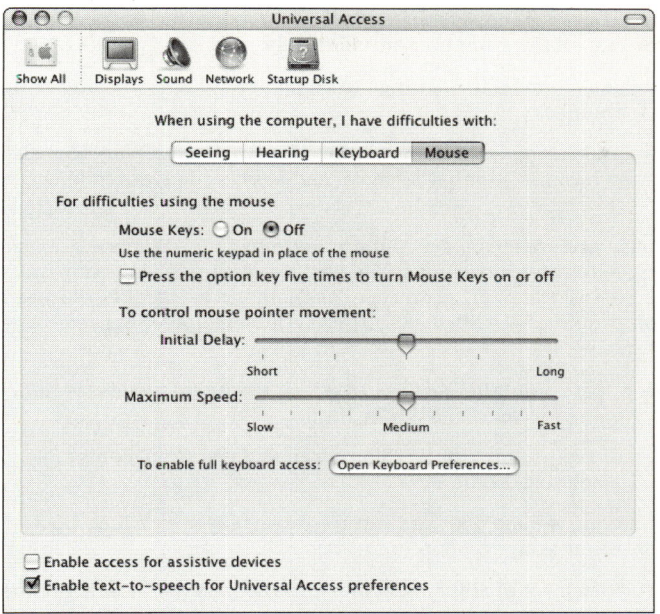

Figure 13-56: The Mouse panel also provides a button shortcut to the Keyboard & Mouse preferences pane, aptly titled Open Keyboard Preferences.

When Mouse Keys is on, the 5 key in the keypad acts like a mouse button. Press once to click; press twice to double-click. The eight keys around 5 move the pointer left, right, up, down, and diagonally. Pressing 0 locks the mouse button down until you press the period key in the keypad. You do not have to hold down 0 like you hold down the actual mouse button.

Tip   If the pointer seems unresponsive, make the Initial Delay shorter and the Maximum Speed faster in Universal Access Preferences. Conversely, if you feel like you don't have enough control over the pointer, make the Initial Delay longer and the Maximum Speed slower.

Summary

In this chapter, you learned the following:

✦ The settings in System Preferences application affect all Mac OS X applications.

✦ The CDs & DVDs pane determines behavior of Mac OS X upon optical media insertion.

✦ In the Date & Time preferences pane, you can adjust the majority of your computer's clock and calendar settings.

✦ In the Displays preferences pane, you set screen resolution, number of colors, refresh rate, contrast, and brightness. You also select a color profile and calibrate your display. If you have multiple displays, you may be able to adjust how they work together. With some displays, you can adjust the shape and position of the screen image.

✦ The Energy Saver preferences pane sets timings for sleep mode and options for starting, sleeping, and turning off the computer automatically.

✦ The Ink preferences pane contains the settings to configure Mac OS X's handwriting input/recognition capabilities.

✦ The International preferences pane contains settings for language preference, text behavior, date and time formats, number formats, and keyboard layout in Mac OS X applications.

✦ The Keyboard & Mouse preferences pane contains settings to configure the sensitivity of the keyboard and the mouse or trackpad. You can also set up full keyboard access to use the keyboard to control the mouse and type combination keystrokes one key at a time by setting up Mouse Keys and Sticky Keys in the Universal Access preferences pane.

✦ The Sound preferences pane contains settings to adjust the overall sound volume, the alert sound, and its volume for Mac OS X applications.

✦ The Speech preferences pane allows for configuration of plain verbal communication between humans and Macintosh computers.

✦ The Startup Disk preferences pane contains settings to specify which Mac OS System Folder is used the next time your computer starts up.

✦ Universal Access provides a set of adjustments for the visibility and hearing of the display and audio of OS X.

✦ ✦ ✦

Beyond the Basics of Mac OS X

◆   ◆   ◆   ◆

◆   ◆   ◆   ◆

Managing User Accounts and Privileges

This chapter examines the types of user accounts in Mac OS X. You find out how to create and manage those user accounts using the Accounts preference pane, and how to assign privileges using Get Info.

Unix and Privileges

As discussed in Chapter 1, Mac OS X is Apple's first true multi-user desktop operating system. Because of its Unix underpinnings, Mac OS X provides the ability to employ a Unix-style security model. In Mac OS X, each user is provided with his/her own user account. As we noted, each user account provides a separate customizable workspace/environment for its assigned user. An example of this is that all user accounts contain their own home folder to save their documents in. Additionally, each user account can be customized with its own preference settings. For example, your Appearance preference settings don't affect other users, and vice versa.

Central to Mac OS X's multi-user security model is the concept of *privileges*. Simply stated, privileges (which Unix folk refer to as *permissions*) provide the control mechanism for access to files, folders, and applications within Mac OS X. Because Mac OS X was designed for a single computer to be shared among many users, it requires a means to prevent one user's data from being accessed or deleted by another user. This is where privileges/permissions come into play. In an OS X system, every file, folder, and application is assigned a user and a set of privileges. In fact, even running applications have ownership.

Note Some preference settings affect all users (a global effect) and are typically denoted by a lock in the bottom left-hand corner of their respective preferences panes.

Identifying Types of User Accounts

All user accounts are assigned a series of attributes. These attributes include a long name, short name, password, and UID (User ID). A UID is a behind-the-scenes mechanism that OS X employs to identify users by unique numeric designations. Three types of user accounts can be configured within OS X: root, administrator, and *ordinary* user.

Root

In Unix, the root account, which is sometimes referred to as the system administrator or the superuser account, has complete access to all settings and files within the operating system. When logged in via the root account, you are master of all that is within Mac OS X. The root account has complete control over all folders and files on your Mac, including the contents of the normally off-limits folder named System. Mac OS X is carefully organized so that users shouldn't need to move, delete, rename, or otherwise change the system files and folders that are located in the folder named System and in several hidden folders. All the parts of Mac OS X that users may need to change are located in the main Library folder, where an administrator can change them, or in the Library folder inside each user's home folder, where the user can change them. Additionally, the root account has unfettered access to all users' folders and files. Be extremely careful; the root account operates without the safety net of Mac OS X's security model and is generally used for the express purposes of system administration. Administration via the root account is something to grow into. As useful as the root account may be for administering an OS X system, for the less-skillful user there is an equal chance of really messing things up. Therefore, you're better off working with administrator account if you are unsure of exactly what you are doing.

You don't need to create a root user account, all OS X systems have a preexisting root account, but it is disabled by default. Apple intentionally designed Mac OS X in this fashion to prevent less-adroit users from breaking the OS. In order to gain access to the root account, you must first enable it. This is can be done via the NetInfo Manager, which is covered. In fact, all user accounts can be administered through the NetInfo Manager utility, although to do so is very difficult because Apple *does not provide sufficient* documentation on the operation of the NetInfo utility.

Administrator (Admin)

For day-to-day system administration, the admin account is where it's at. The admin account has enough power to get the majority of the system administration tasks done without the potential liabilities associated with the root account. An admin user account provides access to all of Mac OS X's system preferences and utilities, and it provides the ability to install applications and system-wide resources. An admin account also has the ability to create and manage other user accounts and enable the root account if needed within an OS X system. However, an administrator cannot view the contents of another user's home folder. Table 14-1 lists system preference settings that can be changed only with an administrator account's name and password.

Table 14-1: Protected Settings That Only Administrators Can Change

System Preferences Pane	Protected Settings
Date & Time	All settings except the menu bar clock settings
Energy Saver	All settings
Login	All login window settings but not the list of login items
Network	All settings except choosing a different location
Sharing	All settings
Software Update	Actual installation of updates (changing of update schedule not protected)
Startup Disk	System folder selected for startup
Accounts	All settings except current user's password

As mentioned in Chapter 1, the Mac OS X Installation Setup Assistant walks you through the initial configuration of the first administrator account. Within Mac OS X, there can be multiple admin accounts per OS X system. This is a useful feature in the event that one admin forgets his password and requires a password reset, which can only be accomplished by another accessible admin user account.

User

A user account belongs to a typical end user. A user account does not allow system-wide administration of Mac OS X. In fact, if a user attempts to install software, a screen with a padlock confronts him with the message that any installation requires an administrator's authorization. A normal user account cannot modify system-wide preferences. These include Date & Time, Energy Saver, Login (Window), Network, Startup Disk, and Users. Normal users typically have the ability to modify any other preference that pertains to their own user account.

Groups

Within the Unix security model, groups are typically used to simplify the assignment of system access to a series of users intended to share the same level of system access. There are three preset groups within Mac OS X: admin, staff, and wheel. Mac OS X automatically handles the assignment of groups. The staff is the standard group all user accounts are assigned to. Admin users are also members of the admin and wheel groups. The admin and wheel groups have access to make system-wide changes. Just as users are assigned unique numerical user IDs, all groups have uniquely assigned GID (Group ID) as well. Mac OS X does not provide an easy-to-use GUI for managing groups, although they can be managed through the NetInfo Manager as well as via the command line.

Configuring Account Preferences

As noted, during the installation of Mac OS X or when first starting a Mac with a factory prein-stallation of Mac OS X, the Setup Assistant creates the first account, which is an admin account. Subsequently, within Mac OS X's GUI, day-to-day user account administration is done through the Accounts preferences pane depicted in Figure 14-1. The Accounts prefer-ences pane can create and delete user accounts; it is also the location where you can config-ure home folder encryption, select items to open automatically at startup, restrict system access for a given user account, grant admin privileges, and specify system login options. Depending on the type of account being administered and the current user account that is logged-in, the Accounts preference pane can present up to six panels: Password, Login Options, Picture, Security Startup Items, and Limitations. The Limitations panel contains three additional panels: No Limits, Some Limits, and Simple Finder.

When opening the Accounts preferences pane for the first time, you will notice that the admin account that is generated by the Setup Assistant during the Mac OS X install process is pre-sent. By default, Mac OS X is configured to automatically log in utilizing this admin account. Once an additional user account is created, you are queried as to whether you want to turn off automatic login. If automatic login is disabled, on the next restart you will be presented with a list of user accounts to choose from for logging in. Figure 14-2 shows the Login window with a list of user accounts.

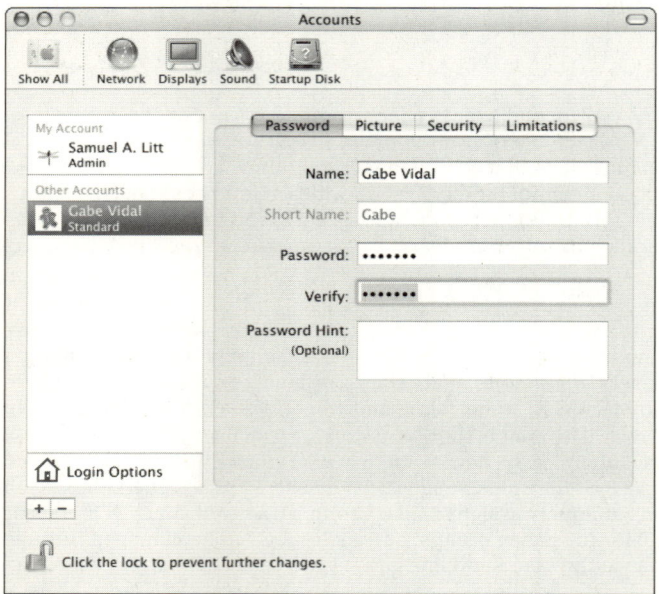

Figure 14-1: The Accounts preferences pane.

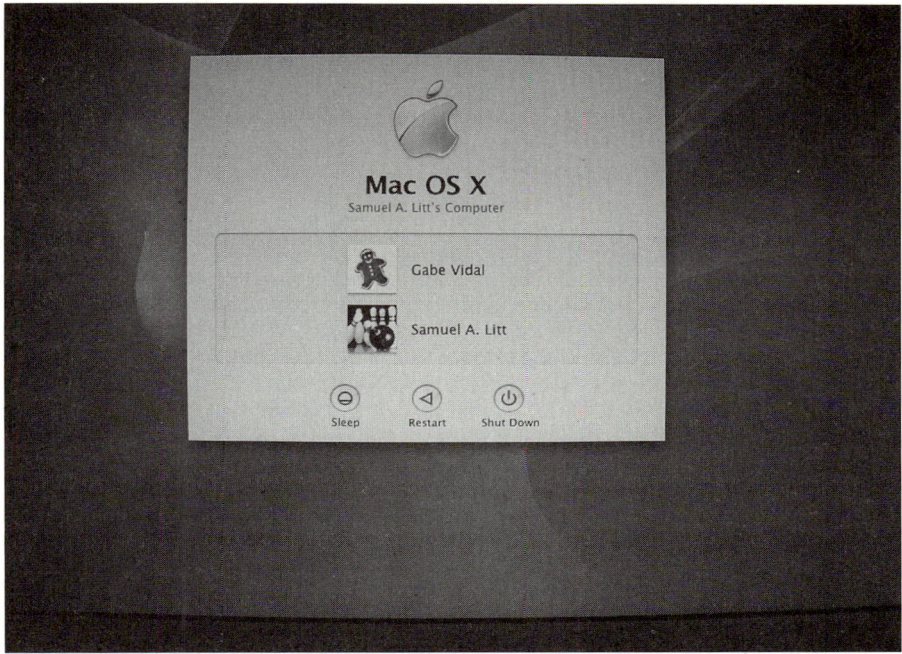

Figure 14-2: The Login window.

As previously stated, you can have more than one admin account on the same machine. Conversely, you can delete an admin account, but you will be prevented from deleting all admin accounts. Every OS X system must have at least one admin account at all times.

When you create a new user account, you also simultaneously create a home directory folder for that user. However, when you delete a user account, that user's home directory is automatically archived into a single file incorporating that user's name with a suffix of .dmg. This file is deposited in a folder titled Deleted Users located inside of the Users folder, as shown in Figure 14-3.

Figure 14-3: The Deleted Users folder.

If, by chance, you change your mind and decide to reinstate a deleted user account, you must first re-create the user's account from scratch. Next, using the account that was assigned ownership of the deleted user's data, manually drag the contents from the deleted user's folder into the new user's folder. An accidental deletion of a user account does not translate into data loss. The deleted user's data still exists. If you decide to reinstate the user account, you will need to manually transfer the data from the archive of the deleted user's home directory to the newly created directory for that account.

Password panel

You create user accounts using the Password panel. Here you assign the user account two unique names: name and a short name. You also give the account a password. Users account holders can use either the full name or short name to login. When assigning full names and short names, use any naming system that you like, but keep in mind these names are case sensitive. When tabbing from the Name field to the Short Name field, a short name is automatically generated. But don't worry; at this point, it still can be changed. A short name has a maximum of eight characters, and cannot contain any spaces or the following characters:

< > ' " * { } [ ] ( ) ^ ! \ # | & $? ~

At any time, the full name and password can be changed, but once the account is created, the short name is permanent. After you have chosen your short name, you will need to provide a password. Although OS X will accept more than eight characters for this field, it only checks the first eight. Finally, the last field allows you to provide yourself an optional password hint if desired.

Caution   Do not assign anyone the user name _root._ This name has a special meaning in all operating systems based on Unix, including Mac OS X. If you create a user named root, problems will result.

Besides the full name and short name, each account has a password. The password can be left blank, but in practice should not be. Although a password can be greater than eight characters, Mac OS X only requires the first eight to be recognized. Passwords may contain upper and lower case letters, blank spaces, and extended characters, but colons should be avoided. Mac OS X does not consistently recognize passwords that contain colons.

Creating a user account

You create a user account in the Accounts pane of the System Preferences application. You do not need to log in using an administrator account. If you log in as an ordinary user, you can unlock the settings in the Accounts pane of System Preferences with an administrator's name and password. To create a user account, follow these steps:

1. **Open System Preferences and choose View ➪ Accounts or click the Accounts button.**

2. **To Unlock the user account settings if they are locked, click the Lock button.** In the dialog that appears, enter an administrator's name, the correct password, and then click OK. If you entered a valid name and the correct password, you return to the Users window with all settings unlocked.

3. **Click the plus button located below the unlabeled column on the left-hand side of the Accounts preferences pane to add a new user account, as shown in Figure 14-1.**

4. **Enter a name and a short name.**

5. **Click in the New Password field and enter a password.** Optionally, you may also enter a password hint.

The password hint is displayed if the user enters the password incorrectly three times in a row during login. If you enter a hint, make it a hint not the actual password! As you enter the password in the New User dialog, you will notice that Mac OS X keeps it secret by displaying dots (Lock Font) instead of what you actually type. Because you can't visually check what you have entered, you have to enter it twice consistently to verify it. If the two entries are not consistent, Mac OS X will prompt you to reenter them.

Subsequently, after the account is created, users can log in and change their password on their own. If at a later date a user's password is changed, a dialog appears stating that the user's Keychain password can't be changed to the new account password that you just entered. The existing Keychain password remains in effect until the user logs in *(using the new account password)* and runs the Keychain Access application to update the Keychain password. You can find information on using the Keychain Access application in Chapter 15.

To delete a user account, follow Steps 1 and 2, but instead of clicking the plus button in step three, select the account to be deleted from the unlabeled column on the left-hand side of the Accounts preferences pane and click the minus button to the right of the plus button. Before an account can be deleted, make sure it is not encrypted with FileVault.

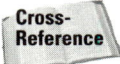
Cross-Reference

For more information on File Vault, turn to Chapter 26

Login Options panel

At the bottom of the list of accounts in the unlabeled column on the left-hand side of the Accounts preferences pane there is a Login Options button. Use this button to configure additional system login options, as shown in Figure 14-4.

✦ **Display Login Window as:** This option changes the login window from a list of users, shown in Figure 14-2, to name and password field.

✦ **Automatically log in as:** Configures Mac OS X for automatic login with a specified user account that is selected within the pop-up menu to the right of this label.

✦ **Hide the Sleep, Restart, and Shut Down buttons:** Determines whether people can restart or shut down the computer by clicking buttons in the login window.

✦ **Enable fast user switching:** Permits more than one user to stay logged in to a computer at the same time without having to quit applications or close documents.

When fast user switching is enabled, the name of the currently logged in user appears in the upper-right corner of the Finder's menu bar as seen in Figure 14-5. To switch between user accounts, click on the menu and select the name of user account you want to switch to. If the selected user account requires a password you will be prompted to enter it as depicted in Figure 14-6, if not, Mac OS X will automatically make the switch. When the transition of user accounts occurs on a Mac that supports Quarts Extreme, the effect will appear as a rotation of a 3-D cube, otherwise the screen will momentarily turn black, before the new account can be used. In order to restart or shutdown a computer that has multiple users logged in utilizing fast user switching, all user accounts must be logged out. If not, you will be prompted with a dialog requesting admin authentication in order to do so. This will result in the loss of unsaved changes in all user accounts that are currently logged in at the time of restart or shutdown.

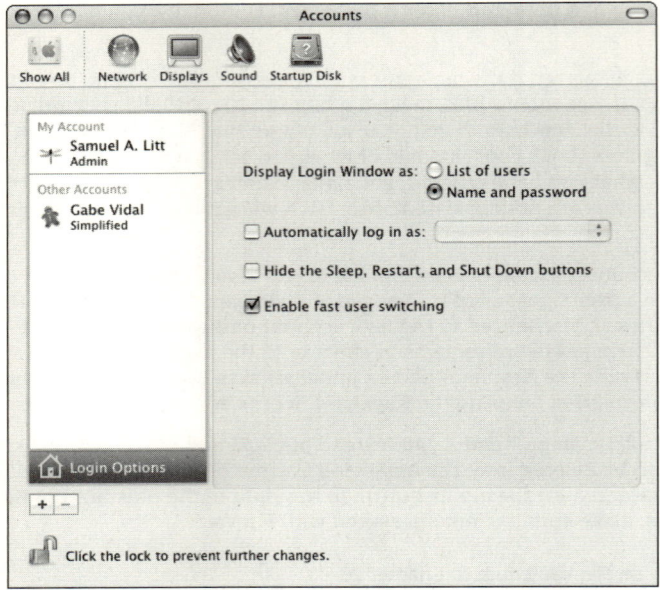

Figure 14-4: Login Options offers additional customization of the login process.

Figure 14-5: Using fast user switching alleviates the need for a logged in user to log out, so another user account can be utilized.

Figure 14-6: Switching to user account that requires the entry of a password will prompt you with a dialog similar in appearance to Mac OS X's initial login screen.

Picture panel

Use the Picture panel, depicted in Figure 14-7, to select a picture or a graphic that will be used as a visual representation of a user account. By default, Mac OS X selects a random picture for each user account. These pictures are used by Mac OS X's login window, as well as by Address Book and iChat applications. Login pictures can be manually chosen as well. By default, Mac OS X provides 30 unsightly selections to choose from. If these do not meet your aesthetic sensibility, use the Edit button as shown in Figure 14-8 to customize your own.

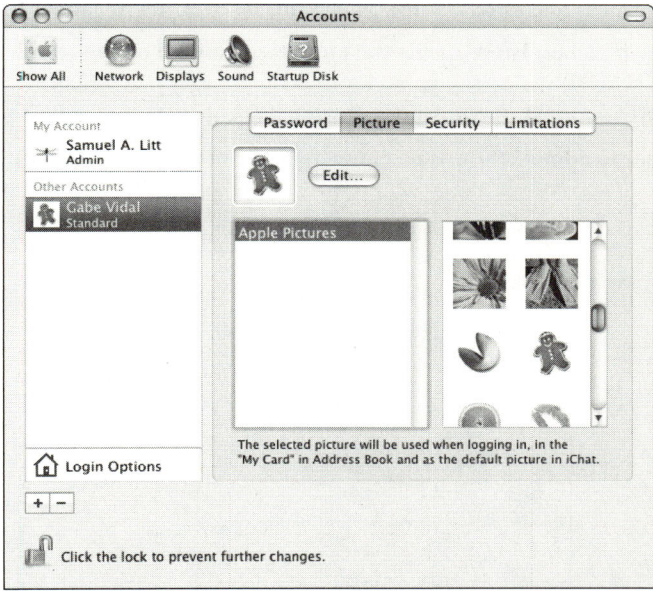

Figure 14-7: Apple provides supplied pictures in the Picture panel.

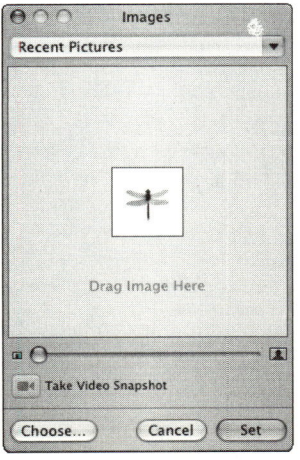

Figure 14-8: Create your own picture selections by taking a video snap shot or using a preexisting image.

Security panel

Use the Security panel to enable home folder encryption and to assign admin privileges to user accounts. FileVault is the name for Mac OS X's on-the-fly home folder encryption mechanism. When enabled, FileVault automatically encodes the data in the home directory into a format that can be accessed by authorized users only. FileVault can be administered via the Security panel as well as the Security preferences pane which is reviewed in Chapter 27.

To set the option to grant a user admin privileges:

1. **Open System Preferences and choose View ➪ Accounts or click the Accounts button.**

2. **Select an account to be administered from the unlabeled column on the left-hand side of the preference pane.**

3. **Click on the Security button at the top of the preference pane.**

4. **Select the Allow user to administer this machine option, as shown in Figure 14-9.**

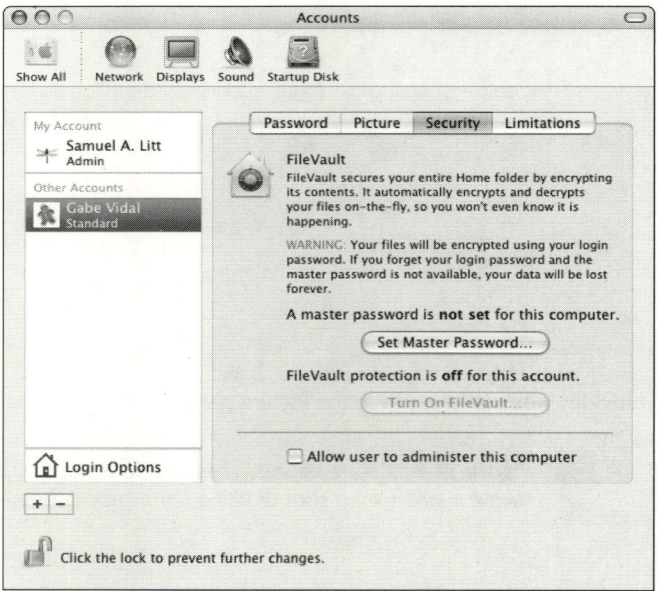

Figure 14-9: Select Allow user to administer this machine, only if you want to grant the account being administered admin privileges; otherwise, makes sure that this option is turned off

Limitations panel

Use the Limitations panel to dictate what users have access to. Limitations can be set for user accounts only. Use the limitations panel as an aid to further enhance Mac OS X's security model. There are three levels of access that a normal user account can be granted: No Limits, Some Limits, and Simple Finder.

✦ **No Limits,** as the name implies, is a user account without any further restrictions other than that of a normal user.

✦ **Some Limits,** as depicted in Figure 14-10, can restrict a user from opening System Preferences, modifying the Dock, changing their password, and burning CDs and DVDs. Access to applications can be restricted on an item-by-item basis.

✦ **Simple Finder** provides a simplified version of the Dock and access to applications solely provided via a My Applications folder in the Dock. As with Some Limits, access to applications can be granted on an item-by-item basis.

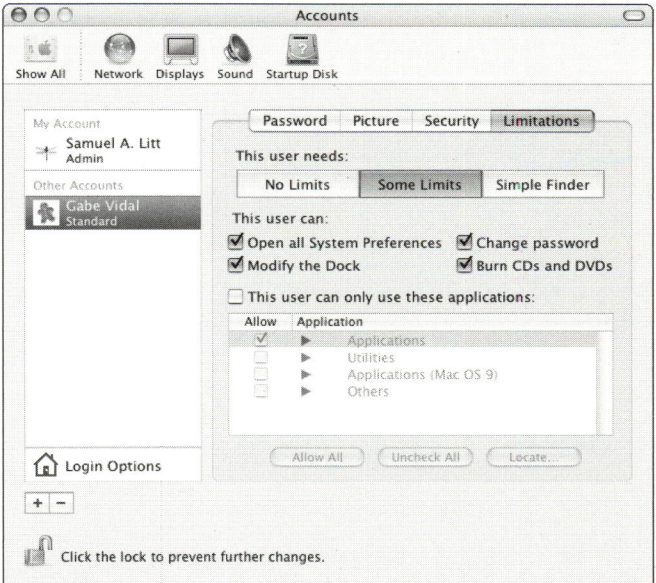

Figure 14-10: Use the Limitations panel to limit the actions of a user account on a Mac OS X system.

Before employing the features of the limitations panel, make sure that are no incompatibilities with any installed third-party applications. To limit a user's capabilities:

1. **Open System Preferences and choose View ➪ Accounts or click the Accounts button.**

2. **Select an account to be administered from the unlabeled column on the left-hand side of the preference pane.**

3. **Click on the Limitations button at the top of the preference pane.**

4. **Grant the user No Limits, Some Limits, Simple Finder by clicking on the corresponding button.**

5. **Select options and capabilities.** You can prevent users from changing their password, from removing items from the Dock, from burning CDs and DVDs, and from opening System Preferences; you can limit users to running specific applications.

6. **Click OK to accept your changes or click Cancel to void them.**

Startup Items panel

The Startup Items panel, shown in Figure 14-11, enables the selection of items that are to be started automatically at the time of login. You can set up a list of documents and applications that you want to open automatically when you log in. You can also designate the order of those items and whether or not they should be hidden. Each user account has its own private list of login items.

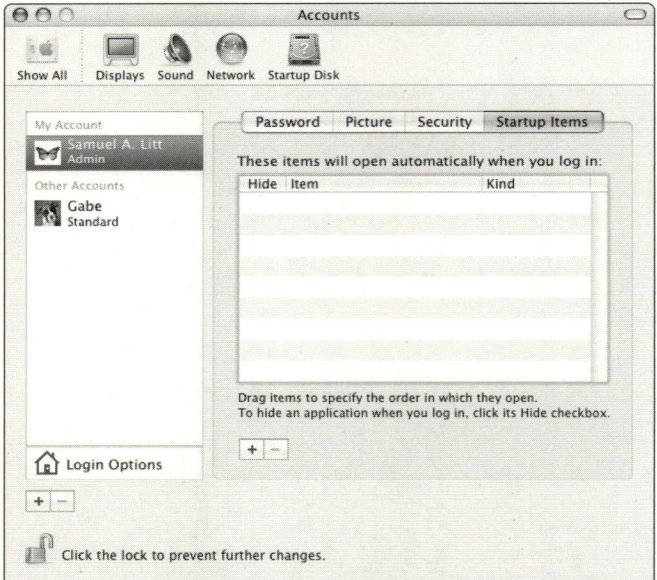

Figure 14-11: Change the list of items opened during login by clicking the Startup Items tab in the Login Preferences window.

 **Tip**   To have the Classic environment start automatically when you log in, use the Classic preferences pane. You can find detailed instructions in Chapter 18.

Adding login items

To have an item to open automatically during login, follow these steps:

1. **Open the Accounts preferences pane inside of the System Preferences application.**

2. **Click on the Startup Items button.**

3. **Click the plus button located below the list of items that will open automatically when you log in.** You can also add items to the Login Items list by dragging their icons from Finder windows or the Desktop to the Login Items list.

4. **In the dialog that appears, select one or more items and click the Open button.** Click once to select one item; Shift-click to select adjacent items; and ⌘-click to select nonadjacent items.

   - **To remove an item:** Select it in the list and click the Remove button.

   - **To rearrange the order in which listed items open during login:** Drag items up or down in the list.

   - **To hide an item automatically when it opens during login:** Click the Hide checkbox next to the application name in the list. A hidden item stays open but doesn't take up any screen space.

Note   If you set an application or a document as a login item and it requires a password to open, it does not open during login. Its icon appears in the Dock, and you must click the icon and enter the password to open the item. Examples of such items include email applications and encrypted documents.

Administering Privileges Using Show Info

Within OS X's GUI, privileges are set via the Finder using the item's Get Info window. Selecting the item within the Finder, and choosing the Get Info command under the File menu or by utilizing the key combination ⌘-I and turning down the chevron adjacent to the label Ownership and Permissions does this.

OS X's GUI groups the assignment of permissions into four selections: Read Only, Write Only (Drop Box), Read & Write, and None. Although folders can be assigned any of the above-specified privileges, files can only be assigned Read Only, Read & Write, or None. When a folder is assigned Write Only, that folder becomes a shared *drop box* for users other than its owner. This means users can drop files onto that folder, but are unable to open that folder or view its contents. Table 14-2 explains the various privileges that can be assigned for an item

Table 14-2: Privilege Settings for Files and Folders

Setting	Privileges Granted for a File	Privileges Granted for a Folder
Read & Write	Open the file. Copy the file. Change, move, and delete the file.	Open the folder. Copy the folder. See enclosed files and folders. Create, change, move, and delete enclosed files and folders.
Read only	Open the file. Copy the file.	Open the folder. Copy the folder. See enclosed files and folders.
Write only	Not applicable.	Drag items into the folder. Save files in the folder.
None	None	None

In Mac OS X, there are three categories for content ownership: owner, group, and other. The owner category is the user account that actually owns the file. In the simplified view this is referred to as You can., but in the detailed view its referred to as owner. By default, Mac OS X displays a simplified view when viewing privileges using the Show Info window. In order to display all of the options you must turn down the chevron adjacent to the details label. Mac OS X does not provide any means of changing group assignment through the GUI. Groups play a greater role within Mac OS X Server. The other assigns privileges for everyone not listed within the owner and group categories.

Note   The movement of files, folders, and applications within an OS X system does not modify privileges. Files do not automatically inherit the privileges of the folder they reside in, and even if you have not been assigned access to a particular file, you can still delete it if you have Read & Write access to the folder it resides in. Locally mounted volumes other than the boot volume can be configured to ignore ownership. When enabled, this will *remove* file security, allowing *all* contents to be accessed by whatever user account is logged in. This feature is enabled by default on external removable media and hard disks. It is controlled via a check-box at the bottom of the Details portion of the Ownership and Permissions section of the Shown Info window for a volume.

Tip   Mac OS 9 does not respect the Mac OS X security model. If an OS X system is rebooted into OS 9, the entire contents of the system including the boot volume are exposed to viewing, modification, and deletion.

You change privileges of a folder or file in the Finder's Info window, shown in Figure 14-12, by following these steps:

1. **Using the Finder click on an item you want to administer privileges for.**

2. **Select Get Info from the Finder's File Menu or use the key combination ⌘-I.**

3. **In the Info window, turn down the chevron adjacent to Ownership & Permissions.**

4. **Turn down the chevron adjacent to Details.**

   Using the selections in the pop-up menus, you can change the owner of the file or the privileges granted to the three categories of ownership. You must be the owner of an item to change its privileges or alternatively you may authenticate using an admin account's name and password.

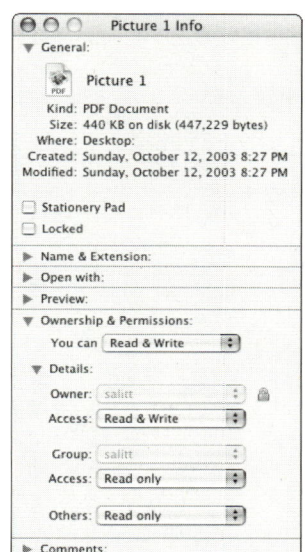

Figure 14-12: Turn down the chevron adjacent to the Details label in order to gain access to all the variables that can be configured within the Ownership and Permissions portion of the Finder's Show Info window.

Summary

Here's what you learned in this chapter:

✦ If you use Mac OS X with an administrator account, you can change all system preference settings and install software in the Applications folder and main Library folder. An administrator can also create, edit, and delete other users' accounts and assign privileges.

✦ If you use Mac OS X with a normal account, you can still administer locked system settings by authenticating with admin user account's name and password.

✦ You create, administer, and delete user accounts in the Accounts preferences pane.

✦ People take turns using Mac OS X by logging in and out. Login can be automatic for one user account, but other user accounts will require manual logging in. Fast user switching allows the simultaneous login of more than one account.

✦ Although some system preferences are global in effect, Mac OS X allows user accounts to be individually customized.

✦ Each user can set up a list of documents and applications to be opened during login, which is configured in the Startup panel of the Accounts preferences pane.

✦ After logging in, users can change their own passwords without the assistance of an admin account.

✦ You can change the privilege settings of your folders and files by using the Finder's Show Info window. You can also set an option to have Mac OS X ignore privilege settings on volumes other than the boot volume.

✦ You should avoid using your Mac with the root account because that account bypasses the safety mechanisms that help maintain Mac OS X's reliability.

✦　　✦　　✦

Setting Up a Local Network

If you have more than one computer in your office or home, you can benefit by connecting them in a network. The idea may seem intimidating, but a simple network is easy to set up and doesn't cost much. Here are some things that you can do with a simple network:

✦ Share one Internet connection among several computers

✦ Share printers

✦ Share files from other computers in your company or home as if their files were on your desktop, and let other computers share files from your computer

✦ Play games designed for multiple players

✦ Access a central database while other computers do likewise

✦ Maintain a group schedule or calendar

✦ Back up hard disks of all networked computers on a central tape drive

✦ Access your hard disk from a remote location over a telephone line or Internet connection

✦ Chat with others on your network or on the Internet

✦ Share your iTunes library

This chapter focuses on setting up a network so that you can use some of these services. We start by discussing the fundamental concepts of a network and how to use these concepts to connect your computer to an Ethernet or AirPort network. You also find out how to configure your network connections in the Network pane of System Preferences and how to easily switch from one configuration to another by using network locations. Additionally, we show you how to set up an AirPort base station and how to share files and connect computers using Bluetooth.

The Networking Concept

Mac OS X is built around the idea of networking. To utilize the power of Mac OS X, you must have a solid understanding of networks and how they work.

Understanding a computer network

The smallest possible network consists of two devices connected directly to each other. For those with broadband Internet access at home, such as DSL or cable modem, you probably connect your computer to your broadband modem using a network cable.

A network's real strength is in its numbers. A network could allow you to share your broadband Internet connection between several computers. This same network could allow you to share a networkable printer as well. You could use iChat to notify someone down the hall that she has a call on line 4. You can use iTunes to listen to your roommate's music collection or even share your own. All sorts of things become possible when you connect your computer to a network. What happens, though, when you want to connect more than just your computer and your cable modem? How do you connect several devices, not just two?

With two devices it was simple: connect them to each other. With several devices, however, we're going to need something else. What we need is a central networking device such as a hub or switch. The network hub or switch connects every device to every other device.

With a hub or switch, you can plug in those two computers along with your networkable printer so that both computers can share the printer. A typical network consists of several devices such as computers and printers connected to each other using a network hub or switch. Connecting your broadband Internet connection to the hub even allows you to share the Internet connection among several computers.

The basic principles of networking are actually fairly simple. However, to build your own network, you need a little more background on how a network actually passes information. Although the basic concept of plugging devices into a hub is very simple, a familiarity with the inner workings of a network as well as basic networking terminology can help you to tailor and optimize your network. If your network ever has any trouble, this working knowledge can help you to troubleshoot those problems. At the very least, having a basic understanding of the vocabulary of networking allows you to find, read, and understand an enormous amount of documentation on the subject.

Understanding layered networks

Computer networks can be broken down into three separate aspects, or *layers:* the physical layer, the communications layer, and the applications layer. These three layers work together seamlessly, one on top of the other, to get your information where it needs to be.

In computer networking theory, these three layers are usually refined into four or more layers. For example, the physical layer discussed in this chapter is usually broken down further into two separate layers: the physical layer and the data link layer. The communications layer can be broken down into three or even four separate layers. Although this refinement is important for an advanced understanding of networking, it is beyond the scope of this book.

The Physical Layer

The first and most obvious aspect of any network is the physical components and how they interact. This is called the *physical layer*. The physical layer is the hardware. It is the wires and all the devices that they connect. Parts of this layer include the network port on your computer or printer, the network cables, network hubs or switches, AirPort Base Stations, an AirPort Card installed in a computer, broadband modems, and much more. Together they make up the physical connection between every device.

These components of the physical layer require a lot of configuration. How fast does your network port send information to the network switch? Which cable leads from the network switch to the printer? What happens when your network card has to send and receive at exactly the same time? It is an incredibly daunting task! Fortunately, all these components can actually configure themselves. They do this by talking to each other using a common language, or protocol. There are several different hardware protocols. However, the Ethernet protocol is the only one that you are likely to see.

Ethernet protocol

For most people, the term Ethernet is synonymous with network, and they aren't far off. Ethernet is by far the most common wired and wireless network in use in homes and offices. An Ethernet network can include computers using Mac OS X, earlier Mac OS versions, Windows, Unix, and many other operating systems. If it can be networked and you've heard of it, you can bet it uses Ethernet.

Token Ring networks are another type of networking. Like Ethernet, the components of a Token Ring network speak to each other. But instead of using the Ethernet protocol, the components use the Token Ring protocol. This makes Ethernet components and Token Ring components incompatible.

Every Ethernet port — whether it is on a computer, printer, cable modem or any other end device — has a unique address called an Ethernet address, or MAC address. (MAC is an acronym for Media Access Control, by the way, not an abbreviation for Macintosh.) This address is a long series of numbers and letters in the form 00:30:65:00:C2:4B. This Ethernet address is how network devices identify each other. Table 15-1 shows OS X 10.3–compatible Macintoshes and their built-in Ethernet capabilities.

Table 15-1: Macs with Built-in Ethernet Capabilities

Mac Model	Gigabit	100Base-T	10Base-T
iMac - all models		✔	✔
eMac - all models		✔	✔
iBook - all models		✔	✔
PowerBook G4 Titanium – (550Mhz-1Ghz)	✔	✔	✔
PowerBook G4 Titanium (400-500Mhz)		✔	✔
PowerBook G4 12″ (867Mhz-1Ghz)		✔	✔

Continued

Table 15-1 *(continued)*

Mac Model	Gigabit	100Base-T	10Base-T
PowerBook G4 15" (Aluminum)	✔	✔	✔
PowerBook G4 17" (1.25-1.33 GHz)	✔	✔	✔
PowerBook G3 Series - Bronze keyboard (Lombard)		✔	✔
PowerBook G3 - FireWire (Pismo)		✔	✔
PowerMac G4 - QuickSilver	✔	✔	✔
Power Mac G4 - Digital Audio	✔	✔	✔
Power Mac G4 - Gigabit Ethernet	✔	✔	✔
Power Mac G4 - AGP Graphics		✔	✔
Power Mac G4 - PCI Graphics		✔	✔
Power Mac G4 Cube		✔	✔
Power Macintosh G3 - Blue and White		✔	✔

Ethernet devices communicate with each other using very small bundles of data called *frames*. Ethernet frames are the Post Office envelopes of your network. Each frame has both the sender's address and the destination's address. Data sent over the network is broken up into pieces that can fit into a frame. Those frames, then, are delivered to the destination. Finally, the destination's network port reassembles these pieces back into the whole.

Making the Ethernet Connection

All Macs that are qualified for Mac OS X are ready to be connected to an Ethernet network. Older Macs commonly used another type of wiring called LocalTalk, but this type of network can't be used with Mac OS X. A LocalTalk to Ethernet adaptor can enable these older Macs for use on an Ethernet network, though.

Ethernet cabling

When you think of an Ethernet network, you probably think of wires. But technically, AirPort wireless networks also use the Ethernet protocol as their physical layer language. AirPort networks are actually wireless Ethernet networks. However, they are rarely, if ever, called that. The common practice is to refer to wired networks as Ethernet networks and wireless networks as AirPort networks or wireless networks.

Looking at Ethernet cables

Ethernet networks may be wired with several types of cable, the most popular being unshielded twisted-pair (UTP). This type of cable looks like telephone cable and uses RJ-45 connectors that look like modular phone connectors, only a little larger. Other kinds of cable include Thinnet, thick coax, and fiber-optic Ethernet cables.

Twisted-pair cable is used in three different capacity networks: 10baseT, 100baseT (also called Fast Ethernet), and 1000baseT (also called Gigabit). All twisted-pair cable is graded according to how well it protects against electrical interference. Category 3 (Cat 3) cable is adequate for 10baseT networks, which have a maximum data transfer rate of 10 Mbps (megabits per second). While adequate for many small networks, this type of network is considered slow by today's standards.

100baseT networks require at least Category 5 (Cat 5) cable, properly installed. These networks have a maximum data transfer rate of 100 Mbps. The rules for installing cable on a 100baseT network, however, are more stringent than for 10baseT. For example, sharp bends in the cable are not allowed.

Gigabit networking requires at least Category 5e (Cat 5e) cable and can sometimes require Category 6 (Cat 6) cable. Gigabit networks have a maximum data transfer rate of 1000 Mbps, or 1 Gigabit per second (Gbps). The rules for installing cable on a Gigabit network are stringent as well.

Some have successfully used Cat 5 cable to run a Gigabit network. While this may work for them, don't count on it. The costs of any cable are insignificant when compared to the costs of installing it properly. If you are going through the trouble of installing the cabling properly, do not waste your time and money on the hope that Cat 5 will suffice. Get the right stuff: Cat 5e or Cat 6.

Using crossover cables

Twisted-pair cables actually contain eight separate wires, twisted into four pairs (hence the name). 10baseT and 100baseT networks use only two of the four pairs, while the other two pairs lie unused. Gigabit uses all four pairs. In each case, however, half of the wires in use are for inbound traffic while the other half are for outbound traffic. Your computer sends data on the outbound wires only and it receives data on the inbound wires only.

Connecting two computers using a standard Ethernet cable does not usually work. All the *outbound* connectors on one computer end up going right into the *outbound* connectors on the other. This won't work! You need some way to cross over the wire somewhere along the line so that outbound goes into inbound.

Hubs, switches, and sometimes devices such as broadband modems and routers do crossing over for you inside the port. To reflect this fact, for example, the ports on a 100baseT switch are designated 100baseTX — the *X* indicates that the port performs this crossover. Sometimes using a hub or switch between two computers isn't an option, though. For example, what if your friend brought her laptop over and wanted to connect it to your computer for a while? In that case, you need a special cable called a *crossover cable*. These are specially made cables that crossover on one end, turning outbound wires into inbound wires.

Most devices that are designed to plug into your computer do so by using a standard Ethernet cable. Put more technically, connecting a 100baseT network port to a 100baseTX network port requires a standard Ethernet cable. The same is true for both 10baseT and Gigabit. Connecting a computer (100baseT) to a cable modem or a network hub (100baseTX) is a good example of this very common kind of configuration.

But when you want to connect two similar devices, such as two computers or two hubs, you need a crossover cable. Put more technically, connecting two 100baseT devices to each other or two 100baseTX devices to each other requires a crossover cable. Connecting a computer (100baseT) to a computer (100baseT) or a hub (100baseTX) to a hub (100baseTX) are good examples of this kind of configuration.

Tip If you try to connect a computer to a hub or switch using a crossover cable, you've just double-crossed yourself! Keep crossover cables clearly labeled so that you don't make this mistake.

Smart network ports

Wouldn't it be nice if each network port could just switch automatically? Then, every cable could be a standard cable. Well, someone figured it out. Some devices now have network ports that automatically change from 100baseT to 100baseTX or 1000baseT to 1000baseTX whenever they need to. Any Macintosh model with built-in 1000baseT (Gigabit) Ethernet has this feature, as do certain versions of Apple's AirPort Base Station. Some of the more expensive network switches will also do this. This feature typically requires at least a standard, four-pair Category 5 cable.

Hubs and switches

At the center of a network is the hub or switch. Both devices serve the same purpose: to connect the various devices on your network at a central point. For many purposes, the subtle differences between a hub and a switch are not important. You could take a hub or a switch and plug in a few computers, a printer or two, a router, and a broadband connection without needing to know the difference between the two devices. The subtle differences, however, quickly become important — even critical — as the demand on your network grows. The wrong device in an otherwise fast network will bring your network to its knees in short order.

Remember that when you send information on an Ethernet network, it is broken down into frames for the journey. Each frame has both the sender's address and the destination's address. So, when your computer sends your document to the printer, that information is broken down into frames and sent down your Ethernet cable to the hub or switch. The hub or switch, then magically sends your frames down the correct cable to the printer. The difference between hubs and switches lies in how they get the right information down the right cable to the right place.

When a hub needs to get the right frame down the right cable, it takes a very simple, brute force approach: just send that frame down *every* cable. When you send an Ethernet frame through a hub to your printer, the hub duplicates that frame and sends it to every single device on the network. Only the destination device, however, recognizes the destination address of the frame and lets it in. Everything else on your network just ignores it.

This works remarkably well for small networks. The problem with this approach is that it generates a lot of extra network traffic because each frame needs to be duplicated for every device on your network. As your network grows, this problem gets worse — and fast. As the network becomes more and more crowded, the Ethernet frames start colliding. Your network is quite capable of dealing with these collisions. The problem is, these network collisions dramatically reduce the efficiency and speed of your network. Even on networks with only a handful of computers, something as ordinary as backing up a computer over the network could cause a very large number of collisions, noticeably reducing the speed of your network. Hubs, therefore, are only appropriate on small networks.

Switches are smart. Instead of broadcasting every single frame to every single device, switches send each Ethernet frame only where it needs to go, creating private paths between devices on your network. Without all of those duplicate frames that a hub generates, your switch can accomplish the same task with significantly less network traffic. More importantly, however, a switch dramatically reduces the number of collisions on your network, even under heavy traffic. This makes switches far more efficient on busy networks or any medium or large network.

It also makes them more secure. The astute or paranoid might have noticed something disconcerting about the nature of a hub. That is that everything you send over the network ends up going to every single device — including every single computer and printer on the network. How can you be sure they aren't reading the information that you send? In short, you can't. This type of network assumes that every other device is going to dutifully ignore your information. And they do, usually. It is possible, albeit difficult, to set up a computer to listen to all the data it receives. If this computer is connected to a hub, receiving every frame on the network, the computer is able to listen to all the traffic on the network. This is called *sniffing* a network. A network switch, on the other hand, sends the information only where it needs to go. From a security standpoint, this makes it significantly harder to listen to all the traffic on a network because your computer is receiving exactly what you are being sent only. But chances are if you are using a hub, your network is very small. So, if your network uses a hub and you have a hacker on your network sniffing around, the problem is the hacker in your bedroom, and not your insecure hub.

Hubs and switches come in many different sizes, measured by the number of network ports they have. The most common sizes are 4-port, 8-port, and 16-port, although you can also find 24-port and 48-port sizes readily. Even larger configurations are available, but these tend to be expensive and very sophisticated. Prices start at about $20 for a generic 4-port 10baseT hub and rise with the number of ports. 100baseT hubs cost more than 10baseT hubs, and switches cost more than hubs. Generally, if a hub or switch supports 100baseT it also supports 10baseT. A hub or switch that supports both speeds will say that it is a dual speed or 10/100 hub or switch. Generally, only switches support Gigabit. Switches that support Gigabit will say so. These switches may or may not support both Gigabit and the slower speeds. Some Gigabit switches offer full support for all three speeds. This is usually indicated by the phrase "10/100/1000." Some Gigabit switches offer only one or two Gigabit-only ports while the rest offer the more standard 10/100 ports. You will often have to look very carefully at the documentation for a switch to determine which ports support Gigabit.

Connecting hubs and switches

If you use up all the ports on one hub or switch, you can connect another hub or switch to it. You can even use hubs and switches together. Connecting hubs is called *daisy chaining*. Up to four hubs can be daisy-chained with twisted-pair cable. Switches are not subject to this restriction.

If you want to connect two hubs or switches, you can do so easily using a crossover cable between any two network ports. Most hubs and switches, however, have a specially designated port for this kind of connection called an *uplink port*.

You don't need a crossover cable if your hub or switch has an uplink port or a port that you can make into an uplink port by setting a switch. Plugging a regular cable into an uplink port has the same effect as using a crossover cable, because the uplink port's wiring is reversed. On some hubs and switches, the uplink port and the port next to it cannot be used at the same time because they are actually the same port, only with two different jacks. Choose one and use it. On other hubs and switches, the uplink port has a button or switch that allows you to change the port from a regular port to an uplink port. In either case, simply use a regular cable to connect the *uplink* port on one hub or switch to any *regular* port on the other hub or switch. Note that connecting two uplink ports would require a crossover cable.

Understanding the lights on a hub or switch

All hubs and switches have lights on them indicating all sorts of information. The most important lights on any switch or hub — aside from the power light, of course, are the *link lights*. Each port has a link light associated with it. Link lights are usually either right next to each port or listed all together on one end of the hub or switch. When two network ports on either end of a cable are connected properly, they automatically establish a *link*. When this happens, the port's link light turns on. Multiple speed hubs and switches show you what speed a port is using. Hubs and switches also indicate traffic and collisions by using lights to indicate such occurrences. Look at the front panel of your device or check the documentation.

The Communications Layer

As strange as it may seem, your Web browser and your email program on your computer don't speak Ethernet. Programs on a computer require a far more sophisticated language than Ethernet to meet their needs. Macintoshes typically use one of two different languages, or protocols: AppleTalk and TCP/IP. These two protocols, in addition to several other less common protocols, are central to the *communications layer*.

In our layered approach to understanding networks, each layer uses the layer below it to achieve its goal. The communications layer, therefore, depends on the physical layer to do its work. In this case, Ethernet frames are responsible for ferrying TCP/IP and AppleTalk packets from place to place.

AppleTalk

AppleTalk has been used on the Macintosh for a long time. Designed in the early 1980s, AppleTalk was intended to allow small workgroups of computers to exchange files, share printers, and remote access. Often called LocalTalk, this early protocol was actually a combination of both the Physical and Communications layers of the network. These networks used LocalTalk cables rather than Ethernet cables to connect devices. Due to limitations built into this early version of AppleTalk, early AppleTalk networks could have no more than 254 devices on them.

In 1989, with the growing prevalence of Ethernet and Token Ring networks, Apple introduced AppleTalk Phase 2. This new version of AppleTalk supported more sophisticated service discovery and a far greater address range of over 16 million possible network devices.

AppleTalk is by far the easiest network protocol to use on a small or medium-sized Macintosh-based network because it is completely autoconfiguring. There is literally nothing to do. Simply connect your devices, make sure that AppleTalk is active, and they will automatically configure themselves to use AppleTalk. But that's not all. When it's time to find a printer or file server on the network, there is no need to remember some ID number or strange name. AppleTalk supports automatic and dynamic discovery of these services on a network. The only way to make AppleTalk any easier to use on a small to medium-sized network would be if the cables plugged themselves in.

As easy as AppleTalk is to use, however, it has its limitations. Windows-based PCs don't talk AppleTalk without additional software. In addition, some of the more sophisticated networking equipment no longer supports AppleTalk. And while AppleTalk supports up to 16 million network devices on a network, it doesn't scale well to very large networks. AppleTalk networks often run into problems far before they reach the 16 million-device barrier.

TCP/IP

TCP/IP is the king of network protocols. It is the most widely used network protocol in use today. It is the language of the Internet. Web pages, email servers, FTP servers, the iTunes Music Store, Instant Messenger programs, and so much more all use TCP/IP. The very name has the word *Internet* in it; IP actually stands for Internet Protocol.

What's in a name?

TCP/IP stands for Transport Control Protocol/Internet Protocol. If that sounds like two protocols instead of just one, you're right. Both *TCP* and *IP* are actually subprotocols of the *Internet Protocol Suite*. Most people, however, refer to the Internet protocols as TCP/IP. So we will, too.

TCP/IP has many strengths. It can handle incredibly large networks. (AppleTalk cannot handle the vast number of computers on the Internet.) TCP/IP was designed from the ground up to handle a virtually unlimited number of computers. This ability to handle incredibly large networks turns out to be good and makes possible TCP/IP's second strength: it's everywhere. Whether it's a Macintosh, a Linux workstation, a network printer, a Windows-based PC, or a cell phone, chances are it uses TCP/IP.

TCP/IP's weakness, however, is usability. It requires configuration and lots of cooperation. Not surprisingly, however, Apple has been hard at work turning TCP/IP into as friendly a protocol as AppleTalk ever was. By working closely with the IETF (Internet Engineering Task Force) on projects such as SLP and ZeroConf, Apple is bringing easy-to-use networking to the rest of us.

How TCP/IP works

Every device on a TCP/IP network needs a unique IP address. The standard form for noting an IP address is in the standard *dotted decimal number* format, which looks like this:

```
192.168.216.105
```

Each IP address has two parts: a *network* address and a *host* address. Every address on a single network must have the same network address. Then, each address has a unique host address. Together, these two parts make up a unique address.

But which part of this address is the network address and which is the host address? Well, that depends on the needs of your network. Because the network address and the host address both come from the same number, the longer one is, the shorter the other one is. Remember, too, that the longer a binary number is, the more possible unique numbers it can make. If your network address consists only of the first few bits, then your host address is very long. In this case, you have a smaller number of possible network addresses but a huge number of possible host addresses for each one of those network address. This would be useful for a huge, international corporation with a gigantic network. They will need a lot of addresses all on one network.

Ethernet Is Multilingual

Ethernet networks support multiple protocols simultaneously. So, you can print to your printer using AppleTalk while you surf the Web using TCP/IP. Modern AppleTalk and TCP/IP can coexist very peacefully. In fact, for several years now Macintoshes have supported AFP over IP, which is the AppleTalk protocol for file sharing (Apple File Protocol) using TCP/IP instead of AppleTalk.

TCP/IP is at the heart of Mac OS X and is tightly integrated. Although AppleTalk is well supported in Mac OS X, many of the services it performs are being replaced by similar functions in TCP/IP. Given its central role in Mac OS X, the following section takes an in-depth look at TCP/IP and how it works.

For example, if you define the first octet as being the network address, then the remaining three octets are used to define the host addresses for each network address. Because the first octet cannot be 0, the theoretical maximum number of network addresses is 255. For technical reasons, this number is actually much smaller, only 126. The host address, then, consists of three octets. So while the total number of possible network addresses is tiny, the possible number of host addresses for each of those network addresses is staggering: over 16 million addresses each!

On the other hand, if your network address consists of most of the first bits of the IP address, then the host address is very short. In this case, you have a very large number of possible network addresses but a small number of possible host addresses for each network address. This would be perfect, for example, for an Internet Service Provider (ISP) with hundreds of customers who each have very small networks. Each customer needs only a few host addresses for their small networks (at home or in a small office). But the ISP needs a very large number of network addresses, one for each customer.

For example, if the network address consists of the first three octets, then the remaining octet is used to define the host addresses for each network address. This means that there are millions of possible network addresses but only 255 possible host addresses for each network address.

Subnets and the subnet mask

Each device on a TCP/IP network needs a unique IP address. This address consists of two parts: the network address and the host address. If all you have is an IP address, however, there is no way to know which part is the network address and which is the host address. So, you need a way of specifying which bits of the address are for what. To do this, you use a setting called the *subnet mask*. The subnet mask is a 32 bit binary number broken down into four 8-bit octets, very similar to the IP address. The subnet mask defines the network address part of the IP address by masking it out. For every bit in the IP address that is used for the network address, the subnet mask's corresponding bit is set to 1. For every bit that is used for the host address, the subnet mask's corresponding bit is set to 0.

For example, if your IP address is 192.168.216.105 and your subnet mask is 255.255.255.0, this is what they look like in their native binary:

Subnet Mask: 11111111.11111111.11111111.00000000

IP Address: 11000000.10101000.11011000.01101001

Table 15-2 shows the subnet mask and IP address broken into network address and host address components.

Table 15-2: Components

	Network Address	Host Address
Subnet mask:	11111111.11111111.11111111.	00000000
IP address:	11000000.10101000.11011000.	01101001

Translated back into dotted decimal form:

	Network Address	*Host Address*
Subnet mask:	255.255.255.	0
IP address:	192.168.216.	105

Now you can determine the network address and the host address of your own IP address. Your network address is 192.168.216 and your host address is 105. More importantly, however, you can also determine which other host addresses are on the same range of addresses as you are. A range of host addresses that all share the same network address is called a *subnet*.

For technical reasons, both first and last addresses in a range are not useable. So, the possible host addresses for your network address are from 1 to 254. So knowing the IP address and the subnet mask of your computer, you can determine which IP addresses are on your subnet and which are outside of your subnet. This determination is central to delivering information from one computer to another regardless of whether they are right next to each other or across the entire planet.

When your computer wants to send data via IP to another device, it must make only one decision: is the destination address on the local network or not. If the destination address *is* on the local subnet, then your computer delivers the information directly to that destination. If the destination address *is not* on the local network, however, your computer delivers the information to a special device on your network called a *router*.

Routers

Routers route. Whether you are from New York City, Los Angeles, or anywhere in between, regardless of how you would otherwise pronounce the word "route," on a network it always rhymes with the word "shout" not "boot." (For those of you from Australia, this makes it much less fun than it might otherwise be.) In a sense, routers are very uncomplicated devices. A simple router has two network ports. These ports are often called the LAN (or Local Area Network) port and WAN (or Wide Area Network) port. The LAN port is connected to your network and has an IP address within the range of your network's subnet. The WAN network port is connected to a second network and has an IP address within the range of that other network's subnet. In the router is a table of information telling the router exactly which addresses are on which side of the router. All this router has to do is direct traffic in the appropriate direction.

When your computer determines that a destination address is not on the local subnet, it passes that data, in the form of an IP packet, to the router. Your computer knows the address of the router from the TCP/IP settings on your computer. This setting is called the *router* or *gateway* address. The router then makes the same decision: is the destination address of this packet on the local subnet of this second network or not. If so, the packet is delivered. If not, the packet is forwarded to the next router.

IP addresses

In order for a device to work on the Internet, it needs an IP address that has been assigned from a pool of available addresses. IP addresses are usually assigned by your ISP or your local network administrator. Whatever the case, however, IP addresses are not arbitrary.

Public and private

There are two classes of IP addresses: public and private. Public IP addresses are standard, fully functional addresses. If there were enough of them, there would be little need for private IP addresses. As it is, however, we are running out of public addresses. So to conserve addresses, private addresses were created.

Private IP addresses are not fully functional addresses. Without any help, in fact, a private IP address could never communicate with any device out on the Internet at all. This is because private IP addresses are not routable. In order to use a private IP address on the Internet, your router has to be configured to do so. This feature of a router to route private IP addresses is called Network Address Translation, or NAT. With NAT, your router's WAN port gets one real IP address. Your network, however, gets private IP addresses. When a device on your network wants to get information from the Internet, it asks the router for help. The router pretends to be that device for a moment and makes the request for you. When the router receives a reply, it then forwards that reply back to that device. From the outside world, then, the only device that ever makes a request for information is the router. For the purposes of a transaction, your private IP address is *translated* into a public address and then back again on the return trip. Through this method, you can have thousands or even millions of devices all accessing the Internet without using more than a single real IP address.

From the Internet's point of view, however, your network is mostly invisible. The only part of your network that anyone else can see is the WAN port of your router. This is both a blessing and a curse. The blessing is that this makes your network very difficult to hack. The curse is that some network services don't work very well with private addresses. If you had a server, for example, such as a Web server, FTP server, or even a hosted network game such as Quake or Unreal Tournament, no one from the Internet would ever see your computer.

Private IP addresses are easily identified because they fall into one of three different ranges:

> 10.0.0.0 through 10.255.255.255

> 172.16.0.0 through 172.31.255.255

> 192.168.0.0 through 192.168.255.255

There is a fourth range of addresses that is not a public set of addresses. While it is not classified as a private range either, it is private in effect. Here it is:

> 169.254.0.0 through 169.254.255.255

This range is special and is discussed in the following section.

TCP/IP configuration

Devices can be configured to use TCP/IP in many different ways. In this section we will cover the reasons for each method. At the end of the chapter, we will walk you through actually setting up the method you choose.

Manual configuration

The most obvious method for configuring a device is to do it by hand. This is called *manual configuration*. In this method, you are prompted to enter all the pertinent information in appropriate places. Each device that needs to be configured in this manner needs to be done individually.

DHCP and BootP configuration

While this would be a simple matter for a small network, configuring a large network this way would be too time consuming. Fortunately, there is a more automated way to configure a device to use TCP/IP. A device may be able to obtain its TCP/IP configuration from a special server on a network called a *DHCP server*. DHCP stands for Dynamic Host Configuration Protocol and is often used to configure the TCP/IP settings of a whole network of computers automatically. Some DHCP servers require that the client have a *DHCP Client ID* specified in order to obtain the configuration settings. BootP servers are also capable of automatically configuring devices on a network.

When a computer that is set up to receive its TCP/IP configuration from a DHCP server cannot contact that server, it configures itself by choosing a random IP address from the range:

169.254.0.0 through 169.254.255.255

In theory, an entire network of computers set to use DHCP to configure themselves would work together perfectly in the absence of a DHCP server. This, however, could cause problems depending on the different services your network provides, such as Internet Access and file servers.

PPP and PPPoE configuration

Dial-up modem communications are also able to automatically configure the connecting device with the appropriate TCP/IP settings. Standard modem connections to the Internet use a protocol called PPP, or Point-to-Point Protocol, to establish the connection. The PPP connection is responsible for configuring the TCP/IP settings of your computer in this case.

Many DSL providers use a protocol called PPPoE for connecting you to the Internet. PPPoE stands for PPP over Ethernet. In this case, your DSL connection creates an Ethernet network over the telephone line all the way to your ISP. PPPoE is a version of PPP for Ethernet networks. Just as with a dial-up modem connection, PPPoE is responsible for configuring the TCP/IP settings of your computer.

Lastly, AOL modem connections have their own proprietary method for configuring TCP/IP.

Static versus dynamic IP addresses

If your computer is configured to obtain its TCP/IP configuration from a DHCP server, it does so automatically whenever you need to connect to the Internet. When it contacts the DHCP server it asks for a lease on an IP address. If the DHCP server grants the lease, that lease is good for a certain predefined time. At the end of that time, your computer will have to get a new lease. This happens automatically whenever it needs to happen. There is no guarantee, however, that you will always get the same address each time your computer asks for an address. This is called a dynamic IP address because it can change.

Not all DHCP servers give out dynamic IP addresses, although it is very common. It is possible for a DHCP server to be set up so that it always gives the same address to the same device. In this case, the DHCP server would be giving out static IP addresses, even though it would be doing so automatically whenever they were needed. But typical DHCP servers give out dynamic IP addresses. So do most BootP servers and PPP servers. The only kind of TCP/IP configuration that is always static is a manually assigned IP address.

Domain name service servers

Every device on the Internet is identified by a unique IP address. But when you open your Web browser and go to a Web site, you don't type in the IP address of the Web site you want to go to. Who could remember all those numbers? To make it easier to get around, the Internet has a naming scheme to help. Now instead of having to remember that Apple's Web site is at the IP address 17.112.152.32, all we have to remember is www.apple.com.

But how does your browser (or your email software or your FTP client) know that www.apple.com equals 17.112.152.32? The answer is that your computer asks a domain name service server, also called a DNS server. DNS servers are responsible for keeping a comprehensive list of which names go with which addresses. In order to function properly then, every computer must know the address of at least one DNS server. If your computer cannot contact a DNS server to resolve a name into an address, you will not be able to contact the destination. To prevent this kind of problem, most computers will hold a list of several DNS servers if you want them to. If the first DNS server in the list does not respond, the computer automatically asks the next server in the list.

Rendezvous

Rendezvous is a collection of technologies that work together to provide automatic network configuration and service discovery. In particular, Rendezvous uses three core technologies: link-local addressing, Multicast DNS, and DNS service discovery. All these technologies are open projects of the Internet Engineering Task Force. Apple's code for Rendezvous is open source.

Rendezvous can automatically configure a device to use TCP/IP *without* a DHCP or BootP server. When a device is added to a network without any means of automatic configuration, such as a DHCP or BootP server, Rendezvous automatically configures the device *link-local addressing*. In link-local addressing, the device randomly chooses an address from a range of addresses set aside by the Internet Assigned Numbers Authority (IANA) for link-local addressing and assigns that address to itself. It then broadcasts a message over the network to determine if that address is in use. If it is, then it randomly chooses another address and tries again until it finds an address that is not in use. After the device has assigned itself an unused address, it is ready to send and receive IP traffic.

Rendezvous can also automatically and dynamically discover new services on a network, such as printers and servers. To do this, Rendezvous uses a combination of Multicast DNS and DNS service discovery to advertise servers on a network and then to find those services when needed.

The two functions of Rendezvous, automatic network configuration and service discovery, may sound familiar. This isn't the first time us Macintosh folk have been able to just turn on a computer, plug in into a network and find all the servers on a network without having to configure anything. That's because AppleTalk can already do these things. But AppleTalk didn't do it as well as Rendezvous does.

First, Rendezvous is far more efficient about it. Whether it is AppleTalk or Rendezvous doing the work, all of this automatic configuration and service discovery generates network traffic. Rendezvous is much more intelligent, however. Rendezvous is also very extensible. AppleTalk really worked only for finding printers and file servers. Adding completely different kinds of services would have been daunting. Rendezvous supports just about any service you can imagine. But most importantly, Rendezvous manages to do what AppleTalk did using TCP/IP instead.

IPv6

The IP address range that we've discussed so far is called IPv4. IP addresses in this range are 32-bit addresses. There are approximately 4.2 billion possible addresses in this range, although many of those addresses are not useable. While this may sound nearly infinite, it is barely enough. Some estimates suggest that we are using about 65% of the useable addresses already. Consider how quickly the remaining 35% will go when every cell phone, every T.V., every refrigerator, and every air conditioner also have their own IP addresses. Or, more importantly, imagine what will happen when all of China goes online in the next decade. Suddenly 4.2 billion doesn't sound so big any more.

To alleviate this problem, the people that brought you IPv4 have been hard at work designing an upgrade. This upgrade is called IPv6. Among the many benefits incorporated into IPv6, the most obvious is the size of the new IP addresses. Instead of using 32-bit addresses, each address is now 128-bits long. A 128-bit long binary number as a lot of possible combinations: 2^{128} possible combinations. This works out to be: 340,282,366,920,938,463,463,374,607,431,768, 211,456.

Understanding the size of that number really isn't possible by just looking at that string of numbers. So consider this: according to the U.S. Census Bureau, the population of this planet as of mid-year 2003 is approximately 6,302,486,693. If we were to divide up the IPv6 addresses giving each person on the face of the Earth an equal number of addresses, each person would get 53,991,762,854,316,031,771,016,167,424! Each of us could have our own IPv4 Internet to ourselves without having to share a single IP address with anybody else on the planet. Even then, each of us would still have more than 12 million billion entire Internets we aren't using!

For years now, manufacturers of network devices such as routers have been working to add support for IPv6 into their products. Apple added support for IPv6 into Mac OS X quite some time ago. But Mac OS X 10.3 adds an easy-to-use graphical user interface for configuring those settings. Currently, most networks do not use IPv6. Getting an IPv6 network to work with the rest of the Internet requires some configuration on the network level. If your network uses IPv6, your network administrator will be able to tell you what settings to make on your computer. But whenever the rest of the world decides to move to IPv6, Mac OS X will be ready.

The Application Layer

The final layer of a network is the *application layer*. When a Web browser gets a Web site to display for you, when your email program checks for new email messages, or when you print, your computer uses the communications layer to get the information to and from the destination. The application layer is responsible for coordinating communications.

It is possible for a computer to be a Web server and an email server at the same time using the same IP address. But how does your browser know to download a Web page, and your email program know to download your new email? It turns out that each IP address is broken down into something called *ports*. These ports are numbered 1 through 65,535. Only one service can use a port at a time. For example, Web servers use port 80 by default. Technically, when you type in the address for Apple's Web site, you should have to specify not only the IP address but the port as well. So, Apple's Web server is at 172.112.152.32 port 80. The shorthand for specifying the full IP address would be 172.112.152.32:80. Web browsers, however, know that most Web sites are on port 80. So, unless you specify otherwise, they will assume that you mean port 80.

Every service you use on a network has at least one port associated with it. When your email software checks for email, it checks a POP email server using port 110. Sending email is usually done using an SMTP server on port 25. When you log into an FTP server and browse the contents, your FTP software connects to the server using port 21. Downloading files from an FTP server is usually done using port 20, however.

Using Firewall Protection

A firewall is a protective gateway for network traffic, preventing and allowing traffic based on a set of rules. Firewalls are typically in one of two places: they are either installed on your computer as software to protect your computer or they are hardware devices on your network that protect your whole network from outside attacks.

In this sense, a NAT-enabled router is a kind of firewall by default: it only allows certain packets back through to the inside. But NAT-enabled devices are not very good firewalls. A good firewall analyzes each packet as it comes or goes and either accepts or rejects it based on a set of rules that you define.

For example, if you had a Web server on your network and a firewall protecting your network, you would want to set up a rule that allowed any traffic going to your Web server on port 80 to pass through while traffic to any other address and any other port is denied. Managing a firewall can be tricky, however. Depending on the services you need to use, you may find that a firewall will prevent certain services from working through it. When in doubt, check the documentation for the service in question. If you are trying to use Timbuktu through a firewall for example, check the Timbuktu Web site for help on configuring a firewall for use with Timbuktu, for example. There are usually detailed instructions about which ports the service uses. Another good references is the Internet Assigned Numbers Authority (IANA). The IANA keeps a list of well known ports for reference at `www.iana.org/assignments/port-numbers`.

The Network Preference Pane

Although at first it is easiest to use tools like the Internet Connect application and the Setup Assistant, as your OS X and networking prowess increase, you'll want to begin to poke around in the Network pane of System Preferences. Doing so provides you with more advanced troubleshooting and more accurate information than the simpler methods, and gives you full manual customization and control over your Mac's network related behavior. After setting up or connecting to your network, it's possible that you'll want to change or add some settings here. Because Mac OS X does do a phenomenal job of automatically handling and sensing network connections, it's also possible that you won't need to make any changes at all. Access the Network Preference Pane by opening the System Preferences and clicking on the Network icon.

Understanding ports and locations

Max OS X handles your network connections through a kind of hierarchy. The first stage is your computer's *location*. Setting up a location implies that you will really be connecting from different physical locations, but it can be simply creating a specific preference set for a specific connection type that you have. You don't have to have a portable machine to set up locations. For example, let's say your cable connection also gives you a free dial-up connection. You can set up a separate dial-up location for use if your cable service is ever out. The next stage is the network ports. Under each location, you can configure multiple ports for connections. A port is a way you connect to a network, like your Ethernet port, or your AirPort card. The default is to have different ports active on a single location, thereby allowing you to use more than one connection per location. The final stage we'll call priority. Within an individual location, OS X lets you specify the *priority* in which ports are used. For example, it is possible to have your modem, your AirPort, and your Ethernet port all configured for one location. But, if you've got a good AirPort signal, you wouldn't want your Mac to start dialing up! To avoid this, OS X lets you choose which port to use first. If you have Ethernet set for first priority, after the Mac senses a good Ethernet signal, it will still take IP addresses from, say, an AirPort connection, but it won't connect to the Internet with that IP unless the top-priority one, the Ethernet, drops off. Then OS X will *fall over* to the other connection, more than likely without you even noticing. Because your Mac can actually have multiple IP addresses at the same time (from different ports), it might seem difficult to determine how, indeed, you are actually connected. A bit later we discuss the first thing that you see when you open the Network preference pane, the Network Status screen, which helps you determine just how you are connected. You can also change locations from this initial screen, by selecting different ones from the Location menu. You can edit and create new ones from this menu as well. Notice that the default location of a new Mac is always the Automatic setting, a preconfigured hierarchy of ports to make automatic sensing of a connection as effective as possible. Port-order/hierarchy and locations are discussed later in this chapter.

Tip 💡 You can have OS X assist you in configuring network settings. Clicking on the Assist Me button brings up a specialized version of the Mac OS Setup Assistant for aiding in the setup of a network. It is similar to the Setup Assistant covered in Chapter 6, but more in tune with the Network preference pane.

Network status display

Open the System Preferences application by choosing it in the Apple menu. The System Preferences application is located in the Applications folder. It is also in the Dock, if you haven't dragged it out of there. After System Preferences is open, choose the Network pane by clicking on its icon. The first thing you see is called the Network Status area. (See Figure 15-1.) This is an overview of what's going on, network-connection-wise, in your Mac's world. You'll notice two different pull-down menus. One is for choosing your location (we get to that later) and the other is entitled Show. What's being shown in the network status screen is a list of all your active network ports and their status as related to Internet connectivity.

When looking at the Network Status screen, you see three columns, one with an iChat-style colored status indicator dot, one with the name of the network port, and one with a brief summary of how the port is connected. A green dot means that the port is active, that is, you've got an IP address, and you are connected to the Internet. Next to the port name (for example, AirPort), OS X gives you a summary of exactly how you are connected. In Figure 15-1, the Mac in question tells you that it's connected through a Base Station called Warri's Wireless, and that it's getting a DHCP address from it. A red dot indicates that the port is inactive. For example, a red dot next to an Ethernet port (Built-In Ethernet) indicates that the cable is not physically plugged in, and your Mac tells you this in the summary area. A red dot next to a modem port indicates that you are not dialed up. A red light next to an AirPort port indicates that there is no wireless signal. An orange dot is an in-between state. In Figure 15-1, the Ethernet DHCP port has an orange dot, and OS X tells you exactly why this is so: The Ethernet cable is plugged in, but the Mac does not have an IP address. Further troubleshooting reveals that the TCP/IP settings were incorrectly set for a manual address.

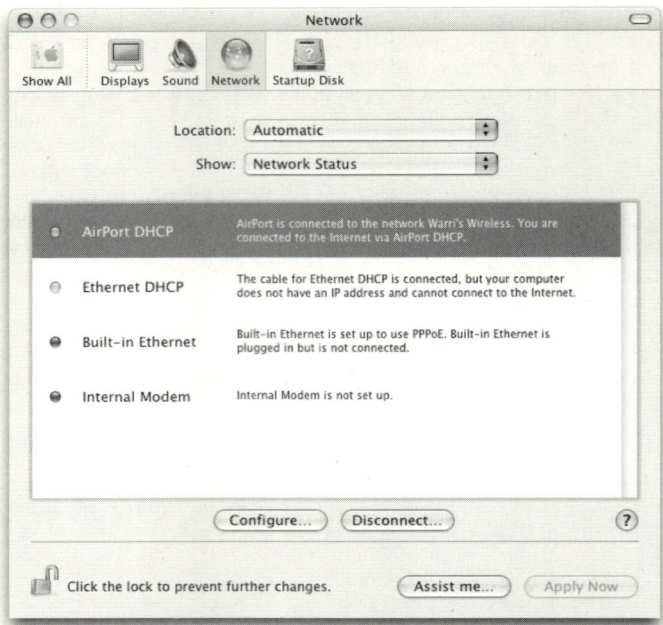

Figure 15-1: The Network Status display provides a quick display of your network connectivity.

The order in which the ports appear in the list are important, because they designate in which order your Mac prefers a connection. In Figure 15-1, AirPort is first in the list, and thus the Mac connects over AirPort if a signal that yields an IP address is present. If that is not the case, then the Mac defaults to the next available connection, and so forth down the list. In this way, it is possible to have many different IP addresses at the same time. You could be connected to an AirPort Base Station and have a valid IP address from it, have an Ethernet cable plugged in and have a valid IP from that network, *and* be dialed up with your internal modem and have an IP address from that connection as well. Each port would show up in the Network Status as having a valid IP address, and thus display a green light in the left column. Although you can have multiple IPs, you can only be connected with one at a time, and again, the Network Status will tell you which port you are actually connected to the Internet with, even though there are multiple ports with IP addresses. In Figure 15-2, both Ethernet and AirPort have valid IP addresses, but because the AirPort connection is first in the list, your Mac tells you that it is actually connected to the Internet with AirPort. If for some reason the AirPort signal fades out, the Ethernet connection takes over.

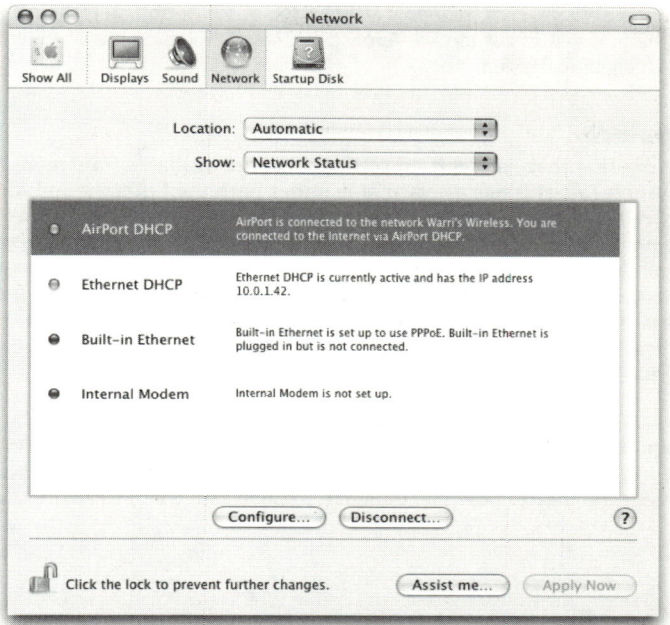

Figure 15-2: Let the colored dots be your guide. The Network Status display pictured here indicates how you are connected; in this case, both AirPort and Ethernet are being given IP addresses, and AirPort takes priority as it is first in the list.

Configuring the port settings

Now that you're aware of your network status, you can configure your ports, your connection methods. It might be that after viewing the Network Status, you've determined that your Mac is set up and accessing the Internet with reckless abandon. For AirPort and Ethernet, the default connection types are DHCP. Therefore, all you should have to do is plug the cable in or select the AirPort network, and if your network is set up to do so, your Mac will automatically take an address, plug and play, no configuration necessary. Whether this is the case, you should become familiar with all the wonderful things that Network preferences has to offer. The following section covers configuring AirPort, Ethernet, Modem, Bluetooth, and Infrared ports.

Unlocking Network preferences settings

Before you can change any settings, you may need to unlock the Network preference pane. If you are not an administrator of the machine, you'll need to get an admin name and password before you can make changes.

Note After changing network settings, click the Apply Now button at the bottom of Network preferences to retain them. If you forget to click Apply Now, Mac OS X asks you whether you want to save your changes as needed.

Common setting panes

It is important to recognize that there are certain settings that are available from more than one port. For example, AppleTalk settings are available under both the Ethernet and AirPort settings. Proxies and TCP/IP are also available under multiple ports, and moreover, can be configured individually per port. This multiple-availability is due to the fact that different connection methods still call upon some similar configurations. Because of this arrangement, we first look at the nonport-specific panel settings, and then move on to configuring the individual ports. You can access the network port settings either by clicking on one from the Network Status list and clicking the Configure button, or by scrolling to the one you wish to choose in the Show menu.

TCP/IP

The TCP/IP configuration is available under every port — AirPort, Ethernet, Modem, and USB Bluetooth Modem Adaptor, because your TCP/IP settings are the very numbers by which you are granted Internet access, no matter how you connect. Typical Ethernet TCP/IP settings are shown in Figure 15-3.

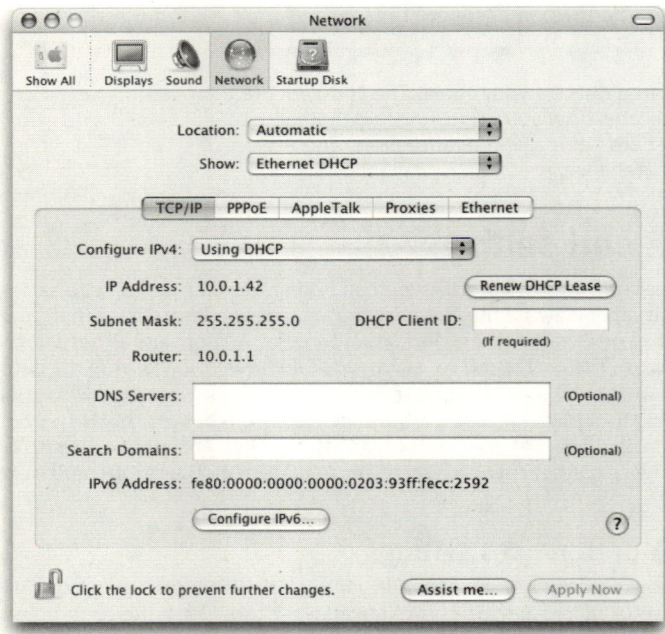

Figure 15-3: Every port has TCP/IP settings. These belong to an Ethernet port.

The connection choices in the TCP/IP pane differ based on the port you have chosen, but, in order to connect, your Mac always needs certain information, whether provided to it or manually set. An IP address, subnet mask, router address, and DNS servers are the minimum settings you'll need. When using Ethernet and AirPort ports, simply enter the relevant information in the appropriate fields or choose a dynamic connection method. When using a modem, PPP is the usual configure option. In the following list, you find the options that are present in the TCP/IP configuration screen.

✦ **Configure:** The method for obtaining some of the other TCP/IP settings for the network connection, such as Manually, Using PPP, Using DHCP, Using DHCP with a fixed IP address, or Using BOOTP.

✦ **DHCP client ID:** May be required by your Internet provider to authorize access to your account, especially if you have a cable modem. This setting is present only when the Configure method includes DHCP.

✦ **IP Address:** The numerical address for the network connection. This address is a set of four numbers separated by periods, such as 17.254.0.91. This setting is provided automatically by some Configure methods.

✦ **Subnet Mask:** Works in tandem with the IP address.

✦ **Router:** The IP address of a machine that connects your local network to other networks or the Internet. This setting can be changed only when the Configure method is Manually. Leave this setting blank if your network has no router or gateway.

✦ **Domain Name Servers:** One or more IP addresses of computers that translate alphabetic addresses, such as `www.apple.com` to IP addresses. Put each address on a separate line. This setting is provided automatically by some Configure methods. Domain Name Servers is usually abbreviated DNS.

✦ **Search Domains:** One or more domain names, such as nps.gov or berkeley.edu that Mac OS X uses to resolve a partial Internet or network address. For example, if Search Domains contains apple.com, then Mac OS X resolves the partial Internet address www as `www.apple.com`, livepage becomes `livepage.apple.com`, store becomes `store.apple.com`, developer becomes `developer.apple.com`, and so forth.

AppleTalk

AppleTalk is available under the AirPort and Ethernet connection methods. If you need to use AppleTalk (you might have a network printer or a file server that requires it), you can enable it by checking its box in the AppleTalk pane, as shown in Figure 15-4.

If your computer is connected to a network that's divided into multiple AppleTalk zones, the AppleTalk tab of Network preferences also specifies the zone in which your computer resides. If your computer is connected to a network with only one zone, you won't have any zones from which to choose.

You should leave the Configure setting at Automatically unless you are an AppleTalk expert. If you are an expert, you know how to set the AppleTalk Node ID and Network ID, which are the settings that appear when you change the Configure setting to Manually.

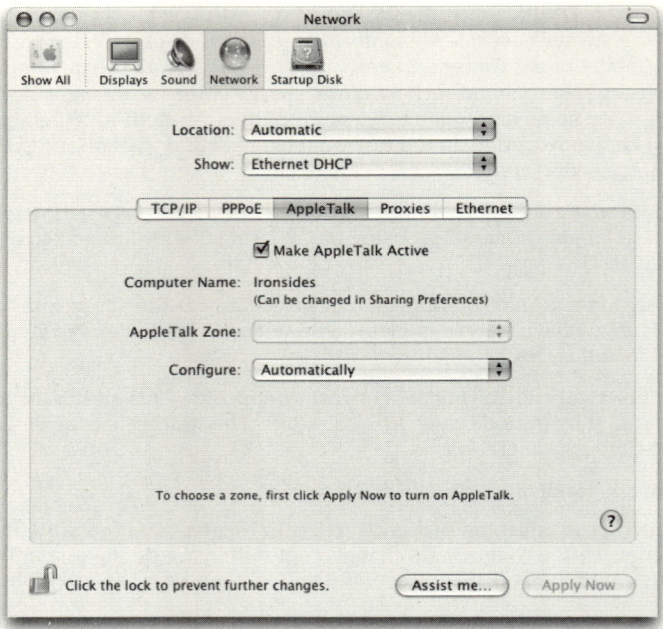

Figure 15-4: Activate AppleTalk with a single click.

Proxies

The Proxies pane looks the same from every port. If your computer connects to a local network that is protected from the Internet by a firewall, you may need to configure a port's Proxies settings. Here, you can specify the proxy servers, which some firewalls use as buffers between a local network and the Internet for privacy, security, and speed. Figure 15-5 shows the Proxies pane.

If your Internet connectivity is fine, and you can access everything you need to, then you don't need to worry about proxies. A network that does have proxy servers almost certainly has a network administrator who can tell you how to configure the Proxies settings. On the left side, you select the proxy server to configure. Check the box if you need to use it. On the right side is a space to type in the Proxy server address; the colon separates the port number that the proxy is set for. Some proxy servers need a password, which can be set by clicking the relevant button. Towards the bottom of the pane you can type in hosts and domains whose proxy settings you want to bypass, for example, if you are on the same network that your email server is on, you might not want to go through the proxy server to access your own local network.

The Proxies pane also lets you choose whether or not to use Passive FTP Mode. When you start an FTP connection, the connection is initiated over the FTP port (20 or 21). In Passive mode, instead of monopolizing the port for the length of your file transfer, the file transfer is done over a different, unused port, which frees up the FTP port for more connections. However, if an FTP site has a firewall in place, Passive FTP usually won't work, because the unused port intended for the file transfer is usually blocked by said firewall. If you are unable to make a successful FTP connection, turn off Passive FTP mode and try again.

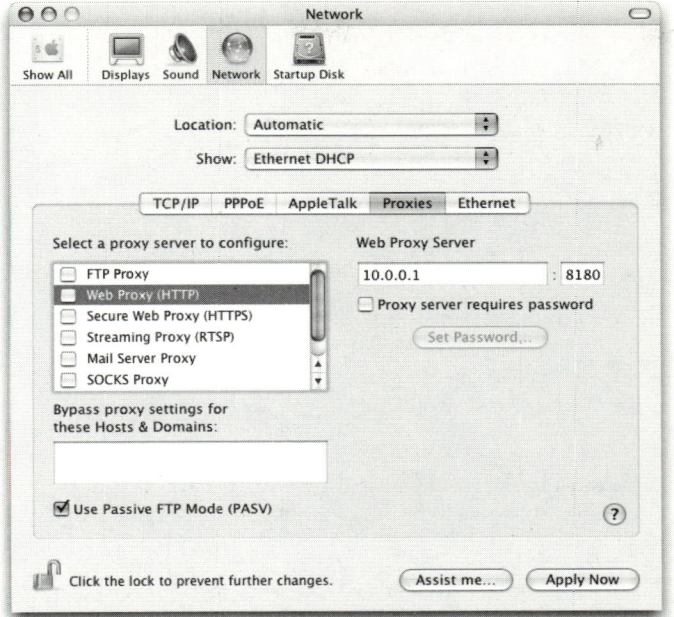

Figure 15-5: Bypass proxy restrictions in the Proxies pane.

Configuring AirPort

Click the Configure button from the Network Status screen after clicking on AirPort in the list, or use the Show menu to choose it. Under the AirPort section are four panels. Figure 15-6 shows the AirPort configuration screen.

AirPort

This pane shows your AirPort card's hardware address, also called a MAC address. In certain situations, such as a secure wireless network that recognizes computers by their hardware address, you'll need to know how to find yours. In this pane, you can specify the behavior of your AirPort connection, that is, which network to join by default. Leaving the setting at Automatic will cause your Mac to try to connect to the nearest network it can find. Choose a specific network by pulling the menu down and changing it to join a specific network. Enter a password if necessary. If you've got a bunch of locations, or switch networks frequently, setting a specific default connection is a good idea.

At the bottom of the window are two checkboxes. Check the first one if you want your Mac to be able to create its own network, such as a computer-to-computer network. Check the second one if you want to display the AirPort status icon in the menu bar and it is not there. Click Apply Now to save your changes.

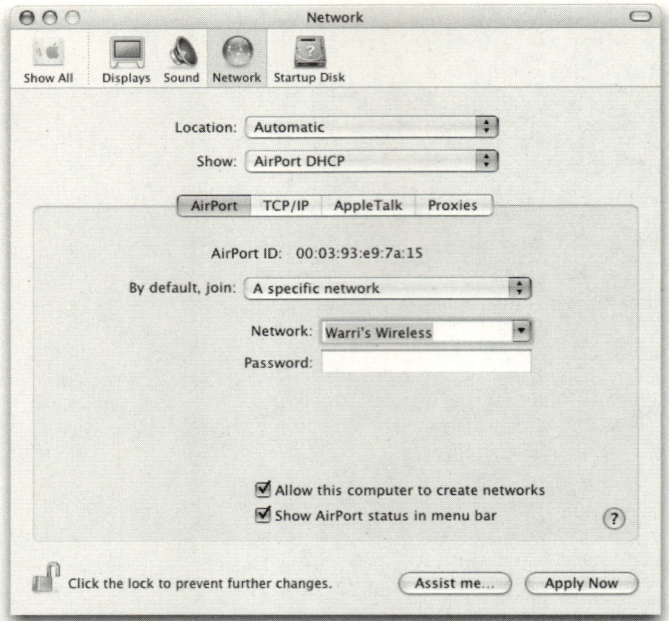

Figure 15-6: Take charge of your AirPort settings here.

TCP/IP

This is the place. Time to type in or select your Internet configuration settings. These terms should all be familiar, as we discuss them in the beginning of this chapter. Choose the appropriate information and type it all in, or make your selections for receiving a dynamic address. If you are having trouble getting a DHCP address, try clicking the Renew DHCP Lease button. This requests a new lease on the address that you have signed out, or if you have no address, a new one altogether. You also have the option to configure IPv6 (as opposed to IPv4), which is a new form of IP addressing that allows for a greater number of total addresses. As of now, it's pretty rare, and you may have to have a network admin tell you how to configure it, if necessary. Click on the button to turn it from automatic, to manual, or to turn it off.

AppleTalk

Click the AppleTalk box to make AppleTalk active. As it seems certain that it is slowly being phased out, you might not need to use it; in fact, the default is that it is turned off.

Proxies

Configure your AirPort connection to use proxy servers in the Proxies pane. Click the Apply Now button to save changes.

Tip   You can move most menu bar icons by pressing the Command key and dragging the icon. Drag the icon left or right to change its position relative to other icons on the right side of the menu bar. Drag the icon off the menu bar to make it vanish in a puff of smoke.

Configuring Ethernet settings

If you need to configure your Ethernet port, click on Built-In Ethernet from the Status menu, or scroll to it in the Show menu. The Ethernet option, within the Ethernet configuration screen, is displayed as shown in Figure 15-7.

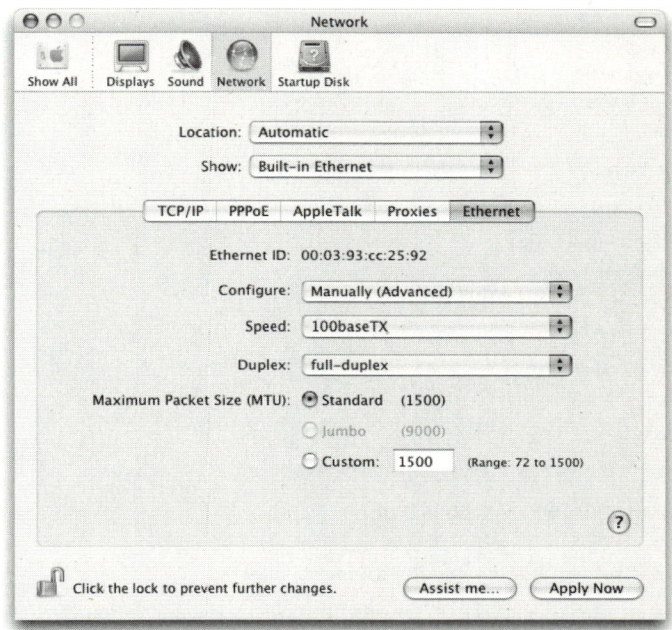

Figure 15-7: Take charge of your Ethernet-specific settings here.

TCP/IP

Same deal here as with AirPort. Configure as necessary, whether it be for a manual IP address, or a dynamic one. Hit the appropriate button to renew your DHCP lease if you need to. If you need to use IPv6, do so.

PPPoE

If your computer connects to the Internet via DSL, your Internet provider probably requires that you use PPPoE to start each Internet session. You can enter your account name, password, and other information by clicking the PPPoE pane. If the Connect Using PPPoE option is selected, Network preferences displays a PPPoE Options button, and clicking this button displays a dialog in which you can set options that affect the PPPoE session. Figure 15-8 shows the additional settings in the PPPoE Options dialog.

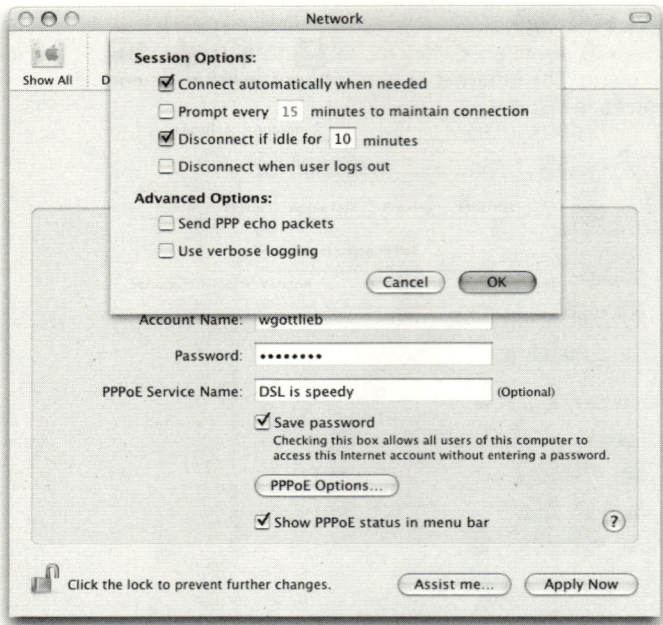

Figure 15-8: Take charge of your PPPoE options here.

The settings in the PPPoE Options dialog have the following effects:

✦ **Connect automatically when needed:** Starts a PPPoE session when an application, for example Safari or iChat, attempts to access the Internet.

✦ **Prompt every *x* minutes to maintain connection:** A dialog appears periodically asking if you want to stay connected, and ends the PPPoE session if no one responds to the dialog.

✦ **Disconnect if idle for *x* minutes:** Automatically stops the PPPoE session if no Internet activity occurs on the PPPoE connection during the specified time interval. Because most connections are unlimited (they don't charge you per minute or hour), it's good to make the specified time interval fairly sizeable, or to not use this option at all.

✦ **Disconnect when user logs out:** Automatically stops the PPPoE session when you log out of Mac OS X, so the next person to log in can't inherit your PPPoE session.

✦ **Send PPP echo packets:** This option makes Mac OS X periodically ask your Internet provider's computer to respond and ends the PPPoE session if your Internet provider's computer stops responding. If your Internet provider doesn't support PPP echoing, then turning on this option may cause your PPPoE sessions to end prematurely.

✦ **Use verbose logging:** Creates a detailed log for troubleshooting. A detailed log uses more disk space.

You can show or hide the PPPoE status icon in the menu bar by selecting or deselecting the option labeled Show PPPoE status in menu bar. You see the effect of changing this setting immediately. If the PPPoE status icon is hidden and you click this checkbox, the PPPoE status icon appears to the left of other icons on the right side of the menu bar. You can use the PPPoE icon to connect to the Internet, disconnect from the Internet, and monitor the connection status, as described in Chapter 6.

AppleTalk

Same as usual. Check the box if you need it. Leave it alone if you don't. Interestingly, AppleTalk cannot be enabled on an Ethernet port if PPPoE is active. Creating new ports is covered later in the chapter.

Proxies

If you need it, you'll know it. Configure as necessary.

Ethernet

A special Ethernet section (within the Ethernet section) lurks. The first thing that is displayed is your Mac's hardware Ethernet address, or MAC address. Most commonly, Ethernet will be set to Configure: Automatically and doesn't need to be changed. If you are troubleshooting a network issue, or tinkering around, you might want to switch from automatic to manual. Doing so gives you the ability to select the speed of your Ethernet port manually (you might want to set it slower, at 10BaseT, to test stability on a problem-prone network) and to control the size of the packets that your Mac sends over the Network.

Click Apply Now to save changes made to your Ethernet Settings.

Configuring Modem settings

Select the Internal Modem port to configure settings for dial-up Internet Access. Figure 15-9 shows the Modem configuration area.

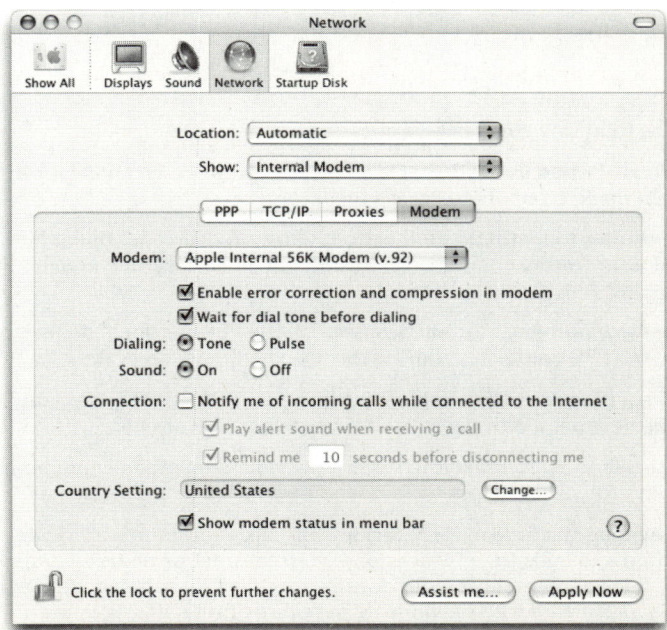

Figure 15-9: Take charge of your Internal Modem settings here.

PPP (Point to Point Protocol)

Click the PPP pane in Network preferences to configure a modem connection to the Internet or a remote network. You can enter the name and password required for connecting to your Internet account, the telephone number that your computer must call to get connected, an alternate telephone number to call if the main number is busy, and the name of the service provider. To display a dialog of additional options that affect a PPP session, click the PPP Options button. Figure 15-10 shows the additional settings in the PPP Options dialog.

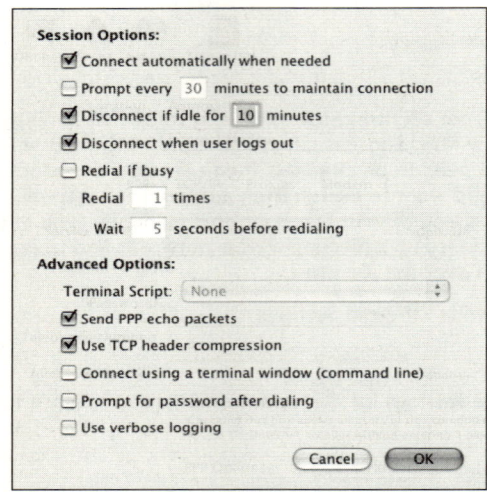

Figure 15-10: The wealth of PPP connection options.

The PPP options have the following effects:

✦ **Connect automatically when needed:** Starts a PPP session when an application, for example Mail or Sherlock, attempts to access the Internet.

✦ **Prompt every *x* minutes to maintain connection:** Causes a dialog to appear periodically, asking if you want to stay connected, and ends the PPP session if no one responds to the dialog.

✦ **Disconnect if idle for *x* minutes:** Automatically stops the PPP session if no Internet activity occurs on the PPP connection during the specified time interval.

✦ **Disconnect when user logs out:** Automatically stops the PPP session when you log out of Mac OS X, so the next person to log in can't inherit your PPP session.

✦ **Redial if busy:** Specifies how to redial the service provider's telephone number if it is busy.

✦ **Send PPP echo packets:** Makes Mac OS X periodically ask your Internet provider's computer to respond and ends the PPP session if your Internet provider's computer stops responding. If your Internet provider doesn't support PPP echoing, then turning on this option may cause your PPP sessions to end prematurely.

✦ **Use TCP header compression:** Makes Mac OS X try to compress TCP header information for efficiency. Leave this option turned on because the service provider can refuse header compression without causing a problem.

✦ **Connect using a terminal window (command line):** Causes a terminal window to appear while you're connecting so that you can type commands and enter requested information for your service provider.

✦ **Use verbose logging:** Creates a detailed connection log for troubleshooting purposes. A detailed log uses more disk space.

TCP/IP

For a dial-up connection, the TCP options are quite different. Most commonly, TCP/IP is set to use PPP to dial up. If you are using an AOL connection, choose the AOL option. In rare cases your ISP will need you to configure a dial-up connection manually, and the option to do so is present.

Proxies

Configure as you would for either AirPort or Ethernet. Because most dial-up connections are commonly away from offices and firewalls, configuring Proxies while using a dial-up connection is rare, but sometimes necessary.

Modem

Click the Modem pane to identify the type of modem you have and to set certain dialing options. Your Mac should default to the correct modem type, but you can find out just what type of modem you have by viewing the modem area of the Apple System Profiler, as shown in Figure 15-11. (Find Apple System Profiler in the Utilities folder, or by going to the Apple Menu and choosing "About This Mac" and clicking on the "More Info" button.) The *V* number that comes after the modem type represents the speed and features supported by the modem. Newest modems use the V.92 protocol, which supports 56K connection speeds and can use call-waiting to receive voice calls even if you are dialed up to the Internet. The V.90 script supports the 56K speeds, but not call-waiting. Lower numbers are for lower speeds. If you're not sure which to use, try the higher one first and work your way down.

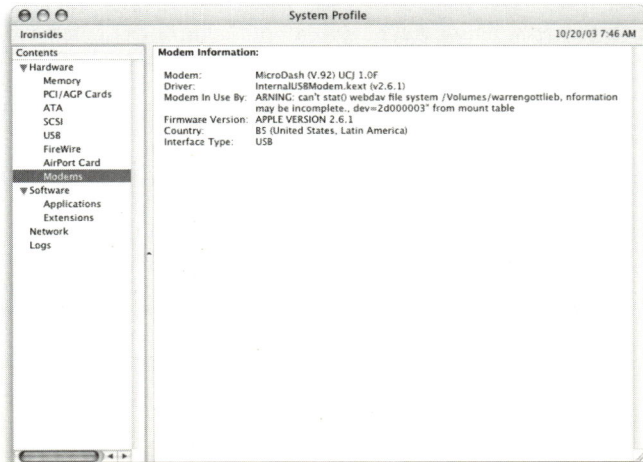

Figure 15-11: Use the System Profiler if you are unsure of your modem type.

The first checkbox is for enabling error correction and compression. If you wish to use speeds above 33.6K, you'll need to have this box checked. If you are having trouble maintaining a faster dial-up speed, unchecking this box can lead to more stability. The second checkbox tells the computer to wait for the dial tone before dialing. If your phone doesn't always give a clean dial tone (such as a voicemail system whose dial tone changes to alert you of new messages) you'll want to uncheck this box.

If your phone is a pulse-dialing model, you'll need to select that option. Almost all phones are tone, so you should probably not select this option.

If you want the modem sound off, you can select the sound off option. Leaving the sound on is usually a good idea, as an aural indicator that your Mac is dialing-up properly.

If you have call-waiting, you can set your Mac to warn you when an incoming call is received when you are dialed up. You can choose to have an alert sound play, and to be warned before being disconnected.

If you change countries, you should alter the modem settings to reflect your new location.

You can show or hide the Modem status icon in the menu bar by selecting or deselecting the option labeled Show Modem status in menu bar. You see the effect of changing this setting immediately. If the Modem status icon is hidden and you select this option, the Modem status icon appears to the left of other icons on the right side of the menu bar. You can use the Modem icon to connect to the Internet, disconnect from the Internet, and monitor the connection status, as described in Chapter 6.

If you have a slightly older Mac, you might have an infrared port. All the PowerBook G3s have them, as well as the earlier PowerBook G4s, and the original Bondi Blue iMac. You can use the infrared, or IR, port to connect to the Internet through an IR-equipped Palm device or cell phone. Configuration is almost identical to both the regular internal modem and a Bluetooth modem (which we cover in the next section). IR is much slower and requires a direct line of sight between the devices.

Configuring the USB Bluetooth modem adaptor

One of the niftier features of OS X is the ability to use a Bluetooth-enabled mobile phone to dial your Mac up to the Internet. This is especially cool (although a bit slow) if you have a PowerBook and are without Internet, whether you're in a cab riding through Central Park, or are actually *in* Central Park. You'll need to set up your phone using the Bluetooth Setup Assistant first (Chapter 6). After you are dialed up through your cell phone, you can even go as far as to set your computer to share its connection over AirPort (see Chapter 10) and broadcast an Internet signal to other computers.

The Bluetooth modem is configured identically as the internal modem would be with respect to the TCP/IP, PPP, and Proxies panels. The unique panel is the Bluetooth Modem panel. Instead of choosing a modem script to reflect your Mac's internal modem, the modem script needs to reflect your cellular phone model. If it's not present, you can go to www.apple.com/bluetooth for information and downloads. You are also given the option to show the Bluetooth status in the menu bar. Otherwise, you initiate a connection just like you would a regular dial-up. You can click Dial Now right from the PPP panel, or use the Internet Connect application, or use the modem menu bar icon. See Figure 15-12 for the Bluetooth Modem setup.

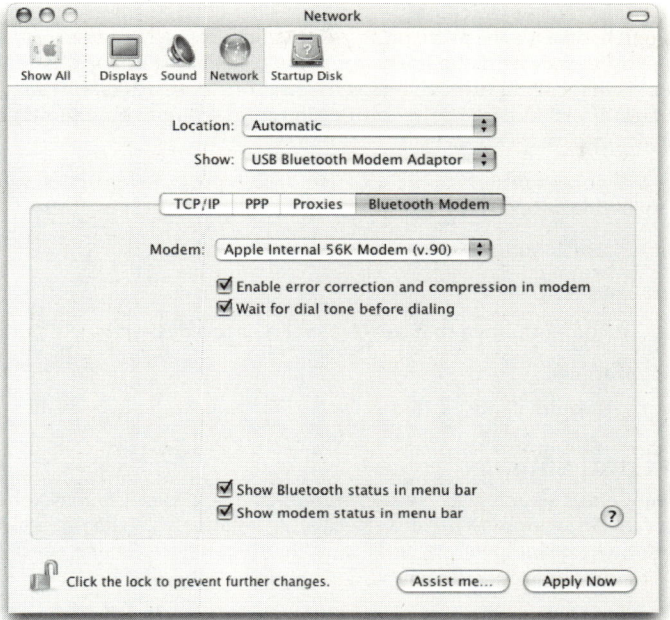

Figure 15-12: The unique settings for your Bluetooth modem adaptor.

Tip   A port exists, called 6 to 4, that does not show up by default in OS X 10.3. In order to create it, you have to view the port list and create a new one, under the Network Port Configurations area. A 6 to 4 is used when you, on an IPv6 network, need to access another IPv6 network, over the Internet, which is still IPv4 based.

Configuring network ports

Mac OS X lets your computer have more than one network port active at the same time. Therefore, as previously stated, your computer can have concurrently active configurations of AirPort, Ethernet, and modem connections. You can even have multiple configurations of the same port, all of them operating in conjunction.

Multiple port configurations can provide overlapping services. On a PowerBook that you use in different locations, Ethernet can provide fast Internet access from the local network at your desk. AirPort can provide wireless Internet access when you're in meetings. A modem can provide Internet access when you're at home. On this PowerBook, the Ethernet, AirPort, and modem configurations are active all the time, and Mac OS X is able to determine which configuration to use for Internet access at any given time and/or location.

Somehow, Mac OS X has to determine which of the available port configurations to use when you start to check your email, browse the Web, print, or use some other network service. Mac OS X has a simple method of prioritizing port configurations. It goes down a list of available port configurations, trying each in turn, and uses the first one that works. By default, Mac OS X tries port configurations in the following order: internal modem, built-in Ethernet, and AirPort. (This is the Automatic location.)

You can change settings in Network preferences that affect which port configuration Mac OS X uses. You can do the following:

✦ Change the priority of port configurations.

✦ Turn each port configuration on or off.

✦ Create additional port configurations that use the same ports as existing configurations.

✦ Rename port configurations.

✦ Delete port configurations.

Displaying network port settings

To display the settings that affect which port configuration Mac OS X uses, choose Network Port Configurations from the Show pop-up menu in Network preferences. If the Location pop-up menu lists more than one network location, make sure that it is set to the one whose port configurations you want to see. Figure 15-13 shows an example of Network Port Configurations settings.

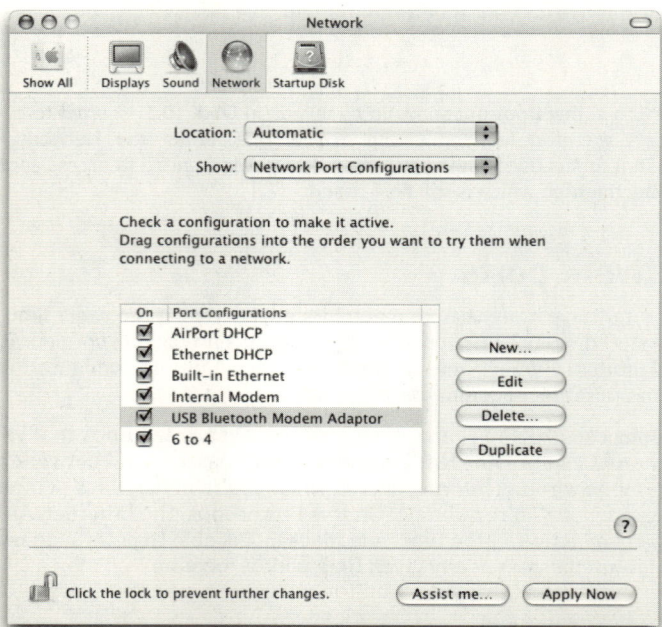

Figure 15-13: Change the Network Port Configurations settings in Network preferences to affect which port configuration Mac OS X uses.

The Network Port Configurations settings of Network preferences include a list of all port configurations. This list shows the order in which Mac OS X tries the port configurations. You can give a port configuration a higher priority by dragging it higher on the list. You can give a port configuration a lower priority by dragging it lower on the list.

Tip   Drag the port configuration you use most often to the top of the Port Configurations list. Now Mac OS X won't waste time checking less-used port configurations.

You can turn a port configuration on or off by selecting or clearing the checkbox next to its name in the Port Configurations list. When a port configuration is turned off, Mac OS X doesn't try to use it.

Tip   Turn off port configurations that you never use so that Mac OS X won't waste time checking them.

Working with port configurations

You can create additional port configurations by making new ones or duplicating existing ones.

To make a new port configuration

Click the New button in the Network Port Configurations settings of Network preferences. In the dialog that appears, enter a name for the new configuration and choose the new configuration's port from the pop-up menu.

To duplicate a port configuration

Select a port configuration in the Network Port Configurations settings of Network preferences and then click the Duplicate button. As shown in Figure 15-4 a dialog appears in which you can edit the name that Mac OS X proposes for the duplicate port configuration.

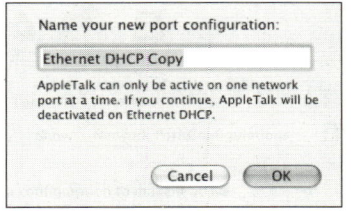

Figure 15-14: Choosing to duplicate a port presents you with the dialog, which gives you the option to name your duplicate.

To rename a port configuration

Double-click on the port name that you wish to edit and type in what you wish to call it. Hitting return selects the next name in the list.

To delete a port configuration

You delete a port configuration by selecting it in the Network Port Configurations settings of Network preferences and then clicking the Delete button. An alert appears asking you to confirm that you really want to delete the port configuration.

When you create a new or duplicate port configuration, Mac OS X puts it at the bottom of the list. You can drag it higher to raise its priority.

Working with network locations

You may find that you need to make regular changes to settings in Network preferences. For example, you may use your computer in locations that need to have different network settings. Every time you change locations, you have to remember what changes to make and then click and type repetitiously to make the changes. You can simplify the process of changing locations by letting Mac OS X do the repetitive part.

You learned how to view the status of the entire network, then how to configure and work with individual ports. This section covers how to create locations of different groups of ports, or a single port. You can create network locations in Network preferences to facilitate making regular changes to network settings. Each network location is simply one specific arrangement of all the various Network preferences settings. When you create a network location, you give it a name. The names of network locations appear in the Apple menu and in the Location pop-up menu at the top of Network preferences. In fact, the network locations appear in these places for all users of your computer; they are system-wide settings. (User accounts don't have private network locations.)

After you create a network location for a particular arrangement of network settings, you can quickly change to that arrangement by choosing the network location by name from the Apple menu. This method of reconfiguring the Network preferences settings is much quicker and simpler than changing all the individual settings involved in the reconfiguration.

Here are some situations in which you may want to create network locations:

✦ **You use the computer in more than one place,** such as at home and at work or school, with different port configurations at each place.

✦ **You connect to different networks from the same port,** such as a modem connection to your Internet provider and a modem connection to your network at work or school.

✦ **You set different port priorities** to determine which port configuration your computer will use for network services that are available on more than one network port, such as file sharing on Ethernet or AirPort.

You use the Location pop-up menu near the top of Network preferences to create, rename, and delete network locations. You use this same pop-up menu to select a network location that you need to reconfigure. You can also use this pop-up menu to switch network locations, but the Apple menu is usually more convenient.

Creating new network locations

You can create additional network locations by making new ones or by duplicating existing ones. To make a new network location, choose New Location from the location pop-up menu, and enter the name in the dialog box that appears. Click OK to save the name, and click Apply Now to retain the new Location. To duplicate a network location, choose edit from the Location pop-up menu, select the location that you want to duplicate and click the Duplicate button. The duped location now appears in the list with the suffix Copy, and its name highlighted, ready to be changed. Change the name and hit the Done button. Click the Apply Now button to retain the settings.

Switching network locations

We already revealed the easiest way to switch to another network location, which is to use the Apple menu. Specifically, you choose the network location by name from the Location submenu in the Apple menu.

You can also switch the network location by choosing the one you want from the Location pop-up menu in Network preferences, but you must click the Apply Now button at the bottom of Network preferences to make the switch take effect. This allows you to view your different locations without changing your current network settings at the same time.

Reconfiguring network locations

Location settings can be changed at any time, by going into the Network preferences and changing the port settings, or the ports themselves. Network locations can also be renamed, or deleted by using the edit option under the Location pop-up menu.

AirPort

The following section is a more in-depth look at AirPort networking, including installation of the card in your machine, and setting up a base station to use. AirPort now comes in two flavors, AirPort (802.11b) and AirPort Extreme (802.11g). AirPort Extreme is faster, and available only on Macs manufactured after January 2003. An AirPort Extreme card is small and silvery. An original AirPort card is white and the size of a regular PCMCIA card. When we speak of an AirPort capable/equipped Mac, unless otherwise specified, it won't matter if it's AirPort or AirPort Extreme.

Installing AirPort cards

Macs that are ready for AirPort have a built-in antenna and a special slot for Apple's AirPort card, but if your Mac doesn't have one of these cards installed, you may need to obtain one, connect the antenna to it, and install it in the slot. Of course, you don't need to install an AirPort card if you order one with the computer or if someone else already installed a card.

All iBooks and all slot-loading and flat panel iMacs are AirPort compatible, except for the 350Mhz models that lack FireWire ports. The new iBook G4s are AirPort Extreme compatible. For the most part, iMacs produced after February of 2003 support AirPort Extreme. Table 15-3 shows the AirPort capabilities of all 10.3-compatible Macs.

Table15-3: AirPort Capabilities

Macintosh Model	*AirPort Capable*	*AirPort Extreme Capable*
Blue and White G3	—	—
PowerBook G3 (Lombard)	—	—
PowerBook G3 (Pismo)	✔	—
PowerMac G4 PCI	—	—
PowerMac G4 AGP	✔	—
PowerMac G4 Gigabit Ethernet	✔	—
PowerMac G4 Digital Audio	✔	—
PowerMac G4 Quicksilver	✔	—

Continued

Table15-3 *(continued)*

Macintosh Model	AirPort Capable	AirPort Extreme Capable
PowerMac G4 Mirrored Drive Doors (2002)	✔	—
PowerMac G4 Mirrored Drive Doors (2003)	—	✔
PowerBook G4 Titanium (400-1GHz)	✔	—
PowerBook G4 Aluminum (12″, 15″, 17″)	—	✔
iBook G3 (Clamshell and White)	✔	—
IBook G4	—	✔
iMac Tray-Load	—	—
IMac Slot Load 350 MHz No FireWire	—	—
iMac Slot Load	✔	—
iMac G4	✔	—
iMac G4 17″ 1GHz	—	✔
iMac G4 (USB 2.0)	—	✔
PowerMac G5	—	✔

All PowerBook G4s are AirPort-compatible. Only the Aluminum G4 PowerBooks are compatible with AirPort Extreme. The PowerBook G3 Pismo with FireWire ports is the only G3 PowerBook that is AirPort compatible. Earlier models need a third-party PCMCIA card.

All PowerMac G4's that have an AGP graphics slot are AirPort compatible (this excludes the original "PCI" G4). G4s made after 2003 are AirPort Extreme compatible. All the G5s are AirPort extreme compatible.

Not surprisingly, the procedure for installing an AirPort card is different for each Mac model. Instructions for installing an AirPort card in your computer are in the manual that came with it. You can also find detailed, illustrated instructions for your Mac model in Apple's Knowledge Base (www.info.apple.com).

Creating a computer-to-computer AirPort network

If you have two or more computers with AirPort cards installed, you can create an ad hoc wireless network. Apple calls this a *computer-to-computer network*. This network connects the AirPort-equipped computers without an AirPort base station. One computer creates a computer-to-computer network, and other computers within about 150 feet can join it.

Note
Any computer with a wireless card that complies with revision b or g of the IEEE 802.11 standard should be able to join a computer-to-computer network created by Mac OS X. The IEEE 802.11b and g standards cover ad hoc wireless networks called *IBSS* (Independent Basic Service Set), and the Mac OS X AirPort software complies with IBSS.

Computers connected to an ad hoc wireless network can share files and participate in multi-player games. They can also access multiuser databases and use other software designed for multiple users.

The easiest way to create a computer-to-computer network is to choose the Create Network option under the AirPort menu bar icon. If you don't have the AirPort icon displayed, you can always launch the Internet Connect application and choose the same option from the Network pull-down menu. Figure 15-15 displays the result of choosing to create a computer-to-computer network.

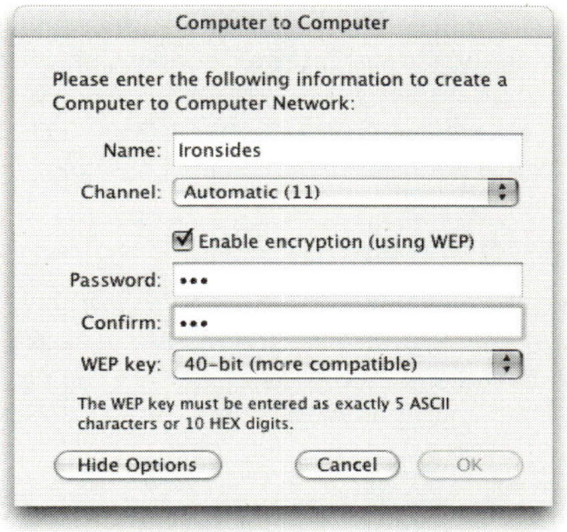

Figure 15-15: Behold, the birth of a computer-to-computer wireless network.

Click the Show Options button (which changes to the Hide Options button shown in Figure 15-15). This gives you the ability to set a password for your network. Check the box to enable WEP encryption. Setting a password for your network is a good habit to get into, for security reasons. Type the name and the password in the appropriate fields. You must retype your password in the Confirm field for verification.

You may need to change the Channel setting if there are other wireless networks in the vicinity. Each wireless network listed in the Network pop-up menu should use a different channel. When two networks share the same channel, their performance decreases. Because adjacent channels actually overlap, you should leave two unused channel numbers between each used channel for best network performance. Also, because 2.4-GHz cordless telephones use the same frequency range as 802.11b wireless Ethernet devices, they can interfere if they are on the same or a adjacent channel.

After you have created your network, users on other computers can join it. If you have set a password, they'll need to type it in. See Chapter 10 for more on sharing files and Chapter 6 for how to join and leave an AirPort Network.

Setting Up an AirPort Base Station

The computer-to-computer AirPort network we described earlier has some limitations. For one, it doesn't inherently let you share an Internet connection. What's more, a computer-to-computer network is transitory. It ceases to exist after all computers have left it.

An AirPort base station has neither of these limitations. It lets all AirPort-equipped computers share an Internet connection, share files, participate in multiplayer games, and use other multiuser software. Additionally, it can bridge a wireless network and an Ethernet network, which adds many potential benefits. Wireless computers gain access to network services on the Ethernet network, such as network printers. Computers on the Ethernet network gain access to services on the wireless network, such as the shared Internet connection. Computers on either network can share files, participate in multiplayer games, and use other multiuser software with computers on the other network. An AirPort base station has all the benefits of a computer-to-computer wireless network and more.

Setting up an AirPort base station device

An AirPort base station device can connect to the Internet via its built-in 56K modem or its WAN Ethernet port. The Ethernet port enables the AirPort base station to connect via a cable modem, DSL modem, or a local network that has an Internet gateway or router. The AirPort base station shares its one Internet connection with up to ten wireless computers concurrently. The computers must have AirPort cards or other wireless equipment that is compatible with the 802.11b standard. For example, an iBook or PowerBook G4 with an AirPort card can access the Internet completely untethered. Adding an AirPort base station to your wireless network is the easiest and most efficient way to provide wireless Internet access, but it is not the cheapest way.

Preparing for base station setup

When you set up an AirPort base station, you need to know all the details about how your base station will connect to the Internet. The details you need to know depend on how the base station connects to the Internet, as follows:

✦ **Base station internal modem:** You must know the name and password for your ISP account, ISP phone number, country, and dialing method (tone or pulse). You also specify whether to dial automatically as needed and how long to wait idle before disconnecting automatically. Additionally, you can enter one or more IP addresses of name servers (also known as DNS addresses) and default domain names.

✦ **Local network (Ethernet):** For a manual configuration, you need to know the base station's IP address and subnet mask on the local network. You also need to know the IP address of your network's Internet router or gateway. For a DHCP configuration, you need to know the DHCP client ID, if the DHCP server requires one. For either type of configuration, you can also enter one or more IP addresses of name servers (also known as DNS addresses) and default domain names.

✦ **Cable modem or DSL using DHCP or a static IP address:** For a manual configuration, you need to know the static IP address, subnet mask, and router IP address assigned by your ISP. For a DHCP configuration, you need to know the DHCP client ID, if your ISP requires one. For either type of configuration, you can also enter one or more IP addresses of name servers (also known as DNS addresses) and default domain names.

✦ **Cable modem or DSL using PPPoE:** You must know the name and password for your ISP account. You also specify whether to connect automatically as needed and how long to wait idle before disconnecting automatically. In addition, you can specify your ISP name and PPPoE service name, and you can enter one or more IP addresses of name servers (also known as DNS addresses) and default domain names.

You can learn the details of a modem, DSL, or cable modem connection from your ISP. You should know the details of a local network connection if you set up your local network. If you didn't set up your own local network, consult the person who set up or administers the network.

Using the AirPort Setup Assistant

With the details about your base station's Internet connection in hand, you are ready to configure the base station settings. You can configure an AirPort base station device by using the AirPort Setup Assistant program that's included with Mac OS X. The Airport Setup Assistant can be found in the Applications/Utilities folder. Proceed as follows:

1. **Plug in the base station's power adapter**. The base station flashes its lights as it starts up, which takes about 30 seconds. The middle light glows white when it is ready. (It's okay if you plugged in the base station ahead of time.)

2. **Make sure that the base station's middle light is glowing white. Then start the AirPort Setup Assistant program and follow the onscreen instructions.** The AirPort Setup Assistant asks you to enter the following information:

   • **Network password:** The Setup Assistant asks for this password only if the base station has been set up previously with a network password.

   • **Base station password:** The Setup Assistant does not ask for this password if the base station has the default password, which is *public*.

   • **Type of network connection:** The base station can connect to the Internet via its built-in modem, DSL, cable modem, or local Ethernet network as described previously. Figure 15-16 illustrates this stage of the AirPort Setup Assistant.

   • **Internet connection details:** The details you enter depend on the type of Internet connection, as described previously.

   • **Network name and password:** You give the base station network a name and password. The password is optional but strongly recommended.

   • **Base station password:** The base station can use the same password as its network or you can give it a different password. A person must know this password to change base station settings.

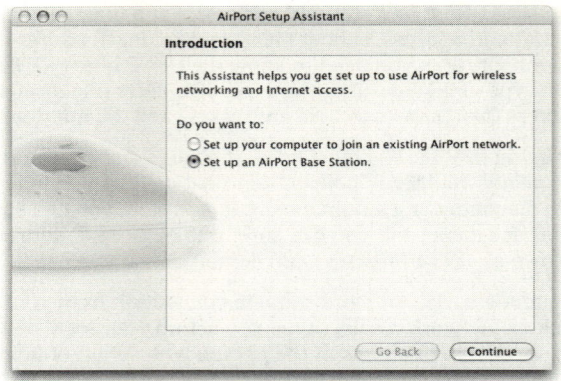

Figure 15-16: The AirPort Setup Assistant leads you through setting up a base station device.

Apple has released three versions of the AirPort base stations. The first version was graphite (gray) with three multicolored status lights. The second version is snow (white) with three white status lights. The third, the Extreme version, is white with a silver Apple. Accordingly, the status is displayed in different ways on the three versions of the base stations. Apple has an article in the Knowledge Base defining the differences in Airport base station light status. A simple way to search the AppleCare Knowledge Base is the Apple channel in Sherlock, which is covered in Chapter 7.

Administering an AirPort base station

Both the AirPort base station device and the AirPort base station software have advanced features that the AirPort Setup Assistant application doesn't set up. These features include the ability to do the following:

✦ **Provide Internet access to computers on an Ethernet network** in addition to wireless computers.

✦ **Turn on a DHCP server to automatically assign private IP addresses** to computers on your AirPort network and optionally on an Ethernet network.

✦ **Change individual Internet connection settings,** such as the phone number for a modem connection.

✦ **Allow computers on the Internet to penetrate your local network** to access Web sites, FTP sites, and other services hosted by computers on your network.

✦ **Limit base station access** to computers with specific AirPort cards so that unauthorized computers can't join the base station's wireless network.

✦ **Change individual base station settings** such as the network password, channel number, and encryption.

To configure the advanced features of a base station device, you use the AirPort Admin Utility program, found in the Utilities folder. Figure 15-17 shows the Admin Utility and some of the settings that can be changed by using it.

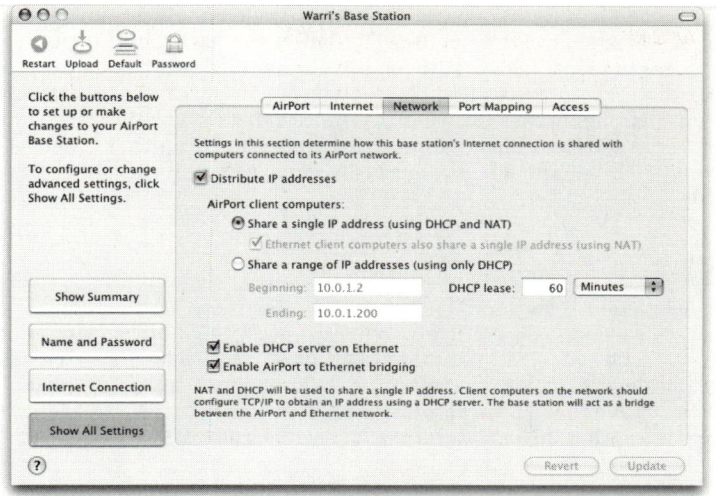

Figure 15-17: Change many settings on an AirPort base station device by using the AirPort Admin Utility application.

Going into full AirPort setup detail is beyond the scope of this book. Use the very capable built-in Help, or go to Apple's online support area for further information.

Bluetooth Networking

Although Bluetooth is better suited for connecting peripherals, like cell phones and mice (think of it as a wireless USB), OS X does have quite a full set of features for connecting computers over the Bluetooth protocol. This is a simple way to create a computer-to-computer network. It provides a direct connection and the ability to browse the files on other machines. Bluetooth is slower than AirPort, so you'll want to use AirPort for wireless file transfers if you can. Open the Bluetooth preference pane by first opening the System Preferences and clicking on Bluetooth.

Settings panel

The Bluetooth pane has three areas, and the first, the Settings panel, deals with general Bluetooth behavior. The first option you have is to turn Bluetooth off or on. If you never use Bluetooth, you should turn it off, it will marginally increase your computer's performance. If you decide to use it later, you can always turn it back on again. If you have a portable, you should turn Bluetooth off when you are not using it — it will save you battery life.

The rest of the Panel is fairly self-explanatory. You can choose to make your computer discoverable or not, making you easily visible to other Bluetooth users. You can choose to require authentication or not, and to encrypt the connection or not. Authentication means that a user must use a password. When the data is encrypted, it's nearly impossible for someone who is sniffing the airwaves to read any of it. Choosing to support nonconforming phones helps if you have an older (relatively) Bluetooth phone. If there are no Bluetooth devices configured, you can set your Mac to always open the Bluetooth Setup Assistant (Chapter 6) when the Bluetooth preferences are launched. Lastly, you can choose to show the Bluetooth status in the menu bar. A solid black *B* indicates that Bluetooth is on, but no devices are paired. A grayed out *B* indicates that Bluetooth is turned off. A *B* with a dashed line through it indicates that a device is paired with the Mac, and a gray *B* with a jagged line through it usually indicates that the external USB Bluetooth adaptor has been unplugged, or for whatever reason is not being recognized.

File exchange

The file exchange panel dictates how your Mac behaves for Bluetooth file sharing. You can choose to prompt before each incoming file, or to refuse or accept all. You can also choose whether to ask when Palm devices (PIMs) or other items (say from a cell phone) try to send your computer files. Clicking the choose folder button chooses the default folder that accepted files are downloaded to. You can also choose whether to allow other computers to browse your own, and if so, what folder they have guest access (no password required) to.

Pair devices

If you are a Bluetooth aficionado, you'll be spending a lot of time in the Pair Devices area. Whether it is another computer, a mouse, a cell phone, or a printer, you always need to *pair* the device with your Mac before you can use it. In the instance of Figure 15-18, the computer in use has found two devices; one is Microsoft's Bluetooth mouse (yeah, but it's an awesome mouse) and the other is Silversides, a G4 Cube with an external USB Bluetooth adaptor. Clicking the Set Up New Device button launches the Setup Assistant, covered in Chapter 6. After you have a successful pairing, you are given the option of adding or removing it from your favorites (depending if it's already there or not), deleting the pairing, disconnecting from the device but not deleting it, or pairing a new device.

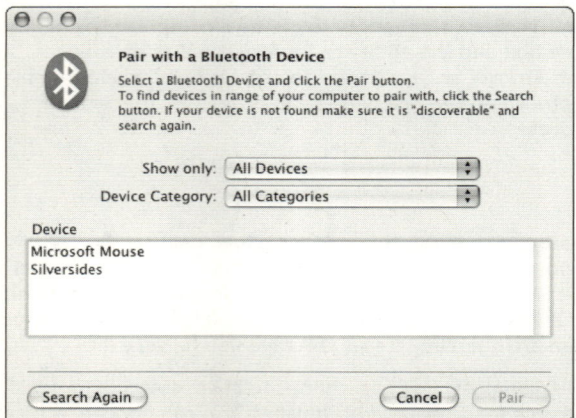

Figure 15-18: When you choose to pair a device, available Bluetooth devices show up in the list displayed. In this case, Silversides, a computer, and a Bluetooth mouse are available.

Bluetooth menu bar icon

If you've set the Bluetooth menu bar icon to be displayed, pulling it down gives you a few new options. Choosing the Send File command lets you send your files another Bluetooth device, like another computer. You can also choose to browse a device for files to take from it. Figure 15-19 shows a file being sent over Bluetooth. Figure 15-20 shows another computer's contents being browsed over Bluetooth.

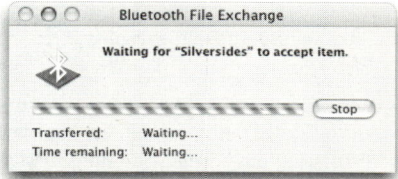

Figure 15-19: You can use Bluetooth to send files to other devices.

Figure 15-20: You can take files from other devices with Bluetooth as well.

Summary

Here's what you know about setting up networks after reading this chapter:

✦ Setting up a network makes it possible for your computers to share an Internet connection, share printers, share files, participate in multiplayer games, and use other multiuser software.

✦ Wiring an Ethernet network involves running a twisted-pair cable from each computer and other network device to a hub or switch.

✦ Establishing an AirPort wireless network involves installing an AirPort card in each computer. Then you can create a computer-to-computer wireless network. An AirPort base station is optional, but allows AirPort-equipped computers to share an Internet connection and to communicate with computers on a wired Ethernet network, if you also have one of these.

✦ After making a network connection—Ethernet, AirPort, or modem—you may need to configure some settings in the Network pane of System Preferences. You configure settings for each network connection separately. Each network connection has several groups of related settings, and you switch between groups by clicking tabs in Network preferences. The tabs include AirPort, TCP/IP, AppleTalk, PPPoE, Proxies, PPP, and Modem.

✦ The Active Network Ports settings of Network preferences lets you change the priority of network port configurations, turn each port configuration on or off, create additional configurations that use the same ports as existing configurations, rename port configurations, and delete port configurations.

✦ Network locations facilitate making regular changes to network settings. Each network location is one specific arrangement of all network settings. You can switch to any network location by choosing it from the Apple menu.

✦ An AirPort base station can be a free-standing device or software running on an AirPort-equipped Mac. A base station lets all AirPort-equipped computers share an Internet connection, and it can bridge a wireless network and an Ethernet network. You set up either kind of base station with a setup assistant application.

✦ You can share files between computers using the Bluetooth protocol.

✦ ✦ ✦

Deploying More Network Services

You know from previous chapters that with Mac OS X you can
share files and some USB printers with other computers on your
local network. In this chapter, we look at the following additional services that Mac OS X can provide on your network or the Internet:

- ✦ Web sharing for hosting a Web site from your computer
- ✦ FTP access for unprotected file copying between your computer and others
- ✦ Remote login for protected file copying between your computer and others and for control of your computer from others
using encrypted Unix commands

In addition to all these network services, your computer can respond
to messages sent from other computers on your network. These messages, called remote Apple events, are sent by AppleScript programs
that are running on other computers. We cover this capability along
with AppleScript in Chapter 24.

Making Network Services Available

All network services described in this chapter require a local network, an Internet connection, or both. The local network can be an
Ethernet network or an AirPort wireless network. If you're not sure
how to set up a local network or an Internet connection, look back at
Chapter 15.

When a network service is enabled on your computer, it is available
as soon as your computer is powered up. While a service is available,
other computers on the Internet or your local network can access it,
depending on firewall rules. The service remains available until someone deliberately turns off the service or shuts down your computer. If
you enable a network service while you are logged into the machine
and then log out, the service remains available. Network services are
even available while no one is logged in; that is, while the login window is displayed. Logging in as another user does not affect availability, because network service settings are not in any way tied to user
account settings or privileges.

Shutting down your computer ends its network services, but only temporarily. The next time the computer is started up, Mac OS X automatically turns on network services that are configured to be available.

If your computer goes into sleep mode, it's the same as shutting down the computer with regards to network services. For this reason, if you are configuring your Mac OS X computer to offer any network services, you will want to use the Energy Saver preference pane to disable sleep functionality as described in Chapter 13. If another computer is connected to your computer for Web sharing, FTP access, or remote login and your computer goes to sleep, the other computer is unable to access that service until your computer wakes from sleep. When your computer wakes up, computers with existing connections to your computer's network services may resume access.

Your computer's IP addresses

Other computers need to know your computer's network identity to access the network services that it provides. For Web sharing, FTP access, and remote login, your computer can always be identified by a numeric IP address. You can think of your computer's IP address as its telephone number.

Actually, your computer can have more than one IP address. It has different IP addresses for each network port that it's connected to. Your computer could be connected to an Internet provider via modem, an Ethernet network via its built-in Ethernet port, and an AirPort wireless network. Each connection has its own IP address.

Displaying your computer's IP address

To see the IP address of the port currently used to provide Web sharing, FTP access, and remote login, open System Preferences and then click the Network button or (choose Location ➪ Network Preferences from the Apple Menu). Click the Show pop-up menu near the top of Network preferences and choose the network port whose IP address you want to see. Then click the TCP/IP tab. The IP address is displayed below the Configure pop-up menu, as shown in Figure 16-1.

Punching holes in your firewall

If your computer is at home and is connected via broadband (DSL, Cable) you likely have an Internet gateway or router that shares a single public IP address among the computers on the network using special reserved private IP addresses. If your IP address is 192.168.x.x, 10.x.x.x, 169.254.x.x, or 172.16.x.x, it is likely a private IP address. You'll have to check your gateway or router to be completely sure. Computers on the Internet see only the shared public IP address. They can't see the private IP addresses of computers on the local network. Therefore, they have no way of contacting computers on the local network for Web, FTP, or remote login services. Because the gateway keeps Internet computers out, it provides a kind of firewall for your local network. If you want to let Internet computers through your firewall, you need to punch holes in the firewall. Each type of service — Web sharing, FTP access, and remote login — needs a separate hole in the firewall.

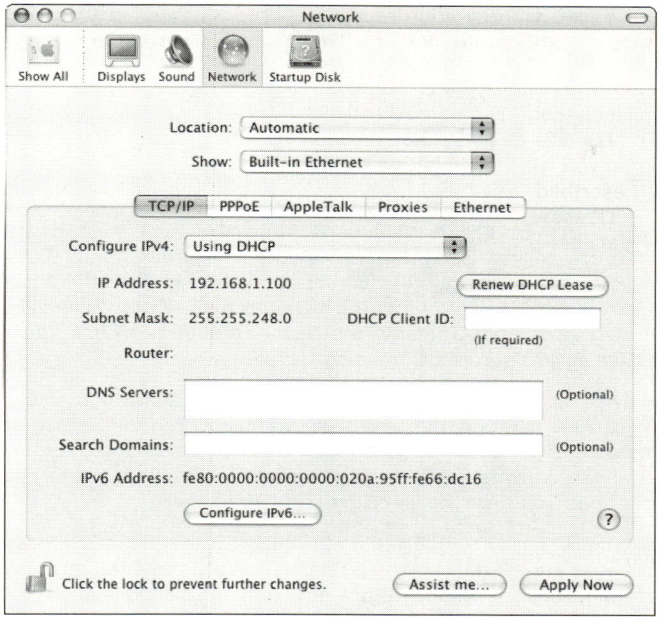

Figure 16-1: See the IP address of any network port in the Network pane of System Preferences.

You may be able to configure your Internet gateway so that it directs all incoming requests for a particular service, such as FTP access, from the shared public IP address to one computer's private IP address. This scheme is usually called *inbound port mapping*. This scheme is like an office with a main phone number and a receptionist who routes incoming calls to a different private extension for each department. Within the company, departments call each other by using the private extension numbers. With inbound port mapping, your local network has one public IP address and a gateway that routes incoming service requests to private IP addresses according to the type of service request. Computers on your local network use your private IP address to access your computer's network services.

The details of configuring inbound port mapping are different for each gateway product. Consult your Internet gateway's manual for specific instructions.

Dynamic and static IP address

Your computer's IP address may be dynamic or static. A *dynamic IP address* may change each time you begin an Internet session or each time your computer starts up. A *static IP address* doesn't change. Your computer probably has a dynamic IP address if it connects to the Internet via modem or DSL with PPPoE. Some cable modem connections also provide a dynamic IP address.

A computer on a local network, Ethernet or AirPort, may get an IP address from a DHCP server on the local network each time the computer starts up. The IP address could be different each time, so it is a dynamic IP address. (The *D* in DHCP stands for Dynamic.) The AirPort base station includes a DHCP server, as do many Internet gateway and router products.

Having a dynamic IP address makes your computer hard for other computers to find, which means that your network services are hard to find. It's like a business whose phone number changes every day.

Getting your computer a name

Although your Mac has an IP address for the Web sharing, FTP access, and remote login services that it provides, an IP address is not as convenient as the names that people normally use to access Web sites and FTP servers on the Internet. In addition to its IP address, your computer can have a name for the services that it provides on the Internet and on your local network. The name is actually just another way of referring to your computer's IP address. When another computer tries to contact your computer by name, a name server on your local network or on the Internet looks up the name in a directory and finds your IP address. These name servers are known as *DNS servers* (Dynamic Name Server).

Mac OS X does not include a DNS server, nor can Mac OS X help get a name assigned to your computer and listed with DNS servers on the Internet or your local network. How you get your computer a name address for its Web sharing, FTP access, and remote login services depends on how it connects to the Internet and whether it is on a local network. The details are beyond the scope of this book, but here are some general guidelines:

✦ You will need to register a domain name, if you do not already have access to one. Traditionally Network Solutions (www.networksolutions.com) provides this service in the United States for the major domains (.com, .net, .org, etc.), however now many other companies provide this service. If you are looking for a domain name you would be well served to spend some time comparison shopping as there are many lower-cost alternatives, which offer different feature packages from Web hosting to email services, that may appeal to you. A good place to start would be to feed the following term to your favorite search engine: domain name registrars.

✦ Most Internet service providers provide name based hosting, such as www.mydomain.com for a fee.

✦ If you have a static IP address and have your own domain name, you can get free DNS service from Granite Canyon Group, LLC (www.granitecanyon.com).

✦ If you don't need your own domain name, you can get a free name like myname.dnsalias.com from an organization that provides dynamic DNS service, such as Dynamic DNS Network Services (www.dyndns.org). If you have a dynamic IP address, you also need to install software on your computer that notices each time you get a different IP address and automatically sends your new IP address to your dynamic DNS service provider. An example of this software is the free Dynamic DNS Client by James Sentman (www.sentman.com/dyndns/).

✦ If you want to use names instead of private IP addresses on your local network, set up a DNS server on the network. Some Internet gateway products include DNS, and DNS software is available for Mac OS 9. Your Mac OS X installation actually includes BIND, the Internet standard DNS server for Unix, however it is not recommended to run DNS on your personal workstation. Configuring the included DNS server is out of the scope of this book, however if you are curious enter man bind at a shell prompt in the Terminal application. Also a trip to your favorite search engine with the query Mac OS X bind will provide a plethora of results.

 **Note** A computer name is displayed above the IP address in the Sharing preference pane. This name is used for file sharing and other AppleTalk services, not for such TCP/IP services as Web sharing, FTP access, and remote login.

Hosting Your Own Web Site

Ever wanted to host your own Web site? All you need, other than a network or Internet connection, is Web server software and some Web pages. Mac OS X includes the Apache Web server, which is in use at many commercial sites hosting large, active sites. This industrial-strength Web server is easy to set up thanks to Mac OS X's Web sharing feature. It gets your Web site on the Internet or your local network in about a minute. (No, this does not include the time it takes to actually create your Web pages!)

Although you could use Web sharing to host a large Web site, you probably wouldn't want to. Web sharing is best suited to hosting a personal Web site. Your Web site is as sturdy as large Web sites, thanks to the Apache server software and Mac OS X's Unix core. System resources, not reliability, are the limiting factor. Unlike administrators of large Web sites, you probably don't want to dedicate your computer to hosting a Web site. Most likely, you want to host some Web pages for other's use or convenience, or perhaps you would like to have access to some pages on your computer from any location, be it home, work, or elsewhere. However, this being your personal computer, you will probably use other applications at the same time. If you use Web sharing to host a large, busy Web site, you'll probably find that your computer is not responsive enough when you use other applications at the same time. Web sharing is ideally suited for distributing information to coworkers on a local network or to family and friends on the Internet.

If you want to host a Web site on the Internet, your computer needs a continuous, high-capacity Internet connection. A DSL or cable modem connection should be adequate for a personal Web site. However, many DSL and cable modem connections *upload* files (send to the Internet) much slower than they *download* files (receive from the Internet). For example, your computer may download files at over 140KB per second but only be permitted to upload at less than 14KB per second. If this is the case with your connection, then visitors to your Web site will receive Web pages from your computer at the slower upload rate. Nevertheless, DSL and cable modem connections are much faster than a modem connection. You don't want to frustrate your Web site visitors with spotty, slow service via a modem connection.

Starting Web sharing

You can get a Web site set up on your local network or your Internet connection in a minute or less. Simply open System Preferences and choose View ➪ Sharing (or click the Sharing button). Click the Services tab, and then click the Start button that is below the words Web Sharing Off. Web sharing takes a few seconds to start up. Then the Start button becomes a Stop button and the text above it reads Personal Web Sharing On. Clicking the Stop button turns off Web sharing. Figure 16-2 shows the Sharing preference pane with Web sharing ready to be turned on.

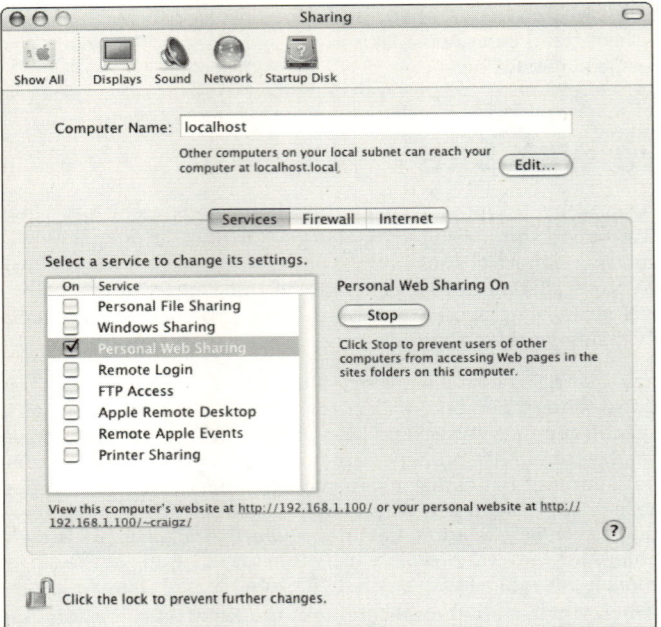

Figure 16-2: Start Web sharing in the Sharing pane of System
Preferences.

If the Sharing preference pane settings are locked, you must unlock them before you can start
Web sharing. When the settings are locked, they are dim and the lock button at the bottom of
the window looks locked. To unlock the settings, click the lock button and enter an administrator's user account name and password in the dialog that appears.

Loading Web site files

Turning on Web sharing in the Sharing preference pane gets a Web site on the air, but it's not
your Web site until you put your site's files into the right folder. In the meantime, you have an
introductory site supplied with Mac OS X, as shown in Figure 16-3.

Loading a personal Web site

You can put files for a Web site in two places. Files for a personal Web site should go in the
Sites folder in your home folder, where other users of your computer can't change them.
Naturally, other users of your computer can create their own personal Web sites, and you
can't change them. Each user's personal Web site has a unique URL.

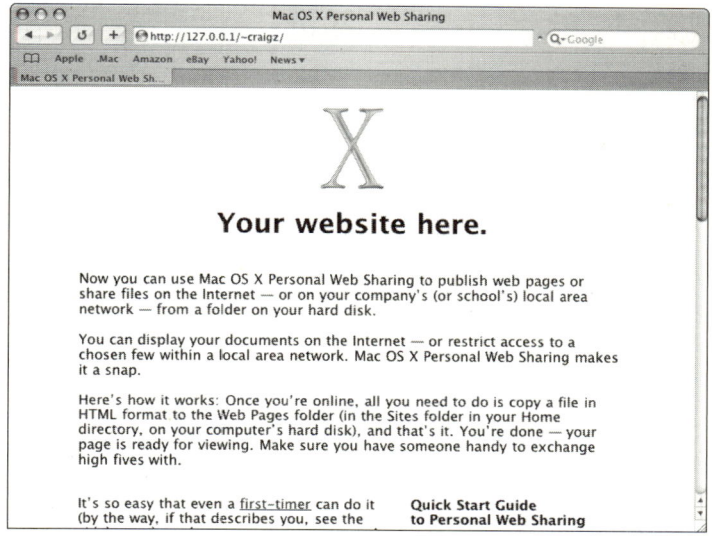

Figure 16-3: Visitors to your personal Web site see a provisional home page until you place your Web site's files in your home folder's Sites folder.

Loading the common Web site

Files for a joint Web site that all users of your computer can change go in the Documents folder in the WebServer folder in the main Library folder; the path is /Library/WebServer/Documents/. This folder initially contains a provisional home page in several languages. Each language has a separate HTML file. These files all have names beginning with index.html and ending with a suffix that indicates the language. For example, index.html.en is the English version and index.html.es is the Spanish (Español) version. You can make any of these HTML files the provisional home page for your Web site by removing the language-designation suffix so that the file name is just index.html. (You do not need to rename the index.html.en file because the Mac OS X Apache Web server automatically uses it if no files are named index.html.) Figure 16-4 shows the joint Web site's provisional home page in English.

Tip

If you have no other use for your computer's common Web site, make it an index to your computer's personal Web sites. This index can be a simple Web page containing a list of links to the personal Web sites. For example, if users Ender and Laz both have personal Web sites, the index page would have a link to /~ender/ and another link to /~laz/.

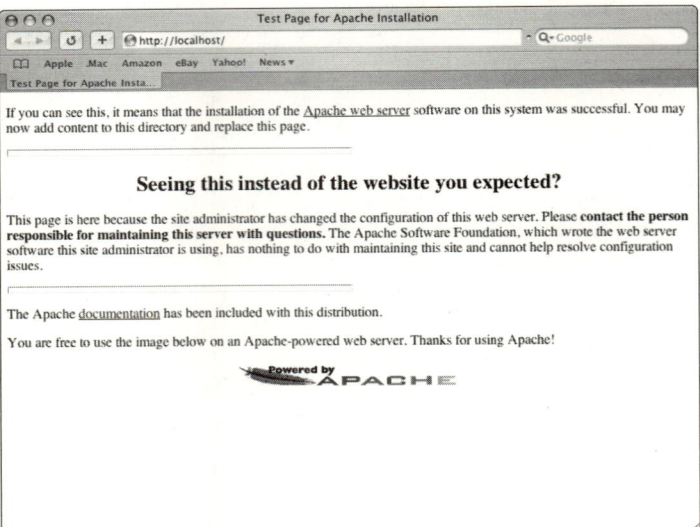

Figure 16-4: Visitors to your computer's common Web site see another provisional Web page until someone using your computer puts Web site files in the /Library/WebServer/Documents/ folder.

Designing and Creating a Web Site

Designing a Web site and creating all the files that go into it can be a lot of work. If your needs are simple, you may be able to produce a satisfactory Web site with a word processing application. For example, recent versions of Microsoft Word and AppleWorks can convert a word processing document to an HTML file. Word or AppleWorks word processing documents can include formatted text, tables, graphics, and links to places in the same document or to other documents. If the original word processing document includes graphics, the graphics are converted to separate image files. You must put the image files together with the HTML file in your Sites folder or the /Library/WebServer/Documents/ folder.

Both Microsoft Word and AppleWorks convert simple documents more accurately than complex documents. You can experiment to see whether your word processing application can generate Web site files that meet your needs.

Of course if you have experience with HTML authoring, you'll be comfortable using TextEdit to create raw html files, or you can use either Adobe's GoLive or Macromedia's Dreamweaver for a more WYSIWYG approach to authoring.

Setting up a file listing

Instead of displaying a home page, your Web site can display a list of the files in your Sites folder or in the Documents folder of the WebServer folder (path Library/WebServer/ Documents/). To make this happen, simply remove the file named index.html or index.html.en from the folder. If the folder doesn't contain a file by either of these names, the Mac OS X Web server creates a Web page that is a list of the folder's contents, as shown in Figure 16-5.

Figure 16-5: If your Web site folder has no home page, visitors see a listing of the folder's contents.

Visiting your Web site

People visit your personal Web site (the one in your Sites folder) at an Internet address (URL) like one of these:

✦ `http://192.168.0.1/~craigz/`

✦ `http://mycomputer.mydomain.com/~craigz/`

Substitute your computer's IP address or name, and substitute the short name of your user account at the end of the Internet address. Be sure to include the ending slash (/) or Apache will not know exactly which file to deliver, and an error message will be displayed. Notice that neither of these Internet addresses has a www prefix. Your Web site's Internet address doesn't include the www prefix unless it is part of the name you have obtained for your computer as described at the beginning of this chapter.

The joint Web site (the one with files in Library/WebServer/Documents/) has an Internet address like one of these:

✦ `http://192.168.0.1`

✦ `http://mycomputer.mydomain.com`

Substitute your computer's IP address or name. Here again, your Web site's Internet address doesn't include the www prefix unless it is part of the name you have obtained for your computer.

Tip   If your computer has only an IP address, put a note on your home page advising people who connect to add a bookmark for your page so that they don't have to remember and retype the IP address to visit again.

Allowing FTP Access

The Mac OS X Web sharing feature is of little help when what you want to share are files, rather than Web pages. Another feature that Mac OS X inherits from Unix, known as *FTP* (file transfer protocol), enables other computers on your local network or the Internet to copy files to and from your computer.

Turning FTP access on or off

The software that provides FTP service is built into Mac OS X, and you can turn it on or off quite easily. First, open System Preferences and choose View ➪ Sharing (or click the Sharing button). When the Sharing preference pane appears, click the Services tab, click on FTP Access in the list box, and then click the Start button to turn it on or off. Figure 16-6 shows FTP ready to be turned on in the Sharing preference pane.

If the Sharing preference pane settings are locked, you must unlock them before you can turn FTP access on or off. The settings are dim when they are locked, and the lock button looks locked. To unlock the settings, click the security button and enter an administrator's user account name and password in the dialog that appears.

Comparing FTP and File Sharing

If you've never used FTP before, you may think that it sounds like Mac OS X's file-sharing feature, which is described in Chapter 16. Actually, FTP differs from file sharing in a couple of significant ways. For one, file sharing is mainly for Macs, but FTP works across platforms. Computers running Windows and Unix operating systems can copy files to and from your computer using a native FTP client program.

Another key difference concerns how people use your files on other computers. With file sharing, other computer users see your shared files in Finder windows and Open dialogs. These computer users can open and save files directly on your computer. With FTP, other computer users see your files in FTP client applications, and these other users must copy files between your computer and theirs. They work with copies of your files on their computers.

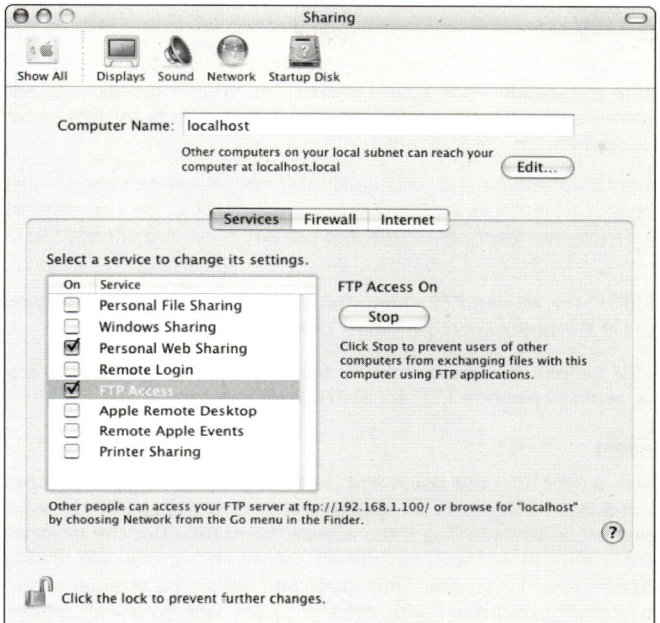

Figure 16-6: Turn the built-in FTP server on or off in the Sharing pane of System Preferences.

Avoiding file damage

FTP was designed to transfer plain text files. Other kinds of files such as pictures, software, and formatted text files lose vital information unless first encoded as binary files before being transferred. Files that must be encoded before being sent over the Internet are known as *binary* files. Encoding Mac files also preserves information used by the Finder, such as the type of file and which application created it. Encoded files must be decoded after being received before they can be used. Read below for information regarding encoding and decoding.

Unlike other FTP software for Macs, the FTP server in Mac OS X is not able to automatically encode Mac files before sending them to another computer. Nor does the Mac OS X FTP server recognize encoded Mac files and automatically decode them when it receives them from another computer.

Because the Mac OS X FTP server doesn't handle any encoding or decoding automatically, you should encode files that you want other users to download from your computer by using FTP. Conversely, if other users upload encoded files to your computer by using FTP, you must decode the files before you can use them. You can use the StuffIt Expander utility application included with Mac OS X to decode files. You can encode files by using the StuffIt Deluxe application or the DropStuff application, both from Aladdin Systems (www.aladdinsys.com).

A future version of Mac OS X may include an FTP server that automatically encodes and decodes transferred files.

Considering security

Although convenient, allowing FTP access to your computer poses a serious security risk. Anyone who knows the name and password of a user account on your computer can connect to your computer from anywhere on your local network, and if your computer has an active Internet connection, from anywhere on the Internet.

Additionally FTP transfers both username and password information used to connect to your server. If someone is listening in to network traffic, either on your side or on the network you're connecting to, then he can see your username and password as you connect to the server.

Additional information on SFTP, the secure FTP client distributed as part of OpenSSH and installed by default on Mac OS X computers is provided later in this chapter.

Please refer to Chapter 26 for further discussion on FTP security, and information on configuring the SFTP server if you wish to provide FTP access to your machine.

Unprotected passwords

FTP's authentication method, a user account name and password, protects your computer against casual snooping, but it is no defense at all against a skilled attacker. FTP does not encrypt the name and password before sending them across the network or the Internet. An attacker can use well-known tools and methods to capture names and passwords of everyone who connects to your computer for FTP access. Your name and password are just as vulnerable as those of other users of your computer. If you use FTP to get files from your computer while you're away from it, then your name and password can be captured.

Tip   If you allow FTP access to your computer, change your password frequently and have all other users of your computer do likewise. Never use the same password for FTP that you use for anything else, such as online banking!

Unprotected file transfers

Similarly, FTP does nothing to protect files transferred to and from your computer. Sure, you can encrypt files on your computer, and encrypted files are secure from snoops if they are transferred as encrypted files. If you follow this route, remember to give the key to the person you are sharing files with, or else they will be unable to open your documents.

Protecting with privilege settings

You don't have to encrypt files inside several of the folders in your home folder to keep other users from seeing them. Other users can see and change folders and files on your computer according to the privileges set for each folder and file. In this regard, FTP access is the same as being logged in locally. For example, the preset privileges of your home folder's Desktop, Documents, Library, Movies, Music, and Pictures folders allow only you to see their contents. Anything you put in these six places, and in other folders you create with the same privilege settings, are safe from FTP access unless someone gets your user account name and password.

The preset privileges of your Public and Sites folders allow other users to see and copy their contents. Other users can't put files in these folders, although they can put files in the Drop Box folder that's inside your Public folder.

Outside your home folder and other users' home folders, the privileges of most other folders and files allow everyone with FTP access to see and copy them. In fact, many folders and files that are hidden in Finder windows can be seen by everyone with FTP access to your computer.

Everyone with FTP access to your computer can see and make changes in several of your top-level folders. Anyone with an administrator account can make changes in additional folders. People who log in to your FTP server don't see your top-level folders at first; they see their own home folder on your computer initially but they can easily navigate to your top-level folders. Thus an attacker who captures a user account name and password for your computer could upload files to a folder where you may not notice them, such as the Volumes folder.

Back door to network volumes

The Volumes folder is actually an insidious security problem on a network where people use file sharing or file servers. The Volumes folder gives everyone who logs in to a computer's FTP server a back door entrance to all network volumes mounted on the computer. For example, suppose your computer has FTP access turned off but file sharing is turned on. Someone named Sue connects to your computer as a file-sharing guest, and your Public folder is mounted on Sue's computer. Our friend Sue has FTP access turned on. Using a third computer, Tim logs in to the FTP server on Sue's computer, goes to Sue's Volumes folder, and through it can access your Public folder. If Sue connects to your computer as a file-sharing administrator and mounts your hard drive as a network volume, then Tim would have access to your entire hard drive through Sue's Volumes folder.

Prevent FTP Access Outside Home Folders

The FTP server normally allows remote users to go outside their home folders, but it can be configured to restrict users individually to their own home folders. This configuration requires the use of the Terminal application and the System Administrator (root user) account.

First, you create a text file containing a list of user accounts that you want to restrict. You put the short name of each user account on a separate line, making sure to press return after the last name. For example, the following list restricts users craigz and ender to their home folders when they log in for FTP access:

```
craigz
ender
```

In addition to restricting FTP access for individual users, you can restrict access for groups of users. For each group that you want to restrict, you simply add a line to the text file consisting of an at-sign (@) symbol followed by the group name. Because all Mac OS X user accounts belong to the staff group, a file containing the following lines (the last line being blank) restricts all users to their home directories when they log in for FTP access to your computer:

```
@staff
```

When you save the text file, name it ftpchroot and put it in your home folder. This file must be plain text. If you want to use the TextEdit application to create this file, you must choose Format ➪ Make Plain Text before saving the file. After saving the file, change the file name so that it does not end with .txt.

After saving the file ftpchroot in your home folder, open the Terminal application and type the following command:

```
sudo mv ~/ftpchroot /etc/ftpchroot
```

When you are prompted in the Terminal window to enter a password, enter your own account password.

Allowing anonymous guest access

Considering the security problems that FTP access has, you may understandably balk at allowing guests to connect without user account names and passwords. Yet ironically, anonymous FTP access is arguably more secure than FTP access with a name and password. One reason is that anyone who connects anonymously is restricted to the contents of one folder. They can't ransack your other folders as users with passwords can. Furthermore, if everyone connects anonymously, their names and passwords aren't being sent over the network or Internet; what isn't there can't be captured. With that said, providing anonymous guest access to your machine can make your computer a very attractive target to some of the more unscrupulous users on the Internet. It is very likely that an unmonitored anonymous FTP server will be used for a purpose not intended by its owner. Although you may not think there is anything special about your home computer, its disk space and bandwidth are very attractive to file swappers, and other network hoodlums.

Although it is possible to use the FTP Server provided by Apple in a default Mac OS X installation to enable and provide anonymous ftp access, we recommend replacing the Apple-provided FTP Server with one that allows greater control over access to the server, and one with much greater logging facilities. This is discussed in Chapter 26.

Connecting to your FTP server

If your computer has FTP access turned on, people can use any FTP client application to connect to your computer's FTP server. They can also use a Web browser, although Web browsers have limited abilities with FTP.

Connecting with an FTP client

The FTP client needs to know the identity of the server or host, and this is just your computer's IP address or name. The client also needs to know the user's account name and password on your computer. If you have set up anonymous FTP access on your computer, the user can specify anonymous as the name (also called username or user ID) or leave the name blank.

There are many FTP clients available for Mac OS X. For this chapter, we use Transmit by Panic Software. Transmit is available at www.panic.com/transmit. Transmit has a very simple two-pane interface, as shown in Figure 16-7. When you open the program, the left window is labeled Your Stuff, and it shows you your home directory. You can navigate through your hard drive in this window. The right side initially is waiting for you to type in login information for a remote server. This typically is the server address, your username, and password, as described previously. There is a space to enter the initial path, if you wish to start somewhere other than your home directory. Additionally Transmit offers a choice between traditional FTP and secure FTP, which is described later in the chapter.

Connecting with a Web browser

Instead of connecting to your FTP server with an FTP client, people can use a Web browser, such as Safari, Internet Explorer or Netscape Communicator. A Web browser can download files from your computer but can't upload files to it. With a Web browser, people connect to your FTP server with an Internet address (URL) like one of these:

✦ `ftp://192.168.0.1`

✦ `ftp://mycomputer.mydomain.com`

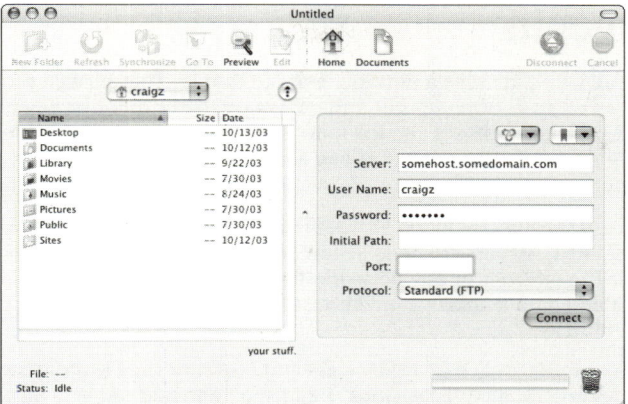

Figure 16-7: Using Transmit to log into a remote FTP server.

Substitute your computer's IP address or name. As the Web browser is connecting to your computer, it displays a dialog asking for a user account name (also called the username or user ID) and password. For FTP access to your computer from a Web browser, specify `ftp://` and your computer's IP address or name as the Internet address; then enter a user account name and password in the resulting dialog. Figure 16-8 shows Safari with the Internet address for an FTP server and the dialog for entering name and password.

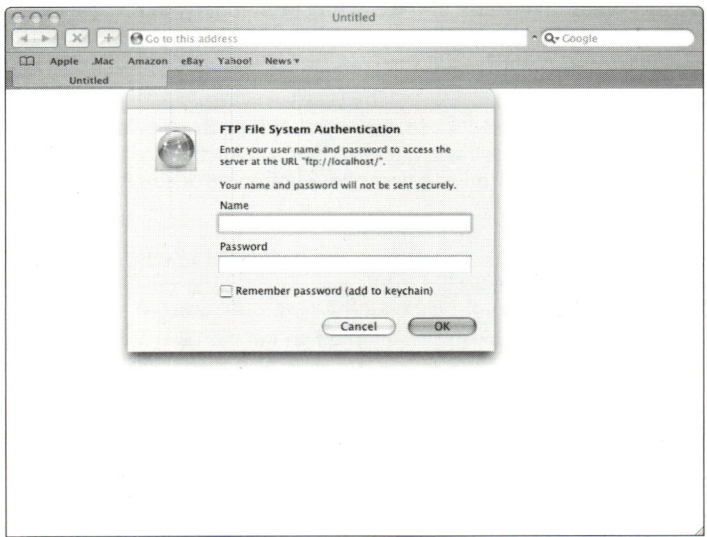

Figure 17-8: FTP File System Authentication.

Allowing Remote Login

Although FTP isn't secure, Mac OS X includes a different service that is. This service provides encrypted communications between your computer and others on the Internet or any network that is not secure. Other computer users can log in to your computer and copy files back and forth. These remote users of your computer can also control it with Unix commands that they type on their computers.

Mac OS X provides remote login through included OpenSSH server software. OpenSSH is a public version of SSH (secure shell), which provides secure, encrypted communications between two computers over the Internet or any network that is not secure. OpenSSH encrypts all communications and data transfer, preventing eavesdropping, hijacking of connections, and other network attacks.

OpenSSH is actually several software tools that replace several insecure Unix tools. The ssh tool provides remote login and command-line sessions, replacing login and telnet. The scp tool provides file copying, replacing rcp and some FTP functions. The sftp tool provides easier file transfer, replacing FTP.

Because OpenSSH is better for file transfer than FTP, you may wonder why more and better FTP client applications are available. The reason is simple: FTP has been around for decades and OpenSSH has been around only a few years.

Turning remote login on or off

You can turn remote login on or off easily. First, open System Preferences and then choose View ➪ Sharing (or click the Sharing button). In the Sharing preference pane, click the Services tab and then select Remote Login in the Service list. Then click the Start button to turn it on or off. Figure 16-9 shows remote login ready to be turned on in the Sharing preference pane.

If the Sharing preference pane settings are locked, you must unlock them before you can turn remote login on or off. The settings are dim when locked, and the lock button looks locked. To unlock the settings, click the lock button and enter an administrator's user account name and password in the dialog that appears.

Note   The first time you turn on the Remote Login option, you may have to wait a minute or so before a check mark appears in the checkbox. While you're waiting for the OpenSSH service to start up, don't become impatient and click in the checkbox repeatedly, or you may induce the condition where remote login appears to be turned on but the OpenSSH service is not actually started. If this happens, remote login may appear to be turned on yet no one is able to connect to your computer by using an SSH client application on another computer. In this case, you can fix the problem by restarting your computer.

Connecting for remote login

When your computer has remote login turned on, other computer users can connect to your computer using SSH client software.

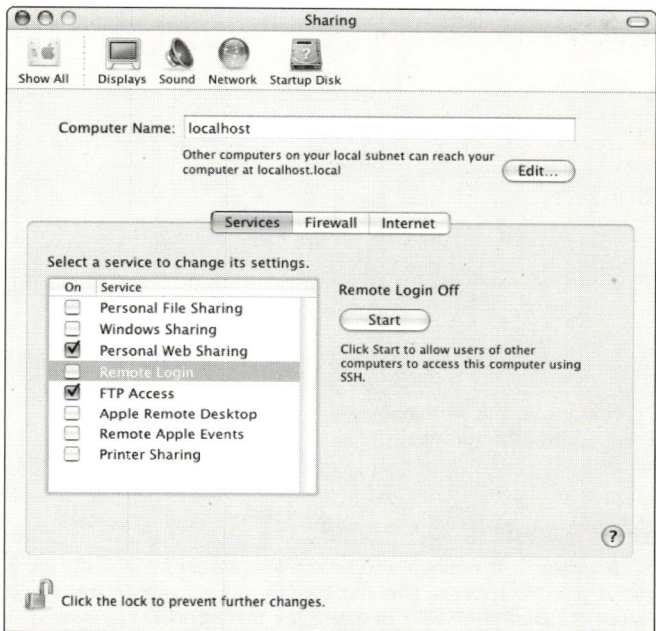

Figure 16-9: Turn Mac OS X's remote login services on or off in the Sharing pane of System Preferences.

Connecting with the Terminal application

Mac OS X includes an SSH client that can be used from the Terminal window. This means another Mac OS X user can log in to your computer by opening the Terminal application and typing a Unix command similar to the following:

```
ssh -lusername 192.168.0.1
```

In this command, -lusername must be replaced with the remote user's short name on your computer, for example -lcraigz. The -l stands for login; it passes that username to ssh. The -lusername part of the command can be omitted if the remote user has the same short name on your computer and on the remote computer he or she is using.

The IP address must be your computer's IP address or your computer's name, if you have obtained one for it as described at the beginning of this chapter.

Note   You may need to wait a moment or so after entering an ssh command for the remote computer to respond, depending upon the speed of the network between your computer and the remote computer.

After logging in to your computer, the remote user can type additional Unix commands in the Terminal application to control your computer. Figure 16-10 shows a Terminal session in which craigz connects remotely to the computer whose IP address is 192.168.2.200 and then uses the w command to see who is using the remote computer.

Figure 16-10: Use the ssh command in the Terminal window to log in remotely and control the remote computer with Unix commands.

Using Transmit For SFTP Transfers

SFTP is part of the OpenSSH package. It is designed to be a replacement for a standard FTP client. SFTP uses an encrypted ssh transport to transfer files from your computer to an SFTP server. Think of SFTP as a safer alternative to FTP. Because the transport is encrypted, neither your login information nor the files you are transferring are visible to an outsider. If someone does sniff the network traffic all they will see is encrypted noise rather than clear text information. SFTP is installed as /usr/bin/sftp and is available as a command line client from the Terminal application.

If you wish to use a GUI front end to SFTP, Transmit includes an SFTP mode for copying files between computers via SFTP using Transmit's familiar FTP browser interface. Simply select Secure (SFTP) from the protocol pop-up menu item in the right pane of the Transmit window, where you enter your login information. See Figure 16-11.

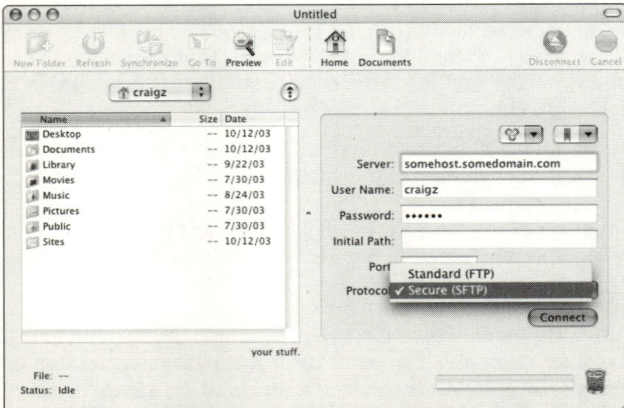

Figure 16-11: Transmit, can log into another computer's SFTP server and securely copy files by using the same two-pane view as it uses for FTP.

Summary

Here's what you know about Web sharing, FTP access, and remote login after reading this chapter:

✦ Every computer on a network or the Internet has an IP address. With Mac OS X, a computer can have a different IP address for Ethernet, modem, AirPort, and other network ports.

✦ If you have a public IP address, then computers on the Internet can use your computer's network services. If you have a private IP address, then Internet computers must go through a gateway on your network to use your computer's network services.

✦ A dynamic IP address may change each time you begin an Internet session or each time your computer starts up. A static IP address doesn't change.

✦ You can get your computer a name, which a name server on your network or the Internet looks up to get your IP address.

✦ You can host a Web site by turning on Web sharing in the Sharing preference pane. Your Web site files go in the Sites folder inside your home folder. Files for a joint Web site shared by all users of your computer go in the Documents folder of the WebServer folder in the main Library folder (path /Library/WebServer/Documents/).

✦ The URL for your personal Web site has the form `http://192.168.0.1/~user/` or `http://mycomputer.mydomain.com/~user/`. The URL for your computer's joint Web site has the form `http://192.168.0.1` or `http://mycomputer.mydomain.com`. (Substitute your computer's address or name and the short name of your user account.)

✦ If you turn on the FTP access option in the Sharing preference pane, other computer users can transfer files to and from your computer. Binary files must be encoded before FTP transfers them. FTP does not protect user account names, passwords, or file transfers from network attackers.

✦ Mac OS X does not normally allow anonymous FTP access, but you can enable it.

✦ For FTP access to your computer, other computer users specify your computer's IP address or name and their user account name and password.

✦ SFTP is secure FTP and is superior to FTP in terms of security. If the remote host supports SFTP then you should use an SFTP client if possible.

✦ Turning on the Remote Login option in the Sharing preference pane enables other computer users to securely log in to your computer, copy files, and send Unix commands.

✦ For remote login, other computer users specify your computer's IP address or name and their user account name and password.

✦   ✦   ✦

Using Classic

In the world of OS X, Classic is what is referred to as an *application environment*. Apple developed Classic as a means to permit Macintosh users to run software that is not capable of running natively in Mac OS X as a Carbon or Cocoa application (see Chapter One for more information on the Carbon and Cocoa application environments). What's good about Classic is that you will be able to run most of your old software. Because the Classic application environment itself runs on top of Mac OS X, if a Classic application crashes, the Classic environment can be restarted without rebooting your computer. The downsides of Classic are that Classic applications don't take advantage of Mac OS X's modern OS features and Classic applications generally do not have extensive hardware support.

So, who needs Classic? It is important to look at Classic as little more than a convenient stopgap to run your old programs while you transition to Mac OS X. The benefits of upgrading your applications to native versions abound: advanced memory management, protected memory space, true multitasking, and symmetric multiprocessing, to name but a few. With Mac OS 10.3's release, just about every major application has been updated to run natively. However, in the event that one of your applications isn't updated, or you just need to run an old version in an emergency and your Mac does not support Mac OS 9 booting, you will have to rely on Classic.

This Chapter is meant to familiarize you with the ins and outs of the Classic application environment — what it is, when and why you would need to use it, and how to configure it from a general standpoint.

Using the Classic Application Environment

Classic applications look and feel, well... classic. When you run a Classic application, you see the application in the Platinum look of the venerable Mac OS 9. Side by side with OS X applications, Classic applications really feel old to you. A Classic application's windows, menus, buttons, and all other controls have the Platinum look, and they work like Mac OS 9 windows, menus, buttons, and so forth.

The reason that Classic applications have the look and feel of Mac OS 9 is that the Classic application environment allows Mac OS X to concurrently run a booted copy of Mac OS 9. Before a Classic application can run, the Classic application environment must start up. This startup process is very similar to booting a Mac under Mac OS 9:

You actually see the "Welcome to Mac OS 9" message and the march of startup items (extensions and control panels), but these things appear within a Mac OS X window. (You can shrink the Classic startup window to show only a progress bar.) After the startup process completes, the startup window goes away and a strange yet systematic mélange of Platinum and Aqua GUI elements coexist on the screen. You see a gray Mac OS 9-style menu bar when you use a Classic application and an Aqua menu bar when you use a Mac OS X application. The Dock is still available at the bottom or the side of the screen, and your Classic application's icons appear there. Because Mac OS 9 does not support the 128 x 128–pixel icons that Mac OS X does, your Classic icons do not look as crisp next to Mac OS X icons. Figure 17-1 shows an example of a Classic application in Mac OS X.

Figure 17-1: Classic Applications like Scrapbook run alongside Mac OS X applications (Safari), but have the old Platinum look down to the jagged icon in the Dock.

Classic limitations

If you have more than one Classic program open at the same time, they share the Classic application environment using cooperative multitasking exactly as they do in Mac OS 9. Because of this, a Classic application can become sluggish when you have other Classic applications working in the background.

Classic applications don't benefit from Mac OS X's protected memory within the Classic application environment. This lack of protected memory means that if one Classic application fails, it may make other Classic programs that are open fail as well (or make the environment unstable). When a Classic program crashes, you may need to restart the entire Classic application environment and all the Classic programs you were using, much like when you were running Mac OS 9. Although individual Classic applications don't benefit from protected memory and preemptive multitasking, the Classic application environment as a whole does. If the Classic application environment crashes, it won't crash your entire computer. To Mac

OS X, the entire Classic application environment (and all its running applications) is a single OS X process. If a Classic application quits unexpectedly, you have to restart the Classic application environment only, not the whole computer. Conversely, a problem in a Mac OS X application does not affect the Classic application environment or any Classic applications.

Perhaps the biggest limitation of the Classic application environment is a lack of support for most third-party hardware. This is because Mac OS X doesn't allow Classic to access hardware directly, the way Mac OS 9 did. In fact, Mac OS X doesn't give any application direct control of hardware, in order to maintain a stable environment. If you have any legacy peripherals that you need to use, make certain you update any applications or drivers your devices require for Mac OS X. If you don't update them, you either have to reboot your machine and run Mac OS 9 when you want to access those devices, or upgrade to newer peripherals.

Classic preference pane

In Mac OS X's System Preferences application, you find the Classic preference pane (see Figure 18-2). This preference pane is used to configure Classic preferences, allows you to start and stop the Classic environment, and gives you troubleshooting information and controls. The Classic preference pane has three panels: Start/Stop, Advanced, and Memory/Versions. The Classic preference pane is found in the System grouping of the System Preferences application.

Using the Start/Stop panel

The Start/Stop panel contains the main controls of the Classic application environment. If you have multiple System Folders (on the same disk, different partitions, or even a completely different disk), you can choose which copy of Mac OS 9 you want the Classic application environment to run. Below this selection, you can choose to manually start or stop the Classic application environment. You can also restart, or even force the entire Classic application environment to quit, should the need arise.

Caution   Forcing the Classic application environment to quit is a drastic measure equivalent to pulling the power cord on a computer with Mac OS 9. You do not have an opportunity to save changes in open Classic documents. Before forcing Classic to quit, try clicking the Stop button in Classic Preferences. If that doesn't stop Classic, switch to each open Classic application, and choose File ➪ Quit to quit the application. You should consider clicking Force Quit in Classic Preferences only after attempting to quit each open Classic application properly.

In the same panel, you can configure Classic to launch when you login, hide the startup screen from you, or warn you that Classic is about to start using the checkboxes to the right of the system selection.

A new addition to Mac OS 10.3 is the Show Classic status in menu bar checkbox. This great new feature places a Classic menu item in your menu bar at the top of the screen. From this menu, you can quickly see if Classic is running, start and stop the process, and even access the old Apple Menu Items folder from Mac OS 9, as shown in Figure 17-2. This menu also shows you the status of the Classic application environment at a glance: a light gray *9* means Classic is inactive, a dark *9* on a white background means Classic is sleeping, and a dark *9* with the left half of the square behind it colored black designates a fully active Classic. The icon also animates while Classic launches.

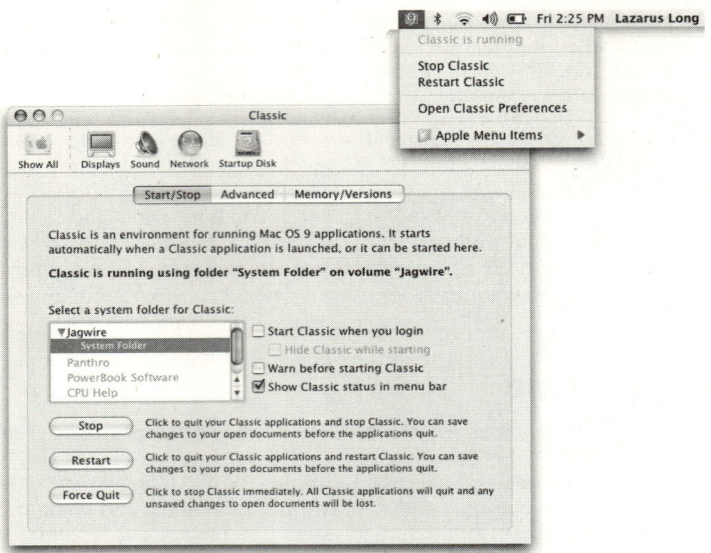

Figure 17-2: The Classic preference pane allows you to control and set up the Classic application environment. In the top-right of the figure, note the new Classic status menu item.

Using the Advanced panel

The Advanced panel in the Classic preference panel allows you to further customize and troubleshoot the Classic application environment. Under Startup and Other Options, you can tell Classic to open the Extensions Manager (either automatically, or using a key combination) as Classic starts. However, it is important to remember that this setting applies *only* when you launch Classic from the Advanced panel of the Classic preference pane. At any other time, Classic loads normally, with the set of extensions you have preset in the Extensions Manager. For more on the Extensions Manager and how to control extensions, see the section "Extensions Manager control panel" later in this chapter. Figure 17-3 shows the Advanced panel.

Well-behaved Classic applications store their preferences in the Preferences folder of the System Folder. This is one place where the compartmentalization of ownership and individualized preferences can break down in Mac OS X. While Mac OS X is a true multiuser operating system, Mac OS 9 is not. Mac OS X allows you to create different Classic system preference folders for each user. In the Advanced panel, select Use Mac OS 9 preferences from your home. This creates new folders in your home folder, corresponding to the old Mac OS 9 Apple Menu Items, Favorites, Internet Search Sites, Launcher Items, Preferences, and the Startup and Shutdown Items (Disabled, too) in the folder of each user with the following path: ~/Library/Classic. The next time you launch Classic, it asks you if you want to copy the contents of the Mac OS 9 System Folder to the corresponding newly created folders as shown in Figure 17-4. Each user can then custom configure their Mac OS 9 preferences without getting in anyone else's way.

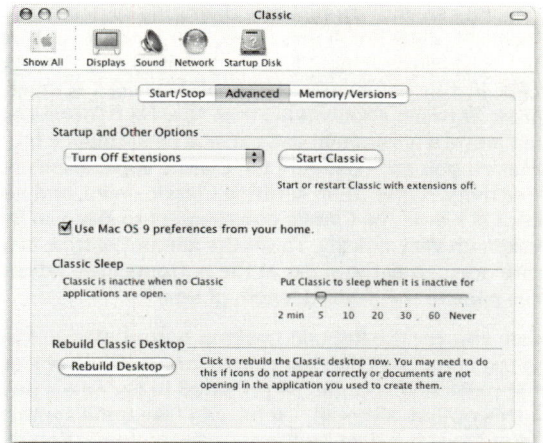

Figure 17-3: The Advanced panel provides access to controls that let you troubleshoot Classic, as well as configure the amount of time before Classic sleeps.

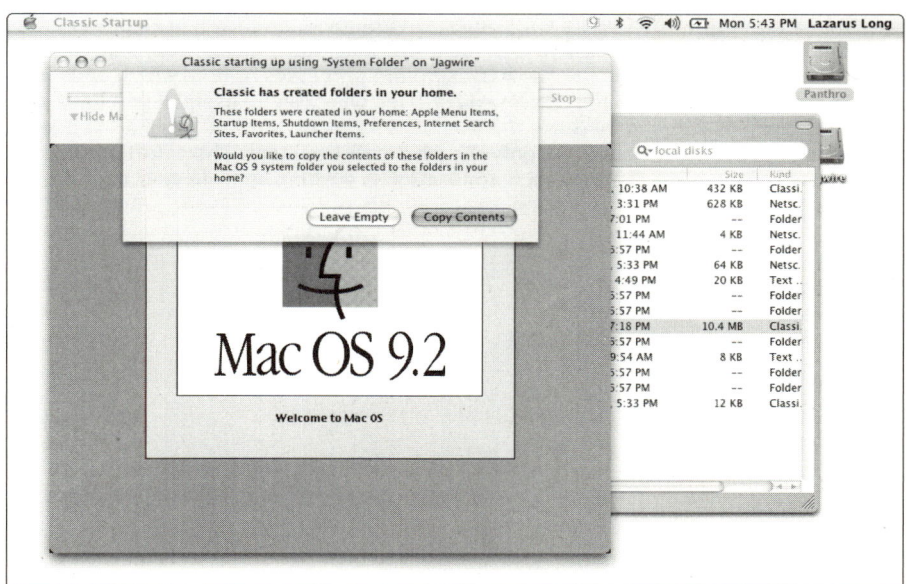

Figure 17-4: The first time you start the Classic application environment for a given user, you will be asked if you want to copy the contents of the Mac OS 9 Apple Menu Items, Favorites, Internet Search Sites, Launcher Items, Preferences, and the Startup and Shutdown Items to the user's home folder.

For all intents and purposes, you are running an entirely separate operating system while Classic is running under Mac OS X. Therefore, even if you don't have any running applications, Classic is using system resources. The Classic environment is using physical and virtual memory and even taking up processor cycles, just by being open. Although Mac OS X is much better at dividing your computer's resources between applications than Mac OS 9 (because of preemptive multitasking), running the Classic environment can cause a performance hit. To maximize the use of your system resources, you can configure the Classic application environment to go to sleep after a period of inactivity. Rather than shutting Classic down, and having to restart it every time you need it, Mac OS X puts the Classic environment to sleep so that it uses minimal resources, yet can be woken up very quickly. To set the amount of time before Classic sleeps, when no applications are open, drag the slider at the bottom of the Advanced panel of the Classic System Preferences pane to the desired length of time.

Near the bottom of the Advanced panel, you see the Rebuild Desktop button. Within Mac OS 9, a volume's desktop file contains the metadata (the descriptive information) of icons and document application bindings for that particular volume. Be prepared to become a professional progress bar watcher, because this option, although useful, can take quite some time to execute even with a limited amount of Mac OS 9 data on the specified volume. Rebuilding the desktop has no affect on Mac OS X, but can be helpful when you're having problems with the Classic application environment.

Using the Memory/Versions panel

The Memory/Versions panel in Classic Preferences shows you detailed information about the applications running in the Classic application environment, as shown in Figure 17-5. This view gives you similar information to the About this Macintosh dialog from Mac OS 9. A major improvement over that view is the Show background processes option, which adds normally invisible system processes to the displayed list. This pane can be useful if you have several Classic applications running, because the Mac OS X's Process Viewer application does not show individual Classic processes — only the whole environment. This information can help you determine how much memory each application is sucking up from your computer's resources.

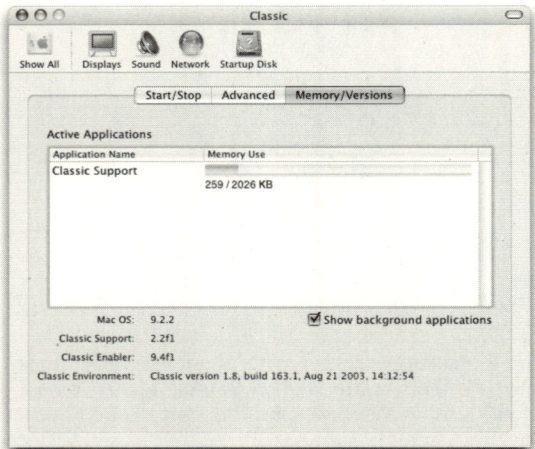

Figure 17-5: The Memory/Versions panel of Classic Preferences, with the Show background applications option checked, allowing you to view the Classic support process.

The Classic startup process

On your computer, Mac OS X may be configured to start the Classic application environment automatically after login. If so, you see a gauge that measures the progress of the Classic application environment starting. This progress gauge appears in a window titled Classic is starting. This window may appear behind other windows because starting the Classic application environment does not monopolize the computer. While Classic starts, you can use the computer for other tasks. As soon as the Classic application environment starts, this progress window disappears. While the Classic application environment starts, you can expand the progress window by clicking the triangle on the left side of the window. The expanded progress window's title also expands to reveal the names of the Classic system folder and the startup disk.

The expanded window also reveals that Mac OS 9 is in fact behind the Classic curtain. In the expanded window, you see the Mac OS 9 welcome message and a sequence of icons marching across the bottom of the window. These icons represent system extensions being loaded as Mac OS 9 gets under way. Clicking the triangle again collapses the window. You can stop Classic before it gets started by clicking the Stop button on the right of the Classic application environment starting window. Avoid forcing Classic to stop because doing so may lead to problems in the Classic application environment, much like unplugging your computer during startup. If you do click Stop, Mac OS X displays a warning and asks if you're sure you want to stop Classic in the midst of starting. Click the Continue Startup button unless you are sure that you need Classic to stop. The Startup window is shown in Figure 17-6.

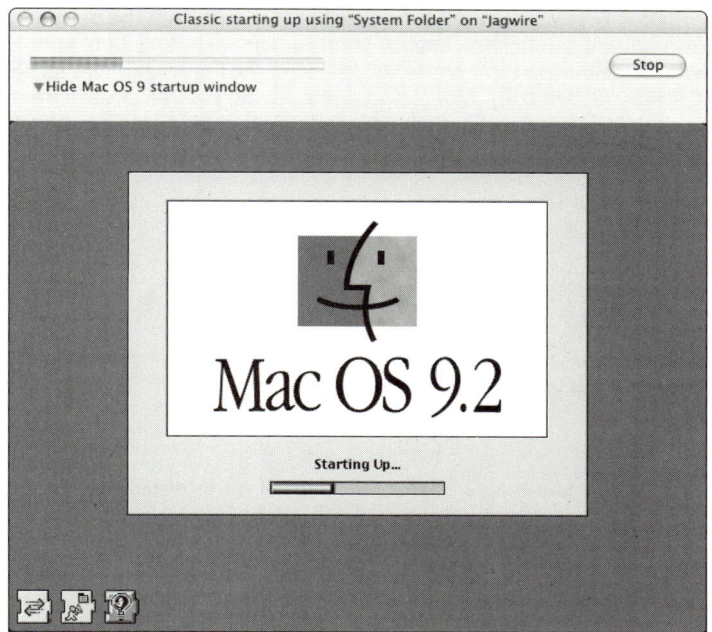

Figure 17-6: The Classic application environment starting up, click the triangle under the progress bar to collapse the view.

Don't be concerned if the Classic application environment does not start automatically after Mac OS X starts up. If the Classic environment hasn't already been started, it automatically starts when it's needed. When you launch a Classic application, the operating system knows that it can't run this application without the Classic environment, so it starts the process for you.

Force quitting Classic applications

Sometimes a Classic application just stops behaving correctly or it locks up on you; in such a case, you can try to force quit the application. Force quitting a Classic application works the same way as force quitting a Mac OS X application, see Chapter 5 for detailed instructions on force quitting an application.

As noted in Chapter 1, the Classic application environment uses does not take advantage of Mac OS X's protected memory and uses shared memory space. Apple very strongly recommends that you save any work in other Classic applications and restart the Classic application environment after force quitting a Classic application. See Figure 17-7 for an example of force quitting a Classic application.

Caution　Be aware that by choosing to force quit a Classic application, you run the risk of bringing the whole Classic application environment down with the single click.

You may remember reading earlier in the chapter about force quitting the Classic application environment from the Classic preference pane. Choosing to force quit from the preference pane, will force the entire Classic application environment to quit, including all of your Classic applications with no chance to save any work. By using the Force Quit dialog, you can attempt to bring a single misbehaving application down, giving you the possibility of trying to save work in your other Classic applications before restarting the Classic application environment.

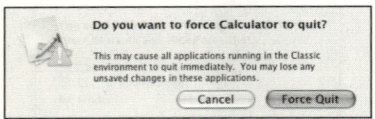

Figure 17-7: Because force quitting an application is a drastic measure, Apple asks you to confirm that this is your true intention.

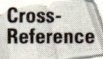

Cross-Reference　See Chapters 21 and 24 for a few more ways that don't require you to restart your computer in Mac OS 9 to delete stubborn files. In Chapter 21 you will find examples of applications that will help you delete stubborn files, and in Chapter 25 you find detailed instructions on how to delete files using the terminal application.

Tips for Using the Classic Application Environment

✦ While you can use the Advanced panel to rebuild the Classic Desktop, Apple recommends rebooting into Mac OS 9 (if your machine supports dual boot) and rebuilding the Desktop file by holding down the Command and Option keys during startup. (See Knowledge Base article 10182 for more information.)

✦ The Classic application environment appears as TruBlueEnvironme in the Mac OS X Activity Monitor.

✦ If a Classic application crashes, Apple recommends that you restart Classic to maintain the stability of the Classic application environment.

✦ Often overlooked, another way to start the Classic application environment is to set a Classic application as a startup item. The launching of the Classic application in the startup item's sequence triggers the start of the Classic application environment. You can add Classic applications to the startup item sequence by using the Startup Items panel of the Accounts preference pane in the System Preferences application.

✦ Rebooting your computer into Mac OS 9 breaks the Mac OS X security model, because Mac OS 9 can't see Mac OS X permissions to obey them. This is often suggested as a means to remove files that Mac OS X refuses to let you delete, but it is also considered a security issue.

✦ Changes you make in control panels, the System Folder, preferences, and extensions while booted into Mac OS 9 affect the Classic application environment when you boot back into Mac OS X, and vice versa. The exception to this is if you have checked the home folders option in the Advanced panel of the Classic preference pane.

✦ Apple recommends against installing and running Classic (or Mac OS 9 for that matter) on a UFS-formatted volume.

Using Classic window controls

Windows in the Classic application environment have most of the same controls as the Aqua windows, but Classic window controls have different appearances and locations. Figure 17-8 shows examples of Classic window controls.

The Classic window controls have these effects:

✦ **Title bar:** Drag to move the window. Double-clicking the title bar may collapse or expand the window the same as the collapse box described later.

✦ **Close box:** Click to make the window go away. Pressing Option and clicking may close all windows in the same application.

✦ **Zoom box:** Click to make the window as large as it needs to be to show all its contents, up to the size of the screen. (A zoomed window usually leaves a margin on the right side of the screen.) Click again to make the window resume its previous size and location.

✦ **Collapse box:** Click to hide all but the window's title bar, or if the window is collapsed, click to show the entire window. Pressing Option and clicking may collapse (or expand) all windows in the same application.

✦ **Scroll arrows, scroller, and scroll track:** Click a scroll arrow to move the window's contents a little; press an arrow to move smoothly; click the scroll track above or below the scroller to move in chunks; drag the scroller to bring another part of the window's contents into view quickly. The scroll bar controls do not appear if scrolling would not bring anything else into view.

✦ **Resize control:** Drag to adjust the size of the window.

✦ **Window frame:** Drag to move the window.

As with Aqua windows, you won't find all the window controls on every Classic window. Document windows have all or most of the available controls, movable dialogs have fewer controls, and immovable dialogs have no controls built into their borders.

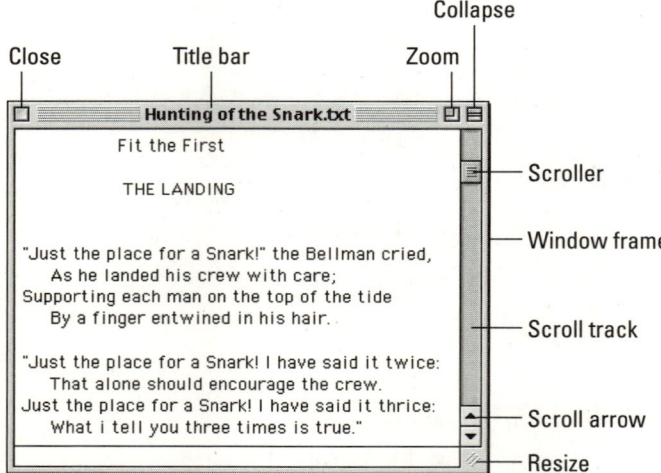

Figure 17-8: Classic windows have many controls.

Using Classic Control Panels

Unlike Mac OS X, Mac OS 9 didn't have a single System Preferences application with different panes to configure the system preferences, there were control panels. All control panels that you use for setting preferences for the Classic application environment are separate applications. These applications are located in the Control Panels folder of the System Folder that's used for starting the Classic application environment on your computer. In addition, these applications are normally listed in a Control Panels submenu of the Classic Apple menu.

You can open Classic control panels in three ways:

✦ You can open a Classic control panel by double-clicking its icon in a Finder window. If the Classic application environment is not currently running, Mac OS X starts it automatically before opening the control panel.

✦ If a Classic application is already open, switch to the Classic application and choose the control panel that you want to open from the Control Panels submenu of the Classic Apple menu.

✦ If you have the Classic Menu active, you can access the Control Panels folder from the Apple Menu Items submenu.

As a rule, the settings in Mac OS X's System Preferences application have an overriding effect on the Classic application environment and Classic applications. Conversely, Mac OS 9 control panels have no effect on Mac OS X. System Preferences replaces many of the control panels that you use for preference settings in Mac OS 9. Only about a third of the Mac OS 9 control panels retain functionality in the Classic application environment. Table 17-1 specifies which Mac OS 9 control panels are obsolete in the Classic application environment and what to use instead in Mac OS X. The control panels listed in Table 17-1 will not even launch in Classic — you must boot in Mac OS 9 to even attempt to take advantage of them. This chapter solely covers Mac OS 9 Control panels that retain functionality in the Classic application environment. For those systems that still retain Mac OS 9 boot capability, besides affecting the Classic application environment, changes that you make with control panels also have an effect on the computer when the system is booted in OS 9.

Table 17-1: Obsolete Control Panels in Classic Application Environment

Mac OS 9 Control Panel	Mac OS X Replacement
AppleTalk	Network pane of System Preferences, no effect in Mac OS 10.3
ColorSync	ColorSync pane of System Preferences, configures color management for Classic application environment only
Control Strip	Icon menus in the menu bar and some Dock icons, no effect in Mac OS 10.3
DialAssist	Configure dialing options in the Network preference pane, or Internet Connect application
Energy Saver	Energy Saver pane of System Preferences
File Exchange	No longer needed
File Sharing	Sharing pane of System Preferences (Lets you change some settings, but better set in Mac OS X preferences.)
Infrared	No real equivalent, but can use Network Preference pane to configure as port and turn on menu item
Keychain Access	Keychain Access application
Location Manager	No equivalent in Mac OS X, although you can change network locations with the Apple menu
Map	Date & Time pane of System Preferences

Continued

Table 17-1 *(continued)*

Mac OS 9 Control Panel	Mac OS X Replacement
Memory	Not applicable in Mac OS X
Modem	Network pane of System Preferences, no effect in Mac OS 10.3
Monitors	Use Displays pane of System Preferences; this control panel is the only part of Classic that can affect Mac OS 10.3 settings
Mouse	Keyboard and Mouse pane of System Preferences, no effect in Mac OS 10.3
Multiple Users	Users pane of System Preferences
Password Security	Account Preference pane and Security Preference pane
PowerBook SCSI Disk Mode	No equivalent control panel in Mac OS X. Use FireWire Target Disk Mode instead; to configure SCSI Disk Mode, first boot into Mac OS
Remote Access	Internet Connect utility (and the Network pane of System Preferences)
Software Update	Reboot into Mac OS 9 to update Classic
Sound	Sound Preference pane
Startup Disk	Startup Disk pane of System Preferences
TCP/IP	Network pane of System Preferences
Trackpad	Mouse pane of System Preferences
USB Printer Sharing	Sharing preference pane, and Print and Fax preference pane
Web Sharing	Sharing pane of System Preferences

Keyboard control panel

The Keyboard control panel enables you to choose a keyboard layout for Classic applications only. You use this option when you want to type in a different language in a Classic application. If you want to switch keyboard layouts in Classic applications by pressing Command-Option-Spacebar, click the Options button in the Keyboard control panel and turn on the option in the dialog that appears. You can always cycle through the language scripts that are installed (if more than one script is installed) by pressing Command-Spacebar. Figure 17-9 shows the general view of the Keyboard control panel.

Appearance control panel

The Appearance control panel has a variety of settings that affect the appearance and behavior of Classic applications. The Appearance control panel also has many settings that do not affect the Classic application environment but do take effect if you restart your computer with Mac OS 9. Naturally, none of the settings in the Appearance control panel has any effect on Mac OS X applications. The Appearance control panel contains Themes, Appearance, Fonts, Desktop, Sounds, and Options panels.

Themes tab

Click the Themes tab of the Appearance control panel to switch all the Appearance control panel's settings to predefined combinations (called *themes*). You can choose from among several themes, and you can save your own additional themes. Switching to a different theme may change some settings that don't affect the Classic application environment, but do take effect if you restart your computer with Mac OS 9. Figure 17-9 shows the Themes tab of the Appearance control panel.

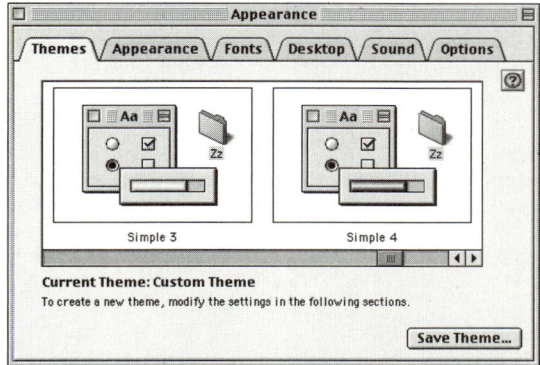

Figure 17-9: The Themes tab of the Appearance control panel lets you switch all the control panel's settings at once in the Classic application environment.

If you click Save Theme, the Appearance control panel displays a dialog in which you can type a name for the theme you're creating. You can change the name of any theme that you created by selecting its preview and choosing Theme Name from the Edit menu. You can't change the names of preconfigured themes.

To remove a theme, select its preview in the Appearance control panel and choose Clear from the Edit menu.

Appearance tab

The Appearance tab of the Appearance control panel has three settings:

✦ **Appearance:** In theory, you can change this setting to give the Classic application environment a different overall look than the gray *platinum appearance* it inherits from Mac OS 9 and its predecessors. While Apple never released any alternate appearances, you can find third-party themes on the Internet.

✦ **Highlight Color:** Determines the color used to highlight text that you select in Classic applications.

✦ **Variation:** Determines the color used to highlight Classic menus and controls.

Fonts tab

In the Fonts tab of the Appearance control panel, you can set the font used for menus, window titles, button names, and some text in dialogs. You can also turn font smoothing on or off, and set a minimum font size for smoothing. Two settings, Small System Font and Views Font, have no effect in the Classic application environment but take effect if you restart your computer with Mac OS 9.

Desktop tab

The Desktop tab of the Appearance control panel affects the look of the Desktop only if you start up the computer with Mac OS 9. These settings have no effect in Mac OS X or the Classic application environment. To change the appearance of the Finder, use the Desktop and Screensaver preference pane.

Sound tab

Click the Sound tab of the Appearance control panel to set sound effects that can play in Classic applications. You can choose a sound set and specify the types of actions that you want sound effects to accompany. Mac OS 9 comes only with a sound set called Platinum Sounds. Other sound sets are available on the Internet. The sound track plays only while you are in the Classic application environment.

Options tab

The final tab of the Appearance control has two options that affect the functionality of the Classic windowing system. If Smart Scrolling is checked, both up and down scroll arrows appear only at one end of the scroll bar. In addition, the length of the scroll box indicates how much you can see without scrolling. The longer the scroll box, the more you can see without scrolling. If you deselect Smart Scrolling, the up arrow appears at one end of the scroll bar, the down arrow appears at the other end, and the scroll box has a fixed length. Checking the Double-click title bar to collapse windows option causes the Classic window to minimize in place, and shutter up and display only the title bar.

General Controls control panel

The General Controls control panel allows you to set whether the Launcher control panel opens automatically when the Classic application environment starts up. Two other settings regulate the blinking rates for the text insertion point and menus. Another setting determines which folder you see first in a dialog for opening or saving a document in a Classic application. The two dim settings are always turned on and can't be changed in the Classic application environment. Figure 17-10 shows the settings in the General Controls control panel.

Apple Menu Options control panel

Settings in the Apple Menu Options control panel determine whether the Apple menu in the Classic application environment has submenus and remembers recently used items. If the Submenus option is turned on and you highlight a folder in the Classic Apple menu, then a submenu lists the contents of the folder. Checking the option to remember recently used items creates folders in the Apple menu for tracking the documents, applications, and servers used most recently. You can set the number of documents, applications, and servers to track. If you want to suppress the tracking of one type of item only, set the number to be remembered to 0 (zero).

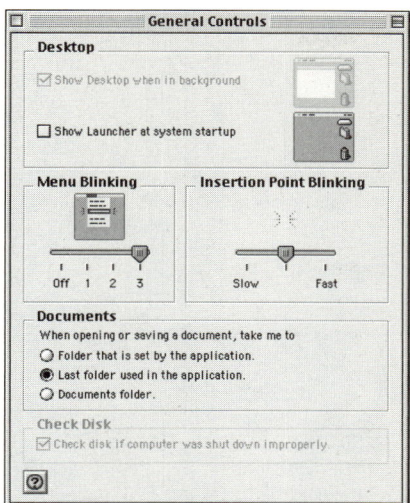

Figure 17-10: The General Controls control panel allows you to configure settings like insertion point blinking.

Extensions Manager control panel

The Extensions Manager control panel can individually deactivate extensions and other startup files in the Mac OS 9 System Folder and in its Control Panels, Extensions, Startup Items, and Shutdown Items folders. The Extensions Manager window has a scrolling list of these items. For each listed item, the Extensions Manager displays its status (on or off), name, size, version, and the package it was installed with. You can also display each item's type and creator codes by selecting options with the Preferences command (in the Edit menu). Figure 17-11 is an example of the Extensions Manager.

Reorganizing the Extensions Manager list

It can sometimes be difficult to find the items you are looking for in the Extensions Manager. Apple has made it possible to organize the list of Extensions, Control Panels, and System Items for easier viewing. You can reorganize the Extensions Manager list as follows:

✦ View items grouped by the folders they're in, grouped by the package they were installed with, or ungrouped. Choose a view from the View menu.

✦ Collapse and expand a group by clicking the disclosure triangle next to the group name or by double-clicking the name.

✦ Sort the list within each group by clicking any column heading to set the sort order.

✦ Adjust the widths of the Name and Package columns by dragging the right boundary line of the Name column heading or the left boundary line of the Package column heading. (You can't adjust the other column widths.)

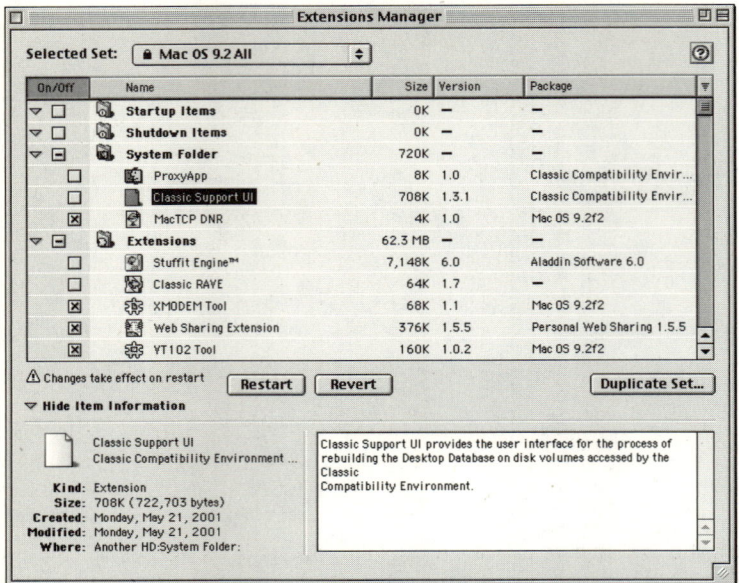

Figure 17-11: Use the Extensions Manager control panel to easily deactivate and activate Classic startup items.

Seeing detailed information about an item

The names of extensions, shared libraries, and control panels do not always provide much information about their purpose. You can view the detailed information about an item in two ways:

✦ See more information about an item by clicking the item's name to select it and then clicking the disclosure triangle labeled Show Item Information at the bottom-left corner of the Extensions Manager window.

✦ Open the folder that contains an item by clicking the item's name to select it and then choosing Find Item from Extensions Manager's Edit menu. (The Get Info command in Extension Manager's Edit menu does not work in the Classic application environment.)

Activating and deactivating items

You deactivate or activate an extension or other item by selecting or deselecting the checkbox next to the item's name. Activating or deactivating a group affects all the items in the group. You can save the current configuration of the Extensions Manager as a named set by choosing New Set from the File menu. Your named sets appear in the Selected Set pop-up menu in alphabetical order, and choosing a set from that pop-up menu changes Extensions Manager to the configuration saved for that set.

Changes you make to the status of any items take place when you restart the Classic application environment (or when you restart the computer with Mac OS 9). To restart Classic immediately, click the Restart button in Extensions Manager. To restart Classic after quitting Extensions Manager, open the Classic pane of System Preferences and click the Restart button there. To cancel the changes you've made, click Revert in the Extensions Manager window.

Note Deactivating items removes features from the Classic application environment. If you deactivate items that are required for the Classic application environment, Mac OS X notices they are missing the next time you start Classic and displays an alert in the Classic startup window offering to replace the missing items.

Extensions Manager puts items that you deactivate into special folders inside the Mac OS 9 System Folder as follows:

✦ Deactivated items from the Extensions folder go into the Extensions (Disabled) folder.

✦ Deactivated control panels go into the Control Panels (Disabled) folder.

✦ Deactivated items from the System Folder go into the System Extensions (Disabled) folder.

✦ Deactivate Startup and Shutdown Items are placed in Startup and Shutdown (Disabled) folders.

An alternative way to disable the items in the Extension manager is by removing the items from the corresponding folders in the System Folder you use for the Classic application environment. See the section titled Examining the Essentials of the Mac OS 9 System Folder later in this chapter for more information.

Using preconfigured sets of extensions

Extensions Manager comes with two preconfigured sets of extensions: Mac OS 9.1 All and Mac OS 9.1 Base. (The version number is higher if you are using Mac OS 9.2.1 or later for the Classic application environment.) These sets are locked so that you can't change them.

You may think that Extensions Manager's preconfigured, locked sets would keep all the items turned on that are required for the Classic application environment. This is the case with Mac OS 9.2.1, but not with Mac OS 9.1. In Mac OS 9.1, both the All and the Base sets turn off some essential items.

If you want to use one of the preconfigured Mac OS 9.1 extension sets when starting the Classic application environment, you need to make a copy of the set and make sure that it has all items turned on that are required for the Classic application environment. You can use Extensions Manager to determine which of the items that Classic requires are turned off when you choose Mac OS 9.1 All or Mac OS 9.1 Base. Follow these steps:

1. **Choose Mac OS 9.1 All or Mac OS 9.1 Base from the Selected Set pop-up menu.** See Figure 17-12 for an example.

2. **Choose File ➪ Duplicate Set.** Extensions Manager makes a copy of the set.

3. **Choose View ➪ As Items and click the On/Off column heading**. This sorts the startup items by their on/off condition so that all items that are turned off are listed together.

4. **Scroll the list looking for items that are turned off and have Classic in their item name or show Classic Compatibility Environment in the Package column.**

5. **Make sure all the Classic items are turned on and then use this set instead of the original locked set when you start the Classic application environment.**

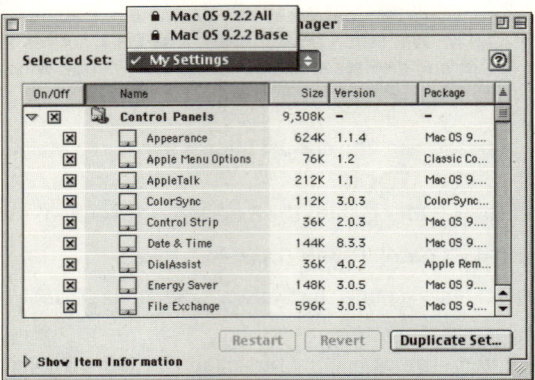

Figure 17-12: Access the Selected Set popup menu from the top of the Extensions Manager window.

Date & Time control panel

Although the current time and date that you set in the Date & Time preferences of Mac OS X also affect the Classic application environment, the settings for the clock in the Mac OS X menu bar don't affect the Classic menu bar. You configure the clock for the Classic menu bar in the Date & Time control panel. You can also set date formats for Classic applications in the Date & Time control panel. To set the date format, click the Date Format button. In the dialog that appears, you can choose a region whose customary formats you want to use, or you can create a custom format by changing individual settings. You set time formats for Classic applications in the Date & Time control panel. First, you click the Time Formats button. In the dialog that appears, you can choose a region whose customary formats you want to use, or you can create a custom format by changing individual settings.

Choosing text behaviors and setting number formats

The Text control panel allows you to choose a text behavior for Classic applications. Choose a language script from the Script pop-up menu, and then choose a regional language from the Behavior pop-up menu. By default only the Roman Script will be available, unless you install other packages such as Japanese language support from the Mac OS 9 installer CD. Regional Languages are only available for the specific Script they apply to.

You can set number formats for Classic applications in the Numbers control panel. You can choose a preconfigured number format for a region of the world, or you can specify a custom format by entering the punctuation marks to use as separators and the currency symbol.

Checking for Mac OS 9 software updates

The Software Update pane of System Preferences does not monitor for updates to Classic software. The Mac OS 9 control panel named Software Update does this. It is likely that you will never use this control panel, because the Software Update control panel does not function in the Classic application environment. You must restart your computer with Mac OS 9 to take advantage of this feature (if your computer supports it). It is also important to realize that Apple ceased development of Mac OS 9 several years ago, so there are likely no updates for you to download anyway. The control panel is simple to use, just open it and click Update Now. A control panel confirms your choice; click OK to continue. If you are connected to the Internet, the control panel contacts Apple's software servers and finds out whether there are any updates available for your Mac. If the control panel finds any available updates, it lists them. Select the updates you'd like to download, and then click Install.

Classic Applications and the Dock

When a Classic application is running, its icon appears in the Dock right next to your native Mac OS X applications. While Mac OS X attempts to make the icon look its best, you'll notice that it looks fuzzy compared to the crispness of a Mac OS X icon (this is due to antialiasing), Figure 17-1 shows an example of this. Mac OS 9 only supports icons that are 32 x 32 pixels, while Mac OS X supports icon sizes up to 128 x 128.

Just as with Mac OS X applications, Classic applications in your Dock can utilize Dock pop-up menus. To access the Dock pop-up menu either Control-click, or click and hold on the application's icon in the Dock and a small pop-up menu appears. You can choose to keep the icon in the Dock, show the application in the Finder, and hide or quit the application. Because Classic applications were not designed with the Dock in mind and run inside of the Classic application environment, you cannot access information that other Mac OS X native applications can provide from the Dock's contextual menu. Mac OS X applications often display a list of open windows in the application — playlists or media controls (iTunes) — usually you can just quit or force quit a Classic application from the Dock.

Managing Fonts in Classic

Although Classic handles font display and printing automatically, you can set a few options that affect how fonts look. You can set a font-smoothing option in the Appearance control panel, for example. If you use ATM with Classic, you can adjust how it scales PostScript fonts.

Adobe Type Manager (ATM)

You can set several options that affect how the optional Adobe Type Manager (ATM) software scales PostScript fonts for Classic applications. The ATM font smoothing appears onscreen and on printers that don't use PostScript. In addition, you can set options that affect ATM's performance. You make these settings in the ATM control panel. The next sections explain all the settings and what they do. Figure 17-13 shows the ATM control panel.

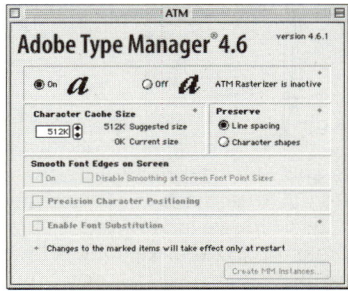

Figure 17-13: Set smoothing and performance options for PostScript fonts in Classic applications by using the ATM control panel.

Note   Adobe Type Manager is required only if you're using PostScript fonts and want to see them rendered properly on a non-PostScript device (such as your screen or most inkjet printers). If you don't find ATM in your Classic Control Panels menu, you can find it on the Mac OS 9 installation CD. Note that ATM Version 4.5.2 or higher is required with Classic—other versions crash and keep Classic from starting if installed. The ATM Deluxe control panel also crashes Classic if it hasn't been updated to Version 4.5.2 or higher. At the time we write this, ATM 4.6.1 is the version included on the Mac OS 9 CD.

Character Cache Size option

The Character Cache Size option affects performance. If applications seem to scroll more slowly with ATM turned on, try increasing this size.

Preserve option

The Preserve option determines whether ATM preserves line spacing or character shapes when it scales text. Preserving line spacing keeps line breaks and page breaks from changing with and without ATM, but this setting may clip the bottoms of some letters and vertically compress some accented capital letters. Preserving character shapes reduces the clipping but may change line breaks. The clipping occurs only onscreen and on output devices that don't use PostScript. No clipping occurs on a PostScript printer.

Smooth Font Edges on Screen option

The Smooth Font Edges on Screen option smoothes font edges onscreen in the same way the Appearance control panel does—by blending their jagged edges with the background color. Whereas Appearance works with all TrueType fonts, ATM works on Type 1 PostScript fonts. ATM can implement anti-aliasing of color text only when the monitor is set to display thousands or millions of colors. If the monitor is set to display 256 colors, ATM can implement anti-aliasing on black-and-white text only.

Precision Character Positioning option

The Precision Character Positioning option displays more accurate spacing, especially at small font sizes. Turning on this option causes ATM to calculate character positions on a fractional pixel basis, which may slow text display of some documents on slower computers.

Enable Font Substitution

By checking the Enable Font Substitution you are allowing ATM to substitute a standard font when a specified font is unavailable. This feature will prevent jagged fonts from being displayed or printed, but will change the look of your document.

Font Activation in Classic

The simplest way to activate fonts in Classic is to place a copy of the font in the Fonts folder of the active Classic System Folder. However, if you are a designer, or deal with many fonts on a daily basis, it becomes very tedious to activate and deactivate fonts manually in this manner. Mac OS 10.3 is the first Macintosh OS that ships with an Apple-supplied application that provides some font management tools. Font Book enables you to activate and deactivate fonts on the fly, and makes the active fonts available to Classic. However, third-party font utilities, which have been around for a while, allow you to organize and activate fonts with more automated controls (see Chapter 12 for more information on Font Book and some of the third party font utilities). Here are a few options:

✦ **ATM Deluxe** is a Classic-only application that extends the features of ATM, and activates fonts dynamically when you open a Classic document that contains fonts your system doesn't have. Other ATM Deluxe features facilitate reviewing, organizing, adding, and removing large numbers of Classic fonts as well as diagnosing some font problems. Fonts that are activated by ATM Deluxe are only seen by Classic applications. Look to www.adobe.com for more information on ATM Deluxe

✦ Both **Extensis Suitcase** and **Extensis FontReserve** are Mac OS X–native applications (they are Carbon, so they run in Mac OS 9 as well) that have similar functionality to ATM Deluxe. They allow you to manage your fonts and even auto-activate them in some applications (auto-activation features usually require a plug-in for some applications such as Illustrator or Quark Xpress. Plug-ins are provided by the Font utility Manufacturer). A great feature of both of these applications is that they make your fonts available in both Mac OS X and Classic. Professionals in a group environment benefit from FontReserve's server package, which allows groups to share the same font sets. Extensis's Web site, www.extensis.com, has trial downloads and more information on these products.

✦ Alsoft's **Master Juggler** has been updated for Mac OS X, and can activate fonts in the Classic application environment. You can find more information about Master Juggler at www.alsoft.com.

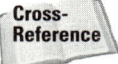

Cross-Reference   See Chapter 12 for additional coverage of font management in the Classic environment.

Printing from Classic Applications

Classic applications do not have access to Mac OS X printer drivers or their range of options, such as outputting PDF or previewing your output. Classic applications use the printer drivers available in the Extensions folder of the Classic application environment's System Folder. You can't print to Mac OS X printers from Classic applications and the same is true in reverse. The general procedures for printing, however, are the same in Classic applications as in Mac OS X applications.

This section is geared toward printing from Classic applications for users without that experience. In particular, it covers printing to networked printers because there are far more variations than we can possibly hope to cover in this space. Coverage for USB printers is brief — install your printer driver (if it's not already there) into the Extensions folder of Classic's System Folder using whatever installer your printer manufacturer includes.

Configuring an AppleTalk printer

Most printing is configured from a legacy program called the Chooser. The Chooser is (by default) kept in the Apple Menu Items folder of your Classic System folder. To launch the Chooser, you can either go to the Classic Menu ⇨ Apple Menu Items ⇨ Chooser, or, if you are already in the Classic System folder's, Apple Menu ⇨ Chooser. See Figure 17-14 for an example of what the Chooser looks like. The left side of the Chooser window displays an icon for each Classic printer driver that you have installed. After you select your printer driver on the left, the right side of the Chooser window displays a list of available printers or ports. You select the printer you want to use or the port to which the printer is connected. After selecting a printer, close the Chooser. Then, in your various Classic applications, make your Page Setup and Print selections.

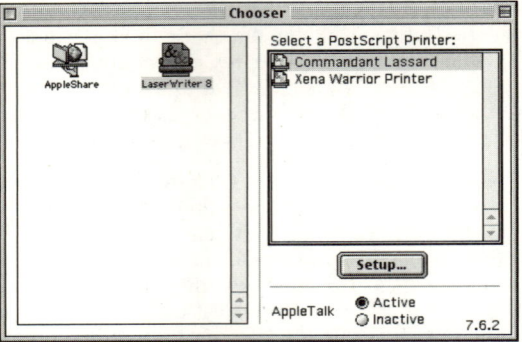

Figure 17-14: Use the Chooser to access printers in the Classic application environment.

Configuring an LPR printer

Not all printers or networks support AppleTalk; in some environments, you may find it impor-tant to configure one of your printers via IP address over a protocol called LPR. (LPR stands for Line Printer, and is a old Unix printer communication protocol) To configure an LPR printer in the Classic application environment you must use a program called the Desktop Printer Utility. This application is installed by default (in a Classic install) in the Utilities folder in your Applications (Mac OS 9) folder. To create an LPR printer, follow theses steps:

1. **Launch the Desktop Printer Utility.** The New Desktop Printer dialog appears (see Figure 17-15).

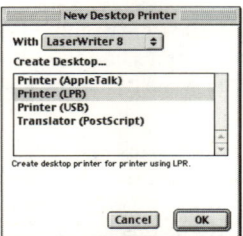

Figure 17-15: Though unsupported, the main screen of the Desktop Printer Utility allows you to configure LPR- and USB-attached PostScript printers in the Classic application environment.

2. **Select: Printer (LPR) and click OK.** Another dialog appears (see Figure 17-16). The top half of the dialog, Postscript Printer Description File, allows you to set the PPD for your printer, which contains information about the options and capability of the printer.

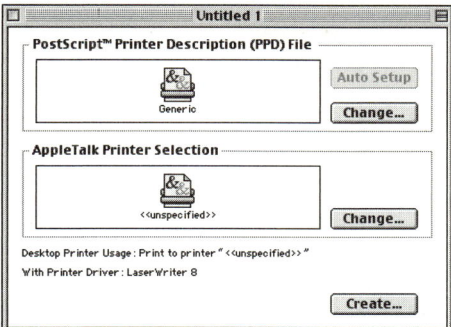

Figure 17-16: Click Change in the top half of the window to set the printer description file.

3. **Click Change in the Postscript Printer Description File section.** A list of installed PPDs appears. You can select from this list. If you do not have the proper PPD file installed, check your printer manufacturer's Web site, and install it into your Classic System Folder. In a pinch, however, you can choose to use the generic PPD; while it may not have all of the options your printer supports, it should at least allow you to get printing (see Figure 17-17).

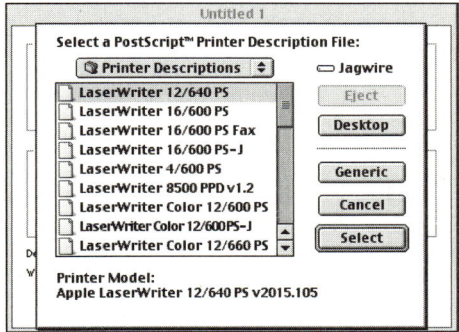

Figure 17-17: Select the printer description that matches the printer you want to use. In a pinch, choose Generic.

4. **Click Change in the bottom half of the window under LPR Printer Selection.** A dialog appears allowing you to enter the IP address and queue name (if there is one) for the printer and then click OK (see Figure 17-18).

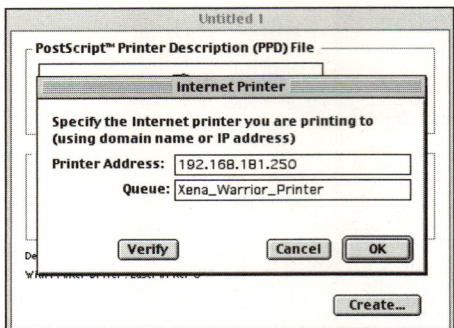

Figure 17-18: It is very important to be certain of the IP address of your printer, so you can use the Verify button to check if you have entered a valid address.

5. **Click Create.** The Printer Name dialog appears, and you are asked to name the printer (see Figure 17-19).

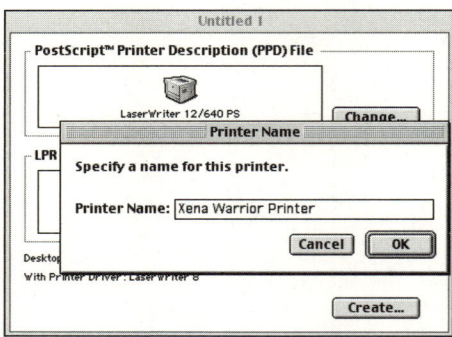

Figure 17-19: Names are important.

6. **Enter a name for the printer and click OK.** Your printer is created.

Note   Although we just discussed using the Desktop Printer Utility, it is important to be aware that Desktop Printing as you know it from Mac OS 9 is nonfunctional. Because the Classic application environment doesn't use the Mac OS 9 Finder, Classic Desktop Printers aren't visible anymore, although you can access all of your desktop printers from the Print dialog box. Printers created using the Desktop Printer Utility are also not visible in the Chooser, and you cannot reconfigure a desktop printer after you create it. To delete a desktop printer, open the Desktop Printer Utility and go to File ➪ Delete. A Delete Printer dialog box will appear and prompt you to select from a list of configured printers allowing you to delete any that you no longer need.

Printing to a networked printer from Classic

Networked printers recognized by the Classic are PostScript printers, and they use the LaserWriter 8 printer driver. If you are unsure whether your printer supports Postscript, check your printer's manual for more information.

To select your default printer, follow these steps:

1. **Launch the Classic application you want to use so that the Classic menu bar is at the top of your screen.**

2. **Choose Apple ⇨ Chooser.** The Chooser will launch in the Classic application environment.

3. **Click the LaserWriter 8 driver.** A list of printers appears on the right. (See Figure 17-14 for an example of a listing of printers.)

4. **Select your desired printer from the list on the right side of the Chooser.** If you only have one printer on your network that supports Appletalk, you will only see one printer listed.

5. **Close the Chooser.** Your printer is now selected as the default.

You can also access the Chooser from the Classic menu (if you have it enabled) under Apple Menu Items, and skip the first two steps.

Fortunately, the Apple LaserWriter 8 Print dialog box is almost as smart as the Mac OS X Print dialog box. While it won't list all your printers in the Printer pop-up menu, it does list all your available LaserWriter-compatible printers, so you can switch between the LaserWriter-compatible printers there. The Print dialog box is accessible from within Classic applications from the File menu, and normally has a keyboard shortcut of Command-P.

Setting LaserWriter 8 Page Setup options

Selecting the Page Setup command for a printer using LaserWriter 8 presents a dialog box with settings for Page Attributes, which is very similar in function to the Mac OS X version in its choices although it looks different (see Figure 17-20). You usually find the Page Setup Command under the File menu of a Classic application.

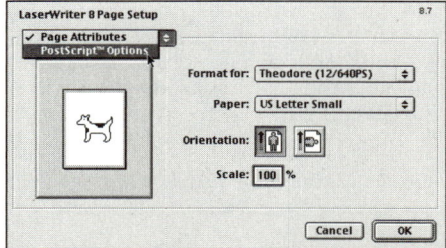

Figure 17-20: The LaserWriter 8 Page Setup allows you to format the page attributes for the specific printer you are printing to.

The Page Attributes options are almost identical to the Mac OS X choices, with the following exceptions:

✦ Orientation provides only two choices — portrait or landscape. You cannot specify the leading edge for landscape documents.

✦ Generic Printer is not available as a choice.

✦ Scaling is limited to a range of 25% to 400%.

Due to Classic's less-capable graphics engine and font support, you have fewer PostScript options than in OS X, as shown in Figure 17-21. The following options are available:

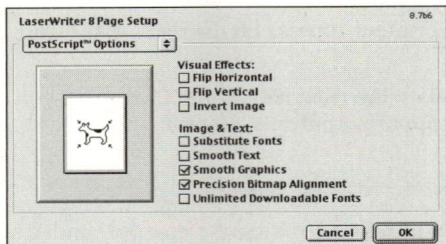

Figure 17-21: The pull-down menu allows you to access the PostScript Options for LaserWriter 8 Page Setup.

✦ **Flip Horizontal/Flip Vertical:** This option creates mirror images of your document. Your selected option appears in the illustration in the dialog box. Flip Horizontal flips the image right to left, which is useful if you are creating a film image on a Linotronic imagesetter for a transparency or if the pages have to be emulsion side down.

✦ **Invert Image:** This option makes all the black parts of a page print white, and vice versa. You probably won't have much use for this parlor trick unless you create film negatives on a slide printer that has no method of its own for creating negative images.

✦ **Substitute Fonts:** This option substitutes PostScript fonts for any fixed-sized screen fonts for which no PostScript or TrueType equivalent is available. For example, Geneva becomes Helvetica, Monaco becomes Courier, and New York becomes Times. The one drawback of font substitution is that although the variable-size font is substituted for its fixed-sized cousin, the spacing of letters and words on a line does not change, and the printed results often are remarkably ugly. For the best results, do not use fixed-size fonts that lack TrueType or PostScript equivalents, and leave the Substitute Fonts option off.

✦ **Smooth Text:** This option smoothes the jagged edges of fixed sizes that have no matching PostScript fonts or TrueType fonts. For best results, avoid such fonts, and leave the Smooth Text option off.

✦ **Smooth Graphics:** This option smoothes the jagged edges of bitmap graphic images created with painting programs. Smoothing improves some images, but blurs the detail out of others. Try printing with Smooth Graphics set both ways, and go with the one that looks best to you. This option has no effect on graphics created with drawing programs, such as FreeHand and Illustrator.

✦ **Precision Bitmap Alignment:** This option reduces the entire printed image to avoid minor distortions in bitmap graphics. The distortions occur because of the nature of the dot density of bitmap graphics. For example, 72 dpi (dots-per-inch), the standard screen-image size, does not divide evenly into 300 dpi, 400 dpi, or 600 dpi (the dot density of many laser printers). When you print to a 300-dpi printer, for example, turning on this option reduces page images by 4 percent, effectively printing them at 288 dpi (an even multiple of 72 dpi). The reductions align the bitmaps properly to produce crisper output.

✦ **Unlimited Downloadable Fonts:** This option enables you to use more fonts than your printer's memory can hold at one time. The printing software does this by removing fonts from the printer's memory after use, making way for other fonts. Be aware that the constant downloading and flushing of font files takes time and, thus, slows printing. Of note is that EPS (Encapsulated PostScript) graphics using fonts that are not present elsewhere on the page do not print correctly because the printer substitutes Courier for those orphan fonts. If you see Courier in a graphic where you did not want it, make sure that this option is turned off.

Setting LaserWriter 8 print options

When you choose the Print command for a printer that uses the LaserWriter 8 driver, you see a dialog box with settings for the number of copies, page numbers to print, paper source, output destination, and more. You switch among several groups of options by choosing a group from the unlabeled pop-up menu near the top of the dialog box. Figure 17-22 illustrates the pop-up menu for switching among groups of options in the Print dialog box for LaserWriter 8.

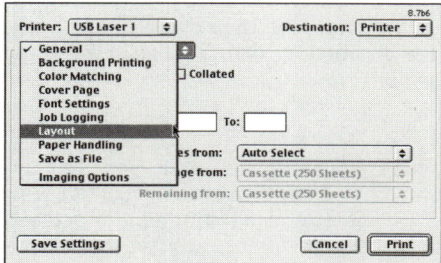

Figure 17-22: The LaserWriter 8 Print dialog box is similar to the Mac OS X print dialog box, but you can't switch among all of your printers, only those that use the LaserWriter 8 PostScript driver.

You'll notice that these print settings are almost identical to the choices described earlier for AppleTalk printers under Mac OS X. The differences are as follows:

✦ **Destination pop-up menu:** This menu enables you to choose whether your output is sent to the printer or saved to disk. The ability to select the print job's destination is similar in concept to the Output Options choice under Mac OS X, with the exceptions that the default save format is PostScript rather than PDF and that a variety of options is available in the Save as File panel. If you have the Acrobat Distiller software installed, you can select Acrobat PDF as the output format on the Save as File panel.

✦ **Save Settings:** This feature applies only to the current printer and does not allow you to name the set. The last-used settings become the default settings for that printer.

✦ **Background Printing:** This feature enables you to determine whether printing should function as a multitasking operation or whether all other Classic activity should be subordinate to the printing task.

✦ **Cover Page:** This feature enables you to direct the printer to produce a cover page and, if so, whether it should print before or after the document. The cover page reports the document name, your user name, and when it was printed.

✦ **Font Settings:** This option enables you to annotate your PostScript output with comments where font changes are made. It also lets you specify which fonts are downloaded.

✦ **Job Logging:** This feature is the equivalent of the Error Handling choice under Mac OS X.

Managing the Classic printing queue

The PrintMonitor application handles printing of waiting print requests while you continue working with other applications. PrintMonitor opens in the background automatically whenever there are print requests in the PrintMonitor Documents folder (inside the System Folder), deletes each print request that it prints, and quits automatically when the PrintMonitor Documents folder is empty.

Some printers made by companies other than Apple come with their own applications for managing the queue of waiting print requests. For instructions on using one of these applications, check the documentation that came with your printer.

Viewing the print queue

While PrintMonitor is open in the background, you can make it the active application by clicking its icon in the Dock. You also can open it at any time by double-clicking its icon, which is located in the Extensions folder of Classic's System Folder. Making PrintMonitor active or opening it displays its window. The PrintMonitor window identifies the print request that is printing, lists the print requests waiting to be printed, and displays the status of the current print request. Figure 17-23 shows the PrintMonitor window.

PrintMonitor automatically hides its window when you switch to another application, but PrintMonitor remains open in the background as long as it has print requests to process.

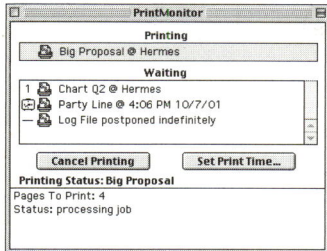

Figure 17-23: View queued print requests from Classic applications in the PrintMonitor window.

Changing the printing order

PrintMonitor ordinarily processes print requests in chronological order, oldest first. You can change the order by dragging print requests in the PrintMonitor window. You drag a print request by its icon, not by its name or sequence number.

Scheduling printing requests

You can schedule when PrintMonitor processes a print request, or you can postpone a print request indefinitely. First, select the print request you want to schedule (by clicking it) in the PrintMonitor window. You can select the print request being printed or any print request waiting to be printed. Then click Set Print Time. Figure 17-24 shows the dialog in which you set a time and date for processing a print request or postpone it indefinitely.

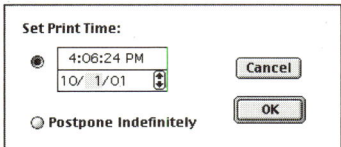

Figure 17-24: In a busy work environment when you need to print a 400-page document, it's courteous to schedule it to begin after every one leaves so that it will be ready when you arrive in the morning.

A print request scheduled for later printing appears in PrintMonitor's waiting list with an alarm-clock icon in place of a sequence number. A print request postponed indefinitely appears in the waiting list with a dash in place of a sequence number, and it will not be printed until you schedule a print time for it.

Stopping and starting printing

You can suspend all background printing by choosing Stop Printing from PrintMonitor's File menu. Before PrintMonitor stops printing, it finishes the request currently printing. To resume printing, choose Resume Printing from the File menu.

Setting PrintMonitor preferences

PrintMonitor can notify you when something happens that requires your attention during background printing. For example, PrintMonitor can notify you when you need to manually feed paper for background printing. An alert box, a blinking PrintMonitor icon in the Classic menu bar, or both, can notify you. To specify how you want to be notified, use the Preferences command in PrintMonitor's File menu.

You can also use the Preferences command to specify how you want to be notified about printing errors, such as PrintMonitor not being able to locate a printer that is supposed to print a print request. PrintMonitor can just display a diamond symbol next to its name in the Application menu at the right end of the menu bar, or it can display the symbol and blink its icon in the menu bar. It can also do both of those things plus display an alert. You can turn off everything except the diamond in the Application menu.

Note   Regardless of the notification settings that you make in PrintMonitor's Preferences dialog box, you are always notified that PrintMonitor requires your attention by the PrintMonitor icon bouncing high out of the Dock.

Examining the Essentials of the Mac OS 9 System Folder

The heart of Mac OS 9 is the System file located in the OS 9 System Folder. This file contains the code that makes Mac OS 9 possible — it provides the basic system services and protocols through which everything else communicates.

In the early days of Mac OS, the System file contained almost everything — fonts, sounds, desk accessories (the original Apple menu items), keyboards, you name it. Due to architectural and space limitations, many of these resources were moved out of the System file to stand alone as files in your System Folder. From this reorganization arose a new problem — System Folder clutter. All of a sudden, there were so many files and folders inside System Folders that most users couldn't find what they were looking for.

Apple addressed this by introducing specialized folders for classes of System support files — Extensions, Control Panels, Fonts, Preferences, and so forth. Of course, even this organizational setup grew unwieldy as more and more capabilities became available, each capability requiring its own collection of support files in the System Folder. Then, there was the problem of users putting the right files in the right folders when installing new software or accidentally dragging a file to a folder where it didn't belong.

Adding items to the System Folder

In response to the location difficulties, Apple provided *autorouting* intelligence to the Finder — you can drop certain file types on the System Folder, and the Finder places them in the correct subfolder for you. Control panels and some applications that have been typed to make them work like control panels are placed in the Control Panels folder; extensions, printer drivers, shared libraries, and the like are routed to the Extensions folder; Sherlock plug-in files are placed in Internet Search Sites; fonts are placed in the Fonts folder; and so forth.

In general, if you have a file that you want in the System Folder, just drag it onto the System Folder's icon (not into a window that is displaying the System Folder), and it is usually placed where it is supposed to be. As shown in Figure 17-25, the Mac OS X Finder has the same feature as Mac OS 9 did, and will let you know that it is about to autoroute the item (and ask for confirmation that this is what you want it to do). On a rare occasion, you might have a need to place a file in a specific location within the System Folder — such as when you want to add something to your Classic Apple menu. When that is the case, open the System Folder in a Finder window and drag the file to the folder where it needs to be.

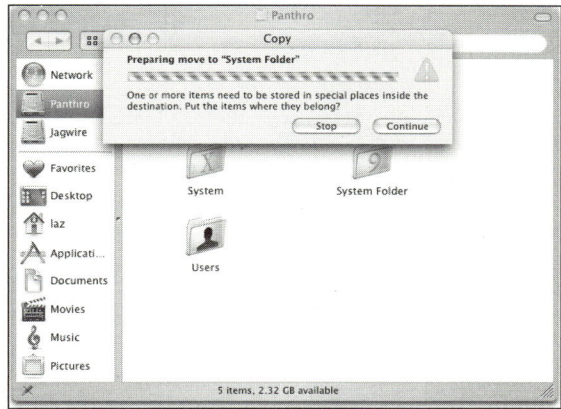

Figure 17-25: You don't have to know where everything in the Classic Folder belongs, or even what you're putting there — Mac OS X can autoroute the item for you by type, just drop it on the System Folder.

Removing items from the System Folder

Unfortunately, Apple has never developed an automated process for removing items from the System Folder or its subfolders, nor does there exist a really intelligent uninstaller that can determine which items can safely be removed without compromising the usability of existing applications. Some third-party solutions come close, for example Aladdin Systems' Spring Cleaning, but they do not cover all contingencies and can make serious mistakes, often leaving your system in worse condition that it was before you used them.

To manage extensions and control panels, you should employ the Extensions Manager that comes with Mac OS 9 (see earlier in this chapter for more information). Deactivate the items you want to remove, and restart the Classic application environment. The deactivated items are now in folders named Extensions (Disabled) and Control Panels (Disabled), and you can safely remove them if you want to free up some disk space. Of course, you can remove items from the Classic application environment's System Folder when Classic application environment isn't running without going through these steps. You can remove (or add) fonts while the Classic application environment is running, but it is best that no Classic applications are running to ensure that they are properly recognized.

Configuring Classic applications to start up automatically

Like Mac OS X's Startup Items (Startup Items is a panel in the Accounts preference pane of the System Preferences application, see Chapter 2 for more info), Classic allows you to specify applications and documents you want to open automatically when Classic starts up or shuts down.

You place the items (in general, it's better to place aliases to the items) into the System Folder's Startup Items and Shutdown Items folders. By placing aliases into the folders, you don't have to worry about navigating into or out of your System Folder hierarchy for changed documents or applications, nor do you have to place support files that need to be located with their applications in the folder with the application items.

Now, each time you start Classic, the applications and documents in your Startup Items folder open. Similarly, each time you quit Classic, the items in your Shutdown Items folder open. Be careful with Shutdown Items. If you set an application that requires user input as a Shutdown Item and you are not around to baby-sit the process, the shutdown of your computer or the shutdown of the Classic application environment will probably "time out" (or fail to complete).

You can use the Extensions Manager, as discussed earlier in this chapter, to toggle these Startup Items on and off.

Summary

When you start actually living in the Classic application environment, your next ambition will quickly become *how to stop using it*. Apple has done a great job making the Classic application environment work side by side with the Mac OS X environment. However, it's so inconvenient to have to deal with the slow Classic screen redraws, menus switching color and placement, and visibly antiquated underpinnings, that you'll soon realize how much easier your life would be if you left Classic behind. Four generations into Mac OS X (five if you count the public beta release), so many applications have been updated, built from scratch, or ported from other operating systems, that you'll find that there are now enough options that you should not be forced to rely on the Classic application environment in your daily life.

In this chapter, you've learned the following:

✦ That the Classic application environment is a version of Mac OS 9 running on top of Mac OS X.

✦ The Classic application environment is useful when you need to run old applications that haven't yet been updated for Mac OS X.

✦ The Classic application environment doesn't take full advantage of Mac OS X's advanced memory protection, multitasking, and multiuser environment.

✦ How to use Classic control panels, manage fonts in Classic, configure printers (even unsupported LPR printers), and the Classic System Folder.

✦   ✦   ✦

Using .Mac Internet Services Suite

At the July 2002 MacWorld Expo in New York, Apple CEO Steve Jobs announced that the free suite of Mac-only Internet-based applications and services previously known as iTools would now be fee-based, and its name would be changed to .*Mac* (Pronounced "dot Mac").

The .Mac services greatly expand on iTools, and have evolved into a remarkably powerful combination of software and services that help you easily store, share, and protect your files as well as communicate in text, voice, or video. As a result, the number of users willing to pay $99 for .Mac is steadily growing.

Mac OS X 10.2 was designed to work with the .Mac service, and provided a tab in the Internet System Preference pane to configure it. Mac OS X 10.3 integrates .Mac further, by now providing a separate .Mac System Preference pane, as well as including in its installation package several applications that can take advantage of .Mac services.

In this chapter, you find out about the Internet services .Mac has to offer, including .Mac mail, iCards, and the HomePage service. We discuss the applications included with Mac OS X 10.3 that interoperate with each other and the .Mac service, but can also be used without it: Address Book, iCal, iChat AV, and iSync. You also explore the main utilities you can download as part of your .Mac membership: Backup, Slides Publisher, and Virex.

Figure 18-1 shows the .Mac welcome Web page.

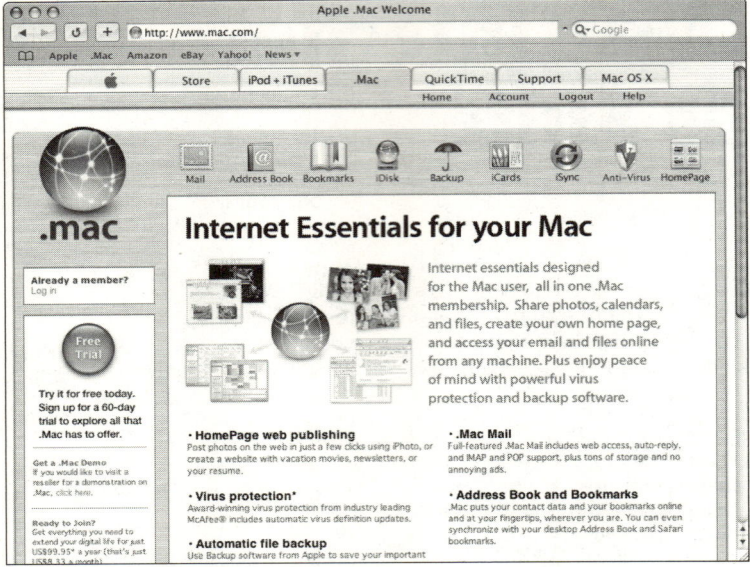

Figure 18-1: Apple's .Mac welcome page.
(Web page courtesy of Apple Computer, Inc.)

About the .Mac Service

Note A membership to .Mac costs US $99.95 for one year. If you don't live in the United States, Apple accepts payment in nine other currencies. You can try a limited version of .Mac free for two months.

For the membership fee, you receive the following services:

✦ **Mac.com Mail:** provides email service from Apple's servers with an initial 15 megabytes of storage, featuring a nifty `membername@mac.com` address, and Web mail access from any computer with a supported Web browser. You have the option to purchase additional storage.

✦ **.Mac Web mail:** access your Mac.com email account from any Web browser.

✦ **.Mac Address Book:** store your contact information on the Web so you can access email addresses whenever you use .Mac Mail via the Web.

✦ **iDisk:** file storage space on Apple's Internet servers, which can be used to share files with anyone you wish, transfer files between computers, or back up your computer's files. The initial storage space of 100MB can be upgraded to a maximum of 1 gigabyte of space.

✦ **iDisk Utility:** allows users of Mac OS X 10.2 to quickly open their iDisk, view or add to their iDisk storage, assign a password and read-write access to their Public folder, or connect to the Public folder of another member. Mac OS X 10.3 users can use the same functionality built in to the new .Mac System Preferences pane.

✦ **iChatAV:** an application that provides instant text messaging to other .Mac or AOL members using AIM, and voice or video messaging to .Mac members using iChatAV.

✦ **Backup:** a utility that copies the files you choose from your hard disk to a CD, DVD, or your iDisk.

✦ **Virex:** a utility that protects your Mac against computer viruses.

✦ **HomePage:** simplifies the creation of personal Web sites to publish text, photos from iPhoto, or movies.

✦ **iCards:** digital greeting cards for email, with a wide range of photos or messages to choose from. Standard iCards can be sent without a .Mac membership, but Create-your-own iCards, using your own images, requires .Mac membership.

✦ **Slides Publisher:** an application that creates a slideshow of photos on your iDisk that can be viewed over the Internet by anyone with Mac OS X 10.2 and above as a slideshow screen saver.

✦ **Member Benefits:** a constantly changing assortment of free downloads, discounted software, and special offers.

✦ **iCal application:** allows users to publish their calendars to their iDisk so others can view them over the Internet.

✦ **iSync application:** allows users to synchronize Address Book contacts, iCal calendars, and Safari bookmarks between Macs.

Requirements to use .Mac

Apple's stated requirements to use the .Mac service are provided in the following list:

✦ You must be age 13 or older.

✦ From a Macintosh computer, you must use Mac OS 9 or Mac OS X.

✦ From a Windows computer, you must use Microsoft Windows 98, Windows 2000, or Windows XP. You can only access the .Mac Web mail, a Web page created by a .Mac user using HomePage on a Macintosh, or see a .Mac member's Public Folder in their iDisk.

✦ Unix or Linux-based computers can access your iDisk or a Public Folder using the Internet file sharing protocol WebDAV.

✦ Web browsers: Mac OS X Safari recommended or Mac OS 9 or Windows.

✦ Microsoft Internet Explorer Version 5.0 or later

✦ Netscape Communicator Version 4.7x; Netscape 6.0 is not supported.

✦ E-mail applications: Mac OS X Mail, Microsoft Outlook Express, and Netscape Navigator or Communicator are recommended.

Figure 18-2 shows the page where .Mac members can log in to the services.

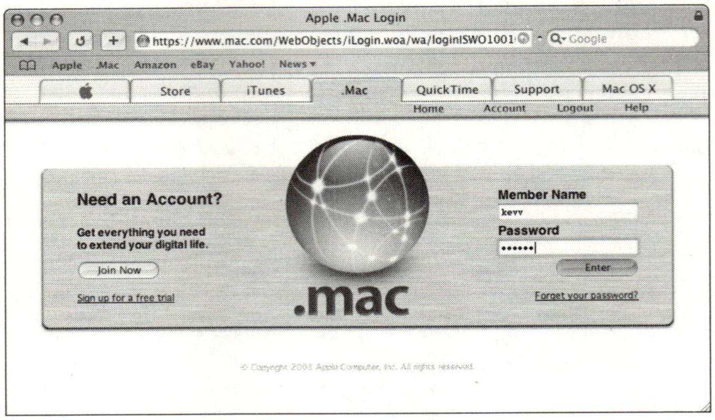

Figure 18-2: The .Mac log in Web page.
(Web page courtesy of Apple Computer, Inc.)

Signing up for a .Mac account

Apple has made signing up for .Mac membership very easy; in fact, we count four different ways to join. Take your pick.

The retail box option

You can buy a .Mac account at any Apple Store, or at certain other retailers. You get a shrink-wrapped cardboard box that contains a CD, a "Getting Started" instruction card with a .Mac activation key sticker, and two Apple logo stickers.

The CD contains the Backup, iDisk, iSync, and Virex utilities and iPhoto, along with some more in depth instructions. This software either comes with Mac OS X 10.3 or can be readily downloaded, usually in more recent versions.

To activate the membership, go to www.mac.com/activate, where you enter your activation key, create a new account or upgrade a trial account, and pick your member name and password. You are also asked to provide your contact information, and you have the option to renew your membership automatically by entering credit card information.

The .Mac retail package is a nice way to give a .Mac membership as a gift, but if you already use Mac OS X 10.2 or above, and have Internet access, you can join .Mac immediately, without having to go to a store.

The online sign-up option

To become a .Mac member by signing up online from any computer with an Internet connection, go to either www.mac.com, or to Apple's home page at www.apple.com and click the .Mac tab. You will see a Web page detailing the benefits of a .Mac membership. Here you can sign up for the free 60-day trial. To become a member, click Ready to Join?

The Mac OS X installation option

Signing up for a .Mac account is possible during the initial setup process that follows installation of Mac OS X. If you already have a .Mac account at that time, the Setup Assistant program offers to configure Mac OS X to use your account. If you don't already have a .Mac account, the Setup Assistant offers to create one on the spot. You can also choose to skip either choice, and not sign up.

The .Mac System Preferences option

If you are already running Mac OS X and did not create a .Mac account during installation, or if you'd like another .Mac account, you can easily create one at any time. To do this, perform the following steps:

1. **Start System Preferences by choosing Apple ⇨ System Preferences or by clicking the System Preferences icon in the Dock.**

2. **Click the .Mac icon or choose View ⇨ .Mac.**

3. **Click the .Mac tab button and then click the Sign Up button.** Your Web browser opens and displays the .Mac sign-up page.

Details about signing up

Whichever option you use to join .Mac, you end up at the .Mac sign-up page, shown in Figure 18-3. This page's format could change slightly, but should look very much like what you see here.

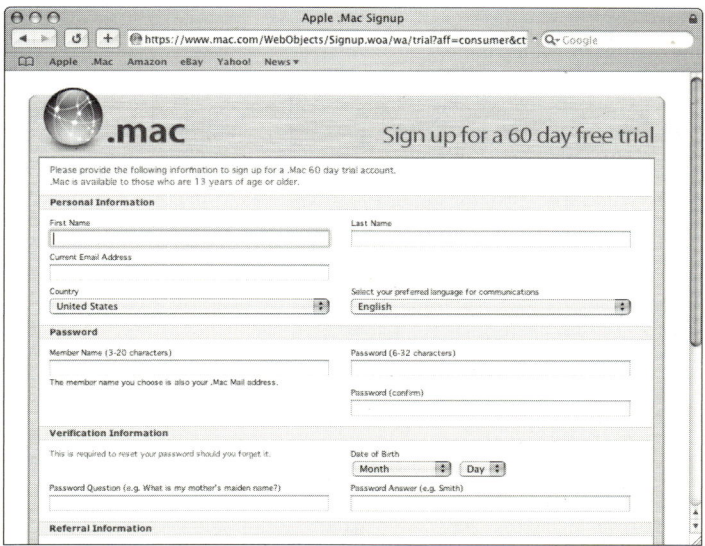

Figure 18-3: The .Mac sign-up page.
(Web page courtesy of Apple Computer, Inc.)

You are asked to fill in personal information and select a member name and password. Your member name is what will precede @mac.com in your .Mac email address. For example, if you choose Jdoe as your member name, your email address will be `jdoe@mac.com`.

Your member name cannot be changed after your account is established. The password you select can be changed at any time.

After you fill out and submit the form, you are informed if your account request was accepted. If you failed to provide some required information, you are asked to resubmit the form with the missing information included. Another possible reason for a rejected request is if your selected member name is already in use. If that problem arises, you are asked to try a different member name, and .Mac suggests some variations of the one you originally proposed.

Next, you are asked to pay for your membership with a credit card (unless you already entered the activation key from the retail package). Your account automatically renews each year using your credit card information unless you deselect the Auto-Renew checkbox.

After your account exists, you're informed that a copy of your sign-up information is sent to your new email account. (See Chapter 6 for a discussion of using Mac OS X Mail to access your .Mac e-mail.) Following that, you are asked whether you want to send announcement iCards (electronic greeting cards) to people informing them of your new email address.

Figure 18-4 shows the .Mac welcome Web page that members see after logging in.

Figure 18-4: Apple's .Mac welcome page.
(Web page courtesy of Apple Computer, Inc.)

Updating or upgrading your .Mac membership

You can update your address, billing information, or password at any time by going to www.mac.com and clicking Account on the .Mac tab. At the same place, you can upgrade your account to include additional iDisk or email storage space, or additional email-only accounts.

You can buy up to 200 megabytes of email storage, 1 gigabyte of iDisk storage, and up to 10 additional 5 megabyte email accounts, whose storage cannot be increased.

The amount you pay to upgrade depends on how much time is left in your yearly membership.

Configuring Mac OS X for your .Mac account using the .Mac System Preference pane

When you get a new .Mac account, you can (and should) configure Mac OS X to use that particular .Mac account. Configuring Mac OS X to use a .Mac account enables you to connect easily to that account's iDisk in the Finder. Doing so also sets up the Mail application to use the account for e-mail.

To configure Mac OS X for a .Mac account, follow these steps:

1. **Start System Preferences.** Either choose Apple ➪ System Preferences or click the System Preferences icon in the Dock.

2. **Click the .Mac icon or choose View ➪ .Mac.**

3. **Click the .Mac button and then enter your .Mac member name and password.** Figure 18-5 shows the .Mac panel.

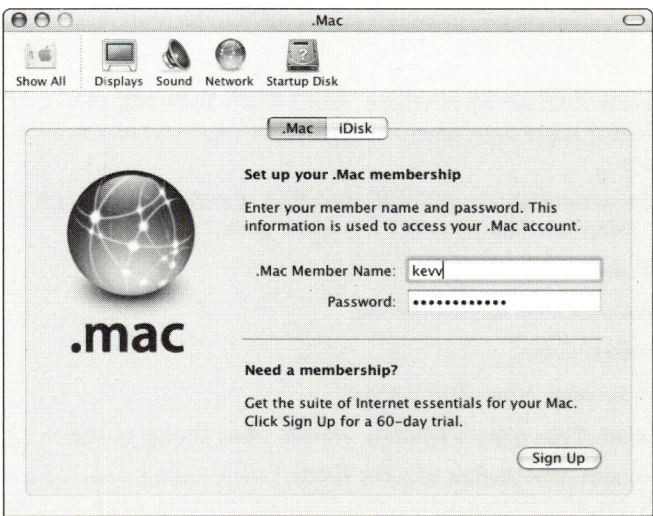

Figure 18-5: Set up your membership at the .Mac panel.

If you enter your .Mac member name and password in the Setup Assistant following the installation of Mac OS X, this information is automatically entered into the .Mac System Preference pane.

Note   If you change your .Mac password, you must enter the new password in the .Mac System Preference pane.

Mac.com email service

.Mac Mail Mac.com (also known as Mac.com) is .Mac's premium email service. The following list provides the service's key features:

✦ A Web-based email account which is ISP (Internet Service Provider) independent; you can keep your Mac.com address if you change your ISP.

✦ Your email address is your .Mac member name followed by @mac.com.

✦ Use any standard email program to read your mail.

✦ Send and receive your email from any Mac or Windows machine with an Internet connection via .Mac Mail on the Web.

✦ 15 megabyte mailbox, expandable up to 200 megabytes.

✦ Auto-reply to incoming email.

✦ Message forwarding to an alternate email address.

✦ Add a text or photo signature to outgoing emails.

You have two choices to read your .Mac Mail messages. You can configure your email program to receive .Mac Mail messages, or you can use your Web browser to access .Mac Mail on the Web.

Setting up Mac OS X Mail to receive .Mac Mail messages

Mac OS X's included Mail application must be set up to receive messages from .Mac Mail. Follow this procedure:

1. Follow the instructions above under the heading "Configuring Mac OS X for your .Mac account using the .Mac System Preference pane."

2. Open the Mail application.

3. Choose Preferences from the Mail menu.

4. Click the Accounts icon.

5. Click the Add Account (plus sign) button.

6. From the Account Type pop-up window, choose .Mac, shown in Figure 18-6.

7. Enter your account information into the fields. Your email address is entered automatically from the information in the .Mac System Preference pane.

8. Click OK.

9. Close the Accounts window.

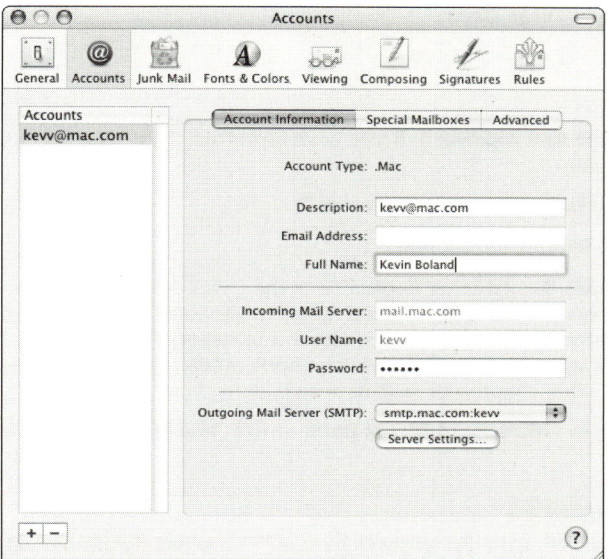

Figure 18-6: The Mail application's Accounts sheet at the Account Information panel.

.Mac Mail on the Web

You can access you .Mac mail account with any Web browser on any Internet connected computer via its Web interface, shown in Figure 18-7.

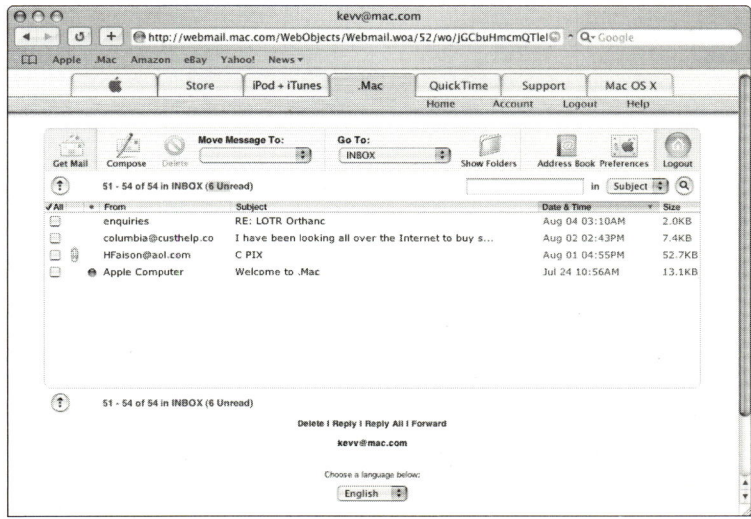

Figure 18-7: The .Mac mail on the Web interface.
(Web page courtesy of Apple Computer, Inc.)

To use Mac.com Web mail, follow these steps:

1. **Go to the .Mac Web page at** `www.mac.com`

2. **Click .Mac Mail.**

3. **Enter your member name and password.** If you have forgotten them, they were sent to you in your welcome email.

4. **The .Mac Mail Web interface opens (see Figure 18-7).**

5. **Click the Address Book icon in the toolbar.**

6. **Enter email addresses into the Address Book.** Check the Quick Address checkbox in right column for those you use the most to have them conveniently appear in a 10-item pop-up menu next to address field when you compose a message. You can also sync this online address book with the Mac OS X Address book application using iSync (see the iSync section later in this chapter for instructions).

7. **Click the Compose icon in either the Address Book or the .Mac Mail interface to create a new email.**

Setting .Mac Mail preferences

To set preferences for .Mac Mail, click the Preferences icon in the toolbar. Figure 18-8 shows the Preferences interface.

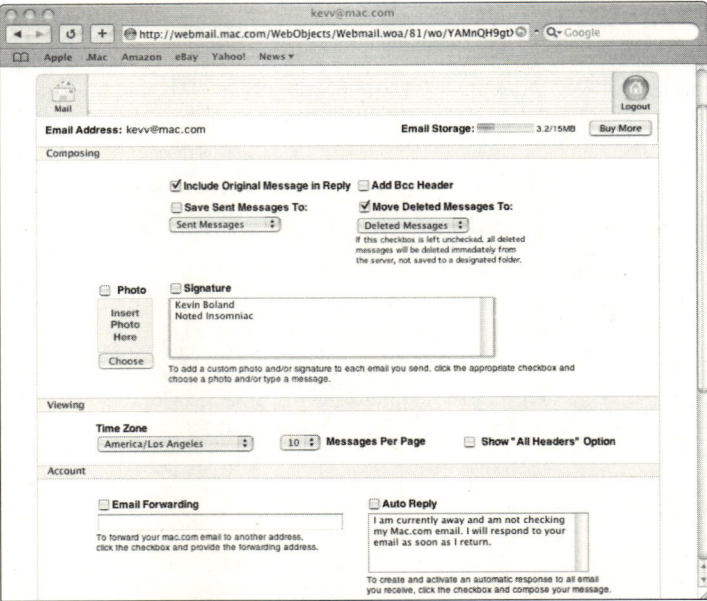

Figure 18-8: The .Mac Mail on the Web Preferences page.
(Web page courtesy of Apple Computer, Inc.)

At the top right, a bar shows the email storage you have used compared to how much is available. Click the Buy More button to upgrade your email storage.

In the Composing section, you can choose an image from your hard drive to use as your photo signature, to appear on outgoing emails. The image looks best if you use iPhoto to create a 64 x 64-pixel image. You can also enter text in the Signature field to add to each email you send; many type their name and contact information here, and sometimes a favorite quotation or saying.

In the Viewing section, set your time zone, the number of messages to appear on the page, and set the Show All Headers option.

In the Account section, click the Email Forwarding checkbox to forward your mac.com email to another address; enter the destination address in the field below. This affects all incoming email, whether you read it using a desktop email program or .Mac Mail on the Web. If you are going away and cannot check your email for awhile, check the Auto Reply checkbox and compose your outgoing message in the field below.

Tips for Using .Mac Mail on the Web

The following list provides you with helpful tips on using .Mac mail:

✦ A .Mac Mail message must be 3 megabytes or smaller to be sent successfully, including any attachments.

✦ You can create new folders to organize your messages by clicking Show Folders and then clicking the New icon. The folders you create will appear in the Go To pop-up menu; select the folder here to view its contents.

✦ To move messages to a particular folder, open the message or select its checkbox and then choose the destination folder from the Move To Folder pop-up menu.

✦ Deleted messages are moved to the Deleted messages folder, where it is saved for 30 days before it is permanently deleted. You can manually empty the folder anytime you wish by choosing Show Folders, clicking the checkbox next to the Deleted Messages folder, and clicking Empty. Permanently delete messages without saving them for 30 days, by clicking Preferences and deselecting the "Moved Deleted Messages To" checkbox.

✦ You can change the folder where deleted messages are saved. Click Preferences and choose a folder from the "Move Deleted Messages To" pop-up menu.

✦ Search for a specific message in the current folder using the Search field. Pick Subject, From, To, or CC from the "in" pop-up menu. Click the button with the magnifying glass to start the search.

✦ To search for a word or phrase in the body of an open message, use your browser's Find feature.

✦ To format a message so that the printed version only contains header information and body text, open the message and then click Print Ready. Otherwise, your Web browser will print the .Mac tabs and the .Mac Mail toolbar.

In the section below the Account section, under the Check Other POP Mail heading, you can enter the email address, Incoming Mail server, User Name, and Password of an email account you want to view along with your .Mac Mail account. Choose a folder to import the mail into from Import POP to: pop-up menu; the default is INBOX. Click the Leave Messages on Server checkbox to do just that, in order to retain the availability of the messages to email programs that are set to check this account. Click the Get Other Mail button to add another account to be checked.

Tip   AOL's email program cannot be used to view .Mac Mail messages directly, but you can set your .Mac Mail account to forward email to your AOL account.

.Mac Address Book

The .Mac Address Book exists on the Web for your use when addressing a message in .Mac Mail on the Web. You can add addresses manually, or have iSync synchronize it with the Address Book application on your Macintosh.

Figure 18-9 shows the page that appears the first time you click the Address Book icon in .Mac mail on the Web.

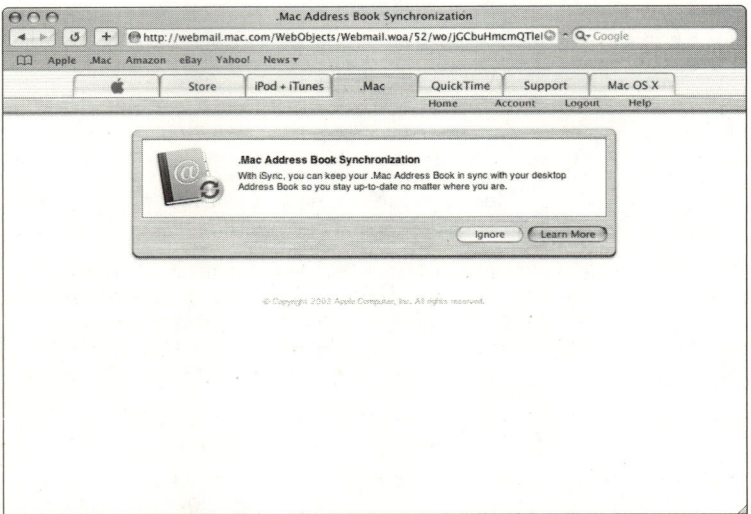

Figure 18-9: The .Mac Address Book Synchronization Learn More page appears the first time you click the Address Book icon in .Mac mail on the Web.
(Web page courtesy of Apple Computer, Inc.)

Add addresses manually to the .Mac Address Book by using the following procedure:

1. **Go to** www.mac.com

2. **Click Address Book.**

3. **Click New.**

You can easily add the sender of a message to your .Mac Address Book from .Mac Mail by opening the message and clicking the Add Sender icon.

To insert an address from the .Mac Address Book to a message you are composing:

1. **Click the Address Book icon on the composing page.**

2. **Choose an address field from the Destination pop-up menu of each email address you want to use.** The choices are: To, CC, Bcc. That address will be inserted into the field you choose.

3. **Click Apply.**

Using iDisk

An iDisk is 100 megabytes or more of storage space on Apple's Internet Servers that can be mounted on your desktop just like another hard drive on your local system.

Apple calls iDisk "Your personal hard disk on the Internet." You can use iDisk to hide sensitive information you don't want others to find, because iDisk is password protected. You can use iDisk to transfer files between computers that are not otherwise connected. Your iDisk contains, for your convenience, the latest Macintosh software. And iDisk is an integral part of other .Mac services.

iDisk is tightly integrated into Mac OS X 10.3. The functionality of iDisk Utility, which works with Mac OS X 10.1 or 10.2, has now been integrated into the Mac OS X 10.3 .Mac System Preference pane. You can now even create a local copy of your iDisk and synchronize it with the Internet iDisk automatically.

All you need to use an iDisk in Mac OS X is the Finder that is specially designed to work with iDisks.

Connecting to iDisks with Mac OS X

After configuring Mac OS X for your .Mac account (see above), you can connect to your iDisk with the Finder. You can connect to another iDisk if you know the name and password of the corresponding .Mac account. You can also connect to an iDisk with a Web browser. In addition, you can connect to iDisks by using aliases or Favorites that you have created.

Connecting to your iDisk with the Finder

If you have configured Mac OS X with your .Mac member name and password, you can open your iDisk with the Finder, which mounts its icon on your desktop, and allows you see its contents and copy files to or from it.

To open your iDisk in Mac OS X 10.3:

1. **Switch to the Finder.**

2. **From the Go menu, click and hold on iDisk.** The iDisk submenu appears.

3. **Choose My iDisk.** Note that you have options to open another user's iDisk or Public Folder in the submenu. See Figure 18-10.

After a short time, the iDisk icon appears on the desktop. Its name is your .Mac member name. A window showing its contents should automatically open.

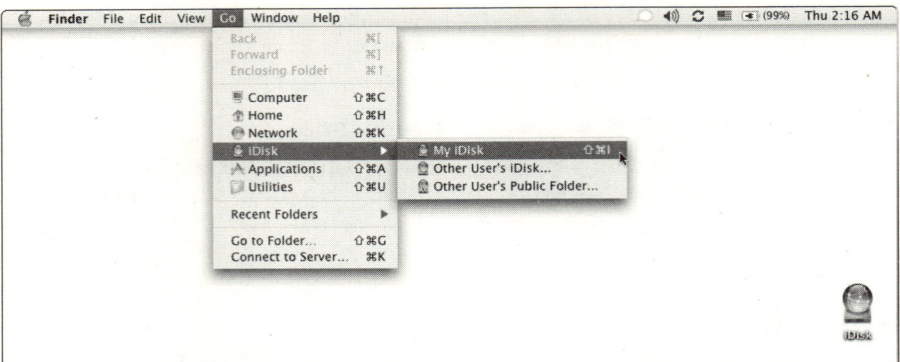

Figure 18-10: Choose My iDisk from the Finder's Go menu to connect to your iDisk.

Alternatively, you can click the iDisk button in the sidebar of any Finder window.

Connecting to another member's iDisk with the Finder

If you want to connect to the iDisk of another .Mac member, they need to provide you with their .Mac Member Name and Password. This is a good way to allow someone you trust to transfer files to you. Follow these steps:

1. **Switch to the Finder.**

2. **From the Go menu, click and hold on iDisk.** The iDisk submenu appears.

3. **Choose Other User's iDisk.** The Connect to iDisk dialog opens.

4. **Enter the Member Name and Password.**

5. **Click Connect.**

After a moment, the iDisk icon will appear on the desktop. Its name is the .Mac member's name. A window showing its contents should automatically open.

Connecting to another member's Public Folder with the Finder

Each iDisk contains a Public Folder that can usually be easily accessed by others without entering your .Mac password. All they need to know is your .Mac member name, unless you change your Public Folder's default settings in the .Mac System Preference pane(described below) to require a password.

The Public folder of your iDisk is interesting because it enables you to share files with other Internet users — both Mac and PC. Anything you place in this folder is automatically available to users who access it. Only you can change the contents of your Public folder. Conversely, you can see and copy, but can't change, files in the Public folder of anyone else's iDisk.

Follow these steps to connect to another member's Public Folder:

1. **Switch to the Finder.**

2. **From the Go menu, click and hold on iDisk. The iDisk submenu appears.**

3. **Choose Other User's Public Folder.** The Connect to iDisk Public Folder dialog opens.

4. **Enter the Member Name.**

5. **Click Connect.**

After a short delay, the Public Folder icon appears on the desktop. You see an iDisk icon with an additional yellow diamond-shaped sign with a walking figure on it named: *membername-*Public. A window showing its contents should automatically open.

Connecting to an iDisk with a Web browser

Although the Finder is the most convenient means of connecting to an iDisk, you can also connect by using a Web browser. In the Web browser, go to the .Mac page of the Apple Web site (www.mac.com). Click the iDisk link, sign in with your .Mac member name and password, and then click the Open Your Disk button. Your iDisk appears in the Finder.

Connecting to an iDisk with an alias

While connected to an iDisk, you can create an alias of the iDisk, as described in Chapter 4. After creating an alias of an iDisk, you can connect to the iDisk again by double-clicking its alias. You can also drag the mounted iDisk icon into the Dock, and click it when you would like to open your iDisk. In either case, you have to enter the .Mac member name and password.

Viewing an iDisk

If you double-click an iDisk, it opens and you see a regular Finder window containing several folders, some of which have the same names as the standard folders of your home folder. You also see a document that you can open to read what Apple has to say about iDisks.

You may notice that items appear slowly in an iDisk window. The iDisk performance is limited by the speed of your Internet connection. However, Mac OS X improves subsequent performance of the iDisk by caching a directory of the iDisk contents. Figure 18-11 shows the folders of an iDisk.

Figure 18-11: The folders inside an iDisk. Notice the syncing progress bar at the bottom of the window.

The eight folders that your iDisk contains are:

   ✦ **Documents:** Anything can be stored in this folder. Only you have access to items inside it.

   ✦ **Pictures:** JPEG or GIF files copied here can be used to create custom iCards, or display them on your Web pages via HomePage.

   ✦ **Movies:** QuickTime movies copied here can be displayed on your Web pages via HomePage.

✦ **Public:** Files copied here can be shared with others who know your .Mac member name. HomePage can create a file-sharing Web page that permits any and all Internet users to copy items from your Public folder. You can also password protect this folder, assign read only or read and write access to it.

✦ **Sites:** HomePage stores your Web pages in this folder. You can also put Web pages you create with other applications in this folder to publish them.

✦ **Music:** Can be used to store your music files.

✦ **Backup:** (read only) Contains files copied here by the Backup utility. Files can be copied from this folder, but can only be deleted with the Backup utility.

✦ **Software:** (read only) Contains Apple's changing selection of the latest software for downloading. Files cannot be copied to this folder, and its contents are not included in your iDisk capacity.

Copying items to and from an iDisk

You can copy files and folders to and from an iDisk just as you copy files to and from any other disk. For example, you can copy an item by dragging it from one Finder window that shows your home folder to another Finder window that shows a folder on an iDisk. Be prepared for the copying to take a while. Copying to or from an iDisk goes only at the speed of your Internet connection, which is far slower than the speed of your computer's hard drive or CD-ROM drive.

Opening files

Rather than copying files from an iDisk and then opening the copies from your home folder, you can open files directly from an iDisk. An iDisk is just another disk, and files on it can be opened using the usual methods for opening files from your home folder. Opening a file from an iDisk takes longer than opening the same file from your hard drive because the file contents are transferred at the speed of your Internet connection. Therefore, you should avoid opening applications or large documents directly from an iDisk.

Getting software from an iDisk

One folder in every iDisk, the Software folder, doesn't actually take up any of the 100MB allotted to the iDisk. The Software folder works like an alias, giving you access to a number of applications from Apple and third-party software developers, which you may find useful.

Because the contents of this folder are constantly changing, it is not possible here to enumerate the files in it. Just remember that it is a handy place to look for software—from games to productivity tools. To use an application from the Software folder, copy the application's disk image or installer file to your Applications folder or your home folder. Then double-click the copied file to install the software.

Caution   Be aware that many of the applications from the Software folder are without any warranty of fitness and can even be preliminary or limited versions of commercial products. Read the accompanying documentation files before installing the application.

Using your iDisk with Mac OS 9

Even if you normally use Mac OS X, you may occasionally need to use your iDisk on a Mac OS 9 computer. With Mac OS 9, you can connect to your iDisk by using the Chooser or the Network Browser.

✦ In the Chooser, click the AppleShare icon and then click the Server IP Address button. Next enter `idisk.mac.com` as the server address. Then enter the .Mac member name and password.

✦ In the Network Browser, choose Connect to iDisk from the Shortcuts pop-up menu or choose Connect To Server from the Shortcuts pop-up menu and enter `idisk.mac.com` as the server address. Then enter the .Mac member name and password.

Using your iDisk with Microsoft Windows

If you're not near a Mac and need a file from your iDisk, you can open your iDisk on a computer with Microsoft Windows XP, Windows ME, Windows 98, or Windows 2000.

✦ In Windows XP, open My Network Places and under Network Tasks, click Add a network place. The Add Network Place Wizard leads you through the process of creating a shortcut to a Web Folder. As the location of the Web Folder, enter `http://idisk.Mac.com/itoolsname` where *itoolsname* is your .Mac member name.

✦ In Windows ME or Windows 98, double-click the My Computer icon, double-click the Web Folders icon, and double-click Add Web Folder. As the location to add, enter `http://idisk.Mac.com/itoolsname` where *itoolsname* is your .Mac member name.

✦ In Windows 2000, open My Computer, choose Map Network Drive from the Tools menu, and click Web folder or FTP site. As the location to add, enter `http://idisk.Mac.com/itoolsname` where *itoolsname* is your .Mac member name.

Disconnecting an iDisk

When you finish using an iDisk, you can disconnect it by dragging its icon to the Trash. When you drag an iDisk in Mac OS X, the Trash icon changes to look like an Eject symbol (a triangle with a line below it) and its name changes to Disconnect. Disconnecting an iDisk removes it from the Finder.

You can leave an iDisk connected as long as you like. Connection time is unlimited in Mac OS X. (In Mac OS 9, connection time is limited to one hour, or 30 minutes of inactivity.)

iDisk .Mac System Preference settings

The .Mac System Preference pane contains two buttons: one for .Mac (covered earlier this chapter) and one for iDisk. The iDisk settings are adapted and expanded from the iDisk Utility used with Mac OS X 10.2. Figure 18-12 shows the iDisk panel.

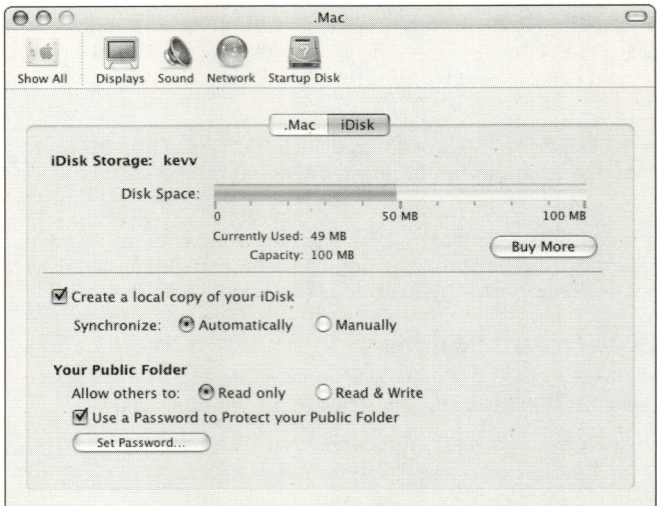

Figure 18-12: The .Mac System Preference pane's iDisk panel.

In the iDisk panel, you can:

✦ Check the amount of iDisk space you are using with the bar display. Also present are readouts of the space currently used, and the iDisk capacity.

✦ Purchase additional iDisk space by clicking the Buy More button.

✦ Create a local copy of your iDisk, and set it to be Synchronized automatically or manually. (The default setting is off.)

✦ Configure your Public Folder to allow others Read only or Read & Write access. (The default setting is Read only.) Figure 18-13 shows the icon for an iDisk Public Folder.

✦ Configure your Public Folder to use a password you set to protect your Public Folder.

Figure 18-13: The icons for a mounted iDisk Public Folder and a local iDisk.

Making a local copy of your iDisk

Mac OS X 10.3 has a new feature that makes it possible to have your iDisk permanently visible and accessible on your desktop, even when you are not connected to the Internet. You make this possible by creating a local copy of your iDisk on your hard drive, and automatically synchronizing it with the remote iDisk when you are connected.

To create a local copy of your iDisk, open the .Mac System Preference pane to the iDisk panel and click the Create a local copy of your iDisk checkbox. Then close the System Preferences window; the process of copying immediately begins, and the window in Figure 18-14 appears.

Working with this Instant iDisk has a few key advantages. Now you can make changes to your iDisk anytime, even from a PowerBook as you travel. The changes you make happen faster because your Internet connection speed is no longer a factor. The changes can be synced with the remote iDisk whenever you next connect to the Internet.

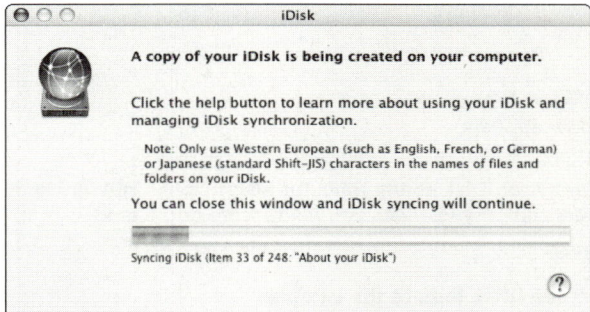

Figure 18-14: This window appears as you are creating a local copy of your iDisk.

After the copying process begins, you cannot cancel it. The length of time it takes to make the local copy depends on your Internet connection speed.

When the process of copying is complete, the iDisk icon appears on your desktop, in the left sidebar of a Finder window, and in a Save dialog represent the iDisk on your computer. When the icon represented the online iDisk, it bore your .Mac Member name; now the local copy is just called iDisk. This is the way to tell the difference between them on a computer you did not configure.

After you have a local copy of your iDisk, you never see the online copy again. Apple wants you to consider the local and remote iDisks as a single entity. Also be aware after you create a local copy of your iDisk, it is apparently permanent. Dragging its icon to the Trash has no effect, and no mechanism in the Mac OS X 10.3 user interface deletes it.

iDisk synchronization

After you have created a local copy of your iDisk, any changes you make to it are automatically synchronized with the remote iDisk at set intervals when you are connected to the Internet. If you log out, restart, or shut down your Mac during the syncing process, it continues after you log in again.

You can check when your iDisk was last synchronized in a Finder window. Click on the iDisk icon in the sidebar, and information at the bottom of the window shows the date and time of last synchronization. If your iDisk is in the process of syncing, a progress bar appears. Figure 18-15 shows the window that appears when your local iDisk is synchronized with your remote iDisk.

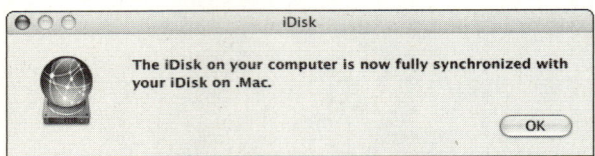

Figure 18-15: When your local iDisk is fully synchronized with your remote iDisk, this window appears.

You can also manually synchronize your iDisk at any time, for instance before you log out or shut down the computer, to ensure that any changes you made were duplicated.

To manually synchronize your iDisk:

1. **In a Finder window, select the iDisk icon in the sidebar.**

2. **Click the Sync button (rotating arrows) to the right of the iDisk icon.**

You can turn off automatic synchronization if you are on a low-bandwidth network and need the processor power for other tasks.

To turn off automatic synchronization:

1. **In a Finder window, select the iDisk icon in the sidebar.**

2. **Click the Action button (with the gear icon) and choose Automatic Syncing to remove the checkmark.**

Repeat this procedure to make the checkmark appear and turn Automatic Syncing back on. Apple recommends that Automatic Syncing be left on as much as possible to ensure that the local and remote iDisks contain the same files.

A synchronization conflict can occur when you make different changes to the same file on your iDisk from more than one computer. You are asked which version of the file you want to save. To replace the file on the remote iDisk with the version on the local iDisk of the Mac you are using, select This Computer, and click Keep Selected. To keep the version on the remote iDisk, select .Mac and click Keep Selected. You can save both versions of the file to your iDisk by clicking Keep Both.

You can compare the files on the local and remote iDisks in order to decide which choice to make, by opening each version of the file. In the Finder's Go menu, choose iDisk, and My iDisk in the submenu. Double-click the file to open it.

iDisk Tips

✦ Check the amount of storage available in your iDisk on a regular basis. If you exceed your iDisk storage quota, you will receive a warning message in your Mac.com email account. If you do not promptly delete enough files to be within your quota, iDisk automatically deletes the excess files! Or, you might want to buy more storage space at this point.

✦ You may experience alarm if you are not prompted to enter a password when opening your iDisk. Not to worry; this is actually normal. The password information is automatically pulled from the .Mac System Preference iDisk panel, and is stored in the keychain, so you don't need to enter it. If you are concerned that others can fiddle with your iDisk while you are away from your computer, log out, or set the screen saver to prompt for a password when waking.

✦ If you are trying to open the .Mac System Preference pane to the iDisk panel, a message can appear that says "There's a problem connecting to the iDisk server at this time. Please try again later." However, you iDisk seems fine. If you get this message, check to see if the date and time settings are correct in System Preferences. These settings can change by themselves under certain circumstances, and this can interfere with the iDisk's communications with System Preferences.

✦ If you cannot delete a folder you have created in one of the iDisk folders, or the Backup folder cannot be seen, it may be because you have connected to the iDisk via the AppleTalk Filing Protocol (AFP). This is the protocol used when you choose Connect to Server from the Finder's Go menu, and enter afp://idisk.mac.com. All other way to connect to an iDisk from Mac OS X 10.3 use the WebDAV protocol. The Backup utility uses the WebDAV protocol to transfer files to and from an iDisk, as does the Finder, and you must connect using WebDAV to delete folders or see the Backup folder. Note that Mac OS 9 uses AFP with iDisk.

✦ You may experience trouble connecting to an iDisk from Mac OS 9. If so, use the Extensions Manager control panel to check that the following required extensions are enabled: AppleShare, Shared Library Manager, Shared Library Manager PPC. If your computer is behind a firewall or a proxy server, they must be set up to allow outbound connections on TCP port 548, and ICMP echo must be enabled. Tell the network administrator this techno-speak, and he or she may be able to help you, and may look at you with new respect.

✦ If you connect to an iDisk from a Windows or Unix computer, or from the Mac OS X Terminal application, you may see two .HSicon files on your iDisk that you do not recognize. Don't delete them! They provide the iDisk icon images for Mac OS 9 users.

HomePage

HomePage is a .Mac online service that easily creates professional looking, personalized Web sites that you can use to share photos, movies, text, or files. Anyone with a computer with an Internet connection and Web browser can access your sites, unless you password protect them. To open your HomePage, follow these steps:

1. **From your Web browser, go to** www.mac.com.

2. **At the .Mac home page, click HomePage on the left sidebar.**

3. **Log in using your member name and password.**

The HomePage welcome page appears, as shown in Figure 18-16.

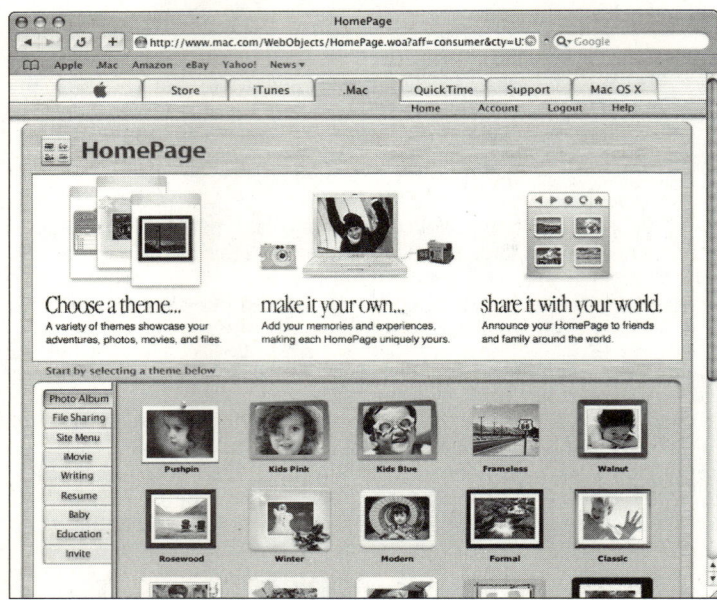

Figure 18-16: The HomePage welcome page.
(Web page courtesy of Apple Computer, Inc.)

On the HomePage welcome page, note the category tabs on the left. These are the categories of Web site designs you can choose from. Each tab is connected to the large area to its right that shows thumbnails of the theme pages available in the selected category.

Creating a Web page with HomePage

If you are making a Photo Album, first drag your pictures to the Pictures folder on your iDisk. If you are making a file sharing page, first drag the files you want to share to the Public Folder on your iDisk. To create a Web page using HomePage, follow these steps:

1. **From the HomePage welcome page, click the category tabs and look at the thumbnails until you find a theme design that you like.**

2. **Click on the desired theme thumbnail.**

3. **Depending on the theme you choose, you will usually be taken to a full-sized Edit your page theme page.** The Photo Album themes take you to a Choose your folder page first that asks you to identify the photos your new page will contain; clicking Choose when you are done with your selection takes you to the Edit your page theme page with your chosen images already appearing.

   If you don't like what you see in the full-sized theme page, click the Themes icon on the upper right, and you will be returned to select another them from that category. If you do like the theme page, click the Edit icon to continue.

4. **Click the Edit icon, so you can edit and personalize the page.** You will see self-explanatory instructions and labels to help you identify various text entry fields, such as image captions and page titles. Some theme pages allow you to select from a choice of layouts.

5. **To add photos and movies, click the small Choose button on each placeholder. Make your selection from the Choose a file page and then click Choose.**

6. **Drag images to the correct positions.**

7. **Choose to display a visitor counter or a Send me a message button that enables visitors to send you an iCard with their feedback. Click the Show checkbox next these features to include them in your Web page.** Some pages allow you to type in links so your visitors can view your other pages.

   If at any time you would like to start over, click the word HomePage in the title bar. You will be returned to the HomePage welcome page.

8. **When the page looks the way you want, click the Publish icon at the top right.** Your page is placed on the Web.

   The Congratulations page appears, as shown in Figure 18-17. You have the option to click on the link and see your page, send and iCard to tell your friends about the page, or click the Return to Homepage button to do just that.

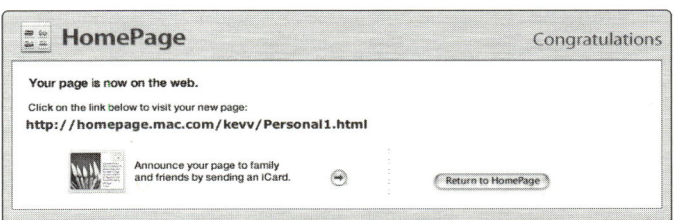

Figure 18-17: The HomePage congratulations page.
(Web page courtesy of Apple Computer, Inc.)

If you click the Return to HomePage button, you notice that the HomePage welcome page now features a new area at its top that is customized for your Web site. See Figure 18-18. Here you will find the new URL to reach this page (it changed when you published your first page). There is a list of pages you have published, and you can add, delete, or edit the pages using the buttons under the list. With the buttons on the right, you can announce your site, learn about new features, protect this site, or add another site.

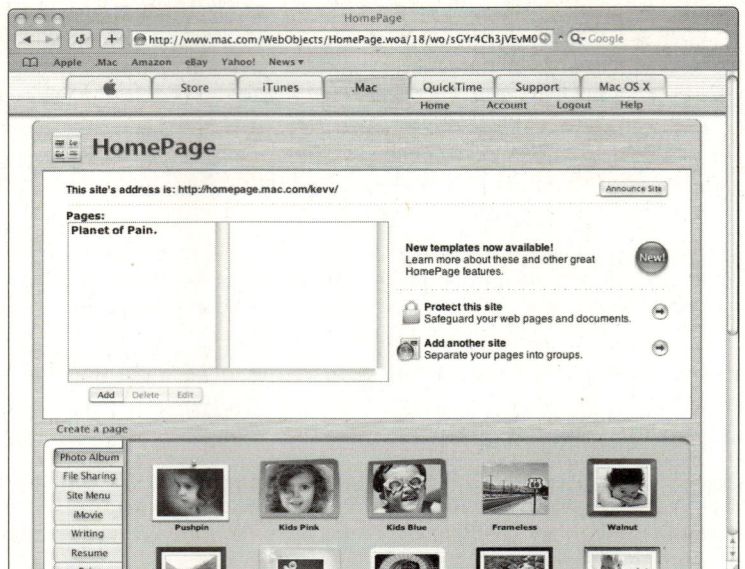

Figure 18-18: The HomePage welcome page is now customized for your Web site.

(Web page courtesy of Apple Computer, Inc.)

Updating a Web page

You can make changes to any of your Web pages at any time. Follow these steps:

1. **From the HomePage welcome page, select the site that contains the page you want to change from the Site list.**

2. **Select the page you want to change from the Page list.**

3. **Click the Edit button below the lists.** The page appears in Edit mode.

4. **Make your desired changes.**

5. **Click Publish when you are done.** The updated page will be available on the Web immediately.

To update a Photo Album page, first put the new pictures in the folder on your iDisk that contains the original pictures.

To set up or edit Web links or email links, in Edit mode find the link you want to edit. To set up a Web link, click the Edit Link button. The Edit your links page appears, as shown in Figure 18-19. Click on the tab for what you would like to do: My Pages allows you to pick another of your pages to link to; Other Pages allows you to type the URL for a page outside of your site; and Email allows you to enter an email address. Click Apply when done.

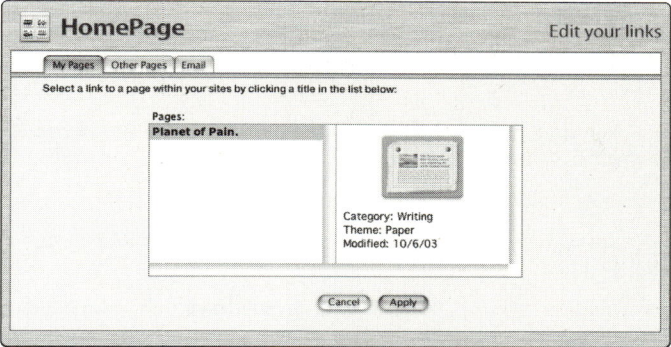

Figure 18-19: The HomePage "Edit your links" page.
(Web page courtesy of Apple Computer, Inc.)

Creating another Web site

You can create more than one Web site in HomePage. A Web site is a collection of Web pages with a designated start page (which visitors see first) and its own Web address.

1. **From the HomePage welcome page, click the Add another site button.** (The name of this button changes to Add if you already have more than one site.) The Create a site page appears, as shown in Figure 18-20.

2. **Type a name for the site.** If you want the site to have password protection, click the On checkbox and enter the password you want.

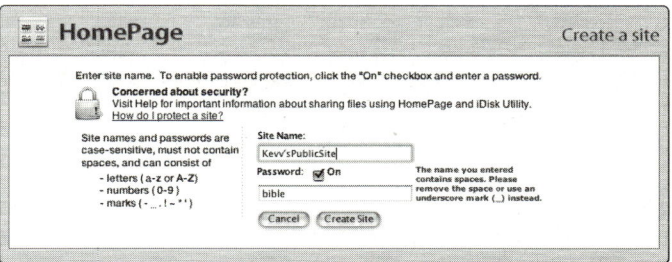

Figure 18-20: The HomePage Create a site page.
(Web page courtesy of Apple Computer, Inc.)

3. **Click the Create Site button.** The site is created.

4. **You are returned to the HomePage welcome page, where you can now see the new site name in the Sites list and the new URL at the top.**

Tip

Creating additional Web sites creates subfolders inside your Sites folder to hold them, bearing the name of the site within. The contents of these folders may be viewed in the Finder, but any attempt to modify the folder or its contents will result in an alert. If you wish to store files or Web pages in you Sites folder, you can store them at the root level of the Sites folder, or create new subfolders with the Finder.

Deleting a page or site

You can remove pages from your Web site or delete the entire site whenever you want. Follow this procedure:

1. **From the HomePage welcome page, select the page you wish to delete in the Page list, or the site you want to delete in the Site list.**

2. **Click the Delete button below the lists.** The selected items disappear.

Deleting a site also deletes all that site's pages. If you only have one site, delete all the pages in the site to delete the site.

Don't forget to remove pictures from the Pictures folder after you have deleted a page containing them in order to conserve space on your iDisk.

The first site you create with HomePage cannot be deleted like any of the other sites you create, because it is the "root" site. If you no longer wish to use it, leave it empty, and the Start Site automatically changes to a site containing published pages.

HomePage Tips

✦ Use iPhoto to quickly and easily create a .Mac HomePage photo album Web page. After the Web page is created, you can edit or delete it using HomePage.

✦ If others frequently must access your iDisk's Public Folder to retrieve files you have left for them, consider creating a .Mac HomePage file-sharing Web page. To do so, in the HomePage welcome page, click the File Sharing tab. If you do not password protect the page, anyone on the Internet can see and download the files in your Public Folder from this page.

✦ You can change the order of the links to other pages in your site that HomePage automatically puts at the top of each Web page you create. Just drag the page titles in the Pages list into the order you want. The page at the top of the list is the start page for the site, and is listed in bold type.

✦ Before you put files, pictures, or movies on you Web pages, you should prepare them in the following ways.

• **Files:** Special characters in some file names may be incompatible with naming conventions on other computers accessing the files. So to be safe, alter the file names to conform to these rules. Use only uppercase letters (A–Z), lowercase letters (a–z), numbers (0–9), and the underscore (_) in your file names. Never begin a file name with a period (.), or the file will become invisible, and only use the period to separate a file name extension from the rest of the name. Include these extensions (such as Report.doc or Photo.jpg) in the file name, so all computers will know how to open them. Since some computers use short file name, use 8 or few characters to name them — 12 if you count the three letter extension. Don't forget to copy the files to your iDisk's Public Folder.

- **Pictures:** Save your pictures in JPEG or GIF format, and add the extension ".jpg" or ".gif" to the end of the file name. Name the pictures files in accord with the rules listed above in the Files section. Don't forget to copy the pictures to your iDisk's Pictures folder.

- **Movies:** Export your iMovie as a QuickTime file, and add ".mov" to the end of its file name. Don't forget to copy the movie to your iDisk's Movies folder.

✦ You don't have to use the HomePage service; you can use any HTML authoring tool to create your .Mac Web site pages. For instance, you can use applications such as BBEdit (BareBones Software, www.barebones.com), GoLive (Adobe Systems, www.adobe.com), or Dreamweaver (Macromedia, www.macromedia.com). After you prepare the Web pages, put them in the Sites folder on your iDisk, in a subfolder if there is already more than one site there.

✦ You can password protect your HomePage Web sites so that they are only accessible to people with a password you have provided. On the HomePage welcome page, if you have only one Web site, click "Protect this site." If you have more than one site, select the site in the Sites list, and click Edit below the list. On the Edit your site page, put a check in the password checkbox, type a password, and click Apply Changes. Change the password any time using the same steps. Don't forget to also password protect your Public Folder!

Visitors will see this page when you password protect your HomePage Web site.
(Web page courtesy of Apple Computer, Inc.)

.Mac Slides Publisher

.Mac Slides Publisher is an application you can use, if you are a .Mac member, to share your digital photos as a slideshow screen saver using your iDisk. Anyone using Mac OS X 10.2 or higher can view the slideshow after it downloads from the Internet. When they subscribe to your slideshow, they will automatically receive updates to your slideshow whenever you change it and publish it.

Download .Mac Slides Publisher from the .Mac Web site at `www.mac.com`, and run the Installer. The application is installed to the Applications folder. You may want to put an alias of it in the Dock to drag photos to it more easily.

If you attempt to launch .Mac Slides Publisher, you will see that it has no interface; it will show you a window with simplified instructions. You just drag photos to it and it does the rest.

To share your photos in a slideshow, follow these steps.

1. **Make sure that all your photos are in the JPEG file format.** It is helpful to first put the photos in a folder.

2. **Select the photos you want.** Remember that you can make a multiple selection by holding down the ⌘ key as you click on each photo, or by holding down the shift key and clicking the first and last photos to select them and all the photos listed in between.

3. **Drag the selected photos on at a time or all at once to the .Mac Slides Publisher icon.**

4. **Click Publish.** The photos are copied to your iDisk.

5. **When the photos are copied, click the Announce Slideshow button to tell others how to subscribe to your slideshow.**

A .Mac membership is not required to subscribe to the slideshows.

To subscribe to a slideshow, follow these steps:

1. **You must be using Mac OS X 10.2 or higher; these instructions are for Mac OS X 10.3.**

2. **Open System Preferences.**

3. **Click Desktop & Screen Saver.**

4. **Click the Screen Saver button.**

5. **Select .Mac in the Screen Savers list.**

6. **Click the Options button.** The Subscriptions and Display Options sheet drops down, as shown in Figure 18-21.

7. **Select the slide shows you want to see, enter the .Mac member name in the box, and check the Display Options you want.**

8. **Click OK.** The slideshow is downloaded to your computer.

After the slideshow has been downloaded, it will appear when the screen saver is activated. An Internet connection is no longer necessary and is only used when available to check for updates.

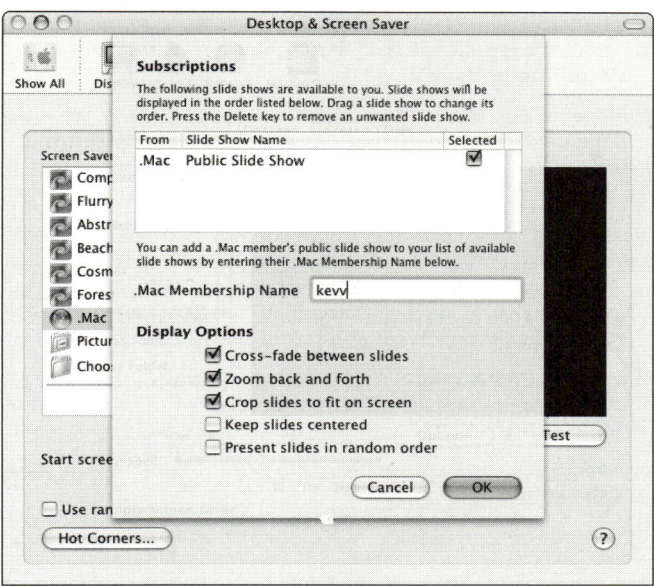

Figure 18-21: The Desktop and Screen Saver System Preference Subscriptions and Display Options sheet.

To unsubscribe from a slideshow:

1. **Open System Preferences.**

2. **Click Desktop & Screen Saver.**

3. **Click the Screen Saver button.**

4. **Select .Mac in the Screen Savers list.**

5. **Click the Options button.** The Subscriptions and Display Options sheet drops down, as shown in Figure 18-21.

6. **To temporarily disable a slideshow, uncheck the "Selected" checkbox to the right of the Slide Show name.**

7. **To remove a slideshow from the list, select it and press the Delete key.**

iChatAV

In recent years, the use of instant messaging (IM) has rapidly increased. Millions of people enjoy its unique advantages. IM lets you type a short message and send it instantly to a recipient, who sees it onscreen and can respond with a message of their own. With IM, you are having a live conversation, called a chat.

America Online enabled the popularity of instant messaging with its AOL Instant Messenger (AIM) system. Because of its great success, it has had many emulators. Apple's iChat brings instant messaging to Mac OS X and supports AIM.

At the 2003 World Wide Developers Conference, Steve Jobs announced iChatAV, which adds live voice and video connections to iChat's text messaging capabilities. He also introduced the iSight video camera, the first Web camera to bear the Apple logo, which works seamlessly with iChatAV.

The result is that you can easily use your Mac as a telephone or video phone, and the call is free; it takes place over your broadband Internet connection. The quality of the sound and picture is impressive, and in typical Apple fashion, everything is beautifully designed and could not be easier to use. No longer do you have to manipulate the hardware and the software that was an integral part of earlier live-video-over-Internet setups.

In particular, a live video chat using iChatAV and the iSight camera is one of the more remarkable experiences you can have with your computer. These features are useful to far-flung friends, grandparents and grandchildren, and travel-weary businesspeople.

iChatAV is included with Mac OS X 10.3, although when you look for it in the Applications folder, you find it is still just called iChat.

iChat Setup

To use iChat with the Internet, you need to have a *screen name,* also known as an instant messaging address. If you are a .Mac member, your screen name is your .Mac email address: `username@mac.com`. If you have an America Online or AIM screen name, it will work with iChat, and is available for free. However, iChat does not work with other instant messaging systems, such as MSN or Yahoo, so you cannot use screen names from them.

You can also use iChat on a local network only, such as a classroom, home, or small office network, without needing screen names for the users. In this situation, iChat automatically locates other iChat users on the network via Rendezvous, and lets you chat or send files to them.

To use iChat's audio capabilities, you need a microphone connected or built in to your computer. If you have a Web camera with a built in microphone, such as iSight, iChat selects the camera microphone automatically. If not, you need to select the microphone in iChat ⇨ Preferences ⇨ Video.

To use iChat's video capabilities, you need a FireWire video camera connected to your computer, and a broadband Internet connection. You can use a Digital Video (DV) camcorder with a FireWire cable; oddly enough, you must turn the camera on for it to work — it does not take its power from your computer's FireWire port.

If you don't have a Web camera yet, do yourself a favor and buy an iSight, shown in Figure 18-22. It is designed to work with iChat, and, in our opinion, is superior to other Web cams in every way. It has a high-resolution chip, automatic exposure, built in microphone, and a white iris you can open or close to ensure your privacy. (The iris is white so you can tell at a glance if it is closed or open.) Perhaps most importantly, its perforated aluminum cylinder looks great perched on top of your Mac's display.

Figure 18-22: Apple's iSight Web camera.
(Image courtesy Apple Computer, Inc.)

When you connect the iSight camera, iChat automatically launches. You can also launch iChat manually at any time.

iChat guides you through its configuration process with an assistant. After the Welcome to iChat AV panel, you go to the Set Up New iChat Account panel, shown in Figure 18-23.

Figure 18-23: The iChat Setup Assistant's Set Up New iChat Account panel.

The Account Type pop-up menu allows a choice between .Mac and AIM accounts.

The Get an iChat Account button opens your browser to a Web page called Try iChat that describes the various irresistible benefits of .Mac membership and suggests you register for an iChat account. If you do so, you will get a 60-day trial of .Mac services, and can keep your iChat account after the 60 days. Please note that this account only allows instant messaging; as stated above, you must pay for a .Mac membership to use audio or video chat capabilities.

After you have entered your information and clicked Continue, the Assistant asks if you want Rendezvous on or off. You will want it on if you will be iChatting with others on a local network; Rendezvous will automatically find them. If you are only connected to the Internet, say through a cable modem at home, leave Rendezvous off.

If you have a webcam attached, the next panel shows the image from it to verify that it is working. If there is no camera attached, this panel tells you to get one if you want to video chat.

When you finish the Assistant setup, iChat opens its Buddy List window, shown in Figure 18-24. When you enter someone's screen name into iChat, it appears in the Buddy List. The entries in your Buddy List are stored on the Internet, so if you log into iChat for the first time on a newly installed copy of Mac OS X, you will see all your previously entered buddy names!

Figure 18-24: iChat's Buddy List.

In Figure 18-25, the Buddy List appears showing the user (My Name) and one buddy (blurofinsanity) ready for a video chat, one buddy (alfred h) ready for an audio chat, and two buddies ready for a text chat (herman m using AIM, sauron using .Mac). All have their Available status marked with a green jewel, except sauron, marked as Away with a red jewel.

Contact your friends to get their screen names. Follow these steps to add people to your Buddy List:

1. **Choose Buddies ➪ Add A Buddy or click the plus sign button in the lower -left corner of the Buddy List window. A sheet drops down, showing the contents of the Address Book.**

2. **Select someone's name and click Select Buddy; the name will be added to your Buddy List.**

3. **Click New Person to see another sheet asking for the Account Type and Account Name and then click Add.** You can also have the option to enter the person's First and Last names and email address. The information is copied to the Address Book, and the name is added to your Buddy List.

Tip If you want to chat with someone, but you don't want to add their name to your Buddy List, choose File ➪ New Chat with Person and enter their screen name.

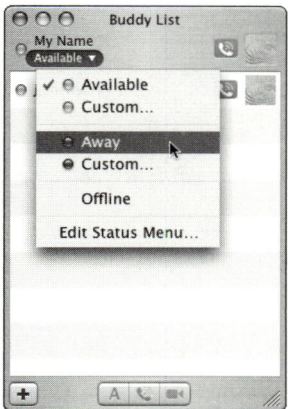

Figure 18-25: iChat's Buddy List, showing the user (My Name) pulling down the Available pop-up menu to mark their status as Away.

iChat Status

The Buddy List window shows the screen names of the people you have added, with some visual indicators to let you know when they are online and if they are available for chatting.

To the left of their name is the status indicator, which looks like a red or green jewel.

The green jewel means they have set their status to Available, meaning they are online and ready to chat.

The red jewel means they have set their status to "Away," meaning they are online, but don't want to chat. You can send a message to them, but they may not answer it.

If their status is Offline, meaning iChat is not running, no jewel appears and their name is grayed out. You cannot send them a message.

Buddies shown as online, but idle, have not used their computers in a while. You can see how long they have been idle. You can send them a message, which will be waiting onscreen for them when they return to the computer.

At the top of the Buddy List window, your name appears. Under it is a pop-up menu where you can set your own status. If you think the default status messages are boring, you can choose Edit Status Menu or Custom next to one of the jewels, and make up your own message.

You can see status information and change your own status setting without opening iChat by using the iChat status menu in the menu bar. The status menu is off by default; you can turn it on by choosing iChat ➪ Preferences ➪ General, and checking Show status in menu bar.

Buddy List features

If a buddy has a video camera icon next to their name, it means that they have a FireWire video camera attached, and you can have a video chat with them if they are available. A telephone icon means they are set up to have an audio chat. No icon means you can only text message them.

Your friends can choose to have a picture display next to their names on your buddy list. This same picture, the buddy icon, will appear in the chat window next to their messages.

You can edit your own picture by clicking on the one next to your name at the top of the window and selecting Edit Picture from the pop-up menu. This opens the Buddy Picture window, where you can drag a picture, choose a picture, or take a video snapshot using your Web camera. Click Set to change your picture.

You can also drag a picture to your name.

Tip   For best results, use a picture for your buddy icon that is 64 x 64 pixels in size. If you drag a larger picture to the Buddy Picture window, or to your name, you can resize and crop the image to the right size.

To edit your buddy's information, select his name and then choose Buddies ➪ Get Info.

You can sort your Buddy list by name, availability, or hide names that are offline, by choosing an option from the View menu.

At the bottom of the Buddy List window are four buttons:

✦ **Plus sign:** Adds a buddy the list.

✦ **A button:** Starts a text chat with the selected buddy.

✦ **Telephone button:** Starts an audio chat with the selected buddy.

✦ **Video camera button:** Starts a video chat with the selected buddy.

The three buttons that start chats will be grayed out until you first select an online buddy in the list.

Tip   To send a file, picture, or movie to a buddy, drag it to the buddy's name. You can also select their name and choose Buddies ➪ Send A File, to navigate to the file you want. Only one file can be sent at a time.

Instant text messaging

To send an instant message to someone on your Buddy List:

1. **Double-click the buddy's name.** A chat window opens.

2. **Type a short message.**

3. **Press the Return key to send the message.**

4. **If your buddy responds, the response appears in the chat window below your message.** Have a conversation with your buddy by sending messages and back and forth.

To send a file or picture with your message, drag it to the message entry area. Pictures will be displayed beside your text in the chat window; buddies must accept a file, which is then viewed separately.

Local network chats

If you would like to use your Mac to chat with other Mac users on a local network, you do not need an instant messaging account or Internet access.

Chatting Tips

Chatting is fun and easy. The following list provides tips for chatting:

✦ You can have many chat windows open at once, instant messaging several people at the same time.

✦ You can choose to invite multiple people to participate in a chat in a single window, by choosing View ⇨ Show Chat Participants. To add participants, click the plus sign button and choose a person from your Buddy List, or choose Other to invite someone who is not in your Buddy List. You can also add participants by dragging them from your Buddy List.

✦ You can change the appearance of your text chats.

✦ To view a chat as plain text, choose View ⇨ Show as Text.

✦ To change the font or balloon color used in your messages, choose iChat ⇨ Preferences, then click the Messages icon. These settings affect how your messages look on both your screen and your recipient's screens.

✦ To override other people's font and color settings, select Reformat Incoming Messages.

✦ To set an image to show in the background, choose View ⇨ Set Chat Background, then select an image file.

✦ To send a hyperlink to a Web site in your message, type a name for the link, highlight the text, and choose Edit ⇨ Add Hyperlink. The Insert Hyperlink window opens; enter the URL (you can copy it from the Web browser). Click OK, complete your message, and press the Return key to send it.

✦ You can send or receive files, and unlike email, there is no limit to the file size. Select a recipient in your Buddy List, choose Buddies ⇨ Send a File, select the file, and click Send. Or, just drag the file to the buddy's name in the Buddy List. Only one file can be sent at a time. Large files can take a large amount of time to transfer.

Rendezvous is Apple's networking technology that automatically recognizes other computers on the network, enabling iChat to communicate with them. Rendezvous is on by default in iChat; if you wish to turn it off, you can do so in the Accounts pane of iChat Preferences.

To chat on a local network:

1. **Choose Window ⇨ Rendezvous.** In the window appear other iChat users on the same subnet (network segment) as you.

2. **To send an invitation to chat, double-click a person in the list.**

   If the person accepts your invitation to chat, by default they can see you type each character of the message, unlike in Internet chatting, where the entire message is sent only when you press the Return key. You can change this default setting, Send Text As I Type, in the Messages pane of iChat Preferences.

Tip If you connect to the Internet with a cable modem, you may see other iChat users via Rendezvous, because you will be on a shared network segment. You will not see other users if you connect to the Internet via modem or DSL.

Tip   If firewall protection is turned on in the Network pane of System Preferences, you may be unable to chat with other Rendezvous users. If you need the firewall on but would like to chat, allow activity on port 5298. See Chapter 26 for instructions on how to configure your firewall settings.

Video chats

You can invite anyone in your Buddy List to a video chat if a camera icon appears next to their name. Figure 18-26 shows and example of iChat's video window. To start a video chat:

1. **Click the camera icon or select the buddy and click the camera button at the bottom of the list.**

2. **If you are already in a text chat with someone who has a camera icon next to their name, choose Buddies ⇨ Invite to Video Chat.** A preview window opens momentarily, showing your video image as seen by your camera.

   If your buddy accepts the invitation, their image appears in the chat window, and your preview image shrinks to a corner. You can move your image to another corner by clicking where you want it to go.

3. **Resize the video chat window, if you wish, by dragging the bottom-right corner. To fill the entire screen with the image, choose Video ⇨ Full Screen.** Use the button with double arrows at the bottom of the video chat window to toggle between normal and full-screen modes.

Figure 18-26: iChat's video chat window, showing remote image (man unaware Christmas lights in background seem like foolish antenna), and the user in the small screen in the lower right (obviously trying not to be too rude about it). Such problems are only possible through iChat.

You can mute the audio during a video chat by choosing Video ⇨ Mute. Or, you can click the microphone button at the bottom of the chat window. When the audio is muted, a microphone icon with a slash appears in your preview image window. (But remember, they may read your lips!)

Pause a video chat by choosing Video ⇨ Pause Video. Alternatively, Option-click The microphone button in the video chat window. This button becomes highlighted during a pause, and the audio is muted. Click the microphone button to resume the chat.

Tip By default, the video chat will take up as much of your Internet connections bandwidth as possible. If you want to share your connection with others on your network, or with another application such as a Web browser, you can adjust the speed at which your video chat is transmitted. Choose iChat ⇨ Preferences, click the Video icon, and choose a speed from the Bandwidth Limit pop-up menu. The slowest setting is 100 Kbps (Kilobits per second) and the fastest is 2 Mbps (Megabits per second).

Tip You can invite a buddy who does not have a camera to a one-way video chat by choosing Buddies ⇨ Invite to One-Way Video Chat. Your buddy will see and hear you, and you will hear them if they have a built-in or attached microphone configured.

The Address Book Application

Mac OS X includes an Address Book application to manage contact information.

Address Book is located on your hard disk in the Applications folder, and should not be confused with the .Mac Address Book, which is located on your iDisk.

You can use iSync to synchronize your Address Book contacts with your .Mac Address Book, your handheld PDA, or your cell phone.

Mail, iCal, iChat, Safari, and Sherlock use the information from Address Book to address emails, invite contacts to chats or events, autofill online forms, and customize driving instructions.

You can use Address Book to:

✦ Store and look up contact information.

✦ Organize and change the formatting of contact information.

✦ Print phone lists or mailing labels.

✦ Send contact information by email to an individual or group.

✦ Automatically merge duplicate contacts.

✦ Back up your contact information.

Address Book setup

The main Address Book window displays three columns. The first column shows the directories and groups defined in the Address Book. The second column shows the names in the selected group, one name per line. The third column shows the card selected in the second column.

Figure 18-27 shows the Address Book window as it appears when you first open the application.

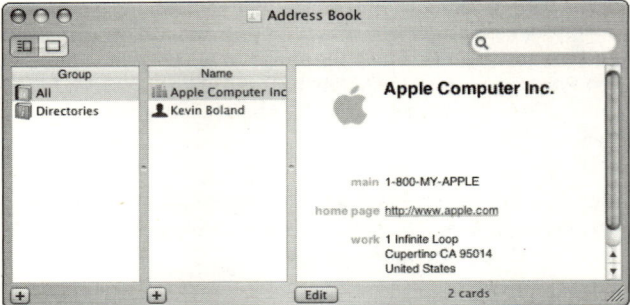

Figure 18-27: The Address Book window.

Notice that your name already appears in the Name list. If you click on your name, you will see your address card, which may be filled with information from the .Mac System Preference pane, if you have entered it there.

Tip Even if you do not use .Mac, and even if you do not intend to manage contacts with Address Book, it's still a good idea to enter your personal information on this card, which is marked "me" in the lower-left corner of your user picture. As mentioned above this information is used by other applications.

To set up your Contact Information:

1. **Select your card.**

2. **Click the Edit button below the card display area.**

3. **Add your contact information to the empty fields.** Press Tab to move from field to field. You can return additional lines to the address field only by pressing Return.

4. **If one of the fields does not apply, skip it; it will not be shown on the final card.**

5. **To add more fields for additional phone numbers, click the green plus button next to the field's name.** This button appears after you have used the initial fields provided. To remove a field, click the red minus button.

6. **Choose Card ⇨ Make This My Card.**

Using the main Address Book window

You can work with contacts in the Address Book window as follows:

✦ Select contacts in the list. Click the name or any other information listed for a contact to select the card. ⌘-click additional contacts to select them also or Shift-click to select a range of contacts. If you select one contact, its basic information appears in the third column of the Address Book window.

✦ View the list by group. Choose a group from the Group column.

✦ Filter the list. Type in the Search box. The Address Book looks for the search text in the information listed for each contact and hides all contacts whose listed information doesn't include the search text. In other words, the Address Book lists only address cards that have the search text in at least one column in the list.

✦ Resize columns. Drag a column heading's right borderline left or right to make the column narrower or wider.

✦ Set View. Switch between single contacts view or the lists plus contact view by clicking on the buttons in the upper-right corner of the address book window. You can also choose View ➪ Card Only or View ➪ Card and Columns. When viewing a single card, advance to the next or previous card with the arrow buttons in the lower left of the window.

Setting Address Book Preferences

The Address Book's Preferences window's General pane shown in Figure 18-28 displays options for display order, sort order, address format, and font size. The checkbox to Notify people when my card changes is grayed out and unavailable unless a group has been created.

Figure 18-28: The Address Book Preferences window's General pane.

The Synchronize with Exchange checkbox enables the Configure button, leading to a sheet where you can set up Address Book to synchronize with Microsoft Exchange.

In the toolbar, note the icons for other preference panes. The Template pane enables you to set the configuration of fields and labels for new address cards. The Phone pane turns on and off automatic formatting of phone numbers, selected from a pop-up menu; use this to conform your phone numbers to the standards used in a particular country.

The vCard format is a common standard used in many applications and uses, from mail programs to PDAs such as Palm Pilots and Handspring Visors, and many newer models of cellular phones. The vCard pane sets the version of the vCard format used, enables a private "Me" card, and enables notes from your address cards to be included in your exported vCards.

The LDAP pane is for setting up Address Book to access contact information on a server that uses the Lightweight Directory Access Protocol. LDAP is an Internet protocol used by email programs to look up contact information on a network directory server. Such servers are often used by larger companies. Contact your network administrator for the information to enter here. Click the plus sign button to drop down a sheet with fields for name, server, search base, port, scope, and authentication details to be entered.

Once this information is entered, click on Directories in the Group column of the Address Book main window, and type in the search field to lookup results from the network directory.

Working with Address Book contacts

To add a contact to Address Book:

1. **Open Address Book.**

2. **Choose File ➪ New Card. A new card is created.**

3. **Add the contact information to the empty fields. Press Tab to move from field to field.** You can add additional lines to the address field only, by pressing Return.

4. **If one of the fields does not apply, skip it; it will not be shown on the final card.**

5. **To add more fields for additional phone numbers, click the green plus button next to the field's name.** This button appears after you have used the initial fields provided. To remove a field, click the red minus button.

6. **If you want to change the field labels, click the label, choose Custom from the pop-up menu, and enter the new label name.** The custom label appears on this contact only. If you want to add a label to all contacts, choose Address Book ➪ Preferences and click Template.

7. **Add notes of any kind to the contact field at the bottom of the card.**

8. **You can add a picture by dragging a picture file to the square box at the top of the card. Or, you can double-click the picture area, click Choose, and navigate to a picture file. Use the slider to enlarge and crop the picture. Click the video camera button to use a connected video camera to take a snapshot.** The resulting picture is used by other applications that access Address Book information, but will never be seen by the person it represents (except for your own picture).

9. **When done, click the Edit button to see the completed card — something like Figure 18-29. Click this same button to edit the card at any time, using the techniques above.**

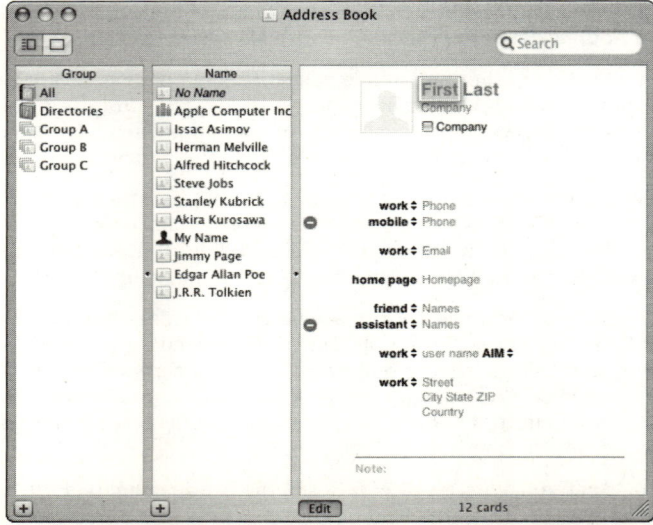

Figure 18-29: A new card has just been created in Address Book.

Tip

The Notes field at the bottom of each card can be set up with keywords associating that contact with a specific group. You can then use the Search field to enter the keyword and quickly locate all the members of this group. For example, if you search for "enemy," all contacts with the keyword "enemy" in the Notes field would be listed.

To remove a contact from the Address Book, select the contact you want to remove and press the Delete key or choose Edit ➪ Delete Person. Click the Yes button when asked if you are sure that you want to delete the card for "contact name."

The contact is removed from the name list, and from any groups it might belong to.

Importing contacts

It is possible to import contacts from another application you may be currently using to store them only if the application supports exporting in vCard or LDIF format (LDAP Interchange Format Files). LDIF is the format an LDAP server uses to exchange information with other LDAP servers.

To import contacts into the Address Book, first check your application's manual to see if it supports exporting addresses in vCard of LDIF formats and then follow these steps:

1. **Export your addresses from the other application as either vCards or an LDIF file.**

2. **In Address Book, choose File ➪ Import, revealing a submenu.**

3. **Choose the format from the Import submenu.**

4. **Select the file that contains the exported addresses.**

You can view the last batch of addresses imported to Address by clicking Last Import in the Group column. This list is updated when you import addresses.

Creating and working with groups

After you add a few contacts to the Address Book, you can create groups to make mailing to several people at once easier. To add a new group, do one of the following:

✦ Click the plus sign button at the bottom of the Group column.

✦ Choose File ➪ New Group.

✦ In the Name column, select several contacts that you want to be in the new group and then choose File ➪ New Group From Selection.

Any of these actions displays a new Group Name in the Group column. Type the name for the new group and then press Return.

You can add contacts to a group by selecting them in the Names column and dragging the selected names to the group.

To drag a contact successfully, position the mouse pointer over the contact's icon in the Names list, hold down the mouse button, and then drag. As you drag, a small address card icon follows the pointer, and a green plus sign icon appears, indicating what you are dragging will be added to the destination.

You can remove a contact from a group by selecting the group, selecting the contact, and pressing Delete. You can also choose Edit ➪ Remove From Group. A sheet drops down that asks, "Are you sure you want to delete *contact name* or simply remove it from the group *Group Name*?" Click the Remove From Group button. The contact is not removed from the name list using this technique. Click the Delete button to remove the contact from all groups and lists.

Delete a group by selecting its name and pressing the Delete key, or choosing Edit ➪ Delete Group. A sheet drops down that asks, "Are you sure you want to delete the selected group?" Click the Yes button.

You can even set up a group to contain other groups. Drag the groups you want to include to the destination group.

To see which group or groups a contact belongs to, hold down the Option key while selecting the contact's name in the Name column. The groups the contact belongs to will appear highlighted in the Group column.

If group members have multiple email addresses, choose which email address to use when sending mail to the group. Choose Edit ➪ Edit Distribution List. Select the group in the left column. The email address listed in bold on the right is the one which will be used when sending mail to the group. Change the email address used by clicking on the one you want to use; this address is now shown in bold. You can also change the phone numbers, fax numbers, or mailing addresses used when printing a distribution list by selecting a choice from the pop-up menu at the column heading of the right column. Click OK when done.

Exchanging contacts

You can copy contacts as vCards to the desktop, to the body of an email message as an attachment, or to a chat window to send to the person you are chatting with. Select the contacts you want to copy in the Name column, and drag them to their destination.

Multiple selected contacts will be copied into a single vCard, unless you hold down the Option key while dragging them, resulting in separate individual vCards. You can also make your selections and choose File ➪ Export vCard.

To keep certain information private before you send your vCard:

1. **Choose Address Book ➪ Preferences.**

2. **Click vCard.**

3. **Select Enable Private 'Me' Card.**

4. **Close the Preferences window.**

5. **Select your card in the Name column.**

6. **Click Edit.**

   Select only the checkboxes next to the information that will be sent.

To send a group an update of the information on your vCard, choose File > Send Updates. In the Send Updates dialog, select the group, type a subject and message (including if you wish a request to be sent their latest vCards), and click Send. A group email message goes out via Mail containing your updated vCard. If you wish this process to happen automatically whenever a change is made to your vCard, select "Notify people when my card changes" in the General pane of Address Book preferences.

When someone sends you a vCard, first save it to any location you choose, then double-click it. Address Book will launch if it is not already running, and a sheet will drop down from the Address Book window, giving you one of the following sets of choices:

✦ If the contact is not a duplicate of a contact already in your Address Book, you are asked to OK or Cancel its addition.

✦ If the contact is a duplicate, you have three choices. You can click OK to update the existing card with the new card, click Cancel, or click Review Duplicates to bring up a window showing the new card with a red Update ribbon at the top right. Compare this card to the one already in your Address Book, and click a button to Keep Old, Keep New, Keep Both, or Update the old card with the new information. If you select Update, the information to be updated is displayed in red, and newly added information is blue.

✦ If you are sent a vCard with multiple duplicate contacts, the Review Duplicates window shows them sequentially after clicking the Next button. You can apply your chosen action to all the contacts by clicking the Apply to All checkbox (see Figure 18-30).

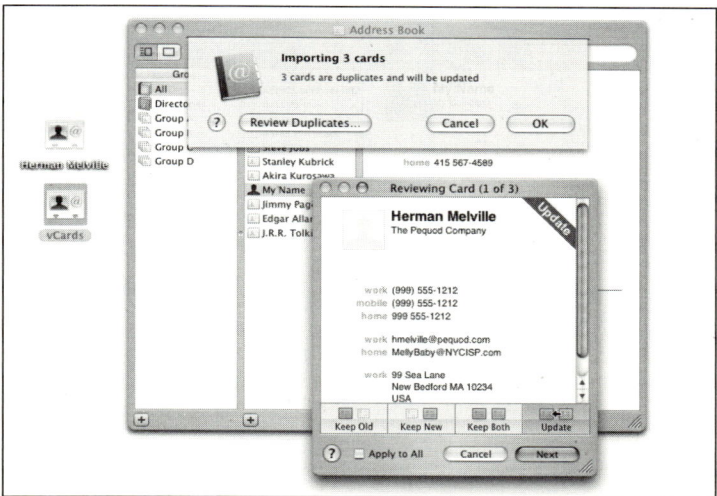

Figure 18-30: A single vCard (upper left) bears the contact's name, but a vCard with multiple contacts (lower left) is called "vCards." Double-clicking "vCards" brings down the "Importing cards" sheet and clicking Review Duplicates brings up the Reviewing Card window.

Combine duplicate contacts to retain all their information on a single card. Use the Search field to get the dupes to show in the Names column. Hold down the ⌘ key as you select the contacts you want to combine. Then choose Card ➪ Merge Cards. Review the resulting card to delete any unwanted information.

Printing address lists and labels

Address Book can print address lists and mailing labels from its contacts database. You can format them to look just right for your purposes using Address Book's sophisticated Print dialog.

To print an address list:

1. **Choose File ➪ Print. Address Book's Print dialog opens as shown in Figure 18-31.**

2. **From the Style pop-up menu, choose List.**

3. **In the Attributes window, select the fields you want to see listed.**

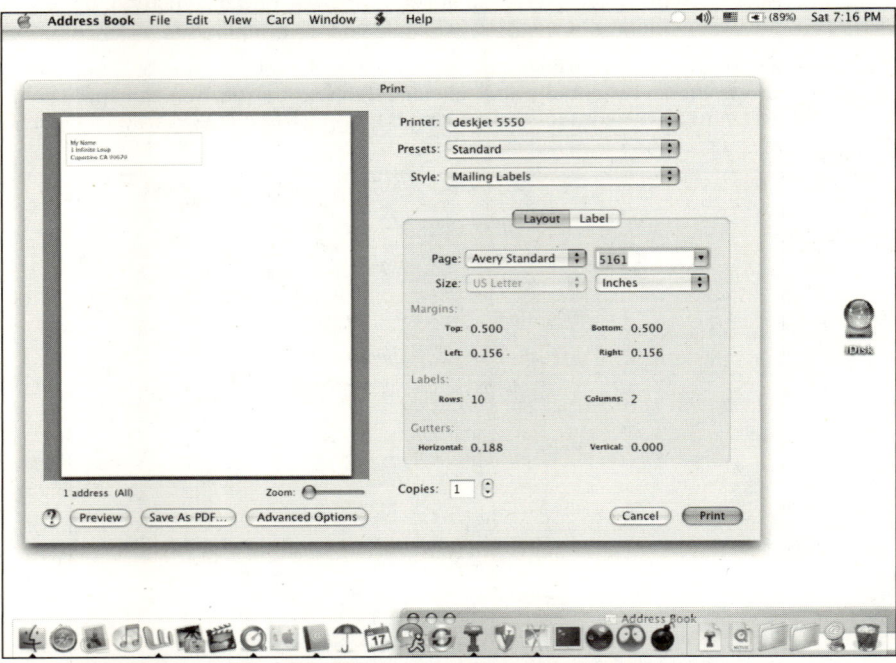

Figure 18-31: The Address Book print dialog, set to the Layout panel.

To print a mailing label:

1. **Choose File ➪ Print.** Address Book's Print dialog opens.

2. **From the Style pop-up menu, choose Mailing Labels.**

3. **Click Layout.**

4. **From the Page pop-up menu, choose a type of label.**

5. **Choose Define Custom from the Page pop-up menu to set up how many labels to print on a page, the page margins, and the gutter space between labels.**

6. **From the Address pop-up menu, choose the type of address.**

7. **From the Sorting pop-up menu, choose Last Name or Postal Code to sort the labels based on one or the other.**

8. **Use the checkboxes to Print Country and Except My Country, or leave them empty.**

9. **If you want, change the font, color, and drag any image you want to print on the label to the well.**

10. **As you make changes, the print preview on the left shows what the labels will look like.**

11. **Select the number of copies and click Print.**

Backing up Address Book

Once you start using Address Book, the information it contains becomes very valuable. It's a good idea to make frequent backups, which can be done with Address Book's Back Up Database command.

To create a backup of Address Book information:

1. **Choose File ⇨ Back Up Database.** A location selection sheet drops down.

2. **Choose a location for the backup file.**

3. **Click Save.** The backup file appears as a document icon with the Address Book icon and the acronym ABBU, for Address Book Back Up.

To restore your Address Book information from a backup file:

1. **Choose File ⇨ Revert to Database Backup.** A Panther navigation sheet will drop down.

2. **Navigate to the desired backup file.**

3. **Click Open.** An alert appears: Reverting will cause your current database to be overwritten. Note that the operation cannot be undone.

4. **Click OK.**

Also note that the Revert operation *can* be undone, in effect, if you first make a backup file; then you can revert to that file if you want to undo the previous revert.

If you have a .Mac account, you can use iSync to backup your Address Book to your iDisk. For more information, see the iSync section of this chapter.

Address Book Tips

Using the Address Book is an easy way to manage your contact information. The following list provides you with tips on using the Address Book feature.

✦ You can tell if a contact is currently available via iChat. A circle next to the contact's picture indicates their status; if the circle is green, they are available. Click the circle to invite the contact to a chat.

✦ If a contact has a .Mac account name email address, there is a easy way to send them an email, start an iChat, open their Public Folder on their iDisk, visit their HomePage, or send them a vCard, right from their address card. Click the field label (for example, home or work) next to the .Mac email address. The resulting pop-up menu will offer the choices Send Email, iChat, Visit HomePage, Open iDisk, or Send Update. Choose what you would like to do, and the appropriate application will be launched, taking you right to what you wanted to do.

✦ Copy an address as a mailing label to paste into another application by clicking on the address field label and choosing Copy Mailing Label from the pop-up menu.

✦ Get a map showing an address's location (if you are connected to the Internet) by clicking on the address field label and choosing Map Of from the pop-up menu.

✦ Keep track of birthdays by choosing Card ➪ Add Field ➪ Birthday. To track anniversaries or other important dates, choose Card ➪ Add Field ➪ Dates.

✦ If a contact has more than one instant messaging account, you can add them all to their address card. Click the Edit button, then add the first address. Select the type of address from the pop-up menu to the right of the address. Click the green add button to add another address. Repeat until all the addresses are entered, and then click the Edit button to view the results; next to each address, the name of the service appears in parentheses.

iCal

iCal is the Mac OS X calendar application (see Figure 18-32). You may assume that it is a basic application that lets you schedule appointments and events on a calendar and not much else.

iCal is simple to use, but its capabilities are quite astonishing, especially when used with the .Mac service. In fact, like the other "iApps," iCal makes a play to be the ultimate application of its kind, at the very least attempting to exceed your expectations by quite a bit.

Check out this summary of what you can do with iCal:

✦ Create digital calendars containing your schedule, viewed by day, week, or month, to keep track of events, appointment, meetings, deadlines, birthdays, anniversaries, reminders, and other time-related information.

✦ Create separate, color-coded calendars for different aspects of your life, like work, home, school, kids, sports, etc. The calendars can be viewed all at once or in any combination, superimposed transparently on each other.

✦ Invite others to events automatically by email sent by Mac OS X Mail.

✦ Create To Do lists.

✦ Search for events, with the results listed so you can click on an event to go directly to it.

✦ Set alarms to notify you of upcoming events, by sounds, onscreen messages, emails, launching applications, playing a song, or running a script.

✦ Share your calendar with other iCal users on the same computer, or over the Internet, using .Mac or your company's WebDAV server.

✦ Subscribe to the calendars of other iCal users that have been published on the Internet.

✦ Synchronize calendars on more than one computer or device using iSync.

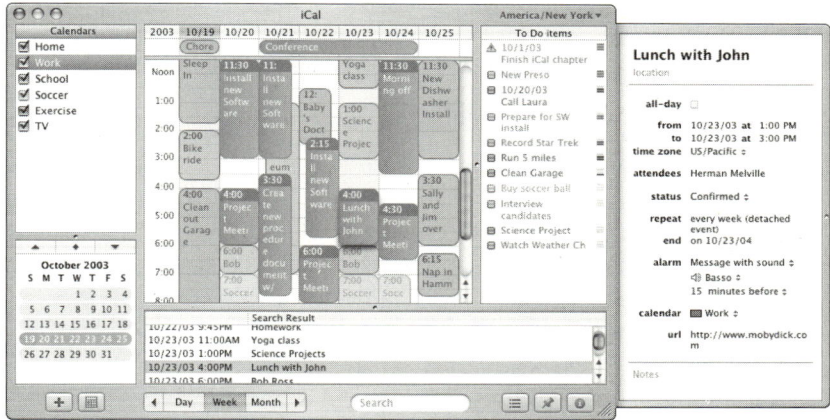

Figure 18-32: The iCal interface.

Working with calendars

iCal gives you two default calendars, Home and Work. You can create other calendars for different aspects of your life or areas of interest.

To create a new calendar, follow these steps:

1. **Click the plus sign button at the bottom left of the iCal window or double-click the white area below the calendars listed in the Calendars list.**

2. **A new calendar appears in the Calendars list, with its name, Untitled, highlighted.**

3. **Type a name for the calendar.**

4. **Press the Return key.**

You can rename a calendar at any time by double-clicking its name and typing a new one.

To delete a calendar:

1. **Click the name of the calendar in the Calendars list.**

2. **Press the Delete key.**

Use a different procedure to delete a calendar that you have published over the Internet; see the instructions for this later in this section.

Working with events

Any item that appears on an iCal calendar is called an event. Once an event is created, its details can be set or later edited in the Info drawer that you can slide out from the right side of the iCal window or hide as necessary.

To add events to a calendar, follow these steps:

1. **In the Calendars list, click the name of the calendar you want to add an event to.**

2. **In Day or Week view, drag from the start time to the end time of the new event.** As you do so, a colored rectangle forms, with the start and end time appearing. When you release the drag, the name New Event becomes highlighted.

   In Month view, double-click the blank area of the day you want the new event to appear. The event appears as a colored bar with its name, New Event, highlighted.

3. **Type a name for the new event.**

4. **Press the Return key.**

To edit an event:

1. **Create a new event or select an existing event.**

2. **Click the Info button at the bottom-right corner of the window.** The Info drawer slides out to the right of the window, listing the editable details of the event.

   In the Day and Week views, you can also double-click the event's start-time bar at the top of its rectangle to show the Info drawer.

3. **Edit the details of the event. You can**

   - Change or delete an event.

   - Change the time or day by dragging the event to a new position in the calendar view.

   - Change the duration, in Day or Week view, by dragging the event's top or bottom edge. If it is an all day event, drag its right or left side.

   - Change the name of the event by double-clicking its name, and type a new name.

   - Delete an event by selecting it and pressing the Delete key.

To automatically delete events after they are due, choose iCal ➪ Preferences. The iCal Preferences window appears, as shown in Figure 18-33. Select the Automatically delete events and To Do items checkbox. Enter the number of days after which the items will be deleted, click Yes in the alert box which appears, and close the Preferences window (see Figure 18-33).

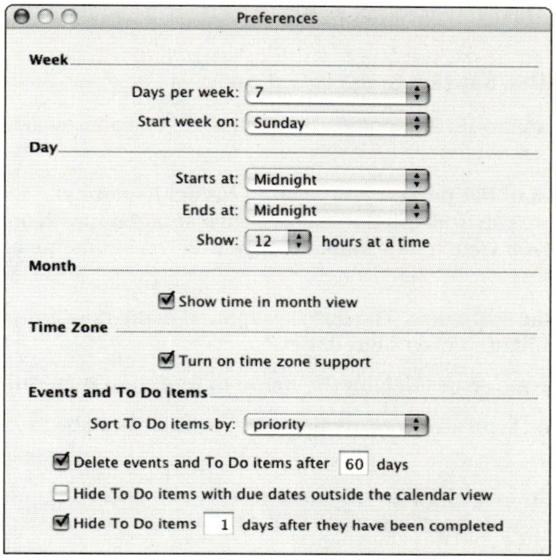

Figure 18-33: iCal's Preferences window.

To create, edit, or view an event that will take place in a different time zone, follow these steps:

1. **Choose iCal ⇨ Preferences.**

2. **Click on the Turn on time zone support checkbox to turn on the feature.**

3. **From the time zone pop-up menu which now appears in the Info drawer, choose Other.** A world time zone map appears.

4. **Click on the location the event will take place in.** A menu appears with the names of big cities in that time zone.

5. **Select a city closest to where the events will take place.** Note that the exact details of time zones change in different areas; for example, some areas keep only a half-hour difference between neighboring time zones, instead of a full hour; iCal knows which ones.

6. **Click OK.** The time zone you selected appears next to the time zone label, and will appear in the pop-up menu from now on.

The event appears in your calendar at the time the event will take place, adjusted for your time zone (based on your computer's settings in the Date & Time System Preference).

To view all your iCal events adjusted for a different time zone, choose a time zone from the pop-up menu in the upper-right corner of the iCal window. If the desired time zone does not appear, choose Other, and repeat Steps 4–6 above to add a new time zone to this menu.

Events created in a particular time zone automatically shift to the correct adjusted time when you change the calendar's time zone.

ICal makes it easy to invite someone, or several people, to an event via email. You might want to do this if you are planning a meeting or a party.

Inviting someone to an event is easy when you use iCal. To create and send an invite follow these steps:

1. **Select the event so its information appears in the Info drawer.**

2. **Next to the label attendees, click None.** It becomes selected and you can now edit the label.

3. **Begin to type the email address of the person you want to invite.** As you type the first letters, any matching names from the Address Book appear in a submenu, with any associated email addresses. (If you want a new name to appear in the submenu, add it to the Address Book.)

4. **Select an email address from the submenu.** The auto-completed name now appears next to the attendees label, highlighted in a colored oval.

5. **Click elsewhere to deselect the name or click on the name to highlight it again.**

6. **To invite more than one person, type a comma or press the Return key after each name.**

7. **Click on the triangle to the right of a highlighted name to reveal a pop-up menu with the associated email addresses, and the commands Edit Attendee, Remove Attendee, Open in Address Book, or Send Email.**

8. **You can also add attendees by dragging names from Address Book to an event in the iCal window.** Click the attendees label and choose Open Address Book from the pop-up menu.

9. **Drag the contacts you want to invite from Address book to the event in the iCal calendar view.**

10. **After you have added all of the attendees, click attendees and choose Send Invitations from the pop-up menu.** Emails are sent by Mac OS X Mail with the details of the event to the people listed.

Question mark icons now appear before each name to show the attendees have not yet confirmed. These icons change to checkmarks when the invitation is accepted, and X marks when declined.

iCal keeps track of the status of events — Tentative, Confirmed, or Cancelled — with status indicators that appear on the events in the Day and Week views.

You can use iCal to set up weekly meetings. Follow these steps to set up recurrent events:

1. **Select the event so its information appears in the Info drawer.**

2. **Next to the label repeat, click None.** A pop-up menu appears with the choices None, Every Day, Every Week, Every Month, Every Year, and Custom.

3. **Select the repeat interval you want to use.**

    If you choose Custom, a box opens to help you configure the repeat interval.

4. **From the Frequency pop-up menu, choose Daily, Weekly, Monthly, or Yearly.** The box changes to reflect each choice.

5. **Make your Custom selections and then click OK.** Your selection appears next to the repeat label. A new end label appears under the repeat label.

6. **Click on the word to the right of the end label to see the choices Never, After, and On date.**

7. **Make your selection for when the repeat will end.** Your choice will be displayed. If you choose "on date", the date will appear; click on the date to edit it.

If you make any other changes to a recurring event, a dialog box opens, asking if you want to change only this occurrence of the event, or all occurrences.

You can set an alarm to warn you of an impending event with an onscreen message, an email, or by opening a file of your choice. To receive an alarm before an event:

1. **Select the event so its information appears in the Info drawer.** You can only set an alarm for an event that has a due date.

2. **Next to the label alarm, click None.** A pop-up menu appears with the choices None, Message, Message with sound, Email, and Open file.

3. **Make your selection for the type of alarm you want.**

   Depending on your selection, other pop-up menus appear, enabling you to set the details of the alarm. Below the details you see a pop-up menu allowing you to set the alarm time before the start time of the event. You can choose to do the following:

   • Select Open file to enable iCal to open an application before the event occurs. Select the application in the Navigation dialog, and the application's name appears in a pop-up menu.

   • To add another alarm, click on the label alarm and choose Add Alarm from the pop-up menu. Then repeat Step 3.

   • To remove an alarm, click on the label alarm and choose Remove Alarm from the pop-up menu.

Note When the alarm goes off, you can choose to "Snooze" it (temporarily silence it and remind you again later) by choosing an item from the "repeat" pop-up menu in the upper- right corner of the iCal Alarm window.

Adding a URL to an event is a way of attaching additional information that is on the Web to an event. This feature is especially helpful for online calendars. To add an associated URL to an event follow these steps:

1. **Select the event so that its information appears in the Info drawer.**

2. **Next to the label url, click None.** The word becomes highlighted and editable.

3. **Type a URL. To add more than one URL, separate each with commas. Or, drag a URL from you Web browser's address field.**

4. **Click on a URL to go to the web page in your browser.**

To Do Lists

In our busy modern world, it always seems that and keeping track of what needs to be done is a difficult chore. iCal can help. To create a To Do List and work with To Do items:

1. **Click the To Do button (with the push-pin icon) in the bottom right corner of the iCal window.** The To Do list appears to the right of the calendar. To hide it, click the To Do button again.

2. **Double-click anywhere in the white area of the To Do list.** A New To Do item appears with its name selected and editable.

3. **Type your desired name for the To Do item and press the Return key.**

4. **If you want to assign settings to the To Do item, click the Info button at the bottom right of the iCal window.** The Info drawer slides out.

5. **When you complete the item, click the completed checkbox.** The word Today appears to the right. When viewing previously completed To Do items, the date of completion appears here. You can also click the checkbox next to the item in the To Do list.

6. **To give the To Do item a priority rating, click the word None to the right of the label priority.** A pop-up menu appears with the choices None, Very Important, Important, Not Important. Select the priority you desire.

7. **To give the To Do item a due date, select the "due date" checkbox, and edit the date, month, day or year.** The due date appears above the item in the To Do list. If the due date passes before you mark the item as completed, the checkbox in the list becomes an alert icon (a triangle with an exclamation point).

8. **To receive an alarm before the due date passes, click the word "None" to the right of the label alarm.** Select from the choices None, Message, Message with Sound, Email, or Open file. If you previously had set a file to open, it will appear below these choices on the menu. You can only set an alarm for items that have a due date.

9. **After the type of alarm has been selected, select the details from the pop-up menus below your selection.** Select the amount of time before the item is due.

10. **To switch the calendar the To Do item appears on, click the name of the present calendar to the right of the calendar label. Select from the calendars listed.** The To Do item changes its color to match the calendar.

Sharing calendars

You can use iCal to share your calendars with others, and to see calendars others have chosen to share. Calendars published on the Internet can be viewed by anyone with a web browser, or viewed in iCal once they are subscribed to. You can also export your events and send them to someone else, who can import them into iCal.

Publishing a calendar puts a copy of it on a Web server, to be accessed by a URL that you send to those you wish to share it with. If you are a .Mac member, you can publish your calendar to your iDisk. If you have access to a private Web server that is running WebDAV, you can publish your calendar using it, to be shared with other users who have access to the server. Users viewing your published calendar cannot make changes to it; it is "read only" to them.

Exporting a calendar creates a file containing your event information which can be sent to the people you want to share it with, so they can import it into iCal. Once imported, the events can be edited; the users have "read/write" access to them. Changes they make on the imported copy are not duplicated on your original calendar.

You can also use the exported information to backup your calendar or transfer your iCal information to another computer.

If you are a .Mac member, you can share your calendar with anyone you wish via the Internet. Imagine allowing your friends, family members, and business associates to check your availability themselves instead of having them contact you.

To publish a calendar on the Internet follow these steps:

1. **Connect to the Internet.** In the Calendars list, click the name of the calendar to be published.

2. **Choose Calendar ➪ Publish.** A sheet drops down.

3. **In the Publish Name field, type the name of the calendar visitors will see.**

4. **Click the Publish changes automatically checkbox if you want changes you make to your calendar to be automatically copied to the published version.**

5. **Click the other checkboxes to control which information will be published.**

6. **From the pop-up menu, choose where you want to publish your calendar, either on .Mac or on a WebDAV server.** If you choose WebDAV the sheet lengthens, providing fields for entering the server's URL and the login name and password.

7. **Click Publish.** Figure 18-34 shows the iCal Publish sheet.

8. **Watch the Status bar to see the progress as your calendar is uploaded to the Web server.**

   The Calendar Published alert appears, informing you that your calendar was published successfully, and providing you with the URL for it. Click Visit Page to go to it, Send Mail to inform others and give them the URL, or click OK.

   After it is published, a broadcast icon (a dot with three short curving lines) appears next to the calendar in the Calendars list.

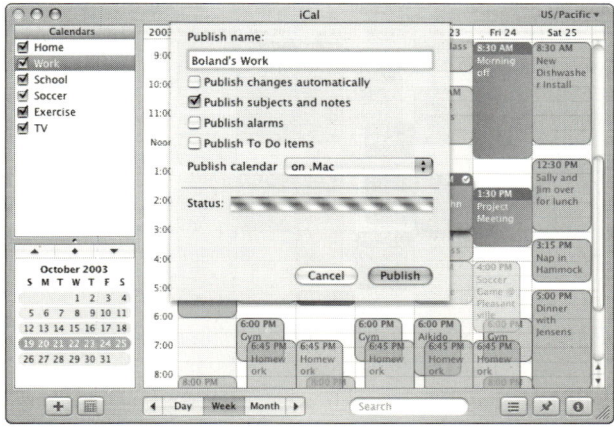

Figure 18-34: iCal's Publish sheet.

If you want to stop publication of your calendar, select the name of the calendar, choose Calendar ➪ Unpublish, and then click Unpublish. The calendar's broadcast icon disappears. It remains available on your computer. People who subscribed to it will still be able to see the last published copy, but no one will be able to subscribe to it.

To subscribe to and update someone else's Calendar:

1. **Connect to the Internet.**

2. **Choose Calendar ➪ Subscribe.** A sheet drops down.

3. **Enter the URL for the calendar you want to subscribe to.**

4. **If you want your copy of the calendar to be automatically updated when changes to it are published, put a click in the Refresh checkbox.** You can also set the calendar to auto-update in the Info drawer: select the calendar and from the Auto-publish pop-up menu, choose after each change. (To update the calendar manually, select it, and choose Calendar ➪ Refresh at any time you wish.)

5. **Check the other checkboxes to control whether you will receive alarms or see To Do items.**

6. **Click Subscribe.**

Watch the Status bar, shown in Figure 18-35, to see the progress as the calendar is downloaded from the Web server. The calendar you have subscribed to appears in the Calendars list with a curved arrow icon next to it. If you want to rename the new calendar, double-click its name. You cannot make any other changes to it.

You can also subscribe to any of the general interest calendars available at iCalShare.com. These include holidays, professional sports team schedules, Movie openings, DVD releases, rock band tour dates, TV schedules, moon phases, and Apple Store events. If you create your own general interest calendar, you can upload it to this site to share it with the world.

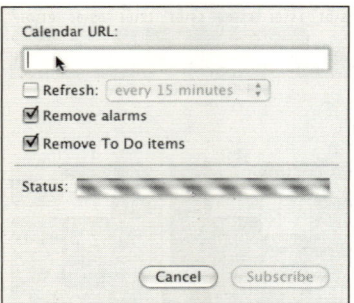

Figure 18-35: iCal's Subscribe sheet.

You can export your calendar information as a file which can then be imported by any iCal user you send it to. This is another way of sharing your calendar. Figure 18-36 shows the iCal's Export command.

To export your calendar information:

1. **In the Calendar list, click the name of the calendar.**

2. **Choose File ⇨ Export.**

3. **Select a name for the file and a destination for it to be saved to.**

4. **Click Export.** The exported file appears as an .ics file (for iCal Standard).

5. **Send the file to the person you want to share it with, transfer it to the Mac you want to import it on, or store it in a archive folder as a backup.**

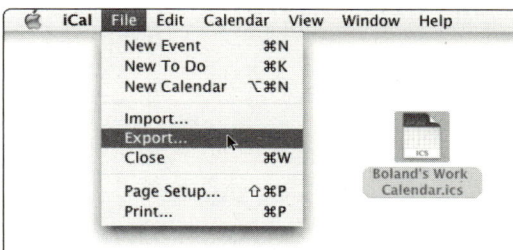

Figure 18-36: Using iCal's Export command produces an .ics file.

You can also import calendar information. Follow these steps:

1. **Choose File ⇨ Import.**

2. **Navigate to the .ics calendar file you want to import.** The Add Events dialog appears.

3. **Select the calendar you want to add the imported events to.**

4. **Click OK.**

5. **You may briefly see a progress bar as the events are imported.** The new events appear in the calendar you chose.

Printing calendars

You may find you have a need to print calendars to distribute them to others in a format that does not require a computer. You can also put them in an organizational notebook, scribble updates on them, and transfer the changes when you get back to your computer.

To print a calendar or a To Do list:

1. **In the Calendars list, check the calendars you wish to print.**

2. **Choose File ⇨ Print.** The Print dialog opens as shown in Figure 18-37.

3. **From the third pop-up menu, choose iCal.**

4. **Set the dates, times, and items you want to print.** You can print calendars, To Do lists, and the mini-month view.

5. **Click Preview to check what you will print.**

6. **Click Print.**

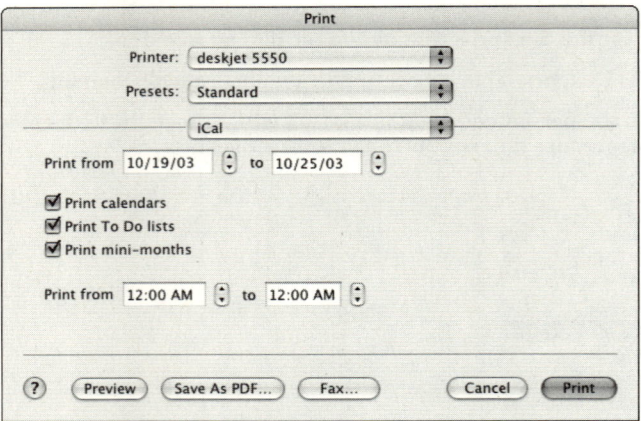

Figure 18-37: iCal's Print dialog.

iCal Tips

✦ In iCal 1.5.1 and later, you can quickly perform the most common actions with an enhanced set if iCal specific keyboard shortcuts. For example, you can skip to the next day, week, or month by pressing ⌘ + Right Arrow. Or, to duplicate a selected event, press ⌘ + D. Anyone who uses iCal frequently may save quite a bit of time by using the shortcuts. You can print a comprehensive list of them from iCal Help, and post them nearby until you learn them. As Apple says on its Web site, "Efficiency is iCal's highest priority."

✦ To change the order of calendars in the Calendars list, drag them to where you want them.

✦ You can copy and paste events in the main calendar window. To select multiple events for copying, hold down the Shift key as you make your selections. Press ⌘+C to copy, as usual. Click where you want to place the first event, and press ⌘+V to paste. The original time difference between the events is maintained.

✦ To see a handy shortcut menu by holding the Control key while you click on an event. You can choose Cut, Copy, Paste, Duplicate, switch the event to any calendar, make an All Day Event, Stop Recurrence, or Email Event. Selecting this last choice opens Mail to a message which looks like Figure 20-39. All you need to do is supply an address, and all the recipient needs to do is click on the .ics file included as an attachment to have it added to his or her calendar.

✦ In Month view, if you see an ellipsis (...) at the top of the day, it means all the events in the day could not be shown due to size limitations. Double-click the ellipsis to see all the events in the Day view.

✦ Events that span several days can be created by dragging an All Day Event across the desired days.

iSync

iSync is the Mac OS X synchronization software. It synchronizes contact and calendar information between different Mac OS X computers, and also devices such as mobile phones, a Palm OS PDA, or an iPod.

What exactly does synchronization mean? In this case, iSync *compares* the information on separate computers or devices and then *changes* the information to be the same on them all. iSync knows to ask you how to resolve conflicting information so that nothing is lost. Anything deleted on one device is deleted on all the other devices after they are synced.

Use iSync to synchronize contact information from the Address Book and calendar and to-do information from iCal. Figure 18-38 shows the iSync window as it first appears.

You can use iSync on the four following choices:

✦ A Bluetooth enabled mobile phone (from a Bluetooth enabled Macintosh)

✦ An iSync-compatible USB mobile phone

✦ A Palm OS handheld PDA via USB, or via Bluetooth (from a Bluetooth enabled Macintosh)

✦ An Apple iPod via a FireWire, one-way, Mac to iPod synch

If you have a .Mac membership, iSync can also synchronize:

✦ Contact information from Address Book

✦ Calendar and To Do information from iCal

✦ Bookmarks from Safari

With (via the Internet):

✦ Multiple Mac OS X computers

✦ The .Mac Address Book for use with .Mac Web Mail

✦ iCal calendars published on the Internet for use by your friends using iCal on their Macs

✦ .Mac Bookmarks for use via any Web browser

 Tip You should plan on only syncing a device with a single computer. For example, if you have three computers, one at home, one at work, and a PowerBook, you cannot sync the device with any of them; you have to pick one. You can change which one later by removing the device from iSync and then adding it to iSync on another machine; see the instruction below for removing a device. Information may not sync correctly when you violate this rule.

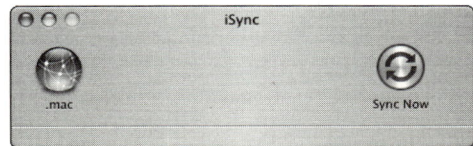

Figure 18-38: The iSync window as it first appears.

Setting up devices for syncing

Before you can use iSync, you need to set up your computers or devices to work with it.

The first step in setting up your device is to check to see if it is iSync-compatible. Visit www.apple.com/isync/devices.html to view an up-to-the minute list of all compatible devices. The list is growing all the time.

Instructions for setting up devices may change with each new revision of iSync. For the most up-to-date information on how do set up your device, refer to the specific instructions in the "Setting up your computers and devices" section of iSync Help.

Although the details vary, in general the setup process for phones goes like this. First ensure connectivity between your Mac and the phone, via Bluetooth or USB. Second, open iSync, choose Devices ⇨ Add Device, and double-click the phone in the add device window to add it to iSync. When the phone is added, a phone icon will appear on the iSync interface. You only need to add the phone once.

To set up a Palm OS device, you need to install the latest iSync Palm Conduit software on your Mac. Download this software from www.apple.com/isync.

After the software is installed, follow the instructions in iSync Help to add your Palm OS device to iSync, which only needs to be done once.

In general, you must first ensure that you have compatible versions of Palm Desktop (at this writing, version 4.0 or later), iCal (1.02 or later) and the latest Palm Conduit. Open the Palm HotSync Manager utility, and choose HotSync ⇨ Conduit Settings. Double-click the iSync Conduit, then select Enable iSync for this Palm device. Click OK, and your Palm device will appear in the iSync window. The Palm Address Book, Date Book, and To Do will now sync with information from the Mac OS X Address Book and iCal. The Palm Notes will still sync as before with the Palm Desktop application.

After you have the iPod software Version 2.0 installed, follow these steps to set up an iPod to work with iSync:

1. **Connect your iPod to your Mac with its FireWire cable.**

2. **Open iSync.**

3. **Choose Devices ⇨ Add Device.** The Add Device window opens.

4. **Double-Click iPod.** The iPod icon appears in the iSync window.

iSync transfers to your iPod your contacts from Address Book, and your calendar events and To Do lists from iCal. iSync will not transfer information from the iPod to your computer.

To set up a Mac to sync with another Mac via iSync and .Mac, connect to the Internet and then follow these steps:

1. **Open the .Mac System Preference to the .Mac panel to ensure your .Mac member name and password are properly entered.**

2. **Open iSync and click the .Mac button.** The .Mac settings appear.

3. **Click the Register button.**

4. **Enter a name to identify this computer with the .Mac synchronization service.** The name must be different from the name of any other computer you register or iSync will not work. The name that is pre-entered is taken from the computer name in the Sharing pane of System Preferences; use this name, or any other unique name.

5. **Repeat the above steps on any other Mac you wish to sync.**

The registered computers will sync with .Mac whenever you perform a sync while connected to the Internet.

Synchronizing your information

After you have set up all the devices and computers you wish to sync, and icons for them appear in the iSync window, you are ready to synchronize!

1. **The first time you synchronize a device, click its icon in the iSync window. From the For first sync pop-up menu, choose Merge to combine the information from all computers and devices, or Replace to replace the information on the current computer or devices with synced information from your other computers or devices.**

   If you want to choose what information will be synchronized, click on the .Mac or a device icon in the iSync window, and make your selections. Selecting less information here will speed up the sync process.

2. **To start the sync between all computers or devices (for everything but a Palm OS device), click Sync Now in the iSync window.**

3. **To do a sync between all computers or devices, including a Palm OS device, perform a Hot Sync operation on the device. To do this, push the Hot Sync button on the device's cradle or on the device's screen, select the Hot Sync application and press the Hot Sync button.**

   Starting the Hot Sync operation when a Palm device has been added to iSync is equivalent to pushing the Sync Now button, in that all the added devices and computers will be synchronized. When the sync starts, the iSync window temporarily hides your settings. If more than 5 percent of the information on any device will be changed by the synchronization, a "Safeguard window" appears to inform you of how much information is going to be changed, and gives you an opportunity to cancel the sync process. (You can change the setting for this window in iSync Preferences.)

All registered computers and added devices are synchronized, as long as they are connected either by wire, within Bluetooth range, or over the Internet. The first sync will take longer than subsequent syncs, because all the information is being synchronized and not just the changes.

If any of the registered computers or added devices are not connected or available at the time of the sync, iSync saves the information meant for them, and updates them as soon as a connection to them becomes available.

If iSync detects that the same record has been changed on different source computers or devices and the changes are not identical, iSync will ask you to resolve the conflict. In the dialog that appears, select the source which will be used. If there is more than one conflict between sources, you will see a message to this effect. To resolve all conflicts with your selected source, click the checkbox next to this message. You can also click Later to resolve the conflicts at your next sync.

Tip   After a sync, you may notice a new calendar in iCal called Unfiled. iSync creates an Unfiled calendar to hold date-related information from a mobile phone or Palm device that you have not specified should be added to one of your iCal calendars. You can keep the Unfiled calendar, or delete it after transferring its events to another iCal calendar.

Automatic synchronization

If you are a .Mac member, you can choose to synchronize the following information automatically, every hour:

✦ Address Book

✦ .Mac Address Book

✦ iCal calendars and To Do lists

✦ Safari bookmarks

When Automatic Synchronization is turned on, and a Bluetooth phone or USB has been added to iSync, they will also be synced when they are connected or in range.

Note that Palm OS devices cannot be automatically synchronized, because they depend upon the Hot Sync software.

Follow these steps to turn on Automatic Synchronization:

1. **Choose iSync ⇨ Preferences.** (See Figure 18-39.)

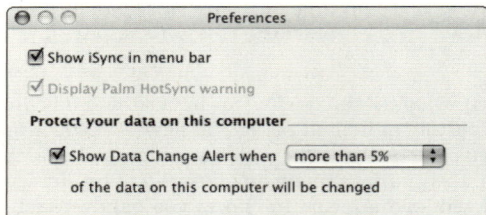

Figure 18-39: The iSync Preferences window.

Make sure that the Show data change alert when...pop-up menu is set to an option other than Any. If you do not do this, you will see a window later asking you to change your Safeguard settings. Close the Preferences window when done.

2. **Click the .Mac icon in the iSync window and select the Automatically synchronize every hour option.**

While you are connected to the Internet, every hour your computers will by synchronized with the .Mac synchronization server. If you are not connected to the Internet, iSync will save your information every hour and will perform the synchronization the next time you are connected to the Internet.

Resetting synchronized information

You can undo a synchronization if you don't like its results, or if you had problems during the process, by performing a reset. You have three choices of how to do this:

1. To revert *only your computer* to the information that was on it just before your last sync, choose Devices ➪ Revert to Last Sync. You will lose any changes made since your last synchronization.

2. To transfer the information currently on your computer to all computers or devices, choose Devices ➪ Reset All Devices. Then select the This computer option from the pop-up menu and click Reset All.

3. To transfer the information currently on the .Mac sync server to all computers or devices, choose Devices ➪ Reset All Devices (see Figure 18-40). Then choose .Mac from the pop-up menu and click Reset All.

If you have turned on syncing for your .Mac Address Book, the information it contains will also be reset. You will lose any information that is stored only in your .Mac Address Book, such as quick-tos and nicknames.

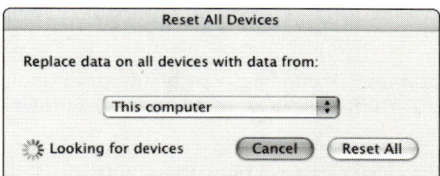

Figure 18-40: iSync's Reset All Devices window.

Turning off synchronization

You can temporarily turn off synchronization off for any of your registered computers or added devices. You can also turn off synchronization for a particular type of information on that computer or device.

To turn synchronization off, click the .Mac icon, or the device's icon, so that the settings appear. Deselect the Turn on Synchronization checkbox to remove the check mark.

To turn off a particular type of information on the computer or device, deselect the information you don't want to synchronize.

Removing computers and devices from iSync

If you no longer want to sync a computer or device with iSync, you can remove it.

You must remove a device if you want to sync it with another computer, because information may not sync correctly if a device that has been added to iSync on two different computers is synchronized first with one, and then the other. As a rule, you should only have the device added to one computer's iSync at a time.

✦ To remove the computer you are working on from iSync, click on the .Mac icon in the iSync window, and click Unregister This Computer.

✦ To remove a registered computer you are not working on from the .Mac synchronization service, click on the .Mac icon in the iSnyc window, select the computer, and click Unregister Selected Computer.

✦ To remove a device from iSync, select the device icon in the iSync window and choose Devices ➪ Remove device. The device icon disappears from the iSync window.

Using the Backup Application

Backup is the .Mac service's backup application, and provides a convenient way to back up important information on your computer to your iDisk or to recordable CD or DVD discs.

To use Backup, you must be a .Mac member.

Backing up

A backup is just a copy of a file or files, but the copy is made to safeguard the data. If something bad happens to the original, the backup copy should still be fine, especially if it is on a different disk.

The hard drive mechanism in your computer will fail at some point; drives are typically rated for 5 years of constant use but can fail *at any time*. And the magnetic medium which holds your precious data becomes demagnetized spontaneously as time progresses; at this very moment, your data is *deteriorating*!

Any time your computer crashes, data corruption may occur. Files can be unintentionally erased. A computer virus may damage your data. Your computer could be lost or stolen or simply die.

The Backup application is the very model of a modern personal backup application. It is easy to understand , easy to use, and free with your $99 .Mac subscription.

You need to manually or automatically make back up copies of your important files to a folder on your hard drive, an external FireWire hard disk, your iPod and iDisk, and a recordable CD or DVD.

With Backup, you can:

✦ Use the QuickPicks feature to automatically suggest groups of important files to back up

✦ Easily add files to be backed up by dragging them to the Backup window

✦ Quickly buy more storage space for your iDisk

✦ Schedule automatic backups

✦ Restore files from a backup

Setting up Backup

If you did not by the .Mac shrink-wrapped box, which contains a CD with the Backup application, you must download it from the .Mac website, and install it on your hard disk.

Put an alias of Backup in your Dock; its purple umbrella will remind you to use it often.

When you first launch Backup, be sure to be connected to the Internet. If you are not connected, Backup will not even open. Instead, you will see the dialog shown in Figure 18-41.

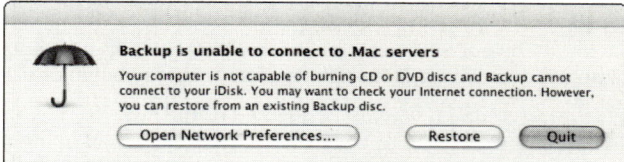

Figure 18-41: This window appears when Backup is first launched and is unable to connect to the .Mac servers via the Internet.

The Backup interface

When you first open backup, you see something like Figure 18-42. The Info drawer on the right will be hidden; to see it, click on an item in the backup list and then click the Info button in the lower left of the window.

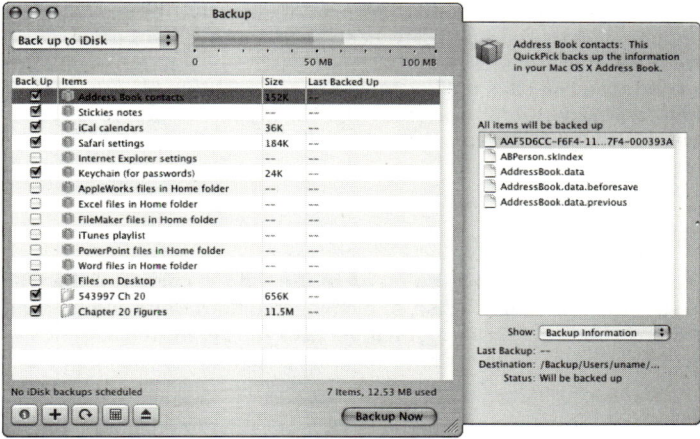

Figure 18-42: The Backup interface.

The items you see in the main window known as the backup list. You can add whichever files you like here, but you will see some have been added by default. These files, marked with package icons, are known as QuickPicks. QuickPicks are groups of important related files that Apple has decided would be most helpful to back up. Take a quick look down the list and you will quickly understand the concept. The QuickPicks include files in Mac OS X that most users would not think of or know to back up.

To see the individual files in a QuickPicks package, click on one to highlight it, and look in the main window of the Info drawer. Click on each of these individual files to view vital information about it in the area below. The Show pop-up menu allows you to choose between General Information (the kind you would find in a Get Info window in the Finder) or Backup Information (when the last backup of this file occurred, the path where it will be backed up to, and its Status — whether it will be backed up or not).

Choosing a destination disk

A destination disk for your backup to be copied to can be chosen from the pop-up menu in the top-left corner of the Backup window. Here are the merits of your three choices:

✦ **Back up to iDisk:** This is a good option if you are connected to the Internet, have enough space on your iDisk, and would like to have access to your backed up files from any Internet-connected Macintosh. However, you must buy more space than the 100 megabytes that comes with your .Mac membership. See the iDisk section of this chapter for more details.

✦ **Back up to CD/DVD:** A good choice if you would like to back up a lot of information. A recordable CD holds 650 megabytes; a recordable DVD holds 4.7 gigabytes. If you have more information than will fit on a single CD or DVD disc, you can use more than one to hold your backup. Backup will inform you of how many discs your backup will use. You can use a combination of CD or DVD disks, if you wish. The last disk in a set is called the master disk, because it contains the information needed to restore files Backup has split between discs.

✦ **Back up to a Drive:** A hard drive can hold the most data and give the fastest access of these storage options. The hard drive you use can be an internal hard drive, or an external FireWire drive; this includes the iPod, which must be mounted on the desktop before it can be used. You can back up files to a folder or partition of your main hard disk, although this largely defeats the purpose of a backup and is not really recommended; but Backup will do it. You can also selected a folder on a mounted network server as the destination.

Backing up your files

To prepare your files and perform a backup:

1. **Select a destination disk from the pop-up menu in the top-left corner of the window.** You can choose your iDisk, a CD/DVD disc, or a connected hard drive, either internal or external. If you choose Back up to Drive, you must click the Set button and pick a location to copy your backup files to. In order to click the Save button, you must type a name for the backup at the top of the window.

2. **Look down the list of QuickPicks and put a check mark next to each one you would like to back up.** When in doubt about whether to include a QuickPick in the backup, choose it; it's better to be safe than sorry.

3. **Add any other files and folders you want to back up to the backup list by simply dragging them to the backup window.** They are automatically marked with a check-mark for backup. If you would like to search for the files from within Backup, click the plus sign button in the lower left of the window; a navigation sheet will drop down enabling you to find what you are looking for. You can also access all the vast power of the Finder's Find feature by choosing File ➪ Find. You can drag the files you want straight from the Find Results window to the backup list.

4. **To remove items from your backup list, select the items and choose Edit ➪ Remove from List or press the Delete key.**

Fine-tune your selections by checking the details of files and folders you have added by selecting them in the backup list, and then examining them with the Info drawer. You can deselect files you don't want to include in the backup by removing the checkmark next to them in the Info drawer window. Verify the files you want will be backed up. Folders with partial contents checked in the Info drawer for backup are marked in the main Backup window with a dash instead of a checkmark.

Tip

As you add files, keep an eye on the storage capacity of your destination disk. The meter in the top right of the main window shows how much space is left in your iDisk if it is selected as the destination disk. Dark green means how much is already on the iDisk now, before the back up. Light green means how much space the current backup will use.

If you choose Backup to CD/DVD in the pop-up menu, you will see the number of discs needed to record your backup in the lower-left corner of the window.

5. **When everything looks good, click the Backup Now button to start the backup process.**

Backups to your iDisk or a hard drive will begin immediately. The iDisk window will shrink to the one seen in Figure 18-43. The file name copying at the moment is shown above the status bar.

Figure 18-43: During a backup to your iDisk, the Backup window shrinks to look like this.

Scheduled backups

You can schedule a backup to all destinations except a CD or DVD disk. The backup can be unattended (you don't have to be there) and the Backup application does not need to be open.

At the time you schedule the backup for, ensure that your computer is turned on, not set to go to sleep, the Backup application is not open, and the destination you have set is connected or available.

To schedule a backup:

1. **From the destination pop-up menu, choose Back up to iDisk or Back up to Drive.**

2. **Click the Schedule button in the lower right of the window.** It's the one with the calendar icon. The schedule sheet drops down (see Figure 18-44).

3. **Select the backup frequency from the radio buttons: Daily or Weekly.** Never leaves the scheduling function off.

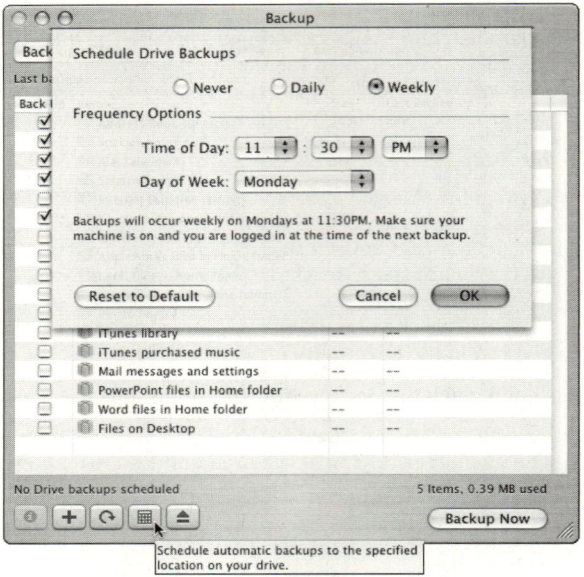

Figure 18-44: The Backup Schedule sheet.

4. **Choose the time of day the backup will occur from the pop-up menus.** If you chose a weekly backup, choose the day of the week it will occur on.

5. **Click OK.**

To verify a scheduled backup took place, check the Backup log by choosing File ➪ Show Log.

Restoring backed-up files

To restore backed up files to your hard disk:

1. **From the destination pop-up menu, choose the location to restore from: Restore from iDisk, Restore from CD/DVD, or Restore from Drive.** As you make your selection, the contents of the backup window will change to include only items that have been backed up to that location. The Backup column is now called Restore.

2. **Click a checkbox in the Restore column to mark the items to be restored.**

3. **Click the Restore Now button.**

   Backup asks you if you want to replace any files on your hard drive that duplicate the ones it is restoring

4. **You can click Yes to all, and Backup will replace all them all.**

To stop an install in progress, click Cancel. Only the files that were restored up to that moment will appear on your hard disk.

Backup Tips

Backing up is vital. Follow these tips when backing up your files.

✦ Do not try to use Backup to copy files from one computer to another. Apple says Backup is meant for personal backups from a single computer only. If you try to use Backup to copy files to a location (like your iDisk) that already contains files put there by Backup running from another computer, the older files will be completely erased.

✦ If you spot an alert icon (a triangle containing an exclamation point) next to an item in the backup list, it means that Backup can't locate the item; it may have been moved, renamed, or deleted. To back up the item, delete it from the backup list, and add it again.

✦ If you deleted one or several QuickPicks, and you change your mind and want them back, choose Edit ▷ Restore All QuickPicks.

✦ File that you copied to a location using Backup can only be deleted using Backup! If you want to remove them to save space, choose the restore location (iDisk or Drive), select the items to be removed, and choose Edit ▷ Remove from List, or click the minus sign button in the lower left of the window.

If the item is in a folder, select the folder, and delete the item from the Info drawer window.

✦ If you want to remove all the files from the Backup folder on your iDisk, Backup must be used to clear the folder's contents. From the destination pop-up menu, choose Back up to iDisk or Restore from iDisk. Choose Edit ▷ Clear iDisk Backup Folder. Click OK.

✦ Backup cannot be used to back up applications.

✦ You must be a paid .Mac member to back up your files to a CD or DVD disk.

✦ You need to have at least the same amount of space free on your hard drive as the size of the recordable media you will use for your backup. For example, if you are backing up to a DVD-R disc, you would need at least 4.7 gigabytes free on you hard drive to perform the backup. Backup uses this space to temporarily assemble the backup before it copies it to the disc.

✦ For a restore, Backup cannot recognize files on a CD or DVD put there by another application, or dragged there manually. Backup can only see files it has backed up.

✦ Restores will not work to files that are write protected. To change a file's privileges, to Read & Write, select the file in the Finder, choose File ▷ Get Info, click the disclosure triangle for Ownership and permissions, and select Read and Write from the Owner and Others pop-up menu.

Virex

Virex is the anti-virus software that Apple includes with your .Mac membership. Virex scans your Mac for viruses and Trojan horses using a frequently updated virus definitions file that can be downloaded automatically over the Internet. It then cleans an infected file, folder, or volume of viruses, and attempts to repair of any file damage resulting from the infection. You can view and print a report of the results

Virex setup

.Mac members can download Virex from the .Mac Web site. Although a version of it is included with the .Mac package, for the latest and greatest version, stick with the downloadable one.

Install Virex on just after you have downloaded the installer and are still connected to the Internet, so it can access the latest virus definitions files. If you have .Mac membership, you don't have to pay for separate copies of the software for all your computers.

As soon as the installer completes, (and by default, any time you launch it) Virex opens and attempts to scan for viruses. It also attempts to connect to the Internet to download the latest virus definitions file from a .Mac Internet server. Virex asks for your administrator password before it tries to download the definitions, as shown in Figure 18-45.

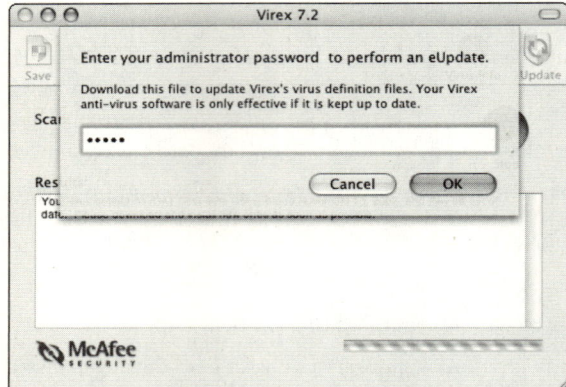

Figure 18-45: When first launched, Virex asks for an administrator's password to perform an eUpdate, a download of the latest virus definition files.

If it cannot connect to the Internet, you will see an alert to that effect, but you can still use Virex without the latest definitions. However, you should make every effort to download these definitions, since they include information about how to protect you machine from the latest crop of viruses. The main Virex window, shown in Figure 18-46.

Using Virex

Virex is an easy-to-use utility. Before scanning for the first time, review the settings in the Virex Preferences sheet. Figure 18-46 shows the main Virex window.

To start a virus scan, launch Virex or press the Scan button. As mentioned above, the scan from a launch will be interrupted if you are not connected to the Internet, and after dismissing the ensuing alert, press the Scan button to continue.

You can also initiate a scan by dragging any number of files or folders onto the Virex application icon or its alias (including the alias in the Dock, if you have put one there), or if Virex is open, onto the Scan button.

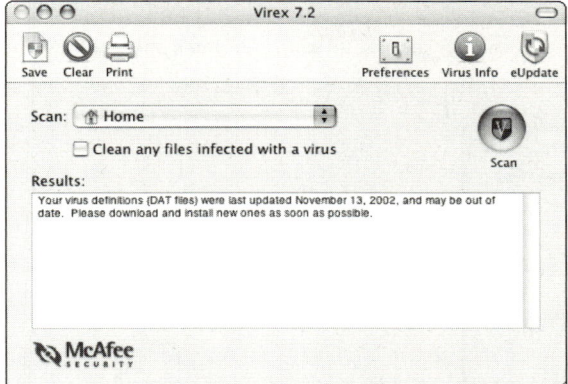

Figure 18-46: The main Virex window.

Virex scans only the home folder of the logged in user by default. To change the location, make a selection from the Scan pop-up menu. If you select Choose you can navigate to the file or folders you want.

By default, Virex conducts Diagnose scan—that is, a scan without automatic virus cleaning.

Figure 18-47 shows the Virex window during a Diagnose scan.

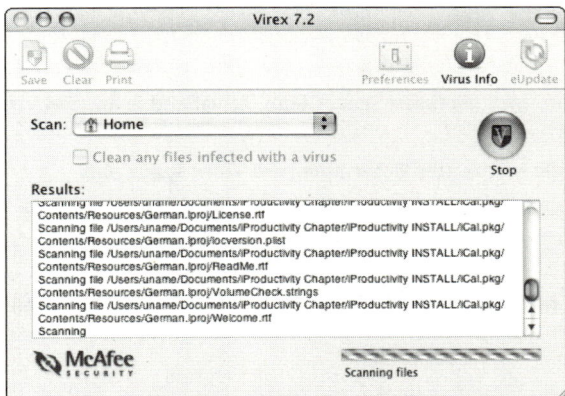

Figure 18-47: A Virex Diagnose scan in progress.

Most of the toolbar buttons are deactivated, the progress bar shows the scan is in progress, and the files being checked are shown in the results window.

When the scan is complete, the red Stop button converts to the blue Scan button, and the last entry in the Results field reads Diagnose scan complete at (followed by the date and time).

If any viruses were found during the scan, they will be displayed in the Results dialog. If this occurs, you should conduct a cleaning scan; set this to happen by checking the Clean any files infected with a virus checkbox, and clicking the Scan and Clean button.

Virex preference settings

Press the Preferences button on the toolbar to see the Virex Preferences sheet, shown in its default state in Figure 18-48.

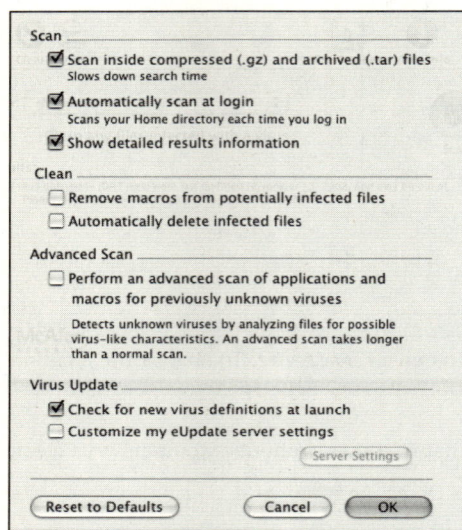

Figure 18-48: The default settings in the Virex Preferences sheet.

The preferences sheet is divided into four sections: Scan, Clean, Advanced Scan, and Virus Update.

✦ **Scan preferences:** The options in this area determine how Virex scans files.

- **Scan inside compressed (.GZ) and archived (.TAR) files:** Active by default, this option enables scans inside compressed and archived files where viruses can lurk, but increases scan time.

- **Automatically scan at login:** Active by default, this option enables an automatic scan whenever the user logs in, which is a good idea unless the user needs to get right to work.

- **Show detailed results information:** Active by default, this option enables detailed information to appear in the Results area and in printed results. If you want less information, deselect this option.

✦ **Clean preferences:** The options in this area determine how Virex cleans infected files.

- **Remove macros from potentially infected files:** this option strips macros from Microsoft Office documents being cleaned to remove any chance of a macro virus. However, these macros (similar to scripts) can provide important functionality. It's your call.

- **Automatically delete infected files:** this option deletes an infected file if the cleaning process fails. Some viruses alter the files they infect so badly, it is impossible to return them to their original state. In this case it may be best to select this option and delete the file.

✦ **Advanced scan preference:** This option determines how Virex scans for unknown viruses.

- **Perform an advanced scan of applications and macros for previously unknown viruses:** this option enables Virex to scan for "virus-like activity." It is very thorough and very slow.

✦ **Virus Update preferences:** These options determine how Virex updates its virus definition files.

- **Check for new virus definitions at launch:** Active by default, this option enables Virex to attempt to download new DAT virus definition files each time you log in or launch Virex.

- **Customize my auto-update server settings:** this option lets you specify the DAT virus definitions download site server you want Virex to use. This option is deselected when you open Virex Preferences. To change the server setting, select this checkbox, then click the Server Settings button. The eUpdate Server Settings dialog box will open, shown in Figure 18-49.

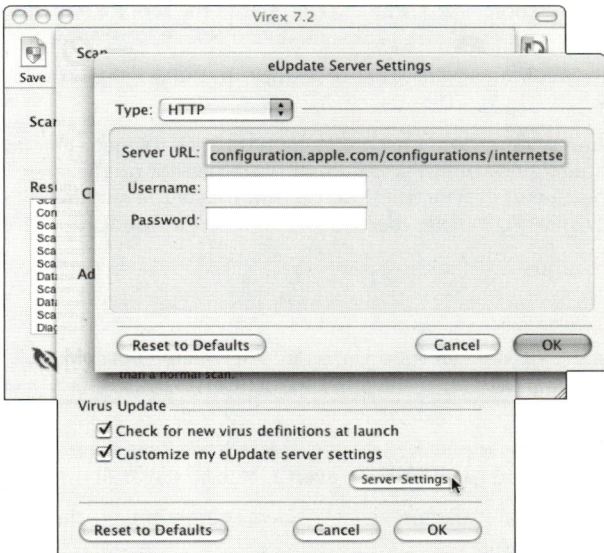

Figure 18-49: When the Server Settings button is clicked, Virex's eUpdate Server Settings dialog opens.

In the eUpdate Server Settings dialog, from the Type pop-up menu, select HTTP to use the Apple .Mac DAT virus definitions server, or select FTP to use the McAfee Network Associates virus definitions server.

The default setting is for the .Mac server, and it is recommended that you do not change the setting unless you know what you are doing. In particular, do not change the entered URL, as Virex will then have no way to get to the DAT server. However, if you do this by accident, you can always click the Reset to Defaults button to re-enter the proper URL.

Usually, you should not need to even enter your .Mac username and password, as Virex takes these from the .Mac pane of Systems Preferences. (Virex versions 7.2.1 and below look to the Internet pane of System Preferences in Jaguar, and therefore will not be able to find your login information in Panther. It is recommended you upgrade your version of Virex, but in a pinch you could manually enter your login information here.)

The Server Settings dialog is mainly meant for non-.Mac members, particularly corporate users of Virex, who have purchased a site license from McAfee and would use this dialog to direct Virex to use McAfee's DAT server, or enter the settings to direct Virex to use a company DAT server location.

To have your Preferences settings take effect, click OK.

The Virex command-line scanner

Virex includes and installs a command-line anti-virus scanner that can be run from the Terminal application. If you prefer working in a Unix command-line environment, or if you want to integrate virus scanning functions into a PERL script, this is the tool for you. It can also be useful if you have booted your Mac into the command-line interface for troubleshooting.

The command-line scanner offer an identical set of features to the graphical interface scanner: no more, no less.

Although the command-line scanner provides online help through its man (manual) pages, Virex also provides a product guide in PDF format that is a bit easier on the eyes. The product guide is almost completely devoted to instructions on how to use the command-line scanner. You can find the Product Guide PDF inside the Virex folder in your Applications folder.

iCards

iCards are digital postcards that you can send via email. Your recipients see the iCard appear right in the email message body, and don't need to click a link to visit a Web site in order to see the card as in similar services.

iCards is the only part of the .Mac services that is completely free (see Figure 18-50). You don't need to be a .Mac member to use iCards, or even a .Mac 60 day trial tire-kicker.

iCards can be sent or viewed on any Macintosh or Windows computer, via the default Web browser and standard email programs.

Over 400 designed iCards are available from the iCard Web site, organized into categories such as Birthday, Love, and Holidays, to name a few.

If you are a .Mac member, you can also create your own custom cards featuring digital photos or artwork from your iDisk. If you design a really beautiful iCard, you can submit it to the

Member's Portfolio, and Apple will review it and consider adding it to the public selection. If you are an artist, you can offer your artwork for others to send by submitting it to the Featured Artist category.

Figure 18-50: The iCards welcome page.
(Web page courtesy of Apple Computer, Inc.)

To send an iCard:

1. **Visit the iCards Web site by setting your web browser to** `www.mac.com`**, and in the .Mac menu bar, click iCards.** The iCards welcome page, Main Categories, appears.

2. **Choose an image category you want to explore by clicking on a category image**. See Figure 18-51.

3. **Choose an image from the category by clicking it.** Some categories have more than one page of images to explore, and you will see links to additional pages in the top-right corner. Also notice that your path through the process is displayed from the top left; to go back, click on the path you want to return to.

4. **Compose a message in the Write your message here field on the Edit page,** shown in Figure 18-52. **Select a font from the list on the right. When done, click Continue.** On the Address Card page shown in Figure 18-53, you see your card at the bottom, complete with your message as it will appear to your recipients.

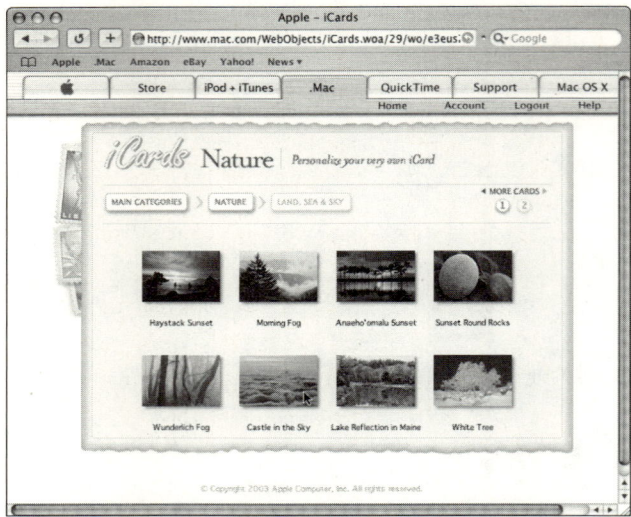

Figure 18-51: Clicking on an iCards category leads to its collection of images.

(Web page courtesy of Apple Computer, Inc.)

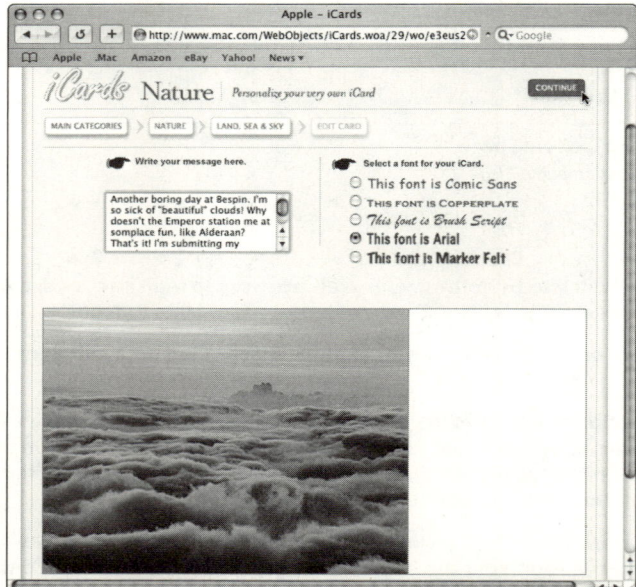

Figure 18-52: The iCards edit card page.

(Web page courtesy of Apple Computer, Inc.)

5. **Enter your name and email address in the fields on the left, and check Send a copy to myself if you want a copy. Check Hide Distribution List if you don't want your recipients to see your other recipients.**

   To send a card to one recipient, type their email address into the field on the top right.

   To send a card to several recipients, type the first person's email address in the field. Then click Add Recipient. Repeat until the Recipient list contains all the addresses you want.

   Remove an address from the Recipient list by selecting it and clicking Remove Recipient.

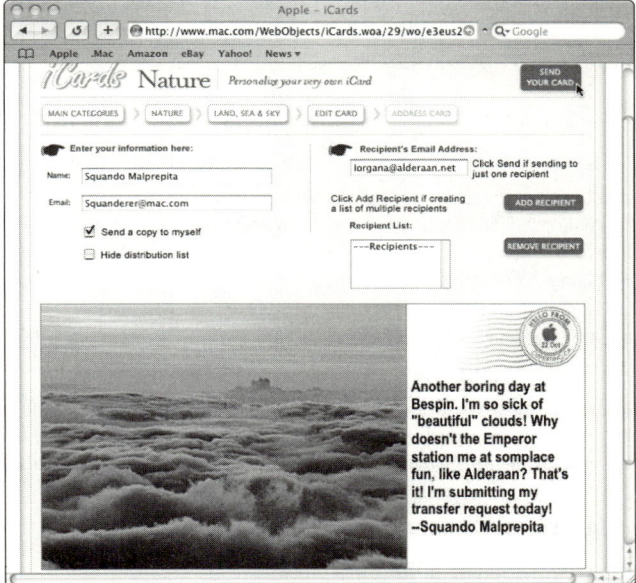

Figure 18-53: The iCards Address Cards page.
(Web page courtesy of Apple Computer, Inc.)

6. **Click Send Your Card.**

   The Thank You page appears, as shown in Figure 18-54.

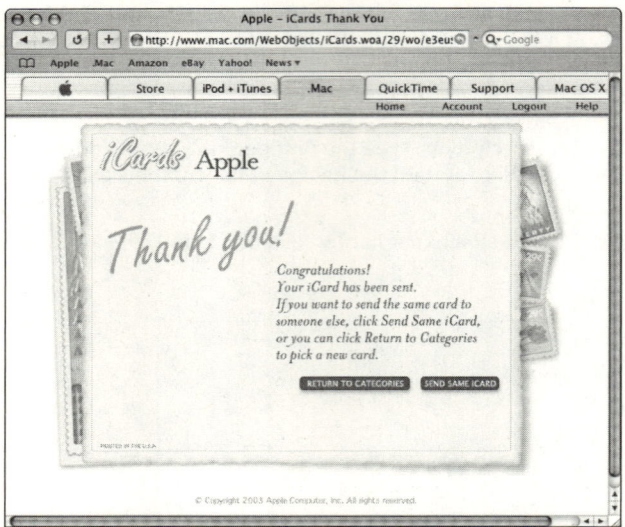

Figure 18-54: The iCards Thank you page appears after you have sent your iCard.

(Web page courtesy of Apple Computer, Inc.)

You can return to the Main Categories page from here by clicking the Return to Categories button, or Send Same Card to send the same card to someone else.

You must be a .Mac member to use your own image on an iCard. You might want to do this to send a holiday photo of your family, share a favorite vacation photo, or show grandparents a scan of your kid's latest artistic scribblings. To place your image on an iCard, follow these steps:

1. **Save your image in either JPEG or GIF format.**

2. **Name the image following these guidelines:**

   • End the file name with a .jpg or .gif extension.

   • Use only uppercase letters (A-Z), lowercase letters (a-z), numbers (0-9) or the underscore (_) in the file name.

   • Don't use spaces, accented letters, or special characters or symbols.

   • Don't start a file name with a period (.)

3. **Copy the file into the Pictures folder on your iDisk or into a folder within the Pictures folder.** The folder name must also follow the naming guidelines in the previous step.

4. **On the iCards Main Categories page, click Create Your Own.** (See Figure 18-55).

5. **Enter your password if necessary and press the Return key.**

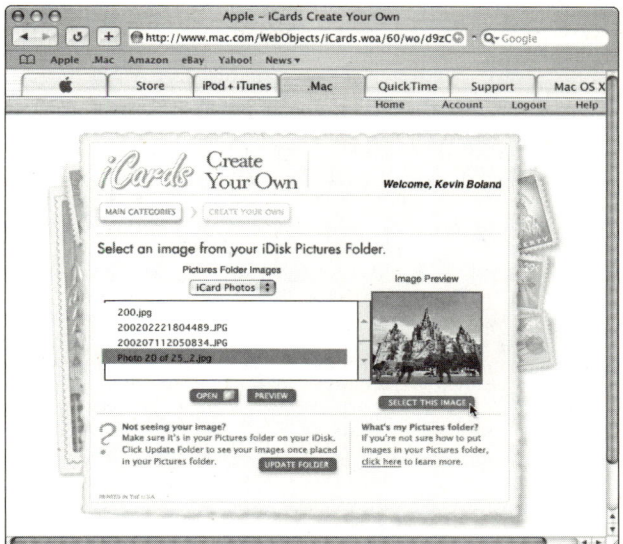

Figure 18-55: A folder called iCard Photos, has been copied to the iDisk, where its contents can be selected and previewed in the iCards Create Your Own page.

(Web page courtesy of Apple Computer, Inc.)

On the Create Your Own page, you see the contents of your iDisk pictures folder in the list on the left. If you need to add other images to the pictures folder of your iDisk, do so and then click Update Folder. Select a new folder from the pop-up menu, look inside a folder by selecting it and clicking the Open button, or select an image and click Preview to see a thumbnail on the right. When you find the image you want, click Select This Image.

6. Send the iCard. (Refer to Steps 4 through 6 in the first list in this section.)

If a recipient cannot view the iCard (which is a JPEG attachment to the email message), his email application may not display attached images automatically. Ask them to open the JPEG file attached to the message to view it.

Summary

In this chapter, we examined Mac OS X's optional .Mac services suite, available for $99.95 from Apple.

We took a detailed look at each of the .Mac services, as well as the included Mac OS X applications that work with .Mac, and programs you can download from .Mac once you are a member.

✦   ✦   ✦

Making the Most of Mac OS X

IV

◆ ◆ ◆ ◆

In This Part

◆ ◆ ◆ ◆

Working with Included Programs

✦ ✦ ✦ ✦

In This Chapter

A Tour of the Mac OS X
Applications Folder

A Tour of the Mac OS X
Utilities Folder

✦ ✦ ✦ ✦

This chapter gives a quick introduction to each of the programs that Apple provides in Mac OS X's Applications and Utilities folders. These programs incorporate a large chunk of the operating system's functionality, and it is important to be familiar with them; even if you never have to use some of them, it's good to be aware of what each of them can do, in case the need arises.

Although at first glance the contents of these folders may seem unchanged from Mac OS X 10.2, a closer look reveals that 10.3 provides a few new items, and newly revised versions of programs you may be familiar with. You will also notice items that are no longer included. Here's a good example: where is Disk Copy? You will look in vain for this vital utility, which previously was used to create, work with, and burn disk images. In Panther, Disk Copy has been incorporated into Disk Utility. But there is no way to know this just by looking through the Utilities folder! The information in this chapter may prevent such moments of unpleasant confusion.

As we take a look at each included Application or Utility, we will often zero in on details we feel would be most helpful to review. Many items are covered in detail in other chapters, but you will find them listed here for your convenience, with a reference pointing you to the chapter that includes them.

A Tour of the Mac OS X Applications Folder

This section lists the applications you can find in the Applications folder and briefly describes them and their use or points you to another chapter where we cover the application in greater detail.

Address Book

The Mac OS X Address Book, shown in Figure 19-1, not only functions as a personal card file, but it is integrated with the Mail application. Read about how Address Book works with Mail, iCal, and iSync, as well as the .Mac service, in Chapter 20.

Figure 19-1: A big step forward from the traditional little black book.

AppleScript (folder)

AppleScript can record your actions into a script that can be run in the future to automate the same tasks. The AppleScript folder contains four applications with self-explanatory names: Folder Actions Setup, Install Script Menu, Remove Script Menu, and Script Editor. A folder of example AppleScripts is also provided. Refer to Chapter 23 for complete coverage of these items, and all about AppleScript.

Calculator

This spiffy onscreen calculator has a Basic mode for the most commonly used functions. The Advanced button adds a wide range of advanced math functions, and the Paper Tape button produces a separate window emulating a scrolling paper tape, which can be printed. Figure 19-2 shows the expanded version of the Calculator.

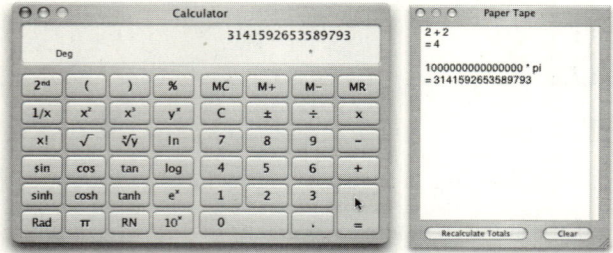

Figure 19-2: The Calculator shows off its Advanced functions and Tape window.

Calculator's frequently overlooked measurement conversion functions are nicely implemented and very helpful. Under the Convert menu, you will find a list of conversion categories: Area, Currency, Energy or Work, Temperature, Length, Speed, Pressure, Weights and Masses, Power, and Volume. Selecting any one brings up a sheet which allows you to select the units of measurement you are converting from and to. First, enter the "from" value into the calculator; then choose your category and the "from" and "to" units. Click OK, and the answer appears on the display. You can even update the currency exchange rates, and read when the last update was performed.

If you think that's cool, check out Calculator's Speech menu. You can turn on Speak Button Pressed and Speak Total. As you press each key, you will hear the voice confirm it; when you press the equals sign key, the voice will speak the result. This is especially helpful if you are entering figures from a printed document, because there is no need to keep looking to see that you have entered the right number. It also impresses kids.

Chess

Panther comes with a newly refurbished chess program, with features that will interest avid players. The default onscreen chess set now looks something like a ritzy wooden Jaques Staunton set, complete with algebraic notation along the edge. You can rotate the board in any direction, or view it from any angle, by dragging an edge, as shown in Figure 19-3.

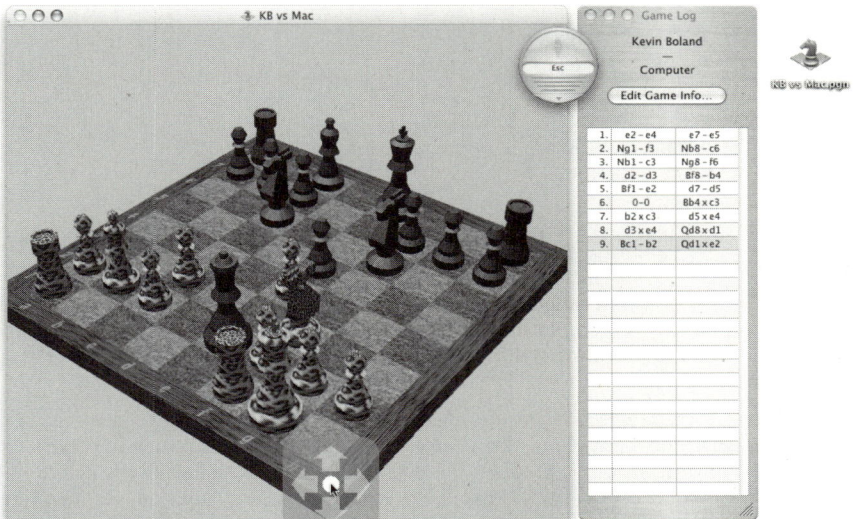

Figure 19-3: The Chess program showing a grass board, fur pieces, the Speech bug, the Game Log, a saved game file, and how to drag an edge.

If you don't like wood, in Preferences you may choose to have the board appear in metal, marble, or even restful grass. The pieces can appear in wood, metal, marble, or — get this — fur! Also in Preferences, you can set a slider to make the computer play faster or stronger.

Chess can read the computer's moves out loud (it does this by default) and also obey your voice commands. You can turn either capability on or off in Preferences. The Speech bug appears onscreen by default to allow you to hold down the Escape key, speak your move, and see if it was understood. With some practice, you can usually get the computer to accept your diction. We are getting perilously close here to the spoken chess scene with HAL in *2001: A Space Odyssey*. In Preferences, you can also set the last move to appear in the title bar.

If you like to keep track of your moves to review and study games, Chess will record each move in its Game Log, which is shown by choosing Game ⇨ Game Log. Games can be exported by choosing Game ⇨ Export; they are saved as .png files that can be opened in another chess program that supports coordinate notation imports.

DVD Player

If your Mac has an optical drive that can read DVDs, you can use the Mac OS X DVD Player to watch DVD video discs on your computer screen. Newly redesigned for Panther, the DVD player is covered in Chapter 20.

Font Book

Font Book (shown in Figure 19-4) is a new application, included with Panther for the first time. It allows you to search for, find, view, turn on or off, and organize your fonts, without depending on a third-party application. Font Book is described in detail in Chapter 12.

Figure 19-4: The Font Book interface.

iCal

Shown in Figure 19-5, iCal is a calendar application that lets you enter appointments, view multiple calendars at the same time, and share you calendar information with others. You can invite anyone in your Address Book to an iCal event, and set iCal to automatically send them an email invitation via the Mail application. If you use Apple's .Mac service, you can have iCal publish your calendar over the Internet, so other people can use a standard Web browser to view it. You can subscribe to calendars that have been published over the Internet. By using iCal with iSync, you can synchronize your calendars on several computers. iCal is covered in detail in Chapter 18.

iChat AV

iChat AV is an Instant Messaging client which can be used with AOL's AIM service, or with Apple's .Mac chat service. If you use .Mac, and connect a webcam such as Apple's iSight, you can have face-to-face video chats with any Mac user who has the same setup, provided you have a broadband Internet connection. Finally, your futuristic videophone has arrived! If you only have a dial-up connection, you can still have an audio chat with any Mac user with a built-in or USB microphone. iChat AV is described in detail in Chapter 18.

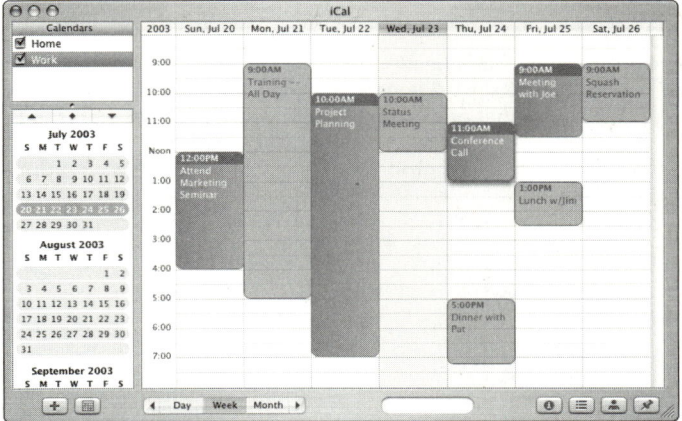

Figure 19-5: iCal's week view.

iMovie

Use iMovie to turn raw video footage from a digital camcorder into a movie by removing unwanted footage, rearranging scenes, and adding titles, transitions, visual effects, sound effects, and other audio. We describe iMovie in more detail in Chapter 20. Figure 19-6 shows iMovie's easy to use interface.

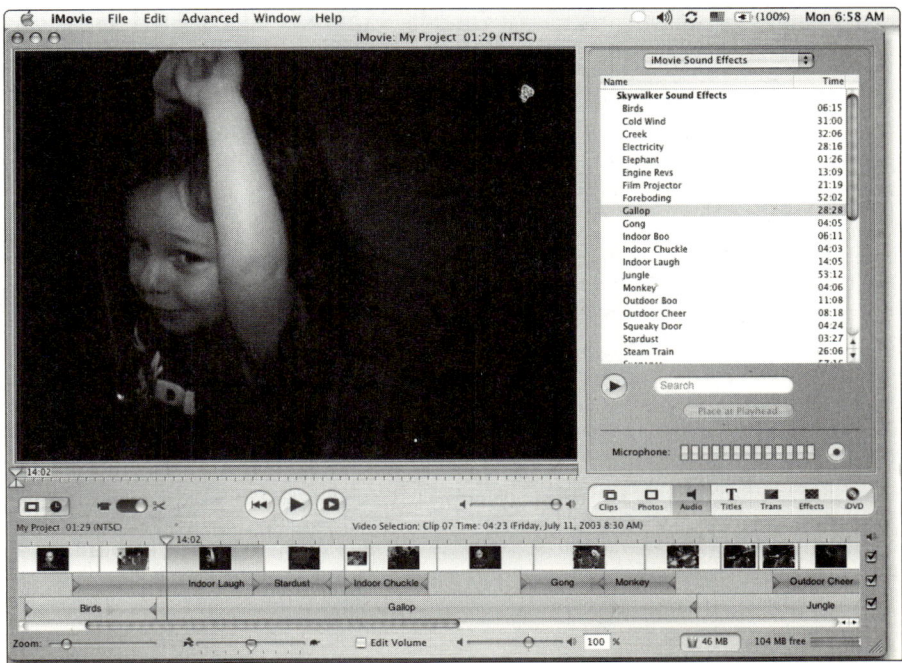

Figure 19-6: Amaze your friends and influence people with the movies you create using iMovie and a digital camcorder.

iSync

iSync synchronizes information between applications on your Mac and devices such as a Bluetooth mobile phone, an iPod, or a Palm OS device (see Figure 19-7). ISync compares your Address Book contacts, your iCal calendar and to do list, and your Web bookmarks in Safari to the information on your devices, and then updates everything to have the same information. If you have a .Mac account, iSync will synchronize this information across multiple computers. iSync is examined in Chapter 19.

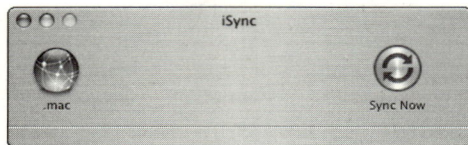

Figure 19-7: Devices can be added to the iSync interface.

Image Capture

You can use Image Capture to download pictures from your digital camera to your disk, scaling to particular sizes if desired. Image Capture can automatically create a Web page of these photos via an AppleScript. You can transfer images from a Kodak Picture CD.

But wait — can't you do basically the same thing with iPhoto? Indeed you can. Why then does Apple include Image Capture? Because many people, especially professional photographers, do not need the extra features of iPhoto. They do not need iPhoto's image database because they use other methods of archiving their work. For them, Image Capture is more convenient. It may be for you also. Using Image Capture, you can transfer only some of the pictures from your camera, instead of all of them as iPhoto does.

Image Capture's Preferences window is where you tell Mac OS X what to do when you connect a digital camera: open Image Capture, open iPhoto, open no application, or open another application of your choice (see Figure 19-8).

Although not all USB camera models are recognized (according to reports on the Internet and Apple's Web-based user forums), Image Capture will recognize mainstream cameras that store their images in an accepted format such as JPEG. Plug your USB camera into the Mac, turn it on if necessary, and its icon appears in the Finder like the icon of a removable disk.

Image Capture can also work with a scanner. You can set Image Capture to open when you press the scan-and-save button that many scanners feature, to open another application of your choice, or to not open any application at all. You can also set Image Capture to use TWAIN software with the scanner wherever possible. You can preview and crop the image before scanning.

Via Image Capture, you can now share cameras and scanners over a local network using Rendezvous (as long as they are on the same subnet). If you have a certain type of digital camera connected to a remote Mac using Image Capture to share images, you can control it over the Internet to monitor an area photographically every 60 seconds. If your camera records video clips, or records sounds as MP3 files, Image Capture can transfer them to your computer.

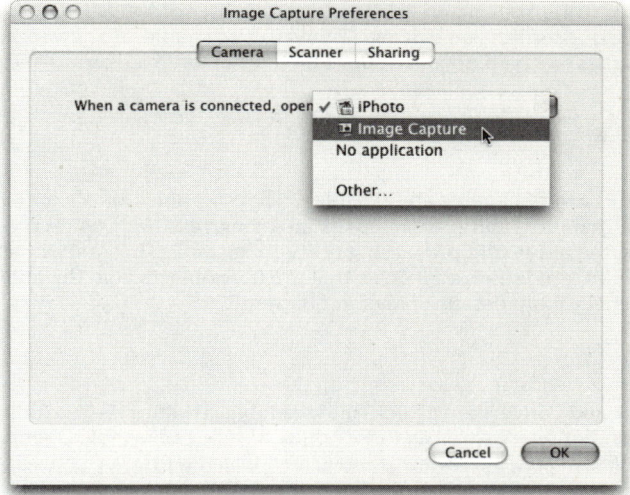

Figure 19-8: Image Capture's Preferences window.

Internet Connect

If you have a dial-up connection to the Internet, or even if you use PPPoE (Point-to-Point Protocol over Ethernet) on a DSL connection, Internet Connect is the tool to use to initiate, control, and monitor your connection. You can also use it to connect to an Airport network or to have your AirPort base station connect to the Internet. Refer to Chapter 6 for detailed coverage of Internet Connect.

Internet Explorer

Internet Explorer, Microsoft's Web browser, is included with your Mac OS X software. Version 5.2.3 was shipped with Mac OS X for 10.3. Internet Explorer is still useful even in the age of Safari because every once in a while, you may encounter a Web page that does not work with Safari; if so, try Internet Explorer.

iPhoto

iPhoto lets you import pictures from a digital camera into your Mac and then view, organize, label, edit, and categorize the images. You can easily create albums, onscreen slideshows, Mail messages, Desktop backgrounds, prints, and Webpage slide galleries. Please turn to Chapter 20 to learn more about iPhoto.

iTunes

With iTunes, you can manage and listen to digital audio from many sources, including audio CDs, MP3files from the Internet or from your own CDs, an MP3 player, or Internet radio stations. ITunes provides the interface for browsing and purchasing music over the Internet from the Apple iTunes Music Store. You can create your own playlists of songs from CD and MP3, and if your Mac has a CD recorder, you can use iTunes to burn audio CDs. If you have an Apple iPod, you can copy songs to it and organize songs on it. Chapter 20 covers iTunes in detail.

Mail

Mac OS X's Mail application is a very capable and flexible email program. It offers excellent integration with the "iApps," handles multiple mailboxes including your .Mac email account, and lets you define rules for the automatic processing of incoming mail. The Panther version of Mail adds Safari-speed HTML rendering, addresses that are now objects, and the ability to manage email threads. We cover more details of Mail in Chapter 6.

Preview

Preview enables you to view and convert any QuickTime-readable graphics file, including JPEG, TIFF, GIF, PICT, PNG, and others, as well as PDF (Adobe Acrobat's Portable Document Format) files. As described in Chapter 9, Preview is integrated into the printing process, enabling you to preview any Mac OS X print job, and save it as a PDF. Choosing the File ➪ Export command enables you to save a graphics file in TIFF format or any other graphics format QuickTime recognizes. Preview can also zoom in and out, rotate the image to left and right, or flip it. The version of Preview installed with Panther has been dramatically improved. Apple claims Preview is now the fastest PDF reader. Searching for text within a PDF document is fast and easy, with a search field that almost instantly finds all matching text as you type each letter. You can now use Preview to read PostScript and EPS files.

Multi-page PDF files can now be viewed with their table of contents, as shown in Figure 19-9 This works only if the document contains a table of contents; otherwise, thumbnails of the pages are shown in the drawer.

Also new to Preview is the ability use links in a PDF file to go to a new location in the document, or open a Web page. Text in a PDF file can now be saved, even with paragraph breaks.

Preview has a new toolbar that is customizable. Choose View ➪ Customize Toolbar to drop down a sheet displaying your choices, shown in Figure 19-10.

Note that with Panther, Apple no longer includes Adobe Acrobat Reader in the Applications Folder. Although you may download and use Acrobat Reader for Mac OS X, Apple feels that it has improved Preview to the point where it is all you need.

Tip   If an image or PDF does not look clear in Preview, choose View ➪ Actual Size. This shows the image pixel for pixel instead of reducing it to fit your display. If you do this a lot, you can change Preview's setting by choosing Preferences ➪ Images and choosing the Actual Size radio button.

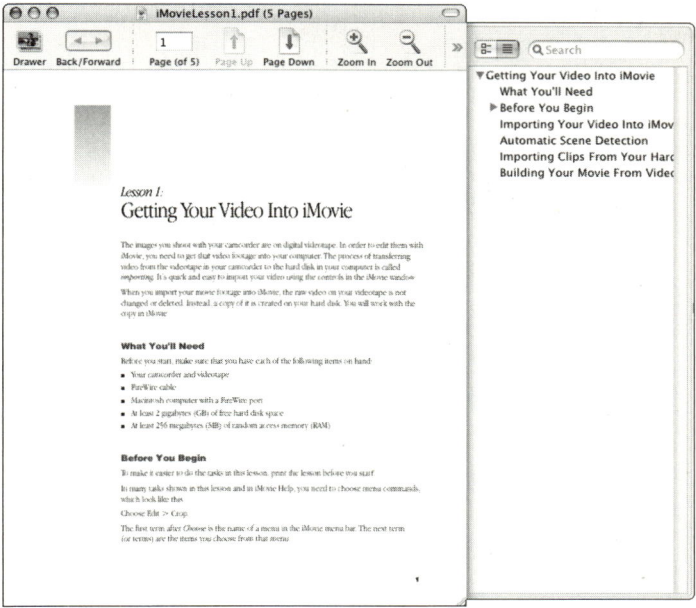

Figure 19-9: The Preview application with a PDF document open. On the right, the cursor points to the button that displays the document's table of contents, shown below it.

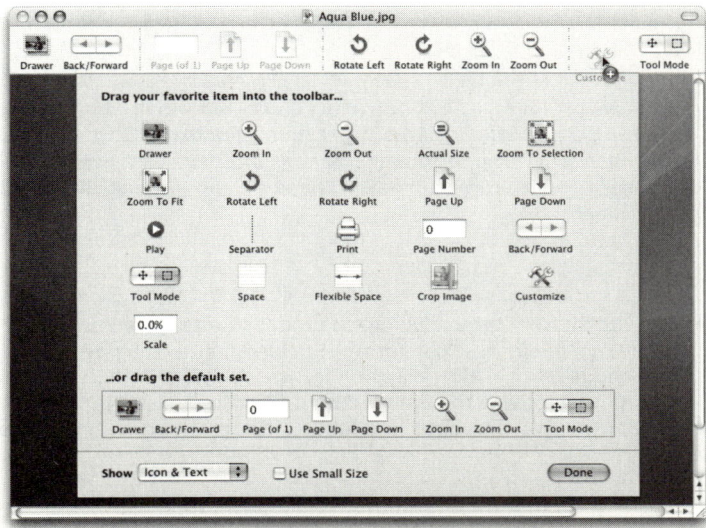

Figure 19-10: Preview's Customize Toolbar sheet, showing the Customize tool being dragged to the toolbar.

QuickTime Player

QuickTime is Apple's award-winning cross-platform multimedia technology. The QuickTime Player application plays digital movie files, QuickTime TV and other streaming QuickTime media from the Internet, QuickTime VR (virtual reality) panoramas and objects, and MP3 and other audio files. Apple provides QuickTime Player and the technology behind it with Mac OS X and as a free download for any interested Mac or Windows user. You can read all about QuickTime and QuickTime Player in Chapter 20. The QuickTime Player interface is shown in Figure 19-11.

Figure 19-11: The QuickTime Player interface.

Safari

Safari is Apple's new Web browser for Mac OS X, introduced in beta form in January of 2003, and in version 1.0 the following June. Safari utilizes the resources of Mac OS X better than any other browser to date, giving it superior performance. Safari's interface can be set to show Web pages in tabs, which many feel is more convenient than opening window after window. Read more about Safari in Chapter 6.

Sherlock

Sherlock helps you search the Internet for useful information, and organizes it in a more useful way than a Web browser can. It features "channels" to help you find Web pages, pictures, stock quotes, movie times and locations, airline flight information, AppleCare Knowledge Base articles, and the like. Sherlock can also help you track eBay auctions. The "channels" are downloaded from Apple when you first open Sherlock. Chapter 7 details what Sherlock can do — check it out.

Stickies

Stickies is the digital equivalent of the ubiquitous Post-it Note. Stickies supports multiple fonts and styles and can even contain embedded graphics, and be made transparent. Best of all, they lend themselves to Cocoa applications as a Service. The welcome notes you see when you first launch Stickies are shown in Figure 19-12. In the figure, the bottom note has been made transparent, and the cursor points to the drag bar at the top of a note, revealing an info box containing its creation and modified dates.

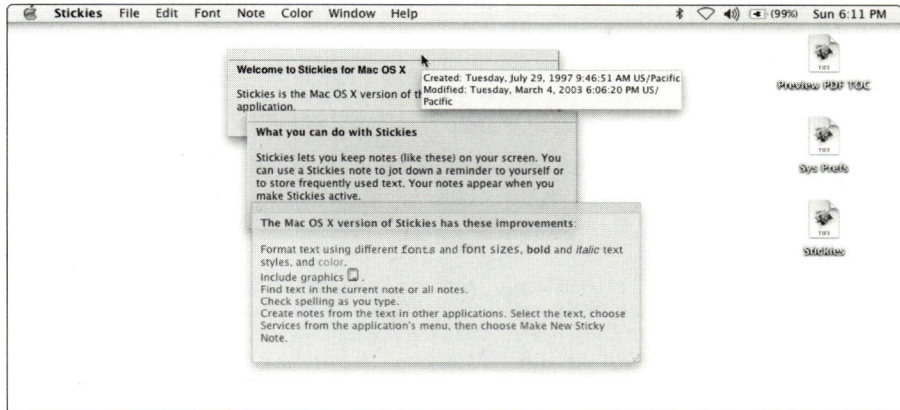

Figure 19-12: The Stickies welcome notes contain basic information about using the application.

System Preferences

Chapter 13 is devoted to covering this essential application, which allows you to have control over Mac OS X's many system settings. The System Preferences pane is shown in Figure 19-13.

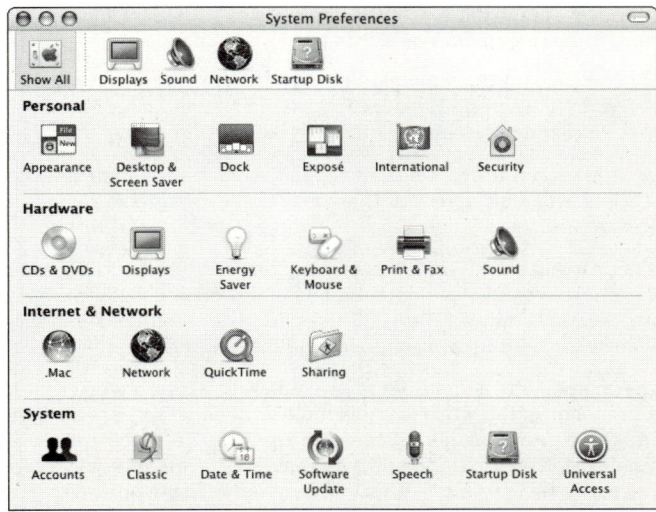

Figure 19-13: The System Preferences pane showing the default icons.

TextEdit

TextEdit is a text editor, as its name implies. When you double-click a Mac OS X ReadMe file, this is the application set by default to open it. Most people only use TextEdit for this purpose, as they may have used Mac OS 9's SimpleText, or, if they are old enough, the ancient TeachText used by prehistoric versions of the Mac OS.

But TextEdit is also a simple but effective word-processor. No, it's not competitive with Microsoft Word or with AppleWorks, but it is all the word-processor many people ever need, and it has the distinct advantage of being free.

TextEdit is a Cocoa application, and can do many tricks. You can create a document in multiple languages, use Unicode fonts such as Zapfino, with advanced typographic features, and view HTML code as text or as it appears in a Web browser. Text in TextEdit can be read aloud by your computer.

Perhaps the coolest tricks TextEdit can now do are open and create files in Microsoft Word format. Yes, you no longer need Microsoft Word to open any file with a .doc extension. (However, not all features in a Microsoft Word file are supported; for instance, you cannot view tables properly.) TextEdit also opens and creates plain text files (.txt), and Rich Text Format (.rtf) files.

The Text Edit ruler, shown in Figure 19-14, provides a quick means of controlling text styles, alignment, line spacing, and tab stops.

TextEdit's Preferences, shown in Figure 19-15 and outlined in the following list, give an idea of its flexibility.

✦ **New Document Attributes:** Allows you specify whether the default document format is in plain text or rich text (which includes formatting information). There is also a check box, Wrap to Page, where you can specify that the window's contents will rewrap when the length matches that of a printed page. The default setting (off) has TextEdit wrapping at the window's width, somewhat like a Web page. All of these settings are adjustable on a document-by-document basis.

✦ **Default Fonts:** Allows you to establish the default font to use for both rich text and plain text documents. Initially, TextEdit defaults to 12-point Helvetica for rich text and 10-point Monaco for plain text documents.

✦ **Rich text processing:** Allows you to tell TextEdit to ignore embedded Rich Text commands in opened HTML or RTF files. Ignoring these commands results in plain text being read and figures ignored.

✦ **Default Plain Text Encoding:** Allows you to specify the text encoding (character set mapping) for files you open or save. Automatic is the default choice for both, but can be changed. When Automatic is chosen, TextEdit uses either Unicode or the default encoding for your System, depending upon the document's contents.

✦ **Editing:** Lets you turn on spell-checking-as-you-type. When you type a word that the spell-checker doesn't recognize, the word is underlined with small red dots. Control-click on the word, and the contextual menu, shown in Figure 19-16, gives you a choice of possible corrections as well as the opportunity to have the word added to your dictionary or for the spelling to be ignored for this instance only. These options are also available from the Spelling window, opened by choosing Edit ⇨ Spelling ⇨ Spelling.

Page margin marker

Ruler with default markings   Decimal tab stop

First line of paragraph indentation marker   Left tab stop

Text alignment   Center tab stop

Set text styles   Set line spacing   Right tab stop

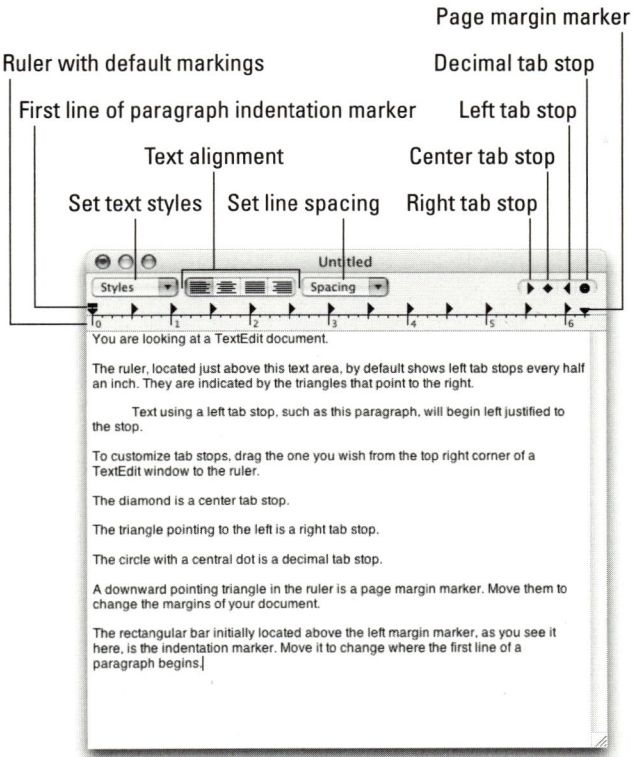

Figure 19-14: The TextEdit interface, showing the ruler.

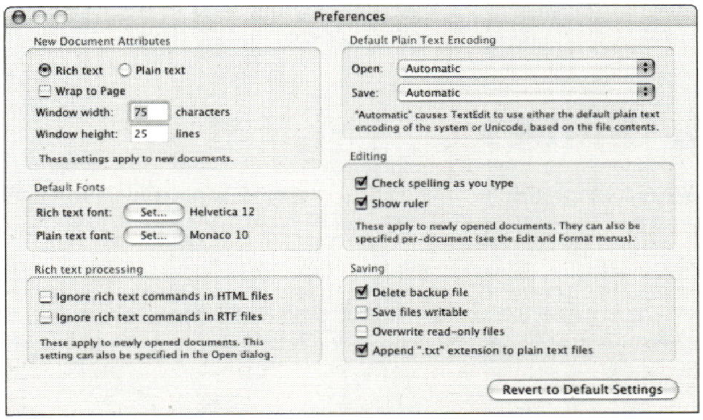

Figure 19-15: TextEdit's Preferences window, showing the default settings.

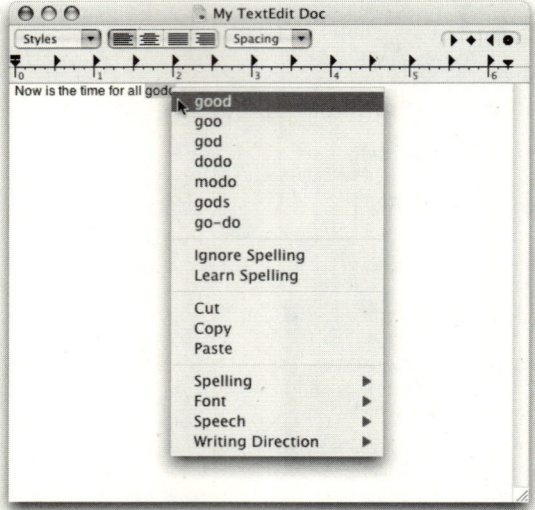

Figure 19-16: Use the contextual menu to correct s
pelling errors in TextEdit.

✦ **Saving:** Lets you set preferences for actions to be taken when you save a document. Delete backup file tells TextEdit not to save the previous version as a backup file. Save files writable sets write privileges on for everyone, not just the owner or group. Overwrite read-only files reverses the standard behavior of not letting you edit and save changes to read-only files. Appending the ".txt" extension to plain text files tells TextEdit to put the extension on the file name for plain text files. Although not necessary for Mac OS X users, this option comes in handy for cross-platform users and is a good visual clue as to the file's character.

✦ **Revert to Default Settings:** The button at the bottom of the dialog that sets all preferences back to their defaults.

A Tour of Mac OS X Utilities

The Utilities folder is located within the Applications folder. It contains a collection of programs to help you set up and work with various subsystems of hardware and software on, or connected to, your Mac.

Tip

If you find yourself frequently going into the Utilities folder, drag it into the Dock or Panther's Finder window sidebar; otherwise those wasted seconds really add up!

Activity Monitor

Activity Monitor, shown in Figure 19-17, is a new-for-Panther utility which replaces and combines the functionality of the utilities CPU Monitor and Process Viewer, which were included with previous versions of Mac OS X. Activity Monitor also has lots of new bells and whistles to explore.

You can use Activity Monitor to watch what your computer is doing behind the scenes, in great detail. Activity Monitor shows you what is running on your computer, how much memory is being used and for what, how the hard disk is being used, and the speed and throughput of the network.

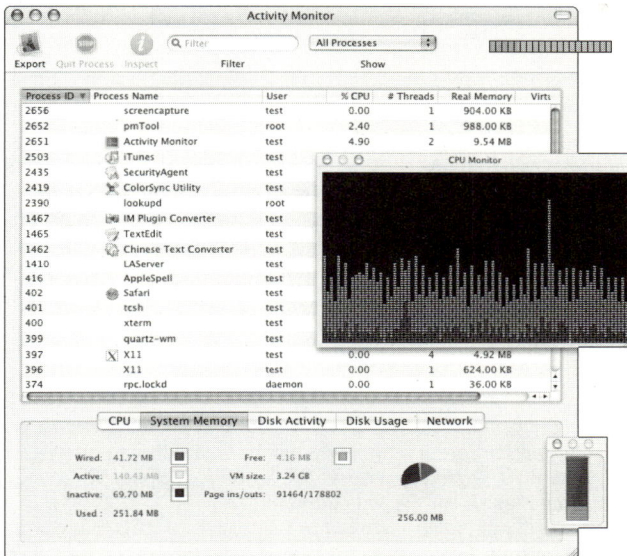

Figure 19-17: The Activity Monitor window, showing the three available CPU graph styles in front of it.

The large window lists the processes that are presently active on your Mac. A process is an instance of a program running in a computer; so this list shows all the applications, utilities, other programs that are running, including some that run without you otherwise being aware of them (called background processes). Examining this list is particularly useful if, for instance, you are troubleshooting the performance of an application which seems too slow. Here you can find out if another process is hogging all the processor time.

The list now has seven columns, up from the five that were shown in Jaguar's Process Viewer. The columns have the following headings:

✦ **Process ID:** This is a unique number assigned by the Unix underpinnings of Mac OS X in order to simplify identifying, interacting with, or terminating the process in the command line interface (the Terminal utility).

✦ **Process Name:** Just as you would expect, this is the name of the process or application. You will see some that are familiar and some that are not familiar — these latter are likely background processes. You will notice the icon of the process, if it has one, precedes the name — a nice touch.

✦ **User:** This is the user name of the account that launched the process.

✦ **%CPU:** This is the percentage of available CPU (Central Processing Unit) time that the process is using.

✦ **# of Threads:** A thread is a computer programming term referring to the information in a program which is used to serve one individual user or one particular service request, when the program is capable of handling more than one user or request. Such a program is said to be multithreaded; in layman's terms, this just means the program can do more than one thing at a time. Mac OS X, to its great benefit, is a multithreaded operating system, and so are the programs made to work with it. This column displays how many of these threads are in use.

✦ **Real Memory:** This is the amount of actual RAM memory being used by the process, as opposed to virtual memory.

✦ **Virtual Memory**: This is the amount of virtual memory being used by the process, as opposed to real RAM memory. Virtual memory, as certain users of Mac OS 9 and before may recall, allows the computer to use some of the free space on the hard drive as if it were RAM; even though it is much slower than RAM, the benefit is that you no longer had to be constrained by the amount of RAM installed in your computer. In Mac OS 9, you could turn virtual memory on and off in the Memory control panel. Mac OS X has and needs no such setting because virtual memory is always "on," and the operating system is constantly, automatically, and intelligently managing memory usage to maximize performance. And this column is where Mac OS X shows you what it is doing with each process.

Note   For those who are interested in seeing the Unix command line way of doing things, if you open the Terminal utility, enter *top* and press return, you will be treated to a non-graphical, but more detailed version of Activity Monitor's process list. To help decipher what you are seeing, enter *man top* to see the manual for the *top* command.

In the toolbar at the top of the Activity Monitor window are the following three icons.

✦ **Export:** Clicking this icon (same as the Mail application) or pressing Command+E exports the current list of processes as an XML file with the default name of Exported Processes.plist. You can view the file with Apple's XML editor, available on the Developer Tools CD.

✦ **Quit Process:** Clicking this icon or pressing Option+Command+Q quits the selected processes. You cannot quit a process unless you are the owner of it. Be warned: if you quit certain processes, you will suddenly be logged out of the system!

✦ **Inspect:** Clicking this icon or pressing Command+I will open a window which gives additional details of memory, statistics, and a listing of the files the system believes are open in the process. Using buttons at the bottom, you can quit the process or get a sample of the calls the process is making at that moment. The results are shown frame by frame, displayed in any one of five ways, with options to hide or unhide particular frames, refresh the sample, or save the sample as a text file. Most of this information is of use to developers or highly technical types, for which these provisions are very convenient and exciting.

Also in the toolbar at the top of the Activity Monitor window you will find a Filter field, with which you can quickly find particular processes by typing their names. There is also a Show pop-up menu, which filters the process list to only display processes in one of the eight categories in the menu. Note that the default view, My Processes, only shows the processes owned by the present user. If you do not see what you are looking for, select All Processes from the pop-up menu.

At the bottom of the Activity Monitor window is an area that shows details selected by the row of five buttons marked CPU, System Memory, Disk Activity, and Network.

✦ **CPU:** Shows a tiny graph (or graphs for dual processor machines) of processor activity.

Tip

Don't worry, you can display the same graphs as the old CPU Monitor did; they can be found under the Monitor menu. Show CPU Usage calls up the small blue vertical LED-style display. Floating CPU Window calls up the green and gray bar, which can be chosen to be horizontal or vertical — but can no longer be positioned over the menu bar, or made transparent, as before. CPU History calls up the expanded view graph, but you can no longer choose what the colors mean, as you could in CPU Monitor. Now, system processes are red, user processes green, niced processes are blue, and the background is gray. By the way, a *niced* process is one that has been adjusted in the Terminal to have more or less access to CPU time than normal.

✦ **System Memory:** Reveals a pie chart of memory usage, color coded to a key on the left (and yes, in case you were wondering, you can change the colors on the graphs by clicking on the key color box to summon the OS X Cocoa color picker).

✦ **Disk Activity:** Shows data in and out on a line graph, along with disk statistics.

✦ **Disk Usage:** Shows a pie chart of utilized and free space on your hard disk partitions. A pop up menu allows you to select the partition.

✦ **Network:** Shows a line graph of data in and out rates as well as statistics on the left.

Under the Monitor menu you can select any of these graphs (except Disk Usage) to appear in the Dock instead of the Activity Monitor icon. You can also set the frequency at which Activity Monitor updates its information; the default is every two seconds.

AirPort Admin Utility

If you have an Apple AirPort Base Station, which is a flying saucer shaped device that establishes a wireless network, you can use the AirPort Admin Utility to change settings that are not handled by the AirPort Setup Assistant (described next, and used first). For example, by changing settings with AirPort Admin Utility you can do the following:

✦ Change the AirPort network name, wireless channel number, and so on.

✦ Change individual Internet connection settings, such as the phone number for a modem connection.

✦ Share a single public IP address on your AirPort network and optionally on an Ethernet network.

✦ Turn on a built-in DHCP server to automatically assign private IP addresses to computers on your AirPort network, and optionally on an Ethernet network.

✦ Restrict use of the wireless network to computers that you identify.

✦ Designate computers on your network to provide particular Internet services, such as Web server (Web sharing) and FTP server.

AirPort Setup Assistant

The AirPort Setup Assistant leads you through the process of setting up or reconfiguring an AirPort Base Station. Macs equipped with AirPort cards can join the wireless network, as can other computers that have cards or circuitry that is compatible with the 802.11b standard for wireless networking. The AirPort Setup Assistant can also help you set your computer to join an AirPort wireless network. Chapter 15 covers the AirPort Setup Assistant in more detail.

You can't use the AirPort Setup Assistant included with Mac OS X 10.3 to set up or reconfigure a software base station. In this case, the wireless network is established by turning on Sharing in the Internet tab of the Sharing pane of System Preferences.

Asia Text Extras

This folder is installed with Mac OS X if you do an Easy Install, which by default includes multiple language files. The folder contains the utilities Chinese Text Converter and IM Plugin Converter, along with a folder containing sample text.

Chinese Text Converter is used to do encoding conversion between Simplified Chinese and Traditional Chinese, as well as supporting other encoding conversions.

IM Plugin Converter converts a text file to a Chinese Input Method Plug-in data file.

Obviously, unless you are planning to be working with Chinese, you can ignore or even delete this folder.

AudioMIDI Setup

The AudioMIDI Setup utility, shown in Figure 19-18, provides control of the audio and MIDI inputs and outputs on the various ports of your computer. Audio can be routed between the CD/DVD drive, the headphone port, the built-in speakers (if present), attached USB devices, and so on.

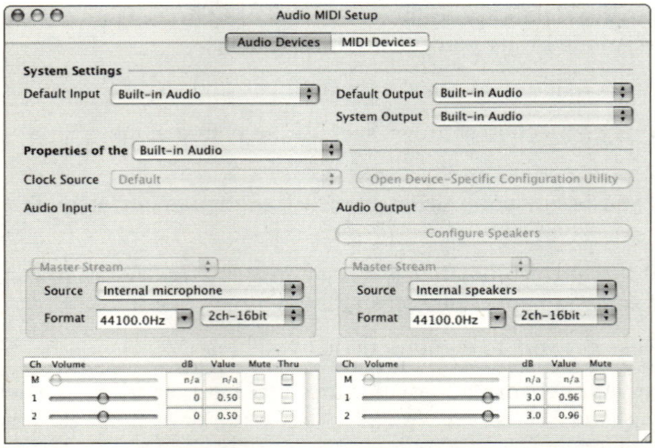

Figure 19-18: The AudioMIDI Setup utility provides control of the audio and MIDI inputs and outputs on the computer.

Bluetooth File Exchange

Bluetooth is essentially a short range, wireless form of USB, intended to eliminate cables between devices. Bluetooth has a range of about 30 feet. You need Bluetooth hardware built into your computer and your device; you can also use an approved USB Bluetooth adapter such as the D-Link DBT-120 on your computer.

To set up a device to use Bluetooth with your computer (known as "pairing"), open Bluetooth Setup Assistant (described later in this chapter) and follow the onscreen instructions. Devices your computer is paired with are listed in the Bluetooth System Preference pane's Devices panel.

Bluetooth File Exchange is used to set up the transmission of files to other Bluetooth devices.

Before you use Bluetooth File Exchange, you can go to the Bluetooth System Preference pane's File Exchange panel to configure your Mac's settings for the file exchange.

Bluetooth File Exchange features two interface windows, Browse Device (shown in Figure 19-19) and Select File to Send, shown in Figure 19-20. You can call them up only one at a time from the File Menu. You can call either one up first.

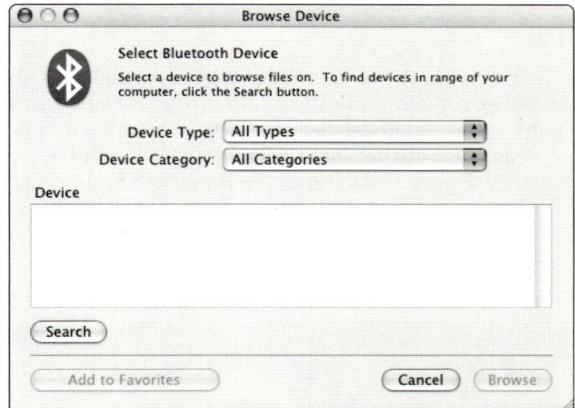

Figure 19-19: The Browse Device window of Bluetooth File Exchange.

Use Browse Device to select a device within range of your computer to browse files on. Hold the device close to the computer and click the Search button; the device should appear in the Device field. Selecting the device reveals a list of the services supported by the device. Click the Browse button to continue.

Select File to Send to navigate to the file you would like to send to the Bluetooth Device; click the Send button to accomplish this.

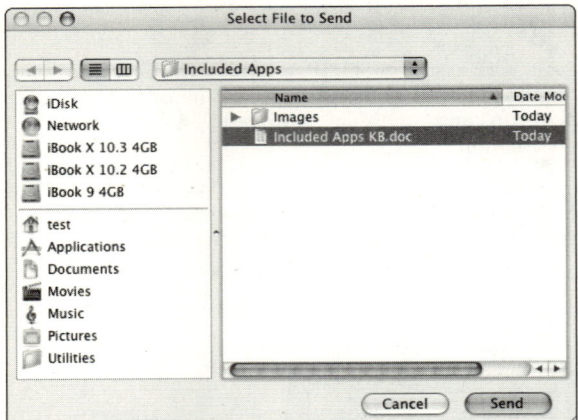

Figure 19-20: The Select File to Send window of Bluetooth File Exchange.

Bluetooth Serial Utility

Use the Bluetooth Serial Utility to set up Bluetooth services for paired devices. When Mac OS X 10.2.4 was released, Apple removed the configuration settings for virtual serial ports from the Bluetooth System Preferences pane to the Bluetooth Serial Utility. This utility allows you to add, name, configure, activate, or deactivate virtual serial ports to your computer, enabling communication with the Bluetooth device. Figure 19-21 shows the Bluetooth Serial Utility interface.

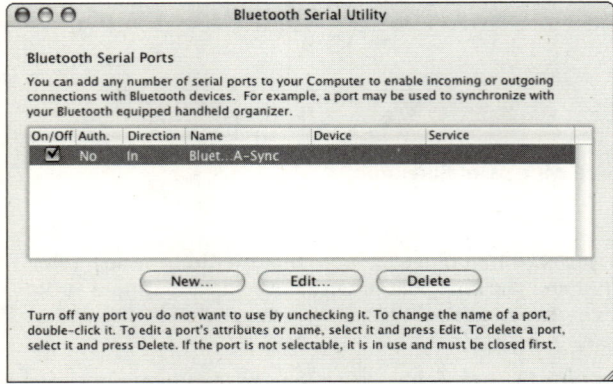

Figure 19-21: The Bluetooth Serial Utility interface.

The only time you need to set up a virtual serial port is if the device you are connecting to does not have a port.

To set up a virtual serial port, click New. Enter the port's name and select options for it. If you are setting up an outgoing port, click the Select Device button to select a device.

Bluetooth Setup Assistant

You use Bluetooth Setup Assistant, shown is Figure 19-22, to perform the initial configuration of Bluetooth hardware, called *pairing*. You must pair a Bluetooth device with your computer before exchanging information over the Bluetooth network. Paired devices are listed in the Devices panel of the Bluetooth System Preferences pane.

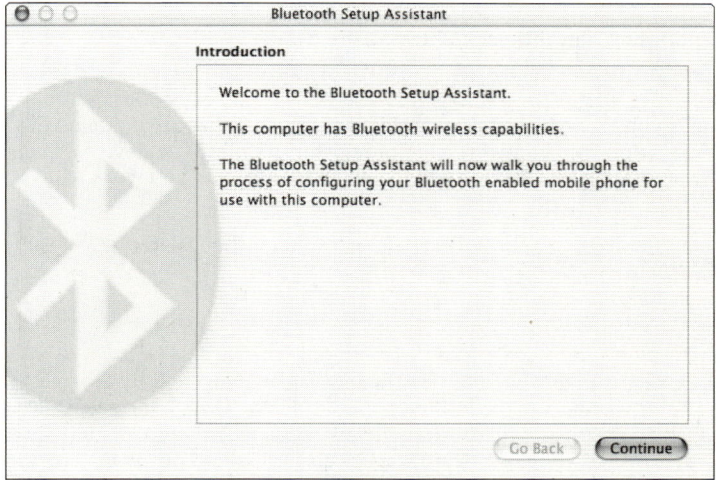

Figure 19-22: The Bluetooth Setup Assistant.

To pair your computer with the device, follow the onscreen instructions.

ColorSync Utility

Use the ColorSync Utility (shown in Figure 19-23) to view, modify, verify, and repair the ICC (International Color Consortium) profiles installed on your computer. These ColorSync profiles coordinate the color spaces employed by different devices, such as a printer and your screen, so that the colors you see are rendered consistently and correctly. The profiles are increasingly used in professional graphic design and publishing.

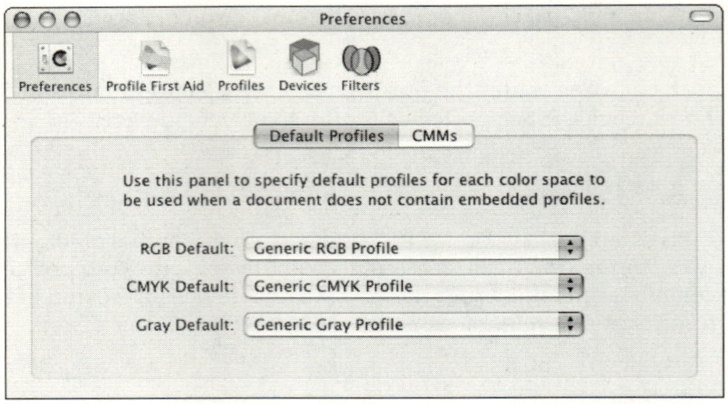

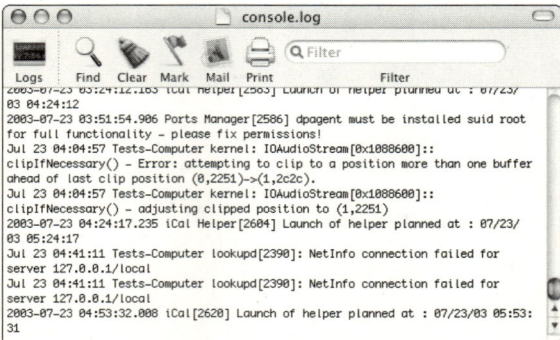

Figure 19-23: The ColorSync Utility interface, showing the default profiles for each color space.

ColorSync Utility allows you to view a list of all ColorSync profiles that are installed in your system, organized by location. You can view a list of registered ColorSync devices, such as Scanners, Cameras, Displays, and Printers. There is also a tool to help you work with ColorSync Filters.

A ColorSync tutorial and additional information can be found on the ColorSync Web site at `www.apple.com/colorsync`.

Console

The Console is a monitoring tool that displays all the messages being sent by applications and system processes to the Unix console hidden behind the Mac OS X interface. Unless you are experienced with Unix system administration, these messages are unlikely to be of any interest or help to you; however, they can be utilized to discern where problems are arising, or if you're a programmer, they can be helpful in debugging your software. Figure 19-24 shows an example of a Console window full of messages.

Figure 19-24: The Console displays all the error and informational messages sent by applications and processes.

DigitalColor Meter

This utility is similar to a Photoshop function in that it tells you what color is beneath the pointer, as shown in Figure 19-25. The frame on the left of the window shows a zoomed-in view of the area around your pointer. You can view the color information as RGB in percentage, decimal (Actual Value), or hexadecimal format; CIE 1931, CIE 1976, or CIE L*a*b (CIE is short for Commission Internationale de l'Eclairage, which is the French title of the international commission on light), or *tristimulus* (a three-dimensional color space in X, Y, and Z coordinates). Not all devices provide color translation tables for CIE or tristimulus — for example, the Color LCD in the figure does not.

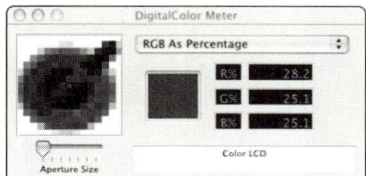

Figure 19-25: Know what color is under your pointer anywhere on the screen. Here a pixel in the DigitalColor Meter icon is being measured.

Directory Access

Mac OS X, and some applications, obtain information about users, servers, and other entities that may be located on a network from directories that are listed in the Directory Access utility. You can use Directory Access to change the directory that Mac OS X uses to authenticate users during login, define LDAP data and attribute mapping, configure search policies, select NetInfo domains, and so on.

Directory Access is primarily for the use of a network administrator. If your computer is connected to a home network or a small office network, you don't need to touch the settings in Directory Access. If your computer is connected to a corporate or school network, ask the network administrator whether you need to make changes in Directory Access. The Directory Access interface is shown in Figure 19-26.

Directory services within Mac OS X are based on a plug-in architecture. With Panther, Apple ships plug-ins for the following Directory Services:

- ✦ Active Directory
- ✦ AppleTalk
- ✦ BSD Flat File and NIS
- ✦ Lightweight Directory Access Protocol version 3 (LDAPv3)
- ✦ NetInfo
- ✦ Rendezvous
- ✦ SLP
- ✦ SMB

This list is a great improvement over Jaguar, which only included plug-ins for NetInfo and LDAP. By default in Panther, they are all enabled except Active Directory and AppleTalk.

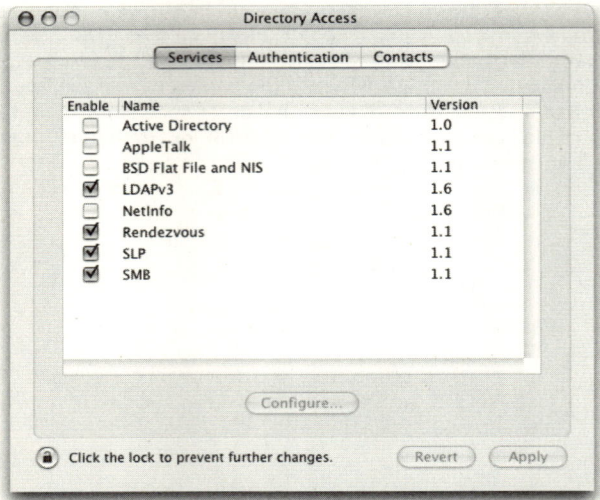

Figure 19-26: The Directory Access interface, showing the default state of the plug-ins.

The Services pane lists all available directory service plug-ins installed. To configure a directory service, you will first need to click the padlock icon in the lower-left corner of the Directory Services pane and authenticate with an Admin login and password. To enable a service, place a check mark in the Enable column next to the desired service. To configure a service, select the service and click the Configure button. Each plug-in has its own setup interface and will need to be configured, as appropriate, for the intended network.

The Authentication pane allows you to choose in what Directory Node to search for user authentication information. The Contacts pane provides a similar choice for contact information. By default, both are set to the /NetInfo/root directory node.

When configured correctly, directory access–capable applications can reference the Directory Setup utility for appropriate configurations, although some applications, such as email clients and OS X's Address Book, have a built-in facility for accessing directory services and do not utilize the Directory Setup utility.

Disk Utility

Use Disk Utility for repairing, erasing, formatting, and partitioning hard drives, rewritable CDs, and other storage devices. Disk Utility can also set up multiple hard drives as a RAID set, repair Mac OS X permissions, and restore a disk image to a destination disk.

Disk Utility combines the functionality of the Mac OS 9 programs Drive Setup, Disk First Aid, and Disk Copy. In Panther, Disk Utility now includes the functionality of the Disk Copy utility included with previous versions of Mac OS X, and the interface has been overhauled. Simplified instructions now appear on the different panels.

From a list on the left side of the window, you first select the storage device or volume that you want to work on. If you have partitioned disks, the partition volumes are listed under the physical hard drive; the buttons at the top of the window change appropriately depending on what you click on, as does the information at the bottom of the window.

Next, select the type of operation that you want to perform by clicking a button.

First Aid panel

Click the First Aid button in the Disk Utility window to check the condition of a volume directory. The First Aid panel, shown in Figure 19-27, provides you with a volume directory to keep track of which files are on the volume and where they are stored. The volume directory is susceptible to corruption. If you have any problems with a volume directory, Disk Copy's First Aid can often fix them. It's good to run First Aid every once in a while — say once a month — to make sure your volume directory is in good shape.

To have First Aid check a volume, select the volume on the left side of the window and click the Verify Disk button. If First Aid discovers problems, it informs you of them, and you can click the Repair Disk button to try to remedy matters.

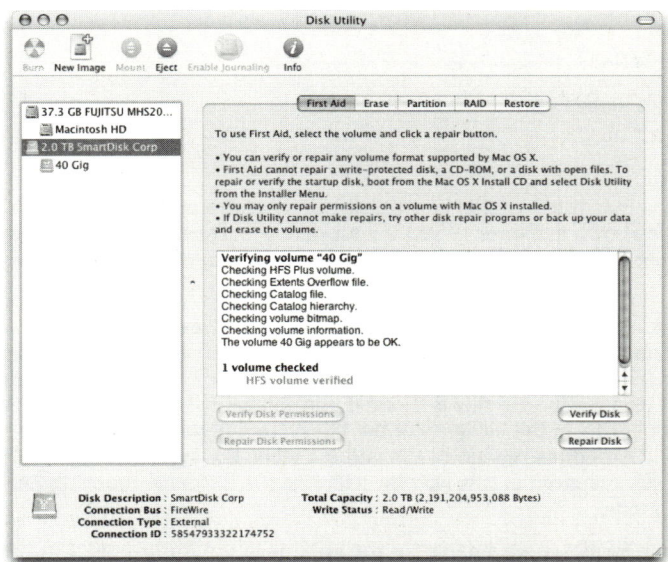

Figure 19-27: Disk Utility's First Aid panel, after the selected disk has been verified.

The Verify Disk Permissions button and the Repair Disk Permissions button allow you to check for and correct incorrect Mac OS X file permissions, which can cause files to which you should have rights to become inaccessible. This has a tendency to happen far too often. (For more about Unix file permissions in Mac OS X, see Chapter 24). Run Verify Disk Permissions first, as shown in Figure 19-28. Progress notices such as "Determining correct file permissions" and "Permissions differ on…" will appear in the window. If problems are discovered, they will be described in detail. To stop the process, click the same button, which now reads Stop Verify Permissions. To perform the repairs, click the Repair Disk Permissions button.

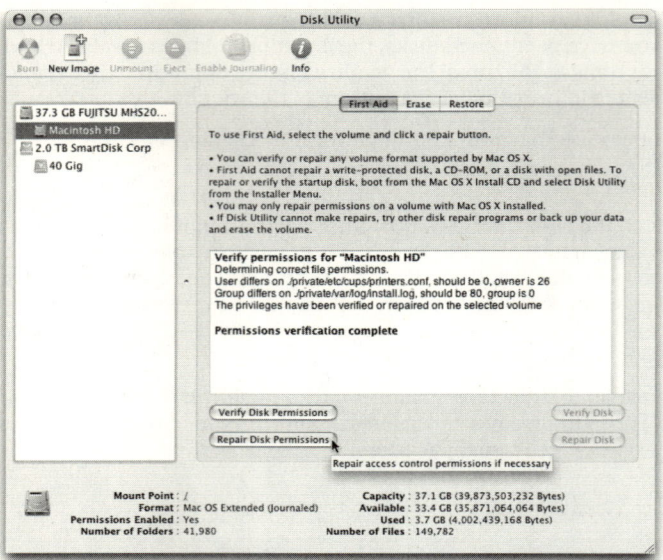

Figure 19-28: Disk Utility's Verify Permissions function at work.

Erase panel

Click the Erase button to erase the contents of a volume or an entire unpartitioned disk. (The Disk Utility Erase panel is shown in Figure 19-29.) If your disk is partitioned, you can only erase the partition volume, not the physical disk (the controls will appear grayed-out when the disk is selected).

Select the volume or disk on the left side of the Disk Copy window. Next, choose a volume format from the pop-up menu: MS DOS File System (for installing a Microsoft Windows operating system to an entire disk only), Mac OS Extended, or the default, Mac OS Extended (Journaled) (recommended for most users). Choose this last one if you will be installing Mac OS X Server on the volume; journaling protects the integrity of the file system in the event of an unplanned shutdown, and expedites repairs to the volume when the system restarts. You can enable Journaling on a disk prepared in this way by selecting the disk and choosing Enable Journaling from the File menu.

After choosing the volume format, type a name for the volume in the Name field. Click the checkbox if you want OS 9 drivers to be installed; as noted below the checkbox, they are necessary to use the volume to boot Mac OS 9, and are not necessary for running Classic under Mac OS X.

When you click the Erase button, the volume will be formatted, permanently deleting all files.

Caution   You can't recover the contents of a volume or disk after erasing it unless you have the resources of the FBI. Make sure you have an up-to-date backup copy of all important files on a volume before you erase it.

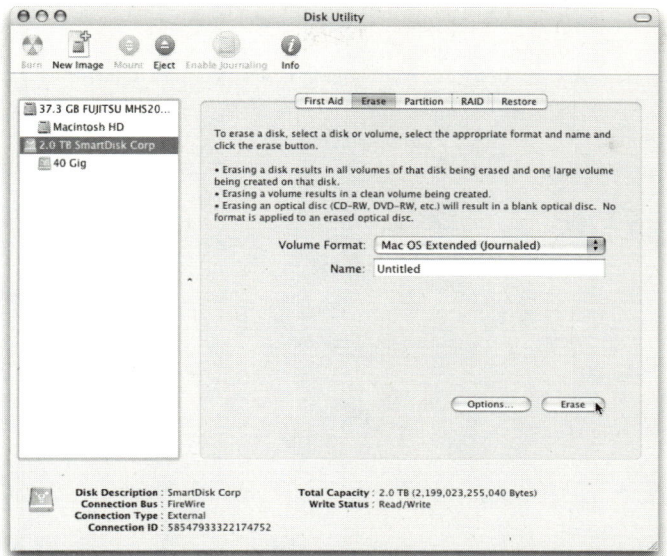

Figure 19-29: Disk Utility's Erase panel.

Partition panel

Partitioning splits a disk into separate volumes, each of which appears on your desktop with its own icon, as if it were a separate disk. Partitions are useful for loading different versions of the Mac OS, or for organizing your information. Click the Partition button in the Disk Utility window to change the number of volumes or the sizes of volumes on the currently selected disk.

The partitioning of the startup disk or a read-only disk cannot be changed. You can choose the number of volumes you desire from the Volume Scheme pop-up menu. You can adjust volume sizes either by dragging the divider handles in the boxes on the left or by typing numbers into the Size text box. When you select a volume on the left, you can use the Split and Delete buttons to, respectively, split that volume in two or delete it from the scheme. The Revert button returns you to the settings you had before you made any changes — Revert is disabled until you've made a change. Figure 19-30 shows the Partition button, which tells Drive Setup to proceed with the settings you've made.

RAID panel

If your computer has multiple hard drives, Disk Utility can create a RAID (Redundant Array of Independent Disks) set. A RAID set coordinates two or more hard drives to optimize storage capacity, improve performance, or increase reliability.

In the RAID panel, you must designate which disks you want to be part of the RAID set by dragging the icons of the physical hard disks to the Disk field which initially reads, "Drag disks here to add to set." Only when you have dragged the second disk will the items above the field become selectable and stop being grayed out. If you drag the wrong disk to the field, simply drag it off.

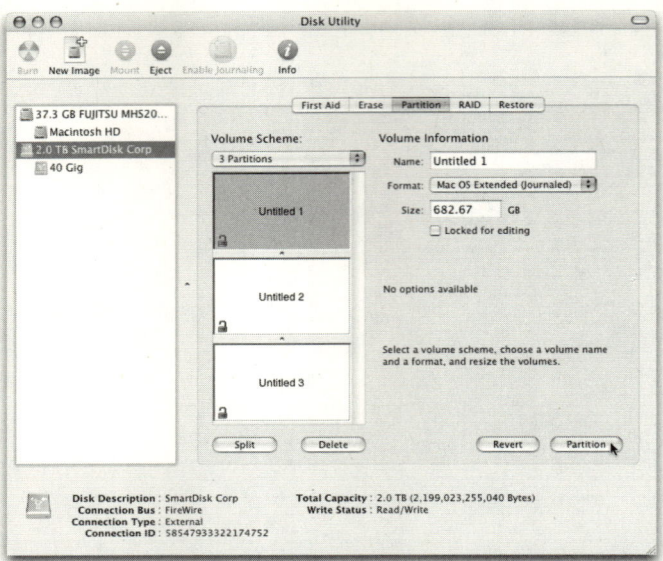

Figure 19-30: Partition a disk into multiple volumes by clicking Disk Utility's Partition button.

In the RAID Scheme pop-up menu, you can choose Stripe or Mirror. Stripe will cause the multiple disks to look and act like a single disk with the combined capacity of all the disks, but with dramatically improved performance due to the redundancy of drive heads. Mirror will cause one disk to automatically duplicate the other to ensure redundant data if one of the disks should fail.

Enter the name of the RAID set in the field, and below that choose the volume format for the disks from the pop-up menu. The estimated size (capacity) of the set appears. Click the Create button to create the RAID set.

Restore panel

Use the Restore panel, shown in Figure 19-31, to copy the contents of a disk image onto a destination volume. You cannot drag copy the contents of a Mac OS X disk to another disk, like you could with Mac OS 9, so you should make an image of the disk first (see the instructions for the Images menu below) and then restore it using this feature.

As the onscreen instructions mention, you must prepare a disk image for the restore process by first "attaching" it so it can be seen in the Disk Utilities volumes list (see the Image menu instructions below). When it can be seen, select it. Then select "Scan Image for Restore" from the Images menu. When the image has been checksummed, drag it to the Source field, or browse for it with the Image... button. Drag a disk to restore onto the Destination field, check the box if you would like to erase the destination first, and check or uncheck the Skip Checksum box (it is recommended that you leave this box unchecked). Click the Restore button to complete the process.

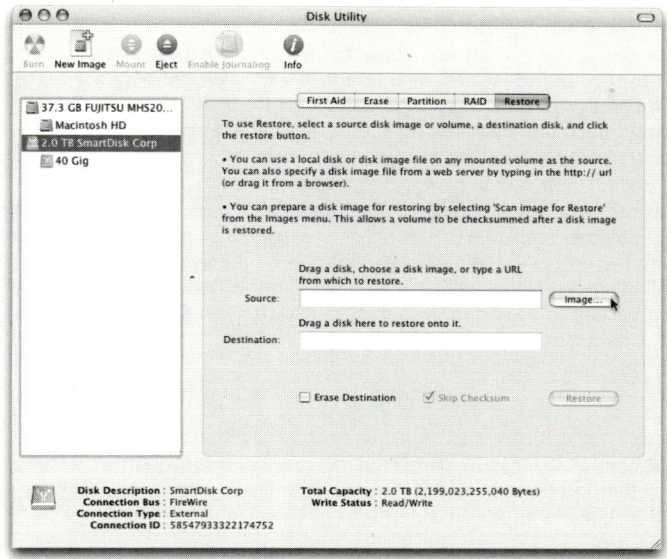

Figure 19-31: The Restore panel of Disk Utility.

Images menu

The Images menu contains much of the functionality of Jaguar's Disk Copy.

A disk image is a file that contains the contents of a disk. A disk image file's icon looks like a document with a picture of a hard disk, and the file name is followed by a ".dmg" extension. Double-clicking a disk image file causes an icon of a removable drive to appear on the desktop (the image is "mounted"), and double-clicking this icon reveals the contents of the file. Once the image is mounted, your computer treats it like a hard drive; you can drag files to and from it, or run installers to or from it. You drag it to the Trash to "eject" it (unmount it).

To create a disk image choose New from the Images menu. From the submenu, choose Blank Image, Image from Folder, or Image from disk. Blank Image will create an empty disk image which you can add files to. Image from Folder will create an image from any folder you choose. Image from Disk will create an image containing the contents of any disk you choose. When creating an image, you can choose its size, format (Mac OS, MS DOS, or Unix), and encryption.

The Checksum command calculates a checksum for any disk you choose in the list. A checksum changes when any character in the volume or disk is changed, so it is a good way of insuring an image has not been corrupted. Most images use a UDIF-CRC32 checksum.

Verify checks the integrity of the disk image file you select first in the list. After choosing this command, the verification begins immediately; a progress bar appears in the lower right of the Disk Utility window. The results are shown in both in a sheet and to the left of the progress bar.

Convert allows you to convert the image format and encryption scheme of a disk image.

Burn lets you burn a disk image onto a CD or DVD disk.

Toolbar

The Disk Utility toolbar, a new feature, contains some handy icon buttons. Burn has the same functionality as the burn button in the Finder. New Image is a convenient way to create a new disk image. Unmount and Eject performs those operations on the selected disk. Enable Journaling turns journaling on for the selected disk. Info produces a rundown of information about the device or volume.

Tip

Most hard disk drives can warn you if they are going to fail, using their S.M.A.R.T. hardware to test themselves for problems. The S.M.A.R.T. status of a selected disk is shown at the bottom of the Disk Utility window, and in the Info window that opens when you click the Info button in the toolbar. "Verified" means all is well. "About to Fail" in red letters means you should immediately make a backup of your disk, and then replace it. "Not Supported" means the drive has no S.M.A.R.T hardware.

Grab

Grab facilitates capturing images from your computer screen. Grab really doesn't have much of an interface, but that is good because there is not much to get in the way of viewing the screen. And Grab is admirably self-explanatory. Grab's capture menu is shown in Figure 19-32.

Grab specializes in helping with trickier screen captures. Simple captures are best done without Grab by pressing Command+Shift+3 to image the entire screen, and Command+Shift+4 to turn the cursor into a cross-hair you can use to draw a shaded selection rectangle around what you want. Images produced in this way appear on the Panther desktop as PDF files, viewable in Preview.

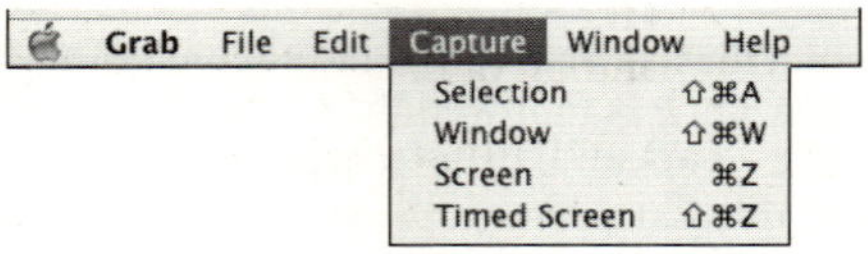

🍎 **Grab** File Edit **Capture** Window Help

Selection	⇧⌘A
Window	⇧⌘W
Screen	⌘Z
Timed Screen	⇧⌘Z

Figure 19-32: This image of Grab's Capture menu is an example of what you can produce with a Timed Screen Grab.

Grab's Capture menu reveals four kinds of capture:

✦ **Selection Grab** (Command+Shift+A): Similar to the Command+Shift+4, mentioned in the previous paragraph, in that you drag the cursor to make a rectangle around what you want to image. The rectangle is red and gives screen pixel coordinates at the start and end of the drag.

For all four kinds of capture Grab performs, a small notice opens in the center of the screen to remind you what to do. The notice floats in front of all windows and is not imaged.

✦ **Window Grab** (Command+Shift+W): Allows you to capture one window of any size. The notice tells you when you have the window you want ready, click the Choose Window button, then click the window to capture it.

✦ **Screen Grab** (Command+Z): Similar to Command+Shift+4 mentioned above. Click outside the notice window to image the entire screen. You can cause a cursor image to appear exactly where you click, if you have first chosen one from the File ⇨ Preferences window. Grab's Preferences are shown in Figure 19-33.

✦ **Timed Screen** (Command+Shift+Z): Capture the screen ten seconds after you click the Start Timer button. Click the button and the cursor turns into a little camera with which you can manipulate things on screen; you can, for instance, get images of menus pulled down, much like the figure which shows Grab's Capture menu. At the end of the ten seconds, the flash of the camera icon goes off, and the screen image is captured.

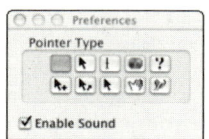

Figure 19-33: Grab's Preferences and Image Inspector windows represent the height of interface minimalism.

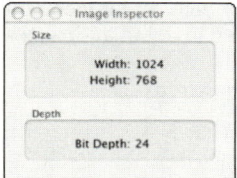

After you make a capture with Grab, the image appears in a Untitled window smaller than the screen; you must name the image and save it. Grab saves these images as TIFF files. The Image Inspector window also appears, detailing the size and bit depth of the resulting image.

Grab is available from applications as a Mac OS X Service under the File menu (turn to Chapter 11 to learn more about Services).

Installer

The Installer is a utility that installs software packages, such as System Updates, which are assembled in a specific format. Software vendors will usually use disk images when all you need to do is place the proffered application in your Applications folder; however, if support files (such as frameworks) also need to be installed, the software company may choose to provide an installer package.

Java (folder)

The Java folder contains Applet Launcher, Input Method Hotkey, Java 1.3.1 Plugin Settings, and Java 1.4.1 Plugin Settings.

Java is a programming language developed by Sun Microsystems which is used to create small, platform-independent applications, called *applets* that your browser can automatically retrieve from a Web page, thereby extending the functionality of that Web page. The divergence from original platform-independent intent (particularly by Microsoft) has made this vision less than fully realized, resulting in Java applets being one of the principal causes of browser instability and crashes.

Other than being able to run applets in Web pages, how important is Java? So far, not very important; however, Mac OS X goes to great lengths to make Java a partner in developing full-featured applications.

If you want to run Java applets without a Web browser's interaction, you can do it with Applet Launcher. After you launch Applet Launcher, you can open an applet's HTML file and launch the applet.

Input Method Hotkey allows Java developers to assign a key combination of their choice to bring up a pop up menu that lists input methods to choose from.

Java 1.3.1 Plugin Settings and Java 1.4.1 Plugin Settings allow Java developers to control settings that pertain to the Java Plugin.

Keychain Access

Keychain Access, shown in Figure 19-34, allows you to manage your collections of user IDs and passwords that you don't want to have to remember individually and type in repeatedly. You need only remember the passphrase that opens the Keychain, and it feeds the information required to any Keychain-aware application, as described in detail in Chapter 11.

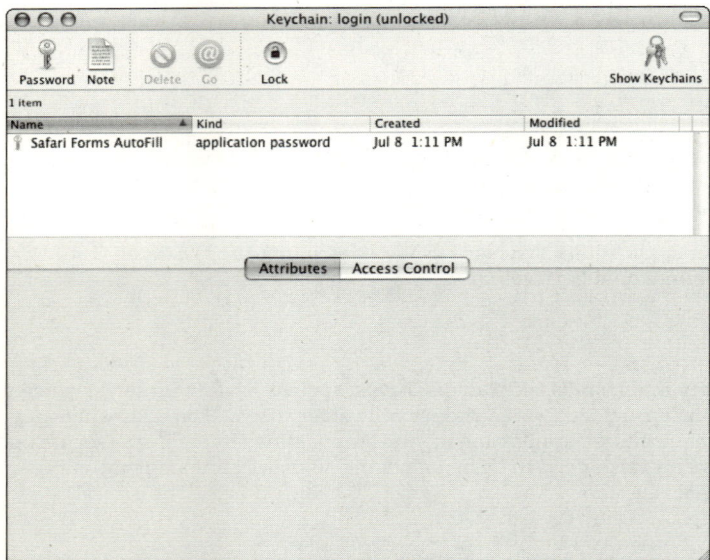

Figure 19-34: The Keychain Access interface.

NetInfo Manager

NetInfo is Mac OS X's directory system, which stores and finds important information about users and resources on your computer (or a network of computers) in a special database, and makes it available to application or system processes that need to use it.

You have already used NetInfo, perhaps without realizing it. When you first set up Mac OS X, you were asked to enter your name and a password to create a user account. This name and password were recorded in the NetInfo database, along with the information that this first user account, by default, has administrator rights to the machine. Whenever you log in to Mac OS X (if you have enabled login), you are authenticating your identity against the records in the NetInfo database.

NetInfo Manager, shown in Figure 19-35, is the graphical interface to this NetInfo database, allowing you to control the details of its contents directly. Most users of Mac OS X will never need to do this, so they will never use NetInfo Manager. In fact Apple advises that you should only use NetInfo Manager if you know what you are doing — similar to the Terminal.

However, if you are a little savvier than the average user, you may find yourself using the NetInfo Manager now and then in order to achieve a particular objective. Perhaps the most common task you might use NetInfo Manager for would be to give yourself access to the root user account, to do something you are ordinarily prevented from doing. The root account is the most powerful account in Mac OS X, with unlimited control over system settings, file access, user accounts, and so on.

To enable the root account within the NetInfo Manager application, unlock the padlock icon in the lower-left corner of the NetInfo Manager pane and authenticate with an Admin login and password. Continue by selecting Security from the Domain menu and Enable Root from the submenu. After acknowledging the warning message that appears, you will be prompted to supply the root account with a password. (By the way, the password cannot be "root"). You will then be prompted to verify the password in order to complete the procedure.

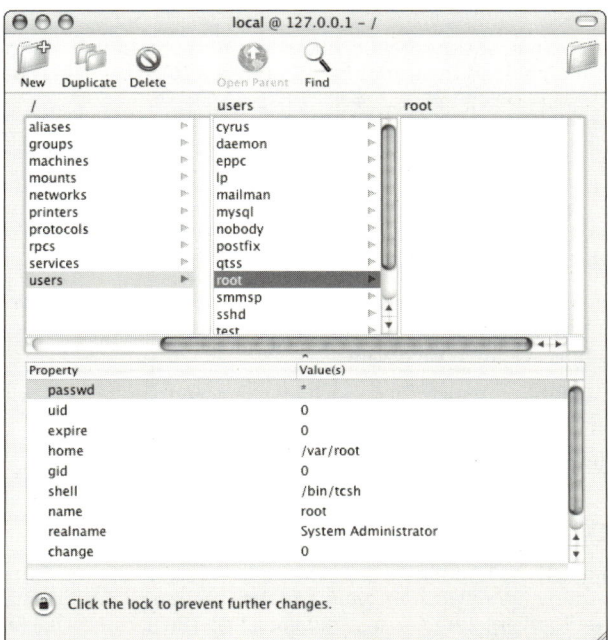

Figure 19-35: The Netinfo Manager interface, with the root user selected.

When you log out, and log back in with the root user name and password, there will be nothing you cannot do to your system. In Mac OS X, this is actually quite dangerous if you don't know what you are doing. You can irrevocably disable your system and lose your data if you, say, delete the wrong files. Do not dabble or linger; do what you must and then log out. Even power users do it this way.

The same stern warning applies if you boot from Mac OS 9 on your Mac OS X machine. Because you are not in Mac OS X, there are no constraints on your actions, and if you start playing around with your Mac OS X system files you can do serious damage. It is interesting to note that in Mac OS 9, you have and always have had root powers; it's just that before the advent of Mac OS X, you could not be as dangerous. If you are intimidated by the process of enabling and logging on as the root user in Mac OS X, you can actually achieve the same end by booting into Mac OS 9 and doing what you have to do.

One other point to clarify about root: this same word applies to both the "superuser" account we have been talking about, and the top level of a hard drive. The first is the root user account, and the second is the root directory or the root level of the disk hierarchy "tree."

Network Utility

Network Utility incorporates several tools that are helpful in working with networks. By using its various tabs (shown in Figure 19-36), you can perform such tasks as:

✦ **Netstat:** Provides a statistical summary of the network activity on your Mac.

✦ **Ping:** Lets you send answer-back messages to another IP address to discern how long it takes to communicate with that location.

✦ **Lookup:** Enables you to ascertain various details about an Internet address, for example, what server hosts it and its IP address after resolution by a *DNS* (Domain Name Server).

✦ **Traceroute:** Reports back to you the route taken to get a message between your Mac and the address entered.

✦ **Whois:** Communicates with the servers where Internet domains are registered and returns to you the information as to who has registered a given domain name, when they registered it, and what its name servers are.

✦ **Finger:** Feed this Internet lookup tool a username and domain name, and it queries the host for that domain to retrieve any published information about that account. Not all domains provide finger information on their users.

✦ **Port Scan:** Scans a domain for open ports. You can limit the scan to only ports within a given range.

✦ **Info:** Tells you about your particular network connection.

ODBC Administrator

The ODBC (Open DataBase Connectivity) Administrator, shown in Figure 19-37, was introduced in Jaguar to allow users to configure ODBC drivers and data sources. ODBC is a programming interface that enables applications to access data in a SQL (Structured Query Language) database. Databases that use SQL are very popular in corporations, and this utility enables Mac OS X to access them.

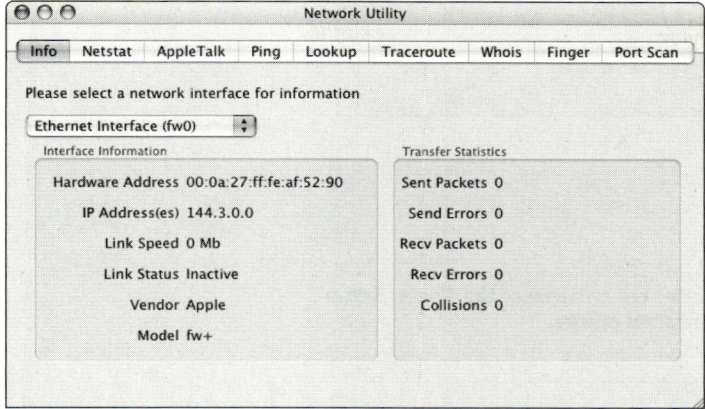

Figure 19-36: Network Utility provides a graphic interface to a collection of Unix-based network search commands.

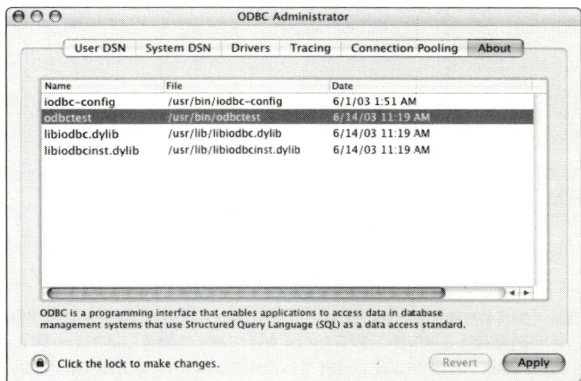

Figure 19-37: The ODBC Administrator interface.

Printer Setup Utility

Printer Setup Utility in Panther replaces the Jaguar-and-before Print Center. Using Printer Setup Utility, you can add or delete printers, monitor the progress of print jobs, start and stop print jobs, and manage a printer's options. The Printer List window is shown in Figure 19-38. New in Panther is a convenient feature: the print jobs appear as an icon in the dock while they are being sent to the printer. Also new is the Fax List, shown if Figure 19-39, which part of Mac OS X's build-in fax capabilities. Printer Setup Utility is described in Chapter 9.

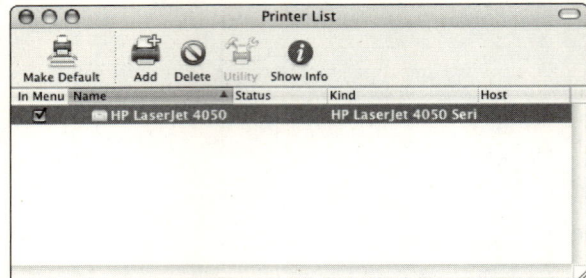

Figure 19-38: The Printer List window of the Printer Setup Utility, showing one installed printer.

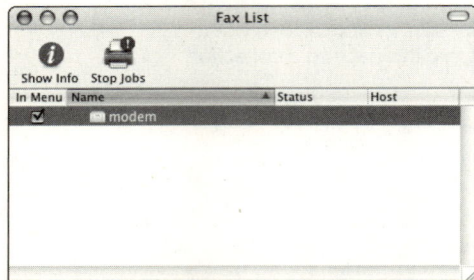

Figure 19-39: The Fax List window of the Printer Setup Utility, showing its default state.

StuffIt Expander

StuffIt Expander is an excellent little tool provided to Apple for free redistribution by Aladdin. StuffIt Expander decodes and decompresses a wide variety of formats used on Mac, Windows, and Unix computers. Many of the files you download from the Internet are automatically decoded and decompressed by StuffIt Expander; it opens, does its work, and quits. You can also use StuffIt Expander with files that aren't processed automatically. Just drag the files over the StuffIt Expander icon shown in Figure 19-40 and let go; Expander decodes and decompresses them for you. If you receive many encoded or compressed files, we recommend keeping StuffIt Expander in your Dock for quick and easy use.

Figure 19-40: If you double-click the StuffIt Expander icon, you will see this larger image to drop your files on top of.

System Profiler

System Profiler, shown in Figure 19-41, which prior to Panther was called Apple System Profiler, tells you what you may need to know if you ever need to call Apple Computer (or some other hardware or software vendor) for technical assistance. You can find out what your processor type is, exactly which version of Mac OS you're running (including any updates), which bus your startup drive is on, how much RAM is present and where it is located, and what frameworks, extensions, and applications are installed.

System Profiler's new interface makes Apple System Profiler seem primitive. On the left is the Contents list, containing the following items: under the heading Hardware: Memory, PCI/AGP Cards, IDE (ATA), SCSI, USB, FireWire, AirPort Card, Modems; under the heading Software: Applications, Frameworks, Extensions, and the headings Network and Logs.

As you click on each item in the contents list, the large area on the right of the window changes to accommodate the details. At times there is a second list at the top of this area, and clicking on the items brings up their information below. The whole utility is pretty self-explanatory.

From the view menu, you can choose a report length of Short, Standard, or Extended, and you can Refresh the results.

The results can be saved as a System Profiler 4.0 document, which is identical to what you see in the window; or, with the File ➪ Export command, as Plain or Rich text documents.

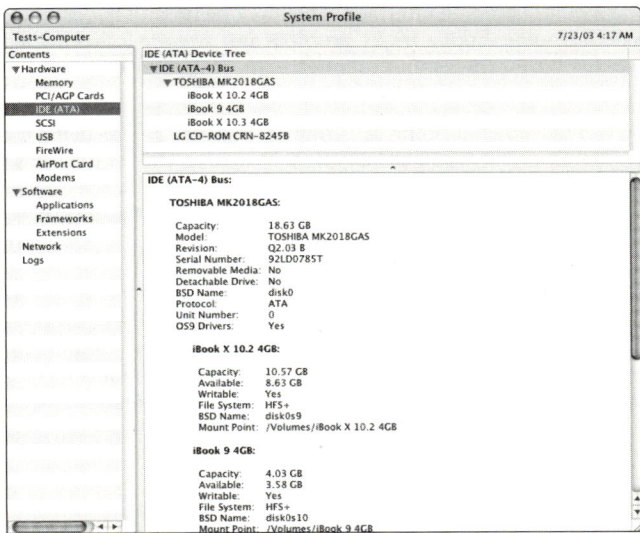

Figure 19-41: System Profiler tells you more than ever wanted to know about your hardware and software.

The About This Mac window features a helpful shortcut to System Profiler. Select the Apple menu, then the About This Mac... command from the Apple menu. The More Info... button shown in Figure 19-42 opens the System Profiler. This is faster than digging through the hierarchy to get to the Utilities folder.

Figure 19-42: The System Profiler can be opened by clicking the More Info... button in the About This Mac window.

Terminal

The Terminal utility, shown in Figure 19-43, allows you to communicate directly with the Unix underpinning of Mac OS X via a command-line interface. This may be helpful in certain situations, for instance if you have to troubleshoot a tricky problem and you are following a procedure in one of Apple's Knowledge Base articles. But otherwise, most typical Mac users would never need to use Terminal.

If you are a Unix person, you will feel right at home in Terminal, and may prefer using it to using the Aqua graphic user interface. But if you are a typical Mac user, the thought of going into Terminal may give you something approximating a severe anxiety attack. Not to worry! If this sounds like you, but you are curious, check out Chapter 24, Commanding Unix, where we will demystify Terminal and all you can do with it.

X11

Before Mac OS X came along, virtually the only way developers could create a graphical application in a Unix-based operating system was with the X Window System, which is more commonly known as X11. Thousands of these applications were created for Unix and Linux, and many have become indispensable. Apple's X11 utility, shown in Figure 19-44, offers the ability to run these applications on Mac OS X. We discuss X11 further in Chapter 25.

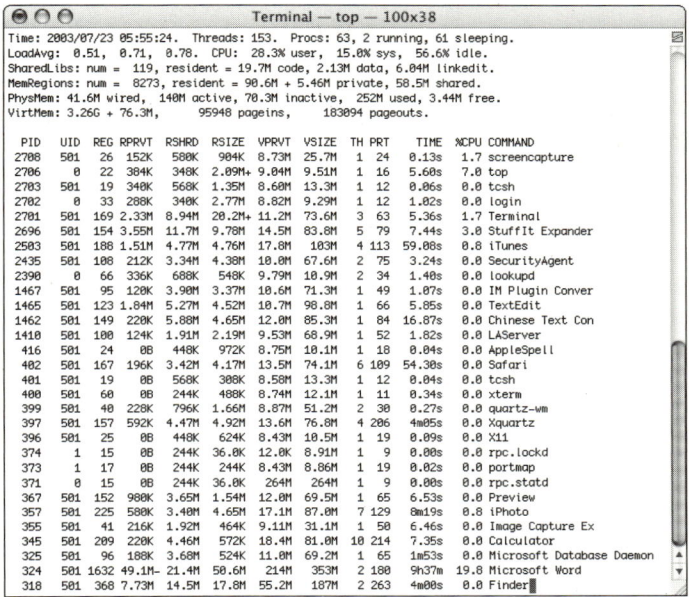

```
                    Terminal — top — 100x38
Time: 2003/07/23 05:55:24.  Threads: 153.  Procs: 63, 2 running, 61 sleeping.
LoadAvg: 0.51, 0.71, 0.78. CPU: 28.3% user, 15.0% sys, 56.6% idle.
SharedLibs: num = 119, resident = 19.7M code, 2.13M data, 6.04M linkedit.
MemRegions: num = 8273, resident = 90.6M + 5.46M private, 58.5M shared.
PhysMem: 41.6M wired, 140M active, 70.3M inactive, 252M used, 3.44M free.
VirtMem: 3.26G + 76.3M,    95948 pageins,    183094 pageouts.

  PID  UID  REG RPRVT  RSHRD  RSIZE  VPRVT  VSIZE TH PRT  TIME   %CPU COMMAND
 2708  501   26  152K   580K   904K  8.73M  25.7M  1  24  0.13s  1.7  screencapture
 2706    0   22  384K   348K 2.09M+ 9.04M  9.51M  1  16  5.60s  7.0  top
 2703  501   19  340K   568K  1.35M  8.60M  13.3M  1  12  0.06s  0.0  tcsh
 2702    0   33  288K   340K  2.77M  8.82M  9.29M  1  12  1.02s  0.0  login
 2701  501  169 2.33M  8.94M 20.2M+ 11.2M  73.6M  3  63  5.36s  1.7  Terminal
 2696  501  154 3.55M  11.7M  9.78M  14.5M  83.8M  5  79  7.44s  3.0  StuffIt Expander
 2503  501  188 1.51M  4.77M  4.76M  17.8M   103M  4 113 59.08s  0.8  iTunes
 2435  501  108  212K  3.34M  4.38M  10.0M  67.6M  2  75  3.24s  0.0  SecurityAgent
 2390    0   66  336K   688K   548K  9.79M  10.9M  2  34  1.40s  0.0  lookupd
 1467  501   95  120K  3.90M  3.37M  10.6M  71.3M  1  49  1.07s  0.0  IM Plugin Conver
 1465  501  123 1.84M  5.27M  4.52M  10.7M  98.8M  1  66  5.85s  0.0  TextEdit
 1462  501  149  220K  5.88M  4.65M  12.0M  85.3M  1  84 16.87s  0.0  Chinese Text Con
 1410  501  100  124K  1.91M  2.19M  9.53M  68.9M  1  52  1.82s  0.0  LAServer
  416  501   24    0B   448K   972K  8.75M  10.1M  1  18  0.04s  0.0  AppleSpell
  402  501  167  196K  3.42M  4.17M  13.5M  74.1M  6 109 54.30s  0.0  Safari
  401  501   19    0B   568K   308K  8.58M  13.3M  1  12  0.04s  0.0  tcsh
  400  501   60    0B   244K   488K  8.74M  12.1M  1  11  0.34s  0.0  xterm
  399  501   40  228K   796K  1.66M  8.87M  14.2M  2  30  0.27s  0.0  quartz-wm
  397  501  157  592K  4.47M  4.92M  13.6M  76.8M  4 206  4m05s  0.0  Xquartz
  396  501   25    0B   448K   624K  8.43M  10.5M  1  19  0.09s  0.0  X11
  374    1   15    0B   244K  36.0K  12.0K  8.91M  1   9  0.00s  0.0  rpc.lockd
  373    1   17    0B   244K   244K  8.43M  8.86M  1  19  0.02s  0.0  portmap
  371    0   15    0B   244K  36.0K   264M   264M  1   9  0.00s  0.0  rpc.statd
  367  501  152  980K  3.65M  1.54M  12.0M  69.5M  1  65  6.53s  0.0  Preview
  357  501  225  580K  3.40M  4.65M  17.1M  87.0M  7 129  8m19s  0.8  iPhoto
  355  501   41  216K  1.92M   464K  9.11M  31.1M  1  50  6.46s  0.0  Image Capture Ex
  345  501  209  220K  4.46M   572K  18.4M  81.0M 10 214  7.35s  0.0  Calculator
  325  501   96  188K  3.60M   524K  11.0M  69.2M  1  65  1m53s  0.0  Microsoft Database Daemon
  324  501 1632 49.1M- 21.4M  50.6M   214M   353M  2 180  9h37m 19.8  Microsoft Word
  318  501  368 7.73M  14.5M  17.8M  55.2M   187M  2 263  4m00s  0.0  Finder
```

Figure 19-43: The Terminal window after the command *top* has been entered (see the description of Activity Monitor for an explanation of *top*).

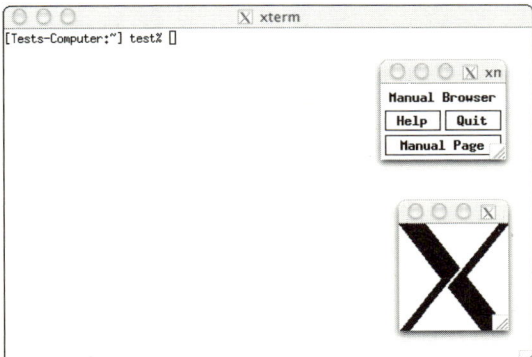

Figure 19-44: The X11 interface with its default command prompt. Two auxiliary windows are also seen here, the xman and xlogo windows.

Summary

This chapter provided brief descriptions of every Application and Utility that is installed with Mac OS X 10.3. If the Application or Utility is covered in detail elsewhere in the book, that chapter was referenced.

✦   ✦   ✦

QuickTime and the iLife Suite

The beginnings of QuickTime were understandably humble, with the first version focusing mainly on providing the ability to watch small, jumpy videos in a "player" window on your Mac.

Twelve years later QuickTime is now the foundation of the amazing multimedia capabilities of Mac OS X and a widely used cross-platform Internet file format standard. Thanks to QuickTime, you can use your Mac as an audio jukebox with the iTunes application, buy music online with the iTunes Music Store, and take it with you in your iPod. You can store and work with the images from your digital camera with iPhoto. You can take raw digital videos from your camcorder and convert them into edited, polished home movies with iMovie. And you can take photos from iPhoto and movies from iMovie and save them on an impressive, slick-looking DVD, with the iDVD application (and an Apple SuperDrive).

These four applications, iTunes, iPhoto, iMovie, and iDVD, are part of what Apple markets as the iLife suite. They are at the center of the digital hub, Steve Jobs' concept of the Macintosh facilitating work with handheld digital devices; and QuickTime is its core.

QuickTime also gives you the ability to watch video DVDs on your Macintosh, or play video files over the Internet (even on a Windows PC), or view video streamed from a QuickTime Streaming Server. You can even view or create virtual reality files with QuickTime VR.

In this chapter, you find out about QuickTime technology, and how it works in Panther. We also give you a concise overview of the four iLife applications — an in-depth how-to for them is beyond the scope of this book.

About QuickTime

QuickTime is also a file format that is a pervasive Internet standard. QuickTime files, often called QuickTime movies, can combine sound and video in a single file, or hold only sound or only video. QuickTime files can have file name extensions of .qt, .mov, or .moov, with .mov being the most common.

QuickTime files can include the following content, technologies, and capabilities:

✦ **Motion pictures:** What you watch on TV or at the movies.

✦ **Digitized sound recordings:** Music and other sounds that play in CD-quality sound (44.1kHz, 18-bit stereo).

✦ **Synthesized music:** Based on the MIDI (Musical Instrument Digital Interface) standard, that takes far less disk space to store than digitized sound, yet sounds realistic and plays in CD-quality.

✦ **Text:** For closed-caption viewing, karaoke sing-a-longs, or text-based searches of movie content.

✦ **Sprites:** Sprites are graphic objects that move independently, like actors moving on a stage with a motion-picture backdrop.

✦ **MPEG:** Movies that use the common MPEG-1 and new MPEG-4 video and audio standards. MPEG-2 playback is an additional component available for a small fee.

✦ **AVI:** Movies that are common on Windows. The file type actually covers a broad range of movie codecs. (Although not all varieties of AVI are currently supported by QuickTime—for example, Intel has not ported the Indeo 2.63 codec to the Mac.)

✦ **Graphics:** QuickTime 6 includes support for Macromedia Flash 5 and JPEG 2000.

✦ **Panoramas and objects:** Permits viewing objects in 360 degrees using QuickTime VR methods.

✦ **Timecode information:** Displays elapsed hours, minutes, seconds, and frames at the bottom of a playing movie.

✦ **Functional information:** Information that tells QuickTime how other tracks interact.

QuickTime is built into Mac OS X as one of its three graphics technologies (the other two being OpenGL and Quartz). QuickTime makes multimedia ubiquitous in Mac OS X. The Finder lets you view QuickTime files as thumbnails without even opening an application. You don't need a special application to watch QuickTime movies. Many applications (such as the Microsoft Office applications) let you copy and paste movies into documents as easily as you copy and paste graphics, and you can play a QuickTime movie wherever you encounter one in a document.

Compressed Images

QuickTime not only handles time-based and interactive media, but it also extends the Macintosh PICT graphics format, which is the standard graphics format in Mac OS 9 and earlier, to handle compressed still images and image previews. An application that recognizes QuickTime can compress a graphic image by using any QuickTime-compatible software or hardware compressor that is available on your computer. All applications that can open uncompressed PICT images are also capable of opening compressed PICT images. QuickTime automatically decompresses a compressed PICT image without requiring changes to the application program.

What's in a movie

The motion pictures, sound, and other types of time-based data in a QuickTime movie file exist in separate tracks. A simple movie may consist of one video track and one sound track. A more complex movie may have several video tracks, several audio tracks, and closed-caption text tracks for text subtitles. Each video track can be designed for playback with a specified number of available colors (for example, 256 colors, thousands of colors, or millions of colors), each audio track can provide dialog in a different language (English, Spanish, Japanese, and so on), and each closed-caption text track can provide subtitles in a different language.

If a QuickTime movie contains MIDI-synthesized music, sprites, or a QuickTime VR scene or object, then each item is in a separate track. QuickTime takes care of synchronizing all tracks so that they play at the proper time.

Getting QuickTime software

You get the basic QuickTime software as a part of the standard installation of Mac OS X. You can upgrade to QuickTime Pro, unleashing many additional editing features, for $29.95 by phone (1-888-295-0648) or from Apple's QuickTime site on the Web (www.apple.com/quicktime/). In some cases, you can get a free upgrade to QuickTime Pro when you purchase a retail version of the Mac OS or various software packages, such as Final Cut Pro.

Note   You can enter your QuickTime Pro registration information in the Registration sheet by choosing the QuickTime System Preferences and clicking the Registration button.

What's in QuickTime Pro?

What do you get when you purchase an upgrade from the basic edition of QuickTime to QuickTime Pro? The upgrade enables the PictureViewer Pro application to save still images (in BMP, JPEG, Photoshop, PICT, or QuickTime Image format). The upgrade similarly enables the QuickTime plug-in for Web browsers to save movies from the Web.

Moreover, the upgrade brings many improvements to the QuickTime Player application. Here's some of what QuickTime Player Pro can do that the basic QuickTime Player cannot:

✦ Create new movies

✦ Open a sequence of still images as a movie (a slide show)

✦ Import and export to and from a large number of additional video formats

✦ Export sound tracks to several additional sound formats

✦ Apply video and audio compression

✦ Edit movies by drag-and-drop editing and with Cut, Copy, and Paste commands

✦ Extract individual tracks from a movie

Continued

Continued

   ✦ Show and set the movie poster frame

   ✦ Present a movie centered on a black screen

   ✦ Play a movie at full-screen size

   ✦ Play a movie in a continuous loop

   ✦ Play only the selected part of a movie

   ✦ Adjust the size and orientation of each video track in the movie frame

   ✦ Show and set the following additional movie, video track, and sound track information

For more detailed information on the differences between QuickTime 6 and QuickTime Pro, visit Apple's QuickTime Pro Web site at `www.apple.com/quicktime/upgrade/`.

Playing QuickTime Movies

QuickTime makes it possible to play movies in all kinds of applications, and it establishes standard methods for controlling playback in all applications. You can use a standard QuickTime movie controller and other standard methods for controlling playback when the controller is absent. The QuickTime Player application included with QuickTime has additional features used to play movies. If you play movies that contain MIDI-synthesized music, you may be able to affect how they sound by setting some options in the QuickTime Settings control panel.

Using the QuickTime movie controller

You usually control playback of a QuickTime movie in an application other than QuickTime Player with a standard collection of buttons and sliders along the bottom edge of the movie. With this controller, you can play, stop, browse, or step through the movie. If the movie has a soundtrack, you can use the controller to adjust the sound level. The controller also gauges where the current scene is in relation to the beginning and end of the movie. By pressing certain keys while operating the controller, you can turn the sound on and off, copy and paste parts of the movie, play in reverse, change the playback rate, and more. Figure 20-1 illustrates the functions of a standard QuickTime movie controller for a music file. (Some applications have variants of the standard controller and may put the controller in a palette that floats above the document window.)

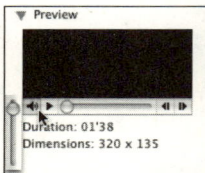

Figure 20-1: Use controls below a movie file to play, pause, browse, or step through it and adjust its sound volume.

Playing and pausing

To start a movie playing, click the Play button. This button has a right-pointing triangle like the play button on a tape recorder or VCR. While a movie is playing, this button becomes a pause button (with two vertical lines on it).

Stepping forward and backward

The two arrow buttons to the right of the play bar step backward and forward at the rate of one frame per click. The step buttons have different effects on movies that don't have frames. For example, in a movie that has only sound or music tracks, each click of a step button skips ahead or back a quarter of a second.

Going to another part of the movie

The gray play bar in the middle of the movie controller shows the position of the currently playing frame relative to the beginning and end of the movie. To go to a different place in the movie, you can drag the playhead in the play bar or simply click the play bar (at or near the location of the movie segment that you want to see).

You can also go immediately to the beginning or end of the movie. Option-click the backward-step button to go to the beginning of a movie. Option-click the forward-step button to go to the end of a movie.

Adjusting the sound

To adjust the sound level, use the button labeled with the speaker. Click and hold down this button to pop up a slider (shown in Figure 20-1) that you can use to raise or lower the sound level. You can turn the sound off and on by Option-clicking the speaker button. You can set the sound level to up to three times louder than its normal maximum by holding down Shift while adjusting the level with the slider. If the speaker button is absent, the movie has no sound.

Changing playback direction and speed

To play the movie backward, ⌘-click the backward-step button. In some applications, you can Control-click either step button to reveal a jog shuttle that controls the direction and play-back rate. Dragging the jog shuttle to the right gradually increases the forward playback rate from below normal to twice normal speed. Dragging the jog shuttle to the left has the same effect on playback speed, but makes the movie play backward.

QuickTime Controller Shortcuts

The QuickTime movie controller responds to all kinds of keyboard shortcuts. Pressing Return or Spacebar alternately starts and pauses play forward. Pressing ⌘-Period (.) also pauses playing. You can press ⌘-Right Arrow (→) to play forward and ⌘-Left Arrow (←) to play backward. Press the Right Arrow (→) to step forward and the Left Arrow (←) to step backward. To raise or lower the sound level, press the Up Arrow (↑) or the Down Arrow (↓). Shift-Up Arrow (↑) raises the sound level beyond its normal maximum.

Choosing a chapter

A text area appears to the left of the step buttons in the movie controller for some movies. This chapter list button lets you go to predetermined points in the movie, in the same way that index tabs let you turn to sections of a binder. Pressing the chapter list button pops up a menu of chapter titles and choosing a chapter title takes you quickly to the corresponding part of the movie. If the chapter list button is absent, either the movie window is too small to show the chapter list or the movie has no defined chapters.

Playing movies without controllers

Applications may display movies without controllers. In this case, a badge in the lower-left corner of the movie distinguishes it from a still graphic. To play a movie that has a badge and no controller, double-click the movie. If you press Shift while double-clicking the movie, it plays backward. Clicking a playing movie stops it. You can also display a standard movie controller by clicking the badge. Figure 20-2 shows a QuickTime movie with a badge.

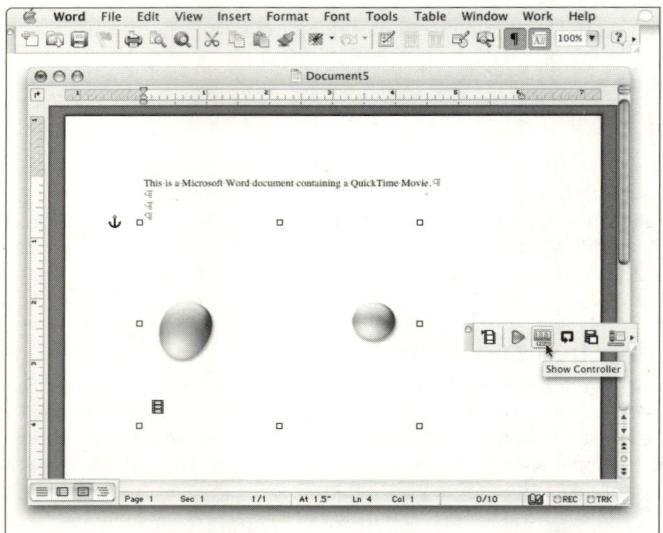

Figure 20-2: A badge identifies a movie without a controller, here seen in a Microsoft Word document.

Note   Badge is a term for a distinguishing mark superimposed on an icon or image to indicate that it isn't a standard icon or image—such as the little arrow to indicate an alias icon.

Viewing with QuickTime Player

Although you don't need a special application to view QuickTime movies, QuickTime includes one called QuickTime Player. With the QuickTime Player menu commands, you have more control than in some other applications over playing a movie. In some cases, however, you have less control over a movie. That's because the QuickTime Player application sports a sleek interface that has traded some features to look more like a consumer device. Some of the controls are more like those found on a VCR.

The controls of QuickTime Player are enhanced when you upgrade to QuickTime Pro. The following descriptions of QuickTime Player commands indicate the QuickTime Player versions in which the described command is available.

Using QuickTime Player controls

When you open a movie in the QuickTime Player application, you find a number of slight differences from the QuickTime controls found in other applications, as Figure 20-3 shows.

Figure 20-3: QuickTime Player has the controls for movie playback seen on most VCRs.

Most of the differences in QuickTime Player controls are cosmetic. The play bar and playhead are located above the play/pause and step controls, which are larger in QuickTime Player than in the QuickTime controller of other applications. QuickTime Player has separate controls for going to the start or end of the movie, and it has a button with the QuickTime logo for accessing QuickTime TV channels, which we discuss later in this chapter. QuickTime Player also displays some extra information, including the elapsed time display to the left of the play bar and the audio equalizer display to the left of the play bar. A few features are missing. For example, you can't ⌘-click the step buttons to bring up a shuttle jog control.

Tip   After clicking the QuickTime logo button to see QuickTime TV channels, you can return to the QuickTime movie that was previously displayed in the window by clicking the TV button again.

In addition to the clearly visible volume control, QuickTime Player has several hidden audio controls. To reveal the hidden controls — Balance, Bass, and Treble — choose Movie ➪ Show Sound Controls or simply click the audio equalizer at the right end of the play bar. See Figure 20-4.

Tip   You can change the volume quickly by clicking in the slider track instead of dragging the slider. For example, to set full volume, click at the right end of the slider track. When the Balance, Bass, and Treble controls are showing, you can drag the mouse over the settings instead of clicking the plus and minus buttons. To raise the sound level beyond its normal maximum, press Shift-Up Arrow (↑).

Figure 20-4: QuickTime Player has hidden audio controls.

Using QuickTime Player Favorites

QuickTime Player can keep track of your favorite movies to make playing them more convenient. You designate which movies are your Favorites, and then you can play one by choosing it from a menu or clicking an item in a list window as shown in Figure 20-5.

Figure 20-5: QuickTime Player can display your favorite movies in its Favorites list.

To see a list of your favorite movies in a window choose Favorites ➪ Show Favorites. The Favorites window is empty until you add movies as Favorites. To make a movie a Favorite, drag its movie file from the Finder to the Favorites window. You can drag several movie files at the same time to make Favorites of them all. You can make a Favorite of a movie that's open in QuickTime Player by bringing the movie to the front and choosing Favorites ➪ Add Movie As Favorite.

To play a favorite movie, click its icon in the Favorites window or choose it from the Favorites submenu.

You can rearrange the Favorites window by dragging icons to different positions in the window. You can remove a Favorite by Control-clicking its icon in the Favorites window and choosing Delete Favorite from the contextual menu that appears.

Using controls within movies

For the most part, you'll probably confine your mouse clicks to the QuickTime Player controls. Occasionally, you may find it useful to actually click inside the movie window. For example, QuickTime can display Macromedia Flash documents, which may include buttons and links that can be clicked in the movie window. If you're viewing an image (especially one that's available via a streaming QuickTime connection over the Internet), you may be able to click a button or link in the QuickTime Player movie window.

Changing the QuickTime Player window size

Unlike many other applications that can show QuickTime movies, the QuickTime Player application displays QuickTime movies in windows with resize controls. If you resize a movie window, QuickTime resizes the movie to fill the window. A resized movie generally plays less smoothly if you change its proportions. As a precautionary measure, QuickTime normally forces movie windows to maintain their original proportions. To resize without this constraint, press Shift while dragging the resize control.

A movie looks best at an even multiple of its original size, such as half-size or double size. QuickTime Player constrains a movie to an optimal multiple of its original size if you press Option while dragging the movie window's resize control. To quickly change a window to the nearest even multiple of its original size, Option-click its resize control.

In addition to dragging a movie window's size box, you can use QuickTime Player menu commands to resize it. The basic edition of QuickTime Player has Half Size, Double Size, and Normal Size commands.

Presenting a movie

Instead of displaying a movie in a window, you can present it centered on a completely black screen. In QuickTime Player Pro, choose Movie ➪ Present Movie (⌘-M). (The Present Movie command is not available in the basic edition of QuickTime Player.)

The Present Movie command displays a dialog in which you can set the movie size and specify whether you want to play the movie normally or in slide show fashion (one frame at a time, for example). If your computer has more than one display, this dialog lets you select the display on which you want the movie presented. Setting a movie's presentation size in this dialog to Double or Full Screen usually produces better results than resizing the movie manually before presenting it.

To stop a movie presentation, click the mouse button. With a slide show presentation, clicking the mouse button advances to the next movie frame; double-clicking goes back one frame. Pressing Esc or ⌘-period stops a slide show presentation.

Searching for a text track

While viewing a movie that contains a text track, you can search for specific text in the movie. In QuickTime Player Pro, choose Edit ➪ Find (⌘-F) — if there are no text tracks, Find is disabled (grayed-out). (Text searching is not available in the basic edition of QuickTime Player.)

The Find command displays a dialog in which you search forward or backward to find text. If QuickTime Player finds the text you're looking for, it immediately shows the corresponding part of the movie and highlights the found text. You can search for another occurrence of the same text by choosing Find Again from the Edit menu.

Choosing a language

QuickTime movies can have sound tracks in several languages. To select the language you want to hear, choose Movie ➪ Choose Language. QuickTime Player displays a dialog that lists the available languages. If the Choose Language command is disabled (grayed out), the movie doesn't have sound tracks in multiple languages.

Playing continuously (looping)

You can set QuickTime Player Pro to play a QuickTime movie in a continuous loop, either always playing forward or playing alternately forward and backward. Choose Loop or Loop Back and Forth from the Movie menu. (These commands are available in the basic edition of QuickTime Player.)

Selecting part of a movie and playing it

In QuickTime Player Pro, you can select part of a movie and then play only the selected part. (You can't select part of a movie in the basic edition of QuickTime Player.)

To select part of a movie while playing that part, follow these steps:

1. **Drag both of the selection triangles to the far-left edge of the play bar.**

2. **Move the playhead to the place in the movie where you want to begin selecting.**

3. **Shift-click the play button to start the movie and begin selecting the movie segment.**

4. **Release Shift to end the selection and stop playing.** The selected part of the movie appears gray in the play bar.

To select part of a movie without playing it, use these steps:

1. **Drag the left selection triangle to the first frame you'd like to select.**

2. **Drag the right selection triangle to the last frame you'd like to select.**

3. **Adjust the selection by doing either of the following:**

   - Drag a selection triangle.

   - Click a selection triangle; then use the Left (←) and Right (→) Arrow keys to adjust the selection frame by frame.

To play the selected part of a movie, follow these steps:

1. **Choose Movie ➪ Play Selection Only (⌘-T).**

2. **Click the Play button.** When a check mark is next to Play Selection Only in the Movie menu, all the movie controls and QuickTime Player commands apply only to the selected part. For example, the Loop command causes only the selected part to play continuously, and the first-frame and last-frame buttons go to the beginning and end of the selection.

To cancel a selection: Drag both selection arrows to the far-left side of the play bar.

Playing every frame

In QuickTime Player Pro, you can prevent QuickTime from dropping any video frames to keep the video and audio tracks synchronized. If you want to see every frame, even if it means playing the movie more slowly and without sound, choose Movie ➪ Play All Frames. (The Play All Frames command is not available in the basic edition of QuickTime Player and is disabled if there is no video track.)

Playing all movies

You can have QuickTime Player Pro play all movies that are currently open by choosing Movie ➪ Play All Movies. (This command is not available in the basic edition of QuickTime Player.)

Saving QuickTime Movies from a Web Browser

When you view a QuickTime movie in a Web browser window, the movie is downloaded from Internet but is not saved permanently on your hard drive. You may be able to save the movie from the Web browser as a movie file on your hard drive so that you can watch the movie again in QuickTime Player without downloading it again. You can save a QuickTime movie from a Web browser only if you have QuickTime Pro and only if the author of the movie allows saving the movie.

To save a QuickTime movie that's displayed in a Web browser, Control-click the movie and choose Save As QuickTime Movie from the contextual menu that appears. You can also make the contextual menu appear by clicking a movie in the browser window and holding the mouse button down for a few seconds. (The Save As QuickTime Movie choice does not appear in the contextual menu if you do not have QuickTime Pro or if the author of the movie does not allow saving the movie.)

Configuring and Updating QuickTime

QuickTime is highly configurable to suit your situation and use. This section will cover some of the settings you can adjust in QuickTime.

QuickTime System Preferences

Many settings are located in the QuickTime pane of System Preferences, shown with the Connection panel selected in Figure 20-6.

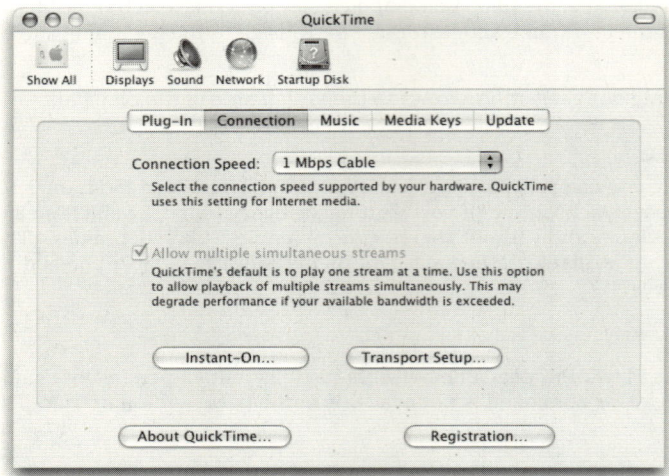

Figure 20-6: The QuickTime pane showing the Connection tab.

Set your system's connection speed with the pop-up menu so that QuickTime knows how fast to request data and at what rate to display the audio or video so as to avoid creating gaps while you wait for the next part of the data to download. If you have a fast connection, you may select the "Allow multiple simultaneous streams" checkbox, or click the Instant-On... button to shorten the wait at the beginning.

In the Plug-In tab, shown in Figure 20-7, the settings allow you to set the way QuickTime functions with your Web browser. You can use the checkboxes to choose whether or not to play a movie automatically, to save a movie in the Web browser's disk cache, and to enable kiosk mode, which reduces the amount of control someone has available. If you click on the MIME Settings button you see the MIME sheet shown in Figure 20-8. Here you can decide what media types the QuickTime browser plug-in will handle. Most people will want to stick with the default selections, which you can return to by clicking the Use Defaults button.

The Music panel allows you to assign the default QuickTime synthesizer or a different music synthesizer (if you have one) to play music and MIDI files.

The Media Keys panel lets you view an encrypted movie by entering the media key supplied by the creator.

Click the Update panel to view the information shown in Figure 20-9.

If you click the Update Now... button on the Update panel, QuickTime checks for new codecs and other QuickTime software. This QuickTime update feature is separate from the Software Update in System Preferences for OS X.

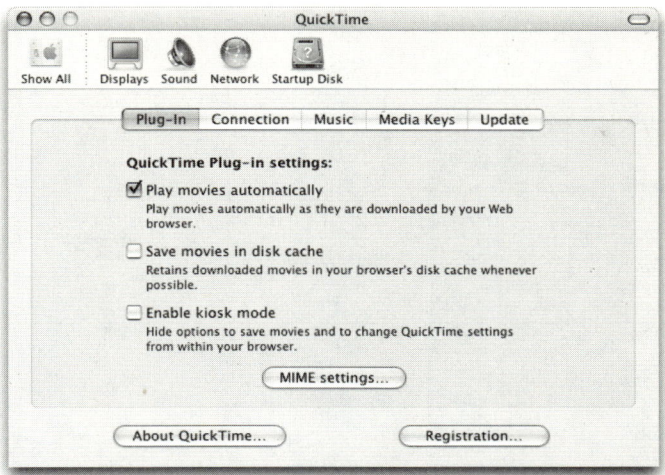

Figure 20-7: Use the Plug-In panel to alter QuickTime's behavior within a Web browser.

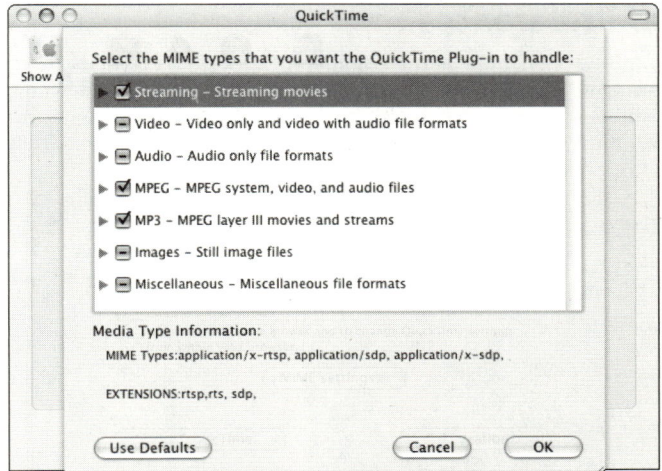

Figure 20-8: Choose the types of media formats QuickTime handles in a Web browser with the MIME sheet of the Plug-In panel.

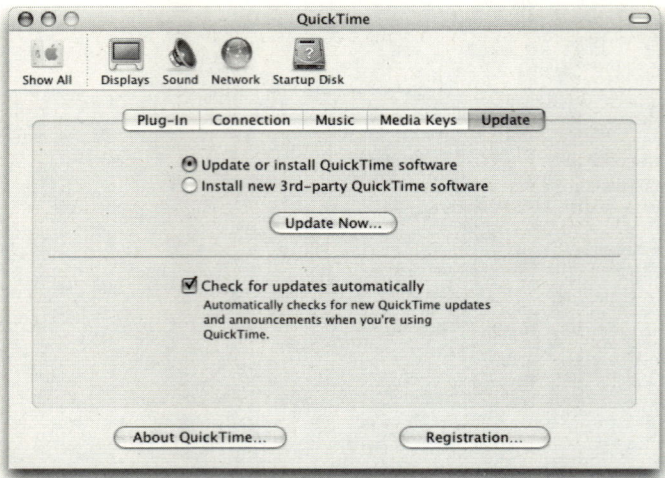

Figure 20-9: Use the Update panel to find and install new QuickTime components and applications.

QuickTime Player Preferences

With a QuickTime Player window open, choose the command QuickTime Player ➪ Preferences ➪ Player Preferences. Here you can alter the settings pertaining to the QuickTime Player for movies, sound, showing Apple's Hot Picks movie, and for pausing a movie when logged out in Fast User Switching. Again, the default settings will be best for most people. Figure 20-10 shows Player Preferences.

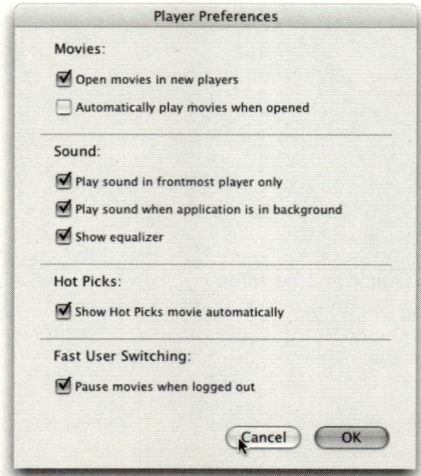

Figure 20-10: Set the behavior of the QuickTime Player application in Player Preferences.

Watching Streaming QuickTime Media

QuickTime 4.0 introduced a new technology to the world of QuickTime—*streaming media*. QuickTime 6, the version included with Mac OS X 10.3, has significantly improved the performance of streaming media. With streaming media, QuickTime movie files (whether they contain video, audio, text, or other elements) are sent over the Internet a piece at a time. Those pieces are reassembled in QuickTime Player and played back almost as quickly as the data arrives over the Internet. In this way, movies can be viewed (or listened to) more quickly over the Internet. Likewise, live events can be displayed in real time over the Web.

Tip   For optimum streaming, QuickTime Player consults the settings on the Connection tab in your QuickTime System Preferences. Make sure these settings match the speed of your connection so that you get better playback from streaming movies.

With some streaming media movies, you can pause, play, and move back and forth within the movie file by using the play bar or the forward and reverse controls. In others, especially live events, you won't have as much control—pausing and playing again takes you to the current moment in the live event instead of picking up where you left off.

QuickTime streaming media uses an Internet protocol known as RTP (real-time transport protocol). RTP is similar to the familiar HTTP protocol used for Web pages, but RTP is designed specifically for the special requirements of streaming media. With RTP, movies are not downloaded to your computer. Instead a continuous data stream is sent to your computer, and QuickTime plays it immediately.

QuickTime movies can also be sent to your computer via the HTTP or FTP protocols. With HTTP or FTP, the entire movie is downloaded to your computer. (If you don't have QuickTime Pro, the movie may be downloaded to a temporary file that is deleted automatically.) You don't necessarily have to wait for the entire movie to finish downloading before it begins playing. Many QuickTime movies use a technology called *fast start* or *progressive download*. In practice, fast-start movies may seem like streaming video. In fact, QuickTime begins playing the first part of the movie while it continues to download the remainder.

Interacting with QuickTime VR Images

You can do more with QuickTime than play linear movies. Apple's QuickTime VR software lets you explore places as if you were really there and examine objects as if they were with you. When you view a QuickTime VR panorama of a place, you can look up, look down, turn around, zoom in to see detail, and zoom out for a broader view. When you view a QuickTime VR object, you can manipulate it to see a different view of it. As you explore a panorama, you can move from it into a neighboring panorama or to an object in it. For example, you could move from one room to another room and then examine an object there.

You can interact with a QuickTime VR panorama or object from any application in which you can view a linear QuickTime movie. You can use QuickTime Player, a Web browser, TextEdit, AppleWorks, or any other application that can play QuickTime movies.

When you view a QuickTime VR panorama or object, a QuickTime VR controller sometimes appears at the bottom of the window. It's in the same place as the controller for a regular QuickTime movie (especially those viewed with the conventional controller in applications like AppleWorks). As with regular QuickTime movies, the QuickTime VR controller in QuickTime Player looks different than the VR controller in other applications. The cosmetic differences don't affect the functions of the controller buttons.

Actually, you don't use the QuickTime VR controller as the primary means of interacting with a QuickTime VR image. You simply drag the mouse pointer to explore a QuickTime VR panorama or investigate a QuickTime VR object. The remainder of this section describes how to use the mouse pointer and the VR controller to interact with a QuickTime VR image.

Exploring VR panoramas

To look around a QuickTime VR panorama, you click the picture and drag left, right, up, or down. The picture moves in the direction that you drag, and the pointer changes shape to indicate the direction of movement. Figure 20-11 shows a QuickTime VR panorama being moved to the left.

Figure 20-11: When you pan a QuickTime VR panorama, the pointer indicates the direction of movement.

Investigating VR objects

To manipulate a QuickTime VR object, you drag it left, right, up, or down. As you drag, the object, or some part of it, moves. For example, it may turn around so that you can see all sides of it, or it may open and close. The author of the VR picture determines the effect.

When viewing a QuickTime VR object, you can also place the pointer near an inside edge of the VR window and press the mouse button to move the object continuously. Figure 20-12 shows two views of QuickTime VR object.

Revealing the VR controller

When you view a QuickTime VR image in a Web browser window, the VR controller may not appear at the bottom of the image. If you have QuickTime Pro, you can view the VR image with a VR controller by saving the VR image as a QuickTime movie file on your hard drive and opening the movie file in QuickTime Player. The method for saving a VR image is the same as the method described earlier for saving a regular QuickTime movie. To recap: Control-click the movie or click the movie and hold the mouse button until the contextual menu appears, and choose Save As QuickTime Movie from the contextual menu. (The Save As QuickTime Movie choice does not appear in the contextual menu if you do not have QuickTime Pro or the author of the VR image does not allow saving it.)

 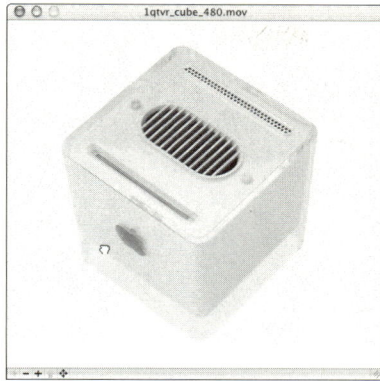

Figure 20-12: Drag a QuickTime VR object in any direction to see another view of the object.
(Images courtesy of John Greenleigh/Flipside Studios.)

Zooming in and out

While viewing a QuickTime VR panorama or object, you can zoom in or out.

✦ **To zoom in:** Click the VR controller button that looks like a plus sign or press the Control key.

✦ **To zoom out:** Click the button that looks like a minus sign or press the Shift key.

As you zoom in on a VR object, it eventually becomes too large to see all at once in the QuickTime VR window. You may be able to view another part of a zoomed-in VR object by clicking the controller button labeled with a four-way arrow and then dragging the object or by pressing Option while dragging. Either way, the object holds its pose as it moves around in the window. To resume normal operation, click the button again or release the Option key. (You don't need to use the four-way drag button or the Option key with a VR panorama, which you can pan just by dragging across it.)

Interacting with hot spots

A QuickTime VR panorama or object can contain hot spots. You click these areas of the picture to cause some action to occur. Typically, the action involves going to another panorama or object. A hot spot can trigger another kind of action, such as displaying text in the empty area of the VR controller or taking you to a Web page.

Hot spots are normally unmarked. One way to find them is to move the pointer around the panorama or object. When the pointer is over a hot spot, the pointer's shape changes. A variety of different pointer shapes may indicate a hot spot. One common shape is a large white arrow pointing up.

You can also have QuickTime VR show the hot spots in the picture. To highlight the hot spots with shaded rectangles, click the VR controller button labeled with an up arrow and question mark. If you double-click this button, it stays down and you can see all hot spots as you drag the pointer to move the picture. Figure 20-13 is an example of an outlined hot spot in a QuickTime VR panorama.

Figure 20-13: Hot spots are revealed in a QuickTime VR panorama (the highlighted area).

If clicking a hot spot takes you to another panorama or object, you can go back to your previous location by clicking the back button, which is labeled with a left arrow in the VR controller. If you've progressed through several hot spots, you can retrace your steps by clicking the back button repeatedly.

Making a QuickTime Slide Show

Telling a story or delivering a message through a sequence of pictures — as they say, a picture is worth a thousand words — is a very common use of computers. Major applications, such as Apple's Keynote or Microsoft's PowerPoint, are devoted to this task. Presenting slide shows from images on your disks is also a major feature of such applications as GraphicConverter and iView Multimedia.

QuickTime allows you to create slide shows from images on your disk, as well. However, QuickTime combines them into a platform-independent file that you can view on any computer with QuickTime support.

Of course, going to the effort of importing multiple image files, placing and orienting them just so, and then saving the result as a QuickTime file in PowerPoint seems like an awful lot of effort. QuickTime Pro makes the task a whole lot easier, as follows:

1. **Collect the image files you want in your slide show in a single folder.**

2. **Give them a common name followed by a sequential number.**

3. **In QuickTime Player, choose File ⇨ Open Image Sequence and select the first file in your sequence of pictures.**

4. **Choose a Frame rate in the Image Sequence Settings dialog that appears.** The default of 15 frames per second is useful for animations, but you will probably want something a bit slower for a slide show.

QuickTime Player Pro then creates a movie, showing each picture in sequence. If you want to save this QuickTime movie, choose File ⇨ Save As and then name the movie in the Save dialog that appears. The default radio button selection, Save normally (allowing dependencies), requires you to transport the folder of images along with the QuickTime movie.

Tip   We recommend, unless you're always going to show the slide show from the machine on which you created it, that you make the movie self-contained to avoid having a piece or pieces missing when you make your presentation.

Tip   If the audio sequence is longer than your slide show, its play is sped up to fit the length of your show; conversely, if it is shorter than your slide show, the clip is slowed down to fit the slide show's length. You should choose a clip as close in length to that of your slide show as possible. You can find the length required by choosing Movie ➪ Get Movie Properties (⌘-J) and choosing Time from the right-hand pop-up menu.

Basic QuickTime Movie Editing

As is usually the case if you want to use QuickTime for much more than a viewer, editing your QuickTime movies and tracks requires an update to QuickTime Pro. One of the first changes you may notice if you've upgraded to QuickTime Pro is that the play bar has two markers at the bottom — you use these to mark the beginning and end of a selection. Another change is that the Edit menu has added a slew of extra options, including the ability to Delete Tracks, Extract Tracks, and more. The Movie menu has added a Present Movie option so that you can have your QuickTime movie take over the whole screen.

The selection markers and additional Edit menu options give you the tools to do a significant amount of editing — either to create a new movie or to modify an existing movie. With these options you can add, eliminate, and rearrange scenes and then save the movie under the same or a new name.

Fine-tuning a selection

Of course, you can drag the selection triangles to the point where you want them. However, this sort of gross movement tends to make positioning on a particular frame of your movie somewhat difficult. Use the drag technique to get the triangle into the general vicinity of the frame, then click a selection triangle and press the Left- or Right-Arrow keys to move the selection triangle one frame in that direction or hold down the appropriate arrow key to move the selection triangle in that direction in slow motion.

Working with selections

After you've made your selection, you can play just the selection by choosing Movie ➪ Play Selection Only (⌘-T). You can even drag the picture from the movie screen to the Desktop or a Finder window to create a movie clipping — just double-click it to view the clip.

You can cut, copy, or clear the contents of a selection using the corresponding Edit menu commands or trim everything but the selection from the movie by choosing Edit ➪ Trim.

To paste a cut or copied selection in another location within your movie (or even in a different movie), position the playhead where you want the insertion to occur and choose Edit ➪ Paste (⌘-V). The pasted information appears, and the selection markers show you where it begins and ends.

Tip   A quick way to add a title or silent-movie style text block is to paste text in at the current frame. This inserts a two-second block of white text against a black background — QuickTime makes use of any font and style information that was with the text on the clipboard. This also works to insert still pictures. You can even drag text files directly to the QuickTime Player screen to get the two-second inserts.

These editing techniques work with all editable QuickTime movies — even sound files such as AIFF.

Note   Some media types, such as MPEG-1 files, which are playable in QuickTime Player, are not editable with these tools. If the movie is in one of these non-editable formats, all the Edit menu choices are disabled.

Adding a Sound Track to Your Movie

By using QuickTime Player Pro's editing capabilities, you can add an audio (sound) track to your movie before saving it. Import the audio file to a new movie and copy the desired portion (or all of it) to the Clipboard. Now, select the slide show movie and choose Edit ⇨ Add Scaled.

Adding QuickTime Text Tracks

QuickTime lets you include multiple tracks in a single movie. One of these track types is the *text track*. Text can be used for credits, subtitles, title screens, or teleprompter text.

You can create text tracks very easily in any word-processor or editor that allows you to save as plain text (sometimes called *ASCII* text). If you use TextEdit, be sure to choose Format ⇨ Make Plain Text (⌘-Shift-T). To create a text track, follow these steps:

1. **Create and save your plain text file.**

2. **Copy the text to the Clipboard.**

3. **In QuickTime Player Pro, position the playhead where you want the track to begin.**

4. **Choose Edit ⇨ Add (⌘-Option-V) to position the text file at that point, overlaying the image.** The default duration for a text track inserted in this manner is two seconds. If you want a different duration, make a selection covering the duration and choose Edit ⇨ Add Scaled (⌘-Option-V). The text track is added with each paragraph of your text file covering its own sequence of frames.

Occasionally, you might want something other than white text on a black background. You might want different colors to better coordinate with the movie frames. To adjust the text color, proceed as follows:

1. **Choose Movie ⇨ Get Movie Properties (⌘-J) to open the Properties window for your movie.**

2. **From the pop-up menu on the left, choose the text track.**

3. **From the pop-up menu on the right, choose Graphics Mode.**

Applying QuickTime Effects

Concealed in the Export dialog (File ➪ Export, ⌘-E), QuickTime Pro includes a number of *filters* (special effects) that you can apply to your movie. You find these filters by first setting the Export dialog's Export pop-up menu to Movie to QuickTime Movie, next clicking the Options button in the Export dialog and then click the Filter button in the Movie Settings dialog that appears. See Figure 20-14 for the Movie Settings dialog and Figure 20-15 for the Choose Video Filter dialog.

QuickTime Pro even enables you to save filter settings for later use via the Save and Load buttons in the Choose Video Filter dialog. Unfortunately, you can only apply one filter to a movie on export. Therefore, if you want to accumulate effects, you need to export with one effect, load that movie, and apply another effect when exporting it, and so on—cumbersome, but possible.

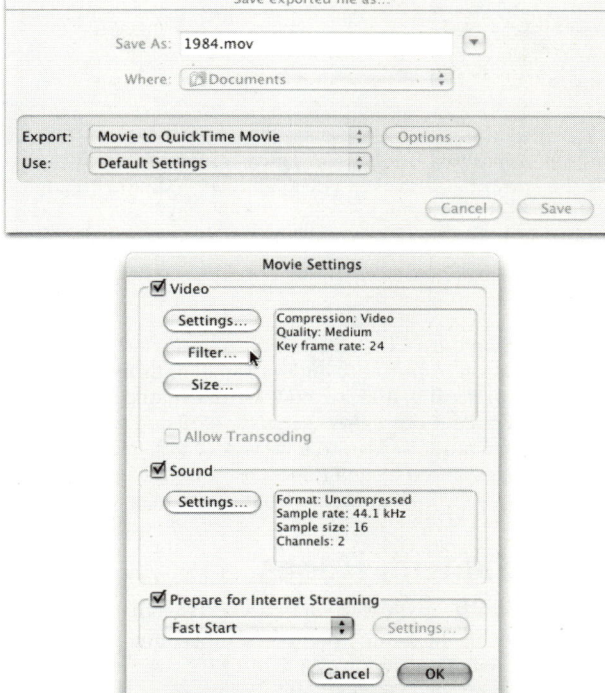

Figure 20-14: The QuickTime Export Movie Settings dialog allows you to apply video special effects to a movie as you export it.

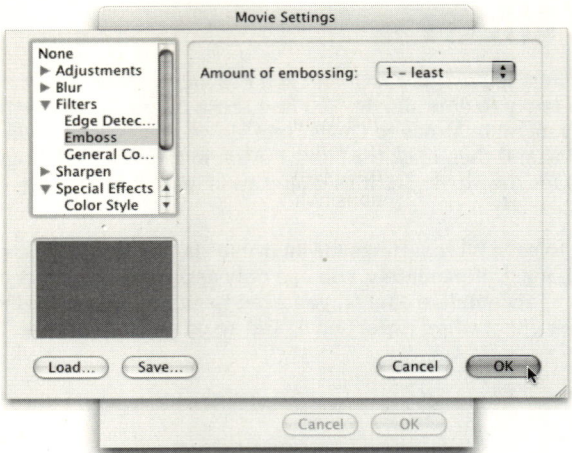

Figure 20-15: The Filters dialog lets you choose and preview filters for your movie.

The available filters (13 of them) let you adjust brightness, color, and contrast; apply blurs or sharpen, add film noise (simulating scratches and dust) or a lens flare (similar to what happens when you have the sun in front of the lens).

iTunes

The free iTunes application enables you to burn CDs, which makes purchasing third-party software tools less necessary if all you want to burn are audio CDs. In addition to *ripping* (recording audio CDs and encoding them in MP3, AIFF, or WAV format) audio from CDs, iTunes also writes audio CDs from MP3 collections called *playlists,* by using a compatible CD-RW drive. Additionally, you can download MP3 files to a variety of MP3 players, such as the Nomad and the Rio and play streaming audio from a huge assortment of Internet radio stations. You can also purchase songs in AAC format online from the iTunes Music Store.

Playing MP3 and CD audio with iTunes

The iTunes window, as shown in Figure 20-16, is divided into panes. The tall, slender pane on the left of the window is the *Source* pane. In the Source pane, you determine from where you select your audio. You can make audio selections from your iTunes Library, Internet radio, a mounted audio CD, a connected MP3 player, or a playlist.

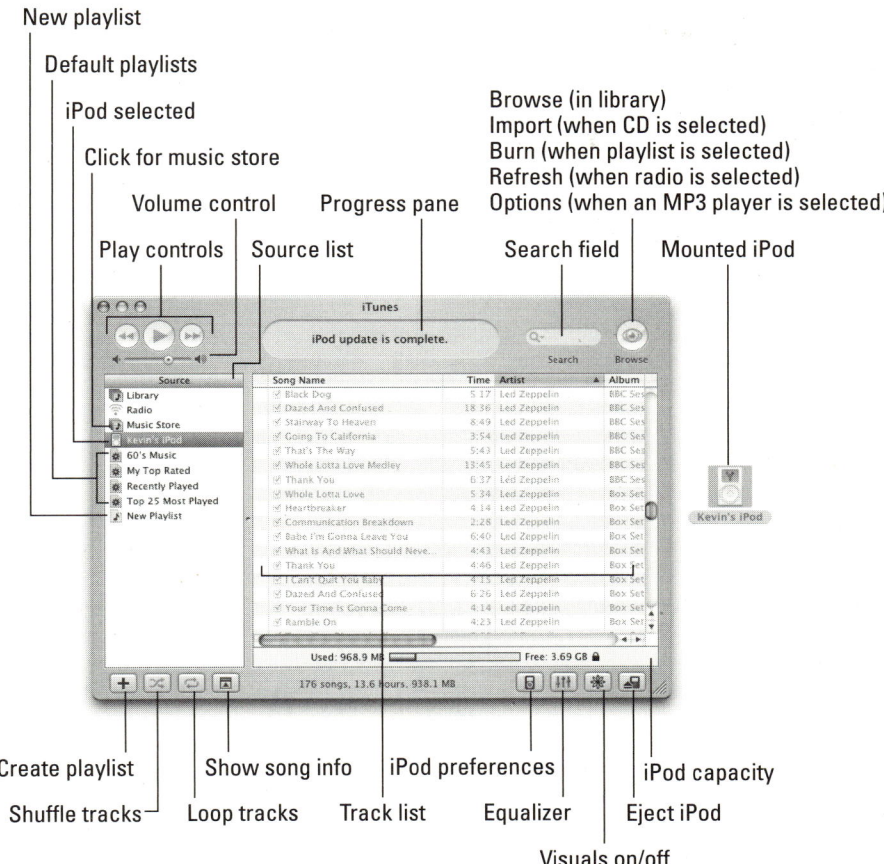

New playlist

Default playlists

iPod selected

Click for music store

Browse (in library)
Import (when CD is selected)
Burn (when playlist is selected)
Refresh (when radio is selected)
Options (when an MP3 player is selected)

Volume control   Progress pane

Play controls   Source list   Search field   Mounted iPod

Create playlist   Show song info   iPod preferences   iPod capacity

Shuffle tracks   Loop tracks   Track list   Equalizer   Eject iPod

Visuals on/off

Figure 20-16: The iTunes interface.

Playing songs

To play songs, you can do the following:

✦ Double-click the song.

✦ Select the song and press Return or Enter.

✦ Select the song and click the Play button.

You can also move between adjacent songs by using one of the following methods:

✦ Press ⌘-← (previous song) and ⌘-→ (next song).

✦ Choose Controls ⇨ Previous Song or Controls ⇨ Next Song.

When a song is playing, iTunes displays your choice of a progress bar or equalizer display. The progress bar is shown in Figure 20-17—you can position or reposition playing to any point in a song by dragging the progress bar playhead (the diamond) to the desired location. To view the equalizer display in this area, all you need to do is click the little arrowhead to which the arrow pointer is pointing in the figure.

Figure 20-17: The iTunes progress bar lets you position the playhead anywhere within a song, if you only wish to listen to a part of the tune, or if you wish to replay a passage.

In Figure 20-17, you see the song title displayed at the top of the progress area. Click this line of text to switch between song title, artist, and album name. Over time, this information automatically cycles between the three possibilities.

Note iTunes takes title, artist, and album information from what are called ID3 tags—textual information stored within an MP3 file. A number of other fields are also described by ID3 tags, which are discussed later in this chapter.

Below the title-artist-album line is the timeline, which you can also click, switching between Total Time, Elapsed Time, and Remaining Time.

The equalizer display gives you a light show depicting what is happening on the two output channels (left and right speakers). If you hear an imbalance in the sound, you can utilize it to see if your problem is because of one of your speakers or if the recording is unbalanced. You can adjust the equalization with the Equalizer window. The button to display the Equalizer is shown in Figure 20-16. Clicking the Equalizer button shows the Equalizer window shown in Figure 20-18. Clicking the pop-up menu shows a wide range of preset equalization options.

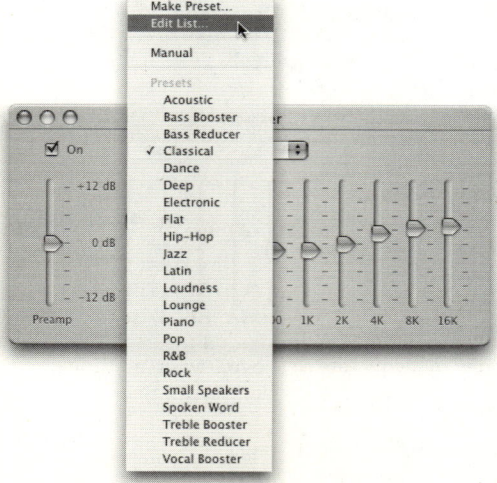

Figure 20-18: The iTunes Equalizer window adjusts balance of audio ranges.

Tip

Clicking the iTunes window zoom button (+) reduces the window to just the controls at the top left and the progress area. Further, the buttons are now positioned vertically at the left edge of the window with close (X) on top, minimize to dock (−) in the middle, and zoom (+) on the bottom. Clicking zoom again pops you back to the original size, which is an easy way to keep the window around in an unobtrusive manner.

Managing your iTunes Library

The *iTunes Library* is the collection of all the MP3 songs you've played in iTunes (less those you've deleted from the iTunes Library), plus all those you've added using File ➪ Add to iTunes Library or by using the Import button when a CD is selected. The iTunes feature adds the song to your iTunes Library whether you've double-clicked an MP3 file on your Desktop or in a Finder window or imported it from an audio CD. If you look in your home folder's Documents folder, you see an iTunes folder. This folder contains a database file, which keeps information on the 32,000 songs that iTunes can handle. This iTunes folder also contains an iTunes Music folder, and inside it are more folders that contain the songs in your iTunes Library. The folders inside the iTunes Music folder are named for performers, and each performer's folder contains folders with the names of album titles.

If you download MP3 files from the Internet, you can add them to your iTunes Library by performing the following steps:

1. **Choose File ➪ Add to Library.**

2. **Locate the item (folder or file) you want to add.**

3. **Click the Choose button.**

Listening to Internet Radio

iTunes supports an ever-changing and growing list of Internet radio stations, divided into categories. Just click the disclosure triangle next to the genre of interest and then select the radio station of interest. You need to have an active Internet connection first as iTunes doesn't make one for you. Of course, if you have an always-on broadband connection, such as a T1, DSL, or cable modem connection, remembering to make an Internet connection isn't a problem. (Chapter 6 explains how to make an Internet connection.)

Tip

Select stations where the Bit Rate field is lower than your connection speed. For example, if your modem cannot actually get a 56K connection, then you should avoid 56kbps streams.

Downloading to digital MP3 players

Digital MP3 players are well supported by iTunes. As long as your MP3 player is on the list of supported devices (see Apple's iTunes Web page because this list grows constantly), you can hook it up by using the supplied USB cable and have it show up in your source list. Select your MP3 player in the source list and see its contents, from which you can delete or add items. Adding items to your MP3 player is very simple — just select the songs you want to add from the iTunes Library or a playlist and then drag the songs to the MP3 player in the source list. You cannot play items on the MP3 player in iTunes or move items from the MP3 player to iTunes.

Using Apple's iPod MP3 player

The iPod MP3 player is tightly integrated with iTunes. If an iPod is connected to a Firewire-equipped Macintosh and the iPod is selected in the Source list of iTunes, an iPod window appears, as shown in Figure 20-19, and the Eject button becomes an Eject iPod button. Clicking the iPod button displays the iPod Preferences window, shown in Figure 20-19.

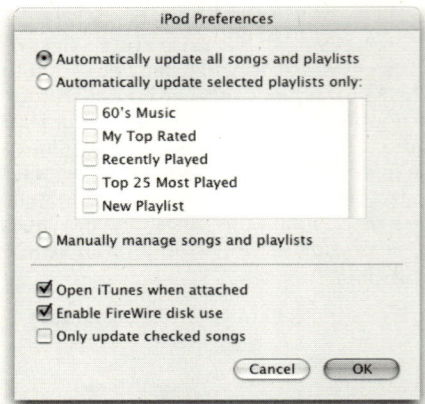

Figure 20-19: Use the iPod Preferences window to change how iTunes and an iPod work together.

Making use of playlists

The playlist is a powerful and useful feature in iTunes. A *playlist* is like a folder containing aliases to your audio songs. You can create a playlist by clicking the "Create a playlist" button (the plus sign button in Figure 20-16 shown earlier) and then naming it in the source list. Playlists let you group songs that you like to hear together and put them in the order you want to hear them. Just select them from the iTunes Library and drag them to the playlist group in the source list.

Note   An alternate and often easier method of creating a playlist involves selecting the songs in the iTunes Library list and choosing File ➪ New Playlist from Selection (⌘-Shift-N). iTunes creates a new playlist entry with the name selected for your editing pleasure. When you then select the playlist, the selected songs are displayed in the song list window. Doing this is a great way to create a playlist containing songs by a particular artist.

Clicking the Shuffle button, the Playlist button with the crossed arrows, you can randomize the order of items in a playlist. Clicking it again reverts you to the original order. You can also click the Repeat button to *loop* a playlist.

You can also work with subsets of a playlist without creating a new playlist just by deselecting the boxes next to the names of the songs you don't want played.

If you want your playlist to open in its own window, just double-click the playlist's icon. To delete a playlist, for example after burning your own CD of it (see the next topic), just click the playlist's icon to select it and press Delete or choose Edit ➪ Clear.

Smart Playlists are a new feature of iTunes in version 3 and up. With Smart Playlists, you can have iTunes automatically create and update playlists as you add and remove music from your iTunes Library.

Recording your own audio CDs

Possibly the most useful feature of a playlist is that it, combined with a compatible CD-RW drive, lets you write audio CDs suitable for use in most standard CD players. Just create your playlist by dragging the songs into the order you want them to appear, checking the time at the bottom of the window to make sure that your material fits on a CD (usually either 74 minutes or 80 minutes), and clicking the Burn CD aperture in the upper-right corner of the window. iTunes asks you to insert a recordable CD into your CD burner and then to click the Burn CD button. At that point, just sit back and relax while iTunes creates your CD. You can listen to music while iTunes burns the CD. The burning process is shown in Figure 20-20.

Figure 20-20: iTunes creates audio CDs for you from your MP3 playlists, if you have a compatible CD burner.

Note   You can set iTunes to automatically start whenever a blank CD or DVD is inserted into the drive with the CDs and DVDs pane of System Preferences, covered in Chapter 13.

Although you can record to a CD-R or a CD-RW and have no difficulties reading the disc on your computer, your experiences using such discs in commercial audio CD players can vary widely. Many standard CD players, especially those made more than three or four years ago, have problems reading CD-R media. Even more have difficulty with CD-RW media. The reasons for these difficulties are rooted in the methods used to record the data on the different media. Standard CDs have physical pits in an aluminum (or other metallic) surface, below the transparent layer encasing the metallic disc. A player's laser detects those deviations in the surface to read the stored data. A CD-R emulates this pitting with charged layers of a photosensitive dye. A CD-RW emulates this pitting with a chemical compound, which crystallizes when heated to the correct temperature, but returns to its liquid state when heated even more and then allowed to cool. In any event, the lasers in many older CD players do not operate at a wavelength that allows them to read CD-R or CD-RW media. Before purchasing a CD player, check to see whether its specifications are CD-R compatible.

Blank CD-R media typically has two sizes listed — one in minutes and one in megabytes. The two most common sizes are 74 min/640 MB and 80 min/700 MB. When you're recording audio to a CD, only look at the time figure. The megabytes figure refers to data CDs.

Note   Another type of CD player can play both audio CDs and what are called MP3 CDs. These MP3 CDs are actually data discs, which are written in a format known as ISO 9660 and can contain literally hundreds of MP3 files. iTunes can create these CDs, but not all CD players will play them. You can play them on your Macintosh computer. You may also archive music to DVDs with iTunes if you have a DVD burner such as Apple's SuperDrive.

Working with iTunes song and album information

The iTunes window (refer to Figure 20-16) has a large pane dedicated to displaying information about the songs in the currently selected source — playlist, audio CD, MP3 player, or iTunes Library. By choosing Edit ➪ View Options, you can control which of the 13 tag fields defined in the ID3 standard are displayed.

With the exception of the song field, which iTunes keeps on the left, you can rearrange the order of the other columns by dragging a column header over another column header. The column with the dark header is the column by which the display is sorted. The small arrow at the right of the selected column header indicates whether it is an ascending (A–Z) or descending (Z–A) sort, and you can reverse the order by clicking the header.

Looking up album information

The *i* in iTunes stands for the Internet. Not only can it stream radio from the Internet, but it can make use of the CDDB (Compact Disc Data Base) at www.gracenote.com to look up information about your CDs, retrieve song names, album title, artist information, and other pertinent information.

If you select the Connect To Internet When Needed box in your iTunes Preferences (on the General tab), iTunes automatically connects to the Internet when you insert an audio CD. If you want iTunes to check manually, choose Advanced ➪ Get CD Track Names.

Note   The information in the CDDB has been submitted by various people and sometimes more than one person submits album information for a CD, resulting in slightly different entries (spelling differences and the like) for the same CD. CDs are recognized by the number of songs and the respective lengths of those songs. Thus, if two different CDs have the same number of songs and each corresponding song is the same length, you may have to choose the appropriate entry. The CDDB is a useful tool, but it isn't infallible.

Entering song information manually

You can enter or edit song information manually by using in-place editing or a dialog for songs that are on your hard disk. You can even edit song information for songs on CD-ROMs and other locked sources. iTunes holds the information you enter in its database, overriding any information previously obtained from the Internet. Naturally, iTunes can't change the song information on the CD-ROM or other locked source itself. You may have some songs stored in locations that prevent you from editing their information. Songs on noneditable media, such as CD-ROMs, are not editable in this way because iTunes cannot write the information back to the read-only media. For example, you can't edit the information of songs that are located in a folder to which you have read-only access, such as the Public folder of someone else's home folder.

In-place editing is a straightforward Macintosh editing operation. Just click to select the record; then click in the text field to select it and start typing. To avoid the typing hassle, you can select a song and choose File ➪ Get Info (⌘-I) to display the Song Information panel, as shown in Figure 20-21. You can navigate to adjacent songs by using the Prev Song and Next Song buttons.

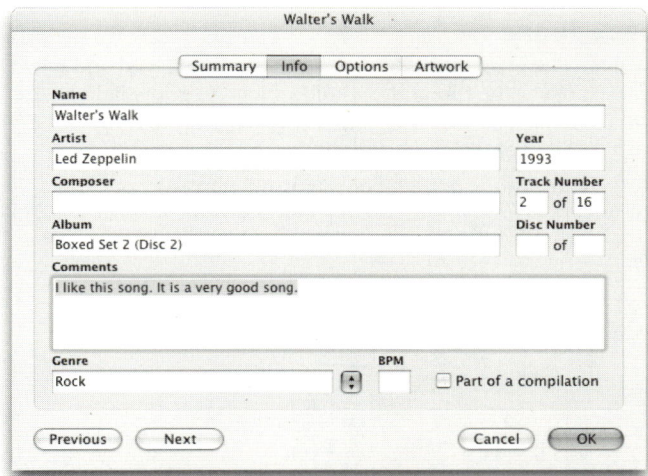

Figure 20-21: Use the iTunes Get Info window's Info panel to enter information about a song.

Watching iTunes visual effects

If you find the iTunes song lists boring while you're listening to your favorite tunes or a book on disk, you can replace the window's contents with iTunes Visual Effects.

You start and stop the show by clicking the Visuals On/Off button, which is located in the lower-right corner of the iTunes window (review Figure 20-16). Alternatively, you can choose Visuals ➪ Turn Visual On or Visuals ➪ Turn Visual Off (⌘-T). You can also use the Visuals menu to set the size of the visual effects show. Three sizes are available for show within the iTunes window (Small, Medium, and Large) as well as a Full Screen (⌘-F) mode.

Special iTunes Symbols

iTunes employs some graphic symbols for specific purposes. The following table describes the ones you're most likely to encounter and gives a description of what they mean.

Moving waveform	Indicates the song is being currently being imported
Circled exclamation point	Indicates the song can't be located
Speaker	Indicates the song being played

Pressing the I key while the effects are on displays information about the song, which gradually fades out. Pressing the ? key presents a list of some of the key options. This list is not comprehensive — maybe that's why it's called *Basic* Visualizer Help. Some other keys that affect the Visualizer are Q, W, A, S, Z, and X — all of which switch among the effects being used. The first two cycle forward and backward through the lists of first effects, the next two through the list of secondary effects, and the last two through the list of tertiary effects.

Searching your iTunes Library

As we described earlier, you have control over which columns are displayed and how the song list is sorted. The Search area at the top of the window (seen previously in Figure 20-16) acts as a filter. Any text you enter there limits the songs presented in the song list area to those that contain the text in one of the displayed columns.

When the iTunes Library is selected in the Source pane, a Browse button appears in the upper-right corner of the iTunes window (where the Burn button is for a Playlist). Clicking the Browse button reveals extra filtering control lists, as shown in Figure 20-22.

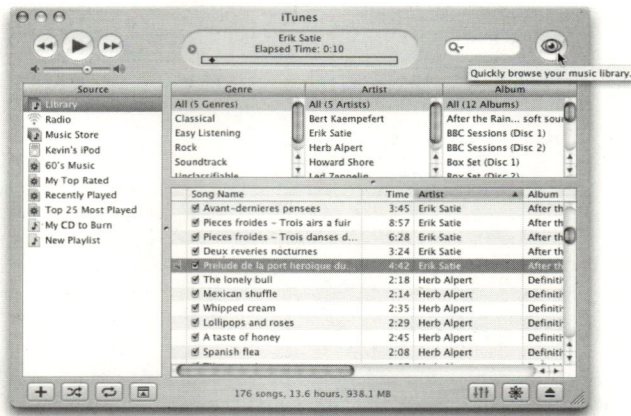

Figure 20-22: Click the Browse button to filter by genre, artist, or album.

Note For the Genre column to appear, you must select the Show Genre When Browsing checkbox on the iTunes Preferences General tab.

Making a choice in one list restricts the choices to only those for the given selection in lists to the right. For example, selecting Comedy under Genre narrows the choices in Artist to only those artists who have songs with Comedy in the Genre tag field. If you select an artist, only the albums for that artist are listed in the Albums column. For this reason, filling in the ID3 Tags is very important if you want to browse your iTunes Library effectively. Only the genres, artists, and albums you have in your iTunes database appear in the various lists. We discuss ID3 tags in more detail shortly.

Removing songs from your iTunes Library

Removing a song from your iTunes Library is simplicity itself. All you need to do is select the song in the Library's song list and press the Delete or Clear key. Doing so does not remove the song from your disk, though.

If you want to remove the song from both the disk and the Library, the easiest method is to perform the following:

1. **Select the song in the Library's song list.**

2. **Control-click it and choose Show Song File from the contextual menu to display the file in a Finder window.**

3. **Now, just drag the file into the Trash (⌘-Delete).**

4. **Return to iTunes and press the Delete key with the song highlighted.**

Managing ID3 tags

Songs you download from the Internet may appear in iTunes with incorrect or unreadable titles and other information. This can be due to the file having been created with a program that stores song information differently than iTunes. Song information is stored in MP3 files in what is called ID3 tags, and you may be able to convert them into a version iTunes can use.

If no tag data exists, as is all-too-often the case with music obtained over the Internet, iTunes displays the file name in place of the title information and the other fields are blank. Enter the song information manually, as described earlier in this chapter.

The ID3 Tag format has gone through a number of versions, and each is slightly different from its predecessors. iTunes can convert the data format between the different versions of ID3 when you select songs and choose Advanced ➪ Convert ID3 Tags. If you're going to exchange MP3 files with Windows users, you should be aware that many of the Windows users are using MP3 player software that does not handle ID3 Version 2 tags well, and you may want to convert to an appropriate Version 1 variant.

The iTunes Music Store

Once upon a time, you had to buy music on the media it was encoded on: player piano rolls, then phonograph records, then tapes, then compact discs. And then along came MP3 and a little outfit called Napster. There was an instant explosion of trading of MP3s via the Internet, which made the record companies very, very angry. But no one seemed to know what to do. Except Apple.

And so it came to pass that in April of 2003 Apple introduced the iTunes Music Store, and sold over one million songs in the first week — and that was only to Mac users, for no others could access the iTunes Music Store. Suddenly, it was easy, legal, and affordable to download and use digital music files. There was a revolution in the way people thought about music distribution — again. Soon there were several sites selling music on the Internet in emulation of the iTunes Music Store. But none of them were as successful. Still, said the critics, Mac users are just 3 percent of computer users — small potatoes.

Then in October of 2003, Apple announced that Windows users could now access the iTunes Music store via iTunes 4.1 and QuickTime 6.4 for Windows. Soon the 25 million members of America Online would gain access to the iTunes Music Store. And so it seemed that the iTunes Music Store was poised to conquer the online music selling business. A real fairy tale!

Figure 20-23 shows the home page of the iTunes Music Store.

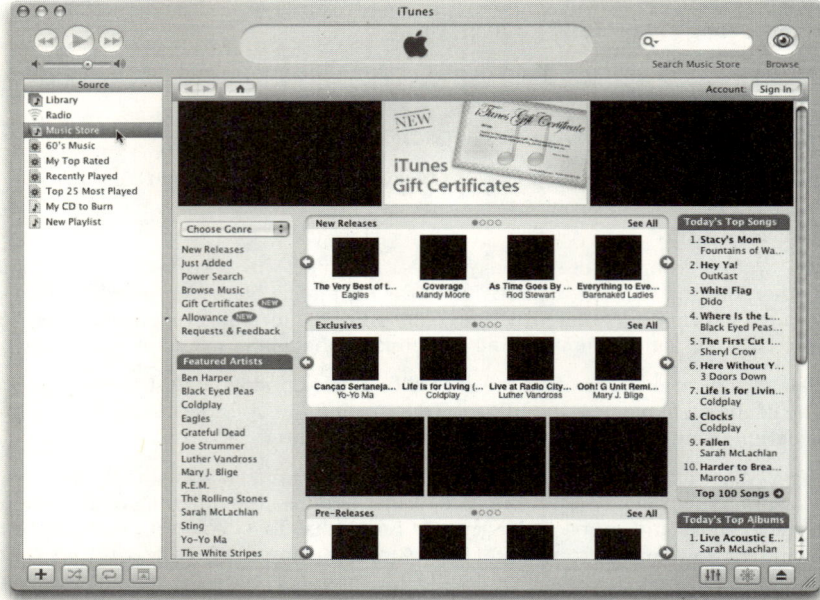

Figure 20-23: Visit the iTunes Music Store.

If you have iTunes and an Internet connection, and you are not one of those people who doesn't like music, you would be doing yourself a grave disservice to not visit the iTunes Music Store and at least browse around.

To visit the Music Store, in iTunes, simply click on Music Store in the Source list. There you will find over 200,000 songs from virtually every category of music, from the five major U.S. labels, and over 200 independent labels, and getting larger every day.

The music is encoded in a format called AAC (for Advanced Audio Coding). The AAC format is part of the MPEG-4 specification, and it features more efficient compression and better quality than MP3 format. In fact, the quality of AAC encoding rivals that of uncompressed CD audio. If you have iTunes 4 and QuickTime 6.2 or higher, you are in.

If you are sick of most of the popular offerings of the large labels, you are not alone. The iTunes Music Store offers music from independent labels that is not available elsewhere online, and is virtually impossible to find anywhere offline. You will also find exclusive tracks from major artists that are available only through the Music Store.

You can spend endless hours browsing to your hearts content, or zero in quickly if you know what you want. There are simple search and Power Search options. Editorial write-ups, reviews, and lists of recommendations can guide you, as well as playlists picked by celebrities. And all from the comfort of your own home, or wherever you have a computer connected to the Internet.

And there is not just music. A large library of audiobooks — more than 5,000 titles — is available. There are also episodes of a variety of interesting radio shows.

At the Music Store, you can preview for free whatever you are interested in, then buy a song or an album with a single click. Songs cost 99 cents each. You can listen to your purchase as soon as it downloads — instant gratification. After you buy the audio, you own it — no monthly fees or tricky rules to follow. You can burn songs onto an unlimited number of CDs. You can use your audio on up to 3 different computers at once. You can also use iTunes to share music with Macs and PCs on a local area network. Allowance accounts can be set up for kids, and gift certificates are available.

iPhoto 2

Mac OS X includes iPhoto, an application for organizing and sharing your digital photo collection. Like iTunes, iPhoto is a kind of database application with lots of bells and whistles to help you use and manipulate the data — in this case, digital images.

What follows is a brief overview of iPhoto's features, including basic hints of how to use it. Figure 20-24 shows the iPhoto 2 interface.

iPhoto 2 gives you the following capabilities:

✦ Import images from a digital camera with a USB connection, or from the camera's memory card reader via USB. You can set iPhoto to open automatically as soon as you connect the camera. Click the Import button to start the process.

✦ Import photos stored on a CD or a hard disk by simply dragging them to iPhoto's main window.

✦ Organize the imported pictures via thumbnail versions which appear in iPhoto's main window, the Library. You can keep track of thousands of images, limited only by the storage space on your drive and your RAM memory. Each "film roll" in the list on the left of the window symbolizes a separate import batch; the time and date of the import are recorded automatically and displayed in the lower-left corner of the window. You can create albums in the list on the left by clicking the plus sign button below, naming the album, and dragging to it the photos you wish it to contain. You can add new titles, alter dates, type comments, and include keywords to making searching easier. View the images at different sizes by moving the Size slider. Double-click an image to see it fill the whole main window.

✦ Search for the photos by a keyword, or text in a file name, title, or comment.

Info section

Albums

Album list

Main window showing thumbnails

Mode buttons

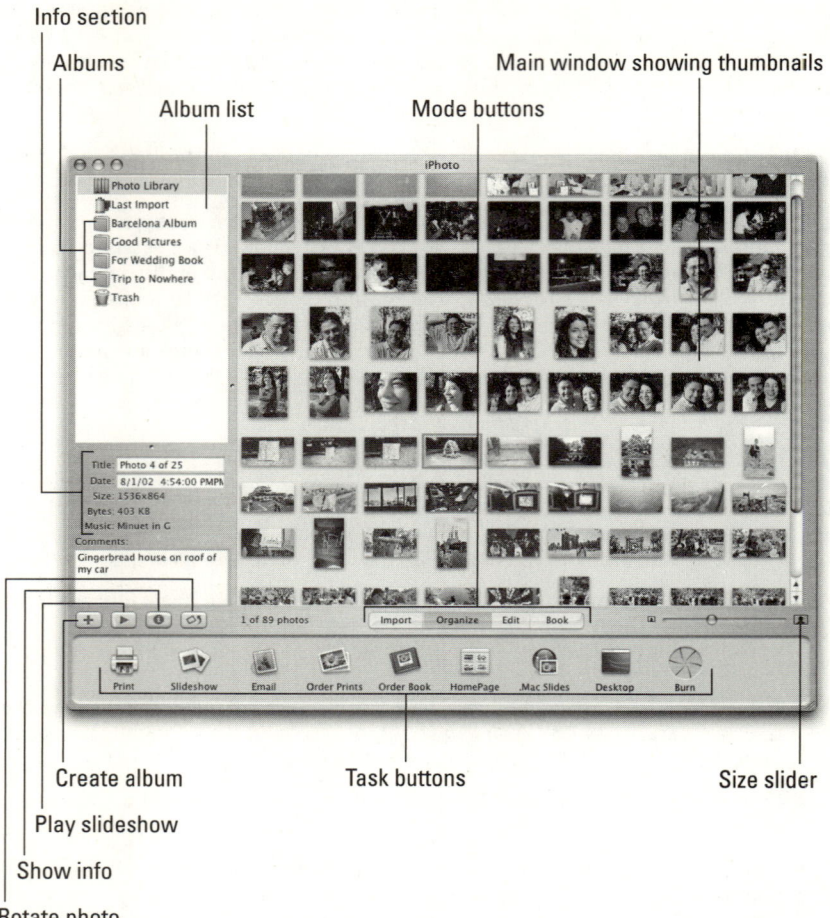

Create album

Play slideshow

Show info

Rotate photo

Task buttons

Size slider

Figure 20-24: The iPhoto 2 interface.

✦ Edit your photos by cropping them as shown in Figure 20-25, rotating them, removing blemishes, wrinkles, shadows, and red-eye, enhance the color, and adjust the contrast and brightness.

✦ Create a book layout from an album by choosing from one of the included layouts and customizing it, adding captions. Use this layout to order a professionally printed hardcover book via the Internet, or print the pages of the book on a color printer. The Book panel is shown in Figure 20-26.

Figure 20-25: The Edit panel of iPhoto, with an image crop in progress.

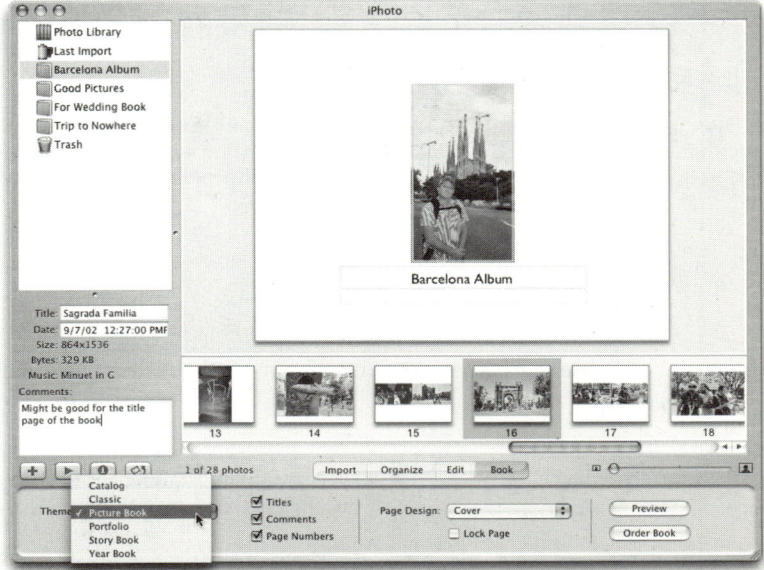

Figure 20-26: The Book panel of iPhoto, showing one of several possible layouts.

✦ Create a slideshow, with a musical soundtrack selected from iTunes, which plays inside of iPhoto, or can be exported as a QuickTime movie or copied to iDVD.

✦ Create a slideshow that appears as your desktop picture.

✦ Email your selected photos to family and friends via the Mail application, AOL, Entourage, or Eudora.

✦ Print your pictures to a color printer. You have the option to use iPhoto's templates for full-page prints, standard-size prints, greeting cards, and others.

✦ Order professionally processed prints via the Internet.

✦ Create a Web page containing your photos via the .Mac HomePage service, and send friends and family the URL for it via email. You must be a .Mac member.

✦ Create a slideshow that others can download from the Internet to use as a screen saver, with the .Mac Slides Publisher application (downloadable by members only from the .Mac Web site).

✦ Burn CDs or DVDs containing your selected pictures, to archive or share the content. You need a CD or DVD burner to do this.

iMovie 3

With iMovie 3 and a compatible digital camcorder, you can create digital video at least the equal of many B-movies and approaching some substantial films in quality. We can't give a full course on the use of iMovie 3 in the space available here, but we show you the basics.

Getting started with iMovie 3

When you launch iMovie 3, its window takes over your whole screen. If your Dock isn't hidden, we recommend that you turn on Dock hiding by choosing Apple ➪ Dock ➪ Turn Hiding On (⌘-Option-D). Click the New Project button, name your project in the Create New Project dialog, and you are ready to start, as shown in Figure 20-27.

iMovie's three main panes are the following:

✦ **Monitor:** Where you watch and edit clips

✦ **Shelf:** Where you store clips and apply effects to them

✦ **Clip and timeline viewers:** Where you arrange clips and construct your movie

The monitor

You use the monitor to view clips or the entire movie, edit clips, and switch between camera and view modes. When a camera is connected, iMovie tells you your location within the tape.

Note　Time in iMovie is measured in hours, minutes, seconds, and frames. If you are using NTSC video (the standard within the United States and Canada), there are 30 frames (really 29.97) per second of video. If your video format is PAL (Europe and most of Asia), there are 25 frames per second.

Figure 20-27: The iMovie 3 interface as it looks when you start a new project with a camera connected.

The buttons along the bottom of the monitor vary depending upon whether the toggle switch to the left of the buttons is in the camera or editing position. In camera mode, the buttons are Reverse, Pause, Play, Stop, and Fast Forward. The Import button tells iMovie to start the camera playing and to import the video coming over the FireWire cable.

When you're in editing mode, the buttons are go to beginning, play/pause, and present full screen.

The shelf

When you import clips from your camera, each individual clip first appears on the shelf, shown in Figure 20-28. New clips start at scene breaks (where your camera stopped and restarted recording), where you stop and then restart importing, and when the clip gets to 2GB in length (a little over nine minutes).

When you click one of the buttons at the bottom of the shelf, its appearance changes to show controls for adding transitions, titles, special effects, and working with audio.

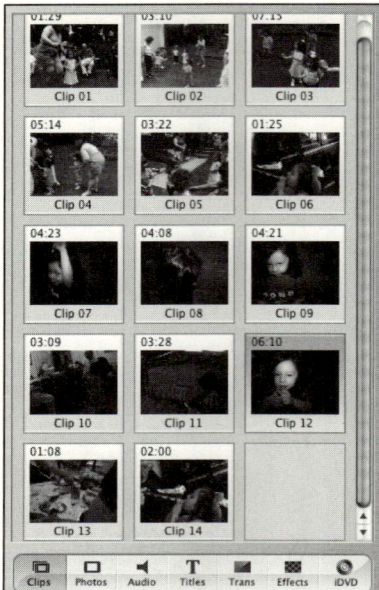

Figure 20-28: iMovie's shelf, populated with auto-separated clips.

The Transitions panel

When you click the Transitions button at the bottom of the shelf, the Transitions panel appears, as shown in Figure 20-29. In it, you see a list of possible transitions. In addition to the transitions and effects included with iMovie, you can obtain more from Apple's iMovie Web pages (www.apple.com/imovie) or by purchasing collections from a third party such as GeeThree (www.geethree.com).

These transitions affect the clips selected in the clip viewer. In most cases, you can also control the speed (duration) of the transition, as well as the direction in which it moves.

After you have created the transition you want in the Transitions panel, make the clip viewer (covered later) active and drag the icon for the desired transition from the Transitions panel to the clip it affects (or between the two clips) in the clip viewer. When the appropriate spacing appears in the clip viewer, release the mouse button. This will apply the transition you created. Until you do this, you're just experimenting.

The Titles panel

Similar to the Transitions panel, the Titles panel lets you create titles and credits to show in your iMovie. If you find the little Preview pane in the Titles panel too small, you can click the Preview button and watch your credits in the monitor, as shown in Figure 20-30.

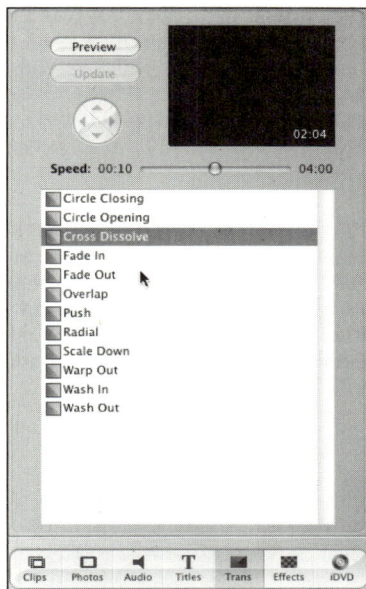

Figure 20-29: You select a transition here, and it will preview in the small pane at the upper right.

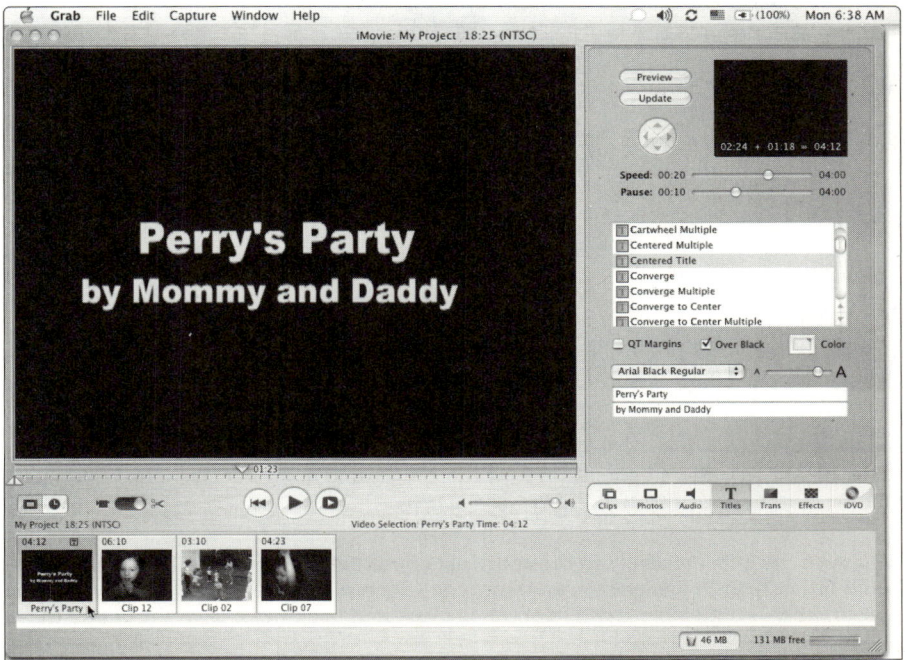

Figure 20-30: You can preview your credits or titles in the monitor if you wish.

The Title panel gives you control over direction, duration (speed), text color, font, and font size. The Over Black checkbox lets you specify that the text appears over a black background. iMovie creates a clip with a black background for you to insert in your clip viewer rather than overlaying it on a selected clip. The QT Margins checkbox tells iMovie to keep the text within a TV set's viewable area so that nothing gets cropped if you play it on a television set. TV sets operate in an overscan mode, in that there is more of the picture than is displayed on the screen.

The Effects panel

Special effects can be applied to clips. You can select from included effects (more are available for download or purchase, as described earlier), each of which has its own set of parameters and controls. With effects, you can change the colors, contrast, and brightness of your clips. You can also create interesting effects, such as a fade from sepia to the normal coloration of your video to give that old-photograph-to-real-life effect so often seen in movies and on television. The Effects panel is shown in Figure 20-31.

Figure 20-31: Set effects options, preview the effects, and apply effects in the Effects panel. Note the Mirror effect shown in the Preview screen.

If you want the effect to apply to the entire clip, both the Effect In and Effect Out sliders should be set to 0:00. If, however, you want the effect to gradually take place, set the sliders appropriately — remember that Effect Out is measured backwards from the end of the clip.

One example of using these staged effects is to go from a sepia-toned still frame to full-color live action (as was done so well in the classic movie, *The Sting*), as follows:

1. **Place a sepia-toned still image of the first frame of your clip just before the clip.**

2. **Select the Sepia Tone effect.**

3. **Move the Effect Out slider to the left to mark the point where you want the effect to end (almost to the beginning of the clip).** By putting the still clip at the end and using the Effect In slider, you can also dissolve to a sepia-tone still.

The Audio panel

The Audio panel is where you add sound effects to your movie. You can simply drag one of the sounds from the list (shown in Figure 20-32) to one of the audio tracks in the timeline viewer.

You can use the Record Voice button (and your Mac's microphone) to create narrative to do voice-overs during your movie. Similarly, the Record Music button enables you to capture music from a CD. When an audio CD is inserted in your CD or DVD drive, a list of tracks appears in this section's list box. Select the one you want to import, click the Record Music button, and iMovie converts the track to an AIFF file and imports it onto the lower audio track of your timeline viewer.

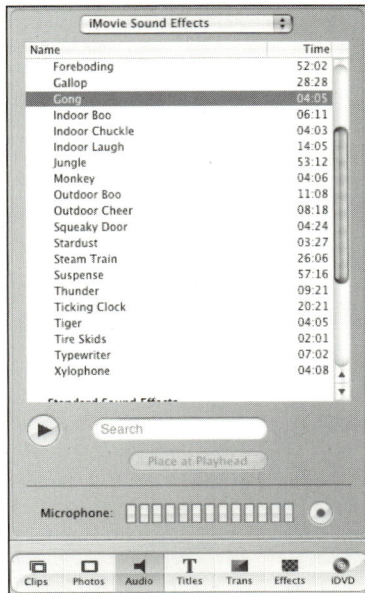

Figure 20-32: Add sound effects, narrative, or a background score using the Audio panel.

The clip and timeline viewer

The wide pane at the bottom of your iMovie screen houses the clip viewer or the timeline viewer, depending on the selection you make with the Clip Viewer button: The film frame icon selects the clip viewer, and the clock icon selects the timeline.

You can drag clips and transitions from the shelf to either the clip viewer or timeline viewer, but much of your editing (particularly cut and paste) will probably be easier in the clip viewer. The timeline viewer is handy for editing individual tracks of your movie—you have a video track and two audio tracks, as shown in Figure 20-33.

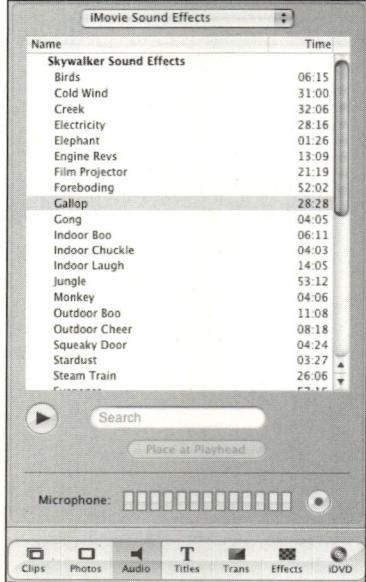

Figure 20-33: You can edit individual tracks in the timeline viewer.

Tip   You can extract the audio portion of your video clip onto one of the timeline viewer's audio tracks by choosing Advanced ➪ Extract Audio (⌘-J). Then, you can turn the volume for the original video track off or down low using the volume control at the bottom of the viewer and move the audio tracks around to give effects similar to those of a television news broadcast where you continue to hear the newscaster speak while you're being shown footage taken in the field.

Editing your movie clips

The monitor provides a playhead and two selection triangles, identical in function to those described earlier in the discussion of QuickTime Pro. iMovie shows you a lot more, though, when you drag the playhead—the video in the monitor fast-forwards and reverses so that you can see exactly where you are at any time. This technique of dragging the playhead is called *scrubbing*. You can also position the playhead to any point by clicking on that point in the timeline viewer. Just as in QuickTime Player Pro, you can advance or reverse a frame at a time by using the arrow keys — ← to go back a frame and → to go forward a frame. Holding down the Shift key when pressing the Left- or Right-Arrow keys moves you 10 frames at a time.

The selection triangles are called *crop markers* in iMovie. Just as with the playhead, you can move the crop markers by clicking on them and then using the arrow keys. You can then choose Edit ➪ Clear to remove the selected portion of the clip or Edit ➪ Crop (⌘-K) to remove everything but the selected portion from the clip.

Tip If you want to remove crop markers, just click on the clip's icon on the shelf. This immediately clears all crop markers. Additionally, until you empty iMovie's Trash, you can recover deleted material by repeatedly choosing Edit ➪ Undo until you get back to where you wanted to be.

Saving your iMovie

Generally, you want to save your iMovie either back to the camera to play on a TV or to QuickTime so that you can put it on the Web, send it in an e-mail, or burn it to a CD. If your Mac has the Apple SuperDrive DVD drive or a compatible product, you can also include your iMovie on a DVD that you create with iDVD. All these actions are initiated by choosing File ➪ Export Movie (⌘-E) and then choosing from the Export pop-up menu shown in Figure 20-34. In iMovie 3, it is no longer necessary to save your project for iDVD, as this is done automatically every time your project is saved. The selection "For iDVD" brings up a notice to this effect.

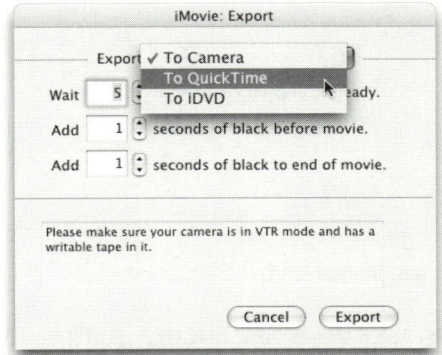

Figure 20-34: Choose how you want to save your movie in the Export Movie dialog.

iDVD

With iDVD and an Apple SuperDrive, you can design and create your own video DVDs, which can be played on any commercial DVD player or DVD-compatible optical drive. iDVD offers DVD authoring made easy.

For content, you can use movies you created with iMovie or any other editing application that can export to a QuickTime file. You can also put a slideshow of digital pictures from iPhoto or elsewhere onto your DVD. You can use music from iTunes to play during the slideshow.

iDVD does not allow you to work with these files, only add them to the DVD project. iDVD does allow you to set up the interactive interface a DVD needs so viewers can navigate them. To this end, iDVD features a variety of built-in themes that allow you to design the backgrounds, menus, and buttons that make up the interface.

When you have designed your DVD, iDVD burns the disc in your SuperDrive. Note that iDVD can only be used with an Apple SuperDrive, and not a third party DVD burner. iDVD comes free with Macs that have SuperDrives, and otherwise it the only one of the iLife apps that you cannot get for free. When Apple sells the iLife suite, it is really selling you iDVD, in a package with the other apps for convenience. The intended customer is the user of an older Mac that has a SuperDrive that came with an earlier version of iDVD, and who wants to upgrade to version 3, as well as the versions of the other iLife applications that work with it.

iDVD is the easiest to use of the iLife apps, and it attains a simplicity in its interface design that makes it an aiming point for software developers. It is possible to pretty much fly it by the seat of one's pants, with just a few hints; here they are.

When you launch iDVD, you see the splash screen shown in Figure 20-35.

Figure 20-35: The splash screen you see when you launch iDVD.

Notice the buttons. Open Tutorial is the one to click if this is your first time, and if you have a little time on your hands to learn iDVD the right way. Click Open Project to do some more work on a project you already began, and New Project to create a new project.

If you open the tutorial, you will see the interface open to an animated red curtain with the title "IDVD Tutorial," and iDVD Help will open to the first page of the Tutorial instructions, as seen in Figure 20-36.

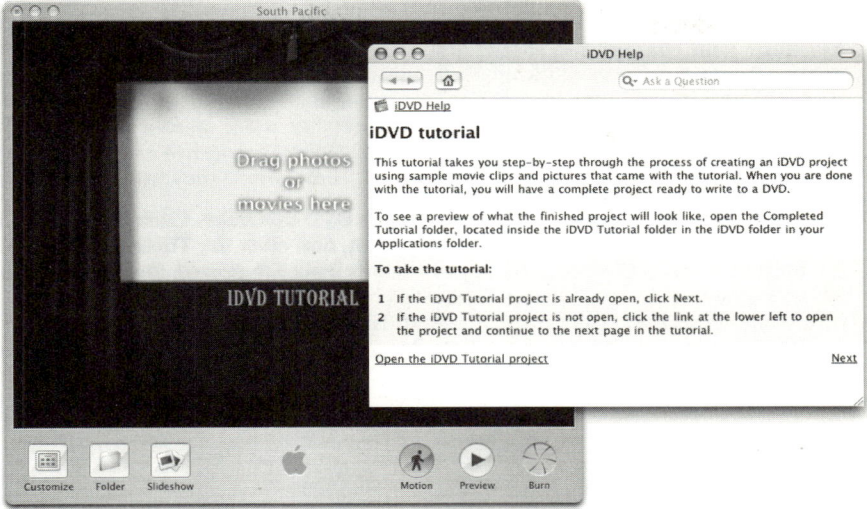

Figure 20-36: The iDVD tutorial.

The Tutorial takes you through the process of designing a DVD, and sample movies and pictures are provided for you to use. Figure 20-37 shows the Settings panel in the Customize drawer.

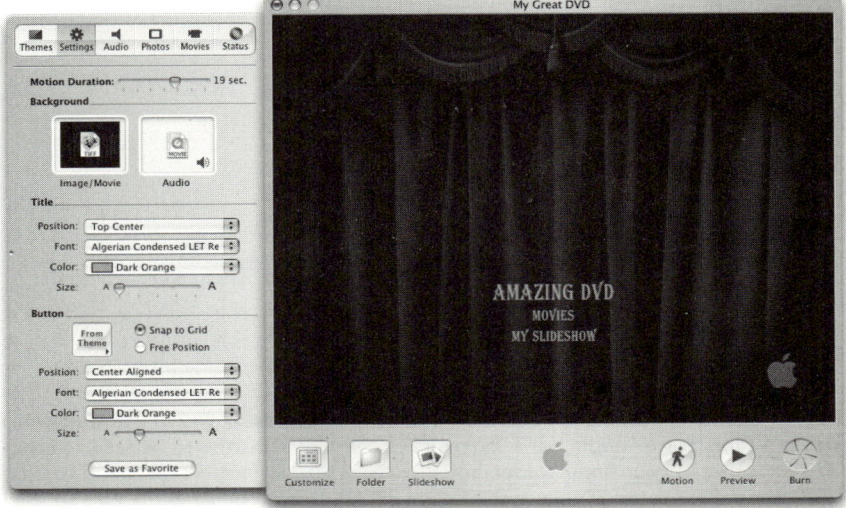

Figure 20-37: The iDVD interface, with the Settings panel showing in the Customize drawer.

Follow these steps to start and complete an iDVD project.

1. **Assemble your content**. You should first gather and organize all the media will need to do the project. If you are following the Tutorial, its movie and picture files are all gathered in the Media folder inside the Tutorial folder inside the iTunes folder, and you should do the same for your project's files. Remember, these movies and pictures should need no more work and be finalized. Any QuickTime movie can be added to your DVD, except for MPEG files, QuickTime VR, and Sprites; they will not work.

2. **Choose a theme to determine the look of your DVD interface. Click the Customize button to make the Customize drawer slide out, and click the Themes button to see the built-in themes. Choose category of themes from the pop-up menu (see Figure 20-38)**. Some themes have motion (indicated by the walking man icon), music, and Drop Zones (areas you can drag a movie, stills, or a slideshow by dragging it). If you want to see the theme's motion, click the Motion button (with the walking man icon) under the main window; but keep if off as much as possible to conserve performance.

Figure 20-38: The iDVD themes panel.

3. **To add media, click on the button the top of the Customize drawer that matches the media's type.** For example, for a Movie, click the Movie button to be taken to the Movies folder in your home folder. You can also choose Photos (takes you to iPhoto 2) or Audio (takes you to iTunes 3; see Figure 20-39). When you drag the files to the DVD menu, buttons that link to the files are created. In Drop Zone themes they appears as text; in other themes, they appear as a still or moving image.

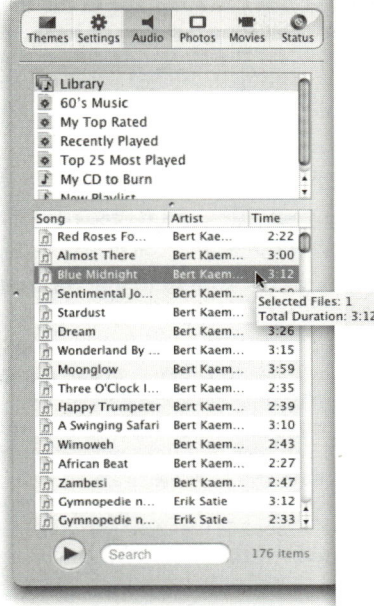

Figure 20-39: The iDVD Audio panel, showing information from iTunes.

4. **To customize a motion button, if you don't like the first frame it shows by default, click it once to select it, and drag the slider until you see a frame you like. In the Customize drawer, click Settings, and set the Motion Duration slider to the time period you want the movie to loop.**

5. **To add a custom button image, drag a photo or a movie to the button.**

6. **Enter the name of your buttons by clicking on their label and typing.** Also change the title of the menus by clicking on it.

7. **Rearrange the positions of the buttons by clicking Settings in the Customize drawer, and then click Free Position. Choose Advanced ⇨ Show TV Safe area to see the outer boundary of TV screens; position everything so it lies within this boundary so it can be seen.**

8. **To add a submenu, click the Folder button, and a new button appears on the menu.** When the viewer clicks on this button, they will see another menu that can hold more media or buttons, with a back button for viewers to return the previous menu. Keep this limitation in mind: a menu can only have six buttons.

9. **To create a scene selection menu, add a movie that already has chapter markers added to it during editing.** Two buttons are created: one with the title of the movie, and one linking to a scene selection submenu. When viewers click the title button, the whole movie will play. When they click the scene selection button, they can click on a scene to play it. The submenu has a Back and Next Scenes button to link to the next scenes submenu, if any.

10. **Pick a new background for your menu if you don't like the one in the theme. In the Customize drawer, click the Settings button, and drag a movie or image to the Background Image/Movie well.** If it is a movie, set the Motion Duration slider to the time period you want the movie to loop. To get rid of the image or movie, drag it from the well to outside the iDVD window and drop it there; it disappears in a puff of smoke, and the menu reverts to its default.

11. **Pick an audio file to play while the viewer sees the menu. Drag it to the Audio well.**

12. **Use the Settings pane to change the look of your titles and buttons.** Click and hold the From Theme pop-up menu to pick a new button style.

13. **If you like your theme, save it with the Save as Favorite button at the bottom of the Settings pane.** After you name it, it will be displayed in the Themes list.

14. **To create a slideshow on your DVD, drag the pictures you want to the Slideshow button. A slideshow button appears on the menu; double-click it to see the Slideshow editor.** You can also create the slideshow and double-click the button; after you are in the editor, go to the Customize drawer's Photos pane. If you have iPhoto running, you can see the list of Libraries and Albums, and can pick and drag photos to the main window (see Figure 20-40). Use the controls beneath the window to show navigation arrows, add the files to the DVD so they can be copied by the viewers to their hard disks, set the Slide Duration and size of the thumbnails, drag an audio file to play during the slideshow. Click the Preview button to view the slideshow; click it again to return to the editor. When done, click Return to go back to the DVD menu.

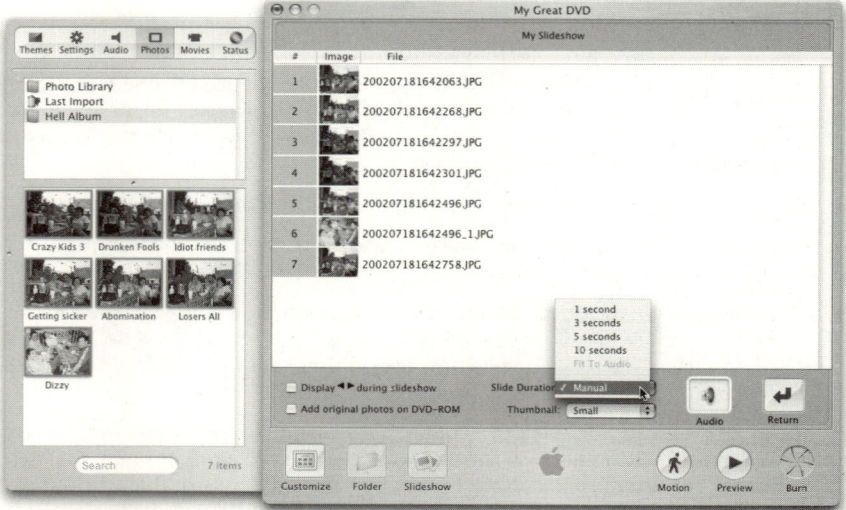

Figure 20-40: The iDVD Slideshow editor, showing in the drawer the list of Libraries and Albums from iPhoto, as well as thumbnails of the photos in an album.

15. **Click the Motion button at any time to preview motion menus and buttons.**

See how the project will appear to the viewer anytime you want by pressing the Preview button. In preview mode, navigate your DVD menus with the onscreen remote control (see Figure 20-41).

Figure 20-41: The onscreen remote used to test the navigation of your DVD project before you burn it to a disc.

16. **To burn the project to a blank DVD disc, first turn on the motion button if you want the DVD to have motion. Click the burn button once, then again to begin the process. Follow the onscreen instructions.** It takes an average of 2 to 3 minutes to encode and write a minute of video to the disc. You can watch the progress in the Status panel of the drawer.

DVD Player

Use the DVD Player application to watch DVD video discs on your Mac, whether they be from Hollywood or from your own SuperDrive via iDVD.

If you know how to use a DVD remote, you already know how to use DVD Player, because the application is controlled with an onscreen remote. It is a little more elaborate than the onscreen remote in iDVD, and better looking, too. Take a look at the horizontal, default version of it in Figure 20-42. There is also a vertically oriented remote if you so prefer.

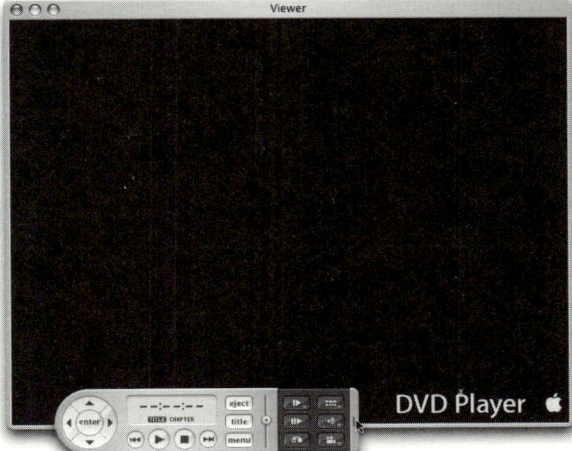

Figure 20-42: The DVD Player interface.

When you insert a DVD video disc, DVD player will automatically launch. Pick the size of the image from the Video menu; most times you may prefer to choose "Enter Full Screen" — it looks best. To enter or exit full screen, press ⌘+0 (zero).

While watching the DVD, the remote will disappear about five seconds after the cursor last touches it; to see it again, move your mouse. Should you wish to access the DVD menu, just use the mouse to bring your cursor close to the top of the screen, and it will appear.

Commands entered on the onscreen remote appear for confirmation in green in the upper-left corner of the screen.

Summary

This chapter covered QuickTime, Apple's multimedia technology, and the applications which use it, known as the iLife suite.

✦ QuickTime is a powerful technology that brings time-based media to the Macintosh. It is built into Mac OS X, so that you can view QuickTime movies without an application.

✦ iTunes is a digital jukebox, and enables you to rip and burn CDs, listen to music on your computer, and access your iPod and the iTunes Music Store.

✦ iPhoto lets you import, view, organize, edit, and share your digital still pictures.

✦ iMovie allows you to edit your digital home videos.

✦ With iDVD, you can create interactive menus to control your media after it is burned onto a DVD and played in any commercial DVD player.

✦ DVD Player allows you to watch DVD video discs on your Mac.

✦   ✦   ✦

Enhancing Your System with Utility Software

Every major operating system revision, including Mac OS 10.3, brings with it significant enhancements in performance and ease of use over previous versions. Nevertheless, Apple can't think of everything. Developers step in to create software that enhances Mac OS X in novel ways that can increase your productivity and computer experience. This chapter presents some of the tools and packages available to enhance your computing experience. You will also discover some of the different licenses that developers use to release their software, and find some useful places to begin your search for new software packages.

Finding Utility Software

The Internet has truly changed the way software is distributed. Because most software is distributed over the Internet in demo form, without dropping a dime or leaving your house you can easily find and test several different products that all perform the same function. Web sites have sprung up whose sole purpose is to track software for different platforms and provide download links so that you don't have to go elsewhere. Most software developers, even noncommercial ones, have their own Web sites where you can learn about their products, download the latest versions, and even obtain demo copies.

The software mentioned in this chapter is just a small fraction of what you can find. The multifaceted environment that Mac OS X brings to the table has drawn thousands of developers, and you too can discover many interesting products while you're visiting a developer's Web site to obtain one of the utilities listed in this chapter.

There are some great places to find useful utilities, hacks, and software packages on the Internet if you know where to look. Here are some places to start:

✦ **Software folder of your iDisk: If you have a .Mac membership,** this folder has Mac OS X software from Apple and many other developers. To check your iDisk, switch to the Finder and choose Go ➪ iDisk ➪ My iDisk (if you haven't set your iDisk up for autosyncronization). To access the software folder, your .Mac account information must be entered in the Internet pane of System Preferences. This is a good place to start, but there is no information about the package you're downloading, and the selection is limited.

✦ **Mac OS X Downloads pages:** Apple provides an extensive collection of current software that you can download for Mac OS X. This site has shareware, software updates, demo versions of commercial software, and free software in every category. The site is well organized, with a search function. You will find information on each piece of software offered for download, but no reviews. Go to `www.apple.com/downloads/macosx/`.

✦ **Apple's Mac OS X Applications page:** This Web page is also hosted by Apple, and has a database that you can use to search for Mac OS X applications and hardware. While a good resource, there are no downloads available, it is still a good place to find great software. Its main thrust is commercial software. Find it at `http://guide.apple.com/macosx/`.

✦ **VersionTracker Online:** One of the best software resources available online, VersionTracker is a great Web site that keeps tabs on the latest versions of Macintosh software. You'll find Mac OS X, Mac OS 9, Windows, and Palm software in different tabs, and the database is updated throughout the day with the most recent updates appearing right on the front page. You can search for a particular software title or by using keywords that describe a something about the type of software you're trying to find. There is also a pro version of the Web site (subscription fee required), which will alert you to updates of the software packages you specify, as well as provide more advanced searching capabilities. It's at `www.versiontracker.com`.

✦ **CNET's software library:** This library offers extensive shareware, demo software, and freeware. Go to `www.download.com`.

If you can't find what you're looking for at this site, you may find a shareware or freeware title at its sister site, Shareware.com, at `www.shareware.com`.

✦ **Info-Mac Archive:** This archive is a major storehouse of shareware, freeware, and demo versions of retail software. All software is submitted to a central location and redistributed to mirror sites throughout the world, such as Apple's FTP mirror site (`ftp://mirror.apple.com/mirrors/Info-Mac.Archive/`). At most mirror sites, you browse for files by category. MIT's HyperArchive mirror (`http://hyperarchive.lcs.mit.edu/HyperArchive.html`) has an Info-Mac search facility, but little information is available on software packages.

✦ **Applelinks.com:** Another, less well-known, stockpile of shareware, freeware, and demo versions of retail software. Go to `http://search.applelinks.com`.

Trying Out Shareware and Freeware

Most of the software available for download from the sites listed above cannot be found in retail stores or ordered from mail-order companies. This software is most often created by individuals who program in their free time, usually for fun, but mainly because they have an idea that they want to share with others. Such products are usually distributed as *shareware* or *freeware,* and sometimes even as *postcardware.* Shareware titles are generally distributed on a trial basis. Aside from the cost of your Internet connection, you pay nothing to obtain and try out shareware; the authors generally only ask for payment if you find the product useful and decide to keep it. Authors of shareware encourage you to try their software and to share copies with your friends and coworkers. Some shareware authors accept payment directly. Many authors accept payment on the Internet through a clearinghouse, such as Kagi (www.kagi.com). Look for payment instructions in the Read Me file or other documentation files that come with the software.

In some cases, the shareware has a couple of key features removed, or it expires after some time. When you pay for the software, you get a registration code that you enter to remove the restrictions. Crippled, demonstration versions of shareware are becoming more commonplace as authors try to cope with the failings of the honor system.

Freeware, on the other hand, is completely free of these types of restrictions. The author is providing the world at large with the fruit of his or her labors and asks nothing in return. Usually software, released as freeware performs a specific task, and doesn't have a very large scope. Other authors ask that you send them a note or a postcard to acknowledge the freeware; this type of freeware has been dubbed postcardware.

A mounting current in the developer community is referred to as *open source* software. It fits in with freeware, in the sense that all of the software that is released under an open source license doesn't cost money, but it does have some interesting twists. Open source software is distributed with the *source code* to the program. The user can get at the inner programming of the software, see how the author designed it, make changes, and release the software himself with any changes he likes. Depending on the license that the original software was released under, the new author usually has to reference the original program, and must distribute the new source code under a similar license (i.e., with the same restrictions that the original license provided). Most open source software is released under the GNU Public License (GPL). More information about open source software can be found at www.opensource.org.

Understanding that free software and shareware do not become your property is important. Most freeware authors (and all shareware authors) retain the copyrights to their work. Their products are not in the public domain. You have a license to use the software, and you are generally encouraged to pass it around, but you can't sell it. For specific rules about distributing a particular product, read the license agreement that comes with the product.

Support Shareware Authors

Shareware depends on the honor and honesty of the people who use it. If you decide to keep shareware installed on your disk, the Honorable Society of Civilized People politely insists that you immediately send payment to the author. The fees that you pay for the shareware you use today (often between $5 to $50) help fund development of even greater shareware by giving the authors incentive to continue coding. For detailed information about the amount of payment requested for a particular shareware product and where to send payment, check each product's Read Me file, About menu command, onscreen help menu, or Web site.

Using shareware and freeware

Although this chapter describes shareware and free software, it does not include detailed operating instructions. This chapter is only intended to be a starting point because there is such a wealth of software to be found, and there is not enough space to describe more than a few choice tools. Because such software can often only be downloaded from the Internet, it doesn't come with printed manuals. Instead, this software usually comes with a text document, frequently named the Read Me file. You can also check for onscreen help in the Help menu while the software is running.

Shareware and freeware programs aren't always as stable as commercial software. Be sure to follow the instructions and discussions provided by the authors in their Read Me or Help files before using any of these programs.

Caution   You use shareware and freeware at your own risk. Authors of any software package can make mistakes, and shareware and freeware authors are no different. Because the developers of shareware and freeware are usually individuals and not gigantic mega-corporations, they often can not beta test their packages as thoroughly as commercial software. Make certain that your system is supported by the requirements outlined in the Read Me file, and that you read the guidelines set forth by the author. This can often help you prevent data loss, or the instability of your system.

Getting support for shareware and freeware

Shareware and freeware are typically developed by a single individual, rather than a whole company full of programmers and support staff. These individuals can afford neither the time nor the money required to provide technical support by telephone. Most developers do, however, provide support by email.

Although the developers of shareware and free software may not be able to hold your hand, they tend to release new versions of their products frequently. Each new version may introduce minor improvements and fix a few bugs that users reported via email.

If you're having trouble with shareware or free software, check the developer's Web site for a new version. Look for a description of what has changed since the version of the software you're using was released. You may find that the problem you're experiencing has been fixed in a newer version of the software. You may also find a list of frequently asked questions (FAQs) and other information that was not included with the software. You'll probably find an email address where you can submit a bug report describing a problem you've discovered that doesn't appear to have been fixed in the latest version. If you do find a bug, the author will usually welcome your input, as it will better the program for everyone.

Utilities List

Apple, commercial developers, and shareware and freeware authors offer thousands of utility programs to the Macintosh community. Many new programs become available every day. The software listed in this chapter is not meant to be all-inclusive, but rather to be examples of the types of software that are available to enhance the performance of your computer, and your enjoyment of it.

The variation in computer models and configurations makes predicting accurately whether a particular shareware or free software product works on your system impossible. Authors of shareware and free software don't typically have the facilities to test their products with every type of software combination and computer model. Instead, they fix the problems reported by people who try out the software.

Note
Some Read Me files and documentation reference the minimum systems and software configurations required and if there are any known conflicts, but others do not. If you decide to try some software, check the Read Me file or any included documentation for compatibility information. If the compatibility information doesn't assure you that the software you want to try is compatible with your computer model and Mac OS version, you should take the precaution of making a backup of your hard drive before trying the software. (Chapter 22 discusses backups.)

The software items described in this chapter are listed alphabetically, with a short description of each of their features. Software is updated often, and you may find that newer versions of programs have features not described here.

You'll find that some of the features provided by the software listed below can be found in some form, somewhere in the Mac OS X operating system. The authors of these products have recognized that there are ways to make things better, give you more control, or even just wanted to provide a different way to go about your business. On the other hand, some of the software described does vastly different things than Apple ever intended.

Alfred

Mac OS 9 had a great feature called *autorouting* that would aid the user in installing and managing system items. Drop a Control Panel on the System Folder, for example, and the OS would know where to put it for you.

Cross-Reference
See Chapter 17 for more information about Mac OS 9's autorouting feature.

While Mac OS X did away with Extensions and Control Panels as we knew them, there are kernel extensions, screensavers, preference panes, contextual menus and the like to contend with. On top of this, as you have seen in earlier chapters, there are at least three different places to install these types of software packages. Alfred (shown in Figure 21-1) restores the autorouting feature to Mac OS X, and aids in enabling and disabling third-party software, offering similar functionality to the Mac OS 9 Extensions Manager. Find Alfred at www.inferiis.com.

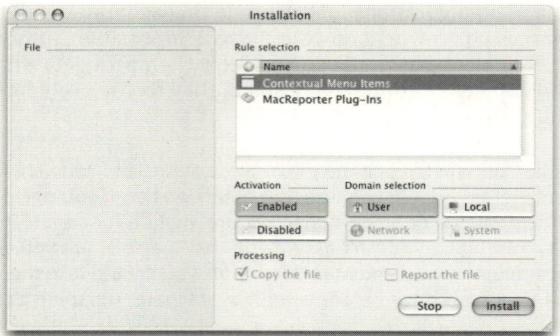

Figure 21-1: When you drop a contextual menu plug-in, kernel extension, screensaver, or preference pane onto the Alfred application (or use the contextual menu plug-in provided) Alfred provides a dialog box that allows you to install locally (for the user) or system wide and to decide whether to enable or disable the package.

Audio Hijack and Detour

Two cool applications by Rogue Amoeba software complement each other rather nicely. Audio Hijack is a sound hack that lets you record the sounds that are created by any of your running applications. In essence, hijacking the sound as it's coming out of the application and allowing you to record it without having to use a microphone in front of your speakers. Detour gives you ultimate control over the sound output ports on your computer. You can send the music from your iTunes out to your headphone jack, while routing your system sounds to the internal speaker of your Mac. It will recognize any output that the system recognizes as a valid sound port — the more ports available, the more flexibility you have. Find demos on line at (www.rogueamoeba.com)

Back Up User Prefs

Backing up your software and documents is an easy thing, but backing up your user preferences folder isn't all that painless. You have to worry about permissions and invisible files. Back Up User Prefs takes care of everything for you and even has an Auto-Pilot feature that will walk you through everything. Go to www.m-t-software.com.

BatchMOD

An application with a silly name, BatchMOD (see Figure 21-2) is a GUI front end for the chmod Unix command. (Though it uses a bit of chgrp as well.) While you can tweak permissions settings directly in the finder using the Get Info command, the Apply to enclosed items button doesn't always succeed. BatchMOD, on the other hand, excels at applying permissions recursively; it also lets you change specific privileges or ownerships without messing with any others. As an added benefit, it will let you force empty the trash for those sticky situations where it refuses to make it to the dumpster. All in all, a good tool to have in your arsenal. Find it at http://macchampion.com/arbysoft.

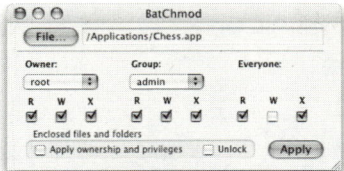

Figure 21-2: BatchMOD is a great little application that lets you change permissions on files and folders (recursively) using a drag-and-drop GUI. It comes complete with a Matrix/Batmanesque icon for your viewing enjoyment.

BootCD

BootCD allows you to create a bootable Mac OS X CD that has a working Finder and Dock. You can add any applications you need to the build, however, space on the disc is limited after your Mac OS X install is complete, so be careful what applications you are trying to add. Another important factor to take into account is that by their very nature, CD-ROM drives are slow and booting can take a long time. Online at `www.charlessoft.com`.

BrickHouse

Basic network security is provided in Mac OS X's Sharing preference pane, under the Firewall tab. For those of you who would prefer more control over your network security, BrickHouse is a much more full-featured front end to the Unix firewall built-in to Mac OS X. It offers, among other things, 3,500 labeled services for easy identification, advanced filter options, IP sharing at startup, and even a network monitoring tool. While a hardware firewall is usually a better option as it doesn't depend on your computer to function (also sucking up some CPU cycles while it's at it), for single users and people on a budget who require network security, BrickHouse is a good offering. Find it at `http://personalpages.tds.net/~brian_hill`.

Other products to look at are FireWalk X and Symantec's Norton Personal Firewall.

Carbon Copy Cloner

Mac OS 10.3 provides the Restore command in the Disk Utility, which allows you to make backup images of volumes, or even just make a bootable clone of a Mac OS X volume. Prior to version 10.3, this feature wasn't available, and those of us who needed to copy Mac OS X volumes turned to Carbon Copy Cloner (see Figure 21-3). Carbon Copy Cloner does just what its name suggests, it clones a volume onto another disk, allowing you to have a bootable backup in the case of emergency. It is also terribly convenient when making disaster recovery disks, or general use build disks. In addition to all of this, Carbon Copy Cloner allows you to synchronize disks as well as schedule clones (these features require you to install a command-line utility called pSync), something that Mac OS 10.3 doesn't provide. Carbon Copy Cloner will clone local disks only. For network disk installations, look at NetRestore, also by Bombich Software, in combination with Apple Software Restore. Find them both at `www.bombich.com/software/index.html`.

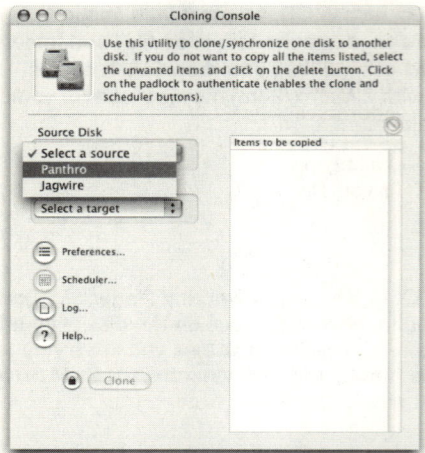

Figure 21-3: Carbon Copy Cloner has a very simple, easy to understand interface, just choose the source disk, then the target disk and then click the clone button. The preferences button reveals advanced features, even providing an easy means to install pSync.

Cocktail

If ever there were a Swiss Army knife tool of utility software, it would be Cocktail. Written entirely in AppleScript Studio (see Chapter 23 for more info), Cocktail is a definite must-have piece of software. Cocktail gives you a very-easy-to-use GUI look into the commands at the fingertips of Unix pros, and some tools to play with the interface of Mac OS X. You can update prebinding, mess with Finder and Dock interface elements (even make the Dock appear at the top of the screen, under the menu bar), optimize your network configuration, and clear out cache files, among many other options. Online at www.macosxcocktail.com.

CodeTek Virtual Desktop

The concept of a virtual desktop is not a new one—organize groups of running applications together to create separate *workspaces*. The only applications visible are those you are currently using and you can quickly switch to another set of running applications on the fly. CodeTek Virtual Desktop brings this functionality to the Macintosh with style and tons of features. A small floating window holds representations of each virtual desktop you have set up. You switch between them by clicking on each one, or by using the menu item provided. On the Web at www.codetek.com.

CronniX

CronniX is a GUI front end for the Unix command cron, a Unix system service that allows you to schedule the execution of scripts, programs, and applications from the command line. Well written and easy to use, CronniX brings scheduled operations to the normal Macintosh user. Find it online at www.koch-schmidt.de/cronnix/.

DragThing

DragThing has been tidying up Mac Desktops since 1995 and knows how to do it right. Use Drag-Thing to create as many docks as you like, and populate each dock with your choice of applications, files, folders, disks, file servers, and Internet addresses. Click a docked application to open it or bring it to the front. You can customize the look of your docks with icons, folder tabs, or just text. DragThing provides some of the same features as Drop Drawers X and PocketDock. Be sure to look at all of them and see which works better for you. DragThing, shown in Figure 21-4, is $25 shareware from TLA Systems at `www.dragthing.com`.

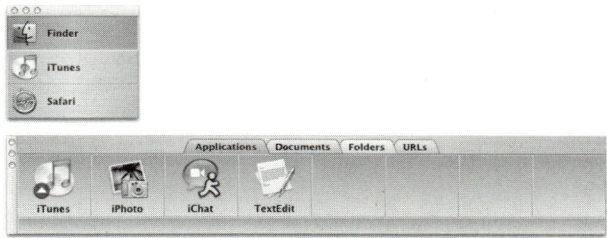

Figure 21-4: DragThing allows you to organize shortcuts to the documents and applications you access the most frequently. Its appearance and customization is very flexible.

Drop Drawers X

Drop Drawers X provides handy places to keep snippets of text, Web addresses, and other URLs, pictures, sounds, movies, and more. The drawers can hold aliases of applications, documents, and so forth. You can also have a drawer that lists applications and processes that are currently running on your computer. The drawers pull out conveniently from the sides of your screen, so their contents are always at hand. You can configure each drawer to your liking, and you can even protect drawers with passwords. The Dock is nowhere near as versatile as Drop Drawers X. Drop Drawers X provides some of the same features as DragThing and PocketDock. Be sure to look at all of them and see which works better for you. Drop Drawers X, shown in Figure 21-5, is shareware from Sig Software at `www.sigsoftware.com`.

Felt Tip Sound Studio

So, you want to record and edit audio on your Mac, on a budget. Felt Tip Sound Studio features one- or two-channel sound editing, effects filters, and pitch shifting. It is the perfect application to use when converting all of those old LPs to CD. It supports many file formats, including AIFF, Sound Designer II, System 7 sound, WAV, CD track, as well as any formats that QuickTime supports. Check out this $50 shareware from Lucius Kwok of Felt Tip Software at `www.felttip.com/products/soundstudio/`. A competing (and cheaper) piece of software is Amadeus II, found at `www.hairersoft.com/amadeus.html`.

GeekTool

A system preference pane for the geek in all of us, GeekTool puts a transparent (if you want it to be) console log viewer on your desktop. Very useful for servers and the criminally inquisitive, it can be a convenient means of keeping tabs on the goings on of your system. Take a look at it at `http://projects.tynsoe.org/en/geektool/`—it's freeware.

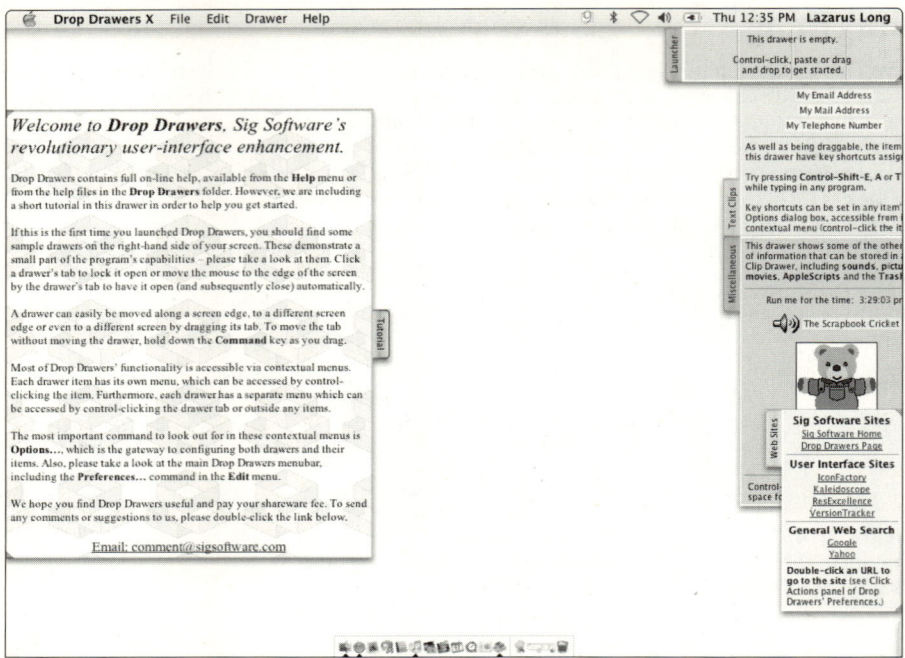

Figure 21-5: Drop Drawers provides handy places to keep a wide variety of objects at the tips of your fingers.

GraphicConverter X

One of the most highly touted, noncommercial image editors of all time GraphicConverter X, seen in Figure 21-6, is an amazing image editing bargain. The number of graphics formats that GraphicConverter can open and save to is unheard of — virtually every format found on Mac, Windows, Unix, Amiga, and Atari computers. GraphicConverter imports over 100 file formats and exports more than 40 file formats — and these numbers keep growing. Even better, the program has tools and filters for editing pictures. Even professional photo editors buy this program for its image conversion utility. Get this $35 graphical can-opener by Thorsten Lemke at www.lemkesoft.com.

Haxies

Mac OS X as it was released, drops a number of features that hardened old Macintosh Users have quite gotten used to — windows that shuttered closed in place, or maybe an audio soundtrack. Unsanity has created a set of programs called Haxies, so-named because, Unsanity contends, they are minihacks of the Mac OS. Window Shade X is a program that restores the minimize-in-place functionality of Mac OS 9. Fruit Menu grants you control over the Apple Menu, by allowing you to place your own items there. Xounds brings the soundtrack concept back to the Macintosh, and even lets you use all your old soundtrack files from Mac OS 9. These haxies and more can be found at www.unsanity.com.

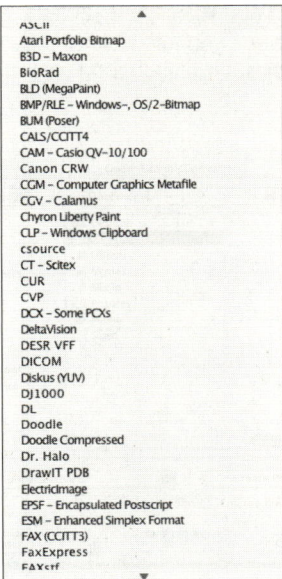

ASCII
Atari Portfolio Bitmap
B3D – Maxon
BioRad
BLD (MegaPaint)
BMP/RLE – Windows–, OS/2–Bitmap
BUM (Poser)
CALS/CCITT4
CAM – Casio QV–10/100
Canon CRW
CGM – Computer Graphics Metafile
CGV – Calamus
Chyron Liberty Paint
CLP – Windows Clipboard
csource
CT – Scitex
CUR
CVP
DCX – Some PCXs
DeltaVision
DESR VFF
DICOM
Diskus (YUV)
DJ1000
DL
Doodle
Doodle Compressed
Dr. Halo
DrawIT PDB
ElectricImage
EPSF – Encapsulated Postscript
ESM – Enhanced Simplex Format
FAX (CCITT3)
FaxExpress
FAXcrf

Figure 21-6: GraphicConverter can open so many formats they can't even all be shown in one screenshot, note the up and down arrows on *both* ends of the pop-up.

Logorrhea

iChat is a great way to connect with friends and family, but many people have overlooked its ability to log chats to your documents folder. (Go to iChat preferences, and check the Automatically save transcripts box under the Messages tab.) You'll find it's quite nice to have a transcript of your conversations for later perusal. The problem with this is that it is very difficult to actually find something in a saved chat. Well, Logorrhea to the rescue. It allows you to quickly flip through old chats by user and date, and previews them in a pane below (see Figure 21-7). Even more convenient is the Search tab when you can't even remember who said it. Check it out at http://spiny.com/software/.

MacTracker

A handy tool for the collector and Macintosh aficionado in all of us, MacTracker is a database with information on all of the Macintosh computers ever built. It is updated as new machines are released, has icon images for all of the models, and contains detailed information about original shipping configurations, maximum RAM and Hard Disk capacities, and much, much more. Find information on MacTracker at www.mactracker.ca.

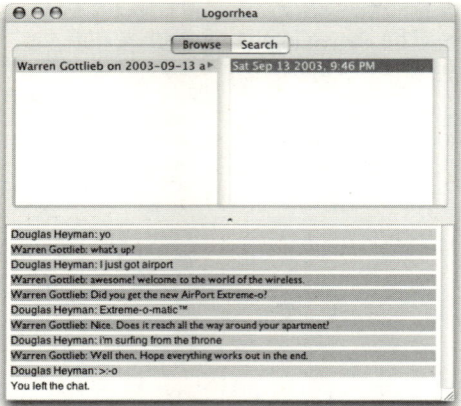

Figure 21-7: Logorrhea is perfect for those cases when you just have to prove how ridiculous sounding your IM was.

NetNewsWire

NetNewsWire, shown in Figure 21-8, by Ranchero Software is a full-featured RSS newsfeed reader. If there are Web sites that you frequent and they get updated throughout the day, it can be inconvenient to have to keep going back to check. NetNewsWire will poll the Web sites you subscribe to as often as every 30 minutes, and update its database with the latest headlines. Double-clicking on a headline launches your default browser right to the headline page of the Web site. It contains presets for a ton of news sites from the most known front page news outlets (the BBC, *Wired* magazine), tech havens (Slashdot, the Register, and CNET), lots of Macintosh news sites (MacNN, MacSlash, and MacCentral), and a whole host of personal blogs. You can find more information on NetNewsWire at `www.ranchero.com`.

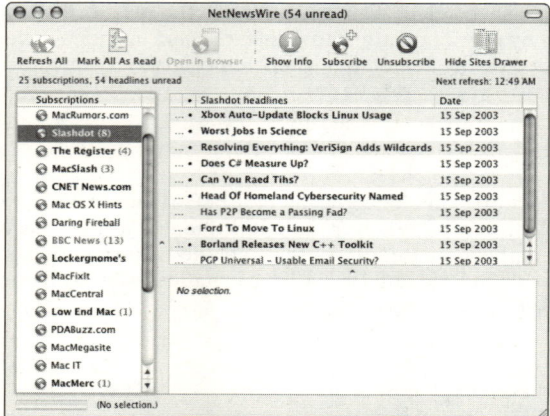

Fig. 21-8: Ranchero Software's NetNewsWire is a great application for keeping up to date with the Web sites you visit regularly. It comes with preconfigured feeds you can subscribe to, as well as those you input on your own.

Process Wizard

Mac OS 9 was based on *cooperative multitasking,* the front-most running process decided how much of the CPU power it wanted to give up. In preemptive multitasking, the OS has a hand, though the task scheduler, in the divvying up of the clock cycles, and can *preempt* another process, if it decides it is more needy of the CPU. Generally, the OS does a good job of making sure every process has what it needs. Process Wizard places a menu item that provides you with access to all the processes currently running and gives you the ability to modify their priority, using the Unix command renice. This is especially useful when you are rendering something that is CPU intensive in the background, and want to give it priority over checking your mail. You can also use the Process Wizard menu to force quit a process by Control-clicking on it. Information on Process Wizard can be found at www.theinteractivething.com.

Pseudo

Pseudo is an application that allows you to launch other applications as root.

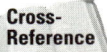

Cross-Reference   See Chapters 24 through 26 for more on the root user.

This can be useful for mucking about where you're not supposed to, as you'll have access to all of the files and folders on the computer. On the flipside, care is of the essence when using this application, as it is terribly easy to modify something that shouldn't have been, and completely confound the operating system. Pseudo was written by the same author as BrickHouse, Brian Hill, and you can find out more about this application at http://personalpages.tds.net/~brian_hill/.

QuickImageCM

QuickImageCM (see Figure 21-9) is perhaps one of the coolest little timesavers this side of minute rice. As its name suggests, QuickImage is a really quick way to preview images. Because it is a contextual menu, all you have to do is either Control-click or right-click on an image and it will open in its own window. Because no application is launched, the preview is almost instantaneous, on snappy Macs at least. There are some nice menu options in the little toolbar along the top of the window. While it breaks with Apple's interface guidelines, that's forgivable based on how dang convenient the program is. Download and find more information about QuickImage at www.pixture.com/macosx.php.

QuicKeys X2

A venerable program, QuicKeys has been around for ages, helping people bring macros into their daily lives. QuicKeys has evolved over the years into a very full-featured macro building, scripting package. You can time-delay, schedule, script, and assign just about any OS action to a button. In essence, it is a very powerful tool (much like AppleScript) that brings the world of automation to the consumer level. Using the intuitive interface, you can compress multistep tasks into shortcuts that comprise one keystroke. If you don't know anything about creating macros, QuickKeys X2 can record your actions and play them back. The Clips Shortcuts is useful for storing frequently used media for use later at the touch of a key. Use Typing Shortcuts to automate the entry of commonly used text. Menu Action Shortcuts let you select menu items via the keyboard that do not normally have key equivalents. See QuicKeys X2 in action in Figure 21-10, and discover what QuicKeys has to offer at www.cesoft.com.

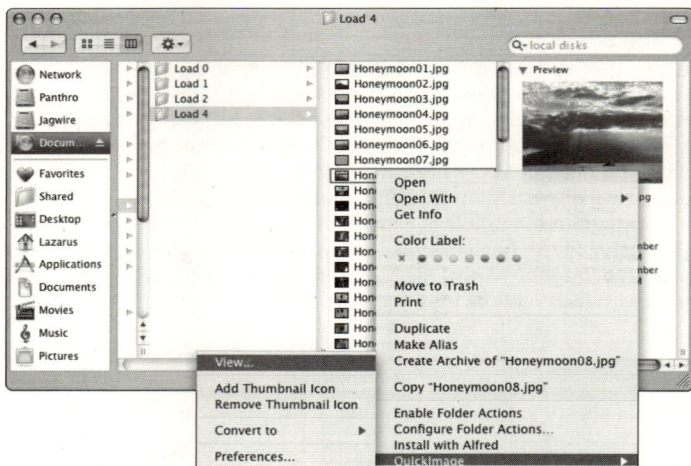

Figure 21-9: It's a lot easier to see the image when it's not a tiny preview in the paned view of the finder. Using QuickImageCM from the finder is easy and fast.

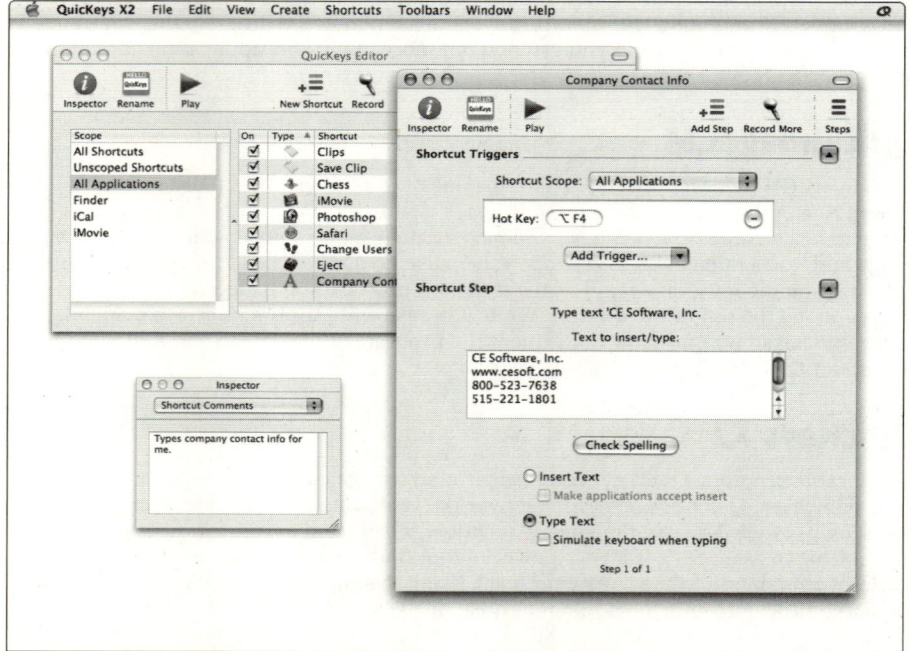

Figure 21-10: QuicKeys X2 helps you enter commonly used text at the touch of a button.

Salling Clicker

Salling Clicker is one of the coolest little preference panes in terms of sheer show off factor. Clicker interfaces with a Bluetooth phone or Palm Pilot (currently only Sony Ericsson phones are supported) and allows you to control your Macintosh wirelessly. If you've got a keynote presentation to give, fire up Salling Clicker, and while you're walking around the room, you'll be able to control the slideshow without any other tools but your phone. It's extensible, as you can set it to engage custom AppleScripts at the push of a button. Even more impressive is the ability to set iChat's status depending on whether your phone is in range. (If you walk away with the phone, iChat will change your status to away.) Find out more about Salling Clicker at www.salling.com.

A competing freeware product is Romeo by Arboreal (http://irowan.com/arboreal).

SharePoints

One of the limitations of Mac OS X as compared to both Mac OS 9 and Mac OS X Server, is that you don't have complete control over the share points you want to make available to the rest of your network. The only folder you can share is the /Users/Public folder. SharePoints is a free Preference pane that restores your ability to have complete control over what folders are shared across the network. Any folder on your hard drive can be shared via Apple Filing Protocol, for Macs, or SMB, for PCs. You are even able to create users and groups again. (See Chapter 15 for more information on setting up file sharing.) SharePoints is created by HornWare, and can be found at www.hornware.com.

SnapzPro

While you can use the built-in screenshot functionality of the Mac OS (Command-Shift-3 for the whole screen, or Command-Shift-4 to select an area of the screen), SnapzPro adds considerably to your ability to take a snapshot of your screen. SnapzPro allows you to save your screenshots in many formats (rather than just the PDF of the Mac OS). It also allows you to take QuickTime Movie snapshots of a process. The new Fatbits feature allows you to zoom in on images as you create them. There is also a delayed execution feature, so you can have the screenshot taken in the middle of an event that you normally wouldn't be able to capture. See more at www.ambrosiasoftware.com.

StuffIt (Standard/Deluxe)

StuffIt Expander ships with Mac OS X, but to actually create StuffIt archives you need either StuffIt Standard or StuffIt Deluxe. StuffIt Standard is a full package that takes over where expander leaves off, it provides droplet programs, which allow you to create Zip, Tar, and StuffIt archives by dropping anything you want onto them. Aladdin has created an even more powerful interface in StuffIt Deluxe. Among its most impressive features, StuffIt Deluxe integrates directly into the Finder, allowing you to append a .sit to the end of a document or folder name, and have that folder archived. This function works for all supported archive formats, and also in reverse. StuffIt Standard and Deluxe retail for $49.95, and $79.99 respectively. Find them online at www.aladdinsys.com.

SubEthaEdit

SubEthaEdit is one of the many applications that have sprung up around Apple's zero-config networking technology, Rendezvous (see Chapter 18). SubEthaEdit is a full featured (but not bloated), text editor that lets users on a network collaborate on documents with almost no configuration of the software. You share a document, and then other people on your network who have SubEthaEdit installed can see your documents with zero configurations using Rendezvous.

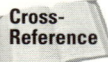

Cross-Reference   See Chapter 15 for more information on Rendezvous and its use as a zero configuration IP protocol.

You can even share documents over the Internet to other people using SubEthaEdit across the country. SubEthaEdit uses Safari's Web core engine to display HTML, and is a great collaborative tool for programmers. Go to www.codingmonkeys.de/.

Timbuktu/Apple Remote Desktop/VNC

Netopia's Timbuktu is *the* remote control application for the Macintosh. It has been around for years and it definitely shows its refinement. One of its greatest features is that it is cross-platform, so that you can control a Windows PC from a Mac and vice versa. It has a nice built-in user database where you can set up a number of different users with different privileges, and a very fast file transfer tool. Check it out at www.netopia.com.

Apple has its own remote control application called, of all things, Apple Remote Desktop (ARD). The ARD server is built in to Mac OS 10.3, and is great for managing a computer lab or classroom, as it has more administration features than Timbuktu. You know where to go: www.apple.com.

If you're interested in remote control on the cheap, look at AT&T's Virtual Network Computing or VNC for short. VNC is bare-bones, but is completely free and has been ported to a number of different operating systems. Find it at www.realvnc.com. Because VNC is open source software, you will also find several implementations if you search on www.versiontracker.com for VNC — "Chicken of the VNC" scores points for stupid name of the century.

TinkerTool

With TinkerTool, you can activate hidden options of Mac OS X. You can control font smoothing, select default fonts used in Cocoa applications, activate transparent Terminal windows, display the Trash on the Desktop, and more. None of these options requires typing Unix commands. Instead you use familiar Aqua controls such as checkboxes and pop-up menus, as you can see in Figure 21-11. TinkerTool is free software from Marcel Bresink Software-Systeme and can be downloaded from www.bresink.com/osx/TinkerTool.html.

Toast Titanium 6

Mac OS X's Disk Burner and Disk Utility are great for the beginner in terms of ease of use, but for those who really desire control over their CD/DVD burning, Roxio Toast is the way to go. With support for HFS+, Hybrid, ISO9660, VCD, and multisession discs, Toast lets you create discs easily and often supports more CDRW features than the Mac OS. One of the new features of version 6 lets you burn a CD-R or DVD-R directly from a FireWire-enabled video camera. If you take a few extra minutes, Toast even provides you with the tools to throw some titles in right before you burn it. The coolest new feature has to be ToastAnywhere, which lets you burn to a CD-RW drive attached to a different computer on your network that is also running Toast (uses Rendezvous). To find out how well it integrates with iMovie, go to www.roxio.com/toast.

Transmit

Transmit by Panic software, is a full-featured, clean FTP program. The first thing you'll notice about Transmit is that it has a familiar looking interface, with some well executed iconography. Transmit supports both the standard FTP protocol, and the more secure sFTP. You can find Transmit at www.panic.com.

The venerable Fetch is showing its age in Mac OS X, but is still a good, easy-to-use FTP client. Go to www.fetchsoftworks.com.

USB Overdrive X

Have you ever seen a mouse, trackball, joystick, or gamepad you just *had* to have, but there were no drivers for the Mac for it? Enter USB Overdrive, a truly universal, Universal Serial Bus (USB) driver for Mac OS X. USB Overdrive can handle all sorts of wheels, switches, extra buttons, and will even allow you to customize the function of each on an application-by-application basis. It supports scrolling (even if you don't have a wheelmouse!), keyboard commands, and other more complicated functions with mere mouse clicks. It can be found at www.usboverdrive.com.

VideoLanClient

VideoLanClient (VLC) is a cross-platform, free media player that can handle most video formats, including QuickTime, MPEG (1, 2, and 4), DivX, and Windows Media files. The VideoLAN project as a whole is a multimedia package designed to support the streaming and playing of video along a network across multiple platforms. VLC is released under the GPL, and is free software. More information about the project can be found at www.videolan.org.

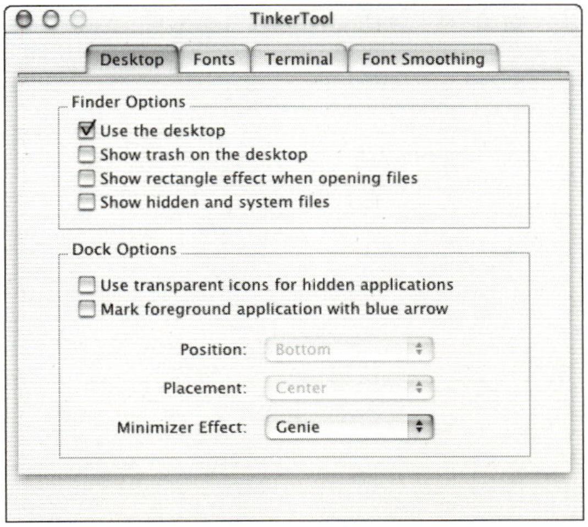

Figure 21-11: TinkerTool provides settings for a host of hidden Mac OS X options.

Webmin

A Web-based tool for configuration of Unix-based services, Webmin has been ported to many operating systems. Using the Web server built into Mac OS X, Webmin provides a graphical interface that helps you administer the Unix underpinnings of Mac OS X, giving you access to file sharing, DNS, user accounts, and more. Rather than your standard Mac OS X application, you access Webmin's interface by using a standard Web browser, and pointing it back towards your own machine. Webmin is freeware, and is released under the open source BSD license. More information and downloads can be found at www.webmin.com.

Xicons

While Xicons is not strictly utility software, having customized icons can certainly enhance your user experience. At the Xicons Web site, you can find countless icons expressly made for Mac OS X. The site has all kinds of replacement icons for applications, folders, disks, games, and hardware, in many different categories. There are some great cult status symbols to be found here, and all of the Icons are free to use. The Web site is located at www.xicons.com/.

Summary

In this chapter, you've been introduced to a few of the shareware , freeware, and commercial programs that are available for Mac OS X. You've learned about some great resources for finding software that fills your needs. You should now know some of the differences between shareware, freeware, and commercial software. While you are encouraged to distribute copies of most shareware and freeware (a sort of grassroots advertising campaign, if you will), authors generally retain copyrights to their software. Shareware authors ask that you send payment for products that you decide to keep, but freeware is free software.

While most of the utilities we've looked at are small programs designed to fulfill specific tasks, there are quite a few well-polished pieces of software that you'd be hard pressed to tell weren't commercial offerings — Alfred, Cocktail, GraphicConverter, Transmit, or VLC to pick just a few. As the Internet has managed to provide a perfect, I-need-it-now software delivery model and commercial software houses are beginning to offer electronic-only downloads, the line between commercial software and shareware is blurring.

✦   ✦   ✦

Maintaining Mac OS X

Although Mac OS X is light years ahead of Mac OS 9 in features and capabilities, it is a much more complex operating system to decipher. New folders are everywhere, no control panels, no extensions as we knew them, fonts everywhere — sometimes it seems as though OS X is a step back. In this chapter, you find out about the structure of the Mac OS X system architecture, some basic system maintenance, and hopefully learn the importance of a good backup.

Exploring the Mac OS X Library Folders

The core of Mac OS X hangs out in the /System folder. You can look in the /System folder hierarchy, but it is generally unwise to touch the files contained inside, a fact which is evidenced by taking a look at the permissions of the folders contained therein. This file hierarchy belongs to the system, and the only visible item is a Library folder. This folder is one of three Library folders you will be introduced to, but also the one that will be discussed the least, as its contents are beyond the scope of this book It hosts a number of important files that are beyond the scope of this book, and is where the code and resources required for core Mac OS X functionality reside. Make changes to this folder at your own risk.

The second Library folder, and perhaps the most easily located one, is found at the top level of your system disk. This folder is modifiable by those users with administrator access, and where such a user would place items in order to make their functionality accessible to all users. It holds the fonts, sounds, screen savers, and so forth that are available to all of the accounts on your computer. Resources that are required by installed applications, as well as drivers for peripheral devices, such as printers are usually found here.

Yet another Library folder can be found in each user's home folder. This one stores personal settings, fonts, sounds, and other configuration objects for each user and can only be accessed by the corresponding user or someone with "root" access. Application support files can be stored here as well as in the /Library folder, but these items will only be available to the specific user whose Library folder it is.

Now that you have some idea of the Library folder, you should understand the concept of search paths. Simply stated, a *search path* is a hierarchically ordered acquisition of system resources. This hierarchy stems from Mac OS X's security model. In general, most search paths work their way from user-specific resources to system-wide resources. The system first checks the local user Library (path ~/Library) for a resource such as a Preference pane, then checks the main Library (path /Library), and then checks the System library (path /System/Library).

Managing the main Library folder

The main Library folder (path /Library) is the repository of all the files required to make your Mac OS X user experience work. This folder is the closest thing you can find to the System Folder of Mac OS 9 or the Windows directory on a PC. It contains all the files that support the applications installed in the Applications folder (path /Applications) as well as any preference settings that apply to the Mac as a whole. The following list is not a complete list of the folders found within the main Library folder, but rather ones that you have the greatest chance of interacting with.

✦ **Address Book Plug-Ins:** This folder is not populated by default but can be used by a third party.

✦ **Application Support:** Contains shared libraries used by installed applications, such as Palm hotsync libraries, Adobe application support files, Shockwave libraries. Applications sometimes store files here so that other applications can share capabilities.

✦ **Audio:** A repository for sounds used systemwide and sound-related plug-ins. If you want to make an alert sound available, save it as an AIFF sound and put it in the Alerts folder of the Sounds folder in this Audio folder (path /Library/Audio/Sounds/Alerts).

✦ **Caches:** Holds temporary and permanent cache files used by applications.

✦ **CFM Support:** Carbon applications will store some plugins and application specific support files here.

✦ **ColorSync:** Holds the ColorSync profiles for a wide variety of devices and monitors in the Profiles subfolder and support AppleScripts in the Scripts subfolder. You can save some space by removing profiles for devices you don't have.

✦ **Contextual Menu Items:** Where you can place contextual menu items, such as QuickImageCM, that third parties have developed to extend the operating system.

✦ **Desktop Pictures:** A collection of the TIFF and JPEG files available for use as a background picture for the Desktop. Items placed in this folder are available to all users. Each user can set a Desktop picture by using the Desktop pane of System Preferences.

✦ **Documentation:** Holds user manuals, help files, and copyright information for installed applications and services.

✦ **Fonts:** Contains the various font files that are not required by the System but that are available to all users of your Mac. As discussed in Chapter 12, Mac OS X supports a wide range of font formats. The Fonts folder (path /Library/Fonts) is where you install fonts you want all users to be able to access, and if there are fonts in here that you do not wish to use, you can remove them. Having said that, certain fonts (such as Arial, Helvetica, Times New Roman, and Courier New) are default fonts for a number of applications, and you should probably leave those in place.

✦ **Frameworks:** Frameworks are another kind of shared library that is dynamic: only loaded into memory when being used. Frameworks are similar to System Extensions in OS 9.

✦ **Image Capture:** Contains a Scripts folder in which the AppleScripts that perform the Image Capture application's hot-plug actions (see Chapter 23) reside.

✦ **Internet Plug-Ins:** Holds the plug-ins that add functionality to Web browsers and other Internet applications. Examples include the QuickTime Plug-in, which allows you to watch QuickTime movies in your Web browser.

✦ **Java:** Contains, by default, an alias to the Java support files and libraries in the Library folder hierarchy of the System folder (path /System/Library). It also contains Java libraries installed for use by various Java applications.

✦ **Keyboard Layouts:** Where keyboard layouts (analogous to keyboard scripts under OS 9) can be stored. Detailed information can be found in Apple Technical Note TN2056, http://developer.apple.com/technotes/tn2002/tn2056.html.

✦ **Logs:** Holds the log histories (viewable with the Console utility — see Chapter 22) for applications that send debug and status information to the system console.

✦ **Modem Scripts:** A collection of files describing the characteristics and capabilities of a wide variety of modems. You can feel free to remove the files for modems you don't have. If you acquire a new modem, you might have to reinstall its modem script into this folder.

✦ **Perl:** Where the scripting language Perl is installed by default on OS X.

✦ **Preference Panes:** Where third-party System Preference panes are stored so that all users can access them. This folder is not created by a default install; an installer or system administrator can create this folder to make extra functionality accessible.

✦ **Preferences:** Holds the .plist (property list) files describing preference and state settings for system-wide services. For example, com.apple.loginwindow.plist contains the user number (as maintained in NetInfo) for the last user to log into Mac OS X, whether that user is currently logged in; and com.apple.PowerManagement.plist contains the settings made for Energy Saver in System Preferences.

✦ **Printers:** Contains the printer drivers and PPD files used by Print Center in recognizing, configuring, and enabling your printers.

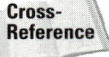

Cross-Reference More on printers in Chapter 9.

✦ **QuickTime:** Where additional codecs and other QuickTime support files should be installed. For example, Roxio Toast includes a QuickTime codec to convert to VCD MPEG (VideoCD-ready MPEG-1) format, and that file is installed here.

✦ **Receipts:** Contains files left by the Installer application describing the changes to your Mac OS X installation after a package has been installed.

✦ **Screen Savers:** A folder you can fill with screen saver modules to be available to all users of your Mac via the Screen Saver pane of Systems Preferences.

✦ **Scripts:** Contains folders of AppleScript scripts that are available to all users of your computer. The scripts in this folder appear in Script Runner's pop-up menu and in the menu of the Script Menu icon, as described in Chapter 23.

✦ **User Pictures:** Contains folders of small pictures suitable for assigning to user accounts. Each user account can have a picture that appears in the login window's list of user accounts. Pictures are assigned to user accounts in the Users pane of System Preferences.

✦ **WebServer:** Holds the *CGI* (Common Gateway Interface) scripts that enable add-on Web server functions, such as forms submittal, for Mac OS X Web Sharing. (Turn on Web Sharing in the Sharing pane of Systems Preferences.) This folder also contains the documentation for Apache, the software that turns your Mac into a Web server.

Exploring your personal Library folder

Located in your home folder you see another folder titled Library. Many of the sub-folders in this folder have the same names as those discussed earlier in this chapter ("Managing the main Library folder"). When you encounter a folder with the same name, it has the same functionality, except that it contains items specific to *your* use of the Mac rather than items for all users. As an example, you install fonts for your personal use in the Fonts folder of the Library folder in your home folder (path ~/Library/Fonts) if you aren't making them available to other users of the Mac. Similarly, alert sounds or screen savers that aren't shared would go in a folder of your personal Library folder.

Some of the other folders you may see in your personal Library folder include:

✦ **Application Support:** Contains shared libraries used by applications you installed when not acting as an administrator. For example, the folder for information from your Address Book was located in Library as Addresses, but in Mac 10.2, the Addresses folder has moved to inside the Application Support folder.

✦ **Assistants:** Contains files used by various Assistants. For example, if you were unable to connect during your initial setup to register Mac OS X, a file named SendRegistration.setup (a .plist file) is saved here with your registration information and preferences.

✦ **Audio:** Sounds and plug-ins you install when not acting as an administrator.

✦ **ColorPickers:** Where you find additional ColorPickers to augment the collection Apple provides.

✦ **Documentation:** Holds user manuals, help files, and copyright information for installed applications and services that you have installed. Like the other files associated with applications installed by you when not acting as an administrator, these are not accessible to other users on the system.

✦ **Favorites:** Where your Favorites are stored.

✦ **FontCollections:** Where your choices for font collections (see Chapter 12) are cached.

✦ **Frameworks:** Where the support frameworks (shared program libraries) for personal applications are stored.

✦ **Internet Search Sites:** Contains folders for each of your Sherlock channels, each containing the search-site plug-in files for that channel. See Chapter 7 for more about Sherlock and its channels. You might not see this folder until you've performed at least one Internet search in Sherlock.

✦ **Keyboards:** Contains any custom keyboard layouts you've installed.

✦ **Keychains:** Holds your Keychain files (see Chapter 10 for more information about the Keychain).

✦ **Mail:** Your personal mail folder. The Mail application (see Chapter 6) keeps its databases and other files here.

✦ **Preferences:** Your personal preferences folder. Where applications store their preferences independently of other users, so that each user can customize the system and his applications to his heart's content.

✦ **Recent Servers:** Contains the URL files to the servers that you've recently used. These are the servers that show up under Recent Servers in the Connect to Server dialog's pop-up menu.

✦ **Scripts:** The repository for your personal AppleScripts, if you have any. This is one of the locations Script Runner and Script Menu check by default when you use them.

✦ **Stickies Database:** Although not a folder, the Stickies database is found in your personal Library folder.

Depending upon what other applications you have installed or run, other folders can be found in your personal Library folder, such as OmniWeb, if you've installed that Web browser.

Tip   You may find at times that an application is not functioning normally. It may not open correctly, or it may just be acting strangely. One of the first actions to take is to go to the ~/Library/Preferences folder, and move any items that look like they pertain to the misbehaving application to the desktop. The application will recreate a preference file according to its default preferences. All of your changes to its settings (such as user names, save locations, or other customizations) will be lost, but the application may be restored to its normally functional state. If the application is still acting strangely, place the removed preferences back where you found them, and try some of the other suggestions found later in this chapter. Most applications follow Apple's preference-naming convention and will look something like com.applicationname.plist, though some create their own folders or use the software maker's name instead of the application name.

One User, Multiple Accounts

Always have at least two—yes, two—user accounts on any machine. Make sure that they are both administrators, especially if there are no other users on the machine.

An important troubleshooting step when things go strange with Mac OS X is to log in as a different user, and see if the problem still occurs. If it doesn't, then you know that the problem lies only with the first user, and is not a system-wide issue.

You may someday (we hope you never do), wake up to find that your user account will not let you log in. It tries to let you in, but you get a blue screen, or perhaps the spinning beachball of death. If you have only one user, it won't be very fun to try and clean the mess up, but if you have another user, you can log in and try cleaning out the broken user's Library (path ~/Library) folder to revive the user. (You can also try restarting from a second hard drive or a CD.)

Practicing Good Housekeeping

As with any disk-based operating system, debris accumulates and storage space becomes fragmented over time. A few basic maintenance operations, performed on a regular basis, provide improved performance and stability.

The most critical of these is to *back up your data*. We cannot stress enough how important a regular backup routine can be — the first time you accidentally delete or overwrite some file(s) you need, you'll be very glad to have a backup from which to restore them. Data recovery is one of the most expensive propositions a company or individual can face. In this case, an ounce of prevention is *definitely* worth a pound of cure.

Backups

A computer user who doesn't make backups is like a parachutist who doesn't check his or her equipment before jumping — they may be lucky for a while, but their luck runs out eventually, usually at a really inopportune time. It's not a matter of *if* you will encounter a problem with one of your files it's merely a matter of *when*.

Software and media

At one time, personal computer users could back up all their files on diskettes — in fact, the first IBM PCs and the first Macs didn't even have hard disks, and everything was kept on floppies. Now that multiple gigabytes are required merely for the Mac OS X system, backing up to floppy is no longer practical or even possible. Even the use of Zip disks is becoming impractical as a general backup medium when you take into consideration the files generated by programs like iMovie. Tape drives, CD-RW, and DVD-R drives are becoming the media of choice. Long the leading purveyor of backup software, Dantz Development (www.dantz.com) produces Mac OS X versions of their Retrospect backup for the casual desktop user to the enterprise. Apple provides .Backup software as part of its .Mac package. .Backup (www.mac.com) allows you to automate backup to CD and DVD, as well as to your .Mac storage space. Roxio Toast 6 (www.roxio.com) now includes Déjà Vu, a Preference pane which provides unattended backup to CDs and DVDs through Toast. There are a number of different backup programs, of which the previously mentioned ones are but a small selection, explore the Web sites indicated in Chapter 22, and you can find a package that suits your needs.

Regardless of the hardware and software you choose, it can't be repeated enough that you should perform backups regularly, and often. A month-old copy of your magnum opus won't be of much use if you've been updating it steadily over the past few weeks, all those changes and additions are lost, and the deadline is tomorrow.

Backup rotation

A useful backup strategy includes regular rotation of your media and periodic archiving of your backups. Writing repeatedly to the same media can frequently be problematic — not only does media degrade under frequent use, but you could easily be overwriting a good copy of a file with a corrupted copy.

If you're backing up data that is of the utmost importance to you or your employer, you'll want to make your plan as fail-safe as possible. Because there is no such thing as a single solution that is completely foolproof, having multiple solutions in place, where each has a minimal chance of failure is best. A good plan requires quite a few sets of backup media, and is only one facet of the overall plan to secure your data. When the data is irreplaceable, there's no such thing as too many backups. Some facets of a good backup are shown in the following sections; use them as a starting guide:

Backing up important data daily is best. You can reuse media for a while, but it is recommended that you archive and replace your media every so often to ensure you've got a good copy. It is a complete waste of time to be backing up your data to a disk that doesn't actually work.

A good reason for using multiple tapes or disks is to be able to keep a copy of your data *somewhere else*. If you are a business owner, think about what would happen to your company if you walked in one morning and the building had fallen down or flooded. Would you be able to continue without any of your files? If you had a copy at home, even if it was a week old, you could turn around, and get things back up in a matter of hours or days, rather than declaring bankruptcy.

You can use incremental backups for daily backups, but creating a full backup to brand new media is best for archival purposes. Think about how far back you want your archive to reach. At a certain point, you can reuse some of your archival media, since they don't get as much wear as daily media.

If you receive a virus or notice disk corruption at some point, you have a number of backups to choose from, including backups that are one day old, three days old, a week old, two weeks old, and so on. (If you find corruption on Thursday, you have Wednesday's backup, Tuesday's backup, Monday's backup, and the previous Friday's archive on top of any previous week's archives you've kept. Hopefully, there is a recent version that lacks the corruption. If your data is less mission critical, you can scale things back to every other day, and possibly only once a week.

For personal backup, the scheme can be a little less arduous depending on the number of files you generate and work on daily. We still recommend that you backup once or twice a week, rotating between at least two different disks or tapes, and archiving your data every month or so, depending on the sensitivity of the data. Entering two weeks worth of Quicken checkbook data is a time-consuming task.

Generally, you don't need to back up applications and system software, because these items are easily reinstalled and replaceable. However, backing up your user's home folders is a good idea because these folders usually contain application preferences, email storage, stickies database, Internet bookmarks, and user documents. A backup of the Classic preferences folder is good to have in the event of a disk crash (/System Folder/Preferences). You should also know where your applications keep their data, so you can be sure that you're backing up what you think you're backing up. You may want an archive of application updates and software downloaded from the Internet, just so you can get to those patches and updates quickly if you need to reinstall. Archive data periodically and keep at least two different backup tapes or disks active at once for some measure of redundancy.

Maintaining the file system

Although Mac OS X can read and write a wide variety of disk formats, it (at least currently) can only start up from two different formats, Mac OS Extended (also known as HFS Plus or HFS+ for *hierarchical file system plus*) and UFS (Unix File System, sometimes called ffs for *fast file system*). Apple recommends the use of the Mac OS Extended format, and so do we. The Classic application environment does not operate from a UFS formatted disk. Most Carbon applications perform better in the Mac OS Extended format because the file system does not have to translate the files to emulate the multiform files to which many Mac applications are accustomed.

Mac OS X comes with a basic disk diagnostic and disk-directory repair tool — Disk Utility, which is covered in depth in Chapter 21. Other vendors of well-regarded disk utilities include Micromat with Drive 10 and TechTool Pro (www.micromat.com), Alsoft with DiskWarrior (www.alsoft.com), and Symantec with Norton Utilities and Norton System Works (System works is a bundle of Utilities and AntiVirus) (www.symantec.com). So far, Alsoft and Norton have shipped Mac OS X versions of their disk utilities, and Micromat promises that TechTool Pro will be released any day now (Drive 10 was the first native Mac OS X disk utility).

Note If you restart in single-user mode (hold down ⌘-S during startup), you can run the Unix command-line tool fsck (File System ChecK), with the -y option, to repair many problems with the directory structures. If you choose this route, you should rerun it repeatedly until it comes back with no errors found.

The directory, sometimes referred to as the catalog of your hard drive, is like a library's card catalog; it is a list of items that provides information to the user regarding where everything in the library can be found. In ideal use, the directory would never have a problem, but with power outages, crashes, reboots, or brownouts, sometimes things in your disk's directory structure get out of order or even broken. Depending on the location of the damage, an incorrect directory structure can cause your computer to act up, lose files, or even refuse to boot to the desktop.

This is where the disk utility software comes in. Norton Utilities, Alsoft DiskWarrior, and Micromat's tools read through the directory structure and compare it to what is actually found in the places they are told to look. If a miscompare occurs, it is noted, and you are prompted to repair it. Norton and Micromat's philosophy of disk repair is to patch the directory — if there is a problem area of the directory, they will remove the incorrect entries and replace just those errors with the correct data. Alsoft on the other hand believes that it is better to create a brand new directory structure from scratch, avoiding any problems that could be created by the patching process. DiskWarrior is generally regarded as the most reliable of the repair tools listed here, though TechTool pro and Norton Utilities have more tools in their bags of tricks, and fix more than just directory damage. You will want to have a few tools at your disposal — sometimes even the most reliable tool will not be able to solve a problem you encounter, and a different utility with a different approach may get the job done.

Note There is a third philosophy when it comes to disk damage — hard drives are cheap these days but your data is expensive to replace, and even a successful repair of the directory doesn't exclude the possibility of further damage. Two companies, Prosoft Engineering (www.prosoftengineering.com) and BinaryBiz (www.www.binarybiz.com), make disk tools that focus on the *recovery* of your data rather than the repair of your disk. DataRescue X (ProSoft) and VirtualLab Data Recovery (BinaryBiz) will even scour a disk that is beyond recovery using the disk utilities listed above, and find your files for you, allowing you to copy them to a new drive, and throw away or replace the damaged disk.

Invisible files and folders

Apple and the graphical user interface try very hard to conceal the sometimes cryptic Unix underpinnings of Mac OS X from you. For example, the standard command-line directories (folders) are hidden from you when you're in the Finder or using an Open or Save dialog.

These directories have such revealing names as .bin (binary executables), .dev (devices), .etc (et cetera, miscellaneous items), .sbin (more binary executables, mostly run at startup time), and .usr (user directory hierarchy).

Now, you may ask, if the Finder hides these from us, how do we ever find out where they are? You can use a few easy ways to find out: use Unix commands in a Terminal window as described in Chapter 25 or use OS X's Find command to search for items whose visibility is off, as shown in Figure 22-1. You can also make use of utilities such as TinkerTool and Cocktail (see Chapter 21 for more information) to turn off the invisibility of all of the files on your Hard Drive, and browse them like any other files.

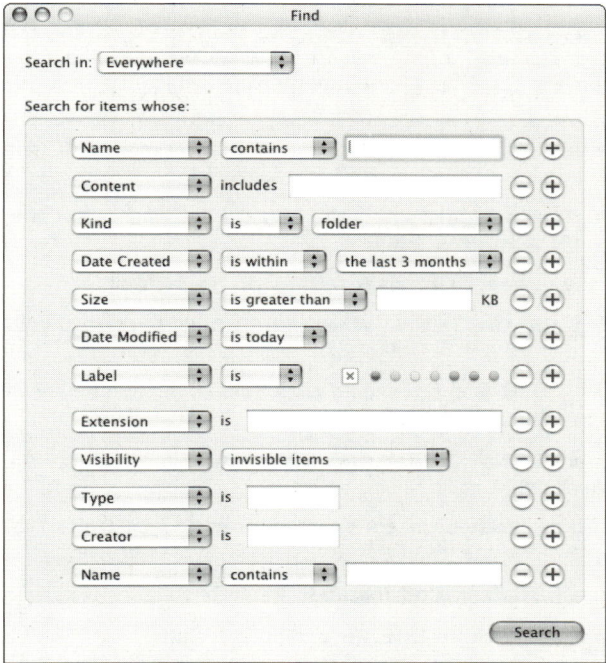

Figure 22-1: Mac OS X's Find command is very powerful and allows you to set many constraints on your file search. You can use the Find command to search for invisible files by selecting the Visibility pull down menu.

Because these folders are invisible, Mac OS X's Find command won't let you double-click them to open them in the Finder. To see what they contain, you will have to make them visible, or be constrained by the use of the Terminal and then enter Unix commands — `ls -F /bin`, for example, gives you a listing of all the files in the /bin directory and indicates whether they are directories (appending a slash), executables (appending an asterisk), or a link (appending an at-sign).

I Forgot my Password and I Can't Get Up

If a user can't remember his or her password on your computer, you can log in as an administrator and reset the user's password. If there are no other accounts, or no one can remember the password of an administrator account on your computer, you can reset passwords of ordinary user and administrator accounts by using the Mac OS X installation CD.

To reset a password when no administrator account passwords are at hand, follow these steps:

1. **Restart the computer with the Mac OS X installation CD.** Insert the CD and choose Apple ➪ Restart.

2. **When you hear the computer's startup chime, hold down the C key until the computer begins starting up from the CD.** You can release the C key when you hear the sounds of activity coming from the CD. After a minute or two, the Installer application opens.

3. **In the Installer, choose Installer ➪ Reset Password.** The Password Reset application opens.

4. **At the top of the Password Reset window, select the Mac OS X disk that has the user account whose password needs resetting.**

5. **For each user account whose password needs resetting, do the following:**

    1. **Click the pop-up menu and choose the user account whose password you want to reset.**

    2. **Type a new password in both text boxes and click Save.** If the two entries are not identical, you are asked to re-enter them.

    3. **In the dialog that appears, click OK. The dialog informs you that the password you entered was saved.**

    4. **When you finish resetting passwords, choose Password Reset ➪ Quit Password Reset.** You return to the Installer.

    5. **In the Installer, choose Installer ➪ Quit Installer.**

    6. **In the dialog that appears, click Restart.** The computer restarts.

Caution   Safeguard your Mac OS X installation CD to prevent someone from using it to gain unrestricted access to your computer. If your data is important to you, secure the computer physically and prevent access to unauthorized users.

Protecting against viruses

Although computer viruses are not nearly as prevalent on Macs as on Microsoft Windows PCs, Mac viruses do exist, and many of the so-called macro viruses developed on PCs (generally infecting Microsoft Office documents) can infect Macs. If you perform a search on one of the popular antivirus sites such as www.symantec.com you'll find millions of viruses, but only a handful of viruses for the Macintosh, many of which don't even apply to Mac OS X. Security through obscurity is not a very strong defense, however, and it is recommended that you take steps to protect yourself.

Viruses invade your computer through documents or applications that you have downloaded from the Internet, through electronic mail attachments, through any type of removable disk (including floppy disks), or network volumes you may use with your computer. Although some viruses may be relatively innocuous, doing little more than taking up space on disk and slowing down your computer a bit, others can be highly destructive, causing crashes and erasing files. The Unix system of file permissions underlying Mac OS X make infection from viruses even less likely to cause extensive damage — at least so long as you don't log in with the System Administrator (root) account.

The only way to protect your Mac from computer viruses is to install an antivirus utility on your computer. Antivirus software warns you if a virus attempts to infect your system, scans your disks for viruses that may be lurking (or may already have caused some damage), and eradicates almost any virus that it finds. Symantec's Norton Antivirus, MacAfee's Virex X, and Sophos Anti-Virus, among others, are available for Mac OS X. If you are a .Mac member, one of the advantages is that Apple provides you with a licensed copy of Virex X with your membership.

Whichever antivirus software package you choose, make sure that you keep it up-to-date; each time a new virus appears, the antivirus packages must generally be updated to recognize it. Most of the time, you receive updates by downloading them from the software publisher's Web site or accessing them in public download Web sites or FTP sites. Usually, you have a limited "subscription" to updates to the virus software itself. With Virex, you can pay an additional fee to have updates e-mailed directly to you. Norton AntiVirus includes a LiveUpdate feature that automatically downloads and applies the latest virus definitions for you. A full year of virus definition updates is normally included in the price of your software package, afterwards you must pay a subscription fee to continue to receive updates. If a newer version of the antivirus software has been released in the past year, it is sometimes a better deal to purchase the newer version rather than subscribe to the update plan. Virex and Norton AntiVirus are targeted at home and small business users, while Sophos Anti-Virus is aimed at the larger networked and cross-platform market. Sophos Anti-Virus generally runs on a server, and can be set to scan files on access, rather than at a set time. MacAfee , Symantec, and Sophos post new virus definitions to their Web sites monthly (normally in the first week of every month), possibly more frequently if a particularly destructive virus is discovered. If you are either a Virex or Norton AntiVirus customer, you should consider marking your calendar to check on the first of the month and to bookmark the company's virus definitions page for easy access.

Mac OS X is mostly free of virus infection, however, viruses in the PC world can affect Mac users. The widespread worms that have been hopping around the Internet, being propagated by insecure Microsoft Windows machines have caused other problems on the Mac. While not an infection, these worms spread themselves by emailing hundreds, sometimes thousands of people in the address books of those computers that are infected. Mac users have been inundated with these virus-containing messages, and while they pose no direct threat of corruption or data loss because they can't infect the Macintosh that receives them, it is quite the pain to get 30 or more spurious messages a day. Even worse, is the fact that some viruses spoof the originator, and Mac users can be incorrectly pegged as virus propagators. Take heart that you haven't been infected, and keep on top of what viruses are rampant in the wild so that you can determine the actual threat to your data.

Computer Viruses, Worms, and Trojan Horses

A *computer virus* is a piece of software designed to spread itself by illicitly attaching copies of itself to legitimate software. Although not all viruses perform malicious actions (such as erasing your hard disk), any virus can interfere with the normal functioning of your computer.

A *macro virus* is a virus written in the *macro language* of an application (a programming language that enables you to automate multiple-step operations in an application). By far, most macro viruses infect Microsoft Word (Version 6.0 and later) and Excel (Version 5.0 and later) documents. Like other viruses, macro viruses can be very destructive.

Viruses, alas, are not the only potentially destructive software that you may encounter. *Worms* are similar to viruses in that they replicate, but they do not attach themselves to files. A worm replaces a legitimate program or file on your system and performs its mischief whenever that legitimate program is run.

A *Trojan horse* is an intentionally destructive program masquerading as something useful, such as a utility, software updater, or game. Although worms and Trojan horses are not viruses, most commercial antivirus programs can detect and remove them.

Keeping software up-to-date

Unfortunately, no software of any consequential size and complexity is completely free of bugs (bugs being improperly programmed instructions). Some bugs may be features that do not function as planned to more serious errors, causing crashes or data corruption. Many bugs are so obscure, requiring an unusual confluence of events that you are likely never to encounter them. But a few bugs may appear to take a nip at you. As one of the largest bodies of code on your Mac, Mac OS X also is not completely bug-free.

Customarily, after software publishers become aware of a problem with their product, they take action to correct the anomaly by either one of the following:

✦ Document a work-around while they work on a new version that fixes the problem.

✦ Provide an *updater* that updates the application to a new version with the problem fixed.

Registering your software (either by sending in the postcard that came with it or via the Internet, as you did when you performed your Mac OS X Setup) and checking the publisher's Web site regularly are two good ways to keep informed of workarounds and updaters. Many software publishers, such as Aladdin Systems, include in their applications the ability to automatically check the publisher for updates just as Apple does with Mac OS X and QuickTime.

Mac OS X, like Mac OS 9 before it, provides a live Software Update capability. The Software Update pane of System Preferences is easily accessible from the System Preference application. Keeping your operating system software up-to-date with the latest enhancements and bug fixes from Apple should be part of your maintenance regimen.

To install software updates:

1. **Launch the System Preferences application.** It can be accessed from the dock, or from the Apple Menu by choosing System Preferences.

2. **In the System section of the System Preferences application, click on the Software update icon.**

3. **Click on the Check Now button (shown in Figure 22-2).** Your computer must be connected to the Internet, and you will see a progress bar in the bottom of the window. If there are any updates to be installed, the Software Update application will launch.

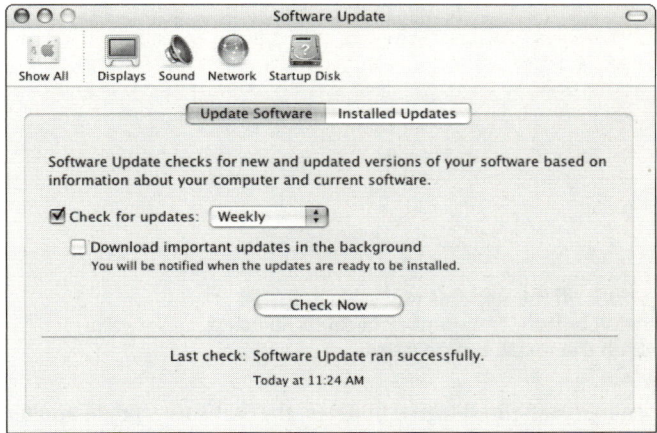

Figure 22-2: The Software Update Preference pane can be configured to automatically check for updates on a daily, weekly, or monthly basis.

4. **Click on an update in the list of available updates to see more information about the update in the lower pane of the window**. Make sure that the updates you want to install are checked and click the install button in the lower-right corner of the window. Some updates require the computer to restart, and they will have an icon next to them that indicates this. Figure 22-3 shows the update list before installation begins.

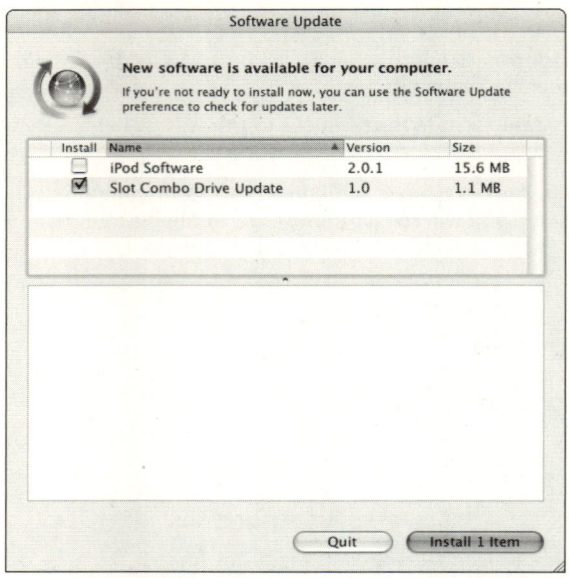

Figure 22-3: Check off the updates you wish to install and click the install button. The number of items selected is displayed within the install button's text.

After you have chosen to install the selected updates, the Software Update application connects to Apple's servers and automatically downloads and installs the updates you have chosen. Some updates can be rather large, if you are on a dial-up account, you should pay attention to the size of the update so you can plan accordingly. Figure 22-4 shows the Software Update application downloading and preparing to install updates.

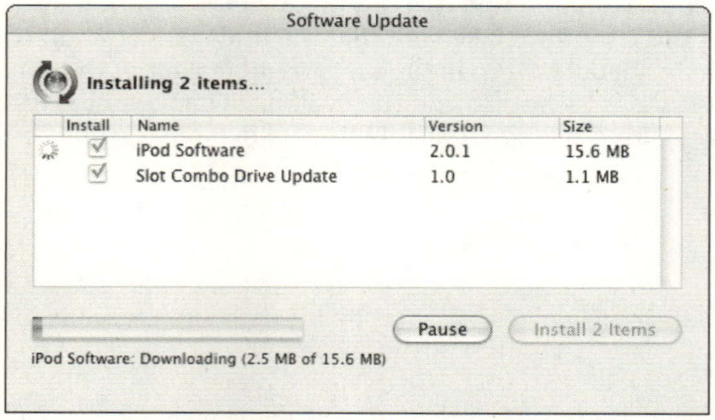

Figure 22-4: The Software Update application conveniently downloads and installs the updates you have selected all at once, saving you the time of downloading and installing each one separately.

Tip

If you chose not to install an update because it doesn't pertain to your system configuration (such as an AirPort update, but your computer doesn't have or support AirPort), you can hide updates so you don't have to see them each time you run the update check. Select an item from the list (do not check the checkbox, merely click on the name of the update), and from the Update menu, select Make inactive. You can show the inactive updates at a later date by going to the Update menu and selecting Show Inactive.

You can also check your iDisk for new and updated applications and utilities from Apple, as discussed in Chapter 10. There, you find such goodies as iTunes, iMovie, and the AppleWorks updaters in addition to new and updated printer drivers for Mac OS X. Here are some excellent sources to check:

✦ Apple's Mac OS X Web site (www.apple.com/macosx/)

✦ Apple's Software Updates library (www.apple.com/swupdates)

✦ VersionTracker (www.versiontracker.com/macosx)

Despite testing by Apple and various software publishers, some older software products are incompatible with the Classic environment. Assuming that you have already verified that they work with Mac OS 9, you should keep them separate and run them only when you start up with Mac OS 9 until a Mac OS X–compatible version becomes available.

Maintenance measures

As you've seen in other chapters, Mac OS X brought with it the concept of permissions. To a certain extent, this security model has grown from the Unix multiuser environment, and is designed to keep users out of places they shouldn't have access to, such as each other's home folders. The system, and all of the documents, applications, and folders contained on your hard drive each have their own permissions which tell the operating system who and what is allowed access to each item. These permissions can get messed up over time, and can cause applications to cease functioning in the way they are supposed to. Fortunately, Apple has provided a means of repairing the permissions on your computer to their proper settings.

Repairing system permissions

The included Disk Utility application provides an automated feature to repair the permissions of the system and the installed applications. If for some reason the permissions of your Disk Utility application are incorrect, it may in some very obscure instances be unable to properly function. In this case, you can boot your computer from a Mac OS X installation CD and repair the permissions using the Disk Utility command under the File menu. Alternatively, boot from an external or separate drive that has Mac OS X installed, and repair permissions from the Disk Utility on that volume. Permissions can only be repaired on drives that have Mac OS X installed; drives that only contain data or are Mac OS 9 boot volumes are not supported.

Disk fragmentation

When the files on a disk become fragmented, disk performance suffers considerably. In addition, files themselves (including applications) can become fragmented on a disk. A single file may be split into several pieces spread around in different locations physically on a disk. Fragmentation degrades disk performance because the drive must take extra time to move from one piece of a file to the next.

A fragmented file is analogous to a single track on an audio CD being split into multiple segments, so that the beginning of the track may be at the beginning of the CD, the middle at the end, and the end of the track some place in the middle with other unrelated files interspersed between. If audio CDs were mastered in that fashion (which, fortunately, they are not), you would likely notice a delay as the CD player's laser moves to play the next segment.

In a disk with no fragmentation, each file physically resides in a single contiguous block. As a disk begins to fill up and new files are created and deleted with increasing frequency, files and the free space start to become fragmented. A heavily fragmented disk is more likely to experience a variety of problems, including corrupted directory structures and damaged files.

Without any special software, you can eliminate fragmentation by copying the entire contents of a disk to another disk, erasing the disk, and copying everything back. An easier solution is to use a commercial disk defragmentation utility, such as the SpeedDisk component of the Norton Utilities from Symantec (www.symantec.com), Plus Optimizer from Alsoft (www.alsoft.com), or Drive 10 from Micromat (www.micromat.com). Note, however, that older disk optimization utilities are not compatible with the Unix File System (UFS) and you should check for compatibility before attempting to run a disk optimizer on a UFS volume.

Before optimizing any disk, take the time to make a full backup, because virtually every byte on the disk can be erased and moved to a different location. If an error occurs during this process you stand the chance of losing some or all of your data.

Scheduling Maintenance

Taken together, all of the maintenance tasks discussed in the preceding sections — backing up, virus checking, securing your system, repairing permissions, defragmentation of your drive, and periodic cleaning up — can help ensure that your Mac experience is relatively error and hassle free.

✦ **Daily.** You should turn on and shut down your Mac only once per day (at the beginning and end of your work day or Mac session), if you elect to do so at all. You can put your Mac to sleep, spin down the hard disk, and make other energy-saving settings in the Energy Saver pane of System Preferences (see Chapter 13). The most wear and tear on your computer's components occurs during startup and shutdown due to the power draw that those processes require. It is good to leave your computer on overnight once in a while as Mac OS X runs maintenance scripts late at night to tidy up after itself.

You should also check your disk space levels — open the Macintosh HD icon and look at the status section of the window at the top (you may have to choose View ⇨ Show Status Bar to make it visible) to make sure that you have disk space available. In a business setting, you may also want to back up on a daily basis or every other day.

✦ **Weekly.** Scan your computer with virus software if it's not already designed to run in the background. If your machine is for personal use, you may want to back up on a weekly basis, according to the media rotation schedule you have devised.

✦ **Monthly.** Update your virus definitions if your virus software doesn't do this for you automatically. Check for updates to Mac OS X at least once a month. If the Software Update pane of System Preferences isn't set to update automatically, go to this pane at least once a month and click the Check Now button to initiate an update manually. In addition, every few months you should defragment your hard disk. Repair the permissions of your drive monthly, especially after an update to the Mac OS system has been applied.

✦ **Every three to six months.** Run a session from one of the Disk Utility packages mentioned earlier in this Chapter. Clean house — remove applications, preference files, and other software that you no longer need. If you are a light computer user, defragment your hard disk.

Monitoring system performance

Some Mac problems manifest themselves in slow performance rather than in crashes or system errors. If your Mac has been performing more slowly than usual, the following sections discuss a few possible causes and solutions.

Memory problems

If you open memory-consumptive applications or documents, Mac OS X employs *virtual memory* (treating part of your hard disk as memory, also called the *swap space*) to continue to work. If your software has to continually access the disk to retrieve data because of this, you experience a significant performance degradation. Other than dealing with smaller documents or using applications with lesser appetites, the solution here is to purchase and install more RAM. Although Mac OS X recommends at least 128MB of RAM, a realistic minimum is 256–384MB and even more will generally speed your computer up drastically, especially if you work with large files.

Insufficient drive space

Running low on hard drive space can affect performance in various ways. You should archive and delete files that you don't need everyday access to, and remove any applications you no longer need. If you don't regularly leave your computer on overnight, use a utility such as Cocktail to manually run the Mac OS X maintenance scripts that delete over-long log files, and clean out cache space that piles up over time. An application such as the Omni Group's OmniDiskSweeper (`www.omnigroup.com`) can help you figure out which directories are taking up the most space, saving you time in the cleanup process.

If you have purged as much as you can stand but are still low on space, you may need to add additional storage space to your computer. Apple's tower models, such as the PowerMac line, support between two and four internal hard drives in capacities up to 250GB each (at the time of this writing, though hard drive manufacturers are constantly creating more voluminous drives). Check your computer's manual or Apple's support page to determine what type and size drives your computer supports. For computers that do not support multiple internal drives you can, with varying degrees of difficulty depending on the model, replace the internal drive with a bigger model. A third alternative for the faint of heart is to invest in an external drive — Firewire enclosures are becoming increasingly popular due to their extreme ease of use and portability. You can purchase external Firewire drives in capacities ranging from 0GB (just an enclosure, you add your own drive, such as the one you just removed from your computer to make way for a bigger one) to 500GB or more using multiple disks. Hard drives come in different physical sizes, ranging from the very portable 2.5-inch laptop-sized drives to the standard 3.5-inch desktop-sized drives. The 2.5-inch drives make for very portable data storage when coupled with a Firewire enclosure, and can be found at many retailers online and off.

Summary

In this chapter, you learned where different system, application, and personal support and preferences files are stored in Mac OS X. You also learned how to perform preventive and basic maintenance on your hard disk(s). You should now recognize the importance of a good backup system, and should know how to devise a backup strategy to maintain your data and recover in the event of a disk or system problem. Preventative maintenance is a worthy cause to invest in and should not be dismissed lightly. Often users do not recognize the importance of a good maintenance and backup regimen until it is too late and their data is lost to them. Visit www.drivesavers.com and find out the cost of data recovery if your files were ever lost. In addition to the expense of recovery, you will be glad of the downtime you've saved yourself by thinking ahead.

✦   ✦   ✦

Automating with AppleScript

Although computers have been touted for years as the ultimate tool to perform redundant tasks, you may feel as though computers have generated new monotonous tasks. In previous chapters, you learned about technologies in Mac OS X that help you launch documents, edit text, create multimedia, print, and perform hundreds of other tasks. And though you may be impressed by components in all of those technologies, no component does much alone — they tend to require user input. Scripting has long been a way to coordinate the different components of a task, by allowing you to compose a script that plays back a set of commands in order.

The AppleScript scripting language is a simplified programming language, which enables you to control your applications and perform tasks automatically. Scripts range from the simplest to the highly complex, depending on your skill at scripting, your knowledge of AppleScript's nuances, and the requirements of your task. In this chapter, you learn enough about AppleScript that even if you are a scripting novice you will get scripts up and running.

You will begin by learning the underlying technologies that make AppleScript possible — messages and events. After you understand messages and events, it's on to an introduction of AppleScript and a look at the tools that enable you to run, modify, and create scripts of your own. Finally, you run through a few basic scripts, gaining an understanding of the AppleScript language as you go.

Understanding Messages and Events

Macintosh applications perform tasks in response to events. Users originate events with the keyboard and mouse, and applications respond to the events by performing tasks. Similarly, an application can make other applications perform tasks by sending messages about events.

The events that applications send to each other in messages are called *Apple events*. AppleScript makes applications perform tasks by sending them Apple events.

When an application receives a message about an Apple event, the application takes a particular action based on the specific event.

This action can be anything from performing a menu command to taking some data, manipulating it, and returning the result to the source of the Apple event message.

For example, when you choose Shut Down or Restart from the Apple menu, Mac OS X sends an Apple event message to every open application saying a Quit event occurred. For this reason, applications quit automatically when you choose Shut Down or Restart.

When you drop document icons on an application icon, the Finder sends a message to Mac OS X saying this event happened, and the system sends the application an Apple event message that says an Open Documents event occurred. The Open Document message includes a list of all the documents whose icons you dragged and dropped. When you double-click an application icon, the Finder sends the system a message that says this event happened, and the system sends the application an Open Application message. When you double-click a document, the application that created the document gets an Open Documents message with the name of the document you double-clicked.

Virtually all Mac applications respond to at least four Apple events: Open Application, Open Documents, and Quit Application. Applications that print also respond to the Apple event Print Documents. Only very old, very specialized, or poorly engineered Mac applications don't respond to these basic Apple events.

Applications that go beyond the four basic Apple events understand another two dozen core Apple events. These Apple events encompass actions and objects that almost all applications have in common, such as the Close, Save, Undo, Redo, Cut, Copy, and Paste commands. Applications with related capabilities recognize still more sets of Apple events. For example, word processing applications understand Apple events about text manipulation, and drawing applications understand Apple events about graphics manipulation. Application developers can even define private Apple events that only their applications know.

Mac OS X provides the means of communicating Apple event messages between applications. The applications can be on the same computer or on different computers connected to the same network. To understand how Apple event messages work, think of them as a telephone system. Mac OS X furnishes a telephone for each application as well as the wires that connect them. Applications call each other with messages about Apple events.

Apple events offer many intriguing possibilities for the world of personal computing. No longer does one application need to handle every possible function; instead, it can send Apple event messages to helper applications. For example, iTunes handles some commands in its File menu, such as Export Song List, by sending Apple event messages to the Finder, which actually carries out the commands.

Some Classic Programs Cannot Receive Apple Event Messages

In the Classic compatibility environment, only application programs can send and receive Apple event messages; true control panels and desk accessories cannot, although these items are now uncommon. Control panels that are actually applications (listed in the Classic environment's Applications menu when open) are not subject to this limitation. And a desk accessory can work around this limitation by sending and receiving through a small surrogate application that is always open in the background. This background application does not have to appear in the Classic environment's Application menu, and the computer user does not have to know that the application is open.

Introducing AppleScript

Apple event messages aren't just for professional software engineers. Macintosh enthusiasts with little technical training can use Apple event messages to control applications by writing statements in the AppleScript language. For example, suppose that you want to quit all open applications. Mac OS X doesn't have a Quit All command, but you can create one with AppleScript. You can use AppleScript commands to automate simple tasks as well as to automate a more complicated series of tasks, as the rest of this chapter demonstrates.

AppleScript language

AppleScript is a language that you can use to tell applications what to do using natural language. AppleScript is a programming language that is designed especially to make it easy for computer users, not computer engineers, to build their own solutions. (Actually, engineers use it, too.)

You tell applications what to do by writing statements in the AppleScript language. Although AppleScript is an artificial language, its statements look like sentences in a natural language, such as English. You can look at many AppleScript statements and easily figure out what they're supposed to do.

The words and phrases in AppleScript statements resemble English, but they are terms that have special meanings in the context of AppleScript. Some terms are commands, and some terms are objects that the commands act on. Other terms control how AppleScript performs the statements.

A single AppleScript statement can perform a simple task, but most tasks require a series of statements that are performed one after the other. A set of AppleScript statements that accomplishes a task (or several tasks) is called a *script*. A script can rename a batch of files, change an application's preference settings, copy data from a database to another application, or automate a sequence of tasks that you previously performed one at a time by hand. You can develop your own script tools to accomplish exactly what you need.

As an added boon, AppleScript can actually watch you as you work with an application and write a script for you behind the scenes. This process is called *script recording*.

Although AppleScript is designed to be a simple to understand language, it offers all the capabilities of a traditional programming language and won't frustrate programmers and advanced users. You can store information in variables for later use; write if...then statements to perform commands selectively according to a condition that you specify; or repeat a set of commands as many times as you want. AppleScript also offers error checking and object-oriented programming.

Scripting additions

AppleScript has an expandable lexicon of terms. It knows meanings of basic terms, and it augments this knowledge with terms from other sources. Many additional AppleScript terms come from the very applications that AppleScript controls. We explore this source of AppleScript terms in greater detail later in this chapter.

Additional AppleScript terms also come from special files called *scripting additions*. AppleScript looks for scripting addition files in the following folders:

✦ **ScriptingAdditions.** In the Library folder of the System folder (path /System/Library/ScriptingAdditions/) — contains standard scripting additions from Apple that are available to all users of your computer. (This folder may also contain other files that are not scripting additions.)

✦ **Scripts.** In the main Library folder (path /Library/Scripts/) — contains more scripting additions that are available to all users of your computer.

✦ **Scripting Additions.** In the folder named System Folder (path /System Folder/Scripting Additions/ unless you have moved or renamed System Folder) — contains more scripting additions that are available in the Classic environment to all users of your computer.

✦ **Scripting Additions and Scripts.** In the Extensions folder of the folder named System Folder (path /System Folder/Extensions/Scripting Additions/ and path /System Folder/Extensions/Scripts/ unless you have moved or renamed System Folder) — contains more scripting additions that are available in the Classic environment to all users of your computer. (This Scripting Additions folder usually exists only on computers that previously used Mac OS 8.)

You need separate scripting additions for Mac OS X and the Classic environment. Scripting additions made for Mac OS X do not work in the Classic environment. Conversely, scripting additions made for Mac OS 9 and earlier work only in the Classic environment. If you get more scripting additions made for Mac OS X, put them in one of the ScriptingAdditions folders that is inside a Library folder. If you get more scripting additions made for Mac OS 9, put them in one of the Scripting Additions folders that are inside the System Folder used for the Classic environment.

Tip   If the ScriptingAdditions folder doesn't exist in a Library folder where you want to put a scripting addition file, create a new folder and name it ScriptingAdditions (put no spaces in the name). Put your scripting addition file in this new folder.

Introducing Script Editor

For creating and editing AppleScript scripts, you can use the Script Editor application included with Mac OS X. Script Editor can also run scripts, and it can make scripts into self-contained applications that run when you double-click them in the Finder. Script Editor is normally located in the AppleScript in the Applications folder.

Tip   If you end up doing a lot of scripting, you may want to replace Script Editor with a more capable script development application, such as or Script Debugger from Late Night Software (www.latenightsw.com). Make sure you get a version made for Mac OS X.

Scriptable applications and environments

The scripts you create with Script Editor can control any *scriptable application*. A prime example of a scriptable application is the Finder. Other scriptable applications included with Mac OS X include Apple System Profiler, ColorSync Scripting, Internet Connect, iCal, iChat, iPhoto, iSync, iTunes, Internet Explorer, Mail, Print Center, QuickTime Player, Sherlock, StuffIt Expander, Terminal, TextEdit, and URL Access Scripting. Interestingly enough, even the Script Editor is scriptable. In addition, many Mac OS X applications not made by Apple are scriptable.

Plenty of Classic applications are also scriptable. Although a Classic version of Script Editor is included with Mac OS 9, you can use the Mac OS X version of Script Editor to make scripts for the Classic environment as well as for Mac OS X.

Looking at a script window

When you open Script Editor, an empty script window appears. Each script window can contain one script. The top part of the script window is the script editing area, where you type and edit the text of the script just as you type and edit in any text editing application. The bottom part of the window is the script description area. You use this area to type a description of what the script does. Figure 23-1 shows an empty script window.

Figure 23-1: A new script window appears when Script Editor opens.

Tip   You can change the default size of a new script window. First, make the script window the size you want and then choose Save as Default from the Window menu in Script Editor.

The tool bar of a script window has four buttons. You find out more about each of them in later sections, but the following list summarizes their functions:

✦ **Record.** AppleScript goes into recording mode and creates script statements corresponding to your actions in applications that support script recording. You can also press ⌘-D to start recording. You cannot record scripts for every scriptable application because software developers must do more work to make an application recordable than to make it scriptable. You can find out whether an application is recordable by trying to record some actions in it.

✦ **Stop.** Takes AppleScript out of recording mode or stops a script that is running, depending on which action is relevant at the time. Pressing ⌘-period (.) on the keyboard is the same as clicking Stop.

✦ **Run.** Starts running the script that is displayed in the script-editing area. You also can press ⌘-R to run the script.

Before running the script, Script Editor scans the script to see if you changed any part of it since you last ran it or checked its syntax (as described next). If the script has changed, Script Editor checks the script's syntax.

✦ **Compile.** Checks for errors in the script, such as incorrect punctuation or missing parts of commands. If any errors turn up, Script Editor highlights the error and displays a dialog explaining the problem. Script Editor also formats the text to make keywords stand out and the structure of the script more apparent. Script Editor may even change the text, but the changes do not affect the meaning of the script.

If the script's syntax is correct, Script Editor tells AppleScript to *compile* the script, which means it converts the text of the script into codes. These codes are what Apple event messages actually contain and what applications understand. You don't usually see these codes in Script Editor, because AppleScript translates them into words for the enlightenment of human beings.

Note   If you use the Classic version of Script Editor to run or check the syntax of a script that controls an application that isn't open, the script may fail while waiting for the application to open. Wait until the needed application opens and then try the script again.

Creating a Simple Script

An easy way to see how a script looks and works is to type a simple script into a new script window. If Script Editor is not already the active application, open it or switch to it. If you need to create a new script window, choose File ➪ New Script. In the script-editing area at the bottom of the new script window, type the following statements:

```
tell application "Finder"
activate
set the bounds of the first Finder window to {128, 74, 671, 479}
set the current view of the first Finder window to icon view
set the icon size of the icon view options of the first Finder window
to 32
select the first item of the first Finder window
end tell
```

Check your script for typographical errors by clicking the Compile button in the script window. If Script Editor reports an error, carefully compare the statement you typed in the script window to the same statement in the book. Pay particular attention to spelling, punctuation, omitted words, and omitted spaces.

When you click Compile, Script Editor formats your script, changing the text formatting as it compiles the script using different type styles to show different kinds of terms. The statements that you typed probably changed from Courier font to Verdana font after you clicked Compile. Script Editor normally formats text that hasn't been compiled as 10-point Courier. Most other words, including commands from scripting additions and application dictionaries, are normally formatted in plain 10-point Verdana. Verdana 10-point Bold normally indicates native words in the AppleScript language. Figure 23-2 shows how Script Editor formats the script that you typed.

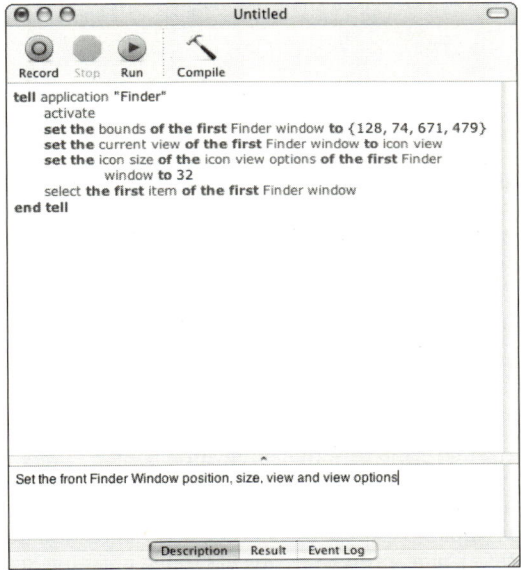

Figure 23-2: Check your script for errors and format it for readability by clicking the Compile button.

Before running this script, return to the Finder and make sure that a Finder window is displayed. If you really want to see the script in action, set the front Finder window to list view and resize the window so that it is very small.

After setting the stage for the script, switch back to Script Editor and click Run in your script's window. AppleScript executes each script statement in turn. When the script finishes running, the Finder window should be a standard size and set to icon view. The item that comes first alphabetically in the window should be selected.

Switch to Script Editor again and examine the script. You find that the script is fairly understandable. It may not be fluent English, but many of the commands should make sense as you read them.

Analyzing a Script

Having looked through the script that you wrote in the previous example, you may be surprised to learn that AppleScript doesn't know anything about the Finder's operations. Although your recorded script contains commands that set the position, size, and view of a Finder window and selects an item in it, AppleScript doesn't know anything about these or other Finder operations. In fact, AppleScript knows how to perform only the six following commands:

✦ Copy

✦ Count

✦ Error

✦ Get

✦ Run

✦ Set

AppleScript learns about moving and resizing Finder windows from the Finder. More generally, AppleScript learns about commands in a script from the application that the script controls. The application has a dictionary of AppleScript commands that work with the application. The dictionary defines the syntax of each command. AppleScript learns about more commands from scripting addition files on your computer. Each scripting addition file contains a dictionary of supplemental AppleScript commands.

Learning application commands and objects

Look at the sample script you created. The first statement says,

```
tell application "Finder"
```

To AppleScript, this statement means "start working with the application named Finder." When AppleScript sees a `tell application` statement, it looks at the dictionary for the specified application and figures out what commands the application understands. For example, by looking at the Finder's dictionary, AppleScript learns that the Finder understands the `select` command. The dictionary also tells AppleScript what objects the application knows how to work with, such as files and windows. In addition, an application's dictionary tells AppleScript how to compile the words and phrases that you write in scripts into Apple event codes that the application understands.

After learning from the `tell application` statement which application it will send event messages to, AppleScript compiles the remaining statements to determine what Apple event messages to send. One by one, AppleScript translates every statement it encounters in your script into an Apple event message based on the application's dictionary. When the script runs, the Apple event messages will be sent to the application named in the `tell` statement. The application will receive the messages and take the appropriate action in response to the Apple events.

AppleScript stops using the application dictionary when it encounters the `end tell` statement at the end of your script.

A complex script may have several `tell application` statements that name different script-able applications. In each case, AppleScript starts using the dictionary of the application named by the `tell application` statement, compiles subsequent statements using this dictionary, and stops using this dictionary when it encounters the next `end tell` statement. Because AppleScript gets all the information about an application's commands and objects from the application itself, you never have to worry about controlling a new application. As long as the application has a dictionary, AppleScript can work with it.

Inspecting a dictionary

Just as AppleScript can get information about an application's commands and objects from its dictionary, so can you. Using Script Editor, you can display the AppleScript dictionary of an application to see what commands the application understands and what objects the commands work with. You can also look at the dictionaries of scripting addition files.

Displaying a dictionary window

In Script Editor, choose Open Dictionary from the File menu. A dialog appears, listing script-able applications and scripting additions. Select an application or scripting addition file in the list and click Open. Script Editor displays a dictionary window for the application or scripting addition you selected, as shown in Figure 23-3.

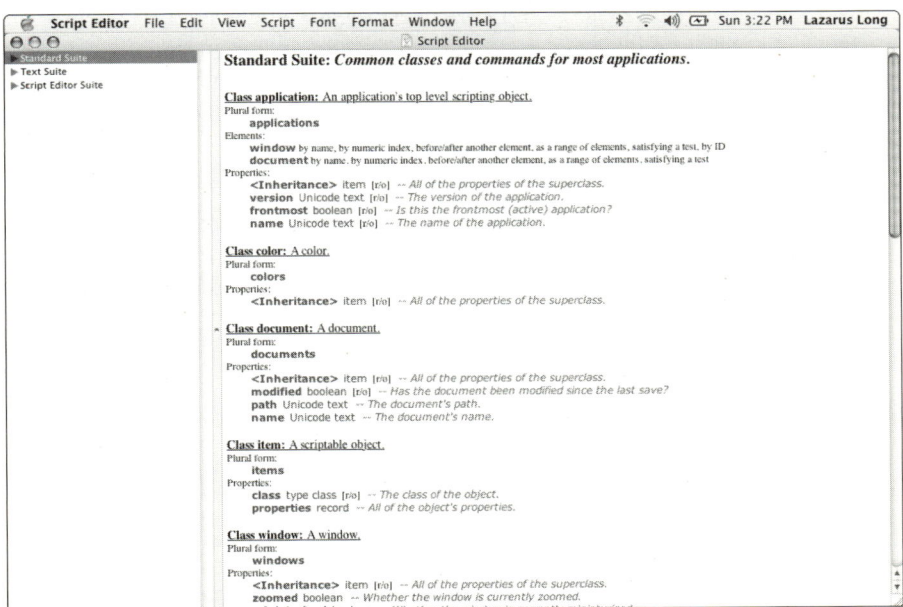

Figure 23-3: An AppleScript dictionary defines suites of commands and objects for a scriptable application or a scripting addition file.

Tip In the Open Dictionary dialog, you can select several applications and scripting additions whose dictionaries you want to display (each in a separate window). To select adjacent items in the list, drag across or Shift-click the items. To select nonadjacent items, ⌘-click each item that you want to select.

Looking at a dictionary window

The left side of a dictionary window displays a list of commands and objects. The commands are displayed in plain text, and objects are displayed in italics. Script Editor groups related commands and objects into suites and displays the names of suites in bold. You don't have to worry about suites when you're scripting.

The right side of a dictionary window displays detailed information about the term or terms selected on the left. To see a detailed description of one term, click it on the left side of the window. To see detailed descriptions of all terms in a suite, click the suite name.

Tip You can also see descriptions of several adjacent terms by dragging across them on the left. You can see descriptions of nonadjacent terms by ⌘-clicking each term on the left.

The description of a command briefly explains what the command does and defines its syntax. In the syntax definition, bold words are command words that you must type exactly as written. Words in plain text represent information that you provide, such as a value or an object for the command to work on. Any parts of a syntax definition that are enclosed in brackets are optional.

The description of an object very briefly describes the object and may list the following:

✦ **Plural Form.** States how to refer to multiple objects collectively. For example, you can refer to a specific window or to all windows.

✦ **Elements.** Enumerates items that can belong to the object. In a script, you would refer to *item* of *object*. For example, you could refer to a file named index.html in the folder named Sites as `file "index.html" of folder "Sites"`.

✦ **Properties.** Lists attributes of an object. Each property has a name, which is displayed in bold, and a value, which is described in plain text. Scripts can get and set property values, except that properties designated [r/o] (means read only) can't be changed.

Saving a Script

In Script Editor, you save a script by choosing Save or Save As. When you choose one of these three commands, Script Editor displays a Save sheet. (The sheet does not appear when you choose Save for a script that has previously been saved.) In the dialog, you can choose any of several different file formats for the saved script. The five options are: Script, Application, Script Bundle, Application Bundle, and Text. Figure 23-4 shows the Save dialog.

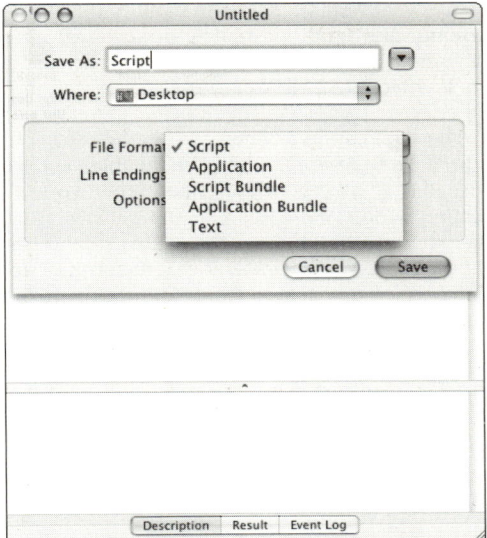

Figure 23-4: Script Editor can save a script in several formats.

Looking at Script File Formats

Script Editor can save a script in three basic file formats. When you save a new script or a copy of a script, you specify a file format by choosing the format from the Format pop-up menu in the Save dialog. Script Editor can save in the following file formats:

✦ **Script/Script Bundle.** Saves the script as Apple event codes rather than plain text. You can open it with Script Editor and then run or change it. You can also run compiled scripts by using the Script Runner application and applications that have a script menu, such as AppleWorks. You can save scripts as run only so they can not be edited, only run.

✦ **Application/Application Bundle.** Saves the script as an application, complete with an icon. Opening the icon (by double-clicking it, for example) runs the script. When you choose the application format, the following two options appear at the bottom of the Save dialog:

  • **Run Only.** Script application can not be edited, only run.

  • **Stay Open.** Causes the application to stay open after its script finishes running. If this option is turned off, the application quits automatically after running its script.

  • **Show Startup Screen.** Displays an identifying window that appears when the application is opened. The Startup screen confirms that the user wishes to run the script.

✦ **Text.** Saves the script as a plain text document. You can open it in Script Editor, in a word processing application, and in many other applications. Although a more portable file, this format is not as efficient as the others, because the script must be compiled before it can be run.

New to AppleScript 1.9.2, the version that ships with Mac OS X.3, is the ability to save scripts as Mac OS X bundles. Cocoa applications are bundles (another name for packages) which, though they appear as a single item or application, are actually a collection of the files and resources that the application needs to run. If you control-click on a cocoa application, you can see inside of an application's bundle by choosing *Show Package Contents*. You'll see all of the necessary files and folders that make up an application's contents. It is the concept of an application bundle that allows developers to make their applications installable via drag and drop, instead of using an installer that places files all over your computer. When you save a script as either a Script Bundle or an Application Bundle, it creates a similar package from your script, and you can control-click on your saved document and see the package contents just like any cocoa application. The differences between a bundle and a standard script or application are beyond the scope of this chapter, and are mainly geared towards developers of applications. See the AppleScript documentation for developers on-line at `http://developer.apple.com/documentation/AppleScript/` if you are interested in more information about bundles and how they can be used. Access to this documentation requires registration with the Apple Developer Connection; you can find information about ADC and sign up at `http://developer.apple.com/index.html`.

Creating a More Complex Script

You now know how to use Script Editor to create a simple AppleScript script. This type of script, however, has limited value. A simple script that doesn't take advantage of the full AppleScript language is not very intelligent.

More frequently, you'll use AppleScript to create more complex scripts. This section explains how to create a full-blown script quickly and use the resulting custom utility to augment an application's capabilities.

Making a Finder utility

Your Mac OS X disk is full of special folders, but when someone sends you a file, it's up to you to figure out where the file belongs. For example, you have to sort TIFF and JPEG files into your Pictures folder, QuickTime files into your Movies folder, and MP3 files into your Music folder. You also have to classify and put away fonts, sounds, and so on. The Finder doesn't help you sort out any of this.

You can, however, write a simple script that recognizes certain types of files and uses the Finder to move files to the folders where you want the files to go. The destination folders can be any folders that you have permission to change. These include all the folders in your home folder. If you log in as a user with administrator privileges, the destination folders can also include folders in the main Library folder.

Beginning the script

To begin writing a new script in Script Editor, choose File ➪ New Script. Then type the following statement in the script editing area of the new script window:

```
choose file
```

This command gives the script user a way to specify the file to be moved. The `choose file` command displays a dialog for choosing a file. This command is part of a scripting addition that is preinstalled in Mac OS X. The name of this scripting addition is Standard Additions.

Changing AppleScript Formatting

You can change the way Script Editor formats text by choosing Script Editor ➪ Preferences... and clicking on the Formatting icon in the toolbar. A dialog appears listing various components of AppleScript commands and the text format of each component. You can change the format of any component by selecting it in the dialog and then choosing different formatting from the Font and Style menus.

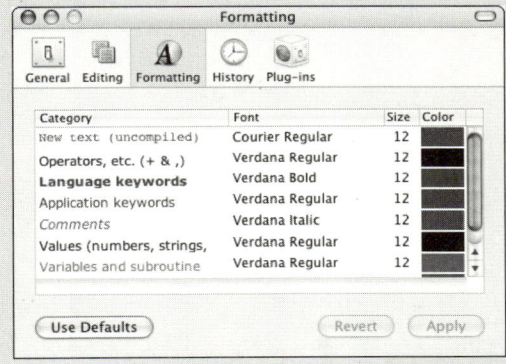

Seeing the script's results

The script isn't finished, but you can run it now to see the results of the one statement you have entered thus far. Click Run to run the script in its current condition. When AppleScript performs the `choose file` statement, it displays a dialog for choosing a file. Go ahead and select any file and click Choose. Because there aren't any more script statements, AppleScript stops the script.

AppleScript shows you the result of the last script action in the result window. If this window isn't open, choose Show Result from the Script Editor Controls menu. The result window contains the word alias and the path through your folders to the file you selected. This wording does not mean that the file is an alias file. In the context of a script, *alias* means the same thing as *file path*. Figure 23-5 is an example of the result window.

Using variables

The result of the `choose file` statement is called a file specification, or *file spec*. A file spec tells Mac OS X exactly where to find a file or folder. You need the file spec later in the script, so you must put it in a *variable,* which is a container for information. You can place data in a variable and then retrieve it whenever you want to before the script finishes running. The data in a variable is called the variable's *value*. You can change a variable's value by placing new data in it during the course of the script.

On the next line of the script, type the following statement:

```
copy the result to thisFile
```

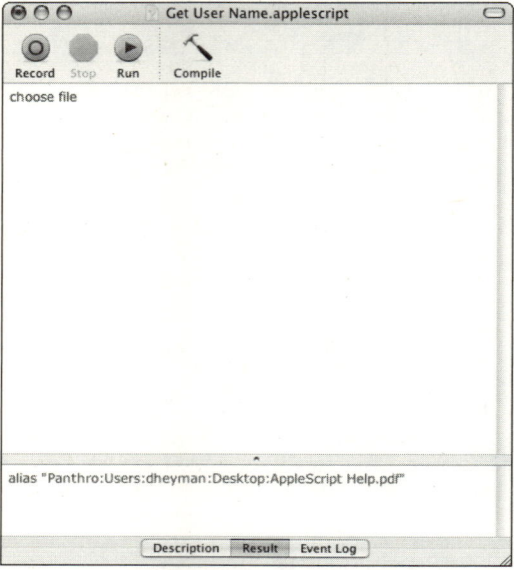

Figure 23-5: Script Editor's result pane shows the result of running a script.

This statement places the result of the `choose file` statement in a variable named `thisFile`. You can include the `thisFile` variable in any subsequent script statements that need to know the file spec of the chosen file. When AppleScript sees a variable name, it uses the current value of the variable. In this case, the value of variable `thisFile` is the file spec you got from the first statement.

When you run the script, you see that the `copy` command doesn't change the result of the script (as displayed in the result window). Because the result is just being copied to a variable, the result doesn't change.

Capitalizing script statements

You may notice the capital `F` in the `thisFile` variable and wonder whether capitalization is important when entering AppleScript statements. In general, you can capitalize any way that makes statements easier to read. Many AppleScript authors adopt the convention of capitalizing each word in a variable name except the first word, hence `thisFile`. This practice helps you distinguish variables from other terms in statements, which are generally all lowercase.

Getting file information

Ultimately, the script you are creating decides where to move a selected file based on the type of file it is. In Mac OS X, a file's type may be indicated by an extension (suffix) at the end of the file's name or by a hidden four-letter code known as the *file type*. Therefore, the script needs to determine the name and the file type of the selected file. You can use another command from the Standard Additions scripting addition to get this information. (Standard Additions is preinstalled in Mac OS X.) Enter the following statements beginning on the third line of the script:

```
copy the info for thisFile to fileInfo
copy the name extension of the fileInfo to nameExtension
copy the file type of the fileInfo to fileType
```

The first of these statements uses the `info for` command to get an information record about the selected file that is now identified by the variable `thisFile`. The first statement also copies the entire information record into a variable named `fileInfo`.

A record in AppleScript is a structured collection of data. Each data item in a record has a name and a value. AppleScript statements can refer to a particular item of a record by name, using a phrase similar to `item of record`. This is the phrasing used in the second two statements above.

Each of the second two statements gets an item of a record and copies it into a variable. The item names in these statements, `name extension` and `file type`, are taken from the AppleScript dictionary definition of the record. In this script, the record was obtained by the `info for` command in a previous statement. Figure 23-6 shows the AppleScript dictionary entries for the `info for` command and the record it provides.

To test the script so far, run it, choose a file, and look at the result. The result window contains the four-letter file type of the file you chose, displayed as a piece of text. Figure 23-7 shows the whole example script so far.

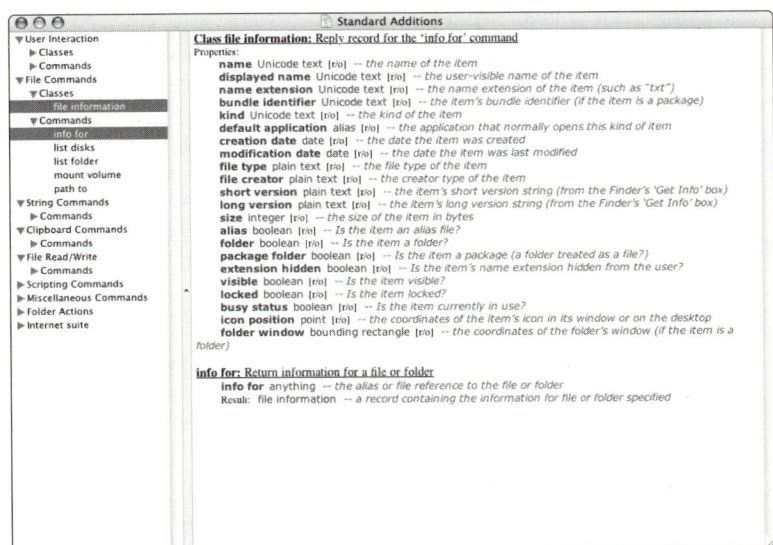

Figure 23-6: An AppleScript dictionary defines the structure of a record provided by an AppleScript command.

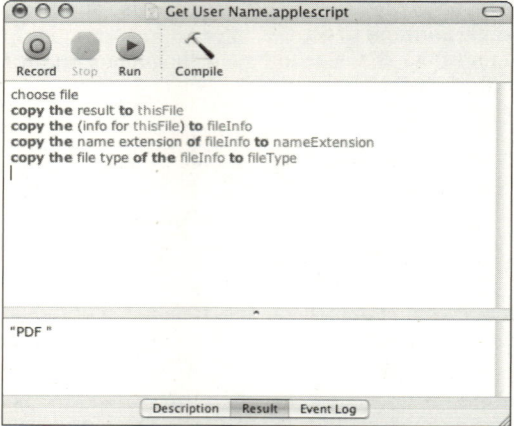

Figure 23-7: This script uses the `info for` command to get file name and file type information.

Using parentheses

You may notice that when AppleScript compiles the example script, which happens when you run the script or check its syntax, AppleScript adds parentheses around `info for thisFile` but does not add parentheses in other statements. AppleScript adds parentheses around a command that returns a value, which any `info for` command does. However, AppleScript does not add parentheses around a command at the end of a statement, such as the `choose file` command in the first statement of the example script. Nor does AppleScript add parentheses around elements that refer to a property, such as `the name extension of the fileInfo` in the example script.

Parentheses group elements of a command together. You can type your own parentheses around elements that you want to group in a statement. Parentheses make a complex AppleScript statement easier to read. Parentheses may also affect the result of a statement, because AppleScript evaluates elements within parentheses before evaluating other elements of a statement.

Working with an application

For the next part of the script, you need to add statements that move the chosen file to the folder where it belongs. The script can use an application—the Finder—to move the file. Add the following statement to have AppleScript start using the Finder:

```
tell application "Finder"
```

After AppleScript encounters this statement, it knows all the commands and objects from the Finder's AppleScript dictionary. This means that subsequent statements use commands and objects that the Finder understands. AppleScript sends these commands and objects to the Finder in Apple event messages. The script doesn't yet include any statements for the Finder, but we add some next. Later we add an `end tell` statement to have AppleScript stop using the Finder.

Performing script statements conditionally

When creating complex scripts you may want to give your script the ability to decide what to do based on the factors you specify. AppleScript, like all programming languages, lets you include a series of conditional statements, or *conditionals* for short. Each conditional begins with an `if` statement, which defines the condition to be evaluated. The `if` statement is followed by one or more other statements to be performed only if the condition is true. The conditional ends with an `end if` statement. In AppleScript, a simple conditional looks like this:

```
if the fileType is "MooV" or the nameExtension is "mov" then
move thisFile to folder "Movies" of home
end if
```

In this example, the `if` statement contains a two-part condition. The first part of the condition determines whether the current value of the `fileType` variable is `MooV`, which is the four-letter file type of QuickTime movie files. The second part of the condition determines whether the file name ends with `mov`, which is the file name extension of a QuickTime movie file. If either part of the condition is true, AppleScript performs the included `move` statement. If both parts are false, AppleScript skips the included `move` statement and goes on to the statement that follows the `end if` statement. Remember that AppleScript sends the `move` command to the Finder because of the `tell application` statement earlier in the script.

Note AppleScript considers the dot, or period, between the file name and the extension to be a separator. The dot is not part of the extension or the file name as far as AppleScript is concerned.

Include as many conditionals in the example script as you want. In each conditional, use the four-character file type and corresponding file name extension for a different type of file, and specify the path of the folder to which you want AppleScript to move files of that type. A quick way to enter several conditionals is to select one conditional (from the `if` statement through the `end if` statement), copy it, paste it at the end of the script, and change the relevant pieces of information. You can repeat this for each conditional you want to include.

Finding a Folder Path

If you don't know the full path of a folder, you can use a script to get this information. Open a new window in Script Editor and type the following script in the script editing area:

```
choose folder
```

Run the script and select a folder. The result is a file spec for the folder you selected. You can copy the text from the result window and paste it in any script.

You may notice that the file spec has a colon after each folder name. AppleScript uses colons in file specs to maintain compatibility with Mac OS 9 and earlier. Outside of AppleScript, Mac OS X generally follows the UNIX and Internet convention of putting a slash after each folder name.

You can make the above script a bit more interesting, by using the choose folder in place of a hard coded folder path:

```
move thisFile to choose folder
```

This will ask the user where to place the file after it is moved.

Breaking long statements

When you type a long statement, Script Editor never breaks it automatically (as a word processor does). You can break a long statement manually by pressing Option-Return. (Do not break a statement in the middle of a quoted text string, however.) AppleScript displays a special symbol (¬) to indicate a manual break. Here's an example:

```
if the fileType is "JPEG" or ¬
the nameExtension is "jpg" or ¬
the nameExtension is "jpeg" then
move thisFile to folder "Pictures" of home
end if
```

In this example, the first statement, which goes from `if` through `then`, takes three lines because it has two manual line breaks.

Ending the use of an application

After the last statement that is directed at the Finder, the script needs a statement that makes AppleScript stop using the application. Type the following statement at the end of the script:

```
end tell
```

This statement doesn't include the name of the application to stop using because AppleScript automatically pairs an `end tell` statement with the most recent `tell` statement. Subsequent statements in the script can't use the commands and objects of that application.

Finding a File's Type

You may not know the file type of the files that you want to move. For example, you may know that you want to put font files in your Fonts folder, but you may not know that the four-letter file type of a font file is FFIL. To make a script that reports the file type, copy the following three-line script to a new Script Editor window:

```
choose file
copy the result to thisFile
copy the file type of the info for thisFile to fileType
```

Run this three-line script and select a file whose four-character file type you need to learn. If the result window is not visible, choose Show Result from the Controls menu. The result of the script is the file type of the selected file. You can copy and paste the result from the result window into a conditional statement in any script window.

If you choose a file that has no file type, one of two things happens. The result window displays an empty value (indicated by quotation marks with nothing between them) or AppleScript reports an error, saying that it can't get the file type.

Now is a good time to recheck the script's syntax. If you tried to compile recently, you got an error message about a missing `end tell` statement. Click Compile now, and after AppleScript compiles the script you see Script Editor neatly indent statements to make the structure of the script more apparent. If AppleScript encounters any errors while compiling your script, Script Editor advises you of them one by one.

Trying out your script

After creating a new script, you must run it and test it thoroughly. To test the script that moves files according to their type, follow these steps:

1. **Run your script.**

2. **When the dialog appears, select a file that is of a type your script should recognize but that is not in the destination folder; then click Choose.**

3. **Switch to the Finder, and make sure that the file you selected actually moved from the source folder to the destination folder.**

4. **Repeat the test, selecting a different file type that your script should recognize.**

Figure 23-8 shows an example of a script with four conditional statements that move a selected file depending on its file type or file name extension.

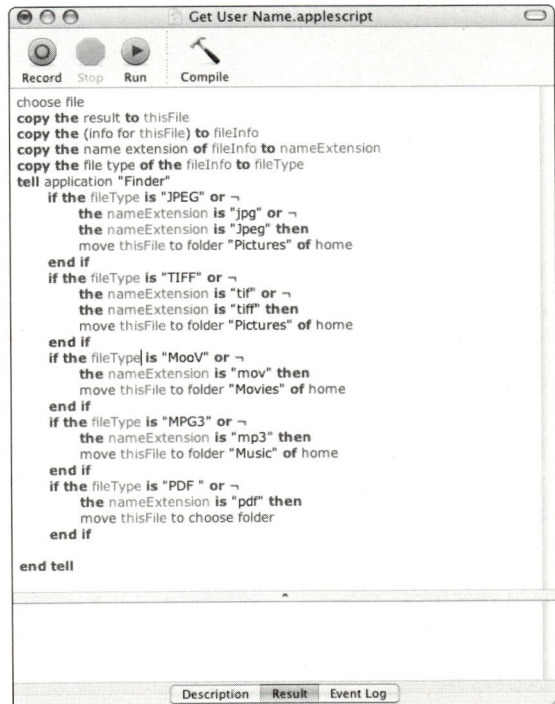

Figure 23-8: This script uses conditional statements to determine where to put a file; it also incorporates user choice for PDF files.

Creating a Drag-and-Drop Script Application

Although the sample script you created is useful, it would be more useful as an application with an icon on your desktop. Then you could drag files that you wanted to sort into folders and drop them on the application's icon. This would cause the application to run and move the files to their appropriate folders. You wouldn't have to open Script Editor every time you wanted to sort files into folders, and you could sort more than one file at a time. Applications respond to this type of drag and drop Apple Event, and so can Apple Scripts.

You already know that AppleScript can save a script as an application. With a little extra work, you can make an application with drag-and-drop capability so that you can simply drag files to it to choose them.

Retrieving dropped files

Remember that when you drop a set of icons on an application in a Finder window, the Finder sends that application an Open Documents message that includes a list of the files you dropped on the icon. This message is sent to all applications, even to applications that you create yourself with AppleScript.

You need to tell your script to intercept that event message and retrieve the list of items that were dropped on to the application icon. Place the following statement at the beginning of your script:

```
on open itemList
```

Now enter the following statement at the end of your script:

```
end open
```

This `on open` statement enables the script to intercept an Open Documents event message and puts the message's list of files in a variable named `itemList`. The `end open` statement helps AppleScript know which statements to perform when the open message is received. Any statements between the `on open` and `end open` statements are performed when the script receives an Open Documents event message.

Save this script by choosing the Save As command from the File menu. From the Format pop-up menu in the Save As dialog, choose the Application option. (You may want to save the script on the desktop, at least for experimental purposes.) If you switch to the Finder and look at the icon of the application you just created, you can see that the icon includes an arrow, which indicates that the icon represents a drag-and-drop application. The application has this kind of icon because its script includes an `on open` statement.

Processing dropped files

The script won't be fully operational until you make a few more changes. As the script stands, it places the list of files in a variable, but it doesn't do anything with that information. If you dropped several files on the application now, the script would still display a dialog asking you to pick a file and then quit, having accomplished nothing.

First, you need to eliminate the script statements that obtain the file to be processed from a dialog. Delete what now are the second and third lines of the script (the ones beginning with the words `choose` and `copy`) and replace them with the following:

```
repeat with x from 1 to the number of items in the itemList
copy item x of the itemList to thisFile
```

Between the end tell and end open statements, which are the last two lines of the script, enter the following statement:

```
end repeat
```

Figure 23-9 shows the complete sample script modified for drag-and-drop operation.

Save the script so that your changes take effect and then switch back to the Finder. You now have a drag-and-drop application that you can use to move certain types of files to specific folders.

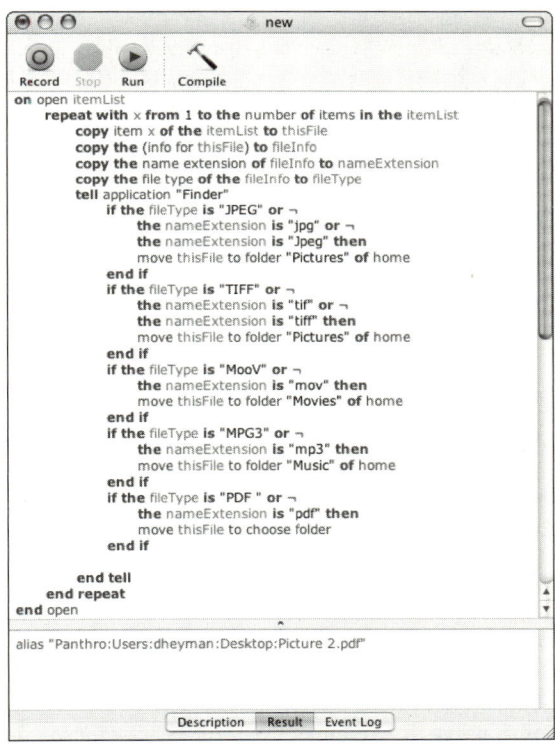

Figure 23-9: This script application processes items dropped on its icon.

Using a repeat loop

In the modified script, AppleScript repeatedly performs the statements between the repeat and end repeat statements for the number of times specified in the repeat statement. This arrangement is called a *repeat loop*. The first time AppleScript performs the repeat statement, it sets variable x to 1, as specified by from 1. Then AppleScript performs statements sequentially until it encounters the end repeat statement.

In the first statement of the repeat loop, variable x determines which file spec to copy from variable itemList to variable thisFile. The rest of the statements in the repeat loop are carried over from the previous version of the script.

When AppleScript encounters the end repeat statement, it loops back to the repeat statement, adds 1 to variable x, and compares the new value of x with the number of items that were dragged to the icon (as specified by the phrase the number of items in the itemList). If the two values are not equal, AppleScript performs the statements in the repeat loop again. If the two values are equal, these statements are performed one last time, and AppleScript goes to the statement immediately following end repeat. This is the end open statement, which ends the script.

Extending the script

Anytime you want the application to handle another type of file, open the script application in Script Editor, add a conditional that covers that type of file, and save the script.

The script in its drag-and-drop form now no longer functions if you double-click on it. You can modify the script to add in this functionality by placing a copy of the original script at the end of the end open statement.

Tip   You can't open a script application by double-clicking it because doing so causes the application to run. To open a script application in Script Editor, choose File ➪ Open in Script Editor or drop the script application on the Script Editor icon in the Finder.

Borrowing Scripts

An easy way to make a script is to modify an existing script that does something close to what you want. You simply duplicate the script file in the Finder, open the duplicate copy, and make changes. You can do this with scripts that have been saved as applications, compiled scripts, or text files. (You can't open a script that has been saved as a run-only script.)

Apple has developed a number of scripts that you can use as starting points or models for your own scripts. You can find some scripts in the Example Scripts folder, which is in the AppleScript folder in the Applications folder. Another place to look is the Scripts folder, which is in the /Library folder. The official AppleScript site has some (www.apple.com/applescript/). Check out the Learn AppleScript, Help & Examples, and Download Scripts areas of this site. Part of the AppleScript site has scripting examples specifically for Mac OS X (www.apple.com/applescript/macosx/).

If you have upgraded to Mac OS X from a previous version of the Mac OS, look for Mac OS 9 scripts in the Automated Tasks folder of the Apple Menu Items folder, which is located in the System Folder. You may find more Mac OS 9 scripts in the AppleScript folder of the Apple Extras folder, which is normally in the folder named Applications (Mac OS 9). Additional Mac OS 9 scripts are located in the AppleScript Extras folder of the CD Extras folder on the Mac OS 9 CD-ROM.

Note Some Mac OS 9 scripts work as-is with Mac OS X, but many require some tweaking. In particular, scripts made to control the Mac OS 9 Finder are likely to require modification, and some parts may not work at all.

Running Scripts

After you've built up a collection of scripts that you run frequently, you're not going to want to switch to Script Editor every time you want to run one. This reason is precisely why Mac OS X includes the Script Menu in 10.2, which replaces the Script Runner application in 10.1 and earlier. The Script Menu sits in the OS toolbar at the top of the screen as shown in Figure 23-10. You can run any of the listed scripts by choosing it from the pop-up menu. To activate the script menu, run the Install Script Menu application from the /Applications/AppleScript folder. If you ever need to remove the menu item, run the Remove Script Menu application from the same folder.

Tip The Script Menu is not limited to just AppleScript, it can be used to launch Perl and shell scripts as well.

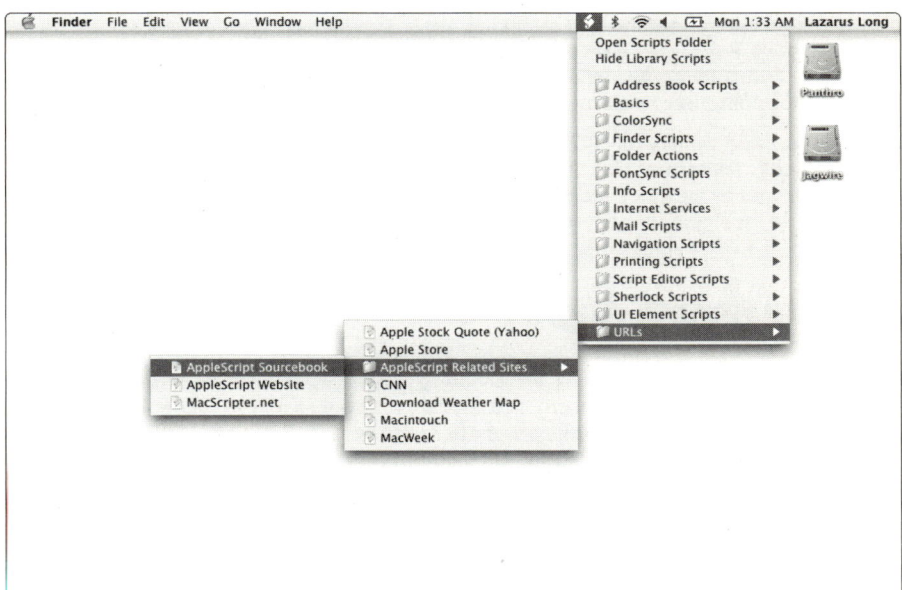

Figure 23-10: Scripts listed in Script Menu's pop-up menu are always available no matter which application is currently active.

Running Scripts from the Menu Bar in OS 9

For a script menu in the Classic environment, you need the OSA Menu software. OSA Menu allows you to quickly run Mac OS 9 scripts while any Classic application is the active application. The scripts are listed in a permanent menu near the right end of the Classic menu bar. You can also use the script menu to start recording a script or open the Classic version of Script Editor. OSA Menu is a system extension for Mac OS 9. It's on the Mac OS 9 CD in the AppleScript Extras folder, which is in the CD Extras folder.

Linking Programs

You have seen how AppleScript can automate tasks on your own computer. Beginning with Mac OS X 10.1, AppleScript can also send Apple events messages to open applications on other Macs in a network. As a result, you can use AppleScript to control applications on other people's computers. Of course, the reverse is also true; other people can use AppleScript to control applications on your computer. To send and receive Apple events over a network your Mac must be running with Mac OS X 10.1, 10.2, or Mac OS 9.

Sharing programs by sending and receiving Apple events messages across a network is called *program linking*. For security reasons, program linking is normally disabled. Computers that you want to control with AppleScript must be set to allow remote Apple events. Likewise you must set your computer to allow remote Apple events.

Mac OS X 10.1 and up use the TCP/IP protocol to send and receive Apple events messages over a network. Therefore, Mac OS X 10.1–10.3 can send and receive Apple events messages over the Internet as well as a local network. Mac OS X 10.1–10.3 can't use the AppleTalk protocol to send or receive Apple events over a remote network as can Mac OS 9 and earlier. Mac OS X 10.0–10.0.4 can't send or receive remote Apple events at all.

Allowing remote Apple events

If you want a Mac OS X computer to receive Apple events from remote computers, you must set it to allow remote Apple events. First, open System Preferences and then choose View ➪ Sharing (or click the Sharing button). In Sharing Preferences, click the Application tab and then turn on the option labeled Allow remote Apple events. If you want the computer to receive Apple events from remote Mac OS 9 computers, turn on the option labeled Allow Mac OS 9 computer to use remote Apple events. If you turn on this option, a dialog appears in which you must enter a password that Mac OS 9 users will have to use when sending Apple events messages to the computer. You can change this password later by clicking Set Password in Sharing Preferences. Figure 23-11 shows remote Apple events turned on in Sharing Preferences.

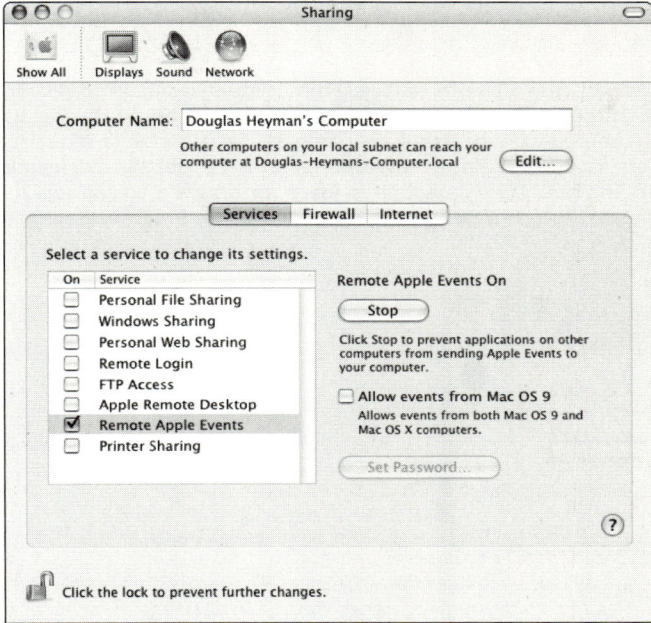

Figure 23-11: Set Mac OS X to receive remote Apple events by using the Sharing pane of System Preferences.

Scripting across a network

Using AppleScript to run a program across the network doesn't take much more work than writing a script to use a program on the same computer. For example, the following script sends commands to the Finder on the computer at IP address 192.168.1.203:

```
set remoteMachine to machine "eppc://192.168.203"
tell application "Finder" of remoteMachine
   using terms from application "Finder"
         activate
         open the trash
   end using terms from
end tell
```

The example script begins by setting the value of variable remoteMachine to the URL of a remote computer. A URL for remote Apple events begins with eppc:// and is followed by the remote computer's IP address or DNS name. (The prefix eppc stands for event program-to-program communication.) Starting with Panther, machines can also be called by their Rendezvous name in scripts (no URL required).

The second statement of the example script names the application, in this case Finder, and uses the variable remoteMachine to identify the remote computer.

Turning On Program Linking in Mac OS 9

If you want a computer that's using Mac OS 9 to receive remote Apple events messages from your computer, the Mac OS 9 computer must have program linking turned on. To do this, open the Mac OS 9 computer's File Sharing control panel and click the Start button in the control panel's Program Linking section. In addition, turn on the option labeled Enable Program Linking clients to connect over TCP/IP. The Mac OS 9 computer is ready for program linking when the button's label changes to Stop and the File Sharing control panel reports "Program Linking on," as shown in the following figure.

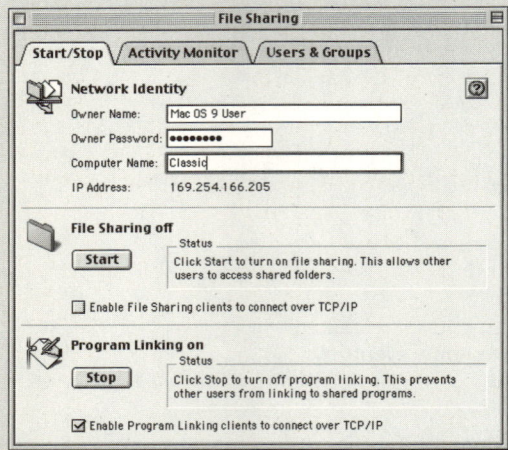

A Mac OS 9 computer can receive remote Apple events when program linking is turned on and set to use TCP/IP.

Mac OS 9 can be configured to receive remote Apple events only from specific users. These access restrictions are set up with the Users & Groups tab in the File Sharing control panel. In addition, each application on a Mac OS 9 computer can be set to not receive any remote Apple events. This restriction is set in each application's Info window in the Finder.

Inside the `tell application...end tell` block is another block that is bracketed by the statements `using terms from` and `end using terms from`. When AppleScript encounters the statement `using terms from`, it compiles subsequent statements using the named application's scripting dictionary but does not send the resulting Apple events to this application. The Apple events from a `using terms from` block are sent to the application named in the enclosing `tell application` block. In the example script, AppleScript compiles the `activate` and `open the trash` statements using terms from the Finder's scripting dictionary on the local computer (your computer) but sends the resulting Apple events to the Finder on the remote computer.

When you run a script that sends remote Apple events, AppleScript has to connect to the remote application. Before doing this, AppleScript displays a dialog in which you must enter a name and password of a user account on the remote computer. If you connect successfully, the script continues. At this point the example script should cause the remote computer's Finder to become the active application and open the Trash in a Finder window.

If you run the script again, you don't have to go through the authentication process. After AppleScript is connected to an application on a particular remote computer, you don't have to go through the authentication dialog each time you want to send an Apple event.

AppleScript Studio

You have seen that AppleScript is a very powerful scripting language, and should now have some ideas as to how you can make your own life more automated. While AppleScript is billed as a scripting language, it is, for all intents and purposes, a programming language as well. Apple knows this, and has built into the developer's tools a means to easily create an application-quality front end to your AppleScripts. Using AppleScript Studio, in concert with Script Editor you can build full-fledged applications with icons, menus and all of the interface elements associated with a complete application. AppleScript Studio has been incorporated into Xcode and Interface Builder and is included free with Mac OS X.3 on the Developer Tools CD. Cocktail and Carbon Copy Cloner, utility applications mentioned in Chapter 21, are two good examples of applications that were written in AppleScript and given a proper Mac OS X interface using AppleScript Studio.

Summary

Here's what you learned in this chapter:

✦ AppleScript makes applications perform tasks by sending them Apple event messages.

✦ AppleScript is a programming language designed with everyday users in mind, but with enough power for advanced users and programmers.

✦ Many AppleScript terms come from the applications it controls. AppleScript terms also come from files called scripting additions.

✦ Use the Script Editor application to create, edit, and run AppleScript scripts. Script Editor can also make scripts into applications.

✦ Script Editor can display the AppleScript dictionary of an application to see what commands an application or scripting addition understands and what objects the commands work with.

✦ You can save a script in any of three formats: text, compiled script, or Application.

✦ You type AppleScript statements into a new Script Editor window, check the syntax for errors using the compile button, and run the script to test it. Your script can use a `copy` statement to set the value of a variable. To start controlling an application, you use a `tell application` statement. A matching `end tell` statement stops controlling the application. With `if` statements, you can have AppleScript perform some operations only when specified conditions are met. Repeat loops execute a group of statements over and over. To make a drag-and-drop script application, you include an `on open` statement and a matching `end open` statement.

✦ Apple has developed a number of scripts that you can use as starting points or models for your own scripts.

✦ You can use Script Runner or Script Menu to run compiled scripts no matter what application is currently active.

✦ AppleScript can control applications over a network or the Internet on computers that are set to allow remote Apple events.

✦   ✦   ✦

Commanding Unix

Mac OS X is built upon a foundation known as Darwin. Apple has made the source to Darwin downloadable on the Internet. Darwin integrates several key technologies including the Mach kernel and services based on BSD Unix. Above Darwin is the Aqua user interface that provides the OS X user experience.

This chapter presents a brief history of Unix and shows you how to use some of its power. Unix is a mature operating system with literally hundreds of commands. You never really need to see many of these commands; however, if your curiosity gets the better of you, this chapter points you to some excellent Unix references.

Introduction to Unix

Unix was developed at Bell Laboratories in 1969. It was designed to be a *multiuser operating system*. The prevalent computers of the time were mainframe systems. On these systems, a single user at a time could use the computing resources made available by creating programs on punch cards and feeding them to the system, then awaiting the output of the program on a nearby printer. This system tended to isolate programmers and users from each other and additionally provided no facility to save data. Unix was designed from the ground up to overcome these and other obstacles. In addition to providing access to more than one program or person at a time, Unix was designed to be interactive, providing output via a terminal or console rather than a printer. Unix went thru many revisions in the 1970s and 1980s. AT&T was prohibited by law from selling computers or software at that time; instead, it granted licenses to many universities, where deployment and development rapidly took place. Even Apple produced a Unix-based system for its Macintosh line, A/UX (Apple Unix), in the late 1980s and early 1990s. Additionally, the NeXT operating system, acquired by Apple with the purchase of NeXT, is a Unix-based operating system. Much of the original NeXTStep or OpenStep operating system concepts are present in Mac OS X.

A standard Unix implementation includes a large variety of commands that enable users to perform a multitude of operations, from editing text to creating multimedia, providing and utilizing network services, and everything in between. Most software one would expect to see on a modern desktop computer is available, including a word processor, Web browser, email client, games, and more.

◆ ◆ ◆ ◆

In This Chapter

Introduction to Unix

Command-line versus graphical interface

Shells

Basic Unix commands

Advanced Unix commands

Commands to investigate on your own

Where to find more information

◆ ◆ ◆ ◆

Command-Line versus Graphical Interface

History, or at least folklore, tells us that Apple's *GUI* (graphical user interface) development arose from a visit to Xerox PARC (Palo Alto Research Center). Apple executives, including Steve Jobs, were impressed with the fledgling foray into a new user experience — the graphical user interface that was implemented on the Xerox Star and Alto workstations. Until that time, the developing personal computer industry was dominated by operating systems and applications directed solely from the keyboard. Pointing devices, such as mice, were virtually unheard of, although some games supported joysticks as optional control devices.

Apple's Lisa was the first consumer line to be introduced with a GUI, but at $10,000 each, a small software base, and limited (and proprietary) development tools, this machine was soon eclipsed by another Apple product, introduced a year later — the Macintosh. From the beginning, traditionalists decried the Mac and its GUI as a toy and opined that "real computer users use the command line." Thus began a religious argument that still flares up today, albeit with slightly less heat and frequency, concerning the relative advantages and disadvantages of the two approaches. The evolution, by Microsoft, from DOS to Windows dragged all but the most vocal opponents of GUIs into the current era, and the advent of windowing systems for Unix has quieted most of the rest.

Whether it is easier to select a desired folder from a Window menu, navigate a file browser to locate it, or type `cd directoryname` depends greatly upon the context, the user's typing ability, and the user's memory.

Note   What we visualize as folders in our graphical interface are generally referred to as directories in a Unix (or almost any other command-line) operating system. Throughout this chapter, we use *folder* when talking about the GUI view and *directory* when dealing with the Command Line Interface or CLI.

The traditional Unix interface is a CLI, although all modern Unix distributions provide GUIs. These GUIs include an assortment of window managers running under the X Window System or X Windows for short. X Windows is a windowing environment for Unix that allows multiple windows on the desktop, much like one would find on any current OS. In fact, most popular window managers enable multiple desktops, a feature which is made available to Mac OS X by means of third-party software, such as CodeTek VirtualDesktop, which is discussed in Chapter 22, or Desktop Manager available at `http://wsmanager.sourceforge.net/`

Note   Apple bundles Xfree86, a freely redistributable open-source implementation of the X Windows System with Panther. Installing X Windows, or X11 as Apple refers to the software, is covered in Chapter 26

Almost without exception, anything that can be accomplished by using one interface is also possible with the other. One example of a CLI's power is to delete all files with a particular extension by typing a single command. Using Finder in Mac OS X, you can launch Sherlock to find all names with the same extension and then drag the found items to the Trash. You achieve the same result by using a different method.

You access the Unix command line in Mac OS X by using the Terminal application (found in the Utilities folder of the Applications folder). The initial Terminal window is shown in Figure 24-1. The Terminal window presents a few clues, if you know how to read them:

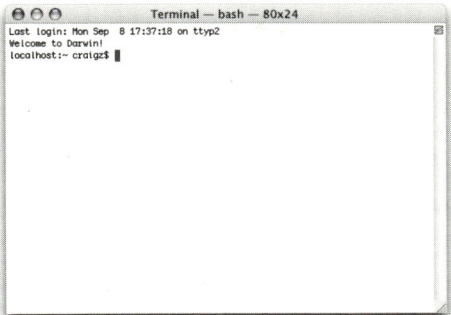

Figure 24-1: The Terminal window doesn't give you many hints on how to proceed.

✦ The path to your current directory (the Unix term for folder) is shown in square brackets to the left of the prompt. In Figure 24-1, localhost followed by the tilde (~) indicates that you are in your home directory on the machine, localhost.

✦ The user ID (short name) of the current user follows—that's you, most often.

✦ The % or $ character at the end of the line indicates that you are not logged in as the System Administrator (the root user) and serves as your command prompt. Depending on the shell you are using, the prompt will be % or $. This is a quick way of identifying the lineage of your shell. C shell and tcsh use the % symbol. Bourne (sh) and Bash (Bourne-Again sh) use the $. If you've installed a fresh copy of Panther you'll have bash as your default shell. If you've upgraded a previous version of Mac OS X to Panther then your default shell will be tcsh.

The command-line interpreter in Unix is called a *shell*. In the next section, we delve a little deeper into the default shell and the other shell choices available to you. Apple has had a shell, called MPW, available as part of a package for Macintosh programmers (and other users) since 1986 (and as a free download for almost a decade) called MPW. The MPW shell differs from the shells available in the Terminal mostly in the following ways:

✦ The command names are different.

✦ The wildcards used are different.

✦ MPW Shell is also a full-featured text-editing environment.

✦ A Unix shell can spawn processes and has more control due to Unix's multitasking model.

Tip Sometimes applications have options available from the command line that aren't necessarily available through the GUI. For an example, open a Terminal window, type the word **screencapture** and press the Return key. Read the options for use of the screencapture command carefully, as they are much more extensive than the options that the Command-Shift-3 and Command-Shift-4 keyboard shortcuts allow you to use.

Shells

The shell is an application that reads user input and reports system or program output. The shell is the primary way a user communicates with a Unix system, and is the primary way the system communicates with a user. Although the kernel does most of the work, the shell is the part that is visible to the user. Various shells are available, such as sh (standard Unix Bourne shell), csh (Berkeley Unix c-shell), and ksh (Korn shell). The Bourne shell, sh, is generally useful in shell scripting, which is discussed further in the next section. For interactive work, or in Unix parlance for login sessions, a more mature featured shell is generally desired. In previous versions of Mac OS X, the default login shell was tcsh, which is a significantly enhanced version of csh. With Panther, the default login shell is bash. Bash is the GNU Project's Bourne Again Shell, which has the same syntax as sh but with features similar to tcsh and zsh, such as command-line editing, job control, brace expansion, and a command history similar to csh. More importantly, bash is the default shell in most Linux distributions. Having the same shell on Mac OS X machines is a great boon for both Linux and Macintosh users. Often, there will be more than one machine on a network, and by becoming familiar with shell usage on the Macintosh, you'll know your way around a Linux system for free.

Tip   For more information on bash, the project's homepage has all the information.

A Mac OS X installation provides five shells in the standard distribution: sh, csh, tcsh, bash, and zsh. Shells fall into two general camps: sh derivatives and csh derivatives. These camps don't differ by much superficially, but they do some things differently. For example, csh derivatives use `setenv` to set environment variables while sh derivatives use a combination of `set` and `export` to set these variables.

As mentioned previously, sh is generally used for shell scripts. The same goes for csh, although the beginning shell scripter should be warned against using csh for shell scripting. For further information on that topic please read "Csh Programming Considered Harmful" by Tom Christiansen, available at `www.faqs.org/faqs/unix-faq/shell/csh-whynot/`. Of interest is that although both sh and csh are available on a Mac OS X system, in fact sh is a copy of bash and csh is a copy of tcsh. Both bash and tcsh behave slightly differently when called by their other names (sh or csh).

In many respects, you can think of the different shells as different dialects of the same language. After you learn one shell, you can pretty much communicate in any of the shells; however, you occasionally find differences in syntax, and you may not command the full power of the new shell's enhancements. For example, if you are fully proficient in every aspect of csh, all of that knowledge is usable in bash. But to get the full power of `bash`, you can take advantage of its command history, command substitution, and other enhancements. Command history lets you recall previous commands using various keyboard shortcuts; Command substitution lets you reuse previous commands in new instances. Moving to zsh, you would learn different techniques for some of these enhancements.

Some common special characters

Unix originated in an era of extremely limited memory and disk space. Conservation of resources was critical; therefore, command names were abbreviated. Commands and file names were case-sensitive, which provided more diversity in short names and eliminated the need to provide code-parsing commands into a consistent case for comparisons.

Additionally, a number of special and punctuation characters were employed as shortcuts or abbreviations. Some are shown in the following list:

~   home directory

.   current directory

..   parent directory to the current directory

/   topmost or root directory

Scripting the shell

All provided shells support *shell scripting*. A shell script is simply a text file containing a list of commands that the shell will execute in order. A shell script supports many programmatic constructs such as variables, conditionals, and loops, as well as supporting a number of *control* and *redirection* operators.

Perhaps you left out the .doc extension on a folder of Microsoft Word files that you want to share with a Windows-using colleague. You can write a very simple shell script to rename all the files in a directory. Your script contains a list of instructions to the shell, using all the constructs listed here. It holds the text string .doc in a *variable,* and uses a *loop* to first create a list of all files in the directory, then to append the variable to each item in the list. Then it writes a logfile using output *redirection*. That is to say that, rather than putting output on the screen, as a command is likely to do, output is redirected to a file. The shell provides a control function that enables you to run this program in the background while you do other things, rather than wait for the program to complete before resuming your own operations.

You can find entire books devoted to Unix shell scripting. All we can give you here are the basics to get you started and pointers to where you can find more information. Read on; later in the chapter, we'll return to this topic, but first we'll need to cover a bit more background. (The man pages for sh, csh, bash, and tcsh are a good place to begin if you are curious.)

Note   The AppleScript Script Menu shown in Chapter 23 will run shell and perl scripts as well as AppleScripts. In addition to shell scripting and AppleScript language interpreters, Mac OS X 10.3 ships with Perl, PHP, Python, Ruby, and Tcl.

Basic Unix Commands

Unix has literally hundreds of standard commands. A basic design philosophy of Unix is to have small commands that do one thing right. For example, a Macintosh Application may be called Super File Friend. Our imaginary application can do all types of things with files: it can duplicate a file, it can rename a file, it can delete a file, and it can even read a file! In Unix, all of these functions are possible via the use of separate programs: cp, mv, rm, cat. All of these small commands can be combined to accomplish any desired result because the small, specialized programs provide an incredible degree of flexibility.

Unix command syntax

The basic form of a Unix command is

```
command-name switches arguments
```

The *command-name* is the Unix name of the command, such as `ls` or `mv`. *Switches* are the options you can specify to modify the default behavior of the command and are usually preceded by a minus sign (-). *Arguments* are strings (frequently, but not always, file names) that provide the command's input and may also specify the output destination.

Unix commands are the CLI equivalent of Mac OS X applications and menu selections. Although Unix commands can be placed anywhere you have permission to access and execute them, traditional organization has them in one of the directories specified by the PATH environment variable. (Type `echo $PATH` in the Terminal to see what directories, separated by colons, are automatically searched for commands.) If the command is not located in one of these directories, its location must be fully specified for the shell to execute the command.

A traditional Unix file system is case-sensitive in the naming of files and directories — that is, the file `INSTALL` is different from the file `Install`, which is also different from the file `install`. Mac OS X modifies this behavior so that file names are not case-sensitive in the GUI, but case-sensitivity is still the rule when you are working in the shell.

Note   Although Mac OS X eliminates case-sensitivity from file names, it does not eliminate case-sensitivity from switches or built-in commands. You must still enter them in the proper case.

Log in and log out

Remember, Unix is a multiuser system. Even if you are the only person who uses the computer, it's still multiuser. As the Process Viewer application shows you (refer to Chapter 22), a user named *root* executes all sorts of system-level processes, even when you're the actual person using the computer.

Specifying File Names

The Macintosh file system is a hierarchy in that you use folders to contain files and other folders, and this process can be carried to an arbitrary depth. You can consider each volume to be a separate hierarchy, or you can consider the Desktop as being the top of the hierarchy, containing the various volumes.

With one significant alteration, Unix takes a Desktop View of your file hierarchy. Viewed as an upside-down tree, the top of the Unix hierarchy is called by a single-character name, /, called the *root* of the tree. The one difference from the Desktop analogy is that in a Unix file system, the mount points are not necessarily mounted directly below the root level — they can reside within folders.

The slash character is also used to separate levels in the *path* from root (or any other reference point) to a given file. For example, the full path to a file named `Diary.rtf` in the Documents folder of a user named Sam would be:

```
/Users/Sam/Documents/Diary.rtf
```

If you omit the leading slash, you are assumed to be specifying a path *relative* to your current directory rather than an *absolute* path specification.

When you first installed Mac OS X, you created an administrator account and gave it a password. To make the process easier for you, this account logs in automatically when you start your computer; however, you can turn that off in the Login pane of System Preferences (refer to Chapter 13) if your computer is going to have multiple users because you might not want your business partner to be logged in as you when he or she restarts the computer.

Just as you are always logged in as a specific user when using the Mac OS X GUI, you are also logged in as a specific user when you use the Terminal application — the CLI. One difference is that you can use Unix commands to change which user identity is in effect for part of your Terminal session. The command used to change users is called su (for switch user). Until you create other accounts or enable root login in NetInfo Manager, no other identities are available to you.

Tip   You can execute a single command as root, even if you haven't enabled the root login by using the sudo command followed by the desired command as an argument to sudo. For example, sudo chown root myfile executes the chown (change owner) command, causing the file, myfile, to belong to root. As a caution, you will be prompted for your own password when using a command through sudo. Access to sudo is configured by a text file etc/sudoers. This file is generally manipulated via a program called visudo. Visudo is a wrapper application, which opens the /etc/sudoers file for editing, but in addition it locks the file so it can not be changed by the system while being edited. For more information on sudo and visudo, including configuring sudo for multiple users consult man sudo, man visudo and man sudoers.

The most visible effect of each user having a distinct identity is that, when each user creates files, the files are marked as belonging to that user. You can see this in the Finder by choosing File ⇨ Show Info and then choosing Privileges in the Info window's pop-up menu. In Terminal, type ls -l thefile (assuming thefile is the file's name).

As shown in Figure 24-1, the default command line includes your username. If you've changed your prompt or are unsure or curious, the whoami command tells you your username.

One big advantage in using Terminal to execute a few commands as another user is that you don't have to log out of the system to run commands as another user. Although Panther offers Fast User Switching which will allow you to keep your session open while you log in as another user to execute a command. You can just su to that user, as shown in Figure 24-2, execute the commands, and terminate their shell session with exit or Control-D. This may be faster than changing users in the GUI.

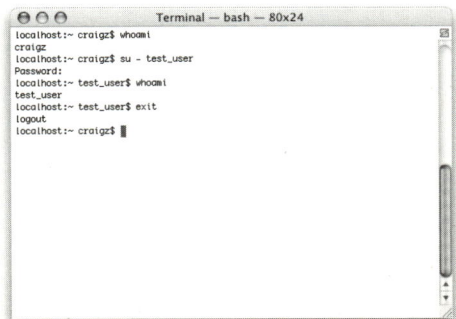

Figure 24-2: Use the su command to temporarily change your identity.

Managing files and directories

Just as you always have an active window in the Finder or a current folder in which an application opens or saves files, you have a *current directory* (also known as *working directory*) when using the Terminal application. As you can see in Figures 24-1 and 24-2, the default shell prompt provides your current directory and user account name. However, you can customize the shell prompt, possibly to make it shorter and still find out your working directory by entering the pwd (print working directory) command.

As was noted earlier in this chapter, some shortcut symbols are used with the shell. In particular, shortcut symbols for directories are ~ (user's home directory), . (current directory), and .. (parent directory to the current directory).

To change your current directory, you use the cd (change directory) command. For example, cd ~ takes you back to your home directory, and cd / takes you to the root of the file system.

Obtaining a list of the files in a directory is as simple as entering the ls command. This command has a number of switches available that you can use to modify its behavior; the more useful and common ones are described in the following list:

-a	Show all files, even invisible (those whose names start with a .) ones.
-F	Append a character to the names of executables (*), directories (/), and links or aliases (@). Characters for sockets are (=), whiteouts (%), and queues (|), which we aren't going to get into here.
-f	Don't sort the output (default is to sort alphabetically).
-L	If the file is a link, resolve the link and list that file.
-l	Long listing, including owner, group, size, permissions.
-n	Use the user and group ID numbers rather than names in a long listing.
-R	Recursively list all subdirectories.
-r	Reverse the sorting order.
-S	Sort by size, largest first.
-s	List the number of 512-byte blocks actually used by each file.
-t	Sort by time modified, most recent first.
-x	Sort multicolumn output across page rather than in columns.
-1	Force output to one item per line (screen output defaults to multicolumn).

Another useful command when dealing with files and directories is the file command. If you type file /Users, the file command attempts to tell you what kind of file /Users is — in this case, a directory. The file command also recognizes other file types, such as TIFF, RTF, text, and so forth.

Using Unix to delete stubborn files

Sometimes Finder is unable to move or delete files in the trash. The error message "The operation cannot be completed because you do not have sufficient privileges for some of the items" is displayed. In this event, you can use two options to remove the file using Terminal. The first way is to use rm. Use the following steps to try both options:

First, try simply removing the file, using `sudo` to have root privileges used for the operation.

1. **Type** `sudo rm filename` **(or** `sudo rm -rf foldername` **if it's a folder).** You are then prompted for your password by sudo.

2. **Type the password,** and the prompt should return. If there is no error, then the file has been removed.

If that fails, it's due to a special file flag which has been set on the file, which marks it to the system as locked or protected.

First, you remove the flag and then you remove the file.

1. **Type** `sudo chflags -R nouchg filename`. After taking your password, the prompt will return.

2. **Type** `sudo rm filename` **to remove the file.** If you simply want to place the file in the trash and delete it later, you can now use the finder to put the file in the trash.

Autocompletion of file names

One of the really nice features of bash and tcsh is that you don't always have to type long file-names. Just as Internet Explorer attempts to complete URLs as you type, these shells attempt to complete the name for you if you press the Tab key while typing a file name. If you have only one choice that completes what you have typed thus far, the shell completes the name; however, if multiple possibilities exist, a list will be printed (as shown in Figure 24-3), and the terminal bell will beep, waiting for you to type more characters and to then press Tab again. This process continues until your typing prior to pressing the Tab uniquely identifies a file or, using wildcards as described shortly, a group of files.

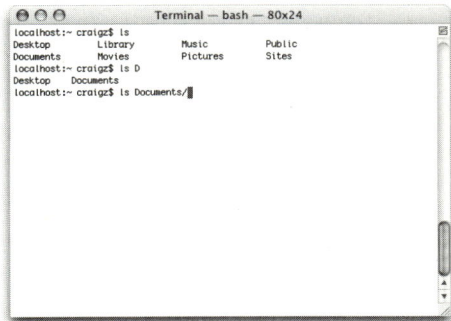

Figure 24-3: Desktop and Documents are offered as possible completions for the letter D as entered. To complete either choice, continue typing either word, then hit tab as soon as it becomes unique.

Unix wildcards and regular expressions

You're probably getting the idea by now that one of Unix's characteristics is to express the most information in the tersest manner. Using *regular expressions,* a shorthand notation for arbitrary strings of characters, the shell buttresses this impression. If you've used BBEdit (BareBones Software, `www.barebones.com`) or any of a number of other applications, you've encountered grep (global regular expression parser), and the power that this shorthand provides in matching patterns and strings.

Regular expressions can be used on the command line in arguments to a command or within applications (particularly editors) to perform searches or find and replace operations.

In its simplest form, an *expression* is a string of characters, such as document name. Two special wildcards are used in regular expressions:

✦ **Asterisk (*),** which stands for any sequence of characters.

✦ **Question mark (?),** which stands for any individual character.

You can also tell the shell to match any character from a list by enclosing the list in square brackets; for example, [aeiou] would indicate that any lowercase vowel would be a matching character. You can even tell the shell to match any character that is not in the list by preceding the list with a caret (^). Additionally, special characters are available if you want it to match at the beginning of a line (^) or end of a line ($).

Note   Yes, the caret is used for both negation and to denote beginning-of-line. Here, you need to be aware of the context. If the caret is the first character within square brackets (a set of characters), it means "anything except the characters enumerated." But, if the caret is outside the brackets and is the first character of the expression, it means "beginning of line."

Giving you even more to remember (but less to type), you can specify ranges of characters, for example [a-z] to specify any lowercase alphabetic character. Now, the obvious question arises, "But what if I want to match a hyphen?" The so-called *escape character* (\) comes into play here—any character following the escape character is to be taken literally, to specify a backslash and to escape it as well. In other words, an \ character is used to escape any special character and to hide it's meaning from the shell. In the case that you want to use a \ character literally you'll escape it as well by using the \ character as in \\.

Tip   Certain escaped characters have special meaning in regular expressions. To denote a line break, you use \n. To specify a tab character, use \t; and to match a page break, type \f.

You can use *metacharacters* to specify how many times a pattern may repeat. The pattern may be a literal character, a wildcard character, a character class, or a special character. The asterisk (*) denotes zero or more occurrences of the pattern—therefore, the pattern is always true. Similarly, the question mark (?) signifies zero or one occurrence of the pattern and also indicates a match for every character scanned. Finally, the plus sign (+) tells the shell to find one or more occurrences of the pattern.

Note   There is actually another repetition indicator. You can enter a {n}, where n is a digit, to indicate matching exactly n occurrences of the pattern. Entering {n,} specifies matching n or more occurrences of the pattern, and entering {n,m} indicates matching at least n but no more than m occurrences of the pattern.

Just as you can combine patterns to form more-complex patterns, you are provided with an *alternate* character (an or operator), enabling you to match any of a collection of patterns. This character is the vertical bar (|).

Table 24-1 illustrates some of the ways that you can use wildcards and regular expressions to find matches.

Table 24-1: Use of Wildcards and Regular Expressions to Find Matches

Pattern	Meaning
[Ff]ile[0-9]	Match anything spelled file, whether or not the f is capitalized and followed by a single digit.
*.rtf	Match any string ending in .rtf.
^From*Spenser$	Find ny line starting with From and ending with Spenser.
^[^a-z]	Find the first character of any line that does not start with a lowercase letter.
1[01]:##[\t][Pp]\.[Mm]\.	Find any time entry starting at 10 p.m., but before midnight.
tom|dick|harry	Find any tom, dick, or harry (not on the command line; only in grep, Unix's *global regular expression parser* command).

You can even create remembered patterns by enclosing the pattern within parentheses. These remembered patterns are often referred to as *tagged regular expressions*. Within the same command, you can specify the remembered patterns by specifying \1 for the first, \2 for the second, and so forth in a subsequent argument. Such references are referred to as *back references*. Back references can take considerable time to evaluate; however, they are of particular advantage when doing search-and-replace operations in an editor.

Note   Operators function in precedence (order) in regular expressions. Repetition operators are evaluated before concatenation operators, and concatenation takes precedence over alternation.

Creating and deleting directories and files

Analogous to the Finder's New Folder command, the shell offers you the mkdir command to create a new directory. You can even create a new (empty) file by using the touch command and specifying a file that does not already exist. The touch command on an existing file changes the file's modification date and time to the current date and time.

Unix doesn't really need a rename command, because it has something just as good; the mv (move) command. If you move a file with a new name rather than copy it into the directory in which it already resides, you have renamed it. Moving a file deletes the original. Of course, you use a cp (copy) command when you don't want to delete the original. Both commands can take one of two forms. They have two arguments (source and destination file names) or they have multiple arguments, the last of which is the directory into which all the other arguments are moved or copied.

Both cp and mv have a number of switches available, and you can read about them by typing man cp or man mv in a Terminal window. The type that we're going to tell you about here is the one that you're probably going to use the most. The -R switch tells the shell to recursively copy or move the contents when a source argument is a directory.

You delete files with the rm (remove) command. Unix shows a different mindset from that typical of the Mac OS or even Windows; the effects of rm are immediate and irrevocable. If you want to provide a little bit of safety while possibly increasing the annoyance factor, you can use the -i option, which interrogates you on every file that the command is going to delete, as shown in Figure 24-4. A y is an affirmative response. Anything else is taken as a negative response.

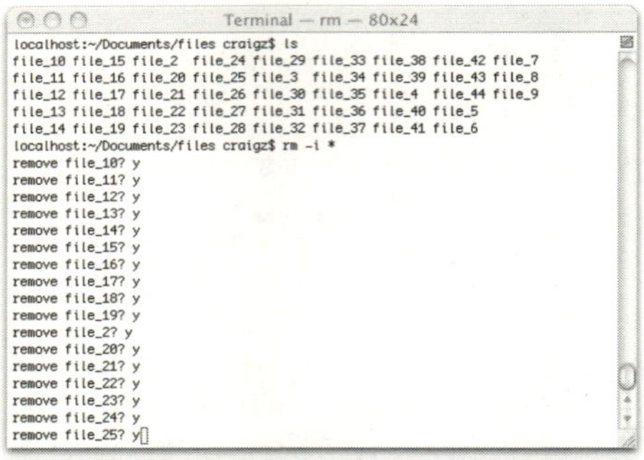

Figure 24-4: Using the -i switch with rm.

To remove an empty directory, you use the rmdir command. If the directory isn't empty, you receive an error message to that effect, and the directory is not deleted. You can, however, use the rm command with either the -R or -r switch to recursively delete a directory and its contents. Again, adding the -i switch causes the shell to interrogate you for each file and directory before deleting it.

Disk and file system statistics

Two commands, du (disk utilization) and df (display free space), let you find out how much space you are using for your files and directories and how much space is available for use.

Displaying free space

By default, the df command gives you a report such as the one shown in Figure 24-5. It gives you a list of all the file systems you have mounted, where they are mounted, how many 512-byte blocks are on the file system, how many are used, how many are still available, and the percentage of capacity utilized. Divide the number of blocks by 2 to get the number of kilobytes or use the -k option to specify that you want the results in kilobytes.

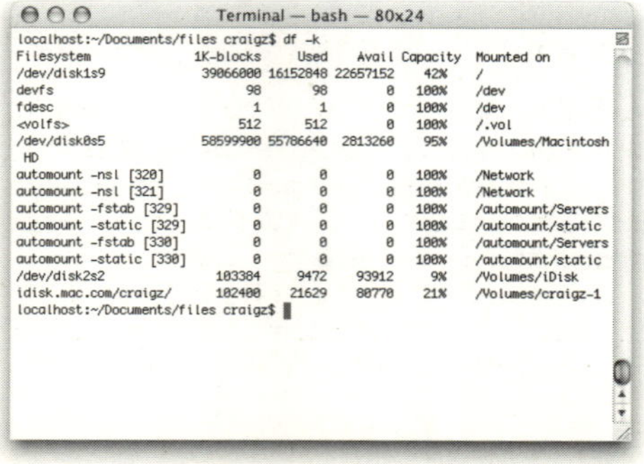

Figure 24-5: df tells you how much space each file system has and how much is being used.

You can give a single file as an argument to df to get statistics for just the file system on which the specified file resides. Notice that the file system names are not normally the names of the volume (such as Macintosh HD) but rather the cryptic device names.

Disk utilization

The du command breaks the information down into finer increments, giving you statistics for files and directories, as shown in Figure 24-6. With no argument(s), du reports on utilization by all files and directories, recursively, from the current directory. With a file for an argument, you get the number of 512-byte blocks used by that file. With a directory as an argument, du gives you the information for that directory and recurses through any directories contained within the directory (see Figure 24-6). Employing the -s option tells du to summarize (not enumerate), also shown in Figure 24-6.

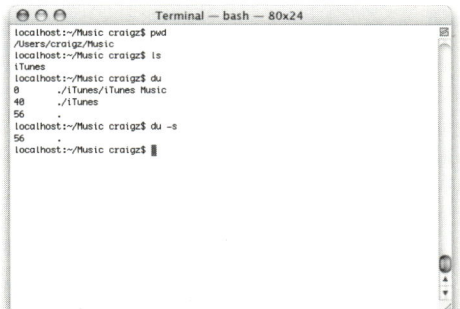

Figure 24-6: To get an itemized breakdown of disk space used, use df without options—the -s option gives a summary. The output shows 40 512-byte blocks in use by the iTunes directory, or 20k of disk space used.

Viewing and Editing Files

Unix's origin as a command-line environment brings with it a number of tools for dealing with files. You have tools to display file contents and many kinds of editors, from ones that execute commands a line at a time, through screen editors, and on to stream editors that process commands against entire files. To use these editors, you type (or store) your commands rather than use a mouse and menus; all editors covered here are keyboard driven.

Standard input, standard output, and pipes

To the shell (and to Unix in general), any place it obtains or places data is a file. The keyboard data stream is a file, the window in which output is displayed is a file, and files on your disk are files. The input stream from your keyboard is the default for a special file called standard input (stdin). The default file for output, your Terminal window, is called standard output. You can redirect standard input to come from some other file by preceding the file name with a less than sign (<). Similarly, you can redirect standard output by using a greater than sign (>). If, for example, you wanted to create a file containing a directory listing of your Documents folder, you could type ls Documents >docdir.txt, as shown in Figure 24-7. A number of commands display the contents of files. Among these commands are cat, more, pr, head, and tail. The meaning for each command is provided in Table 24-2.

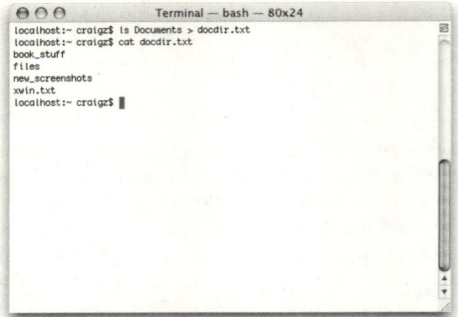

Figure 24-7: Output from the list directory (ls) command is redirected into a text file docdir.txt. The concatenate (cat) command is used to view the file.

Table 24-2: Commands that Display Contents of Files

Command	Meaning
Cat	Concatenate the files given as arguments and display on standard output.
More	Display the arguments on standard output a page (window full) at a time. You type a space to get to the next screen; type b to go back a screen. Typing a return advances one line, and typing q terminates the command.
Pr	Similar to more, but it includes page headers and footers at would-be page breaks if the output were directed to a printer.
Head n	Display the first *n* (10 if n is omitted) lines of a file on standard output.
Tail n	Display the last *n* (10 if n is omitted) lines of a file on standard output.

Tip You can append output to an existing file by using two successive greater than signs. For example, ls Movies >>docdir.txt would append the directory listing for your Movies folder to the file docdir.txt.

You can chain commands together with the pipe symbol, a vertical bar (|), so that the output from the first command is the input to the next. For example, ls -R|more would display a recursive directory listing one screen at a time.

Most commands default to taking their input from standard input. For example, if you omit the file argument from the cat command, cat patiently waits for you to enter it from the keyboard. When you enter data from the keyboard, you need to indicate that you're finished by entering the Unix end-of-input character (Control-D).

Paths and Variables

With few exceptions, such as cd, almost every command you enter at the Unix prompt is a program stored on your disk. The shell is a programming environment, complete with loops, conditionals, and variables. Shell programs are usually called *scripts*. Shell programs are *interpreted* rather than *compiled*. Therefore, when a shell script or command executes, the shell parses the command, evaluates the variables, and then executes rather than having the instructions reduced to binary machine instructions.

You create shell variables by using the set command. For example, set myPath = "~/MyApps" would create a variable named myPath that had the value /Users/craigz/MyApps (assuming that your username is craigz). You can determine the current value of any shell variable by issuing the echo command, with the variable name, preceded by a dollar sign ($), as an argument. One very important shell variable is PATH. PATH is the variable the shell evaluates to determine where it should look for commands you issue. The following figure shows the initial value of PATH for the user craigz.

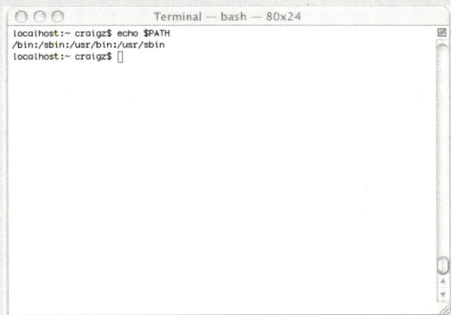

As you can determine, PATH is a series of directory specifications that are separated by colons. Every time you issue a command, such as ls or cp, the shell starts checking each directory in PATH until it finds the command and executes it. If the command cannot be found in any directory in PATH, you receive an error message to that effect. If the program is not in one of the PATH directories, you need to specify a directory path to it. To execute a command in your current directory, you precede it with ./. If you are curious as to which directory holds the command you want to execute, you can use the which command (a built-in shell command). The which command can come in handy if, for example, you are attempting to execute a newly installed command, and the wrong command executes because a command with the same name was located in an earlier PATH directory.

About permissions

In addition to the read and write permissions, you find an execute permission at the file level. Because Unix commands aren't applications with an APPL file type (or a bundle with an .app extension), the shell needs some way to indicate that a particular file is executable, and Unix has used this method of file-based permissions for over three decades now.

Permissions on directories have a slightly different but analogous meaning compared to files as shown in Table 24-3.

Table 24-3: Unix Permissions and Meanings

Permission	Meaning for a file	Meaning for a directory
R read	read a file	list files in ...
W write	write a file	create file in ... rename file in ... delete file ...
x execute	execute a shell script, command, or program	read a file in ... write to a file in ... execute a file in ... execute a shell script in ...

Commands, programs, and shell scripts are examples of files for which execute permission should be enabled. As with any other file, this file has three levels of permission: owner, group, and everybody.

Note   Unix users typically refer to permissions as three (octal) digit numbers. Read permission is worth four points, write permission is worth two, and execute permission is worth one. Therefore, when you hear that a file has 740 permission, the first digit being 7 means that the owner can read, write, and execute the file (4+2+1=7); the second digit being 4 means members of the group can read the file (4+0+0=4); and the third digit being 0 means everyone else has no permissions with respect to the file (0-0+0=0).

Changing permissions

The chmod command enables the owner or root to change the permissions on a file. The simplest form of this command is to follow chmod with the new permissions and then the file or list of files to receive those permissions. For example, chmod 777 myscript.sh would give read, write, and execute permission to everyone for the file myscript.sh.

If you don't want to do the math, you only need to remember six letters — *u* for user, *g* for group, *a* for all, *r* for read, *w* for write, and *x* for execute. You also need to remember three symbols as well: + to add a permission, - to subtract a permission, and = to set permissions. For example, chmod g+w dirdoc.txt would add write permission for members of the group to the file dirdoc.txt without affecting any other permissions.

Changing owner and groups

Only the root user (system administrator) has the authority to change a file's owner. Assuming that you have logged in as root or are running from an administrator account and using the sudo command, the syntax to change a file's owner is chown *newownerid filelist*. The newownerid is either the new owner's login name or her numeric ID, as displayed in NetInfo Manager, and filelist is the file or files whose ownership is to be changed.

If you are a member of the group to which you want to change group ownership and you have write and execute permissions to the files and directories in question, you can change the group ownership of a file with the chgrp command, whose form is the same as chown command except that you use a group name or number rather than a user name or number.

Tip   To determine to which groups you belong, you can enter the groups command. You can also determine to which groups another user belongs by typing groups with their username as an argument.

Advanced Unix Topics

Unix is a highly configurable environment with a wealth of tools. In this section, we introduce some tools and commands available to you when interacting with a shell in Terminal.

Environment and shell variables

Every time you log in, open a new Terminal window, or switch shells, the shell checks its initialization files to establish your environment and your shell variables. Each shell handles its initialization files and environment settings somewhat differently. The default shell (bash) is covered in this section.

First, bash reads files that are referred to as *shell initialization files*. These files set specific behaviors for the shell. There is usually a system-wide shell initialization file located at /etc/profile, this file will be read and used by all users on the system. Generally a user would like to set personal options for their shell. For this reason, the home directory is scanned for the following invisible files: ~/.bash_profile, ~/.bash_login, or ~/.profile. (Remember that by using a period as the first part of a file name, the file will be invisible to an ls command, unless the -a switch is provided.) For introductory purposes, the three files are functionally equivalent. If none of these files are in your home directory and you want to experiment with changing local variables such as your shell prompt, default editor, and so on, you should create a ~/.bash_profile file and make changes in that file.

Note   By convention, environment variables are all uppercase, and shell variables are all lowercase. Thus, the environment variable PATH and the shell variable path can (and usually do) have different values.

Enter the env command to see a list of your current environment variables and the set command to see a list of your current shell variables. Examples of both are shown in Figure 24-8.

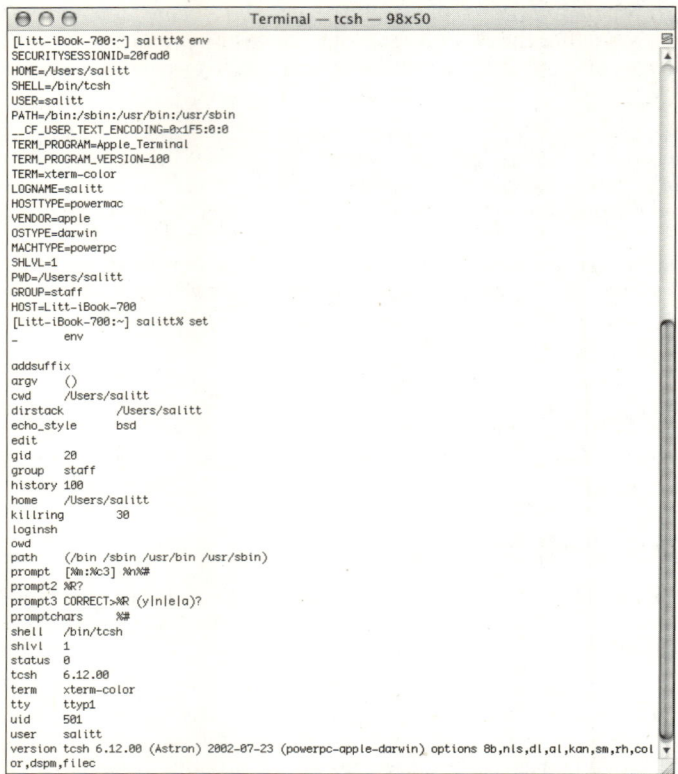

Figure 24-8: The env and set commands display environment and shell variables, respectively.

Changing environment variables

You can change environment variable settings or declare new environment variables for the current session by entering a command of the form: `export VARIABLENAME=new_value` where `VARIABLENAME` is the environment variable you want to change or declare and `new_value` is the value you want to give it. This value persists until you log out or exit the shell in which you're working.

If you want to make the change apply to future sessions, you need to edit the `~/.bash_profile` file (or the `~/.bash_login` or `~/.profile` file). You can do this with a shell editor, such as vi or emacs. You can also do so with Mac OS X or Classic text editor, such as TextEdit, BBEdit, or SimpleText. But you first have to make an unhidden copy in the shell (the Open dialogs won't display hidden files), edit that copy, and make sure to save the result as plain text, and then replace the hidden file with the edited copy. Proceed as follows:

1. **If it is a new variable, add the export command to the .bash_profile file.** If it is a change to an existing variable, find the line where that variable is declared and change the line.

2. **Save the file and exit the editor.**

3. Enter the command `source .bash_profile` **if you want the change to take effect.**

Note   The default location of `.bash_profile` is your home directory.

The source command feeds the contents of the file arguments to the shell as input.

Changing shell variables

To define a temporary value to a shell variable, use the following command:

```
variable_name=value
```

The value of this variable remains set until you exit from this shell. The value of this variable is not exported to other shells when they are invoked.

To give a lasting value to a shell variable, follow these steps:

1. **Use an editor to open your** `~/.bash_profile` **file and add the following line:**

```
variable_name=value
```

2. **Save the file and leave the editor.**

3. **Enter the command**

```
source ~/.bash_profile
```

Doing so adds the value of the shell variable to your shell's present environment. When subsequent shells are invoked, they also have this variable set.

Creating aliases

No, these aren't the same aliases available under Mac OS. Unix aliases are pseudonyms for other Unix commands. To create an alias for use with the bash shell, add the command `alias aliasname=what-it-stands-for` to the `~/.bash_profile` file and enter the `source .bash_profile` command, making the obvious substitutions.

One example of an alias is the following:

```
alias what='ps -aux | grep $USER | more'
```

This command sequence pipes (sends) the output of the process status command as input to grep, which searches that input for the processes you're running and then displays the results a screen at a time.

You can even chain multiple commands together in an alias by separating them with semi-colons. For example, `alias tree 'cd; ls -R'` would display a complete directory hierarchy of a user's home directory when the command tree was entered.

Manipulating text file contents

Just as Unix provides you the cat, pr, head, tail, more, and less commands (mentioned earlier in this chapter) to display files or parts of files, it provides a variety of editors and other tools with which to create, edit, and summarize text file contents. In addition to the ancient command-line editor, ed, you also have vi, pico, and emacs, all of which are screen editors. Screen editors offer functionality between line editors where you entered commands describing the editing action you wanted to take and the direct manipulation windowing editors, such as

TextEdit. In a screen editor, file contents are displayed on a terminal screen, and you move the cursor around via the keyboard and shift modes between overstrike and insert, with the option of still using the commands of the old-line editors. Although multiple editors are available in Mac OS X, among the screen editors, only vi is guaranteed to be included with every Unix distribution, so a knowledge of vi, whether or not it is your editor of choice, is recommended.

Each editor is well documented in its man pages, and full books are written about their use. Which is the best for you is a decision only you can make after trying them out. Each has a devoted, almost religious, following.

Some other tools you can use to work with file contents are listed in Table 24-4.

Table 24-4: Text File Tools

Command	Description
Compress	Reduce the size of files by encoding, similar to StuffIt or Zip, but only compresses individual files. Use uncompress to restore the file to its original state. Convention has it that the .z extension indicates a compressed file. To create compressed archives, use tar to create the archive and then compress to reduce its size.
Cut	Selects portions of each line of a file.
Diff	Compares two files.
Fmt	Reformats the files given to have consistent line lengths — default is 65, maximum is 75 characters. This tool originated primarily for the manipulation of line breaks in email messages.
grep	The (in)famous regular expression parser is used to find all instances of patterns within a file or list of files.
Sed	A stream editor, it reads the file(s) specified, modifying the input based upon the command(s) listed and passing the result to standard output. The editing commands may be stored in a file, one per line.
sort	Reorders the lines of a file into a user-defined order. Sort order can be alphabetical, reverse alphabetical, or other combinations.
split	Divides a file into multiple parts, each (except possibly the last part) of the same size. Use cat to recombine the files..
Tar	Creates (uncompressed) archives of the files given as arguments. Short for tape archiver, it is used to package files together.
uniq	Removes duplicate adjacent lines. Pipe the output of sort to uniq if you want to remove all duplicates.
Wc	Reports the number of characters, words, and lines in a file.

Writing shell scripts

You can do more with the shell than just execute commands. The shell has a built-in programming language so that you can write your own text programs or commands. These programs are called *shell scripts.* The main strength of shell scripts is that you can use them to invoke a possibly long and complex sequence of instructions, with logical branches, as though the sequence were a simple command.

Writing a shell script is similar to entering the commands manually in a Terminal window, with a few significant differences:

✦ You may want your command to accept arguments. The shell automatically assigns any strings following your script's name on the command line to a set of parameters: shell variables named $1 through $9. You don't have to do anything special to obtain arguments from the command line; they're already available in the parameter variables when your script begins its execution. If you need more than nine arguments, you can use the shift operator in your script to access later variables.

✦ You may want your new command to support options. The shell passes options to your script the same as any other arguments: each command-line string is set into the $*n* variables (also accessible in the special shell array variable argv[*n*]).

✦ Usually you enter keyboard commands with all information explicitly stated; however, commands inside shell scripts are often parameterized and can be executed conditionally. You parameterize a command by providing variable references and file name substitutions as the command's arguments instead of literal text. You need to use the shell's if, switch, while, and foreach commands to handle alternative paths of executions. You rarely use these commands at the keyboard, but they occur often in shell scripts.

Regardless of the use to which you're going to put a shell script, almost all shell scripts are developed using the following general plan:

1. **Develop a text file containing the required commands.**

2. **Mark the text file executable,** using the chmod command chmod +x *filename* to make it executable for all users.

3. **Test the shell script.**

4. **Install the script in its permanent location.**

5. **Use it.**

If the script is for your personal use, create a ~/bin directory and add it to your search path, as described earlier in this chapter ("Changing shell variables"). After you create a new script, you can just mark the script executable and drop it in your personal bin directory, and it will be available for use.

When testing a script, you may want to see which commands are being executed so that you can track an unexpected behavior. To do so, invoke your script with the command bash -x *scriptname* or embed a set echo command in your script.

Tip   If you are only interested in a specific range of included commands, you can set echo just before the commands and unset echo immediately after the commands. Remember to remove these set and unset commands after testing.

As with most any other programming language, internal documentation in the form of *comments* — lines that are not executed but are meant to explain what is going on — is considered very good form. Lines beginning with a *splat* (MIT jargon for the sharp or number sign character, *#*) are taken as comments by the shell. In fact, the shell ignores anything starting with a splat to the end of that line as a comment unless the splat is escaped with the backslash character (\).

Where to Find More Information

Unix is a complete operating system, and we can only touch on the surface of it in this book. Fortunately, Unix comes with a lot of internal documentation in the form of man pages. Enter man followed by the name of the command, and you receive chapter and verse about that command. If you aren't quite sure about the name of the command but you know roughly what it does, you may be able to find it by using the apropos command followed by a keyword. First, you should investigate the man command — type man man.

Tip   Instead of displaying man pages in the Terminal window, you can display them in a Mac OS X application such as ManOpen by Carl Lindberg (www.clindberg.org/projects/ManOpen.html). This application has a Find command to help you find the man page that you want to read. You can also select a man page from a list of available pages in another window.

Many applications are already written for Unix. Fink is an open-source project intended to ease the task of installing and managing Unix software on your Mac OS X system. For a thorough explanation of what Fink is and how to install and use it, read the next chapter!

You can find a number of excellent books on Unix. If you want a gentle introduction, we would recommend *Unix For Dummies,* 4th Edition, by John R. Levine and Margaret Levine Young.

As always, the Internet provides a wealth of references. For Unix issues, some Web sites we particularly recommend include

✦ A Unix Guide at www.ed.com/unixguide

✦ Unix is a Four-Letter Word at http://unix.t-a-y-l-o-r.com

You can find literally hundreds of others. Use Sherlock to do an Internet search for Unix, and you will be amazed at the number of sites that have Unix as a keyword.

Summary

In this chapter, you discovered a little bit about how to use the Mac OS X Unix underpinnings, known as Darwin, as well as a little history about Unix in general. You saw how to use the Terminal application, modify your Unix shell environment, enter commands in the shell, switch from one shell to another, and write shell scripts. You also saw that we barely touch the surface of this complex subject, and we've given you some pointers to learn more if you're interested.

✦   ✦   ✦

Making Use of Unix

In this chapter, we move on past the basics of using Unix and start to explore some of the advantages of having a Unix-based system. Now that Apple is the world's leading provider of Unix systems, Macintosh users can get in on the power and flexibility that had been only available to users of high-end workstations in the past.

Apple provides a wealth of applications with a default installation of Mac OS X. However, a plethora of additional software is available for Unix to meet all of your needs and wants. From more flexible network utilities and Internet clients to graphic applications and office suites, they are all available and easily installed. For a discussion of different types of software and licenses, review Chapter 21. We provide an overview of major free software available for Mac OS X and cover the installation of Unix-based software on Mac OS X in this chapter.

More Than Surviving with Unix

The previous chapter provided a rough survival guide for Unix. Now that you are familiar with the underpinnings of the system, it's time to roll up your sleeves and see what you can do with this new Operating System.

When Apple looked for a foundation to build their next generation operating system on, they settled on Unix. Many users will never be aware of the Unix underpinnings of the new system. Aqua will be the interface for the majority of old and new Macintosh users. Aqua is quite powerful and can enable users to do almost anything they desire with their personal computer. However, for those users who want to customize their experience to a greater degree, or who want to tap into the vast software libraries available for Linux and other Unix-based systems, Mac OS X provides just the ticket. Apple has provided a flexible and powerful system where the user has the elegance of Aqua and the raw power of X-Windows and Terminal-based applications available in one place.

On first look, a computer running Mac OS X looks exactly like a traditional Macintosh. However, a quick look through the Applications and Utilities folders shows some unfamiliar programs. Chapter 21 introduces these programs; we go into further detail here.

The programs that are of the most interest as you explore the Unix side of Mac OS X are Terminal and X11. Terminal and X11 are found in the Utilities folder inside the Applications folder. X11 may require a separate installation, depending on how Mac OS X was installed on your computer. (We discuss this later in the chapter.)

What can I do with Unix?

The reason for all the excitement regarding these new applications is that they never were part of an Apple operating system before. Of course, telnet and other terminal emulation applications have been available for ages. However, these programs were used to connect to other computers. Also, X-Windows servers were available for pre–Mac OS X systems; however, these too were used to connect to clients on other computers. Terminal and X11 on Mac OS X focus internally. That is to say, that they connect to your own computer. For anyone who has had access to a Unix machine located elsewhere, for example, at their ISP or in a computer lab, having a full-fledged Unix machine on their own desk can be an exciting prospect.

Note   In the world of X-Windows, traditional concepts of client-server are turned upside down. The program that you use to connect to an application either on your own computer or on a host computer is called a server. The program that runs on a host computer listening for connections and allowing access to authenticated visitors is called a client. More information is available on this subject at `www.x.org/X11_clientdesign.html`.

With access to a Unix system, one can do all kinds of fun and useful things, from working on systems at work or in other locations to providing services to other users. Programs are available on Unix systems that are unavailable for other systems. If you manage other Unix systems, either at work or elsewhere, a home Unix system is indispensable. Most of the Internet is based on Unix systems in some shape or fashion. Having the same system at home opens a lot of doors for exploration and enables you to do a lot of things that you could never do before, either because you would not have administrative access to the system, or just never had it so close at hand.

Network services are transparent using Unix. Most popular Internet services were developed on Unix systems. The protocol TCP/IP, which is used for almost all Internet traffic, was developed on Unix systems. TCP/IP is the native language for Unix systems. Therefore, communicating with other systems is a simple matter. It's easy to connect to other computers, either for Web surfing or for file transfer, or for anything else you may want to accomplish. Files can be copied and even edited in place with very simple commands. Where older operating systems required explicitly enabling networking, or installing additional software, networking is part of the core of Unix. This greatly simplifies networking issues.

More programming languages are compatible with Unix than with any other mainstream operating system. That makes Unix a great asset for anyone who is interested in learning how to program a computer. Programming languages other than AppleScript are out of the scope of this book, but you are using the right operating system, should you decide to pursue any type of programming.

Installing Additional Software

Apple has included a good selection of software with Mac OS X, however sooner or later you'll find yourself wanting to do more with your computer than work with the included applications. You may also wish to avail yourself of the wealth of software available for Unix. In order to install traditional Unix software on your Macintosh you'll first need to ensure that you've got the right tools.

Install Apple Software for Unix

Apple provides several software tools that allow further access to the Unix system than do the applications that come shrink-wrapped with Mac OS X. In order to install additional Unix software, Apple Developer Tools must be installed. Read on for an explanation of the developer tools and why you'll need to have them installed.

When software developers write software, they write it using a computer language. For the Macintosh, traditionally this was Pascal. On Mac OS X, however, there are many more choices for the developer. Popular choices are C, C++, Objective-C (developed by NeXT Computer, and now called Cocoa by Apple), Java, and many others. After code is written, it is run through a piece of software called a *compiler*. The compiler takes the human-readable code that the programmer or programming team wrote, and transforms it to machine-readable code that the computer takes and executes. When the code has been compiled, the result is a binary file, which is no longer human readable. If programmers want to make a change to the program, they would need to make changes to their source code and then recompile the code, producing a new binary program. Generally, when you purchase software for your computer, you are given only the binary application, not the source code. In other words, when you purchase software for your computer, no assembly is generally required.

Working with Unix software is an entirely different experience. Unix has its roots in academic research and its initial user base was mostly programmers. The operating system was designed by programmers and for programmers. The standard way of distributing software for Unix is by distributing the source code. This is considered useful, because the user is now empowered. Don't like the way something works? Change it yourself. Find a bug, fix it, and email the developer with what you did. This active participation means that the user never has to wait for a vendor fix. Of course, most users are busy doing other tasks and don't generally feel compelled to fix bugs in their software. However, knowing that you can fix a bug is a comfort. A user is expected to have the tools installed on their own system to compile or build the software locally, after making changes to the source code. The advantage to this is that the software can be written in one place but can run on a variety of systems. This is immediately visible when you consider that much software has been written to run on Linux, but it can be compiled on a Mac OS X system and run as if it was designed for a Mac. We will cover installing some popular free software utilities later in this chapter. For now we will have to install some tools that will allow us to install software later.

If you have not already done so, you'll have to install the Apple Developer Tools software. The Developer Tools software is part of the new Xcode software for software developers.

In order to install Developer Tools, you need to insert the Xcode Tools CD into your computer. Launch the Install Xcode Tools package and click through the first few screens. When you get to the installation type, choose Custom. Then select at least Developer Tools Software and the BSD SDK as shown in Figure 25-1. Other packages are optional.

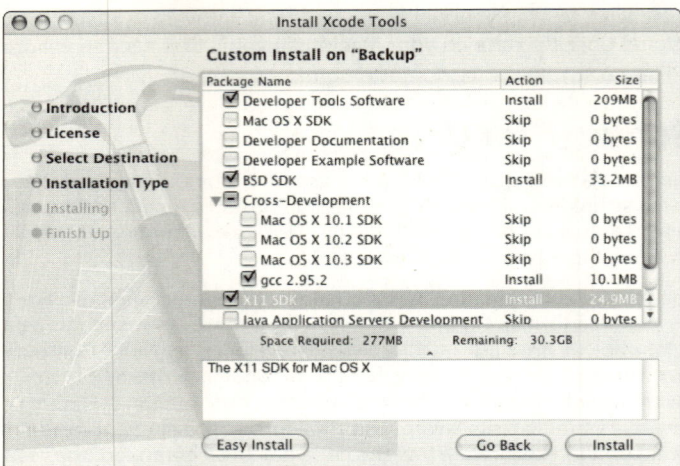

Figure 25-1: Using the Install Xcode Tools package to install Developer Tools Software.

Installing X11 for Mac OS X

Now that you've installed Apple Developer Tools, you can build software for your Mac OS X system. However, you'll be limited to software that displays in text-only mode and is usable only from within the Terminal application. Install X11 in order to run your Unix programs in full-screen mode. Apple has provided a full-featured X-Windows implementation in X11. X11 encompasses an entire graphic environment for a computer. Everything that Aqua does for Mac OS X, X-Windows does for a Unix system. Apple has done a great job of hiding this complexity. X-Windows systems provide what is called a *window manager*. The window manger does exactly what it sounds like it does: it manages windows, including where windows are located on screen, if windows are minimized, window dimensions, and so on. In short, all the things that you see on screen are, in fact, managed.

X11 for Mac OS X also contains a window manager. This one is different than what you would see on a traditional Unix or Linux system. The one that Apple provides is invisible. The elements that it draws are functionally and visually equivalent to their Aqua counterparts. Hence, a window's title bar looks the same whether it is being presented by Aqua or X11. This is a significant achievement, although it looks like nothing. This allows you to seamlessly switch between applications, regardless of which system they were originally designed for. As discussed in Chapter 17, when using Classic, application title bars and menus appear different than they do in Mac OS X–native applications.

If X11 was installed on your computer when you installed or upgraded to Panther, or at the factory, then it will be available in your Applications folder. If X11 has not been installed, then you will need to use the Panther installation disks, and do a customized upgrade. Choose X11 from the list of software and let the installer complete its task.

Third-party installation tools

Now you have ensured that both Apple Developer Tools and X11 are installed, and you're ready to leap into the deep end of software installation. There are two ways to go about installing software on your system. The sure-fire, longer way; and the very easy way, which may sometimes not work quite the way you would like, requiring you to go back to the long way. In this section, you'll set up the system to run third-party software that is designed to aid you in the task of installing additional software. The little bit of effort in installing this software will more than pay off in ease of use for installing software in the future. And, it will keep your installed software up to date. This is an important benefit because most open source software projects are constantly improving; the only way to benefit from these software improvements and security updates is to be running the latest versions.

The day the first Mac OS X system came out of the box, there were thousands of software programs available in the form of source code downloads. Early adapters rushed to build software on Mac OS X, and found that with simple tweaks to the makefiles and other install files, both of which are mostly of use to programmers and compilers only, the software would build and run. Over time, many developers integrated these changes that were made by individual users into their own software distributions, making many programs easier to install on the Mac now. However, each individual program has to be dealt with individually, some have been adapted for Mac OS X, others have not Tracking which software builds out of the box, and which requires little tweaks can be a real chore. And if you are simply looking to use a program that may be useful to you, you probably don't want to spend a lot of time trying to get it to work on your computer. This is where Fink comes in. The developers of Fink have tracked hundreds of software packages and integrated the changes that let this software build on Mac OS X, patching the source code where necessary and doing other busy work so that you don't have to.

The Fink Project

Fink is a project that grew out of the excitement of Mac OS X being based on Unix. Early adapters to Mac OS X realized the power of the new operating system and were eager to mine the wealth of free Unix software available at sites like `http://freshmeat.net/`, `http://sourceforge.net/` and other such repositories. Although building each individual software package was not entirely difficult, each package offered its own unique challenges. The Fink developers, initially Christoph Pfisterer and others started to make notes of what had to be done to each package, and then developed a tool to automate making these changes. Also, most Linux systems have software that automates not only the installation process, but also the upgrade process. After a piece of software is installed on your system, you should be able to upgrade it simply. Often upgrading Unix software can be a chore, the goal was to ease this operation, and make the entire procedure more Mac like in the process. To learn more about Fink and their project goals, please visit their Web site at `http://fink.sourceforge.net`.

From Fink—FAQ—General: `http://fink.sourceforge.net/faq/`

Over time, the Fink project has collected many Unix applications, and has made installing these applications on your Macintosh extremely simple. There are several ways to use Fink, most from the command line. However, you can also use Fink in conjunction with another piece of software called Fink Commander. Fink Commander provides a graphical user interface to the Fink software. This provides all the utility of the command line program with the familiar ease of use of a Macintosh application. First, you install Fink, and then you install Fink Commander.

Installing Fink

Fink can be downloaded from the project homepage at `fink.sourceforge.net`. Follow the download link and click to download the binary installer. The current version is 0.5.3; however, the software is continually updated, so make sure to get the latest version. The binary installer is available as a disk image (.dmg) file. After downloading and expanding the disk image file, you'll have a disk image with several items. The main feature is the Fink Installer.pkg file. Double-click the package file to launch the Fink installer to install Fink on your system, as shown in Figure 25-2.

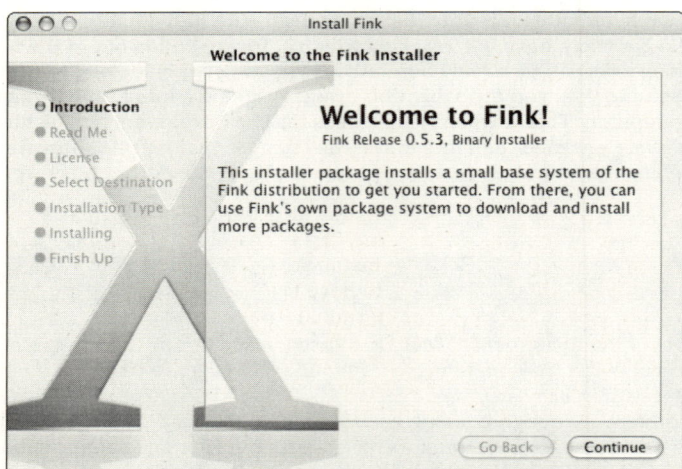

Figure 25-2: Run the Fink installer from the binary installer disk image.

After the installation is complete, a shell script opens in a new Terminal window. The script asks for permission, before changing your shell configuration files to execute the script /sw/bin/init.sh at login. Fink creates a directory at the root of your hard drive called sw. The script /sw/bin/init.sh adds sw to your search path as well as enabling any HTTP or FTP proxies that may be set in the Fink configuration file. Figure 25-3 shows the pathsetup.command script launched in a Terminal window.

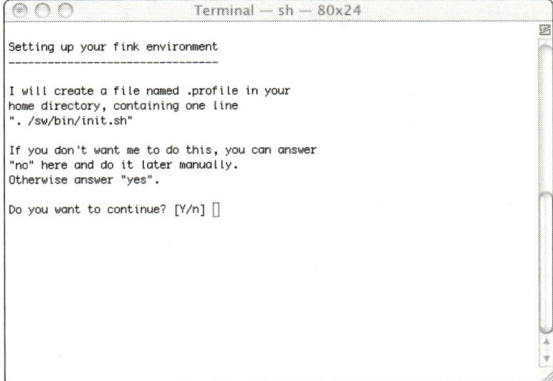

Figure 25-3: When the Fink install is completed the pathsetup.command script is launched in a Terminal window. Enter Y to continue.

You can use Fink in several different ways to browse through available software and install and upgrade software packages on your Mac OS X system. For complete information and instructions, please refer to the Fink documentation provided at the project's home page, `http://fink.sourceforge.net/doc/users-guide/` or follow the links in the included Documentation.html file in the Fink Installer Disk. A brief listing of the available ways to use Fink follows:

✦ **Fink:** This is the catch-all command. It works to download and compile source code on your computer. This no-frills command will generally work when other invocations pose problems. You use the fink command to install software in the following section. In order to use the fink command you'll need to have the developer tools installed. To use the fink command, simply type `fink` in a terminal window.

✦ **dselect:** Dselect is a curses-based text application that runs in Terminal. Curses is a Unix library which controls screen display in a terminal window, providing menus, inverse video, and allow a program to run in full-screen mode (full terminal window mode that is), rather than line-based output. Like other curses-based applications, dselect takes over the entire Terminal window, allows you to use the arrow keys for navigation, and is very friendly to use, as far as command-line-based software goes. Dselect has extensive built-in help pages, and is very simple. You can use dselect to browse the Fink software collection. A useful feature of dselect is that it will show you the version of the software that you have installed, and will show you the latest version available from Fink. This is helpful in order to ensure that the software you are running is the most up to date. If there is a newer version available, upgrading is as simple as selecting the package for installation. Figure 25-4 shows the dselect program running in a Terminal window.

✦ **Apt-get:** Apt-get is the engine that does the heavy lifting for dselect. Apt-get is invoked at the terminal, as are the other utilities. We will not be discussing the use of apt-get. If you are curious however, typing `apt-get -h` in a Terminal window will get you started.

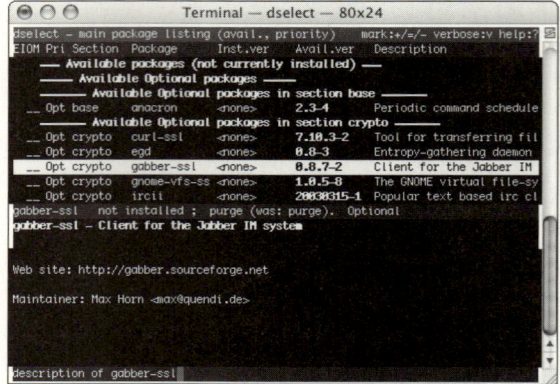

Figure 25-4: Browsing available packages with dselect.

✦ **FinkCommander:** FinkCommander is a GUI for Fink. Its functionality is identical to dselect, except it runs as a full-screen application. FinkCommander is included in the Fink installer disk. Simply drag the application folder from the mounted installer disk to your hard drive, preferably in your Applications folder. To launch the software, double-click the icon in your applications folder. Using FinkCommander to browse available software is shown in Figure 25-5.

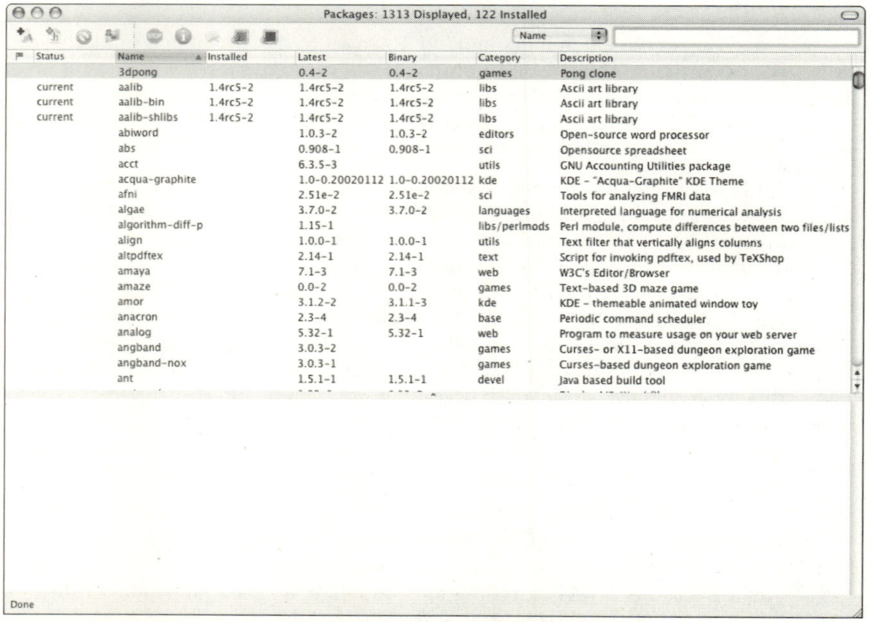

Figure 25-5: Browsing available packages with FinkCommander.

Now that Fink is installed on your system and you are comfortable using it to locate, install, and update software, you need to explore this treasure trove of software.

Useful software

In this section, we give a brief overview of useful software that can be installed on your Mac OS X system, to make your computer a bit more usable, flexible, and fun. All of the software being discussed in this section can be installed in several ways. As the software mentioned is all open source, full source code can be downloaded from the respective project's home pages. For brevity's sake, we used the easiest way to install the following packages, with Fink from the command line. FinkCommander can also be used to install the software if desired.

Lynx

Lynx is a text-mode Web browser, meaning that it runs in a Terminal window. Lynx has no GUI. It doesn't display graphic images as pictures, rather it displays their addresses. This sounds useless but can prove indispensable in troubleshooting Web pages. It's great to see what's going on with a remote site that is proving slow to load. Also, it can be invaluable in tracking down Web bugs either in Web pages or email. Web bugs are generally invisible and cannot be viewed with a traditional Web browser. Figure 25-6 shows the Lynx browser in action.

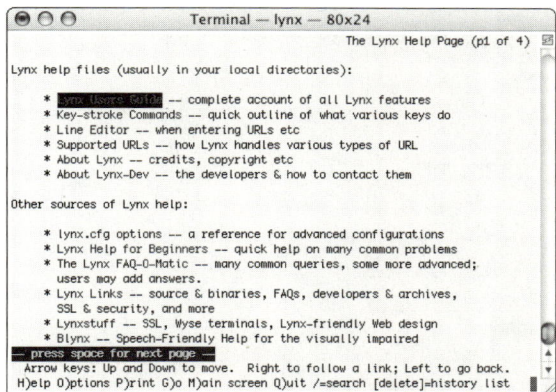

Figure 25-6: Text-based Web browsing with Lynx.

To install Lynx using Fink, simply type `fink install lynx`, as shown in Figure 25-7. For more information on Lynx, visit the project home page at `http://lynx.isc.org/`

NcFTP

Ncftp is a command line FTP client. It's a full-featured FTP client, with many modern features, and is far easier to use than standard FTP. It's got a wealth of features that make using FTP from the command a pleasure. Some of the improvements to the standard FTP client are progress meters, command-line editing, file name completion, auto-resume downloads, bookmarks, host redialing, downloading of whole directories, and more. NcFTP is very much like a Web browser for FTP servers. Figure 25-8 shows the NcFTP help text.

Terminal — sh — 80x24
Last login: Mon Sep 22 12:32:45 on ttyp1
Welcome to Darwin!
pandora:~ craigz$ fink install lynx
sudo /sw/bin/fink install lynx
Password:
Information about 1277 packages read in 1 seconds.
The following package will be installed or updated:
lynx
curl -f -L -s -S -O http://distfiles.opendarwin.org/lynx2.8.4.tar.bz2
mkdir -p /sw/src/lynx-2.8.4-2
bzip2 -dc /sw/src/lynx2.8.4.tar.bz2 | /sw/bin/tar -xf -
./configure --prefix=/sw --enable-nls --with-screen=ncurses --disable-full-paths
--enable-file-upload --enable-internal-links --libdir=/sw/etc --mandir=/sw/shar
e/man
creating cache ./config.cache
checking host system type...

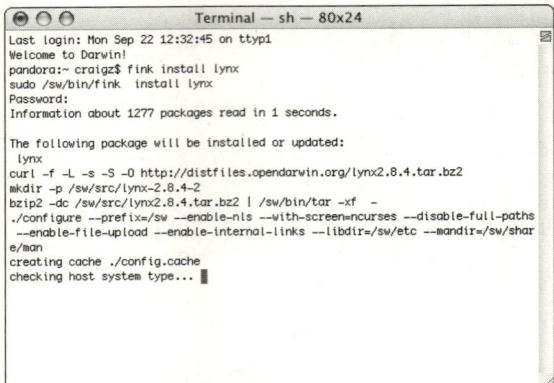

Figure 25-7: Installing Lynx with Fink.

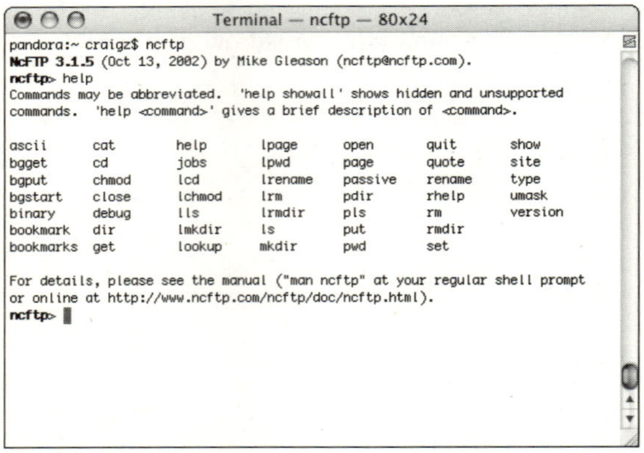

Terminal — ncftp — 80x24
pandora:~ craigz$ ncftp
NcFTP 3.1.5 (Oct 13, 2002) by Mike Gleason (ncftp@ncftp.com).
ncftp> help
Commands may be abbreviated. 'help showall' shows hidden and unsupported
commands. 'help <command>' gives a brief description of <command>.
ascii cat help lpage open quit show
bgget cd jobs lpwd page quote site
bgput chmod lcd lrename passive rename type
bgstart close lchmod lrm pdir rhelp umask
binary debug lls lrmdir pls rm version
bookmark dir lmkdir ls put rmdir
bookmarks get lookup mkdir pwd set
For details, please see the manual ("man ncftp" at your regular shell prompt
or online at http://www.ncftp.com/ncftp/doc/ncftp.html).
ncftp>

Figure 25-8: NcFTP — the better FTP client.

NcFTP also comes with the utility programs, ncftpget and ncftpput. These programs are provided as conveniences for shell scripting. These programs can be used in shell scripts to automate FTP actions, such as downloading logs from a Web server or uploading data to a server on a nightly basis.

For more information on NcFTP please visit the NcFTP client home page at `http://www.ncftpd.com/ncftp/`.

To install NcFTP, simply type `fink install ncftp`, as shown in Figure 25-9.

Wget

GNU Wget is designed for downloading Web content from the command line. Where Lynx is a full-featured Web browser, Wget is specifically designed for when you are trying to downloading files from a Web site. Additionally, Wget can download from FTP servers using the FTP protocol. Wget is very useful for when a server is very busy. You can copy the address from your Web browser into your clipboard and let Wget download the file for you.

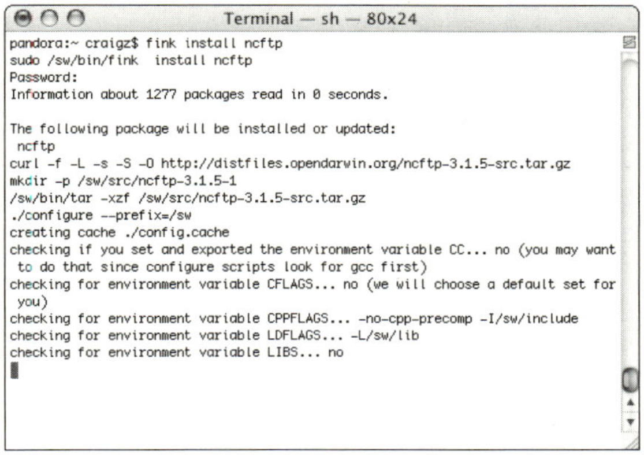

Figure 25-9: Installing Ncftp with Fink.

Wget is easily scripted, making it a perfect tool to use in automated scripts that you run at night via cron. You could run scripts to download nightly builds of Mozilla, or other actively developed software projects.

Wget is very useful when you want to download an entire Web tree — perhaps a documentation section of a Web site, or a site you are working on and want to archive a local copy of the site. For example, you can download the documentation for Wget from `www.gnu.org`. Enter the following command:

```
wget -r --level=0 -p -k
http://www.gnu.org/manual/wget/html_chapter/wget_toc.html
```

> `-r` turns on recursive retrieval.

> `--level=0` sets the depth of recursion to infinite. This will get the entire site.

> `-p` downloads all page requisites, images, and so on, needed to display the page.

> `-k` converts the links in the document to relative links that will work correctly from your hard drive.

This form of usage is very handy if you desire a local mirror of a Web site, or if you want to back up a remote site. Such a command can also be used in a shell script and called by cron nightly.

For additional information on Wget, please visit `http://www.gnu.org/software/wget/wget.html`.

To install Wget, simply type `fink install wget`, as shown in Figure 25-10.

GIMP

GIMP stands for the Gnu Image Manipulation Program. GIMP is free software distributed by GNU. GIMP is basically a free implementation of Adobe Photoshop. Although GIMP is not as complete as Photoshop, it is quite capable. It does most of what you would want from a graphics program and considerably more than converting graphics between formats. It's a handy piece of software to have installed, for those times that something comes in via email or otherwise, and you want to make simple changes to it. Figure 25-11 shows the GIMP at work. The project home page is located at `www.gimp.org`.

Figure 25-10: Installing GNU Wget with Fink.

If you don't have a copy of Adobe Photoshop or Macromedia Fireworks installed on your system, the GIMP is invaluable software. Even if you do already have a full-featured image editor installed on your system, it is worth installing, as it is truly a fantastic offering from the free software community. It is interesting to see just how good free software can be.

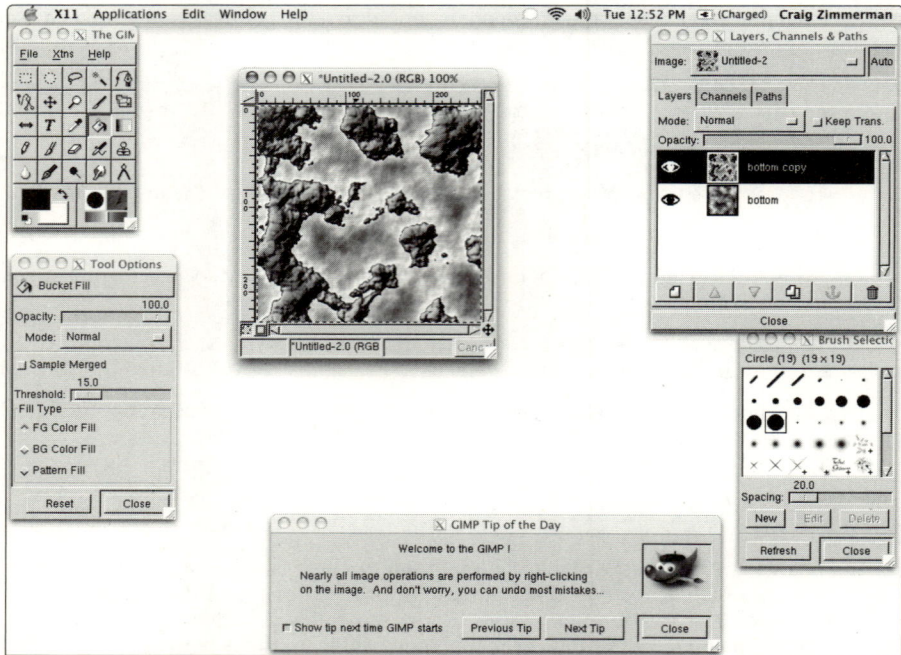

Figure 25-11: The GIMP in action.

Installing the GIMP can be very complicated, as there are many separate pieces of software that need to be built. Thankfully, Fink has GIMP in its library, so although installing GIMP is as simple as typing `fink install gimp`, there are more stages to this install than others we have seen so far This process takes quite a while, as there are a lot of software packages that require download. Though you'll have to wait quite some time, the download process is completely automated by Fink.

Installing the GIMP on your system with Fink is a bit different than other software installs you've encountered so far. As the GIMP relies on many different software packages, you'll have to answer some questions before continuing. Run the (now) traditional `fink install gimp` command.

Fink will need to know the answers to several questions. The first question regards how to handle GIF images. There are two available libraries, one with LZW and the other without. The two packages offer the same functionality; the distinction is due to politics and copyright issues. Either choice will result in a working GIMP. The second question is for Fink to know where and how X-Windows is installed on your system. Before Apple made X11 available for Mac OS X, installing X-Windows was generally a task that Fink would have been used for. In our case, we have installed our own copy, that is one that Fink has nothing to do with So we choose Option 1 which is a placeholder packing for xfree86. This simply tells Fink not to concern itself with the specifics of X-Windows, and to just assume that it is correctly installed. This is illustrated in Figure 25-12.

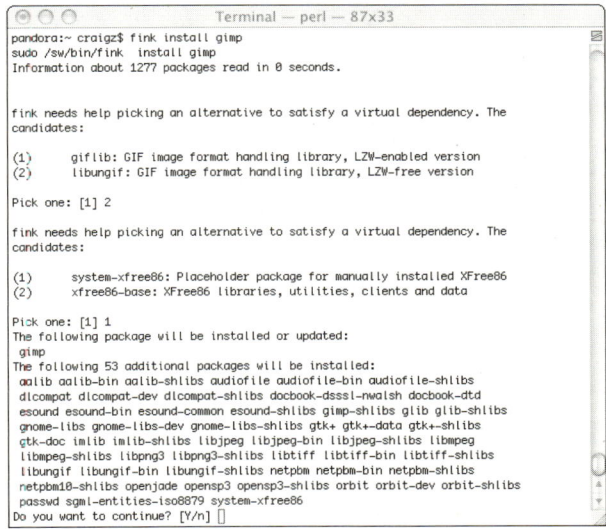

Figure 25-12: Fink needs to have a few questions answered before installing the GIMP.

The GIMP is an X-Windows-based application. Therefore, to run the software, you first have to launch X11. X11 should be installed on your system. If X11 is not already installed, please refer to the section "Installing X11 For Mac OS X" earlier in this chapter. X11 is located in your Applications folder. Launching it will automatically launch an application named xterm. xterm provides a window that looks almost exactly like a terminal window. In the xterm window, a command prompt appears. Type `gimp` at the prompt as shown in Figure 25-13.

Figure 25-13: Launching the GIMP from an xterm.

When the GIMP is launched for the first time, a folder must be created in the user's home directory, and another configuration must be done. the GIMP presents the following series of user installation dialog boxes that you will need to okay. Figures 25-14 through 25-18 show the dialog boxes. Click Continue in each box to confirm.

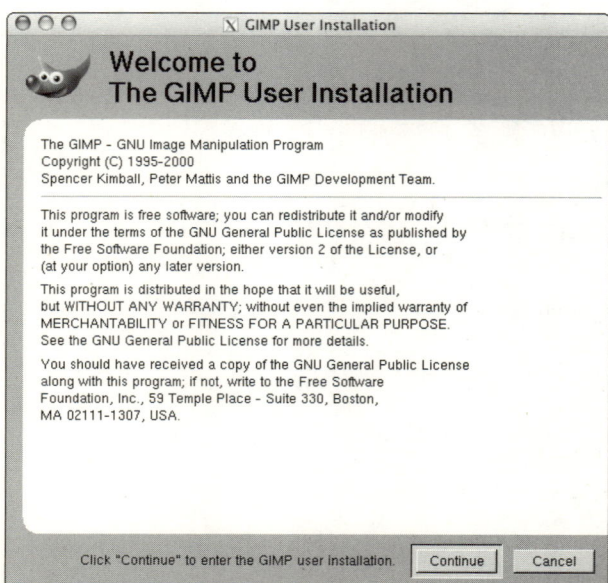

Figure 25-14: The GIMP user installation splash screen.

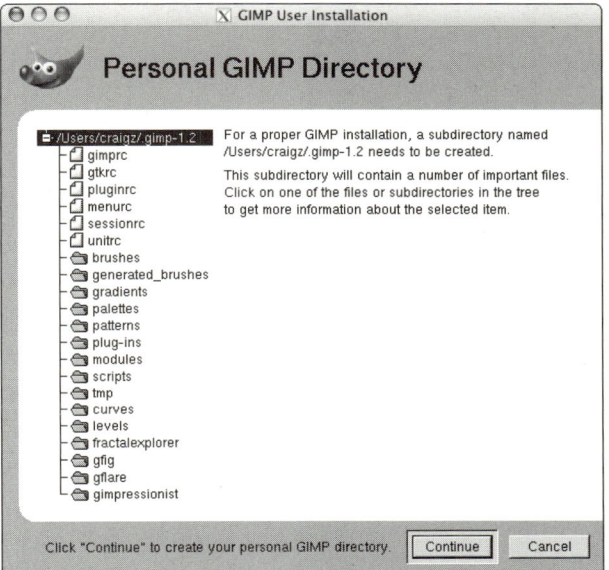

Figure 25-15: Creating your personal GIMP directory.

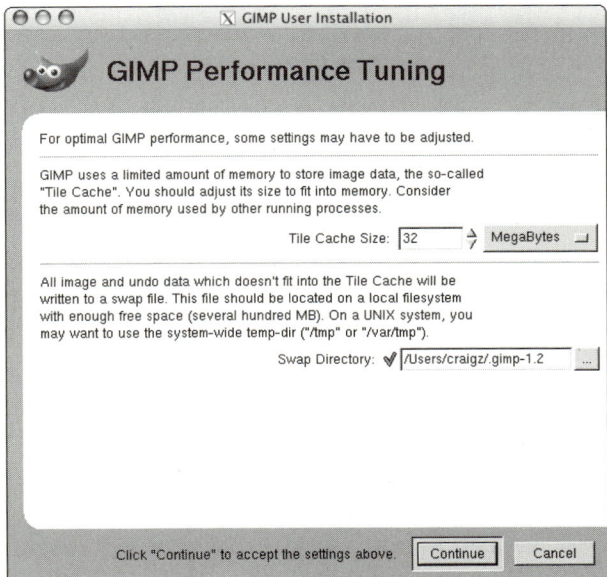

Figure 25-16: Setting GIMP performance tuning options. Leave these at default values.

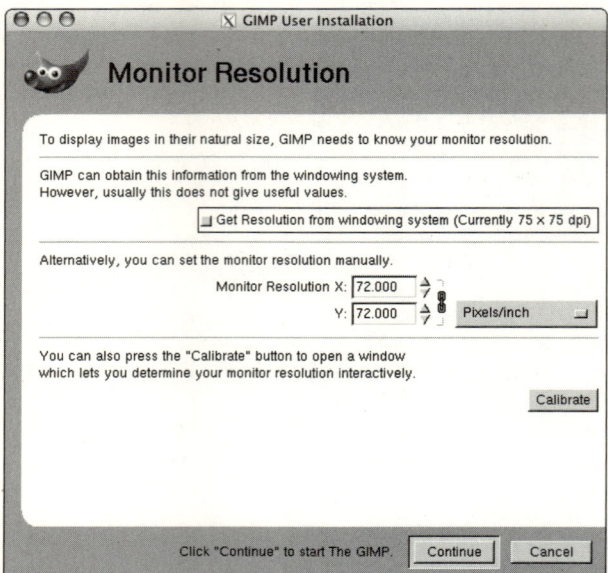

Figure 25-17: Setting monitor resolution information for the GIMP.

When you are finished working with the GIMP, you can type Control-Q or choose Quit from the file menu in the main tool palette as shown in Figure 25-18.

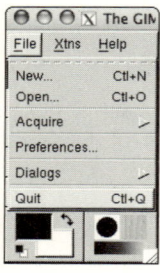

Figure 25-18: Choosing the Quit command from the GIMP's main menu.

CinePaint (filmGimp)

CinePaint is a special version of GIMP, created by and for motion picture professionals. It is designed to work with 35mm film and other high-resolution images. CinePaint displays images in a 32-bit-per-channel color range. This means no resolution is lost from scanning the film and digitizing the footage. CinePaint can work with all standard image formats, and it supports industry-specific formats such as Industrial Light & Magic's OpenEXR (www.openexr.com/) and Kodak's Cineon (www.cineon.com). CinePaint is in use at many major effects studios, on feature films such as *Harry Potter, 2 Fast, 2 Furious, Stuart Little II, Cats & Dogs,* and many more. There is a feature list available at the projects home page at `http://cinepaint.sourceforge.net`:

CinePaint used to be known as filmGimp, and that is how Fink has it listed in its package list. To install CinePaint, simply type `fink install filmgimp`.

Summary

This chapter provides an overview of installing and using additional Unix software on your Mac OS X system. Apple Developer Tools and X11 were installed, bridging the gap between traditional Macintosh functionality and Unix. Fink and the GUI-based FinkCommander were introduced as tools to use for installing Unix software and keeping it up to date. Readers should have a familiarity with some useful Unix programs and know how to install new programs on their own. `http://sourceforge.net` and `http://freshmeat.net` are both great places to find new software to install for a variety of needs and interests.

✦   ✦   ✦

Unix Security

In this chapter we provide an overview of Unix Security. We acquaint the reader with a summary of the types of threats that exist on the Internet and what can be done to protect against external hostilities. We also describe the tools that are built into every Mac OS X computer to help safeguard your computer.

Introduction to Unix Security

When considering computer security it's most important to understand that there is a trade off between ease of use and flexibility versus security. The more secure a system is, the more complex it becomes. Think of your car. You could leave the doors unlocked and keep the key in the ignition. Then you wouldn't ever need to fumble with the keys to open the doors, and with the keys handily stored in the ignition; you wouldn't ever have to remember where you left them at night. As far as ease of use, it couldn't get better. However, you'd be lucky to find your car where you left it; eventually someone else would just open the door, turn the key and drive away with your ride. The same thing goes for your computer. If you are the only user it's easy to assume that nobody would want anything you've got and just leave the "doors" wide open.

The main issue at hand is what you've got to protect, and how much you're willing to put into securing it. The more valuable the asset, the more effort needs to be put into protecting it. In the following chapter, we discuss the types of threats your Mac OS X system faces, and hopefully enlighten you as to just how attractive your Macintosh can be, and along the way, you'll learn some of the tricks of the security trade.

Thinking Securely

Macintosh users have not had to worry much about security matters. Previous versions of the Macintosh Operating System were quite difficult to harm from the outside. In fact, there have been several hack-a-Mac contests, which have not ever produced a winner. The one major issue that has affected legacy Macintosh operating systems was in fact related to misconfigured third-party software. On Macintosh systems offering Web or other Internet services, the appearance of a modal dialog box would divert resources from server programs, and was generally undesirable. A shareware program called Okie Dokie was developed that would simply select the default button in a modal dialog after a user-definable period. This helped servers to do their work rather than wait for user input.

Another popular third-party application is Timbuktu Pro. Timbuktu allows for remote screen control along with other features. A feature of the program is to allow guests to ask permission to use the machine. With Okie Dokie installed, when a guest asked for permission, a modal dialog box was presented, with a default of "allow." Okie Dokie would automatically click the allow button, and the interloper would be allowed access to the system. This unfortunate misconfiguration was quickly identified and rectified by system administrators in short time. Due to the nature of the software involved this problem only affected a very small population of Macintosh users, those who were operating their Macintosh computers as Internet servers. Server configurations aside, there have never been any major attacks on Macintosh computers running the legacy Macintosh Operating System. Today however, things are much different. Today's Macintosh Operating System is Unix based. The Unix operating system brings a lot of major benefits to the Macintosh community, enabling our computers to run the most up-to-date, robust software available from both commercial software companies, and those from the open source software movement. However the trade-off for this great flexibility is that we now have concerns and issues that were never of any consequence to us as Macintosh users before. Using Mac OS X, your personal computer shares a lot more in common with industrial strength servers in use in server rooms, such as database servers and Web and file servers, than it does with a Macintosh running Mac OS 9.

The additional power and flexibility of Unix comes at a price. That price is your consideration of security issues regarding your computer. At a minimum, this comes down to ensuring that your Operating System is kept up to date. Apple will frequently issue software updates that are designed to replace various bits of the system that contain bugs that can allow unauthorized users access to your system. Simply allowing the Software Update mechanism built into Mac OS X to run at regular intervals will keep your software current, and will ensure your machine's basic security.

When considering security there are two angles that need to be covered, Physical and Local security and Network security. Physical security refers to the actual computer and hardware. Local security is like the inside view of your computer, from logging in to the computer, to what users can do on the computer once they are logged in. Network security refers to the outside view of your computer. How is it connected to the network or the Internet, and what can folks who are on other computers see of your computer. Although most serious security concerns focus on network security, that is hardening your computer to the outside, and allowing only authorized and necessary access to your computer from the network, there are several things that need to be taken care of locally and that is how we will start examining the situation.

Physical Security

Physical security means *you* are the security of your actual computer. For some time now, Macintosh desktop computers have been designed to be easy to open, and the internal parts are readily accessible. This ease of use is great for when we need to go into the machine and swap parts, add components, and so on. It also makes it extremely easy for anyone to walk up to your machine and take parts out. Although a user may not know the name and password information required to login to your computer, if they can simply open the machine and walk away with your hard disk, the information contained on your computer is as good as theirs. Most desktop Macintosh computers now come with slots for locks. Adding a lock to your computer, if it's in a public place is a very good idea. Laptop computers of course are easy targets for theft. It's critical to ensure that your machine stays where you expect it to be and isn't simply walked away with. The other major issue with regard to physical security is that the computer stays turned on. If you are providing any services to other users on your computer, and it is inadvertently turned off, those services will be unavailable. For these reasons, server computers are traditionally kept in a locked room. By locking the room, only those who are authorized to access the computer are granted physical access to the power button, keyboard and mouse. Clearly you wouldn't want to keep your personal computer under lock and key, but it is helpful to be aware of the potential issues.

Setting an Open Firmware password

Open Firmware is the processor and system-independent boot firmware used in Apple Macintosh products. More information on Open Firmware and Apple's implementation of the technology is available at `http://bananajr6000.apple.com/`.

Apple provides a utility to set password security in Open Firmware. This utility will disable any key presses at start up that modify how the computer boots. With security set, the computer for example will not boot from a CD when the C key is pressed. In order to use special key sequences at boot, the application must be run again to disable security. To boot off a disk that is not selected in the Startup Disk preferences pane you can hold the option key on start up to access the Startup Manager. From the Startup Manager, you may select an alternate disk or CD, but you will be prompted for the Open Firmware password that you have established.

Follow the steps below to establish an Open Firmware password.

1. **Download the utility from:** `www.apple.com/downloads/macosx/apple/open-firmwarepassword.html`

2. **Mount the resulting .dmg image.**

3. **Launch the Open Firmware Password Application.** Figure 26-1 shows the program window.

4. **Click the Change button and enter your administrator password when prompted.**

5. **Select the require password to change Open Firmware settings checkbox.**

6. **Enter and verify your password.**

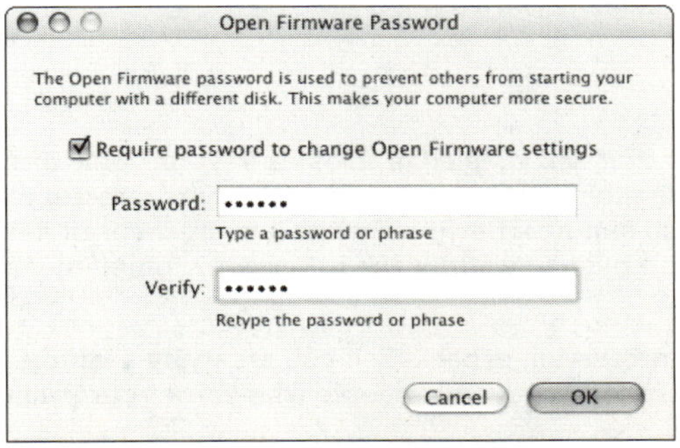

Figure 26-1: Setting an Open Firmware password.

Security preferences pane

The Security preferences pane has several options that can be selected to increase the security of your computer.

The first option you can select is to require a password to resume use of the computer from either the screen saver or sleep. Check this option to enable this feature, as shown in Figure 26-2.

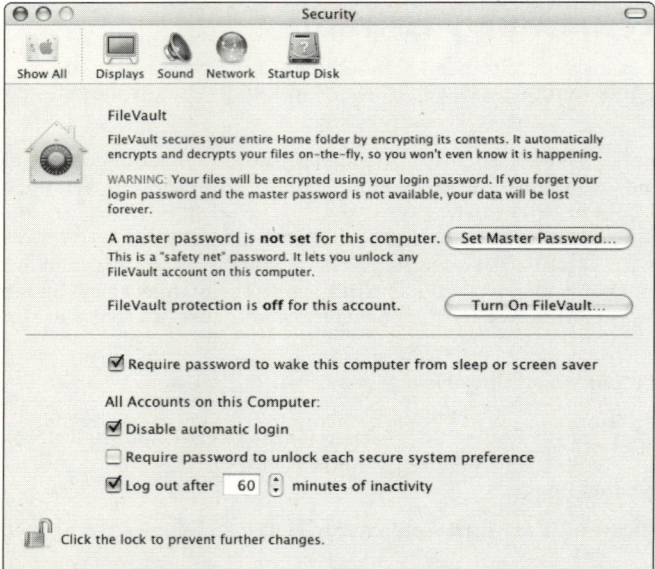

Figure 26-2: Check require password and log out time.

There is another option labeled Log Out based on inactivity. Select this option and set the time interval. These settings are useful for when you leave your computer because they prevent someone from helping themselves to your system, and perhaps stealing your data or changing system settings to their benefit.

FileVault

FileVault is a new feature in Panther that can keep all of the files in your home directory encrypted. FileVault uses AES-128 bit encryption to encrypt your home directory. The initial encryption process can take up to 20 minutes, however, when it is finished, all newly created files will be encrypted, and you won't have to wait for the process to complete. As you open files, they are unencrypted invisibly.

This ability offers a great degree of protection especially if you are using a laptop computer or if you share your computer with other users. Only people who know your password can read or copy your files.

This security means that you must keep track of your password. If you lose your password you will be unable to access your documents in a clear text form. For this reason, Apple has implemented the FileVault Master Password. You can set a master password for the entire computer, which you can use to unlock any users files if they have forgotten their password. To set the FileVault master password, open the Security preference pane, and click the Change button, as shown in Figure 26-3.

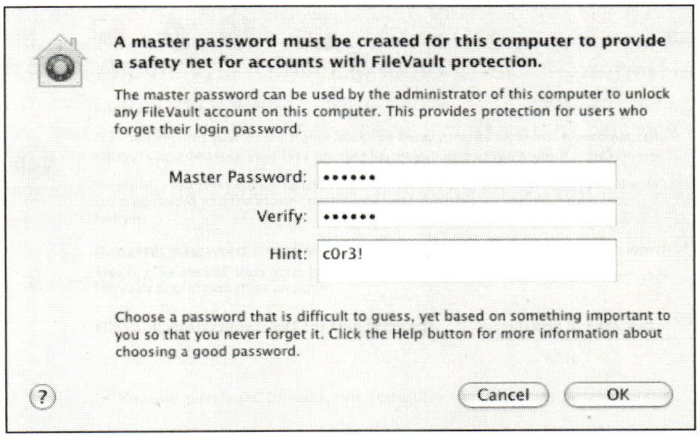

Figure 26-3: Setting Filevault Master Password.

To enable FileVault protection for your home directory open the Security preference pane and click the button labeled Turn On FileVault as shown in Figure 26-4.

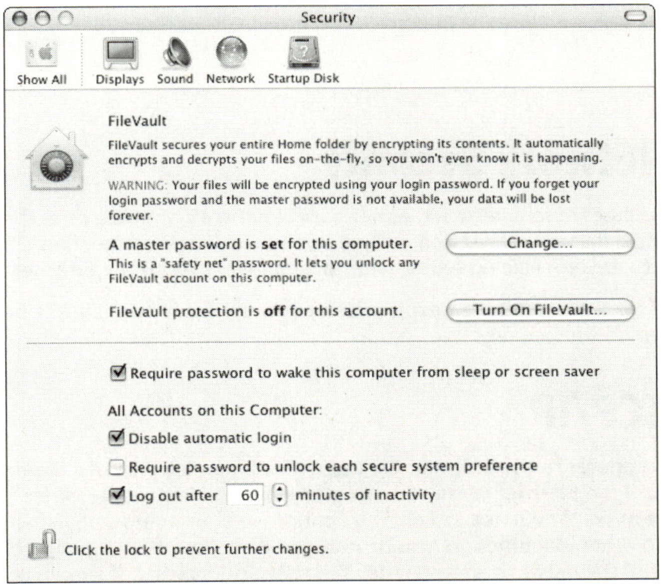

Figure 26-4: Turn on FileVault Protection.

At the time of this writing, November 2003, serious issues regarding data corruption have been reported on support Web sites. We recommend allowing time for the File Vault technology to mature and to be patched by Apple before you use this cutting edge technology.

Secure Empty Trash

A new feature in Panther is Secure Empty Trash. Traditionally, when you place a file in the trash, and choose empty trash the file is not actually deleted. A disk usage file is updated to reflect that the space on the disk occupied by the file that you've "trashed" is now available as free space. Anyone who's run Norton Utilities or other Macintosh disk utilities is aware that frequently you can recover deleted files. This can be quite useful. However, sometimes you want to throw something away and ensure that it will never be recovered. There have been third-party utilities available to fill this task by actually writing zeros or other data over the place in the disk where the file existed. After data is written to the disk your data no longer exists. The Department of Defense has developed guidelines regarding the secure deletion of files, and Apple now includes this feature built in to Panther. Simply select Secure Empty Trash from the Finder menu to erase all traces of that offending file, as shown in Figure 26-5.

Figure 26-5: Secure Empty Trash.

Understanding Network Security

When your computer is connected to a network, either a local network at home or at the office, or to the Internet via a dial-up connection or dedicated broadband connection (DSL or Cable) it becomes visible to anyone else on either your local network or on the Internet.

Please refer to Chapter 15 for a more detailed explanation of Computer Networking. A brief networking primer follows.

Introduction to TCP/IP

When you connect your computer to the Internet, your machine becomes part of a large network. You mostly think of the Internet connection as providing connectivity to other machines, generally Web servers. You'll use a client application on your computer, usually a Web browser to connect to other machines, as you browse the Web. Your Web browser hides the underlying complexity of the network, as you enter Web site addresses; it'll simply present you text, images, and multimedia objects as delivered by the Web servers you connect to.

The Internet is comprised of several layers through which data passes before delivery to your client application. A detailed discussion of the communications protocols involved is out of the scope of this chapter; however, a brief explanation follows. There are many layers of network protocols that are used in combination with each other to provide Internet connectivity. These layers are commonly described as the Internet protocol suite. Below we will sketch out the basic operation of these communication protocols.

There are two separate acronyms in use when we look at TCP/IP communications. Both ends of a connection use both TCP and IP to send and receive data.

TCP stands for Transmission Control Protocol. TCP is responsible for breaking up large sources of data into individual packets on the sending side, and on the receiving side reconnecting the individual packets into a solid chunk of data. Additionally TCP on the receiving side ensures that all segments have been received. In a data network, it is extremely likely that parts will arrive in a different order then that which they were transmitted TCP is responsible for reordering data as it arrives, and ensuring that all parts are intact.

IP stands for Internet Protocol. IP is the layer that is responsible for moving the individual data packets between machines. It helps to think of IP as transport. Where TCP is responsible for ensuring that packets all arrive as they should and in their entirety, IP simply moves the data. The IP protocol has no sense of what it is moving, or if it's arrived, as it should, it just moves the packets.

Understanding Network Security Threats

To protect your computer against network security threats, you must have a basic understanding of the type of threats out there. Although many different types of security vulnerabilities exist, the types of attacks can be distilled into three basic types: denial of service attacks, theft of data attacks, and unauthorized use of computing and network resources. For a more detailed overview and an extensive list of additional resources, please download the following pdf: www.cert.org/archive/pdf/attack_trends.pdf

Denial of service attacks

Denial of service attacks are probably the hardest to protect against, due to the nature of sharing resources. If your system allows access from outside, perhaps by serving Web pages, how do you determine the difference between legitimate requests for data and illegitimate requests, which are designed to simply tie up your resources? Denial of service attacks are extremely easy to implement, requiring little to no technical competence on the behalf of the attacker.

A denial of service attack is a situation where a specific resource is the target of excessive or malformed traffic. Example services are a Web server, ftp server, mail server, and so on. Usually many compromised machines will be used in a denial of service attack. The end result is that if you are victim to such an attack, you will be unable to engage in the communications you expect to, as you will be tied up responding to excessive fake clients.

Denial of service attacks can also cause real headaches when they are directed at a resource that you require in order to do day-to-day tasks. For example a service that is required for most productive work on the Internet is DNS. DNS stands for Domain Name Service. DNS translates numerical IP addresses such as 17.254.0.91 to a friendlier, familiar name based address such as www.apple.com. If we didn't have access to DNS and had to use numbered IP addresses for all communications, such as Web surfing, sending email, and so on, the Internet would be much less useful to us. DNS is a distributed database of numbers to names and is based on a system built of Root Servers. There are currently 13 Root Servers worldwide. These 13 servers are the authoritative servers for global DNS services. These 13 servers point at local DNS servers worldwide. The Root Servers serve information for what are called Top Level Domains, such as .com, .net, .org, and .edu. A successful denial of service attack against these 13 servers would render much of the Internet inaccessible to most users.

Data theft

Theft of data attacks occur when somebody from the outside manages to obtain access to your computer and takes files from your machine. These types of attacks are the most discussed in the media and elsewhere, as they often involve real financial loss. The data stolen can be personal information, such as credit card numbers and bank account information, or can be intellectual property. This kind of attack is much like a bank robbery where your personal property is stolen from you. Unlike in the physical world, you may retain copies of the files, as just copying them does not ensure destruction. Although many times data will be destroyed in the process, it is not necessarily the case. In fact much of the time that data has been stolen, the victim may be completely unaware that the theft has occurred. That is until a later time, when unauthorized financial activity occurs or similar events take place.

Unauthorized use of computing and network resources

Unauthorized use pertains to a situation where your computer or network resources are utilized by unauthorized users. Viruses are frequently responsible for such situations. The recent Nimda and Code Red viruses are examples of unauthorized use violations. The virus, once installed in your computer, then uses your computer to scan the network for other vulnerable hosts, and to attack those computers. Additionally many viruses of these types have as their goal bringing your computer into an ad-hoc network of infected computers. Once your computer is tagged in to the network, it will await further instructions. Frequently the goal is to use your computing and network resources along with those of other such compromised machines to launch denial of service attacks against large high profile Internet hosts. Microsoft is frequently a target of such attacks. Not all types of unauthorized use are virus related. Suppose someone on the Internet finds a way to connect to your computer, and is able to log in via a software bug (called a vulnerability) or a misconfiguration of some network component; the hacker then may be able to configure network services on your machine that you are unaware of. A common situation today is where an unauthorized user will create a directory on your machine and configure FTP access to that directory. You could then be the unwilling host of a treasure trove of pirated music, software, and movies. Many times such access can go unnoticed, as today's hard disks are large enough to contain such additional data without running out of space, and broadband connections provide adequate bandwidth to support these supplementary connections alongside legitimate Internet access.

Understanding Services

In Chapter 11, we discuss various services that could be enabled on your Mac OS X computer. Simply turning on the services will enable various daemons on your computer. In this section, we take a look at what's really going on with your computer when these services are enabled.

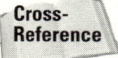

Cross-Reference   Refer to Chapter 18 for more information on Apache, FTPd, and SSH.

Port usage

The Internet is comprised of clients and servers. You the client want some information from the Internet, and it is located on a server. A client uses an application to browse the Internet. All computers that are connected to the Internet have an IP address. The IP address serves as the main address for the machine. Each service on the system has a unique identifier called a port. A port is a unique number between 0 and 65535. A list of ports is available on each Mac OS X system, in the file /etc/services. The ports between 0 and 1023 are referred to as "well-known ports." A small program that runs on the computer called a daemon handles each service that is available on a computer. The daemon launches and binds to a specific port, then waits and listens for connections to come in to that port. When a connection is opened to that port, the daemon wakes up and sends a reply to the client. Arguably, port 80 is the most well-known port. It is the port that is most often used for http, which is Web traffic. When you type the address www.apple.com into your Web browser, the browser first performs a DNS lookup, and then sends a request to the servers IP address, at port 80. However, sometimes your Web browser is redirected to another port. Most common is https on port 443(secure http), which is used for online purchases, banking, and so on. Other popular ports are 25 used for SMTP, Simple Mail Transfer Protocol which handles the sending of email, 110 POP, Post Office Protocol used for checking email, 143 IMAP Interactive Mail Access Protocol an alternative to POP for checking email, 21 used for FTP, and 22 used for ssh (secure shell).

TCP/IP does not dictate what ports are used for which applications. You can operate a Web server on any port you desire. Port 8080 is popular as a default port for the Apache Web server. The well-known ports system is offered as a convenience. Much as DNS is useful to assist in translating hard-to-remember numeric addresses to easily remembered text-based hostnames, the well-known ports serve as a basis for standardization. Rather then having to ask which port to connect to for each individual Web site, we can simply agree to use port 80 for Web servers and get about the business of browsing, rather than searching.

Principle of least privilege

A long-standing guideline in computer security is the principle of least privilege. This states that any given user be given only the privileges that they need to perform their jobs or tasks. Rather than leave everything unlocked, and providing all users all privileges available, which makes administrative tasks simple in the short term because you never have to unlock anything simply to allow administrative access, you take a longer term approach and provide each user with exactly the level of access they require for day-to-day work. In a special situation, you can elevate specific user access rights to provide granular rights to privileges without leaving everything unlocked. A practical example is this: You'd like to share your printer with other users in your office. There is no reason to allow those users to login to your computer and change file-sharing preferences.

Using the principle of least privilege in networking

The same guiding principle applies when it comes to offering network services from your computer. The ideal situation regarding services is to first ensure that your machine is offering no services whatsoever. If you do not intend to share any resources with neighboring users, then there should be nothing enabled on your computer. Often there are services enabled by default, or the installation of third-party software may open ports or add services to your computer's configuration. If you plan to share any resources from your computer, best practices are to start with a clean slate. Turn off all services, and ensure all ports are closed. Then determine which services you wish to offer, turning the services on one by one. As you enable services, check your system and see which ports have been opened, and ensure that only those you require are active. Doing this will add very little additional time to your configuration process, and will ensure that you are not exposing more than you expect to the Internet. In the next section, we will describe how to check which ports are open on your computer.

Monitoring open ports

Run a check on your system each time you install or upgrade any kind of services to ensure that you are only opening ports that you want to have open. The way to do this is to run port scanning software. Port scanners are a major tool in the hacker's arsenal. By running a port scan, they are able to see what your computer is offering, and can then use those openings to penetrate your system. By running a port scan against your own computer, you'll know what the hackers know, and can close off any unintended openings.

To check which ports are open on your system, you'll want to run third-party software, as the Apple-supplied Network Utility is not entirely thorough. Like most things regarding interacting with Unix in Mac OS X, you'll have the choice between using a graphical interface or a command line interface.

If you are curious, Apple provides an application in the Utilities folder, inside the Applications folder, called Network Utility which does provide a rudimentary port scan. To access the port scan, launch the application and choose the port scan tab in the bar on top. Figure 26-6 shows Apples Network Utility.

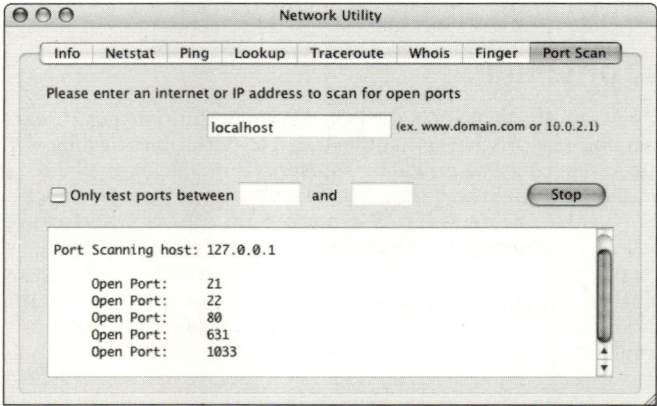

Figure 26-6: The Apple Network Utility Port Scan.

For a quick fix, you can utilize an online service, which port scans, your computer from the outside. The following URL links to a port-scanning service provided by Gibson Research Corporation, a maker of security software for Windows systems: The service can be reached by following the ShieldsUP! link from www.grc.com. The SheildsUP! Page is shown in Figure 26-7. Run the two tests called Test My Shields and Probe My Ports. As always, your results may vary. It's best to install your own software to do this task, but if you're in a hurry, the Web-based check is quite through.

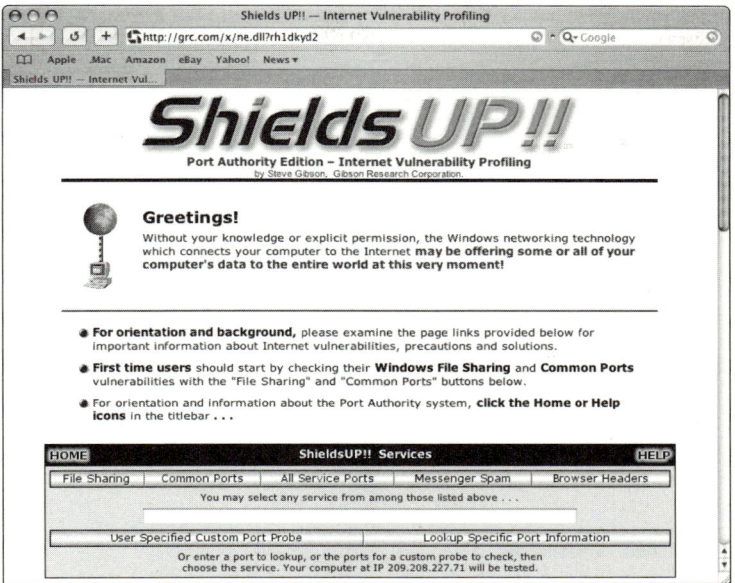

Figure 26-7: Gibson Research Corporation Online Port Scan.

Using a graphical interface to check open ports

Several third-party programs are available that can show you what daemons are running and what ports they are listening on. A description of several popular tools follows.

AysMon (Are You Serving Monitor) is written in Java and is available at http://www.pepsan.com/aysmon/index.html. It is distributed as a disk image file. To mount the image, simply double-click the .dmg file, and then drag the AysMon folder to your Applications folder. AysMon comes with a list of services, and checks your computer for each one and shows you the results. AysMon is shareware and costs $5.

whatPorts v 1.1 is a freeware port scanner available at www.davtri.com/freeware.html

Using the command line to check open ports

Nmap is a full-featured port scanner for Unix systems that runs beautifully on Mac OS X. A full description of the software is available at www.insecure.org/nmap/index.html. Nmap is designed to scan open ports on either a full network (multiple hosts) or a single host. Nmap has many advanced features that are just not available in any of the GUI-based port scanners. Many of the features are aimed at providing stealth, which is frankly of more use to the hacker trying to either evade detection or work around your firewall. However, many of the advanced features are quite helpful to the personal systems administrator (that's you) as well. A sample nmap window is shown in Figure 26-8. Nmap uses an advanced software technique called TCP/IP fingerprinting to guess at the operating system in use. Additionally the latest versions of the software now will query each detected service for version information.

This single feature is of immense use, as typically patches and upgrades are made to various software in order to rectify security issues, however it can be overwhelming to keep up with such information. By running periodic nmap scans against your host, you can ensure that the versions of the software you are running (apache, sshd, FTPd,) are up to date.

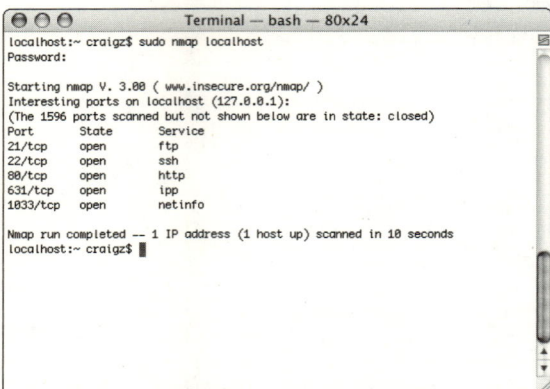

Figure 26-8: Nmap portscan of localhost.

Installing nmap

You can install Nmap on your Mac OS X computer two ways — the easy way using Fink, or the manual way. If you've installed Fink as described in Chapter 25, then you can proceed to the next section. If you've not installed Fink, or if you wish to install a later version of the software than Fink is distributing, then you'll have to follow the manual instructions listed later. Not to worry, either way results in an extremely powerful port scanner at your fingertips!

Installing nmap using Fink

If you've installed Fink, then you can use any method of interacting with Fink to complete the install (FinkCommander, dselect, etc). X11 refers to X-Windows, Apple includes an optional install of X11 with Panther. Installing X11 is covered in Chapter 25. If you have X11 installed on your machine, you will want to install the package called nmap. If you don't have X11 installed then you will install the package nmap-nox.

The X11 version includes the nmap program, which you'll run as a command in Terminal, as well as an additional GUI front end to the software called nmapfe (nmap front end), which provides a graphical interface to the tool. To install this version, open Terminal and type `fink install nmap` at the command prompt.

To install the vanilla version without X Windows support simply open Terminal and type `fink install nmap-nox` at the command prompt.

Either installation will result in an executable program nmap installed in /sw/bin. If you installed the X11 front end it will be installed in /sw/bin as well, and is called nmapfe.

Manually installing nmap

Download the latest version of the source code to a temporary directory. Open the following page in your Web browser: `www.insecure.org/nmap/nmap_download.html` and download the latest source package available. The current version at the time of this writing is nmap-3.48.tgz.

When your download finishes, open the Terminal application and change to the directory where you downloaded the software, using the change directory (cd) command

To install nmap, you must be logged into an account with administrative privileges.

```
tar zxvf nmap-3.48.tgz
cd nmap-3.48
./configure (this command will generate a lot of output)
make sudo
make install (type your password at the prompt)
```

The configure script checks for GTK+. If it finds that software installed, then the X11 front end to nmap nmapfe will be installed in addition to nmap. If GTK+ is unavailable, then only the nmap binary will be installed. If you desire the graphical front end and are manually installing, but don't have GTK+ installed, you must first install GTK+. Information on this procedure is available on the Web at `www.gtk.org/`. However, you may find it much simpler to install fink and allow fink to manage this procedure for you.

Manually installing nmap places the software in /usr/local/bin. If nmapfe is installed, it also will be in /usr/local/bin.

Basic nmap usage

Using nmap for a basic scan is very simple. However, nmap is a very powerful program that can provide a lot of information if you are willing to invest some time learning and playing with the software. For more detailed instruction on using the software, please check `www.insecure.org/nmap/nmap_documentation.html` for links to several articles.

To use nmap, you need to open the Terminal application. Because nmap accesses raw network resources, some of its options require root privileges to run. A basic TCP Connect scan does not require root privileges, and is the default scan type if you do not launch the command with sudo. At a shell prompt type either one of two commands.

Nmap runs one of two default scan types if run without argument. If you enter the command nmap localhost at a shell prompt, nmap will run a TCP Connect Scan. This is the most basic kind of scan possible. It will open connections to all possible ports, and will record those that respond, assuming the rest are closed. This kind of scan requires no special privileges to run. The more powerful SYN scan is frequently referred to as a half-open scan. This type of scan does not open a complete connection to the port as it connects, and is preferred by hackers, as it avoids being logged on, in most cases. It is also valuable to us as it will show ports that are filtered where a Connect Scan would miss those ports. This command requires root privileges to run, so it must be launched with sudo. Enter the command sudo nmap localhost at a command prompt to launch this scan.

Nmap can detect both OS version, and software name and version used on a given port. This means that rather than simply reporting an http server on port 80, nmap will report Apache httpd 1.3.27 ((Darwin)). A scan with version detection can be run without root privileges by entering the following command at a shell prompt nmap -sV localhost. Scanning for both version detection and OS detection provides the most interesting report, but will require root privileges to run. To run a scan with both OS and Version Detection, enter the following command at a shell prompt sudo nmap -sV -O localhost.

Bonus X Windows port scanner

Nmap ships with an X11 based front end called nmapfe. If X11 is installed on your system, and you have the GTK+ software installed as described in the preceding sections, then xmapfe is available. Nmapfe provides a GUI interface to nmap. The scan types remain the same, however it is easer to select the options from the GUI then typing the various arguments to nmap. To launch nmapfe, you'll first have to open X11 from the Applications folder. When X11 launches it will provide a window labeled xterm. Xterm is extremely similar to the Terminal Application, in that it provides a shell prompt where you can enter commands and interact with Mac OS X from the command line interface. Nmapfe has the same restrictions as nmap with regard to requiring root privileges to execute certain scan types and OS Detection. Figure 26-9 shows the Nmap Front End. To launch nmapfe with root privileges type the following command at the xterm shell prompt sudo nmapfe. To launch as a regular user with limited privileges, simply type nmapfe at the xterm shell prompt.

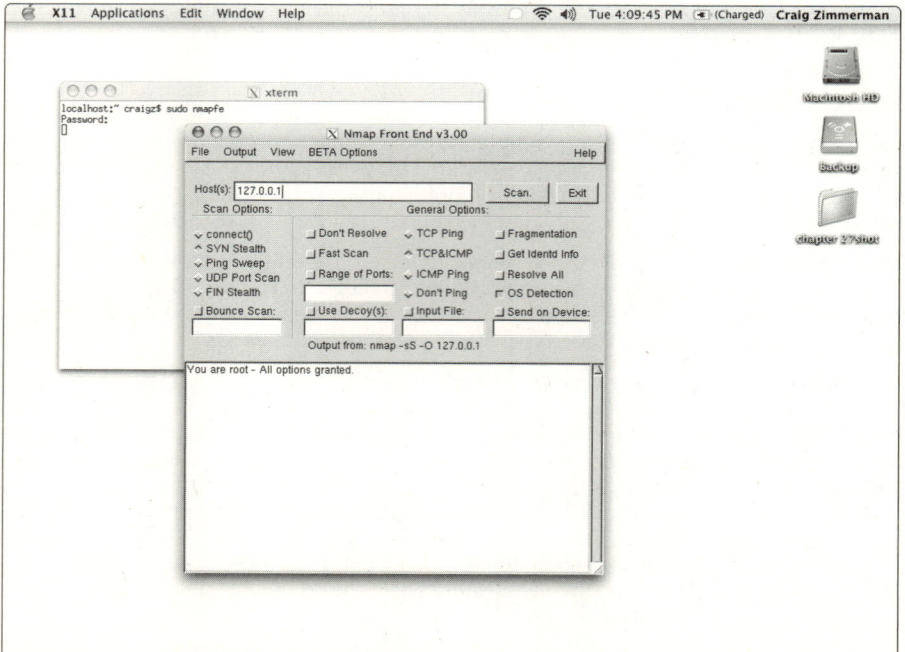

Figure 26-9: nmapfe — the nmap front end.

Built-in Firewall

A computer firewall is either software or hardware that is intended to protect your computer from outside threats, while allowing you to use the Internet and to share specific resources. Firewalls are often installed on corporate computer networks in order to protect inside computers from outside attacks. However, having a firewall on your local computer is of great benefit. With a firewall enabled, you can browse the Internet unhindered, however connections to your machine will be denied, if they are not explicitly allowed. For example if you are providing Web services, you can configure the firewall to only allow access to the Web server, and no other ports on your computer.

Apple has shipped a software firewall as part of a standard Mac OS X installation since Version 10.0. This is just one way that Mac OS X users have benefited from Mac OS X's Unix heritage. The included software is called ipfw for IP Firewall. ipfw is actually a front end to two individual programs called dummynet and ipfirewall.

Inspecting firewall rulesets using Terminal

If you are interested in directly interacting with the firewall, you can do so by opening the Terminal application and using the ipfw command. To learn more about the ipfw command and how to use it open the Terminal application and type the command man ipfw. To see what rulesets are in place, type the command sudo ipfw list. If you've not implemented any rules the only rule listed will be the catchall rule 65535 allow ip from any to any, which lets any ip traffic from any port on any host to any port on your computer. Although further discussion of manual ipfw configuration is out of the scope of this chapter, as you set up various firewall rules using methods discussed later in this section, you can always check the rules that have been created by issuing the command sudo ipfw list in a Terminal widow.

Implementing firewall rulesets using Sharing preferences

Apple includes a simple GUI for configuring ipfw rules with Mac OS X. To access this open the Firewall panel of the Sharing preferences pane. From here you can enable the firewall and select what type of traffic to allow to your computer. Example services are Personal File Sharing, FTP Access, Printer Sharing, and Personal Web Sharing. There are several more to choose from. Figure 26-10 shows the Firewall preferences. You will see that services you have selected to share in the Services panel of the Sharing preferences pane are already selected for you. Any additional ports you wish to open may be checked here as well.

Implementing firewall rulesets using a third-party GUI

There is a shareware program called BrickHouse that acts as a more complete front end to ipfw. BrickHouse can be downloaded from http://personalpages.tds.net/~brian_hill/downloads.html. If you find you've got a service you wish to share, and it's not available in the Firewall panel of the Sharing preferences pane, and you don't wish to create a rule manually, this program can help. Figure 26-11 shows the BrickHouse main window. The program is distributed as a stuffed .dmg file. Simply unstuff the archive and mount the disk image. BrickHouse installs a firewall start up script in /Library/StartupItems/Firewall. Should you wish to run BrickHouse you should ensure that the built in firewall is not enabled, by going to the Firewall panel of the Sharing preferences pane and clicking the stop button if the text in the window says Firewall On. You don't want both the built-in controls and BrickHouse firing at boot time. If you wish to disable the firewall as set by BrickHouse simply click the Remove Startup Script button in BrickHouse. This will return the firewall to the default state of allowing all connections.

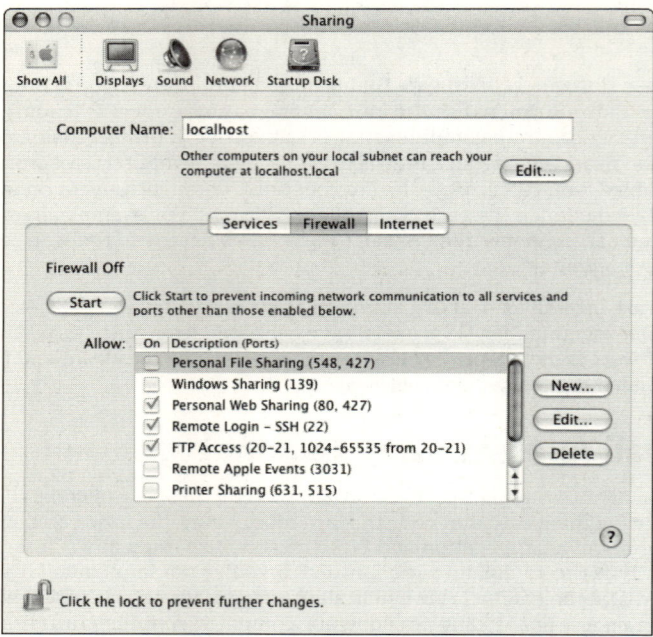

Figure 26-10: Firewall panel of the Sharing preferences pane.

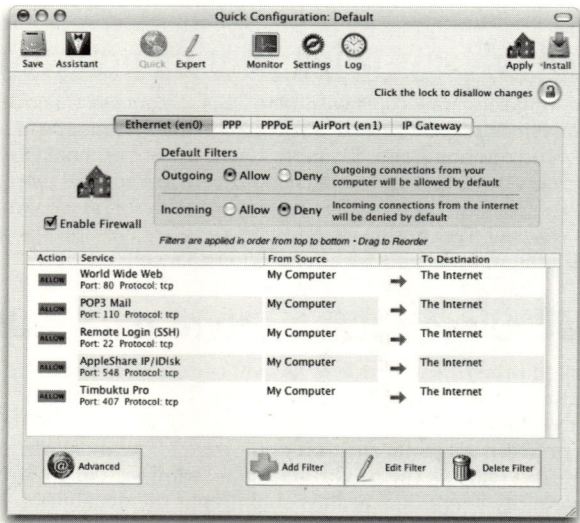

Figure 26-11: Setting firewall rules using BrickHouse.

Necessary Daemons

As we discuss earlier in this chapter, you'll want to ensure that you are only offering services that you intend to provide. In the process of auditing the services you wish to offer, you may find that now is a good time to upgrade some of the daemons from those that are provided by Apple with Mac OS X. Apple does you a real favor by including all the software you need to share services with your local network and the Internet, and if you ever just need to turn on something quickly, it's handy to have that service located only a preference pane away. However, if you've decided that you want to run a service full time from your computer, it's probably a good idea to replace the basic software supplied with Mac OS X with a more configurable and security orientated package.

As we see in Chapter 25 many open-source Unix programs build quite simply on Mac OS X. This is true in the case of Internet server programs as well. There are many server programs to choose from, for any service you can imagine wanting to serve from your computer, and most of them build and run quite easily and well on Mac OS X.

There are also commercial alternatives for most of the servers that are available for Mac OS X. The choice between installing a commercial product versus free software is yours. For the most part both options will work comparably to each other. Often times the commercial products require a bit less work in order to install, as they are usually .pkg files that install with a simple double-click.

A multitude of servers are available for Mac OS X, but in this section, focus only on replacing the default FTP server. Other servers can be replaced using similar procedures, however FTP is one of the more exposed services, and it is important to system security to ensure that you are only offering access to the files and folders that you want shared.

Replacing FTPd

The default FTP server is very good for simple needs. One shortcoming of using the built-in FTP server is that for users to access your server they will require an account on your system. Perhaps you don't want to give out accounts, have to manage security for multiple users on your system, nor ensure that every new user you create for FTP sharing has shell access revoked, etc. Several replacement servers offer FTP access utilizing a separate users and groups database. Additionally the default FTP server can only listen on your given IP address or hostname. With ProFTPd you can create several virtual FTP servers, allowing for a good bit of flexibility. Additionally the configuration file is very similar to Apache's config file, which will help you leverage any knowledge you have from one or the other product. While there are many very good FTP servers to choose from, I recommend ProFTPd. The main reason for this recommendation is that this server is included in the Fink package database. That means that you can use Fink for the installation, as well as for updating the software. Please keep in mind is that by replacing the Apple-supplied software, you will no longer receive the benefits of Apple Software Update keeping your server software up to date. If you install any third-party server software, I urge you to join the respective mailing lists, and keep up to date with software updates and security updates. As you are opening your computer to the Internet, you must be aware of the risks involved. Security experts (and hackers) constantly find bugs in software, for which the developers release bug fixes. Your system is only immune to these bugs if you keep your software up to date. If you would prefer not to spend the time keeping your software at the latest revision, then I suggest that you do not replace the software that Apple has provided you. If you're still intrigued, then read on, we've got some work to do!

Installing ProFTPd using fink

Fink supports and builds ProFTPd properly. However at the current time the software is not included in fink's stable build directory. This will probably change at some time in the near future. For now there is some additional work required in order to use fink to install ProFTPd. First we have to move the installation files to a place where they are available to fink. Open the Terminal application and type the following commands at a prompt:

```
sudo cp /sw/fink/dists/unstable/main/finkinfo/net/proftpd* \
/sw/fink/dists/local/main/finkinfo
sudo cp /sw/fink/10.2/unstable/main/finkinfo/base/ftpfiles* \
/sw/fink/dists/local/main/finkinfo
fink install proftpd
```

Fink will give the following output:

```
fink needs help picking an alternative to satisfy a virtual dependency.
The candidates:
(1)      proftpd-pam: Incredibly configurable and secure FTP daemon
(Default)
(2)      proftpd-ldap: Incredibly configurable and secure FTP daemon
(LDAP)
(3)      proftpd-mysql: Incredibly configurable and secure FTP daemon
(MySQL) (4)      proftpd-pgsql: Incredibly configurable and secure FTP
daemon (PostgreSQL)
```

Enter number 1 to use proftpd-pam.

Fink will then request permission to install three additional packages, anacron, ftpfiles and proftpd-pam. Grant permission by entering Y or hitting enter.

```
The following package will be installed or updated: proftpd The
following 3 additional packages will be installed: anacron ftpfiles
proftpd-pam Do you want to continue? [Y/n]
```

Fink will then ask for permission to set up anacron. Anacron is used by proftpd to do log rotation. You will want to grant this permission by entering Y or hitting enter.

```
Anacron is not currently set up to be run periodically by cron. Would
you like for anacron to be run automatically? In most cases, you
probably want to say yes to this option. [Y/n]
```

Skip the following section and continue to Configuring ProFTPd below.

Installing ProFTPd manually

If you wish to manually install ProFTPd, download the source from http://www.proftpd.org/ to a temporary directory. You'll have to extract the archive, run the configure script, make the software then install the software. This whole process goes very smoothly on Mac OS X. Open the Terminal Application and type the following at a shell prompt.

```
tar -zxvf proftpd-1.2.8p.tar.gz
cd proftpd-1.2.8
make
sudo make install
```

Configuring ProFTPd

ProFTPd's configuration file is installed at /sw/etc/proftpd.conf, if ProFTPd was installed using fink. Otherwise the file can be found at /etc/proftpd.conf. Either way the same changes will be made to the file. Some changes are necessary to get our server up and running. You'll notice when looking at the file that there are two kinds of directives. The first kind of directive is a single line directive such as ServerName and ServerType. The second type of directive is a container directive such as <Directory> and <Limit>. The container directives are much like html tags where a container is opened with a <Directive> and closed with a </Directive>.

The first section of the file defines how the server will run. There are two choices, either stand-alone or inetd. A stand-alone server launches when the machine boots and is always running. If your machine is a dedicated FTP server this is the best choice. The other option is to use inetd, the Internet superserver. Apple ships xinetd an improved version of the basic inetd server, inetd listens on all configured ports on your computer and when a request comes in on a port that it is listening to, it launches the application configured for that port and hands the connection to that application. This is the best solution for a low-volume part-time server, as system resources are not tied up by the server program except for when it is actually in use. We will configure the server as inetd. If you wish to run as stand-alone you will need to create a StartupItem for the FTP server.

Open the configuration file in your favorite editor and make the following changes:

```
ServerName                                    "Your Server's name goes
here" ServerType                                          inetd
# Set the user and group under which the server will run.
User                          nobody
Group                         nobody
```

Note the change in group to nobody from nogroup.

Uncomment the DefaultRoot ~ line below for security purposes. This will make the user's home directory appear as the root volume when they connect. In other words users can not navigate up past their own home directory. This makes the system far more secure as users are not allowed to see anything that has not been explicitly given to them. In order to uncomment the line remove the # character that begins the line, so that it looks like the line below.

```
# To cause every FTP user to be "jailed" (chrooted) into their home
# directory, uncomment this line.
DefaultRoot ~
```

The configuration file as it is shipped allows for anonymous access for a user named FTP. If you truly want to offer anonymous access, you'll need to create an FTP user on your computer. Apple ships with an FTP group pre-installed, but not a user FTP. To create the user go into the Accounts preferences pane and create a user FTP. For a more secure server, you'll want to disable anonymous access by commenting out the following section of the configuration file

Comment out the section by adding # marks at the beginning of each line so that it looks like the lines below:

```
#<Anonymous ~ftp>
#  User                       ftp
#  Group                      ftp
```

Comment out the file by adding a # mark to the beginning of all three lines.

By commenting out the anonymous user your server will only allow users who have accounts on your computer to connect..

ProFTPd can also use its own password file, in lieu of consulting your existing system users. In order to create the password file for ProFTPd, you'll use the provided ftpasswd utility, then configure proFTPd to use that password file for access to the server.

Depending how you installed ProFTPd you'll find ftpasswd in /sw/sbin/ or /usr/local/sbin. Create a new password file /etc/ftp_passwd by opening the Terminal application and typing the following command:

```
sudo /sw/sbin/ftpasswd --passwd --file /etc/ftp_passwd \
--name craigz --home /Users/ftp/ --shell /usr/bin/false \
 --uid 1000 --gid 1000 --des
ftpasswd: using alternate file: /etc/ftp_passwd
ftpasswd: creating passwd entry for user craigz

Please be aware that only the first 8 characters of a DES password are
relevant.  Use the --md5 option to select MD5 passwords, as they do not
have this limitation.

Password:
Re-type password:

ftpasswd: entry created
```

Repeat the command for each user you wish to add. List the newly created file by typing the following command at a shell prompt:

```
sudo more /etc/ftp_passwd
craigz:qXkl3YMWB/Zvg:1000:1000::/Users/ftp:/usr/bin/false
```

There are many more options to ftpasswd. To read about them all please visit the following Web site: http://www.castaglia.org/proftpd/contrib/ftpasswd.html.

Next we'll need to configure our server to use the newly created password file located at /etc/ftp_passwd.

Add the following line to the configuration file proftpd.conf

```
AuthUserFile                /etc/ftp_passwd
```

The final step is to configure xinetd to launch the ProFTPd server when FTP connections are opened. To do this, use sudo to open the file /etc/xinetd.d/ftp

Change the line server   = /usr/libexec/ftpd

To server   = /sw/sbin/proftpd

if proftpd was installed by fink , or

```
server              = /usr/local/sbin/proftpd
```

if proftpd was installed by hand.

In order to force xinetd to reread it's configuration we'll need to restart it. Type the following command:

```
sudo kill -HUP `/bin/cat /var/run/xinetd.pid`
```

System Logs

Out of the box a Mac OS X computer logs much of the activity that happens on the system. Most events that involve sharing in any way over the network such as Web or FTP server, and most events that involve changes happening on the system are logged by the system. Logs are often overlooked and are only consulted in the event of a system failure, security breach or other catastrophic event. Familiarize yourself with the types of items your system logs, and the content of those logs when things are normal. If you have a good idea of what goes on under normal circumstances, you will know when things are happening that are out of the ordinary. The log files are simply text files, and there are a variety of ways of interacting with these logfiles. We will explain how the system decides what to log and where, and make some changes to the defaults to highlight important security related events. We'll discuss both traditional Unix tools to view and parse the logs, as well as the included Console Application and some third party GUI tools for reading logfiles.

Introducing Syslog

Syslog is the System Event Logger originally written by Eric Allman. Syslog is a standard component of Unix and other *nix systems. Rather than making each application author worry about where how and when to log, and burdening users with the concern about finding each individual program's log files, syslog offers developers simple logging routines to access from their programs in the form of openlog and other libraries. Syslogd is the logging daemon which is launched at system startup by the startup item /System/Library/StartupItems/SystemLog. The file /etc/syslog.conf is read by the syslog daemon as it starts up, and configures how the daemon processes incoming messages. There is also a user command called logger that can be used interactively or by shell scripts to create entries in the system log.

Programs that take advantage of syslog for logging, and this includes the Mach Kernel, write their messages to a special file, which only the syslog daemon reads. Syslog parses the incoming messages according to its configuration file and takes one or more of these four actions:

✦ Forward the message to a syslog daemon running on a different host

✦ Append the message to a specified file

✦ Output the message to /dev/console

✦ Output it to the screen of defined users if they are logged in

The syslog.conf file defines how messages are handled based on two specific criteria called levels and facilities. The levels refer to the severity of an event, and the facility refers to the specific program running. Both the levels and facilities supported by Mac OS X are described in the man page for syslogd.conf.

Configuring Syslog to separate interesting messages

The directory /var/log is where most logfiles are kept on a Mac OS X system. Syslog is configured by default to log most messages to the file /var/log/system.log. Separate logfiles are created by default for authorization actions (generally logins), lpr printer messages, mail, ftp and netinfo errors. This is a reasonable set of defaults. However, in the interest of securing your system, and as a way of example we'll make modifications to the configuration to isolate messages from both sudo and ssh.

All lines in the /etc/syslog.conf take the form of : selector <TAB> action. It is critical that in the examples below and in any changes you make to the file that you use a tab between items on a line, or unpredictable results may occur. Before making any changes to the syslog.conf file, make a backup of the original file, just in case. To backup the file open the Terminal application and enter the following command : sudo cp /etc/syslog.conf /etc/syslog.orig.conf.

Separating sudo messages

Sudo is configured to log messages to a facility called local2. It just so happens that sudo is the only program installed in a default system that uses the facility local2. This makes it a trivial matter to isolate messages generated by sudo. Open /etc/syslog.conf in your favorite editor and make the following addition to the file:

```
local2.*            /var/log/sudo.log
```

In this example, we've told syslog to select all messages from the facility local2 at all severity levels and write those messages to the file /var/log/sudo.log.

Syslog will not create a file by itself, so we'll have to create the logfile. Additionally we'll set the proper permissions on the file, and finally we'll restart syslog to force it to reread its configuration file. Open the Terminal application and type the following commands:

```
sudo touch /var/log/sudo.log
sudo chmod 640 /var/log/sudo.log
sudo kill -HUP `/bin/cat /var/run/syslog.pid`
```

Separating ssh messages

If you are allowing connections to your system via ssh, you'll want to log those connections so you can monitor them. In order to do this we'll need to modify both the sshd configuration file and the syslog configuration file.

First open the ssh server configuration file located at /etc/sshd_config with sudo and your favorite editor and change the value of SyslogFacility from AUTH to LOCAL7. Ensure that you've removed the # character from the beginning of the line. Then remove the # character from the LogLevel line immediately below. Save the file and close it.

Next, open /etc/syslog.conf in your favorite editor and make the following addition to the file:

```
local7.*            /var/log/sshd.log
```

In this example we've told syslog to select all messages from the facility local7 at all severity levels and write those messages to the file /var/log/sshd.log.

Again, syslog can not create files in the /var/log directory for us, so we'll go create the logfile with proper permissions, then we'll restart syslog to force it to reread the configuration file. Open the Terminal application and type the following commands:

```
sudo touch /var/log/sshd.log
sudo chmod 640 /var/log/sudo.log
sudo kill -HUP `/bin/cat /var/run/syslog.pid`
```

Viewing system logs

Now that we're familiar with syslog and the configuration of system messages written to log files, we'll need to examine these files to see what kind of events are occurring on our computer and ensure that everything is going the way we expect it to be. Here we have several options. We can browse the log files in the Terminal application or use the Console application to view log messages. For debugging new services, and other system occurrences, looking at the log file in real time can be extremely helpful. A new feature in Panther is that Apple System Profiler also includes a log file viewer , as shown in Figure 26-12. This is useful if you need to provide copies of log files for technical support types.

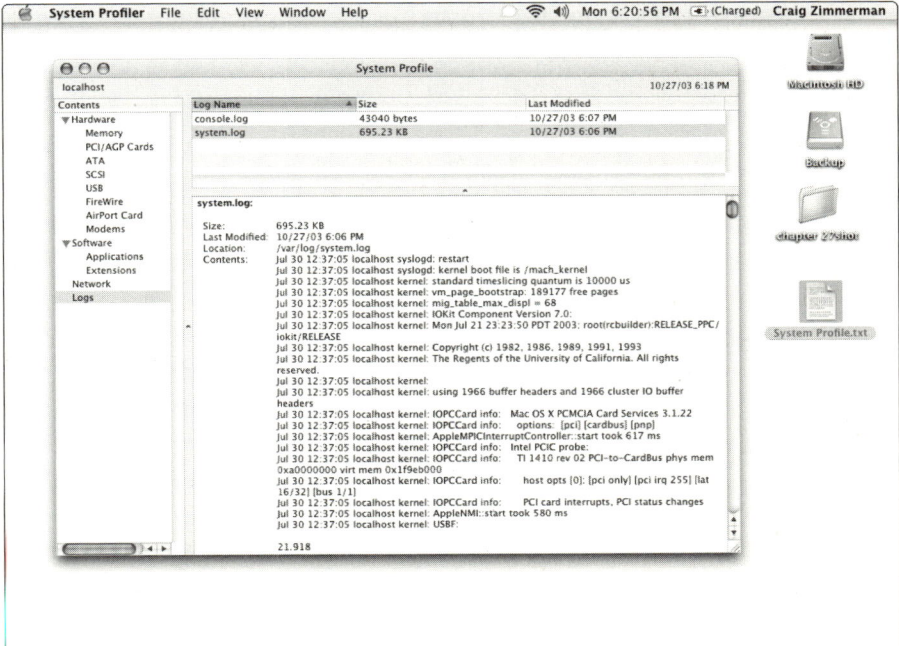

Figure 26-12: Using Apple System Profiler to view system logfiles.

Using Terminal to view logfiles

Tail, less, cat and grep are all very useful when it comes to viewing and searching logfiles.

Use the tail command to view the end of a logfile by typing tail /var/log/system.log. Tail can be used to continuously monitor a file by using the -f switch. When tail is invoked with the -f switch, it will not stop when the EOF (end of file) marker is reached, but will wait for additional input. To open and watch a logfile use the command tail -f /var/log/system.log. Replace /var/log/system.log with the logfile you are watching.

Use the less command to scroll through a logfile page by page. You can search within the file you are reading by typing the / character followed by your search string ie: /craigz. The first occurrence of your search term will be highlighted. You can jump to the next occurrence by typing the n key on your keyboard, and continue typing n to move through found items. You can also move line by line down the file by using either the return key or the down arrow. The up arrow can also be used to scroll upwards line by line. To move through the document page by page use the space bar.

If you want to check on a specific text string in your logfile, you can use the cat command in conjunction with grep. For example to search for the string craigz in the system log file, type the following command `cat /var/log/system.log | grep craigz`.

Using the Console application to view logfiles

The Console application is located in the folder Utilities inside the Applications folder. The left side of the application displays two stand-alone files: console.log and system.log as well as three folders where logs are located, /Library/Logs ~Library/Logs and /var/log. Each of these folders has disclosure triangles next them that can be expanded to show individual log files within. This window is shown in Figure 26-13.Once a file is selected on the left, its contents will populate the right side of the window. The search box on the top right is labeled filter. You can type text in that window, and only lines containing that text string will be left in the content window. Clicking the Clear icon will clear the window. Using the Reload button will refresh the window content, and the Mark button will insert a line with a timestamp. The Mark button is quite useful if you are watching a file for a specific event as you can insert timestamps to mark your place, and note between similar looking lines.

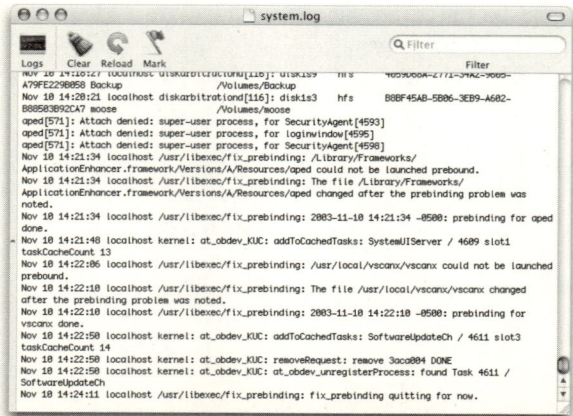

Figure 26-13: Using the Console application to view system logfiles.

Summary

In this chapter, we've introduced you to the major concepts involved in computer security in general, and specifically how they relate to Mac OS X. We've looked at both the physical security of your computer and its files, and the network security of your computer, or how other computers can connect to your computer. We've learned what kinds of threats exist on the Internet, and developed an understanding of the issues that can affect us. We've learned how to replace the provided FTP server with a more secure and configurable server, and have looked at the built in firewall and learned how to manage and monitor system logs.

We've covered a lot of ground in this chapter, and truthfully have barely scratched the tip of the iceberg. Entire books are written on the subject of security. Hopefully this introduction has given you a sense of the issues surrounding security and will help you think about security and how it relates to using your computer and safely sharing resources with other users.

As was stated in the beginning of the chapter, computer security is a fast-moving target. You'd do well to read up on current events in the security world. The Web site http://www.securityfocus.com is a tremendous resource, with many mailing lists dedicated to the issue of computer security.

The best way to secure your system is to keep all software you are running current. Do this through Apple Software Update, and by maintaining current versions of all third-party software you install. Consider using package managers like Fink whenever possible to maintain and keep third-party software up to date.

Appendix

◆ ◆ ◆ ◆

In This Part

Appendix
Installing Applications

◆ ◆ ◆ ◆

Installing Applications

◆   ◆   ◆   ◆

In This Appendix

Installing applications using the Installer utility

Installing applications from disk images

Installing applications from compressed archives

Installing applications with custom installers

◆   ◆   ◆   ◆

With Mac OS X, Apple includes an Installer program, and many applications take advantage of it by distributing packages that Installer opens and distributes to the appropriate folders. Early releases of this Installer had some problems, the most serious of which was deleting folders when it removed old versions of a file before installing the new one. These issues have since been resolved in subsequent updates — another reason to use the Software Update pane of System Preferences periodically to make sure that your system software is up-to-date. Meanwhile, MindVision and Aladdin have carbonized their installers so that they run natively under Mac OS X.

First, one of the things you need to know about installing an application is that, if you want to install it in the Applications folder so that all users of your Mac can access it, you need to be logged in with an administrator account.

Using the Installer Utility

Unless Mac OS X was preinstalled on your Mac or somebody else installed Mac OS X for you, you have seen the Mac OS X Installer in action. Apple uses the Installer for installing Mac OS X, updating Mac OS X via the Software Update pane of System Preferences, and using applications.

The Installer utility is located in, ta-da, the Utilities folder of the Applications folder. The Installer's documents are installer *packages* and generally have a .PKG extension on their file name and an icon similar to the one shown in Figure A-1. The Installer application's icon is also seen in Figure A-1.

Installer   Essentials.pkg

Figure A-1: The Installer (left) and a typical Installer package (right).

A typical installation follows these steps:

1. **Double-click the Installer icon, and initiate the installation process.**

2. **The Installer will ask to run a program that verifies that it can run (shown in Figure A-2).**

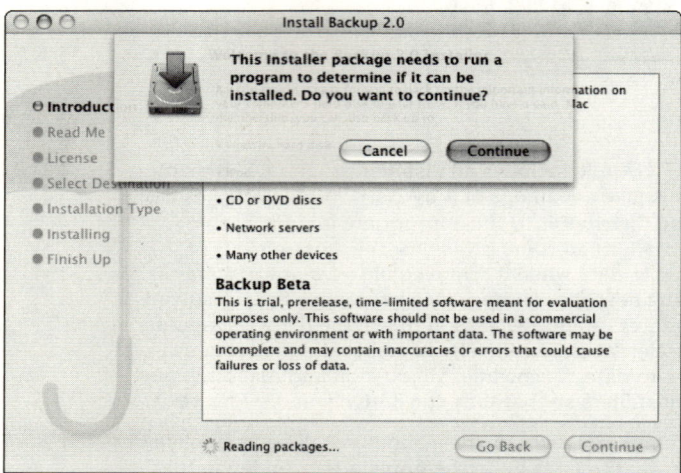

Figure A-2: The Installer needs to run software to determine if the installation procedure can continue.

3. **After the Installer has run its check, you see an Introduction screen, as shown in Figure A-3.**

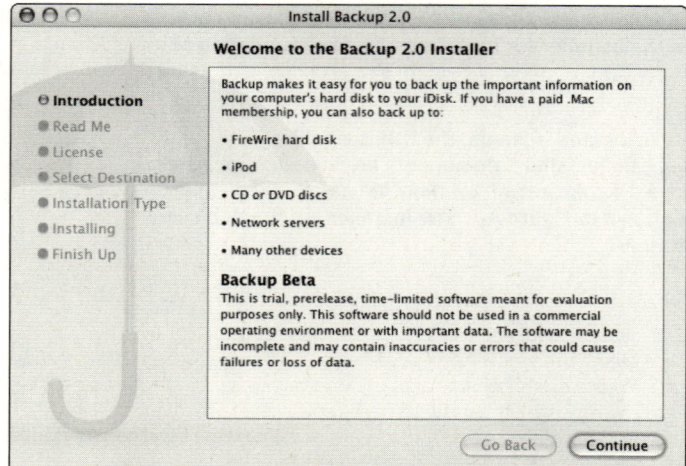

Figure A-3: Greetings from the Installer. Click Continue to proceed.

4. **Click the Continue button to proceed to the next step.** The screen reveals important information (the Read Me document) about the software product and adds four buttons along the bottom of the window, as shown in Figure A-4.

The Read Me document often includes directions on things you need to do or know before you install. You can print the Read Me file (click the Print button at the bottom), or save it to your disk (click the Save button) if you want to refer to it at a later time. The Go Back button allows you to retrace your steps, in case you want to change an earlier selection (although there isn't much point in that, yet).

Note

On the left of the Installer window is a task bar listing the steps taken during the installation process. Although you cannot use it to navigate the installation process, it is a handy reference for where you are and which steps remain.

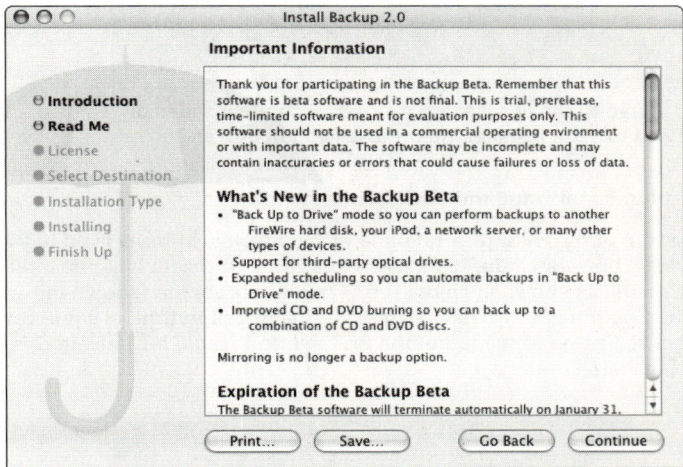

Figure A-4: Release notes provided by the software provider in the Read Me file.

5. **Click Continue.** The software license agreement appears. In most cases (at least for software from Apple), you need to agree to the license before the installation takes place.

6. **After reading the license agreement (and you'll read every word, won't you?), click Continue.** The Install screen appears, asking you to agree or disagree to the terms of the license agreement, as shown in Figure A-5.

7. **Click Agree to continue with the installation. If you do not agree with the license, click Disagree and you return to the previous screen.** Usually, if you disagree with the license, you cannot install the software. Assuming that you agreed to the terms of the license agreement, you are asked to choose the volume on which you want the software installed. The available volumes appear in the destination window. (Because there is no more documentation, the Print and Save buttons have disappeared.)

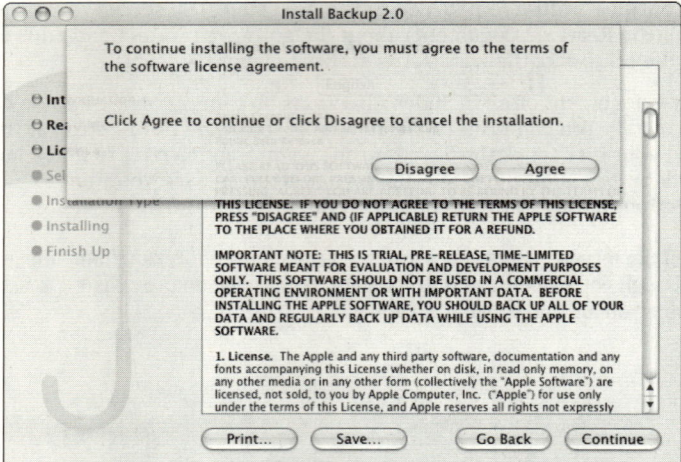

Figure A-5: Agree to the license and proceed with the installation, or disagree and exit the Installer after it takes you back a step.

8. Select the volume you want and click Continue.

Near the bottom of the window, where the Print and Save buttons used to be, the Installer reveals how much disk space is required to do the installation after selecting the volume's icon, as shown in Figure A-6. A fairly bare screen (shown in Figure A-7) appears. The Continue button has changed to the Install button. In some cases you will see a Customize button to the left of the Go Back and Install buttons; in this case there are no custom install options.

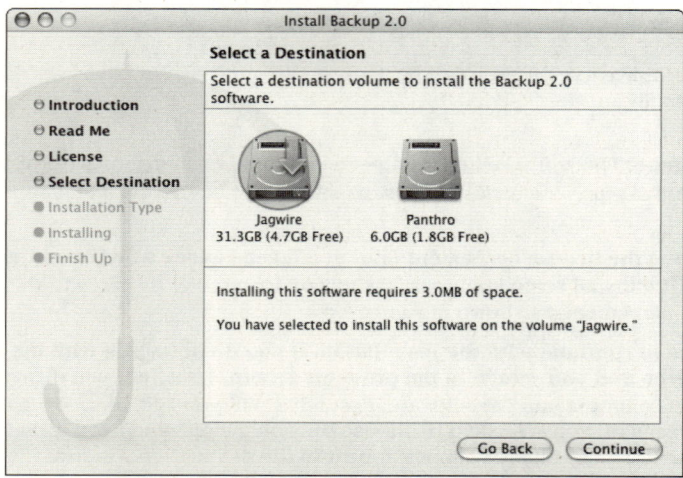

Figure A-6: Select the destination of your software installation.

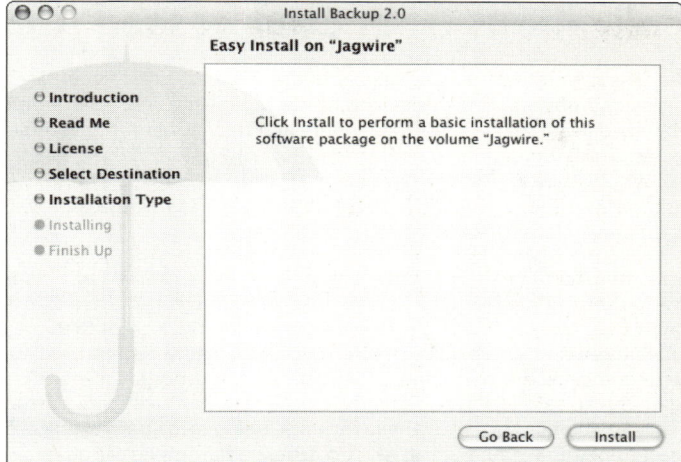

Figure A-7: The point of no return — time to install.

9. **Click Install.** A progress bar appears in the right pane of the window. When the installation is complete, you are notified and you can quit from the Installer. Some installations, particularly many involving updates to the System, require you to restart. When that is the case, the Installer tells you that you need to restart (via a dialog) and restarts the Mac when you dismiss the dialog.

Installing Applications from Disk Images

With the advent of packages, many applications do not require installation of additional components in scattered locations. In fact, it is now normal for an application to be just one file, a package (a special folder type that the Mac OS X presents to you like a single file), or a small group of files maintained in the same folder as the application. Thus, the ease of the drag install is currently the norm for Mac OS X applications.

Because of the ease of drag installations, shipping applications as disk image files is one of the most common distribution methods for applications. In fact, Apple uses it for distribution of Mac OS X applications, such as iTunes, iMovie, and AppleWorks.

Disk image files are usually obtained via download from the Internet, which includes the software folder of your iDisk where Apple provides a veritable cornucopia of software for Mac OS X — both from Apple and from third-party developers.

Copy the disk image file to your hard disk and double-click it. The disk image usually has a .IMG, .DMG, or .SMI file name extension (suffix). If the image has an .SMI extension, you may want to just drag it to the Disk Copy window (after launching Disk Copy, of course). Why? Because double-clicking an .SMI file may launch the Classic version of Disk Copy if it is present.

Disk image files mount just like external hard disks, CD-ROMs, or the venerable floppy — ready for you to install your software. To install the application in the Applications folder, you need to be logged in with an administrator account. Just drag the file to the folder where you want it to reside, and you'll be able to run it from there.

Installing Applications from Compressed Archives

Just as you use Disk Copy to mount disk images, you use a decompression utility to make the contents of compressed archives installable. Until quite recently, a Mac user would rarely encounter a compressed archive in any format other than that of Aladdin Systems' StuffIt Deluxe. In the rare situation where a user encountered a WinZip file, the free StuffIt Expander would decompress WinZip as well. While there were other compressors and archivers (Disk Doubler and Compact Pro, to name two), anything other than .SIT (StuffIt) or .ZIP (WinZip) was extremely uncommon.

Thanks to the Unix underpinnings of Mac OS X, a couple of other formats are becoming semi-standard. As noted in Chapter 26, `tar` files are the Unix standard for archiving, and compression is achieved with `compress` or `gzip`. `gzip` files typically have a .gz file name extension and compressed files have a .z extension. The multitalented StuffIt Expander also recognizes these formats and decompresses and expands `tar` archives, although some other utilities, such as OpenUp — a freeware offering by Scott Anguish, obtained from `www.stepwise.com/Software/OpenUp/` — also decompresses these formats. If you have both StuffIt Expander and OpenUp, you should be ready for just about any compressed archive that comes your way.

To install from a compressed archive, decompress the archive and then extract the archive's contents. If there are installation instructions (such as a Unix script to run in a Terminal shell), follow them. If there are no installation instructions, just drag the application where you want it, remembering that you might need administrator privileges to install it in the Applications folder.

Installing Applications with Custom Installers

Some application providers decided to "roll their own" installation utility or script. When you encounter one of these situations, just follow the instructions that accompany the custom installer — every one will be different. Other than telling you to follow the accompanying instructions, no general rule applies.

✦   ✦   ✦

Glossary

absolute pathname A pathname that specifies the exact location of a single directory. An *absolute pathname* begins at the root directory, a slash (/), and traverses through the Unix file system, ending at the desired directory or file, and naming each directory that is passed through. Each directory that is passed through is named and separated by a slash. /Users/warren/Documents is the *absolute pathname* of my Documents folder. This contrasts to the relative pathname.

Active application The application that is visible in the foreground. If iTunes is the *Active application,* its name is visible in bold in the menu bar, directly to the right of the Apple menu.

admin See *administrator account*

administrator account Admin is one type of Mac OS X user account in which the user has access to system-wide resources, including abilities to modify the System Preferences, create and edit other user accounts, and install applications. When OS X is initially set up, the first user created is an admin.

adopted ownership When a Mac OS X user account is deleted, its contents can be transferred to an existing admin account. The admin user is said to be adopting ownership of the previous user's files.

Advanced Memory Management Automatically and dynamically assigns and handles the allocation of both physical RAM and virtual memory to applications and processes as needed.

AirPort Apple's name for its implementation of the IEEE 802.11 standard for wireless networking. This includes AirPort, (802.11b) at speeds of 11Mbs, and AirPort Extreme, (802.11g) at speeds up to 54Mbs.

AirPort Base Station An Apple hardware device that provides a wireless signal to 802.11-equipped computers, Macintosh or otherwise. A base station can be connected to the Internet and transmit a wireless net connection, and can dial up directly through its own internal modem. "Extreme" versions can wirelessly share USB printers and can be connected to an external antenna.

alias Also known as a shortcut, an alias is a representative file that can dynamically locate its target file or folder. The pathway will not be lost if either the original or the alias is moved to a different location on the same volume. Under the Mac file system, each file has a unique identifier, which can be traced even if the file has moved.

antialiasing A technique that causes text and graphics to appear smoother and easier to read when displayed using the relatively low resolution of a computer screen. Shading and blending of otherwise jagged lines are used to fool the eye into seeing a cleaner image.

Apache An open source Web server that is provided within every copy of Mac OS X and Mac OS X Server. Apache is the most widely used Web server (over 60 percent of Web sites) on the Internet and runs on a variety of platforms, including Unix-based operating systems and Windows servers.

API See *Application Programming Interface*

AppleCare Knowledge Base Located at `www.apple.com/support`, the Knowledge Base is Apple's official Web-based library of articles and information pertaining to the usage and support of its products.

Apple Menu Located at the top left-most corner of the screen, it is a menu in the shape of an Apple logo, either gray or blue depending on the configuration. The Apple Menu contains commands that affect the machine on a system-wide level, such as changing the settings of the Dock, or shutting down the machine.

AppleScript A programming language that is used for automating tasks and customizing application features, as well as creating stand-alone applets. The language is heavily English based, more so than most, making it easy to learn and decipher. AppleScript is included with every copy of OS X; a third-party application that is able to be affected by an AppleScript is said to be "scriptable."

applet A mini-Application program that is usually Java or AppleScript based. Java applets are often embedded within Web pages (like an Internet search engine), and AppleScripts are often integrated within a larger application to perform a certain function. For example, within Apple's DVD Player application, one can pull down the scripts menu and access a specific time within a movie.

AppleTalk A networking protocol created by Apple that dates back to the early Macintosh days in the mid-1980s. It was (is) popular due to its ease of use and the fact that network devices easily make themselves known on a network. It was the primary method of networking Macs and peripherals for many years and only now is being phased out in favor of less "chatty" protocols, such as TCP/IP networking and *Rendezvous,* Apple's new "zero-config" networking protocol.

application A complete and self-contained program that when launched (for example, double-clicked on) will perform certain functions for a human being. The Finder, iTunes, and the Print Center are all examples of applications.

Application Programming Interface (API) The method by which an operating system can make certain requests of an application, or by which an application can make certain requests of an operating system in order to call upon and perform specific tasks. For example, the Quicktime API would be called upon to add movie and sound features to an application.

applications folder The default location for all of the user-accessible programs. For example, if one installs FileMaker Pro for the first time, it is automatically placed inside the applications folder. Applications do not have to be placed here, but it is a good idea to keep them here for organizational purposes.

Aqua Apple's name for the look and feel of the graphical user interface that makes up OS X. The pulsating OK buttons, the huge photorealistic icons, and the fancy "genie" animation that occurs when a window is minimized to the Dock are all examples of what Aqua is.

archive A single compressed file containing files and folders, ready for emailing or backing up.

argument Is the piece of a Unix command line on which the command is being acted. Arguments are usually filenames or directory names. For example:

```
% chown warren:staff /Users/warren/Documents
```

In this command, the argument is the documents folder.

ASCII (American Standard Code for Information Interchange) The most basic character set used by almost all modern computers. US-ASCII uses 0-127 to represent upper and lowercase letters, punctuation, space, and numbers. More advanced ASCII sets, like Unicode, use more characters and can represent accented letters and more complicated punctuation.

authentication The process of verifying that someone is, in actuality, who he or she claims to be. Under Mac OS X, when one types a correct password into the login screen, that person is being authenticated to log in to the system.

authoritative DNS server An authoritative DNS server is a computer that holds the definitive DNS records for a given domain name. A DNS server that can hold the DNS entries for IP-aware entities connected to the Internet.

autoscrolling When scrolling is accomplished by dragging an item to the edge of a window (which will cause the window's contents to scroll in that direction) and not by manually clicking on the scrollbar or arrows, then the window is said to autoscroll.

background program A program that while running is usually not visible to the user of the system. Launch the Process Viewer to see examples of this. The iChat Agent is one such instance. This process runs in the background and can sign the user onto AOL's Instant Messenger service even if the iChat application is not open yet.

backup A backup is created to guard against data loss that occurs due to hardware failure, corruption, viruses, natural disasters, theft, and human error. Essentially a backup is a copy of existing information so that if the original is lost, a copy exists. A backup can be a burned CD of some digital pictures, or a system in which an entire office of computers is automatically backed up via network to a central server every night, using programs like Retrospect.

binary The base two number system that computers use. It is unlike the number system humans use, which is base ten. In binary, there are two number choices, a one or a zero. A single binary digit is called a bit. A group of eight bits is called a byte. For convenience's sake, a kilobyte is considered to be 1000 bytes, but more accurately, because it is within a base two system and is 2^{10}, a single kilobyte is 1024 bytes. Thus, a gigabyte of RAM is really 1024 megabytes.

binary file A type of compressed and encoded file, usually containing the .bin suffix. MacBinary files are encoded so that the data contained in them can be stored on other operating systems (like Microsoft Windows) and transferred back and forth without issue. Stuffit Expander can decode these files.

BinHex A method of encoding and compressing binary files for download and transfer. BinHex files have an .hqx suffix and is the most common format to receive Macintosh software downloads in. Stuffit Expander can decompress these files.

bit Stands for Binary Digit. A bit is the smallest unit of storage, a one or a zero, a yes or a no, an on or an off, a true or a false.

bit depth See *color depth* and *pixel depth*

bitmap font Same as *fixed-size font*

Blessed Under Mac OS 9.x, or "Classic," the term *Blessed* refers to a system folder that is active and recognized by the operating system as a valid and bootable OS. It is possible for a good system folder to become unblessed, causing a Mac not to recognize its ability to boot from. Running a utility such as DiskWarrior will re-bless an unblessed system folder.

bookmark Refers to a saved URL (Uniform Resource Locator) within a Web browser. For example, if, when using Safari, one wishes to save MacAddict's Web site (www.macaddict.com) for future viewing, one can go to the Bookmark menu and choose "Add Bookmark" and save the location for easy future access.

boot The act of powering on a machine and having the operating system loaded and started up. If I asked you to "boot up" your Mac, I'd be asking you to power it on and wait until the OS had finished loading.

bridge A piece of hardware that is used to move traffic between two different types of networks or networking hardware. An AirPort Base Station is a bridge when it routes information from a wired Ethernet network to its wireless one.

BSD (Berkeley Software Distribution) There are many different versions, or "flavors," of Unix that exist, including distributions called Linux, Solaris, and AIX. BSD is an umbrella term for the Unix flavor that has been released by UC Berkeley. It is this version that Mac OS X is based upon.

BSD subsystem Together with the Mach Kernel, the BSD subsystem makes up Apple's own flavor of Unix, called Darwin. On top of Darwin, Apple placed its proprietary frameworks like Carbon, Cocoa, and QuickTime, and its Aqua user interface, resulting in Mac OS X.

bug An error within a piece of software (like a program) or hardware (like a printer) that causes an unwanted behavior, usually resulting in a malfunction. A well-known bug was the Y2K bug, which left many computers (Macs excluded) vulnerable to reverting back to the year 1900 instead of the year 2000 due to the two-digit year limitation encoded in most software. Updates, or "bug-fixes," are usually released to repair bugs.

built-in memory Is Apple's terminology for the RAM (Random Access Memory) that is physically installed in the Machine.

bundle Another term for *package*.

burn When information is recorded onto a CD, (compact disc) the disc is said to be burned. The term stems from the way a CD is recorded, which involves using a laser beam to heat a layer of photosensitive dye.

burn-in A condition affecting CRT monitors in which a vestige of an unchanging screen image remains visible after the image changes, and even after the computer has powered off. Today's computer screens are no longer susceptible to burn-in. Flat-panel LCDs (Liquid Crystal Displays) such as those found on Apple's PowerBooks are not affected by this condition.

byte One byte is comprised of 8 bits. A byte is the smallest unit of storage that the Mac OS will recognize. Bytes are commonly measured by many thousands (Kilobytes, or K), millions (Megabytes, or MB), billions (Gigabytes, or GB), and trillions (Terabytes, or TB) at a time.

case-sensitive Means that it matters whether or not letters are capitalized. Passwords in Mac OS X are case-sensitive. In some instances, such as in the screensaver password window, the dialog box will tell you if the caps lock key is pressed, alleviating the frustration of being sure the correct password is being typed in but having it entered unknowingly in all caps.

character A written representation of a letter, digit, or symbol. A single character could be the letter "W" or an exclamation point (!).

checkbox Gives you the option of activating or deactivating a setting presented by the operating system or by a program. A checkbox is literally a box that has three different states, blank, checked, or dashed. A check indicates a setting is chosen, a blank means it has not been chosen, and a dash usually is presented if multiple items are selected with different settings (such as ownership and permissions of files viewed in the Finder) or to indicate that settings will not be changed. In the realm of mathematical logic, a series of checkboxes function as an "AND." That is, out of five boxes, you can select one and two and three. Contrast this to the *radio button*.

clean installation A type of Mac OS X installation in which a new, fresh copy of the system is installed, and the original system folder is left unaltered and moved into a "Previous Systems" folder at the root level of the hard drive. An option for preserving the user folders is available.

CLI See *command-line interface*

click-and-a-half A gesture used to make a disk or folder spring open. To perform the gesture, begin to double-click the disk or folder, but do not release the mouse button after the second click.

click-through The ability to interact directly with an item in an inactive window. For example, you can operate the Close, Minimize, and Zoom buttons in most inactive Aqua windows.

client A program (or a computer running a program) that requests and receives information or services from a *server*.

clipping file A file created by the Finder to hold material that has been dragged from a document to the Desktop or a Finder window.

closed network An AirPort network that requires you to type its name (not simply pick the name from a list) to connect to it.

Cocoa Applications that are specifically developed for Mac OS X. Cocoa applications are incompatible with older Macintosh operating systems. Cocoa applications take advantage of all of Mac OS X's modern OS features, such as advanced memory, preemptive multitasking, symmetric multiprocessing, and the Aqua interface.

codec (compressor-decompressor) Something that compresses data so that it takes less space to store and decompresses compressed data back to its original form for playing or other use. A compressor may consist of software, hardware, or both.

collated Multiple printed copies of a document with each copy having all its pages in the correct order.

color depth The number of bits of information that are required to represent the number of colors available on the screen. For example, a screen that can display thousands of colors is set at a color depth of 16 bits. Compare to *pixel depth*.

Color picker The dialog in which you specify a custom color either by clicking a color wheel, clicking a color sample, or entering color values.

command-line interface A non-GUI method of interacting with the operating system. A means of interacting with and controlling a computer by typing commands into the terminal, one line at a time.

comment An AppleScript line that begins with a hyphen, or a Unix command line that begins with a number sign character (#), which in either case means that the line is descriptive and not a command to be performed.

compile To convert the human-readable text of an AppleScript *script* into command codes that a Mac can execute. As part of this process, AppleScript checks the script for nonconformance with AppleScript grammar, such as a missing parenthesis.

compression algorithm A method for compressing data so that it fits in less space and can be transferred more quickly. Each compression algorithm generally works best with one type of data, such as sound, photographs, video or motion pictures, and computer-generated animation. Three characteristics of a compression algorithm determine how effectively it compresses — *compression ratio,* fidelity to the original data, and speed.

compression ratio Indicates the amount of compression and is calculated by dividing the size of the original source data by the size of the compressed data. Larger compression ratios mean greater compression and generally (although not always) a loss of quality in the compressed data.

conditional A programming command that evaluates a condition (stated as part of the conditional) to determine whether another command or set of commands should be performed. (Also referred to as a *conditional statement.*)

contextual menu A contextual menu lists commands relevant to an item that you Control-click.

Control Panel A small Classic application that you use to set the way some part of the Classic environment looks and behaves. Similar to OS X Preference panes.

cooperative multitasking A scheme of *multitasking* used by Classic applications whereby multiple applications are open in the Classic environment and voluntarily taking turns using the Classic environment's processing time. While each Classic application is idle, it allows other Classic applications to use the processor. Compare *preemptive multitasking.*

crack A means of circumventing a programs serialization and security.

crop markers Small triangles that indicate the beginning and end of a selected part of a movie in iMovie.

crossover cable A cable whose wires are reversed inside the plug at one end of the cable.

custom installation You can selectively install Mac OS X packages. You can also selectively install Mac OS 9 modules for the Classic environment.

daisy chaining The process of connecting one peripheral or network device to another device, linking them so that they can share data. This is often done with Ethernet networking hubs to extend the size of an Ethernet network. It's also how multiple FireWire and SCSI devices are connected to a single Macintosh computer so that they can all be accessed by that computer.

Darwin A joint project between the Open Source community and Apple. The primary objective of the Darwin project is to build an industrial-strength UNIX-based operating system core that provides greater stability and performance compared to the existing iterations of the Mac OS to date.

dead keys The keys that generate accented characters when typed in combination with the Option key and in proper sequence. For example, typing Option-E followed by O generates ó on a U.S. keyboard. The Key Caps program highlights the dead keys when you press Option.

default browser The Web browser application that opens when you click a link to a Web page in Sherlock's list of search results, open an Internet *location file,* or otherwise don't specify a particular browser application.

default button The one button that pulsates in an Aqua dialog or alert box; in a Classic dialog or alert box, the default button has a heavy border. In either case it represents the action you'll most often want to take. If the most common action is dangerous, a button representing a safer action may be the default button. Usually, pressing Return or Enter has the same effect as clicking the default button.

Desktop database Invisible files used by the Finder to associate Classic applications and their documents. Mac OS X keeps the Desktop database hidden because you don't use it directly. You can use the Classic pane of System Preferences to rebuild the Desktop database.

device A piece of hardware attached to a computer, either internally or externally. Some examples include keyboards, scanners, and drives.

device driver Software that controls a device, such as a printer or scanner. The driver contains data that the OS requires to fully utilize the device.

DHCP (Dynamic Host Configuration Protocol) A networking service in which a host device dynamically assigns TCP/IP addresses to client computers to grant them access to the network.

dialog A window that displays options you can set or select. A dialog typically has a button for accepting the changes and another button for canceling the changes. Both buttons close the dialog.

digital signature Functions as a handwritten signature, identifying the person who vouches for the accuracy and authenticity of the signed document.

DIMM A dual in-line memory module is a small circuit board containing memory chips.

directory Another name for folder.

Directory Services Directory Services provide a consolidated user list that can be shared via multiple network services or servers for authentication. Directory Services do not provide the user list data itself but rather describe how they are set up and enable the communication of the data.

disclosure triangle A displayed control that regulates how much detail you see in a window. When the window is displaying minimal detail, clicking a disclosure triangle reveals additional detail and may automatically enlarge the window to accommodate it. Clicking the same triangle again hides detail and may automatically shrink the window to fit.

disk cache Improves system performance by storing recently used information from disk in a dedicated part of memory. Accessing information in memory is much faster than accessing information on disk.

disk image A file that, when mounted using Disk Copy or a similar utility, appears on the Desktop as if it were a removable disk.

display mirroring See *video mirroring*

DNS (Domain Name System) A service that resolves domain names to IP addresses, and vice versa.

DogCow Also known as Clarus, it is the official mascot of Mac enthusiasts. It looks vaguely like a dog (or a cow, thus the name) and is pictured in the Page Setup Options dialog of Classic applications.

domain name The part of a *URL* that identifies the owner of an Internet location. A domain name has the form `companyname.com`, `organizationname.net`, `schoolname.edu`, `militaryunitname.mil`, `governmentagencyname.gov`, and so forth.

double-click speed The rate at which you have to click so that Mac OS X perceives two clicks in a row as a single event.

download The process of receiving software or other computer files from another computer, over the Internet or a local network.

dpi (dots per inch) A measure of how fine or coarse the dots are that make up a printed image. More dots per inch means smaller dots, and smaller dots mean finer (less coarse) printing.

drag To move the mouse while holding down the mouse button.

drag-and-drop editing To copy or move selected text, graphics, and other material by dragging it to another place in the same window, a different window, or on the desktop. Some applications do not support drag-and-drop editing.

drag-and-drop open To drag a document to a compatible application in the Finder, thereby highlighting the application, and then releasing the mouse button, causing the application to open the document.

drop box A shared folder located inside a user's Public folder in which other users may place items (when peer-to-peer file sharing is enabled), but only the folder's owner can see them.

DSL (Digital Subscriber Line) An add-on for standard telephone service that enables you to maintain a constant, high-speed Internet connection over a standard telephone line.

duplex A method of printing on both sides of the page that does not need a person there to flip the pages.

dynamic IP address See *DHCP*

dynamic RAM allocation An operating system technology that allows the operating system to respond to an application's request for more or less memory as needed.

Easter eggs Cute or funny animations or other surprising actions hidden in a program. You reveal them by performing secret combinations of keystrokes and mouse clicks.

edition A file that contains a live copy of the material in the *publisher* portion of a document belonging to a Classic application. When the publisher changes, the edition is updated. *Subscribers* contain copies of editions.

enclosing folder The enclosing folder contains another folder.

encryption The process of making messages or files unrecognizable; for example, to keep someone from reading a sensitive document.

escape character A backslash (\) in a Unix command. Used to indicate that the next character is to be used literally, not interpreted as a *wildcard* or other special character.

Ethernet A high-speed standard for connecting computers and other devices in a network. Ethernet ports are built into all Macs that can use Mac OS X and in many network printers. Ethernet networks can be wireless, as exemplified by AirPort wireless networks.

event message A means of *interprocess communication*. Applications can send event messages to one another. When an application receives an event message, it takes an action according to the content of the message. This action can be anything from executing a particular command to taking some data, working with it, and then returning a result to the program that sent the message.

Exposé Apple's new window management function. Designed to afford users easy access to all open applications, windows, or the desktop.

extension The last part of a file's name, typically three or four letters, following a period. The extension helps to designate an item's parent application. Also referred to as a file name suffix.

fair use Defines the criteria that must be considered before using another person's copyrighted work (printed or recorded materials).

Favorites Often-accessed items. Aliases can be added to the Favorites folder, which then appear on the Favorites menu in the Finder's Go menu and in Open and Save dialogs of Mac OS X applications.

file ID number The number that Mac OS X uses internally to identify the original item to which an alias is attached even if you have renamed or moved that original item.

file mapping The technique used by Mac OS X of treating a program file as part of *virtual memory* so that fragments of a program are only loaded into memory as needed.

file name extension See *extension*

file server A computer running a program that makes files centrally available for other computers on a network.

file sharing Enables you to share files in your Public folder with people whose computers are connected to yours in a network.

file spec (specification) Tells Mac OS X exactly where to find a file or folder.

file system A method of organizing data on a volume. Macintosh OS X uses either HFS+ or the UFS file system.

file type A four-letter code that identifies the general characteristics of a file's contents, such as plain text, formatted text, picture, or sound.

File Vault A secure file storage method added to OS 10.3.

filter A technology that applies special effects to an image, such as a visual effect to a QuickTime movie.

Finder The core system application that allows users to graphically interact with the operating system.

firewall A device or software that prevents Internet users from getting access to computers on a local network. A firewall may also stop local network users from sending sensitive information out.

firmware Low-level programming that tells the hardware of a computer (or device) how to behave.

fixed-size font Contains exact pictures of every letter, digit, and symbol for one size of a font. Fixed-size fonts are called *bitmap fonts* because each picture precisely maps the dots, or *bits,* to be displayed or printed for one character.

folder-action script An AppleScript script that is attached to a folder so that it can watch and respond to user interaction with that folder in the Finder.

font A set of *characters* that have a common and consistent design.

font family A collection of differently styled variations (such as bold, italic, and plain) of a single *font*. Many *fixed-size, TrueType,* and *PostScript* fonts come in the four basic styles: plain, bold, italic, and bold italic. Some PostScript font families include 20 or more styled versions.

fonts folder Located in the System Folder used for the Classic environment, this folder includes all *fixed-size, PostScript,* and *TrueType* fonts available in the Classic environment.

font suitcase A folder-like container specifically for *fixed-size* and *TrueType* fonts in the Classic environment.

fork Part of a Mac OS file. Many Mac OS files include a data fork and a resource fork where different types of information are stored.

fps (frames per second) Measures how smoothly a motion picture plays. More frames per second means smoother playback. This measurement is used when discussing the *frame rate* of time-based media.

frame One still image that is part of a series of still images, which, when shown in sequence, produce the illusion of movement.

frame rate The number of frames displayed in one second. The TV frame rate is 30 fps in the United States and other countries that use the NTSC broadcasting standard; 25 fps in countries that use the PAL or SEACAM standard. The standard movie frame rate is 24 fps. See also *fps.*

frameworks Mac OS X frameworks contain dynamically loading code that is shared between applications. Frameworks alleviate the need for applications that utilize identical code to load multiple iterations of the same code simultaneously.

freeware Free software primarily distributed over the Internet and from person to person. Most freeware is still copyrighted by the person who created it. You can use it and give it to other people, but you can't sell it. See also *shareware.*

FTP (File Transfer Protocol) A data communications *protocol* used by the Internet and other TCP/IP networks to transfer files between computers.

FTP site A collection of files on an FTP server available for downloading.

full motion Video displayed at frame rates of 24 to 30 fps. The human eye perceives fairly smooth motion at frame rates of 12 to 18 fps. See also *fps* and *frame rate.*

gamma The relationship between the intensity of color and its luminance. Also the type of radiation wave that converted Dr. Banner into the Hulk.

gamma correction A method of compensating for the loss of detail that the human eye perceives in dark areas.

glyph A distinct visual representation of one character (such as a lowercase *z*), multiple characters treated as one (such as the ligature æ), or a nonprinting character (such as a space).

grid fitting The process of modifying characters at small point sizes so that they fit the grid of dots on the relatively coarse display screen. The font designer provides a set of instructions (also known as *hints*) for a *TrueType* or *PostScript* font that tells Mac OS X how to modify character outlines to fit the grid.

group Used to simplify the assignment of system privileges for clusters of users that have identical levels of access.

guest A network user who is not identified by a name and password.

GUI (Graphical User Interface) A means of interacting with and controlling a computer by manipulating graphical objects shown on the display, such as windows, menus, and icons. The opposite of CLI.

hack A programming effort that accomplishes something resourceful or unconventional. Often used as a disparaging term for a quick-fix or for a poorly skilled technician.

hacker A person who likes to tinker with computers and especially with computer software code. Some hackers create new software, but many hackers use programs such as ResEdit to make unauthorized changes to existing software. Largely an interchangeable term with *cracker.*

handler A named set of *AppleScript* commands that you can execute by naming the handler elsewhere in the same script. Instead of repeating a set of commands several times in different parts of a script, you can make the set of commands a handler and invoke the handler each place you would have repeated the set of commands. This is also sometimes called a subroutine.

helper application A program that handles a particular kind of media or other data encountered on the Internet.

help tag A short description of the object under the mouse pointer in a Mac OS X application. The description appears in a small yellow box near the object. Many objects do not have help tags. The equivalent in Classic applications is *Balloon Help.*

HFS+ (Hierarchical File System Plus) An extended file format designed for high-capacity hard drives.

Home Folder The folder in which a user stores all personal files. The Mac OS X system also preserves settings for the user in the user's Home Folder Library.

Home page This term refers to the main page of a Web site, and it is also the page that a Web browser displays when you first open it.

hot spots Places in a QuickTime VR panorama that you can click to go to another scene in the panorama or to a QuickTime VR object.

hub A device on an Ethernet network that passes signals from any device connected to one of the hub's RJ-45 ports to all other devices connected to the hub.

hyperlink Underlined text or an image on a *Web page* that takes you to another page on the same or a different Web site when clicked.

icon A small picture that represents an entity such as a program, document, folder, or disk.

iDisk A service within the .Mac service that provides remote storage accessible via the Internet.

inbound port mapping A scheme for directing all requests coming into a local network from the Internet for a particular service, such as a Web server, to a particular computer on the local network.

inherited permissions Privileges that propagate from a parent folder to child folders and all files within.

initialization A process that creates a blank disk directory. The effect is the same as erasing the disk. Initialization actually wipes out the means of accessing the existing files on the disk without actually touching the content of files.

insertion point A blinking vertical bar that indicates where text is inserted when you start typing.

installation The process of putting a new or updated version of software on your disk.

Internet A worldwide network that provides email, Web pages, news, file storage and retrieval, and other services and information.

Internet gateway A device or software that enables all the computers on a local network to connect to the Internet, optionally sharing a single public IP address on the Internet.

Internet Service Provider (ISP) A company that gives you access to the Internet via your modem.

interpreted The technique used by Unix shells and other scripting languages such as Perl to perform each command as it is encountered rather than converting all commands to machine instructions in advance.

interprocess communication The technology that enables programs to send each other messages requesting action and receiving the results of requested actions. Mac OS X has several forms of interprocess communication, one of which is *Apple events,* which is the basis of *AppleScript.*

IP address A 32-bit binary number, such as 192.168.0.1, that uniquely identifies a computer or other device on a network.

ISDN (Integrated Services Digital Technology) A special telephone technology that allows for medium-speed network transmissions over long distances.

Jaguar Mac OS 10.2. Replaced by *Panther,* the newest Mac OS.

Java A programming language developed by Sun Microsystems. Java is platform independent, allowing its applications to function within any platform as long as the Java Virtual Machine software is available and installed.

kernel The kernel is the core of Mac OS X. The kernel provides services for all other elements of the operating system. See Mach 3.0 Microkernel.

kerning Adjusting the space between pairs of letters so that the spacing within the word looks consistent.

keychain Technology that enables you to store passwords and passphrases for network connections, file servers, some types of secure Web sites, and encrypted files.

label A means of color-coding files, folders, and disks. Each of the eight label types has its own color and title.

LAN (Local Area Network) See *local network*

landscape A printed page that is wider than it is tall.

language script system Software that enables the Mac OS to use an additional natural language, such as Japanese. Multiple languages can use one language script system (for example, the Roman script is used for English, French, Italian, Spanish, and German).

launch The act of getting an application started.

LDAP (Lightweight Directory Access Protocol) A software protocol that enables the location of individuals, groups, and other resources such as files or devices on a network.

Library folder Contains resources and preferences for Mac OS X. Library folders located within a user's Home Folder are user-customizable.

ligature A glyph composed of two merged characters. For example, *f* and *l* can be merged to form *fl*.

link See *hyperlink*

little arrows Displayed controls that let you raise or lower a value incrementally. Clicking an arrow changes the value one increment at a time. Pressing an arrow on the keyboard continuously changes the value until it reaches the end of its range.

localhost The standard generic name of a machine linked to an IP address.

localization The development of software whose dialogs, screens, menus, and other screen elements use the language spoken in the region in which the software is sold.

local network A system of computers that are interconnected for sharing information and services and are located in close proximity such as in an office, home, school, or campus. Compare to WAN.

LocalTalk An Apple proprietary networking topology. Effectively obsolete.

location file A file that, when opened, takes you to a location on the Internet or a local network.

log in The process of entering a username and password to begin a session with Mac OS X or another secured resource such as a network connection.

log out A command to quit current user settings and return the OS X system back to the login screen.

loop To repeat a command, a movie, a song, or an entire *playlist.*

lossless A type of compression algorithm that regenerates exactly the same data as the uncompressed original.

LPR (Line Print Remote) printer A printer that contains a protocol that allows it to print via TCP/IP.

MacBinary A scheme for encoding the special information in a Macintosh file's data and resource forks into a file format appropriate for transmission over the Internet.

Mach 3.0 Microkernel Developed at Carnegie-Mellon University, the Mach 3.0 Microkernel has a closely tied history to BSD (Berkeley Software Distribution) UNIX. Mach gives OS X the features of protected memory architecture, preemptive multitasking, and symmetric multi-processing.

man pages Documentation for some of the Mac OS X Unix commands (which are actually Unix programs) and other Unix components.

memory protection An operating system technology that makes it impossible for one active application to read and write data from another active application's space in memory. Memory protection helps applications run with fewer crashes.

MIDI The acronym for Musical Instrument Digital Interface. Developed in 1983 by several of the music industry's electronics manufacturers, MIDI is a data transmission protocol that permits devices to work together in a performance context. MIDI doesn't transfer music, it transfers information about the notes and their characteristics in a format another MIDI device can reconstruct the music from.

modem A device that connects a computer to telephone lines. It converts digital information from the computer into sounds for transmission over phone lines and converts sounds from phone lines to digital information for the computer. (The term *modem* is a shortened form of *modulator-demodulator*.) This term is also used informally for devices that connect computers by using digital technologies — for example, TV cable, DSL, and ISDN connections.

modem script Software consisting of the modem commands necessary to start and stop a remote access connection for a particular type of modem.

mount To mount means to connect to and access the contents of a disk or other volume. After mounting, the stored items in the mounted volume are then available to the local computer. In the case of internal hard drives, mounting is automatic and occurs every time you start up the computer.

movie Any time-related data, such as video, sound, animation, and graphs, that change over time; Apple's format for organizing, storing, and exchanging time-related data.

multimedia A presentation combining text or graphics with video, animation, or sound, and presented on a computer.

multitasking The capability to have multiple programs open and executing concurrently.

multithreading An operating system technology that allows tasks in an application to share processor time.

navigate To open disks and folders until you have opened the one that contains the item you need; to go from one *Web page* to another.

NetInfo The native directory service for Mac OS X. A NetInfo database/directory is referred to as a domain. The NetInfo database is hierarchical and contains both information on local and network users in addition to group authentication information.

network A collection of interconnected, individually controlled computers, printers, and other devices together with the hardware, software, and protocols used to connect them. A network lets connected devices exchange messages and information.

network administrator Someone who sets up and/or maintains a centralized file server and other network services.

networking protocol See *protocol*

network interface card (NIC) An internal adapter card that provides a network port.

network location A specific arrangement of all the various Network Preferences settings that can be put into effect all at once (for example, by choosing from the Location submenu of the Apple menu).

network time servers Computers on a network or the Internet that provide the current time of day.

Newsgroup A subject on the Internet's *Usenet*. It is a collection of people and messages pertaining to that particular subject.

NFS (Network File System) The Unix equivalent of personal file sharing. NFS allows users to view and store files on a remote computer.

nonblocking alert An alert from a background Classic application that appears in a floating window so that the current application's activities are not halted.

object A kind of information, such as words, paragraphs, and characters, that an application knows how to work with. An application's *AppleScript* dictionary lists the kinds of objects it can work with under script control.

Open GL (Open Graphics Library) An industry standard for three-dimensional graphics rendering. It provides a standard graphics API by which software and hardware manufacturers can build 3D applications and hardware across multiple platforms on a common standard.

open source Typically refers to software developed as a public collaboration and made freely available.

operating system Software that controls the basic activities of a computer system. Also known as *system software*.

original item A file, folder, or disk to which an *alias* points, and which opens when you open its alias.

orphaned alias An *alias* that has lost its link with its original item (and, therefore, Mac OS X cannot find it).

outline font A font whose *glyphs* are outlined by curves and straight lines that can be smoothly enlarged or reduced to any size and then filled with dots.

owner The user who can assign access *privileges* to a file or folder.

package A folder that the Finder displays as if it were a single application file. The Finder normally hides the files inside a package so users can't change them. A package is also a logical grouping of files that are related, such as all of the items that make up fax software or all of the parts of QuickTime. Sometimes referred to as a *bundle*.

palette An auxiliary window that contains controls or tools or displays information for an application. A palette usually floats above regular windows of the same application.

pane An Aqua GUI element comprised of separate screens within a single window, typically accessed via a pulldown menu or tab. Panes and their sub-panes when selected redraw within a single window, displaying alternate information and controls.

Panther The latest version of Macintosh OS X. Version 10.3 or higher. The replacement for *Jaguar*.

partition Noun: An identifiable logical division of a hard disk. Also referred to as a volume. Verb: To divide a hard drive into several smaller volumes, each of which the computer treats as a separate disk.

passphrase Like a password, but generally consisting of more than one word. (The larger a password or passphrase, the more difficult it is to guess or otherwise discover.)

password A combination of letters, digits, and symbols that must be typed accurately to gain access to information or services on the Internet or a *local network*.

path A way of writing the location of a file or folder by specifying each folder that must be opened to get at the file. The outermost folder name is written first, and each folder name is followed by a slash (/). See also *absolute path* and *relative path*.

PCMCIA (People Can't Memorize Computer Industry Acronyms) Also known as Cardbus, PCMCIA is a hardware interface typically found in laptops. Small credit-card sized devices are easily installed and removed from the laptop to expand functionality.

PDF (Portable Document Format) A platform-independent file format developed by Adobe. PDF files are often used in lieu of printed documents, as electronic transmission methods get more and more commonly accepted.

peer-to-peer file sharing A technology for allowing other client computers to access folders located on your client computer rather than a central file server. Less powerful than server-client file sharing, it is cheaper and easier to configure.

peripheral See *device*

permissions See *privileges*

ping A support tool that can be used to verify and validate the connectivity status of IP-aware network devices.

pipe A means of directing the output of one Unix command to the input of the next Unix command. Expressed in a Unix command line with a vertical bar symbol (|).

pixel Short for picture element, a pixel is the smallest dot that the computer and a display can show.

pixel depth The number of memory bits used to store each pixel of an image. The number of bits determines the number of different colors that could be in the image. For example, thousands of colors require 16 bits per pixel. Compare to *color depth*.

playhead A marker that tracks movie frames as they are shown, always indicating the location of the current frame in relationship to the beginning and end of the movie.

playlist A collection of songs arranged for playing in a particular sequence.

plug-ins Software that works with an application to extend its capabilities. For example, plug-ins for the Sherlock application enable it to search additional Internet sites.

POP 1. (Post Office Protocol) A client/server store-and-forward protocol for the receipt of email. 2. (Point Of Presence) A telephone number that gains access to the Internet through an Internet service provider. An entry point to the Internet.

pop-up menu A menu that is not in the menu bar, but that is marked with an arrowhead and pops open when you click it.

port As referred to within the Network preference pane, a port is some form of physical connection to a data network.

portrait A printed page that is taller than it is wide. For example, a normal letter–sized page in portrait mode is 8.5" wide x 11" high.

PostScript font An outline font that conforms to the specifications of the PostScript page description language. PostScript fonts can be smoothly scaled to any size, rotated, and laid out along a curved path. (Compare *TrueType*.)

PostScript printers Printers that interpret Adobe-developed PostScript language to create printable images. Commonly used in environments where precise and accurate printing is a must.

PPD (PostScript Printer Description) A file that contains the optional features of a PostScript printer, such as its resolution and paper tray configuration.

PPP (Point-To-Point Protocol) An industry standard for the communication between computing devices over dial-up connections.

PPPoE (Point-To-Point Protocol over Ethernet) An implementation of PPP over Ethernet, used by ISPs that want to regulate access or meter usage of its subscribers, like DSL (Digital Subscriber Line) connections.

PRAM (parameter RAM) A small amount of battery-powered memory that stores system settings, such as time and date.

preemptive multitasking Prioritizes processor tasks by order of importance. Preemptive multitasking allows the computer to handle multiple tasks simultaneously. This method of managing processor tasks more efficiently allows the computer to remain responsive, even during the most processor-intensive tasks.

Preferences folder Holds files that contain the settings you make in System Preferences and with the Preferences commands of application programs.

primary script The *language script system* used by system dialogs and menus. If you are working on a computer that is set up for English, Roman is your primary script; your secondary script can be any other installed language script, such as Japanese.

printer driver Software that prepares pages for and communicates with a particular type of printer.

print job A file of page descriptions that is sent to a particular type of printer. Also called a *print request* or *spool file*.

print request See *print job*

print server A device or software that manages one or more shared printers on a network.

private IP address An *IP address* for use on a local network. Compare *public IP address*.

privileges Privileges provide the control mechanism for regulating user access to files, folders, and applications within Mac OS X.

process Programs or threads (tasks) within a program that are currently running on the computer.

program A set of coded instructions that direct a computer in performing a specific task.

program linking The process of sharing programs by sending and receiving *event messages* across a network.

protected memory Isolates applications in their individual memory workspaces. In the event of an application crash, the program can be terminated without having a negative effect on other running applications or requiring a restart of the computer.

protocol A set of rules for the exchange of data between computer systems.

proxy icon A little icon next to the title of a Finder window. It represents the folder whose contents are currently displayed in the window. You can drag the proxy icon to any folder, volume, or the Trash.

proxy server A device that acts as an intermediary between a user's workstation and the Internet. When a request is made for Internet content, the request is passed along to the proxy server. The proxy server acts on behalf of the client and forwards the request on to the Internet. It then relays the retrieved response to the user.

public IP address An *IP address* for use on the Internet. Compare *private IP address.*

publisher A section of a document that is saved as an *edition,* which can appear as *subscribers* in other documents. The documents all belong to Classic applications.

push button A displayed control that when clicked causes an action to take place. A label on the button indicates the action that the button performs. The label may be text or graphic. Push buttons with text labels are generally rectangular with rounded ends. Buttons with graphic labels may be any shape.

Quartz A powerful two-dimensional graphics rendering system. Quartz has built-in support for PDF, on-the-fly rendering, compositing, and antialiasing. It supports multiple font formats, including True Type, Postscript Type 1, and OpenType. Quartz supports Apple's ColorSync color-management technology, allowing for consistent and accurate color in the print/graphics environment.

Quicktime Apple's proprietary, cross-platform multimedia authoring and distribution engine. Quicktime is both a file format and a suite of applications.

radio buttons A group of displayed controls that let you select one setting from a group. They work like the station presets on a car radio. Just as you can select only one radio station at a time, you can select only one radio button from a group.

RAM (Random Access Memory) Physical dynamic memory built into the computer in the form of electronic chips or small circuit boards called DIMMs or SODIMMs.

RAM disk Memory that is set aside to be used as if it were a very fast hard drive.

raster image An image made of lines of discrete dots for the display screen or the printer. Compare to *vector image.*

record A structured collection of data in AppleScript (and in other programming languages), in which each data item has a name and a value.

regular expression A shorthand method of expressing a string of characters or various permutations of a string of characters. Used in Unix command lines.

relative path A *path* that does not begin with a slash character (/) and is therefore assumed to start in the current folder.

Rendezvous A networking technology requiring zero configuration. Turn on the device, and your computer can see it and use it. As it is a new technology, older devices typically will not have support for Rendezvous available.

repeat loop An arrangement of *AppleScript* commands that begins with a Repeat command and ends with an End Repeat command. AppleScript executes the commands between the Repeat and End Repeat commands for the number of times specified in the Repeat command.

resolution The horizontal and vertical dimensions of a display, measured in pixels. Also refers to the perceived smoothness of a displayed or printed image. Printed resolution is measured in dots per inch *(dpi).* A high-resolution image has more dots per inch than a low-resolution image.

resolve an alias What Mac OS X does to find the original item that is represented by an *alias.*

resources Information such as text, menus, icons, pictures, or patterns used by Mac OS X, an application, or other software. Also refers to a computer's processing power, memory, and disk space.

rip To convert tracks from audio CDs typically into MP3 or AAC format. The first step to really irritating the RIAA.

RIP (Raster Image Processor) Software that translates PostScript code into an image made of lines of dots.

ROM (Read Only Memory) Non-editable information, typically located within a hardware device, with specifications as to the device's behavior. Compare to *RAM*.

root The name of the user account that has control over all folders and files on a computer, including the contents of the normally off-limits System folder. Root is also used as a term for the top-level directory of a file system.

root level The main level of a disk, which is what you see when you open the disk icon.

router See *Internet gateway*.

screen saver Software that protects against *burn-in* by showing a constantly changing image on the display while the computer is idle.

script A collection of *AppleScript* commands that perform a specific task. Also, short for *language script system*, which is software that defines a method of writing (vertical or horizontal, left-to-right, or right-to-left). A language script also provides rules for text sorting, word breaking, and the formatting of dates, times, and numbers.

scriptable application An application that can be controlled by *AppleScript* commands.

script applet *AppleScript* scripts saved as applets or small applications.

scripting additions Files that add commands to the *AppleScript* language, such as plug-ins add features to applications.

script recording A process in which *AppleScript* watches as you work with an application and automatically writes a corresponding *script*.

scrolling list Displays a list of values in a box with an adjacent scroll bar. Clicking a listed item selects it. You may be able to select multiple items by pressing Shift or ⌘ while clicking.

scrub To move quickly forward or backward through a movie by dragging the *playhead*.

search path An ordered search for resources within a Mac OS X System.

selection rectangle A dotted-line box that you drag around items to select them all.

server Software or a device that provides information or services to *clients* on demand.

shared folder The place where local user accounts can share files among themselves locally on the system.

shareware Software distributed over the Internet and from person to person on a trial basis. You pay for it if you decide to keep using it. See also *freeware*.

sheet A *dialog* that applies to and is attached to another window, ensuring you won't lose track of which window the dialog applies to.

shell Part of the Unix operating system that interprets command lines.

Sidebar A new feature of *Panther,* the Sidebar is located at the left side of all Finder windows and contains shortcuts to mounted volumes and commonly used folders.

single-user mode Entered during the system startup by holding down ⌘-S during the boot process (just after the startup chime). Single-user mode goes straight to the command line, eliminating the GUI until a reboot occurs. This mode is typically used for troubleshooting.

slider A displayed control consisting of a track that displays a range of values or magnitudes and the slider itself, also known as the thumb, which indicates the current setting. You can change the setting by dragging the slider.

smoothing See *antialiasing*

SMTP (Simple Mail Transfer Protocol) A protocol typically used in sending email.

software One or more programs that consist of coded instructions that direct a computer in performing tasks.

soundtrack The audible part of a movie.

splat Unix jargon for the number sign symbol (#).

spool file See *print job*

spooling A printer-driver operation in which the driver saves page descriptions in a file (called a *spool file*) for later printing.

SSH (Secure SHell) A protocol for securely accessing a remote computer.

standard input The source of Unix commands, which is the keyboard by default.

standard output The destination for the result of Unix commands, which is the terminal window by default.

startup disk A disk that contains the software needed for the computer to begin operation.

static IP address An *IP address* that doesn't change when you begin an Internet session or when your computer starts up.

stationery pad A template document that contains preset formatting and contents.

status bar A strip in the top part of a Finder window that shows how much free space is available on the volume that contains the currently displayed folder.

streaming media Movies designed to be played over the Internet as they are downloaded.

stuffed file A file (or group of files) that has been compressed in the StuffIt file format from Aladdin Systems.

submenu A secondary menu that pops out from the side of another menu. A submenu appears when you place the pointer on a menu item that has an arrowhead at the right side of the menu. Submenus are sometimes referred to as hierarchical menus.

subnet mask A 32-bit binary number that is used to identify a segment of a network.

subscriber A copy of an *edition* that has been placed in a document belonging to a Classic application. A subscriber can be updated automatically when the edition is updated by its *publisher*.

suite In *AppleScript,* a group of related commands and other items.

superuser The user who has complete control over all folders and files on a computer, including the contents of the normally off-limits System folder.

switch A central device on an Ethernet network that passes signals from any device connected to one of its RJ-45 ports to one of the other devices connected to it. Also refers to options you can specify as part of a Unix command.

symbolic link A representative file that contains exact information as to where a file or folder resides.

symmetric multiprocessing The technology that allows the operating system to take advantage of two processors by assigning applications to a specific processor or by splitting an application's tasks between multiple processors simultaneously.

system administrator A person who has the knowledge and authority to make changes to settings that affect the fundamental operation of a computer's operating system.

system extension A software module loads when the Classic environment starts up. It adds features or capabilities to Mac OS 9 for the Classic environment.

system file Contains sounds, keyboard layouts, and language script systems, as well as the basic Mac OS 9 software for the Classic environment.

System Folder Stores the Mac OS 9 software used by the Classic environment.

system software Software that controls the basic activities of a computer system. Also known as the *operating system*.

tabs Controls that look like the tabs on dividers used in card files. They divide the contents of a window into discrete pages called panes, with each tab connected to one pane of window content.

TCP/IP (Transmission Control Protocol/Internet Protocol) The basic communication language of the Internet.

Telnet An application that allows *remote* users to interact with Mac OS X's command line over TCP/IP, assuming they can gain authorization.

Terminal An application that allows *local* users to interact with Mac OS X's command line.

text behavior The set of rules used in a particular language for alphabetizing, capitalizing, and distinguishing words.

theme A group of all the settings in the Classic environment's Appearance control panel.

thread A string of messages about the same subject in a newsgroup. Also refers to a single task being executed within an application that may have multiple threads.

thumb The movable part of a *slider* control that indicates the current setting.

topology A description of a physical arrangement or layout of networking hardware.

track One channel of a QuickTime movie, containing video, sound, closed-captioned text, MIDI data, time codes, or other time-related data.

tracking The overall spacing between letters in an entire document or text selection. Text with loose tracking has extra space between the characters in words. Text with tight tracking has characters squeezed close together.

tracking speed The rate at which the pointer moves as you drag the mouse.

Translator A program that translates your documents from one file format to another file format, such as a PICT graphic to a GIF graphic.

Tristimulus A three-dimensional color space expressed in terms of X, Y, and Z coordinates.

Trojan horse Destructive software that masquerades as something useful, such as a utility program or game. Compare to *virus* and *worm*.

TrueType The outline font technology built into the Mac OS (and Microsoft Windows). TrueType fonts can be smoothly scaled to any size onscreen or to any type of printer.

Type 1 font A PostScript font that includes instructions for grid fitting so that the font can be scaled to small sizes and low printer resolutions with good results.

UFS (Unix File System) An alternative to the HFS+ file system format for Mac OS X.

UNIX (UNiplexed Information and Computing System, originally UNICS) A complex and powerful operating system whose TCP/IP networking protocol is the basis of the Internet.

unmount To remove a disk's icon from the Desktop and make the disk's contents unavailable without deleting the items in that disk permanently.

unshielded twisted-pair (UTP) The type of cable used in a 10Base-T, 100Base-T, or Gigabit Ethernet network.

upload The process of sending files from your computer to another computer.

URL (Uniform Resource Locator) An *Internet* address. This can be the address of a *Web page*, a file on an *FTP* site, or anything else that you can access on the Internet.

Usenet A worldwide *Internet* bulletin board system that enables people to post messages and join discussions about subjects that interest them.

user Someone who can log into your computer with a unique name and a password. A non-techie whose continued existence is tied to the economic survival of geeks everywhere.

user group An organization that provides information and assistance to people who use computers. For the names and phone numbers of user groups near you, check Apple's Web page (`www.apple.com/usergroups/find.html`).

username A name that can be used to log into a Mac OS X system.

user preferences Unique settings where users configure the behavior and appearance of applications and system software.

variable A container for information in a *script*. You can place data in a variable and then use it elsewhere in the script.

vector image A form of computer artwork comprised of lines and shapes, each defined by its start and end points. Unlike *raster images,* vector art can be resized to any dimension with no loss of quality, since it is not comprised of a finite amount of dots, but rather geometric lines and shapes.

verbose mode Displays all system activity in text format during the boot process. Useful for troubleshooting.

video mirroring The duplication of one screen image on two displays connected to a computer.

virtual memory Additional memory made available by Mac OS X treating part of a hard drive as if it were built-in memory.

virus Software designed to spread itself by illicitly attaching copies of itself to legitimate software. Some viruses perform malicious actions, such as erasing your hard drive. Even seemingly innocuous viruses can interfere with the normal functioning of your computer. Compare to *Trojan horse* and *worm*.

volume A disk or a part of a disk that the computer treats as a separate storage device. Each volume can have an icon on the Desktop. See partition.

WAN (Wide Area Network) Typically a network comprised of two or more *LANs*, a WAN is a network that is not compressed into one geographic location, but rather spread out over a larger area.

Web browser A program that displays *Web pages* from the Internet.

Web page A basic unit that the Web uses to display information (including text, pictures, animation, audio, and video clips). A Web page can also contain *hyperlinks* to the same page or to other Web pages (on the same or a different Web server).

Web server A computer or a program running on a computer that provides information to a Web browser program.

white point A setting that determines whether colors look warm (reddish) or cool (bluish). Measured in degrees Kelvin, with warm white points having lower temperatures than cool white points.

white space A run of blank spaces, tab characters, or both.

wildcard A character that represents a range of characters in a *regular expression*. For example, an asterisk stands for any individual character.

worm Software that replicates like a virus but without attaching itself to other software. It may be benign or malicious. Compare to *Trojan horse* and *virus*.

write-protect The process of locking a disk so that it cannot be erased, have its name changed, have files copied to it or duplicated from it, or have files or folders it contains moved to the Desktop or trash.

.zip file A file (or group of files) that has been compressed by using Mac OS X's *Archive* command. Windows and UNIX systems create .zip files as well, using WinZip or gzip, respectively.

Index

Continued

Continued